Organization of OSCM: The Intergration of Strategy, Processes, and Planning

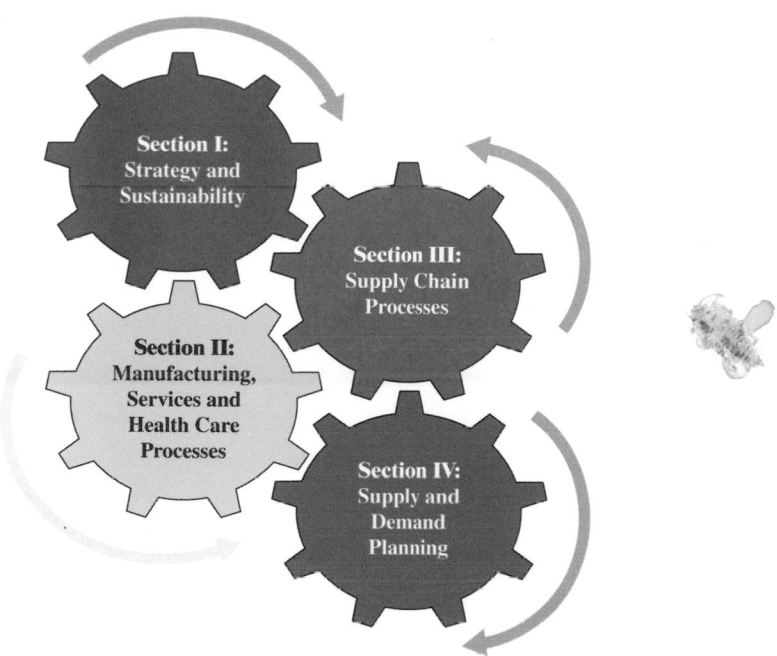

The Triple Bottom Line

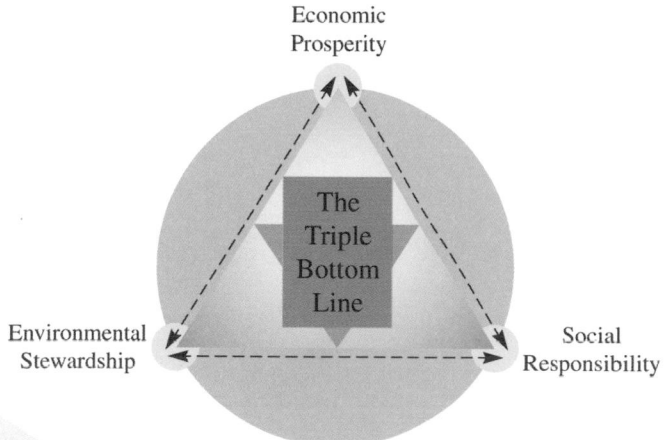

OPERATIONS AND
SUPPLY CHAIN MANAGEMENT

THE MCGRAW-HILL/IRWIN SERIES

Operations and Decision Sciences

OPERATIONS MANAGEMENT

Beckman and Rosenfield
Operations, Strategy: Competing in the 21st Century
First Edition

Benton
Purchasing and Supply Chain Management
Second Edition

Bowersox, Closs, and Cooper
Supply Chain Logistics Management
Third Edition

Brown and Hyer
Managing Projects: A Team-Based Approach
First Edition

Burt, Petcavage, and Pinkerton
Supply Management
Eighth Edition

Cachon and Terwiesch
Matching Supply with Demand: An Introduction to Operations Management
Second Edition

Finch
Interactive Models for Operations and Supply Chain Management
First Edition

Fitzsimmons and Fitzsimmons
Service Management: Operations, Strategy, Information Technology
Seventh Edition

Gehrlein
Operations Management Cases
First Edition

Harrison and Samson
Technology Management
First Edition

Hayen
SAP R/3 Enterprise Software: An Introduction
First Edition

Hill
Manufacturing Strategy: Text & Cases
Third Edition

Hopp
Supply Chain Science
First Edition

Hopp and Spearman
Factory Physics
Third Edition

Jacobs, Berry, Whybark, and Vollmann
Manufacturing Planning & Control for Supply Chain Management
Sixth Edition

Jacobs and Chase
Operations and Supply Management: The Core
Second Edition

Jacobs and Chase
Operations and Supply Chain Management
Thirteenth Edition

Jacobs and Whybark
Why ERP?
First Edition

Larson and Gray
Project Management: The Managerial Process
Fifth Edition

Leenders, Johnson, Flynn, and Fearon
Purchasing and Supply Management
Thirteenth Edition

Nahmias
Production and Operations Analysis
Sixth Edition

Olson
Introduction to Information Systems Project Management
Second Edition

Schroeder, Goldstein, and Rungtusanatham
Operations Management: Contemporary Concepts and Cases
Fifth Edition

Seppanen, Kumar, and Chandra
Process Analysis and Improvement
First Edition

Simchi-Levi, Kaminsky, and Simchi-Levi
Designing and Managing the Supply Chain: Concepts, Strategies, Case Studies
Third Edition

Sterman
Business Dynamics: Systems Thinking and Modeling for Complex World
First Edition

Stevenson
Operations Management
10th Edition

Swink, Melnyk, Cooper, and Hartley
Managing Operations Across the Supply Chain
First Edition

Thomke
Managing Product and Service Development: Text and Cases
First Edition

Ulrich and Eppinger
Product Design and Development
Fourth Edition

Zipkin
Foundations of Inventory Management
First Edition

QUANTITATIVE METHODS AND MANAGEMENT SCIENCE

Hillier and Hillier
Introduction to Management Science: A Modeling and Case Studies Approach with Spreadsheets
Fourth Edition

Stevenson and Ozgur
Introduction to Management Science with Spreadsheets
First Edition

OPERATIONS AND SUPPLY CHAIN MANAGEMENT

thirteenth edition

F. ROBERT JACOBS
Indiana University

RICHARD B. CHASE
University of Southern California

OPERATIONS AND SUPPLY CHAIN MANAGEMENT

ISBN   978-0-07-352522-8
MHID   0-07-352522-7

Vice president and editor-in-chief: *Brent Gordon*
Editorial director: *Stewart Mattson*
Publisher: *Tim Vertovec*
Executive editor: *Richard T. Hercher, Jr.*
Director of development: *Ann Torbert*
Managing development editor: *Gail Korosa*
Vice president and director of marketing: *Robin J. Zwettler*
Marketing director: *Sankha Basu*
Senior marketing manager: *Melissa S. Caughlin*
Vice president of editing, design, and production: *Sesha Bolisetty*
Lead project manager: *Christine A. Vaughan*
Lead production supervisor: *Michael R. McCormick*
Lead designer: *Matthew Baldwin*
Cover Image: *© Getty Images*
Senior photo research coordinator: *Jeremy Cheshareck*
Photo researcher: *Allison Grimes*
Lead media project manager: *Kerry Bowler*
Typeface: *10/12 Times Roman*
Compositor: *MPS Limited, A Macmillan Company*
Printer: *R. R. Donnelley*

Library of Congress Cataloging-in-Publication Data

Jacobs, F. Robert.
    Operations and supply chain management / F. Robert Jacobs, Richard B. Chase.
— Thirteenth ed.
       p. cm. — (The McGraw-Hill/Irwin series operations and decision sciences)
    Rev. ed. of: Operations and supply management.
    Includes index.
    ISBN-13: 978-0-07-352522-8 (alk. paper)
    ISBN-10: 0-07-352522-7 (alk. paper)
    1. Production management. I. Chase, Richard B. II. Jacobs, F. Robert. Operations
and supply management. III. Title.
TS155.J27 2011
658.5—dc22
                                                    2010003515

www.mhhe.com

To my parents Joan and Jake and my children
Jennifer and Suzy

To my wife Harriet and to our children
Laurie, Andy, Glenn, Robb, and Christine

PREFACE

Operations and supply chain management (OSCM) is a key element in the improvement in productivity in business around the world. Establishing a *creative advantage* through operations requires an understanding of how the operations and supply chain functions contribute to productivity growth. However, our intent in this book is to do more than just show you what companies are doing to create a competitive advantage for you in the marketplace by conveying a set of skills and tools that you can actually apply.

Hot topics in business today that relate to operations and supply chain management are sustainability, lean supply chains, and improving the efficiency of supply chain processes. These topics are studied in the book with up-to-date, high-level managerial material to clarify the "big picture" of what these topics are and why they are so important to business today.

Three significant new features of this book are the incorporation of material covering sustainability in supply chain processes, a new chapter on health care processes, and the use of value stream mapping. In the case of sustainability, we have woven the topic in the book with new material in the introduction and the chapters on strategy, global sourcing and procurement, and lean and sustainable supply chains. Our new health care processes chapter is the first time this topic has been included in a book intended for the introductory operations and supply chain educational market. The value stream mapping material is again a first relative to the depth of coverage of the topic.

Global

Service

Supply Chain

Excel: Spreadsheet

Operations and Supply Chain Management requires a global perspective for many of the topics. The reality of global customers, global suppliers, and global supply chains has made the global firm recognize the importance of being both lean and green to ensure competitiveness. Applications that range from high-tech manufacturing to high-touch service are used in the balanced treatment of the traditional topics of the field. Success for companies today requires successfully managing the entire supply flow, from the sources of the firm, through the value-added process of the firm, and on to the customers of the firm. To highlight our emphasis on globalization, services, and supply chain integration, we've used the logos you see here in the text margin next to these discussions.

Each chapter includes information about how operations and supply chain–related problems are solved. There are concise treatments of the many decisions that need to be made in designing, planning, and managing the operations of a business. Many spreadsheets are available from the book Web site to help clarify how these problems are quickly solved. We have indicated those spreadsheets with the spreadsheet logo shown here in the margin.

OSCM should appeal to individuals who want to be directly involved in making products or providing services. The entry-level operations specialist is the person who determines how best to design, supply, and run the processes. Senior operations managers are responsible for setting the strategic direction of the company from an operations and supply chain standpoint, deciding what technologies should be used and where facilities should be located, and managing the facilities that make the products or provide the services. OSCM is an interesting mix of managing people and applying sophisticated technology. The goal is to efficiently create wealth by supplying quality goods and services.

Features to aid in your understanding of the material include the following:

- Solved problems at the end of chapters to serve as models that can be reviewed prior to attempting problems.
- Key terms highlighted in the chapter outline and their definitions at the end of each chapter.

- Answers to selected problems in Appendix D.
- Super Quiz questions at the end of each chapter. These are special questions designed to require a deeper understanding of the material in the chapter. They are similar to the type of short-answer questions that might be given on a test.
- The book Web site, which includes PowerPoint slide outlines of each chapter, Excel spreadsheets for the solved problems and other examples, practice quizzes, ScreenCam tutorials, Internet links, and video segments that illustrate the application of operations concepts in companies such as Xerox, Zappos.com, Six Flags, Caterpillar, Burton Snowboards, Honda, Disney, Ford, and many others.
- Breakthrough Boxes and boxed inserts provide short overviews of how leading-edge companies are applying OSCM concepts today.

Our aim is to cover the latest and the most important issues facing OSCM managers as well as basic tools and techniques. We supply many examples of leading-edge companies and practices. We have done our best to make the book interesting reading and give you a competitive advantage in your career.

We hope you enjoy it.

PLAN OF THE BOOK

This book is about methods to effectively produce and distribute the goods and services sold by a company. To develop a better understanding of the field, this book is organized into four major sections: Strategy and Sustainability; Manufacturing, Service, and Health Care Processes; Supply Chain Processes; and Supply and Demand Planning. In the following paragraphs, we quickly describe the major topics in the book.

Strategy and sustainability are important and recurring topics in the book. Any company must have a comprehensive business plan that is supported by a marketing strategy, operations strategy, and financial strategy. It is essential for a company to ensure that the three strategies support each other. Strategy is covered from a high-level view in Chapter 2 (Strategy and Sustainability), and more details are covered in three chapters: Chapter 4 (Strategic Capacity Management), Chapter 11 (Global Sourcing and Procurement), and Chapter 13 (Lean and Sustainable Supply Chains). Our reason for spreading the strategy material throughout the book is to make things more interesting while placing them in an appropriate context. In general, we try to give you the "big picture" and then fill in the details with the following chapters.

The lifeline of the company is a steady stream of innovative products that are offered to the marketplace at the lowest cost possible. Product and Service Design (Chapter 3) includes a view of how products are designed in the context of having to actually produce and distribute the product over its life cycle. The chapter includes material on how to manage and analyze the economic impact of a stream of products that are developed over time.

The second section of the book, titled Manufacturing, Services, and Health Care Processes, focuses on the design of internal processes. Chapter 4, Strategic Capacity Management, develops the big picture of how firms reap economies of scale, how they learn over time, and the related cost implications. Chapter 5, Process Analysis, is a nuts-and-bolts chapter on process flow charting and static process analysis using some easily understood "real-life" examples. Chapters 6 and 7 cover the unique characteristics of production and service processes. Important technical material that relates to design activities is covered in Chapters 6A (Facility Layout) and 7A (Waiting Line Analysis).

Health Care Processes (Chapter 8) is a new chapter designed to show how health care processes have features of both production and services, depending on the type of task involved. Health care represents a great area of business that is ripe for the application of the concepts and tools that are fundamental to operations and supply chain management.

An essential element of process design is quality. Six-Sigma Quality is the topic of Chapter 9. Here we cover total quality management concepts, Six-Sigma tools, and ISO 9000 and 14000. Technical details covering all the statistical aspects of quality are in Chapter 9A (Process Capability and Statistical Process Control).

Businesses have to change to remain competitive. Working on projects is very common and even a predominant organizing approach in companies now. The success of any project is invariably measured by our ability to complete the project in time and within budget. How can we be confident we will meet the objective? Becoming proficient in managing projects is important to success in OSCM.

The third section of the book, titled Supply Chain Processes, expands our focus to the entire distribution system from the sourcing of material and other resources to the distribution of products and services. Many different transformation processes are needed to put together a supply chain. There are critical decisions such as: Where should we locate our facility? What equipment should we buy or lease? Should we outsource work or do it in-house? These are the topics of Chapters 11 and 12 that relate to sourcing, procurement, location of facilities, and distribution. All of these decisions have a direct financial impact on the firm. We discuss the concepts behind lean manufacturing and just-in-time processes in Chapter 13. These are ideas used by companies throughout the world and are key drivers for efficient and quick-responding supply systems.

Section Four, titled Supply and Demand Planning, covers the techniques required to actually run the system. This is at the heart of OSCM. The basic building blocks are Demand Management and Forecasting (Chapter 15), Sales and Operations Planning (Chapter 16), Inventory Control (Chapter 17), Material Requirements Planning (Chapter 18), and Scheduling (Chapter 19). These daily processes are often partially automated with computer information systems. Coverage of Enterprise Resource Planning Systems is the topic of Chapter 14.

Making fact-based decisions is what OSCM is all about, so this book features extensive coverage of decision-making approaches and tools. One useful way to categorize decisions is by the length of the planning horizon, or the period of time that the decision maker must consider. For example, building a new plant would be a long-term decision that a firm would need to be happy with for 10 to 15 years into the future. At the other extreme, a decision about how much inventory for a particular item should be ordered for tomorrow typically has a much shorter planning horizon of a few months or, in many cases, only a few days. Such short-term decisions are usually automated using computer programs. In the intermediate term are decisions that a company needs to live with for only 3 to 12 months. Often these decisions correspond to yearly model changes and seasonal business cycles.

As you can see from this discussion, this material is all interrelated. A company's strategy dictates how operations are designed. The design of the operation dictates how it needs to be managed. Finally, because businesses are constantly being presented with new opportunities through new markets, products, and technologies, a business needs to be very good at managing change.

ACKNOWLEDGMENTS

Many very talented scholars have made major contributions to specific chapters in this edition of the book. We are pleased to thank the following individuals:

Rhonda Lummus of Indiana University for her many ideas for improving the Supply Chain material in the book. Gene Fliedner of Oakland University for his help with the Sustainability material. Craig Froehle of the University of Cincinnati for his review of the Health Care chapter.

Chris Albright, Goker Aydin, Doug Blocher, Kyle Cattani, Seb Hesse, Gilvan Souza, Ash Soni, and Wayne Winston of the ODT department at the Kelley School of Business, Indiana University, for all the time spent discussing ideas.

In the past, major contributions have been made to this book by the following people:

Luca Bencini, Rath & Strong; Barb Flynn, Indiana University/Purdue; Mark Ippolito, Indiana University/Purdue; and John R. M. Gordon, Queens University.

Supplements are a great deal of work to write, and we appreciate the efforts that make teaching the course easier for everyone who uses the text. Rex Cutshall of Indiana University prepared the ScreenCam tutorials. Patrick Johanns of Purdue University revised the Excel spreadsheets. Bill Berry of Queens College updated the test bank. Ronny Richardson of Southern Polytechnic State University prepared the PowerPoint slides and the step-by-step solutions to the examples in the book. Christopher Kelly of the University of Indianapolis revised the Solutions Manual and checked the text problems for accuracy.

We wish to express our gratitude to the reviewers of the twelfth edition who provided many helpful suggestions for this thirteenth edition:

Nazim Ahmed, *Ball State University*
Tony Arreola-Risa, *Texas A&M University*
Craig Froehle, *University of Cincinnati*
Craig Hill, *Georgia State University*
Mehdi Kaighobadi, *Florida Atlantic*
Sham Kekre, *Carnegie Mellon University*
David Lewis, *University of Massachusetts, Lowell*
Marie Matta, *George Washington University*
Roy Nersesian, *Monmouth University*
Shrikant Panwalkar, *Purdue University*
Marc Schniederjans, *University of Nebraska, Lincoln*
Theresa Wells, *University of Wisconsin, Eau Claire*
Yuehwern Yih, *Purdue University*

Special thanks to participants in McGraw-Hill/Irwin's focus groups:

Joy Field, *Boston College*
Daniel Heiser, *DePaul University*
James Ho, *University of Illinois, Chicago*
Mary Holcomb, *University of Tennessee*
Hsiu-Yueh Hsu, *University of Louisiana, Lafayette*
Rahul Kale, *University of North Florida*
Jian Li, *Northeastern Illinois University*
Nagesh Murthy, *University of Oregon*
Fariborz Partovi, *Drexel University*
Eddy Patuwo, *Kent State University*
Willard Price, *University of the Pacific*
Paul Schikora, *Indiana State University*
Don Smith, *California State University, Fullerton*
Harm-Jan Steenhuis, *Eastern Washington University*
Tekle Wanorie, *Northwest Missouri State*

We also wish to thank the following individuals whose input over past editions has helped the book to evolve to its present form: Ajay Aggarwal, *Millsaps College*; Frank Barnes, *University of North Carolina–Charlotte*; Marie-Laure Bougnol-Potter, *Western Michigan University*; Ajay Das, *Baruch College*; Art Duhaime, *Nichols College*; Frank Montabon, *Iowa State University*; Zinovy Radovilsky, *California State University–East Bay*; Kaushik Sengupta, *Hofstra University*; Kimberly Snyder, *Winona State University*; Jeremy Stafford, *University of North Alabama*; James Stewart, *University of Maryland, University College*; Ina Van Loo, *West Virginia University Institute of Technology*; David Alexander, *Angelo State University*; John Aloysius, *University of Arkansas*; Uday Apte, *Naval Postgraduate School*; Yasemin Askoy, *Tulane University*; Saba Bahouth, *University of Central Oklahoma*; Frank Barnes, *University of North Carolina–Charlotte*; Uttarayan Bagchi, *University of Texas*; Ravi Behara, *Florida Atlantic University*; Injazz J. Chen, *Cleveland State University*; Susan Cholette, *San Francisco State University*; Bruce Christensen, *Weber State University*; Chen-Hua Chung, *University of Kentucky*; Robert F. Conti, *Bryant College*; David Cook, *Old Dominion University*; Lori Cook, *DePaul University*; Bill Cosgrove, *California Polytechnic State University*; Henry Crouch, *Pittsburgh State University*; Dinesh Dave, *Appalachian State University*; Eddie Davila, *Arizona State University*; Renato de Matta, *University of Iowa*; Steven Dickstein, *The*

Ohio State University; Chris Ellis, *Florida International University*; Farzaneh Fazel, *Illinois State University*; Mark Ferguson, *Georgia Institute of Technology*; Jonathan Furdek, *Purdue University–Calumet*; Michael R. Godfrey, *University of Wisconsin–Oshkosh*; Robert H. Greinier, *Augustana College*; D. M. Halemane, *Erasmus University, Rotterdam*; Marijane Hancock, *University of Nebraska–Lincoln*; Paul Hong, *University of Toledo*; John Jensen, *University of Southern Maine*; Seung-Lae Kim, *Drexel University*; Vinod Lall, *Minnesota State University, Moorhead*; Dennis Krumwiede, *Idaho State University*; Paul J. Kuzdrall, *University of Akron*; David Levy, *Bellevue University*; Patrick McDonald, *University of Arizona*; Frank Montabon, *Iowa State University*; Alysse Morton, *University of Utah, Salt Lake City*; Buchi Felix Offodile, *Kent State University*; Özgür Özlük, *San Francisco State University*; Andru Peters, *San Jose State University*; Sharma Pillutla, *Towson University*; Anita Lee Post, *University of Kentucky*; Fred Raafat, *San Diego State University*; Drew Rosen, *University of North Carolina–Wilmington*; Edie K. Schmidt, *Purdue University*; Ruth Seiple, *University of Cincinnati*; Joao Neves, *College of New Jersey*; Sue Siferd, *Arizona State University*; Gilvan C. Souza, *University of Maryland*; Carl Steiner, *University of Illinois–Chicago*; Donna H. Stewart, *University of Wisconsin–Stout*; Gregory Stock, *Northern Illinois University*; Ronald Tibben-Lembke, *University of Nevada–Reno*; Vera Tilson, *Case Western Reserve University*; Vicente A. Varga, *University of San Diego*; Jay Varzandeh, *California State University–San Bernardino*; Rohit Verma, *Cornell Hotel School*; Bill L. Ward, *University of Western Alabama*; Helio Yang, *San Diego State University*; G. Peter Zhang, *Georgia State University*.

We also want to thank former doctoral students who have contributed to the book over the years, including Mahesh Nagarajan, *University of British Columbia*; Hiroshi Ochiumi, Wayne Johannson, and Jason Niggley, *USC*; Douglas Stewart, *University of New Mexico*; Anderas Soteriou, *University of Cyprus*; Arvinder Loomba, *University of Northern Iowa*; Deborah Kellogg, *University of Colorado–Denver*; Blair Berkeley, *California State University–Los Angeles*; and Bill Youngdahl, *Thunderbird American Graduate School of International Management*.

We sincerely appreciate the amazing dedication of our executive editor, Dick Hercher. Over the years his brilliant guidance and all-out support have provided the solid foundation on which the entire team associated with this book is built.

Gail Korosa, our developmental editor, has done a great job editing our scribbling and nudging us to hit those due dates. Thanks for the patience. It's great working with you.

Thanks to the McGraw-Hill/Irwin marketing and production team who make this possible—Melissa Caughlin, marketing manager; Stewart Mattson, editorial director; Christine Vaughan, project manager; Jill Traut, project manager; Michael McCormick, production supervisor; Matt Baldwin, designer; Kerry Bowler, media project manager; and Greg Bates, media producer.

Last but certainly not least, we thank our families, who for the thirteenth time let the life cycle of the book disrupt theirs.

F. Robert Jacobs

Richard B. Chase

NOTE TO INSTRUCTORS— DISCUSSION OF 13TH EDITION REVISIONS

In developing the revisions for the 13th edition, we have been careful to make the sections and chapters as modular as possible. This allows you to drop material or rearrange topics as you see fit. Our discussions concerning the current lineup of chapters were extensive. But we realize that no matter how we organized the book, it was a compromise. We know from experience that the current lineup works well.

A totally new feature of this book is the addition of the Health Care Processes chapter. Given the strong acceptance of operations and supply chain concepts in this industry, we felt that developing this chapter was needed. There are great opportunities for operations and supply chain professionals in this industry. One might view this chapter as a "matrix" chapter in that it cuts across many of the topics of the book. Depending on the application, health care processes share features of manufacturing, services, and supply chains. Our hope is that students can see that generic concepts, such as process analysis, quality management, and inventory control, can be applied in many different business contexts. We feel that many students will see the exciting opportunities that are available in this industry for those who have expertise in operations and supply chain management.

A second new feature of this book is the emphasis on sustainability as it relates to operations and supply chain management. To incorporate this feature in the book, we elected to weave sustainability into many areas including strategy, quality management and value stream mapping, purchasing and global sourcing, and lean supply chain analysis. Sustainability is a topic that fits well within operations and supply chain management due to the strong tie between being green and being efficient. This is sometimes a synergistic relationship, but often involves a difficult trade-off that needs to be considered. The reality of global customers, global suppliers, and global supply chains has made the global firm recognize the importance of being both lean and green to ensure competitiveness.

In this 13th edition, we have significantly strengthened the supply chain management material. This is particularly true in the areas of purchasing and strategic sourcing, and in lean supply chain analysis. Our view is that operations management, as a field of study, has significantly changed over the past few years. Due to the emphasis on integration across suppliers, the entities of the firm, and customers, we can no longer consider processes as isolated from other processes. Rather, the supply chain is an integrated whole that requires the synchronization of transportation, warehousing, and distribution together with internal product and service producing processes. This new integrated supply chain view even includes the important concepts involved with product returns and eventual recycling. We feel that titling this book *Operations and Supply Chain Management* captures the importance of the integration of this whole set of internal and external processes.

A major new feature is a "Super Quiz" included at the end of each chapter. This is designed to allow students to see how well they understand the material using a format that is similar to what they might see in an exam. The questions are designed in a short-answer fill-in-the-blank format. Many of the questions are straightforward, but in each chapter we have included insightful questions that require depth of understanding of the material. You may want to go over these questions with your students as part of a review session prior to an exam.

The following list outlines the major revisions in each chapter:

- Chapter 1—Operations and Supply Chain Management—Here we refocused this chapter on understanding what operations and supply chain management is all about, its origins, and how it relates to current business practice. Now we introduce the SCORE "Plan, Source, Make, Deliver, Return" framework for understanding how the processes in the supply chain must integrate.

- Chapter 2—Strategy and Sustainability—The chapter has an introduction to sustainability and triple-bottom-line material (people, planet, and profit). We have also included new material on the "process" for creating a strategy.
- Chapter 3—Product and Service Design—Related to our sustainability theme, we have added material on ecodesign to the chapter. Ecodesign is the incorporation of environmental consideration in the design and development of products or services.
- Chapter 4—Strategic Capacity Management—In this chapter, we updated our descriptions of focus factory and plant-within-a-plant concepts.
- Chapter 5—Process Analysis—In this chapter the explanation of Little's Law has been rewritten so that it can be applied to the analysis of integrated supply chain processes.
- Chapter 6—Production Processes—Note here that we have retitled this chapter to "Production" processes, rather than "Manufacturing." This is an important change as it generalizes the chapter. We have added material from the SCORE model (Make-Source-Deliver) and added the concept of "customer order decoupling point" to the chapter.
- Chapter 7—Service Processes—We have added new material on "virtual services" and updated "service blueprinting" in the chapter.
- Chapter 8—Health Care Processes—This is a totally new chapter that describes processes that are used in hospitals, clinics, and other health care facilities. The scope of the chapter is broad and includes workflow analysis, layout, quality, purchasing, and supply chain concepts.
- Chapter 9—Six-Sigma Quality—Here we added c-charts to the material. This was requested by a number of reviewers. Some notation was cleaned up in the chapter.
- Chapter 10—Projects—On the basis of suggestions from some reviewers, this chapter was moved to a later position in the book. We updated the explanation of crashing.
- Chapter 11—Global Sourcing and Procurement—A new introduction on the "green supply chain" was added. Information on different types of sourcing processes, including vendor-managed inventory, has been added. A "green sourcing" process, which includes material on the total cost of ownership with an example and new problems, was added.
- Chapter 12—Location, Logistics, and Distribution—The chapter has been streamlined and a new puzzle-type problem called "Supply and Demand" has been added.
- Chapter 13—Lean and Sustainable Supply Chains—New material on "green supply chains" has been added and we show how this relates to being "lean." A major new section on value stream mapping including examples and new problems has been added to the chapter. All the "lean" material has been consolidated into this chapter including discussion of the Toyota Production System concepts, "pull" concepts, and developing supplier networks to support lean processes.
- Chapter 14—Enterprise Resource Planning Systems—Material on "cloud" computing has been added to the chapter.
- Chapter 15—Demand Management and Forecasting—Here we have updated CPFR and moved it up in the chapter so that it can be used to discuss the importance of an integrated process for managing demand. In terms of actual forecasting techniques, regression is now the first technique discussed due to its general applicability. We have also added "decomposition" techniques (seasonal indexes) to this discussion. Examples and problems have been added to support this material.

Other than these changes, there have been literally hundreds of other small changes to the book. Many of these changes are based on the extensive feedback that we got from you, the users of the book. Please do not hesitate to send us an e-mail or to call if you have comments or questions related to the book.

F. Robert Jacobs
Richard B. Chase
January 2010

McGRAW-HILL CONNECT™ OPERATIONS MANAGEMENT

Less Managing. More Teaching. Greater Learning.

 McGraw-Hill *Connect™ Operations Management* is an online assignment and assessment solution that connects students with the tools and resources they'll need to achieve success. McGraw-Hill *Connect™ Operations Management* helps prepare students for their future by enabling faster learning, more efficient studying, and higher retention of knowledge.

McGraw-Hill *Connect™ Operations Management* features

Connect™ Operations Management offers a number of powerful tools and features to make managing assignments easier so faculty can spend more time teaching. With *Connect™ Operations Management* students can engage with their coursework anytime and anywhere making the learning process more accessible and efficient. *Operations Management* offers you the features described below.

Simple assignment management

With *Connect™ Operations Management,* creating assignments is easier than ever, so you can spend more time teaching and less time managing. The assignment management function enables you to:

- Create and deliver assignments easily with selectable end-of-chapter questions and test bank items.
- Streamline lesson planning, student progress reporting, and assignment grading to make classroom management more efficient than ever.
- Go paperless with the eBook and online submission and grading of student assignments.

Smart grading

When it comes to studying, time is precious. *Connect™ Operations Management* helps students learn more efficiently by providing feedback and practice material when they need it, where they need it. When it comes to teaching, your time also is precious. The grading function enables you to:

- Have assignments scored automatically, giving students immediate feedback on their work and side-by-side comparisons with correct answers.
- Access and review each response; manually change grades or leave comments for students to review.
- Reinforce classroom concepts with practice tests and instant quizzes.

Instructor library

The *Connect™ Operations Management* Instructor Library is your repository for additional resources to improve student engagement in and out of class. You can select and use any asset that enhances your lecture. The *Connect™ Operations Management* Instructor Library includes:

- PowerPoint slides
- Text Figures
- Instructor's Solutions Manual
- Instructor's Resource Manual
- Test Bank

Student study center

The *Connect™ Operations Management* Student Study Center is the place for students to access additional resources. The Student Study Center:

- Offers students quick access to study and review material.

Student progress tracking

Connect™ Operations Management keeps instructors informed about how each student, section, and class is performing, allowing for more productive use of lecture and office hours. The progress-tracking function enables you to:

- View scored work immediately and track individual or group performance with assignment and grade reports.
- Access an instant view of student or class performance relative to chapter headings.

McGRAW-HILL CONNECT™ PLUS OPERATIONS MANAGEMENT

McGraw-Hill reinvents the textbook learning experience for the modern student with *Connect™ Plus Operations Management*. A seamless integration of an eBook and *Connect™ Operations Management*, *Connect™ Plus Operations Management* provides all of the *Connect™ Operations Management* features plus the following:

- An integrated eBook, allowing for anytime, anywhere access to the textbook.
- Dynamic links between the problems or questions you assign to your students and the location in the eBook where that problem or question is covered.
- A powerful search function to pinpoint and connect key concepts in a snap.

For more information about Connect, go to www.mcgrawhillconnect.com, or contact your local McGraw-Hill sales representative.

TEGRITY CAMPUS: LECTURES 24/7

Tegrity Campus is a service that makes class time available 24/7 by automatically capturing every lecture in a searchable format for students to review when they study and complete assignments. With a simple one-click start-and-stop process, you capture all computer screens and corresponding audio. Students can replay any part of any class with easy-to-use browser-based viewing on a PC or Mac. Educators know that the more students can see, hear, and experience class resources, the better they learn. In fact, studies prove it. With Tegrity Campus, students quickly recall key moments by using Tegrity Campus's unique search feature. This search helps students efficiently find what they need, when they need it, across an entire semester of class recordings. Help turn all your students' study time into learning moments immediately supported by your lecture.

To learn more about Tegrity watch a 2-minute Flash demo at http://tegritycampus.mhhe.com.

OPERATIONS MANAGEMENT AND THE AACSB
ASSURANCE OF LEARNING READY

Many educational institutions today are focused on the notion of *assurance of learning,* an important element of some accreditation standards. *Operations and Supply Chain Management* is designed specifically to support your assurance of learning initiatives with a simple, yet powerful solution.

Each test bank question for *Operations and Supply Chain Management* maps to a specific chapter learning outcome/objective listed in the text. You can use our test bank software, EZ Test and EZ Test Online, or in *Connect Operations Management* to easily query for learning outcomes/objectives that directly relate to the learning objectives for your course. You can then use the reporting features of EZ Test to aggregate student results in similar fashion, making the collection and presentation of assurance of learning data simple and easy.

AACSB STATEMENT

The McGraw-Hill Companies is a proud corporate member of AACSB International. Understanding the importance and value of AACSB accreditation, *Operations and Supply Chain Management* recognizes the curricula guidelines detailed in the AACSB standards for business accreditation by connecting selected questions in the test bank to the six general knowledge and skill areas in the AACSB standards Assessment of Learning Standards.

The statements contained in *Operations and Supply Chain Management* are provided only as a guide for the users of this textbook. The AACSB leaves content coverage and assessment within the purview of individual schools, the mission of the school, and the faculty. While *Operations and Supply Chain Management* and the teaching package make no claim of any specific AACSB qualification or evaluation, we have within the Test Bank labeled questions according to the six general knowledge and skill areas.

McGRAW-HILL CUSTOMER CARE
CONTACT INFORMATION

At McGraw-Hill, we understand that getting the most from new technology can be challenging. That's why our services don't stop after you purchase our products. You can e-mail our Product Specialists 24 hours a day to get product training online. Or you can search our knowledge bank of Frequently Asked Questions on our support Web site. For Customer Support, call **800-331-5094**, e-mail hmsupport@mcgraw-hill.com, or visit www.mhhe.com/support. One of our Technical Support Analysts will be able to assist you in a timely fashion.

Walkthrough

The following section highlights the key features developed to provide you with the best overall text available. We hope these features give you maximum support to learn, understand, and apply operations concepts.

Chapter Opener →

Opening Vignettes →

Each chapter opens with a short vignette to set the stage and help pique students' interest in the material about to be studied. A few examples include:

- The GAP, Chapter 1, page 3

- IKEA, Chapter 2, page 21

- Mayo Clinic, Chapter 8, page 269

GREEN IS THE NEW BLACK[1]

SURVEY SUGGESTS THAT ENVIRO-CONSCIOUS MANUFACTURERS ARE THE BEST RISK FOR INVESTORS

Many manufacturers still have a long way to go to address the risks and opportunities posed by the push toward more environment-friendly production processes, according to a new study conducted by RiskMetrics Group, a provider of risk management services. Those risks include higher energy costs due to tighter

After reading this chapter you will:

1. Describe how Green and Lean can complement each other.
2. Explain how a production pull system works.
3. Understand Toyota Production System concepts.
4. Summarize important attributes of a lean supply chain.
5. Analyze a supply chain process using value stream mapping.
6. Know the principles of supply chain design.

greenhouse gas (GHG) emissions standards, and the opportunities include growing global demand for more energy-efficient products.

The report ranks large manufacturers and other companies on their effectiveness in such areas as reducing GHG emissions, introducing energy-efficient projects, expanding renewable energy purchases, and integrating climate factors into product designs. However, perhaps reflecting

UNDERSTANDING THE GLOBAL SUPPLY CHAIN

At an iron-ore mine in Western Australia, I once stood and watched as a young man worked an excavator to claw bucketfuls of deep-red ore from the ground. For a project, I wanted to follow the ore on its journey from raw material to finished product. So I went on a train that took it to a port, then traveled on the Chinese ship that carried it to Japan. There it was refined into steel ingots, which were sent to a factory outside Tokyo and fashioned into a Toyota Corolla. Next I got on a mighty ship carrying thousands of Toyota imports across the Pacific Ocean to Seattle.

The car made from my ore—small, red, sporty—was unloaded in Washington and put on a truck. I rode with it to a dealer in San Francisco, where I bought the car. Then I drove it to a port and put it, and me as well, onto a Norwegian passenger liner bound for Australia. Ten days later, I unloaded and drove the car to the cliff face and the young excavator operator.

"Here," I said to him, pointing at the car. "This is what your bucketful of iron ore made." He was astonished. Astonished

that I had come back to see him. Astonished that his pile of ore had been made into a car. But most astonished of all to learn that so many people—Chinese, Japanese, American, Norwegian—from so many countries had been involved in the process. "I guess we are all linked," he said. "Even if we never think we are."

SOURCE: ADAPTED FROM SIMON WINCHESTER, "HOW AMERICA CAN MAINTAIN ITS EDGE," *PARADE*, DECEMBER 21, 2008, P. 8.

Boxes

The boxes provide examples or expansions of the topics presented by highlighting leading companies practicing new, breakthrough ways to run their operations. Examples include:

- Understanding the Global Supply Chain, Chapter 1, page 6

- J. D. Power and Associates Initial Quality Study of New Cars, Chapter 9, page 291

- Capability Sourcing at 7-Eleven, Chapter 11, page 384

- Mr. Rounder Is On-Call at Hackensack University, Medical Center, Chapter 8, page 280

Examples with Solutions

Examples follow quantitative topics and demonstrate specific procedures and techniques. Clearly set off from the text, they help students understand the computations.

A series of detailed, worked-out solutions for every example in the text can be found on the text Web site which provides another level of detailed support for students.

EXAMPLE 4.1: Determining Capacity Requirements

The Stewart Company produces two flavors of salad dressings: Paul's and Newman's. Each is available in bottles and single-serving plastic bags. Management would like to determine equipment and labor requirements for the next five years.

Step by Step

SOLUTION

Step 1. Use forecasting techniques to predict sales for individual products within each product line. The marketing department, which is now running a promotional campaign for Newman's dressing, provided the following forecast demand values (in thousands) for the next five years. The campaign is expected to continue for the next two years.

	YEAR				
	1	2	3	4	5
Paul's					
Bottles (000s)	60	100	150	200	250
Plastic bags (000s)	100	200	300	400	500

Global

Global icons identify international examples and text discussion.

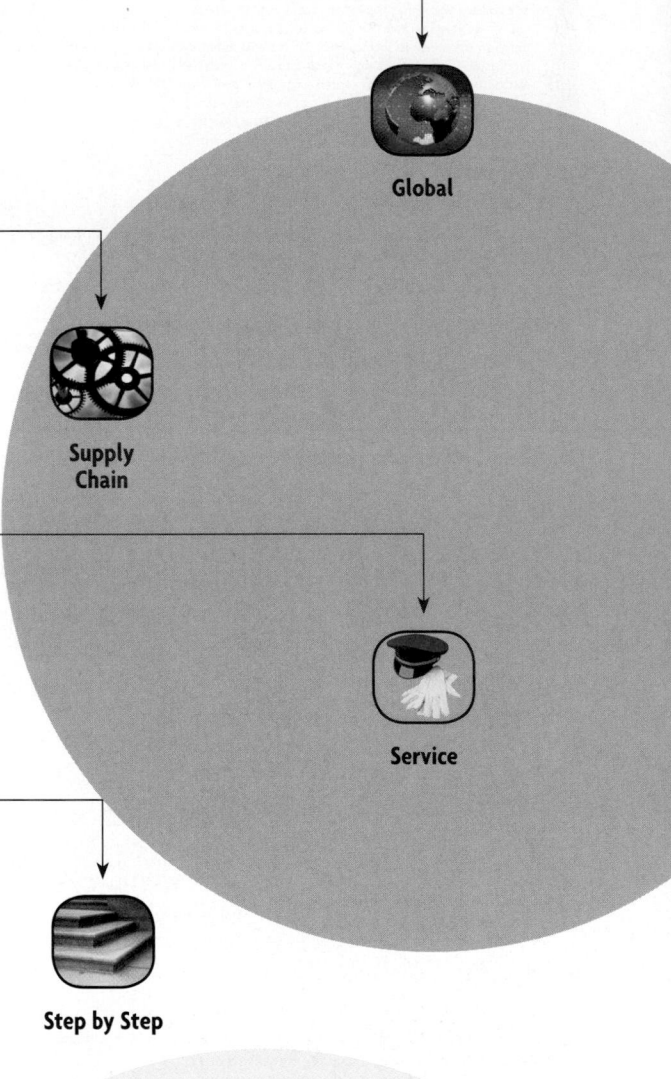

Global

Supply Chain

Supply chain icons highlight areas with a direct link to supply chain management.

Supply Chain

Services

Service icons alert students to examples that relate to services and service companies.

Service

Step by Step

Every example and solved problem in the book includes a step-by-step icon. They draw attention to detailed, worked-out solutions on the text Web site.

Step by Step

Excel

Excel icons point out concepts where Excel templates are available on the text Web site.

Excel

Tutorials

The tutorial icons highlight links to the ScreenCam tutorials on the text Web site.

Tutorial

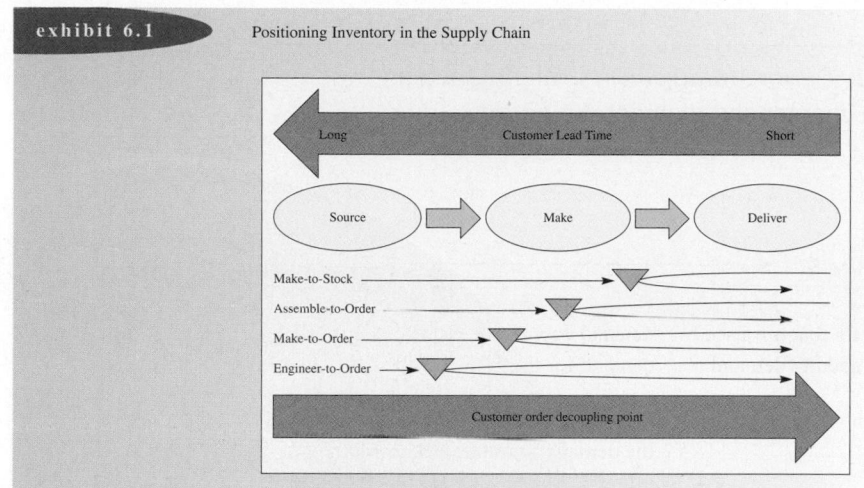

exhibit 6.1   Positioning Inventory in the Supply Chain

Photos and Exhibits

Over sixty photos and two hundred exhibits are included in the text to enhance the visual appeal and clarify text discussions. Many of the photos illustrate additional examples of companies that utilize the operations and supply chain concepts in their business.

TOYOTA'S DESIGN TEAM AT THEIR CALTY DESIGN RESEARCH FACILITIES IN CALIFORNIA. FROM CONCEPT TO COMPETITION VEHICLES, EACH TEAM MEMBER IS CONSIDERED AS IMPORTANT AS THE VEHICLES THEY DESIGN. CALTY PROVIDES DESIGN SOLUTIONS FOR TOYOTA, LEXUS AND SCION PRODUCT DEVELOPMENT.

Solved Problems

Representative problems are placed at the end of appropriate chapters. Each includes a worked-out solution giving students a review before solving problems on their own.

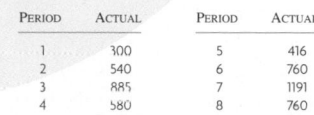

SOLVED PROBLEMS

SOLVED PROBLEM 1

Here are quarterly data for the past two years. From these data, prepare a forecast for the upcoming year using decomposition.

Excel:
Forecasting

PERIOD	ACTUAL	PERIOD	ACTUAL
1	300	5	416
2	540	6	760
3	885	7	1191
4	580	8	760

Solution

(Note that the values you obtain may be slightly different due to rounding. The values given here were obtained using an Excel spreadsheet.)

(1) PERIOD x	(2) ACTUAL y	(3) PERIOD AVERAGE	(4) SEASONAL FACTOR	(5) DESEASONALIZED DEMAND

Key Terms

The vocabulary of *Operations and Supply Chain Management* is highlighted in the Key Terms section at the end of each chapter and includes definitions.

KEY TERMS

Strategic forecasts Medium and long-term forecasts that are used to make decisions related to design and plans for meeting demand.

Tactical forecasts Short-term forecasts used as input for making day-to-day decisions related to meeting demand.

Dependent demand Requirements for a product or service caused by the demand for other products or services. This type of internal demand does not need a forecast, but can be calculated based on the demand for the other products or services.

Independent demand Demand that cannot be directly derived from the demand for other products.

Time series analysis A type of forecast in which data relating to past demand are used to predict future demand.

Formula Reviews

These lists at the end of chapters summarize formulas in one spot for easy student access and review.

FORMULA REVIEW

Least squares regression

$$Y = a + bx \qquad\qquad [15.1]$$

$$a = \bar{y} - b\bar{x} \qquad\qquad [15.2]$$

$$b = \frac{\Sigma xy - n\bar{x}\cdot\bar{y}}{\Sigma x^2 - n\bar{x}^2} \qquad\qquad [15.3]$$

Standard error of estimate

$$S_{yx} = \sqrt{\frac{\sum_{i=1}^{n}(y_i - Y_i)^2}{n - 2}} \qquad\qquad [15.4]$$

Super Quiz

Designed to allow students to see how well they understand the material using a format that is similar to what they might see in an exam. The super quiz includes many straightforward review questions, but also has a selection which tests for mastery and integration/application level understanding, that is, the kind of questions that make an exam challenging. The super quizzes include short answers at the bottom so students can see how they perform.

SUPER QUIZ

1   The level of capacity for which a process was designed and at which it operates at minimum cost.

2   A facility has a maximum capacity of 4,000 units per day using overtime and skipping the daily maintenance routine. At 3,500 units per day, the facility operates at a level where average cost per unit is minimized. Currently, the process is scheduled to operate at a level of 3,000 units per day. What is the capacity utilization rate?

3   The concept that relates to gaining efficiency through the full utilization of dedicated resources such as people and equipment.

4   A facility that limits its production to a single product or a set of very similar products.

5   Term that describes when multiple (usually similar) products can be produced in a facility less expensively than a single product.

6   We have this when we have the ability to serve more customers than we expect to have to serve.

7   In considering a capacity expansion we have two alternatives. The first alternative is expected to cost $1,000,000 and has an expected profit of $500,000 over the next three years. The second alternative has an expected cost of $800,000 and expected profit of $450,000 over the next three years. Which alternative should we select and what is the expected value of the expansion? Assume a 10 percent interest rate.

8   In a service process such as the checkout counter in a discount store, a good target for capacity utilization is about this percent.

1. Best operating level 2. 85% 3. Economies of scale 4. Focused factory 5. Economies of scope 6. Capacity cushion 7. Alternative 1 Present Value = 500,000 × (.909 + .826 + .751) − 1,000,000 = $243,000, Alternative 2 Present Value = 450,000 × (.909 + .826 + .751) − 800,000 = $318,700, Alternative 2 is best 8. 70 percent

Text Web Site

 The text Web site, our Online Learning Center (OLC), can be found at www.mhhe.com/jacobs13e. It includes a variety of material to help students succeed in the course. These assets include:

- Excel templates

- Online quizzes

- PowerPoint presentations

- Step-by-step solutions to examples

- ScreenCam tutorials

- Chapter outlines

- Updates

- Interactive Operations Management

- Web links

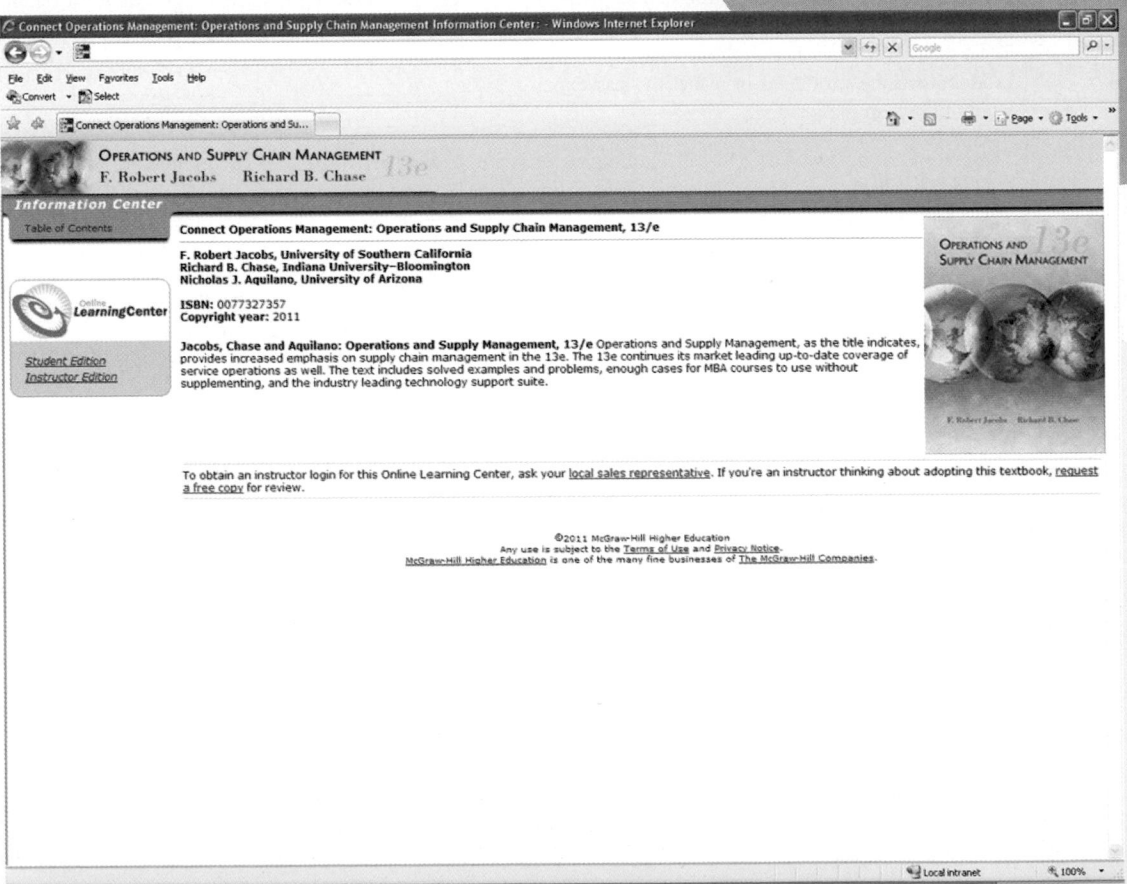

For Instructors

Instructor CD-ROM

The Instructor Resource CD provides PowerPoint slides, Excel templates, text figures, Operations Supply Chain Framework PowerPoint slides, and digital versions of the teaching supplements including the Test Bank (in Word) and the E-Z Test Computerized Testing System, Instructor's Solutions Manual, and Instructor's Resource Manual.

Text Web Site

Text Online Learning Center (OLC) at www.mhhe.com/jacobs13e. The text Web site includes a variety of material for instructors and students.

Student Web Site

Online quizzes
Excel templates
PowerPoint presentations
ScreenCam tutorials
Chapter outlines
Step-by-step solutions to text examples
Updates
Interactive Operations Management

Instructor Site

Instructor's Resource Manual
Test Bank
Instructor PowerPoint Slides
Instructor Solutions Manual
Map to Harvard Cases
OSCM Framework PowerPoints

OMC

The Operations Management Center at www.mhhe.com/pom offers a wealth of
edited and organized OM resources including links to Operations Management
BusinessWeek articles, OM Organizations, and virtual tours of operations in real
companies.

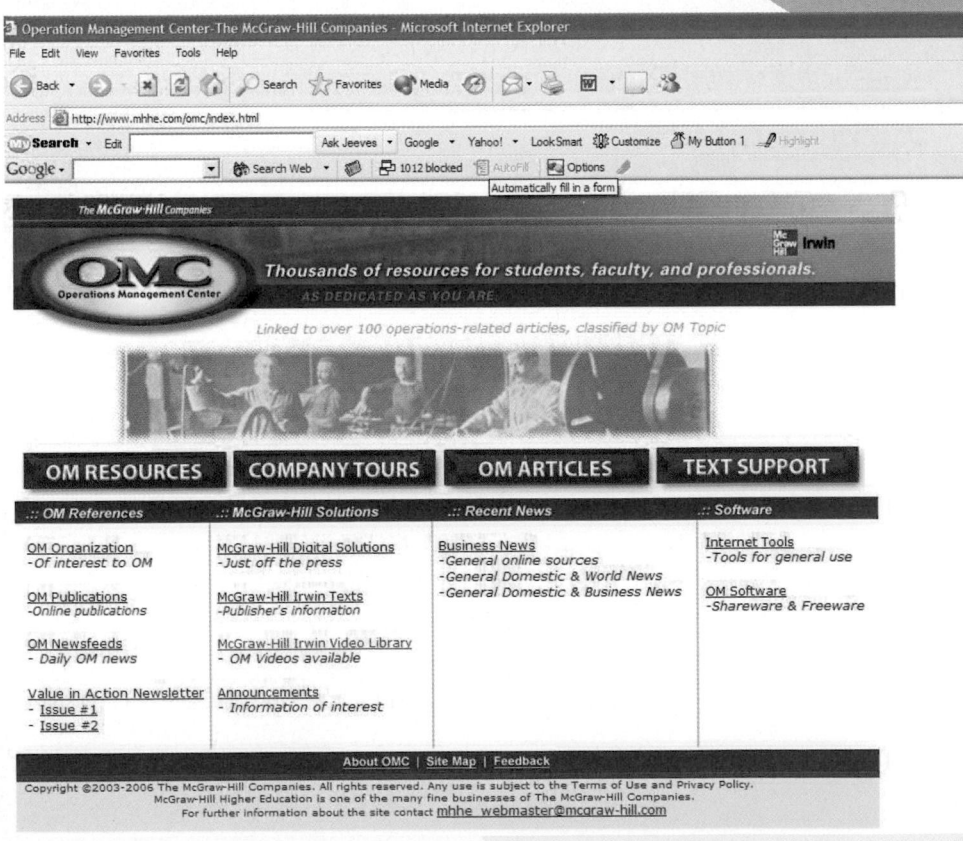

Student Operations Management Video DVD

These fifteen videos cover topics such as service at Zappos.com, project management at Six Flags, supply chain management and supplier partnering at Ford, Burton Snowboards, and Noodles and Company, special services at FedEx, the development of Honda's new "green" Civic, and several others. This DVD can be packaged free with the text.

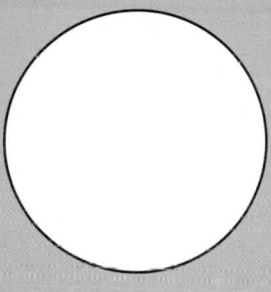

Student Operations Management Video DVD to accompany

Operations and Supply Chain Management

F. ROBERT JACOBS | RICHARD B. CHASE
Thirteenth Edition

Installation Instructions:
This DVD will autostart on most machines equipped with viable DVD player and system applications.

System Requirements:
DVD drive with software capable of playing a DVD-Video disc or a DVD-Video player that is capable of playing DVD+/−R, DVD+/−RW, or DVD+DL discs

OPERATIONS AND
SUPPLY CHAIN MANAGEMENT
13e

F. Robert Jacobs   Richard B. Chase

ISBN 978-0-07-732740-8
MHID 0-07-732740-3

McGraw-Hill Irwin   DVD VIDEO

ScreenCam Tutorials

These screen "movies" and voice over tutorials demonstrate chapter content using Excel and other software platforms.

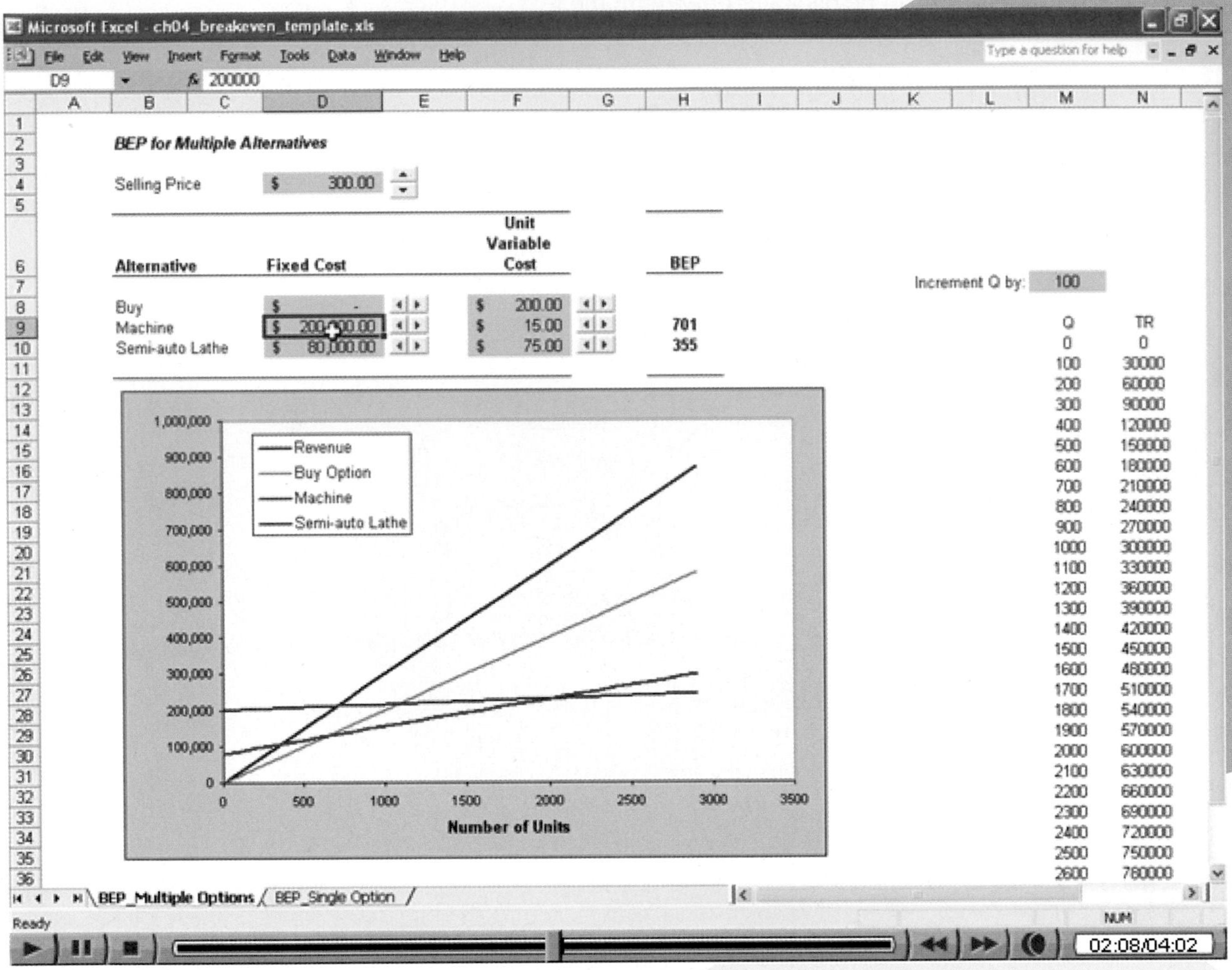

**Tutorial:
Break-Even
Analysis**

Step by Step

EXAMPLE 6.1: Break-Even Analysis

Suppose a manufacturer has identified the following options for obtaining a machined part: It can buy the part at $200 per unit (including materials); it can make the part on a numerically controlled semiautomatic lathe at $75 per unit (including materials); or it can make the part on a machining center at $15 per unit (including materials). There is negligible fixed cost if the item is purchased; a semiautomatic lathe costs $80,000; and a machining center costs $200,000.

The total cost for each option is

$$\text{Purchase cost} = \$200 \times \text{Demand}$$

$$\text{Produce-using-lathe cost} = \$80,000 + \$75 \times \text{Demand}$$

$$\text{Produce-using-machining-center cost} = \$200,000 + \$15 \times \text{Demand}$$

Excel Icon

An icon in the margin indicates there is a spreadsheet available on the text Web site.

Break-Even Chart of Alternative Processes

exhibit 6.3

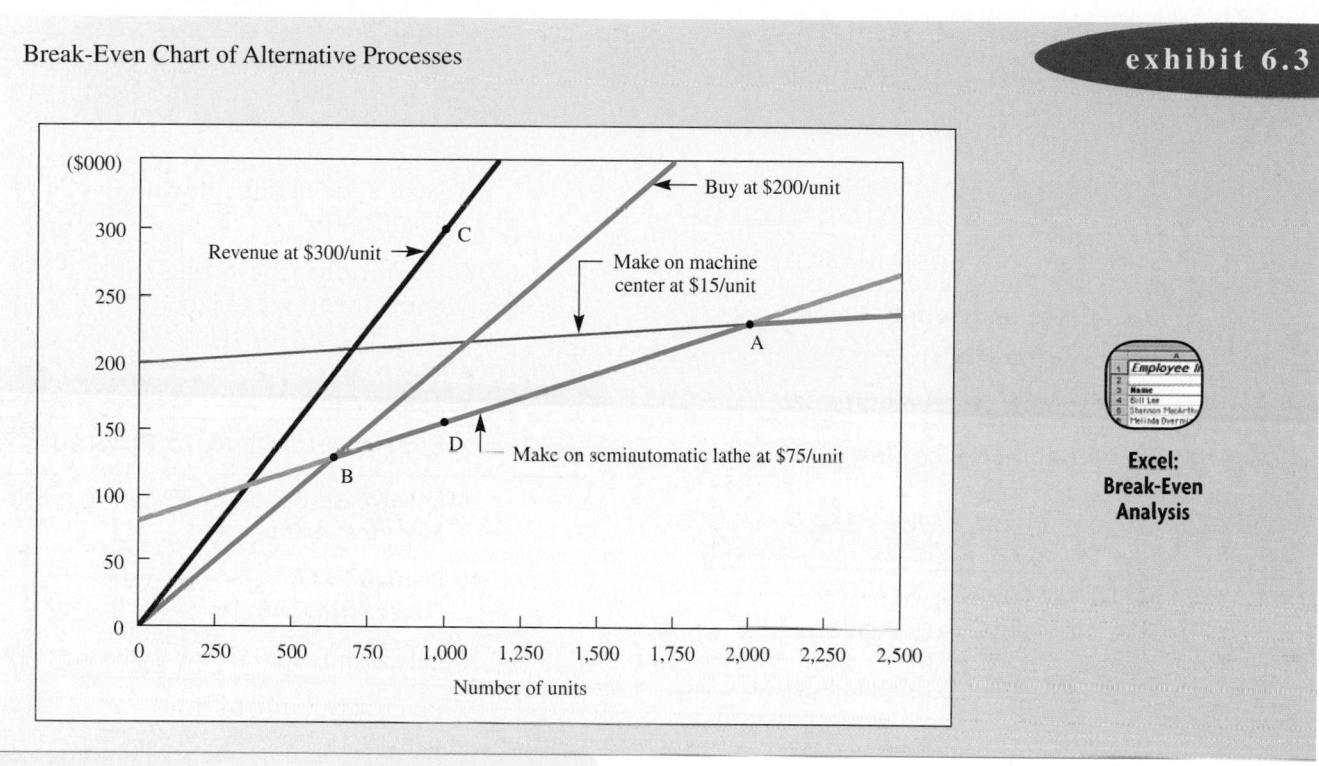

Excel:
Break-Even
Analysis

CONTENTS IN BRIEF

Contents

Section Two

Manufacturing, Service, and Health Care Processes

SECTION THREE

SUPPLY CHAIN PROCESSES

SECTION FOUR

SUPPLY AND DEMAND PLANNING

Section Five

Scheduling

APPENDICES

section 1

STRATEGY AND SUSTAINABILITY

TWENTY-FIRST-CENTURY OPERATIONS AND SUPPLY MANAGEMENT

Managing a modern supply chain involves specialists in manufacturing, purchasing, and distribution, of course. However, today it is also vital to the work of chief financial officers, chief information officers, operations and customer service executives, and chief executives. Changes in operations and supply management have been truly revolutionary, and the pace of progress shows no sign of moderating. In our increasingly interconnected and interdependent global economy, the process of delivering supplies and finished goods from one place to another is accomplished by means of mind-boggling technological innovation, clever new applications of old ideas, seemingly magical mathematics, powerful software, and old-fashioned concrete, steel, and muscle.

In the first section of *Operations and Supply Management,* we lay a foundation for understanding the dynamic field of operations and supply management. This book is about designing and operating processes that deliver a firm's goods and services in a manner that matches customers' expectations. Really successful firms have a clear and unambiguous idea of how they intend to make money. Be it high-end products or services that are custom-tailored to the needs of a single customer or generic inexpensive commodities that are bought largely on the basis of cost, competitively producing and distributing these products is a great challenge.

chapter 1

OPERATIONS AND SUPPLY CHAIN MANAGEMENT

QUICK SUPPLY CHAINS ENABLE RETAILERS TO GET FASHIONS TO MARKET QUICKLY

Retailers now know that to keep earnings high they need to get the latest fashions into their stores as quickly as possible. Chains ranging from JC Penney to J. Crew scramble to make their orders more precise, so they can stock just enough of the hottest styles for today's increasingly fickle and tight-fisted consumers. Advances in software and technology allow stores to offer the latest trends weeks or even months faster than before and give these retailers more stable profitability. The analysts at Piper Jaffray, a consulting company, say that profit margins have improved at such retailers as Abercrombie & Fitch, Gap, Aéropostale, and Kohl's due to these technology advances.

After reading this chapter you will:

1. Understand why it is important to study operations and supply chain management.
2. Define efficient and effective operations.
3. Categorize operations and supply chain processes.
4. Contrast differences between services and goods producing processes.
5. Identify operations and supply chain management career opportunities.
6. Describe how the field has developed over time.

Efficient logistics have taken on a whole new level of importance. Until recently, many stores were still using the phone and fax machines to place big orders, a very manual and slow, error-prone process. Now, software lets designers, buyers, and manufacturers view the same fabric swatch or color at the same time, thereby eliminating the need to fly designers around the globe or to send overnight packages. By quickly moving the most desirable items into stores, retailers can also ease their reliance on price markdowns, which cut into earnings. They can also order less merchandise and order more often. This lets them adjust orders more easily once certain styles or sizes fail to sell.

SOURCE: ADAPTED FROM JAYNE O'DONNELL, "STORES GET FASHIONS TO MARKET LICKETY-SPLIT," *USA TODAY*, MAY 29, 2000, P. 1B.

The goal is to have the right product at the right place at the right time. In these competitive times, fashion retailers, in particular, need to be agile and flexible. They cannot afford to carry excess inventory, and thus the ability to react to what is selling is as important as customers demand the most innovative and current products. So today's leading retailers are using operations and supply chain management techniques to match supply and demand as closely and quickly as possible. They refer to the strategy as minimizing "concept-to-cash" time and work to minimize the time between the appearance of a fashion concept and the time they start receiving revenue from the sales of that concept.

WHAT IS OPERATIONS AND SUPPLY CHAIN MANAGEMENT?

Operations and supply chain management (OSCM)

Service

Operations and supply chain management (OSCM) is defined as the design, operation, and improvement of the systems that create and deliver the firm's primary products and services. Like marketing and finance, OSCM is a functional field of business with clear line management responsibilities. OSCM is concerned with the management of the entire system that produces a good or delivers a service. Producing a product such as the Men's Nylon Supplex Parka or providing a service such as a cellular phone account involves a complex series of transformation processes.

Exhibit 1.1 shows a supply network for a Men's Nylon Supplex Parka sold on Web sites such as L.L. Bean or Land's End. We can understand the network by looking at the four color-coded paths. The blue path traces the activities needed to produce the Polartec insulation material used in the parkas. Polartec insulation is purchased in bulk, processed to get the proper finish, and then dyed prior to being checked for consistency—or grading—and color. It is then stored in a warehouse. The red path traces the production of the nylon Supplex used in the parkas. Using petroleum-based polymer, the nylon is extruded and drawn into a yarnlike material. From here the green path traces the many steps required to fabricate the clothlike Supplex used to make the parkas. The yellow path shows the Supplex and Polartec material coming together and used to assemble the lightweight and warm parka. The completed parkas are sent to a warehouse and then on to the retailer's distribution center. The parkas are then picked and packed for shipment to individual customers. Think of the supply network as a pipeline through which material and information flows. There are key locations in the pipeline where material and information is stored for future use: Polartec is stored near the end of the blue pipeline; Supplex is stored near the end of the red pipeline. In both cases, fabric is cut prior to merging with the yellow pipeline. At the beginning of the yellow path, bundles of Supplex and Polartec are stored prior to their use in the fabrication of the parkas. At the end of the yellow path are the distribution steps which involve storing to await orders, picking according to actual customer order, packing, and finally shipping to the final customer.

Networks such as this can be constructed for any product or service. Typically each part of the network is controlled by different companies including the nylon Supplex producer, the Polartec producer, the parka manufacturer, and the catalog sales retailer. All of the material is moved using transportation providers, ships

exhibit 1.1

Process Steps for Men's Nylon Supplex Parka

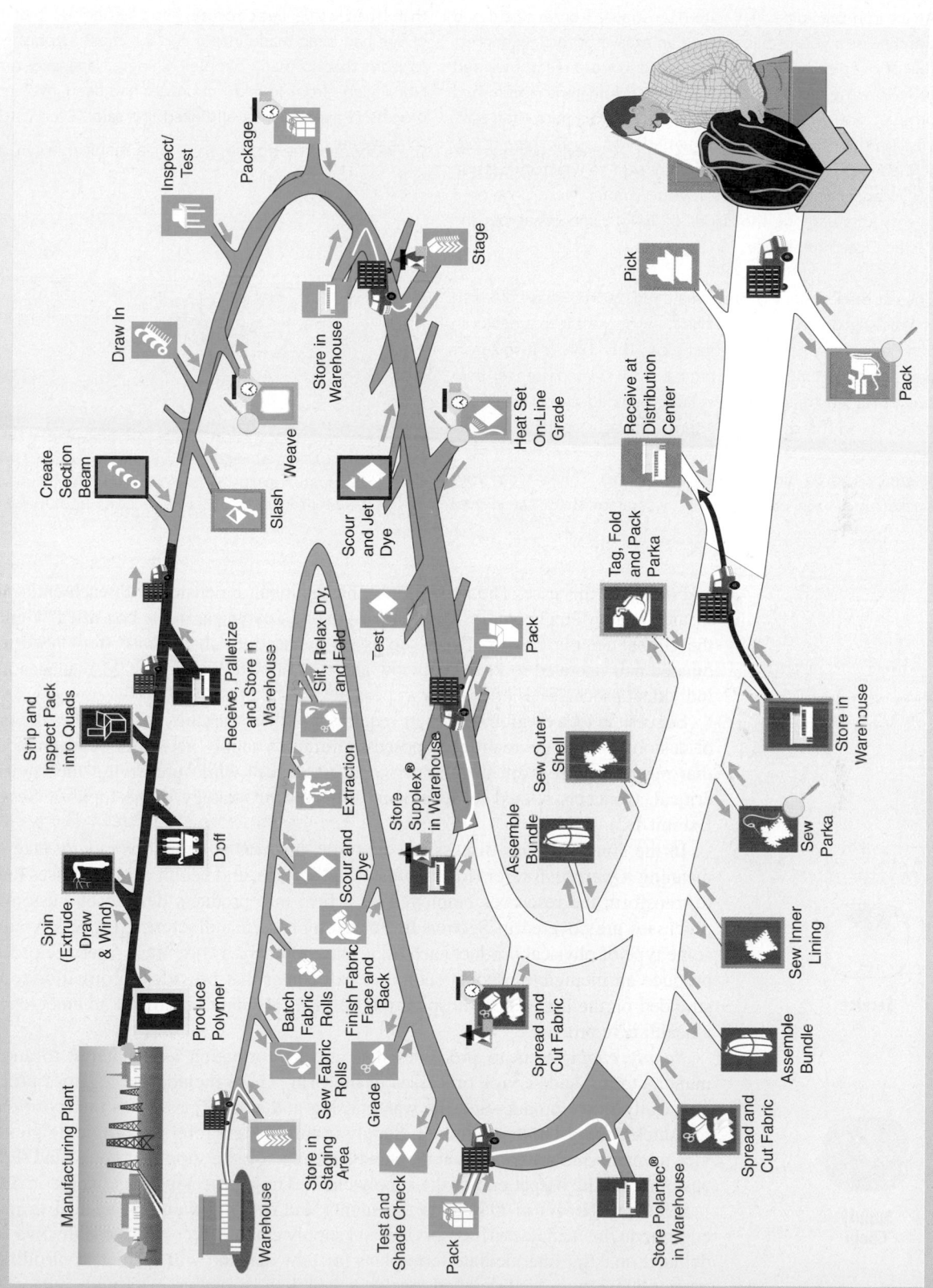

UNDERSTANDING THE GLOBAL SUPPLY CHAIN

At an iron-ore mine in Western Australia, I once stood and watched as a young man worked an excavator to claw bucketfuls of deep-red ore from the ground. For a project, I wanted to follow the ore on its journey from raw material to finished product. So I went on a train that took it to a port, then traveled on the Chinese ship that carried it to Japan. There it was refined into steel ingots, which were sent to a factory outside Tokyo and fashioned into a Toyota Corolla. Next I got on a mighty ship carrying thousands of Toyota imports across the Pacific Ocean to Seattle.

The car made from my ore—small, red, sporty—was unloaded in Washington and put on a truck. I rode with it to a dealer in San Francisco, where I bought the car. Then I drove it to a port and put it, and me as well, onto a Norwegian passenger liner bound for Australia. Ten days later, I unloaded and drove the car to the cliff face and the young excavator operator.

"Here," I said to him, pointing at the car. "This is what your bucketful of iron ore made." He was astonished. Astonished that I had come back to see him. Astonished that his pile of ore had been made into a car. But most astonished of all to learn that so many people—Chinese, Japanese, American, Norwegian—from so many countries had been involved in the process. "I guess we are all linked," he said. "Even if we never think we are."

SOURCE: ADAPTED FROM SIMON WINCHESTER, "HOW AMERICA CAN MAINTAIN ITS EDGE," *PARADE*, DECEMBER 21, 2008, P. 8.

and trucks in this case. The network also has a global dimension with each entity potentially located in a different country. Trace the origin of a Toyota car in the box titled "Understanding the Global Supply Chain." For a successful transaction, all of these steps need to be coordinated and operated to keep costs low and to minimize waste. OSCM manages all of these individual processes as effectively as possible.

Success in today's global markets requires a business strategy that matches the preferences of customers with the realities imposed by complex supply networks. A sustainable strategy that meets the needs of shareholders and employees while preserving the environment is critical. Concepts related to developing this type of strategy is the topic of Section I (see Exhibit 1.2).

In the context of our discussion, the terms *operations* and *supply chain* take on special meaning. *Operations* refers to manufacturing, service, and health care processes that are used to transform the resources employed by a firm into products desired by customers. These processes are covered in Section II. For example, a manufacturing process would produce some type of physical product such as an automobile or a computer. A service process would produce an intangible product such as a call center that provides information to customers stranded on the highway. A hospital that services accident victims in an emergency room is a health care process.

Supply chain refers to processes that move information and material to and from the manufacturing and service processes of the firm. These include the logistics processes that physically move product and the warehousing and storage processes that position products for quick delivery to the customer. Supply in this context refers to providing goods and service to plants and warehouses at the input end, and also the supply of goods and service to the customer on the output end of the supply chain. These processes are covered in Section III.

Another element of OSCM is the supply and demand planning needed to manage and coordinate the manufacturing, service, and supply chain processes. These involve forecasting demand, making intermediate-term plans for how demand will be met, controlling different types of inventory, and detailed weekly scheduling of processes. Topics related to this are covered in Section IV.

All managers should understand the basic principles that guide the design of transformation processes. This includes understanding how different types of processes are organized,

Service

Supply Chain

Organization of OSCM: The Integration of Strategy, Processes and Planning

exhibit 1.2

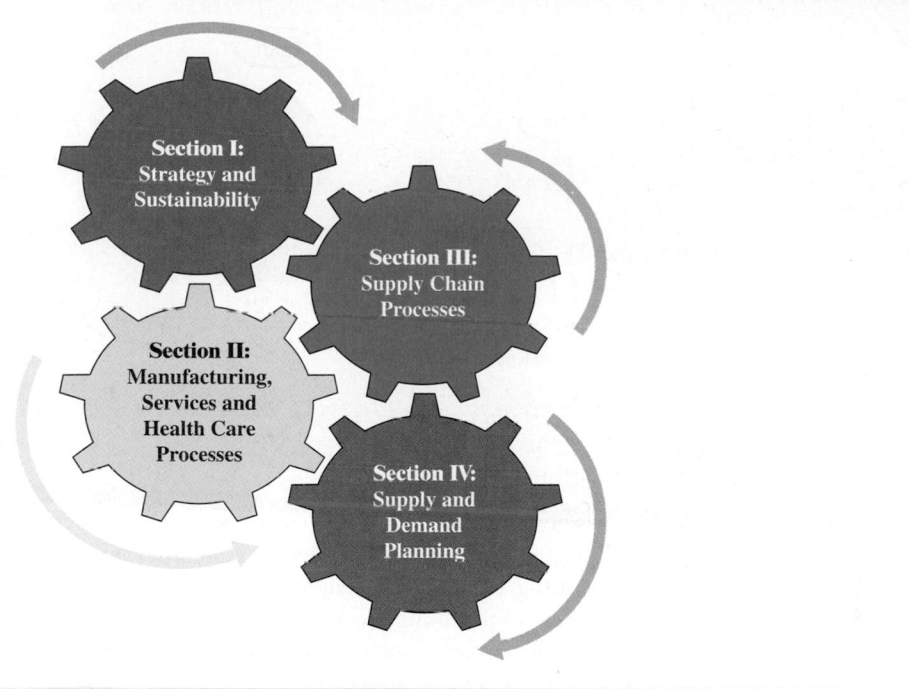

how to determine the capacity of a process, how long it should take a process to make a unit, how the quality of a process is monitored, and how planning information systems are used to coordinate these processes.

The field of operations and supply management is ever changing due to the dynamic nature of competing in global business and the constant evolution of information technology. So while many of the basic concepts have been around for many years, their application in new and innovative ways is exciting. Internet technology has made the sharing of reliable real-time information inexpensive. Capturing information directly from the source through such systems as point-of-sale, radio-frequency identification tags, bar-code scanners, and automatic recognition has changed the focus to one of understanding what all the information is saying and how good decisions can be made using it.

OPERATIONS AND SUPPLY CHAIN PROCESSES

Operations and supply chain processes can be conveniently categorized, particularly from the view of a producer of consumer products and services, as planning, sourcing, making, delivering, and returning. Exhibit 1.3 depicts where the processes are used in different parts of a supply chain. The following describes the work involved in each type of process.

1. **Planning** consists of the processes needed to operate an existing supply chain strategically. Here a firm must determine how anticipated demand will be met with available resources. A major aspect of planning is developing a set of metrics to monitor the supply chain so that it is efficient and delivers high quality and value to customers.
2. **Sourcing** involves the selection of suppliers that will deliver the goods and services needed to create the firm's product. A set of pricing, delivery, and payment processes is needed together with metrics for monitoring and improving the relationships between

exhibit 1.3   Supply Chain Processes

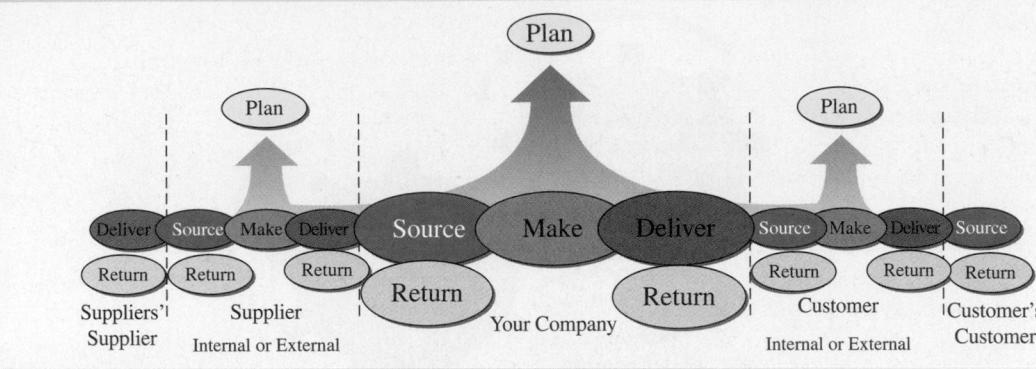

partners of the firm. These processes include receiving shipments, verifying them, transferring them to manufacturing facilities, and authorizing supplier payments.

3. **Making** is where the major product is produced or the service provided. The step requires scheduling processes for workers and the coordination of material and other critical resources such as equipment to support producing or providing the service. Metrics that measure speed, quality, and worker productivity are used to monitor these processes.

4. **Delivering** is also referred to as logistics processes. Carriers are picked to move products to warehouses and customers, coordinate and schedule the movement of goods and information through the supply network, develop and operate a network of warehouses, and run the information systems that manage the receipt of orders from customers, and invoicing systems to collect payments from customers.

5. **Returning** involves the processes for receiving worn-out, defective, and excess products back from customers and support for customers who have problems with delivered products. In the case of services, this may involve all types of follow-up activities that are required for after-sales support.

To understand the topic it is important to consider the many different players that need to coordinate work in a typical supply chain. The aforementioned steps of planning, sourcing, making, delivering, and returning are fine for manufacturing and can also be used for the many processes that do not involve the discrete movement and production of parts. In the case of a service firm such as a hospital, for example, supplies are typically delivered on a daily basis from drug and health care suppliers and require coordination between drug companies, local warehouse operations, local delivery services, and hospital receiving. Patients need to be scheduled into the services provided by the hospital such as operations and blood tests. Other areas, such as the emergency room, need to be staffed to provide service on demand. The orchestration of all of these activities is critical to providing quality service at a reasonable cost.

Service

DIFFERENCES BETWEEN SERVICES AND GOODS

Service

There are five essential differences between services and goods. The first is that a service is an *intangible* process that cannot be weighed or measured, whereas a good is a tangible output of a process that has physical dimensions. This distinction has important business implications since a service innovation, unlike a product innovation, cannot be patented. Thus, a company with a new concept must expand rapidly before competitors copy its procedures. Service intangibility also presents a problem for customers since, unlike with a physical product, they cannot try it out and test it before purchase.

The second is that a service requires some degree of *interaction with the customer* for it to be a service. The interaction may be brief, but it must exist for the service to be complete. Where face-to-face service is required, the service facility must be designed to handle the customer's presence. Goods, on the other hand, are generally produced in a facility separate from the customer. They can be made according to a production schedule that is efficient for the company.

The third is that services, with the big exception of hard technologies such as ATMs and information technologies such as answering machines and automated Internet exchanges, are inherently *heterogeneous*—they vary from day to day and even hour by hour as a function of the attitudes of the customer and the servers. Thus, even highly scripted work such as found in call centers can produce unpredictable outcomes. Goods, in contrast, can be produced to meet very tight specifications day-in and day-out with essentially zero variability. In those cases where a defective good is produced, it can be reworked or scrapped.

The fourth is that services as a process are *perishable and time dependent,* and unlike goods, they can't be stored. You cannot "come back last week" for an air flight or a day on campus.

And fifth, the specifications of a service are defined and evaluated as a *package of features* that affect the five senses. These features are

- Supporting facility (location, decoration, layout, architectural appropriateness, supporting equipment).
- Facilitating goods (variety, consistency, quantity of the physical goods that go with the service; for example, the food items that accompany a meal service).
- Explicit services (training of service personnel, consistency of service performance, availability and access to the service, and comprehensiveness of the service).
- Implicit services (attitude of the servers, atmosphere, waiting time, status, privacy and security, and convenience).

THE GOODS–SERVICES CONTINUUM

Most any product offering is a combination of goods and services. In Exhibit 1.4, we show this arrayed along a continuum of "pure goods" to "pure services." The continuum captures the main focus of the business and spans from firms that just produce products to those that only provide services. Pure goods industries have become low-margin commodity businesses, and in order to differentiate, they are often adding some services. Some examples are providing help with logistical aspects of stocking items, maintaining extensive information databases, and providing consulting advice.

Service

The Goods–Services Continuum

exhibit 1.4

Pure Goods	Core Goods	Core Services	Pure Services
Food products	Appliances	Hotels	Teaching
Chemicals	Data storage systems	Airlines	Medical advice
Book publishing	Automobiles	Internet service providers	Financial consulting

Goods ◄───► Services

SOURCE: ANDERS GUSTOFSSON AND MICHAEL D. JOHNSON, *COMPETING IN A SERVICE ECONOMY* (SAN FRANCISCO: JOSSEY-BASS, 2003), P. 7.

Core goods providers already provide a significant service component as part of their businesses. For example, automobile manufacturers provide extensive spare parts distribution services to support repair centers at dealers.

Core service providers must integrate tangible goods. For example, your cable television company must provide cable hookup and repair services and also high-definition cable boxes. Pure services, such as may be offered by a financial consulting firm, may need little in the way of facilitating goods, but what they do use—such as textbooks, professional references, and spreadsheets—are critical to their performance.

SERVITIZATION STRATEGIES

Service

Servitization refers to a company building service activities into its product offerings for its current users, that is, its installed base. Such services include maintenance, spare part provisioning, training, and in some cases, total systems design and R&D. A well-known pioneer in this area is IBM, which treats its business as a service business and views physical goods as a small part of the "business solutions" it provides its customers. Companies that are most successful in implementing this strategy start by drawing together the service aspects of the business under one roof in order to create a consolidated service organization. The service evolves from a focus on enhancing the product's performance to developing systems and product modifications that support the company's move up the "value stream" into new markets. A servitization strategy might not be the best approach for all product companies, however. A recent study found that while servitized firms generate higher revenues, they tend to generate lower profits as a percentage of revenues when compared to focused firms. This is because they are often unable to generate revenues or margins high enough to cover the additional investment required to cover service-related costs.

GROWTH OF SERVICES

Service

The dominance of services throughout the world economies is clearly evident in Exhibit 1.5. Looking first at the United States, in 1800, 90 percent of the labor force was working on farms doing agriculture production. Today only 3 percent of the U.S. labor force is involved in agriculture production. This represents over a one-million-times productivity increase in about 200 years. Manufacturing peaked in the 1950s and, due to automation and outsourcing, now employs only about 27 percent of the U.S. labor force.

The shift toward services is not simply a U.S. phenomenon, or a developed nation's phenomenon—the chart shows the top 10 nations of the world by size of their labor force: China is 21 percent of the world's labor force, and Germany is 1.4 percent of the world's labor force. China has seen its service sector grow by 191 percent in the last 25 years. Germany has seen its service sector grow by 44 percent in the last 25 years. The shift to services represents the single largest labor force migration in human history. Global communications, business and technology growth, urbanization, and low labor costs in the developing world are all responsible for this dramatic shift. The world is becoming a giant service system, composed of six billion people, millions of businesses, and millions of technology products connected into service networks.

TWO OF THE LEADING EUROPEAN BANKS EXEMPLIFY THE GROWTH OF THE SERVICE INDUSTRY WORLDWIDE.

International Growth in Service

exhibit 1.5

Service

Global

Nation	Percent Worldwide Labor	Percent Agriculture	Percent Manufacturing	Percent Services	25-Year Growth in Services
China	21.0%	50.0%	15.0%	35.0%	191.0%
India	17.0	60.0	17.0	23.0	28.0
U.S.	4.8	3.0	27.0	70.0	21.0
Indonesia	3.9	45.0	16.0	39.0	35.0
Brazil	3.0	23.0	24.0	53.0	20.0
Russia	2.5	12.0	23.0	65.0	38.0
Japan	2.4	5.0	25.0	70.0	40.0
Nigeria	2.2	70.0	10.0	20.0	30.0
Bangladesh	2.2	63.0	11.0	26.0	30.0
Germany	1.4	3.0	33.0	64.0	44.0

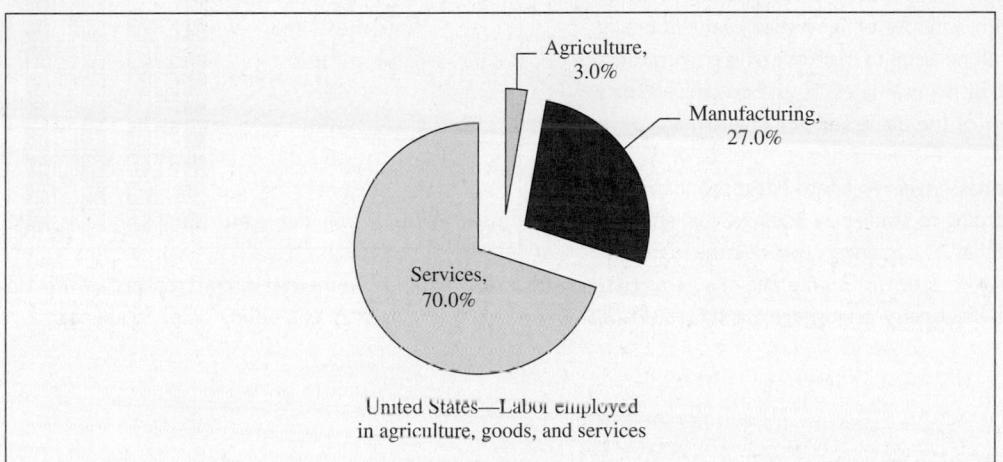

Agriculture, 3.0%

Manufacturing, 27.0%

Services, 70.0%

United States—Labor employed in agriculture, goods, and services

EFFICIENCY, EFFECTIVENESS, AND VALUE

Compared with most of the other ways managers try to stimulate growth—technology investments, acquisitions, and major market campaigns, for example—innovations in operations are relatively reliable and low cost. As a business student, you are perfectly positioned to come up with innovative operations-related ideas. You understand the big picture of all the processes that generate the costs and support the cash flow essential to the firm's long-term viability.

Through this book, you will become aware of the concepts and tools now being employed by companies around the world as they craft efficient and effective operations. Efficiency means doing something at the lowest possible cost. Later in the book we define this more thoroughly, but roughly speaking the goal of an efficient process is to produce a good or provide a service by using the smallest input of resources. Effectiveness means doing the right things to create the most value for the company. Often maximizing effectiveness and efficiency at the same time creates conflict between the two goals. We see this trade-off every day in our lives. At the customer service counter at a local store or bank, being efficient means using the fewest people possible at the counter. Being effective, though, means minimizing the amount of time customers need to wait in line. Related to efficiency and effectiveness is the concept of value, which can be metaphorically defined as quality divided by price. If you

Efficiency

Effectiveness

Service

Value

UNDERSTAND OPERATIONS

EFFICIENCY: IT'S THE DETAILS THAT COUNT

Getting passengers on a plane quickly can greatly affect an airline's costs. Southwest says that if its boarding times increased by 10 minutes per flight, it would need 40 more planes at a cost of $40 million each to run the same number of flights it does currently.

Not all the innovation in the airline industry is from Southwest. US Airways, working with researchers at Arizona State University, has developed an innovative boarding system called "reverse pyramid." The first economy-class passengers to get on the plane are those with window seats in the middle and rear of the plane. Then US Airways gradually fills in the plane, giving priority to those with window or rear seats, until it finally boards those seated along aisles in the front. This is in contrast to the approach used by many airlines of just boarding all seats starting from the back of the plane and working forward.

The time it takes for passengers to board has more than doubled since 1970, according to studies by Boeing Co. A study in the mid-1960s found that 20 passengers boarded the plane per minute. Today that figure is down to nine per minute as passengers bring along heftier carry-on luggage. Both Boeing and

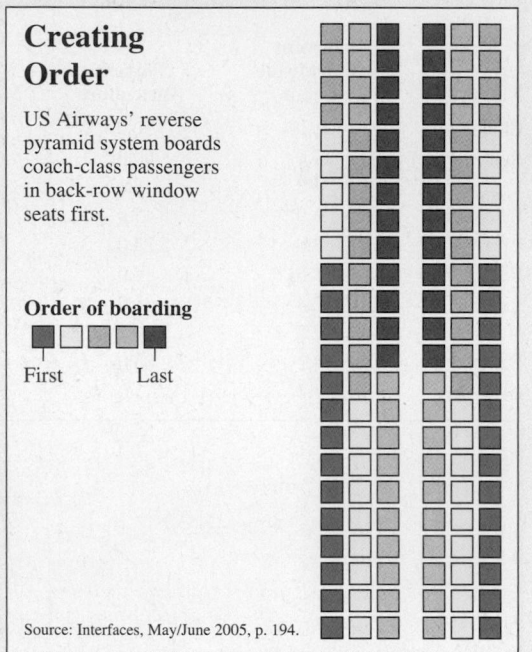

Creating Order

US Airways' reverse pyramid system boards coach-class passengers in back-row window seats first.

Order of boarding

First   Last

Source: Interfaces, May/June 2005, p. 194.

Airbus, the two top commercial-aircraft makers, are working on improving boarding time as a selling point to airlines.

can provide the customer with a better car without changing price, value has gone up. If you can give the customer a better car at a *lower* price, value goes way up. A major objective of this book is to show how smart management can achieve high levels of value.

CAREERS IN OPERATIONS AND SUPPLY CHAIN MANAGEMENT

Service

So what do people who pursue careers in operations and supply chain management do? Quite simply, they specialize in managing the production of goods and services. Jobs abound for people who can do this well since every organization is dependent on effective performance of this fundamental activity for its long-term success.

It is interesting to contrast entry-level jobs in operations and supply management to marketing and finance jobs. Many marketing entry-level jobs focus on actually selling products or managing the sales of products. These individuals are out on the front line trying to push product to potential customers. Often a significant part of your income will depend on commissions from these sales. Entry-level finance (and accounting) jobs are often in large public accounting firms. These jobs often involve working at a desk auditing transactions to ensure the accuracy of financial statements. Other assignments often involve the analysis of transactions to better understand the costs associated with the business.

Contrast the marketing and finance jobs to operations and supply chain management jobs. The operations and supply chain manager is out working with people to figure out the best way to deliver the goods and services of the firm. Sure, they work with the marketing folks, but rather than being on the selling side, they are on the buying side: trying to select the best materials and hiring the greatest talent. They will use the data generated by the finance people and analyze processes to figure out the best way to do things. Operations and supply chain management jobs are hands-on, working with people and figuring out the best way to do things.

The following are some typical management and staff jobs in operations and supply chain management:

- Plant manager—Oversees the workforce and physical resources (inventory, equipment, and information technology) required to produce the organization's product.
- Hospital administrator—Oversees human resource management, staffing, and finances at a health care facility.
- Branch manager (bank)—Oversees all aspects of financial transactions at a branch.
- Department store manager—Oversees all aspects of staffing and customer service at a store.
- Call center manager—Oversees staffing and customer service activities at a call center.
- Supply chain manager—Negotiates contracts with vendors and coordinates the flow of material inputs to the production process and the shipping of finished products to customers.
- Purchasing manager—Manages the day-to-day aspects of purchasing such as invoicing and follow-up.
- Business process improvement analyst—Applies the tools of lean production to reduce cycle time and eliminate waste in a process.
- Quality control manager—Applies techniques of statistical quality control such as acceptance sampling and control charts to the firm's products.
- Lean improvement manager—Trains organizational members in lean production and continuous improvement methods.

B R E A K T H R O U G H   B I O

TIMOTHY D. COOK, CHIEF OPERATING OFFICER, APPLE

Timothy D. Cook is Apple's chief operating officer and reports to Apple's CEO. Cook is responsible for all of the company's worldwide sales and operations, including end-to-end management of Apple's supply chain, sales activities, and service and support in all markets and countries. He also heads Apple's Macintosh division and plays a key role in the continued development of strategic reseller and supplier relationships, ensuring flexibility in response to an increasingly demanding marketplace.

Before joining Apple, Cook was vice president of corporate materials for Compaq and was responsible for procuring and managing all of Compaq's product inventory. Previous to his work at Compaq, Cook was the chief operating officer of the reseller division at Intelligent Electronics.

Cook also spent 12 years with IBM, most recently as director of North American fulfillment, where he led manufacturing and distribution functions for IBM's Personal Computer Company in North and Latin America. Cook earned an M.B.A. from Duke University, where he was a Fuqua Scholar, and a Bachelor of Science degree in Industrial Engineering from Auburn University.

- Project manager—Plans and coordinates staff activities such as new-product development, new-technology deployment, and new-facility location.
- Production control analyst—Plans and schedules day-to-day production.
- Facilities manager—Assures that the building facility design, layout, furniture, and other equipment are operating at peak efficiency.

CHIEF OPERATING OFFICER

So how far can you go in a career in operations and supply management? One goal would be to become the chief operating officer of a company. The chief operating officer (COO) works with the CEO and company president to determine the company's competitive strategy. The COO's ideas are filtered down through the rest of the company. COOs determine an organization's location, its facilities, which vendors to use, and how the hiring policy will be implemented. Once the key decisions are made, lower-level operations personnel carry them out. Operations personnel work to find solutions and then set about fixing the problems.

Managing the supply chain, service, and support are particularly challenging aspects of a chief operating officer's job at such innovative companies as Apple Computer. (See Breakthrough Bio on Timothy D. Cook of Apple.) Career opportunities in operations and supply management are plentiful today as companies strive to improve profitability by improving quality and productivity and reducing costs. The hands-on work of managing people is combined with great opportunities to leverage the latest technologies in getting the job done at companies around the world. No matter what you might do for a final career, your knowledge of operations and supply management will prove to be a great asset.

HISTORICAL DEVELOPMENT OF OPERATIONS AND SUPPLY CHAIN MANAGEMENT

Our purpose in this section is not to go through all the details of OSCM; that would require us to recount the entire Industrial Revolution. Rather, the focus is on major OSCM-related concepts that have been popular since the 1980s. Where appropriate, how a supposedly new idea relates to an older idea is discussed. (We seem to keep rediscovering the past.)

Lean Manufacturing, JIT, and TQC   The 1980s saw a revolution in the management philosophies and technologies by which production is carried out. Just-in-time (JIT) production was the major breakthrough in manufacturing philosophy. Pioneered by the Japanese, JIT is an integrated set of activities designed to achieve high-volume production using minimal inventories of parts that arrive at the workstation exactly when they are needed. The philosophy—coupled with total quality control (TQC), which aggressively seeks to eliminate causes of production defects—is now a cornerstone in many manufacturers' production practices, and the term "lean manufacturing" is used to refer to the set of concepts.

Of course, the Japanese were not the first to develop a highly integrated, efficient production system. In 1913, Henry Ford developed an assembly line to make the Model-T automobile. Ford developed a system for making the Model-T that was constrained only by the capabilities of the workforce and existing technology. Quality was a critical prerequisite for Ford: The line could not run steadily at speed without consistently good components. On-time delivery was also critical for Ford; the desire to keep workers and machines busy with materials flowing constantly made scheduling critical. Product, processes, material, logistics, and people were well integrated and balanced in the design and operation of the plant.[1]

Manufacturing Strategy Paradigm   The late 1970s and early 1980s saw the development of the manufacturing strategy paradigm by researchers at the Harvard Business School. This work by professors William Abernathy, Kim Clark, Robert Hayes, and Steven Wheelwright (built on earlier efforts by Wickham Skinner) emphasized how manufacturing executives could use their factories' capabilities as strategic competitive weapons. Central to their thinking was the notion of factory focus and manufacturing trade-offs. They argued that because a factory cannot excel on all performance measures, its management must devise a focused strategy, creating a focused factory that performs a limited set of tasks extremely well. This required trade-offs among such performance measures as low cost, high quality, and high flexibility in designing and managing factories. Ford seems to have realized this about 60 years before the Harvard professors.

Service Quality and Productivity   The great diversity of service industries—ranging from airlines to zoos, with many different types in between—precludes identifying any single pioneer or developer that has made a major impact in these areas. However, McDonald's unique approach to quality and productivity has been so successful that it stands as a reference point in thinking about how to deliver high-volume standardized services.

Service

Total Quality Management and Quality Certification   Another major development was the focus on total quality management (TQM) in the late 1980s and 1990s. All operations executives are aware of the quality message put forth by the so-called quality gurus: W. Edwards Deming, Joseph M. Juran, and Philip Crosby. It's interesting that these individuals were students of Shewhart, Dodge, and Romig in the 1930s (sometimes it takes a generation for things to catch on). Helping the quality movement along is the Baldrige National Quality Award, which was started in 1987 under the direction of the National Institute of Standards and Technology. The Baldrige Award recognizes companies each year for outstanding quality management systems.

The ISO 9000 certification standards, created by the International Organization for Standardization, now plays a major role in setting quality standards for global manufacturers. Many European companies require that their vendors meet these standards as a condition for obtaining contracts.

Global

Business Process Reengineering   The need to become lean to remain competitive in the global economic recession in the 1990s pushed companies to seek innovations in the processes by which they run their operations. The flavor of business process reengineering (BPR) is conveyed in the title of Michael Hammer's influential article in *Harvard Business Review:* "Reengineering Work: Don't Automate, Obliterate." The approach seeks to make revolutionary changes as opposed to evolutionary changes (which are commonly advocated in TQM). It does this by taking a fresh look at what the organization is trying to do in all its business processes, and then eliminating non–value-added steps and computerizing the remaining ones to achieve the desired outcome.

Hammer actually was not the first consultant to advocate eliminating non–value-added steps and reengineering processes. In the early 1900s, Frederick W. Taylor developed principles of scientific management that applied scientific analysis to eliminating wasted effort from manual labor. Around the same time, Frank and Lillian Gilbreth used the new technology of the time, motion pictures, to analyze such diverse operations as bricklaying and medical surgery procedures. Many of the innovations this husband-and-wife team developed, such as time and motion study, are widely used today.

Six-Sigma Quality   Originally developed in the 1980s as part of total quality management, six-sigma quality in the 1990s saw a dramatic expansion as an extensive set of diagnostic tools was developed. These tools have been taught to managers as part of "Green and Black Belt Programs" at many corporations. The tools are now applied to not only the well-known manufacturing applications, but also to nonmanufacturing processes such as accounts receivable, sales, and research and development. Six-sigma has been applied to

**Supply
Chain**

Mass customization

environmental, health, and safety services at companies and is now being applied to research and development, finance, information systems, legal, marketing, public affairs, and human resources processes.

Supply Chain Management   The central idea of supply chain management is to apply a total system approach to managing the flow of information, materials, and services from raw material suppliers through factories and warehouses to the end customer. Recent trends such as outsourcing and mass customization are forcing companies to find flexible ways to meet customer demand. The focus is on optimizing core activities to maximize the speed of response to changes in customer expectations.

Electronic Commerce   The quick adoption of the Internet and the World Wide Web during the late 1990s was remarkable. The term *electronic commerce* refers to the use of the Internet as an essential element of business activity. The Internet is an outgrowth of a government network called ARPANET, which was created in 1969 by the Department of Defense of the U.S. government. The use of Web pages, forms, and interactive search engines has changed the way people collect information, shop, and communicate. It has changed the way operations managers coordinate and execute production and distribution functions.

Service Science   A direct response to the growth of services is the development of a major industry and university program called Service Science Management and Engineering (SSME). SSME aims to apply the latest concepts in information technology to continue to improve service productivity of technology-based organizations. An interesting question raised by Jim Spohrer, leader of the IBM team that started the effort, is where will the labor go, once productivity improves in the service sector? "The short answer is new service sector industries and business—recall the service sector is very diverse and becoming more so every day. Consider the growth of retail (franchises, ecommerce, Amazon, eBay), communication (telephones, T-Mobile, Skype), transportation (airlines, FedEx), financial (discount ebrokers, Schwab), as well as information (television, CNN, Google) services. Not to mention all the new services in developing nations of the world. The creative capacity of the service sector for new industries and business has scarcely been tapped."[2]

Service

CURRENT ISSUES IN OPERATIONS AND SUPPLY CHAIN MANAGEMENT

**Supply
Chain**

Operations and supply chain management is a dynamic field, and challenges presented by global enterprise suggest exciting new issues for operations managers. Looking forward to the future, we believe the major challenges in the field will be as follows:

1. **Coordinating the relationships between mutually supportive but separate organizations.** Recently there has been a dramatic surge in the outsourcing of parts and services that had previously been produced internally. This has been encouraged by the availability of fast, inexpensive communications. A new breed of *contract manufacturers* that specialize in performing focused manufacturing activities now exists. The success of this kind of traditional outsourcing has led companies to consider outsourcing other major corporate functions such as information systems, product development and design, engineering services, packaging, testing, and distribution. The ability to coordinate these activities is a significant challenge for the operations manager of the future.

2. **Optimizing global supplier, production, and distribution networks.** The implementation of global enterprise resource planning systems, now common in large

companies, has challenged managers to use all of this information. This requires a careful understanding of where control should be centralized and where autonomy is important, among other issues. Companies have only begun to take advantage of the information from these systems to optimally control such resources as inventory, transportation, and production equipment.

Global

3. **Managing customer touch points.** As companies strive to become superefficient, they often scrimp on customer support personnel (and training) required to effectively staff service departments, help lines, and checkout counters. This leads to the frustrations we have all experienced such as being placed in call-center limbo seemingly for hours, getting bad advice when finally interacting with a company rep, and so on. The issue here is to recognize that making resource utilization decisions must capture the implicit costs of lost customers as well as the direct costs of staffing.

4. **Raising senior management awareness of operations and supply chain management as a significant competitive weapon.** As we stated earlier, many senior executives entered the organization through finance, strategy, or marketing and built their reputations on work in these areas and, as a result, often take operations for granted. As we will demonstrate in this book, this can be a critical mistake when we realize how profitable companies such as Toyota, Dell, Taco Bell, and Southwest Airlines are. These are companies where executives have creatively used operations and supply chain management for competitive advantage.

5. **Sustainability and the triple bottom line.** Sustainability is the ability to maintain balance in a system. Management must now consider the mandates related to the ongoing economic, employee, and environmental viability of the firm (the triple bottom line). Economically the firm must be profitable. Employee job security, positive working conditions, and development opportunities are essential. Nonpolluting and non–resource-depleting products and processes bring new challenges to operations and supply managers.

Sustainability

Triple bottom line

KEY TERMS

Operations and supply chain management (OSCM) Design, operation, and improvement of the systems that create and deliver the firm's primary products and services.

Servitization Building service activities to support a firm's product offerings.

Efficiency Doing something at the lowest possible cost.

Effectiveness Doing the right things to create the most value for the company.

Value Ratio of quality to price paid. Competitive "happiness" is being able to increase quality and reduce price while maintaining or improving profit margins. (This is a way that operations can directly increase customer retention and gain market share.)

Mass customization Producing products to order in lot sizes of one.

Sustainability The ability to maintain balance in a system.

Triple bottom line Relates to the economic, employee, and environmental impact of the firm's strategy.

REVIEW AND DISCUSSION QUESTIONS

1 Look at the want ads in *The Wall Street Journal* and evaluate the opportunities for an OSCM major with several years of experience.

2 What factors account for the resurgence of interest in OSCM today?

3 Using Exhibit 1.3 as a model, describe the source-make-deliver-return relationships in the following systems:
   a. An airline.
   b. An automobile manufacturer.
   c. A hospital.
   d. An insurance company.

INTERNET EXERCISE: HARLEY-DAVIDSON MOTORCYCLES

Harley-Davidson has developed a Web site that allows potential customers to customize their new motorcycles. Working from a "basic" model, the customer can choose from an assortment of bags, chrome covers, color schemes, exhausts, foot controls, mirrors, and other accessories. The Web-based application is set up so that the customer cannot only select from the extensive list of accessories but also see exactly what the motorcycle will look like. These unique designs can be shared with friends and family by printing the final picture or transferring it via e-mail. What a slick way to sell motorcycles!

Go to the Harley-Davidson (HD) Web site (*www.Harley-Davidson.com*). From there select "Parts & Apparel" and "Genuine Motor Accessories," then select "The Customizer." This should get you into the application.

1. How many different bike configurations do you think are possible? Could every customer have a different bike? To make this a little simpler, what if HD had only two types of bikes, three handlebar choices, four saddlebag combinations, and two exhaust pipe choices? How many combinations are possible in this case (assume they need to select one item from each set of options)?
2. To keep things simple, HD has the dealer install virtually all these options. What would be the trade-off involved if HD installed these options at the factory instead of having the dealers install the options?
3. How important is this customization to HD's marketing strategy? Concisely describe HD's operations and supply strategy.

CASE: FAST-FOOD FEAST

Visit at least two different fast-food restaurants that make hamburgers. For example, in the United States McDonald's, Wendy's, and Burger King are good choices. For some of you fast-food junkies, this will not be difficult; vegans may have to take a friend for product testing. Observe the basic operational differences between these stores. Note the differences in the following processes:

3 How are special orders handled?
4 How are the hamburgers cooked?
5 How are the hamburgers assembled?
6 Is a microwave oven used in the process?
7 How are other common items, such as french fries and drinks, handled?

QUESTIONS

1 How are in-store orders taken?
2 Are the hamburgers prepared to order, or are they prepared ahead of time and delivered from a storage bin?

SUPER QUIZ

1 The pipelinelike movement of the materials and information needed to produce a good or service.
2 A strategy that meets the needs of shareholders, employees, and preserves the environment.
3 The processes needed to determine the set of future actions required to operate an existing supply chain.
4 The selection of suppliers.
5 A type of process where the major product is produced or service provided.
6 A type of process that moves products to warehouses or customers.
7 Processes that involve the receiving of wornout, defective, and excess products back from customers and support for customers who have problems.

8 A business where the major product is intangible, so that it cannot be weighed or measured.
9 Refers to when a company builds service activities into its product offerings.
10 Means doing something at the lowest possible cost.
11 Means doing the right things to create the most value for the company.
12 Metaphorically defined as quality divided by price.
13 A philosophy which aggressively seeks to eliminate causes of production defects.
14 An approach that seeks to make revolutionary changes as opposed to evolutionary changes (which is advocated by total quality management).

15 An approach that combines TQM and JIT.
16 Tools that are taught to managers in "Green and Black Belt Programs."

17 A program to apply the latest concepts in information technology to improve service productivity.

1. Supply (chain) network 2. Triple bottom line strategy 3. Planning 4. Sourcing 5. Making 6. Delivery 7. Returning 8. Service 9. Servitization 10. Efficiently 11. Effectively 12. Value 13. Total quality control 14. Business process reengineering 15. Lean manufacturing 16. Six-Sigma Quality 17. Service science management and engineering.

SELECTED BIBLIOGRAPHY

APICS The Association for Operations Management. www.APICS.org.

Journal of Operations Management. Washington, DC: American Production and Inventory Control Society, 1980 current.

Manufacturing & Service Operations Management: M&SOM. Linthicum, MD: Institute for Operations Research and the Management Sciences, 1999–current.

Production and Operations Management: An International Journal of the Production and Operations Management Society/POMS. Baltimore: Production and Operations Management Society, 1992–current.

Production and Operations Management Society. www.poms.org.

FOOTNOTES

1 See J. Wilson, "Henry Ford: A Just-in-Time Pioneer," *Production & Inventory Management Journal* 37 (1996), pp. 26–31.

2 Jim Spohrer, "Service Science, Management, and Engineering (SSME): A Next Frontier in Education, Employment, Innovation, and Economic Growth," IBM India, teleconference to India from Santa Clara, CA, December 2006.

chapter 2

STRATEGY AND SUSTAINABILITY

HOW IKEA DESIGNS ITS SEXY PRICES

Competitive strategy is about being different. It means deliberately choosing a different set of activities to deliver a unique mix of value. IKEA, the Swedish retailer of home products, dominates markets in 43 countries, and is poised to conquer North America.

Global

Above all else, one factor accounts for IKEA's success: good quality at a low price. IKEA sells household items that are cheap but not cheapo, with prices that typically run 30 to 50 percent below those of the competition. While the price of other companies' products tends to rise over time, IKEA says it has reduced its retail prices by a total of about 20 percent during the last four years. At IKEA the process of driving down costs starts the moment a new item is conceived and continues relentlessly throughout the life of the product.

After reading the chapter you will:

1. Compare how operations and supply chain strategy relates to marketing and finance.

2. Understand the competitive dimensions of operations and supply chain strategy.

3. Identify order winners and order qualifiers.

4. Understand the concept of strategic fit.

5. Describe how productivity is measured and how it relates to operations and supply chain processes.

6. Explain how the financial markets evaluate a firm's operations and supply chain performance.

IKEA has always had a 50-cent coffee mug. Prior to the new TROFÉ mug, the company offered the "Bang" mug, which had been redesigned three times, in ways to maximize the number of mugs that could be stored on a pallet. Originally, only 864 mugs would fit. A redesign added a rim such as you would find on a flowerpot so that each pallet could hold 1,280 mugs. Another redesign created a shorter mug with a new handle, allowing 2,024 to squeeze onto a pallet. These changes reduced shipping costs by 60 percent.

The latest version of the 50-cent coffee mug has been made even more useful with a simple notch on the bottom that prevents water from pooling up around the base during a dishwasher run. Further refinements have optimized the speed at which the cup can pass through the machines forming the cups and enable IKEA to fit the maximum number into kilns, saving on the expensive firing process. Simple changes in the shape of the mug have reduced the cost to produce the mug significantly while creating more value for customers purchasing this simple 50-cent coffee mug.

This is the essence of operations supply chain management: creating great value to the customer while reducing the cost of delivering the good or service.

A SUSTAINABLE STRATEGY

Strategy should describe how a firm intends to create and sustain value for its current shareholders. By adding "sustainability" to the concept, we add the requirement to meet these current needs without compromising the ability of future generations to meet their own needs. *Shareholders* are those individuals or companies that legally own one or more shares of stock in the company. Many companies today have expanded the scope of their strategy to include stakeholders. *Stakeholders* are those individuals or organizations who are influenced, either directly or indirectly, by the actions of the firm. This expanded view means that the scope of the firm's strategy must not only focus on the economic viability of its shareholders but should also consider the environmental and social impact on key stakeholders.

Triple bottom line

To capture this expanded view the phrase **triple bottom line** has been coined.[1] The triple bottom line, Exhibit 2.1, considers evaluating the firm against social, economic, and environmental criteria. Many companies have developed this expanded view through goals that relate to sustainability along each of these dimensions. Some alternative phrases for the same concept are "People, Planet, and Profit" used by Shell Oil Company, and "Folk, Work, and Place" which originated with the 20th-century writer Patrick Geddes. The following expands on the meaning of each dimension of the triple bottom line framework.

- **Social** Pertains to fair and beneficial business practices toward labor, the community, and the region in which a firm conducts its business. A triple bottom line company seeks to benefit its employees, the community, and other social entities that are impacted by the firm's existence. A company should not use child labor, should pay fair salaries to its workers, maintain a safe work environment with tolerable working hours, and not otherwise exploit a community or its labor force. A business can also give back by contributing to the strength and growth of its community through health care, education, and other special programs.

exhibit 2.1   The Triple Bottom Line

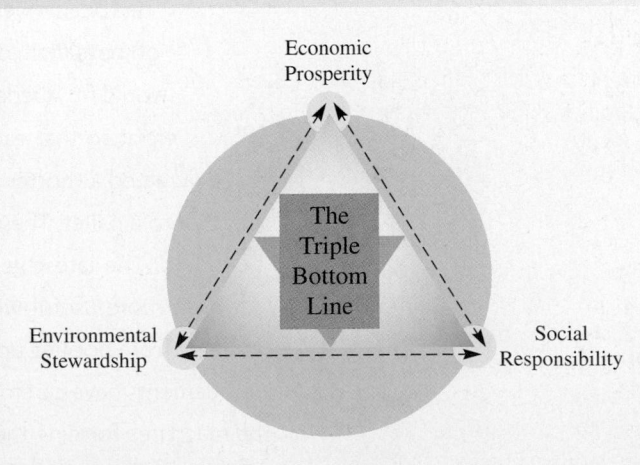

- **Economic** The firm is obligated to compensate shareholders who provide capital through stock purchases and other financial instruments via a competitive return on investment. Company strategies should promote growth and grow long-term value to this group in the form of profit. Within a sustainability framework, this dimension goes beyond just profit for the firm but also provides lasting economic benefit to society.
- **Environmental** This refers to the firm's impact on the environment. The company should protect the environment as much as possible—or at least cause no harm. Managers should move to reduce a company's ecological footprint by carefully managing its consumption of natural resources and by reducing waste, as well as ensuring that the waste is less toxic before disposing of it in a safe and legal manner. Many businesses now conduct "cradle-to-grave" assessments of products to determine what the true environmental costs are—from processing the raw material to manufacture to distribution to eventual disposal by the final customer.

Conventional strategy focuses on the economic part of this framework. Because many of the processes that fall under the domain of operations and supply chain management have social and environment impact, it is important these criteria be considered as well. Some proponents argue that in many ways European Union countries are more advanced due to the standardized reporting of ecological and social losses that came with the adoption of the euro.

Although many company planners agree with the goals of improving society and preserving the environment, many others disagree. Dissenting arguments relate to the potential loss of efficiency due to the focus on conflicting criteria. Others argue that these goals may be appropriate for rich societies that can afford to contribute to society and the environment. A company in a poor or developing society/nation must focus on survival. The economic benefit derived from the use of abundant local resources may be viewed as worth their destruction.

In this chapter we take a customer-centered focus; issues associated with people and the environment are left to an individual case approach. Depending on the country, industry, and scope of the firm, these other issues vary widely and thus are not amenable to a general approach for analysis. The issues and their relationship to operations and supply chain management are very real, however, and we anticipate they will become even more relevant in the future.

WHAT IS OPERATIONS AND SUPPLY CHAIN STRATEGY?

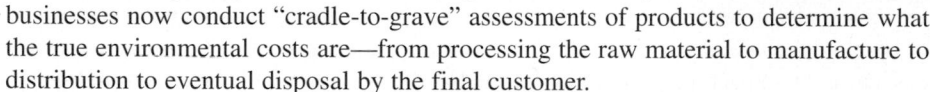
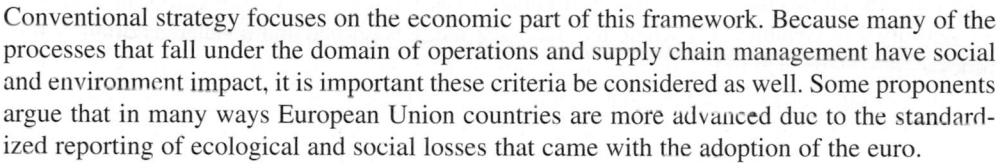

Operations and supply chain strategy is concerned with setting broad policies and plans for using the resources of a firm and must be integrated with corporate strategy. So, for example, if the high-level corporate strategy includes goals related to the environment and social responsibility, then the operations and supply chain strategy must consider this. A major focus to the operations and supply chain strategy is operations effectiveness. *Operations effectiveness* relates to the core business processes needed to run the business. The processes span all the business functions from taking customer orders, handling returns, manufacturing, managing the updating of the Web site, to shipping products. Operational effectiveness is reflected directly in the costs associated with doing business. Strategies associated with operational effectiveness, such as quality assurance and control initiatives, process redesign, planning and control systems, and technology investments, can show quick, near-term (12 to 24 months) results.

Operations and supply chain strategy can be viewed as part of a planning process that coordinates operational goals with those of the larger organization. Since the goals of the larger organization change over time, the operations strategy must be designed to anticipate future needs. A firm's operations and supply chain capabilities can be viewed as a portfolio best suited to adapt to the changing product and/or service needs of the firm's customers.

Operations and supply chain strategy

Planning strategy is a process just like making a product or delivering a service. The process involves a set of activities that are repeated at different intervals over time. Just as products are made over and over, the strategy planning activities are repeated. A big difference is that these activities are done by executives in the board room!

Exhibit 2.2 shows the major activities of a typical strategic planning process. Activity 1 is performed at least yearly and is where the overall strategy is developed. A key part of this step is the "strategic analysis," which involves looking out and forecasting how business conditions that impact the firm's strategy are going to change in the future. Here such things as changes in customer preferences, the impact of new technologies, changes in population demographics, and the anticipation of new competitors are considered. A successful strategy will anticipate change and formulate new initiatives in response. *Initiatives* are the major steps that need to be taken to drive success in the firm. Many of these initiatives are repeated from year to year such as the updating of existing product designs and the operation of manufacturing plants in different regions of the world. New initiatives that innovatively respond to market dynamics are extremely important to company success. Initiatives that develop innovative new products or open new markets, for example, drive future revenue growth. Other initiatives that reduce costs directly impact the profitability of the firm. Companies with triple bottom line strategies may have initiatives that reduce waste or enhance the welfare of the local communities.

Activity 2 in Exhibit 2.2 is where the overall strategy is refined and updated as often as four times a year. Here each initiative is evaluated and appropriate budget estimates for the next year or more are developed. Measures that relate to the performance of each initiative are needed so that success or failure can be gauged in an unbiased and objective way. Because of the quickly changing nature of global business, many businesses must revise plans several times per year.

exhibit 2.2   Closed-Loop Strategy Process

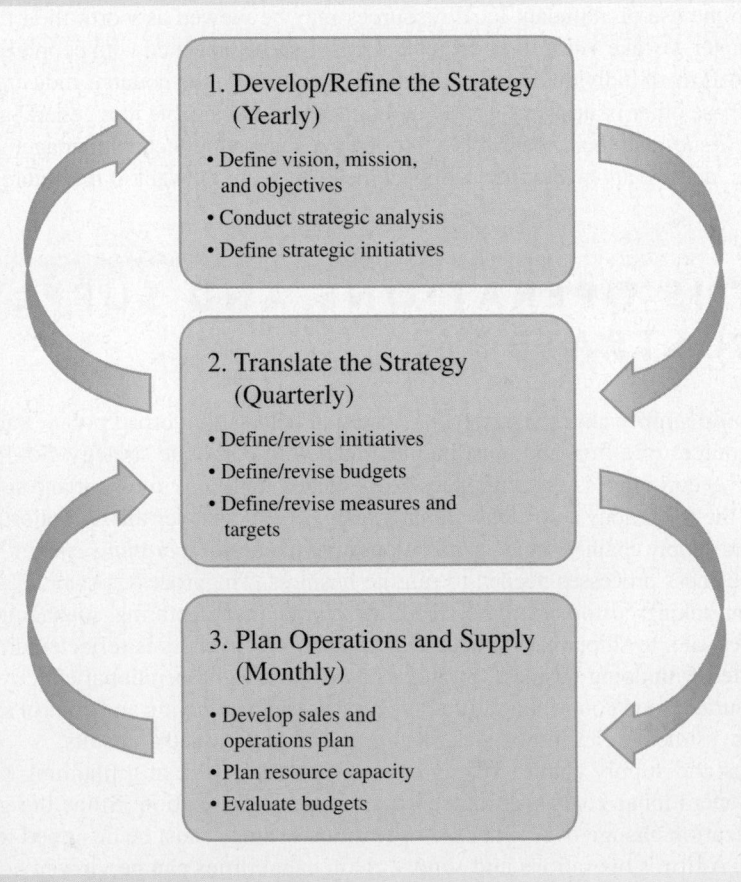

1. Develop/Refine the Strategy (Yearly)
   • Define vision, mission, and objectives
   • Conduct strategic analysis
   • Define strategic initiatives

2. Translate the Strategy (Quarterly)
   • Define/revise initiatives
   • Define/revise budgets
   • Define/revise measures and targets

3. Plan Operations and Supply (Monthly)
   • Develop sales and operations plan
   • Plan resource capacity
   • Evaluate budgets

The operations and supply chain planning activity shown in the third box is where operational plans that relate to functional areas such as marketing, manufacturing, warehousing, transportation, and purchasing are coordinated for six months up to a year and a half. The functional areas involved in the coordination can vary greatly depending on the needs of the firm. A hospital requires coordination across the operating room, intensive care units, and auxiliary units such as radiation and chemotherapy. Similarly, the coordination for a retailer such as Walmart may be very different compared to an automobile manufacturer such as Ford. These coordination efforts are largely focused on adjusting capacity and resource availability based on anticipated demand scenarios.

In the next section, we focus on integrating operations and supply chain strategy with a firm's operations capabilities. This involves decisions that relate to the design of the processes and infrastructure needed to support these processes. Process design includes selecting the appropriate technology, sizing the process over time, determining the role of inventory in the process, and locating the process. The infrastructure decisions involve the logic associated with the planning and control systems, quality assurance and control approaches, work payment structure, and organization of the operations and supply chain functions. A firm's operations capabilities can be viewed as a portfolio best suited to adapt to the changing product and/or service needs of a firm's customers.

COMPETITIVE DIMENSIONS

Given the choices customers face today, how do they decide which product or service to buy? Different customers are attracted by different attributes. Some customers are interested primarily in the cost of a product or service and, correspondingly, some companies attempt to position themselves to offer the lowest prices. The major competitive dimensions that form the competitive position of a firm include the following.

Cost or Price: "Make the Product or Deliver the Service Cheap"   Every industry usually includes a segment of the market that buys solely on the basis of low cost. To successfully compete in this niche, a firm must be the low-cost producer, but even this does not always guarantee profitability and success. Products and services sold strictly on the basis of cost are typically commoditylike; in other words, customers cannot distinguish the product or service of one firm from those of another. This segment of the market is frequently very large, and many companies are lured by the potential for significant profits, which they associate with the large unit volumes. As a consequence, however, competition in this segment is fierce—and so is the failure rate. After all, there can be only one lowest-cost producer, who usually establishes the selling price in the market.

Price, however, is not the only basis on which a firm can compete. Other companies, such as BMW, seek to attract those who want *higher quality*—in terms of performance, appearance, or features—than that available in competing products and services, even though accompanied by a higher price.

Quality: "Make a Great Product or Deliver a Great Service"   Two characteristics of a product or service define quality: design quality and process quality. Design quality relates to the set of features the product or service contains. This relates directly to the design of the product or service. Obviously a child's first two-wheel bicycle is of significantly different quality than the bicycle of a world-class cyclist. The use of special aluminum alloys and special lightweight sprockets and chains is important to the performance needs of the advanced cyclist. These two types of bicycle are designed for different customers' needs. The higher-quality cyclist product commands a higher price in the marketplace due to its special features. The goal in establishing the proper level of design quality is to focus on the requirements of the customer. Overdesigned products and services with too many or inappropriate features will be viewed as prohibitively expensive.

In comparison, underdesigned products and services will lose customers to products that cost a little more but are perceived by customers as offering greater value.

Process quality, the second characteristic of quality, is critical because it relates directly to the reliability of the product or service. Regardless of whether the product is a child's first two-wheeler or a bicycle for an international cyclist, customers want products without defects. Thus, the goal of process quality is to produce defect-free products and services. Product and service specifications, given in dimensional tolerances and/or service error rates, define how the product or service is to be made. Adherence to these specifications is critical to ensure the reliability of the product or service as defined by its intended use.

Delivery Speed: "Make the Product or Deliver the Service Quickly"   In some markets, a firm's ability to deliver more quickly than its competitors is critical. A company that can offer an on-site repair service in only 1 or 2 hours has a significant advantage over a competing firm that guarantees service only within 24 hours.

Service

Delivery Reliability: "Deliver It When Promised"   This dimension relates to the firm's ability to supply the product or service on or before a promised delivery due date. For an automobile manufacturer, it is very important that its supplier of tires provide the needed quantity and types for each day's car production. If the tires needed for a particular car are not available when the car reaches the point on the assembly line where the tires are installed, the whole assembly line may have to be shut down until they arrive. For a service firm such as Federal Express, delivery reliability is the cornerstone of its strategy.

Coping with Changes in Demand: "Change Its Volume"   In many markets, a company's ability to respond to increases and decreases in demand is important to its ability to compete. It is well known that a company with increasing demand can do little wrong. When demand is strong and increasing, costs are continuously reduced due to economies of scale, and investments in new technologies can be easily justified. But scaling back when demand decreases may require many difficult decisions about laying off employees and related reductions in assets. The ability to effectively deal with dynamic market demand over the long term is an essential element of operations strategy.

Flexibility and New-Product Introduction Speed: "Change It"   Flexibility, from a strategic perspective, refers to the ability of a company to offer a wide variety of products to its customers. An important element of this ability to offer different products is the time required for a company to develop a new product and to convert its processes to offer the new product.

Service

Other Product-Specific Criteria: "Support It"   The competitive dimensions just described are the most common. However, other dimensions often relate to specific products or situations. Notice that most of the dimensions listed next are primarily service in nature. Often special services are provided to augment the sales of manufactured products.

1. **Technical liaison and support.** A supplier may be expected to provide technical assistance for product development, particularly during the early stages of design and manufacturing.
2. **Meeting a launch date.** A firm may be required to coordinate with other firms on a complex project. In such cases, manufacturing may take place while development work is still being completed. Coordinating work between firms and working simultaneously on a project will reduce the total time required to complete the project.
3. **Supplier after-sale support.** An important competitive dimension may be the ability of a firm to support its product after the sale. This involves availability of replacement parts and, possibly, modification of older, existing products to new performance levels. Speed of response to these after-sale needs is often important as well.

4. **Environmental impact.** A dimension related to criteria such as carbon dioxide emissions, use of nonrenewable resources, or other factors that relate to sustainability.

5. **Other dimensions.** These typically include such factors as colors available, size, weight, location of the fabrication site, customization available, and product mix options.

THE NOTION OF TRADE-OFFS

Central to the concept of operations and supply chain strategy is the notion of operations focus and trade-offs. The underlying logic is that an operation cannot excel simultaneously on all competitive dimensions. Consequently, management has to decide which parameters of performance are critical to the firm's success and then concentrate the resources of the firm on these particular characteristics.

For example, if a company wants to focus on speed of delivery, it cannot be very flexible in its ability to offer a wide range of products. Similarly, a low-cost strategy is not compatible with either speed of delivery or flexibility. High quality also is viewed as a trade-off to low cost.

A strategic position is not sustainable unless there are compromises with other positions. Trade-offs occur when activities are incompatible so that more of one thing necessitates less of another. An airline can choose to serve meals—adding cost and slowing turnaround time at the gate—or it can choose not to, but it cannot do both without bearing major inefficiencies.

Straddling

Straddling occurs when a company seeks to match the benefits of a successful position while maintaining its existing position. It adds new features, services, or technologies onto the activities it already performs. The risky nature of this strategy is shown by Continental Airlines' ill-fated attempt to compete with Southwest Airlines. While maintaining its position as a full-service airline, Continental set out to match Southwest on a number of point-to-point routes. The airline dubbed the new service Continental Lite. It eliminated meals and first-class service, increased departure frequency, lowered fares, and shortened gate turnaround time. Because Continental remained a full-service airline on other routes, it continued to use travel agents and its mixed fleet of planes and to provide baggage checking and seat assignments.

Service

Trade-offs ultimately grounded Continental Lite. The airline lost hundreds of millions of dollars, and the chief executive officer lost his job. Its planes were delayed leaving congested hub cities or slowed at the gate by baggage transfers. Late flights and cancellations generated a thousand complaints a day. Continental Lite could not afford to compete on price and still pay standard travel agent commissions, but neither could it do without agents for its full-service business. The airline compromised by cutting commissions for all Continental flights. Similarly, it could not afford to offer the same frequent-flier benefits to travelers paying the much lower ticket prices for Lite service. It compromised again by lowering the rewards of Continental's entire frequent-flier program. The results: angry travel agents and full-service customers. Continental tried to compete in two ways at once and paid an enormous straddling penalty.

ORDER WINNERS AND ORDER QUALIFIERS: THE MARKETING–OPERATIONS LINK

A well-designed interface between marketing and operations is necessary to provide a business with an understanding of its markets from both perspectives. The terms *order winner* and *order qualifier* describe marketing-oriented dimensions that are key to competitive success. An **order winner** is a criterion that differentiates the products or services of one firm from those of another. Depending on the situation, the order-winning criterion may be the cost of the product (price), product quality and reliability, or any of the other dimensions developed earlier. An **order qualifier** is a screening criterion that permits a firm's products to even be considered as possible candidates for purchase. Oxford

Order winner

Order qualifier

Global

Professor Terry Hill states that a firm must "requalify the order qualifiers" every day it is in business.

It is important to remember that the order-winning and order-qualifying criteria may change over time. For example, when Japanese companies entered the world automobile markets in the 1970s, they changed the way these products won orders, from predominantly price to product quality and reliability. American automobile producers were losing orders through quality to the Japanese companies. By the late 1980s, product quality was raised by Ford, General Motors, and Chrysler; today they are "qualified" to be in the market. Consumer groups continually monitor the quality and reliability criteria, thus requalifying the top-performing companies. Today the order winners for automobiles vary greatly depending on the model. Customers know the set of features they want (such as reliability, design features, and gas mileage), and they want to purchase a particular combination at the lowest price, thus maximizing value.

STRATEGIC FIT: FITTING OPERATIONAL ACTIVITIES TO STRATEGY

Service

All the activities that make up a firm's operation relate to one another. To make these activities efficient, the firm must minimize its total cost without compromising customers' needs. IKEA targets young furniture buyers who want style at a low cost. IKEA has chosen to perform activities differently from its rivals.

Consider the typical furniture store, where showrooms display samples of the merchandise. One area may contain many sofas, another area displays dining tables, and many other areas focus on particular types of furniture. Dozens of books displaying fabric swatches or wood samples or alternative styles offer customers thousands of product varieties from which to choose. Salespeople escort customers through the store, answering their questions

and helping them navigate through the maze of choices. Once a customer decides what he or she wants, the order is relayed to a third-party manufacturer. With a lot of luck, the furniture will be delivered to the customer's home within six to eight weeks. This is a supply chain that maximizes customization and service but does so at a high cost.

In contrast, IKEA serves customers who are happy to trade service for cost. Instead of using sales associates, IKEA uses a self-service model with roomlike displays where furniture is shown in familiar settings. Rather than relying on third-party manufacturers, IKEA designs its own low-cost, modular, ready-to-assemble furniture. In the store there is a warehouse section with the products in boxes ready for delivery. Customers do their own picking from inventory and delivery. Much of its low-cost operation comes from having customers service themselves, yet IKEA offers extra services such as in-store child care and extended hours. Those services align well with the needs of its customers, who are young, not wealthy, and likely to have children, and who need to shop at odd hours.

Activity-system maps

Exhibit 2.3 shows how IKEA's strategy is implemented through a set of activities designed to deliver it. Activity-system maps such as the one for IKEA show how a company's strategy is delivered through a set of tailored activities. In companies with a clear strategy, a number of higher-order strategic themes (in darker green) can be identified and implemented through clusters of tightly linked activities. This type of map can be useful in understanding how good the fit is between the system of activities and the company's strategy. Competitive advantage comes from the way a firm's activities fit with and reinforce one another.

Mapping Activity Systems

exhibit 2.3

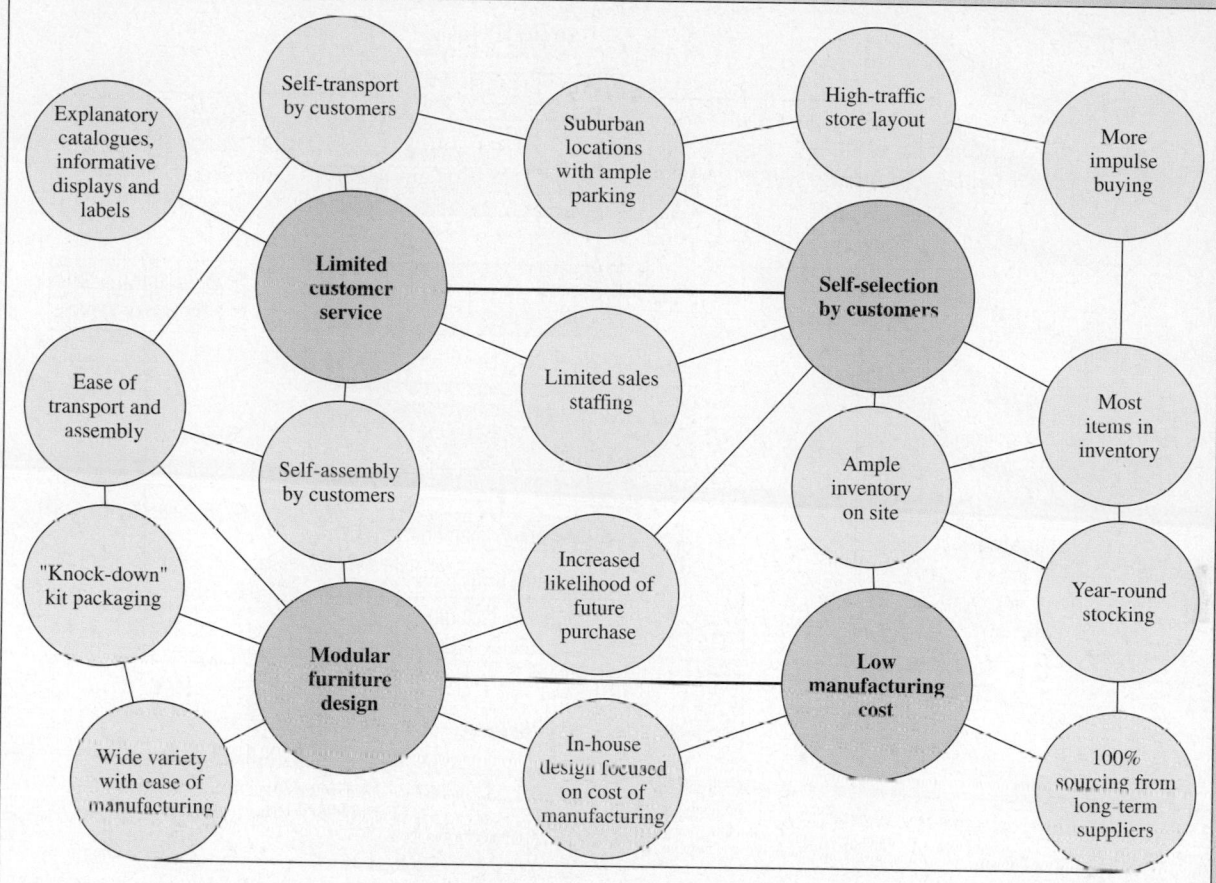

Activity-system maps, such as this one for IKEA, show how a company's strategic position is contained in a set of tailored activities designed to deliver it. In companies with a clear strategic position, a number of higher-order strategic themes (in darker green circles) can be identified and implemented through clusters of tightly linked activities (in lighter circles).

SOURCE: M. E. PORTER, ON COMPETITION (BOSTON: HBS, 1998), P. 50.

A FRAMEWORK FOR OPERATIONS AND SUPPLY CHAIN STRATEGY

Operations strategy cannot be designed in a vacuum. It must be linked vertically to the customer and horizontally to other parts of the enterprise. Exhibit 2.4 shows these linkages among customer needs, their performance priorities and requirements for manufacturing operations, and the operations and related enterprise resource capabilities to satisfy those needs. Overlying this framework is senior management's strategic vision of the firm. The vision identifies, in general terms, the target market, the firm's product line, and its core enterprise and operations capabilities.

The choice of a target market can be difficult, but it must be made. Indeed, it may lead to turning away business—ruling out a customer segment that would simply be unprofitable or too hard to serve given the firm's capabilities. An example here is clothing manufacturers not making half-sizes in their dress lines. **Core capabilities** (or competencies) are the skills that differentiate the service or manufacturing firm from its competitors.

Core capabilities

exhibit 2.4   Operations and Supply Chain Strategy Framework: From Customer Needs to Order Fulfillment

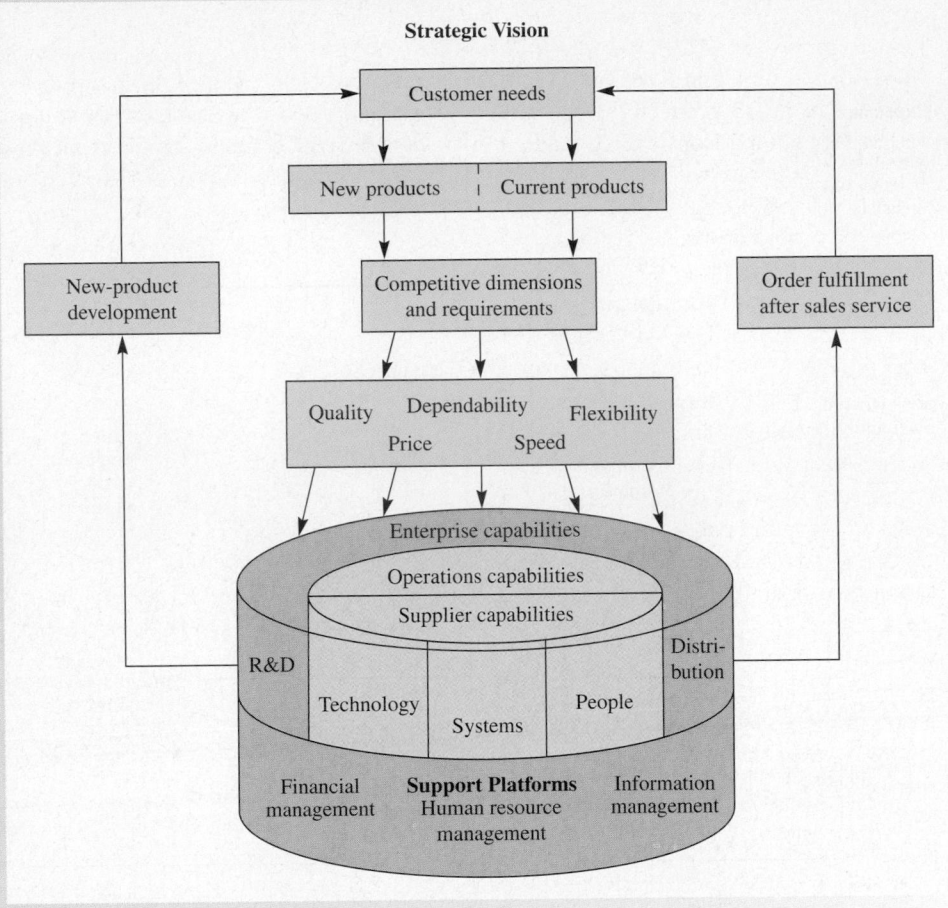

Possibly the most difficult thing for a firm to do is part with tradition. Top-level managers often make their mark based on innovations made 15 to 20 years ago. These managers are often too comfortable just tinkering with the current system. All the new advanced technologies present themselves as quick fixes. It is easy to patch these technologies into the current system with great enthusiasm. While doing this may be exciting to managers and engineers working for the firm, they may not be creating a distinctive core competence—a competence that wins future customers. What companies need in this world of intense global competition is not more techniques but a way to structure a whole new product realization system differently and better than any competitor.

PRODUCTIVITY MEASUREMENT

Productivity

Productivity is a common measure of how well a country, industry, or business unit is using its resources (or factors of production). Since operations and supply chain management focuses on making the best use of the resources available to a firm, productivity measurement is fundamental to understanding operations-related performance. In this section, we define various measures of productivity. Throughout the rest of the book, many other performance measures will be defined as they relate to the material.

In its broadest sense, productivity is defined as

$$\text{Productivity} = \frac{\text{Outputs}}{\text{Inputs}}$$

To increase productivity, we want to make this ratio of outputs to inputs as large as practical.

Productivity is what we call a *relative measure*. In other words, to be meaningful, it needs to be compared with something else. For example, what can we learn from the fact that we operate a restaurant and that its productivity last week was 8.4 customers per labor hour? Nothing!

Productivity comparisons can be made in two ways. First, a company can compare itself with similar operations within its industry, or it can use industry data when such data are available (e.g., comparing productivity among the different stores in a franchise). Another approach is to measure productivity over time within the same operation. Here we would compare our productivity in one time period with that in the next.

As Exhibit 2.5 shows, productivity may be expressed as partial measures, multifactor measures, or total measures. If we are concerned with the ratio of output to a single input, we have a *partial productivity measure*. If we want to look at the ratio of output to a group of inputs (but not all inputs), we have a *multifactor productivity measure*. If we want to express the ratio of all outputs to all inputs, we can use a *total factor measure of productivity* to describe the productivity of an entire organization or even a nation.

A numerical example of productivity appears in Exhibit 2.5. The data reflect quantitative measures of input and output associated with the production of a certain product. Notice that for the multifactor and partial measures, it is not necessary to use total output as the numerator. Often it is desirable to create measures that represent productivity as it relates to some particular output of interest. For example, as in Exhibit 2.5, total units might be the output of interest to a production control manager, whereas total output may be of key interest to the plant manager. This process of aggregation and disaggregation of productivity measures provides a means of shifting the level of the analysis to suit a variety of productivity measurement and improvement needs.

Examples of Productivity Measures

exhibit 2.5

Partial measure	$\dfrac{\text{Output}}{\text{Labor}}$ or $\dfrac{\text{Output}}{\text{Capital}}$ or $\dfrac{\text{Output}}{\text{Materials}}$ or $\dfrac{\text{Output}}{\text{Energy}}$
Multifactor measure	$\dfrac{\text{Output}}{\text{Labor} + \text{Capital} + \text{Energy}}$ or $\dfrac{\text{Output}}{\text{Labor} + \text{Capital} + \text{Materials}}$
Total measure	$\dfrac{\text{Output}}{\text{Inputs}}$ or $\dfrac{\text{Goods and services produced}}{\text{All resources used}}$

INPUT AND OUTPUT PRODUCTION DATA ($)		PRODUCTIVITY MEASURE EXAMPLES
OUTPUT		Total measure
1. Finished units	$10,000	$\dfrac{\text{Total output}}{\text{Total input}} = \dfrac{13,500}{15,193} = 0.89$
2. Work in process	2,500	
3. Dividends	1,000	Multifactor measures:
4. Bonds		
5. Other income		$\dfrac{\text{Total output}}{\text{Human} + \text{Material}} = \dfrac{13,500}{3,153} = 4.28$
Total output	$13,500	
		$\dfrac{\text{Finished units}}{\text{Human} + \text{Material}} = \dfrac{10,000}{3,153} = 3.17$
INPUT		Partial measures:
1. Human	$ 3,000	
2. Material	153	$\dfrac{\text{Total output}}{\text{Energy}} = \dfrac{13,500}{540} = 25$
3. Capital	10,000	
4. Energy	540	$\dfrac{\text{Finished units}}{\text{Energy}} = \dfrac{10,000}{540} = 18.52$
5. Other expenses	1,500	
Total input	$ 15,193	

**Excel:
Productivity Measures**

exhibit 2.6

Partial Measures of Productivity

BUSINESS	PRODUCTIVITY MEASURE
Restaurant	Customers (meals) per labor hour
Retail store	Sales per square foot
Chicken farm	Lb. of meat per lb. of feed
Utility plant	Kilowatts per ton of coal
Paper mill	Tons of paper per cord of wood

Exhibit 2.5 shows all units in dollars. Often, however, management can better understand how the company is performing when units other than dollars are used. In these cases, only partial measures of productivity can be used, as we cannot combine dissimilar units such as labor hours and pounds of material. Examples of some commonly used partial measures of productivity are presented in Exhibit 2.6. Such partial measures of productivity give managers information in familiar units, allowing them to easily relate these measures to the actual operations.

HOW DOES WALL STREET EVALUATE OPERATIONS PERFORMANCE

Comparing firms from an operations view is important to investors since the relative cost of providing a good or service is essential to high earnings growth. When you think about it, earnings growth is largely a function of the firm's profitability, and profit can be increased through higher sales and/or reduced cost. Highly efficient firms usually shine when demand drops during recession periods since they often can continue to make a profit due to their low-cost structure. These operations-savvy firms may even see a recession as an opportunity to gain market share as their less-efficient competitors struggle to remain in business.

Take a look at the automobile industry, where efficiency has been such an important factor. Exhibit 2.7 shows a comparison of some of the major companies. These ratios reflect late 2008 performance, prior to the restructuring of General Motors and Chrysler in 2009. As you can see, Toyota dominates the group. Toyota's net income per employee is five times greater than that of Ford and Chrysler, truly an amazing accomplishment. Toyota also shines in receivables turnover, inventory turnover, and asset turnover. Ford and General Motors have worked hard at implementing the inventory management philosophy that was pioneered by Toyota in Japan. True efficiency goes beyond inventory management and requires an integrated product development, sales, manufacturing, and supply system. Toyota is very mature in its approach to these activities, and that clearly shows on its bottom line.

Each summer, *USA Today* publishes annual reports of productivity gains by the largest U.S. firms. Productivity has been on the rise for the past few years, which is very good for the economy. Productivity often increases in times of recession; as workers are fired, those remaining are expected to do more. Increases also come from technological advances. Think of what the tractor did for farm productivity.

In the evaluation of the largest productivity winners and losers, it is important to look for unusual explanations. For example, energy companies have had big productivity gains due almost exclusively to higher oil prices, which boosted the companies' revenue without forcing them to add employees. Pharmaceutical companies such as Merck and Pfizer have not done well recently. Their productivity plunges were due primarily to one-time events, Merck because it spun off a company and Pfizer because it bought a company. Such one-time quirks create a lot of noise for anybody who wants to know how well companies are run. It is best to examine multiyear productivity patterns.

Efficiency Measures Used by Wall Street

exhibit 2.7

A COMPARISON OF AUTOMOBILE COMPANIES					
MANAGEMENT EFFICIENCY MEASURE	TOYOTA	FORD	GENERAL MOTORS	CHRYSLER	INDUSTRY
Income per employee	$40,000	$8,000	$10,000	$8,000	$15,000
Revenue per employee	$663,000	$535,000	$597,000	$510,000	$568,000
Receivables turnover	4.0	1.5	1.0	2.2	2.1
Inventory turnover	12.0	11.5	11.7	5.9	11.0
Asset turnover	0.8	0.6	0.4	0.8	0.8

SUMMARY

In this chapter we have stressed the importance of the link between operations and supply chain management and the competitive success of the firm. The topics in this book include those that all managers should be familiar with. The operations and supply activities of the firm need to strategically support the competitive priorities of the firm. IKEA's entire integrated process, including the design of products, design of the packaging, manufacturing, distribution, and retail outlets, is carefully wired toward delivering functionally innovative products at the lowest cost possible.

In this chapter we show how the overall strategy of the firm can be tied to operations and supply chain strategy. Important concepts are the operational competitive dimensions, order winners and qualifiers, and strategic fit. The ideas apply to virtually any business and are critical to the firm's ability to sustain a competitive advantage. For a firm to remain competitive, all of the operational activities must buttress the firm's strategy. Wall Street analysts are constantly monitoring how efficient companies are from an operations view. Companies that are strong operationally are able to generate more profit for each dollar of sales, thus making them attractive investments.

KEY TERMS

Triple bottom line A business strategy that includes social, economic, and environmental criteria.

Operations and supply chain strategy Setting broad policies and plans for using the resources of a firm to best support the firm's long-term competitive strategy.

Straddling Occurs when a firm seeks to match what a competitor is doing by adding new features, services, or technologies to existing activities. This often creates problems if certain trade-offs need to be made.

Order winner A dimension that differentiates the products or services of one firm from those of another.

Order qualifier A dimension used to screen a product or service as a candidate for purchase.

Activity-system maps A diagram that shows how a company's strategy is delivered through a set of supporting activities.

Core capabilities Skills that differentiate a manufacturing or service firm from its competitors.

Productivity A measure of how well resources are used.

SOLVED PROBLEM

A furniture manufacturing company has provided the following data. Compare the labor, raw materials and supplies, and total productivity of 2009 and 2010.

		2009	2010
Output:	Sales value of production	$22,000	$35,000
Input:	Labor	10,000	15,000
	Raw materials and supplies	8,000	12,500
	Capital equipment depreciation	700	1,200
	Other	2,200	4,800

Solution

	2009	2010
Partial productivities		
Labor	2.20	2.33
Raw materials and supplies	2.75	2.80
Total productivity	1.05	1.04

REVIEW AND DISCUSSION QUESTIONS

1   Can a factory be fast, dependable, and flexible; produce high-quality products; and still provide poor service from a customer's perspective?
2   Why should a service organization worry about being world-class if it does not compete outside its own national border? What impact does the Internet have on this?
3   What are the major priorities associated with operations strategy? How has their relationship to one another changed over the years?
4   For each priority in question 3, describe the unique characteristics of the market niche with which it is most compatible.
5   Find examples where companies have used features related to environmental sustainability to "win" new customers.
6   A few years ago, the dollar showed relative weakness with respect to foreign currencies such as the yen, euro, and pound. This stimulated exports. Why would long-term reliance on a lower-valued dollar be at best a short-term solution to the competitiveness problem?
7   In your opinion, do business schools have competitive priorities?
8   Why does the "proper" operations strategy keep changing for companies that are world-class competitors?
9   What is meant by the expressions *order winners* and *order qualifiers*? What was the order winner(s) for your last major purchase of a product or service?
10   What do we mean when we say productivity is a "relative" measure?

PROBLEMS*

1   As operations manager, you are concerned about being able to meet sales requirements in the coming months. You have just been given the following production report.

	JAN	FEB	MAR	APR
Units produced	2,300	1,800	2,800	3,000
Hours per machine	325	200	400	320
Number of machines	3	5	4	4

Find the average monthly productivity (units per hour).

*Special thanks to Bill Ruck of Arizona State University for the problems in this section.

2   Sailmaster makes high-performance sails for competitive windsurfers. Below is information about the inputs and outputs for one model, the Windy 2000.

Units sold	1,217
Sale price each	$1,700
Total labor hours	46,672
Wage rate	$12/hour
Total materials	$60,000
Total energy	$4,000

Calculate the productivity in **sales revenue/labor expense.**

3   Acme Corporation received the data below for its rodent cage production unit. Find the **total** productivity.

OUTPUT	INPUT	
50,000 cages	Production time	620 labor hours
Sales price: $3.50 per unit	Wages	$7.50 per hour
	Raw materials (total cost)	$30,000
	Component parts (total cost)	$15,350

4   Two types of cars (Deluxe and Limited) were produced by a car manufacturer. Quantities sold, price per unit, and labor hours follow. What is the labor productivity for each car? Explain the problem(s) associated with the labor productivity.

	QUANTITY	$/UNIT
Deluxe car	4,000 units sold	$8,000/car
Limited car	6,000 units sold	$9,500/car
Labor, Deluxe	20,000 hours	$12/hour
Labor, Limited	30,000 hours	$14/hour

5   A U.S. manufacturing company operating a subsidiary in an LDC (less developed country) shows the following results:

	U.S.	LDC
Sales (units)	100,000	20,000
Labor (hours)	20,000	15,000
Raw materials (currency)	$20,000	FC 20,000
Capital equipment (hours)	60,000	5,000

a. Calculate partial labor and capital productivity figures for the parent and subsidiary. Do the results seem misleading?

b. Compute the multifactor productivity figures for labor and capital together. Are the results better?

c. Calculate raw material productivity figures (units/$ where $1 = FC 10). Explain why these figures might be greater in the subsidiary.

6   Various financial data for 2009 and 2010 follow. Calculate the total productivity measure and the partial measures for labor, capital, and raw materials for this company for both years. What do these measures tell you about this company?

		2009	2010
Output:	Sales	$200,000	$220,000
Input:	Labor	30,000	40,000
	Raw materials	35,000	45,000
	Energy	5,000	6,000
	Capital	50,000	50,000
	Other	2,000	3,000

7   An electronics company makes communications devices for military contracts. The company just completed two contracts. The navy contract was for 2,300 devices and took 25 workers two weeks (40 hours per week) to complete. The army contract was for 5,500 devices that were produced by 35 workers in three weeks. On which contract were the workers more productive?

8   A retail store had sales of $45,000 in April and $56,000 in May. The store employs eight full-time workers who work a 40-hour week. In April the store also had seven part-time workers at 10 hours per week, and in May the store had nine part-timers at 15 hours per week (assume four weeks in each month). Using sales dollars as the measure of output, what is the percentage change in productivity from April to May?

9   A parcel delivery company delivered 103,000 packages in 2009, when its average employment was 84 drivers. In 2010 the firm handled 112,000 deliveries with 96 drivers. What was the percentage change in productivity from 2009 to 2010?

10 A fast-food restaurant serves hamburgers, cheeseburgers, and chicken sandwiches. The restaurant counts a cheeseburger as equivalent to 1.25 hamburgers and chicken sandwiches as 0.8 hamburger. Current employment is five full-time employees who work a 40-hour week. If the restaurant sold 700 hamburgers, 900 cheeseburgers, and 500 chicken sandwiches in one week, what is its productivity? What would its productivity have been if it had sold the same number of sandwiches (2,100) but the mix was 700 of each type?

CASE: THE TAO OF TIMBUK2*

"Timbuk2 is more than a bag. It's more than a brand. Timbuk2 is a bond. To its owner, a Timbuk2 bag is a dependable, everyday companion. We see fierce, emotional attachments form between Timbuk2 customers and their bags all the time. A well-worn Timbuk2 bag has a certain patina—the stains and scars of everyday urban adventures. Many Timbuk2 bags are worn daily for a decade, or more, accompanying the owner through all sorts of defining life events. True to our legend of 'indestructibility,' it's not uncommon for a Timbuk2 bag to outlive jobs, personal relationships, even pets. This is the Tao of Timbuk2."

What makes Timbuk2 so unique? Visit their Web site at **www.timbuk2.com** and see for yourself. Each bag is custom designed by the customer on their Web site. After the customer selects the basic bag configuration and size, colors for each of the

various panels are presented; various lines, logos, pockets, and straps are selected so that the bag is tailored to the exact specifications of the customer. A quick click of the mouse and the bag is delivered directly to the customer in only two days. How do they do this?

This San Francisco–based company is known for producing high-quality custom and classic messenger bags direct to customer order. They have a team of approximately 25 hardworking cutters and sewers in their San Francisco plant. Over the years, they have fine-tuned their production line to make it as efficient as possible while producing the highest-quality messenger bags available.

The local manufacturing is focused on the custom messenger bag. For these bags, orders are taken over the Internet. The customers are given many configuration, size, color, pocket, and strap options. The bag is tailored to the exact specifications of the

customer on the Timbuk2 assembly line in San Francisco and sent via overnight delivery directly to the customer.

Recently, Timbuk2 has begun making some of its new products in China, which is a concern to some of its long-standing customers. The company argues that it has designed its new products to provide the best possible features, quality, and value at reasonable prices and stresses that these new products are designed in San Francisco. Timbuk2 argues that the new bags are much more complex to build and require substantially more labor and a variety of very expensive machines to produce. They argue that the San Francisco factory labor cost alone would make the retail price absurdly high. After researching a dozen factories in China, Timbuk2 found one that it thinks is up to the task of producing these new bags. Much as in San Francisco, the China factory employs a team of hardworking craftspeople who earn good wages and an honest living. Timbuk2 visits the China factory every four to eight weeks to ensure superior quality standards and working conditions.

On the Timbuk2 Web site, the company argues they are the same hardworking group of bag fanatics designing and making great bags, and supporting our local community and increasingly competitive global market. The company reports that demand is still strong for the custom messenger bags made in San Francisco and that the new laptop bags sourced from China are receiving rave reviews. The additional business is allowing them to hire more people in all departments at the San Francisco headquarters—creating even more jobs locally.

QUESTIONS

1 Consider the two categories of products that Timbuk2 makes and sells. For the custom messenger bag, what are the key competitive dimensions that are driving sales? Are their competitive priorities different for the new laptop bags sourced in China?

2 Compare the assembly line in China to that in San Francisco along the following dimensions: (1) volume or rate of production, (2) required skill of the workers, (3) level of automation, and (4) amount of raw materials and finished goods inventory.

3 Draw two diagrams, one depicting the supply chain for those products sourced in China and the other depicting the bags produced in San Francisco. Show all the major steps, including raw material, manufacturing, finished goods, distribution inventory, and transportation. Other than manufacturing cost, what other costs should Timbuk2 consider when making the sourcing decision?

*SPECIAL THANKS TO KYLE CALTANI OF INDIANA UNIVERSITY FOR THIS CASE.

SUPER QUIZ

1 A strategy that is designed to meet current needs without compromising the ability of future generations to meet their needs.

2 The three criteria included in a triple bottom line.

3 It is probably most difficult to compete on this major competitive dimension.

4 Name the seven operations and supply competitive dimensions.

5 This occurs when a company seeks to match what a competitor is doing while maintaining its existing competitive position.

6 A criterion that differentiates the products or services of one firm from those of another.

7 A screening criterion that permits a firm's products to be considered as possible candidates for purchase.

8 A diagram showing the activities that support a company's strategy.

9 A measure calculated by taking the ratio of output to input.

1. Sustainable 2. Social, economic, environmental 3. Cost 4. Cost, quality, delivery speed, delivery reliability, coping with changes in demand, flexibility and new-product introduction speed, other product-specific criteria 5. Straddling 6. Order winner 7. Order qualifier 8. Activity-system map 9. Productivity

SELECTED BIBLIOGRAPHY

Blanchard, David. *Supply Chain Management Best Practices*. New York: John Wiley & Sons, 2006.

Hayes, Robert; Gary Pisano; David Upton; and Steven Wheelwright. *Operations, Strategy, and Technology: Pursuing the Competitive Edge*. New York: John Wiley & Sons, 2004.

Hill, T. J. *Manufacturing Strategy—Text and Cases*. Burr Ridge; IL: Irwin/McGraw-Hill, 2000.

Slack, N., and M. Lewis. *Operations Strategy*. Harlow, England, and New York: Prentice Hall, 2002.

FOOTNOTE

1 J. Elkington, "Toward the Sustainable Corporation: Win-Win-Win Business Strategies for Sustainable Development," *California Management Review* 36, no. 2 (1994), pp. 90–100.

chapter 3

PRODUCT AND SERVICE DESIGN

IDEO, A DESIGN AND INNOVATION FIRM

IDEO is the world's most celebrated design and innovation consultancy. Its ultimate creation is the process of creativity itself. For co-founder David M. Kelley and his colleagues, work is play, brainstorming is a science, and the most important rule is to break the rules (**www.ideo.com**).

"IDEO is a zoo—oh, lovely metaphor for this age of the nanosecond! Experts of all flavors commingle in 'offices' that look more like rowdy kindergarten classrooms than home to one of America's (and the world's) most successful design firms. Desks are littered with works-in-progress and the remains of midnight fast-food binges. Models of futuristic lamps and movie special-effects devices and high-tech blood-chemistry analyzers, in all

After reading this chapter you will:

1. Understand the product development process for both manufactured and service products.

2. Demonstrate how the development of products can have significant economic impact on the firm.

3. Align design with the desires of the customer by using quality function deployment (QFD) concepts.

4. Explain how design can significantly impact manufacturing cost.

5. Be introduced to product development performance measures.

stages of development, lie about here and there—and are the cause of nonstop kibitzing. The planet's most advanced software programs, running on the world's most advanced workstations, networked with heaven-knows-whom from heaven-knows-where, hum 24 hours a day.

"Clients and other outsiders pop in and out without ado. Chatter is ceaseless. Brainstorming sessions, pitting a dozen minds from different disciplines against one another in raucous pursuit of zany ideas, are called on a moment's notice. Bikes line the halls. Joke prizes, along with impressive awards, hang on every wall. The bottom line: IDEO gets the job done on time, on budget, and with exceptional imagination."[1]

IDEO's novel design process centers on two activities that are repeated over and over:

1. **Brainstorming.**   IDEO enforces some strict rules during these sessions.
   a. Defer judgment so that the flow of ideas is not interrupted.
   b. Build on the ideas of others because this is far more productive than hogging the glory for your own insights.
   c. Stay focused on the topic; tangents are not allowed.
   d. One person at a time so that you do not drown out that quiet, brilliant mumbler in the corner of the room.
   e. Go for quantity—150 ideas in 30–45 minutes is good.
   f. Encourage wild ideas.
   g. Be visual; for example, sketch ideas to help others understand them.
2. **Rapid prototyping.**   The idea is that it is easier to discuss a model of something, no matter how primitive, than to talk about a bunch of abstract ideas. Rapid prototyping consists of three R's: rough, rapid, and right. The first two R's are fairly self-explanatory—make your models rough and make them rapidly. In the early stages, perfecting a model is a waste of time. Right does not mean your model needs to work. Instead, it refers to building lots of small models that focus on specific problems. For example, when a group at IDEO designed a phone, they cut out dozens of pieces of foam and cradled them between their heads and shoulders to find the best shape for a handset.

Designing new products and getting them to market quickly is the challenge facing manufacturers in industries as diverse as computer chips and potato chips. Customers of computer chip manufacturers, such as computer companies, need ever-more-powerful semiconductors for their evolving product lines. Food producers need to provide their grocery store customers with new taste sensations to sustain or enlarge their retail market share. How manufactured products are designed and how the process to produce them is selected are the topics of this chapter.

THE PRODUCT DESIGN PROCESS

Companies continuously bring new products to market as customer needs and wants change. Product design is integral to the success of many companies. Product design differs significantly depending on the industry. For consumer products, understanding consumer preferences and market testing prospective products are very important activities. For pharmaceuticals, extensive clinical tests are often required that involve carefully controlled experiments to test both the safety and the effectiveness of a potential product. Companies that specialize in the design of products have highly developed processes to support the activities needed for an industry.

In today's world, companies often outsource major functions rather than supporting these functions in-house, including product design. Companies that specialize in designing and manufacturing products for other companies have become very successful. The producing companies are called **contract manufacturers**, and they have become successful in industries such as electronic products, clothing, drug, plastics, and custom manufacturing. A simple definition of a contract manufacturer is an organization capable of manufacturing and/or purchasing all the components needed to produce a finished product or device.

Contract manufacturer

The use of contract manufacturers has dramatically changed the way traditional manufacturing companies now operate. Depending on the situation, contract manufacturers will take various roles for a company. For example, in the automobile industry, contract manufacturers produce many of the parts and subassemblies, such as the seats and other interior parts, the headlight and taillight assemblies, and the electronic equipment such as radio/CD and GPS navigation systems. The actual automobiles are often built regionally in the countries where the products will be sold to reduce transportation cost and manage currency exchange risk. Close coordination is required to manage the network of assembly plants and contract manufacturing partners for success.

Given the potential advantages of using contract manufacturers for producing products and specialized design firms for designing their products, a firm must decide what its core competency should be. A company's **core competency** is the one thing that it can do better than its competitors. A core competency can be anything from product design to sustained dedication of a firm's employees. The goal is to have a core competency that yields a long-term competitive advantage to the company.

Core competency

As an example, consider Honda's expertise in engines. Honda has been able to exploit this core competency to develop a variety of quality products from lawn mowers and snow blowers to trucks and automobiles. To take another example from the automotive industry, it has been claimed that Volvo's core competency is safety.

A core competency has three characteristics:

1. It provides potential access to a wide variety of markets.
2. It increases perceived customer benefits.
3. It is hard for competitors to imitate.

A good example is Black and Decker, the U.S. manufacturer of tools. Black and Decker's core technological competency is in 200- to 600-watt electric motors. All of its products are modifications of this basic technology (with the exception of workbenches, flashlights, battery-charging systems, toaster ovens, and coffee percolators). The company produces products for three markets:

1. The home workshop market. In the home workshop market, small electric motors are used to produce drills, circular saws, sanders, routers, rotary tools, polishers, and drivers.
2. The home cleaning and maintenance market. In the home cleaning and maintenance market, small electric motors are used to produce dust busters, vacuum cleaners, hedge trimmers, edge trimmers, lawn mowers, leaf blowers, and pressure sprayers.
3. The kitchen appliance market. In the kitchen appliance market, small electric motors are used to produce can openers, food processors, blenders, breadmakers, and fans.

The real challenge for a firm is to decide exactly how the various functions critical to success will be handled. At one extreme is the fully vertically integrated firm where all activities from the design to the fabrication of the individual parts are handled in-house. At the other extreme is a company that only sells products and outsources all the design and manufacturing functions.

The following are a few examples of what some highly successful companies are doing:

• Sun Microsystems designs the SPARC chips used in its high-performance workstations but subcontracts the fabrication of those chips to specialized chip makers (while maintaining ownership of the intellectual property).
• A pharmaceutical company may purchase information on genetic targets from a genomics company, contract with a specialist in combinatorial chemistry for rapid synthesis and screening of candidate compounds, and even utilize a contract research organization to conduct clinical trials but retain ownership of the intellectual property (patents, experimental data, trademarks, etc.) of the drug that eventually comes to market.

- Dell has developed a set of highly specialized systems that support its make-to-order operating strategy. Dell has created a set of proprietary logistical processes that range from the design of its Web page through its information systems infrastructure (a process that has proved difficult for others to imitate). Dell owns the data about what people are buying and in which combinations. It also has been vertically integrated into final assembly facilities that are designed to efficiently produce in lot sizes of one. Finally, while it outsources components, Dell uses longer-term relationships with its suppliers and links them into its information system to support quick response.

In this chapter we first discuss a generic product design process. Here we develop a generic process and show how this can be adapted to various types of common products. Next, we show how the economic impact of new products can be evaluated. Later in the chapter we discuss how customer preferences are considered in product design. Then we show how the design of the product impacts manufacturing and assembly processes. Finally, we discuss measures of product development performance.

THE PRODUCT DEVELOPMENT PROCESS[2]

We begin by defining a generic product development process that describes the basic steps needed to design a product. This process represents the basic sequence of steps or activities that a firm employs to conceive, design, and bring a product to market. Many of these tasks involve intellectual rather than physical activities. Some firms define and follow a precise and detailed development process, while others may not even be able to describe their processes. Every organization employs a process that is different from that of every other organization; in fact, the same organization may follow different processes for different product groups.

Our generic product development process consists of six phases, as illustrated in Exhibit 3.1. The process begins with a planning phase, which is the link to advanced research and technology development activities. The output of the planning phase is the project's mission statement, which is the input required to begin the concept development phase and serves as a guide to the development team. The conclusion of the product development process is the product launch, at which time the product becomes available for purchase in the marketplace. Exhibit 3.1 identifies the key activities and responsibilities of the different functions of the firm during each development phase. Because of their continuous involvement in the process, we articulate the roles of marketing, design, and manufacturing. Representatives from other functions, such as research, finance, field service, and sales, also play key roles at points in the process.

The six phases of the generic development process are

Phase 0: Planning.   The planning activity is often referred to as "phase zero" since it precedes the project approval and launch of the actual product development process. This phase begins with corporate strategy and includes assessment of technology developments and market objectives. The output of the planning phase is the project mission statement, which specifies the target market for the product, business goals, key assumptions, and constraints.

Phase 1: Concept development.   In this phase, the needs of the target market are identified, alternative product concepts are generated and evaluated, and one or more concepts are selected for further development and testing. A concept is a description of the form, function, and features of a product and is usually accompanied by a set of specifications, an analysis of competitive products, and an economic justification of the project.

Phase 2: System-level design.   The system-level design phase includes the definition of the product architecture and the decomposition of the product into subsystems and components. The final assembly scheme (which we discuss later in the chapter) for the production system is usually defined during this phase as well. The output of this phase usually includes a geometric layout of the product, a functional specification of each of the product's subsystems, and a preliminary process flow diagram for the final assembly process.

The Generic Product Development Process.
Six phases are shown, including the tasks and responsibilities of the key functions of the
organization for each phase.

exhibit 3.1

	PHASE 0: PLANNING	PHASE 1: CONCEPT DEVELOPMENT	PHASE 2: SYSTEM-LEVEL DESIGN	PHASE 3: DETAIL DESIGN	PHASE 4: TESTING AND REFINEMENT	PHASE 5: PRODUCTION RAMP-UP
MARKETING	• Articulate market opportunity. • Define market segments.	• Collect customer needs. • Identify lead users. • Identify competitive products.	• Develop plan for product options and extended product family. • Set target sales price point(s).	• Develop marketing plan.	• Develop promotion and launch materials. • Facilitate field testing.	• Place early production with key customers.
DESIGN	• Consider product platform and architecture. • Assess new technologies.	• Investigate feasibility of product concepts. • Develop industrial design concepts. • Build and test experimental prototypes.	• Generate alternative product architectures. • Define major subsystems and interfaces. • Refine industrial design.	• Define part geometry. • Choose materials. • Assign tolerances. • Complete industrial design control documentation.	• Reliability testing. • Life testing. • Performance testing. • Obtain regulatory approvals. • Implement design changes.	• Evaluate early production output.
MANUFACTURING	• Identify production constraints. • Set supply chain strategy.	• Estimate manufacturing cost. • Assess production feasibility.	• Identify suppliers for key components. • Perform make-buy analysis. • Define final assembly scheme. • Set target costs.	• Define piece-part production processes. • Design tooling. • Define quality assurance processes. • Begin procurement of long-lead tooling.	• Facilitate supplier ramp-up. • Refine fabrication and assembly processes. • Train workforce. • Refine quality assurance processes.	• Begin operation of entire production system.
OTHER FUNCTIONS	• Research: Demonstrate available technologies. • Finance: Provide planning goals. • General Management: Allocate project resources.	• Finance: Facilitate economic analysis. • Legal: Investigate patent issues.	• Finance: Facilitate make-buy analysis. • Service: Identify service issues.		• Sales: Develop sales plan.	

Phase 3: Design detail.   This phase includes the complete specification of the geometry,
materials, and tolerances of all the unique parts in the product and the identification of
all the standard parts to be purchased from suppliers. A process plan is established, and
tooling is designed for each part to be fabricated within the production system. The output
of this phase is the drawings or computer files describing the geometry of each part and
its production tooling, the specifications of purchased parts, and the process plans for the
fabrication and assembly of the product.

Phase 4: Testing and refinement.   The testing and refinement phase involves the construction and evaluation of multiple preproduction versions of the product. Early prototypes are usually built with parts with the same geometry and material properties as the production version of the product but not necessarily fabricated with the actual processes to be used in production. Prototypes are tested to determine whether the product will work as designed and whether the product satisfies customer needs.

Phase 5: Production ramp-up.   In the production ramp-up phase, the product is made using the intended production system. The purpose of the ramp-up is to train the workforce and to work out any remaining problems in the production processes. Products produced during production ramp-up are sometimes supplied to preferred customers and are carefully evaluated to identify any remaining flaws. The transition from production ramp-up to ongoing production is usually gradual. At some point in the transition, the product is *launched* and becomes available for widespread distribution.

The development process described in Exhibit 3.1 is generic, and particular processes will differ in accordance with a firm's unique context. The generic process is most like the process used in a *market-pull* situation. This is when a firm begins product development with a market opportunity and then uses whatever available technologies are required to satisfy the market need (i.e., the market "pulls" the development decisions). In addition to the generic market-pull processes, several variants are common and correspond to the following: *technology-push* products, *platform* products, *process-intensive* products, *customized* products, *high-risk* products, *quick-build* products, and *complex systems*. Each of these situations is described below. The characteristics of these situations and the resulting deviations from the generic process are summarized in Exhibit 3.2.

Technology-Push Products   In developing technology-push products, a firm begins with a new proprietary technology and looks for an appropriate market in which to apply this technology (that is, the technology "pushes" development). Gore-Tex, an expanded Teflon sheet manufactured by W. L. Gore & Associates, is a good example of technology

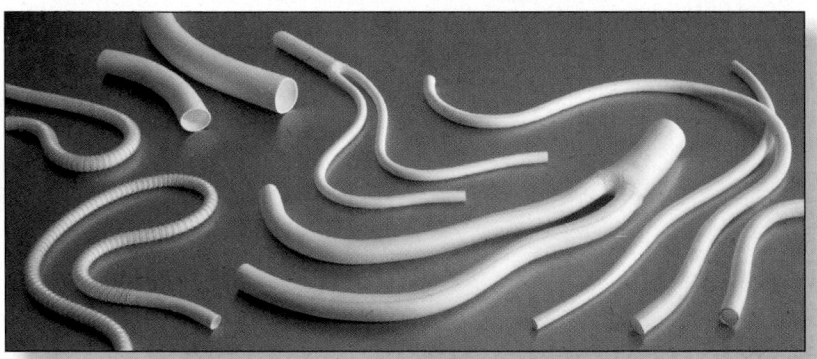

push. The company has developed dozens of products incorporating Gore-Tex, including artificial veins for vascular surgery (see photo this page), insulation for high-performance electric cables, fabric for outerwear, dental floss, and liners for bagpipe bags.

Platform Products   A platform product is built around a preexisting technological subsystem (a technology *platform*). Examples include the hybrid motor used in the Toyota Prius, the Microsoft Vista operating system, and the video imaging system used in Canon cameras. Huge investments were made in developing these platforms, and therefore every attempt is made to incorporate them into several different products. In some sense, platform products are very similar to technology-push products in that the team begins the development effort with an assumption that the product concept will embody a particular technology. The primary difference is that a technology platform has already demonstrated its usefulness in the marketplace in meeting customer needs. The firm, in many cases, can assume that the technology also will be useful in related markets. Products built on technology platforms are much simpler to develop than if the technology were developed from scratch. For this reason, and because of the possible sharing of costs across several products, a firm may be able to offer a platform product in markets that could not justify the development of a unique technology.

Process-Intensive Products   Examples of process-intensive products include semiconductors, foods, chemicals, and paper. For these products, the production process has

Summary of Variants of Generic Product Development Process   **exhibit 3.2**

PROCESS TYPE	DESCRIPTION	DISTINCT FEATURES	EXAMPLES
Generic (market-pull products)	The team begins with a market opportunity and selects appropriate technologies to meet customer needs	Process generally includes distinct planning, concept development, system-level design, detail design, testing and refinement, and production ramp-up phases	Sporting goods, furniture, tools
Technology-push products	The team begins with a new technology, then finds an appropriate market	Planning phase involves matching technology and market; concept development assumes a given technology	Gore-Tex rainwear, Tyvek envelopes
Platform products	The team assumes that the new product will be built around an established technological subsystem	Concept development assumes a proven technology platform	Consumer electronics, computers, printers
Process-intensive products	Characteristics of the product are highly constrained by the production process	Either an existing production process must be specified from the start or both product and process must be developed together from the start	Snack foods, breakfast cereals, chemicals, semiconductors
Customized products	New products are slight variations of existing configurations	Similarity of projects allows for a streamlined and highly structured development process	Motors, switches, batteries, containers
High-risk products	Technical or market uncertainties create high risks of failure	Risks are identified early and tracked throughout the process. Analysis and testing activities take place as early as possible	Pharmaceuticals, space systems
Quick-build products	Rapid modeling and prototyping enables many design–build–test cycles	Detail design and testing phases are repeated a number of times until the product is completed or time/budget runs out	Software, cellular phones
Complex systems	System must be decomposed into several subsystems and many components	Subsystems and components are developed by many teams working in parallel, followed by system integration and validation	Airplanes, jet engines, automobiles

an impact on properties of the product so that product design cannot be separated from the production process design. In many cases, process-intensive products are produced at very high volumes and are bulk, rather than discrete, goods. Often, the new product and new process are developed simultaneously. For example, creating a new shape of breakfast cereal or snack food requires both product and process development activities. In other cases, the existing process will constrain the product design by the capabilities of the process. This might be true of a new paper product to be made in a particular paper mill or a new semiconductor device to be made in an existing wafer fabrication facility, for example.

Customized Products   Customized products are slight variations of standard configurations and are typically developed in response to a specific order by a customer. Examples include switches, motors, batteries, and containers. Developing these products consists primarily of setting values of design variables such as physical dimensions and materials. Companies can become very good at quickly producing these custom products using a highly structured design and development process structured around the capabilities of the process to be used.

High-Risk Products   High-risk products are those that entail unusually large uncertainties related to the technology or market so that there is substantial technical or market risk. The generic product development process is modified to face high-risk situations by taking steps to address the largest risks in the early stages of product development. This usually requires completing some design and test activities earlier in the process. For example, if there is high uncertainty related to the technical performance of the product, it makes sense to build working models of the key features and to test these earlier in the process. Multiple solution paths may be explored in parallel to ensure that one of the solutions succeeds. Design reviews must assess levels of risk on a regular basis, with the expectation that risk is being reduced over time and not postponed.

Quick-Build Products   For the development of some products, such as software and many electronic products, building and testing prototype models has become such a rapid process that the design–build–test cycle can be repeated many times. Following concept development in this process, the system-level design phase entails decomposition of the product into high-, medium-, and low-priority features. This is followed by several cycles of design, build, integrate, and test activities, beginning with the highest-priority items. This process takes advantage of the fast prototyping cycle by using the result of each cycle to learn how to modify the priorities for the next cycle. Customers may even be involved in the testing process. When time or budget runs out, usually all of the high- and medium-priority features have been incorporated into the evolving product, and the low-priority features may be omitted until the next product generation.

Complex Systems   Larger-scale products such as automobiles and airplanes are complex systems composed of many interacting subsystems and components. When developing complex systems, modifications to the generic product development process address a number of system-level issues. The concept development phase considers the architecture of the entire system, and multiple architectures may be considered as competing concepts for the overall system. The system-level design becomes critical. During this phase, the system is decomposed into subsystems and these further into many components. Teams are assigned to develop each component. Additional teams are assigned the special challenge of integrating components into the subsystems and these into the overall system. Detail design of the components is a highly parallel process, often referred to as concurrent engineering, with many separate development teams working at once. System engineering specialists manage the interactions across the components and subsystems. The testing and refinement phase includes not only system integration but extensive testing and validation of the product.

Concurrent engineering

ECONOMIC ANALYSIS OF PRODUCT DEVELOPMENT PROJECTS[3]

A product development team at Polaroid Corporation was in the midst of developing a new photograph printer, the CI-700. The CI-700 would produce instant full-color photographs from digital images stored in a computer. The primary markets for the product are the graphic arts, insurance, and real estate industries. During the CI-700's development, the Polaroid team was faced with several decisions that it knew could have a significant impact on the product's profitability:

- Should the team take more time for development in order to make the product available on multiple computer "platforms" or would a delay in bringing the CI-700 to market be too costly?
- Should the product use print media (instant film) from Polaroid's consumer camera business or new and specialized premium-quality print media?

- Should the team increase development spending in order to increase the reliability of the CI-700?

It is important to remember that economic analysis can capture only those factors that are measurable and that projects often have both positive and negative implications that are difficult to quantify. Also, it is difficult for an economic analysis to capture the characteristics of a dynamic and competitive environment. Economic analysis is useful in at least two different circumstances:

1. Go/no-go milestones. For example, should we try to develop a product to address a new market opportunity? Should we proceed with the implementation of a selected concept? Should we launch the product we have developed? These decisions typically arise at the end of each phase of development.
2. Operational design and development decisions. Operational decisions involve questions such as: Should we spend $100,000 to hire an outside firm to develop this component in order to save two months of development time? Should we launch the product in four months at a unit cost of $450 or wait six months, when we can reduce the cost to $400?

We recommend that a base-case financial model be initially built to understand the financial implications of a product development project. In the following, we describe how to construct this model.

BUILD A BASE-CASE FINANCIAL MODEL

Constructing the base-case model consists of estimating the timing and magnitude of future cash flows and then computing the net present value (NPV) of those cash flows. The timing and magnitude of the cash flows are estimated by merging the project schedule with the project budget, sales volume forecasts, and estimated production costs. The level of detail of cash flows should be coarse enough to be convenient to work with, yet contain enough detail to facilitate effective decision making. The most basic categories of cash flow for a typical new-product-development project are

- Development cost (all remaining design, testing, and refinement costs up to production ramp-up).
- Ramp-up cost.
- Marketing and support cost.
- Production cost.
- Sales revenue.

The financial model we use is simplified to include only the major cash flows that are typically used in practice, but conceptually it is identical to more complex models. The numerical values of the cash flows come from budgets and other estimates obtained from the development team, the manufacturing organization, and the marketing organization. We will illustrate the approach by using data similar to what might have been used by the Polaroid team developing the CI-700.

The following are cost estimates that we will use for our sample model:

Development cost	$5 million
Ramp-up cost	$2 million
Marketing and support cost	$1 million/year
Unit production cost	$400/unit
Sales and production volume	20,000 units/year
Unit price	$800/unit

For our model, we assume that all revenue and expenses that have occurred prior to today are sunk costs and are irrelevant to NPV calculations. For those of you not familiar with NPV calculations, see Appendix C at the end of the book.

exhibit 3.3   CI-700 Project Schedule from Inception through Market Withdrawal

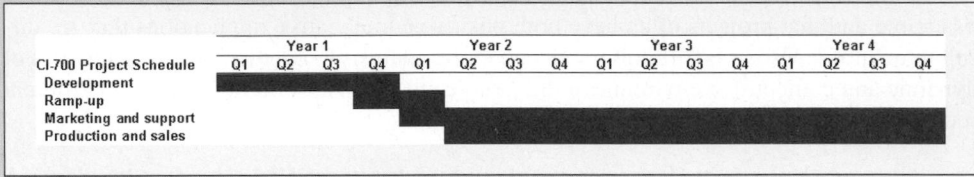

To complete the model, the financial estimates must be merged with timing information. This can be done by considering the project schedule and sales plan. Exhibit 3.3 shows the project timing information in Gantt chart form for the CI-700. For most projects, a time increment of months or quarters is most appropriate. The remaining time to market is estimated to be five quarters, and the product sales are anticipated to last 11 quarters.

A simple method of organizing project cash flow is with a spreadsheet. The rows of the spreadsheet are the different cash flow categories, while the columns represent successive time periods. To keep things simple, we assume that the rate of cash flow for any category is constant across any time period. For example, total development spending of $5 million over one year is allocated equally to each of the four quarters. In practice, of course, the values can be arranged in any way that best represents the team's forecast of the cash flows. We multiply the unit sales quantity by the unit price to find the total product revenues in each period. We also multiply the unit production quantity by the unit production cost to find the total production cost in each period. Exhibit 3.4 illustrates the resulting spreadsheet.

Computing the NPV requires that the net cash flow for each period be determined, and then that this cash flow be converted to its present value (its value in today's dollars), as

exhibit 3.4   Merging the Project Financials and Schedule into a Cash Flow Report

Microsoft Excel - Ch5 - Economic Analysis.xls

File Edit View Insert Format Tools Data Window Help

	A	B	C	D	E	F	G	H	I	J	K	L	M	N	O	P	Q
1		Year 1				Year 2				Year 3				Year 4			
2	CI-700 Project Schedule	Q1	Q2	Q3	Q4	Q1	Q2	Q3	Q4	Q1	Q2	Q3	Q4	Q1	Q2	Q3	Q4
3	Development																
4	Ramp-up																	
5	Marketing and support																	
6	Production and sales																	
7																		
8		Year 1				Year 2				Year 3				Year 4			
9	($ values in thousands)	Q1	Q2	Q3	Q4	Q1	Q2	Q3	Q4	Q1	Q2	Q3	Q4	Q1	Q2	Q3	Q4
10																		
11	Development cost	-1,250	-1,250	-1,250	-1,250												
12	Ramp-up cost				-1,000	-1,000												
13	Marketing and support cost					-250	-250	-250	-250	-250	-250	-250	-250	-250	-250	-250	-250
14	Production volume						5,000	5,000	5,000	5,000	5,000	5,000	5,000	5,000	5,000	5,000	5,000
15	Unit production cost						-0.4	-0.4	-0.4	-0.4	-0.4	-0.4	-0.4	-0.4	-0.4	-0.4	-0.4
16	Production cost						-2,000	-2,000	-2,000	-2,000	-2,000	-2,000	-2,000	-2,000	-2,000	-2,000	-2,000
17	Sales volume						5,000	5,000	5,000	5,000	5,000	5,000	5,000	5,000	5,000	5,000	5,000
18	Unit price						0.8	0.8	0.8	0.8	0.8	0.8	0.8	0.8	0.8	0.8	0.8
19	Sales revenue						4,000	4,000	4,000	4,000	4,000	4,000	4,000	4,000	4,000	4,000	4,000
20																		
21	Period cash flow	-1,250	-1,250	-1,250	-2,250	-1,250	1,750	1,750	1,750	1,750	1,750	1,750	1,750	1,750	1,750	1,750	1,750
22	PV Year 1, r = 10%	-1,220	-1,190	-1,161	-2,038	-1,105	1,509	1,472	1,436	1,401	1,367	1,334	1,301	1,269	1,239	1,208	1,179
23																		
24	Project NPV	8,003																

Economic Analysis

CI-700 Development Cost Sensitivity

exhibit 3.5

CHANGE IN DEVELOPMENT COST (%)	DEVELOPMENT COST ($ THOUSANDS)	CHANGE IN DEVELOPMENT COST ($ THOUSANDS)	CHANGE IN NPV (%)	NPV ($ THOUSANDS)	CHANGE IN NPV ($ THOUSANDS)
50	7,500	2,500	−29.4	5,791	−2,412
20	6,000	1,000	−11.8	7,238	−964
10	5,500	500	−5.9	7,721	−482
Base case	5,000	Base case	0.0	8,203	0
−10	4,500	−500	5.9	8,685	482
−20	4,000	−1,000	11.8	9,167	964
−30	2,500	−2,500	29.4	10,615	2,412

shown in the last few rows of Exhibit 3.5. Consider, for example, the calculations for year 3, first quarter:

1. The period cash flow is the sum of inflows and outflows.

Marketing cost	$ −250,000
Product revenues	4,000,000
Production cost	−2,000,000
Period cash flow	$1,750,000

2. The present value of this period cash flow discounted at 10 percent per year (2.5 percent per quarter) back to the first quarter of year 1 (a total of nine quarters) is $1,401,275. (The concepts and spreadsheet functions for calculating present value, net present value, and discount rate are reviewed in Supplement A.)

$$\frac{\$1,750,000}{1.025^9} = \$1,401,275$$

3. The project NPV is the sum of the discounted cash flows for each of the periods, or $8,002,819. (Note that in the spreadsheet we have rounded the numbers to the nearest $1,000.)

The NPV of this project, according to the base-case model, is positive, so the model supports and is consistent with the decision to proceed with development. Such modeling also can be used to support major investment decisions. Say, for example, that Polaroid was deciding between two different production facilities with different ramp-up, production, and support costs. The team could develop a model for each of the two scenarios and then compare the NPVs. The scenario with the higher NPV would better support the investment decision. We now consider sensitivity analysis as a technique for studying multiple scenarios for ongoing product development decisions.

SENSITIVITY ANALYSIS TO UNDERSTAND PROJECT TRADE-OFFS

Sensitivity analysis uses the financial model to answer "what if " questions by calculating the change in NPV corresponding to a change in the factors included in the model. As an example, consider the sensitivity of NPV to changes in development cost. By making incremental changes to development cost while holding other factors constant, we can see the incremental impact on project NPV. For example, what will be the change in NPV if the development cost is decreased by 20 percent? A 20 percent decrease would lower the total development spending from $5 million to $4 million. If development time remains one year, then the spending per quarter would decrease from $1.25 million to $1 million. This change is simply entered in the model, and the resulting NPV is calculated.

A 20 percent decrease in development cost will increase NPV to $9,167,000. This represents a dollar increase of $964,000 and a percentage increase of 11.8 in NPV. This is an extremely simple case: we assume we can achieve the same project goals by spending $1 million less on development and we therefore have increased the project value by the present value of $1 million in savings accrued over a one-year period of time. The CI-700 development cost sensitivity analysis for a range of changes is shown in Exhibit 3.5.

Many other scenarios can be developed for the project, including the following:

1. **Project development time.** Consider the impact of a 25 percent increase in the project development time. This would raise the development time from four to five quarters and delay the start of the production ramp-up, marketing efforts, and product sales.

2. **Sales volume.** Increasing sales is a powerful way to increase profit. Of course, a decrease in sales can result in significant loss. Consider, for example, the impact of a 25 percent increase and a 25 percent decrease on the profitability of the new product.

3. **Product cost or sales price.** Consider that a $1 increase in price or a $1 decrease in cost results in a $1 increase in profit. Of course, the $1 increase in price may have a significant impact on demand. Scenarios relating to these parameters are often useful to study.

4. **Development cost.** A dollar spent or saved on development cost is worth the present value of that dollar to the value of the project.

Financial modeling and sensitivity analysis are powerful tools for supporting product development decisions, but these techniques have important limitations. Many argue that rigorous financial analyses are required to bring discipline and control to the product development process. Others argue that financial analysis only focuses on measurable quantities and that it is often extremely difficult to predict these values accurately. The analysis is only as good as the assumptions built into the model, so these limitations must be considered. Possibly more significant are those that argue that activities associated with economic modeling can be very expensive and may significantly reduce the productivity associated with the real product development activities. Their point is that potentially productive development time is devoted to preparation of analyses and meetings and the cumulative effect of this planning and review time can significantly increase development costs.

Development teams must understand the strengths and limitations of the techniques and refrain from developing a stifling bureaucracy around the development of new products. New-product development should be a process that nurtures innovation and creativity. The purpose of economic modeling is simply to ensure that the team is making decisions that are economically sound.

DESIGNING FOR THE CUSTOMER

Before we detail the hows and whys of designing and producing products, it is useful to reflect (or, perhaps more accurately, to editorialize) on the issue of product design from the user's standpoint. In recent years, companies have been so caught up with technological efforts and advances—especially in the field of electronics—that somewhere along the line, consumers were forgotten. Designing for aesthetics and for the user is generally termed *industrial design.* IDEO is one of the most successful industrial design firms in the world. The unique process used at the company is described in the chapter's opening vignette titled "IDEO, A Design and Innovation Firm."

Industrial design is probably the area most abused by manufacturers. When frustrated with products—setting options on the cell phone, working on the car, adjusting a computerized furnace thermostat, or operating a credit card telephone at the airport—most of us have said to ourselves, "The blankety-blank person who designed this should be made to use it!" Often parts are inaccessible, operation is too complicated, or there is no logic to setting or controlling the unit. Sometimes even worse conditions exist: metal edges are sharp and consumers cut their hands trying to reach for adjustment or repairs. Many products have too many technological features—far more than necessary. Most purchasers of electronic products cannot fully operate them and use only a small number of the available features. This has occurred because computer chips are inexpensive and adding more controls has negligible cost. Including an alarm clock or a calculator on a microwave oven costs little. But do you need it? What happens when you lose the operator's manual to any of these complex devices? Why is it that the "Help" icon on your computer provides so little help? Where is the voice of the customer?

QUALITY FUNCTION DEPLOYMENT

One approach to getting the voice of the customer into the design specification of a product is **quality function deployment (QFD)**.[4] This approach, which uses interfunctional teams from marketing, design engineering, and manufacturing, has been credited by Toyota Motor Corporation for reducing costs on its cars by more than 60 percent by significantly shortening design times.

Quality function deployment (QFD)

The QFD process begins with studying and listening to customers to determine the characteristics of a superior product. Through market research, the consumers' product needs and preferences are defined and broken down into categories called *customer requirements*. One example is an auto manufacturer that would like to improve the design of a car door. Through customer surveys and interviews, it determines that two important customer requirements in a car door are that it "stays open on a hill" and is "easy to close from the outside." After the customer requirements are defined, they are weighted based on their relative importance to the customer. Next the consumer is asked to compare and rate the company's products with the products of competitors. This process helps the company determine the product characteristics that are important to the consumer and to evaluate its product in relation to others. The end result is a better understanding and focus on product characteristics that require improvement.

Customer requirement information forms the basis for a matrix called the **house of quality** (see Exhibit 3.6). By building a house of quality matrix, the cross-functional QFD team can use customer feedback to make engineering, marketing, and design decisions. The matrix helps the team translate customer requirements into concrete operating or engineering goals. The important product characteristics and goals for improvement are jointly agreed on and detailed in the house. This process encourages the different departments to work closely together, and it results in a better understanding of one another's goals and issues. However, the most important benefit of the house of quality is that it helps the team focus on building a product that satisfies customers.

House of quality

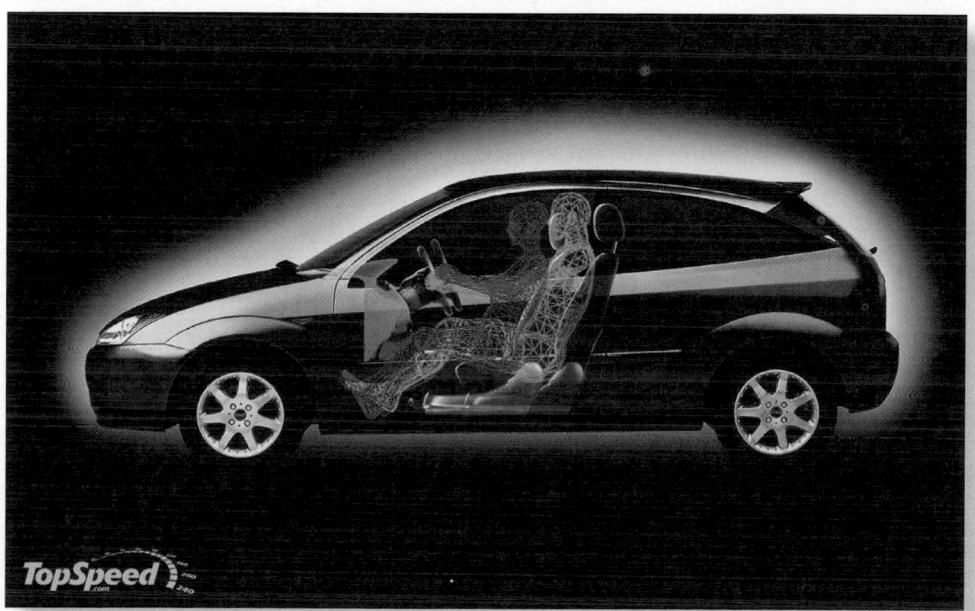

QFD INVOLVES CONVERTING THE EXPECTATIONS AND DEMANDS OF THE CUSTOMERS INTO CLEAR OBJECTIVES, WHICH ARE THEN TRANSLATED INTO THE VEHICLE SPECIFICATION. FOR EXAMPLE, TOPSPEED FOUND THAT PASSENGERS BECAME UNCOMFORTABLE IF THE CAR ROLLED MORE THAN 2 DEGREES AND SIDE ACCELERATION EXCEEDED 13.2 FEET PER SECOND SQUARED. THESE DATA WERE USED TO HELP DEFINE DESIGN CRITERIA FOR THE CHASSIS ENGINEERS.

TopSpeed.com

exhibit 3.6   Completed House of Quality Matrix for a Car Door

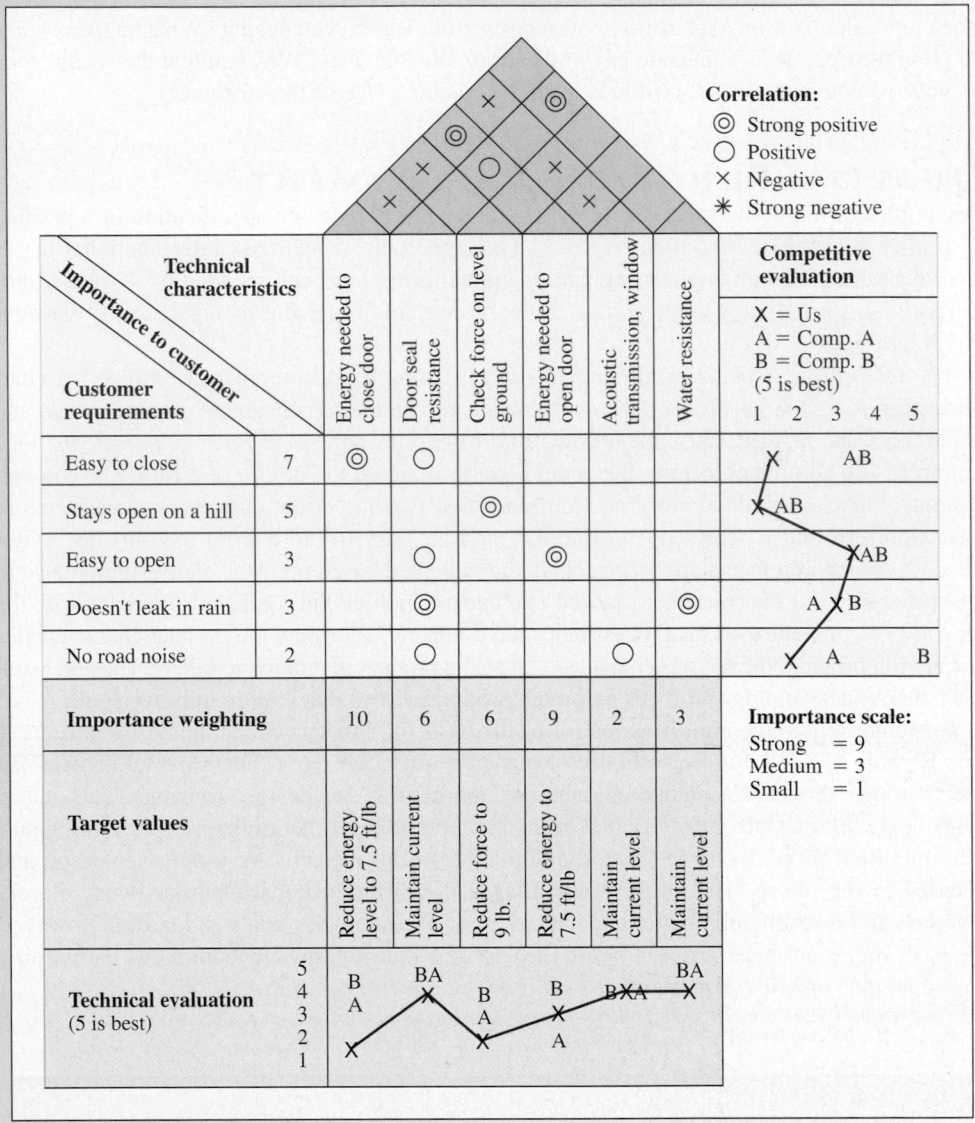

SOURCE: BASED ON J. R. HAUSER AND D. CLAUSING. "THE HOUSE OF QUALITY," *HARVARD BUSINESS REVIEW*, MAY–JUNE 1988, PP. 62–73.

The first step in building the house of quality is to develop a list of customer requirements for the product. These requirements should be ranked in order of importance. Customers are then asked to compare the company's product to the competition. Next a set of technical characteristics of the product is developed. These technical characteristics should relate directly to customer requirements. An evaluation of these characteristics should support or refute customer perception of the product. These data are then used to evaluate the strengths and weaknesses of the product in terms of technical characteristics.

VALUE ANALYSIS/VALUE ENGINEERING

Value analysis/value engineering (VA/VE)

Another way to consider the customers in designing products is by analyzing the "value" they see in the end product. Because it is so important that value be designed into products, we briefly describe value analysis and value engineering. The purpose of **value analysis/ value engineering (VA/VE)** is to simplify products and processes. Its objective is to achieve equivalent or better performance at a lower cost while maintaining all functional requirements defined by the customer. VA/VE does this by identifying and eliminating unnecessary cost. Technically, VA deals with products already in production and is used to analyze product specifications and requirements as shown in production documents and purchase requests. Typically, purchasing departments use VA as a cost reduction technique. Performed before the production stage, value engineering is considered a cost-avoidance method. In practice, however, there is a looping back and forth between the two for a given product. This occurs because new materials, processes, and so forth, require the application of VA techniques to products that have previously undergone VE. The VA/VE analysis approach involves brainstorming such questions as

Does the item have any design features that are not necessary?

Can two or more parts be combined into one?

How can we cut down the weight?

Are there nonstandard parts that can be eliminated?

In the following section, we describe a more formal approach that is often used to guide the process of designing and improving the design of products.

DESIGNING PRODUCTS FOR MANUFACTURE AND ASSEMBLY

The word *design* has many different meanings. To some it means the aesthetic design of a product, such as the external shape of a car or the color, texture, and shape of the casing of a can opener. In another sense, design can mean establishing the basic parameters of a system. For example, before considering any details, the design of a power plant might mean establishing the characteristics of the various units such as generators, pumps, boilers, connecting pipes, and so forth.

Yet another interpretation of the word *design* is the detailing of the materials, shapes, and tolerance of the individual parts of a product. This is the concern of this section. It is an activity that starts with sketches of parts and assemblies and then progresses to the computer-aided design (CAD) workstation (described in the supplement on Operations Technology at the end of the book), where assembly drawings and detailed part drawings are produced. Traditionally, these drawings are then passed to the manufacturing and assembly engineers, whose job it is to optimize the processes used to produce the final product. Frequently, at this stage manufacturing and assembly problems are encountered and requests are made for design changes. Often these design changes are major and result in considerable additional expense and delays in the final product release.

Traditionally, the attitude of designers has been "We design it; you build it." This has now been termed the "over-the-wall approach," where the designer is sitting on one side of the wall and throwing the design over the wall to the manufacturing engineers. These manufacturing engineers then have to deal with the problems that arise because they were not involved in the design effort. One way to overcome this problem is to

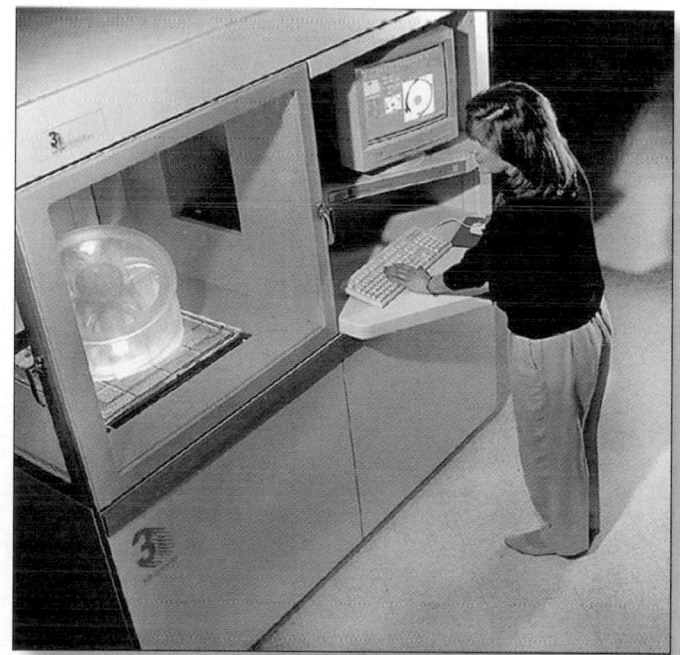

RAPID PROTOTYPING COMBINED WITH DFMA TOOLS NOT ONLY CAN DETERMINE IF A PRODUCT WILL PERFORM ITS DESIGNED FUNCTIONS, BUT HOW WELL AND FOR HOW LONG. USED EARLY IN THE DESIGN CYCLE, IT LEADS TO MORE ROBUST DESIGNS FOR MANUFACTURE, ASSEMBLY, AND PRODUCT USE, AND ALLOWS CRITICAL CHANGES TO BE MADE BEFORE EXPENSIVE TOOLING IS APPLIED. A PRODUCT'S ESTHETICS AND FUNCTIONALITY ARE CONSIDERED JOINTLY AND RESULT IN PRODUCTS CONSTRUCTED WITH OPTIMAL FUNCTIONALITY, CORRECT MATERIALS, AND EFFICIENT ASSEMBLY.

consult the manufacturing engineers during the design stage. The resulting teamwork avoids many of the problems that will arise. These concurrent engineering teams require analysis tools to help them study proposed designs and evaluate them from the point of view of manufacturing difficulty and cost.

HOW DOES DESIGN FOR MANUFACTURING AND ASSEMBLY (DFMA) WORK?

Let's follow an example from the conceptual design stage.[5] Exhibit 3.7 represents a motor drive assembly that is required to sense and control its position on two steel guide rails. This might be the motor that controls a power window in a drive-through window at McDonald's, for example. The motor must be fully enclosed and have a removable cover for access to adjust the position sensor. A major requirement is a rigid base designed to slide up and down the guide rails, which will both support the motor and locate the sensor. The motor and sensor have wires connecting to a power supply and control unit.

A proposed solution is shown in Exhibit 3.8. The base has two bushing inserts so that the holes will not wear out. The motor is secured to the base with two screws, and a hole accepts the cylindrical sensor, which is held in place with a set screw. To provide the required covers, an end plate is screwed to two stand-offs, which are screwed into the base. To keep the wires from shorting out on the metal cover, should they become worn, a plastic bushing is fitted to the end plate, through which the wires pass. Finally, a box-shaped cover slides over the whole assembly from below the base and is held in place by four screws, two passing into the base and two passing into the end cover.

The current design has 19 parts that must be assembled to make the motor drive. These parts consist of the two subassemblies—the motor and the sensor—an additional eight main parts (cover, base, two bushings, two stand-offs, a plastic bushing, and the end plate), and nine screws.

The greatest improvements related to DFMA arise from simplification of the product by reducing the number of separate parts. In order to guide the designer in reducing the part

exhibit 3.7   Configuration of Required Motor Drive Assembly

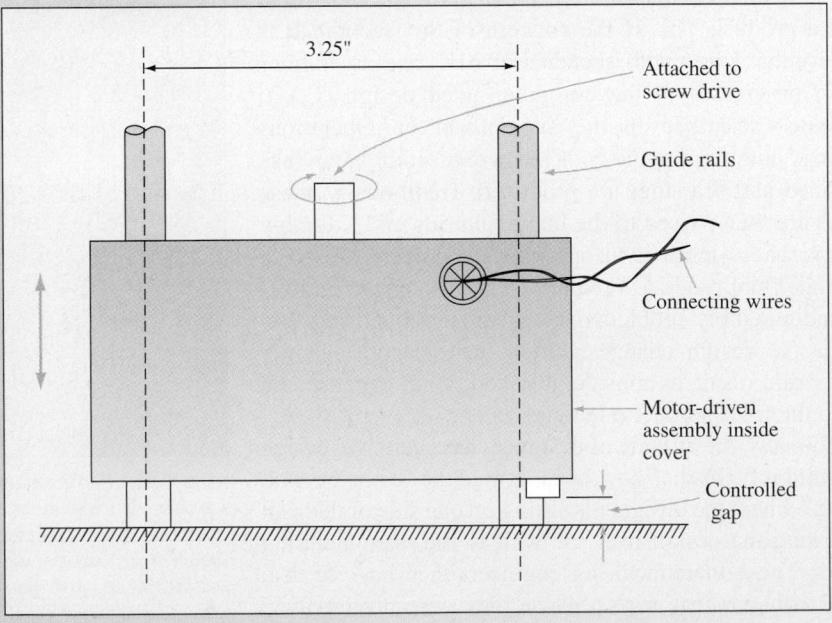

Proposed Motor Drive Design

exhibit 3.8

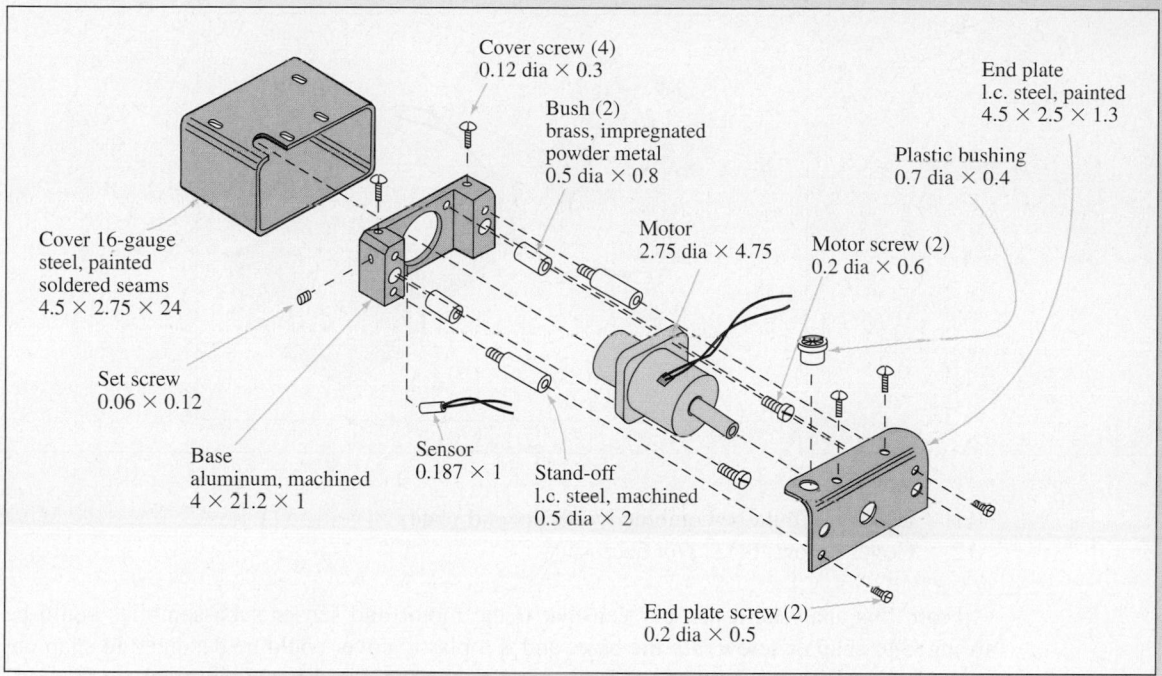

count, the methodology provides three criteria against which each part must be examined as it is added to the product during assembly:

1. During the operation of the product, does the part move relative to all other parts already assembled?
2. Must the part be of a different material than or be isolated from other parts already assembled?
3. Must the part be separate from all other parts to allow the disassembly of the product for adjustment or maintenance?

Application of these criteria to the proposed design would proceed as follows:

1. **Base.** Because this is the first part to be assembled, there are no other parts with which to combine, so it is theoretically a necessary part.
2. **Bushings (2).** These do not satisfy the second criterion. Theoretically, the base and bushings could be of the same material.
3. **Motor.** The motor is a subassembly purchased from a supplier. The criteria do not apply.
4. **Motor screws (2).** In most cases, separate fasteners are not needed, because a fastening arrangement integral to the design (for example, snapping the part into place) is usually possible.
5. **Sensor.** This is another standard subassembly.
6. **Set screw.** Similar to 4, this should not be necessary.
7. **Standoffs (2).** These do not meet the second criterion; they could be incorporated into the base.
8. **End plate.** This must be separate to allow disassembly (apply criterion three).
9. **End plate screws (2).** These should not be necessary.
10. **Plastic bushing.** Could be of the same material as, and therefore combined with, the end plate.

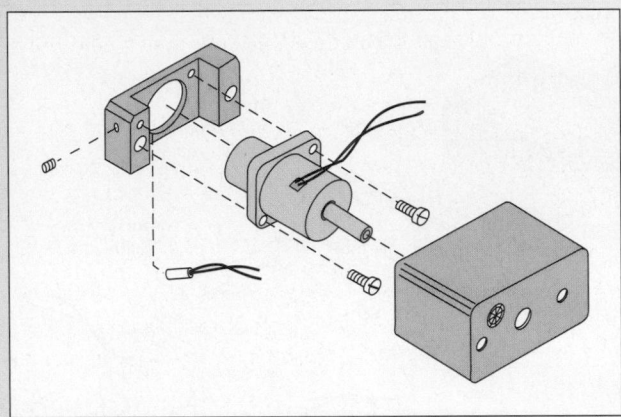

11. **Cover.**   Could be combined with the end plate.
12. **Cover screws (4).**   Not necessary.

From this analysis, it can be seen that if the motor and sensor subassemblies could be arranged to snap or screw into the base, and if a plastic cover could be designed to snap on, only 4 separate items would be needed instead of 19. These four items represent the theoretical minimum number needed to satisfy the constraints of the product design.

At this point, it is up to the design team to justify why the parts above the minimum should be included. Justification may be based on practical, technical, or economic considerations. In this example, it could be argued that two screws are needed to secure the motor and that one set screw is needed to hold the sensor, because any alternatives would be impractical for a low-volume product such as this. However, the design of these screws could be improved by providing them with pilot points to facilitate assembly.

Exhibit 3.9 is a drawing of a redesigned motor drive assembly that uses only seven separate parts. Notice how the parts have been eliminated. The new plastic cover is designed to snap on to the base plate. This new product is much simpler to assemble and should be much less expensive due to the reduced number of parts.

DESIGNING SERVICE PRODUCTS

A SERVICE EXPERIENCE FIT: DISNEYLAND VISITORS HAVE THEIR PHOTO TAKEN BY AN
EMPLOYEE OF THE PARK.

Service

As we saw in the last section, the detailed design of manufactured products is focused on reducing the number of parts in the item and designing the item in such a way that it can be efficiently produced. Service products are very different because direct customer involvement in the process introduces significant variability in the process in terms of both the time that it takes to serve a customer and the level of knowledge required of the firm's employees. Questions that should be addressed in the design of a service include: How will this variability be addressed? and What are the implications for operational cost and the customer service experience?

An important issue in developing a new service or modifying an existing one is the question of fit. Frei identifies the following three general factors for determining this: the service experience fit, the operational fit, and the financial impact.[6]

1. **Service experience fit.**   This means that the new service should fit into the current service experience for the customer. For example, Disneyland has started positioning employees with cameras around the park at memorable locations offering to take pictures of visitors that can be viewed online later. As a part of the greater service experience of making dreams come true and recording them, this has a good service experience fit. However, some services, like a car wash with a restaurant in the waiting area, are less complementary.

2. **Operational fit.**   Even the greatest service ideas require operational support to execute. One example of this is when grocery stores decided to offer home delivery. Even though this seemed like a logical extension of the service experience, it required completely new operational skills, such as selecting perishables for customers and delivering frozen foods.

3. **Financial impact.**   Designing and implementing a new service is costly and should be financially justified. Although this is often thought of in a positive sense of making a profit, it can just as well be introducing a new service in order to keep from losing valued customers.

Complexity and Divergence   A useful way of analyzing the operational fit for new service development is by specifying the *complexity* and *divergence* of the proposed service process relative to the basic service process. Complexity is the number of steps involved in a service and possible actions that can be taken at each step. Divergence is the number of ways a customer/service provider interaction can vary at each step according to the needs and abilities of each. The result may be a combination of higher complexity/divergence on some steps and lower complexity/divergence on others. This can be used to determine different resource requirements such as worker skills, layout, and process controls. For example, the hypothetical family restaurant shown in Exhibit 3.10 is considering whether to change the service to create a new process format. Relative to the current process, a minimum service format would have lower complexity/divergence, while an upscale format would have higher complexity/divergence.

Structural Alternatives for a Family Restaurant[7]

exhibit 3.10

PROCESS NAME	LOWER COMPLEXITY/ DIVERGENCE	CURRENT PROCESS	HIGHER COMPLEXITY/ DIVERGENCE
Reservations	No reservations	Take reservation	Specific table selection
Seating	Guests seat themselves	Host shows guests the table	Maitre d' escorts guests to seats, pulls out chairs, and places napkins in their laps
Menus	No menu	Menus on the table	Recite menu; describe entrees and specials
Bread	No bread offered at the table	Serve bread and butter	Assortment of hot breads and hors d'oeuvres
Ordering	Guests pick their food from buffet line	Take orders	At table; taken personally by maitre d'
Salads	Salad bar	Prepare orders	Individually prepared at table
Entrees	Entrees offered on the buffet	Entree (15 choices)	Expand to 20 choices; add flaming or sizzling dishes, deboning fish at the table
Desserts	Dessert bar	Dessert (6 choices)	Expand to 12 choices
Beverages	Guests get their drinks from the drink station	Beverage (6 choices)	Add exotic coffees, wine list, liqueurs
Service during the meal	No service	Serve orders	Separate-course service; hand-grind pepper
Payment	Paid at entry to buffet	Collect payment	Choice of payment, including house accounts
Table clearing	Guests are asked to bus the table themselves	Bus boy clears table at the end	Bus boy clears table throughout the meal

ECODESIGN[8]

Ecodesign

Ecodesign is the incorporation of environmental considerations in the design and development of products or services. Ecodesign is an extension of the other important requirements considered in the design process such as quality, costs, manufacturability, functionality, durability, ergonomics, and aesthetics. As a result, ecodesigned products are innovative, have better environmental performance, and are of a quality at least equal to the market standard. This makes the use of ecodesign increasingly important for business and leads to clear advantages for those companies incorporating ecodesign. Ecodesign adopts an integrated approach to the relationship between products and services and the environment on three levels:

*   The whole life cycle of the product or service is considered. The environmental impacts of a product arise not only during its manufacturing and use or when it has become waste, but throughout its entire life cycle. It includes the extraction and transport of resources needed to manufacture the product, the manufacturing processes, distribution, use and maintenance, reuse, and the treatment of its waste.
*   The product is considered as a system. All the elements needed to develop the product's function (consumables, packaging, energy networks) must also be taken into account.
*   A multicriteria approach is considered. All different environmental impacts that can be generated by a product system

THE NEW, EFFICIENT ECOBOOST ENGINE FROM FORD AT THE FRANKFURT MOTOR SHOW IN 2009.

along its life cycle are assessed in order to avoid trade-offs between different impact categories (for example, resource depletion, greenhouse effect, and toxicity). This is discussed in more depth in Chapter 11 as it relates to the sourcing of material.

The application of ecodesign can benefit business, users, and society at the same time because it responds to the common interest of obtaining more efficient products in an economic as well as environmental dimension. The producer manufactures a product using fewer materials; using less water, energy, and so on; and generating less waste to be managed. Consequently, the manufacturing costs are reduced. The user buys a more reliable and durable product that will need less energy or consumables to function and can be easily repaired when necessary. Society will benefit by increasing the future availability of resources for other products or services and by preventing possible environmental damage, thereby saving any corresponding treatment or remediation costs.

In addition, European regulations recognize and emphasize producers' responsibility in minimizing the environmental impacts of their products and services. Ecodesign can help producers to manage that responsibility and comply with product-related legislation.

Global

MEASURING PRODUCT DEVELOPMENT PERFORMANCE

There is strong evidence that generating a steady stream of new products to market is extremely important to competitiveness. To succeed, firms must respond to changing customer needs and the moves of their competitors. The ability to identify opportunities, mount the development effort, and bring to market new products and processes quickly is critical. Firms also must bring new products and processes to market efficiently. Because the number

Performance Measures for Development Projects

exhibit 3.11

PERFORMANCE DIMENSION	MEASURES	IMPACT ON COMPETITIVENESS
Time to market	Frequency of new product introductions	Responsiveness to customers/competitors
	Time from initial concept to market introduction	Quality of design—close to market
	Number started and number completed	Frequency of projects—model life
	Actual versus plan	
	Percentage of sales coming from new products	
Productivity	Engineering hours per project	Number of projects—freshness and breadth of line
	Cost of materials and tooling per project	
	Actual versus plan	Frequency of projects—economics of development
Quality	Conformance—reliability in use	Reputation—customer loyalty
	Design—performance and customer satisfaction	Relative attractiveness to customers— market share
	Yield—factory and field	
		Profitability—cost of ongoing service

of new products and new process technologies has increased while model lives and life cycles have shrunk, firms must mount more development projects than previously, and these projects must use substantially fewer resources per project.

In the U.S. automobile market, for example, the growth of models and market segments over the last 25 years has meant that an auto firm must initiate close to four times as many development projects simply to maintain its market share position. But smaller volumes per model and shorter design lives mean resource requirements must drop dramatically. Remaining competitive requires efficient engineering, design, and development activities.

Measures of product development success can be categorized into those that relate to the speed and frequency of bringing new products online, to the productivity of the actual development process, and to the quality of the actual products introduced (see Exhibit 3.11). Taken together, time, quality, and productivity define the performance of development, and in combination with other activities—sales, manufacturing, advertising, and customer service— determine the market impact of the project and its profitability.

SUMMARY

Product development is a major challenge that directly impacts the long-range success of a firm. Effectively managing the process requires an integrated effort involving all the functional areas of the firm. In this chapter, a generic process for developing products has been discussed. How this generic process is modified for various types of products is considered. An economic plan that ties the timing of the various product development activities to the project budget is essential for making good decisions as the process progresses. In the chapter, we also gave some insight into how the customer view may be incorporated into the product design process. Designing a product that can be produced efficiently is an interesting engineering exercise that we briefly introduced in the chapter. We also discussed how operational fit of a new or modified service can be evaluated in developing new service products as well as new developments in ecodesign. Finally, we considered various measures that are useful for monitoring a firm's product design activities.

KEY TERMS

Contract manufacturer An organization capable of manufacturing and/or purchasing all the components needed to produce a finished product or device.

Core competency The one thing that a firm can do better than its competitors. The goal is to have a core competency that yields a long-term competitive advantage to the company.

Concurrent engineering Emphasizes cross-functional integration and concurrent development of a product and its associated processes.

Quality function deployment (QFD) A process that helps a company determine the product characteristics important to the consumer and to evaluate its own product in relation to others.

House of quality A matrix that helps a product design team translate customer requirements into operating and engineering goals.

Value analysis/value engineering (VA/VE) Analysis with the purpose of simplifying products and processes by achieving equivalent or better performance at a lower cost.

Ecodesign The incorporation of environmental considerations into the design and development of products or services. These concerns relate to the entire life cycle including materials, manufacturing, distribution and the eventual disposal of waste.

SOLVED PROBLEM

VidMark, a manufacturer of cell phones, is currently developing a new model (VidPhone X70) that will be released on the market when development is complete. This phone will be revolutionary in that it will allow the user to place video phone calls. VidMark is concerned about the development cost and time. They are also worried about market estimates of the sales of the new VidPhone X70. The cost estimates and forecast are given in the table below.

Development Cost	$2,00,000
Development Time	2 years
Ramp-up Cost	$750,000
Marketing and Support Cost	$500,000/year
Unit Production Cost	$75
Unit Price	$135
Sales and Production Volume	
Year 3	40,000
Year 4	50,000
Year 5	40,000

Use the data above to develop a base-case analysis. The project schedule is shown below with timings of the cash flows.

PROJECT SCHEDULE VIDPHONE X70	YEAR 1	YEAR 2	YEAR 3	YEAR 4	YEAR 5
Development					
Ramp-up					
Marketing and Support					
Production and Sales					

There are several questions that need to be answered for VidMark on this project:

a. What are the yearly cash flows and their present value (discounted at 12%) of this project? What is the net present value?

b. What is the impact on VidMark if sales estimates are off by 20%?

c. What is the impact on VidMark if unit production cost is $85?

d. VidMark thinks that it can cut the development time in half by spending an extra $1,500,000 on development for this project. If the product is launched a year earlier, then the product will still have a 3-year life but the forecast starting in year 2 will be 48,000, 60,000, and 50,000. Is it worth it to VidMark to spend the extra money on development?

Solution

a. Start by building the base-case scenario (analysis is in 000).

PROJECT SCHEDULE VIDPHONE X70	YEAR 1	YEAR 2	YEAR 3	YEAR 4	YEAR 5
Development	−$1,000	−$1,000			
Ramp-up		−$750			
Marketing and Support		−$500	−$500	−$500	−$500
Production Volume			40	50	40
Unit Production Cost (dollars)			−$75	−$75	−$75
Production Costs			−$3,000	−$3,750	−$3,000
Sales Volume			40	50	40
Unit Price (dollars)			$135	$135	$135
Sales Revenue			$5,400	$6,750	$5,400
Period Cash Flow	−$1,000	−$2,250	$1,900	$2,500	$1,900
PV Year 1 (r = 12%)	−$1,000	−$2,009	$1,515	$1,779	$1,207
Project NPV	$1,493				

The cash flows and present value of the cash flows are shown. The project NPV under the base case is $1.493 million.

b. If sales are reduced by 20%, then project NPV drops to $378,000.

PROJECT SCHEDULE VIDPHONE X70	YEAR 1	YEAR 2	YEAR 3	YEAR 4	YEAR 5
Period Cash Flow	−$1,000	−$2,250	$1,420	$1,900	$1,420
PV Year 1 (r = 12%)	−$1,000	−$2,009	$1,132	$1,352	$902
Project NPV	$378				

If sales are increased by 20%, then project NPV goes up to $2.607 million. A change of 20% either way has a large impact on the NPV.

PROJECT SCHEDULE VIDPHONE X70	YEAR 1	YEAR 2	YEAR 3	YEAR 4	YEAR 5
Period Cash Flow	−$1,000	−$2,250	$2,380	$3,100	$2,380
PV Year 1 (r = 12%)	−$1,000	−$2,009	$1,897	$2,207	$1,513
Project NPV	$2,607				

c. Increased unit production costs.

PROJECT SCHEDULE VIDPHONE X70	YEAR 1	YEAR 2	YEAR 3	YEAR 4	YEAR 5
Period Cash Flow	−$1,000	−$2,250	$1,500	$2,000	$1,500
PV Year 1 (r = 12%)	−$1,000	−$2,009	$1,196	$1,424	$953
Project NPV	$564				

The cash flows are severely affected by the increased unit production cost. Increased future cash outflow of $1.3 million (130,000 units * $10 increase) causes a decrease in net present value of $929,000 ($1.493 million − $.564 million). However, it still appears to be worth developing the new phone.

d. Here are the changes proposed by VidMark:

Development Cost	$3,500,000
Development Time	1 year
Ramp-up Cost	$750,000
Marketing and Support Cost	$500,000/year
Unit Production Cost	$75
Unit Price	$135
Sales and Production Volume	
Year 2	48,000
Year 3	60,000
Year 4	50,000

Use the data above to develop a base-case analysis. The project schedule is shown below with timings of cash flows.

PROJECT SCHEDULE VIDPHONE X70	YEAR 1	YEAR 2	YEAR 3	YEAR 4
Development				
Ramp-up				
Marketing and Support				
Production and Sales				

It appears that VidMark is better off to take two years to develop its new VidPhone X70 because the NPV of the base case is $1.493 million versus the fast development NPV of $1,625,000 (see table below).

PROJECT SCHEDULE VIDPHONE X70	YEAR 1	YEAR 2	YEAR 3	YEAR 4
Development	−$3,500			
Ramp-up	−$750			
Marketing and Support	−$500	−$500	−$500	−$500
Production Volume		48	60	50
Unit Production Cost (dollars)		−$75	−$75	−$75
Production Costs		−$3,600	−$4,500	−$3,750
Sales Volume		48	60	50
Unit Price (dollars)		$135	$135	$135
Sales Revenue		$6,480	$8,100	$6,750
Period Cash Flow	−$4,750	$2,380	$3,100	$2,500
PV Year 1 (r = 12%)	−$4,750	$2,125	$2,471	$1,779
Project NPV	$1,625			

REVIEW AND DISCUSSION QUESTIONS

1   Describe the generic product development process described in the chapter. How does the process change for "technology-push" products?

2   Discuss the product design philosophy behind industrial design and design for manufacture and assembly. Which one do you think is more important in a customer-focused product development?

3   Discuss design-based incrementalism, which is frequent product redesign throughout the product's life. What are the pros and cons of this idea?

4   What factors must be traded off by product development before introducing a new product?

5   How does the QFD approach help? What are some limitations of the QFD approach?

6   Do the concepts of complexity and divergence apply to an online sales company such as Dell Computer?

INTERNET ENRICHMENT EXERCISE

Consider a product or service currently produced that you are interested in purchasing. Based on the concepts of quality function deployment (QFD), develop a 3 by 3 house of quality matrix (three customer requirements translated into three technical requirements) for this product or service, completing all the appropriate sections of the matrix. For reference and help with the exercise, access the interactive tutorial provided at http://www.gsm.mq.edu/au/cmit/.

PROBLEMS

1 The Tuff Wheels was getting ready to start its development project for a new product to be added to their small motorized vehicle line for children. The new product is called the Kiddy Dozer. It will look like a miniature bulldozer, complete with caterpillar tracks and a blade. Tuff Wheels has forecasted the demand and the cost to develop and produce the new Kiddy Dozer. The table below contains the relevant information for this project.

Development Cost	$1,000,000
Estimated Development Time	9 months
Pilot Testing	$200,000
Ramp-up Cost	$400,000
Marketing and Support Cost	$150,000 per year
Sales and Production Volume	60,000 per year
Unit Production Cost	$100
Unit Price	$170
Interest Rate	8%

Tuff Wheels also has provided the project plan shown below. As can be seen in the project plan, the company thinks that the product life will be three years until a new product must be created.

PROJECT SCHEDULE KIDDY DOZER	YEAR 1				YEAR 2				YEAR 3				YEAR 4			
	Q_1	Q_2	Q_3	Q_4	Q_1	Q_2	Q_3	Q_4	Q_1	Q_2	Q_3	Q_4	Q_1	Q_2	Q_3	Q_4
Development																
Pilot Testing																
Ramp-up																
Marketing and Support																
Production and Sales																

a. What are the yearly cash flows and their present value (discounted at 8%) of this project? What is the net present value?

b. What is the impact on NPV for the Kiddy Dozer if the actual sales are 50,000 per year or 70,000 per year?

c. What is the effect caused by changing the discount rate to 9%, 10%, or 11%?

2 Perot Corporation is developing a new CPU chip based on a new type of technology. Its new chip, the Patay2 chip, will take two years to develop. However, because chip manufacturers will be able to copy the technology, it will have a market life of two years after it is introduced. Perot expects to be able to price the chip higher in the first year, and it anticipates a significant production cost reduction after the first year as well. The relevant information for developing and selling the Patay2 is given below.

PATAY2 CHIP PRODUCT ESTIMATES

Development Cost	$20,000,000
Pilot Testing	$5,000,000
Debug	$3,000,000
Ramp-up Cost	$3,000,000
Advance Marketing	$5,000,000
Marketing and Support Cost	$1,000,000 per year
Unit Production Cost Year 1	$655.00
Unit Production Cost Year 2	$545.00
Unit Price Year 1	$820.00
Unit Price Year 2	$650.00
Sales and Production Volume Year 1	250,000
Sales and Production Volume Year 2	150,000
Interest Rate	10%

PATAY2 CHIP PROJECT TIMING

PROJECT SCHEDULE	YEAR 1		YEAR 2		YEAR 3		YEAR 4	
	1ST	2ND	1ST	2ND	1ST	2ND	1ST	2ND
PATAY2 CHIP	HALF	HALF	HALF	HALF	HALF	HALF	HALF	HALF
Development								
Pilot Testing								
Debug								
Ramp-up								
Advance Marketing								
Marketing and Support								
Production and Sales								

a. What are the yearly cash flows and their present value (discounted at 10%) of this project? What is the net present value?

b. Perot's engineers have determined that spending $10 million more on development will allow them to add even more advanced features. Having a more advanced chip will allow them to price the chip $50 higher in both years ($870 for year 1 and $700 for year 2). Is it worth the additional investment?

c. If sales are only 200,000 the first year and 100,000 the second year, would Perot still do the project?

3 Pick a product and list issues that need to be considered in its design and manufacture. The product can be something like a stereo, telephone, desk, or kitchen appliance. Consider the functional and aesthetic aspects of design as well as the important concerns for manufacturing.

4 The chart below is a partial house of quality for a golf country club. Provide an importance weighting from your perspective (or that of a golfing friend) in the unshaded areas. If you can, using the QFD approach, compare it to a club where you or your friends play.

WHATs versus HOWs Strong Relationship: ● Medium Relationship: ○ Weak Relationship: △	Physical Aspects	Course location	Grounds maintenance	Landscaping	Pin placement	Course tuning	Tee placement	Service Facilities	Customer-trained attendants	Top-quality food	Highly rated chefs	Attractive restaurant	Tournament Activities	Calloway handicapping	Exciting door prizes	Perception Issues	Invitation only	Types of guests	Income level	Celebrity
Physical Aspects																				
Manicured grounds																				
Easy access																				
Challenging																				
Service Facilities																				
Restaurant facilities																				
Good food																				
Good service																				
Good layout																				
Plush locker room																				
Helpful service attendants																				
Tournament Facilities																				
Good tournament prize																				
Types of players																				
Fair handicapping system																				
Perception Issues																				
Prestigious																				

CASE: IKEA: DESIGN AND PRICING

The Swedish retailer dominates markets in 32 countries, and now it's poised to conquer North America. Its battle plan: Keep making its offerings less expensive, without making them cheap.

Above all else, one factor accounts for IKEA's success: good quality at a low price. IKEA sells household items that are cheap but not cheapo, at prices that typically run 30 to 50 percent below the competition's. While the price of other companies' products tends to rise over time, IKEA says it has reduced its retail prices by a total of about 20 percent during the past four years. At IKEA the process of driving down costs starts the moment a new item is conceived and continues relentlessly throughout its production run. The price of a basic Pöang chair, for example, has fallen from $149 in 2000 to $99 in 2001 to $79 today. IKEA expects the most recent price cut to increase Pöang sales by 30 to 50 percent.

IKEA's corporate mantra is "Low price with meaning." The goal is to make things less expensive without ever making customers feel cheap. Striking that balance demands a special kind of design, manufacturing, and distribution expertise. But IKEA pulls it off in its own distinctive way: tastefully, methodically, even cheerfully, and yet somehow differently than any other company anywhere. Here's a step-by-step guide to how IKEA designs, builds, and distributes the items that the entire world wants to buy.

The Trofé mug is one of the most popular IKEA products. The story of the mug is an example of how IKEA works, from a coworker's bright idea through to production and sales. It is also a story about all the demands that we and our customers place on IKEA. A low price tag is the obvious one, but other requirements include function, modern design, environmental considerations, and making sure products have been manufactured under acceptable working conditions. Both customers and coworkers must be able to rely on IKEA.

STEP 1. PICK A PRICE

Product Development—A sketch for a new product? Yes, but it's also a calculation of what that product will cost. The low price begins at the drawing board.

The team behind each product consists of designers, product developers, and purchasers who get together to discuss design, materials, and suitable suppliers. Everyone contributes with their specialist knowledge. Purchasers, for example, use their contacts with suppliers all over the world via IKEA Trading Service Offices. Who can make this at the best quality for the right price at the right time?

When product developer Pia Eldin Lindstén was given the task of creating a new mug over five years ago, she was also told how much it should cost in the stores. In the case of Trofé, the price had to be incredibly low—five Swedish kronor! This mug had to have a real knock-out price.

To produce the right mug at the right price, Pia and her colleagues had to take into account materials, colors, and design. For example, the mug is made in green, blue, yellow, or white as these pigments cost less than other shades, such as red.

STEP 2. CHOOSE A MANUFACTURER

Suppliers and Purchasing—The task of developing products never ends. Working with suppliers, the mug was shortened and the handle changed so it stacks more efficiently, saving space for transport, warehousing, and store display—and, not least, in the customers' cupboards at home. IKEA is always keen to banish as much air as possible from its packaging. Packages should preferably be flat for efficient transport and storage.

One supplier, a factory in Romania, has worked with IKEA for 15 years. Long-term relationships help both parties to build up a huge fund of knowledge about demands and expectations. That is why products are often developed in close cooperation with suppliers. In the case of Trofé, for example, the new size has rationalized production by making better use of the space in the kiln during the firing process. That's cost-effective and saves time.

IKEA has introduced a code of conduct governing working conditions and environmental awareness among suppliers. This deals with matters such as health and safety in the workplace and forbids the use of child labor. The practical work of implementing this code of conduct is carried out by coworkers in IKEA Trading Service Offices worldwide. Many suppliers already meet the demands; others are working together with IKEA to carry out the necessary improvements. IKEA also works closely with external quality control and audit companies who check that IKEA and its suppliers live up to the requirements of the code of conduct.

The low price tag is crucial to the vision IKEA has of creating a better everyday life for many people. That is why IKEA works non-stop to reduce costs. But it's also a question of saving raw materials and, ultimately, the environment. The low-cost mug is one example of how environmental considerations can influence the development of products. For example, the new mug is lighter in color—a move that cuts costs and is more environmentally friendly. The less pigment that is used, the better. The mug is also lead and cadmium free.

STEP 3. DESIGN THE PRODUCT

With a price point and a manufacturer in place, IKEA once again uses internal competition to find a designer and select a design for production. The designer begins the design process by writing a brief that explains the product's price, its function, the materials to be used, and the fabricator's capabilities. The designer then sends the brief to IKEA's staff designers and freelancers, and refines promising designs until settling on the one to produce. The designer wants products to be like Swiss Army knives—to get maximum functionality at minimum cost.

STEP 4. SHIP IT

Distribution and logistics are the lifeblood of IKEA and important pieces of the puzzle on their road to a low price. IKEA strives to deliver the right number of goods to the right stores at the right time. They calculate the goods requirements and make sure that deliveries are efficient.

Each pallet holds 2,024 mugs, which are transported from Romania by rail, road, and sea to IKEA distribution centers around the world. Transportation does, of course, have an effect on the environment, but IKEA is working toward reducing environmental impact.

Many of IKEA's products are bulky, for example, tables and chairs. IKEA pioneered the concept of flat. The company's eureka moment occurred in 1956, when one of IKEA's first designers watched a customer trying to fit a table into his car. There was only one way to do it: Remove the legs. From that day forward, most IKEA products have been designed to ship disassembled, flat enough to be slipped into the cargo hatch of a station wagon or safely tied down on an auto's roof rack.

In IKEA's innately frugal corporate culture, where waste has been declared a "deadly sin," the flat package is also an excellent way to lower shipping costs by maximizing the use of space inside shipping containers. The company estimates transport volume would be six times greater if its items were shipped assembled. From the design studio to the warehouse floor, IKEA employees' mantra is always the same: "We don't want to pay to ship air."

Making things flat is an IKEA obsession. How many times can you redesign a simple fired-clay coffee mug? IKEA's mug was redesigned three times—simply to maximize the number of them that can be stored on a pallet. Originally, only 864 mugs would fit. A redesign added a rim such as you'd find on a flowerpot, so that each pallet could hold 1,280 mugs. Yet another redesign created a shorter mug with a new handle, allowing 2,024 to squeeze onto a pallet. While the mug's sales price has remained at 50 cents, shipping costs have been reduced by 60 percent, which is a significant savings, given that IKEA sells about 25 million of the mugs each year. Even better, the cost of production at IKEA's Romanian factory also has fallen because the more compact mugs require less space in the kiln.

When you ship 25 million cubic meters of goods all over the globe, flat-pack frugality adds up. IKEA now uses a 65 percent average fill-rate target for all the containers it ships, and it hopes to increase that to 75 percent. Meeting that goal will require further design changes and sometimes even sucking the air out of items (like IKEA's shrink-wrapped pillows, which look like giant crackers on store shelves). And, of course, flat packing shifts the cost of product assembly to the customer, saving even more.

As IKEA has shifted more of its buying from Europe to the Far East, shipping time and costs have become an even more critical concern. Last year China tied Sweden atop IKEA's list of supplier countries. The company has responded by creating a global network of distribution centers, most of which are near container ports and major truck and rail routes. There are 18 IKEA distribution centers worldwide—which handle about 70 percent of IKEA's total product line—and 4 more are under construction. The other 30 percent of IKEA's products travel directly from supplier to store.

Sometimes, however, product components actually come together for the first time in the store. In the case of the Pöang chair, the cushion comes from Poland and the frame from China. The two pieces are united only when the customer pulls each one off the shelf.

STEP 5. SELL IT

IKEA sells a lot of expensive furniture, and in a traditional store this is relatively easy: Put a piece in a lush setting, let the customer fall prey to visions of wealth and comfort, then offer plenty of easy credit. But to keep prices low, IKEA needs to sell furniture and other products such as the mug without salespeople or conspicuous price reductions. The company asks customers to assemble their furniture themselves. And IKEA doesn't want to ship it to you either. By any conventional measure, these are formidable hurdles to overcome. Yet they also explain why IKEA has worked so hard to create a separate world inside its stores—a kind of theme park masquerading as a furniture outlet—where normal rules and expectations don't apply.

The Trofé mugs arrive at IKEA stores packed on pallets. Any transportation packaging is collected for recycling. Price tags have already been placed on the mugs at the suppliers. In-store display is important. It's not just a question of displaying mugs and other products. It's also about providing inspiration for smart interior solutions. Customers contribute to the low prices at IKEA by selecting and collecting the products from the self-serve area, taking them home, and using the instructions enclosed to assemble them. Many will have already chosen the products from the IKEA catalogue, of which 110 million copies are printed in 34 different language versions.

When you walk through the door of an IKEA store, you enter a meticulously constructed virtual Sweden. The first thing you encounter is a company-sponsored child-care facility. Hungry? Have some of those Swedish meatballs and lingonberries. The layout of an IKEA store guides shoppers in a predetermined path past several realistic model homes, which convey an eerily lived-in impression but are open for customers to sit in. Information kiosks provide advice on home decor. Color-coordinated cards offer plenty of suggestions on offbeat uses for products.

But the emphasis is always on price. Low-priced products that IKEA calls BTIs ("breathtaking items") are often perched on risers, framed by a huge yellow price tag. Nearby, shoppers will find other products—pricier, more design-oriented—as substitutes for the BTI.

The model homes suggest cheerful young people throwing dinner parties in hallways, using mismatched office chairs and narrow side tables. These aren't the aspirational images you'll find at Pottery Barn or Crate & Barrel. These are people who are living well in modest circumstances—frugal folks who know the value of a comfortable place to sit.

IKEA says its biggest selling point is the price tag, but it can't hurt that getting through one of IKEA's huge stores takes a lot of time. The layout is blatantly manipulative—though in a friendly, knowing way, not unlike at Disneyland—but when customers finally arrive at the checkout counter, they've had plenty of time to fully consider their purchases.

IKEA products broadcast an ethos for living in the modern world: Don't buy an ugly pitcher if you can get a stylish one for the same price. If you organize your plastic bags, you'll feel more in control of your life. It's left-brain logic applied to the right-brain art of living well. And if happiness involves dragging a cumbersome flat package off the shelf, standing in line at the checkout, hauling the box home, and spending hours assembling a kitchen cabinet, well, 260 million customers a year are willing to make that trade-off.

And, of course, next year it will be even cheaper.

QUESTIONS

1   What are IKEA's competitive priorities?
2   Describe IKEA's process for developing a new product.
3   What are additional features of the IKEA concept (beyond their design process) that contribute to creating exceptional value for the customer?
4   What would be important criteria for selecting a site for an IKEA store?

SOURCE: INFORMATION ABOUT THE TROFÉ COFFEE MUG WAS OBTAINED FROM HTTP://WWW.IKEA.COM.

CASE: DENTAL SPA

Would a warm paraffin hand treatment during your dental cleaning or dental treatment put you at ease and make the process more bearable? That is the idea behind the new "dental spa" services opening in major cities throughout the United States. Beyond calming music and comfortable chairs and flat screen TVs mounted on the ceiling with sound from the noise-canceling headphones that block unpleasant dental noises, foot scrubs, pedicures, or other spa services are sometimes possible at the same time. Two major trends have helped fuel the growth of dental spas: improving the painful associations of dentistry and the increased cosmetic focus of dentistry that goes along with other spa treatments.

QUESTIONS

1. Which one of the three new service requirements would a dental spa least likely pass: service experience fit, operational fit, or financial impact? Why?
2. What are some of the main areas of complexity and divergence in this kind of operation relative to the standard dental clinic?

SUPER QUIZ

1. This is an organization capable of manufacturing or purchasing all the components needed to produce a finished product or device.
2. This is the one thing that a company can do better than its competitors.
3. These are the six phases of the product development process.
4. A useful tool for the economic analysis of a product development project is this.
5. An approach that uses interfunctional teams to get input from the customer in design specification is this.
6. This is a matrix of information that helps a team translate customer requirements into operating or engineering goals.
7. The greatest improvements from this arise from simplification of the product by reducing the number of separate parts.
8. This is the incorporation of environmental considerations into the design and development of products or services.

1. Contract manufacturer 2. Core competency 3. Planning, concept development, system-level design, detail design, testing, production ramp-up 4. Net present value 5. Quality function development 6. House of quality 7. Design for manufacturing and assembly 8. Ecodesign

SELECTED BIBLIOGRAPHY

Boothroyd, G.; P. Dewhurst; and W. Knight. *Product Design for Manufacture and Assembly.* 2nd ed. New York: Marcel Dekker, 2002.

Cooper, R. G. *Winning at New Products: Accelerating the Process from Idea to Launch.* Reading, MA: Perseus Books, 2001.

Morgan, James M., and Jeffrey K. Liker. *The Toyota Product Development System: Integrating People, Process, and Technology.* New York: Productivity Press, 2006.

Ulrich, Karl T., and Steven D. Eppinger. *Product Design and Development.* 3rd ed. New York: McGraw-Hill/Irwin, 2004.

FOOTNOTES

1 Excerpt from T. Peters, "Beating the Great Blight of Dullness," *Forbes ASAP* (undated).

2 Adapted from Karl T. Ulrich and Steven D. Eppinger, *Product Design and Development,* 3rd ed. (New York: McGraw-Hill/Irwin, 2004), pp. 12–25.

3 Adapted from ibid., pp. 308–19.

4 The term *quality* is actually a mistranslation of the Japanese word for qualities, because QFD is widely used in the context of quality management.

5 Example adapted from G. Boothroyd, P. Dewhurst, and W. Knight, *Product Design for Manufacture and Assembly* (New York: Marcel Dekker, 1994), pp. 5–10.

6 Frances Frei, "Designing New Service Models," HBS No. 606-031 (Boston: Harvard Business School Publishing, 2006).

7 Example adapted from G. Lynn Shostack, "Service Positioning through Structural Change," *Journal of Marketing* 51 (January 1987), p. 41.

8 Adapted from http://www.ecosmes.net.

section 2

MANUFACTURING, SERVICE, AND HEALTH CARE PROCESSES

MANUFACTURING, SERVICE, AND HEALTH CARE PROCESSES

The second section of *Operations and Supply Chain Management* is centered on the design and analysis of business processes. Have you ever wondered why you always have to wait in line at one store but another one seems to be on top of the crowds? The key to serving customers well, whether with products or with services, is having a great process.

Companies also need to develop a quality philosophy and integrate it into their processes. Actually, quality and process efficiency are closely related. Have you ever done something but then had to do it again because it was not done properly the first time? This section considers these subjects in manufacturing, service, and health care industries.

chapter 4

STRATEGIC CAPACITY MANAGEMENT

SHOULDICE HOSPITAL: HERNIA SURGERY INNOVATION

Service

After reading the chapter you will:

1. Recognize the concept of capacity and how important it is to "manage" capacity.

2. Explain the impact of economies of scale on the capacity of a firm.

3. Understand how to use decision trees to analyze alternatives when faced with the problem of adding capacity.

4. Describe the differences in planning capacity between manufacturing firms and service firms.

During World War II, Dr. Edward Earle Shouldice, a major in the army, found that many young men willing to serve their country had to be denied enlistment because they needed surgical treatment to repair hernias before they could be pronounced physically fit for military training. In 1940, hospital space and doctors were scarce, especially for a nonemergency surgery that normally took three weeks of hospitalization. So, Dr. Shouldice resolved to do what he could to alleviate the problem. Contributing his services at no fee, he performed an innovative method of surgery on 70 of those men, speeding their induction into the army.

The recruits made their success stories known, and by the war's end, more than 200 civilians had contacted the doc-

tor and were awaiting surgery. The limited availability of hospitals beds, however, created a major problem. There was only one solution: Dr. Shouldice decided to open his own hospital.

In July 1945, Shouldice Hospital, with a staff consisting of a nurse, a secretary, and a cook, opened its doors to its waiting patients. In a single operating room, Dr. Shouldice repaired two hernias per day. As requests for this surgery increased, Dr. Shouldice extended the facilities, located on Church Street in Toronto, by eventually buying three adjacent buildings and increasing the staff accordingly. In 1953, he purchased a country estate in Thornhill, where a second hospital was established.

Today all surgery takes place in Thornhill. Repeated development has culminated in the present 90-bed facility. Shouldice Hospital has been dedicated to the repair of hernias for over 55 years, using the "Shouldice Technique." The "formula," although not a secret, extends beyond the skill of

SOURCE: SUMMARIZED FROM www.shouldice.com.

surgeons and their ability to perform to the Shouldice standard. Shouldice Hospital is a total environment. Study the capacity problems with this special type of hospital in the case at the end of this chapter.

Manufacturing and service capacity investment decisions can be very complex. Consider some of the following difficult questions that need to be addressed:

- How long will it take to bring new capacity on stream? How does this match with the time that it takes to develop a new product?
- What will be the impact of not having sufficient capacity in the supply chain for a promising product?
- How large a facility should we build?
- When and how much capacity should we add to our existing facility?
- Should the firm use third-party contract manufacturers? How much of a premium will the contract manufacturer charge for providing flexibility in manufacturing volume?

In this chapter, we look at these tough strategic capacity decisions. We begin by discussing the nature of capacity from an OM perspective.

CAPACITY MANAGEMENT IN OPERATIONS

Service

A dictionary definition of capacity is "the ability to hold, receive, store, or accommodate." In a general business sense, it is most frequently viewed as the amount of output that a system is capable of achieving over a specific period of time. In a service setting, this might be the number of customers that can be handled between noon and 1:00 P.M. In manufacturing, this might be the number of automobiles that can be produced in a single shift.

When looking at capacity, operations managers need to look at both resource inputs *and* product outputs. For planning purposes, real (or effective) capacity depends on what is to be produced. For example, a firm that makes multiple products inevitably can produce more of one kind than of another with a given level of resource inputs. Thus, while the managers of an automobile factory may state that their facility has 6,000 production hours available per year, they are also thinking that these hours can be used to make either 150,000 two-door models or 120,000 four-door models (or some mix of the two- and four-door models). This reflects their knowledge of what their current technology and labor force inputs can produce and the product mix that is to be demanded from these resources.

An operations management view also emphasizes the time dimension of capacity. That is, capacity must also be stated relative to some period of time. This is evidenced in the common distinction drawn between long-range, intermediate-range, and short-range capacity planning.

Capacity planning is generally viewed in three time durations:

Long range—greater than one year. Where productive resources (such as buildings, equipment, or facilities) take a long time to acquire or dispose of, long-range capacity planning requires top management participation and approval.

Intermediate range—monthly or quarterly plans for the next 6 to 18 months. Here, capacity may be varied by such alternatives as hiring, layoffs, new tools, minor equipment purchases, and subcontracting.

Short range—less than one month. This is tied into the daily or weekly scheduling process and involves making adjustments to eliminate the variance between planned and actual output. This includes alternatives such as overtime, personnel transfers, and alternative production routings.

Although there is no one person with the job title "capacity manager," several managerial positions are charged with the effective use of capacity. *Capacity* is a relative term; in an operations management context, it may be defined as *the amount of resource inputs available relative to output requirements over a particular period of time.*

The objective of strategic capacity planning is to provide an approach for determining the overall capacity level of capital-intensive resources—facilities, equipment, and overall labor force size—that best supports the company's long-range competitive strategy. The capacity level selected has a critical impact on the firm's response rate, its cost structure, its inventory policies, and its management and staff support requirements. If capacity is inadequate, a company may lose customers through slow service or by allowing competitors to enter the market. If capacity is excessive, a company may have to reduce prices to stimulate demand; underutilize its workforce; carry excess inventory; or seek additional, less profitable products to stay in business.

Strategic capacity planning

CAPACITY PLANNING CONCEPTS

The term capacity implies an attainable rate of output, for example, 480 cars per day, but says nothing about how long that rate can be sustained. Thus, we do not know if this 480 cars per day is a one-day peak or a six-month average. To avoid this problem, the concept of best operating level is used. This is the level of capacity for which the process was designed and thus is the volume of output at which average unit cost is minimized. Determining this minimum is difficult because it involves a complex trade-off between the allocation of fixed overhead costs and the cost of overtime, equipment wear, defect rates, and other costs.

Capacity

Best operating level

An important measure is the capacity utilization rate, which reveals how close a firm is to its best operating level:

Capacity utilization rate

$$Capacity\ utilization\ rate = \frac{Capacity\ used}{Best\ operating\ level} \qquad [4.1]$$

So, for example, if our plant's *best operating level* were 500 cars per day and the plant was currently operating at 480 cars per day, the *capacity utilization rate* would be 96 percent.

$$Capacity\ utilization\ rate = \frac{480}{500} = .96\ or\ 96\%$$

The capacity utilization rate is expressed as a percentage and requires that the numerator and denominator be measured in the same units and time periods (such as machine hours/day, barrels of oil/day, dollars of output/day).

ECONOMIES AND DISECONOMIES OF SCALE

The basic notion of economies of scale is that as a plant gets larger and volume increases, the average cost per unit of output drops. This is partially due to lower operating and capital cost, because a piece of equipment with twice the capacity of another piece typically does not cost twice as much to purchase or operate. Plants also gain efficiencies when they become large enough to fully utilize dedicated resources (people and equipment) for information technology, material handling, and administrative support.

Economies of scale

At some point, the size of a plant becomes too large and diseconomies of scale become a problem. These diseconomies may surface in many different ways. For example, maintaining the demand required to keep the large facility busy may require significant discounting of the product. The U.S. automobile manufacturers continually face this problem. Another typical example involves using a few large-capacity pieces of equipment. Minimizing equipment

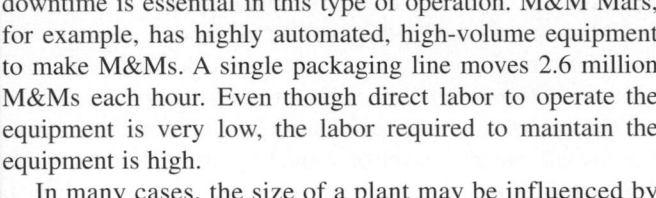

Global

downtime is essential in this type of operation. M&M Mars, for example, has highly automated, high-volume equipment to make M&Ms. A single packaging line moves 2.6 million M&Ms each hour. Even though direct labor to operate the equipment is very low, the labor required to maintain the equipment is high.

In many cases, the size of a plant may be influenced by factors other than the internal equipment, labor, and other capital expenditures. A major factor may be the cost to transport raw materials and finished product to and from the plant. A cement factory, for example, would have a difficult time serving customers more than a few hours from its plant. Similarly, automobile companies such as Ford, Honda, Nissan, and Toyota have found it advantageous to locate plants within specific international markets. The anticipated size of these intended markets will largely dictate the size and capacity of the plants.

Jaguar, the luxury automobile producer, recently found it had too many plants. Jaguar was employing 8,560 workers in three plants that produced 126,122 cars, about 14 cars per employee. In comparison, Volvo's plant in Torslanda, Sweden, was more than twice as productive, building 158,466 cars with 5,472 workers, or 29 cars per employee. By contrast, BMW AG's Mini unit made 174,000 vehicles at a single British plant with just 4,500 workers (39 cars per employee).

CAPACITY FOCUS

Focused factory

The concept of a focused factory holds that a production facility works best when it focuses on a fairly limited set of production objectives. This means, for example, that a firm should not expect to excel in every aspect of manufacturing performance: cost, quality, delivery speed and reliability, changes in demand, and flexibility to adapt to new products. Rather, it should select a limited set of tasks that contribute the most to corporate objectives. Typically the focused factory would produce a specific product or related group of products. A focused factory allows capacity to be focused on producing those specific items.

Plant within a plant (PWP)

The capacity focus concept can be operationalized through the mechanism of plant within a plant—or PWP. A focused factory (see Exhibit 4.1) may have several PWPs, each of which may have separate suborganizations, equipment and process policies, workforce management policies, production control methods, and so forth for different products—even if they are made under the same roof. This, in effect, permits finding the best operating level for each department of the organization and thereby carries the focus concept down to the operating level.

CAPACITY FLEXIBILITY

Capacity flexibility means having the ability to rapidly increase or decrease production levels, or to shift production capacity quickly from one product or service to another. Such flexibility is achieved through flexible plants, processes, and workers, as well as through strategies that use the capacity of other organizations. Increasingly, companies are taking the idea of flexibility into account as they design their supply chains. Working with suppliers, they can build capacity into their whole systems.

Flexible Plants   Perhaps the ultimate in plant flexibility is the *zero-changeover-time* plant. Using movable equipment, knockdown walls, and easily accessible and reroutable utilities, such a plant can quickly adapt to change. An analogy to a familiar service business captures the flavor well: a plant with equipment "that is easy to install and easy to tear down and move—like the Ringling Bros.–Barnum and Bailey Circus in the old tent-circus days."

Focused Factories—Plant-Within-Plant

exhibit 4.1

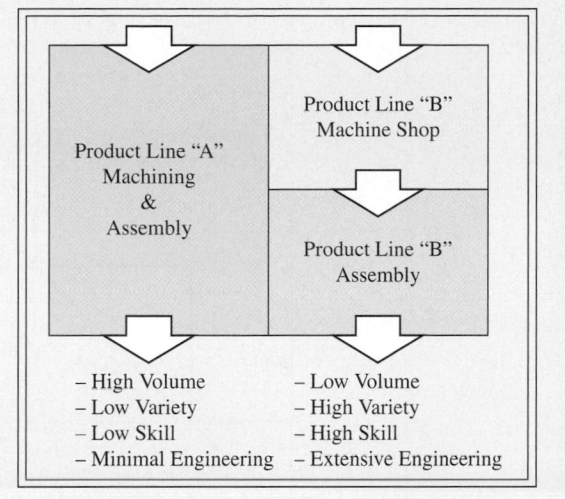

A FACILITY THAT IS ILL-DESIGNED, ATTEMPTS TOO MUCH, OR IS OPTIMIZED FOR THE WRONG TASK CAN BE A MILLSTONE.

FACILITY PLANNING CAN HELP ADDRESS THIS STRATEGIC ISSUE USING THE "PLANT-WITHIN-PLANT" CONCEPT.

HERE, THE PLANT LAYOUT HAS REGIONS THAT BECOME, ESSENTIALLY, STAND-ALONE FACTORIES. EACH HAS (AT LEAST SUBSTANTIALLY) ITS OWN AREA AND INFRASTRUCTURE SUCH AS MAINTENANCE, PURCHASING, AND ENGINEERING.

THE FIGURE ILLUSTRATES THIS WITH AN EXAMPLE. TWO MAJOR PRODUCT LINES HAD CONFLICTING DEMANDS FROM CUSTOMERS AND CONFLICTING DEMANDS ON THE FACTORY'S INFRASTRUCTURE. IN ADDITION, ONE OF THE PRODUCT LINES HAD HIGHLY DISSIMILAR PROCESSES. THE FACTORY WAS SPLIT INTO THREE FOCUSED FACTORIES, AS SHOWN.

Flexible Processes   Flexible processes are epitomized by flexible manufacturing systems on the one hand and simple, easily set up equipment on the other. Both of these technological approaches permit rapid low-cost switching from one product to another, enabling what are sometimes referred to as economies of scope. (By definition, economies of scope exist when multiple products can be combined and produced at one facility, at a lower cost than they can be produced separately.)

Economies of scope

Flexible Workers   Flexible workers have multiple skills and the ability to switch easily from one kind of task to another. They require broader training than specialized workers and need managers and staff support to facilitate quick changes in their work assignments.

CAPACITY PLANNING

CONSIDERATIONS IN CHANGING CAPACITY

Many issues must be considered when adding or decreasing capacity. Three important ones are maintaining system balance, frequency of capacity additions or reductions, and the use of external capacity.

Maintaining System Balance   In a perfectly balanced plant, the output of stage 1 provides the exact input requirement for stage 2. Stage 2's output provides the exact input requirement for stage 3, and so on. In practice, however, achieving such a "perfect" design is usually both impossible and undesirable. One reason is that the best operating levels for each stage generally differ. For instance, department 1 may operate most efficiently over a range of 90 to 110 units per month, whereas department 2, the next stage in the process, is most efficient at 75 to 85 units per month, and department 3 works best over a range of 150 to 200 units per month. Another reason is that variability in product demand and the processes themselves may lead to imbalance.

exhibit 4.2   Frequent versus Infrequent Capacity Expansion

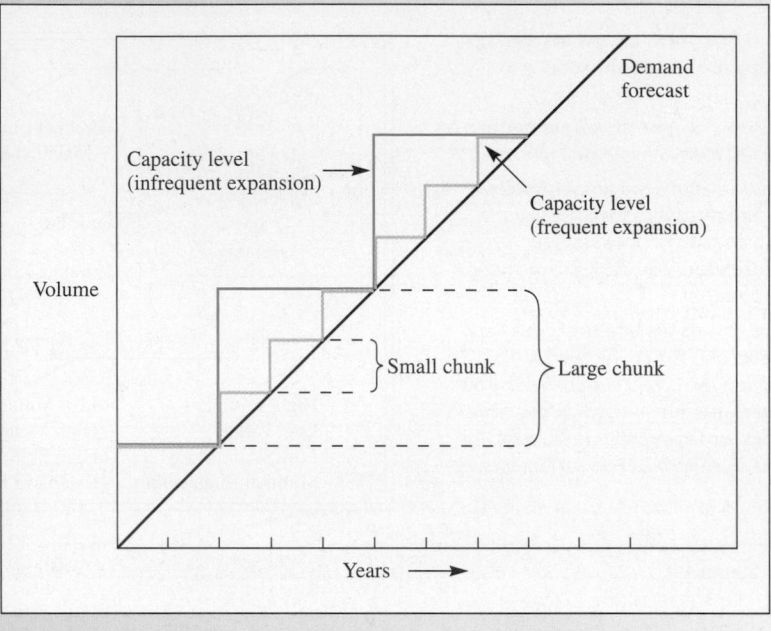

**Supply
Chain**

There are various ways of dealing with imbalance. One is to add capacity to stages that are bottlenecks. This can be done by temporary measures such as scheduling overtime, leasing equipment, or purchasing additional capacity through subcontracting. A second way is through the use of buffer inventories in front of the bottleneck stage to ensure that it always has something to work on. A third approach involves duplicating or increasing the facilities of one department on which another is dependent. All these approaches are increasingly being applied to supply chain design. This supply planning also helps reduce imbalances for supplier partners and customers.

Frequency of Capacity Additions   There are two types of costs to consider when adding capacity: the cost of upgrading too frequently and that of upgrading too infrequently. Upgrading capacity too frequently is expensive. Direct costs include removing and replacing old equipment and training employees on the new equipment. In addition, the new equipment must be purchased, often for considerably more than the selling price of the old. Finally, there is the opportunity cost of idling the plant or service site during the changeover period.

Conversely, upgrading capacity too infrequently is also expensive. Infrequent expansion means that capacity is purchased in larger chunks. Any excess capacity that is purchased must be carried as overhead until it is utilized. (Exhibit 4.2 illustrates frequent versus infrequent capacity expansion.)

External Sources of Operations and Supply Capacity   In some cases, it may be cheaper to not add capacity at all, but rather to use some existing external source of capacity. Two common strategies used by organizations are outsourcing and sharing capacity. An example of outsourcing is Dell Computer using a Chinese company to assemble its notebook computers. An example of sharing capacity is two domestic airlines flying different routes with different seasonal demands exchanging aircraft (suitably repainted) when one's routes are heavily used and the other's are not. A new twist is airlines sharing routes—using the same flight number even though the airline company may change through the route. Outsourcing is covered in more depth in Chapter 11.

Global

Decreasing Capacity   Although we normally think in terms of expansions, shedding capacity in response to decreased demand can create significant problems for a firm. Temporary strategies such as scheduling fewer hours or scheduling an extended shutdown period are often used. Permanent reductions in capacity would typically require the sale of equipment or possibly even the liquidation of entire facilities.

DETERMINING CAPACITY REQUIREMENTS

In determining capacity requirements, we must address the demands for individual product lines, individual plant capabilities, and allocation of production throughout the plant network. Typically this is done according to the following steps:

1. Use forecasting techniques (see Chapter 15) to predict sales for individual products within each product line.
2. Calculate equipment and labor requirements to meet product line forecasts.
3. Project labor and equipment availabilities over the planning horizon.

Often the firm then decides on some capacity cushion that will be maintained between the projected requirements and the actual capacity. A capacity cushion is an amount of capacity in excess of expected demand. For example, if the expected annual demand on a facility is $10 million in products per year and the design capacity is $12 million per year, it has a 20 percent capacity cushion. A 20 percent capacity cushion equates to an 83 percent utilization rate (100%/120%).

Capacity cushion

When a firm's design capacity is less than the capacity required to meet its demand, it is said to have a negative capacity cushion. If, for example, a firm has a demand of $12 million in products per year but can produce only $10 million per year, it has a negative capacity cushion of 16.7 percent.

We now apply these three steps to an example.

EXAMPLE 4.1: Determining Capacity Requirements

The Stewart Company produces two flavors of salad dressings: Paul's and Newman's. Each is available in bottles and single-serving plastic bags. Management would like to determine equipment and labor requirements for the next five years.

Step by Step

SOLUTION

Step 1. Use forecasting techniques to predict sales for individual products within each product line. The marketing department, which is now running a promotional campaign for Newman's dressing, provided the following forecast demand values (in thousands) for the next five years. The campaign is expected to continue for the next two years.

	YEAR				
	1	2	3	4	5
Paul's					
Bottles (000s)	60	100	150	200	250
Plastic bags (000s)	100	200	300	400	500
Newman's					
Bottles (000s)	75	85	95	97	98
Plastic bags (000s)	200	400	600	650	680

Step 2. Calculate equipment and labor requirements to meet product line forecasts. Currently, three machines that can package up to 150,000 bottles each per year are available. Each machine requires two operators and can produce bottles of both Newman's and Paul's dressings. Six bottle machine operators are available. Also, five machines that can package up to 250,000 plastic bags each per year

are available. Three operators are required for each machine, which can produce plastic bags of both Newman's and Paul's dressings. Currently, 20 plastic bag machine operators are available.

Total product line forecasts can be calculated from the preceding table by adding the yearly demand for bottles and plastic bags as follows:

Excel: Capacity

	YEAR				
	1	2	3	4	5
Bottles (000s)	135	185	245	297	348
Plastic bags (000s)	300	600	900	1,050	1,180

We can now calculate equipment and labor requirements for the current year (year 1). Because the total available capacity for packaging bottles is 450,000/year (3 machines × 150,000 each), we will be using 135/450 = 0.3 of the available capacity for the current year, or 0.3 × 3 = 0.9 machine. Similarly, we will need 300/1,250 = 0.24 of the available capacity for plastic bags for the current year, or 0.24 × 5 = 1.2 machines. The number of crew required to support our forecast demand for the first year will consist of the crew required for the bottle and the plastic bag machines.

The labor requirement for year 1's bottle operation is

$$.9 \text{ bottle machines} \times 2 \text{ operators} = 1.8 \text{ operators}$$
$$1.2 \text{ bag machines} \times 3 \text{ operators} = 3.6 \text{ operators}$$

Step 3. Project labor and equipment availabilities over the planning horizon. We repeat the preceding calculations for the remaining years:

	YEAR				
	1	2	3	4	5
Plastic Bag Operation					
Percentage capacity utilized	24	48	72	84	94
Machine requirement	1.2	2.4	3.6	4.2	4.7
Labor requirement	3.6	7.2	10.8	12.6	14.1
Bottle Operation					
Percentage capacity utilized	30	41	54	66	77
Machine requirement	.9	1.23	1.62	1.98	2.31
Labor requirement	1.8	2.46	3.24	3.96	4.62

A positive capacity cushion exists for all five years because the available capacity for both operations always exceeds the expected demand. The Stewart Company can now begin to develop the intermediate-range or sales and operations plan for the two production lines. (See Chapter 16 for a discussion of sales and operations planning.) ●

USING DECISION TREES TO EVALUATE CAPACITY ALTERNATIVES

A convenient way to lay out the steps of a capacity problem is through the use of decision trees. The tree format helps not only in understanding the problem but also in finding a solution. A *decision tree* is a schematic model of the sequence of steps in a problem and the conditions and consequences of each step. In recent years, a few commercial software packages have been developed to assist in the construction and analysis of decision trees. These packages make the process quick and easy.

Decision trees are composed of decision nodes with branches to and from them. Usually squares represent decision points and circles represent chance events. Branches from decision points show the choices available to the decision maker; branches from chance events show the probabilities for their occurrence.

In solving decision tree problems, we work from the end of the tree backward to the start of the tree. As we work back, we calculate the expected values at each step. In calculation of the expected value, the time value of money is important if the planning horizon is long.

Once the calculations are made, we prune the tree by eliminating from each decision point all branches except the one with the highest payoff. This process continues to the first decision point, and the decision problem is thereby solved.

We now demonstrate an application of capacity planning for Hackers Computer Store.

EXAMPLE 4.2: Decision Trees

The owner of Hackers Computer Store is considering what to do with his business over the next five years. Sales growth over the past couple of years has been good, but sales could grow substantially if a major proposed electronics firm is built in his area. Hackers' owner sees three options. The first is to enlarge his current store, the second is to locate at a new site, and the third is to simply wait and do nothing. The decision to expand or move would take little time, and, therefore, the store would not lose revenue. If nothing were done the first year and strong growth occurred, then the decision to expand would be reconsidered. Waiting longer than one year would allow competition to move in and would make expansion no longer feasible.

The assumptions and conditions are as follows:

1. Strong growth as a result of the increased population of computer fanatics from the new electronics firm has a 55 percent probability.
2. Strong growth with a new site would give annual returns of $195,000 per year. Weak growth with a new site would mean annual returns of $115,000.
3. Strong growth with an expansion would give annual returns of $190,000 per year. Weak growth with an expansion would mean annual returns of $100,000.
4. At the existing store with no changes, there would be returns of $170,000 per year if there is strong growth and $105,000 per year if growth is weak.
5. Expansion at the current site would cost $87,000.
6. The move to the new site would cost $210,000.
7. If growth is strong and the existing site is enlarged during the second year, the cost would still be $87,000.
8. Operating costs for all options are equal.

Step by Step

Service

Tutorial: Decision Trees

SOLUTION

We construct a decision tree to advise Hackers' owner on the best action. Exhibit 4.3 shows the decision tree for this problem. There are two decision points (shown with the square nodes) and three chance occurrences (round nodes).

The values of each alternative outcome shown on the right of the diagram in Exhibit 4.4 are calculated as follows:

ALTERNATIVE	REVENUE	COST	VALUE
Move to new location, strong growth	$195,000 × 5 yrs	$210,000	$765,000
Move to new location, weak growth	$115,000 × 5 yrs	$210,000	$365,000
Expand store, strong growth	$190,000 × 5 yrs	$87,000	$863,000
Expand store, weak growth	$100,000 × 5 yrs	$87,000	$413,000
Do nothing now, strong growth, expand next year	$170,000 × 1 yr + $190,000 × 4 yrs	$87,000	$843,000
Do nothing now, strong growth, do not expand next year	$170,000 × 5 yrs	$0	$850,000
Do nothing now, weak growth	$105,000 × 5 yrs	$0	$525,000

Excel: Capacity

Excel: Decision Trees

Working from the rightmost alternatives, which are associated with the decision of whether to expand, we see that the alternative of doing nothing has a higher value than the expansion alternative. We therefore eliminate the expansion in the second-year alternatives. What this means is that if we do nothing in the first year and we experience strong growth, then in the second year it makes no sense to expand.

| exhibit 4.3 | Decision Tree for Hackers Computer Store Problem |

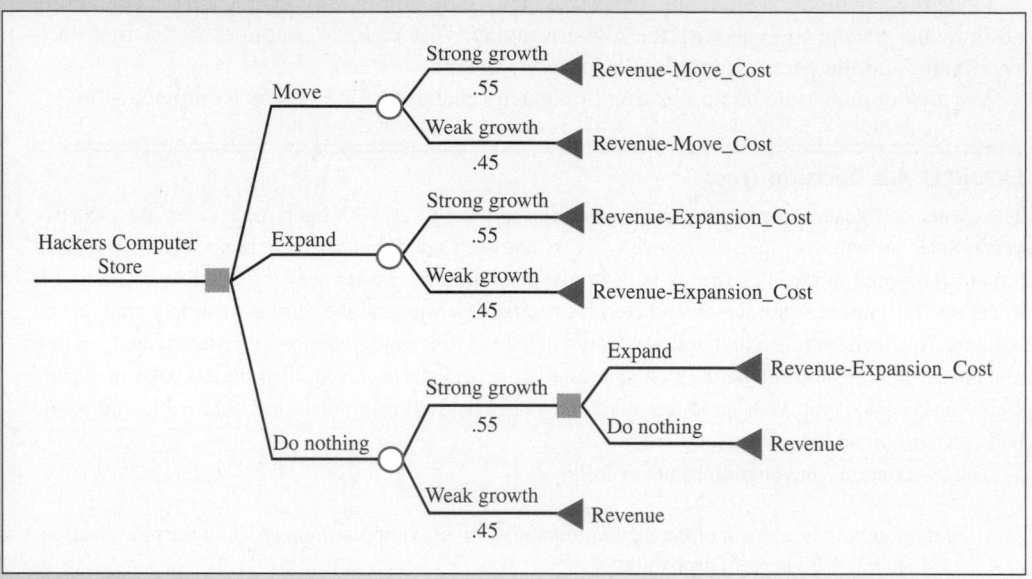

| exhibit 4.4 | Decision Tree Analysis |

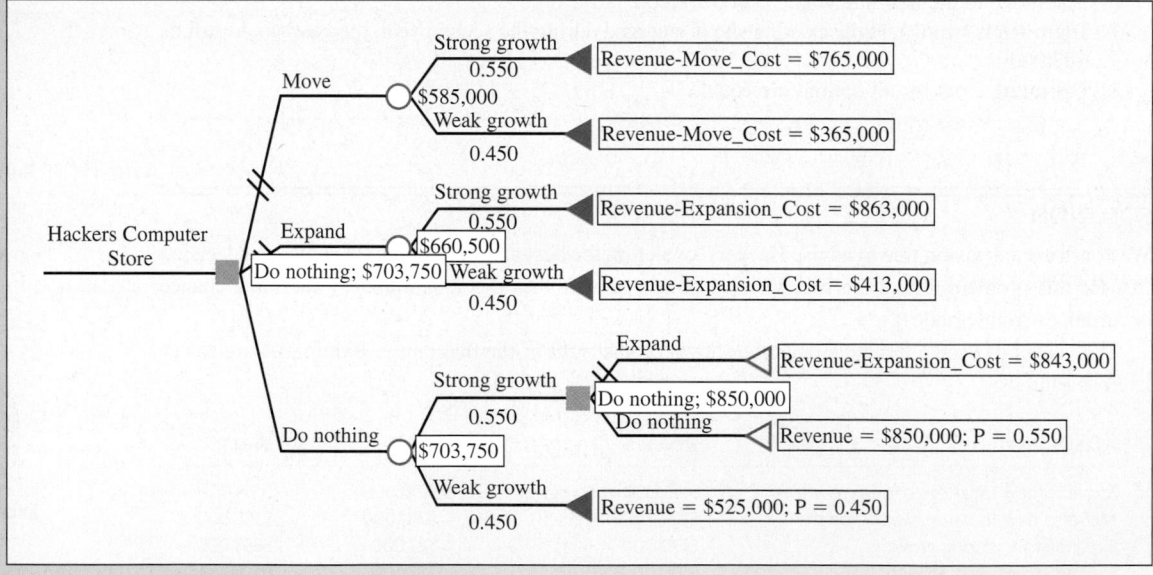

Now we can calculate the expected values associated with our current decision alternatives. We simply multiply the value of the alternative by its probability and sum the values. The expected value for the alternative of moving now is $585,000. The expansion alternative has an expected value of $660,500, and doing nothing now has an expected value of $703,750. Our analysis indicates that our best decision is to do nothing (both now and next year)!

Due to the five-year time horizon, it may be useful to consider the time value of the revenue and cost streams when solving this problem. If we assume a 16 percent interest rate, the first alternative

Decision Tree Analysis Using Net Present Value Calculations

exhibit 4.5

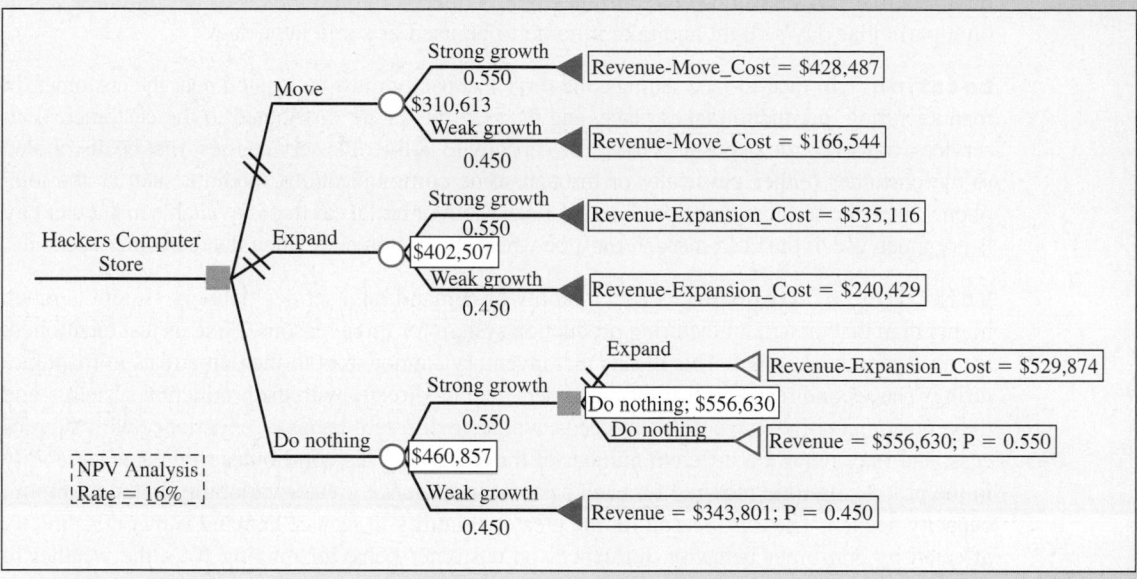

outcome (move now, strong growth) has a discounted revenue valued at $428,487 (195,000 × 3.274293654) minus the $210,000 cost to move immediately. Exhibit 4.5 shows the analysis considering the discounted flows. Details of the calculations are given below. The present value table in Appendix E can be used to look up the discount factors. In order to make our calculations agree with those computed by Excel, we have used discount factors that are calculated to 10 digits of precision. The only calculation that is a little tricky is the one for revenue when we do nothing now and expand at the beginning of next year. In this case, we have a revenue stream of $170,000 the first year, followed by four years at $190,000. The first part of the calculation (170,000 × .862068966) discounts the first-year revenue to the present. The next part (190,000 × 2.798180638) discounts the next four years to the start of year two. We then discount this four-year stream to present value.

ALTERNATIVE	REVENUE	COST	VALUE
Move to new location, strong growth	$195,000 × 3.274293654	$210,000	$428,487
Move to new location, weak growth	$115,000 × 3.274293654	$210,000	$166,544
Expand store, strong growth	$190,000 × 3.274293654	$87,000	$535,116
Expand store, weak growth	$100,000 × 3.274203654	$87,000	$240,429
Do nothing now, strong growth, expand next year	($170,000 × .862068966 + $190,000 × 2.798180638 × .862068966)	($87,000 × .862068966)	$529,874
Do nothing now, strong growth, do not expand next year	$170,000 × 3.274293654	$0	$556,630
Do nothing now, weak growth	$105,000 × 3.274293654	$0	$343,801

Excel: Decision Trees

PLANNING SERVICE CAPACITY

CAPACITY PLANNING IN SERVICE VERSUS MANUFACTURING

Although capacity planning in services is subject to many of the same issues as manufacturing capacity planning, and facility sizing can be done in much the same way, there are several important differences. Service capacity is more time- and location-dependent, it is subject to more volatile demand fluctuations, and utilization directly impacts service quality.

Service

Time   Unlike goods, services cannot be stored for later use. As such, in services managers must consider time as one of their supplies. The capacity must be available to produce a service when it is needed. For example, a customer cannot be given a seat that went unoccupied on a previous airline flight if the current flight is full. Nor could the customer purchase a seat on a particular day's flight and take it home to be used at some later date.

Location   In face-to-face settings, the service capacity must be located near the customer. In manufacturing, production takes place, and then the goods are distributed to the customer. With services, however, the opposite is true. The capacity to deliver the service must first be distributed to the customer (either physically or through some communications medium such as the telephone); then the service can be produced. A hotel room or rental car that is available in another city is not much use to the customer—it must be where the customer is when that customer needs it.

Volatility of Demand   The volatility of demand on a service delivery system is much higher than that on a manufacturing production system for three reasons. First, as just mentioned, services cannot be stored. This means that inventory cannot smooth the demand as in manufacturing. The second reason is that the customers interact directly with the production system—and these customers often have different needs, will have different levels of experience with the process, and may require a different number of transactions. This contributes to greater variability in the processing time required for each customer and hence greater variability in the minimum capacity needed. The third reason for the greater volatility in service demand is that it is directly affected by consumer behavior. Influences on customer behavior ranging from the weather to a major event can directly affect demand for different services. Go to any restaurant near your campus during spring break and it will probably be almost empty. This behavioral effect can be seen over even shorter time frames such as the lunch-hour rush at a bank's drive-through window. Because of this volatility, service capacity is often planned in increments as small as 10 to 30 minutes, as opposed to the one-week increments more common in manufacturing.

Service

CAPACITY UTILIZATION AND SERVICE QUALITY

Planning capacity levels for services must consider the day-to-day relationship between service utilization and service quality. Exhibit 4.6 shows a service situation using waiting line terms (arrival rates and service rates). The term arrival rate refers to the average number of customers

---

exhibit 4.6   Relationship between the Rate of Service Utilization (ρ) and Service Quality

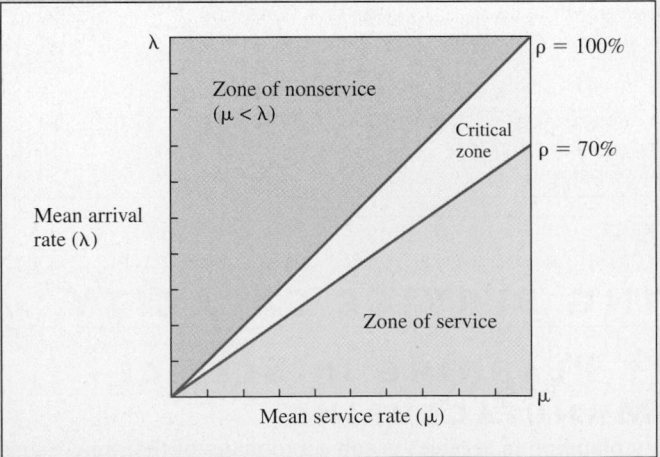

SOURCE: J. HAYWOOD-FARMER AND J. NOLLET, *SERVICES PLUS: EFFECTIVE SERVICE MANAGEMENT* (BOUCHERVILLE, QUEBEC, CANADA: G. MORIN PUBLISHER LTD. 1991), p. 59.

that come to a facility during a specific period of time. The service rate is the average number of customers that can be processed over the same period of time when the facility is operating at maximum capacity. The best operating point is near 70 percent of the maximum capacity. This is enough to keep servers busy but allows enough time to serve customers individually and keep enough capacity in reserve so as not to create too many managerial headaches. In the critical zone, customers are processed through the system, but service quality declines. Above the critical zone, the line builds up and it is likely that many customers may never be served.

The optimal utilization rate is very context specific. Low rates are appropriate when both the degree of uncertainty and the stakes are high. For example, hospital emergency rooms and fire departments should aim for low utilization because of the high level of uncertainty and the life-or-death nature of their activities. Relatively predictable services such as commuter trains or service facilities without customer contact, such as postal sorting operations, can plan to operate much nearer 100 percent utilization. Interestingly, there is a third group for which high utilization is desirable. All sports teams like sellouts, not only because of the virtually 100 percent contribution margin of each customer, but because a full house creates an atmosphere that pleases customers, motivates the home team to perform better, and boosts future ticket sales. Stage performances and bars share this phenomenon. On the other hand, many airline passengers feel that a flight is too crowded when the seat next to theirs is occupied. Airlines capitalize on this response to sell more business-class seats.

SUMMARY

Strategic capacity planning involves an investment decision that must match resource capabilities to a long-term demand forecast. As discussed in this chapter, factors to be taken into account in selecting capacity additions for both manufacturing and services include

- The likely effects of economies of scale.
- The impact of changing facility focus and balance among production stages.
- The degree of flexibility of facilities and the workforce in the operation and its supply system.

Service

For services in particular, a key consideration is the effect of capacity changes on the quality of the service offering.

KEY TERMS

Strategic capacity planning Determining the overall capacity level of capital-intensive resources that best supports the company's long-range competitive strategy.

Capacity The amount of output that a system is capable of achieving over a specific period of time.

Best operating level The level of capacity for which the process was designed and the volume of output at which average unit cost is minimized.

Capacity utilization rate Measures how close a firm is to its best operating level.

Economies of scale The notion is that as a plant gets larger and volume increases, the average cost per unit drops.

Focused factory A facility with a fairly limited set of production objectives. Typically the focus would relate to a specific product or product group.

Plant within a plant (PWP) A concept that can be used to operationalize a focused factory by designating a specific area in a larger plant.

Economies of scope Exist when multiple products can be produced at a lower cost in combination than they can separately.

Capacity cushion Capacity in excess of expected demand.

FORMULA REVIEW

Capacity utilization rate

$$Capacity\ utilization\ rate = \frac{Capacity\ used}{Best\ operating\ level}$$ [4.1]

SOLVED PROBLEM

E-Education is a new start-up that develops and markets MBA courses offered over the Internet. The company is currently located in Chicago and employs 150 people. Due to strong growth the company needs additional office space. The company has the option of leasing additional space at its current location in Chicago for the next two years, but after that will need to move to a new building. Another option the company is considering is moving the entire operation to a small Midwest town immediately. A third option is for the company to lease a new building in Chicago immediately. If the company chooses the first option and leases new space at its current location, it can, at the end of two years, either lease a new building in Chicago or move to the small Midwest town.

The following are some additional facts about the alternatives and current situation:

1   The company has a 75 percent chance of surviving the next two years.
2   Leasing the new space for two years at the current location in Chicago would cost $750,000 per year.
3   Moving the entire operation to a Midwest town would cost $1 million. Leasing space would run only $500,000 per year.
4   Moving to a new building in Chicago would cost $200,000, and leasing the new building's space would cost $650,000 per year.
5   The company can cancel the lease at any time.
6   The company will build its own building in five years, if it survives.
7   Assume all other costs and revenues are the same no matter where the company is located.

What should E-Education do?

Solution

Step 1: Construct a decision tree that considers all of E-Education's alternatives. The following shows the tree that has decision points (with the square nodes) followed by chance occurrences (round nodes). In the case of the first decision point, if the company survives, two additional decision points need consideration.

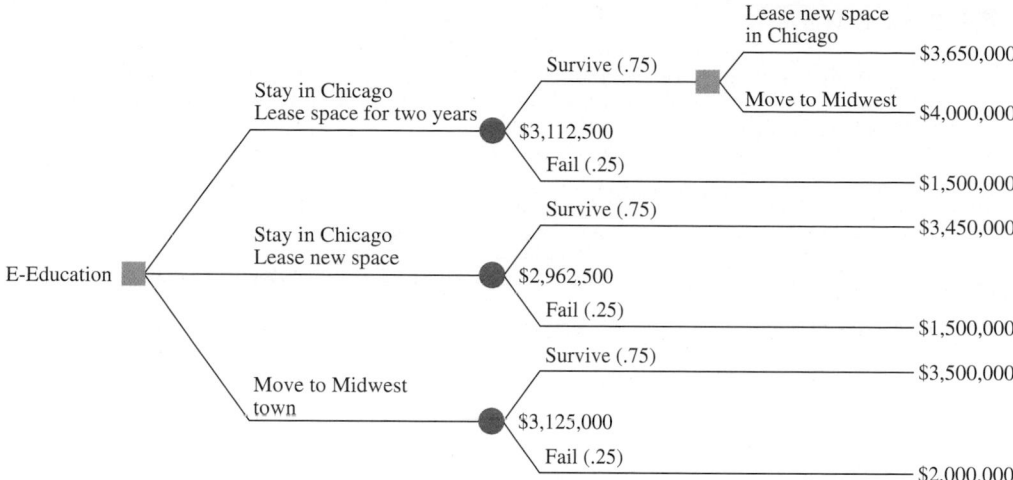

Step 2: Calculate the values of each alternative as follows:

ALTERNATIVE	CALCULATION	VALUE
Stay in Chicago, lease space for two years, survive, lease new building in Chicago	(750,000) × 2 + 200,000 + (650,000) × 3 =	$3,650,000
Stay in Chicago, lease space for two years, survive, move to Midwest	(750,000) × 2 + 1,000,000 + (500,000) × 3 =	$4,000,000
Stay in Chicago, lease space for two years, fail	(750,000) × 2 =	$ 1,500,000
Stay in Chicago, lease new building in Chicago, survive	200,000 + (650,000) × 5 =	$3,450,000
Stay in Chicago, lease new building in Chicago, fail	200,000 + (650,000) × 2 =	$ 1,500,000
Move to Midwest, survive	1,000,000 + (500,000) × 5 =	$3,500,000
Move to Midwest, fail	1,000,000 + (500,000) × 2 =	$2,000,000

Working from our rightmost alternatives, the first two alternatives end in decision nodes. Because the first option, staying in Chicago and leasing space for two years, is the lowest cost, this is what we would do if for the first two years we decide to stay in Chicago. If we fail after the first two years, represented by the third alternative, the cost is only $1,500,000. The expected value of the first option of staying in Chicago and leasing space for the first two years is .75 × 3,650,000 + .25 × 1,500,000 = $3,112,500.

The second option, staying in Chicago and leasing a new building now, has an expected value of .75 × 3,450,000 + .25 × 1,500,000 = $2,962,500.

Finally, the third option of moving to the Midwest immediately has an expected value of .75 × 3,500,000 + .25 × 2,000,000 = $3,125,000.

From this, it looks like the best alternative is to stay in Chicago and lease a new building immediately.

REVIEW AND DISCUSSION QUESTIONS

1   What capacity problems are encountered when a new drug is introduced to the market?
2   List some practical limits to economies of scale; that is, when should a plant stop growing?
3   What are some capacity balance problems faced by the following organizations or facilities?
    a. An airline terminal.
    b. A university computing lab.
    c. A clothing manufacturer.
4   What are some major capacity considerations in a hospital? How do they differ from those of a factory?
5   Management may choose to build up capacity in anticipation of demand or in response to developing demand. Cite the advantages and disadvantages of both approaches.
6   What is capacity balance? Why is it hard to achieve? What methods are used to deal with capacity imbalances?
7   What are some reasons for a plant to maintain a capacity cushion? How about a negative capacity cushion?
8   At first glance, the concepts of the focused factory and capacity flexibility may seem to contradict each other. Do they really?

PROBLEMS

1   AlwaysRain Irrigation, Inc., would like to determine capacity requirements for the next four years. Currently two production lines are in place for making bronze and plastic sprinklers. Three types of sprinklers are available in both bronze and plastic: 90-degree nozzle sprinklers, 180-degree nozzle sprinklers, and 360-degree nozzle sprinklers. Management has forecast demand for the next four years as follows:

	YEARLY DEMAND			
	1 (IN 000s)	2 (IN 000s)	3 (IN 000s)	4 (IN 000s)
Plastic 90	32	44	55	56
Plastic 180	15	16	17	18
Plastic 360	50	55	64	67
Bronze 90	7	8	9	10
Bronze 180	3	4	5	6
Bronze 360	11	12	15	18

Both production lines can produce all the different types of nozzles. The bronze machines needed for the bronze sprinklers require two operators and can produce up to 12,000 sprinklers. The plastic injection molding machine needed for the plastic sprinklers requires four operators and can produce up to 200,000 sprinklers. Three bronze machines and only one injection molding machine are available. What are the capacity requirements for the next four years? (Assume that there is no learning.)

2   Suppose that AlwaysRain Irrigation's marketing department will undertake an intense ad campaign for the bronze sprinklers, which are more expensive but also more durable than the plastic ones. Forecast demand for the next four years is

	YEARLY DEMAND			
	1 (IN 000s)	2 (IN 000s)	3 (IN 000s)	4 (IN 000s)
Plastic 90	32	44	55	56
Plastic 180	15	16	17	18
Plastic 360	50	55	64	67
Bronze 90	11	15	18	23
Bronze 180	6	5	6	9
Bronze 360	15	16	17	20

What are the capacity implications of the marketing campaign (assume no learning)?

3   In anticipation of the ad campaign, AlwaysRain bought an additional bronze machine. Will this be enough to ensure that enough capacity is available?

4   Suppose that operators have enough training to operate both the bronze machines and the injection molding machine for the plastic sprinklers. Currently AlwaysRain has 10 such employees. In anticipation of the ad campaign described in Problem 2, management approved the purchase of two additional bronze machines. What are the labor requirement implications?

5   Expando, Inc., is considering the possibility of building an additional factory that would produce a new addition to its product line. The company is currently considering two options. The first is a small facility that it could build at a cost of $6 million. If demand for new products is low, the company expects to receive $10 million in discounted revenues (present value of future revenues) with the small facility. On the other hand, if demand is high, it expects $12 million in discounted revenues using the small facility. The second option is to build a large factory at a cost of $9 million. Were demand to be low, the company would expect $10 million in discounted revenues with the large plant. If demand is high, the company estimates that the discounted revenues would be $14 million. In either case, the probability of demand being high is .40, and the probability of it being low is .60. Not constructing a new factory would result in no additional revenue being generated because the current factories cannot produce these new products. Construct a decision tree to help Expando make the best decision.

6   A builder has located a piece of property that she would like to buy and eventually build on. The land is currently zoned for four homes per acre, but she is planning to request new zoning. What she builds depends on approval of zoning requests and your analysis of this problem to

advise her. With her input and your help, the decision process has been reduced to the following costs, alternatives, and probabilities:

Cost of land: $2 million.

Probability of rezoning: .60.

If the land is rezoned, there will be additional costs for new roads, lighting, and so on, of $1 million.

If the land is rezoned, the contractor must decide whether to build a shopping center or 1,500 apartments that the tentative plan shows would be possible. If she builds a shopping center, there is a 70 percent chance that she can sell the shopping center to a large department chain for $4 million over her construction cost, which excludes the land; and there is a 30 percent chance that she can sell it to an insurance company for $5 million over her construction cost (also excluding the land). If, instead of the shopping center, she decides to build the 1,500 apartments, she places probabilities on the profits as follows: There is a 60 percent chance that she can sell the apartments to a real estate investment corporation for $3,000 each over her construction cost; there is a 40 percent chance that she can get only $2,000 each over her construction cost. (Both exclude the land cost.)

If the land is not rezoned, she will comply with the existing zoning restrictions and simply build 600 homes, on which she expects to make $4,000 over the construction cost on each one (excluding the cost of land).

Draw a decision tree of the problem and determine the best solution and the expected net profit.

Service   **Excel: Shouldice Hosp**

CASE: SHOULDICE HOSPITAL—A CUT ABOVE

"Shouldice Hospital, the house that hernias built, is a converted country estate which gives the hospital 'a country club' appeal."

A quote from *American Medical News*

Shouldice Hospital in Canada is widely known for one thing—hernia repair! In fact, that is the only operation it performs, and it performs a great many of them. Over the past two decades this small 90-bed hospital has averaged 7,000 operations annually. Last year, it had a record year and performed nearly 7,500 operations. Patients' ties to Shouldice do not end when they leave the hospital. Every year the gala Hernia Reunion dinner (with complimentary hernia inspection) draws in excess of 1,000 former patients, some of whom have been attending the event for over 30 years.

A number of notable features in Shouldice's service delivery system contribute to its success. (1) Shouldice accepts only patients with the uncomplicated external hernias, and it uses a superior technique developed for this type of hernia by Dr. Shouldice during World War II. (2) Patients are subject to early ambulation, which promotes healing. (Patients literally walk off the operating table and engage in light exercise throughout their stay, which lasts only three days.) (3) Its country club atmosphere, gregarious nursing staff, and built-in socializing make a surprisingly pleasant experience out of an inherently unpleasant medical problem. Regular times are set aside for tea, cookies, and socializing. All patients are paired up with a roommate with similar background and interests.

THE PRODUCTION SYSTEM

The medical facilities at Shouldice consist of five operating rooms, a patient recovery room, a laboratory, and six examination rooms. Shouldice performs, on average, 150 operations per week, with patients generally staying at the hospital for three days. Although operations are performed only five days a week, the remainder of

the hospital is in operation continuously to attend to recovering patients.

An operation at Shouldice Hospital is performed by one of the 12 full-time surgeons assisted by one of seven part-time assistant surgeons. Surgeons generally take about one hour to prepare for and perform each hernia operation, and they operate on four patients per day. The surgeons' day ends at 4 P.M., although they can expect to be on call every 14th night and every 10th weekend.

THE SHOULDICE EXPERIENCE

Each patient undergoes a screening exam prior to setting a date for his or her operation. Patients in the Toronto area are encouraged to walk in for the diagnosis. Examinations are done between 9 A.M. and 3:30 P.M. Monday through Friday, and between 10 A.M. and 2 P.M. on Saturday. Out-of-town patients are mailed a medical information questionnaire (also available over the Internet), which is used for the diagnosis. A small percentage of the patients who are overweight or otherwise represent an undue medical risk are refused treatment. The remaining patients receive confirmation cards with the scheduled dates for their operations. A patient's folder is transferred to the reception desk once an arrival date is confirmed.

Patients arrive at the clinic between 1 and 3 P.M. the day before their surgery. After a short wait, they receive a brief preoperative examination. They are then sent to an admissions clerk to complete any necessary paperwork. Patients are next directed to one of the two nurses' stations for blood and urine tests and then are shown to their rooms. They spend the remaining time before orientation getting settled and acquainting themselves with their roommates.

Orientation begins at 5 P.M., followed by dinner in the common dining room. Later in the evening, at 9 P.M., patients gather in the lounge area for tea and cookies. Here new patients can talk with

exhibit 4.7   Operations with 90 Beds (30 patients per day)

	BEDS REQUIRED						
CHECK-IN DAY	MONDAY	TUESDAY	WEDNESDAY	THURSDAY	FRIDAY	SATURDAY	SUNDAY
Monday	30	30	30				
Tuesday		30	30	30			
Wednesday			30	30	30		
Thursday				30	30	30	
Friday							
Saturday							
Sunday	30	30					30
Total	60	90	90	90	60	30	30

patients who have already had their surgery. Bedtime is between 9:30 and 10 P.M.

On the day of the operation, patients with early operations are awakened at 5:30 A.M. for preoperative sedation. The first operations begin at 7:30 A.M. Shortly before an operation starts, the patient is administered a local anesthetic, leaving him or her alert and fully aware of the proceedings. At the conclusion of the operation, the patient is invited to walk from the operating table to a nearby wheelchair, which is waiting to return the patient to his or her room. After a brief period of rest, the patient is encouraged to get up and start exercising. By 9 P.M. that day, he or she is in the lounge having cookies and tea and talking with new, incoming patients.

The skin clips holding the incision together are loosened, and some are removed, the next day. The remainder are removed the following morning just before the patient is discharged.

When Shouldice Hospital started, the average hospital stay for hernia surgery was three weeks. Today, many institutions push "same day surgery" for a variety of reasons. Shouldice Hospital firmly believes that this is not in the best interests of patients, and is committed to its three-day process. Shouldice's postoperative rehabilitation program is designed to enable the patient to resume normal activities with minimal interruption and discomfort. Shouldice patients frequently return to work in a few days; the average total time off is eight days.

"It is interesting to note that approximately 1 out of every 100 Shouldice patients is a medical doctor."

FUTURE PLANS

The management of Shouldice is thinking of expanding the hospital's capacity to serve considerable unsatisfied demand. To this effect, the vice president is seriously considering two options. The first involves adding one more day of operations (Saturday) to the existing five-day schedule, which would increase capacity by 20 percent. The second option is to add another floor of rooms to the hospital, increasing the number of beds by 50 percent. This would require more aggressive scheduling of the operating rooms.

The administrator of the hospital, however, is concerned about maintaining control over the quality of the service delivered. He thinks the facility is already getting very good utilization. The doctors and the staff are happy with their jobs, and the patients are satisfied with the service. According to him, further expansion of capacity might make it hard to maintain the same kind of working relationships and attitudes.

QUESTIONS

Exhibit 4.7 is a room-occupancy table for the existing system. Each row in the table follows the patients that checked in on a given day. The columns indicate the number of patients in the hospital on a given day. For example, the first row of the table shows that 30 people checked in on Monday and were in the hospital for Monday, Tuesday, and Wednesday. By summing the columns of the table for Wednesday, we see that there are 90 patients staying in the hospital that day.

1   How well is the hospital currently utilizing its beds?
2   Develop a similar table to show the effects of adding operations on Saturday. (Assume that 30 operations would still be performed each day.) How would this affect the utilization of the bed capacity? Is this capacity sufficient for the additional patients?
3   Now look at the effect of increasing the number of beds by 50 percent. How many operations could the hospital perform per day before running out of bed capacity? (Assume operations are performed five days per week, with the same number performed on each day.) How well would the new resources be utilized relative to the current operation? Could the hospital really perform this many operations? Why? (Hint: Look at the capacity of the 12 surgeons and the five operating rooms.)
4   Although financial data are sketchy, an estimate from a construction company indicates that adding bed capacity would cost about $100,000 per bed. In addition, the rate charged for the hernia surgery varies between about $900 and $2,000 (U.S. dollars), with an average rate of $1,300 per operation. The surgeons are paid a flat $600 per operation. Due to all the uncertainties in government health care legislation, Shouldice would like to justify any expansion within a five-year time period.

SUPER QUIZ

1 The level of capacity for which a process was designed and at which it operates at minimum cost.

2 A facility has a maximum capacity of 4,000 units per day using overtime and skipping the daily maintenance routine. At 3,500 units per day, the facility operates at a level where average cost per unit is minimized. Currently, the process is scheduled to operate at a level of 3,000 units per day. What is the capacity utilization rate?

3 The concept that relates to gaining efficiency through the full utilization of dedicated resources such as people and equipment.

4 A facility that limits its production to a single product or a set of very similar products.

5 Term that describes when multiple (usually similar) products can be produced in a facility less expensively than a single product.

6 We have this when we have the ability to serve more customers than we expect to have to serve.

7 In considering a capacity expansion we have two alternatives. The first alternative is expected to cost $1,000,000 and has an expected profit of $500,000 over the next three years. The second alternative has an expected cost of $800,000 and expected profit of $450,000 over the next three years. Which alternative should we select and what is the expected value of the expansion? Assume a 10 percent interest rate.

8 In a service process such as the checkout counter in a discount store, a good target for capacity utilization is about this percent.

1. Best operating level 2. 85% 3. Economies of scale 4. Focused factory 5. Economies of scope 6. Capacity cushion 7. Alternative 1 Present Value = 500,000 × (.909 + .826 + .751) − 1,000,000 = $243,000, Alternative 2 Present Value = 450,000 × (.909 + .826 + .751) − 800,000 = $318,700, Alternative 2 is best 8. 70 percent

SELECTED BIBLIOGRAPHY

Wright, T. P. "Factors Affecting the Cost of Airplanes." *Journal of Aeronautical Sciences,* February 1936, pp. 122–128.

Yu-Lee, R. T. *Essentials of Capacity Management.* New York: Wiley, 2002.

chapter 4A

LEARNING CURVES

After reading this chapter you will:

1. Understand what learning curves are and how they can be estimated.

2. Apply learning curves to estimate the cost to produce products in the future.

3. Describe how companies improve based on individual and organization learning.

APPLICATION OF LEARNING CURVES

A **learning curve** is a line displaying the relationship between unit production time and the cumulative number of units produced. Learning (or experience) curve theory has a wide range of application in the business world. In manufacturing, it can be used to estimate the time for product design and production, as well as costs. Learning curves are important and are sometimes overlooked as one of the trade-offs in just-in-time (JIT) systems, where sequencing and short runs achieve lower inventories by forfeiting some benefits of experience from long product runs. Learning curves are also an integral part in planning corporate strategy, such as decisions concerning pricing, capital investment, and operating costs based on experience curves.

Learning curve

Learning curves can be applied to individuals or organizations. **Individual learning** is improvement that results when people repeat a process and gain skill or efficiency from their own experience. That is, "practice makes perfect." **Organizational learning** results from practice as well, but it also comes from changes in administration, equipment, and product design. In organizational settings, we expect to see both kinds of learning occurring simultaneously and often describe the combined effect with a single learning curve.

Individual learning

Organizational learning

Learning curve theory is based on three assumptions:

1. The amount of time required to complete a given task or unit of a product will be less each time the task is undertaken.
2. The unit time will decrease at a decreasing rate.
3. The reduction in time will follow a predictable pattern.

Each of these assumptions was found to hold true in the airplane industry, where learning curves were first applied.[1] In this application, it was observed that, as output doubled, there was a 20 percent reduction in direct production worker-hours per unit between doubled units. Thus, if it took 100,000 hours for Plane 1, it would take 80,000 hours for Plane 2, 64,000 hours for Plane 4, and so forth. Because the 20 percent reduction meant that, say, Unit 4 took only 80 percent of the production time required for Unit 2, the line connecting the coordinates of output and time was referred to as an "80 percent learning curve." (By convention, the percentage learning rate is used to denote any given exponential learning curve.)

A learning curve may be developed from an arithmetic tabulation, by logarithms, or by some other curve-fitting method, depending on the amount and form of the available data.

There are two ways to think about the improved performance that comes with learning curves: time per unit (as in Exhibit 4A.1A) or units of output per time period (as in 4A.1B). *Time per unit* shows the decrease in time required for each successive unit. *Cumulative average time* shows the cumulative average performance times as the total number of units increases. Time per unit and cumulative average times are also called *progress curves* or

---

Learning Curves Plotted as Times and Numbers of Units

exhibit 4A.1

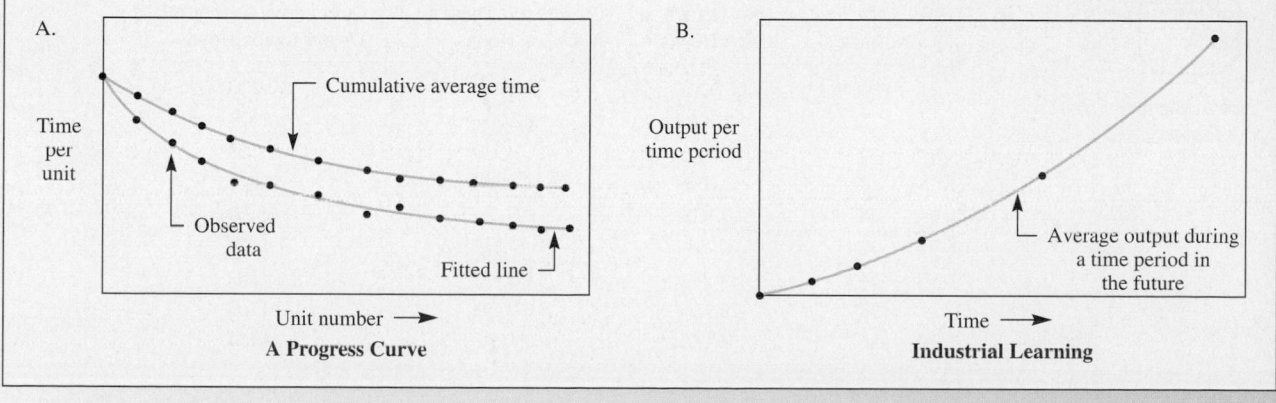

A Progress Curve

Industrial Learning

product learning and are useful for complex products or products with a longer cycle time. *Units of output per time period* is also called *industry learning* and is generally applied to high-volume production (short cycle time).

Note in Exhibit 4A.1A that the cumulative average curve does not decrease as fast as the time per unit because the time is being averaged. For example, if the time for Units 1, 2, 3, and 4 were 100, 80, 70, and 64, they would be plotted that way on the time per unit graph, but would be plotted as 100, 90, 83.3, and 78.5 on the cumulative average time graph.

PLOTTING LEARNING CURVES

There are many ways to analyze past data to fit a useful trend line. We will use the simple exponential curve first as an arithmetic procedure and then by a logarithmic analysis. In an arithmetical tabulation approach, a column for units is created by doubling, row by row, as 1, 2, 4, 8, 16 . . . The time for the first unit is multiplied by the learning percentage to obtain the time for the second unit. The second unit is multiplied by the learning percentage for the fourth unit, and so on. Thus, if we are developing an 80 percent learning curve, we would arrive at the figures listed in column 2 of Exhibit 4A.2. Because it is often desirable for planning purposes to know the cumulative direct labor hours, column 4, which lists this information, is also provided. The calculation of these figures is straightforward; for example, for Unit 4, cumulative average direct labor hours would be found by dividing cumulative direct labor hours by 4, yielding the figure given in column 4.

Exhibit 4A.3A shows three curves with different learning rates: 90 percent, 80 percent, and 70 percent. Note that if the cost of the first unit was $100, the 30th unit would cost $59.63 at the 90 percent rate and $17.37 at the 70 percent rate. Differences in learning rates can have dramatic effects.

In practice, learning curves are plotted using a graph with logarithmic scales. The unit curves become linear throughout their entire range, and the cumulative curve becomes linear after the first few units. The property of linearity is desirable because it facilitates extrapolation and permits a more accurate reading of the cumulative curve. This type of scale is an option in Microsoft Excel. Simply generate a regular scatter plot in your spreadsheet and then select each axis and format the axis with the logarithmic option. Exhibit 4A.3B shows the 80 percent unit cost curve and average cost curve on a logarithmic scale. Note that the cumulative average cost is essentially linear after the eighth unit.

Although the arithmetic tabulation approach is useful, direct logarithmic analysis of learning curve problems is generally more efficient because it does not require a complete enumeration of successive time–output combinations. Moreover, where such data are not available, an analytical model that uses logarithms may be the most convenient way of obtaining output estimates.

exhibit 4A.2   Unit, Cumulative, and Cumulative Average Direct Labor Worker-Hours Required for an 80 Percent Learning Curve

Excel: Learning Curves

(1) UNIT NUMBER	(2) UNIT DIRECT LABOR HOURS	(3) CUMULATIVE DIRECT LABOR HOURS	(4) CUMULATIVE AVERAGE DIRECT LABOR HOURS
1	100,000	100,000	100,000
2	80,000	180,000	90,000
4	64,000	314,210	78,553
8	51,200	534,591	66,824
16	40,960	892,014	55,751
32	32,768	1,467,862	45,871
64	26,214	2,392,453	37,382
128	20,972	3,874,395	30,269
256	16,777	6,247,318	24,404

Learning Curve Plots

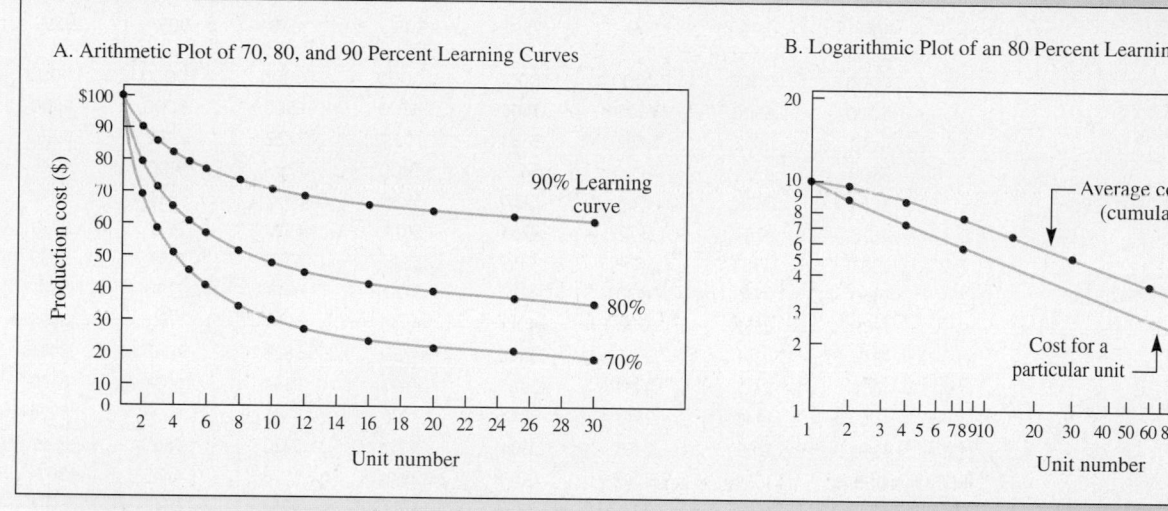

A. Arithmetic Plot of 70, 80, and 90 Percent Learning Curves

B. Logarithmic Plot of an 80 Percent Learning Curve

LOGARITHMIC ANALYSIS

The normal form of the learning curve equation is[2]

$$Y_x = Kx^n \qquad \text{[4A.1]}$$

where

x = Unit number

Y_x = Number of direct labor hours required to produce the xth unit

K = Number of direct labor hours required to produce the first unit

n = log b/log 2, where b = Learning percentage

We can solve this mathematically or by using a table, as shown in the next section. Mathematically, to find the labor-hour requirement for the eighth unit in our example (Exhibit 4A.2), we would substitute as follows:

$$Y_8 = (100,000)(8)^n$$

Using logarithms:

$$Y_8 = 100,000(8)^{\log 0.8/\log 2}$$

$$= 100,000(8)^{-0.322} = \frac{100,000}{(8)^{0.322}}$$

$$= \frac{100,000}{1.9535} = 51,192$$

Therefore, it would take 51,192 hours to make the eighth unit. (See the spreadsheet "Learning Curves.")

LEARNING CURVE TABLES

When the learning percentage is known, Exhibits 4A.4 and 4A.5 can be used to easily calculate estimated labor hours for a specific unit or for cumulative groups of units. We need only multiply the initial unit labor hour figure by the appropriate tabled value.

To illustrate, suppose we want to double-check the figures in Exhibit 4A.2 for unit and cumulative labor hours for Unit 16. From Exhibit 4A.4, the unit improvement factor for Unit 16 at 80 percent is .4096. This multiplied by 100,000 (the hours for Unit 1) gives 40,960, the same as in Exhibit 4A.2. From Exhibit 4A.5, the cumulative improvement factor for cumulative hours for the first 16 units is 8.920. When multiplied by 100,000, this gives 892,000, which is reasonably close to the exact value of 892,014 shown in Exhibit 4A.2.

Excel: Learning Curves

exhibit 4A.4

Excel: Learning Curves

Improvement Curves: Table of Unit Values

UNIT	UNIT IMPROVEMENT FACTOR							
	60%	65%	70%	75%	80%	85%	90%	95%
1	1.0000	1.0000	1.0000	1.0000	1.0000	1.0000	1.0000	1.0000
2	.6000	.6500	.7000	.7500	.8000	.8500	.9000	.9500
3	.4450	.5052	.5682	.6338	.7021	.7729	.8462	.9219
4	.3600	.4225	.4900	.5625	.6400	.7225	.8100	.9025
5	.3054	.3678	.4368	.5127	.5956	.6857	.7830	.8877
6	.2670	.3284	.3977	.4754	.5617	.6570	.7616	.8758
7	.2383	.2984	.3674	.4459	.5345	.6337	.7439	.8659
8	.2160	.2746	.3430	.4219	.5120	.6141	.7290	.8574
9	.1980	.2552	.3228	.4017	.4930	.5974	.7161	.8499
10	.1832	.2391	.3058	.3846	.4765	.5828	.7047	.8433
12	.1602	.2135	.2784	.3565	.4493	.5584	.6854	.8320
14	.1430	.1940	.2572	.3344	.4276	.5386	.6696	.8226
16	.1290	.1785	.2401	.3164	.4096	.5220	.6561	.8145
18	.1188	.1659	.2260	.3013	.3944	.5078	.6445	.8074
20	.1099	.1554	.2141	.2884	.3812	.4954	.6342	.8012
22	.1025	.1465	.2038	.2772	.3697	.4844	.6251	.7955
24	.0961	.1387	.1949	.2674	.3595	.4747	.6169	.7904
25	.0933	.1353	.1908	.2629	.3548	.4701	.6131	.7880
30	.0815	.1208	.1737	.2437	.3346	.4505	.5963	.7775
35	.0728	.1097	.1605	.2286	.3184	.4345	.5825	.7687
40	.0660	.1010	.1498	.2163	.3050	.4211	.5708	.7611
45	.0605	.0939	.1410	.2060	.2936	.4096	.5607	.7545
50	.0560	.0879	.1336	.1972	.2838	.3996	.5518	.7486
60	.0489	.0785	.1216	.1828	.2676	.3829	.5367	.7386
70	.0437	.0713	.1123	.1715	.2547	.3693	.5243	.7302
80	.0396	.0657	.1049	.1622	.2440	.3579	.5137	.7231
90	.0363	.0610	.0987	.1545	.2349	.3482	.5046	.7168
100	.0336	.0572	.0935	.1479	.2271	.3397	.4966	.7112
120	.0294	.0510	.0851	.1371	.2141	.3255	.4830	.7017
140	.0262	.0464	.0786	.1287	.2038	.3139	.4718	.6937
160	.0237	.0427	.0734	.1217	.1952	.3042	.4623	.6869
180	.0218	.0397	.0691	.1159	.1879	.2959	.4541	.6809
200	.0201	.0371	.0655	.1109	.1816	.2887	.4469	.6757
250	.0171	.0323	.0584	.1011	.1691	.2740	.4320	.6646
300	.0149	.0289	.0531	.0937	.1594	.2625	.4202	.6557
350	.0133	.0262	.0491	.0879	.1517	.2532	.4105	.6482
400	.0121	.0241	.0458	.0832	.1453	.2454	.4022	.6419
450	.0111	.0224	.0431	.0792	.1399	.2387	.3951	.6363
500	.0103	.0210	.0408	.0758	.1352	.2329	.3888	.6314
600	.0090	.0188	.0372	.0703	.1275	.2232	.3782	.6229
700	.0080	.0171	.0344	.0659	.1214	.2152	.3694	.6158
800	.0073	.0157	.0321	.0624	.1163	.2086	.3620	.6098
900	.0067	.0146	.0302	.0594	.1119	.2029	.3556	.6045
1,000	.0062	.0137	.0286	.0569	.1082	.1980	.3499	.5998
1,200	.0054	.0122	.0260	.0527	.1020	.1897	.3404	.5918
1,400	.0048	.0111	.0240	.0495	.0971	.1830	.3325	.5850
1,600	.0044	.0102	.0225	.0468	.0930	.1773	.3258	.5793
1,800	.0040	.0095	.0211	.0446	.0895	.1725	.3200	.5743
2,000	.0037	.0089	.0200	.0427	.0866	.1683	.3149	.5698
2,500	.0031	.0077	.0178	.0389	.0806	.1597	.3044	.5605
3,000	.0027	.0069	.0162	.0360	.0760	.1530	.2961	.5530

Improvement Curves: Table of Cumulative Values

Excel: Learning Curves

	CUMULATIVE IMPROVEMENT FACTOR							
UNIT	60%	65%	70%	75%	80%	85%	90%	95%
1	1.000	1.000	1.000	1.000	1.000	1.000	1.000	1.000
2	1.600	1.650	1.700	1.750	1.800	1.850	1.900	1.950
3	2.045	2.155	2.268	2.384	2.502	2.623	2.746	2.872
4	2.405	2.578	2.758	2.946	3.142	3.345	3.556	3.774
5	2.710	2.946	3.195	3.459	3.738	4.031	4.339	4.662
6	2.977	3.274	3.593	3.934	4.299	4.688	5.101	5.538
7	3.216	3.572	3.960	4.380	4.834	5.322	5.845	6.404
8	3.432	3.847	4.303	4.802	5.346	5.936	6.574	7.261
9	3.630	4.102	4.626	5.204	5.839	6.533	7.290	8.111
10	3.813	4.341	4.931	5.589	6.315	7.116	7.994	8.955
12	4.144	4.780	5.501	6.315	7.227	8.244	9.374	10.62
14	4.438	5.177	6.026	6.994	8.092	9.331	10.72	12.27
16	4.704	5.541	6.514	7.635	8.920	10.38	12.04	13.91
18	4.946	5.879	6.972	8.245	9.716	11.41	13.33	15.52
20	5.171	6.195	7.407	8.828	10.48	12.40	14.61	17.13
22	5.379	6.492	7.819	9.388	11.23	13.38	15.86	18.72
24	5.574	6.773	8.213	9.928	11.95	14.33	17.10	20.31
25	5.668	6.909	8.404	10.19	12.31	14.80	17.71	21.10
30	6.097	7.540	9.305	11.45	14.02	17.09	20.73	25.00
35	6.478	8.109	10.13	12.72	15.64	19.29	23.67	28.86
40	6.821	8.631	10.90	13.72	17.19	21.43	26.54	32.68
45	7.134	9.114	11.62	14.77	18.68	23.50	29.37	36.47
50	7.422	9.565	12.31	15.78	20.12	25.51	32.14	40.22
60	7.941	10.39	13.57	17.67	22.87	29.41	37.57	47.65
70	8.401	11.13	14.74	19.43	25.47	33.17	42.87	54.99
80	8.814	11.82	15.82	21.09	27.96	36.80	48.05	62.25
90	9.191	12.45	16.83	22.67	30.35	40.32	53.14	69.45
100	9.539	13.03	17.79	24.18	32.65	43.75	58.14	76.59
120	10.16	14.11	19.57	27.02	37.05	50.39	67.93	90.71
140	10.72	15.08	21.20	29.67	41.22	56.78	77.46	104.7
160	11.21	15.97	22.72	32.17	45.20	62.95	86.80	118.5
180	11.67	16.79	24.14	34.54	49.03	68.95	95.96	132.1
200	12.09	17.55	25.48	36.80	52.72	74.79	105.0	145.7
250	13.01	19.28	28.56	42.05	61.47	88.83	126.9	179.2
300	13.81	20.81	31.34	46.94	69.66	102.2	148.2	212.2
350	14.51	22.18	33.89	51.48	77.43	115.1	169.0	244.8
400	15.14	23.44	36.26	55.75	84.85	127.6	189.3	277.0
450	15.72	24.60	38.48	59.80	91.97	139.7	209.2	309.0
500	16.26	25.68	40.58	63.68	98.85	151.5	228.8	340.6
600	17.21	27.67	44.47	70.97	112.0	174.2	267.1	403.3
700	18.06	29.45	48.04	77.77	124.4	196.1	304.5	465.3
800	18.82	31.09	51.36	84.18	136.3	217.3	341.0	526.5
900	19.51	32.60	54.46	90.26	147.7	237.9	376.9	587.2
1,000	20.15	31.01	57.40	96.07	158.7	257.9	412.2	647.4
1,200	21.30	36.59	62.85	107.0	179.7	296.6	481.2	766.6
1,400	22.32	38.92	67.85	117.2	199.6	333.9	548.4	884.2
1,600	23.23	41.04	72.49	126.8	218.6	369.9	614.2	1001
1,800	24.06	43.00	76.85	135.9	236.8	404.9	678.8	1116
2,000	24.83	44.84	80.96	144.7	254.4	438.9	742.3	1230
2,500	26.53	48.97	90.39	165.0	296.1	520.8	897.0	1513
3,000	27.99	52.62	98.90	183.7	335.2	598.9	1047	1791

The following is a more involved example of the application of a learning curve to a production problem.

Step by Step

EXAMPLE 4A.1: Sample Learning Curve Problem

Captain Nemo, owner of the Suboptimum Underwater Boat Company (SUB), is puzzled. He has a contract for 11 boats and has completed 4 of them. He has observed that his production manager, young Mr. Overick, has been reassigning more and more people to torpedo assembly after the construction of the first four boats. The first boat, for example, required 225 workers, each working a 40-hour week, while 45 fewer workers were required for the second boat. Overick has told them that "this is just the beginning" and that he will complete the last boat in the current contract with only 100 workers!

Overick is banking on the learning curve, but has he gone overboard?

SOLUTION

Because the second boat required 180 workers, a simple exponential curve shows that the learning percentage is 80 percent (180 ÷ 225). To find out how many workers are required for the 11th boat, we look up Unit 11 for an 80 percent improvement ratio in Exhibit 4A.4 and multiply this value by the number required for the first boat. By interpolating between Unit 10 and Unit 12, we find the improvement ratio is equal to .4629. This yields 104.15 workers (.4269 interpolated from table × 225). Thus, Overick's estimate missed the boat by four people. ●

Step by Step

EXAMPLE 4A.2: Estimating Cost Using Learning Curves

SUB has produced the first unit of a new line of minisubs at a cost of $500,000—$200,000 for materials and $300,000 for labor. It has agreed to accept a 10 percent profit, based on cost, and it is willing to contract on the basis of a 70 percent learning curve. What will be the contract price for three minisubs?

SOLUTION

Cost of first sub		$ 500,000
Cost of second sub		
Materials	$200,000	
Labor: $300,000 × .70	210,000	410,000
Cost of third sub		
Materials	200,000	
Labor: $300,000 × .5682	170,460	370,460
Total cost		1,280,460
Markup: $1,280,460 × .10		128,046
Selling price		$1,408,506

If the operation is interrupted, then some relearning must occur. How far to go back up the learning curve can be estimated in some cases. ●

ESTIMATING THE LEARNING PERCENTAGE

If production has been under way for some time, the learning percentage is easily obtained from production records. Generally speaking, the longer the production history, the more accurate the estimate. Because a variety of other problems can occur during the early stages of production, most companies do not begin to collect data for learning curve analysis until some units have been completed.

If production has not started, estimating the learning percentage becomes enlightened guesswork. In such cases, the analyst has these options:

1. Assume that the learning percentage will be the same as it has been for previous applications within the same industry.
2. Assume that it will be the same as it has been for the same or similar products.

3. Analyze the similarities and differences between the proposed start-up and previous start-ups and develop a revised learning percentage that appears to best fit the situation.

The following guidelines are useful for estimating the impact of learning on manufacturing tasks.[3] These guidelines use estimates of the percentage of time spent on manual work (i.e., hand assembly) versus the time spent on machine-controlled work (i.e., machining).

- 75 percent hand assembly/25 percent machining = 80 percent learning
- 50 percent hand assembly/50 percent machining = 85 percent
- 25 percent hand assembly/75 percent machining = 90 percent

Another set of guidelines based on what is seen in specific industries is the following:

- Aerospace, 85 percent
- Shipbuilding, 80–85 percent
- Complex machine tools for new models, 75–85 percent
- Repetitive electronics manufacturing, 90–95 percent
- Repetitive machining or punch-press operations, 90–95 percent
- Repetitive electrical operations (wiring and circuit board fabrication), 75–85 percent
- Repetitive welding operations, 90 percent
- Raw materials manufacturing, 93–96 percent
- Purchased parts fabrication, 85–88 percent

There are two reasons for disparities between a firm's learning rate and that of its industry. First, differences in operating characteristics between any two firms, stemming from the equipment, methods, product design, plant organization, and so forth, are inevitable. Second, procedural differences are manifested in the development of the learning percentage itself, such as whether the industry rate is based on a single product or on a product line, and the manner in which the data were aggregated.

HOW LONG DOES LEARNING GO ON?

Does output stabilize, or is there continual improvement? Some areas can be shown to improve continually even over decades (radios, computers, and other electronic devices; and, if we allow for the effects of inflation, also automobiles, washing machines, refrigerators, and most other manufactured goods). If the learning curve has been valid for several hundreds or thousands of units, it will probably be valid for several hundreds or thousands more. On the other hand, highly automated systems may have a near-zero learning curve because, after installation, they quickly reach a constant volume.

GENERAL GUIDELINES FOR LEARNING

In this section, we offer guidelines for two categories of "learners": individuals and organizations.

INDIVIDUAL LEARNING

A number of factors affect an individual's performance and rate of learning. Remember that two elements are involved: the rate of learning and the initial starting level. To explain this more clearly, compare the two learning curves in Exhibit 4A.6. Suppose these were the times for two individuals who performed a simple mechanical test administered by the personnel department as part of their application for employment in the assembly area of manufacturing.

Which applicant would you hire? Applicant A had a much lower starting point but a slower learning rate. Applicant B, although starting at a much higher point, is clearly the better choice. This points out that performance times are important—not just the learning rate by itself.

exhibit 4A.6   Test Results of Two Job Applicants

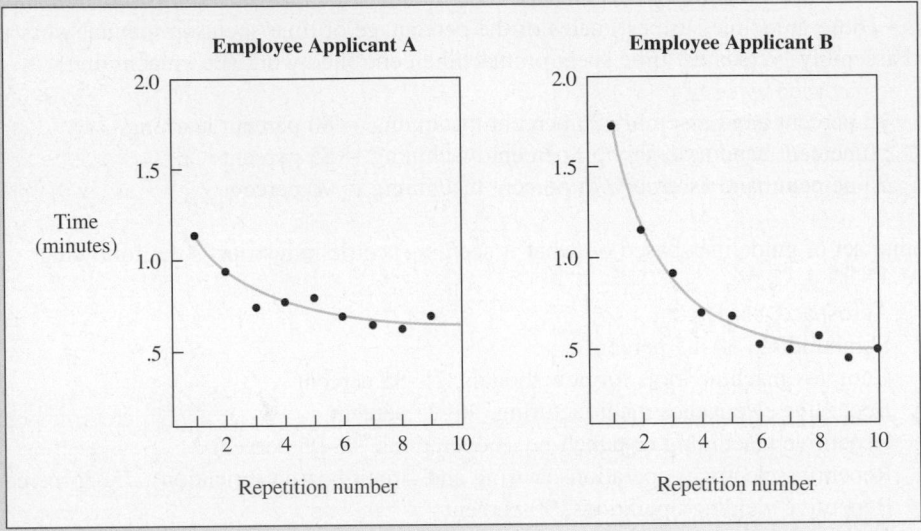

Some general guidelines to improve individual performance based on learning curves include the following:

1. **Proper selection of workers.**   A test should be administered to help choose the workers. These tests should be representative of the planned work: a dexterity test for assembly work, a mental ability test for mental work, tests for interaction with customers for front office work, and so on.
2. **Proper training.**   The more effective the training, the faster the learning rate.
3. **Motivation.**   Productivity gains based on learning curves are not achieved unless there is a reward. Rewards can be money (individual or group incentive plans) or nonmonetary (employee of the month awards, etc.).
4. **Work specialization.**   As a general rule, the simpler the task, the faster the learning. Be careful that boredom doesn't interfere; if it does, redesign the task.
5. **Do one or very few jobs at a time.**   Learning is faster on each job if completed one at a time, rather than working on all jobs simultaneously.
6. **Use tools or equipment that assists or supports performance.**
7. **Provide quick and easy access for help.**   The benefits from training are realized and continue when assistance is available.
8. **Allow workers to help redesign their tasks.**   Taking more performance factors into the scope of the learning curve can, in effect, shift the curve downward.

ORGANIZATIONAL LEARNING

Organizations learn as well. It has been argued that organizational learning is critical to sustaining a competitive advantage. For the individual, it is easy to conceptualize how knowledge is acquired and retained and how this results in an individual learning effect. Certainly, a main source of organizational learning is the individual learning of the employees. An organization also acquires knowledge in its technology, its structure, documents that it retains, and standard operating procedures.[4] For example, as a manufacturing unit becomes experienced, knowledge is embedded in software and in tooling used for production. Knowledge also can be embedded in the organization's structure. For example, when an organization shifts its industrial engineering group from a functional organization centralized in one area to a decentralized organization where individuals are deployed to particular parts of the plant floor, knowledge about how to become more productive is embedded in the organization's structure.

Knowledge can depreciate if individuals leave the organization. When Lockheed had problems in the production of the L-1011 airplane, the company's hiring of 2,000 inexperienced employees to quickly ramp up production was blamed. These employees were put through a four-week training program in aircraft construction. Initial costs rose rather than fell during the initial production of the plane due to the inexperienced workers.

Knowledge also can depreciate if technologies become inaccessible or difficult to use. An example of this is the difficulty in accessing data collected by Landsat, an Earth surveillance program. Ninety percent of the data collected before 1979 is now inaccessible because the data were recorded by equipment that no longer exists or cannot be operated. Knowledge can also depreciate if a company's records and routine processes are lost. When Steinway Piano Company decided to put a discontinued piano back into production, the plant discovered it no longer had records or blueprints for the piano.

LEARNING CURVES APPLIED TO HEART TRANSPLANT MORTALITY

Learning curves provide an excellent means to examine performance. The best comparison for one's performance would be the learning rates for competitors in the industry. Even when a standard or expected level is unknown, much can still be learned by simply using and plotting data in a learning curve fashion. As an illustration of this ability to learn about one's performance, we present the experience of a heart transplant facility in a hospital.[5]

Service

The learning curve model in the heart transplant analysis was of the form

$$Y_i = B_0 + B_1 x^{-B_2}$$

where Y_i is the cumulative average resource consumption (the total number of deaths, costs, and so on, divided by the number of transplants), B_0 is the asymptote (the minimum), B_1 is the maximum possible reduction (the difference between the first unit and minimum B_0), x is the total number of units produced, and B_2 is the rate of change for each successive unit as it moves toward the lower bound.

Exhibit 4A.7A shows the coefficients that were obtained for the model. Exhibit 4A.7B shows the cumulative death rate. This seems to follow an industrial learning curve with a rate just over 80 percent. Seven of the first 23 transplant patients died within a year after transplant surgery. Only 4 of the next 39 patients died within a year. For the cumulative average length of stay, shown in Exhibit 4A.7C, the reduction rate is approximately 9 percent.

The least sloping curve (the lowest learning rate) is the cost of heart transplants. Exhibit 4A.7D shows that the initial costs were in the vicinity of $150,000. After 51 surviving

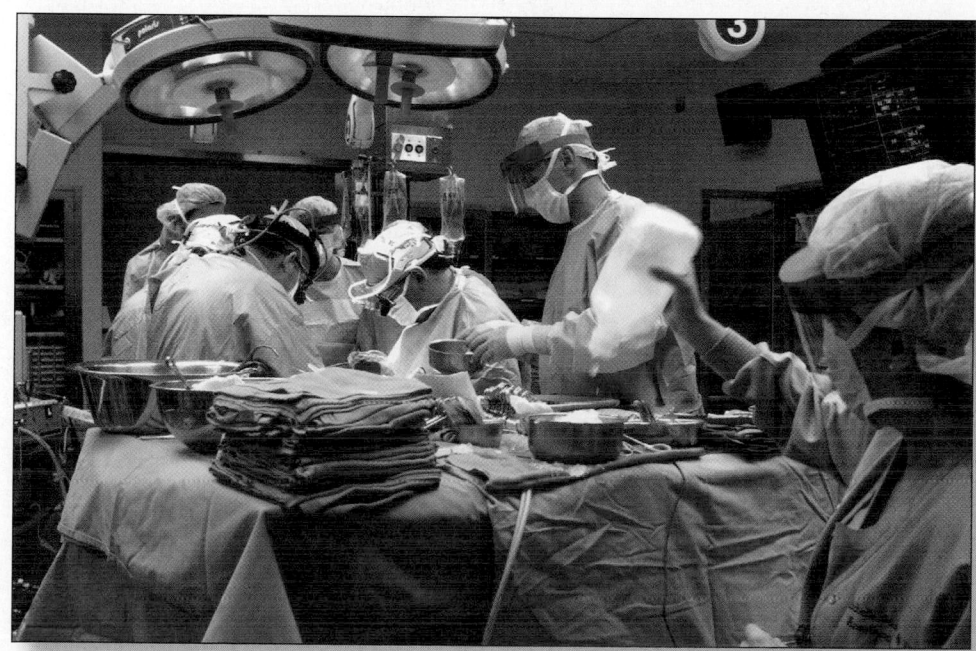

A. Consumption Coefficients for Heart Transplant Learning Model

	B_0 (ASYMPTOTE)	B_1 (RANGE)	B_2 (RATE)	PERCENTAGE DECREASE
Death rate	.2329	.8815	.2362	21.04%
Length of stay	28.26	23.76	.0943	9.00
Units of service	1,282.84	592.311	.0763	7.35
Adjusted charges	$96,465.90	$53,015.80	.0667	6.45

B. Death Rates, Less Than One Year Survival

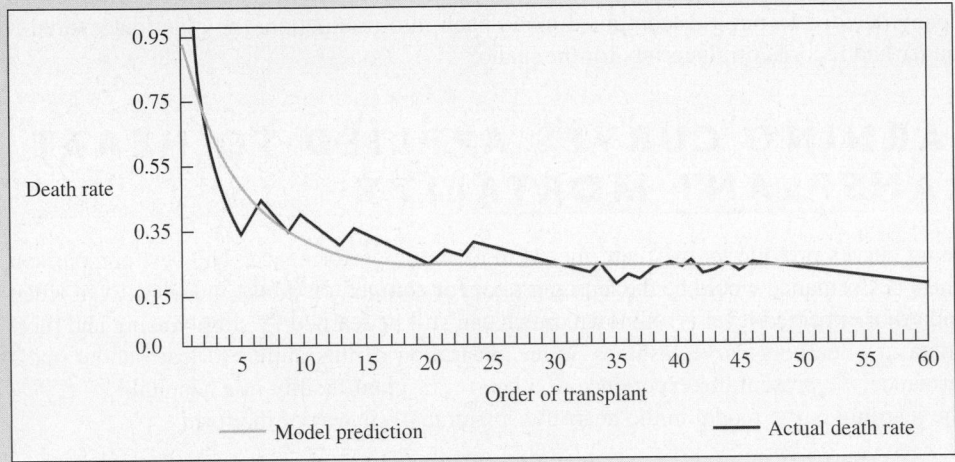

C. Average Length of Stay (ALOS) for Heart Transplant Survivors

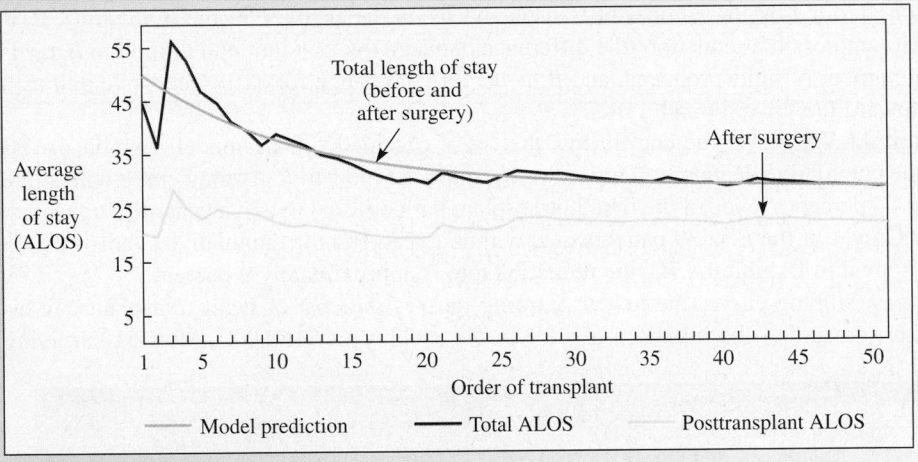

D. Cost for Heart Transplant Survivors

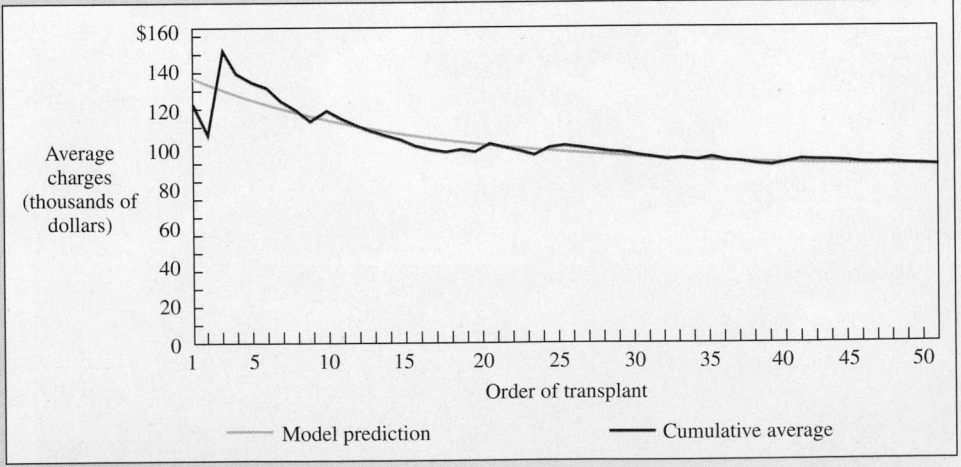

NOTE: FOR TRANSPLANT ADMISSION ONLY, ACTUAL COSTS ARE APPROXIMATELY 50 PERCENT OF CHARGES.

patients (62 procedures, 11 died), the average cost was still close to $100,000. (A learning rate of 80 percent would result in an average cost of $40,000; a 90 percent rate would result in a cost of $80,000.)

Why are learning rates high in death rate reduction and low in average length of stay, with the lowest rate in cost reduction? Smith and Larsson question whether the low learning rates may be related to conservatism in dealing with human lives. Or could it be due to the power and insulation of the heart transplant team from pressure to reduce cost? The purpose of this study on learning curves was to make institutions and administrators aware of learning. Institutions need to behave according to learning curve logic—that is, in pricing as well as in motivation for continuous improvement.

KEY TERMS

Learning curve A line displaying the relationship between unit production time and the cumulative number of units produced.

Individual learning Improvement that results when people repeat a process and gain skill or efficiency from their own experience.

Organizational learning Improvement that comes both from experience and from changes in administration, equipment, and product design.

FORMULA REVIEW

Logarithmic curve:

$$Y_x = Kx^n \qquad\qquad \text{[4A.1]}$$

SOLVED PROBLEMS

SOLVED PROBLEM 1

A job applicant is being tested for an assembly-line position. Management feels that steady-state times have been approximately reached after 1,000 performances. Regular assembly-line workers are expected to perform the task within four minutes.

  a. If the job applicant performed the first test operation in 10 minutes and the second one in 9 minutes, should this applicant be hired?
  b. What is the expected time that the job applicant would take to finish the 10th unit?
  c. What is a significant limitation of this analysis?

Solution

  a. Learning rate = 9 minutes/10 minutes = 90%
     From Exhibit 4A.4, the time for the 1,000th unit is .3499 × 10 minutes = 3.499 minutes. Yes, hire the person.
  b. From Exhibit 4A.4, unit 10 at 90% is .7047. Therefore, the time for the 10th unit = .7047 × 10 = 7.047 minutes.
  c. More data should be collected on the job applicant's performance.

SOLVED PROBLEM 2

Excel: Learning Curves

Boeing Aircraft collected the following cost data on the first 8 units of its new business jet.

UNIT NUMBER	COST ($ MILLIONS)	UNIT NUMBER	COST ($ MILLIONS)
1	$100	5	60
2	83	6	57
3	73	7	53
4	62	8	51

  a. Estimate the learning curve for the new business jet.
  b. Estimate the average cost for the first 1,000 units of the jet.
  c. Estimate the cost to produce the 1,000th jet.

Solution

a. First, estimate the learning curve rate by calculating the average learning rate with each doubling of production.

$$\text{Units 1 to 2} = 83/100 = 83\%$$
$$\text{Units 2 to 4} = 62/83 = 74.7\%$$
$$\text{Units 4 to 8} = 51/62 = 82.26\%$$
$$\text{Average} = (83 + 74.4 + 82.6)/3 = 80\%$$

b. The average cost of the first 1,000 units can be estimated using Exhibit 4A.5. The cumulative improvement factor for the 1,000th unit at 80 percent learning is 158.7. The cost to produce the first 1,000 units is

$$\$100M \times 158.7 = \$15,870M$$

The average cost for each of the first 1,000 units is

$$\$15,870M/1,000 = \$15.9M$$

c. To estimate the cost to produce the 1,000th unit, use Exhibit 4A.4.
The unit improvement factor for the 1,000th unit at 80 percent is .1082.
The cost to produce the 1,000th unit is

$$\$100M \times .1082 = \$10.82M$$

REVIEW AND DISCUSSION QUESTIONS

1. If you kept any of your old exam grades from last semester, get them out and write down the grades. Use Exhibits 4A.4 and 4A.5, use log-log graph paper, or use a spreadsheet to find whether the exponential curve fits, showing that you experienced learning over the semester (insofar as your exam performance is concerned). If not, can you give some reasons why not?

2. How might the following business specialists use learning curves: accountants, marketers, financial analysts, personnel managers, and computer programmers?

3. As a manager, which learning percentage would you prefer (other things being equal), 110 percent or 60 percent? Explain.

4. What difference does it make if a customer wants a 10,000-unit order produced and delivered all at one time or in 2,500-unit batches?

PROBLEMS

1. A time standard was set as 0.20 hour per unit based on the 50th unit produced. If the task has a 90 percent learning curve, what would be the expected time of the 100th, 200th, and 400th units?

2. You have just received 10 units of a special subassembly from an electronics manufacturer at a price of $250 per unit. A new order also has just come in for your company's product that uses these subassemblies, and you wish to purchase 40 more to be shipped in lots of 10 units each. (The subassemblies are bulky, and you need only 10 a month to fill your new order.)

   a. Assuming a 70 percent learning curve by your supplier on a similar product last year, how much should you pay for each lot? Assume that the learning rate of 70 percent applies to each lot of 10 units, not each unit.

   b. Suppose you are the supplier and can produce 20 units now but cannot start production on the second 20 units for two months. What price would you try to negotiate for the last 20 units?

3. Johnson Industries received a contract to develop and produce four high-intensity long-distance receiver/transmitters for cellular telephones. The first took 2,000 labor hours and $39,000 worth of purchased and manufactured parts; the second took 1,500 labor hours and $37,050 in parts; the third took 1,450 labor hours and $31,000 in parts; and the fourth took 1,275 labor hours and $31,492 in parts.

   Johnson was asked to bid on a follow-on contract for another dozen receiver/transmitter units. Ignoring any forgetting factor effects, what should Johnson estimate time and parts costs to be for the dozen units? (Hint: There are two learning curves—one for labor and one for parts.)

4. Lambda Computer Products competed for and won a contract to produce two prototype units of a new type of computer that is based on laser optics rather than on electronic binary bits.

The first unit produced by Lambda took 5,000 hours to produce and required $250,000 worth of material, equipment usage, and supplies. The second unit took 3,500 hours and used $200,000 worth of materials, equipment usage, and supplies. Labor is $30 per hour.

a. Lambda was asked to present a bid for 10 additional units as soon as the second unit was completed. Production would start immediately. What would this bid be?

b. Suppose there was a significant delay between the contracts. During this time, personnel and equipment were reassigned to other projects. Explain how this would affect the subsequent bid.

5 You've just completed a pilot run of 10 units of a major product and found the processing time for each unit was as follows:

UNIT NUMBER	TIME (HOURS)
1	970
2	640
3	420
4	380
5	320
6	250
7	220
8	207
9	190
10	190

a. According to the pilot run, what would you estimate the learning rate to be?
b. Based on a, how much time would it take for the next 190 units, assuming no loss of learning?
c. How much time would it take to make the 1,000th unit?

6 Lazer Technologies Inc. (LTI) has produced a total of 20 high-power laser systems that could be used to destroy any approaching enemy missiles or aircraft. The 20 units have been produced, funded in part as private research within the research and development arm of LTI, but the bulk of the funding came from a contract with the U.S. Department of Defense (DoD).

Testing of the laser units has shown that they are effective defense weapons, and through redesign to add portability and easier field maintenance, the units could be truck-mounted.

DoD has asked LTI to submit a bid for 100 units.

The 20 units that LTI has built so far cost the following amounts and are listed in the order in which they were produced:

UNIT NUMBER	COST ($ MILLIONS)	UNIT NUMBER	COST ($ MILLIONS)
1	$12	11	$3.9
2	10	12	3.5
3	6	13	3.0
4	6.5	14	2.8
5	5.8	15	2.7
6	6	16	2.7
7	5	17	2.3
8	3.6	18	3.0
9	3.6	19	2.9
10	4.1	20	2.6

a. Based on past experience, what is the learning rate?
b. What bid should LTI submit for the total order of 100 units, assuming that learning continues?
c. What is the cost expected to be for the last unit under the learning rate you estimated?

7 Jack Simpson, contract negotiator for Nebula Airframe Company, is currently involved in bidding on a follow-up government contract. In gathering cost data from the first three units, which Nebula produced under a research and development contract, he found that the first unit took 2,000 labor hours, the second took 1,800 labor hours, and the third took 1,692 hours.

In a contract for three more units, how many labor hours should Simpson plan for?

8 Honda Motor Company has discovered a problem in the exhaust system of one of its automobile lines and has voluntarily agreed to make the necessary modifications to conform with government safety requirements. Standard procedure is for the firm to pay a flat fee to dealers for each modification completed.

Honda is trying to establish a fair amount of compensation to pay dealers and has decided to choose a number of randomly selected mechanics and observe their performance and learning rate. Analysis demonstrated that the average learning rate was 90 percent, and Honda then decided to pay a $60 fee for each repair (3 hours × $20 per flat-rate hour).

Southwest Honda, Inc., has complained to Honda Motor Company about the fee. Six mechanics, working independently, have completed two modifications each. All took 9 hours on the average to do the first unit and 6.3 hours to do the second. Southwest refuses to do any more unless Honda allows at least 4.5 hours. The dealership expects to perform the modification to approximately 300 vehicles.

What is your opinion of Honda's allowed rate and the mechanics' performance?

9   United Research Associates (URA) had received a contract to produce two units of a new cruise missile guidance control. The first unit took 4,000 hours to complete and cost $30,000 in materials and equipment usage. The second took 3,200 hours and cost $21,000 in materials and equipment usage. Labor cost is charged at $18 per hour.

The prime contractor has now approached URA and asked to submit a bid for the cost of producing another 20 guidance controls.

a. What will the last unit cost to build?

b. What will be the average time for the 20 missile guidance controls?

c. What will the average cost be for guidance control for the 20 in the contract?

10   United Assembly Products (UAP) has a personnel screening process for job applicants to test their ability to perform at the department's long-term average rate. UAP has asked you to modify the test by incorporating learning theory. From the company's data, you discovered that if people can perform a given task in 30 minutes or less on the 20th unit, they achieve the group long-run average. Obviously, all job applicants cannot be subjected to 20 performances of such a task, so you are to determine whether they will likely achieve the desired rate based on only 2 performances.

a. Suppose a person took 100 minutes on the first unit and 80 minutes on the second. Should this person be hired?

b. What procedure might you establish for hiring (i.e., how to evaluate the job applicant's two performances)?

c. What is a significant limitation of this analysis?

11   A potentially large customer offered to subcontract assembly work that is profitable only if you can perform the operations at an average time of less than 20 hours each. The contract is for 1,000 units.

You run a test and do the first one in 50 hours and the second one in 40 hours.

a. How long would you expect the third one to take?

b. Would you take the contract? Explain.

12   Western Turbine, Inc., has just completed the production of the 10th unit of a new high-efficiency turbine/generator. Its analysis showed that a learning rate of 85 percent existed over the production of the 10 units. If the 10th unit contained labor costs of $2.5 million, what price should Western Turbine charge for labor on units 11 and 12 to make a profit of 10 percent of the selling price?

13   FES Auto recently hired Meg the mechanic to specialize in front-end alignments. Although she is a trained auto mechanic, she had not used FES's brand of equipment before taking this job. The standard time allocated for a front-end alignment is 30 minutes. Her first front-end alignment took 50 minutes and her second 47.5 minutes.

a. What is the expected time for Meg's 10th front-end alignment?

b. What is the expected time for Meg's 100th front-end alignment?

14   An initial pilot run of 10 units produces the following times:

UNIT NUMBER	TIME (MINUTES)
1	39
2	29
3	23
4	19
5	17
6	16
7	15
8	13
9	13
10	12

a. According to this pilot run, what is your estimate of the learning rate?

b. How much time will it take for the next 90 units?

c. How much time will it take to make the 2,000th unit?

15 A new bank clerk needed an hour to encode his first 500 checks, 51 minutes for the second 500, and 46 minutes for the third 500. After how many batches of 500 checks will he be able to work at the standard rate of 1,000 checks per hour?

16 A fast-food trainee takes an hour to prepare his first 20 sandwiches, 45 minutes for the second 20, and 38 minutes for the third 20. What will his production rate be after 24 hours of experience?

17 Capital City Flowers received a request for 20 corsages. The first one took 15 minutes to assemble. An 85 percent learning percentage has been observed in the past while assembling similar corsages. What is the total time in minutes to assemble all 20 corsages? What is the total time in minutes to assemble the last 10 corsages?

18 U.S. Subs, builder of the new Phoenix 1000 private submarine, is making 25 yellow mini-submarines for a new movie and wants to know how long it will take to build the last 15 yellow subs. The company strongly believes that the time to build a sub follows the learning curve model, but has only the following information:

Time to build the second sub = 63 hours
Time to build the third sub = 53.26 hours
Time to build the fourth sub = 47.25 hours

SUPER QUIZ

1 This is a line that shows the relationship between the time to produce a unit and the cumulative number of units produced.
2 Improvement that derives from people repeating a process and gaining skill or efficiency is called this.
3 Improvement that comes from changes in administration, equipment, and product design is called this.

4 Assuming an 80 percent learning rate, if the 4th unit takes 100 hours to produce, the 16th unit should take how long to produce?
5 The resulting plot of a learning curve when logarithmic scales are used is this.
6 Systems that have this characteristic usually have near-zero learning.

1. Learning curve 2. Individual learning 3. Organizational learning 4. 64 hours 5. A straight line 6. They are highly automated systems

SELECTED BIBLIOGRAPHY

Argote, L. "Organizational Learning Curves: Persistence, Transfer and Turnover." *International Journal of Technology Management* 11, nos. 7/8 (1996), pp. 759–69.

Argote, L., and D. Epple. "Learning Curves in Manufacturing." *Science* 247 (February 1990), pp. 920–24.

Bailey, C. D. "Forgetting and the Learning Curve: A Laboratory Study." *Management Science* 35, no. 3 (March 1989), pp. 340–52.

Chambers, S., and R. Johnson. "Experience Curves in Services: Macro and Micro Level Approaches." *International Journal of Operations & Production Management* 20, no. 4, 2000, pp. 852–59.

Smunt, T. L. "A Comparison of Learning Curve Analysis and Moving Average Ratio Analysis for Detailed Operational Planning." *Decision Sciences* 17, no. 4 (Fall 1986), pp. 475–95.

Wright, T. P. "Factors Affecting the Cost of Airplanes." *Journal of Aeronautical Sciences*, February 1936, pp. 122–28.

Yelle, L. E. "The Learning Curves: Historical Review and Comprehensive Survey." *Decision Sciences* 10, no. 2 (April 1979), pp. 302–28.

FOOTNOTES

1 See the classic paper by T. P. Wright, "Factors Affecting the Cost of Airplanes," *Journal of the Aeronautical Sciences,* February 1936, pp. 122–28.

2 This equation says that the number of direct labor hours required for any given unit is reduced exponentially as more units are produced.

3 Rodney D. Stewart, Richard M. Wyskida, and James D. Johannes (eds.), *Cost Estimator's Reference Manual,* 2nd ed. (New York: John Wiley & Sons, 1995).

4 See L. Argote, "Organizational Learning Curves: Persistence, Transfer and Turnover," *International Journal of Technology Management* 11, nos. 7/8 (1996), pp. 759–69.

5 D. B. Smith, and J. L. Larsson, "The Impact of Learning on Cost: The Case of Heart Transplantation," *Hospital and Health Sciences Administration* 34, no. 1 (Spring 1989), pp. 85–97.

chapter 5

PROCESS ANALYSIS

CUSTOMER-DRIVEN SERVICE FOR McDONALD'S

SELF-ORDERING KIOSKS

IDEO collaborated with McDonald's on the first generation of a new service system in their Lone Tree restaurant, south of Denver. The new system allows McDonald's customers to place their orders without assistance, providing improved flexibility, speed, accuracy, and convenience to McDonald's customers as well as its crews. The system consists of touch-screen self-order kiosks at the front counter and in the children's PlayPlace area that have been fully integrated into the McDonald's physical environment, operational flow, and brand message.

Service

After reading this chapter you will:

1. Recognize three basic types of processes: a serial flow process, parallel processes (such as what happens in a restaurant), and logistics processes.

2. Understand basic flowcharting of processes.

3. Explain how to analyze processes using Little's law.

4. Understand how to calculate process performance measures.

Customers place their orders using an icon-based system and pay at the kiosk or at the pick-up counter. After placing their orders, customers pick up their food at the counter by showing the order number on their printed receipts. In the PlayPlace area, parents can place and pay for their orders while supervising their children. A McDonald's crewmember then delivers the food to their table.

This new model needed to work within the popular and highly efficient system in use today. The completed design spanned the entire ordering experience and not just the kiosks themselves. The team updated the restaurant's graphics, signage, counters, and crew uniforms, and created nine self-order kiosks with a fully developed icon-based menu system. All design elements plus the in-store layout of the new service experience were arranged to complement the traditional experience of ordering at the counter.

The work began with a national survey of all kinds of quick-serve and self-serve experiences and distilled behavioral patterns of McDonald's customers to guide the design work. Since its launch and after thousands of transactions, the new service has had a high customer adoption rate with virtually no lines.

PROCESS ANALYSIS

Process

Understanding how processes work is essential to ensuring the competitiveness of a company. A process that does not match the needs of the firm will punish the firm every minute that the firm operates. Take, for example, two fast-food restaurants. If one restaurant can deliver a quarter-pound hamburger to the customer for $0.50 in direct costs and a second restaurant costs $0.75, no matter what the second restaurant does, it will lose $0.25 in profit for every hamburger it sells compared to the first restaurant. Many factors need to be considered when one sets up the process to make those hamburgers. These factors include the cost of the raw materials, the costs associated with how the hamburger is prepared, and the cost of taking the order and delivering it to the customer.

Service

What is a process? A **process** is any part of an organization that takes inputs and transforms them into outputs that, it is hoped, are of greater value to the organization than the original inputs. Consider some examples of processes. Honda Motors assembles the Accord in a plant in Marysville, Ohio. The assembly plant takes in parts and components that have been fabricated for the plant. Using labor, equipment along an assembly line, and energy, these parts and components are transformed into automobiles. McDonald's, at each of its restaurants, uses inputs such as hamburger meat, lettuce, tomatoes, and potatoes. To these inputs, trained labor is added in the form of cooks and order takers, and capital equipment is used to transform the inputs into hamburgers, french fries, and other foods.

In both of these examples, the process produces products as output. However, the outputs of many processes are services. In a hospital, for example, specialized equipment and highly trained doctors, nurses, and technicians are combined with another input, the patient. The patient is transformed through proper treatment and care into a healthy patient. An airline is another example of a service organization. The airline uses airplanes, ground equipment, flight crews, ground crews, reservation personnel, and fuel to transport customers between locations all over the world.

This chapter describes how to analyze a process. Analyzing a process allows some important questions to be answered, such as these: How many customers can the process handle per hour? How long will it take to serve a customer? What change is needed in the process to expand capacity? How much does the process cost? A difficult, but important, first step in process analysis is to clearly define the purpose of the analysis. Is the purpose to solve a problem? Is it to better understand the impact of a change in how business will be done in the future?

Clearly understanding the purpose of the analysis is critical to setting the level of detail in modeling the process. The analysis must be kept as simple as possible. The following sections of this chapter discuss the details of constructing flowcharts and measures that are appropriate for different types of processes. But first, consider a simple example.

ANALYZING A LAS VEGAS SLOT MACHINE

The slot machine is common in casinos around the world. Let's use this machine to illustrate how a simple process is analyzed.

Assume that we work for the casino and management is considering a new type of electronic slot machine that is much faster than the current mechanical machine. Management has asked how much we can expect to make from the new electronic machine over a 24-hour period compared to the old mechanical machine.

Step 1. Analyzing the Mechanical Slot Machine   Begin by analyzing a mechanical slot machine. The slot machine is activated when the customer puts one or more coins in the machine and then pulls the arm on the machine (slot machines are often called "one-armed bandits"). Three wheels spin, and after a time each wheel stops and displays a particular symbol. The machine pays money when certain combinations of symbols simultaneously appear. For those not familiar with how a slot machine works, we have included a slot machine simulation program on the text Web site. Sorry, but it does not pay real money.

Service

Slot machines are designed to pay back a certain percentage of what they take in. Typical paybacks would be 90 to 95 percent of what is taken in; the casino keeps 5 to 10 percent. These payback percentages are a function of the number of different symbols that are on each wheel. Each symbol is repeated on each wheel a certain number of times. For example, if a wheel has 10 symbols, one might be a single bar, one a double bar, and one a lemon; two might be cherries, three lucky sevens, and two liberty bells. Because the wheels stop on a random symbol, the probability of lucky sevens coming up on all three wheels is $\frac{3}{10} \times \frac{3}{10} \times \frac{3}{10} = 0.027$, or 2.7 percent of the time. The probability of certain combinations of symbols coming up, combined with the payout for each combination, sets the average percentage that the machine is expected to pay out.

Consider a mechanical slot machine that pays out 95 percent of the coins played. With this machine, assume the average player feeds coins into the machine at a pace of one coin each 15 seconds. This 15-second interval is called the *cycle time* of the process. The cycle time of a repetitive process is the average time between completions of successive units. In the case of the slot machine, the unit is a silver dollar. With a 15-second cycle time, our

Cycle time

mechanical slot machine can process $4 (60 seconds/15 seconds) per minute, or $240 ($4/minute × 60 minutes) per hour. Because our slot machine has a payout of 95 percent, we would expect the machine to give the customer 228 (240 × 0.95) of the silver dollars that it took in and keep $12 for the casino for each hour that it is in operation. If we started with $100, we could expect to play for about 8.3 hours ($100/$12 per hour) before we would run out of silver dollars. We might be lucky and win the jackpot, or we might be unlucky and lose it all in the first hour; but, on average, we would expect to lose the entire $100 in 8.3 hours.

Step 2. Analyzing the New Electronic Slot Machine   Now consider the new electronic slot machine. It operates in exactly the same manner; the only difference is that it uses "electronic" coins and it takes only 10 seconds to process each bet. With a 10-second cycle time, the machine processes $6 (60 seconds/10 seconds) per minute, or $360 ($6/minute × 60 minutes) per hour. With a 95 percent payout, the machine would give the customer back 342 (360 × 0.95) silver dollars and keep $18 for the casino each hour. This machine would take our $100 in only 5.5 hours ($100/$18 per hour).

Step 3. Comparison   So how much does the electronic slot machine make for the casino in 24 hours compared to the mechanical slot machine? One more critical piece of information is needed to answer this question: How long will the slot machine operate over the 24 hours? The casino feels that the machine will be used 12 out of the 24 hours; this 12 out of 24 hours is the expected utilization of the machine. Utilization is the ratio of the time that a resource is actually activated relative to the time that it is available for use. Adjusting for utilization, the expected revenue from the mechanical machine is $144/day ($12/hour × 24 hours × 0.5) compared to revenue of $216/day ($18/hour × 24 hours × 0.5) for the electronic machine. When an analysis is performed, it is important to qualify the analysis with

Utilization

the assumptions made. In this comparison, we assumed that the operator only bets one silver dollar at a time and that the utilization would be the same for the mechanical and electronic slot machines.

Step 4. The Slot Machine Is One of Many Casino Processes   The speed of the slot machine can have a major impact on the casino's revenue. The single slot machine is only a small part of the casino. To really understand how much revenue the casino can generate, we need to consider all of the other revenue-generating processes, such as the blackjack and poker tables, keno games, craps, and the other games in the casino. Many times analyzing an enterprise involves evaluating a number of independent activities, like our slot machine. The aggregate performance of each individual activity may be all that is needed to understand the overall process. On the other hand, often there is significant interaction between individual activities or processes that must be considered.

Think about our gambling casino. Many casinos offer great deals on food, which is served right in the casino. What do you think would be the main priority of the food operation manager in one of these casinos? Would great-tasting food be important? How important is the cost of the food? Is speed of service important? Good food certainly is important. If the food is unpleasant, the customer will not even consider eating at the casino. This is bad for the casino because if the customers leave, they take their money with them. Remember, the casino makes money based on how long the customers gamble. The more time spent gambling, the more money the casino makes. What about cost? If the customers think the meals are too expensive, they might leave. So it is important to keep the cost of the meals down so that they can be priced inexpensively. Many casinos even give meals away. How important is it to serve the customer quickly? Think about it this way: Every minute that the customers are sitting in the restaurant, they are not feeding silver dollars into a slot machine. So speed is important because it impacts the revenue generated at the games in the casino.

PROCESS FLOWCHARTING

Often the activities associated with a process affect one another so that it is important to consider the simultaneous performance of a number of activities, all operating at the same time. A good way to start analyzing a process is with a diagram showing the basic elements of a process—typically tasks, flows, and storage areas. Tasks are shown as rectangles, flows as arrows, and the storage of goods or other items as inverted triangles. Sometimes flows through a process can be diverted in multiple directions depending on some condition. Decision points are depicted as a diamond with the different flows running from the points on the diamond. Exhibit 5.1 displays examples of these symbols. Separating a diagram into different horizontal or vertical bands sometimes is useful because it allows the separation of tasks that are part of the process. For example, with the slot machine, the tasks performed by the customer can be separated from the tasks performed by the slot machine.

In the slot machine example, the level of abstraction considers the slot machine as a simple black box that takes in silver dollars and either keeps them or returns some of them during each cycle. Viewing the slot machine as a black box might be fine if the purpose is just to analyze how much the machine is expected to make for the casino each hour. In reality, more activities are required to support the slot machine. Inside an old style mechanical slot machine are two buckets of silver dollars. One bucket stores coins needed for internal use by the slot machine. When a customer wins, the payout comes from this payout bucket. The slot machine is designed to automatically keep this payout bucket filled during play. When the payout bucket is full, the silver dollars are deposited in a second winnings bucket. The winnings bucket must be periodically emptied to claim the winnings for the casino. The flowchart in Exhibit 5.1 depicts the external activities of the player and the internal movement of the coins within the machine.

Process Flowchart Example

exhibit 5.1

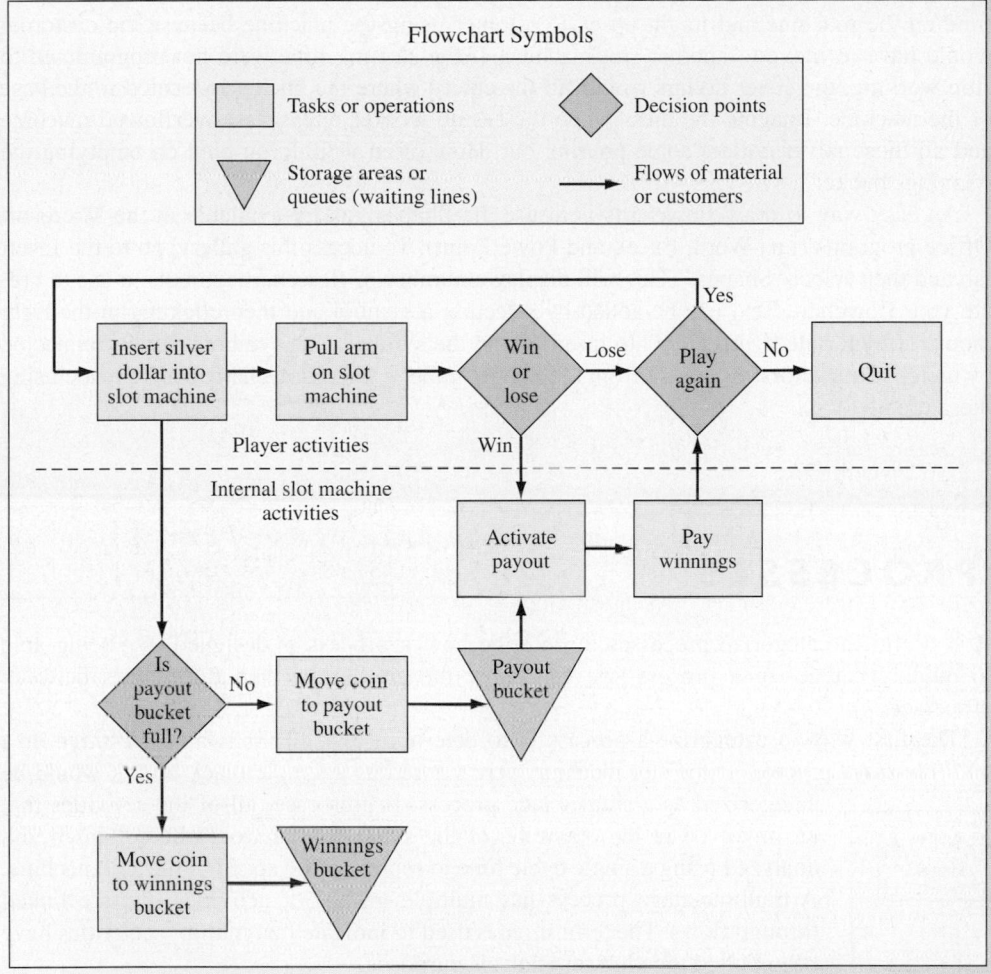

Probably the most interesting thing about the payout bucket is how big it should be. The slot machine is programmed so that if the payout bucket empties, the machine stops and lights on the top of the machine flash, thus notifying casino personnel that a lucky customer has emptied the machine. The payout bucket would be sized to keep this a rare occurrence. Think of the payout bucket as a buffer or intermediate storage area for silver dollars that allows the slot machine to operate on its own. The smaller the payout bucket, the more the casino personnel need to attend to the machine, and the more time the machine is idle for lack of silver dollars. On the other hand, with a larger bucket more money is tied up.

The situation with the winnings bucket in the machine is similar. A small winnings bucket will need to be emptied more often. On the other hand, a large winnings bucket means that the casino does not deposit the money into its bank account as quickly. The advantage of buffering operations with the slot machine is easily seen. Large buffers allow the process to operate independently, whereas small buffers require more attention. In the case of the slot machine, the buffer is composed of the silver dollars. In other situations, where the buffer is other items such as a raw material, these items have a value, so they also represent money.

Consider a slot machine that we expect to deposit $12 into the winnings bucket every hour. If our winnings bucket can hold 1,000 silver dollars, then we expect to need to empty the winnings bucket every 83.3 hours ($1,000/$12 per hour) if the slot machine is used 100 percent of the time. What happens when the winnings bucket fills up? If the slot machine is smart enough to know that the winnings bucket is full, it might be programmed to just stop working with its lights flashing as they do when the payout bucket empties. This would cause downtime on the machine and might upset a customer using the machine because the customer would have to move to another slot machine. If the slot machine were not programmed to stop working, the silver dollars would fill the cavity where the bucket is located in the base of the machine. Imagine the mess when the casino worker opens that overflowed machine and all those silver dollars come pouring out. How often would you plan on emptying the winnings bucket?

An easy way to draw flowcharts is to use the Shapes gallery available in the Microsoft Office programs (i.e., Word, Excel, and PowerPoint). To access this gallery, go to the Insert tab and then select "Shapes." This will display a number of flowchart symbols to use to create your flowchart. Text can be added by selecting a symbol and then clicking on the right mouse button. Select "Add text" to insert text in the symbol. The symbols can be connected by using "Connectors" available from the Shapes gallery. Nice flowcharts can be made using these tools.

TYPES OF PROCESSES

It is useful to categorize processes to describe how a process is designed. By being able to quickly categorize a process, we can show the similarities and differences between processes.

The first way to categorize a process is to determine whether it is a *single-stage* or a *multiple-stage* process. If the slot machine were viewed as a simple black box, it would be categorized as a single-stage process. In this case, all of the activities that are involved in the operation of the slot machine would be collapsed and analyzed using a single cycle time to represent the speed of the slot machine. A multiple-stage process has multiple groups of activities that are linked through flows. The term *stage* is used to indicate that multiple activities have been pulled together for analysis purposes.

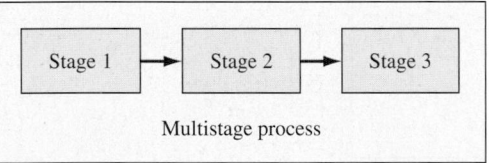
Multistage process

BUFFERING, BLOCKING, AND STARVING

Buffering

A multiple-stage process may be buffered internally. Buffering refers to a storage area between stages where the output of a stage is placed prior to being used in a downstream stage. Buffering allows the stages to operate independently. If one stage feeds a second stage with no intermediate buffer, then the assumption is that the two stages are directly linked. When a process is designed this way, the most common problems that can happen are blocking and starving. Blocking occurs when the activities in the stage must stop because there is no place to deposit the item just completed. Starving occurs when the activities in a stage must stop because there is no work.

Blocking
Starving

Consider a two-stage process where the first stage has a cycle time of 30 seconds and the second a cycle time of 45 seconds. If this process needs to produce 100 units, then for each unit produced, the first stage would be blocked for 15 seconds.

What would happen if an inventory buffer were placed between the two stages? In this case, the first stage would complete the 100 units in 3,000 seconds (30 seconds/unit × 100 units). During these 3,000 seconds, the second stage would complete only 66 units ((3,000 − 30) seconds/45 seconds/unit). The 30 seconds are subtracted from the 3,000 seconds because the second stage is starved for the first 30 seconds. This would mean that the inventory would build to 34 units (100 units − 66 units) over that first 3,000 seconds. All of the units would be produced in 4,530 seconds. The second stage in this case is called a bottleneck because it limits the capacity of the process.

Bottleneck

What would happen if the first stage required 45 seconds and the second stage had the 30-second cycle time? In this case, the first stage would be the bottleneck, and each unit would go directly from the first stage to the second. The second stage would be starved for 15 seconds waiting for each unit to arrive; however, it would still take 4,530 seconds to complete all 100 units. All of this assumes that there is no variability in the cycle time. With the relatively low 67 percent utilization on the second stage, variability would have little impact on the performance of this system, but if the cycle times were closer, some inventory might collect in the buffer.

Often activities, stages, and even entire processes are operated in parallel. For example, operating two identical activities in parallel would theoretically double capacity. Or perhaps two different sets of activities can be done at the same time on the unit being produced. In analyzing a system with parallel activities or stages, it is important to understand the context. In the case where parallel processes represent alternatives, for example, a diamond should show that flows divert and what percentage of the flow moves in each direction. Sometimes two or more processes terminate in a common inventory buffer. This normally indicates that the two processes make identical items that are going into this inventory. Separate inventories should be used in the diagram if the outputs of the parallel processes are different.

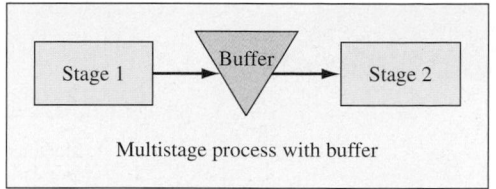

Multistage process with buffer

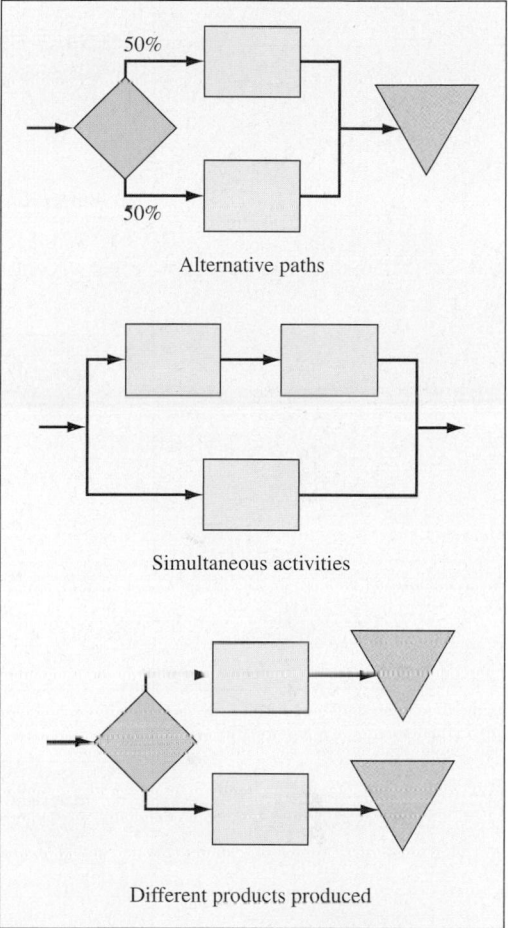

Alternative paths

Simultaneous activities

Different products produced

MAKE-TO-STOCK VERSUS MAKE-TO-ORDER

Another useful way to characterize a process is whether the process *makes to stock* or *makes to order*. To illustrate these concepts, consider the processes used to make hamburgers at the three major fast-food restaurant chains in the United States: McDonald's, Burger King, and Wendy's. In the case of McDonald's, in 1999 the company converted to a new make-to-order process, but the company has now revised that into a "hybrid" system. We begin our tour of the approaches used by the top fast-food restaurants by first reviewing the traditional approach.

Consider a traditional restaurant making hamburgers. Before the era of fast food, hamburgers were always made to order. In the traditional process, the customer places an order specifying the degree of doneness (medium or well done) and requests specific condiments (pickles, cheese, mustard, onions, catsup). Using this specification, the cook takes raw hamburger meat from inventory (typically this inventory is refrigerated and the patties have already been made), cooks the hamburger, and warms the bun. The hamburger is then assembled and delivered to the customer. The quality of the hamburger is highly dependent on the skill of the cook.

This **make-to-order** process is activated only in response to an actual order. Inventory (both work-in-process and finished goods) is kept to a minimum. Theoretically, one would expect that response time would be slow because all the activities need to be completed before the product is delivered to the customer. Services by their very nature often use make-to-order processes.

McDonald's revolutionized the hamburger-making process by developing a high-volume approach. A diagram of McDonald's traditional process is shown in Exhibit 5.2A. With the old process, hamburgers were grilled in batches. Standard hamburgers (for example, the "Big Mac" consists of two beef patties, sauce, lettuce, cheese, pickles, and onion on a sesame seed bun) were then prepared and stored in a holding bin for immediate delivery to the customer. A person that judged current demand and placed orders to keep inventory in the bin at an appropriate level controlled the whole process. This is a highly efficient **make-to-stock** process that produces standard products that can be delivered quickly to the

Service

Make-to-order

Make-to-stock

exhibit 5.2   Making Hamburgers at McDonald's, Burger King, and Wendy's

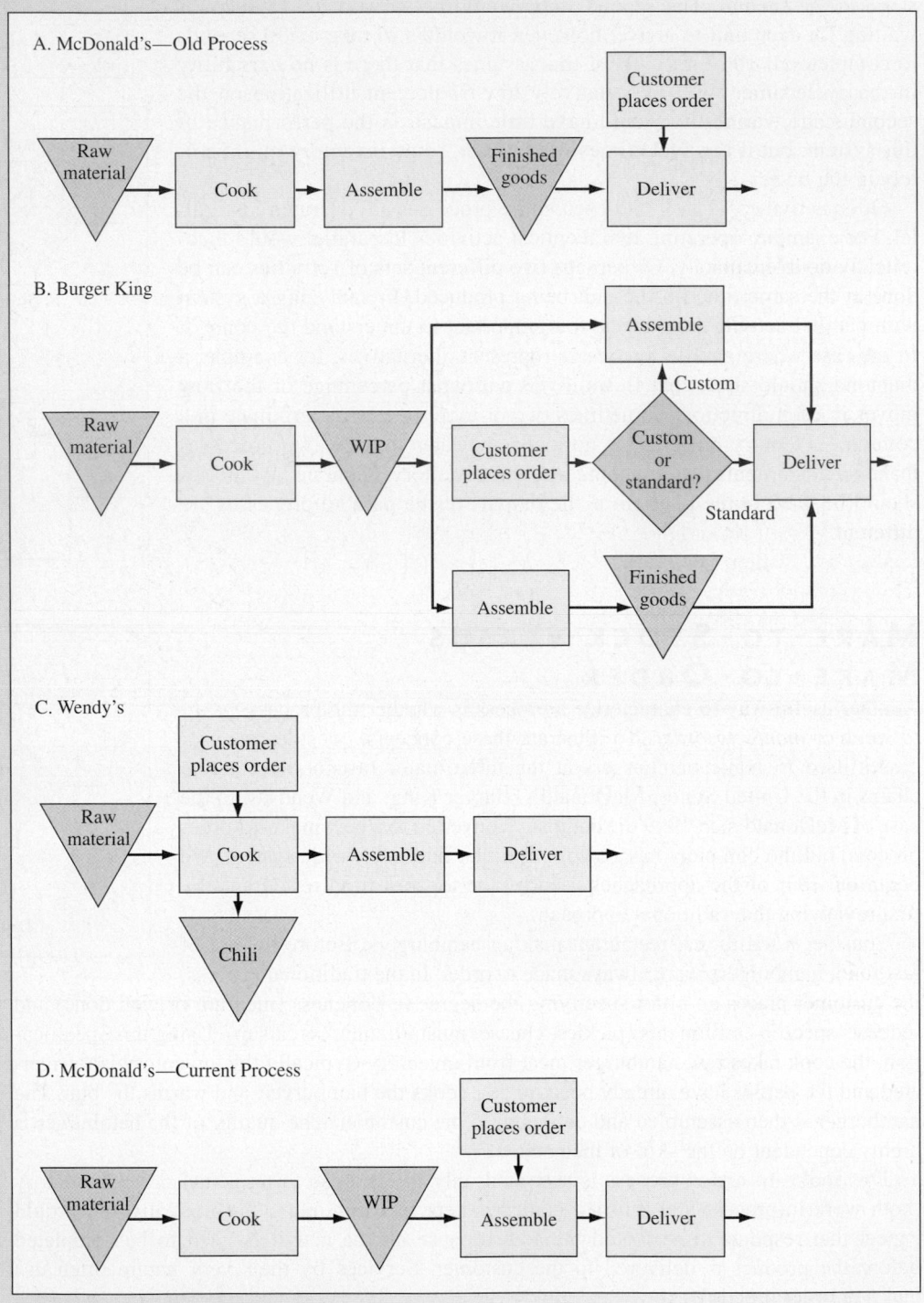

customer. This quick process appeals to families with small children, for whom speed of delivery is important.

In general, a make-to-stock process ends with finished goods inventory; customer orders are then served from this inventory. A make-to-stock process can be controlled based on the actual or anticipated amount of finished goods inventory. A target stocking level, for example, might be set, and the process would be periodically activated to maintain that target stocking level. Make-to-stock processes are also used when demand is seasonal. In this case, inventory can be built during the slow season and used during the peak season, thus allowing the process to run at a constant rate throughout the year.

The unique feature of the Burger King process, shown in Exhibit 5.2B, is a highly specialized conveyor–broiler. Raw hamburger patties are placed on a moving conveyor that runs through a flaming broiler. In exactly 90 seconds, the patties are cooked on both sides with a unique broiler taste. To move a patty through the conveyor–broiler in a fixed time, the thickness of the patties must be the same for all the hamburger products. The buns are also warmed on a conveyor. This system results in a unique, highly consistent product. The cooked patties are stored in a warmed storage container. During periods of high demand, some standard hamburgers are prepared and inventoried for immediate delivery. Custom hamburgers with unique combinations of condiments are prepared to order. This *hybrid* process provides flexibility to respond to customer preferences through the assemble-to-order backend process—thus, the Burger King "have it your way" slogan. In general, **hybrid** processes combine the features of both make-to-order and make-to-stock. Here two types of process are parallel

Hybrid

alternatives at the end of the Burger King process. In the most common hybrid form, a generic product is made and stocked at some point in the process. These generic units are then finished in a final process based on actual orders.

Continuing with our tour, Wendy's uses a make-to-order process (as shown in Exhibit 5.2C) that is in full view of the customer. Hamburger patties are cooked on a grill. During high-volume times, the cook tries to get a little ahead and anticipates the arrival of customers. Patties that are on the grill too long are used in the chili soup. On arrival of a customer order, a patty is taken from the grill and the hamburger is assembled to the exact specifications of the customer. Because the process starts with the cooking of the patty, it is a little slower. The customer can see what is going on, and the perception is of a high-quality custom product.

WENDY'S MAKE-TO-ORDER PROCESS.

Finally, the current McDonald's process introduced in 1999 (Exhibit 5.2D) is a hybrid process. Cooked hamburger patties are inventoried in a special storage device that maintains the moistness of the cooked patties for up to 30 minutes. The process makes extensive use of the latest cooking technologies. Hamburger patties are cooked in less than 45 seconds. Buns are toasted in only 11 seconds. Individual items on each customer order are transmitted immediately to the area where the hamburgers are assembled using a specially designed computer system. The assembly process that includes toasting the buns is designed to respond to a customer order in only 15 seconds. By combining the latest technology and clever process engineering, McDonald's has developed a very quick response process. The product is fresh, delivered quickly, and made to the exact specifications of the customer.

MCDONALD'S ASSEMBLY PROCESS.

Each of the processes used by these companies has its strengths and weaknesses. McDonald's is the high-volume leader, catering to families with young children. Burger King has its unique taste. Wendy's appeals to those who want their hamburgers prepared the old-fashioned way. Each company focuses advertising and promotional efforts toward attracting the segment of the market its process characteristics best support.

One final method for categorizing a process is by whether it is paced or nonpaced. Recall that Burger King uses the conveyor–broiler to cook hamburgers in exactly 90 seconds. **Pacing** refers to the fixed timing of the movement of items through the process. In a serial process, the movement of items through each activity (or stage) is often paced in some

Pacing

mechanical way in order to coordinate the line. An assembly line may, for example, move every 45 seconds. Another mechanism used is a clock that counts down the amount of time left in each cycle. When the clock reaches zero, the parts are manually moved to the next activity. Dividing the time available to produce a certain product by customer demand for the product calculates the required cycle time for a process. For example, if an automobile manufacturer needs to produce 1,000 automobiles during a shift where the assembly line operates 420 minutes, the cycle time is 25.2 seconds (420 minutes/1,000 automobiles × 60 seconds/minute = 25.2 seconds/automobile).

MEASURING PROCESS PERFORMANCE

There is much variation in the way performance metrics are calculated in practice. This section defines metrics in a manner consistent with the most common use in practice. It is vital, though, to understand exactly how a metric coming from a particular company or industry is calculated prior to making any decisions. This would be easier if metrics were calculated more consistently, but this just is not the case. So if a manager says that his utilization is 90 percent or her efficiency is 115 percent, a standard follow-up question is "How did you calculate that?" Metrics often are calculated in the context of a particular process. Metrics used in cases that you are studying may be defined slightly differently from what is given here. It is important to understand, within the context of the case, how a term is being used.

Comparing the metrics of one company to another, often referred to as *benchmarking,* is an important activity. Metrics tell a firm if progress is being made toward improvement. Similar to the value of financial measures to accountants, process performance metrics give the operations manager a gauge on how productively a process currently is operating and how productivity is changing over time. Often operations managers need to improve the performance of a process or project the impact of a proposed change. The metrics described in this section are important for answering these questions. To help in understanding these calculations, Exhibit 5.3 shows how these metrics relate to one another.

exhibit 5.3   Process Performance Metrics

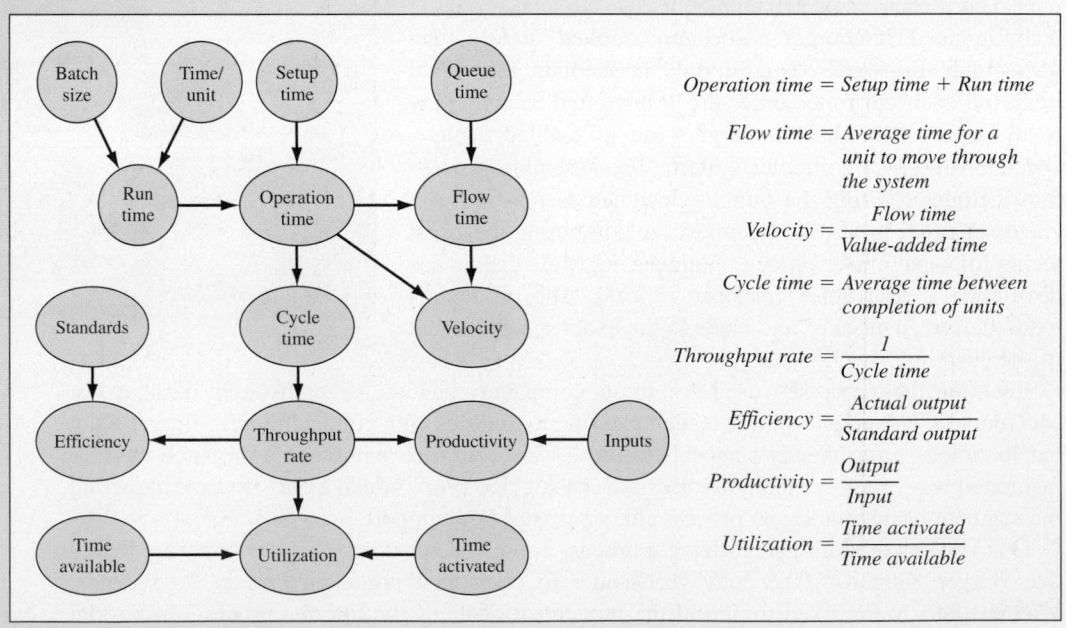

$Operation\ time = Setup\ time + Run\ time$

$Flow\ time = Average\ time\ for\ a\ unit\ to\ move\ through\ the\ system$

$Velocity = \dfrac{Flow\ time}{Value\text{-}added\ time}$

$Cycle\ time = Average\ time\ between\ completion\ of\ units$

$Throughput\ rate = \dfrac{1}{Cycle\ time}$

$Efficiency = \dfrac{Actual\ output}{Standard\ output}$

$Productivity = \dfrac{Output}{Input}$

$Utilization = \dfrac{Time\ activated}{Time\ available}$

Possibly the most common process metric is utilization. As discussed earlier in the chapter, utilization is the ratio of the time that a resource is actually being used relative to the time that it is available for use. Utilization is always measured in reference to some resource—for example, the utilization of direct labor or the utilization of a machine resource. The distinction between productivity and utilization is important. **Productivity** is the ratio of output to input. Total factor productivity is usually measured in monetary units, dollars, for example, by taking the dollar value of the output (such as goods and services sold) and dividing by the cost of all the inputs (that is, material, labor, and capital investment). Alternatively, *partial factor productivity* is measured based on an individual input, labor being the most common. Partial factor productivity answers the question of how much output we can get from a given level of input; for example, how many computers are made per employee working in the computer manufacturing plant? (See Chapter 2 for additional information about productivity.) Utilization measures the actual activation of the resource. For example, what is the percentage of time that an expensive machine is actually operating?

Productivity

Efficiency is a ratio of the actual output of a process relative to some standard. For example, consider a machine designed to package cereal at a rate of 30 boxes per minute. If during a shift the operators actually produce at a rate of 36 boxes per minute, then the efficiency of the machine is 120 percent (36/30). An alternative way that the term *efficiency* is used is to measure the loss or gain in a process. For example, if 1,000 units of energy are put into a process designed to convert that energy to some alternative form, and the process produces only 800 units of energy in the new form, then the process is 80 percent efficient.

Efficiency

Run time is the time required to produce a batch of parts. This is calculated by multiplying the time required to produce each unit by the batch size. The **setup time** is the time required to prepare a machine to make a particular item. Machines that have significant setup time will typically run parts in batches. The **operation time** is the sum of the setup time and run time for a batch of parts that are run on a machine. Consider the cereal-boxing machine that is designed to produce at a rate of 30 boxes per minute. The run time for each box is 2 seconds. To switch the machine from 16-ounce boxes to 12-ounce boxes requires a setup time of 30 minutes. The operation time to make a batch of 10,000 12-ounce boxes is 21,800 seconds (30 minutes' setup × 60 seconds/minute + 2 seconds/box × 10,000 boxes), or 363.33 minutes.

Run time
Setup time
Operation time

In practice, often setup time is not included in the utilization of the process. In essence, setup time is categorized like the downtime caused by repair or some other disruption to the process. This assumption can vary from company to company, so it is important when comparing the utilization of a machine or other resource to understand exactly how the company categorizes setup time.

The cycle time (also defined earlier in this chapter) is the elapsed time between starting and completing a job.[1] Another related term is **flow time**. Flow time includes the time that the unit spends actually being worked on together with the time spent waiting in a queue. As a simple example, consider a paced assembly line that has six stations and runs with a cycle time of 30 seconds. If the stations are located one right after another and every 30 seconds parts move from one station to the next, then the throughput time is three minutes (30 seconds × 6 stations/60 seconds per minute). The **throughput rate** is the output rate that the process is expected to produce over a period of time. The throughput rate of the assembly line is 120 units per hour (60 minutes/hour × 60 seconds/minute ÷ 30 seconds/unit). In this case, the throughput rate is the mathematical inverse of the cycle time.

Flow time

Throughput rate

Often units are not worked on 100 percent of the time as they move through a process. Because there often is some variability in the cycle time of a process, buffers are incorporated in the process to allow individual activities to operate independently, at least to some

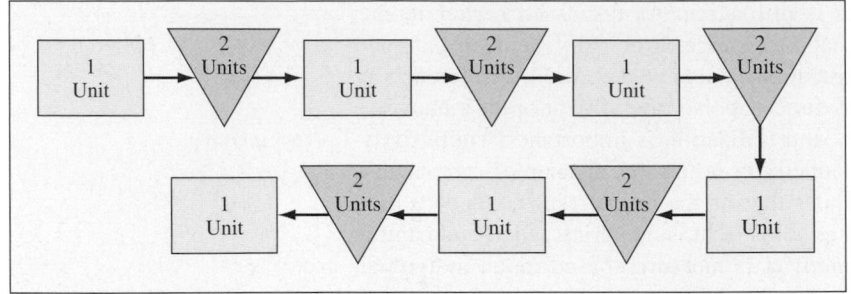

extent. In the six-station assembly line just described, consider the impact of having 10 additional buffer positions along the line. Assume that two of these positions are between the first and second workstations, two are between stations 2 and 3, and so forth. If these positions are always occupied, then the throughput time would be eight minutes (assuming a total of 16 positions along the assembly line and an average cycle time of 30 seconds).

Process velocity (throughput ratio)

Value-added time

Process velocity (also known as **throughput ratio**) is the ratio of the total throughput time to the value-added time. **Value-added time** is the time in which useful work is actually being done on the unit. Assuming that all of the activities that are included in the process are value-added activities, value-added time should be the sum of the activity operation times in the process. The process velocity (or throughput ratio) for our assembly line with the 10 additional buffer positions, assuming the positions are used 100 percent of the time, is 2.66 (8 minutes/3 minutes).

PRODUCTION PROCESS MAPPING AND LITTLE'S LAW

Supply Chain

Next, we look at how to quickly develop a high-level map of a process, which can be useful to understand how material flows and where inventory is held. The approach used here should be the first step in analyzing the flow of material through a production process. This idea will be further developed in "Value Stream Mapping" in Chapter 13.

Consider a simple system that might be typical of many make-to-stock companies. As shown in Exhibit 5.4, material is purchased from a set of suppliers and initially staged in raw material inventory. The material is used in a manufacturing process where the product is fabricated. After fabrication, the product is put into finished goods inventory and from here it is shipped according to orders received from customers.

Focusing on the Make part of the process, it is useful to analyze how this step operates using performance measures that relate to the inventory investment and also how quickly material flows through the process. A simplified way of thinking about material in a process is that it is in one of two states. The first state is where material is moving or "in-transit."

exhibit 5.4   Make-to-Stock Process Map

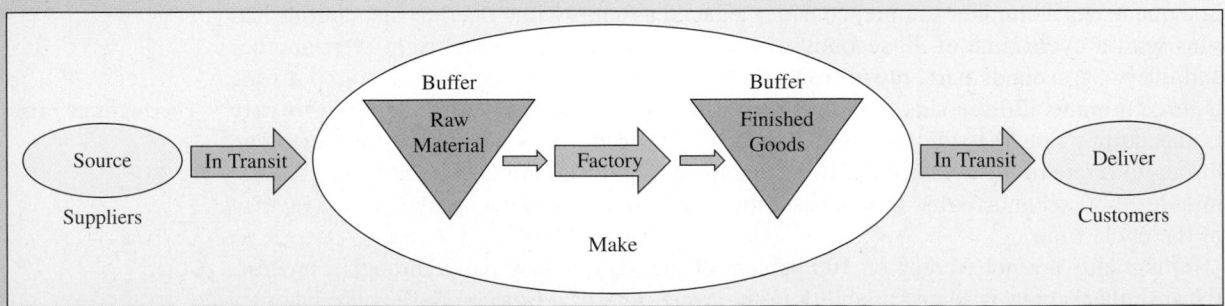

The second state is material that is sitting in inventory and acting as a "buffer" waiting to be used.

In the first state, material is moving in the process. This is material that is in-transit between entities in the process, for example, between the vendor and the raw material inventory at the manufacturer. Material that is in a manufacturing process in a factory can also be considered in-transit. Actually, we refer to this material as "work-in-process" inventory. In the second state, material is held in a storage area and waits until it is needed. In the case of raw material inventory, the need is dependent on the factory usage of the item. This "buffer" inventory allows different entities in the process to operate relatively independently.

A common measure is the **total average value of inventory** in the process. From an accounting view this would be the sum of the value (at cost) of the raw material, work-in-process, and finished goods inventory. This is commonly tracked in accounting systems and reported in the firm's financial statements. In addition to the total value of this inventory, another measure is the firm's **inventory turn**, which is the cost of goods sold divided by the average inventory value. Although useful for accounting purposes, these measures are not particularly useful for evaluating the performance of a process. Consider the total average value of inventory. What is better, a firm that has $2 million worth of inventory on average or one that has $4 million? This depends greatly on the size of the firm, the type of strategy being used (make-to-order or make-to-stock, for example), and the relative cost of the product being produced.

Total average value of inventory

Inventory turn

A better measure than the total value of inventory is inventory turn. Since inventory turn scales the amount of inventory by dividing by the cost of goods sold, this provides a relative measure that has some comparability, at least across similar firms. For two similar consumer products manufacturers, an inventory turn of six times per year is certainly much better than a firm turning inventory two times per year. A measure directly related is **days-of-supply**, which is the inverse of inventory turn scaled to days. For example, if a firm turns inventory six times per year, the days of supply is equal to one-sixth times per year or approximately every 61 days (this is calculated as 1/6 year × 365 days/year = 60.8 days).

Days-of-supply

Simple systems can be analyzed quickly using a principle known as **Little's law**. Little's law says there is a long-term relationship between the inventory, throughput, and flow time of a production system in steady state. The relationship is:

Little's law

$$Inventory = Throughput\ rate \times Flow\ time \qquad [5.1]$$

As noted earlier, throughput rate is the long-term average rate that items are flowing through the process and flow time is the time that it takes a unit to flow through the process from beginning to end. Consider the Factory process in Exhibit 5.4. Raw material is brought into the factory and is transformed and then stored in finished goods inventory. The analysis assumes that the process is operating in "steady state," meaning that over a long enough period of time the amount that is produced by the factory is equal to the amount shipped to customers. The throughput rate of the process is equal to average demand, and the process is not producing any excess or shortage. If this was not true and the amount produced by the manufacturing process was greater than demand, for example, the finished goods inventory would build over time. So if demand averages 1,000 units per day and 20 days are needed for a unit to flow through the factory, then the expected work-in-process in the factory would be 20,000 units.

We can think of Little's law as a relationship between units and time. Inventory is measured in pieces, flow time in days, and throughput in pieces per day. Therefore, if we divide inventory by throughput we get flow time. For example, 20,000 units divided by 1,000 units per day is 20 days. We can also take inventory and divide by flow time and get throughput rate. Here 20,000 units divided by 20 days is equal to 1,000 units a day. This conversion is useful when diagnosing a plant's performance.

To appreciate a major limitation, suppose that a process has just started with no inventory on hand. Some of the initial production will be used to fill the system, thus limiting initial throughput. In this case Little's law will not hold, but after the process has been operating for a while, and there is inventory at every step, the process stabilizes, and then the relationship holds.

Supply Chain

Little's law is actually much more general than a simple way to convert between units. It can be applied to single work stations, multistep production lines, factories, or even entire supply chains. Further, it applies to processes with variability in the arrival rate (or demand rate) and processing time. It can be applied to single or multiple product systems. It even applies to nonproduction systems where inventory represents people, financial orders, or other entities.

For our factory, it is common for accounting systems to capture average work-in-process in terms of the value (at cost) of the inventory that is being worked on in the factory. For our example, say that work-in-process averages $200,000 and that each unit is valued at cost at $10.00. This would imply that there are 20,000 units in the factory (calculated $200,000 ÷ $10.00 per unit = 20,000 units).

The following example shows how these concepts can be applied to quickly analyze simple processes.

Global

Step by Step

EXAMPLE 5.1

An automobile company assembles cars in a plant and purchases batteries from a vendor in China. The average cost of each battery is $45. The automobile company takes ownership of the batteries when they arrive at the plant. It takes exactly 12 hours to make a car in the plant and the plant assembles 200 cars per 8-hour shift (currently the plant operates one shift per day). Each car uses one battery. The company holds on average 8,000 batteries in raw material inventory at the plant as a buffer. Assignment: Find the total number of batteries in the plant on average (in work-in-process at the plant and in raw material inventory). How much are these batteries worth? How many days of supply are held in raw material inventory on average?

SOLUTION

We can split this into two inventories, work-in-process and raw material. For the work-in-process, Little's law can be directly applied to find the amount of work-in-process inventory:

$$Inventory = Throughput \times Flow\ time$$

Throughput is the production rate of the plant, 200 cars per 8-hour shift, or 25 cars per hour. Since we use one battery per car, our throughput rate for the batteries is 25 per hour. Flow time is 12 hours, so the work-in-process is:

$$Work\text{-}in\text{-}process\ inventory = 25\ batteries/hour \times 12\ hours = 300\ batteries$$

We know from the problem there are 8,000 batteries in raw material inventory, so the total number of batteries in the pipeline on average is:

$$Total\ inventory = 8,000 + 300 = 8,300\ batteries$$

These batteries are worth 8,300 × $45 = $373,500.

The days of supply in raw material inventory is the "flow time" for a battery in raw material inventory (or the average amount of time that a battery spends in raw material inventory). Here, we need to assume that they are used in the same order they arrive. Rearranging our Little's law formula:

$$Flow\ time = Inventory/Throughput$$

So, Flow time = 8,000 batteries/(200 batteries/day) = 40 days, which represents a 40-day supply of inventory. ●

In the next section, we look at how the production processes are organized in different environments. This is largely dependent on the variety of products being produced and on the volume. How a company produces airplanes is very different when compared to building computers or making ink pens.

PROCESS ANALYSIS EXAMPLES

In this section, the concepts described thus far in the chapter are illustrated with three examples. These examples are typical of the types of analysis that are performed in manufacturing, services, and logistics businesses. Keep in mind that the analysis used in each example can be applied to many different contexts. Be creative in applying something that you have seen in another context to the problem at hand. The first example analyzes a bread-making process. Following this, a restaurant operation is evaluated. Finally, a typical logistics operation is appraised.

A BREAD-MAKING OPERATION[2]

Step by Step

EXAMPLE 5.2: Bread Making

For the manager of a bakery, a first priority is to understand the products that are made and the process steps required. Exhibit 5.5A is a simplified diagram of the bread-making process. Two steps are required to prepare the bread. The first is preparing the dough and baking the loaves, here referred to as bread making. The second is packaging the loaves. Due to the size of the mixers in the bakery, bread is made in batches of 100 loaves. Bread making completes a batch of 100 loaves every hour, which is the cycle time for the activity. Packaging needs only 0.75 hour to place the 100 loaves in bags.

From this we see that bread making is the bottleneck in the process. A bottleneck is the activity in a process that limits the overall capacity of the process. So if we assume that the bread-making and packaging activities both operate the same amount of time each day, then the bakery has a capacity of 100 loaves per hour. Notice that over the course of the day the packaging operation will be idle for quarter-hour periods in which the next batch of bread is still being made but packaging has already completed bagging the previous batch. One would expect that the packaging operation would be utilized only 75 percent of the time under this scenario.

Bread-Making Processes

exhibit 5.5

A. Bread making on one line

Raw material → Bread making **Cycle time:** 1 hour/100 loaves → WIP → Pack **Cycle time:** $\frac{3}{4}$ hour/100 loaves → Finished Goods

B. Bread making on two parallel lines

Raw material → Bread making **Cycle time:** 1 hour/100 loaves / Bread making **Cycle time:** 1 hour/100 loaves → WIP → Pack **Cycle time:** $\frac{3}{4}$ hour/100 loaves → Finished Goods

Suppose that instead of having only one bread-making operation we now have two, as shown in Exhibit 5.5B. The cycle time for each individual bread-making operation is still one hour per 100 loaves. The cycle time for the two bread-making lines operating together is half an hour. Because the packaging operation takes 0.75 hour to bag 100 loaves, the packaging operation now is the bottleneck. If both bread making and packaging were operated the same number of hours each day, it would be necessary to limit how much bread was made because we do not have the capacity to package it. However, if we operated the packaging operation for three eight-hour shifts and bread making for two shifts each day, then the daily capacity of each would be identical at 3,200 loaves a day (this assumes that the packaging operation starts up one hour after the bread-making operation). Doing this requires building up a shift's worth of inventory each day as work-in-process. Packaging would bag this during the third shift. So what is the flow time of our bakery?

SOLUTION

In the original operation with just the single bread-making process, this is easy to calculate because inventory would not build between the bread-making and packaging processes. In this case the flow time would be 1.75 hours. In the case where we operate the packaging operation for three shifts, the average wait in work-in-process inventory needs to be considered. If both bread-making operations start at the same time, then at the end of the first hour the first 100 loaves move immediately into packaging while the second 100 loaves wait. The waiting time for each 100-loaf batch increases until the baking is done at the end of the second shift.

This is a case where Little's law can estimate the time that the bread is sitting in work-in-process. To apply Little's law, we need to estimate the average work-in-process between bread making and packaging. During the first two shifts, inventory builds from 0 to 1,200 loaves. We can estimate the average work-in-process over this 16-hour period to be 600 loaves (half the maximum). Over the last eight-hour shift inventory drops from the 1,200-loaf maximum down to 0. Again the average work-in-process is 600 loaves. Given this, the overall average over the 24-hour period is simply 600 loaves of bread. The packing process limits the cycle time for the process to 0.75 hour per 100 loaves (assume that the loaves are packaged in a batch), and this is equivalent to a throughput rate of 133.3 loaves/hour ($100/0.75 = 133.3$). Little's law calculates that the average time that loaves are in work-in-process is 4.5 hours (600 loaves/133.3 loaves/hour).

The total flow time is the time that the loaves are in work-in-process plus the operations time for the bread-making and packaging processes. The total flow time then is 6.25 hours (1 hour for bread making + 4.5 hours in inventory + 0.75 hour packaging). ●

A RESTAURANT OPERATION

EXAMPLE 5.3: A Restaurant

Service

Step by Step

Our bakery operates in what is referred to as *steady state,* meaning that the operation is started up and runs at a steady rate during the entire time that it is in operation. The output of this steady state process is adjusted by setting the amount of time that the operation is run. In the case of the bakery, we assumed that bread making worked for three shifts and packaging for two shifts.

A restaurant cannot run in this manner. The restaurant must respond to varying customer demand throughout the day. During some peak times, it may be impossible to serve all customers immediately, and some customers may have to wait to be seated. The restaurant, because of this varying demand, is a *non–steady state* process. Keep in mind that many of the menu items in a restaurant can be pre-prepared. The pre-prepared items, salads and desserts, for example, help speed the processes that must be performed when customers are at the restaurant being served.

Consider the restaurant in the casino that we discussed earlier. Because it is important that customers be served quickly, the managers have set up a buffet arrangement where customers serve themselves. The buffet is continually replenished to keep items fresh. To further speed service, a fixed amount is charged for the meal, no matter what the customer eats. Assume that we have designed our buffet so customers take an average of 30 minutes to get their food and eat. Further, assume that they typically eat in groups (or customer parties) of two or three to a table. The restaurant has 40 tables. Each table can accommodate four people. What is the maximum capacity of this restaurant?

SOLUTION

It is easy to see that the restaurant can accommodate 160 people seated at tables at a time. Actually, in this situation, it might be more convenient to measure the capacity in terms of customer parties because this is how the capacity will be used. If the average customer party is 2.5 individuals, then the average seat utilization is 62.5 percent (2.5 seats/party ÷ 4 seats/table) when the restaurant is operating at capacity. The cycle time for the restaurant, when operating at capacity, is 0.75 minute (30 minutes/table ÷ 40 tables). So, on average, a table would become available every 45 seconds. The restaurant could handle 80 customer parties per hour (60 minutes ÷ 0.75 minute/party).

The problem with this restaurant is that everyone wants to eat at the same time. Management has collected data and expects the following profile for customer parties arriving during lunch, which runs from 11:30 A.M. until 1:30 P.M. Customers are seated only until 1:00 P.M.

TIME	PARTIES ARRIVING
11:30–11:45	15
11:45–12:00	35
12:00–12:15	30
12:15–12:30	15
12:30–12:45	10
12:45–1:00	5
Total parties	110

Because the restaurant operates for two hours for lunch and the capacity is 80 customer parties per hour, the restaurant does not appear to have a problem. In reality, though, the uneven flow of customers into the restaurant is a problem. A simple way to analyze the situation is to calculate how we expect the system to look in terms of number of customers being served and number waiting in line at the end of each 15-minute interval. Think of this as taking a snapshot of the restaurant every 15 minutes.

The key to understanding the analysis is to look at the cumulative numbers. The difference between cumulative arrivals and cumulative departures gives the number of customer parties in the restaurant (those seated at tables and those waiting). Because there are only 40 tables, when the cumulative difference through a time interval is greater than 40, a waiting line forms. When all 40 tables are busy, the system is operating at capacity; and, from the previous calculation, we know the cycle time for the entire restaurant is 45 seconds per customer party at this time (this means that on average a table empties every 45 seconds or 20 tables empty during each 15-minute interval). The last party will need to wait for all of the earlier parties to get a table, so the expected waiting time is the number of parties in line multiplied by the cycle time.

TIME PERIOD	PARTIES ARRIVING DURING PERIOD (CUMULATIVE)	PARTIES DEPARTING DURING PERIOD (CUMULATIVE)	PARTIES EITHER AT TABLE OR WAITING TO BE SERVED (AT END OF PERIOD)	TABLES USED (AT END OF PERIOD)	CUSTOMER PARTIES WAITING (AT END OF PERIOD)	EXPECTED WAITING TIME (AT END OF PERIOD)
11:30–11:45	15	0	15	15		
11:45–12:00	35 (50)	0	50	40	10	7.5 minutes
12:00–12:15	30 (80)	15	65	40	25	18.75 minutes
12:15–12:30	15 (95)	20 (35)	60	40	20	15 minutes
12:30–12:45	10 (105)	20 (55)	50	40	10	7.5 minutes
12:45–1:00	5 (110)	20 (75)	35	35		
1:00–1:30	0 (110)	35 (110)				

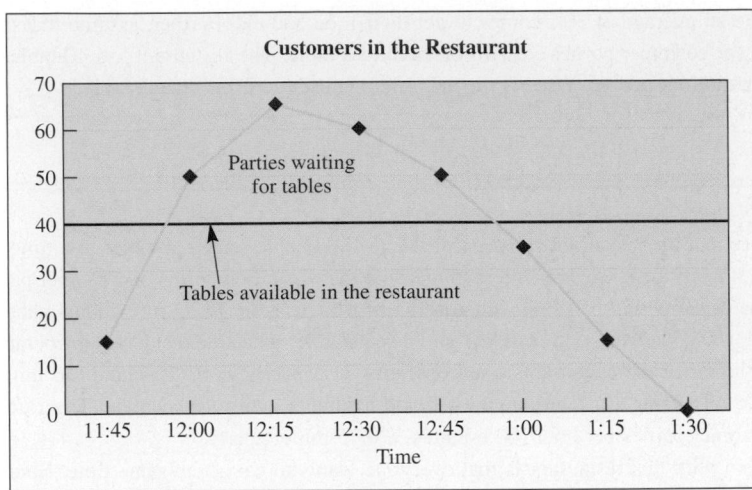

Customers in the Restaurant

Parties waiting for tables

Tables available in the restaurant

The analysis shows that by 12 noon, 10 customer parties are waiting in line. This line builds to 25 parties by 12:15. The waiting line shortens to only 10 parties by 12:45.

So what can we do to solve our waiting line problem? One idea might be to shorten the cycle time for a single table, but customers are unlikely to be rushed through their lunch in less than 30 minutes. Another idea would be to add tables. If the restaurant could add 25 tables, then a wait would not be expected. Of course, this would eat into the space used for slot machines, so this alternative might not be attractive to casino management. A final idea might be to double up parties at the tables, thus getting a higher seat utilization. Doubling up might be the easiest thing to try. If 25 out of the 40 tables were doubled up, our problem would be solved. ●

PLANNING A TRANSIT BUS OPERATION

Service

Step by Step

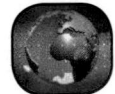

Global

EXAMPLE 5.4: Transit Bus Operation

The final example involves a *logistics* system. The term *logistics* refers to the movement of things such as materials, people, or finished goods. Our example involves a bus route that would be typical of one used on campus or in a metropolitan area. A similar analysis could be used for analyzing plane routes, truck routes, or ships. Similar to the restaurant, a bus transit route does not operate in steady state. There are definite peaks in demand during the day and evening. A good approach to take, the same as was done with the restaurant, is to analyze distinct periods of time that represent the different types of demand patterns placed on the service. These distinct analyses can be referred to as *scenarios*. Depending on the situation, it might be reasonable to develop either a single solution that covers all the relevant scenarios or a set of solutions for the different scenarios.

A great bus route is the Balabus, or "tourist bus," in Paris. This route loops past all the major attractions in Paris. Some of the sights along the route include Notre-Dame, the Louvre, Concorde, Champs-Elysées, the Arc de Triomphe, the Eiffel Tower, and others.

Consider the problem of planning the number of buses needed to service this route. A number of factors need to be considered. Let's assume that a single bus takes exactly two hours to traverse the route during peak traffic. The bus company has designed delays in the route so that even though traffic is busy, the bus can keep on schedule. The route has 60 stops, although the bus stops only when passengers on the bus request a stop or when the driver sees customers waiting to board at a stop. Each bus has seating capacity of about 50 passengers, and another 30 passengers can stand. This route is busy much of the day because visitors to the city tend to start visiting the sites early and continue until dark. Finally, the transit authority wants to give good service and have enough capacity to handle peak customer loads. The following is an analysis of the situation.

SOLUTION

A key measure of service is how long a customer must wait prior to the arrival of a bus. Consider initially the case of only a single bus serving the route. If a person at a random time comes to a bus stop, we know that the maximum time that the customer needs to wait is two hours. Here we assume that the bus is able to cover the route in exactly two hours. If this cycle time varies significantly, the waiting time goes up. We discuss the impact of variability in Chapter 7A. This would be the case when the unlucky customer just missed the bus. If the bus was halfway through the route (relative to where the customer is waiting), then the customer needs to wait one hour. Continuing with this logic, we can estimate the average wait time for the customer to be one hour. In general, we can say that the average wait time would be half the cycle time of the process. If two buses are used, the cycle time is one hour and the average wait is 30 minutes. If we want the average wait to be two minutes, then the required cycle time is four minutes, and 30 buses are needed (120 minutes ÷ 4 minutes/bus = 30 buses).

The next issue relates to the capacity of the system. If we have 30 buses on the route and each bus seats 50 passengers with another 30 standing, we know that we can accommodate 1,500 seated or 2,400 passengers in total at one point in time.

Assume that the following table is an estimate of the number of passengers that travel the route during a typical tourist season day. The table shows calculations of the amount of bus capacity required during each hour. If a customer rides the bus for 45 minutes, then one seat is needed for 45 minutes, or 0.75 hour, to handle that passenger. Of course, 60 minutes, or a full hour's worth of capacity, is available for each seat that we have. At maximum utilization including standing, each bus can handle 80 passenger-hours' worth of load. Dividing the expected passenger load during the hour by the maximum load for a single bus calculates the minimum number of buses needed. Similarly, dividing the expected passenger load by the number of seats on each bus calculates the number of buses needed so that all passengers can be seated.

Time	Number of Customers	Average Time on Bus	Load (Passenger Hours)	Minimum Number of Buses Needed	Buses Needed for All Passengers to Be Seated
8:00–9:00 A.M.	2,000	45 minutes	1,500	18.75	30
9:00–10:00 A.M.	4,000	30 minutes	2,000	25	40
10:00–11:00 A.M.	6,000	30 minutes	3,000	37.5	60
11:00 A.M.–12:00 NOON	5,000	30 minutes	2,500	31.25	50
12:00–1:00 P.M.	4,000	30 minutes	2,000	25	40
1:00–2:00 P.M.	3,500	30 minutes	1,750	21.875	35
2:00–3:00 P.M.	3,000	45 minutes	2,250	28.125	45
3:00–4:00 P.M.	3,000	45 minutes	2,250	28.125	45
4:00–5:00 P.M.	3,000	45 minutes	2,250	28.125	45
5:00–6:00 P.M.	4,000	45 minutes	3,000	37.5	60
6:00–7:00 P.M.	3,000	45 minutes	2,250	28.125	45
7:00–8:00 P.M.	1,500	45 minutes	1,125	14.0625	22.5
TOTALS	42,000		25,875		

From the analysis, if the Paris transit authority uses only 30 buses throughout the day, many people will need to stand. Further, during the morning rush between 10 and 11 A.M. and the evening rush between 5 and 6 P.M., not all of the customers can be accommodated. It would seem reasonable that at least 40 buses should be used between 9 A.M. and 7 P.M. Even with this number of buses, one would expect passengers to be standing most of the time.

If the transit authority decided to use 40 buses between the extended hours of 8 A.M. through 8 P.M., what would be the average utilization of the buses in terms of seats occupied? Over this 12-hour period, 24,000 seat-hours of capacity would be available (40 buses × 12 hours × 50 seats/bus). The table indicates that 25,875 seat-hours are needed. The utilization would be 107.8 percent (25,875/24,000 × 100). What this means is that, on average, 7.8 percent of the customers must stand. Of course, this average value significantly understates the severe capacity problem that occurs during the peak times of the day. ●

Consider in the preceding example how useful this type of analysis is to the Paris transit authority. Data can be collected for each day of the week, and the analysis performed. Interesting questions concerning the design of the route or the capacity of the buses can be evaluated. Consider, for example, what would happen if the route were split into two parts. What if larger buses that could carry 120 passengers were put into service? The analysis can be extended to include the cost of providing the service by considering the wages paid the operators, the cost to maintain and operate the vehicles, and depreciation of the buses. As seen from the above example, designing a transit system involves a trade-off between the convenience of the service, or how frequently buses arrive at each stop, and the capacity utilization of the buses.

PROCESS FLOW TIME REDUCTION

Critical processes are subject to the well-known rule that time is money. For example, the longer a customer waits, the more likely the customer is to switch to a different vendor. The longer material is kept in inventory, the higher the investment cost. There are exceptions in services, where more time in process can lead to more money. See the box "Efficiency Meets Corporate Goals: A Love Story."

Unfortunately, critical processes often depend on specific limited resources, resulting in bottlenecks. Flow time can sometimes be reduced without purchasing additional equipment. The following are some suggestions for reducing the flow time of a process that do not require the purchase of new equipment. Often a combination of ideas is appropriate.[3]

1. **Perform activities in parallel.**   Most of the steps in an operations process are performed in sequence. A serial approach results in the flow time for the entire process being the sum of the individual steps plus transport and waiting time between steps. Using a parallel approach can reduce flow time by as much as 80 percent and produces a better result.

    A classic example is product development, where the current trend is toward concurrent engineering. Instead of forming a concept, making drawings, creating a bill of materials, and mapping processes, all activities are performed in parallel by integrated teams. Development time is reduced dramatically, and the needs of all those involved are addressed during the development process.

2. **Change the sequence of activities.**   Documents and products are often transported back and forth between machines, departments, buildings, and so forth. For instance, a document might be transferred between two offices a number of times for inspection and signing. If the sequence of some of these activities can be altered, it may be possible to perform much of the document's processing when it comes to a building the first time.

3. **Reduce interruptions.**   Many processes are performed with relatively large time intervals between the activities. For example, purchase orders may be issued only every other day. Individuals preparing reports that result in purchase orders should be aware of deadlines to avoid missing them, because improved timing in these processes can save many days of flow time.

To illustrate these ideas, consider an electronics manufacturer that has been receiving customer complaints about a long order lead time of 29 days. As assessment of the order-processing system revealed 12 instances where managers had to approve employees' work.

EFFICIENCY MEETS CORPORATE GOALS: A LOVE STORY

Due to my lack of patience, I gave birth to a beautiful process improvement idea at a local coffee shop. It came to me as I stood in front of coffee servers with pupils the size of bowling balls owing to the high-octane java they had been drinking for six straight hours.

The process improvement idea was to improve the efficiency with which they provide value to their customers. Or, in brew-guy terms, reduce the wait time, reducing the line, delivering coffee faster.

The Problem: Why is it that regular coffee drinkers wait in the same line as drinkers of a double latte cinnamon frappuccino, which takes eons to prepare?

Idea: Give the straight joe Joes and Josephines their own line. Simple, yet brilliant.

So, armed with good intentions and a righteous buzz, I approached the entrepreneurial spirit disguised as the coffee shop owner, ordered my regular drip, and pitched my idea.

Watching him dervish around, it was clear that I underestimated my sponsor's passion for process. As he slung beans, brew, and bucks to their containers, I thought to myself: he would have made a lovely ballerina. And he knew *exactly* what he was doing.

"Mr. Process Analyst," said he, "it is the goal of my corporation to make money. And it is during this pregnant pause provided prior to pouring coffee that patrons peer into the pleasantly populated pastry case, and decide they want a coffee *and* a pastry!" I was amazed, as I hadn't heard such alliteration since Muhammad Ali was in his prime, and equally amazed at his perfect logic and very effective process. It was, in fact, a beautiful thing. We embraced, and I devoured a wedge of pound cake the size of a cat.

So, consultants, managers, process analysts, and general do-gooders alike, take heed. The most efficient process does not always attain your corporate goals; thus, it is imperative that the process and goal be aligned. Also, learn to appreciate the process in front of you, and the business people that designed it. They (whomever "they" may be) do know their stuff much of the time. And it is essential you *listen* and *learn* from these subject matter experts before you open your mouth and propose possible process nonsense.

SOURCE: ADAPTED FROM "EFFICIENCY MEETS CORPORATE GOALS: A LOVE STORY," ANONYMOUS, POSTED JULY 21, 2006, ON www.pavilion.com.

It was determined that the first 10 approvals were not needed. This saved an average of seven to eight days in the order processing.

Many subsystems—each performing the same or similar tasks—had interfered with the process. The logical step was to eliminate redundancy, and a detailed flowchart of the process was created. At close inspection, 16 steps proved very similar to one another. Changing the sequence of activities and creating one companywide order document removed 13 of these steps.

Over four months, the order system was totally redesigned to allow information to be entered once and become available to the entire organization. Due to this adjustment, activities could be handled in a parallel manner. After a value-added analysis (focused on eliminating the non–value-adding activities), the manufacturer was able to reduce the customer order lead time from 29 days to 9 days, save cost and employee time per order, and increase customer satisfaction.

SUMMARY

Process analysis is a basic skill needed to understand how a business operates. Great insight is obtained by drawing a simple flowchart showing the flow of materials or information through an enterprise. The diagram should include all the operating elements and show how they fit together. Be sure to indicate where material is stored or where orders are queued. Often 90 percent or more of the time that is required to serve a customer is spent just waiting. Hence, merely eliminating the waiting time can dramatically improve the performance of the process.

Remember this fundamental concept when analyzing a process: What goes into the process must come out of the process. A process taken as a whole is like the funnel shown in Exhibit 5.6. The outlet of the funnel restricts the amount that can flow through. In a real business process, certain resources limit output. If liquid is poured into the funnel at a rate greater than it can exit, the level in the funnel will continue to grow. As the level of liquid in the funnel grows, the time needed for the liquid to flow through the funnel increases. If too much liquid is poured into the funnel, it just spills over the top and never flows through.

The same is true of a real process. If too many jobs are pumped into the process, the time that it takes to complete a job will increase because the waiting time will increase. At some point, customers will go somewhere else and the business will be lost. When a process is operating at capacity, the only way to take on more work without increasing the waiting time is to add more capacity. This requires finding what activity is limiting the output of the process and increasing the capacity of that activity. In essence, the tube leading out of the funnel needs to be made larger.

exhibit 5.6   What Goes into a Process Must Come Out of the Process. Input Rate Must Be Less Than or Equal to the Output Rate; Otherwise, the System Will Overflow.

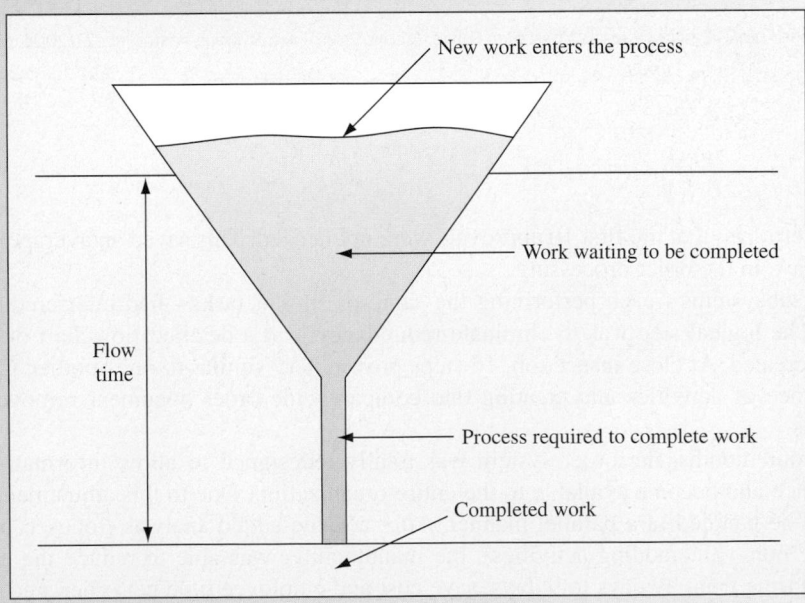

New work enters the process

Work waiting to be completed

Flow time

Process required to complete work

Completed work

KEY TERMS

Process Any set of activities performed by an organization that takes inputs and transforms them into outputs ideally of greater value to the organization than the original inputs.

Cycle time The average time between completions of successive units in a process (this is the definition used in this book). The term is sometimes used to mean the elapsed time between starting and completing a job.

Utilization The ratio of the time that a resource is actually activated relative to the time that it is available for use.

Buffering A storage area between stages where the output of a stage is placed prior to being used in a downstream stage. Buffering allows the stages to operate independently.

Blocking The activities in the stage must stop because there is no place to deposit the item just completed.

Starving The activities in a stage must stop because there is no work.

Bottleneck A resource that limits the capacity or maximum output of the process.

Make-to-order A process that is activated only in response to an actual order.

Make-to-stock A process that produces standard products that are stored in finished goods inventory. The product is delivered quickly to the customer from the finished goods inventory.

Hybrid Combines the features of both make-to-order and make-to-stock. Typically, a generic product is made and stocked at some point in the process. These generic units are customized in a final process to meet actual orders.

Pacing Movement of items through a process is coordinated through a timing mechanism. Most processes are not paced, but assembly lines usually are paced.

Productivity The ratio of output to input. Taking the dollar value of the output and dividing by the dollar value of the inputs usually measures total factor productivity. Alternatively, *partial factor productivity* is measured based on an individual input and often is not calculated using dollar values (an example would be units/person).

Efficiency A ratio of the actual output of a process relative to some standard.

Run time The time required to produce a batch of parts.

Setup time The time required to prepare a machine to make a particular item.

Operation time The sum of the setup time and run time for a batch of parts that are run on a machine.

Flow time The average time that it takes a unit to move through an entire process. Usually the term *lead time* is used to refer to the total time that it takes a customer to receive an order (includes time to process the order, throughput time, and delivery time).

Throughput rate The output rate that the process is expected to produce over a period of time.

Process velocity or throughput ratio The ratio of the total flow time to the value-added time.

Value-added time The time in which useful work is actually being done on the unit.

Total average value of inventory The total average investment in raw material, work-in-process, and finished goods inventory. This is valued at the cost to the firm.

Inventory turn The cost of goods sold divided by the total average value of inventory.

Days-of-supply The number of days of inventory of an item. If an item were not replenished, this would be the numbers of days until the firm would run out of the item (on average). Also, the inverse of inventory turn expressed in days.

Little's law States a mathematical relationship between throughput rate, flow time, and the amount of work-in-process inventory. Flow time is equal to work-in-process divided by the throughput rate.

FORMULA REVIEW

Little's law

$$Inventory = Throughput\ rate \times Flow\ time \qquad \text{[5.1]}$$

SOLVED PROBLEMS

SOLVED PROBLEM 1

Suppose we schedule shipments to our customers so that we expect each shipment to wait for two days in finished goods inventory (in essence we add two days to when we expect to be able to ship). We do this as protection against system variability to ensure a high on-time delivery service. If we ship approximately 2,000 units each day, how many units do we expect to have in finished goods inventory due to allowing this extra time? If the item is valued at $4.50 each, what is the expected value of this inventory?

Solution

Using Little's law the expected finished goods inventory is:

$$\text{Inventory} = 2{,}000 \text{ units per day} \times 2 \text{ days} = 4{,}000 \text{ units}$$

This would be valued at 4,000 units $\times$ $4.50 per unit = $18,000

SOLVED PROBLEM 2

Daffy Dave's Sub Shop makes custom submarine sandwiches to order. They are analyzing the processes at their shop. The general flow of the process is shown below. A different person is working at each of the steps in the process.

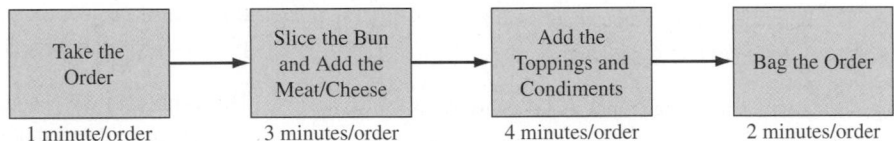

Daffy Dave wants to figure out the following for a typical 8-hour work day.

a. What is the current maximum output of the process?

b. If we add another person, where would we add him or her and what is the benefit?

c. Is there a benefit if we can shift 1 minute from Bun and Meat to Order Taking? Assume we do not make the change in part *b* above.

d. Is there a benefit if we shift 1 minute of work from Condiments to Bagging? Assume we do not make the changes in parts *b* and *c* above.

Solution

a. Maximum output is 120 subs per day.

OPERATION	OUTPUT
Take Orders	(60 min. per hour/1 min. per order) * 8 hours = 480 subs per day
Bun and Meat	(60 min. per hour/3 min. per order) * 8 hours = 160 subs per day
Toppings/Condiments	(60 min. per hour/4 min. per order) * 8 hours = 120 subs per day
Bag the Order	(60 min. per hour/2 min. per order) * 8 hours = 240 subs per day

Output per day is determined by the slowest station; therefore, we can only produce 120 per day because that is the limit of the Toppings/Condiments station.

b. Dave should add the person to the slowest station (Condiments/Toppings) since it is the bottleneck.

OPERATION	OUTPUT
Take Orders	480 subs per day
Bun and Meat	160 subs per day
Toppings/Condiments	120 * 2 = 240 subs per day
Bag the Order	240 subs per day

The impact is not a very big one. Even though the Toppings/Condiments station now can do 240 subs per day, the Bun and Meat station can only do 160, so that is the maximum output.

c. Order Taking station will go from 1 minute to 2 minutes, and Bun and Meat goes from 3 minutes to 2 minutes.

OPERATION	OUTPUT
Take Orders	(60 min. per hour/2 min. per order) * 8 hours = 240 subs per day
Bun and Meat	(60 min. per hour/2 min. per order) * 8 hours = 240 subs per day
Toppings/Condiments	(60 min. per hour/4 min. per order) * 8 hours = 120 subs per day
Bag the Order	(60 min. per hour/2 min. per order) * 8 hours = 240 subs per day

There is no benefit to this change. Dave can still only make 120 subs per day since we can only produce 120 per day because that is the limit of the Toppings/Condiments station.

d. Toppings/Condiments station will go from 4 minutes to 3 minutes, and Bagging goes from 2 minutes to 3 minutes.

OPERATION	OUTPUT
Take Orders	(60 min. per hour/1 min. per order) * 8 hours = 480 subs per day
Bun and Meat	(60 min. per hour/3 min. per order) * 8 hours = 160 subs per day
Toppings/Condiments	(60 min. per hour/3 min. per order) * 8 hours = 160 subs per day
Bag the Order	(60 min. per hour/3 min. per order) * 8 hours = 160 subs per day

There is a benefit to this change. Dave can now make 160 subs per day. This will provide the same benefit as hiring another worker. However, if Dave wants to increase output further, he will have to hire some additional staff.

REVIEW AND DISCUSSION QUESTIONS

1 Compare McDonald's old and current processes for making hamburgers. How valid is McDonald's claim that the new process will produce fresher hamburgers for the customer? Comparing McDonald's current process to the processes used by Burger King and Wendy's, which process would appear to produce the freshest hamburgers?

2 State in your own words what Little's law means. Describe an example that you have observed where Little's law applies.

3 Explain how having more work-in-process inventory can improve the efficiency of a process. How can this be bad?

4 Recently some operations management experts have begun insisting that simply minimizing process velocity, which actually means minimizing the time that it takes to process something through the system, is the single most important measure for improving a process. Can you think of a situation in which this might not be true?

PROBLEMS[4]

1 You are in a line at the bank drive-through and 10 cars are in front of you. You estimate that the clerk is taking about five minutes per car to serve. How long do you expect to wait in line?

2 A firm has redesigned its production process so that it now takes 10 hours for a unit to be made. Using the old process, it took 15 hours to make a unit. If the process makes one unit each hour on average and each unit is worth $1,500, what is the reduction in work-in-process value?

3 An enterprising student has set up an internship clearinghouse for business students. Each student who uses the service fills out a form and lists up to 10 companies that he or she would like to have contacted. The clearinghouse has a choice of two methods to use for processing the forms. The traditional method requires about 20 minutes to review the form and arrange the information in the proper order for processing. Once this setup is done, it takes only two minutes per company requested to complete the processing. The other alternative uses an optical scan/retrieve system, which takes only a minute to prepare but requires five minutes per company for completing the processing. If it costs about the same amount per minute for processing with either of the two methods, when should each be used?

4   Rockness Recycling refurbishes rundown business students. The process uses a moving belt, which carries each student through the five steps of the process in sequence. The five steps are as follows:

Step	Description	Time Required per Student
1	Unpack and place on belt	1.0 minute
2	Strip off bad habits	1.5 minutes
3	Scrub and clean mind	0.8 minute
4	Insert modern methods	1.0 minute
5	Polish and pack	1.2 minutes

One faculty member is assigned to each of these steps. Faculty members work a 40-hour week and rotate jobs each week. Mr. Rockness has been working on a contract from General Eclectic, which requires delivery of 2,000 refurbished students per week. A representative of the human resources department has just called complaining that the company hasn't been receiving the agreed-upon number of students. A check of finished goods inventory by Mr. Rockness reveals that there is no stock left. What is going on?

5   The bathtub theory of operations management is being promoted as the next breakthrough for global competitiveness. The factory is a bathtub with 50 gallons of capacity. The drain is the outlet to the market and can output three gallons per hour when wide open. The faucet is the raw material input and can let material in at a rate of four gallons per hour. Now, to test your comprehension of the intricacies of operations (assume the bathtub is empty to begin with):

a. Draw a diagram of the factory and determine the maximum rate at which the market can be served if all valves are set to maximum. What happens to the system over time?

b. Suppose that instead of a faucet, a five-gallon container is used for filling the bathtub (assume a full container is next to the tub to begin with); it takes two hours to refill the container and return it to the bathtub. What happens to the system over time?

6   A local market research firm has just won a contract for several thousand small projects involving data gathering and statistical analysis. In the past, the firm has assigned each project to a single member of its highly trained professional staff. This person would both gather and analyze the data. Using this approach, an experienced person can complete an average of 10 such projects in an eight-hour day.

The firm's management is thinking of assigning two people to each project in order to allow them to specialize and become more efficient. The process would require the data gatherer to fill out a matrix on the computer, check it, and transmit it to the statistical analysis program for the analyst to complete. Data can be gathered on one project while the analysis is being completed on another, but the analysis must be complete before the statistical analysis program can accept the new data. After some practice, the new process can be completed with a standard time of 20 minutes for the data gathering and 30 minutes for the analysis.

a. What is the production (output per hour) for each alternative? What is the productivity (output per labor hour)?

b. How long would it take to complete 1,000 projects with each alternative? What would be the labor content (total number of labor hours) for 1,000 projects for each alternative?

7   A processor makes two components, A and B, which are then packaged together as the final product (each product sold contains one A and one B). The processor can do only one component at a time: either it can make As or it can make Bs. There is a setup time when switching from A to B.

Current plans are to make 100 units of component A, then 100 units of component B, then 100 units of component A, then 100 units of component B, and so forth, where the setup and run times for each component are given below.

Component	Setup/Changeover Time	Run Time/Unit
A	5 minutes	0.2 minute
B	10 minutes	0.1 minute

Assume the packaging of the two components is totally automated and takes only two seconds per unit of the final product. This packaging time is small enough that you can ignore it. What is the average hourly output, in terms of the number of units of packaged product (which includes one component A and one component B)?

8   The following represents a process used to assemble a chair with an upholstered seat. Stations A, B, and C make the seat; stations J, K, and L assemble the chair frame; station X is where the two subassemblies are brought together; and some final tasks are completed in stations Y and Z. One worker is assigned to each of the stations. Generally there is no inventory kept anywhere in the system, although there is room for one unit between each of the stations that might be used for a brief amount of time.

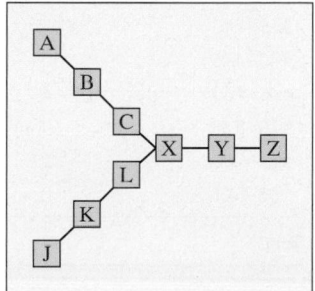

Given the following amount of work in seconds required at each station:

A	38	J	32	X	22
B	34	K	30	Y	18
C	35	L	34	Z	20

a. What is the possible daily output of this "process" if 8 hours of processing time is available each day?

b. Given your output rate in part *a*, what is the efficiency of the process?

c. What is the flow time of the process?

9   Wally's Widget Warehouse takes orders from 7 A.M. to 7 P.M. The manager wants to analyze the process and has provided the process flow diagram shown below. There are three steps required to ship a customer order. The first step is to take the order from a customer. The second step is to pick the order for the customer, and then they have to pack the order ready for shipping. Wally promises that every order placed today gets shipped tomorrow. That means that the picking and packing operations must finish all orders before they go home.

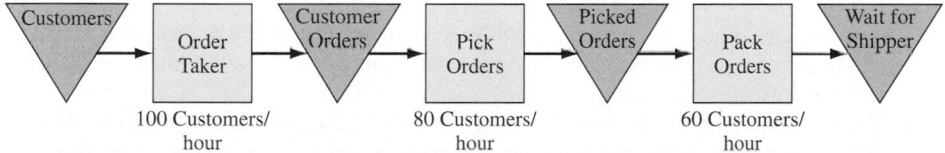

Wally wants to figure out the following.

a. What is the current maximum output of the process assuming that no one works overtime?

b. How long will the picking and packing operations have to work if we have a day where the order taker works at his maximum capacity?

c. Given *b*, what is the maximum number of orders waiting to be picked?

d. Given *b*, what is the maximum number of orders waiting to be packed?

e. If we double the packing capacity (from 60 to 120 orders per hour), what impact does this have on your answers in parts *b*, *c*, and *d*?

10 The National State Bank is trying to make sure that they have enough tellers to handle the Friday afternoon rush of workers wanting to cash their paychecks. They are only concerned

with the last hour of the day from 4:00 to 5:00 P.M. It takes 5 minutes per customer to be processed by the tellers. The average customer arrivals are shown in the table below.

TIME	CUSTOMERS ARRIVING
4:00–4:05	2
4:05–4:10	5
4:10–4:15	6
4:15–4:20	8
4:20–4:25	10
4:25–4:30	12
4:30–4:35	16
4:35–4:40	12
4:40–4:45	10
4:45–4:50	6
4:50–4:55	4
4:55–5:00	2
5:00–5:05	0
Total	93

The bank currently has 8 teller stations, and all are staffed during the Friday afternoon rush hour.
a. What is the current maximum output at the bank during rush hour?
b. Can the bank process all the customers by 5:00 P.M.?
c. What is the maximum waiting time for customers, and what time period does it occur in?

11   I-mart is a discount optical shop that can fill most prescription orders in around 1 hour. The management is analyzing the processes at the store. There currently is one person assigned to each task below. The optometrist assigned to task "B" takes an hour off for lunch and the other employees work the entire day.

TASK	TIME
A. Greet/register the patient	2 minutes/patient
B. Optometrist conducts eye exam	25 minutes/patient
C. Frame/lenses selection	20 minutes/patient
D. Glasses made (process can run 6 pairs of glasses at the same time)	60 minutes/patient
E. Final fitting	5 minutes/patient

For a typical 10-hour retail day (10 A.M.–8 P.M.), the manager would like to calculate the following:
a. What is the current maximum output of the process per day (assuming every patient requires glasses)?
b. If another person was added, where is the logical place?
c. What effect would a mail order lab (where the glasses are made off site and returned in 5–7 days) have on the process?

12   A quoting department for a custom publishing house can complete 4 quotes per day, and there are 20 quotes in various stages in the department. Applying Little's law, the current lead time for a quote is how many days?

13   A small barber shop has a single chair and an area for waiting, where only one person can be in the chair at a time, and no one leaves without getting their hair cut. So the system is roughly:

Entrance → Wait → Haircut → Exit

Assume customers arrive at the rate of 10 per hour and stay an average of 0.5 hour.
What is the average number of customers in the barber shop?

ADVANCED PROBLEM

14   Remember Mr. Rockness in Problem 4? He now retrains college professors. It is a much more challenging task but still involves five steps. He has worked hard to balance the line; however, there is a lot of variability. Each stage in the process now handles between one and six faculty

members per hour depending on how bad the case is. If there is some inventory available for every position (do not worry about the start-up), what is the expected output per hour? (Assume that each stage is independent and that it is equally likely that one, two, three, four, five, or six faculty members get processed each hour at each stage.)[5]

CASE: ANALYZING CASINO MONEY-HANDLING PROCESSES

Retrieving money from a mechanical slot machine is referred to as the *drop process.* The drop process begins with a security officer and the slot drop team leader obtaining the slot cabinet keys from the casino cashier's cage. Getting the keys takes about 15 minutes. The slot drop team consists of employees from the hard count coin room, security, and accounting. The slot drop leader, under the observation of a security officer and a person from accounting, actually removes the drop bucket from the slot machine cabinet. When the drop bucket is pulled from the slot cabinet, a tag with the proper slot machine number is placed on top of the coins to identify where that bucket came from when the weigh process begins. Retrieving the drop bucket takes about 10 minutes per slot machine. Once a cart is filled with buckets from 20 different slot machines, the drop team leader and security and accounting people deliver the buckets to the hard count room. The buckets are securely locked in the hard count room to await the start of the hard count process. Delivering and securing the buckets takes about 30 minutes per cart.

The hard count process is performed at a designated time known to gaming regulatory authorities. The hard count team first tests the weigh scale, which takes 10 minutes. The scale determines the dollar value, by denomination, for set weights of 10 and 25 pounds. These results are compared to calibration results, calculated when the scale was last serviced, to determine if a significant variance exists. If one does exist, the hard count supervisor must contact the contractor responsible for maintaining the scale and the controller's office. If no significant variance is found, the weigh process can continue.

Following the scale check, each drop bucket is emptied into the weigh scale holding hopper. Using information from the identification tag, the specific slot machine number from which the bucket originated is entered into the weigh scale computer. The weigh scale computer is programmed to convert the weight of coins, by denomination, into specific dollar values, which are recorded in the weigh journal along with the slot machine number. This weighing and recording process takes seven minutes per bucket. Once the scale has weighed the contents of the drop bucket, the coins automatically drop onto a conveyor belt, which transports them to wrapping machines. As the coins are wrapped, the rolls of coins drop onto another conveyor belt, which takes them to a canning station. Twenty-five silver dollars are wrapped in each roll at a rate of 10 rolls per minute.

At the canning station, the coin rolls are placed in metal or plastic cans that hold specific dollar amounts based on coin denomination. The cans are stacked to facilitate counting the wrapped coins. Silver dollar cans hold $1,000, or 40 rolls, and take five minutes to fill and stack. When the weigh process is completed, the weigh scale computer runs a summary report totaling the weight by denomination. These totals are recorded on the weigh/wrap verification report, which takes five minutes to produce.

When the wrap portion of the count is completed and all of the rolled coins have been canned and stacked, they are manually counted by denomination. These totals are also recorded on the weigh/wrap verification report. The variance in both dollar amounts and percentages, for each denomination, is calculated. Variances that exceed plus or minus 2 percent or are $1,000 or greater (whichever is less) must be investigated by the hard count supervisor, who writes an explanatory report. If no significant variances exist, all members of the hard count team sign the weigh/wrap verification report. To complete the hard count process, the casino cashier's cage is then notified that the slot drop is ready to be transferred into cage accountability. Manually counting and verifying the counts take on average two minutes per can.

In a process separate from the hard count, a cage cashier performs an independent count and verification, by denomination, of the wrap. If everything balances, the main bank cashier signs the weigh/wrap verification report, accepting the slot drop into cage accountability. It is at this point that the actual slot gross gaming revenue is recognized.

QUESTIONS

1 Draw a diagram of the drop process. How long should it take to empty 300 silver dollar slot machines?
2 Draw a diagram of the hard count process. How long should this process take to complete for 300 silver dollar slot machines? Assume that each slot machine has an average of 750 silver dollars when it is emptied.
3 The casino is considering the purchase of a second coin-wrapping machine. What impact would this have on the hard count process? Is this the most desirable machine to purchase?
4 What would be the impact of purchasing "electronic" slot machines that do not use coins?

CASE: KRISTEN'S COOKIE COMPANY (A)

You and your roommate are preparing to start Kristen's Cookie Company in your on-campus apartment. The company will provide fresh cookies to starving students late at night. You need to evaluate the preliminary design for the company's production process to figure out many variables, including what prices to charge, whether you will be able to make a profit, and how many orders to accept.

BUSINESS CONCEPT
Your idea is to bake fresh cookies to order, using any combination of ingredients that the buyer wants. The cookies will be ready for pickup at your apartment within an hour.

Several factors will set you apart from competing products such as store-bought cookies. First, your cookies will be completely fresh. You will not bake any cookies before receiving the order; therefore, the buyer will be getting cookies that are literally hot out of the oven.

Second, like Steve's Ice Cream,[6] you will have a variety of ingredients available to add to the basic dough, including chocolate chips, M&M's, chopped Heath bars, coconut, walnuts, and raisins. Buyers will telephone in their orders and specify which of these ingredients they want in their cookies. You guarantee completely fresh cookies. In short, you will have the freshest, most exotic cookies anywhere, available right on campus.

THE PRODUCTION PROCESS

Baking cookies is simple: mix all the ingredients in a food processor; spoon out the cookie dough onto a tray; put the cookies into the oven; bake them; take the tray of cookies out of the oven; let the cookies cool; and, finally, take the cookies off the tray and carefully pack them in a box. You and your roommate already own all the necessary capital equipment: one food processor, cookie trays, and spoons. Your apartment has a small oven that will hold one tray at a time. Your landlord pays for all the electricity. The variable costs, therefore, are merely the cost of the ingredients (estimated to be $0.60/dozen), the cost of the box in which the cookies are packed ($0.10 per box; each box holds a dozen cookies), and your time (what value do you place on your time?).

A detailed examination of the production process, which specifies how long each of the steps will take, follows. The first step is to take an order, which your roommate has figured out how to do quickly and with 100 percent accuracy. (Actually, you and your roommate devised a method using the campus electronic mail system to accept orders and to inform customers when their orders will be ready for pickup. Because this runs automatically on your personal computer, it does not take any of your time.) Therefore, this step will be ignored in further analysis.

You and your roommate have timed the necessary physical operations. The first physical production step is to wash out the mixing bowl from the previous batch, add all of the ingredients, and mix them in your food processor. The mixing bowls hold ingredients for up to 3 dozen cookies. You then dish up the cookies, one dozen at a time, onto a cookie tray. These activities take six minutes for the washing and mixing steps, regardless of how many cookies are being made in the batch. That is, to mix enough dough and ingredients for two dozen cookies takes the same six minutes as one dozen cookies. However, dishing up the cookies onto the tray takes two minutes per tray.

The next step, performed by your roommate, is to put the cookies in the oven and set the thermostat and timer, which takes about one minute. The cookies bake for the next nine minutes. So total baking time is 10 minutes, during the first minute of which your roommate is busy setting the oven. Because the oven holds only one tray, a second dozen takes an additional 10 minutes to bake.

Your roommate also performs the last steps of the process by first removing the cookies from the oven and putting them aside to cool for 5 minutes, then carefully packing them in a box and accepting payment. Removing the cookies from the oven takes only a negligible amount of time, but it must be done promptly. It takes two minutes to pack each dozen and about one minute to accept payment for the order.

That is the process for producing cookies by the dozen in Kristen's Cookie Company. As experienced bakers know, a few simplifications were made in the actual cookie production process.

For example, the first batch of cookies for the night requires preheating the oven. However, such complexities will be put aside for now. Begin your analysis by developing a process flow diagram of the cookie-making process.

KEY QUESTIONS TO ANSWER BEFORE YOU LAUNCH THE BUSINESS

To launch the business, you need to set prices and rules for accepting orders. Some issues will be resolved only after you get started and try out different ways of producing the cookies. Before you start, however, you at least want a preliminary plan, with as much as possible specified, so that you can do a careful calculation of how much time you will have to devote to this business each night, and how much money you can expect to make. For example, when you conduct a market survey to determine the likely demand, you will want to specify exactly what your order policies will be. Therefore, answering the following operational questions should help you:

1 How long will it take you to fill a rush order?
2 How many orders can you fill in a night, assuming you are open four hours each night?
3 How much of your own and your roommate's valuable time will it take to fill each order?
4 Because your baking trays can hold exactly one dozen cookies, you will produce and sell cookies by the dozen. Should you give any discount for people who order two dozen cookies, three dozen cookies, or more? If so, how much? Will it take you any longer to fill a two-dozen cookie order than a one-dozen cookie order?
5 How many food processors and baking trays will you need?
6 Are there any changes you can make in your production plans that will allow you to make better cookies or more cookies in less time or at lower cost? For example, is there a bottleneck operation in your production process that you can expand cheaply? What is the effect of adding another oven? How much would you be willing to pay to rent an additional oven?

PROBLEMS FOR FURTHER THOUGHT

1 What happens if you are trying to do this by yourself without a roommate?
2 Should you offer special rates for rush orders? Suppose you have just put a tray of cookies into the oven and someone calls up with a "crash priority" order for a dozen cookies of a different flavor. Can you fill the priority order while still fulfilling the order for the cookies that are already in the oven? If not, how much of a premium should you charge for filling the rush order?
3 When should you promise delivery? How can you look quickly at your order board (list of pending orders) and tell a caller when his or her order will be ready? How much of a safety margin for timing should you allow?
4 What other factors should you consider at this stage of planning your business?
5 Your product must be made to order because each order is potentially unique. If you decide to sell standard cookies instead, how should you change the production system? The order-taking process?

SUPER QUIZ

1   This is a part of an organization that takes inputs and transforms them into outputs.
2   This is the ratio of the time that a resource is activated relative to the time it is available for use.
3   This is when one or more activities stop because of a lack of work.
4   This is when an activity stops because there is no place to put the work that was just completed.
5   This is a step in a process that is the slowest compared to the other steps. This step limits the capacity of the process.
6   What is the difference between McDonald's old and current processes?
7   This refers to the fixed timing of the movement of items through a process.
8   This is when one company compares itself to another relative to operations performance.
9   This is the time that it takes a unit to flow through the process from beginning to end. It includes time waiting in queues and buffers.
10   The relationship between time and units in a process is call this.
11   What is the mathematical relationship between time and units in a process?
12   What is the major assumption about how a process is operating for Little's law to be valid.

1. A process 2. Utilization 3. Starving 4. Blocking 5. Bottleneck 6. Make-to-stock versus make-to-order
7. Pacing 8. Benchmarking 9. Flow time 10. Little's law 11. Inventory = Throughput rate × Flow time
12. Process is operating in steady state

SELECTED BIBLIOGRAPHY

Anupindai, R.; S. Chopra; S. D. Deshmukh; J. A. van Mieghem; and E. Zemel. *Managing Business Process Flows*. 2nd ed. Upper Saddle River, NJ: Prentice Hall, 2005.

Gray, A. E., and J. Leonard. "Process Fundamentals." Harvard Business School 9-696-023.

Jeston, J., and J. Nelis. *Business Process Management: Practical Guidelines to Successful Implementation*. Burlington, MA: Butterworth-Heinemann, 2006.

FOOTNOTES

1   Often the term *cycle time* is used to mean *flow time*. It is important to carefully determine how the term is being used in the context of the process being studied.
2   This example is similar to one given by A. E. Gray in "Capacity Analysis: Sample Problems," Harvard Business School 9-696-058.
3   B. Andersen, "Process Cycle Time Reduction," *Quality Progress*, July 1999, p. 120. For some additional guidelines for improving process, also see Chapter 17.
4   The authors are indebted to D. Clay Whybark of the University of North Carolina for contributing Problems 3–6 and Problem 11.
5   The idea for this problem came from an exercise developed by Dr. Eli Goldratt titled "The Great Manufacturing Crapshoot."
6   Steve's Ice Cream was started in the Boston area by a young entrepreneur to provide make-to-order ice cream, using mix-ins.

chapter 5A

JOB DESIGN AND WORK MEASUREMENT

BRIEFING OUTLINE

After reading this chapter you will:

1. Understand how job design impacts the type of worker needed and the motivation of the worker.

2. Describe how jobs can be made more interesting for workers.

3. Explain how worker performance can be tied to incentive pay.

4. Explain how performance standards are set using various methods.

The operations manager's job, by definition, deals with managing the personnel that create a firm's products and services. To say that this is a challenging job in today's complex environment is an understatement. The diversity of the workforce's cultural and educational background, coupled with frequent organization restructuring, calls for a much higher level of people management skills than has been required in even the recent past.

The objective in managing personnel is to obtain the highest productivity possible without sacrificing quality, service, or responsiveness. The operations manager uses job design techniques to structure the work so that it will meet both the physical and psychological needs of the human worker. Work measurement methods are used to determine the most efficient means of performing a given task, as well as to set reasonable standards for performing it. People are motivated by many things, only one of which is financial reward. Operations managers can structure such rewards not only to motivate consistently high performance but also to reinforce the most important aspects of the job.

JOB DESIGN DECISIONS

Job design may be defined as the function of specifying the work activities of an individual or group in an organizational setting. Its objective is to develop job structures that meet the requirements of the organization and its technology and that satisfy the jobholder's personal and individual requirements. Exhibit 5A.1 summarizes the decisions involved. These decisions are affected by the following trends:

Job design

Service

1. **Quality control as part of the worker's job.** Now often referred to as "quality at the source" (see Chapter 9), quality control is linked with the concept of empowerment. *Empowerment,* in turn, refers to workers being given authority to stop a production line if there is a quality problem, or to give a customer an on-the-spot refund if service was not satisfactory.
2. **Cross-training of workers to perform multiskilled jobs.** As companies downsize, the remaining workforce is expected to do more and different tasks.
3. **Employee involvement and team approaches to designing and organizing work.** This is a central feature in total quality management (TQM) and continuous improvement efforts. In fact, it is safe to say that virtually all TQM programs are team based.

Job Design Decisions   **exhibit 5A.1**

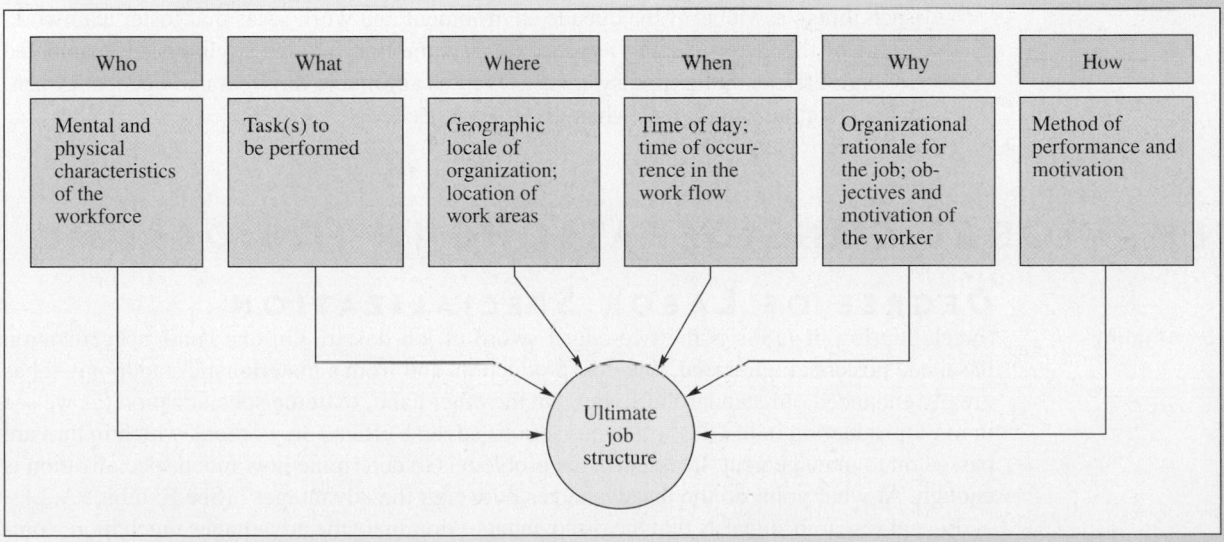

4. **"Informating" of ordinary workers through e-mail and the Internet, thereby expanding the nature of their work and their ability to do it.**   In this context, informating is more than just automating work—it is revising work's fundamental structure. Northeast Utilities' computer system, for example, can pinpoint a problem in a service area before the customer service representative answers the phone. The rep uses the computer to troubleshoot serious problems, to weigh probabilities that other customers in the area have been affected, and to dispatch repair crews before other calls are even received.

5. **Extensive use of temporary workers.**   Manpower, a company specializing in providing temporary employees, has over 4.4 million temporary employees worldwide on its payroll.

6. **Creation of "alternative workplaces" such as shared offices, telecommuting, and virtual offices to supplement or replace traditional office settings.**   These are used to increase productivity, reduce travel and real estate costs, and aid in recruiting and retaining employees. IBM, AT&T, and American Express are major proponents of the approach.[1]

7. **Automation of heavy manual work**.   Examples abound in both services (one-person trash pickup trucks) and manufacturing (robot spray painting on auto lines). These changes are driven by safety regulations as well as economics and personnel reasons.

8. **Organizational commitment to providing meaningful and rewarding jobs for all employees.** Companies featured on *Fortune* magazine's "100 Best Companies to Work For" use creative means to keep employees satisfied, and offer generous severance and compassion when cuts must be made (see **www .fortune.com** for the current list of companies).

SUSTAINABLE WORKPLACE

Sustainable workplace

9. **Development of the sustainable workplace.**   This most recent trend is a natural follow-up to item 8. A sustainable workplace fully supports the individual and the organization without compromising future generations. The characteristics of a sustainable workplace include the use of an integrated design process, collaborative development of the design with the occupants of the workplace, and use of renewable materials. The current focus is on the design of city office buildings to include such things as views of the outside environment and work areas that foster teamwork. Some of the energy-saving features are daytime lighting and skylights supplemented by high-efficiency lighting systems as well as automatic daylight and occupancy sensors, which turn lights off when they're not needed.

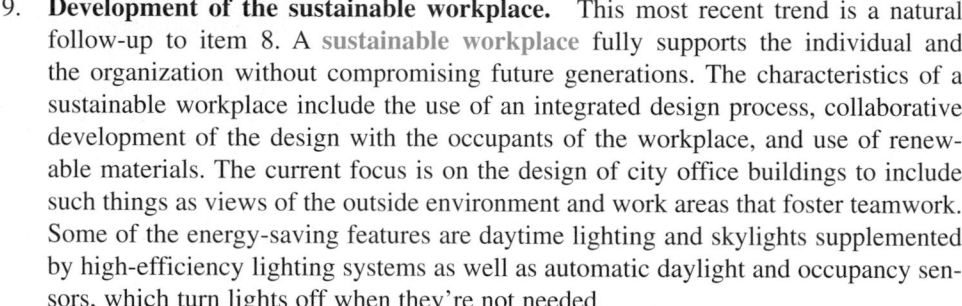

BEHAVIORAL CONSIDERATIONS IN JOB DESIGN

DEGREE OF LABOR SPECIALIZATION

Specialization of labor

Specialization of labor is the two-edged sword of job design. On one hand, specialization has made possible high-speed, low-cost production, and from a materialistic standpoint, it has greatly enhanced our standard of living. On the other hand, extreme specialization (as we see in mass-production industries) often has serious adverse effects on workers, which in turn are passed on to management. In essence, the problem is to determine how much specialization is enough. At what point do the disadvantages outweigh the advantages? (See Exhibit 5A.2.)

Recent research suggests that the disadvantages dominate the advantages much more commonly than was thought in the past. However, simply stating that, for purely humanitarian

Advantages and Disadvantages of Specialization of Labor

ADVANTAGES OF SPECIALIZATION	
TO MANAGEMENT	TO LABOR
1. Rapid training of the workforce	1. Little or no education required to obtain work
2. Ease in recruiting new workers	2. Ease in learning job
3. High output due to simple, repetitive work	
4. Low wages due to ease of substitutability of labor	
5. Close control over work flow and workloads	

DISADVANTAGES OF SPECIALIZATION	
TO MANAGEMENT	TO LABOR
1. Difficulty in controlling quality because no one has responsibility for entire product	1. Boredom stemming from repetitive nature of work
2. Worker dissatisfaction leading to hidden costs arising from turnover, absenteeism, tardiness, grievances, and intentional disruption of production process	2. Little gratification from work itself because of small contribution to each item
3. Reduced likelihood of improving the process because of workers' limited perspective	3. Little or no control over the work pace, leading to frustration and fatigue (in assembly-line situations)
4. Limited flexibility to change the production process to produce new or improved products	4. Little opportunity to progress to a better job because significant learning is rarely possible on fractionated work

reasons, specialization should be avoided is risky. The reason, of course, is that people differ in what they want from their work and what they are willing to put into it. Some workers prefer not to make decisions about their work, some like to daydream on the job, and others are simply not capable of performing more complex work. To improve the quality of jobs, leading organizations try different approaches to job design. Two popular contemporary approaches are job enrichment and sociotechnical systems.

JOB ENRICHMENT

Job enlargement generally entails adjusting a specialized job to make it more interesting to the job holder. A job is said to be enlarged *horizontally* if the worker performs a greater number or variety of tasks, and it is said to be enlarged *vertically* if the worker is involved in planning, organizing, and inspecting his or her own work. Horizontal job enlargement is intended to counteract oversimplification and to permit the worker to perform a "whole unit of work." Vertical enlargement (traditionally termed *job enrichment*) attempts to broaden workers' influence in the transformation process by giving them certain managerial powers over their own activities. Today, common practice is to apply both horizontal and vertical enlargement to a given job and refer to the total approach as job enrichment.

Job enrichment

The organizational benefits of job enrichment occur in both quality and productivity. Quality in particular improves dramatically because when individuals are responsible for their work output, they take ownership of it and simply do a better job. Also, because they have a broader understanding of the work process, they are more likely to catch errors and make corrections than if the job is narrowly focused. Productivity improvements also occur from job enrichment, but they are not as predictable or as large as the improvements in quality. The reason is that enriched work invariably contains a mix of tasks that (for manual labor) causes interruptions in rhythm and different motions when switching from one task to the next. This is not the case for specialized jobs.[2]

SOCIOTECHNICAL SYSTEMS

Consistent with the job enrichment philosophy but focusing more on the interaction between technology and the work group is the sociotechnical systems approach. This approach

Sociotechnical systems

attempts to develop jobs that adjust the needs of the production process technology to the needs of the worker and work group. The term was developed from studies of weaving mills in India and of coal mines in England in the early 1950s. These studies revealed that work groups could effectively handle many production problems better than management if they were permitted to make their own decisions on scheduling, work allocation among members, bonus sharing, and so forth. This was particularly true when variations in the production process required quick reactions by the group or when one shift's work overlapped with other shifts' work.

Since those pioneering studies, the sociotechnical approach has been applied in many countries—often under the heading of "autonomous work groups," "Japanese-style work groups," or employee involvement (EI) teams. Most major international service as well as manufacturing companies use work teams as the basic building block in so-called high employee involvement plants. The benefits of teams are similar to those of individual job enrichment: They provide higher quality and greater productivity (they often set higher production goals than general management), do their own support work and equipment maintenance, and have increased chances to make meaningful improvements.

Global

Service

One major conclusion from these applications is that the individual or work group requires a logically integrated pattern of work activities that incorporates the following job design principles:

1. **Task variety.** An attempt must be made to provide an optimal variety of tasks within each job. Too much variety can be inefficient for training and frustrating for the employee. Too little can lead to boredom and fatigue. The optimal level is one that allows the employee to rest from a high level of attention or effort while working on another task or, conversely, to stretch after periods of routine activity.
2. **Skill variety.** Research suggests that employees derive satisfaction from using a number of skill levels.
3. **Feedback.** There should be some means for informing employees quickly when they have achieved their targets. Fast feedback aids the learning process. Ideally, employees should have some responsibility for setting their own standards of quantity and quality.
4. **Task identity.** Sets of tasks should be separated from other sets of tasks by some clear boundary. Whenever possible, a group or individual employee should have responsibility for a set of tasks that is clearly defined, visible, and meaningful. In this way, work is seen as important by the group or individual undertaking it, and others understand and respect its significance.
5. **Task autonomy.** Employees should be able to exercise some control over their work. Areas of discretion and decision making should be available to them.

WORK MEASUREMENT AND STANDARDS

Work measurement

The fundamental purpose of work measurement is to set time standards for a job. Such standards are necessary for four reasons:

1. **To schedule work and allocate capacity.** All scheduling approaches require some estimate of how much time it takes to do the work being scheduled.
2. **To provide an objective basis for motivating the workforce and measuring workers' performance.** Measured standards are particularly critical where output-based incentive plans are employed.
3. **To bid for new contracts and to evaluate performance on existing ones.** Questions such as "Can we do it?" and "How are we doing?" presume the existence of standards.
4. **To provide benchmarks for improvement.** In addition to internal evaluation, benchmarking teams regularly compare work standards in their company with those of similar jobs in other organizations.

BREAKTHROUGH

USING WORK MEASUREMENT SOFTWARE AT NORTHWEST AIRLINES

Northwest Airlines (NWA) is facing myriad challenges due to record fuel prices, steep competition from low-cost carriers, and high labor costs. These challenges require restructuring NWA's business model to focus on cost reductions while maintaining customer service. NWA relies on its industrial engineering (IE) group to design and evaluate process improvement opportunities. In turn, the IE group relies on time studies to analyze and quantify process improvement opportunities. A basic tool used for this purpose is WorkStudy+, a software product developed by Quetech Ltd. of Canada.

One of the projects for which NWA uses WorkStudy+ is passenger throughput analyses of its seasonal Mexico stations. NWA was planning a significant flight schedule increase to one of its top leisure travel destinations in Mexico. The general manager of customer service wanted to ensure that the station would have the appropriate number of ticket counter positions available to handle the planned rise in passenger traffic so that passengers would not face long queues and wait times upon their arrival to the airport. In engineering terms, what is the throughput capacity per ticket counter position based on process constraints, and how can NWA ensure an acceptable service level for its passengers measured in queue length and wait time?

To solve these challenges, IE had to gather passenger check-in time and passenger arrival rate. Passenger check-in time is the amount of time it takes a customer service agent to check in a passenger or group of passengers for their flight. Passenger arrival rate is the number of passengers arriving at different time intervals before their flight departure. To collect the data, two different studies were developed using a PDA and WorkStudy+ software. "With this software, it is possible to create a study while flying to a location and to analyze the data on a laptop when flying back. This capability has greatly improved our project turnaround time," says NWA industrial engineer Victor Perazzoli.

After the data was collected and summarized, throughput capacity and passenger arrival rate were obtained. The results demonstrated unique differences in arrival rates between this location and other domestic NWA locations. Once quantified, the IE group constructed a model using data collected from WorkStudy+ to determine ticket-counter positions required to maintain the desired service levels of passenger queue length and passenger wait. Then different staffing and flight scenarios were analyzed to make appropriate recommendations aimed at improving the operational efficiency of the airline.

SOURCE: ADAPTED FROM QUETECH WEB SITE, www.quetech.com.

Work measurement and its resulting work standards have been controversial since Taylor's time. Much of this criticism has come from unions, which argue that management often sets standards that cannot be regularly achieved. (To counter this, in some contracts, the industrial engineer who sets the standard must demonstrate that he or she can do the job over a representative period of time at the rate that was set.) There is also the argument that workers who find a better way of doing the job get penalized by having a revised rate set. (This is commonly called *rate cutting*.)

Despite these criticisms, work measurement and standards have proved effective. Much depends on sociotechnical aspects of the work. Where the job requires work groups to function as teams and create improvements, worker-set standards often make sense. On the other hand, where the job really boils down to doing the work quickly, with little need for creativity (such as delivering packages for UPS), tightly engineered, professionally set standards are appropriate.

Service

WORK MEASUREMENT TECHNIQUES

There are four basic techniques for measuring work and setting standards. These consist of two direct observational methods and two indirect methods: The direct methods are **time study**, which uses a stopwatch to time the work, and **work sampling**, which entails recording random observations of a person or teams at work. The two indirect methods are **predetermined motion-time data systems (PMTS)**, which sum data from tables of generic movement times developed in the laboratory to arrive at a time for the job

Time study

Work sampling

Predetermined motion-time data systems (PMTS)

Elemental data

(the most widely used are proprietary systems—Methods Time Measurement [MTM] and Most Work Measurement System [MOST]), and **elemental data**, which sums times from a database of similar combinations of movements to arrive at job time. The choice of techniques depends on the level of detail desired and the nature of the work itself. Highly detailed, repetitive work usually calls for time study and predetermined motion-time data analysis. When work is done in conjunction with fixed-processing-time equipment, elemental data are often used to reduce the need for direct observation. When work is infrequent or entails a long cycle time, work sampling is the tool of choice. (See box "What the Pros Say. . . About Work Measurement Applications in Retailing" for an example of how the different techniques are used in a service setting.)

TIME STUDY

We now turn to a discussion of the technical details of time study. A time study is generally made with a stopwatch, either on the spot or by analyzing a videotape for the job. The job or task to be studied is separated into measurable parts or elements, and each element is timed individually.

Some general rules for breaking down the elements are

1. Define each work element to be short in duration but long enough so that it can be timed with a stopwatch and the time can be written down.
2. If the operator works with equipment that runs separately (meaning the operator performs a task and the equipment runs independently), separate the actions of the operator and of the equipment into different elements.
3. Define any delays by the operator or equipment into separate elements.

Work measurement pioneer Frank Gilbreth holds a physical model of arm motions used to analyze assembly tasks.

After a number of repetitions, the collected times are averaged. (The standard deviation may be computed to give a measure of variance in the performance times.) The averaged times for each element are added, yielding the performance time for the operator. However, to make this operator's time usable for all workers, a measure of speed or *performance rating* must be included to "normalize" the job. The application of a rating factor gives what is called **normal time**. For example, if an operator performs a task in two minutes and the time-study analyst estimates her to be performing about 20 percent faster than normal, the operator's performance rating would be 1.2, or 120 percent of normal. The normal time would be computed as 2 minutes × 1.2, or 2.4 minutes. In equation form,

Normal time = Observed performance time per unit × Performance rating

Normal time

In this example, denoting normal time by *NT,*

$$NT = 2(1.2) = 2.4 \text{ minutes}$$

When an operator is observed for a period of time, the number of units produced during this time, along with the performance rating, gives

$$NT = \frac{\text{Time worked}}{\text{Number of units produced}} \times \text{Performance rating}$$

Standard time is derived by adding to normal time allowances for personal needs (such as washroom and coffee breaks), unavoidable work delays (such as equipment breakdown or lack of materials), and worker fatigue (physical or mental). Two such equations are

Standard time

$$\text{Standard time} = \text{Normal time} + (\text{Allowances} \times \text{Normal time})$$

or

$$ST = NT\,(1 + \text{Allowances}) \qquad\qquad \text{[5A.1]}$$

and

$$ST = \frac{NT}{1 - \text{Allowances}} \qquad\qquad \text{[5A.2]}$$

Equation (5A.1) is most often used in practice. If one presumes that allowances should be applied to the total work period, then equation (5A.2) is the correct one. To illustrate, suppose that the normal time to perform a task is one minute and that allowances for personal needs, delays, and fatigue total 15 percent; then by equation (5A.1)

$$ST = 1(1 + 0.15) = 1.15 \text{ minutes}$$

In an eight-hour day, a worker would produce $8 \times 60/1.15$, or 417 units. This implies 417 minutes working and $480 - 417$ (or 63) minutes for allowances.

With equation (5A.2),

$$ST = \frac{1}{1 - 0.15} = 1.18 \text{ minutes}$$

In the same eight-hour day, $8 \times 60/1.18$ (or 408) units are produced with 408 working minutes and 72 minutes for allowances. Depending on which equation is used, there is a difference of nine minutes in the daily allowance time.

EXAMPLE 5A.1: Time Study for a Four-Element Job

Exhibit 5A.3 shows a time study of 10 cycles of a four-element job. For each element, there is a space for the watch readings that are recorded in 100ths of a minute. Space also is provided for summarizing the data and applying a performance rating.

Step by Step

SOLUTION

The value of $\bar{T}$ is obtained by averaging the observed data. *PR* denotes the performance rating and is multiplied by $\bar{T}$ to obtain the normal time (*NT*) for each element. The normal time for the job is the sum of the element normal times. The standard time, calculated according to equation (5A.1), is given at the bottom of Exhibit 5A.3. ●

exhibit 5A.3   Time-Study Observation Sheet

<table>
<tr><td colspan="18" align="center">Time Study Observation Sheet</td></tr>
<tr><td colspan="2">Identification of Operation</td><td colspan="10" align="center">ASSEMBLE 24" × 36" CHART BLANKS</td><td colspan="6">Date <u>10/9</u></td></tr>
<tr><td colspan="2">Began Timing: 9:26
Ended Timing: 9:32</td><td colspan="4">Operator 109</td><td colspan="4">Approval BgR</td><td colspan="6">Observer f.D.T.</td></tr>
<tr><td colspan="2" rowspan="2">Element Description and
Breakpoint</td><td colspan="10" align="center">Cycles</td><td colspan="4" align="center">Summary</td></tr>
<tr><td>1
0.00</td><td>2</td><td>3</td><td>4</td><td>5</td><td>6</td><td>7</td><td>8</td><td>9</td><td>10</td><td>ΣT</td><td>$\bar{T}$</td><td>PR</td><td>NT</td></tr>
<tr><td>1</td><td>Fold over end
(grasp stapler)</td><td>.07</td><td>.07</td><td>.05</td><td>.07</td><td>.09</td><td>.06</td><td>.05</td><td>.08</td><td>.08</td><td>.06</td><td>.68</td><td>.07</td><td>.90</td><td>.06</td></tr>
<tr><td></td><td></td><td>.07</td><td>.61</td><td>.14</td><td>.67</td><td>.24</td><td>.78</td><td>.33</td><td>.88</td><td>.47</td><td>.09</td><td></td><td></td><td></td><td></td></tr>
<tr><td>2</td><td>Staple five times
(drop stapler)</td><td>.16</td><td>.14</td><td>.14</td><td>.15</td><td>.16</td><td>.16</td><td>.14</td><td>.17</td><td>.14</td><td>.15</td><td>1.51</td><td>.15</td><td>1.05</td><td>.16</td></tr>
<tr><td></td><td></td><td>.23</td><td>.75</td><td>.28</td><td>.82</td><td>.40</td><td>.94</td><td>.47</td><td>.05</td><td>.61</td><td>.24</td><td></td><td></td><td></td><td></td></tr>
<tr><td>3</td><td>Bend and insert wire
(drop pliers)</td><td>.22</td><td>.25</td><td>.22</td><td>.25</td><td>.23</td><td>.23</td><td>.21</td><td>.26</td><td>.25</td><td>.24</td><td>2.36</td><td>.24</td><td>1.00</td><td>.24</td></tr>
<tr><td></td><td></td><td>.45</td><td>.00</td><td>.50</td><td>.07</td><td>.63</td><td>.17</td><td>.68</td><td>.31</td><td>.86</td><td>.48</td><td></td><td></td><td></td><td></td></tr>
<tr><td>4</td><td>Dispose of finished chart
(touch next sheet)</td><td>.09</td><td>.09</td><td>.10</td><td>.08</td><td>.09</td><td>.11</td><td>.12</td><td>.08</td><td>.17</td><td>.08</td><td>1.01</td><td>.10</td><td>.90</td><td>.09</td></tr>
<tr><td></td><td></td><td>.54</td><td>.09</td><td>.60</td><td>.15</td><td>.72</td><td>.28</td><td>.80</td><td>.39</td><td>.03</td><td>.56</td><td></td><td colspan="3" rowspan="2">0.55
normal
minute
for
cycle</td></tr>
<tr><td>5</td><td></td><td></td><td></td><td></td><td></td><td></td><td></td><td></td><td></td><td></td><td></td><td></td></tr>
<tr><td>6</td><td></td><td></td><td></td><td></td><td></td><td></td><td></td><td></td><td></td><td></td><td></td><td></td><td></td><td></td><td></td></tr>
<tr><td>10</td><td></td><td></td><td></td><td></td><td></td><td></td><td></td><td></td><td></td><td></td><td></td><td></td><td></td><td></td><td></td></tr>
<tr><td colspan="18">Normal cycle time <u>0.55</u> + Allowance <u>(0.55 × 0.143) or 0.08</u> = Std. time <u>0.63 min./pc.</u></td></tr>
</table>

How many observations are enough? Time study is really a sampling process; that is, we take relatively few observations as being representative of many subsequent cycles to be performed by the worker. Based on a great deal of analysis and experience, Benjamin Niebel's table shown in Exhibit 5A.4 indicates that "enough" is a function of cycle length and number of repetitions of the job over a one-year planning period.

WORK SAMPLING

A second common technique for measuring a job is called work sampling. As the name suggests, work sampling involves observing a portion or sample of the work activity. Then, based on the findings in this sample, statements can be made about the activity. For example, if we were to observe a fire department rescue squad at 100 random times during the day and found it was involved in a rescue mission for 30 of the 100 times (en route, on site, or returning from a call), we would estimate that the rescue squad spends 30 percent of its time directly on rescue mission calls. (The time it takes to make an observation depends on what is being observed. Many times, only a glance is needed to determine the activity, and the majority of studies require only several seconds' observation.)

Observing an activity even 100 times may not, however, provide the accuracy desired in the estimate. To refine this estimate, three main issues must be decided. (These points are discussed later in this section, along with an example.)

1. What level of statistical confidence is desired in the results?
2. How many observations are necessary?
3. Precisely when should the observations be made?

The three primary applications for work sampling are

1. Ratio delay to determine the activity-time percentage for personnel or equipment. For example, management may be interested in the amount of time a machine is running or idle.

Guide to Number of Cycles to Be Observed in a Time Study

WHEN TIME PER CYCLE IS MORE THAN	MINIMUM NUMBER OF CYCLES OF STUDY (ACTIVITY)		
	OVER 10,000 PER YEAR	1,000–10,000	UNDER 1,000
8 hours	2	1	1
3	3	2	1
2	4	2	1
1	5	3	2
48 minutes	6	3	2
30	8	4	3
20	10	5	4
12	12	6	5
8	15	8	6
5	20	10	8
3	25	12	10
2	30	15	12
1	40	20	15
0.7	50	25	20
0.5	60	30	25
0.3	80	40	30
0.2	100	50	40
0.1	120	60	50
Under 0.1	140	80	60

SOURCE: B. W. NIEBEL, *MOTION AND TIME STUDY*, 9TH ED. (BURR RIDGE, IL: RICHARD D. IRWIN, 1993), P. 390. THE MCGRAW-HILL COMPANIES, INC. USED WITH PERMISSION.

2. Performance measurement to develop a performance index for workers. When the amount of work time is related to the quantity of output, a measure of performance is developed. This is useful for periodic performance evaluation.
3. Time standards to obtain the standard time for a task. When work sampling is used for this purpose, however, the observer must be experienced because he or she must attach a performance rating to the observations.

The number of observations required in a work-sampling study can be fairly large, ranging from several hundred to several thousand, depending on the activity and desired degree of accuracy. Although the number can be computed from formulas, the easiest way is to refer to a table such as Exhibit 5A.5, which gives the number of observations needed for a 95 percent confidence level in terms of absolute error. *Absolute error* is the actual range of the observations. For example, if a clerk is idle 10 percent of the time and the designer of the study is satisfied with a 2.5 percent range (meaning that the true percentage lies between 7.5 and 12.5 percent), the number of observations required for the work sampling is 576. A 2 percent error (or an interval of 8 to 12 percent) would require 900 observations.

Five steps are involved in making a work-sampling study:

1. Identify the specific activity or activities that are the main purpose for the study. For example, determine the percentage of time that equipment is working, idle, or under repair.
2. Estimate the proportion of time of the activity of interest to the total time (e.g., that the equipment is working 80 percent of the time). These estimates can be made from the analyst's knowledge, past data, reliable guesses from others, or a pilot work-sampling study.

Number of Observations Required for a Given Absolute Error at Various Values of p, with 95 Percent Confidence Level

PERCENTAGE OF TOTAL TIME OCCUPIED BY ACTIVITY OR DELAY, p	ABSOLUTE ERROR					
	±1.0%	±1.5%	±2.0%	±2.5%	±3.0%	±3.5%
1 or 99	396	176	99	63	44	32
2 or 98	784	348	196	125	87	64
3 or 97	1,164	517	291	186	129	95
4 or 96	1,536	683	384	246	171	125
5 or 95	1,900	844	475	304	211	155
6 or 94	2,256	1,003	564	361	251	184
7 or 93	2,604	1,157	651	417	289	213
8 or 92	2,944	1,308	736	471	327	240
9 or 91	3,276	1,456	819	524	364	267
10 or 90	3,600	1,600	900	576	400	294
11 or 89	3,916	1,740	979	627	435	320
12 or 88	4,224	1,877	1,056	676	469	344
13 or 87	4,524	2,011	1,131	724	503	369
14 or 86	4,816	2,140	1,204	771	535	393
15 or 85	5,100	2,267	1,275	816	567	416
16 or 84	5,376	2,389	1,344	860	597	439
17 or 83	5,644	2,508	1,411	903	627	461
18 or 82	5,904	2,624	1,476	945	656	482
19 or 81	6,156	2,736	1,539	985	684	502
20 or 80	6,400	2,844	1,600	1,024	711	522
21 or 79	6,636	2,949	1,659	1,062	737	542
22 or 78	6,864	3,050	1,716	1,098	763	560
23 or 77	7,084	3,148	1,771	1,133	787	578
24 or 76	7,296	3,243	1,824	1,167	811	596
25 or 75	7,500	3,333	1,875	1,200	833	612
26 or 74	7,696	3,420	1,924	1,231	855	628
27 or 73	7,884	3,504	1,971	1,261	876	644
28 or 72	8,064	3,584	2,016	1,290	896	658
29 or 71	8,236	3,660	2,059	1,318	915	672
30 or 70	8,400	3,733	2,100	1,344	933	686
31 or 69	8,556	3,803	2,139	1,369	951	698
32 or 68	8,704	3,868	2,176	1,393	967	710
33 or 67	8,844	3,931	2,211	1,415	983	722
34 or 66	8,976	3,989	2,244	1,436	997	733
35 or 65	9,100	4,044	2,275	1,456	1,011	743
36 or 64	9,216	4,096	2,304	1,475	1,024	753
37 or 63	9,324	4,144	2,331	1,492	1,036	761
38 or 62	9,424	4,188	2,356	1,508	1,047	769
39 or 61	9,516	4,229	2,379	1,523	1,057	777
40 or 60	9,600	4,266	2,400	1,536	1,067	784
41 or 59	9,676	4,300	2,419	1,548	1,075	790
42 or 58	9,744	4,330	2,436	1,559	1,083	795
43 or 57	9,804	4,357	2,451	1,569	1,089	800
44 or 56	9,856	4,380	2,464	1,577	1,095	804
45 or 55	9,900	4,400	2,475	1,584	1,099	808
46 or 54	9,936	4,416	2,484	1,590	1,104	811
47 or 53	9,964	4,428	2,491	1,594	1,107	813
48 or 52	9,984	4,437	2,496	1,597	1,109	815
49 or 51	9,996	4,442	2,499	1,599	1,110	816
50	10,000	4,444	2,500	1,600	1,111	816

Note: Number of observations is obtained from the formula $E = Z \sqrt{\dfrac{p(1-p)}{N}}$ and the required sample (N) is $N = \dfrac{Z^2 p(1-p)}{E^2}$

where E = Absolute error

$\quad p$ = Percentage occurrence of activity or delay being measured

$\quad N$ = Number of random observations (sample size)

$\quad Z$ = Number of standard deviations to give desired confidence level (e.g., for 90 percent confidence, Z = 1.65; for 95 percent, Z = 1.96; for 99 percent, Z = 2.23). In this table Z = 2.

3. State the desired accuracy in the study results.
4. Determine the specific times when each observation is to be made.
5. At two or three intervals during the study period, recompute the required sample size by using the data collected thus far. Adjust the number of observations if appropriate.

The number of observations to be taken in a work-sampling study is usually divided equally over the study period. Thus, if 500 observations are to be made over a 10-day period, observations are usually scheduled at 500/10, or 50 per day. Each day's observations are then assigned a specific time by using a random number table.

EXAMPLE 5A.2: Work Sampling Applied to Nursing

There has been a long-standing argument that a large amount of nurses' hospital time is spent on nonnursing activities. This, the argument goes, creates an apparent shortage of well-trained nursing personnel, wastes talent, hinders efficiency, and increases hospital costs because nurses' wages are the highest single cost in the operation of a hospital. Further, pressure is growing for hospitals and hospital administrators to contain costs. With that in mind, let us use work sampling to test the hypothesis that a large portion of nurses' time is spent on nonnursing duties.

Service

Step by Step

SOLUTION

Assume at the outset that we have made a list of all the activities that are part of nursing and will make our observations in only two categories: nursing and nonnursing activities. Actually, there is much debate on what constitutes nursing activity. For instance, is talking to a patient a nursing duty? (An expanded study could list all nursing activities to determine the portion of time spent in each.) Therefore, when we observe during the study and find the nurse performing one of the duties on the nursing list, we simply place a tally mark in the nursing column. If we observe anything besides nursing activities, we place a tally mark in the nonnursing column.

We can now plan the study. Assume that we (or the nursing supervisor) estimate that nurses spend 60 percent of their time in nursing activities. Assume that we would like to be 95 percent confident that findings of our study are within the absolute error range of ±3 percent; that is, if our study shows nurses spend 60 percent of their time on nursing duties, we want to be 95 percent confident that the true percentage lies between 57 and 63 percent. From Exhibit 5A.5, we find that 1,067 observations are required for 60 percent activity time and ±3 percent error. If our study is to take place over 10 days, we start with 107 observations per day.

To determine when each day's observations are to be made, we assign specific numbers to each minute and use a random number table to set up a schedule. If the study extends over an eight-hour shift, we can assign numbers to correspond to each consecutive minute. For this study, it is likely the night shift would be run separately because nighttime nursing duties are considerably different from daytime duties. Exhibit 5A.6A shows the assignment of numbers to corresponding minutes. For simplicity, because each number corresponds to one minute, a three-number scheme is used, with the second and third numbers corresponding to the minute of the hour. A number of other schemes would also be appropriate. If a number of studies are planned, a computer program may be used to generate a randomized schedule for the observation times.

If we refer to a random number table and list three-digit numbers, we can assign each number to a time. The random numbers in Exhibit 5A.6B demonstrate the procedure for seven observations.

This procedure is followed to generate 107 observation times, and the times are rearranged chronologically for ease in planning. Rearranging the times determined in Exhibit 6A.6B gives the total observations per day shown in Exhibit 5A.6C (for our sample of seven).

To be perfectly random in this study, we should also "randomize" the nurse we observe each time. (The use of various nurses minimizes the effect of bias.) In the study, our first observation is made at 7:13 A.M. for Nurse X. We walk into the nurse's area and, on seeing the nurse, check either a nursing or a nonnursing activity. Each observation need be only long enough to determine the class of activity—in

exhibit 5A.6

Sampling Plan for Nurses' Activities
A. Assignment of Numbers to Corresponding Minutes
B. Determination of Observation Times
C. Observation Schedule

A.

TIME	ASSIGNED NUMBERS
7:00–7:59 A.M.	100–159
8:00–8:59 A.M.	200–259
9:00–9:59 A.M.	300–359
10:00–10:59 A.M.	400–459
11:00–11:59 A.M.	500–559
12:00–12:59 P.M.	600–659
1:00–1:59 P.M.	700–759
2:00–2:59 P.M.	800–859

B.

RANDOM NUMBERS	CORRESPONDING TIME FROM THE LIST IN 5A.6A
669	Nonexistent
831	2:31 P.M.
555	11:55 A.M.
470	Nonexistent
113	7:13 A.M.
080	Nonexistent
520	11:20 A.M.
204	8:04 A.M.
732	1:32 P.M.
420	10:20 A.M.

C.

OBSERVATION	SCHEDULE TIME	NURSING ACTIVITY(✓)	NONNURSING ACTIVITY(✓)
1	7:13 A.M.		
2	8:04 A.M.		
3	10:20 A.M.		
4	11:20 A.M.		
5	11:55 A.M.		
6	1:32 P.M.		
7	2:31 P.M.		

most cases only a glance is needed. At 8:04 A.M. we observe Nurse Y. We continue in this way to the end of the day and the 107 observations. At the end of the second day (and 214 observations), we decide to check for the adequacy of our sample size.

Let us say we made 150 observations of nurses working and 64 of them not working, which gives 70.1 percent working. From Exhibit 5A.5, this corresponds to 933 observations. Because we have already taken 214 observations, we need take only 719 over the next eight days, or 90 per day.

When the study is half over, another check should be made. For instance, if days 3, 4, and 5 showed 55, 59, and 64 working observations, the cumulative data would give 328 working observations of a total 484, or a 67.8 percent working activity. For a ±3 percent error, Exhibit 5A.5 shows the sample size to be about 967, leaving 483 to be made—at 97 per day—for the following five days. Another computation should be made before the last day to see if another adjustment is required. If after the 10th day several more observations are indicated, these can be made on day 11.

If at the end of the study we find that 66 percent of nurses' time is involved with what has been defined as nursing activity, there should be an analysis to identify the remaining 34 percent. Approximately 12 to 15 percent is justifiable for coffee breaks and personal needs, which leaves 20 to 22 percent of the time that must be justified and compared to what the industry considers ideal levels of nursing activity. To identify the nonnursing activities, a more detailed breakdown could have been originally built into the sampling plan. Otherwise, a follow-up study may be in order. ●

Deriving a Time Standard Using Work Sampling

INFORMATION	SOURCE OF DATA	DATA FOR ONE DAY
Total time expended by operator (working time and idle time)	Computer payroll system	480 min.
Number of parts produced	Inspection department	420 pieces
Working time in percent	Work sampling	85%
Idle time in percent	Work sampling	15%
Average performance index	Work sampling	110%
Total allowances	Company time-study manual	15%

$$\text{Standard time per piece} = \frac{\left(\begin{array}{c}\text{Total time}\\ \text{in minutes}\end{array}\right) \times \left(\begin{array}{c}\text{Working time}\\ \text{proportion}\end{array}\right) \times \left(\begin{array}{c}\text{Performance}\\ \text{index}\end{array}\right)}{\text{Total number of pieces produced}} \times \frac{1}{1 - \text{Allowances}}$$

$$= \left(\frac{480 \times 0.85 \times 1.10}{420}\right) \times \left(\frac{1}{1 - 0.15}\right) = 1.26 \text{ minutes}$$

As mentioned earlier, work sampling can be used to set time standards. To do this, the analyst must record the subject's performance rate (or index) along with working observations. Exhibit 5A.7 gives a manufacturing example that demonstrates how work sampling can be used for calculating standard time.

WORK SAMPLING COMPARED TO TIME STUDY

Work sampling offers several advantages:

1. Several work-sampling studies may be conducted simultaneously by one observer.
2. The observer need not be a trained analyst unless the purpose of the study is to determine a time standard.
3. No timing devices are required.
4. Work of a long cycle time may be studied with fewer observer hours.
5. The duration of the study is longer, which minimizes effects of short-period variations.
6. The study may be temporarily delayed at any time with little effect.
7. Because work sampling needs only instantaneous observations (made over a longer period), the operator has less chance to influence the findings by changing his or her work method.

When the cycle time is short, time study is more appropriate than work sampling. One drawback of work sampling is that it does not provide as complete a breakdown of elements as time study. Another difficulty with work sampling is that observers, rather than following a random sequence of observations, tend to develop a repetitive route of travel. This may allow the time of the observations to be predictable and thus invalidate the findings. A third factor—a potential drawback—is that the basic assumption in work sampling is that all observations pertain to the same static system. If the system is in the process of change, work sampling may give misleading results.

BREAKTHROUGH

LINKING STANDARDS AND INCENTIVES AT THE GAP DISTRIBUTION CENTERS

Fashion retailer The Gap, Inc., believes strongly in the value of engineered labor standards, which have been implemented in some Gap distribution centers for more than a decade. The retailer has engineered labor standards in place for receiving, stocking, order filling, and shipping. These standards "are our number one means of communication" with warehouse associates, explains Jay Ninah, senior planning engineer for The Gap. Reports on individual and group performance are posted weekly and associates meet with their supervisors on a monthly basis to discuss their performance. As a result, associates always know what level of performance is expected of them and how their individual performance compares to the standard.

Posting individual as well as group performance data keeps with The Gap's open-book policy, Ninah says. "It's not there to intimidate anyone, but to share our findings. It also creates an expectation that the standards are correctly set. If 85 percent to 90 percent are achieving the standard, those not meeting the standard can determine whether they're using a method that's not the best one." The Gap coaches based on its standards. Ninah states, "As we identify lower-performing individuals, we have a structured coaching process," whereby supervisors work with associates on the areas they need to improve. Associates have an extra push to improve their work, thanks to an incentive program tied to performance. The program was pioneered last year, Ninah says, and is getting a good response from associates. "Instead of giving an across-the-board increase, we give it based on performance," he says.

GLOBAL STANDARDS, LOCAL APPLICATION

The Gap's distribution network is made up of 18 facilities that range from brand-new warehouses with the latest technology to others that are 20 years old. To make sure that the labor standards are appropriate for each facility, The Gap's central engineering group in Erlanger, Kentucky, creates global standards. These are then localized to fit each distribution center by engineers that work in that facility. Most of The Gap's labor standards are derived largely by using predetermined labor standards using the MOST system developed by H. B. Maynard Co., Ninah says. They are then validated with stopwatch studies. A handful of standards not included in the predetermined time measures have to be completely developed by the engineering staff.

STANDARDS TO BUILD ON

The standards are a key planning and scheduling tool for The Gap and have proven to be very valuable when setting up new distribution centers. "It gives us a good gauge of how many people we need to hire," Ninah reports. They also use the labor standards to track a new facility's learning curve. "We're able to see how long it takes a new distribution center to get up to speed," he says, and for associates to learn their jobs. The standards have proven to be a powerful communication tool for new facilities. The engineering staff develops labor standards for a new distribution center before it opens. The measures enable associates to "understand what's expected of them, and where they are with respect to where they should be," Ninah says. "We used to expect a six- to eight-month learning curve. Now, it's about half that."

SOURCE: MODIFIED FROM DISTRIBUTION CENTER MANAGEMENT 2002, ALEXANDER COMMUNICATIONS GROUP, INC., www.distributiongroup.com.

SUMMARY

Many people consider job design and work measurement of minor importance to modern businesses, but doing a poor job in these activities can sabotage the most sophisticated operations and marketing strategies. Relative to the range of application, the use of work study techniques is often a more cost-effective approach to continuous improvement than using such currently popular approaches as lean production and Six Sigma. This outcome is even more likely for small companies where having a skilled work study analyst can save the time and effort required to train worker improvement teams to perform job design and work measurement studies themselves.

KEY TERMS

Job design The function of specifying the work activities of an individual or group in an organizational setting.

Sustainable workplace A workplace that fully supports the organization without compromising future generations.

Specialization of labor Simple, repetitive jobs are assigned to each worker.

Job enrichment Specialized work is made more interesting by giving the worker a greater variety of tasks or by getting a worker involved in planning, organization, and inspection.

Sociotechnical systems A philosophy that focuses on the interaction between technology and the work group. The approach attempts to develop jobs that adjust the production process technology to the needs of the worker and work group.

Work measurement Job analysis for the purpose of setting time standards.

Time study Separation of a job into measurable parts, with each element timed individually. The individual times are then combined, and allowances are added to calculate a standard time.

Work sampling Analyzing a work activity by observing an activity at random times. Statements about how time is spent during the activity are made from these observations.

Predetermined motion-time data systems (PMTS) Systems for deriving a time for a job by summing data from tables of generic movement times developed in the laboratory.

Elemental data Used to derive a job time by summing times from a database of similar combinations of movements.

Normal time The time that a normal operator would be expected to take to complete a job without the consideration of allowances.

Standard time Calculated by taking the normal time and adding allowances for personal needs, unavoidable work delays, and worker fatigue.

FORMULA REVIEW

Standard time

$$ST = NT(1 + \text{Allowances})$$ Assumes that allowances are added to normal time.   [5A.1]

$$ST = \frac{NT}{1 - \text{Allowances}}$$ Assumes that allowances are applied to the total work period.   [5A.2]

SOLVED PROBLEMS

SOLVED PROBLEM 1

Brandon is very organized and wants to plan his day perfectly. To do this, he has his friend Kelly time his daily activities. Here are the results of her timing Brandon on polishing two pairs of black shoes using the snapback method of timing. What is the standard time for polishing two pairs? (Assume a 5 percent allowance factor for Brandon to put something mellow on his iPod. Account for noncyclically recurring elements by dividing their observed times by the total number of cycles observed.)

| ELEMENT | OBSERVED TIMES | | | | PERFORMANCE RATING | NT |
	1	2	3	4		
Get shoeshine kit	0.50				125%	
Polish shoes	0.94	0.85	0.80	0.81	110	
Put away kit				0.75	80	

Solution

	ΣT	$\bar{T}$	PERFORMANCE RATING	NT
Get shoeshine kit	0.50	0.50/2 = 0.25	125%	0.31
Polish shoes (2 pairs)	3.40	3.40/2 = 1.70	110	1.87
Put away kit	0.75	0.75/2 = 0.375	80	0.30
Normal time for one pair of shoes				2.48

Standard time for the pair = $2.48 \times 1.05 = 2.60$ minutes.

SOLVED PROBLEM 2

A total of 15 observations has been taken on a head baker for a school district. The numerical breakdown of the baker's activities is

MAKE READY	DO	CLEAN UP	IDLE
2	6	3	4

Based on this information, how many work-sampling observations are required to determine how much of the baker's time is spent in "doing"? Assume a 5 percent desired absolute accuracy and 95 percent confidence level.

Solution

To calculate the number of observations, use the formula at the bottom of Exhibit 5A.5 because the 95 percent confidence is required (that is, $Z \cong 2$).

$$p = \text{"Doing"} = 6/15 = 40\%$$

$$E = 5\% \text{ (given)}$$

$$N = \frac{4p(1 - p)}{E^2} = \frac{4(.4)(1 - .4)}{(.05)(.05)} = \frac{.96}{.0025} = 384$$

REVIEW AND DISCUSSION QUESTIONS

1 Why might practicing managers and industrial engineers be skeptical about job enrichment and sociotechnical approaches to job design?

2 Is there an inconsistency when a company requires precise time standards and encourages job enlargement?

3 You have timed your friend Lefty assembling widgets. His time averaged 12 minutes for the two cycles you timed. He was working very hard, and you believe that none of the nine other operators doing the same job can beat his time. Are you ready to put forth this time as the standard for making an order of 5,000 widgets? If not, what else should you do?

4 Comment on the following:

a. "Work measurement is old hat. We have automated our office, and now we run every bill through our computer (after our 25 clerks have typed the data into our computer database)."

b. "It's best that our workers don't know that they are being time studied. That way, they can't complain about us getting in the way when we set time standards."

c. "Once we get everybody on an incentive plan, then we will start our work measurement program."

d. "Rhythm is fine for dancing, but it has no place on the shop floor."

5 Your company's new process improvement guru is aggressive at providing and requiring online self-service at all levels of management, from making travel arrangements to doing check requests, travel expense reports, and even performance evaluations online. What advice would you give to the guru about this?

PROBLEMS

1 Use the following form to evaluate a job you have held relative to the five principles of job design given in the chapter. Develop a numerical score by summing the numbers in parentheses.

	POOR (0)	ADEQUATE (1)	GOOD (2)	OUTSTANDING (3)
Task variety				
Skill variety				
Feedback				
Task identity				
Task autonomy				

    a. Compute the score for your job. Does the score match your subjective feelings about the job as a whole? Explain.

    b. Compare your score with the scores generated by your classmates. Is there one kind of job that everybody likes and one kind that everybody dislikes?

2 A time study was made of an existing job to develop new time standards. A worker was observed for 45 minutes. During that period, 30 units were produced. The analyst rated the worker as performing at a 90 percent performance rate. Allowances in the firm for rest and personal time are 12 percent.

    a. What is the normal time for the task?

    b. What is the standard time for the task?

3 The Bullington Company wants a time standard established on the painting operation of souvenir horseshoes for the local Pioneer Village. Work sampling is to be used. It is estimated that working time averages 95 percent of total time (working time plus idle time). A co-op student is available to do the work sampling between 8:00 A.M. and 12:00 noon. Sixty working days are to be used for the study. Use Exhibit 5A.5 and an absolute error of 2.5 percent. Use the table of random numbers (Appendix F) to calculate the sampling schedule for the first day (that is, show the times of day that an observation of working/idle should be made). Hint: Start random number selection with the first tour.

4 The final result of the study in Problem 3 estimated working time at 91.0 percent. In a 480-minute shift, the best operator painted 1,000 horseshoes. The student's performance index was estimated to be 115 percent. Total allowances for fatigue, personal time, and so on, are 10 percent. Calculate the standard time per piece.

5 Suppose you want to set a time standard for the baker making her specialty, square doughnuts. A work-sampling study of her on "doughnut day" yielded the following results:

Time spent (working and idle)	320 minutes
Number of doughnuts produced	5,000
Working time	280 minutes
Performance rating	125%
Allowances	10%

What is the standard time per doughnut?

6 In an attempt to increase productivity and reduce costs, Rho Sigma Corporation is planning to install an incentive pay plan in its manufacturing plant. In developing standards for one operation, time-study analysts observed a worker for 30 minutes. During that time, the worker completed 42 parts. The analysts rated the worker as producing at 130 percent. The base wage rate of the worker is $5 per hour. The firm has established 15 percent as a fatigue and personal time allowance.

    a. What is the normal time for the task?

    b. What is the standard time for the task?

    c. If the worker produced 500 units during an eight-hour day, what wages would the worker have earned?

7 Because new regulations will greatly change the products and services offered by savings and loan associations, time studies must be performed on tellers and other personnel to determine the number and types of personnel needed and incentive wage payment plans that might be installed. As an example of the studies that the various tasks will undergo, consider the following problem and come up with appropriate answers.

A hypothetical case was set up in which the teller (to be retitled later as an *account adviser*) was required to examine a customer's portfolio and determine whether it was more beneficial for the customer to consolidate various CDs into a single issue currently offered, or to leave the portfolio unaltered. A time study made of the teller yielded the following findings:

Time of study	90 minutes
Number of portfolios examined	10 portfolios
Performance rating	130 percent
Rest for personal time	15 percent
Teller's proposed new pay rate	$12 per hour

   a. What is the normal time for the teller to do a portfolio analysis for the CDs?
   b. What is the standard time for the analysis?

8   Based on a manager's observations, a milling machine appears to be idle approximately 30 percent of the time. Develop a work-sampling plan to determine the percentage of idle time, accurate within a 3 percent error (±3%) with a 95 percent confidence level. Use the random numbers from Appendix B to derive the first day's sampling schedule (assume that the sample will take place over 60 days and that an eight-hour shift is used from 8:00 to 12:00 and 1:00 to 5:00).

9   In a time study at a producer of LCD televisions, a worker assembled 20 units in 100 minutes. The time study analyst rated the worker a performance rate of 110 percent. An allowance for personal time and fatigue is 15 percent. What are the normal time and standard time?

10   A bank manager wants to determine the percent of time that tellers are working and idle. She decides to use work sampling, and her initial estimate is that the tellers are idle 30 percent of the time. How many observations should the manager take in order to be 95 percent confident that the results will not be more than 2.5 percent away from the true result?

11   Decision Science Institute (DSI) promotes its annual national conference by mailing thousands of letters to various recipients. A time study has been conducted on the task of preparing the letters for mailing. On the basis of the observations below, DSI wants to develop a time standard for the task. The organization's personal, delay, and fatigue allowance factor is 15 percent. Compute the average cycle time and normal time for each element. Then, calculate the standard time for the entire task.

	CYCLE OBSERVED IN MINUTES					
JOB ELEMENT	1	2	3	4	5	PERFORMANCE RATING
(A) Compose letter	8	10	9	11	11	120%
(B) Print address labels	2	3	2	1	3	105%
(C) Stuff, seal, and sort envelopes	2	1	3	2	1	110%

Super Quiz

1   The two-edged sword of job design.
2   The freedom for an employee to give an on-the-spot refund.
3   This is when a job is enlarged vertically.
4   The four basic work measurement techinques.
5   Normal time plus allowances.

6   The purpose of normalizing a job
7   MOST is what kind of a work measurement technique?
8   These are the five job design principles.
9   A potential drawback to work sampling.

1. Specialization 2. Empowerment 3. Workers are given certain managerial powers over their own activities 4. Time study, work sampling, predetermined motion-time data systems, elemental data 5. Standard time 6. Making an operator's time usable for all workers 7. Predetermined motion-time data system 8. Task variety, skill variety, feedback, task identity, task autonomy 9. The assumption that all observations pertain to the same static system

SELECTED BIBLIOGRAPHY

Aft, L. S. *Work Measurement and Methods Improvement (Engineering Design and Automation).* New York: Wiley-Interscience, 2000.

Groover, Mikell P. *Work Systems: The Methods, Measurement & Management of Work.* Upper Saddle River, NJ: Prentice Hall, 2006.

Meyers, F. E., and J. R. Stewart. *Time and Motion Study: For Lean Manufacturing.* 3rd ed. Upper Saddle River, NJ: Prentice Hall, 2001.

Niebel, B. W., and A. Freivalds. *Methods, Standards, and Work Design.* 12th ed. New York: WCB/McGraw-Hill, 2008.

Sakamoto, S. "Return to Work Measurement." *Industrial Engineer* 41, no. 3 (March 2009), p. 24.

FOOTNOTES

1 M. Apgar IV, "The Alternative Workplace: Changing Where and How People Work," *Harvard Business Review* 76, no. 3 (May–June 1998), pp. 121–36.

2 S. Lohr, "Slow Down, Brave Multitasker, and Don't Read This in Traffic," *New York Times*, March, 25, 2007.

chapter 6

PRODUCTION PROCESSES

TOSHIBA: PRODUCER OF THE FIRST NOTEBOOK COMPUTER

Global

Tokyo Shibaura Denki (Tokyo Shibaura Electric Co. Ltd) was formed in 1939 by a merger of two highly innovative Japanese companies: Shibaura Seisaku-sho (Shibaura Engineering Works), which manufactured transformers, electrical motors, hydroelectric generators, and x-ray tubes, and Tokyo Electric Company, which produced lightbulbs, radio receivers, and cathode-ray tubes. The company was soon after known as "Toshiba," which became its official name in 1978. Toshiba became the first company in Japan to make fluorescent lamps (1940), radar (1942), broadcasting equipment (1952), and digital computers (1954). Toshiba also became the first in the world to produce the powerful 1-megabit DRAM chip and the first laptop computer, the T3100, both in 1985.

After reading the chapter, you will:

1. Understand the idea of production process mapping.

2. Demonstrate how production processes are organized.

3. Explain the trade-offs that need to be considered when designing a production processes.

4. Describe the product–process matrix.

5. Recognize how break-even analysis is just as important in operations and supply chain management as it is in other functional areas.

Toshiba has built its strength in the notebook PC market by beating its competitors to the market with aggressively priced, technologically innovative products. Competition in the notebook PC market is fierce, and Toshiba can retain its position as a market leader only by relentlessly improving its manufacturing processes and lowering its costs.

Dell Computer is a formidable competitor and seeks to minimize its costs by assembling to order and selling directly to customers. Toshiba has some significant advantages over Dell that stem largely from huge investments in technologies such as thin-film transistor (TFT) color displays, hard disk drives, lithium-ion batteries,

SOURCE: ADAPTED FROM *TOSHIBA: OME WORKS*, HARVARD BUSINESS SCHOOL (9-696-059) AND www.toshiba.co.jp/worldwide/about/history.html.

and DVD drives. In addition, by forming partnerships and joint ventures with other industry giants, Toshiba can share the risk of developing expensive new technologies.

Put yourself in the position of Toshihiro Nakamura, the production supervisor at Toshiba's Ome Works plant. Production of Toshiba's latest subnotebook computer is scheduled to begin in only 10 days. As he wends his way through a maze of desks, heading to the factory floor, he wonders if it is really feasible to get the line designed in time.

Read the details related to designing the new assembly line in the case at the end of chapter 6A titled "Designing Toshiba's Notebook Computer Assembly Line."

PRODUCTION PROCESSES

Supply Chain

In this chapter we consider how processes used to make tangible goods are designed. Production processes are used to make everything that we buy ranging from the apartment building in which we live to the ink pens with which we write. The high-level view of what is required to make something can be divided into three simple steps. The first step is sourcing the parts we need, followed by actually making the item, and then sending the item to the customer. As discussed in Chapter 1, a supply chain view of this may involve a complex series of players where subcontractors feed suppliers, suppliers feed manufacturing plants, manufacturing plants feed warehouses, and finally warehouses feed retailers. Depending on the item being produced, the supply chain can be very long with subcontractors and manufacturing plants spread out over the globe (such as an automobile or computer manufacturer) or short where parts are sourced and the product made locally (such as a house builder).

Consider Exhibit 6.1, which illustrates the Source step where parts are procured from one or more suppliers, the Make step where manufacturing takes place, and the Deliver

exhibit 6.1   Positioning Inventory in the Supply Chain

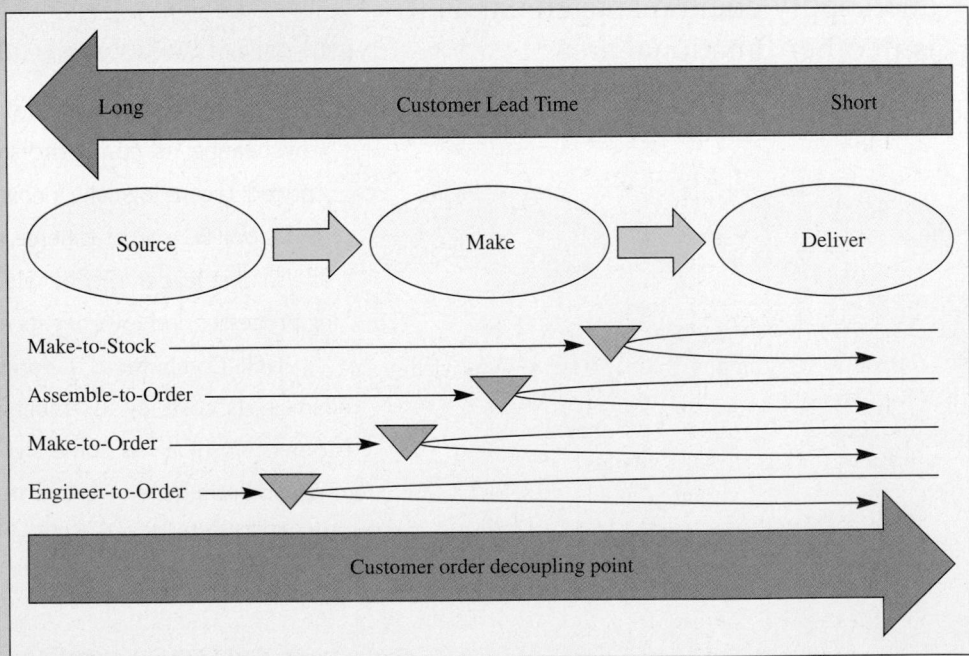

step where the product is shipped to the customer. Depending on the strategy of the firm, the capabilities of manufacturing, and the needs of customers, these activities are organized to minimize cost while meeting the competitive priorities necessary to attract customer orders. For example, in the case of consumer products such as DVDs or clothes, customers normally want these products "on-demand" for quick delivery from a local department store. As a manufacturer of these products, we build them ahead of time in anticipation of demand and ship them to the retail stores where they are carried in inventory until they are sold. At the other end of the spectrum are custom products, such as military airplanes, that are ordered with very specific uses in mind and that need to be designed and then built to the design. In the case of an airplane, the time needed to respond to a customer order, called the lead time, could easily be years compared to only a few minutes for the DVD.

Lead time

A key concept in production processes is the customer order decoupling point, which determines where inventory is positioned to allow processes or entities in the supply chain to operate independently. For example, if a product is stocked at a retailer, the customer pulls the item from the shelf and the manufacturer never sees a customer order. Inventory acts as a buffer to separate the customer from the manufacturing process. Selection of decoupling points is a strategic decision that determines customer lead times and can greatly impact inventory investment. The closer this point is to the customer, the quicker the customer can be served. Typically, there is a trade-off where quicker response to customer demand comes at the expense of greater inventory investment because finished goods inventory is more expensive than raw material inventory. An item in finished goods inventory typically contains all the raw materials needed to produce the item. So from a cost view it includes the cost of the material plus the cost to fabricate the finished item.

Customer order decoupling point

Service

Positioning of the customer order decoupling point is important to understanding production environments. Firms that serve customers from finished goods inventory are known as make-to-stock firms. Those that combine a number of preassembled modules to meet a customer's specifications are called assemble-to-order firms. Those that make the customer's product from raw materials, parts, and components are make-to-order firms. An engineer-to-order firm will work with the customer to design the product, and then make it from purchased materials, parts, and components. Of course, many firms serve a combination of these environments and a few will have all simultaneously. Depending on the environment and the location of the customer order decoupling point, one would expect inventory concentrated in finished goods, work-in-process (this is inventory in the manufacturing process), manufacturing raw material, or at the supplier as shown in Exhibit 6.1.

Make-to-stock
Assemble-to-order
Make-to-order
Engineer-to-order

The essential issue in satisfying customers in the make-to-stock environment is to balance the level of finished inventory against the level of service to the customer. Examples of products produced by these firms include televisions, clothing, and packaged food products. If unlimited inventory were possible and free, the task would be trivial. Unfortunately, that is not the case. Providing more inventory increases costs, so a trade-off between the costs of the inventory and the level of customer service must be made. The trade-off can be improved by better estimates (or knowledge) of customer demand, by more rapid transportation alternatives, by speedier production, and by more flexible manufacturing. Many make-to-stock firms invest in lean manufacturing programs in order to achieve higher service levels for a given inventory investment. Regardless of the trade-offs involved, the focus in the make-to-stock environment is on providing finished goods where and when the customers want them.

Lean manufacturing

In the assemble-to-order environment, a primary task is to define a customer's order in terms of alternative components and options since it is these components that are carried in inventory. A good example is the way Dell Computer makes desktop computers. The number of combinations that can be made may be nearly infinite (although some might not be feasible). One of the capabilities required for success in the assemble-to-order environment is an engineering design that enables as much flexibility as possible in combining components, options, and modules into finished products. Similar to make-to-stock, many assemble-to-order companies have applied lean manufacturing principles to dramatically decrease the time required to assemble finished goods. By doing so they are delivering

DELL'S MANUFACTURING PROCESS COVERS ASSEMBLY, SOFTWARE INSTALLATION, FUNCTIONAL TESTING (INCLUDING "BURN-IN"), AND QUALITY CONTROL. DELL'S JIT APPROACH UTILIZES THE PULL SYSTEM BY BUILDING COMPUTERS ONLY AFTER CUSTOMERS PLACE ORDERS AND BY REQUESTING MATERIALS FROM SUPPLIERS AS NEEDED.

customers' order so quickly that they appear to be make-to-stock firms from the perspective of the customer.

Assembling-to-order derives significant advantages from moving the customer order decoupling point from finished goods to components. The number of finished products is usually substantially greater than the number of components that are combined to produce the finished product. Consider, for example, a computer for which there are four processor alternatives, three hard disk drive choices, four DVD alternatives, two speaker systems, and four monitors available. If all combinations of these 17 components are valid, they can be combined into a total of 384 different final configurations. This can be calculated as follows:

If N_i is the number of alternatives for component I, the total number of combinations of n components (given all are viable) is:

$$\text{Total number of combinations} = N_1 \times N_2 \times \ldots \times N_n \qquad \text{[6.1]}$$
$$\text{Or } 384 = 4 \times 3 \times 4 \times 2 \times 4 \text{ for this example.}$$

It is much easier to manage and forecast the demand for 17 components than for 384 computers.

In the make-to-order and engineer-to-order environments the customer order decoupling point could be in either raw materials at the manufacturing site or possibly even with the supplier inventory. Boeing's process for making commercial aircraft is an example of make-to-order. The need for engineering resources in the engineer-to-order case is somewhat different than make-to-order since engineering determines what materials will be required, and what steps will be required in manufacturing. Depending on how similar the products are it might not even be possible to pre-order parts. Rather than inventory, the emphasis in these environments may be more toward managing capacity of critical resources such as engineering and construction crews. Lockheed Martin's Satellite division uses an engineer-to-order strategy.

HOW PRODUCTION PROCESSES ARE ORGANIZED

Process selection refers to the strategic decision of selecting which kind of production processes to use to produce a product or provide a service. For example, in the case of Toshiba notebook computers, if the volume is very low, we may just have a worker manually assemble each computer by hand. In contrast, if the volume is higher, setting up an assembly line is appropriate.

The formats by which a facility is arranged are defined by the general pattern of work flow; there are five basic structures (project, workcenter, manufacturing cell, assembly line, and continuous process).

Project layout

In a **project layout**, the product (by virtue of its bulk or weight) remains in a fixed location. Manufacturing equipment is moved to the product rather than vice versa. Construction sites (houses and bridges) and movie shooting lots are examples of this format. Items produced with this type of layout are typically managed using the project management techniques described in Chapter 10. Areas on the site will be designated for various purposes, such as material staging, subassembly construction, site access for heavy equipment, and a management area.

A **workcenter** layout, sometimes referred to as a job shop, is where similar equipment or functions are grouped together, such as all drilling machines in one area and all stamping machines in another. A part being worked on travels, according to the established sequence of operations, from workcenter to workcenter, where the proper machines are located for each operation.

Workcenter

A **manufacturing cell** layout is a dedicated area where products that are similar in processing requirements are produced. These cells are designed to perform a specific set of processes, and the cells are dedicated to a limited range of products. A firm may have many different cells in a production area, each set up to produce a single product or a similar group of products efficiently. These cells typically are scheduled to produce "as needed" in response to current customer demand.

Manufacturing cell

An **assembly line** is where work processes are arranged according to the progressive steps by which the product is made. The path for each part is, in effect, a straight line. Discrete products are made by moving from workstation to workstation at a controlled rate, following the sequence needed to build the product. Examples include the assembly of toys, appliances, and automobiles.

Assembly line

A **continuous process** is similar to an assembly line in that production follows a predetermined sequence of steps, but the flow is continuous such as with liquids, rather than discrete. Such structures are usually highly automated and, in effect, constitute one integrated "machine" that may operate 24 hours a day to avoid expensive shutdowns and start-ups. Conversion and processing of undifferentiated materials such as petroleum, chemicals, and drugs are good examples.

Continuous process

The relationship between layout structures is often depicted on a **product–process matrix** similar to the one shown in Exhibit 6.2. Two dimensions are shown. The first dimension relates to the volume of a particular product or group of standardized products. Standardization is shown on the vertical axis and refers to variations in the product that is produced. These variations are measured in terms of geometric differences, material differences, and so on. Standardized products are highly similar from a manufacturing processing point of view, whereas low standardized products require different processes.

Product–process matrix

Product–Process Matrix: Framework Describing Layout Strategies

exhibit 6.2

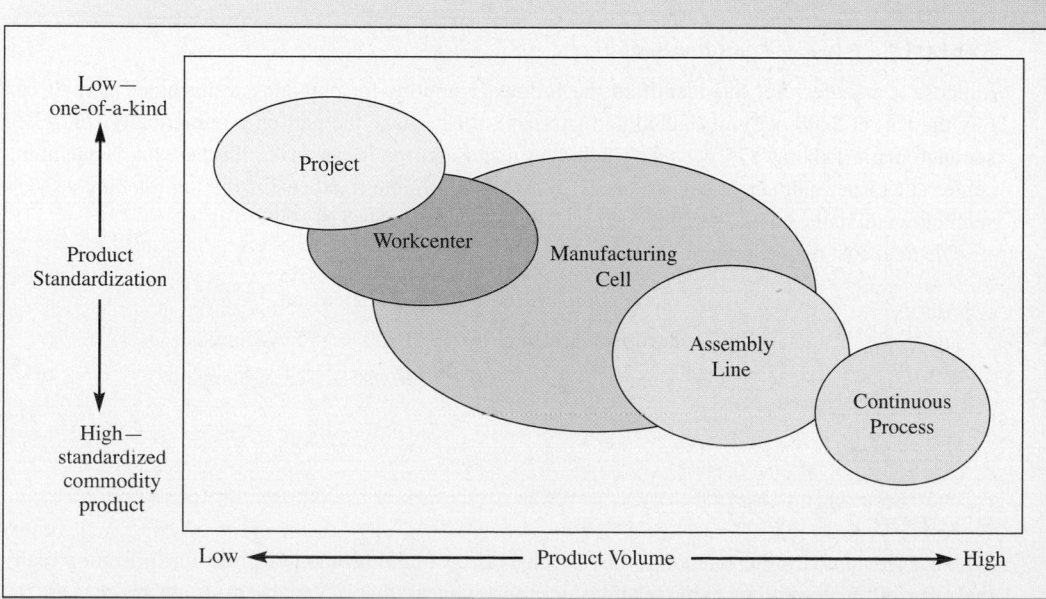

Exhibit 6.2 shows the processes approximately on a diagonal. In general, it can be argued that it is desirable to design processes along the diagonal. For example, if we produce nonstandard products at relatively low volumes, workcenters should be used. A highly standardized product (commodity) produced at high volumes should be produced using an assembly line or a continuous process, if possible. As a result of the advanced manufacturing technology available today, we see that some of the layout structures span relatively large areas of the product–process matrix. For example, manufacturing cells can be used for a very wide range of applications, and this has become a popular layout structure that often is employed by manufacturing engineers.

BREAK-EVEN ANALYSIS

The choice of which specific equipment to use in a process often can be based on an analysis of cost trade-offs. In the product–process matrix (Exhibit 6.2) there is often a trade-off between more and less specialized equipment. Less specialized equipment is referred to as "general-purpose," meaning that it can be used easily in many different ways if it is set up in the proper way. More specialized equipment, referred to as "special-purpose," is often available as an alternative to a general-purpose machine. For example, if we need to drill holes in a piece of metal, the general-purpose option may be to use a simple hand drill. An alternative special-purpose drill is a drill press. Given the proper setup, the drill press can drill holes much quicker than the hand drill can. The trade-offs involve the cost of the equipment (the manual drill is inexpensive, and the drill press expensive), the setup time (the manual drill is quick, while the drill press takes some time), and the time per unit (the manual drill is slow, and the drill press quick).

A standard approach to choosing among alternative processes or equipment is *break-even analysis*. A break-even chart visually presents alternative profits and losses due to the number of units produced or sold. The choice obviously depends on anticipated demand. The method is most suitable when processes and equipment entail a large initial investment and fixed cost, and when variable costs are reasonably proportional to the number of units produced.

**Tutorial:
Break-Even
Analysis**

Step by Step

EXAMPLE 6.1: Break-Even Analysis

Suppose a manufacturer has identified the following options for obtaining a machined part: It can buy the part at $200 per unit (including materials); it can make the part on a numerically controlled semiautomatic lathe at $75 per unit (including materials); or it can make the part on a machining center at $15 per unit (including materials). There is negligible fixed cost if the item is purchased; a semiautomatic lathe costs $80,000; and a machining center costs $200,000.

The total cost for each option is

$$\text{Purchase cost} = \$200 \times \text{Demand}$$

$$\text{Produce-using-lathe cost} = \$80,000 + \$75 \times \text{Demand}$$

$$\text{Produce-using-machining-center cost} = \$200,000 + \$15 \times \text{Demand}$$

SOLUTION

Whether we approach the solution to this problem as cost minimization or profit maximization really makes no difference as long as the relationships remain linear: that is, variable costs and revenue are the same for each incremental unit. Exhibit 6.3 shows the break-even point for each process. If demand is expected to be more than 2,000 units (point A), the machine center is the best choice because this would

Break-Even Chart of Alternative Processes

exhibit 6.3

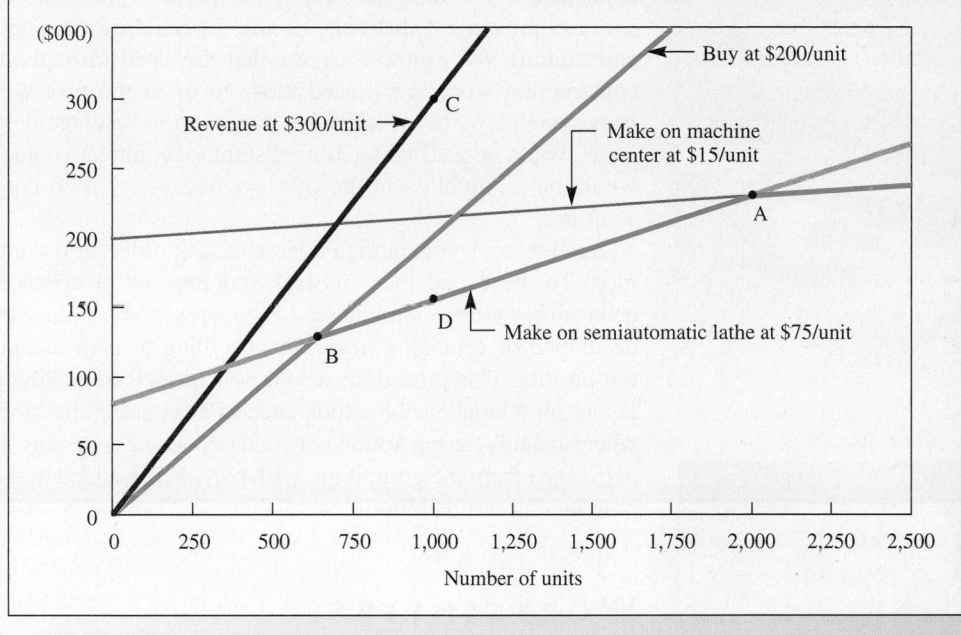

**Excel:
Break-Even
Analysis**

result in the lowest total cost. If demand is between 640 (point B) and 2,000 units, the semiautomatic lathe is the cheapest. If demand is less than 640 (between 0 and point B), the most economical course is to buy the product.

The break-even point A calculation is

$$\$80{,}000 + \$75 \times \text{Demand} = \$200{,}000 + \$15 \times \text{Demand}$$

$$\text{Demand (point A)} = 120{,}000/60 = 2{,}000 \text{ units}$$

The break-even point B calculation is

$$\$200 \times \text{Demand} = \$80{,}000 + \$75 \times \text{Demand}$$

$$\text{Demand (point B)} = 80{,}000/125 = 640 \text{ units}$$

Consider the effect of revenue, assuming the part sells for $300 each. As Exhibit 6.3 shows, profit (or loss) is the distance between the revenue line and the alternative process cost. At 1,000 units, for example, maximum profit is the difference between the $300,000 revenue (point C) and the semiautomatic lathe cost of $155,000 (point D). For this quantity the semiautomatic lathe is the cheapest alternative available. The optimal choices for both minimizing cost and maximizing profit are the lowest segments of the lines: origin to B, to A, and to the right side of Exhibit 6.3 as shown in green. ●

DESIGNING A PRODUCTION SYSTEM

Many techniques are available to determine the actual layouts of the production process. This section gives a quick overview of how the problems are addressed. For each of the layout types, descriptions are given of how the layouts are represented and the main criteria used. The next section takes an in-depth look at process flow design.

PROJECT LAYOUT

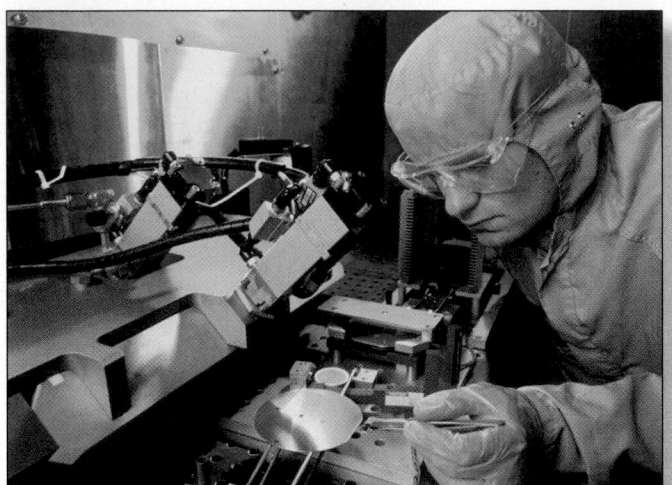

WORKCENTERS

MANUFACTURING CELL

PROJECT LAYOUT

In developing a project layout, visualize the product as the hub of a wheel, with materials and equipment arranged concentrically around the production point in the order of use and movement difficulty. Thus, in building commercial aircraft, for example, rivets that are used throughout construction would be placed close to or in the fuselage; heavy engine parts, which must travel to the fuselage only once, would be placed at a more distant location; and cranes would be set up close to the fuselage because of their constant use.

In a project layout, a high degree of task ordering is common. To the extent that this task ordering, or precedence, determines production stages, a project layout may be developed by arranging materials according to their assembly priority. This procedure would be expected in making a layout for a large machine tool, such as a stamping machine, where manufacturing follows a rigid sequence; assembly is performed from the ground up, with parts being added to the base in almost a building-block fashion.

WORKCENTERS

The most common approach to developing this type of layout is to arrange workcenters in a way that optimizes the movement of material. A workcenter sometimes is referred to as a department and is focused on a particular type of operation. Examples include a workcenter for drilling holes, one for performing grinding operations, and a painting area. The workcenters in a low-volume toy factory might consist of shipping and receiving, plastic molding and stamping, metal forming, sewing, and painting. Parts for the toys are fabricated in these workcenters and then sent to the assembly workcenter, where they are put together. In many installations, optimal placement often means placing workcenters with large amounts of interdepartmental traffic adjacent to each other.

MANUFACTURING CELL

A manufacturing cell is formed by allocating dissimilar machines to cells that are designed to work on products that have similar shapes and processing requirements. Manufacturing cells are widely used in metal fabricating, computer chip manufacture, and assembly work.

ASSEMBLY LINE AND CONTINUOUS PROCESS LAYOUTS

An assembly line is a layout design for the special purpose of building a product by going through a progressive set of steps. The assembly steps are done in areas referred to as "stations," and typically the stations are linked by some form of material handling device. In addition, usually there is some form of pacing by which the amount of time allowed at each station is managed. Rather than develop the process for designing assembly at this time, we will devote the entire next section of this chapter to the topic of assembly-line design since these designs are used so often by manufacturing firms around the world. A continuous or flow process is similar to an assembly line except that the product continuously moves through the process. Often the item being produced by the continuous process is a liquid or chemical that actually "flows" through the system; this is the origin of the term. A gasoline refinery is a good example of a flow process.

ASSEMBLY LINE

MANUFACTURING PROCESS FLOW DESIGN

Manufacturing process flow design is a method to evaluate the specific processes that raw materials, parts, and subassemblies follow as they move through the plant. The most common production management tools used in planning and designing the process flow are assembly drawings, assembly charts, route sheets, and flow process charts. Each of these charts is a useful diagnostic tool and can be used to improve operations during the steady state of the production system. Indeed, the standard first step in analyzing any production system is to map the flows and operations using one or more of these techniques. These are the "organization charts" of the manufacturing system.

An *assembly drawing* (Exhibit 6.4) is simply an exploded view of the product showing its component parts. An *assembly chart* (Exhibit 6.5) uses the information presented in the assembly drawing and defines (among other things) how parts go together, their order of assembly, and often the overall material flow pattern.[1] An *operation and route sheet* (Exhibit 6.6), as its name implies, specifies operations and process routing for a particular part. It conveys such information as the type of equipment, tooling, and operations required to complete the part.

A *process flowchart* such as Exhibit 6.7 denotes what happens to the product as it progresses through the productive facility. Recall, process flowcharting was covered in Chapter 5. The focus in analyzing a manufacturing operation should be the identification

Plug Assembly Drawing   e x h i b i t   6 . 4

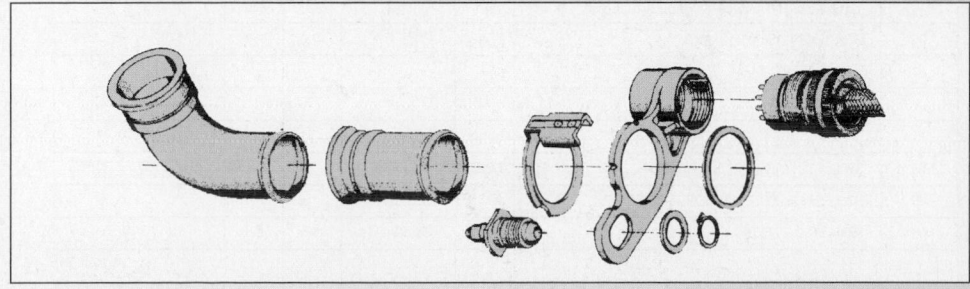

exhibit 6.5   Assembly (or Gozinto) Chart for Plug Assembly

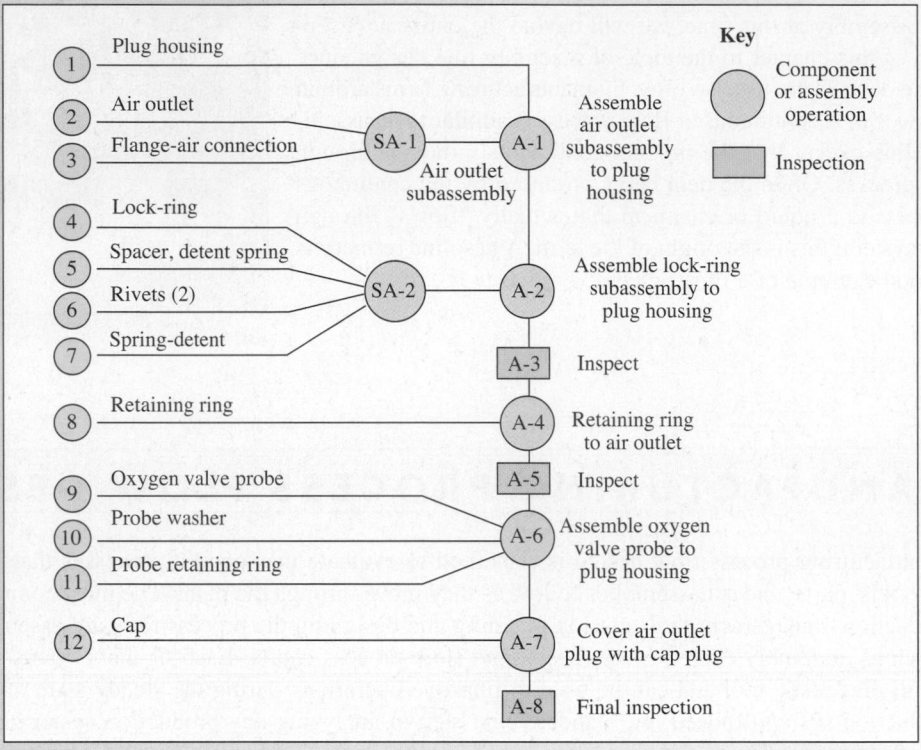

exhibit 6.6   Operation and Route Sheet for Plug Assembly

Material Specs _____	Part Name _____ Plug Housing	Part No. _____ TA 1274
Purchased Stock Size _____	Usage _____ Plug Assembly	Date Issued _____
Pcs. Per Pur Size _____	Assy. No. _____ TA 1279	Date Supplied _____
Weight _____	Sub.Assy. No. _____	Issued By _____

Oper. No.	Operation Description	Dept.	Machine	Setup Hr.	Rate Pc. Hr.	Tools
20	Drill hole .32 $^{+.015}_{-.005}$	Drill	Mach. 513 Drill	1.5	254	Drill fixture L-76 Jig # 10393
30	Deburr .312 $^{+.015}_{-.005}$ dia. hole	Drill	Mach. 510 Drill	.1	424	Multitooth burring tool
40	Chamfer .009/875. bore .878/.875 dia (2 passes). bore .7600/7625 (1 pass)	Lathe	Mach. D 109 lathe	1.0	44	Ramet-1, TPG 221, chamfer tool
50	Tap hole as designated 1/4 min. full thread	Tap	Mach. 517 drill tap	2.0	180	Fixture #CR-353 tap. 4 Flute sp.
60	Bore hole 1.33 to 1.138 dia.	Lathe	H&H E107	3.0	158	L44 turret fixture Hartford
						Superspacer, pl. #45 holder #L46
						FDTW-100, insert #21 chk. fixture
70	Deburr .005 to.010 both sides, hand feed to hard stop	Lathe	E162 lathe	.3	175	Collect CR #179 1327 RPM
80	Broach keyway to remove thread burrs	Drill	Mach. 507 drill	.4	91	B87 fixture, L59 broach tap. .875120 G-H6
90	Hone thread I.D. .822/ .828	Grind	Grinder	1.5	120	
95	Hone .7600/ .7625	Grind	Grinder	1.5	120	

Process Flowchart for the Plug Housing (partial)

exhibit 6.7

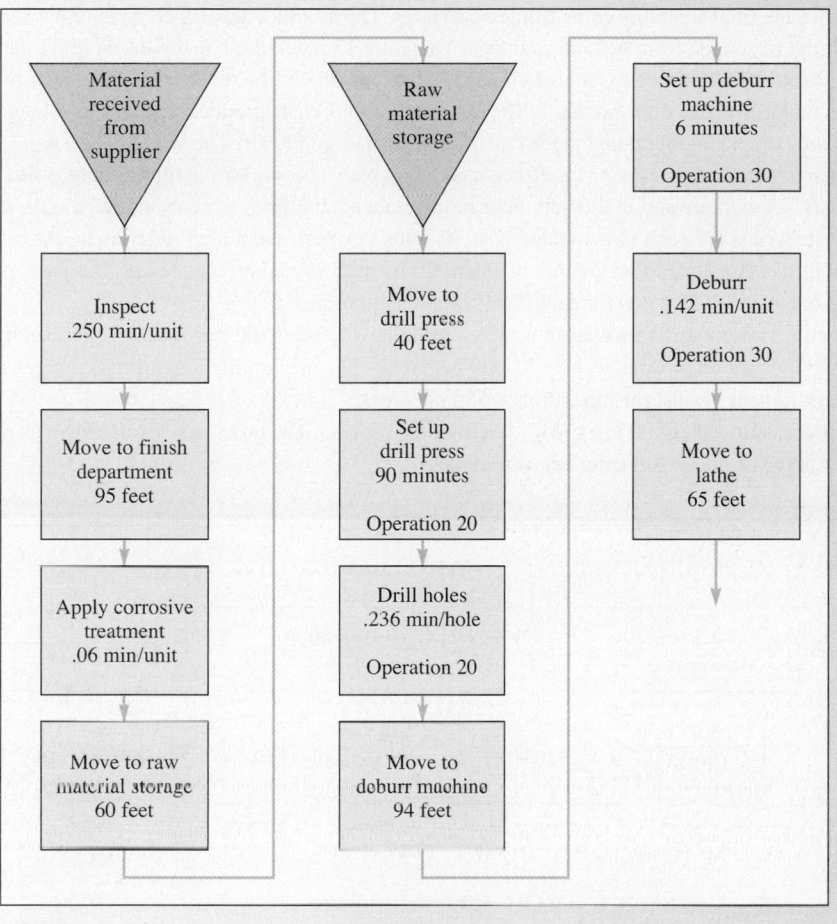

of activities that can be minimized or eliminated, such as movement and storage within the process. As a rule, the fewer the moves, delays, and storages in the process, the better the flow.

EXAMPLE 6.2: Manufacturing Process Analysis

Recall from Chapter 5 that a process usually consists of (1) a set of *tasks,* (2) a *flow* of material and information that connects the set of tasks, and (3) *storage* of material and information.

1. Each task in a process accomplishes, to a certain degree, the transformation of input into the desired output.
2. The flow in a process consists of material flow as well as flow of information. The flow of material transfers a product from one task to the next task. The flow of information helps in determining how much of the transformation has been done in the previous task and what exactly remains to be completed in the present task.
3. When neither a task is being performed nor a part is being transferred, the part has to be stored. Goods in storage, waiting to be processed by the next task, are often called *work-in-process inventory.*

Process analysis involves adjusting the capacities and balance among different parts of the process to maximize output or minimize the costs with available resources. Our company supplies a component to several large auto manufacturers. This component is assembled in a shop by 15 workers working an eight-hour shift on an assembly line that moves at the rate of 150 components per hour. The workers

Step by Step

receive their pay in the form of a group incentive amounting to 30 cents per completed good part. This wage is distributed equally among the workers. Management believes that it can hire 15 more workers for a second shift if necessary.

Parts for the final assembly come from two sources. The molding department makes one very critical part, and the rest come from outside suppliers. There are 11 machines capable of molding the one part done in-house; but historically, one machine is being overhauled or repaired at any given time. Each machine requires a full-time operator. The machines could each produce 25 parts per hour, and the workers are paid on an individual piece rate of 20 cents per good part. The workers will work overtime at a 50 percent increase in rate, or for 30 cents per good part. The workforce for molding is flexible; currently, only six workers are on this job. Four more are available from a labor pool within the company. The raw materials for each part molded cost 10 cents per part; a detailed analysis by the accounting department has concluded that 2 cents of electricity is used in making each part. The parts purchased from the outside cost 30 cents for each final component produced.

This entire operation is located in a rented building costing $100 per week. Supervision, maintenance, and clerical employees receive $1,000 per week. The accounting department charges depreciation for equipment against this operation at $50 per week.

The process flow diagram just below describes the process. The tasks have been shown as rectangles and the storage of goods (inventories) as triangles.

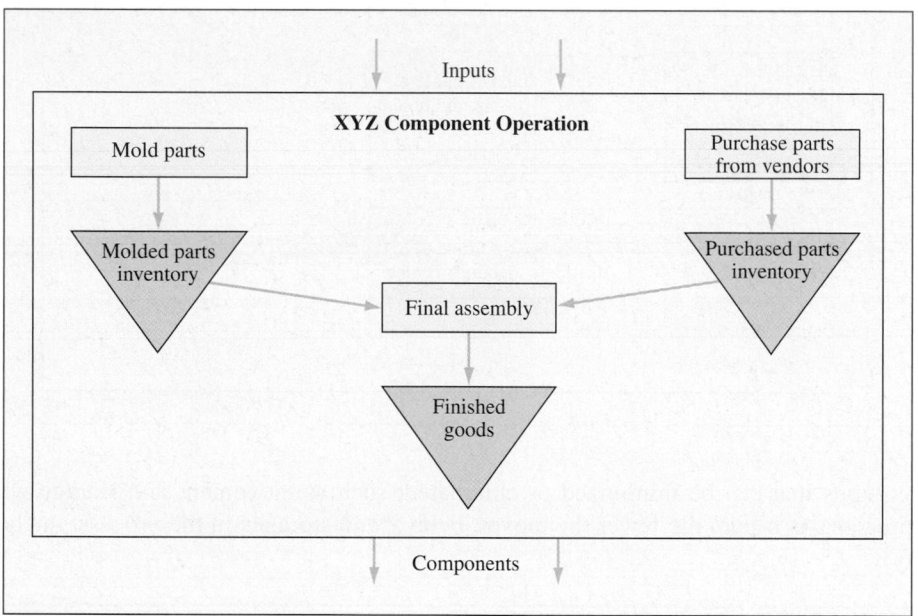

SOLUTION

a. Determine the capacity (number of components produced per week) of the entire process. Are the capacities of all the processes balanced?

Capacity of the molding process:

Only six workers are employed for the molding process, each working as a full-time operator for one machine. Thus, only 6 of the 11 machines are operational at present.

Molding capacity = 6 machines × 25 parts per hour per machine × 8 hours per day × 5 days per week

= 6,000 parts per week

Capacity of the assembly process:

Assembly capacity = 150 components per hour × 8 hours per day × 5 days per week

= 6,000 components per week

Because capacity of both the tasks is 6,000 units per week, they are balanced.

b. If the molding process were to use 10 machines instead of 6, and no changes were to be made in the final assembly task, what would be the capacity of the entire process?

Molding capacity with 10 machines:

Molding capacity = 10 machines × 25 parts per hour per machine × 8 hours per day × 5 days per week

= 10,000 parts per week

Because no change has been made in the final assembly task, the capacity of the assembly process remains 6,000 components per week. Thus, even though the molding capacity is 10,000 per week, the capacity of the entire process is only 6,000 per week because in the long run the overall capacity cannot exceed the slowest task.

c. If our company went to a second shift of eight more hours on the assembly task, what would be the new capacity?

A second shift on the assembly task:

As calculated in the previous section, the molding capacity is 10,000.

Assembly capacity = 150 components per hour × 16 hours per day × 5 days per week

= 12,000 components per week

Here, even though the assembly capacity is 12,000 per week, the capacity of the entire process remains at 10,000 per week because now the slowest task is the molding process, which has a capacity of 10,000 per week. Thus, we can note here that capacity of a process is not a constant factor; it depends on the availability of inputs and the sequence of tasks. In fact, it depends on several other factors not covered here.

d. Determine the cost per unit output when the capacity is (1) 6,000 per week or (2) 10,000 per week.

(1) Cost per unit when output per week = 6,000

First, we calculate the cost of producing all the 6,000 parts per week:

ITEM	CALCULATION	COST
Raw material for molding	$0.10 per part × 6,000 =	$ 600
Parts purchased from outside	$0.30 per component × 6,000 =	1,800
Electricity	$0.02 per part × 6,000 =	120
Molding labor	$0.20 per part × 6,000 =	1,200
Assembly labor	$0.30 per part × 6,000 =	1,800
Rent	$100 per week	100
Supervision	$1,000 per week	1,000
Depreciation	$50 per week	50
Total cost		$6,670

$$\text{Cost per unit} = \frac{\text{Total cost per week}}{\text{Number of units produced per week}} = \frac{\$6,670}{6,000} = \$1.11$$

(2) Cost per unit when output per week = 10,000

Next, we calculate the cost of producing all the 10,000 parts per week:

ITEM	CALCULATION	COST
Raw material for molding	$0.10 per part × 10,000 =	$ 1,000
Parts purchased from outside	$0.30 per component × 10,000 =	3,000
Electricity	$0.02 per part × 10,000 =	200
Molding labor	$0.20 per part × 10,000 =	2,000
Assembly labor	$0.30 per part × 10,000 =	3,000
Rent	$100 per week	100
Supervision	$1,000 per week	1,000
Depreciation	$50 per week	50
Total cost		$10,350

$$\text{Cost per unit} = \frac{\text{Total cost per week}}{\text{Number of units produced per week}} = \frac{\$10,350}{10,000} = \$1.04$$

As you can see, our cost per unit has been reduced by spreading the fixed cost over a greater number of units.

Such process analysis calculations are required for many production decisions discussed throughout this book. ●

SUMMARY

Designing a customer-pleasing product is an art. Building the product is a science. Moving the product from design to the customer is management. World-class manufacturers excel at the speedy and flexible integration of these processes. A key to this is teamwork, not only on the part of marketing, product development, manufacturing, and distribution, but on the part of the supplier and customer as well.

Effective process planning requires clear understanding of what the factory can and cannot do relative to process structures. Many plants use a combination of the structures identified in this chapter—job shops or workcenters for some parts, batch or assembly operations for others. Frequently a choice exists as to when demand seems likely to favor a switch from one to the other. Making such decisions also requires understanding the nuances of each production process to determine if the process really fits new product specifications. On a day-to-day basis, it requires the ability to systematically analyze capacity capabilities of each processing step, as was done in this chapter.

Finally, there is the issue of technology. Although the details of manufacturing processes constitute the world of the engineer, awareness of modern technologies—particularly computer-integrated manufacturing—is now seen as an essential part of a business education. CIM, along with other operations technologies, is discussed in Supplement B, "Operations Technology."

KEY TERMS

Lead time The time needed to respond to a customer order.

Customer order decoupling point The place where inventory is positioned to allow processes or entities in the supply chain to operate independently.

Make-to-stock A production environment where the customer is served "on-demand" from finished goods inventory.

Assemble-to-order A production environment where preassembled components, subassemblies, and modules are put together in response to a specific customer order.

Make-to-order A production environment where the product is built directly from raw materials and components inresponse to a specific customer order.

Engineer-to-order Here the firm works with the customer to design the product, which is then made from purchased materials, parts, and components.

Lean manufacturing The attempt to achieve high customer service with minimum levels of inventory investment.

Project layout The product, because of its sheer bulk or weight, remains fixed in a location. Equipment is moved to the product rather than vice versa.

Workcenter A process structure suited for low-volume production of a great variety of nonstandard products. Workcenters sometimes are referred to as departments and are focused on a particular type of operation

Manufacturing cell An area where simple items that are similar in processing requirements are produced.

Assembly line A process structure designed to make discrete parts. Parts are moved through a set of specially designed workstations at a controlled rate.

Continuous process An often automated process that converts raw materials into a finished product in one continuous process.

Product–process matrix Shows the relationships between different production units and how they are used depending on product volume and the degree of product standardization.

SOLVED PROBLEMS

SOLVED PROBLEM 1

An automobile manufacturer is considering a change in an assembly line that should save money by reducing labor and material cost. The change involves the installation of four new robots that will automatically install windshields. The cost of the four robots, including installation and initial programming, is $400,000. Current practice is to amortize the initial cost of robots over two years on a straight-line basis. The process engineer estimates that one full-time technician will be needed to monitor, maintain, and reprogram the robots on an ongoing basis. This person will cost approximately $60,000 per year. Currently, the company uses four full-time employees on this job and each makes about $52,000 per year. One of these employees is a material handler, and this person will still be needed with the new process. To complicate matters, the process engineer estimates that the robots will apply the windshield sealing material in a manner that will result in a savings of $0.25 per windshield installed. How many automobiles need to be produced over the next two years to make the new robots an attractive investment? Due to the relatively short horizon, do not consider the time value of money.

Solution

Cost of the current process over the next two years is just the cost of the four full-time employees.

$$\$52,000/\text{employee} \times 4 \text{ employees} \times 2 \text{ years} = \$416,000$$

The cost of the new process over the next two years, assuming the robot is completely costed over that time, is the following:

$$(\$52,000/\text{material handler} + \$60,000/\text{technician}) \times 2 + \$400,000/\text{robots} - \$0.25 \times \text{autos}$$

Equating the two alternatives:

$$\$416,000 = \$624,000 - \$0.25 \times \text{autos}$$

Solving for the break-even point:

$$-\$208,000/-\$0.25 = 832,000 \text{ autos}$$

This indicates that to break even, 832,000 autos would need to be produced with the robots over the next two years.

SOLVED PROBLEM 2

A contract manufacturer makes a product for a customer that consists of two items, a cable with standard RCA connectors and a cable with a mini-plug, which are then packaged together as the final product (each product sold contains one RCA and one mini-plug cable). The manufacturer makes both cables on the same assembly line and can only make one a time: either it can make RCA cables or it can make mini-plug cables. There is a setup time when switching from one cable to the other. The assembly line costs $500/hour to operate, and this rate is charged whether it is being set up or actually making cables.

Current plans are to make 100 units of the RCA cable, then 100 units of the mini-plug cable, then 100 units of the RCA cable, then 100 units of the mini-plug cable, and so on, where the setup and run times for each cable are given below.

COMPONENT	SETUP/CHANGEOVER TIME	RUN TIME/UNIT
RCA cable	5 minutes	0.2 minute
Mini-plug cable	10 minutes	0.1 minute

Assume the packaging of the two cables is totally automated and takes only 2 seconds per unit of the final product and is done as a separate step from the assembly line. Since the packaging step is quick and the time required does not depend on the assembly-line batch size, its cost does not vary and need not be considered in the analysis.

What is the average hourly output in terms of the number of units of packaged product (which includes one RCA cable and one mini-plug cable)? What is the average cost per unit for assembling the product? If the batch size were changed from 100 to 200 units, what would be the impact on the assembly cost per unit?

Solution

The average hourly output rate when the batch size is 100 units is calculated by first calculating the total time to produce a batch of cable. The time consists of the setup + the run time for a batch:

$$5 + 10 + 0.2(100) + 0.1(100) = 15 + 30 = 45 \text{ minutes}/100 \text{ units}$$

So if we can produce 100 units in 45 minutes, we need to calculate how many units can be produced in 60 minutes; we can find this with the following ratio:

$$45/100 = 60/X$$

Solving for X:

$$X = 133.3 \text{ units/hour}$$

The cost per unit is then

$$\$500/133.3 = \$3.75/\text{unit}$$

If the batch size were increased to 200 units:

$$5 + 10 + 0.2(200) + 0.1(200) = 15 + 60 = 75 \text{ minutes}/200 \text{ units}$$
$$75/200 = 60/X$$
$$X = 160/\text{hour}$$
$$\$500/160 = \$3.125/\text{unit}$$

REVIEW AND DISCUSSION QUESTIONS

1   What does the product–process matrix tell us? How should the kitchen of a Chinese restaurant be structured?
2   It has been noted that during World War II Germany made a critical mistake by having its formidable Tiger tanks produced by locomotive manufacturers, while the less formidable U.S. Sherman tank was produced by American car manufacturers. Use the product–process matrix to explain that mistake and its likely result.
3   How does the production volume affect break-even analysis?
4   What is meant by a process? Describe its important features.

PROBLEMS

1   Owen Conner works part-time packaging software for a local distribution company in Indiana. The annual fixed cost is $10,000 for this process, direct labor is $3.50 per package, and material is $4.50 per package. The selling price will be $12.50 per package. How much revenue do we need to take in before breaking even? What is the break-even point in units?
2   AudioCables, Inc. is currently manufacturing an adapter that has a variable cost of $.50 per unit and a selling price of $1.00 per unit. Fixed costs are $14,000. Current sales volume is 30,000 units. The firm can substantially improve the product quality by adding a new piece of equipment at an additional fixed cost of $6,000. Variable costs would increase to $.60, but sales volume should jump to 50,000 units due to a higher-quality product. Should AudioCables buy the new equipment?
3   Consider the construction of a simple 8" × 10" wood picture frame. The picture frame consists of four wood pieces that are cut from the wood molding, four staples to hold the frame together,

a piece of glass, a backing board made of cardboard, six points to hold the glass and backing board to the frame, and a clip for hanging the picture frame from the wall.

a. Construct an assembly chart for the picture frame.

b. Construct a flowchart for the entire process from receiving materials to final inspection.

4   The purpose of this system design exercise is to gain experience in setting up a manufacturing process. (We suggest that this be done as a team project.) Assignment:

a. Get one Ping-Pong paddle.

b. Specify the type of equipment and raw materials you would need to manufacture that paddle, from the receipt of seasoned wood to packaging for shipment.

c. Assume that one unit of each type of equipment is available to you. Further assume that you have a stock of seasoned wood and other materials needed to produce and box 100 paddles. Making reasonable assumptions about times and distances where necessary,

(1) Develop an assembly drawing for the paddle.

(2) Prepare an assembly chart for the paddle.

(3) Develop a process flowchart for the paddle.

(4) Develop a route sheet for the paddle.

5   The Goodparts Company produces a component that is subsequently used in the aerospace industry. The component consists of three parts (A, B, and C) that are purchased from outside and cost 40, 35, and 15 cents per piece, respectively. Parts A and B are assembled first on assembly line 1, which produces 140 components per hour. Part C undergoes a drilling operation before being finally assembled with the output from assembly line 1. There are in total six drilling machines, but at present only three of them are operational. Each drilling machine drills part C at a rate of 50 parts per hour. In the final assembly, the output from assembly line 1 is assembled with the drilled part C. The final assembly line produces at a rate of 160 components per hour. At present, components are produced eight hours a day and five days a week. Management believes that if need arises, it can add a second shift of eight hours for the assembly lines.

The cost of assembly labor is 30 cents per part for each assembly line; the cost of drilling labor is 15 cents per part. For drilling, the cost of electricity is 1 cent per part. The total overhead cost has been calculated as $1,200 per week. The depreciation cost for equipment has been calculated as $30 per week.

a. Draw a process flow diagram and determine the process capacity (number of components produced per week) of the entire process.

b. Suppose a second shift of eight hours is run for assembly line 1 and the same is done for the final assembly line. In addition, four of the six drilling machines are made operational. The drilling machines, however, operate for just eight hours a day. What is the new process capacity (number of components produced per week)? Which of the three operations limits the capacity?

c. Management decides to run a second shift of eight hours for assembly line 1 plus a second shift of only four hours for the final assembly line. Five of the six drilling machines operate for eight hours a day. What is the new capacity? Which of the three operations limits the capacity?

d. Determine the cost per unit output for questions *b* and *c*.

e. The product is sold at $4.00 per unit. Assume that the cost of a drilling machine (fixed cost) is $30,000 and the company produces 8,000 units per week. Assume that four drilling machines are used for production. If the company had an option to buy the same part at $3.00 per unit, what would be the break-even number of units?

6   A book publisher has fixed costs of $300,000 and variable costs per book of $8.00. The book sells for $23.00 per copy.

a. How many books must be sold to break even?

b. If the fixed cost increased, would the new break-even point be higher or lower?

c. If the variable cost per unit decreased, would the new break-even point be higher or lower?

7   A manufacturing process has a fixed cost of $150,000 per month. Each unit of product being produced contains $25 worth of material and takes $45 of labor. How many units are needed to break even if each completed unit has a value of $90?

8   Assume a fixed cost of $900, a variable cost of $4.50, and a selling price of $5.50.

a. What is the break-even point?

b. How many units must be sold to make a profit of $500.00?

c. How many units must be sold to average $0.25 profit per unit? $0.50 profit per unit? $1.50 profit per unit?

9   Aldo Redondo drives his own car on company business. His employer reimburses him for such travel at the rate of 36 cents per mile. Aldo estimates that his fixed costs per year such as taxes, insurance, and depreciation are $2,052. The direct or variable costs such as gas, oil, and maintenance average about 14.4 cents per mile. How many miles must he drive to break even?

10   A firm is selling two products, chairs and bar stools, each at $50 per unit. Chairs have a variable cost of $25, and bar stools $20. Fixed cost for the firm is $20,000.
    a. If the sales mix is 1:1 (one chair sold for every bar stool sold), what is the break-even point in dollars of sales? In units of chairs and bar stools?
    b. If the sales mix changes to 1:4 (one chair sold for every four bar stools sold), what is the break-even point in dollars of sales? In units of chairs and bar stools?

11   How would you characterize the most important difference for the following issues when comparing a job shop and a flow shop?

ISSUE	JOB SHOP	FLOW SHOP
Number of changeovers		
Labor content of product		
Flexibility		

12   The diagram below represents a process where two components are made at stations A1 and A2 (one component is made at A1 and the other at A2). These components are then assembled at station B and moved through the rest of the process, where some additional work is completed at stations C, D, and E.

    Assume that one and only one person is allowed at each station. Assume that the times given below for each station represent the amount of work that needs to be done at that station by that person, with no processing time variation. Assume that inventory is not allowed to build in the system.

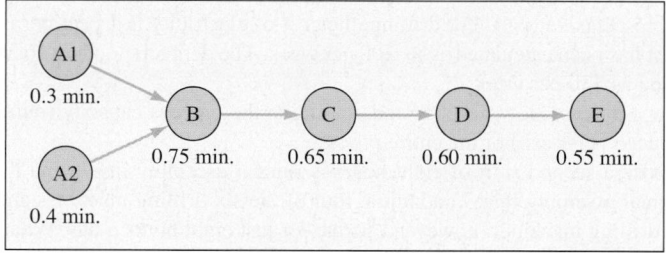

What is the average hourly output of the process when it is in normal operation?

13   A certain custom engraving shop has traditionally had orders for between 1 and 50 units of whatever a customer orders. A large company has contacted this shop about engraving "reward" plaques (which are essentially identical to each other). It wants the shop to place a bid for this order. The volume is expected to be 12,000 units per year and will most likely last four years. To successfully bid (low enough price) for such an order, what will the shop likely have to do?

14   The product–process matrix is a convenient way of characterizing the relationship between product volumes (one-of-a-kind to continuous) and the processing system employed by a firm at a particular location. In the boxes presented below, describe the nature of the intersection between the type of shop (column) and process dimension (row).

	WORKSTATION	ASSEMBLY LINE
Engineering emphasis		
General workforce skill		
Statistical process control		
Facility layout		
WIP inventory level		

15   For each of the following variables, explain the differences (in general) as one moves from a workstation to an assembly line environment.
    a. Throughput time (time to convert raw material into product).
    b. Capital/labor intensity.
    c. Bottlenecks.

CASE: CIRCUIT BOARD FABRICATORS, INC.

Circuit Board Fabricators, Inc. (CBF), is a small manufacturer of circuit boards located in California near San Jose. Companies such as Apple Computer and Hewlett-Packard use the company to make boards for prototypes of new products. It is important that CBF give quick and very-high-quality service. The engineers working on the new products are on a tight schedule and have little patience with sloppy work or missing delivery dates.

Circuit boards are a rigid flat surface where electronic components are mounted. Electronic components such as integrated circuits, resistors, capacitors, and diodes are soldered to the boards. Lines called "traces" are etched on the board and electronically connect the components. Since the electronic traces cannot cross, holes through the circuit board are used to connect traces on both sides of the boards, thus allowing complex circuits to be implemented. These boards often are designed with 40–50 components that are connected through hundreds of traces on a small four- by six-inch board.

CBF has developed a good business plan. It has four standard-size board configurations and has automated much of its process for making these standard boards. Fabricating the boards requires CBF's numerically controlled (NC) equipment to be programmed. This is largely an automated process that works directly from engineering drawings that are formatted using industry standard codes.

Currently, the typical order is for 60 boards. Engineers at customer companies prepare a computer-aided design (CAD) drawing of the board. This CAD drawing precisely specifies each circuit trace, circuit pass-through holes, and component mounting points on the board. An electronic version of the drawing is used by a CBF process engineer to program the NC machines used to fabricate the boards.

Due to losses in the system, CBF has a policy of increasing the size of an order by 25 percent. For example, for a typical order consisting of 60 boards, 75 boards would be started through the process. Fifteen percent of the boards are typically rejected during an inspection that occurs early in the manufacturing process and another 5 percent of the remaining boards are rejected in final test.

BOARD FABRICATION PROCESS

CBF purchases circuit board blanks from a vendor. These boards are made from woven fiberglass cloth that is impregnated with epoxy. A layer of copper is laminated onto each side to form a blank board. The blank board comes from the vendor trimmed to the standard sizes that CBF's numerically controlled equipment can handle.

The following is a description of the steps involved in processing an order at CBF:

1 **Order acceptance.** Check to verify that the order fits within the specification of boards that can be produced with CBF equipment. The process engineer at CBF works with the customer engineer to resolve any problems with the order.
2 **NC machine programming.** CAD information is used to program the machines to produce the order.
3 **Board fabrication.**
   a. **Clean.** Each board is manually loaded into this machine by an operator. The machine then cleans the boards with a special chemical. Each board is then automatically transferred to the coating machine.
   b. **Coat.** A liquid plastic coating is deposited on both sides of the board. Following this process, an operator places the boards on a cart. Each cart, with a complete order of boards, is then moved immediately to the "clean room."
   c. **Expose.** This photographic process makes the exposed plastic coating resistant to dissolving in the areas where the copper traces are needed. An operator must attend to this machine 100 percent of the time, and load and unload each individual board.
   d. **Develop.** Each board is manually loaded onto this machine. The boards are dipped by the machine, one-at-a-time, in a chemical bath that dissolves the plastic and the underlying copper in the proper areas. After dipping, the machine places each board on a conveyor.
   e. **Inspect.** Each board is picked from the conveyor as it comes from the developer. The board is optically checked for defects using a machine similar to a scanner. Approximately 15 percent of the boards are rejected at this point. Boards that pass inspection are placed back on the conveyor that feeds the bake oven. Two inspectors are used at this station.
   f. **Bake.** Boards travel through a bake oven that hardens the plastic coating, thus protecting the traces. Boards are then manually unloaded and placed on a cart. When all the boards for an order are on the cart, it is moved to the drilling machines.
   g. **Drilling.** Holes are drilled using an NC machine to connect circuits on both sides of the board. The boards are manually loaded and unloaded. The machines are arranged so that one person can keep two machines going simultaneously. The cart is used to move the boards to the copper plate bath.
   h. **Copper plate.** Copper is deposited inside the holes by running the boards through a special copper plating bath. This copper connects the traces on both sides of the board. Each board is manually loaded on a conveyor that passes through the plating bath. Two people are needed for this process, one loading and a second unloading the conveyor. On completion of plating, boards are moved on the cart to the final test machines.
   i. **Final test.** Using a special NC machine, a final electrical test of each board is performed to check the integrity of the circuits. On average, approximately 5 percent of the boards fail this test. The boards are manually loaded and unloaded. One person is needed to operate each machine and sort the good and bad boards. The cart is used to move the good boards to the shipping area. The bad boards are scrapped.
4 **Shipping.** The completed order is packed and shipped to the customer.

The plant was designed to run 1,000 boards per day when running five days a week and one eight-hour shift per day. Unfortunately, to date it has not come near that capacity and on a good day it is able to produce only about 700 boards. Data concerning the standard setup and run times for the fabrication process are given in Exhibit 6.8. These times include allowances for morning and afternoon breaks, but do not include time for the half-hour lunch period. In addition, data on current staffing levels also are provided. The CBF process engineer insists that the capacity at each process is sufficient to run 1,000 boards per day.

In order to help understand the problem, CBF hired a consulting company to help solve the problem.

exhibit 6.8

Circuit Board Fabricators—Process Data

Required output per shift	1,000
Average job size (boards)	60
Production hours per day	7.5
Working days per week	5

PROCESS/MACHINE	NUMBER OF MACHINES	NUMBER OF EMPLOYEES	SETUP (MINUTES PER JOB)	RUN (MINUTES PER PART)
Load	1	1	5	0.33
Clean	1			0.5
Coat	1			0.5
Unload	1	1		0.33
Expose	5	5	15	1.72
Load	1	1	5	0.33
Develop	1			0.33
Inspect	2	2		0.5
Bake	1			0.33
Unload	1	1		0.33
Drilling	6	3	15	1.5
Copper plate	1	2	5	0.2
Final test	6	6	15	2.69

Excel: Circuit Board Fabricators

ASSIGNMENT

CBF hired you to help determine why it is not able to produce the 1,000 boards per day.

1   What type of process flow structure is CBF using?
2   Diagram the process in a manner similar to Exhibit 6.7.
3   Analyze the capacity of the process.
4   What is the impact of losses in the process in Inspection and Final Test?
5   What recommendations would you make for a short-term solution to CBF's problems?
6   What long-term recommendations would you make?

SUPER QUIZ

1   A firm that makes predesigned products directly to fill customer orders has this type of production environment.
2   A point where inventory is positioned to allow the production process to operate independently of the customer order delivery process.
3   A firm that designs and builds products from scratch according to customer specifications would have this type of production environment.
4   If a production process makes a unit every two hours and it takes 42 hours for the unit to go through the entire process, then the expected work-in-process is equal to this.
5   A finished goods inventory on average contains 10,000 units. Demand averages 1,500 units per week. Given that the process runs 50 weeks a year, what is the expected inventory turn for the inventory? Assume that each item held in inventory is valued at about the same amount.
6   This is a production layout where similar products are made. Typically it is scheduled on an as-needed basis in response to current customer demand.
7   The relationship between how different layout structures are best suited depending on volume and product variety characteristics is depicted on this type of graph.

1. Make-to-order 2. Customer order decoupling point 3. Engineer-to-order 4. 21 units = 42/2
5. 7.5 turns = (1,500 × 50)/10,000 6. Manufacturing cell 7. Product–process matrix.

SELECTED BIBLIOGRAPHY

Hammer, M. "Reengineering Work: Don't Automate, Obliterate." *Harvard Business Review,* July–August 1990, pp. 104–12.

Hill, T. *Manufacturing Strategy.* 3rd ed. New York: Irwin/McGraw-Hill, 2000.

Hyer, N., and U. Wemmerlöv. *Reorganizing the Factory: Competing through Cellular Manufacturing.* Portland, OR: Productivity Press, 2002.

Schniederjans, M. J., and J. R. Olsen. *Advanced Topics in Just-in-Time Management.* Westport, CT: Quorum Books, 1999.

Womack, J. P., and D. T. Jones. *Lean Thinking: Banish Waste and Create Wealth in Your Corporation.* New York: Simon and Schuster, 1996.

FOOTNOTES

1 Also called a *Gozinto chart,* named, so the legend goes, after the famous Italian mathematician Zepartzat Gozinto.

FACILITY LAYOUT

After reading this chapter you will:

1. Understand how production processes are typically organized and the trade-off between efficiency and flexibility offered by each design.
2. Gain experience with the basic tools used to design workcenters, assembly lines, and manufacturing cells.
3. Recognize typical retail and office layout designs.

Layout decisions entail determining the placement of departments, work groups within the departments, workstations, machines, and stock-holding points within a production facility. The objective is to arrange these elements in a way that ensures a smooth work flow (in a factory) or a particular traffic pattern (in a service organization). In general, the inputs to the layout decision are as follows:

1. Specification of the objectives and corresponding criteria to be used to evaluate the design. The amount of space required and the distance that must be traveled between elements in the layout are common basic criteria.
2. Estimates of product or service demand on the system.
3. Processing requirements in terms of number of operations and amount of flow between the elements in the layout.
4. Space requirements for the elements in the layout.
5. Space availability within the facility itself or, if this is a new facility, possible building configurations.

In our treatment of layout, we examine how layouts are developed under various formats (or work-flow structures). Our emphasis is on quantitative techniques, but we also show examples of how qualitative factors are important in the design of the layout. Both manufacturing and service facilities are covered in this chapter.

THIS SALO OPERATION IN MERIKAARI, FINLAND, IS ONE OF NINE NOKIA MOBILE PHONE FACTORIES WORLDWIDE. THE TOTAL FACTORY AREA IS OVER 15,000 SQUARE METERS, AND IT EMPLOYS OVER 1,200.

Global

BASIC PRODUCTION LAYOUT FORMATS

Workcenter

Service

Assembly line

Manufacturing cell

Project layout

The formats by which departments are arranged in a facility are defined by the general pattern of work flow; there are three basic types (workcenter, assembly line, and project layout) and one hybrid type (manufacturing cell).

A **workcenter** (also called a *job-shop* or *functional layout*) is a format in which similar equipment or functions are grouped together, such as all lathes in one area and all stamping machines in another. A part being worked on then travels, according to the established sequence of operations, from area to area, where the proper machines are located for each operation. This type of layout is typical of hospitals, for example, where areas are dedicated to particular types of medical care, such as maternity wards and intensive care units.

An **assembly line** (also called a *flow-shop layout*) is one in which equipment or work processes are arranged according to the progressive steps by which the product is made. The path for each part is, in effect, a straight line. Assembly lines for shoes, chemical plants, and car washes are all product layouts.

A **manufacturing cell** groups dissimilar machines to work on products that have similar shapes and processing requirements. A manufacturing cell is similar to a workcenter in that cells are designed to perform a specific set of processes, and it is similar to an assembly line in that the cells are dedicated to a limited range of products. (*Group technology* refers to the parts classification and coding system used to specify machine types that go into a cell.)

In a **project layout**, the product (by virtue of its bulk or weight) remains at one location. Manufacturing equipment is moved to the product rather than vice versa. Construction sites and movie lots are examples of this format.

Many manufacturing facilities present a combination of two layout types. For example, a given production area may be organized as a workcenter, while another area may be an assembly line. It is also common to find an entire plant arranged according to product flow—for example, a parts fabrication area followed by a subassembly area, with a final assembly area at the end of the process. Different types of layouts may be used in each area, with workcenters used in fabrication, manufacturing cells in subassembly, and an assembly line used in final assembly.

WORKCENTERS

The most common approach to developing a workcenter layout is to arrange workcenters consisting of like processes in a way that optimizes their relative placement. For example, the workcenters in a low-volume toy factory might consist of the shipping and receiving workcenter, the plastic molding and stamping workcenter, the metal forming workcenter, the sewing workcenter, and the painting workcenter. Parts for the toys are fabricated in these workcenters and then sent to assembly workcenters where they are put together. In many installations, optimal placement often means placing workcenters with large amounts of interdepartment traffic adjacent to one another.

Suppose that we want to arrange the eight workcenters of a toy factory to minimize the interdepartmental material handling cost. Initially, let us make the simplifying assumption that all workcenters have the same amount of space (say, 40 feet by 40 feet) and that the building is 80 feet wide and 160 feet long (and thus compatible with the workcenter dimensions). The first things we would want to know are the nature of the flow between workcenters and how the material is transported. If the company has another factory that makes similar products, information about flow patterns might be abstracted from the records. On the other hand, if this is a new-product line, such information would have to come from routing sheets or from estimates by knowledgeable personnel such as process or industrial engineers. Of course, these data, regardless of their source, will have to be modified to reflect the nature of future orders over the projected life of the proposed layout.

DESIGN STYLING STUDIO I, PRODUCTION LINE, PAINT SHOP, AND PRODUCTION LINE 3 FOR LOTUS ELISE FACILITY IN HETHEL, UNITED KINGDOM.

Let us assume that this information is available. We find that all material is transported in a standard-size crate by forklift truck, one crate to a truck (which constitutes one "load"). Now suppose that transportation costs are $1 to move a load between adjacent workcenters and $1 extra for each workcenter in between. The expected loads between workcenters for the first year of operation are tabulated in Exhibit 6A.1; available plant space is depicted in

Interworkcenter Flow

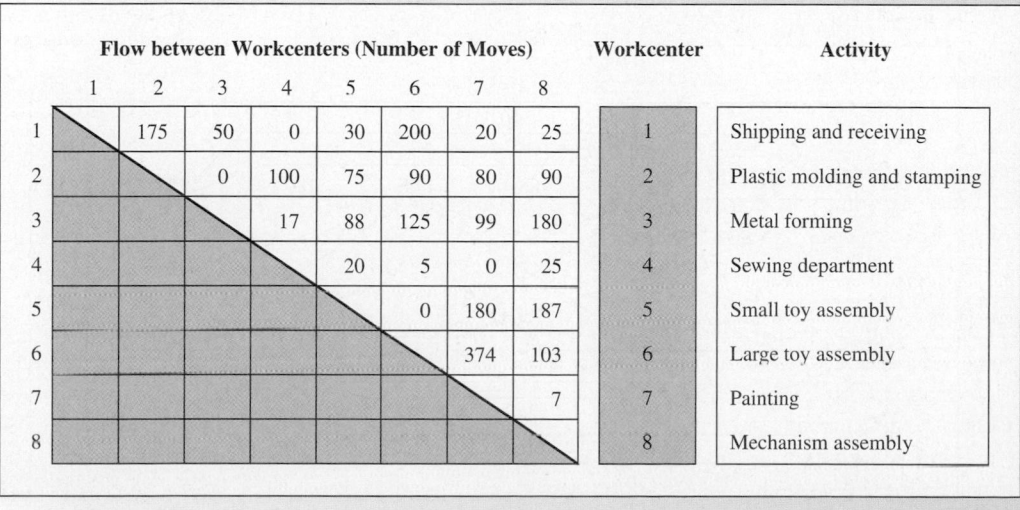

	Flow between Workcenters (Number of Moves)								Workcenter	Activity
	1	2	3	4	5	6	7	8		
1		175	50	0	30	200	20	25	1	Shipping and receiving
2			0	100	75	90	80	90	2	Plastic molding and stamping
3				17	88	125	99	180	3	Metal forming
4					20	5	0	25	4	Sewing department
5						0	180	187	5	Small toy assembly
6							374	103	6	Large toy assembly
7								7	7	Painting
8									8	Mechanism assembly

exhibit 6A.2

exhibit 6A.2   Building Dimensions and Workcenters

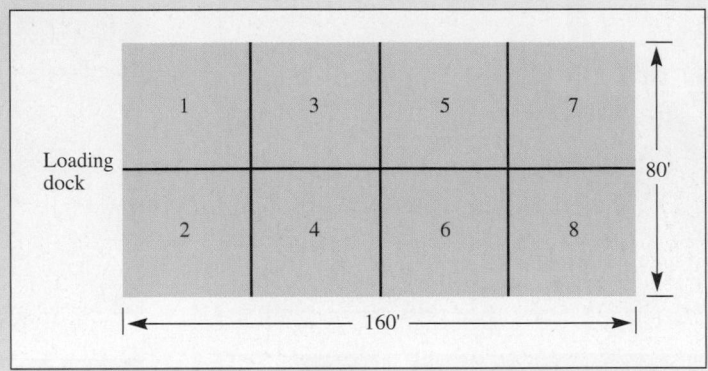

Exhibit 6A.2. Note that, in our example, diagonal moves are permitted so that workcenters 2 and 3, and 3 and 6, are considered adjacent.

Given this information, our first step is to illustrate the interworkcenter flow by a model, such as Exhibit 6A.3. This provides the basic layout pattern, which we will try to improve.

The second step is to determine the cost of this layout by multiplying the material handling cost by the number of loads moved between each pair of workcenters. Exhibit 6A.4 presents this information, which is derived as follows: The annual material handling cost between Workcenters 1 and 2 is $175 ($1 × 175 moves), $60 between Workcenters 1 and 5 ($2 × 30 moves), $60 between Workcenters 1 and 7 ($3 × 20 moves), $240 between diagonal Workcenters 2 and 7 ($3 × 80), and so forth. (The "distances" are taken from Exhibit 6A.2 or 6A.3, not Exhibit 6A.4.)

The third step is a search for workcenter location changes that will reduce costs. On the basis of the graph and the cost matrix, it seems desirable to place Workcenters 1 and 6 closer together to reduce their high move-distance costs. However, this requires shifting several other workcenters, thereby affecting their move-distance costs and the total cost of the second solution. Exhibit 6A.5 shows the revised layout resulting from relocating Workcenter 6 and an adjacent workcenter. (Workcenter 4 is arbitrarily selected for this purpose.) The revised cost matrix for the exchange, showing the cost changes, is given in Exhibit 6A.6. Note the

Excel: Process Layout

exhibit 6A.3   Interworkcenter Flow Graph with Number of Annual Movements

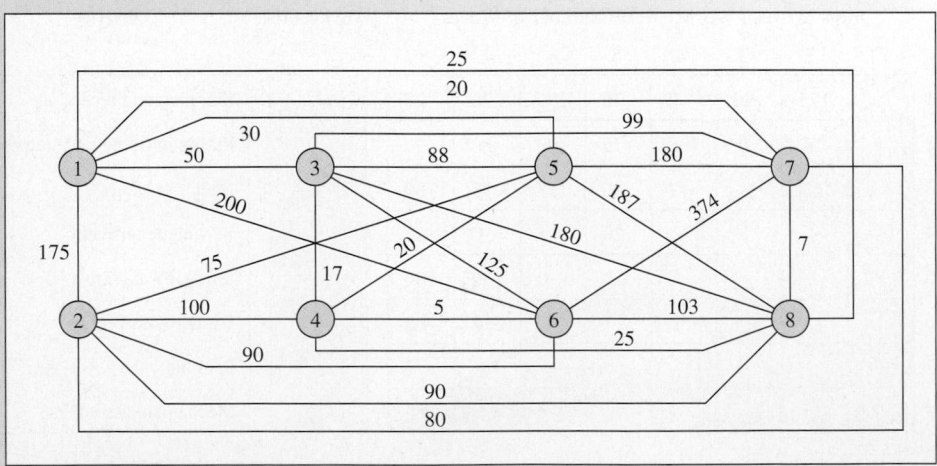

Cost Matrix—First Solution

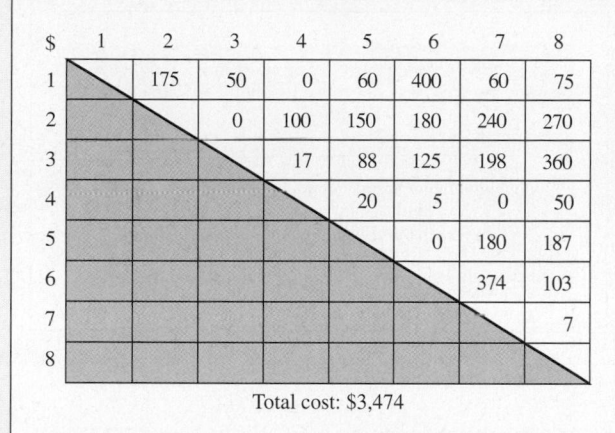

Total cost: $3,474

Revised Interworkcenter Flowchart (Only interworkcenter flow with effect on cost is depicted.)

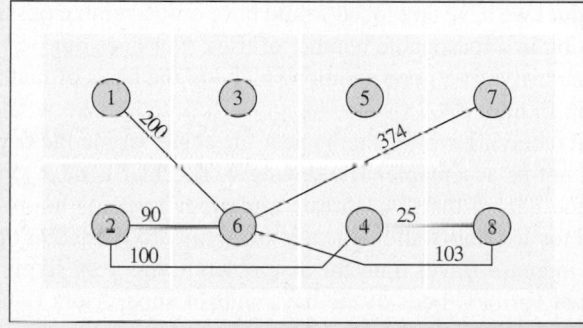

Cost Matrix—Second Solution

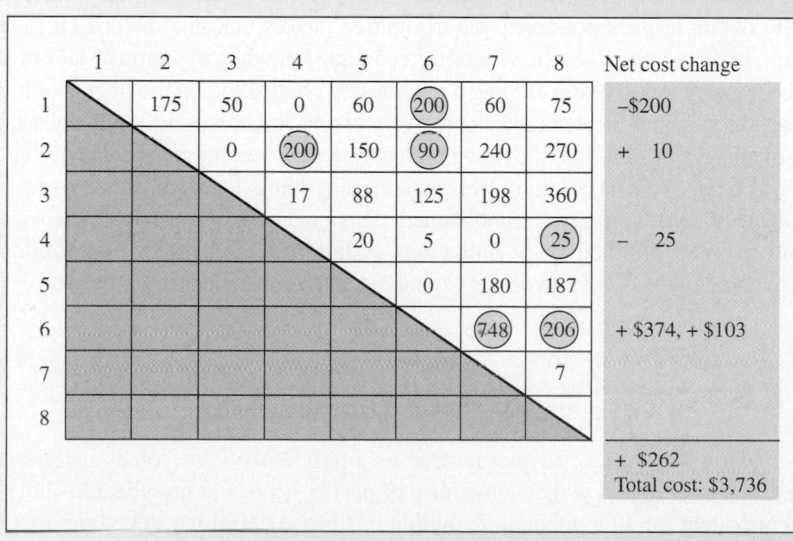

     A Feasible Layout

Small toy assembly	Mechanism assembly	Shipping and receiving	Large toy assembly
5	8	1	6
Metal forming	Plastic molding and stamping	Sewing	Painting
3	2	4	7

total cost is $262 *greater* than in the initial solution. Clearly, doubling the distance between Workcenters 6 and 7 accounted for the major part of the cost increase. This points out the fact that, even in a small problem, it is rarely easy to decide the correct "obvious move" on the basis of casual inspection.

Thus far, we have shown only one exchange among a large number of potential exchanges; in fact, for an eight-workcenter problem, there are 8! (or 40,320) possible arrangements. Therefore, the procedure we have employed would have only a remote possibility of achieving an optimal combination in a reasonable number of tries. Nor does our problem stop here.

Suppose that we *do* arrive at a good solution solely on the basis of material handling cost, such as that shown in Exhibit 6A.7 (whose total cost is $3,550). We would note, first of all, that our shipping and receiving workcenter is near the center of the factory—an arrangement that probably would not be acceptable. The sewing workcenter is next to the painting workcenter, introducing the hazard that lint, thread, and cloth particles might drift onto painted items. Further, small toy assembly and large toy assembly are located at opposite ends of the plant, which would increase travel time for assemblers (who very likely would be needed in both workcenters at various times of the day) and for supervisors (who might otherwise supervise both workcenters simultaneously). Often factors other than material handling cost need to be considered in finalizing a layout.

SYSTEMATIC LAYOUT PLANNING

Systematic layout planning (SLP)

In certain types of layout problems, numerical flow of items between workcenters either is impractical to obtain or does not reveal the qualitative factors that may be crucial to the placement decision. In these situations, the venerable technique known as systematic layout planning (SLP) can be used.[1] It involves developing a relationship chart showing the degree of importance of having each workcenter located adjacent to every other workcenter. From this chart, an activity relationship diagram, similar to the flow graph used for illustrating material handling between workcenters, is developed. The activity relationship diagram is then adjusted by trial and error until a satisfactory adjacency pattern is obtained. This pattern, in turn, is modified workcenter by workcenter to meet building space limitations. Exhibit 6A.8 illustrates the technique with a simple five-workcenter problem involving laying out a floor of a department store.

ASSEMBLY LINES

The term *assembly line* refers to progressive assembly linked by some material handling device. The usual assumption is that some form of pacing is present and the allowable processing time is equivalent for all workstations. Within this broad definition, there are important differences among line types. A few of these are material handling devices (belt or roller conveyor,

Systematic Layout Planning for a Floor of a Department Store

A. Relationship Chart (based on Tables B and C)

From	To 2	To 3	To 4	To 5	Area (sq. ft.)
1. Credit department	I 6	U —	E 4	U —	100
2. Toy department		U —	I 1	A 1,6	400
3. Wine department			U —	X 1	300
4. Camera department				X 1	100
5. Candy department					100

Letter	Closeness rating
Number	Reason for rating

B.

CODE	REASON*
1	Type of customer
2	Ease of supervision
3	Common personnel
4	Contact necessary
5	Share same space
6	Psychology

*Others may be used.

C.

VALUE	CLOSENESS	LINE CODE*	NUMERICAL WEIGHTS
A	Absolutely necessary	≡≡≡	16
E	Especially important	≡≡	8
I	Important	≡	4
O	Ordinary closeness OK	—	2
U	Unimportant		0
X	Undesirable	⋀⋀⋀	−80

*Used for example purposes only.

Initial relationship diagram (based on Tables A and C)

Initial layout based on relationship diagram (ignoring space and building constraints)

Final layout adjusted by square footage and building size

---

overhead crane); line configuration (U-shape, straight, branching); pacing (mechanical, human); product mix (one product or multiple products); workstation characteristics (workers may sit, stand, walk with the line, or ride the line); and length of the line (few or many workers). For many readers, their first exposure to assembly lines is in the *I Love Lucy* episode where Lucy and Ethel are putting candies in paper wrappings on a fast-moving line and, in order to keep up, they resort to sticking them in their pockets and finally in their mouths. While this clearly overstates the pressure of assembly-line work, there is no doubt that speed and dexterity are of the essence in real situations such as automobile lines. For worker insight, see the box titled "What's It Like Working on an Assembly Line?"

WHAT'S IT LIKE WORKING ON AN ASSEMBLY LINE?

Ben Hamper, the infamous "Rivethead" working for General Motors, describes his new job on the Chevy Suburban assembly line with the following:

The whistle blew and the Rivet Line began to crawl. I took a seat up on the workbench and watched the guy I was replacing tackle his duties. He'd grab one end of a long rail and, with the help of the worker up the line from him, flip it over on its back. CLAAAANNNNNNGGGG! He then raced back to the bench and grabbed a four-wheel-drive spring casting and a muffler hanger. He would rivet the pieces onto the rail. With that completed, he'd jostle the rail back into an upright position and grab a cross member off the overhanging feeder line that curled above the bench. Reaching up with his spare arm, he'd grab a different rivet gun while fidgeting to get the cross member firmly planted so that it aligned with the proper set of

holes. He then inserted the rivets and began squashing the cross member into place. Just watching this guy go at it made my head hurt.

"How about takin' a stab at it?" the guy asked me after a while. "You're not gonna get the feel of the job sittin' up there on the bench."

I politely declined. I didn't want to learn any portion of this monster maze before it was absolutely necessary. Once the bossman thought you had a reasonable grasp of the setup, he was likely to step in and turn you loose on your own. I needed to keep delaying in order to give Art some time to reel me back up to Cab Shop.

"Well, you've got three days," the guy replied. "After that, this baby's all yours."

EXCERPT FROM B. HAMPER'S *RIVETHEAD: TALES FROM THE ASSEMBLY LINE* (NEW YORK: WARNER BOOKS, 1992), P. 90.

The range of products partially or completely assembled on lines includes toys, appliances, autos, planes, guns, garden equipment, clothing, and a wide variety of electronic components. In fact, it is probably safe to say that virtually any product that has multiple parts and is produced in large volume uses assembly lines to some degree. Clearly, lines are an important technology; to really understand their managerial requirements, we should have some familiarity with how a line is balanced.

ASSEMBLY-LINE BALANCING

Though primarily a scheduling issue, assembly-line balancing often has implications for layout. This would occur when, for balance purposes, workstation size or the number used would have to be physically modified.

Workstation cycle time

The most common assembly line is a moving conveyor that passes a series of workstations in a uniform time interval called the **workstation cycle time** (which is also the time between successive units coming off the end of the line). At each workstation, work is performed on a product either by adding parts or by completing assembly operations. The work performed at each station is made up of many bits of work, termed *tasks, elements,* and *work units.* Such tasks are described by motion–time analysis. Generally, they are groupings that cannot be subdivided on the assembly line without paying a penalty in extra motions.

Assembly-line balancing

The total work to be performed at a workstation is equal to the sum of the tasks assigned to that workstation. The **assembly-line balancing** problem is one of assigning all tasks to a series of workstations so that each workstation has no more than can be done in the workstation cycle time, and so that the unassigned (that is, idle) time across all workstations is minimized. The problem is complicated by the relationships among tasks imposed by product design and process technologies. This is called the **precedence relationship**, which specifies the order in which tasks must be performed in the assembly process.

Precedence relationship

The steps in balancing an assembly line are straightforward:

1. Specify the sequential relationships among tasks using a precedence diagram. The diagram consists of circles and arrows. Circles represent individual tasks; arrows indicate the order of task performance.

2. Determine the required workstation cycle time (*C*), using the formula

$$C = \frac{\text{Production time per day}}{\text{Required output per day (in units)}} \qquad \text{[6A.1]}$$

3. Determine the theoretical minimum number of workstations (N_t) required to satisfy the workstation cycle time constraint using the formula (note that this must be rounded up to the next highest integer)

$$N_t = \frac{\text{sum of task times } (T)}{\text{Cycle time } (C)} \qquad \text{[6A.2]}$$

4. Select a primary rule by which tasks are to be assigned to workstations and a secondary rule to break ties.
5. Assign tasks, one at a time, to the first workstation until the sum of the task times is equal to the workstation cycle time, or no other tasks are feasible because of time or sequence restrictions. Repeat the process for Workstation 2, Workstation 3, and so on, until all tasks are assigned.
6. Evaluate the efficiency of the balance derived using the formula[2]

$$\text{Efficiency} = \frac{\text{Sum of task times } (T)}{\text{Actual number of workstations } (N_a) \times \text{Workstation cycle time } (C)} \qquad \text{[6A.3]}$$

7. If efficiency is unsatisfactory, rebalance using a different decision rule.

EXAMPLE 6A.1: Assembly-Line Balancing

The Model J Wagon is to be assembled on a conveyor belt. Five hundred wagons are required per day. Production time per day is 420 minutes, and the assembly steps and times for the wagon are given in Exhibit 6A.9. Assignment: Find the balance that minimizes the number of workstations, subject to cycle time and precedence constraints.

Step by Step

Assembly Steps and Times for Model J Wagon

TASK	TASK TIME (IN SECONDS)	DESCRIPTION	TASKS THAT MUST PRECEDE
A	45	Position rear axle support and hand fasten four screws to nuts.	—
B	11	Insert rear axle.	A
C	9	Tighten rear axle support screws to nuts.	B
D	50	Position front axle assembly and hand fasten with four screws to nuts.	—
E	15	Tighten front axle assembly screws.	D
F	12	Position rear wheel #1 and fasten hubcap.	C
G	12	Position rear wheel #2 and fasten hubcap.	C
H	12	Position front wheel #1 and fasten hubcap.	F
I	12	Position front wheel #2 and fasten hubcap.	E
J	8	Position wagon handle shaft on front axle assembly and hand fasten bolt and nut.	F, G, H, I
K	9	Tighten bolt and nut.	J
	195		

exhibit 6A.10   Precedence Graph for Model J Wagon

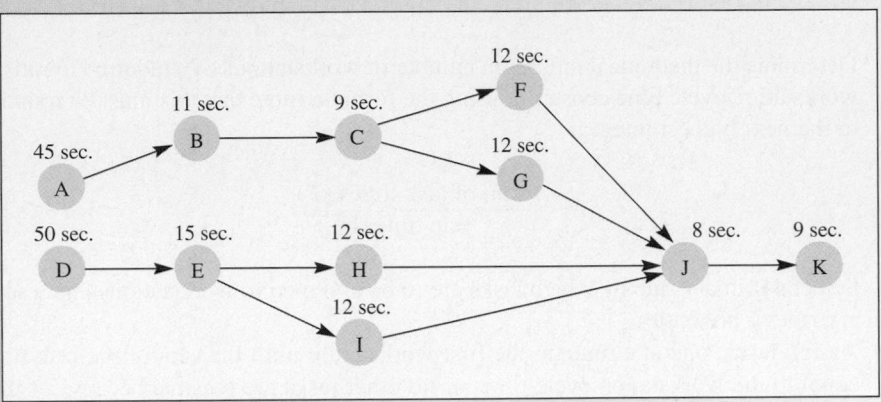

SOLUTION

1. Draw a precedence diagram. Exhibit 6A.10 illustrates the sequential relationships identified in Exhibit 6A.9. (The length of the arrows has no meaning.)
2. Determine workstation cycle time. Here we have to convert to seconds because our task times are in seconds.

$$C = \frac{\text{Production time per day}}{\text{Output per day}} = \frac{60 \text{ sec.} \times 420 \text{ min.}}{500 \text{ wagons}} = \frac{25,200}{500} = 50.4$$

3. Determine the theoretical minimum number of workstations required (the actual number may be greater):

$$N_t = \frac{T}{C} = \frac{195 \text{ seconds}}{50.4 \text{ seconds}} = 3.87 = 4 \text{ (rounded up)}$$

4. Select assignment rules. Research has demonstrated that some rules are better than others for certain problem structures. In general, the strategy is to use a rule assigning tasks that either have many followers or are of long duration because they effectively limit the balance achievable. In this case, we use the following as our primary rule:

    a. Prioritize tasks in order of the largest number of following tasks.

TASK	NUMBER OF FOLLOWING TASKS
A	6
B or D	5
C or E	4
F, G, H, or I	2
J	1
K	0

Our secondary rule, to be invoked where ties exist from our primary rule, is

    b. Prioritize tasks in order of longest task time (shown in Exhibit 6A.11). Note that D should be assigned before B and E assigned before C due to this tiebreaking rule.

5. Make task assignments to form Workstation 1, Workstation 2, and so forth, until all tasks are assigned. The actual assignment is given in Exhibit 6A.11A and is shown graphically in Exhibit 6A.11B. It is important to meet precedence and cycle time requirements as the assignments are made.

A. Balance Made According to Largest-Number-of-Following-Tasks Rule

	TASK	TASK TIME (IN SECONDS)	REMAINING UNASSIGNED TIME (IN SECONDS)	FEASIBLE REMAINING TASKS	TASK WITH MOST FOLLOWERS	TASK WITH LONGEST OPERATION TIME
Station 1	A	45	5.4 idle	None		
Station 2	D	50	0.4 idle	None		
Station 3	B	11	39.4	C, E	C, E	E
	E	15	24.4	C, H, I	C	
	C	9	15.4	F, G, H, I	F, G, H, I	F, G, H, I
	F*	12	3.4 idle	None		
Station 4	G	12	38.4	H, I	H, I	H, I
	H*	12	26.4	I		
	I	12	14.4	J		
	J	8	6.4 idle	None		
Station 5	K	9	41.4 idle	None		

*Denotes task arbitrarily selected where there is a tie between longest operation times.

B. Precedence Graph for Model J Wagon with a Visual Representation of the Workstations

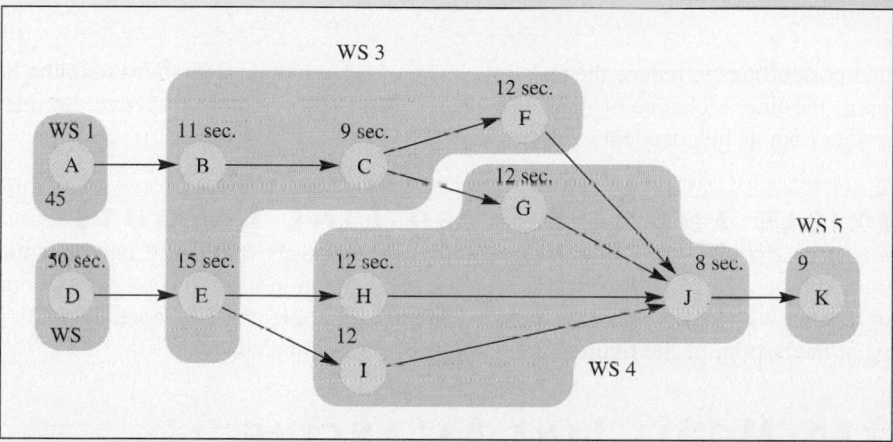

C. Efficiency Calculation

$$\text{Efficiency} = \frac{T}{N_c C} = \frac{195}{(5)(50.4)} = 0.77, \text{ or } 77\%$$

6. Calculate the efficiency. This is shown in Exhibit 6A.11C.
7. Evaluate the solution. An efficiency of 77 percent indicates an imbalance or idle time of 23 percent (1.0 − 0.77) across the entire line. From Exhibit 6A.11A, we can see that there are 57 total seconds of idle time and the "choice" job is at Workstation 5.

Is a better balance possible? In this case, yes. Try balancing the line with rule *b* and breaking ties with rule *a*. (This will give you a feasible four-station balance.) ●

SPLITTING TASKS

Often the longest required task time forms the shortest workstation cycle time for the production line. This task time limits how quickly the assembly line can produce a product unless it is possible to split the task into two or more workstations.

Consider the following illustration: Suppose that an assembly line contains the following task times in seconds: 40, 30, 15, 25, 20, 18, 15. The line runs for $7\frac{1}{2}$ hours per day, and demand for output is 750 per day.

The workstation cycle time required to produce 750 per day is 36 seconds ([$7\frac{1}{2}$ hours × 60 minutes × 60 seconds]/750). Our problem is that we have one task that takes 40 seconds. How do we deal with this task?

There are several ways that we may be able to accommodate the 40-second task in a 36-second cycle. Possibilities are

1. **Split the task.** Can we split the task so that complete units are processed in two workstations?
2. **Share the task.** Can the task somehow be shared so an adjacent workstation does part of the work? This differs from the split task in the first option because the adjacent station acts to assist, not to do some units containing the entire task.
3. **Use parallel workstations.** It may be necessary to assign the task to two workstations that would operate in parallel.
4. **Use a more skilled worker.** Because this task exceeds the workstation cycle time by just 11 percent, a faster worker may be able to meet the 36-second time.
5. **Work overtime.** Producing at a rate of one every 40 seconds would create 675 per day, 75 short of the needed 750. The amount of overtime required to produce the additional 75 is 50 minutes (75 × 40 seconds/60 seconds).
6. **Redesign.** It may be possible to redesign the product to reduce the task time slightly.

Other possibilities to reduce the task time include an equipment upgrade, a roaming helper to support the line, a change of materials, and multiskilled workers to operate the line as a team rather than as independent workers.

FLEXIBLE AND U-SHAPED LINE LAYOUTS

As we saw in the preceding example, assembly-line balances frequently result in unequal workstation times. Flexible line layouts such as those shown in Exhibit 6A.12 are a common way of dealing with this problem. In our toy company example, the U-shaped line with work sharing at the bottom of the figure could help resolve the imbalance.

MIXED-MODEL LINE BALANCING

This approach is used by JIT manufacturers such as Toyota. Its objective is to meet the demand for a variety of products and to avoid building high inventories. Mixed-model line balancing involves scheduling several different models to be produced over a given day or week on the same line in a cyclical fashion.

Step by Step

EXAMPLE 6A.2: Mixed-Model Line Balancing

To illustrate how this is done, suppose our toy company has a fabrication line to bore holes in its Model J wagon frame and its Model K wagon frame. The time required to bore the holes is different for each wagon type.

Assume that the final assembly line downstream requires equal numbers of Model J and Model K wagon frames. Assume also that we want to develop a cycle time for the fabrication line that is balanced for the production of equal numbers of J and K frames. Of course, we could produce Model J frames for several days and then produce Model K frames until an equal number of frames has been produced. However, this would build up unnecessary work-in-process inventory.

If we want to reduce the amount of in-process inventory, we could develop a cycle mix that greatly reduces inventory buildup while keeping within the restrictions of equal numbers of J and K wagon frames.

Process times: 6 minutes per J and 4 minutes per K.

The day consists of 480 minutes (8 hours × 60 minutes).

Flexible Line Layouts

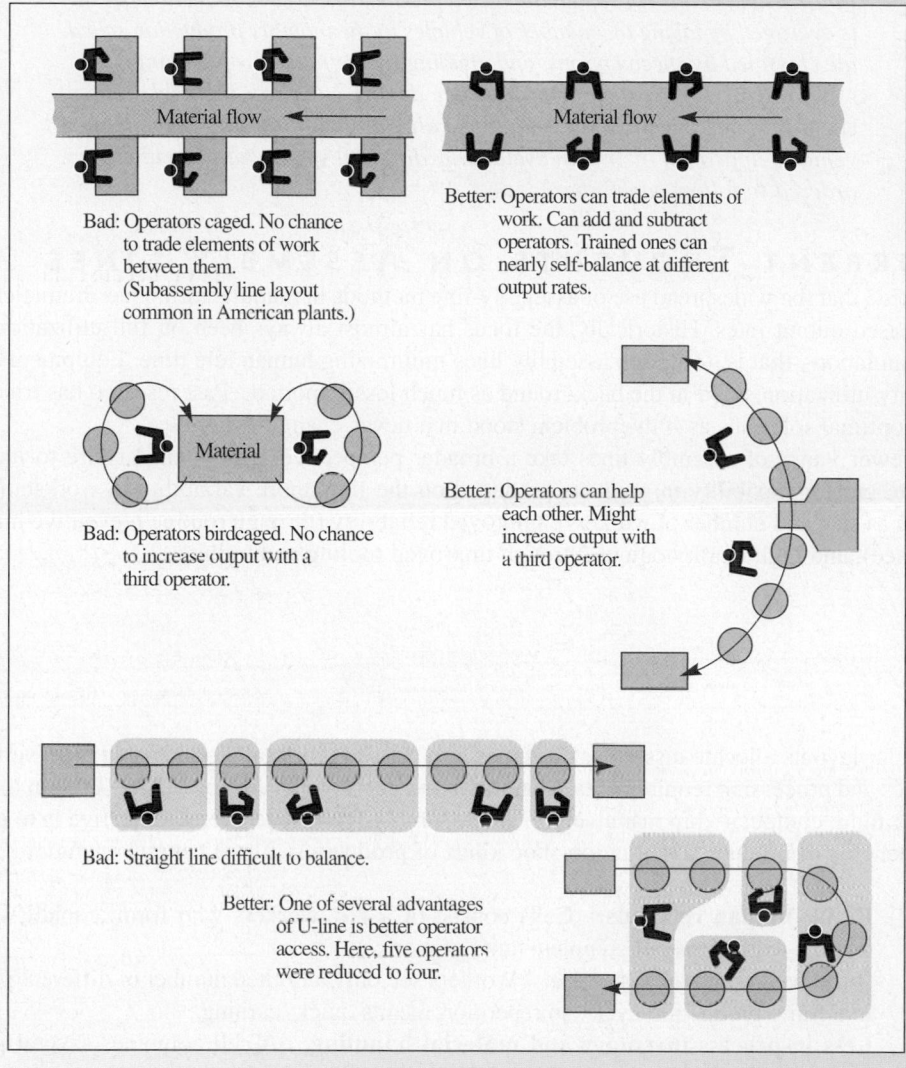

Bad: Operators caged. No chance to trade elements of work between them. (Subassembly line layout common in American plants.)

Better: Operators can trade elements of work. Can add and subtract operators. Trained ones can nearly self-balance at different output rates.

Bad: Operators birdcaged. No chance to increase output with a third operator.

Better: Operators can help each other. Might increase output with a third operator.

Bad: Straight line difficult to balance.

Better: One of several advantages of U-line is better operator access. Here, five operators were reduced to four.

SOLUTION

$$6J + 4K = 480$$

Because equal numbers of J and K are to be produced (or J = K), produce 48J and 48K per day, or 6J and 6K per hour.

The following shows one balance of J and K frames.

Balanced Mixed-Model Sequence

Model sequence	J J	K K K	J J	J J	K K K	
Operation time	6 6	4 4 4	6 6	6 6	4 4 4	Repeats 8 times per day
Minicycle time	12	12	12	12	12	
Total cycle time			60			

This line is balanced at 6 frames of each type per hour with a minicycle time of 12 minutes.

Another balance is J K K J K J, with times of 6, 4, 4, 6, 4, 6. This balance produces 3J and 3K every 30 minutes with a minicycle time of 10 minutes (JK, KJ, KJ). ●

The simplicity of mixed-model balancing (under conditions of a level production schedule) is seen in Yasuhiro Monden's description of Toyota Motor Corporation's operations:

> *Final assembly lines of Toyota are mixed product lines. The production per day is averaged by taking the number of vehicles in the monthly production schedule classified by specifications, and dividing by the number of working days.*
>
> *In regard to the production sequence during each day, the cycle time of each different specification vehicle is calculated. To have all specification vehicles appear at their own cycle time, different specification vehicles are ordered to follow each other.*[3]

CURRENT THOUGHTS ON ASSEMBLY LINES

It is true that the widespread use of assembly-line methods in manufacturing has dramatically increased output rates. Historically, the focus has almost always been on full utilization of human labor—that is, to design assembly lines minimizing human idle time. Equipment and facility utilization stood in the background as much less important. Past research has tried to find optimal solutions as if the problem stood in a never-changing world.

Newer views of assembly lines take a broader perspective. The intentions are to incorporate greater flexibility in products produced on the line, more variability in workstations (such as size and number of workers), improved reliability (through routine preventive maintenance), and high-quality output (through improved tooling and training).

CELLS

Cellular layouts allocate dissimilar machines into cells to work on products that have similar shapes and processing requirements. Manufacturing cell layouts are now widely used in metal fabricating, computer chip manufacture, and assembly work. The overall objective is to gain the benefits of product layout in job-shop kinds of production. These benefits include

1. **Better human relations.** Cells consist of a few workers who form a small work team; a team turns out complete units of work.
2. **Improved operator expertise.** Workers see only a limited number of different parts in a finite production cycle, so repetition means quick learning.
3. **Less in-process inventory and material handling.** A cell combines several production stages, so fewer parts travel through the shop.
4. **Faster production setup.** Fewer jobs mean reduced tooling and hence faster tooling changes.

DEVELOPING A MANUFACTURING CELL

Shifting from process layout to a cellular layout entails three steps:

1. Grouping parts into families that follow a common sequence of steps. This step requires developing and maintaining a computerized parts classification and coding system. This is often a major expense with such systems, although many companies have developed shortcut procedures for identifying parts families.
2. Identifying dominant flow patterns of parts families as a basis for location or relocation of processes.
3. Physically grouping machines and processes into cells. Often there will be parts that cannot be associated with a family and specialized machinery that cannot be placed in any one cell because of its general use. These unattached parts and machinery are placed in a "remainder cell."

Exhibit 6A.13 illustrates the cell development process for four part families. Part A shows the original process layout. Part B shows a routing matrix based on flow of parts. Part C

Development of Manufacturing Cell

A. Original workcenter layout

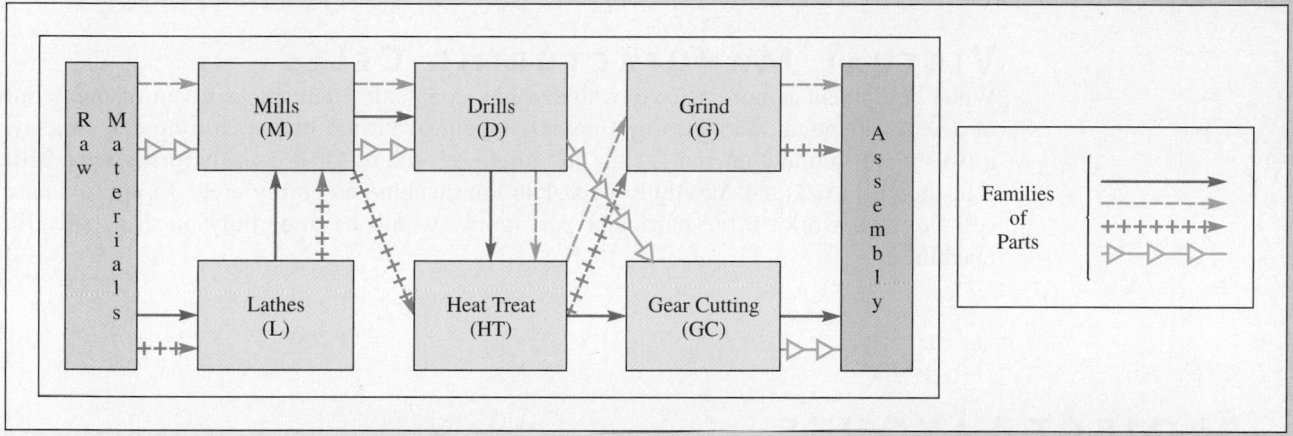

SOURCE: ADAPTED FROM D. FOGARTY AND T. HOFFMAN, *PRODUCTION AND INVENTORY MANAGEMENT* (CINCINNATI: SOUTH-WESTERN PUBLISHING, 1983), P. 472.

B. Routing matrix based upon flow of parts

Raw Materials	Part Family	Lathes	Mills	Drills	Heat Treating	Grinders	Gear Cutting	To	Assembly
---→			X	X	X	X		---→	
→▷–			X	X			X	→▷–	
——→		X	X	X	X		X	——→	
+++→		X	X		X	X		+++→	

C. Reallocating machines to form cells according to part family processing requirements.

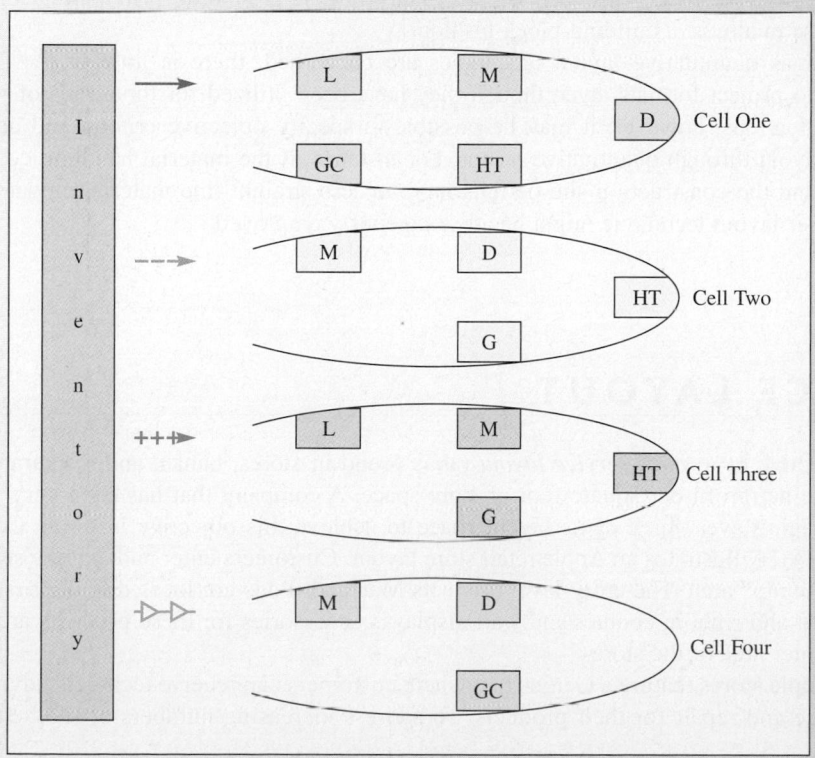

illustrates the final organization of cells, with equipment organized in the traditional U shape. The example assumes that there are multiple lathes, mills, and so forth, so that each cell will have the requisite number of each type physically located within it.

VIRTUAL MANUFACTURING CELLS

When equipment is not easily movable, many companies dedicate a given machine out of a set of identical machines in a process layout. A virtual manufacturing cell for, say, a two-month production run for the job might consist of Drill 1 in the drills area, Mill 3 in the mill area, and Assembly Area 1 in the machine assembly area. To approximate cell flow, all work on the particular part family would be done only on these specific machines.

PROJECT LAYOUTS

Project layouts are characterized by a relatively low number of production units in comparison with workcenter and assembly-line formats. In developing a project layout, visualize the product as the hub of a wheel with materials and equipment arranged concentrically around the production point in their order of use and movement difficulty. Thus, in building custom yachts, for example, rivets that are used throughout construction would be placed close to or in the hull; heavy engine parts, which must travel to the hull only once, would be placed at a more distant location; and cranes would be set up close to the hull because of their constant use.

In a project layout, a high degree of task ordering is common, and to the extent that this precedence determines production stages, a project layout might be developed by arranging materials according to their technological priority. This procedure would be expected in making a layout for a large machine tool, such as a stamping machine, where manufacture follows a rigid sequence; assembly is performed from the ground up, with parts being added to the base in almost a building-block fashion.

As far as quantitative layout techniques are concerned, there is little in the literature devoted to project formats, even though they have been utilized for thousands of years. In certain situations, however, it may be possible to specify objective criteria and develop a project layout through quantitative means. For instance, if the material handling cost is significant and the construction site permits more or less straight-line material movement, the workcenter layout technique might be advantageously employed.

RETAIL SERVICE LAYOUT

Service

The objective of a *retail service layout* (as is found in stores, banks, and restaurants) is to maximize net profit per square foot of store space. A company that has been very successful leveraging every inch of its layout space to achieve this objective is Apple Computer. Exhibit 6A.14 illustrates an Apple retail store layout. Customers enter and exit the store from the "cashwrap" area. The entry-level products Mac and iPods are located in the first section on the left and right in counter and wall displays. Accessories for these products are located in the center area of the store.

All Apple stores feature a Genius bar, where customers can receive technical advice or set up service and repair for their products. To address increasing numbers of iPod customers

Apple Retail Store Layout

Software, books	iPod bar
	iPod
	iPod

Accessories   Cashwrap

Studio bar   Kids

Mac   Mac

Hardware accessories   Genius bar

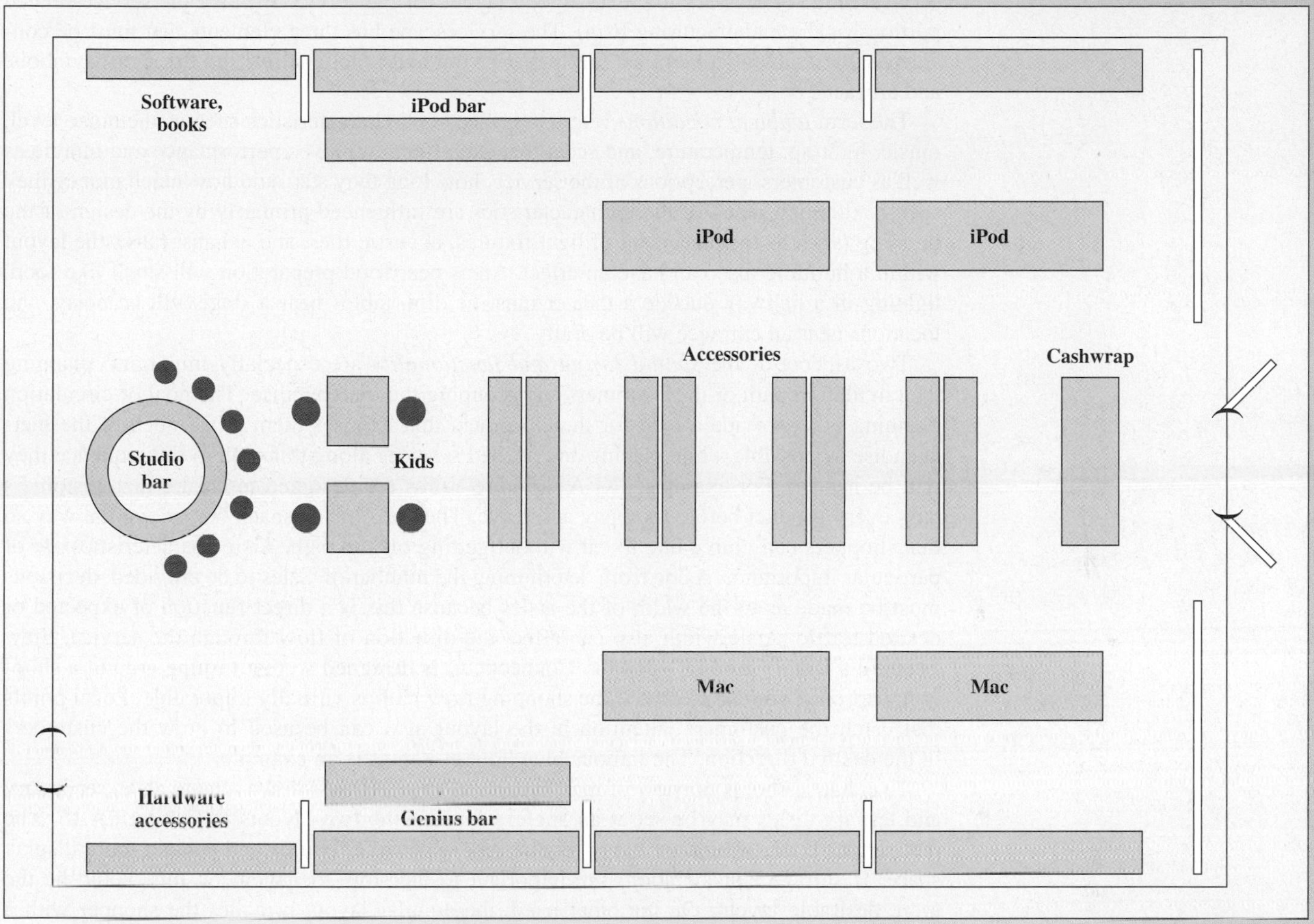

at the Genius bar, some new stores also feature an iPod bar. Most stores feature a station called The Studio, a Genius bar–like setting where customers can meet with a "Creative" and receive help with projects ranging from organizing a photo album to music composition to film editing. The areas for trying out the products and "experimenting" are located toward the rear of the store. Software and books also are located in the rear of the store. A special area for kids with low seating and a round table provides an area for trying out popular products.

SERVICESCAPES

As previously noted, the broad objective of layout in retail services is generally to maximize net profit per square foot of floor space. Operationally, this goal is often translated into such criteria as "minimize handling cost" or "maximize product exposure." However, as Sommers and Kernan observed more than 30 years ago, employing these and similar criteria in service layout planning "results in stores that look like warehouses and requires shoppers to approach the task like order pickers or display case stockers."[4] Of course, Walmart and Home Depot customers gladly accept such arrangements for price savings.

Service

Other, more humanistic aspects of the service also must be considered in the layout. Bitner coined the term *servicescape* to refer to the physical surroundings in which the service takes place and how these surroundings affect customers and employees. An understanding of the servicescape is necessary to create a good layout for the service firm (or the service-related portions of the manufacturing firm). The servicescape has three elements that must be considered: the ambient conditions; the spatial layout and functionality; and the signs, symbols, and artifacts.[5]

The term *ambient conditions* refers to background characteristics such as the noise level, music, lighting, temperature, and scent that can affect employee performance and morale as well as customers' perceptions of the service, how long they stay, and how much money they spend. Although many of these characteristics are influenced primarily by the design of the building (such as the placement of light fixtures, acoustic tiles, and exhaust fans), the layout within a building also can have an effect. Areas near food preparation will smell like food, lighting in a hallway outside a theater must be dim, tables near a stage will be noisy, and locations near an entrance will be drafty.

Two aspects of the *spatial layout and functionality* are especially important: planning the circulation path of the customers and grouping the merchandise. The goal of circulation planning is to provide a path for the customers that exposes them to as much of the merchandise as possible while placing any needed services along this path in the sequence they will be needed. For example, IKEA furniture stores are designed to ensure that customers pass every product before they pay and leave. They also place snack bars along the way so that shoppers can grab a bite to eat without getting off the path. Aisle characteristics are of particular importance. Aside from determining the number of aisles to be provided, decisions must be made as to the width of the aisles because this is a direct function of expected or desired traffic. Aisle width also can affect the direction of flow through the service. Stew Leonard's Dairy Store in Norwalk, Connecticut, is designed so that turning around a shopping cart once you have entered the shopping flow path is virtually impossible. Focal points that catch the customers' attention in the layout also can be used to draw the customers in the desired direction. The famous blue light at Kmart is an example.

To enhance shoppers' view of merchandise as they proceed down a main aisle, secondary and tertiary aisles may be set at an angle. Consider the two layouts in Exhibit 6A.15. The rectangular layout would probably require less expensive fixtures and contain more display space. If storage considerations are important to the store management, this would be the more desirable layout. On the other hand, the angular layout provides the shopper with a much clearer view of the merchandise and, other things being equal, presents a more desirable selling environment.

exhibit 6A.15   Alternative Store Layouts

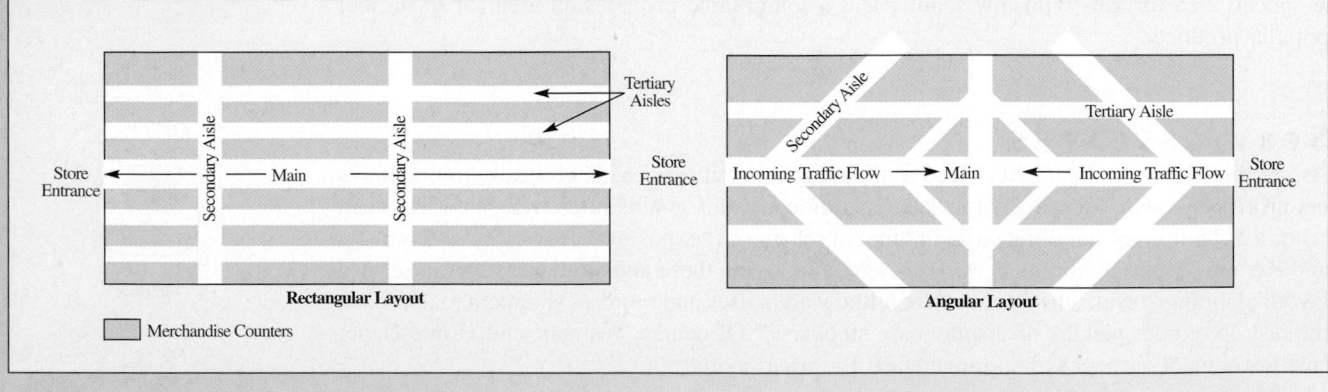

Rectangular Layout

Store Entrance — Secondary Aisle — Main — Secondary Aisle — Store Entrance

Tertiary Aisles

Angular Layout

Store Entrance — Incoming Traffic Flow → Main ← Incoming Traffic Flow — Store Entrance

Secondary Aisle

Tertiary Aisle

Merchandise Counters

It is common practice now to base merchandise groupings on the shopper's view of related items, as opposed to the physical characteristics of the products or shelf space and servicing requirements. This grouping-by-association philosophy is seen in boutiques in department stores and gourmet sections in supermarkets.

Special mention is in order for a few guidelines derived from marketing research and relating to circulation planning and merchandise grouping:

1. People in supermarkets tend to follow a perimeter pattern in their shopping behavior. Placing high-profit items along the walls of a store will enhance their probability of purchase.
2. Sale merchandise placed at the end of an aisle in supermarkets almost always sells better than the same sale items placed in the interior portion of an aisle.
3. Credit and other nonselling departments that require customers to wait for the completion of their services should be placed either on upper floors or in "dead" areas.
4. In department stores, locations nearest the store entrances and adjacent to front-window displays are most valuable in terms of sales potential.

SIGNS, SYMBOLS, AND ARTIFACTS

Signs, symbols, and artifacts refer to the parts of the service that have social significance. As with the ambiance, these are often a characteristic of the design of the building, although the orientation, location, and size of many objects and areas can carry special meaning. As examples,

Service

- In the old days, bank loan officers were easily identified because their desks were located on a raised section of the bank floor called the platform.
- A person seated at the desk closest to the entrance is usually in charge of greeting customers and directing them to their destination.
- In a workcenter store, the tiled areas indicate the aisles for travel, while carpeted areas indicate departments for browsing.
- Some car salespeople have blackboards installed in their offices because a person writing on a blackboard symbolizes someone who should be listened to and trusted (such as a teacher).

As you might have gathered from these examples, the influence of behavioral factors makes the development of hard-and-fast rules for servicescape layout rather difficult. Suffice it to say that making the layout choice is not simply a matter of choosing between display space and ease of operation.

OFFICE LAYOUT

The trend in *office layout* is toward more open offices, with personal work spaces separated only by low divider walls. Companies have removed fixed walls to foster greater communication and teamwork. Signs, symbols, and artifacts, as discussed in the section on service layout, are possibly even more important in office layout than in retailing. For instance, size and orientation of desks can indicate the importance or professionalism of the people behind them.

Service

Global

Central administration offices are often designed and laid out to convey the desired image of the company. For example, Scandinavian Airlines System's (SAS) administrative office complex outside Stockholm is a two-story collection of glass-walled pods that provide the feeling of the open communication and flat hierarchy (few levels of organization) that characterize the company's management philosophy.

Service-Master (the highly profitable janitorial management company) positions its "Know-How Room" at the center of its headquarters. This room contains all of the physical products, operations manuals, and pictorial displays of career paths and other symbols for the key knowledge essential to the business. "From this room, the rest of the company can be seen as a big apparatus to bring the knowledge of the marketplace to its employees and potential customers."[6]

SUMMARY

Facility layout is where the rubber meets the road in the design and operation of a production system. A good factory (or office) layout can provide real competitive advantage by facilitating material and information flow processes. It also can enhance employees' work life. A good service layout can be an effective "stage" for playing out the service encounter. In conclusion, here are some marks of a good layout in these environments:

MARKS OF A GOOD LAYOUT FOR MANUFACTURING AND BACK-OFFICE OPERATIONS
1. Straight-line flow pattern (or adaptation).
2. Backtracking kept to a minimum.
3. Production time predictable.
4. Little interstage storage of materials.
5. Open plant floors so everyone can see what is happening.
6. Bottleneck operations under control.
7. Workstations close together.
8. Orderly handling and storage of materials.
9. No unnecessary rehandling of materials.
10. Easily adjustable to changing conditions.

MARKS OF A GOOD LAYOUT FOR FACE-TO-FACE SERVICES
1. Easily understood service flow pattern.
2. Adequate waiting facilities.
3. Easy communication with customers.
4. Easily maintained customer surveillance.
5. Clear exit and entry points with adequate checkout capabilities.
6. Departments and processes arranged so that customers see only what you want them to see.
7. Balance between waiting areas and service areas.
8. Minimum walking and material movement.
9. Lack of clutter.
10. High sales volume per square foot of facility.

KEY TERMS

Workcenter Also called a *job-shop* or *functional layout*; a format in which similar equipment or functions are grouped together.

Assembly line Equipment or work processes are arranged according to the progressive steps by which the product is made.

Manufacturing cell Groups dissimilar machines to work on products that have similar shapes and processing requirements.

Project layout The product remains at one location, and equipment is moved to the product.

Systematic layout planning (SLP) A technique for solving process layout problems when the use of numerical flow data between departments is not practical. The technique uses an activity relationship diagram that is adjusted by trial and error until a satisfactory adjacency pattern is obtained.

Workstation cycle time The time between successive units coming off the end of an assembly line.

Assembly-line balancing The problem of assigning all the tasks to a series of workstations so that each workstation has no more than

can be done in the workstation cycle time, and so that idle time across all workstations is minimized.

Precedence relationship The order in which tasks must be performed in the assembly process.

FORMULA REVIEW

Workstation cycle time

$$C = \frac{\text{Production time per day}}{\text{Required output per day (in units)}} \quad [6A.1]$$

Minimum number of workstations required to satisfy the workstation cycle time constraint

$$N_t = \frac{\text{Sum of task times } (T)}{\text{Cycle time } (C)} \quad [6A.2]$$

Efficiency

$$\text{Efficiency} = \frac{\text{Sum of task times } (T)}{\text{Actual number of workstations } (N_a) \times \text{Workstation cycle time } (C)} \quad [6A.3]$$

SOLVED PROBLEMS

SOLVED PROBLEM 1

A university advising office has four rooms, each dedicated to specific problems: petitions (Room A), schedule advising (Room B), grade complaints (Room C), and student counseling (Room D). The office is 80 feet long and 20 feet wide. Each room is 20 feet by 20 feet. The present location of rooms is A, B, C, D—that is, a straight line. The load summary shows the number of contacts that each adviser in a room has with other advisers in the other rooms. Assume that all advisers are equal in this value.

Load summary: $AB = 10, AC = 20, AD = 30,$

$BC = 15, BD = 10, CD = 20.$

a. Evaluate this layout according to the material handling cost method.
b. Improve the layout by exchanging functions within rooms. Show your amount of improvement using the same method as in *a.*

Solution

a.

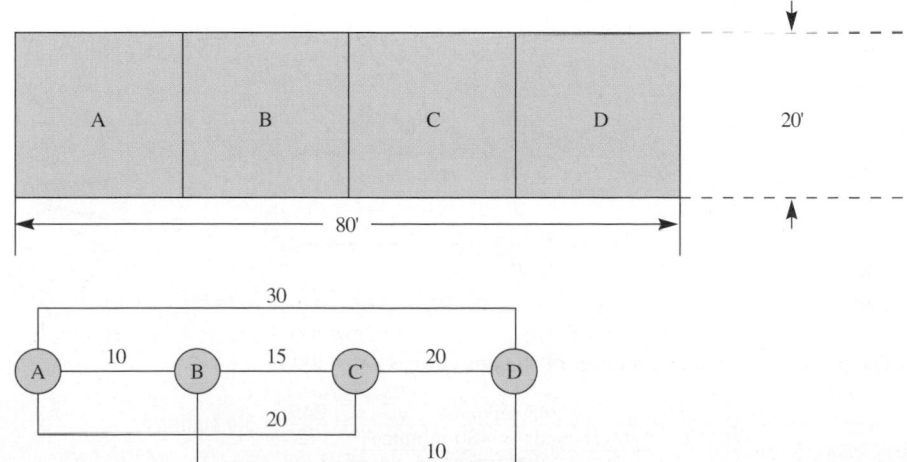

Using the material handling cost method shown in the toy company example (see Exhibits 6A.1–6A.7), we obtain the following costs, assuming that every nonadjacency doubles the initial cost/unit distance:

$$AB = 10 \times 1 = 10$$
$$AC = 20 \times 2 = 40$$
$$AD = 30 \times 3 = 90$$
$$BC = 15 \times 1 = 15$$
$$BD = 10 \times 2 = 20$$
$$CD = 20 \times 1 = 20$$
$$\text{Current cost} = 195$$

b. A better layout would be *BCDA.*

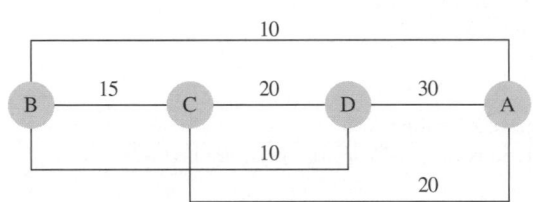

$$AB = 10 \times 3 = 30$$
$$AC = 20 \times 2 = 40$$
$$AD = 30 \times 1 = 30$$
$$BC = 15 \times 1 = 15$$
$$BD = 10 \times 2 = 20$$
$$CD = 20 \times 1 = 20$$
$$\text{Improved cost} = 155$$

SOLVED PROBLEM 2

The following tasks must be performed on an assembly line in the sequence and times specified:

TASK	TASK TIME (SECONDS)	TASKS THAT MUST PRECEDE
A	50	—
B	40	—
C	20	A
D	45	C
E	20	C
F	25	D
G	10	E
H	35	B, F, G

a. Draw the schematic diagram.
b. What is the theoretical minimum number of stations required to meet a forecast demand of 400 units per eight-hour day?
c. Use the longest-task-time rule and balance the line in the minimum number of stations to produce 400 units per day.

Solution

a.

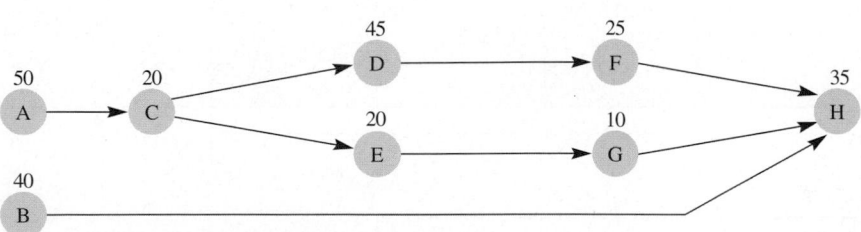

b. The theoretical minimum number of stations to meet $D = 400$ is

$$N_t = \frac{T}{C} = \frac{245 \text{ seconds}}{\left(\dfrac{60 \text{ seconds} \times 480 \text{ minutes}}{400 \text{ units}}\right)} = \frac{245}{72} = 3.4 \text{ stations}$$

c.

	Task	Task Time (Seconds)	Remaining Unassigned Time	Feasible Remaining Task
Station 1	A	50	22	C
	C	20	2	None
Station 2	D	45	27	E, F
	F	25	2	None
Station 3	B	40	32	E
	E	20	12	G
	G	10	2	None
Station 4	H	35	37	None

SOLVED PROBLEM 3

The manufacturing engineers at Suny Manufacturing were working on a new remote-controlled toy Monster Truck. They hired a production consultant to help them determine the best type of production process to meet the forecasted demand for this new product. The consultant recommended that they use an assembly line. He told the manufacturing engineers that the line must be able to produce 600 Monster Trucks per day to meet the demand forecast. The workers in the plant work eight hours per day. The task information for the new Monster Truck is given below:

Task	Task Time (Seconds)	Tasks That Must Precede
A	28	—
B	13	—
C	35	B
D	11	A
E	20	C
F	6	D,F
G	23	F
H	25	F
I	37	G
J	11	G,H
K	27	I,J
Total	236	

a. Draw the schematic diagram.
b. What is the required cycle time to meet the forecasted demand of 600 trucks per day based on an eight-hour workday?
c. What is the theoretical minimum number of workstations given the answer in part *b*?
d. Use longest task time with alphabetical order as the tie breaker and balance the line in the minimum number of stations to produce 600 trucks per day.
e. Use shortest task time with largest number of following tasks as the tie breaker and balance the line in the minimum number of stations to produce 600 trucks per day.

Solution

a.

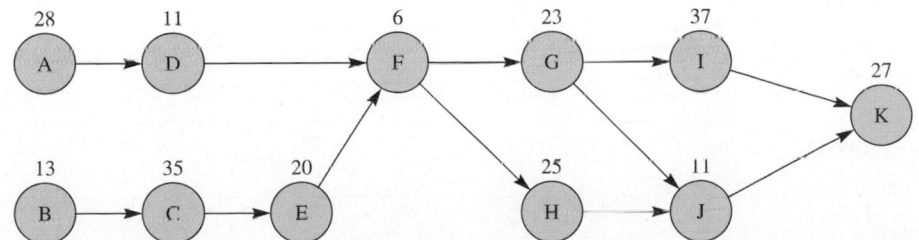

b.
$$C = \frac{\text{Production time per day}}{\text{Output per day}} = \frac{60 \text{ seconds} \times 480 \text{ minutes}}{600 \text{ trucks}} = \frac{28{,}800}{600} = 48 \text{ seconds}$$

c.
$$N_t = \frac{T}{C} = \frac{236 \text{ seconds}}{48 \text{ seconds}} = 4.92 = 5 \text{ (rounded up)}$$

d.

	FEASIBLE TASKS	TASK	TASK TIME (SECONDS)	REMAINING UNASSIGNED TIME
Station 1	A,B	A	28	20
	B,D	B	13	7
Station 2	C,D	C	35	13
	D	D	11	2
Station 3	E	E	20	28
	F	F	6	22
Station 4	G,H	H	25	23
	G	G	23	0
Station 5	I,J	I	37	11
	J	J	11	0
Station 6	K	K	27	21

e.

TASK	NUMBER OF FOLLOWING TASKS
A	7
B	8
C	7
D	6
E	6
F	5
G	3
H	2
I	1
J	1
K	0

	FEASIBLE TASKS	TASK	TASK TIME (SECONDS)	REMAINING UNASSIGNED TIME
Station 1	A,B	B	13	35
	A,C	A	28	7
Station 2	C,D	D	11	37
	C	C	35	2
Station 3	E	E	20	28
	F	F	6	22
Station 4	G,H	G	23	25
	H,I	H	25	0
Station 5	I,J	J	11	37
	I	I	37	0
Station 6	K	K	27	21

REVIEW AND DISCUSSION QUESTIONS

1 What kind of layout is used in a physical fitness center?
2 What is the objective of assembly-line balancing? How would you deal with the situation where one worker, although trying hard, is 20 percent slower than the other 10 people on a line?
3 How do you determine the idle time percentage from a given assembly-line balance?
4 What is the essential requirement for mixed-model lines to be practical?
5 Why might it be difficult to develop a manufacturing cell?
6 In what respects is facility layout a marketing problem in services? Give an example of a service system layout designed to maximize the amount of time the customer is in the system.
7 Consider a department store. Which departments probably should not be located near each other? Would any departments benefit from close proximity?
8 How would a flowchart help in planning the servicescape layout? What sorts of features would act as focal points or otherwise draw customers along certain paths through the service? In a supermarket, what departments should be located first along the customers' path? Which should be located last?

PROBLEMS

1 The Cyprus Citrus Cooperative ships a high volume of individual orders for oranges to northern Europe. The paperwork for the shipping notices is done in the accompanying layout. Revise the layout to improve the flow and conserve space if possible.

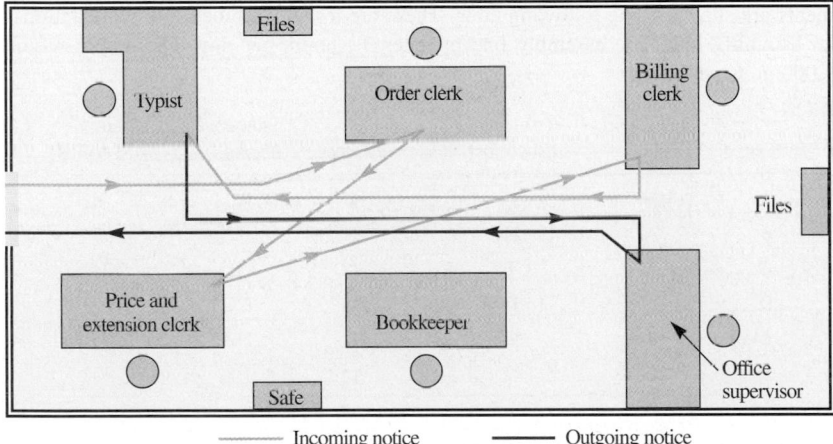

——— Incoming notice   ——— Outgoing notice

2 An assembly line makes two models of trucks: a Buster and a Duster. Busters take 12 minutes each and Dusters take 8 minutes each. The daily output requirement is 24 of each per day. Develop a perfectly balanced mixed-model sequence to satisfy demand.
3 An assembly line is to operate eight hours per day with a desired output of 240 units per day. The following table contains information on this product's task times and precedence relationships:

TASK	TASK TIME (SECONDS)	IMMEDIATE PREDECESSOR
A	60	—
B	80	A
C	20	A
D	50	A
E	90	B, C
F	30	C, D
G	30	E, F
H	60	G

    a. Draw the precedence diagram.
    b. What is the workstation cycle time?
    c. Balance this line using the longest task time.
    d. What is the efficiency of your line balance?

4   The desired daily output for an assembly line is 360 units. This assembly line will operate 450 minutes per day. The following table contains information on this product's task times and precedence relationships:

Task	Task Time (Seconds)	Immediate Predecessor
A	30	—
B	35	A
C	30	A
D	35	B
E	15	C
F	65	C
G	40	E, F
H	25	D, G

    a. Draw the precedence diagram.
    b. What is the workstation cycle time?
    c. Balance this line using the largest number of following tasks. Use the longest task time as a secondary criterion.
    d. What is the efficiency of your line balance?

5   Some tasks and the order in which they must be performed according to their assembly requirements are shown in the following table. These are to be combined into workstations to create an assembly line. The assembly line operates $7\frac{1}{2}$ hours per day. The output requirement is 1,000 units per day.

Task	Preceding Tasks	Time (Seconds)	Task	Preceding Tasks	Time (Seconds)
A	—	15	G	C	11
B	A	24	H	D	9
C	A	6	I	E	14
D	B	12	J	F, G	7
E	B	18	K	H, I	15
F	C	7	L	J, K	10

    a. What is the workstation cycle time?
    b. Balance the line using the longest task time based on the 1,000-unit forecast, stating which tasks would be done in each workstation.
    c. For *b*, what is the efficiency of your line balance?
    d. After production was started, Marketing realized that they understated demand and must increase output to 1,100 units. What action would you take? Be specific in quantitative terms, if appropriate.

6   An initial solution has been given to the following workcenter layout problem. Given the flows described and a cost of $2.00 per unit per foot, compute the total cost for the layout. Each location is 100 feet long and 50 feet wide as shown on the following figure. Use the centers of departments for distances and measure distance using metropolitan-rectilinear distance.

Department

		A	B	C	D
	A	0	10	25	55
Department	B		0	10	5
	C			0	15
	D				0

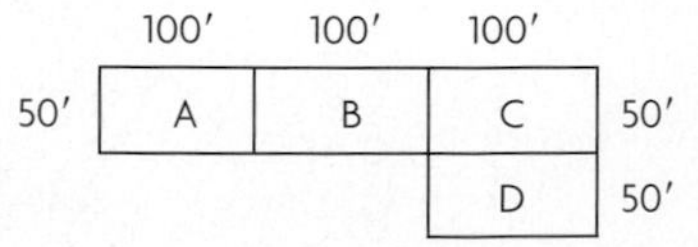

7 An assembly line is to be designed to operate $7\frac{1}{2}$ hours per day and supply a steady demand of 300 units per day. Here are the tasks and their performance times:

Task	Preceding Tasks	Performance Time (Seconds)	Task	Preceding Tasks	Performance Time (Seconds)
a	—	70	g	d	60
b	—	40	h	e	50
c	—	45	i	f	15
d	a	10	j	g	25
e	b	30	k	h, i	20
f	c	20	l	j, k	25

a. Draw the precedence diagram.
b. What is the workstation cycle time?
c. What is the theoretical minimum number of workstations?
d. Assign tasks to workstations using the longest operating time.
e. What is the efficiency of your line balance?
f. Suppose demand increases by 10 percent. How would you react to this? Assume that you can operate only $7\frac{1}{2}$ hours per day.

8 S. L. P. Craft would like your help in developing a layout for a new outpatient clinic to be built in California. From analysis of another recently built clinic, she obtains the data shown in the following diagram. This includes the number of trips made by patients between departments on a typical day (shown above the diagonal line) and the numbered weights (defined in Exhibit 6A.8) between departments as specified by the new clinic's physicians (below the diagonal). The new building will be 60 feet by 20 feet.

a. Develop an interdepartmental flow graph that minimizes patient travel.
b. Develop a "good" relationship diagram using systematic layout planning.
c. Choose either of the layouts obtained in *a* or *b* and sketch the departments to scale within the building.
d. Will this layout be satisfactory to the nursing staff? Explain.

Department	2	3	4	5	6	Area Requirement (sq ft.)
1 Reception	A / 2	O / 5	E / 200	U / 0	O / 10	100
2 X-ray		E / 10	I / 300	U / 0	O / 8	100
3 Surgery			I / 100	U / 0	A / 4	200
4 Examining rooms (5)				U / 0	I / 15	500
5 Lab					O / 3	100
6 Nurses' station						100

9 The following tasks are to be performed on an assembly line:

Task	Seconds	Tasks That Must Precede
A	20	—
B	7	A
C	20	B
D	22	B
E	15	C
F	10	D
G	16	E, F
H	8	G

The workday is seven hours long. Demand for completed product is 750 per day.

a. Find the cycle time.
b. What is the theoretical number of workstations?
c. Draw the precedence diagram.
d. Balance the line using sequential restrictions and the longest-operating-time rule.
e. What is the efficiency of the line balanced as in *d*?
f. Suppose that demand rose from 750 to 800 units per day. What would you do? Show any amounts or calculations.
g. Suppose that demand rose from 750 to 1,000 units per day. What would you do? Show any amounts or calculations.

10 The Dorton University president has asked the OM department to assign eight biology professors (A, B, C, D, E, F, G, and H) to eight offices (numbered 1 to 8 in the diagram) in the new biology building.

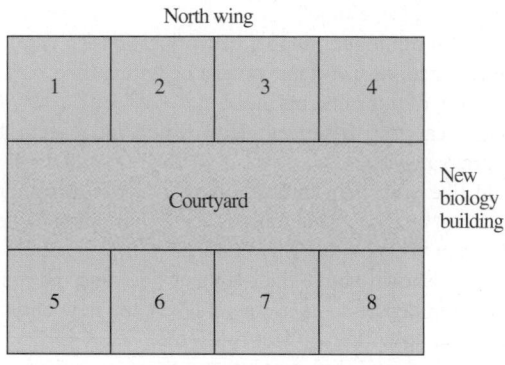

The following distances and two-way flows are given:

DISTANCES BETWEEN OFFICES (FEET)									TWO-WAY FLOWS (UNITS PER PERIOD)							
	1	2	3	4	5	6	7	8		A	B	C	D	E	F	G	H
1	—	10	20	30	15	18	25	34	A	—	2	0	0	5	0	0	0
2		—	10	20	18	15	18	25	B		—	0	0	0	3	0	2
3			—	10	25	18	15	18	C			—	0	0	0	0	3
4				—	34	25	18	15	D				—	4	0	0	0
5					—	10	20	30	E					—	1	0	0
6						—	10	20	F						—	1	0
7							—	10	G							—	4
8								—	H								—

a. If there are no restrictions (constraints) on the assignment of professors to offices, how many alternative assignments are there to evaluate?
b. The biology department has sent the following information and requests to the OSCM department:

Offices 1, 4, 5, and 8 are the only offices with windows.

A must be assigned Office 1.

D and E, the biology department co-chairpeople, must have windows.

H must be directly across the courtyard from D.

A, G, and H must be in the same wing.

F must *not* be next to D or G or directly across from G.

Find the optimal assignment of professors to offices that meets all the requests of the biology department and minimizes total material handling cost. You may use the path flow list as a computational aid.

PATH	FLOW	PATH	FLOW	PATH	FLOW	PATH	FLOW	PATH	FLOW
A–B	2	B–C	0	C–D	0	D–E	4	E–F	1
A–C	0	B–D	0	C–E	0	D–F	0	E–G	0
A–D	0	B–E	0	C–F	0	D–G	0	E–H	0
A–E	5	B–F	3	C–G	0	D–H	0	F–G	1
A–F	0	B–G	0	C–H	3			F–H	0
A–G	0	B–H	2					G–H	4
A–H	0								

11 The flow of materials through eight departments is shown in the table below. Even though the table shows flows into and out of the different departments, assume that the direction of flow is not important. In addition, assume that the cost of moving material depends only on the distance moved.

	1	2	3	4	5	6	7	8
1	—	20						
2	15	—	25				4	
3		5	—	40	5			
4			5	—	10			
5	1			20	—	30		
6						—	20	
7			3				—	10
8						5	—	

DEPARTMENTS

a. Construct a schematic layout where the departments are arranged on a 2 × 4 grid with each cell representing a 10 × 10-meter square area.
b. Evaluate your layout using a distance-times-flow measure. Assume that distance is measured rectilinearly (in this case, departments that are directly adjacent are 10 meters apart and those that are diagonal to one another are 20 meters apart).

12 A firm uses a serial assembly system and needs answers to the following:
a. An output of 900 units per shift (7.5 hours) is desired for a new processing system. The system requires product to pass through four stations where the work content at each station is 30 seconds. What is the required cycle time for such a system?
b. How efficient is your system with the cycle time you calculated?
c. Station 3 changes and now requires 45 seconds to complete. What will need to be done to meet demand (assume only 7.5 hours are available)? What is the efficiency of the new system?

13 The Sun River beverage company is a regional producer of teas, exotic juices, and energy drinks. With an interest in healthier lifestyles, there has been an increase in demand for their sugar-free formulation.

The final packing operation requires 13 tasks. Sun River bottles their sugar-free product 5 hours a day, 5 days a week. Each week, there is a demand for 3,000 bottles of this product. Using the data below, solve the assembly-line balancing problem and calculate the efficiency of your solution. Use the longest task time for your decision criteria.

Task	Performance Time (Minutes)	Task Must Follow
1	0.1	—
2	0.1	1
3	0.1	2
4	0.2	2
5	0.1	2
6	0.2	3, 4, 5
7	0.1	1
8	0.1	7
9	0.2	8
10	0.1	9
11	0.2	6
12	0.2	10, 11
13	0.1	12

14 Consider the following tasks, times, and predecessors for an assembly of set top cable converter boxes:

Task Element	Time (Minutes)	Element Predecessor
A	1	—
B	1	A
C	2	B
D	1	B
E	3	C, D
F	1	A
G	1	F
H	2	G
I	1	E, H

Given a cycle time of four minutes, develop two alternative layouts.
What is the efficiency of your layouts?

ADVANCED PROBLEM

15 Francis Johnson's plant needs to design an efficient assembly line to make a new product. The assembly line needs to produce 15 units per hour, and there is room for only four workstations. The tasks and the order in which they must be performed are shown in the following table. Tasks cannot be split, and it would be too expensive to duplicate any task.

Task	Task Time (Minutes)	Immediate Predecessor
A	1	—
B	2	—
C	3	—
D	1	A, B, C
E	3	C
F	2	E
G	3	E

a. Draw the precedence diagram.
b. What is the workstation cycle time?

c. Balance the line so that only four workstations are required. Use whatever method you feel is appropriate.

d. What is the efficiency of your line balance?

CASE: SOTERIOU'S SOUVLAKI

Soteriou looks up from cleaning the floor—the lights are on. This means that the power has finally been hooked up and soon his restaurant will reopen here in its new location.

Soteriou's Souvlaki is typical of many of the small dining establishments scattered around the perimeter of the university. Specializing in Greek cuisine—souvlaki (lamb kabobs), gyros, tiropita (cheese-filled pastries), and baklava (a honey and pistachio nut dessert)—the restaurant has been very popular with the student body.

The operations are similar to those of most fast-food restaurants. Customers enter and queue near the register to place their orders and pay. Food is prepared and given to the customer over the main counter. Drinks are self-serve and the tables are bused by the customers as they leave. The kitchen is normally run by Soteriou with help from an assistant working the cash register.

Until recently, Soteriou's had been located in a local food court, but earthquake damage, space constraints, and deteriorating sanitary conditions prompted him to move the restaurant to these new quarters. The new facility is a small, free-standing building, formerly a hamburger joint. Although the previous owners have removed all equipment and tables, the large fixed service counter remains, physically marking out the kitchen and dining areas. (See the accompanying figure.)

Aware of students' growing health consciousness (and possibly a little heady with the extra floor space in the new building), Soteriou has decided to add a self-service salad bar to the new restaurant. The salad bar will be much like those in other restaurants, but with a more Mediterranean flair.

The new kitchen does not appear to be much larger than the old one, though it is narrower. To prepare his Greek specialties in this new kitchen, Soteriou will need a grill/oven, a storage refrigerator, a preparation table (with hot and cold bins for the condiments, side dishes, and pita bread), a vertical spit broiler for the gyro meat, and a display case to hold the tiropitas, baklava, and cups for the self-serve drink machines.

The new dining area will include smoking and nonsmoking seating, the salad bar, self-serve drink machines, and an area for the

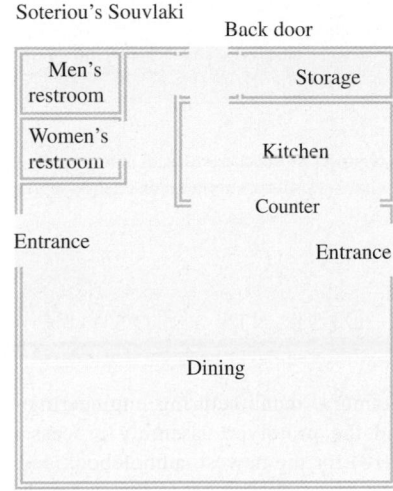

register queues. Of course, the location of the cash register will be important to both the kitchen and dining area layouts.

Leaning against the mop handle, Soteriou looks around the clean, empty floor. Eager to open the new location, he has already ordered all the necessary equipment, but where will he put it? Unfortunately, the equipment will be arriving tomorrow morning. Once it is placed by the delivery crew, it will be hard for Soteriou and his assistant to rearrange it by themselves.

QUESTIONS

The matrices in Exhibits 6A.16 and 6A.17 show the importance of proximity for the kitchen equipment and dining area features. Use systematic layout planning (with numerical reference weightings) to develop a floor layout for the kitchen and the dining area of Soteriou's Souvlaki.

The Kitchen

exhibit 6A.16

	GRILL	PREP. TABLE	REFRIG.	VERTICAL BROILER	DISPLAY CASE
Cash register	X	A	X	U	A
Grill	—	A	A	U	E
Prep. table	—	—	I	A	U
Refrigerator	—	—	—	U	X
Vertical broiler	—	—	—	—	U
Display case	—	—	—	—	—

exhibit 6A.17

The Dining Area

	NO SMOKING	SMOKING	DRINKS	SALAD BAR	WAITING AREA
Cash register	U	U	I	I	A
No smoking	—	X	E	E	U
Smoking	—	—	I	I	U
Drinks	—	—	—	U	U
Salad bar	—	—	—	—	X
Waiting area	—	—	—	—	—

SOURCE: THIS CASE WAS PREPARED BY DOUGLAS STEWART. IT IS NOT INTENDED TO SHOW PROPER OR IMPROPER HANDLING OF FOOD.

CASE: DESIGNING TOSHIBA'S NOTEBOOK COMPUTER ASSEMBLY LINE

Toshihiro Nakamura, manufacturing engineering section manager, examined the prototype assembly process sheet (shown in Exhibit 6A.18) for the newest subnotebook computer model. With every new model introduced, management felt that the assembly line had to increase productivity and lower costs, usually resulting in changes to the assembly process. When a new model was designed, considerable attention was directed toward reducing the number of components and simplifying parts production and assembly requirements. This new computer was a marvel of high-tech, low-cost innovation and should give Toshiba an advantage during the upcoming fall/winter selling season.

Production of the subnotebook was scheduled to begin in 10 days. Initial production for the new model was to be at 150 units per day, increasing to 250 units per day the following week (management thought that eventually production would reach 300 units per day). Assembly lines at the plant normally were staffed by 10 operators who worked at a 14.4-meter-long assembly line. The line could accommodate up to 12 operators if there was a need. The line normally operated for 7.5 hours a day (employees worked from 8:15 A.M. to 5:00 P.M. and regular hours included 1 hour of unpaid lunch and 15 minutes of scheduled breaks). It is possible to run one, two, or three hours of overtime, but employees need at least three days' notice for planning purposes.

exhibit 6A.18

A Prototype Assembly Line for the Subnotebook Computer

**Excel:
Toshiba**

STATION	OPN. #	TIME (SEC)	DESCRIPTION OF OPERATIONS
1	1	100	Lay out principal components on conveyor
110 sec	2	6	Peel adhesive backing from cover assembly
	3	4	Put screws for Opn 8 in foam tray, place on belt
2	4	50	Scan serial number bar code
114 sec	5	13	Connect LCD cable-1 to LCD-printed circuit board (PCB)
	6	16	Connect LCD cable-1 to LCD display panel
	7	13	Connect LCD cable-2 to LCD-PCB
	8	16	Screw LCD-PCB into cover assembly
	9	6	Put screws for Opns 13, 16 in foam tray on belt
3	10	26	Install LCD display panel in cover assembly
101 sec	11	10	Fold and insulate cables
	12	13	Install LCD frame in cover assembly
	13	23	Screw in frame
	14	6	Place PCB-1 in base assembly
	15	6	Install CPU bracket on PCB-1
	16	13	Screw CPU bracket into base assembly
	17	4	Put screws for Opn 23 in foam tray

(Continued)

STATION	OPN. #	TIME (SEC)	DESCRIPTION OF OPERATIONS
4	18	15	Connect ribbon cable to hard disk drive (HDD)
107 sec	19	11	Connect ribbon cable to PCB-1
	20	8	Place insulator sheet on HDD
	21	8	Stack PCB-2 on PCB-1
	22	8	Stack PCB-3 on PCB-1
	23	13	Screw in both PCBs
	24	6	Install condenser microphone in holder
	25	13	Connect microphone cable to PCB-1
	26	8	Tape microphone cable down
	27	13	Connect backup battery to PCB-2 and install in base
	28	4	Put screws for Opn 31 in foam tray
5	29	6	Install support frame on base assembly
103 sec	30	13	Stack PCB-3 on PCB-1
	31	6	Screw in PCB-3
	32	8	Install Accupoint pointing device pressure sensor
	33	11	Connect PCB-5 to PCB-2 and PCB-4
	34	6	Set speaker holder on base
	35	11	Install speaker holder and connect cable to PCB-2
	36	10	Install clock battery on PCB-4
	37	10	Tape down speaker and battery cable
	38	16	Check voltage of clock battery and backup battery
	39	6	Put screws for Opns 44, 46 in foam tray
6	40	13	Install wrist rest over Accupoint buttons
107 sec	41	6	Connect LCD cable to PCB-1
	42	6	Tape cable down
	43	5	Install keyboard support plate to base
	44	23	Screw in support plate
	45	18	Install keyboard, connect cable and set in base
	46	18	Screw in keyboard
	47	8	Install keyboard mask
	48	10	Place cushion pads on LCD mask
7	49	18	Place protective seal on LCD display
108 sec	50	10	Place brand name seal on LCD mask
	51	11	Place brand name seal on outside of cover
	52	8	Connect cable to DVD drive
	53	33	Install DVD on base
	54	22	Install cover on DVD
	55	6	Put screws for Opns 56, 57 in foam tray
8	56	58	Turn over machine and put screws in base
93 sec	57	8	Put in grounding screw
	58	8	Install connector protective flap
	59	8	Install DVD assembly
	60	6	Install battery cover on battery pack
	61	5	Install battery cover
9	62	31	Insert memory card for hardware test and start software
310 sec	63	208	Software load (does not require operator)
	64	71	Test DVD, LCD, keyboard, and pointer; remove memory
10	65	5	Place unit on shock test platform
105 sec	66	75	Perform shock test
	67	10	Scan bar codes
	68	15	Place unit on rack for burn-in

SOURCE: ADAPTED FROM : *TOSHIBA: OME WORKS*, HARVARD BUSINESS SCHOOL (9-696-059).

THE ASSEMBLY LINE

At the head of the assembly line, a computer displayed the daily production schedule, consisting of a list of model types and corresponding lot sizes scheduled to be assembled on the line. The models were simple variations of hard disk size, memory, and battery power. A typical production schedule included seven or eight model types in lot sizes varying from 10 to 100 units. The models were assembled sequentially: All the units of the first model were assembled, followed by all the units of the second, and so on. This computer screen also indicated how far along the assembly line was in completing its daily schedule, which served as a guide for the material handlers who supplied parts to the assembly lines.

The daily schedules were shared with the nearby Fujihashi Parts Collection and Distribution Center. Parts were brought from Fujihashi to the plant within two hours of when they were needed. The material supply system was very tightly coordinated and worked well.

The assembly line consisted of a 14.4-meter conveyor belt that carried the computers, separated at 1.2-meter intervals by white stripes on the belt. Workers stood shoulder to shoulder on one side of the conveyor and worked on the units as they moved by. In addition to 10 assembly workers, a highly skilled worker, called a "supporter," was assigned to each line. The supporter moved along the line, assisting workers who were falling behind and replacing workers who needed to take a break. Supporters also made decisions about what to do when problems were encountered during the assembly process (such as a defective part). The line speed and the number of workers varied from day to day, depending on production demand and the workers' skills and availability. Although the assembly line was designed for 10 workers, the number of workers could vary between 8 and 12.

Exhibit 6A.18 provides details of how the engineers who designed the new subnotebook computer felt that the new line should be organized. These engineers design the line assuming that one notebook is assembled every two minutes by 10 line workers. In words, the following is a brief description of what each operator does:

1   The first operator lays out the major components of a computer between two white lines on the conveyor.
2   The second operator enters the bar codes on those components into a centralized computer system by scanning the bar codes with a hand-held scanning wand. On a shelf above the conveyor, portable computers display the operations that are performed at each station.
3   The next six steps of the assembly process involve a large number of simple operations performed by hand or with simple tools, such as electric screwdrivers. Typical operations involve snapping connectors together or attaching parts with small screws. All tools are hung by a cable above the operators, within easy reach. Although the individual operations are simple, they require manual dexterity and speed.
4   The last two operations are the hardware and shock tests. To prepare for the hardware test, an operator inserts a memory card into the USB port containing software designed to test different components of the computer circuitry. Because it takes nearly four minutes to load the testing software, the cycle time of this operation is longer than the other cycle times on the line. To achieve a lower cycle time for the line, the hardware test is performed in parallel on three different units. The units remain on the moving conveyor, and the tests are staggered so that they can be performed by a single operator. The shock test (the last operation on the assembly line) tests the ability of the computer to withstand vibrations and minor impacts.

The computers are moved to a burn-in area after the assembly-line shock test. Here computers are put in racks for a 24-hour 25°C "burn-in" of the circuit components. After burn-in, the computer is tested again, software is installed, and the finished notebook computer is packaged and placed on pallets.

TWEAKING THE INITIAL ASSEMBLY-LINE DESIGN

From past experience Toshihiro has found that the initial assembly-line design supplied by the engineers often needs to be tweaked. Consider the following questions that Toshihiro is considering:

1   What is the daily capacity of the assembly line designed by the engineers?
2   When it is running at maximum capacity, what is the efficiency of the line?
3   How should the line be redesigned to operate at the target 300 units per day, assuming that no overtime will be used? What is the efficiency of your new design?
4   What other issues might Toshihiro consider when bringing the new assembly line up to speed?

SUPER QUIZ

1   Three terms commonly used to refer to a layout where similar equipment or functions are grouped together.
2   A layout where the work to make an item is arranged in progressive steps and work is moved between the steps at fixed intervals of time.
3   A measure used to evaluate a workcenter layout.
4   This is a way to shorten the cycle time for an assembly line that has a task time that is longer than the desired cycle time. Assume that it is not possible to speed up the task, split the task, use overtime, or redesign the task.
5   This involves scheduling several different models of a product to be produced over a given day or week on the same line in a cyclical fashion.
6   If you wanted to produce 20 percent of one product (A), 50 percent of another (B), and 30 percent of a third product (C) in a cyclic fashion, what schedule would you suggest?
7   A term used to refer to the physical surroundings in which a service takes place and how these surroundings affect customers and employees.
8   A firm is using an assembly line and needs to produce 500 units during an eight-hour day. What is the required cycle time in seconds?

9   What is the efficiency of an assembly line that has   that needs to be completed based on a time study
     25 workers and a cycle time of 45 seconds? Each   completed by engineers at the factory.
     unit produced on the line has 16 minutes of work

1. Workcenter, job-shop, or functional 2. Assembly line 3. Number of annual movements multiplied by
the distance of each movement, and then multiple by the cost 4. Use parallel workstations 5. Mixed-
model line balancing 6. AABBBBBCCC (then repeat) 7. Servicescape 8. 57.6 seconds $= (8 \times 60 \times 60)/500$ 9. 85% $= (16 \times 60)/(25 \times 45)$

SELECTED BIBLIOGRAPHY

Heragu, S. *Facilities Design.* Boston, MA: PWS Publishing Company, 1997.

Hyer, N., and U. Wemmerlöv. *Reorganizing the Factory: Competing through Cellular Manufacturing.* Portland, OR: Productivity Press, 2002.

Tompkins, J. A., and J. A. White. *Facilities Planning.* New York: John Wiley & Sons, 2003.

FOOTNOTES

1 See R. Muther and J. D. Wheeler, "Simplified Systematic Layout Planning," *Factory* 120, nos. 8, 9, 10 (August, September, October 1962), pp. 68–77, 111–19, 101–13.

2 The workstation cycle time used in this calculation should be the actual cycle time used by the assembly line.

3 Y. Monden, *Toyota Production System: Practical Approach to Production Management* (Atlanta, GA: Industrial Engineering and Management Press, Institute of Industrial Engineers, 1983), p. 208.

4 M. S. Sommers and J. B. Kernan, "A Behavioral Approach to Planning, Layout and Display," *Journal of Retailing*, Winter 1965–66, pp. 21–27.

5 M. J. Bitner, "Servicescapes: The Impact of Physical Surroundings on Customers and Employees," *Journal of Marketing* 56 (April 1992), pp. 57–71.

6 R. Norman, *Service Management*, 2nd ed. (New York: John Wiley & Sons, 1991), p. 28.

SERVICE PROCESSES

chapter 7

MY WEEK AS A ROOM-SERVICE WAITER AT THE RITZ

his was to be my first real test. After completing a two-day orientation program and spending the same number of days shadowing Stephen Posner, a veteran Ritz-Carlton room-service waiter, I was going to take the lead on delivering a dinner order. As we headed up the service elevator with a light meal for two—a cheeseburger, a salad, a beer, and a bottle of mineral water—I again went over in my head Steve's instruction on what to say and do. He noticed my furrowed brow. "Don't be so serious," he said, as I awkwardly maneuvered the room-service cart down the hall. "Feel out the guests and try to match their mood."

After reading this chapter you will:

1. Understand the characteristics of service processes and know how they differ from manufacturing processes.

2. Construct a service blueprint.

3. Demonstrate how services are classified.

4. Explain the involvement of the customer in services.

I knocked on the door of Room 1036 and swallowed: "Good evening. In-room dining." A cheerful woman opened the door and I pushed, rather than pulled, the jiggling and tinkling cart over the threshold—nearly tipping over the bottle of San Pellegrino in the process. When the woman, who was watching a game show on television with her husband, learned from Steve that I was in training, she tried to put me at ease with some conversation about the program. But I didn't have the excess mental capacity required for casual banter. I was focused on my task.

"Would you like me to open the water for you?" I asked.
"Oh, sure, if you'd like to," said the woman.

Then I stood there, slightly slack jawed, hands behind my back, surveying the cart and trying to recall what my checklist said to do next.

The woman stood there looking at me expectantly. Steve stood there looking at me quizzically. Ah, I know! Explain what I've brought for them. "You have a Caesar salad and a grilled beef burger with cheese, medium rare," I said, lifting up the warming cover. "And I brought some extra mustard and ketchup, in case you need it." Steve, having finally despaired of my ever opening the San Pellegrino, deftly stepped forward and did it himself. "Please don't hesitate to call us if you need anything else," I said, as we prepared to leave. The woman smiled. I forgot to offer to open the Heineken. As Steve and I stepped into the hallway, he closed the door behind us and said: "We have a few things to talk about on the way downstairs."

Service

The delivery of food at the Ritz-Carlton is just the visible portion of a series of service design decisions that emanate from their service strategy. The best service companies, like the Ritz-Carlton, understand that how well they manage the details of every stage of their operations determines the success of the business.

In this chapter, after some preliminary comments about services, we address the issue of service delivery system design, starting with the notion of customer contact as a way of classifying service operations. Next we discuss service organization design, service strategy, and service focus and describe how marketing and operations interrelate to achieve (or fail to achieve) competitive advantage. We also look at a service-system design matrix that can define the broad features of a service process, and at service blueprints as a way of designing the precise steps of a process. In the latter part of the chapter, we present three service designs used in service industries and discuss how service guarantees can be used as "design drivers." The chapter ends with two service organization case studies.

THE NATURE OF SERVICES

A glance at the management book section in your local bookstore gives ample evidence of the concern for service among practitioners. The way we now view service parallels the way we view quality: The *customer* is (or should be) the focal point of all decisions and actions of the service organization. This philosophy is captured nicely in the service triangle in Exhibit 7.1. Here the customer is the center of things—the service strategy, the systems, and the employees who serve him or her. From this view, the organization exists to serve the customer, and

exhibit 7.1   The Service Triangle

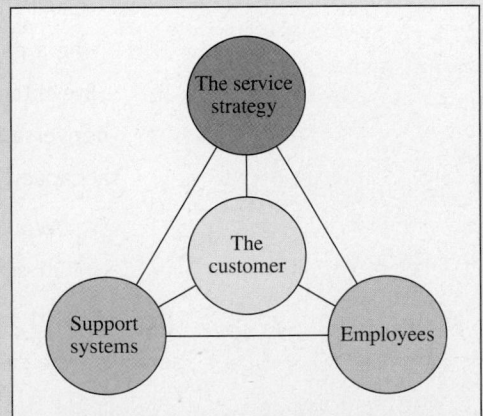

the systems and the employees exist to facilitate the process of service. Some suggest that the service organization also exists to serve the workforce because they generally determine how the service is perceived by the customers. Relative to the latter point, the customer gets the kind of service that management deserves; in other words, how management treats the worker is how the worker will treat the public. If the workforce is well trained and well motivated by management, they will do good jobs for their customers.

The role of operations in the triangle is a major one. Operations is responsible for service systems (procedures, equipment, and facilities) and is responsible for managing the work of the service workforce, who typically make up the majority of employees in large service organizations. But before we discuss this role in depth, it is useful to classify services to show how the customer affects the operations function.

Every service has a **service package**, which is defined as a bundle of goods and services that is provided in some environment. This bundle consists of five features:[1]

Service package

1. *Supporting facility:* The physical resources that must be in place before a service can be offered. Examples are a golf course, a ski lift, an airline, and an auto repair facility.
2. *Facilitating goods:* The material purchased or consumed by the buyer or the items provided by the customer. Examples are golf clubs, skis, beverages, and auto parts.
3. *Information:* Operations data or information that is provided by the customer, to enable efficient and customized services. Examples include tee-off times, weather reports, medical records, seat preferences, parts availability.
4. *Explicit services:* The benefits that are readily observable by the senses and that consist of the essential or intrinsic features of the service. Examples are response time of an ambulance, air conditioning in a hotel room, and a smooth-running car after a tune-up.
5. *Implicit services:* Psychological benefits that the customer may sense only vaguely, or the extrinsic features of the service. Examples are the status of a degree from an Ivy League school, the privacy of a loan office, and worry-free auto repair.

AN OPERATIONAL CLASSIFICATION OF SERVICES

Service organizations are generally classified according to who the customer is, for example, individuals or other businesses, and to the service they provide (financial services, health services, transportation services, and so on). These groupings, though useful in presenting aggregate economic data, are not particularly appropriate for OSCM purposes because they tell us little about the process. Manufacturing, by contrast, has fairly evocative terms to classify production activities (such as intermittent and continuous production); when applied to a manufacturing setting, they readily convey the essence of the process. Although it is possible to describe services in these same terms, we need one additional item of information to reflect the fact that the customer is involved in the production system. That item, which we believe operationally distinguishes one service system from another in its production function, is the extent of customer contact in the creation of the service.

Customer contact refers to the physical presence of the customer in the system, and *creation of the service* refers to the work process involved in providing the service itself. *Extent of contact* here may be roughly defined as the percentage of time the customer must be in the system relative to the

exhibit 7.2

Major Differences between High- and Low-Contact Systems in a Bank

DESIGN DECISION	HIGH-CONTACT SYSTEM (A BRANCH OFFICE)	LOW-CONTACT SYSTEM (A CHECK PROCESSING CENTER)
Facility location	Operations must be near the customer	Operations may be placed near supply, transport, or labor.
Facility layout	The facility should accommodate the customer's physical and psychological needs and expectations.	The facility should focus on production efficiency.
Product design	Environment as well as the physical product define the nature of the service.	The customer is not in the service environment, so the product can be defined by fewer attributes.
Process design	Stages of production process have a direct, immediate effect on the customer.	The customer is not involved in the majority of processing steps.
Scheduling	The customer is in the production schedule and must be accommodated.	The customer is concerned mainly with completion dates.
Production planning	Orders cannot be stored, so smoothing production flow will result in loss of business.	Both backlogging and production smoothing are possible.
Worker skills	The direct workforce constitutes a major part of the service product and so must be able to interact well with the public.	The direct workforce need only have technical skills.
Quality control	Quality standards are often in the eye of the beholder and, thus, are variable.	Quality standards are generally measurable and, thus, fixed.
Time standards	Service time depends on customer needs, so time standards are inherently loose.	Work is performed on customer surrogates (such as forms), so time standards can be tight.
Wage payment	Variable output requires time-based wage systems.	"Fixable" output permits output-based wage systems.
Capacity planning	To avoid lost sales, capacity must be set to match peak demand.	Storable output permits capacity at some average demand level.

total time needed to perform the customer service. Generally speaking, the greater the percentage of contact time between the service system and the customer, the greater the degree of interaction between the two during the production process.

High and low degree of customer contact

From this conceptualization, it follows that service systems with a high degree of customer contact are more difficult to control and more difficult to rationalize than those with a low degree of customer contact. In high-contact systems, the customer can affect the time of demand, the exact nature of the service, and the quality, or perceived quality, of service because the customer is involved in the process.

Exhibit 7.2 describes the implications of this distinction. Here we see that each design decision is impacted by whether the customer is present during service delivery. We also see that when work is done behind the scenes (in this case, in a bank's processing center), it is performed on customer surrogates—reports, databases, and invoices. We can thus design it according to the same principles we would use in designing a factory—to maximize the amount of items processed during the production day.

There can be tremendous diversity of customer influence and, hence, system variability within high-contact service systems. For example, a bank branch offers both simple services such as cash withdrawals that take just a minute or so and complicated services such as loan application preparation that can take in excess of an hour. Moreover, these activities may range from being self-service through an ATM, to coproduction where bank personnel and the customer work as a team to develop the loan application.

DESIGNING SERVICE ORGANIZATIONS

In designing service organizations we must remember one distinctive characteristic of services: We cannot inventory services. Unlike manufacturing, where we can build up inventory during slack periods for peak demand and thus maintain a relatively stable level of employment and production planning, in services we must (with a few exceptions) meet demand as it arises. Consequently, in services capacity becomes a dominant issue. Think about the many service situations you find yourself in—for example, eating in a restaurant or going to a Saturday night movie. Generally speaking, if the restaurant or the theater is full, you will decide to go someplace else. So, an important design parameter in services is "What capacity should we aim for?" Too much capacity generates excessive costs. Insufficient capacity leads to lost customers. In these situations, of course, we seek the assistance of marketing. This is one reason we have discount airfares, hotel specials on weekends, and so on. This is also a good illustration of why it is difficult to separate the operations management functions from marketing in services.

Waiting line models, which are discussed in Chapter 7A, provide a powerful mathematical tool for analyzing many common service situations. Questions such as how many tellers we should have in a bank or how many telephone lines we need in an Internet service operation can be analyzed with these models. These models can be easily implemented using spreadsheets.

Several major factors distinguish service design and development from typical manufactured product development. First, the process and the product must be developed simultaneously; indeed, in services, the process is the product. (We say this with the general recognition that many manufacturers are using such concepts as concurrent engineering and DFM [design for manufacture] as approaches to more closely link product design and process design.)

Second, although equipment and software that support a service can be protected by patents and copyrights, a service operation itself lacks the legal protection commonly available to goods production. Third, the service package, rather than a definable good, constitutes the major output of the development process. Fourth, many parts of the service package are often defined by the training individuals receive before they become part of the service organization. In particular, in professional service organizations (PSOs) such as law firms and hospitals, prior certification is necessary for hiring. Fifth, many service organizations can change their service offerings virtually overnight. Routine service organizations (RSOs) such as barbershops, retail stores, and restaurants have this flexibility.

STRUCTURING THE SERVICE ENCOUNTER: SERVICE-SYSTEM DESIGN MATRIX

Service encounters can be configured in a number of different ways. The service-system design matrix in Exhibit 7.3 identifies six common alternatives.

The top of the matrix shows the degree of customer/server contact: the *buffered core,* which is physically separated from the customer; the *permeable system,* which is penetrable by the customer via phone or face-to-face contact; and the *reactive system,* which is both penetrable and reactive to the customer's requirements. The left side of the matrix shows what we believe to be a logical marketing proposition, namely, that the greater the amount of contact, the greater the sales opportunity; the right side shows the impact on production efficiency as the customer exerts more influence on the operation.

exhibit 7.3   Service-System Design Matrix

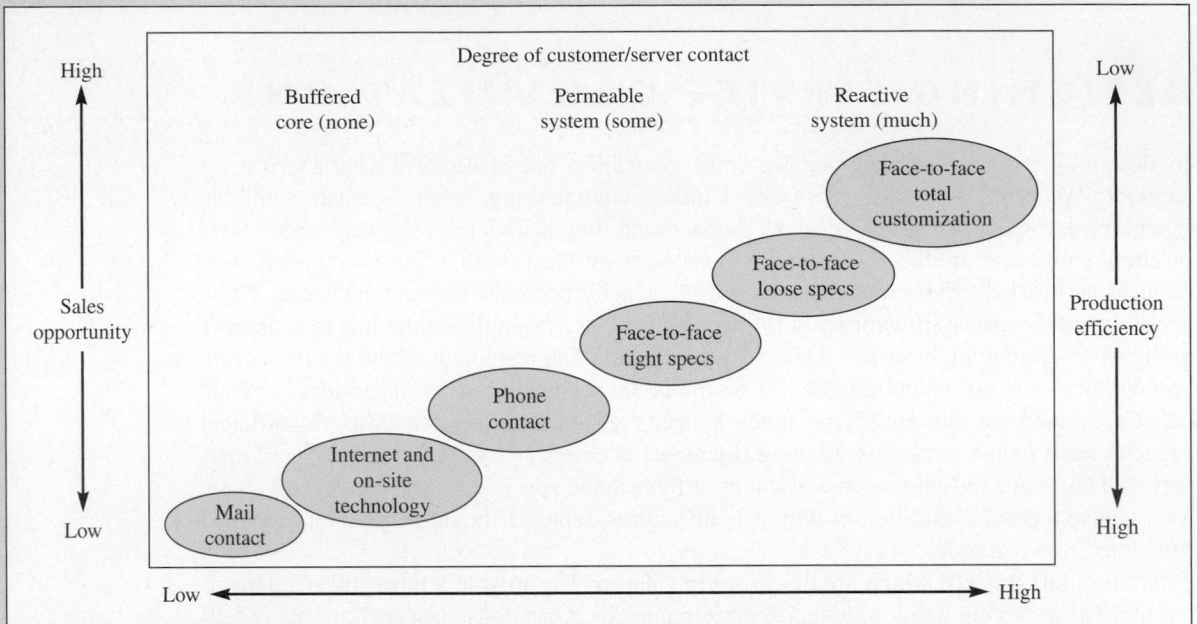

Characteristics of Workers, Operations, and Innovations Relative to the Degree of Customer/Service Contact

Degree of customer/server contact
Low ← — — → High

Worker requirements	Clerical skills	Helping skills	Verbal skills	Procedural skills	Trade skills	Diagnostic skills
Focus of operations	Paper handling	Demand management	Scripting calls	Flow control	Capacity management	Client mix
Technological innovations	Office automation	Routing methods	Computer databases	Electronic aids	Self-serve	Client/worker teams

The entries within the matrix list the ways in which service can be delivered. At one extreme, service contact is by mail; customers have little interaction with the system. At the other extreme, customers "have it their way" through face-to-face contact. The remaining four entries in the matrix contain varying degrees of interaction.

As one would guess, production efficiency decreases as the customer has more contact (and therefore more influence) on the system. To offset this, the face-to-face contact provides high sales opportunity to sell additional products. Conversely, low contact, such as mail, allows the system to work more efficiently because the customer is unable to significantly affect (or disrupt) the system. However, there is relatively little opportunity for additional product sales.

There can be some shifting in the positioning of each entry. For our first example, consider the "Internet and on-site technology" entry in the matrix. The Internet clearly buffers the company from the customer, but interesting opportunities are available to provide relevant information and services to the customer. Because the Web site can be programmed to intelligently react to the inputs of the customer, significant opportunities for new sales may be possible. In addition, the system can be made to interface with real employees when the customer needs assistance that goes beyond the programming of the Web site. The Internet is truly a revolutionary technology when applied to the services that need to be provided by a company.

Another example of shifting in the positioning of an entry can be shown with the "face-to-face tight specs" entry in the matrix. This entry refers to those situations where there is little variation in the service process—neither customer nor server has much discretion in creating the service. Fast-food restaurants and Disneyland come to mind. Face-to-face loose specs refer to situations where the service process is generally understood but there are options in how it will be performed or in the physical goods that are part of it. A full-service restaurant and a car sales agency are examples. Face-to-face total customization refers to service encounters whose specifications must be developed through some interaction between the customer and server. Legal and medical services are of this type, and the degree to which the resources of the system are mustered for the service determines whether the system is reactive, possibly to the point of even being proactive, or merely permeable. Examples would be the mobilization of an advertising firm's resources in preparation for an office visit by a major client or an operating team scrambling to prepare for emergency surgery.

The changes in workers, operations, and types of technical innovations as the degree of customer/service system contact changes are described in the bottom of Exhibit 7.3. For worker requirements, the relationships between mail contact and clerical skills, Internet technology and helping skills, and phone contact and verbal skills are self-evident. Face-to-face tight specs require procedural skills in particular, because the worker must follow the routine in conducting a generally standardized, high-volume process. Face-to-face loose specs frequently call for trade skills (bank teller, draftsperson, maitre d', dental hygienist) to finalize the design for the service. Face-to-face total customization tends to call for diagnostic skills of the professional to ascertain the needs or desires of the client.

STRATEGIC USES OF THE MATRIX

The matrix in Exhibit 7.3 has both operational and strategic uses. The operational uses are reflected in their identification of worker requirements, focus of operations, and innovations previously discussed. The strategic uses include

1. Enabling systematic integration of operations and marketing strategy. Trade-offs become more clear-cut, and, more important, at least some of the major design variables are crystallized for analysis purposes. For example, the matrix indicates that it would make little sense relative to sales for a service firm to invest in high-skilled workers if it plans to operate using tight specs.
2. Clarifying exactly which combination of service delivery the firm is in fact providing. As the company incorporates the delivery options listed on the diagonal, it is becoming diversified in its production process.
3. Permitting comparison with how other firms deliver specific services. This helps to pinpoint a firm's competitive advantage.
4. Indicating evolutionary or life cycle changes that might be in order as the firm grows. Unlike the product–process matrix for manufacturing, however, where natural growth moves in one direction (from workcenter to assembly line as volume increases), evolution of service delivery can move in either direction along the diagonal as a function of a sales–efficiency trade-off.

VIRTUAL SERVICE: THE NEW ROLE OF THE CUSTOMER

The service system design matrix was developed from the perspective of the production system's utilization of company resources. With the advent of virtual services through the Internet, we need to account not just for customer's interactions with a business, but for his or her interaction with other customers as well. As suggested by BYU Professor Scott Sampson, we have two categories of contact: *pure virtual customer contact* where companies such as eBay and SecondLife enable customers to interact with one another in an open environment;

and *mixed virtual and actual customer contact* where customers interact with one another in a server-moderated environment such as product discussion groups, YouTube, and Wikipedia. In these environments the operations management challenge is to keep the technology functioning and up to date, and to provide a policing function through monitoring the encounters that take place.

SERVICE BLUEPRINTING AND FAIL-SAFING

Service blueprint

Just as is the case with manufacturing process design, the standard tool for service process design is the flowchart. Recently, the service gurus have begun calling the flowchart a **service blueprint** to emphasize the importance of process design. A unique feature of the service blueprint is the distinction made between the high customer contact aspects of the service (the parts of the process that the customer sees) and those activities that the customer does not see. This distinction is made with a "line of visibility" on the flowchart.

Exhibit 7.4 is a blueprint of a typical automobile service operation. Each activity that makes up a typical service encounter is mapped into the flowchart. To better show the entity

exhibit 7.4   Fail-Safing an Automotive Service Operation

FAILURE: Customer forgets the need for service.
POKA-YOKE: Send automatic reminders with a 5 percent discount.

FAILURE: Customer cannot find service area, or does not follow proper flow.
POKA-YOKE: Clear and informative signage directing customers.

FAILURE: Customer has difficulty communicating problem.
POKA-YOKE: Joint inspection—service adviser repeats his/her understanding of the problem for confirmation or elaboration by the customer.

FAILURE: Customer does not understand the necessary service.
POKA-YOKE: Preprinted material for most services, detailing work, reasons, and possibly a graphic representation.

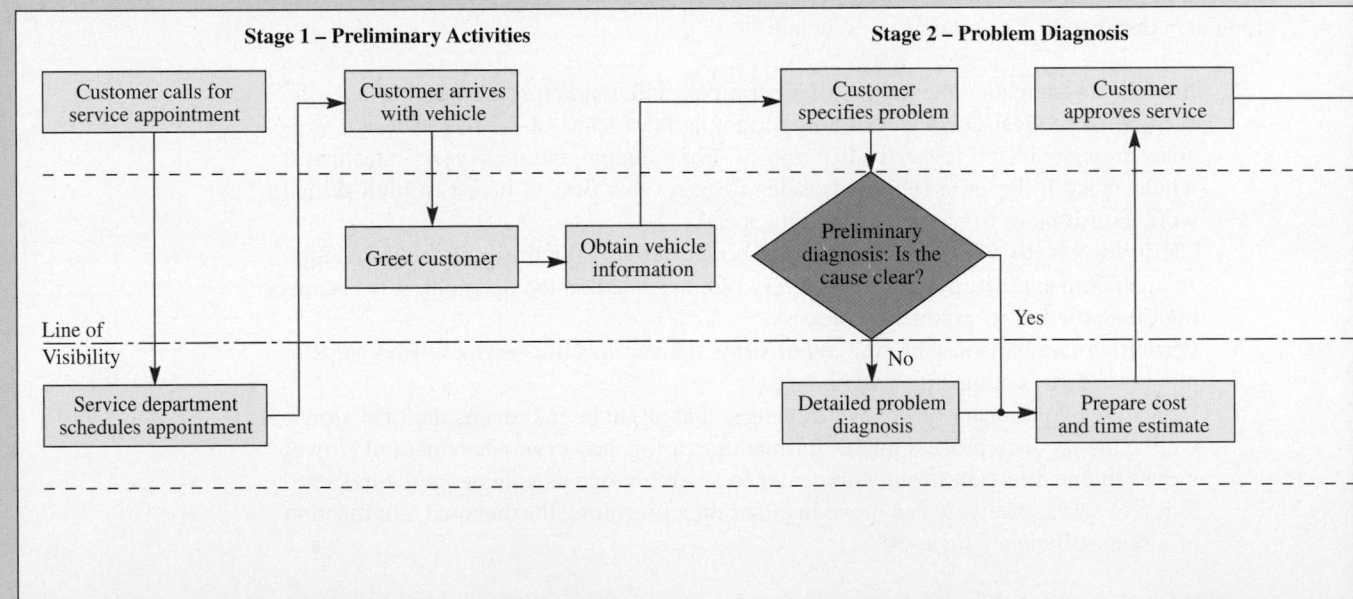

FAILURE: Customer arrival unnoticed.
POKA-YOKE: Use a bell chain to signal arrivals.

FAILURE: Customers not served in order of arrival.
POKA-YOKE: Place numbered markers on cars as they arrive.
FAILURE: Vehicle information incorrect and process is time-consuming.
POKA-YOKE: Maintain customer database and print forms with historical information.

FAILURE: Incorrect diagnosis of the problem.
POKA-YOKE: High-tech checklists, such as expert systems and diagnostic equipment.

FAILURE: Incorrect estimate.
POKA-YOKE: Checklists itemizing costs by common repair types.

that controls the activities, levels are shown in the flowchart. The top level consists of activities that are under the control of the customer. Next are those activities performed by the service manager in handling the customer. The third level is the repair activities performed in the garage; the lowest level is the internal accounting activity.

Basic blueprinting describes the features of the service design but does not provide any direct guidance for how to make the process conform to that design. An approach to this problem is the application of **poka-yokes**—procedures that block the inevitable mistake from becoming a service defect.[2] Poka-yokes (roughly translated from the Japanese as "avoid mistakes") are common in factories (see Chapter 9, "Six-Sigma Quality," for examples) and consist of such things as fixtures to ensure that parts can be attached only in the right way, electronic switches that automatically shut off equipment if a mistake is made, kitting of parts prior to assembly to make sure the right quantities are used, and checklists to ensure that the right sequence of steps is followed.

There are many applications of poka-yokes to services as well. These can be classified into warning methods, physical or visual contact methods, and by what we call the *Three T's*—the Task to be done (Was the car fixed right?), the Treatment accorded to the customer (Was the service manager courteous?), and the Tangible or environmental features of the service

Poka-yokes

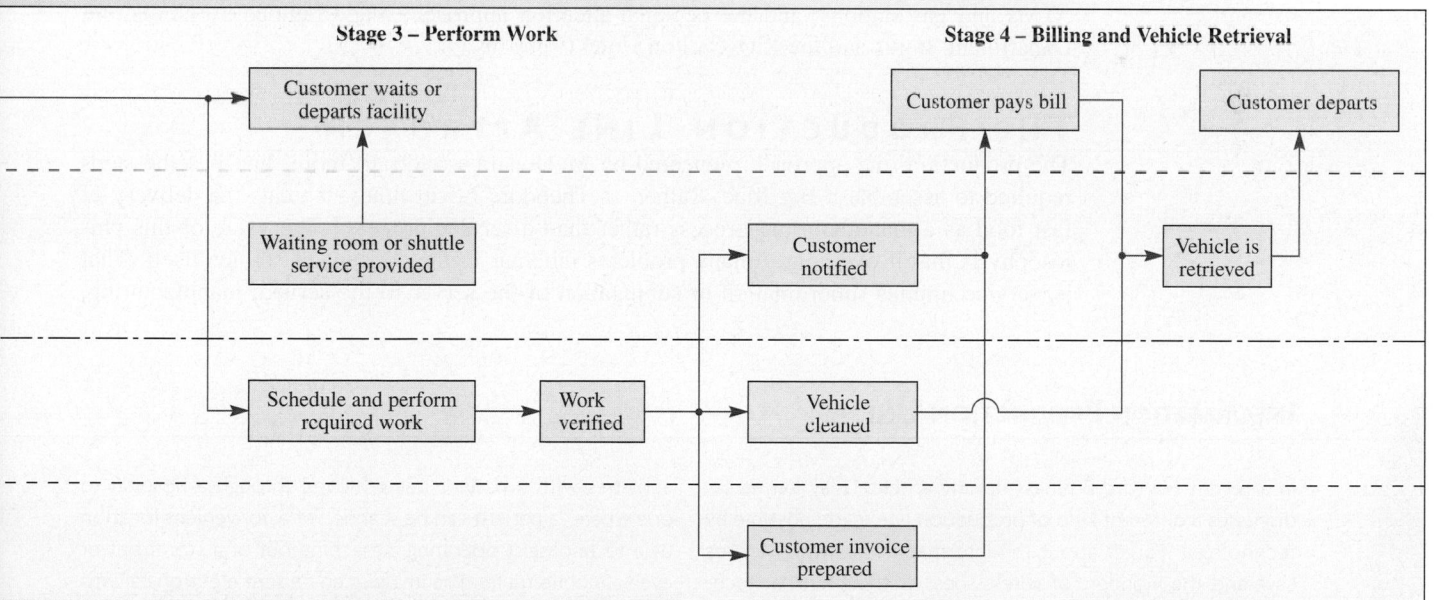

FAILURE: CUSTOMER NOT LOCATED.
POKA-YOKE: ISSUE BEEPERS TO CUSTOMERS WHO WISH TO LEAVE FACILITY.

FAILURE: BILL IS ILLEGIBLE.
POKA-YOKE: TOP COPY TO CUSTOMER, OR PLAIN PAPER BILL.

FAILURE: FEEDBACK NOT OBTAINED.
POKA-YOKE: CUSTOMER SATISFACTION POSTCARD GIVEN TO CUSTOMER WITH KEYS TO VEHICLE.

FAILURE: SERVICE SHUTTLE IS INCONVENIENT.
POKA-YOKE: SEATING IN AVAILABLE SHUTTLES IS ALLOCATED WHEN SCHEDULING APPOINTMENTS. LACK OF FREE SPACE INDICATES THAT CUSTOMERS NEEDING SHUTTLE SERVICE SHOULD BE SCHEDULED FOR ANOTHER TIME.
FAILURE: PARTS ARE NOT IN STOCK.
POKA-YOKE: LIMIT SWITCHES ACTIVATE SIGNAL LAMPS WHEN PART LEVEL FALLS BELOW ORDER POINT.

FAILURE: VEHICLE NOT CLEANED CORRECTLY.
POKA-YOKE: PERSON RETRIEVING VEHICLE INSPECTS, ORDERS A TOUCH-UP IF NECESSARY, AND REMOVES FLOOR MAT IN PRESENCE OF CUSTOMER.

FAILURE: VEHICLE TAKES TOO LONG TO ARRIVE.
POKA-YOKE: WHEN CASHIER ENTERS CUSTOMER'S NAME TO PRINT THE BILL, INFORMATION IS ELECTRONICALLY SENT TO RUNNERS WHO RETRIEVE VEHICLE WHILE THE CUSTOMER IS PAYING.

facility (Was the waiting area clean and comfortable?). Finally (unlike in manufacturing), service poka-yokes often must be applied to fail-safing the actions of the customer as well as the service worker.

Poka-yoke examples include height bars at amusement parks; indented trays used by surgeons to ensure that no instruments are left in the patient; chains to configure waiting lines; take-a-number systems; turnstiles; beepers on ATMs to warn people to take their cards out of the machine; beepers at restaurants to make sure customers do not miss their table calls; mirrors on telephones to ensure a "smiling voice"; reminder calls for appointments; locks on airline lavatory doors that activate lights inside; small gifts in comment card envelopes to encourage customers to provide feedback about a service; and pictures of what "a clean room" looks like for kindergarten children.

Exhibit 7.4 illustrates how a typical automobile service operation might be fail-safed using poka-yokes. As a final comment, although these procedures cannot guarantee the level of error protection found in the factory, they still can reduce such errors in many service situations.

THREE CONTRASTING SERVICE DESIGNS

Three contrasting approaches to delivering on-site service are the production-line approach, made famous by McDonald's Corporation; the self-service approach, made famous by ATMs and gas stations; and the personal-attention approach, made famous by Nordstrom Department Stores and the Ritz-Carlton Hotel Company.

THE PRODUCTION-LINE APPROACH

The production-line approach pioneered by McDonald's refers to more than just the steps required to assemble a Big Mac. Rather, as Theodore Levitt notes, it treats the delivery of fast food as a manufacturing process rather than a service process.[3] The value of this philosophy is that it overcomes many problems inherent in the concept of service itself. That is, service implies subordination or subjugation of the server to the served; manufacturing,

INFORMATION PRODUCTION LINE

In a recent *Harvard Business Review* article, Uday Karmarkar discusses a different kind of production line made possible by technology. "Forget about the information highway, Moore's Law, and the wonders of wirelessness. Rather think of technology as creating an information assembly line—information today can be standardized, built to order, assembled from components, picked, packed, stored, and shipped, all using processes resembling manufacturing." As an example, he describes how the process of diagnostic imaging can be entirely reconfigured from one involving extensive manual activities with a patient being moved through a hospital to one where "a patient can be scanned at a convenient location by a technologist operating a machine out of a storefront or even a mobile trailer. The images can be sent electronically to the diagnosing radiologist, who may be in a clinic many miles away, or directly to the referring physician. Voice recognition software transcribes the diagnosis, or the transcriptions can be performed offshore. Intelligent software tools are being developed to aid in the actual diagnosis, and one day they may even supplant the radiologist for certain problems."

SOURCE: UDAY KARMARKAR, "WILL YOU SURVIVE THE SERVICES REVOLUTION?" *HARVARD BUSINESS REVIEW*, MAY–JUNE 2004, P. 102.

on the other hand, avoids this connotation because it focuses on things rather than people. Thus, in manufacturing and at McDonald's, "the orientation is toward the efficient production of results not on the attendance on others." Levitt notes that besides McDonald's marketing and financial skills, the company carefully controls "the execution of each outlet's central function—the rapid delivery of a uniform, high-quality mix of prepared foods in an environment of obvious cleanliness, order, and cheerful courtesy. The systematic substitution of equipment for people, combined with the carefully planned use and positioning of technology, enables McDonald's to attract and hold patronage in proportions no predecessor or imitator has managed to duplicate."

Levitt cites several aspects of McDonald's operations to illustrate the concepts. Note the extensive use of what we term poka-yokes.

- The McDonald's french fryer allows cooking of the optimum number of french fries at one time.
- A wide-mouthed scoop is used to pick up the precise amount of french fries for each order size. (The employee never touches the product.)
- Storage space is expressly designed for a predetermined mix of prepackaged and premeasured products.
- Cleanliness is pursued by providing ample trash cans in and outside each facility. (Larger outlets have motorized sweepers for the parking area.)
- Hamburgers are wrapped in color-coded paper.
- Through painstaking attention to total design and facilities planning, everything is built integrally into the (McDonald's) machine itself—into the technology of the system. The only choice available to the attendant is to operate it exactly as the designers intended. Using our service-system design matrix (Exhibit 7.3), we would categorize this as a face-to-face tight spec service.

THE SELF-SERVICE APPROACH

In contrast to the production-line approach, C. H. Lovelock and R. F. Young propose that the service process can be enhanced by having the customer take a greater role in the production of the service.[4] Company Web sites, automatic teller machines, self-service gas stations, salad bars, and e-tickets are approaches that shift the service burden to the consumer. Based on our service-system design matrix, these are great examples of the use of Internet and on-site technology. Many customers like self-service because it puts them in control. For others, this philosophy requires some selling on the part of the service organization to convince customers that it helps them. To this end, Lovelock and Young propose a number of steps, including developing customer trust; promoting the benefits of cost, speed, and convenience; and following up to make sure that the procedures are being effectively used. In essence, this turns customers into "partial employees" who must be trained in what to do and, as noted earlier, must be "fail-safed" in case of mistake.

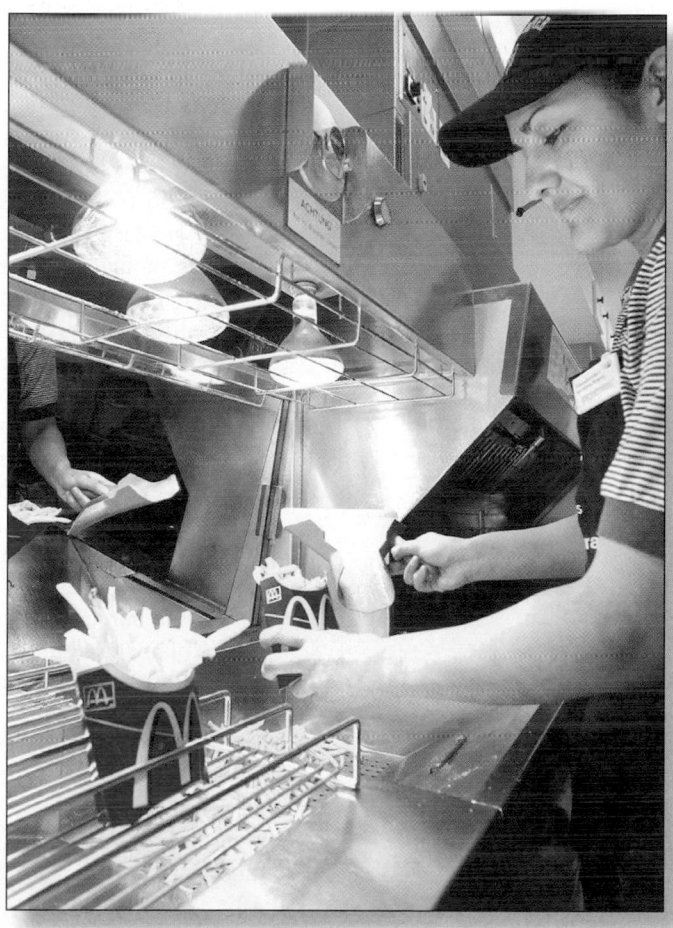

THE PERSONAL-ATTENTION APPROACH

An interesting contrast in the way personal attention is provided can be seen in Nordstrom Department Stores and the Ritz-Carlton Hotel Company.

At Nordstrom, a rather loose, unstructured process relies on developing a relationship between the individual

salesperson and the customer (this is a face-to-face with total customization service). At the Ritz-Carlton, the process is virtually scripted, and the information system rather than the employee keeps track of the guest's (customer's) personal preferences (this is a face-to-face loose spec example). Tom Peters describes Nordstrom's approach here:

> After several visits to a store's men's clothing department, a customer's suit still did not fit. He wrote the company president, who sent a tailor to the customer's office with a new suit for fitting. When the alterations were completed, the suit was delivered to the customer—free of charge.

This incident involved the $8.3 billion, Seattle-based Nordstrom, a specialty clothing retailer. Its sales per square foot are about two times that of a typical department store. Who received the customer's letter and urged the extreme (by others' standards) response? Co-chairman John Nordstrom.

The frontline providers of this good service are well paid. Nordstrom's salespersons earn a couple of bucks an hour more than competitors, plus a 6.75 percent commission. Its top salesperson moves over $2 million a year in merchandise. Nordstrom lives for its customers and salespeople. Its only official organization chart puts the customer at the top, followed by sales and sales support people. Next come department managers, then store managers, and the board of directors at the very bottom.

Salespersons religiously carry a "personal book," where they record voluminous information about each of their customers. The system helps in the goal of getting one new personal customer a day. Each salesperson has a virtually unlimited budget to send cards, flowers, and thank-you notes to customers. They are also encouraged to shepherd his or her customer to any department in the store to assist in a successful shopping trip.

He also is abetted by what may be the most liberal returns policy in this or any other business: Return *anything*, no questions asked. Betsy Sanders, the vice president who orchestrated the company's entry in the California market, says that "trusting customers," or "our bosses" as she repeatedly calls them, is vital to the Nordstrom philosophy. Past president Jim Nordstrom told the *Los Angeles Times*, "I don't care if they roll a Goodyear tire into the store. If they say they paid $200, give them $200 (in cash) for it." Sanders acknowledges that a few customers rip the store off—"rent hose from us," to use a common insider's line. But this is more than offset by goodwill from the 99 percent-plus who benefit from the "No Problem at Nordstrom" philosophy that the company lives up to with unmatched zeal.

No bureaucracy gets in the way of serving the customer. Policy? Sanders explains to a dumbfounded group of Silicon Valley executives, "I know this drives the lawyers nuts, but our whole 'policy manual' is just one sentence, 'Use your own judgment at all times.'" One store manager offers a translation: "Don't chew gum. Don't steal from us."[5]

The Ritz-Carlton approach is described in the following excerpts from the company's Baldrige Award Application Summary and discussions with Scott Long of Ritz-Carlton's Huntington Hotel in Pasadena, California. Exhibit 7.5 shows the formalized service procedure (the Three Steps of Service). Exhibit 7.6 displays the information system used to capture

The Ritz-Carlton Hotel Company (Three Steps of Service)

exhibit 7.5

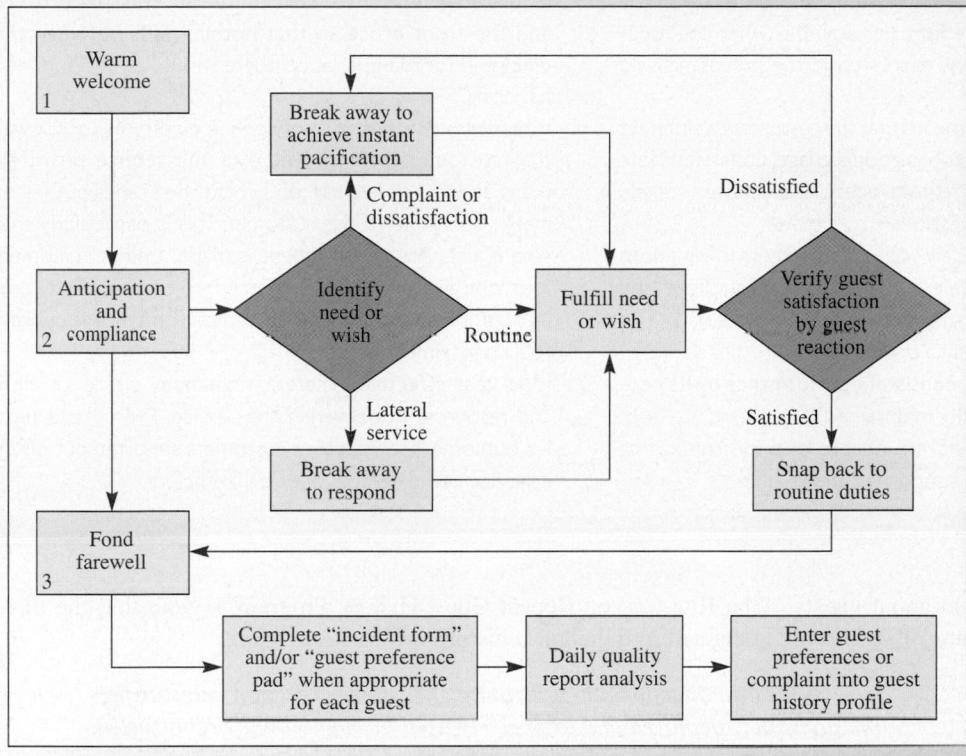

SOURCE: *RITZ-CARLTON.*

The Ritz-Carlton Repeat Guest History Program (As Aid to Highly Personalized Service Delivery)

exhibit 7.6

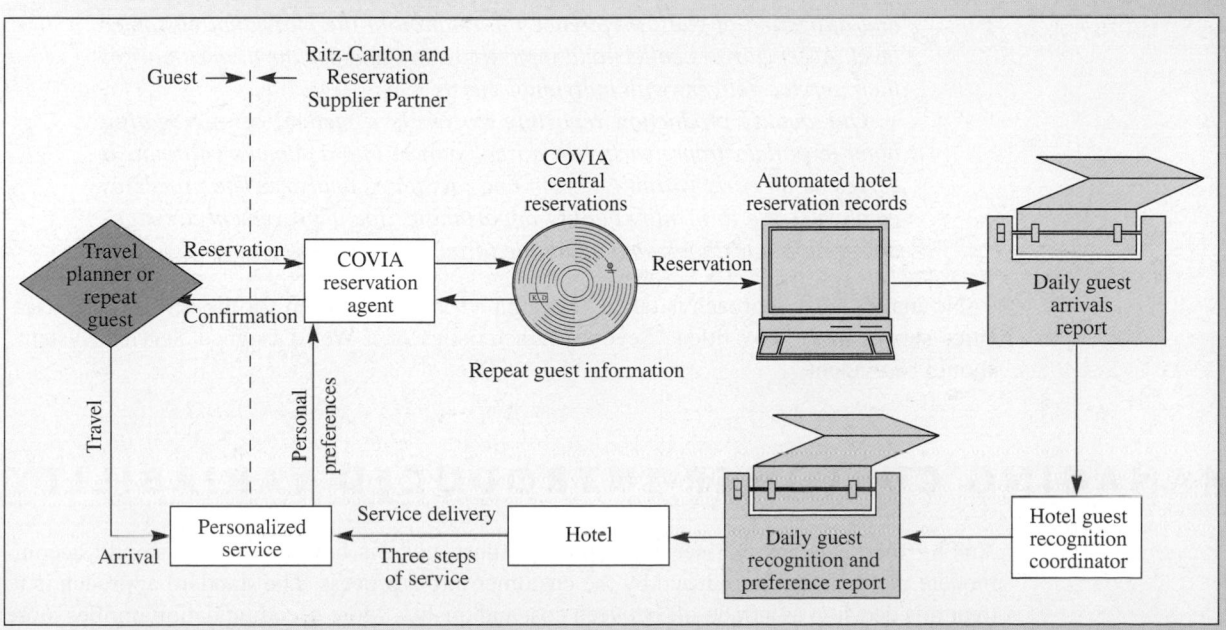

SOURCE: *RITZ-CARLTON MALCOLM.*

SEVEN CHARACTERISTICS OF A WELL-DESIGNED SERVICE SYSTEM

1 **Each element of the service system is consistent with the operating focus of the firm.** For example, when the focus is on speed of delivery, each step in the process should help foster speed.

2 **It is user-friendly.** This means that the customer can interact with it easily—that is, it has good signage, understandable forms, logical steps in the process, and service workers available to answer questions.

3 **It is robust.** That is, it can cope effectively with variations in demand and resource availability. For example, if the computer goes down, effective backup systems are in place to permit service to continue.

4 **It is structured so that consistent performance by its people and systems is easily maintained.** This means the tasks required of the workers are doable, and the supporting technologies are truly supportive and reliable.

5 **It provides effective links between the back office and the front office so that nothing falls between the cracks.** In football parlance, there should be "no fumbled handoffs."

6 **It manages the evidence of service quality in such a way that customers see the value of the service provided.** Many services do a great job behind the scenes but fail to make this visible to the customer. This is particularly true where a service improvement is made. Unless customers are made aware of the improvement through explicit communication about it, the improved performance is unlikely to gain maximum impact.

7 **It is cost-effective.** There is minimum waste of time and resources in delivering the service. Even if the service outcome is satisfactory, customers are often put off by a service company that appears inefficient.

data about guests ("The Ritz-Carlton Repeat Guest History Program"). Note that the three steps of service are integrated into the guest history information system.

> *Systems for the collection and utilization of customer reaction and satisfaction are widely deployed and extensively used throughout the organization. Our efforts are centered on various customer segments and product lines.*
>
> *Our approach is the use of systems which allow every employee to collect and utilize quality-related data on a daily basis. These systems provide critical, responsive data which include:*
> *(1) On-line guest preference information;*
> *(2) Quantity of error free products and services;*
> *(3) Opportunities for quality improvement.*
>
> *Our automated property management systems enable the on-line access and utilization of guest preference information at the individual customer level. All employees collect and input this data, and use the data as part of their service delivery with individual guests.*
>
> *Our quality production reporting system is a method of aggregating hotel level data from nearly two dozen sources into a summary format. It serves as an early warning system and facilitates analysis. The processes employees use to identify quality opportunities for improvement are standardized in a textbook, and available throughout our organization.*[6]

No matter what approach is taken to design a service, the need for the service characteristics shown in the box titled "Seven Characteristics of a Well-Designed Service System" should be evident.

MANAGING CUSTOMER-INTRODUCED VARIABILITY

Among the decisions that service managers must make is how much they should accommodate the variation introduced by the customer into a process. The standard approach is to treat this decision as a trade-off between cost and quality. More accommodation implies more cost; less accommodation implies less-satisfied customers. Francis Frei has suggested that this narrow type of analysis overlooks ways that companies can accommodate the customer while at the same time controlling cost.[7] To develop these, she says that a company must first determine which of five types of variability is causing operational difficulties and then select which of four types of accommodation would be most effective.

The five basic types of variability, along with examples, are *arrival variability*—customers arriving at a store at times when there are too few clerks to provide prompt service (this is the type of variability that is dealt with in the waiting line analysis in Chapter 7A); *request variability*—travelers requesting a room with a view at a crowded hotel; *capability variability*—a patient being unable to explain his or her symptoms to a doctor; *effort variability*—shoppers not bothering to put their shopping carts in a designated area in a supermarket parking lot; and *subjective preference variability*—one bank customer interpreting a teller addressing him by his first name as a sign of warmth, while another customer feels that such informality is unbusinesslike.

The four basic accommodation strategies are *classic accommodation*, which entails, for example, extra employees or additional employee skills to compensate for variations among customers; *low-cost accommodation*, which uses low-cost labor, outsourcing, and self-service to cut the cost of accommodation; *classic reduction*, which requires, for example, customers to engage in more self-service, use reservation systems, or adjust their expectations; and *uncompromised reduction*, which uses knowledge of the customer to develop procedures that enable good service, while minimizing the variation impact on the service delivery system. Exhibit 7.7 illustrates the tactics that are useful in each of the four accommodation categories.

As we can see from Exhibit 7.7, effective management of variability generally requires a company to influence customer behavior. Netflix provides an example of how this was done to deal with the variation in rental times for DVDs. While competitor Blockbuster uses a classic reduction approach of late fees for late returns (which generates tension with the

Strategies for Managing Customer-Introduced Variability

exhibit 7.7

	Classic Accommodation	Low-Cost Accommodation	Classic Reduction	Uncompromised Reduction
Arrival	• Make sure plenty of employees are on hand	• Hire lower-cost labor • Automate tasks • Outsource customer contact • Create self-service options	• Require reservations • Provide off-peak pricing • Limit service availability	• Create complementary demand to smooth arrivals without requiring customers to change their behavior
Request	• Make sure many employees with specialized skills are on hand • Train employees to handle many kinds of requests	• Hire lower-cost specialized labor • Automate tasks • Create self-service options	• Require customers to make reservations for specific types of service • Persuade customers to compromise their requests • Limit service breadth	• Limit service breadth • Target customers on the basis of their requests
Capability	• Make sure employees are on hand who can adapt to customers' varied skill levels • Do work for customers	• Hire lower-cost labor • Create self-service options that require no special skills	• Require customers to increase their level of capability before they use the service	• Target customers on the basis of their capability
Effort	• Make sure employees are on hand who can compensate for customers' lack of effort • Do work for customers	• Hire lower-cost labor • Create self-service options with extensive automation	• Use rewards and penalties to get customers to increase their effort	• Target customers on the basis of motivation • Use a normative approach to get customers to increase their effort
Subjective Preference	• Make sure employees are on hand who can diagnose differences in expectations and adapt accordingly	• Create self-service options that permit customization	• Persuade customers to adjust their expectations to match the value proposition	• Target customers on the basis of their subjective preferences

SOURCE: FRANCIS X. FREI, "BREAKING THE TRADE-OFF BETWEEN EFFICIENCY AND SERVICE," *HARVARD BUSINESS REVIEW* 84, NO. 11 (NOVEMBER 2006), P. 97.

customer), the Netflix subscription model allows customers to keep the DVD for as long as they want. A customer's incentive to return them is being able to get the next movie on his or her request list. This approach thereby accommodates the customer's behavior and at the same time assures revenues.

APPLYING BEHAVIORAL SCIENCE TO SERVICE ENCOUNTERS

Effective management of service encounters requires that managers understand customer perceptions as well as the technical features of service processes. Chase and Dasu[8] suggest applying behavioral concepts to enhance customer perceptions of three aspects of the encounter: *the flow of the service experience* (what's happening), *the flow of time* (how long it seems to take), and *judging encounter performance* (what you thought about it later). Looking at the service encounter from this perspective has led to the following six behaviorally based principles for service encounter design and management.

1. **The front end and the back end of the encounter are not created equal.** It is widely believed that the start and finish of a service or the so-called service bookends are equally weighted in the eyes of the customer. A good deal of research indicates that this is not the case. While it is essential to achieve a base level of satisfactory performance at the beginning so that the customer remains throughout the service, a company is likely to be better off with a relatively weak start and a modest upswing on the end than having a great start and a so-so ending. This ties in with two important findings from behavioral decision theory: the preference for improvement and the dominant effect of the ending in our recollections. The disproportionate influence of the ending gives rise to a corollary principle—that is, end on an up note. Examples of companies that "finish strong": Malaysian Airlines, which lavishes attention on baggage collection and ground transportation, in order to leave the customer with a good feeling; a kitchen cabinet company that ties bright bows on all the installed work, and leaves behind a vase of flowers; cruise lines that end each day with raffles, contests, and shows, end the cruise with the captain's dinner, and pass out keepsakes or bottles of wine upon reaching the home port. All of these strategies are designed to make the final interaction a good one. In a similar vein, relative to unpleasant experiences, researchers have found that prolonging of a colonoscopy by painlessly leaving the colon scope for about a minute after the procedure was completed produced significant improvements in how patients perceived the procedure. (Note here that we are actually extending the duration of discomfort, yet the overall perception is superior to immediate cessation of the procedure!)

2. **Segment the pleasure; combine the pain.** Breaking up may be hard to do, but depending upon the type of encounter, it might be the best thing to do. Events seem longer when they are segmented. This suggests that we want to break pleasant experiences into multiple stages and combine unpleasant ones into a single stage. Thus, it makes sense to, say, reduce the number of stages in a visit to a clinic, even if it extends the time of the visit somewhat, and to provide two 90-second rides at Disneyland rather than one three-minute ride.

3. **Let the customer control the process.** Giving people control over how a process is to be conducted enhances their satisfaction with it. In the medical area, allowing people to choose which arm a blood sample is drawn from reduces the perceived pain of the procedure. For certain repair jobs, allowing people to select a future date they want it to be scheduled may be preferred to doing it right away.

4. **Pay attention to norms and rituals.** Deviations from norms are likely to be overly blamed for failures. This is particularly true for professional services whose processes and outcomes are not clearly ascertainable by the client, and hence adherence to norms is the central basis for evaluation. Consulting firms are expected to make presentations to the boss, even if he or

THE HOTEL MONACO IN CHICAGO AIMS TO IMPRESS ITS GUESTS THROUGHOUT THEIR STAY. GUESTS ARE GIVEN THEIR OWN PET GOLDFISH TO MAKE THEM FEEL AT HOME.

she has little or nothing to do with the problem being studied. At such presentations, all members of the client team are to be lauded for their assistance even if they were less than helpful in accomplishing the work.

5. **People are easier to blame than systems.** When things go wrong, people's gut reaction is to blame the server rather than the system. We want to put a human face on the problem. This is seen especially in complex services where what goes on behind the scenes or in the system is difficult for the customer to untangle. The gate agent is frequently blamed for not allowing a late arrival to get on the plane, even though it is a rule of the airline association that no one can board 15 minutes before departure. (A corollary to this principle is that "a miss is worse than a mile." That is, if someone arrives late for a service, it's better not to say, "too bad, you just missed it.")

6. **Let the punishment fit the crime in service recovery.** How do you make up for an encounter error? Research suggests that the most appropriate recovery action depends upon whether it is a task (outcome) error or a treatment (interpersonal process) error. A botched task calls for material compensation, while poor treatment from a server calls for an apology. Reversing these recovery actions is unlikely to be effective. For example, having a copying job done poorly at a copy store, of course, calls for a quick apology, but more important for quick rework and perhaps some compensation for the customer's inconvenience. On the other hand, if the copying job is done correctly, but the clerk is rude, a sincere apology from the store manager and the clerk is far more likely to result in a satisfied customer than a free coupon or other minor tangible form of compensation.

SERVICE GUARANTEES AS DESIGN DRIVERS

The phrase "Positively, absolutely, overnight" is an example of a service guarantee most of us know by heart. Hiding behind such marketing promises of service satisfaction is a set of actions that must be taken by the operations organization to fulfill these promises.

Thousands of companies have launched service guarantees as a marketing tool designed to provide peace of mind for customers unsure about trying their service. From an operations perspective, a service guarantee can be used not only as an improvement tool but also at the design stage to focus the firm's delivery system squarely on the things it must do well to satisfy the customer.

Service guarantees

Even professional service firms such as Rath and Strong Consulting have service guarantees. (Theirs allows the client to choose from a menu of payouts if they do not—for example—cut lead time by *x* percent. Menu options include refunds and no charge for overtime work to get the job done.)

The elements of a good service guarantee are that it is unconditional (no small print); meaningful to the customer (the payoff fully covers the customer's dissatisfaction); easy to understand and communicate (for employees as well as customers); and painless to invoke (given proactively).[9]

Recent research on service guarantees has provided the following conclusions about them:[10]

1. Any guarantee is better than no guarantee. The most effective guarantees are big deals. They put the company at risk in the eyes of the customer.
2. Involve the customer as well as employees in the design.
3. Avoid complexity or legalistic language. Use big print, not small print.
4. Do not quibble or wriggle when a customer invokes the guarantee.
5. Make it clear that you are happy for customers to invoke the guarantee.

An issue of growing importance in service relates to the ethical and possibly legal responsibility of a company to actually provide the service that is promised. For example, is an airline responsible for transporting a passenger with a guaranteed reservation, even though the flight has been overbooked? Or consider the Internet service provider's responsibility to provide enough telephone lines so that customers do not receive busy signals when they try to connect to the service. These are difficult issues because having excess capacity is expensive. Demand can be nearly impossible to predict with great accuracy, thus making the estimates of needed capacity difficult.

A very powerful tool—waiting line analysis—is available to help better understand the relationships between the factors that drive a service system. These factors include the average number of customers that arrive over a period of time, the average time that it takes to serve each customer, the number of servers, and information about the size of the customer population. Waiting line models have been developed that allow the estimation of expected waiting time and expected resource utilization. This is the topic of Chapter 7A.

SUMMARY

In this chapter, we have shown how service businesses are in many ways very similar to manufacturing businesses, as is the need for trade-offs in developing a focus. Focus, for example, is important to success, just as it was with the design of manufacturing systems.

The service-system design matrix is in many ways similar to the product–process matrix we used to categorize manufacturing operations. Further, the tools of flow diagrams and capacity analysis are similar as well.

Services are, however, very different compared to manufacturing when we consider the high degree of personalization often required, the speed of delivery needed, the direct customer contact, and the inherent variability of the service encounter. The buffering and scheduling mechanisms that we have available to smooth the demand placed on a manufacturing operation are often not available to the service operation. Services generally require much higher levels of capacity relative to demand. In addition, they place a greater need for flexibility on the part of the workers involved in providing the services.

KEY TERMS

Service package A bundle of goods and services that is provided in some environment.

High and low degree of customer contact The physical presence of the customer in the system and the percentage of time the customer must be in the system relative to the total time it takes to perform the service.

Service blueprint The flowchart of a service process, emphasizing what is visible and what is not visible to the customer.

Poka-yokes Procedures that prevent mistakes from becoming defects. They are commonly found in manufacturing but also can be used in service processes.

Service guarantee A promise of service satisfaction backed up by a set of actions that must be taken to fulfill the promise.

REVIEW AND DISCUSSION QUESTIONS

1   What is the service package of your college or university?
2   How have price and variety competition changed McDonald's basic formula for success?
3   Could a service firm use a production-line approach or self-service design and still keep a high customer focus (personal attention)? Explain and support your answer with examples.
4   Why should a manager of a bank home office be evaluated differently from a manager of a bank branch?
5   Identify the high-contact and low-contact operations of the following services:
    a. A dental office.
    b. An airline.
    c. An accounting office.
    d. An automobile agency.
    e. Amazon.com
6   Are there any service businesses that won't be affected by knowledge outsourcing?
7   Relative to the behavioral science discussion, what practical advice do you have for a hotel manager to enhance the ending of a guest's stay in the hotel?
8   List some occupations or sporting events where the ending is a dominant element in evaluating success.

9   Behavioral scientists suggest that we remember events as snapshots, not movies. How would you apply this to designing a service?

10 Some suggest that customer expectation is the key to service success. Give an example from your own experience to support or refute this assertion.

11 Where would you place a drive-in church, a campus food vending machine, and a bar's automatic mixed drink machine on the service-system design matrix?

12 Can a manufacturer have a service guarantee in addition to a product guarantee?

13 Suppose you were the manager of a restaurant and you were told honestly that a couple eating dinner had just seen a mouse. What would you say to them? How would you recover from this service crisis?

14 What strategy do the following organizations seem to use to manage customer-introduced variability?
    a. eBay
    b. Ritz-Carlton Hotels
    c. New airline check-in procedures

PROBLEMS

1   Place the following functions of a department store on the service-system design matrix: mail order (that is, catalog), phone order, hardware, stationery, apparel, cosmetics, customer service (such as taking complaints).

2   Do the same as in the previous problem for a hospital with the following activities and relationships: physician/patient, nurse/patient, billing, medical records, lab tests, admissions, diagnostic tests (such as X-rays).

3   Perform a quick service audit the next time you go shopping at a department store. Evaluate the three T's of service: the Task, the Treatment, and the Tangible features of the service on a scale of 1 (poor), 3 (average), and 5 (excellent). Remember that the tangible features include the environment, layout, and appearance of the store, not the goods you purchased.

4   SYSTEM DESCRIPTION EXERCISE
    The beginning step in studying a productive system is to develop a description of that system. Once a system is described, we can better determine why the system works well or poorly and recommend production-related improvements. Because most of us are familiar with fast-food restaurants, try your hand at describing the production system employed at, say, a McDonald's. In doing so, answer the following questions:
    a. What are the important aspects of the service package?
    b. Which skills and attitudes are needed by the service personnel?
    c. How can customer demand be altered?
    d. Provide a rough-cut blueprint of the delivery system. (It is not necessary to provide execution times. Just diagram the basic flow through the system.) Critique the blueprint. Are there any unnecessary steps or can failure points be eliminated?
    e. Can the customer/provider interface be changed to include more technology? More self-serve?
    f. Which measures are being used to evaluate the service? Which could be used?

5   What are the differences between high and low customer contact service (CCS) businesses, in general, for the dimensions listed below? (Example—Facility Layout: in a high CCS, the facility would be designed to enhance the feelings and comfort of the customer while in a low CCS, the facility would be designed for efficient processing.)

	Low CCS Businesses	High CCS Businesses
Worker skill		
Capacity utilization		
Level of automation		

CASE: PIZZA USA: AN EXERCISE IN TRANSLATING CUSTOMER REQUIREMENTS INTO PROCESS DESIGN REQUIREMENTS

A central theme of contemporary operations management is *focus on the customer.* This is commonly understood to mean that if a company does focus on its customers and if it is able to consistently deliver what the customer wants in a cost-effective manner, then the company should be successful. The hard part is to be able to truly understand what the customer wants. Translating what the customer wants into a deliverable product (meaning some combination of goods and services) and designing a set of processes that will consistently deliver the product in a cost-effective manner are every bit as difficult. Finally, connecting the management of these products and processes to obtain desired business outcomes of the organization is a further challenge.

The following exercise will try to illustrate how difficult all of this can be.

THE SETTING

Pizza USA is a chain of pizza restaurants that currently offers sit-down and take-out service. Many customers have said that they would buy more pizzas from Pizza USA if it offered a delivery service. This exercise is in two parts. In Part I, you play the customer. In Part II, you play the manager at Pizza USA who is responsible for developing the pizza delivery process design requirements.

PART I

To start with, you have to think *like* a customer. This should be easy since you probably have experience with *ordering pizza to be delivered.* Put that experience to work! Make a list of the attributes of *pizza delivery* that are important to you *AS A CUSTOMER!*

As we said, this should be easy. Right? Or is it? In devising your list, consider the following:

> What must a pizza delivery service accomplish so that you are reasonably satisfied? Beyond your being reasonably satisfied, what could a pizza delivery service do that would make it really unique and create a differential advantage? In other words, what could a pizza delivery service do that might cause you to ALWAYS order from one particular service (and, perhaps, to pay more for the privilege)?

As you develop your list, remember that you are considering *only the delivery service* and NOT the pizza itself. Assume that this pizza restaurant can make whatever kind of pizza (and side items) that you want.

PART II

Now, put on your *"Pizza USA manager's hat."* For this part of the exercise, you will be teamed with some other students. First, using the lists of all of your team members, create a master list. Next, try to group the items on your list under a series of major headings; for example, "condition of the delivered pizza" or "quick, on-time delivery" or "order accuracy," and so on. Finally, make a list of the "pizza delivery process design requirements" that your pizza delivery process will have to meet. As you do this, think about measurable standards; in other words, what would you measure in order to ensure that your process is operating effectively and efficiently? Why do you think that these measures will be useful?

Here's an example of how a part of this analysis could go. One customer requirement may be that *the pizza should be hot when it is delivered.* The fact is that as soon as the pizza comes out of the oven, it starts to cool. So, how could you keep the pizza from dropping below some minimum temperature before you hand it to your customer?

ASSIGNMENT

1. Make a list of pizza delivery attributes that are important to you as a customer.
2. Combine your list with the lists of a few other class members and categorize the items under a series of major headings.
3. Make a list of pizza delivery process design requirements. Associate with each requirement a measure that would ensure that the process meets the requirement.
4. Design a process that meets your requirements. Describe it by using a flowchart similar to those shown in Exhibits 7.4, 7.5, and 7.6.

SOURCE: SPECIAL THANKS TO MARK IPPOLITO OF INDIANA UNIVERSITY–PURDUE UNIVERSITY INDIANAPOLIS FOR CONTRIBUTING THIS EXERCISE.

CASE: CONTACT CENTERS SHOULD TAKE A LESSON FROM LOCAL BUSINESSES

There are now three bagel shops in my hometown, two of which are fairly rudimentary in nature: They sell bagels, cream cheese, and coffee. Good bagels, but nothing fancy.

The third store is part of a large, Boston-area chain, and the bagels there are also good. The store often has children's entertainment and has a large seating area with games, free newspapers, and room to spread out and relax. Last, and most important, it has a system that consists of a conveyor belt running across the length of the counter—between the register and the "schmearing" operation—with a huge circular saw in the center. As bagels are ordered, they are tossed onto the conveyor, sliced in half by the saw, and travel at high speed to the end of the conveyor. In other words, store number three isn't just a bagel store; it's entertainment as well.

But that store has lost my business . . . At least 30 percent of the time we order from this store, the order is wrong. And the schmearers at store number three are probably the most stressed cream cheese–appliers ever. The look of terror on their faces from the constant pressure of the sliced bagels whizzing down the conveyor

toward them is similar to the look I've seen on the faces of customer service reps in oh-so-many call centers.

Does this happen in your call center? Think about it. The system that makes store number three so very profitable just cost it what I'd argue is a pretty profitable customer.

There's also a hardware store in my hometown (actually, two). In the next town, there is a Home Depot, which I've frequented many a weekend, but not anymore. Our kitchen sink had been leaking on and off for six months, though the leak had been patched. The prospect of standing in line at Home Depot yet again, waiting for service and searching through what seemed like thousands of O-rings to find the right one, was not what I had planned for the weekend.

So I changed my plan and went to my local hardware store. As expected, the prices were at least two times what Home Depot charges, but the service was fabulous, particularly the part when the plumbing department manager suggested a little trick that would prevent the O-ring from failing. I took my expensive O-ring, went home, tried his suggestion, and five minutes later was finished. Not a drop since.

QUESTIONS

1 What lessons are there from these two examples for contact (call) center managers?

2 What are the dilemmas posed in solving these problems in the context of a call center?

SOURCE: MODIFIED FROM CHRIS SELLAND, *CUSTOMER RELATIONSHIP MANAGEMENT* 8, NO. 4 (APRIL 2004), P. 22.

SUPER QUIZ

1 Service systems can generally be categorized according to this characteristic that relates to the customer.

2 A service triangle consists of these four features.

3 A framework that relates to the customer service system encounter.

4 This is the key feature that distinguishes a service blueprint from a normal flowchart.

5 Having your luggage arrive on time when you land at an airport is what type of service in the service package?

6 SecondLife would be this type of virtual service.

7 This is done to make a system mistake-proof.

8 These are the three steps of service at Nordstrom.

9 What are the four strategies for managing customer-induced variability?

10 The front end and the back end of a service encounter are referred to as what?

1. Customer contact 2. Service strategy, support systems, employees, customer 3. Service system design matrix 4. Line of visibility 5. Implicit service 6. Pure virtual customer contact 7. Poka-yokes 8. Warm Welcome, Anticipation and Compliance, Fond Farewell 9. Classic accommodation, low-cost accommodation, classic reduction, uncompromised reduction 10. Service bookends

SELECTED BIBLIOGRAPHY

Baker, S., and M. Kripalani. "Software: Will Outsourcing Hurt America's Supremacy?" *BusinessWeek,* March 1, 2004, pp. 85–94.

Chase, R. B. "The Customer Contact Approach to Services: Theoretical Bases and Practical Extensions." *Operations Research* 21, no. 4 (1981), pp. 698–705.

Chase, R. B., and U. Apte. "A History of Research in Service Operations: What's the Big Idea?" *Journal of Operations Management,* March 2007, pp. 375–86.

Chase, R. B., and S. Dasu. "Want to Perfect Your Company's Service? Use Behavioral Science." *Harvard Business Review* 72, no. 6 (May–June 2001), pp. 78–84.

Chase, R. B., and D. M. Stewart. "Make Your Service Fail-Safe." *Sloan Management Review,* Spring 1994, pp. 35–44.

Fitzsimmons, J. A., and M. J. Fitzsimmons. *Service Management: Operations, Strategy, Information Technology.* 6th ed. New York: Irwin/McGraw-Hill, 2008.

Frei, F. X. "The Four Things a Service Business Must Get Right." *Harvard Business Review* 86, no. 4 (April 2008), pp. 70–81.

Goldhar, J.; Y. Braunstein; and D. Berg. "Services Innovation in the 21st Century: It All Begins with Defining Services vs. Products and Factory vs. Service Operations." University of California–Berkeley, Service Innovation Conference, April 26–28, 2007.

Karmarkar, U. "Will You Survive the Services Revolution?" *Harvard Business Review,* May–June 2004, pp. 99–107.

Metters, R.; K. King-Metters; and M. Pullman. *Successful Service Operations Management.* 2nd ed. Mason OH: Thomson South-Western Publishing, 2005.

FOOTNOTES

1 J. A. Fitzsimmons and M. J. Fitzsimmons, *Service Management: Operations, Strategy, Information Technology,* 6th ed. (New York: Irwin/McGraw-Hill, 2008), p. 22.

2 R. B. Chase and D. M. Stewart, "Make Your Service Fail-Safe," *Sloan Management Review,* Spring 1994, pp. 35–44.

3 T. Levitt, "Production-Line Approach to Service," *Harvard Business Review* 50, no. 5 (September–October 1972), pp. 41–52.

4 C. H. Lovelock and R. F. Young, "Look to Customers to Increase Productivity," *Harvard Business Review* 57, no. 2 (March–April 1979), pp. 168–78.

5 T. Peters, *Quality!* (Palo Alto, CA: TPC Communications, 1986), pp. 10–12.

6 *Ritz-Carlton Malcolm Baldrige National Quality Award Application Summary,* 1993, p. 6.

7 Francis X. Frei, "Breaking the Trade-Off between Efficiency and Service," *Harvard Business Review* 84, no. 11 (November 2006), pp. 93–101.

8 Richard B. Chase and Sriram Dasu, "Want to Perfect Your Company's Service? Use Behavioral Science," *Harvard Business Review* 72, no. 6 (May–June 2001), pp. 78–84.

9 C. W. L. Hart, "The Power of Unconditional Service Guarantees," *Harvard Business Review* 56, no. 4 (July–August 1988), p. 55.

10 Gordon H. G. McDougall, T. Levesque, and P. VanderPlaat, "Designing the Service Guarantee: Unconditional or Specific?" *The Journal of Service Marketing* 12, no. 4 (1998), pp. 278–93.

chapter 7A

WAITING LINE ANALYSIS

BRIEFING OUTLINE

After reading this chapter you will:

1. Describe what waiting line (queuing) analysis is.

2. Model some common waiting line situations and estimate service utilization, the length of a waiting line, and average customer wait time.

Understanding waiting lines or **queues** and learning how to manage them is one of the most important areas in operations management. It is basic to creating schedules, job design, inventory levels, and so on. In our service economy, we wait in line every day, from driving to work to checking out at the supermarket. We also encounter waiting lines at factories—jobs wait in lines to be worked on at different machines, and machines themselves wait their turn to be overhauled. In short, waiting lines are pervasive.

Queues

We will discuss the basic elements of waiting line problems and provide standard steady state formulas for solving them. These formulas, arrived at through queuing theory, enable planners to analyze service requirements and establish service facilities appropriate to stated conditions. Queuing theory is broad enough to cover such dissimilar delays as those encountered by customers in a shopping mall or aircraft in a holding pattern awaiting landing slots.

ECONOMICS OF THE WAITING LINE PROBLEM

A central problem in many service settings is the management of waiting time. The manager must weigh the added cost of providing more rapid service (more traffic lanes, additional landing strips, more checkout stands) against the inherent cost of waiting.

Service

Frequently, the cost trade-off decision is straightforward. For example, if we find that the total time our employees spend in the line waiting to use a copying machine would otherwise be spent in productive activities, we could compare the cost of installing one additional machine to the value of employee time saved. The decision could then be reduced to dollar terms, and the choice easily made.

On the other hand, suppose that our waiting line problem centers on demand for beds in a hospital. We can compute the cost of additional beds by summing the costs for building construction, additional equipment required, and increased maintenance. But what is on the other side of the scale? Here we are confronted with the problem of trying to place a dollar figure on a patient's need for a hospital bed that is unavailable. While we can estimate lost hospital income, what about the human cost arising from this lack of adequate hospital care?

THE PRACTICAL VIEW OF WAITING LINES

Before we proceed with a technical presentation of waiting line theory, it is useful to look at the intuitive side of the issue to see what it means. Exhibit 7A.1 shows arrivals at a service facility (such as a bank) and service requirements at that facility (such as tellers and loan officers). One

exhibit 7A.1   Arrival and Service Profiles

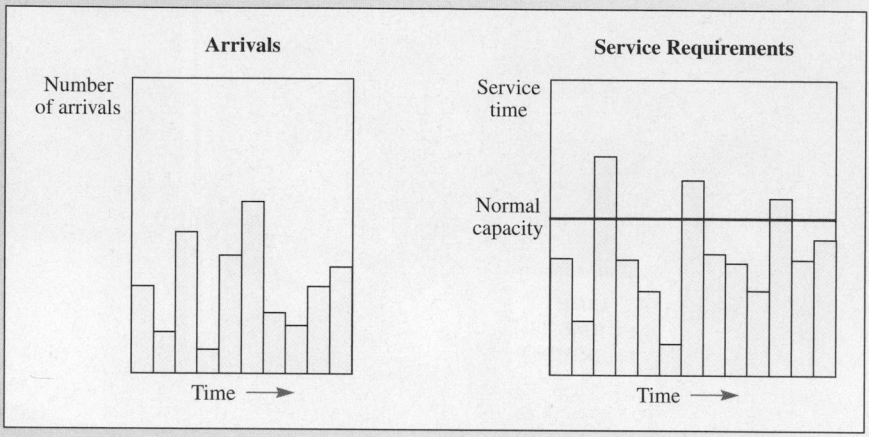

important variable is the number of arrivals over the hours that the service system is open. From the service delivery viewpoint, customers demand varying amounts of service, often exceeding normal capacity. We can control arrivals in a variety of ways. For example, we can have a short line (such as a drive-in at a fast-food restaurant with only several spaces), we can establish specific hours for specific customers, or we can run specials. For the server, we can affect service time by using faster or slower servers, faster or slower machines, different tooling, different material, different layout, faster setup time, and so on.

The essential point is waiting lines are *not* a fixed condition of a productive system but are to a very large extent within the control of the system management and design. Useful suggestions for managing queues based on research in the banking industry are the following:

- **Segment the customers.** If a group of customers need something that can be done very quickly, give them a special line so that they do not have to wait for the slower customers.
- **Train your servers to be friendly.** Greeting the customer by name or providing another form of special attention can go a long way toward overcoming the negative feeling of a long wait. Psychologists suggest that servers be told when to invoke specific friendly actions such as smiling when greeting customers, taking orders, and giving change (for example, in a convenience store). Tests using such specific behavioral actions have shown significant increases in the perceived friendliness of the servers in the eyes of the customer.
- **Inform your customers of what to expect.** This is especially important when the waiting time will be longer than normal. Tell them why the waiting time is longer than usual and what you are doing to alleviate the wait.
- **Try to divert the customer's attention when waiting.** Providing music, a video, or some other form of entertainment may help distract the customers from the fact that they are waiting.
- **Encourage customers to come during slack periods.** Inform customers of times when they usually would not have to wait; also tell them when the peak periods are—this may help smooth the load.

THE QUEUING SYSTEM

Queuing system

Service

The **queuing system** consists essentially of three major components: (1) the source population and the way customers arrive at the system, (2) the servicing system, and (3) the condition of the customers exiting the system (back to source population or not?), as seen in Exhibit 7A.2. The following sections discuss each of these areas.

Components of a Queuing System

CUSTOMER ARRIVALS

Arrivals at a service system may be drawn from a *finite* or an *infinite* population. The distinction is important because the analyses are based on different premises and require different equations for their solution.

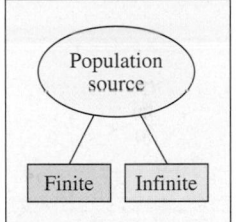

Finite Population   A *finite population* refers to the limited-size customer pool that will use the service and, at times, form a line. The reason this finite classification is important is that when a customer leaves its position as a member for the population (a machine breaking down and requiring service, for example), the size of the user group is reduced by one, which reduces the probability of the next occurrence. Conversely, when a customer is serviced and returns to the user group, the population increases and the probability of a user requiring service also increases. This finite class of problems requires a separate set of formulas from that of the infinite population case.

As an example, consider a group of six machines maintained by one repairperson. When one machine breaks down, the source population is reduced to five, and the chance of one of the remaining five breaking down and needing repair is certainly less than when six machines were operating. If two machines are down with only four operating, the probability of another breakdown is again changed. Conversely, when a machine is repaired and returned to service, the machine population increases, thus raising the probability of the next breakdown.

Infinite Population   An *infinite population* is large enough in relation to the service system so that the population size caused by subtractions or additions to the population (a customer needing service or a serviced customer returning to the population) does not significantly affect the system probabilities. If, in the preceding finite explanation, there were 100 machines instead of 6, then if one or two machines broke down, the probabilities for the next breakdowns would not be very different and the assumption could be made without a great deal of error that the population (for all practical purposes) was infinite. Nor would the formulas for "infinite" queuing problems cause much error if applied to a physician with 1,000 patients or a department store with 10,000 customers.

DISNEY'S **FASTPASS** ALLOWS GUESTS TO MAKE 'RESERVATIONS' FOR A POPULAR RIDE TO AVOID WAITING IN LONG LINES. EACH FASTPASS ATTRACTION HAS TWO DISPLAYS OF TIME. THE FIRST GIVES THE APPROXIMATE WAITING TIME IF YOU WERE TO ENTER THE ATTRACTION RIGHT THEN. THE SECOND SHOWS THE WINDOW OF TIME FOR A RETURN VISIT IF YOU WERE TO GET A FASTPASS. IF THE WAIT IS LONGER THAN YOU FEEL IS REASONABLE THEN GET A FASTPASS FOR A RETURN APPOINTMENT.

DISTRIBUTION OF ARRIVALS

Arrival rate

When describing a waiting system, we need to define the manner in which customers or the waiting units are arranged for service.

Waiting line formulas generally require an **arrival rate**, or the number of units per period (such as an average of one every six minutes). A *constant* arrival distribution is periodic, with exactly the same time between successive arrivals. In productive systems, the only arrivals that truly approach a constant interval period are those subject to machine control. Much more common are *variable* (random) arrival distributions.

In observing arrivals at a service facility, we can look at them from two viewpoints: First, we can analyze the time between successive arrivals to see if the times follow some statistical distribution. Usually we assume that the time between arrivals is exponentially distributed. Second, we can set some time length (*T*) and try to determine how many arrivals might enter the system within *T*. We typically assume that the number of arrivals per time unit is Poisson distributed.

Exponential distribution

Exponential Distribution   In the first case, when arrivals at a service facility occur in a purely random fashion, a plot of the interarrival times yields an **exponential distribution** such as that shown in Exhibit 7A.3. The probability function is

$$f(t) = \lambda e^{-\lambda t} \qquad \text{[7A.1]}$$

where λ is the mean number of arrivals per time period.

The cumulative area beneath the curve in Exhibit 7A.3 is the summation of equation (7A.1) over its positive range, which is $e^{-\lambda t}$. This integral allows us to compute the probabilities of arrivals within a specified time. For example, for the case of single arrivals to a waiting line ($\lambda = 1$), the following table can be derived either by solving $e^{-\lambda t}$ or by using Appendix F. Column 2 shows the probability that it will be more than *t* minutes until the next arrival. Column 3 shows the probability of the next arrival within *t* minutes (computed as 1 minus column 2)

(1)	(2)	(3)
	PROBABILITY THAT THE NEXT ARRIVAL WILL OCCUR IN	PROBABILITY THAT THE NEXT ARRIVAL WILL OCCUR IN
t (MINUTES)	*t* MINUTES OR MORE (FROM APPENDIX F OR SOLVING e^{-t})	*t* MINUTES OR LESS [1− COLUMN (2)]
0	1.00	0
0.5	0.61	0.39
1.0	0.37	0.63
1.5	0.22	0.78
2.0	0.14	0.86

exhibit 7A.3   Exponential Distribution

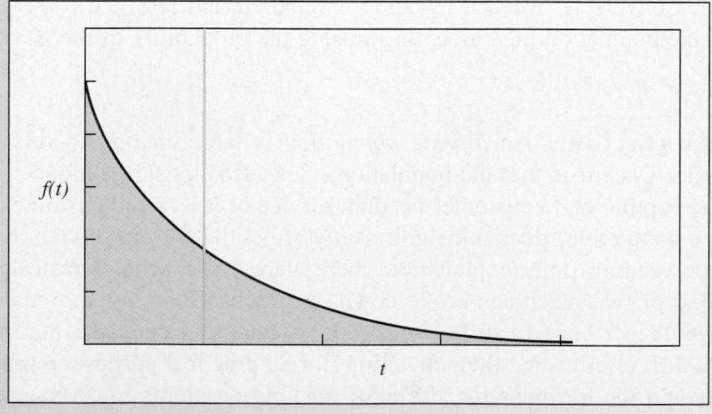

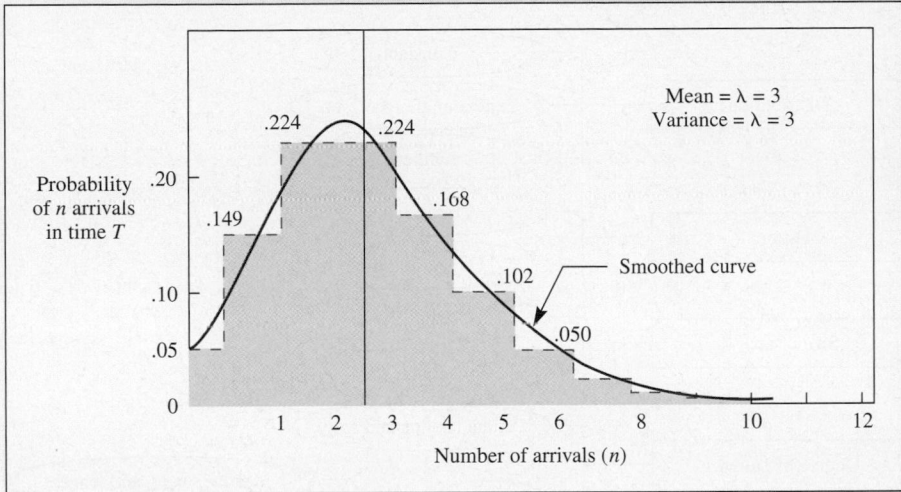

Poisson Distribution   In the second case, where one is interested in the number of arrivals during some time period T, the distribution appears as in Exhibit 7A.4 and is obtained by finding the probability of exactly n arrivals during T. If the arrival process is random, the distribution is the **Poisson**, and the formula is

Poisson distribution

$$P_T(n) = \frac{(\lambda T)^n e^{-\lambda T}}{n!} \qquad [7A.2]$$

Equation (7A.2) shows the probability of exactly n arrivals in time T.[1] For example, if the mean arrival rate of units into a system is three per minute ($\lambda = 3$) and we want to find the probability that exactly five units will arrive within a one-minute period ($n = 5$, $T = 1$), we have

$$P_1(5) = \frac{(3 \times 1)^5 e^{-3 \times 1}}{5!} = \frac{3^5 e^{-3}}{120} = 2.025 e^{-3} = 0.101$$

That is, there is a 10.1 percent chance that there will be five arrivals in any one-minute interval.

Although often shown as a smoothed curve, as in Exhibit 7A.4, the Poisson is a discrete distribution. (The curve becomes smoother as n becomes large.) The distribution is discrete because n refers, in our example, to the number of arrivals in a system, and this must be an integer. (For example, there cannot be 1.5 arrivals.)

Also note that the exponential and Poisson distributions can be derived from one another. The mean and variance of the Poisson are equal and denoted by λ. The mean of the exponential is $1/\lambda$, and its variance is $1/\lambda^2$. (Remember that the time between arrivals is exponentially distributed and the number of arrivals per unit of time is Poisson distributed.)

Other arrival characteristics include arrival patterns, size of arrival units, and degree of patience. (See Exhibit 7A.5.)

Arrival patterns.   The arrivals at a system are far more controllable than is generally recognized. Barbers may decrease their Saturday arrival rate (and supposedly shift it to other days of the week) by charging an extra $1 for adult haircuts or charging adult prices for children's haircuts. Department stores run sales during the off-season or hold one-day-only sales in part for purposes of control. Airlines offer excursion and off-season rates for similar reasons. The simplest of all arrival-control devices is the posting of business hours.

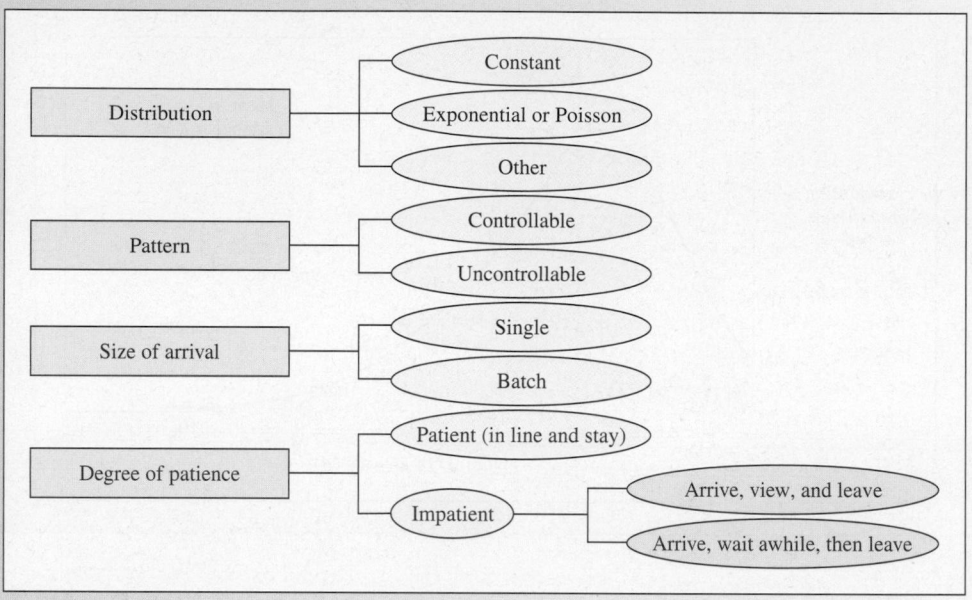

Some service demands are clearly uncontrollable, such as emergency medical demands on a city's hospital facilities. But even in these situations, arrivals at emergency rooms in specific hospitals are controllable to some extent by, say, keeping ambulance drivers in the service region informed of the status of their respective host hospitals.

Size of arrival units.   A *single arrival* may be thought of as one unit. (A unit is the smallest number handled.) A single arrival on the floor of the New York Stock Exchange (NYSE) is 100 shares of stock; a single arrival at an egg-processing plant might be a dozen eggs or a flat of 2½ dozen; a single arrival at a restaurant is a single person.

A *batch arrival* is some multiple of the unit, such as a block of 1,000 shares on the NYSE, a case of eggs at the processing plant, or a party of five at a restaurant.

Degree of patience.   A *patient* arrival is one who waits as long as necessary until the service facility is ready to serve him or her. (Even if arrivals grumble and behave impatiently, the fact that they wait is sufficient to label them as patient arrivals for purposes of waiting line theory.)

There are two classes of *impatient* arrivals. Members of the first class arrive, survey both the service facility and the length of the line, and then decide to leave. Those in the second class arrive, view the situation, join the waiting line, and then, after some period of time, depart. The behavior of the first type is termed *balking*, while the second is termed *reneging*.

THE QUEUING SYSTEM: FACTORS

The queuing system consists primarily of the waiting line(s) and the available number of servers. Here we discuss issues pertaining to waiting line characteristics and management, line structure, and service rate. Factors to consider with waiting lines include the line length, number of lines, and queue discipline.

Length.   In a practical sense, an infinite line is simply one that is very long in terms of the capacity of the service system. Examples of *infinite potential length* are a line of vehicles backed up for miles at a bridge crossing and customers who must form a line around the block as they wait to purchase tickets at a theater.

Gas stations, loading docks, and parking lots have *limited line capacity* caused by legal restrictions or physical space characteristics. This complicates the waiting line problem not only in service system utilization and waiting line computations but also in the shape of the actual arrival distribution. The arrival denied entry into the line because of lack of space may rejoin the population for a later try or may seek service elsewhere. Either action makes an obvious difference in the finite population case.

Number of lines.   A single line or single file is, of course, one line only. The term *multiple lines* refers to the single lines that form in front of two or more servers or to single lines that converge at some central redistribution point. The disadvantage of multiple lines in a busy facility is that arrivals often shift lines if several previous services have been of short duration or if those customers currently in other lines appear to require a short service time.

Queue discipline.   A queue discipline is a priority rule or set of rules for determining the order of service to customers in a waiting line. The rules selected can have a dramatic effect on the system's overall performance. The number of customers in line, the average waiting time, the range of variability in waiting time, and the efficiency of the service facility are just a few of the factors affected by the choice of priority rules.

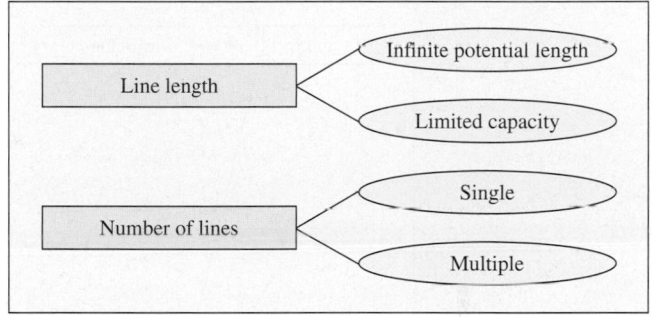

Probably the most common priority rule is first come, first served (FCFS). This rule states that customers in line are served on the basis of their chronological arrival; no other characteristics have any bearing on the selection process. This is popularly accepted as the fairest rule, although in practice it discriminates against the arrival requiring a short service time.

Reservations first, emergencies first, highest-profit customer first, largest orders first, best customers first, longest waiting time in line, and soonest promised date are other examples of priority rules. There are two major practical problems in using any rule: One is ensuring that customers know and follow the rule. The other is ensuring that a system exists to enable employees to manage the line (such as take-a-number systems).

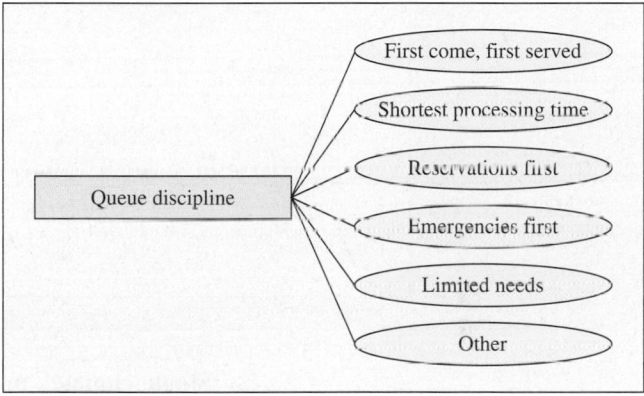

Service Time Distribution   Another important feature of the waiting structure is the time the customer or unit spends with the server once the service has started. Waiting line formulas generally specify **service rate** as the capacity of the server in number of units per time period (such as 12 completions per hour) and *not* as service time, which might average five minutes each. A constant service time rule states that each service takes exactly the same time. As in constant arrivals, this characteristic is generally limited to machine-controlled operations.

Service rate

When service times are random, they can be approximated by the exponential distribution. When using the exponential distribution as an approximation of the service times, we will refer to μ as the average number of units or customers that can be served per time period.

Line Structures   As Exhibit 7A.6 shows, the flow of items to be serviced may go through a single line, multiple lines, or some mixture of the two. The choice of format depends partly on the volume of customers served and partly on the restrictions imposed by sequential requirements governing the order in which service must be performed.

1. **Single channel, single phase.**   This is the simplest type of waiting line structure, and straightforward formulas are available to solve the problem for standard distribution patterns of arrival and service. When the distributions are nonstandard, the problem is easily solved by computer simulation. A typical example of a single-channel, single-phase situation is the one-person barbershop.

exhibit 7A.6   Line Structures

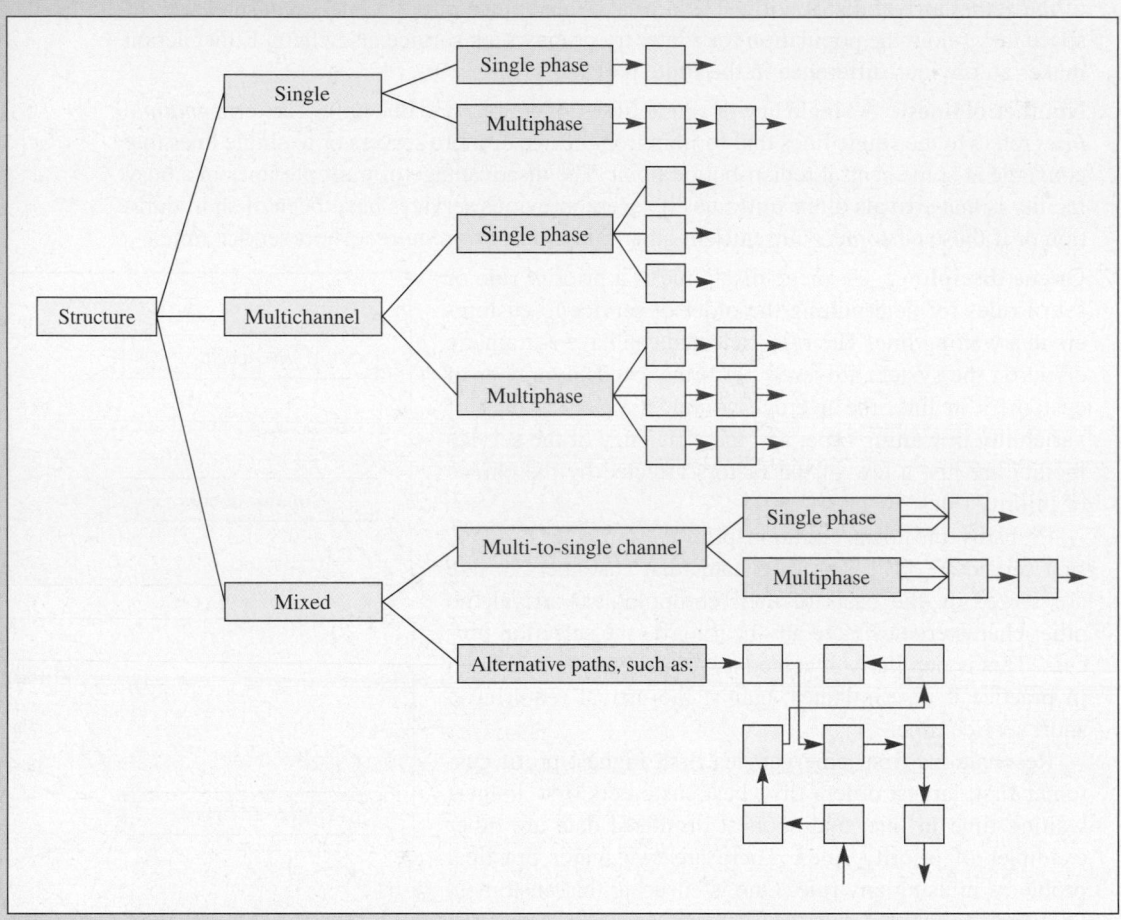

2. **Single channel, multiphase.**   A car wash is an illustration because a series of services (vacuuming, wetting, washing, rinsing, drying, window cleaning, and parking) is performed in a fairly uniform sequence. A critical factor in the single-channel case with service in series is the amount of buildup of items allowed in front of each service, which in turn constitutes separate waiting lines.

3. **Multichannel, single phase.**   Tellers' windows in a bank and checkout counters in high-volume department stores exemplify this type of structure. The difficulty with this format is that the uneven service time given each customer results in unequal speed or flow among the lines. This results in some customers being served before others who arrived earlier, as well as in some degree of line shifting. Varying this structure to ensure the servicing of arrivals in chronological order would require forming a single line, from which, as a server becomes available, the next customer in the queue is assigned.

    The major problem of this structure is that it requires rigid control of the line to maintain order and to direct customers to available servers. In some instances, assigning numbers to customers in order of their arrival helps alleviate this problem.

4. **Multichannel, multiphase.**   This case is similar to the preceding one except that two or more services are performed in sequence. The admission of patients in a hospital follows this pattern because a specific sequence of steps is usually followed: initial contact at the admissions desk, filling out forms, making identification tags, obtaining a room assignment, escorting the patient to the room, and so forth. Because several servers are usually available for this procedure, more than one patient at a time may be processed.

5. **Mixed.**   Under this general heading we consider two subcategories: (1) multiple-to-single channel structures and (2) alternative path structures. Under (1), we find either

lines that merge into one for single-phase service, as at a bridge crossing where two lanes merge into one, or lines that merge into one for multiphase service, such as subassembly lines feeding into a main line. Under (2), we encounter two structures that differ in directional flow requirements. The first is similar to the multichannel–multiphase case, except that (a) there may be switching from one channel to the next after the first service has been rendered and (b) the number of channels and phases may vary—again—after performance of the first service.

EXITING THE QUEUING SYSTEM

Once a customer is served, two exit fates are possible: (1) The customer may return to the source population and immediately become a competing candidate for service again or (2) there may be a low probability of reservice. The first case can be illustrated by a machine that has been routinely repaired and returned to duty but may break down again; the second can be illustrated by a machine that has been overhauled or modified and has a low probability of reservice over the near future. In a lighter vein, we might refer to the first as the "recurring-common-cold case" and to the second as the "appendectomy-only-once case."

It should be apparent that when the population source is finite, any change in the service performed on customers who return to the population modifies the arrival rate at the service facility. This, of course, alters the characteristics of the waiting line under study and necessitates reanalysis of the problem.

WAITING LINE MODELS

In this section we present four sample waiting line problems followed by their solutions. Each has a slightly different structure (see Exhibit 7A.7) and solution equation (see Exhibit 7A.8). There are more types of models than these four, but the formulas and solutions become quite complicated, and those problems are generally solved using computer simulation. Also, in using these formulas, keep in mind that they are steady-state formulas derived on the assumption that the process under study is ongoing. Thus, they may provide inaccurate results when applied to processes where the arrival rates and/or service rates change over time. The Excel Spreadsheet QueueModel.xls, developed by John McClain of Cornell University and included on the book Web site, can be used to solve these problems.

Here is a quick preview of our four problems to illustrate each of the four waiting line models in Exhibits 7A.7 and 7A.8.

Excel: Queue

Properties of Some Specific Waiting Line Models								**exhibit 7A.7**

MODEL	LAYOUT	SERVICE PHASE	SOURCE POPULATION	ARRIVAL PATTERN	QUEUE DISCIPLINE	SERVICE PATTERN	PERMISSIBLE QUEUE LENGTH	TYPICAL EXAMPLE
1	Single channel	Single	Infinite	Poisson	FCFS	Exponential	Unlimited	Drive-in teller at bank; one-lane toll bridge
2	Single channel	Single	Infinite	Poisson	FCFS	Constant	Unlimited	Roller coaster rides in amusement park
3	Multichannel	Single	Infinite	Poisson	FCFS	Exponential	Unlimited	Parts counter in auto agency
4	Single channel	Single	Finite	Poisson	FCFS	Exponential	Unlimited	Machine breakdown and repair in a factory

exhibit 7A.8

Notations for Equations

INFINITE QUEUING NOTATION: MODELS 1–3	FINITE QUEUING NOTATION: MODEL 4
λ = Arrival rate	D = Probability that an arrival must wait in line
μ = Service rate	F = Efficiency factor, a measure of the effect of having to wait in line
$\frac{1}{\mu}$ = Average service time	H = Average number of units being serviced
$\frac{1}{\lambda}$ = Average time between arrivals	J = Population source less those in queuing system $(N - n)$
ρ = Ratio of total arrival rate to service rate for a single server $\left(\frac{\lambda}{\mu}\right)^*$	L = Average number of units in line
L_q = Average number waiting in line	S = Number of service channels
L_s = Average number in system (including any being served)	n = Average number of units in queuing system (including the one being served)
W_q = Average time waiting in line	N = Number of units in population source
W_s = Average total time in system (including time to be served)	P_n = Probability of exactly n units in queuing system
n = Number of units in the system	T = Average time to perform the service
S = Number of identical service channels	U = Average time between customer service requirements
P_n = Probability of exactly n units in system	W = Average waiting time in line
P_w = Probability of waiting in line	X = Service factor, or proportion of service time required

*For single-server queues, this is equivalent to utilization.

Equations for Solving Four Model Problems

Model 1
$$L_q = \frac{\lambda^2}{\mu(\mu - \lambda)} \qquad W_q = \frac{L_q}{\lambda} \qquad P_n = \left(1 - \frac{\lambda}{\mu}\right)\left(\frac{\lambda}{\mu}\right)^n \qquad P_0 = \left(1 - \frac{\lambda}{\mu}\right) \qquad \text{[7A.3]}$$
$$L_s = \frac{\lambda}{\mu - \lambda} \qquad W_s = \frac{L_s}{\lambda} \qquad \rho = \frac{\lambda}{\mu}$$

Model 2
$$L_q = \frac{\lambda^2}{2\mu(\mu - \lambda)} \qquad W_q = \frac{L_q}{\lambda} \qquad\qquad\qquad\qquad \text{[7A.4]}$$
$$L_s = L_q + \frac{\lambda}{\mu} \qquad W_s = \frac{L_s}{\lambda}$$

(Exhibit 7A.9 provides the value of L_q given λ/μ and the number of servers S.)

Model 3
$$L_s = L_q + \lambda/\mu \qquad W_s = L_s/\lambda \qquad\qquad\qquad \text{[7A.5]}$$
$$W_q = L_q/\lambda \qquad P_w = L_q\left(\frac{S\mu}{\lambda} - 1\right)$$

Model 4 is a finite queuing situation that is most easily solved by using finite tables. These tables, in turn, require the manipulation of specific terms.

Model 4
$$X = \frac{T}{T + U} \qquad H = FNX \qquad L = N(1 - F) \qquad n = L + H$$
$$P_n = \frac{N!}{(N - n)!}X^n P_0 \qquad\qquad J = NF(1 - X) \qquad\qquad \text{[7A.6]}$$
$$W = \frac{L(T + U)}{N - L} = \frac{LT}{H} \qquad\qquad F = \frac{T + U}{T + U + W}$$

Problem 1: Customers in line. A bank wants to know how many customers are waiting for a drive-in teller, how long they have to wait, the utilization of the teller, and what the service rate would have to be so that 95 percent of the time there will not be more than three cars in the system at any time.

Problem 2: Equipment selection. A franchise for Robot Car Wash must decide which equipment to purchase out of a choice of three. Larger units cost more but wash cars faster. To make the decision, costs are related to revenue.

Problem 3: Determining the number of servers. An auto agency parts department must decide how many clerks to employ at the counter. More clerks cost more money, but there is a savings because mechanics wait less time.

Problem 4: Finite population source. Whereas the previous models assume a large population, finite queuing employs a separate set of equations for those cases where the calling customer population is small. In this last problem, mechanics must service four weaving machines to keep them operating. Based on the costs associated with machines being idle and the costs of mechanics to service them, the problem is to decide how many mechanics to use.

EXAMPLE 7A.1: Customers in Line

Western National Bank is considering opening a drive-through window for customer service. Management estimates that customers will arrive at the rate of 15 per hour. The teller who will staff the window can service customers at the rate of one every three minutes.

Service

Part 1   Assuming Poisson arrivals and exponential service, find

1. Utilization of the teller.
2. Average number in the waiting line.
3. Average number in the system.
4. Average waiting time in line.
5. Average waiting time in the system, including service.

Step by Step

SOLUTION—Part 1

1. The average utilization of the teller is (using Model 1)

$$\rho = \frac{\lambda}{\mu} = \frac{15}{20} = 75 \text{ percent}$$

2. The average number in the waiting line is

$$L_q = \frac{\lambda^2}{\mu(\mu - \lambda)} = \frac{(15)^2}{20(20 - 15)} = 2.25 \text{ customers}$$

3. The average number in the system is

$$L_s = \frac{\lambda}{\mu - \lambda} = \frac{15}{20 - 15} = 3 \text{ customers}$$

4. Average waiting time in line is

$$W_q = \frac{L_q}{\lambda} = \frac{2.25}{15} = 0.15 \text{ hour, or 9 minutes}$$

5. Average waiting time in the system is

$$W_s = \frac{L_s}{\lambda} = \frac{3}{15} = 0.2 \text{ hour, or 12 minutes}$$

Excel: Queue

EXAMPLE 7A.1: (Continued)

Part 2 Because of limited space availability and a desire to provide an acceptable level of service, the bank manager would like to ensure, with 95 percent confidence, that no more than three cars will be in the system at any time. What is the present level of service for the three-car limit? What level of teller use must be attained and what must be the service rate of the teller to ensure the 95 percent level of service?

SOLUTION—Part 2

The present level of service for three or fewer cars is the probability that there are 0, 1, 2, or 3 cars in the system. From Model 1, Exhibit 7A.8,

$$P_n = \left(1 - \frac{\lambda}{\mu}\right)\left(\frac{\lambda}{\mu}\right)^n$$

at $n = 0$, $P_0 = (1 - 15/20)$ $(15/20)^0 = 0.250$

at $n = 1$, $P_1 = (1/4)$ $(15/20)^1 = 0.188$

at $n = 2$, $P_2 = (1/4)$ $(15/20)^2 = 0.141$

at $n = 3$, $P_3 = (1/4)$ $(15/20)^3 = \underline{0.105}$

0.684 or   68.5 percent

The probability of having more than three cars in the system is 1.0 minus the probability of three or fewer cars $(1.0 - 0.685 = 31.5$ percent).

For a 95 percent service level of three or fewer cars, this states that $P_0 + P_1 + P_2 + P_3 = 95$ percent.

$$0.95 = \left(1 - \frac{\lambda}{\mu}\right)\left(\frac{\lambda}{\mu}\right)^0 + \left(1 - \frac{\lambda}{\mu}\right)\left(\frac{\lambda}{\mu}\right)^1 + \left(1 - \frac{\lambda}{\mu}\right)\left(\frac{\lambda}{\mu}\right)^2 + \left(1 - \frac{\lambda}{\mu}\right)\left(\frac{\lambda}{\mu}\right)^3$$

$$0.95 = \left(1 - \frac{\lambda}{\mu}\right)\left[1 + \frac{\lambda}{\mu} + \left(\frac{\lambda}{\mu}\right)^2 + \left(\frac{\lambda}{\mu}\right)^3\right]$$

We can solve this by trial and error for values of λ/μ. If $\lambda/\mu = 0.50$,

$$0.95 \overset{?}{=} 0.5(1 + 0.5 + 0.25 + 0.125)$$
$$0.95 \neq 0.9375$$

With $\lambda/\mu = 0.45$,

$$0.95 \overset{?}{=} (1 - 0.45)(1 + 0.45 + 0.203 + 0.091)$$
$$0.95 \neq 0.96$$

With $\lambda/\mu = 0.47$,

$$0.95 \overset{?}{=} (1 - 0.47)(1 + 0.47 + 0.221 + 0.104) = 0.95135$$
$$0.95 \approx 0.95135$$

Therefore, with the utilization $\rho = \lambda/\mu$ of 47 percent, the probability of three or fewer cars in the system is 95 percent.

To find the rate of service required to attain this 95 percent service level, we simply solve the equation $\lambda/\mu = 0.47$, where λ = number of arrivals per hour. This gives $\mu = 32$ per hour. That is, the teller must serve approximately 32 people per hour (a 60 percent increase over the original 20-per-hour capability) for 95 percent confidence that not more than three cars will be in the system. Perhaps service may be speeded up by modifying the method of service, adding another teller, or limiting the types of transactions available at the drive-through window. Note that with the condition of 95 percent confidence that three or fewer cars will be in the system, the teller will be idle 53 percent of the time. ●

EXAMPLE 7A.2: Equipment Selection

The Robot Company franchises combination gas and car wash stations throughout the United States. Robot gives a free car wash for a gasoline fill-up or, for a wash alone, charges $0.50. Past experience shows that the number of customers that have car washes following fill-ups is about the same as for a wash alone. The average profit on a gasoline fill-up is about $0.70, and the cost of the car wash to Robot is $0.10. Robot stays open 14 hours per day.

Robot has three power units and drive assemblies, and a franchisee must select the unit preferred. Unit I can wash cars at the rate of one every five minutes and is leased for $12 per day. Unit II, a larger unit, can wash cars at the rate of one every four minutes but costs $16 per day. Unit III, the largest, costs $22 per day and can wash a car in three minutes.

The franchisee estimates that customers will not wait in line more than five minutes for a car wash. A longer time will cause Robot to lose the gasoline sales as well as the car wash sale.

If the estimate of customer arrivals resulting in washes is 10 per hour, which wash unit should be selected?

Service

Step by Step

SOLUTION

Using unit I, calculate the average waiting time of customers in the wash line (μ for unit I = 12 per hour). From the Model 2 equations (Exhibit 7A.8),

$$L_q = \frac{\lambda^2}{2\mu(\mu - \lambda)} = \frac{10^2}{2(12)(12 - 10)} = 2.08333$$

$$W_q = \frac{L_q}{\lambda} = \frac{2.08333}{10} = 0.208 \text{ hour, or } 12\tfrac{1}{2} \text{ minutes}$$

Excel: Queue

For unit II at 15 per hour,

$$L_q = \frac{10^2}{2(15)(15 - 10)} = 0.667$$

$$W_q = \frac{0.667}{10} = 0.0667 \text{ hour, or 4 minutes}$$

If waiting time is the only criterion, unit II should be purchased. But before we make the final decision, we must look at the profit differential between both units.

With unit I, some customers would balk and renege because of the $12\tfrac{1}{2}$-minute wait. And, although this greatly complicates the mathematical analysis, we can gain some estimate of lost sales with unit I by increasing $W_q = 5$ minutes or $\frac{1}{12}$ hour (the average length of time customers will wait) and solving for λ. This would be the effective arrival rate of customers:

$$W_q = \frac{L_q}{\lambda} = \left(\frac{\lambda^2/2\mu(\mu - \lambda)}{\lambda} \right)$$

$$W_q = \frac{\lambda}{2\mu(\mu - \lambda)}$$

$$\lambda = \frac{2W_q\mu^2}{1 + 2W_q\mu} = \frac{2\left(\frac{1}{12}\right)(12)^2}{1 + 2\left(\frac{1}{12}\right)(12)} = 8 \text{ per hour}$$

Therefore, because the original estimate of λ was 10 per hour, an estimated 2 customers per hour will be lost. Lost profit of 2 customers per hour × 14 hours × $\frac{1}{2}$($0.70 fill-up profit + $0.40 wash profit) = $15.40 per day.

Because the additional cost of unit II over unit I is only $4 per day, the loss of $15.40 profit obviously warrants installing unit II.

The original five-minute maximum wait constraint is satisfied by unit II. Therefore, unit III is not considered unless the arrival rate is expected to increase. ●

Service

Step by Step

Excel: Queue

EXAMPLE 7A.3: Determining the Number of Servers

In the service department of the Glenn-Mark Auto Agency, mechanics requiring parts for auto repair or service present their request forms at the parts department counter. The parts clerk fills a request while the mechanic waits. Mechanics arrive in a random (Poisson) fashion at the rate of 40 per hour, and a clerk can fill requests at the rate of 20 per hour (exponential). If the cost for a parts clerk is $6 per hour and the cost for a mechanic is $12 per hour, determine the optimum number of clerks to staff the counter. (Because of the high arrival rate, an infinite source may be assumed.)

SOLUTION

First, assume that three clerks will be used because having only one or two clerks would create infinitely long lines (since $\lambda = 40$ and $\mu = 20$). The equations for Model 3 from Exhibit 7A.8 will be used here. But first we need to obtain the average number in line using the table of Exhibit 7A.9. Using the table and values $\lambda/\mu = 2$ and $S = 3$, we obtain $L_q = 0.8888$ mechanic.

At this point, we see that we have an average of 0.8888 mechanic waiting all day. For an eight-hour day at $12 per hour, there is a loss of mechanic's time worth 0.8888 mechanic × $12 per hour × 8 hours = $85.32.

Our next step is to reobtain the waiting time if we add another parts clerk. We then compare the added cost of the additional employee with the time saved by the mechanics. Again, using the table of Exhibit 7A.9 but with $S = 4$, we obtain

$L_q = 0.1730$ mechanic in line

0.1730 × $12 × 8 hours = $16.61 cost of a mechanic waiting in line

Value of mechanics' time saved is $85.32 − $16.61   = $68.71

Cost of an additional parts clerk is 8 hours × $6/hour =   48.00

Cost of reduction by adding fourth clerk   = $20.71

This problem could be expanded to consider the addition of runners to deliver parts to mechanics; the problem then would be to determine the optimal number of runners. This, however, would have to include the added cost of lost time caused by errors in parts receipts. For example, a mechanic would recognize a wrong part at the counter and obtain immediate correction, whereas the parts runner might not. ●

Service

Step by Step

Excel: Queue

EXAMPLE 7A.4: Finite Population Source

Studies of a bank of four weaving machines at the Loose Knit textile mill have shown that, on average, each machine needs adjusting every hour and that the current servicer averages $7\frac{1}{2}$ minutes per adjustment. Assuming Poisson arrivals, exponential service, and a machine idle time cost of $40 per hour, determine if a second servicer (who also averages $7\frac{1}{2}$ minutes per adjustment) should be hired at a rate of $7 per hour.

SOLUTION

This is a finite queuing problem that can be solved by using finite queuing tables. (See Exhibit 7A.10.) The approach in this problem is to compare the cost of machine downtime (either waiting in line or being serviced) and of one repairer to the cost of machine downtime and two repairers. We do this by finding the average number of machines that are in the service system and multiplying this number by the downtime cost per hour. To this we add the repairers' cost.

Before we proceed, we first define some terms:

N = Number of machines in the population

S = Number of repairers

T = Time required to service a machine

U = Average time a machine runs before requiring service

Expected Number of People Waiting in Line (L_q) for Various Values of S and λ/μ

λ/μ	\multicolumn{15}{c}{NUMBER OF SERVICE CHANNELS, S}

λ/μ	1	2	3	4	5	6	7	8	9	10	11	12	13	14	15
0.10	0.0111														
0.15	0.0264	0.0006													
0.20	0.0500	0.0020													
0.25	0.0833	0.0039													
0.30	0.1285	0.0069													
0.35	0.1884	0.0110													
0.40	0.2666	0.0166													
0.45	0.3681	0.0239	0.0019												
0.50	0.5000	0.0333	0.0030												
0.55	0.6722	0.045	0.0043												
0.60	0.9090	0.0593	0.0061												
0.65	1.2071	0.0767	0.0084												
0.70	1.6333	0.0976	0.0112												
0.75	2.2500	0.1227	0.0147												
0.80	3.2000	0.1523	0.0189												
0.85	4.8165	0.1873	0.0239	0.0031											
0.90	8.1000	0.2285	0.0300	0.0041											
0.95	18.0500	0.2767	0.0371	0.0053											
1.0		0.3333	0.0454	0.0067											
1.2		0.6748	0.0940	0.0158											
1.4		1.3449	0.1778	0.0324	0.0059										
1.6		2.8441	0.3128	0.0604	0.0121										
1.8		7.6731	0.5320	0.1051	0.0227	0.0047									
2.0			0.8888	0.1730	0.0390	0.0090									
2.2			1.4907	0.2770	0.066	0.0158									
2.4			2.1261	0.4205	0.1047	0.0266	0.0065								
2.6			4.9322	0.6581	0.1609	0.0425	0.0110								
2.8			12.2724	1.0000	0.2411	0.0659	0.0180								
3.0				1.5282	0.3541	0.0991	0.0282	0.0077							
3.2				2.3855	0.5128	0.1452	0.0427	0.0122							
3.4				3.9060	0.7365	0.2085	0.0631	0.0189							
3.6				7.0893	1.0550	0.2947	0.0912	0.0283	0.0084						
3.8				16.9366	1.5181	0.4114	0.1292	0.0412	0.0127						
4.0					2.2164	0.5694	0.1801	0.0590	0.0189						
4.2					3.3269	0.7837	0.2475	0.0827	0.0273	0.0087					
4.4					5.2675	1.0777	0.3364	0.1142	0.0389	0.0128					
4.6					9.2885	1.4857	0.4532	0.1555	0.0541	0.0184					
4.8					21.6384	2.0708	0.6071	0.2092	0.0742	0.0260					
5.0						2.9375	0.8102	0.2785	0.1006	0.0361	0.0125				
5.2						4.3004	1.0804	0.3680	0.1345	0.0492	0.0175				
5.4						6.6609	1.4441	0.5871	0.1779	0.0663	0.0243	0.0085			
5.6						11.5178	1.9436	0.6313	0.2330	0.0683	0.0330	0.0119			
5.8						26.3726	2.6481	0.8225	0.3032	0.1164	0.0443	0.0164			
6.0							3.6878	1.0707	0.3918	0.1518	0.0590	0.0224			
6.2							5.2979	1.3967	0.5037	0.1964	0.0775	0.0300	0.0113		
6.4							8.0768	1.8040	0.6454	0.2524	0.1008	0.0398	0.0153		
6.6							13.7992	2.4198	0.8247	0.3222	0.1302	0.0523	0.0205		
6.8							31.1270	3.2441	1.0533	0.4090	0.1666	0.0679	0.0271	0.0105	
7.0								4.4471	1.3471	0.5172	0.2119	0.0876	0.0357	0.0141	
7.2								6.3133	1.7288	0.6521	0.2677	0.1119	0.0463	0.0187	
7.4								9.5102	2.2324	0.8202	0.3364	0.1420	0.0595	0.0245	0.0097
7.6								16.0379	2.9113	1.0310	0.4211	0.1789	0.0761	0.0318	0.0129
7.8								35.8956	3.8558	1.2972	0.5250	0.2243	0.0966	0.0410	0.0168
8.0									5.2264	1.6364	0.6530	0.2796	0.1214	0.0522	0.0220
8.2									7.3441	2.0736	0.8109	0.3469	0.1520	0.0663	0.0283
8.4									10.9592	2.6470	1.0060	0.4288	0.1891	0.0834	0.0361
8.6									18.3223	3.4160	1.2484	0.5236	0.2341	0.1043	0.0459
8.8									40.6824	4.4805	1.5524	0.6501	0.2885	0.1208	0.0577
9.0										6.0183	1.9366	0.7980	0.3543	0.1603	0.0723
9.2										8.3869	2.4293	0.9788	0.4333	0.1974	0.0899
9.4										12.4183	3.0732	1.2010	0.5267	0.2419	0.1111
9.6										20.6160	3.9318	1.4752	0.5437	0.2952	0.1367
9.8										45.4769	5.1156	1.8165	0.7827	0.3699	0.16731
10											6.8210	2.2465	0.9506	0.4352	0.2040

253

exhibit 7A.10   Finite Queuing Tables

POPULATION 4											
X	S	D	F	X	S	D	F	X	S	D	F
.015	1	.045	.999		1	.479	.899	.400	3	.064	.992
.022	1	.066	.998	.180	2	.088	.991		2	.372	.915
.030	1	.090	.997		1	.503	.887		1	.866	.595
.034	1	.102	.996	.190	2	.098	.990	.420	3	.074	.990
.038	1	.114	.995		1	.526	.874		2	.403	.903
.042	1	.126	.994	.200	3	.008	.999		1	.884	.572
.046	1	.137	.993		2	.108	.988	.440	3	.085	.986
.048	1	.143	.992	.200	1	.549	.862		2	.435	.891
.052	1	.155	.991	.210	3	.009	.999		1	.900	.551
.054	1	.161	.990		2	.118	.986	.460	3	.097	.985
.058	1	.173	.989		1	.572	.849		2	.466	.878
.060	1	.179	.988	.220	3	.011	.999		1	.914	.530
.062	1	.184	.987		2	.129	.984	.480	3	.111	.983
.064	1	.190	.986		1	.593	.835		2	.498	.864
.066	1	.196	.985	.230	3	.012	.999	.480	1	.926	.511
.070	2	.014	.999		2	.140	.982	.500	3	.125	.980
	1	.208	.984		1	.614	.822		2	.529	.850
.075	2	.016	.999	.240	3	.014	.999		1	.937	.492
	1	.222	.981		2	.151	.980	.520	3	.141	.976
.080	2	.018	.999		1	.634	.808		2	.561	.835
	1	.237	.978	.250	3	.016	.999		1	.947	.475
.085	2	.021	.999		2	.163	.977	.540	3	.157	.972
	1	.251	.975		1	.654	.794		2	.592	.820
.090	2	.023	.999	.260	3	.018	.998		1	.956	.459
	1	.265	.972		2	.175	.975	.560	3	.176	.968
.095	2	.026	.999		1	.673	.780		2	.623	.805
	1	.280	.969	.270	3	.020	.998		1	.963	.443
.100	2	.028	.999		2	.187	.972	.580	3	.195	.964
	1	.294	.965		1	.691	.766		2	.653	.789
.105	2	.031	.998	.280	3	.022	.99s8		1	.969	.429
	1	.308	.962		2	.200	.968	.600	3	.216	.959
.110	2	.034	.998		1	.708	.752		2	.682	.774
	1	.321	.958	.290	3	.024	.998		1	.975	.415
.115	2	.037	.998		2	.213	.965	.650	3	.275	.944
	1	.335	.954		1	.725	.738		2	.752	.734
.120	2	.041	.997	.300	3	.027	.997		1	.985	.384
	1	.349	.950		2	.226	.962	.700	3	.343	.926
.125	2	.044	.997		1	.741	.724		2	.816	.695
	1	.362	.945	.310	3	.030	.997		1	.991	.357
.130	2	.047	.997		2	.240	.958	.750	3	.422	.905
	1	.376	.941		1	.756	.710		2	.871	.657
.135	2	.051	.996	.320	3	.033	.997		1	.996	.333
	1	.389	.936		2	.254	.954	.800	3	.512	.880
.140	2	.055	.996		1	.771	.696		2	.917	.621
	1	.402	.931	.330	3	.036	.996		1	.998	.312
.145	2	.058	.995		2	.268	.950	.850	3	.614	.852
	1	.415	.926		1	.785	.683		2	.954	.587
.150	2	.062	.995	.340	3	.039	.996		1	.999	.294
	1	.428	.921		2	.282	.945	.900	3	.729	.821
.155	2	.066	.994		1	.798	.670		2	.979	.555
	1	.441	.916	.360	3	.047	.994	.950	3	.857	.786
.160	2	.071	.994		2	.312	.936		2	.995	.526
	1	.454	.910		1	.823	.644				
.165	2	.075	.993	.380	3	.055	.993				
	1	.466	.904		2	.342	.926				
.170	2	.079	.993		1	.846	.619				

X = Service factor, or proportion of service time required for each machine ($X = T/(T + U)$)

L = Average number of machines waiting in line to be serviced

H = Average number of machines being serviced

The values to be determined from the finite tables are

D = Probability that a machine needing service will have to wait

F = Efficiency factor, which measures the effect of having to wait in line to be serviced

The tables are arranged according to three variables: N, population size; X, service factor; and S, the number of service channels (repairers in this problem). To look up a value, first find the table for the correct N size, then search the first column for the appropriate X, and finally find the line for S. Then read off D and F. (In addition to these values, other characteristics about a finite queuing system can be found by using the finite formulas.)

To solve the problem, consider Case I with one repairer and Case II with two repairers.

Case I: One repairer. From problem statement,

$N = 4$

$S = 1$

$T = 7\frac{1}{2}$ minutes

$U = 60$ minutes

$$X = \frac{T}{T + U} = \frac{7.5}{7.5 + 60} = 0.111$$

From Exhibit 7A.10, which displays the table for $N = 4$, F is interpolated as being approximately 0.957 at $X = 0.111$ and $S = 1$.

The number of machines waiting in line to be serviced is L, where

$$L = N(1 - F) = 4(1 - 0.957) = 0.172 \text{ machine}$$

The number of machines being serviced is H, where

$$H = FNX = 0.957(4)(0.111) = 0.425 \text{ machine}$$

Exhibit 7A.11 shows the cost resulting from unproductive machine time and the cost of the repairer.

Case II: Two repairers. From Exhibit 7A.10, at $X = 0.111$ and $S = 2$, $F = 0.998$.

The number of machines waiting in line, L, is

$$L = N(1 - F) = 4(1 - 0.998) = 0.008 \text{ machine}$$

The number of machines being serviced, H, is

$$H = FNX = 0.998(4)(0.111) = 0.443 \text{ machine}$$

The costs for the machines being idle and for the two repairers are shown in Exhibit 7A.11. The final column of that exhibit shows that retaining just one repairer is the better choice. ●

A Comparison of Downtime Costs for Service and Repair of Four Machines   **exhibit 7A.11**

NUMBER OF REPAIRERS	NUMBER OF MACHINES DOWN $(H + L)$	COST PER HOUR FOR MACHINES DOWN $[(H + L) \times \$40/\text{HOUR}]$	COST OF REPAIRERS ($\$7/\text{HOUR EACH}$)	TOTAL COST PER HOUR
1	0.597	$23.88	$ 7.00	$30.88
2	0.451	18.04	14.00	32.04

APPROXIMATING CUSTOMER WAITING TIME[2]

Good news for managers. All you need is the mean and standard deviation to compute average waiting time! Some good research has led to a "quick and dirty" mathematical approximation to the queuing models illustrated earlier in the chapter. What's nice about the approximation is that it does not assume a particular arrival rate or service distribution. All that is needed is the mean and standard deviation of the interarrival time and the service time. We will not burden you with all the details of how the approximations were derived, just how to use the formulas.

First, you will need to collect some data on your service time. The service time is the amount of time that it takes to serve each customer. Keep in mind that you want to collect your data during a period of time that fairly represents what you expect to happen during the period that you are concerned about. For example, if you want to know how many bank tellers you should have to service customers on Friday around the lunch period, collect your data during that period. This will ensure that the transactions being performed are similar to those that you expect in the future. You can use a stopwatch to time how long it takes to serve each customer. Using these data, calculate the mean and standard deviation of the service time.

Recall from your statistics that the mean is

$$\overline{X} = \sum_{i=1}^{N} x_i / N \qquad\qquad \text{[7A.7]}$$

where x_i = observed value and N = total number of observed values.

The standard deviation is

$$s = \sqrt{\frac{\sum_{i=1}^{N}(x_i - \overline{X})^2}{N - 1}} \qquad\qquad \text{[7A.8]}$$

Next, capture data on the amount of time between the arrivals of each new customer during the period of time you are studying. This is called the interarrival time. From the data, calculate the mean and standard deviation of the interarrival time. From these calculations, we have

$\overline{X}_s$ = Mean service time

$\overline{X}_a$ = Mean interarrival time

S_s = Standard deviation of the service time sample

S_a = Standard deviation of the interarrival time sample

Next, define the following:

C_s = Coefficient of variation of service time = $\dfrac{S_s}{\overline{X}_s}$

C_a = Coefficient of variation of interarrival time = $\dfrac{S_a}{\overline{X}_a}$ $\qquad\qquad$ [7A.9]

λ = Customer arrival rate = $\dfrac{1}{\overline{X}_a}$

μ = Customer service rate = $\dfrac{1}{\overline{X}_s}$

Now, we can calculate some statistics about our system. First, define S as the number of servers that we intend to use. Then,

ρ = Utilization of the servers = $\dfrac{\lambda}{S\mu}$

L_q = Expected length of the waiting line = $\dfrac{\rho^{\sqrt{2(S+1)}}}{1 - \rho} \times \dfrac{C_a^2 + C_s^2}{2}$ $\qquad\qquad$ [7A.10]

L_s = Expected number of people in the system = $L_q + S\rho$

W_q = Expected time waiting in line = $\dfrac{L_q}{\lambda}$

W_s = Expected time in the system = $\dfrac{L_s}{\lambda}$

The utilization (ρ) is the percentage of time that the servers are expected to be busy. Often companies that provide high service target this number at between 70 and 80 percent depending on the amount of variance there is in the customer arrival and service rates. L_q is how long the queue is expected to be, and W_q is how long a customer is expected to have to wait in the queue. L_s and W_s are the expected number of customers in the system and the expected time that a customer is in the system. These statistics consider that the total number of customers and the total waiting time must include those that are actually being served.

EXAMPLE 7A.5: Waiting Line Approximation

Let's consider an example of a call center that takes orders for a mail order business. During the peak period, the average time between call arrivals ($\overline{X}_a$) is 0.5 minute with a standard deviation (S_a) of 0.203 minute. The average time to service a call ($\overline{X}_s$) is 4 minutes and the standard deviation of the service time (S_s) is 2.5 minutes. If the call center is using 9 operators to service calls, how long would you expect customers to wait before being serviced? What would be the impact of adding an additional operator?

Step by Step

Service

SOLUTION

W_q is the time that we expect a customer to wait before being served. The best way to do these calculations is with a spreadsheet. The spreadsheet "Queue_Models.xls" can be easily used. The following steps are needed for the calculation of the customer wait time.

Excel: Queue

Step 1. Calculate expected customer arrival rate (λ), service rate per server (μ), and coefficient of variation for the interarrival time (C_a) and service time (C_s).

$$\lambda = \frac{1}{\overline{X}_a} = \frac{1}{0.5} = 2 \text{ customers per minute}$$

$$\mu = \frac{1}{\overline{X}_s} = \frac{1}{4} = 0.25 \text{ customer per minute}$$

$$C_a = \frac{S_a}{\overline{X}_a} = \frac{0.203}{0.5} = 0.406$$

$$C_s = \frac{S_s}{\overline{X}_s} = \frac{2.5}{4} = 0.625$$

Step 2. Calculate the expected server utilization (ρ).

$$\rho = \frac{\lambda}{S\mu} = \frac{2}{9 \times 0.25} = 0.888889 \qquad \text{(Operators are expected to be busy 89 percent of the time.)}$$

Step 3. Calculate the expected number of people waiting (L_q) and the length of the wait (W_q).

$$L_q = \frac{\rho^{\sqrt{2(S+1)}}}{1-\rho} \times \frac{C_a^2 + C_s^2}{2} = \frac{0.888889^{\sqrt{2(9+1)}}}{1 - 0.888889} \times \frac{0.406^2 + 0.625^2}{2} = 1.476064 \text{ customers}$$

(This is the number of customers that we expect to be waiting on hold.)

$$W_q = \frac{L_q}{\lambda} = \frac{1.476064}{2} = 0.738032 \text{ minute}$$

On average, we expect customers to wait 44 seconds (0.738032×60) before talking to an operator.

For 10 operators, the calculations are as follows:

$$\rho = \frac{\lambda}{S\mu} = \frac{2}{10 \times 0.25} = 0.8 \qquad \text{(Operators are expected to be busy 80 percent of the time.)}$$

$$L_q = \frac{\rho^{\sqrt{2(S+1)}}}{1-\rho} \times \frac{C_a^2 + C_s^2}{2} = \frac{0.8^{\sqrt{2(10+1)}}}{1-0.8} \times \frac{0.406^2 + 0.625^2}{2} = 0.487579 \text{ customer}$$

$$W_q = \frac{L_q}{\lambda} = \frac{0.487579}{2} = 0.24379 \text{ minute}$$

With 10 operators, the waiting time is cut one-third to 14.6 seconds. If you add two operators (bringing the total to 11), the waiting time in queue is 6.4 seconds. Adding the first additional operator has a significant impact on customer wait time. ●

This approximation is useful for many typical queuing situations. It is easy to implement using a spreadsheet such as the "Queue_Models.xls" spreadsheet. Keep in mind that the approximation assumes that the population to be served is large and customers arrive one at a time. The approximation can be useful for a quick analysis of a queuing situation.

COMPUTER SIMULATION OF WAITING LINES

Some waiting line problems that seem simple on first impression turn out to be extremely difficult or impossible to solve. Throughout this chapter, we have been treating waiting line situations that are independent; that is, either the entire system consists of a single phase or else each service that is performed in a series is independent. (This could happen if the output of one service location is allowed to build up in front of the next one so that this, in essence, becomes a calling population for the next service.) When a series of services is performed in sequence where the output rate of one becomes the input rate of the next, we can no longer use the simple formulas. This is also true for any problem where conditions do not meet the requirements of the equations, as specified in Exhibit 7A.8. The technique best suited to solving this type of problem is computer simulation. We treat the topic of modeling and simulation in Chapter 19A.

SUMMARY

Waiting line problems both challenge and frustrate those who try to solve them. The basic objective is to balance the cost of waiting with the cost of adding more resources. For a service system, this means that the utilization of a server may be quite low to provide a short waiting time to the customer. One main concern in dealing with waiting line problems is which procedure or priority rule to use in selecting the next product or customer to be served.

Many queuing problems appear simple until an attempt is made to solve them. This chapter has dealt with the simpler problems. When the situation becomes more complex, when there are multiple phases, or where services are performed only in a particular sequence, computer simulation is necessary to obtain the optimal solution.

KEY TERMS

Queue A line of waiting persons, jobs, things, or the like.

Queuing system Consists of three major components: (1) the source population and the way customers arrive at the system, (2) the serving systems, and (3) how customers exit the system.

Arrival rate The expected number of customers that arrive each period.

Exponential distribution A probability distribution often associated with interarrival times.

Poisson distribution Probability distribution often used to describe the number of arrivals during a given time period.

Service rate The capacity of a server measured in number of units that can be processed over a given time period.

FORMULA REVIEW

Exponential distribution

$$f(t) = \lambda e^{-\lambda t} \qquad [7A.1]$$

Poisson distribution

$$P_T(n) = \frac{(\lambda T)^n e^{-\lambda T}}{n!} \qquad [7A.2]$$

Model 1 (See Exhibit 7A.8.)

$$L_q = \frac{\lambda^2}{\mu(\mu - \lambda)} \qquad W_q = \frac{L_q}{\lambda} \qquad P_n = \left(1 - \frac{\lambda}{\mu}\right)\left(\frac{\lambda}{\mu}\right)^n \qquad P_0 = \left(1 - \frac{\lambda}{\mu}\right) \qquad [7A.3]$$

$$L_s = \frac{\lambda}{\mu - \lambda} \qquad W_s = \frac{L_s}{\lambda} \qquad \rho = \frac{\lambda}{\mu}$$

Model 2

$$L_q = \frac{\lambda^2}{2\mu(\mu - \lambda)} \qquad W_q = \frac{L_q}{\lambda}$$

$$[7A.4]$$

$$L_s = L_q + \frac{\lambda}{\mu} \qquad W_s = \frac{L_s}{\lambda}$$

Model 3

$$L_s = L_q + \lambda/\mu \qquad W_s = L_s/\lambda$$

$$[7A.5]$$

$$W_q = L_q/\lambda \qquad P_w = L_q\left(\frac{S\mu}{\lambda} - 1\right)$$

Model 4

$$X = \frac{T}{T + U} \qquad H = FNX \qquad L = N(1 - F) \qquad n = L + H$$

$$P_n = \frac{N!}{(N - n)!} X^n P_0 \qquad J = NF(1 - X) \qquad [7A.6]$$

$$W = \frac{L(T + U)}{N - L} = \frac{LT}{H} \qquad F = \frac{T + U}{T + U + W}$$

Waiting time approximation

$$\bar{X} = \sum_{i=1}^{N} x_i \Big/ N \qquad \text{(mean)} \qquad [7A.7]$$

$$s = \sqrt{\frac{\sum_{i=1}^{N}(x_i - X)^2}{N - 1}} \qquad \text{(standard deviation)} \qquad [7A.8]$$

$$C_s = \frac{S_s}{\bar{X}_s} \qquad C_a = \frac{S_a}{\bar{X}_a} \qquad \lambda = \frac{1}{\bar{X}_a} \qquad \mu = \frac{1}{\bar{X}_s} \qquad [7A.9]$$

$$\rho = \frac{\lambda}{S\mu}$$

$$L_q = \frac{\rho^{\sqrt{2(S+1)}}}{1 - \rho} \times \frac{C_a^2 + C_s^2}{2} \quad L_s = L_q + S\rho$$ [7A.10]

$$W_q = \frac{L_q}{\lambda} \quad W_s = \frac{L_s}{\lambda}$$

SOLVED PROBLEMS

SOLVED PROBLEM 1

Excel: Queue

Quick Lube Inc. operates a fast lube and oil change garage. On a typical day, customers arrive at the rate of three per hour and lube jobs are performed at an average rate of one every 15 minutes. The mechanics operate as a team on one car at a time.

Assuming Poisson arrivals and exponential service, find
a. Utilization of the lube team.
b. The average number of cars in line.
c. The average time a car waits before it is lubed.
d. The total time it takes to go through the system (that is, waiting in line plus lube time).

Solution

$\lambda = 3, \mu = 4$

a. Utilization $\rho = \frac{\lambda}{\mu} = \frac{3}{4} = 75\%$.

b. $L_q = \frac{\lambda^2}{\mu(\mu - \lambda)} = \frac{3^2}{4(4 - 3)} = \frac{9}{4} = 2.25$ cars in line.

c. $W_q = \frac{L_q}{\lambda} = \frac{2.25}{3} = 0.75$ hour, or 45 minutes.

d. $W_s = \frac{L_s}{\lambda} = \frac{\lambda}{\mu - \lambda}/\lambda = \frac{3}{4 - 3}/3 = 1$ hour (waiting + lube).

SOLVED PROBLEM 2

Excel: Queue

American Vending Inc. (AVI) supplies vended food to a large university. Because students often kick the machines out of anger and frustration, management has a constant repair problem. The machines break down on an average of three per hour, and the breakdowns are distributed in a Poisson manner. Downtime costs the company $25 per hour per machine, and each maintenance worker gets $4 per hour. One worker can service machines at an average rate of five per hour, distributed exponentially; two workers working together can service seven per hour, distributed exponentially; and a team of three workers can do eight per hour, distributed exponentially.

What is the optimal maintenance crew size for servicing the machines?

Solution

Case I—One worker:

$\lambda = 3$/hour Poisson, $\mu = 5$/hour exponential
The average number of machines in the system is

$$L_s = \frac{\lambda}{\mu - \lambda} = \frac{3}{5 - 3} = \frac{3}{2} = 1\frac{1}{2} \text{ machines}$$

Downtime cost is $25 × 1.5 = $37.50 per hour; repair cost is $4.00 per hour; and total cost per hour for 1 worker is $37.50 + $4.00 = $41.50.

Downtime (1.5 × $25) = $37.50
Labor (1 worker × $4) = <u>4.00</u>
$41.50

Case II—Two workers:
  $\lambda = 3, \mu = 7$

$$L_s = \frac{\lambda}{\mu - \lambda} = \frac{3}{7 - 3} = 0.75 \text{ machine}$$

Downtime (0.75 × $25)   = $18.75
Labor (2 workers × $4.00) =   8.00
                            $26.75

Case III—Three workers:
  $\lambda = 3, \mu = 8$

$$L_s = \frac{\lambda}{\mu - \lambda} = \frac{3}{8 - 3} = \frac{3}{5} = 0.60 \text{ machine}$$

Downtime (0.60 × $25) = $15.00
Labor (3 workers × $4) = 12.00
                         $27.00

Comparing the costs for one, two, or three workers, we see that Case II with two workers is the optimal decision.

SOLVED PROBLEM 3

American Bank has a single automated teller machine (ATM) located in a shopping center. Data were collected during a period of peak usage on Saturday afternoon, and it was found that the average time between customer arrivals is 2.1 minutes with a standard deviation of 0.8 minute. It also was found it takes an average of 1.9 minutes for a customer to complete a transaction with a standard deviation of 2 minutes. Approximately how long will customers need to wait in line during the peak usage period?

Excel: Queue

Solution

Step 1. Calculate expected customer arrival rate (λ), service rate per server (μ), and coefficient of variation for the arrival distribution (C_a) and service distribution (C_s).

$$\lambda = \frac{1}{\overline{X}_a} = \frac{1}{2.1} = 0.47619 \text{ customer per minute}$$

$$\mu = \frac{1}{\overline{X}_s} = \frac{1}{1.9} = 0.526316 \text{ customer per minute}$$

$$C_a = \frac{S_a}{\overline{X}_a} = \frac{0.8}{2.1} = 0.380952$$

$$C_s = \frac{S_s}{\overline{X}_s} = \frac{2}{1.9} = 1.052632$$

Step 2. Calculate the expected server utilization (ρ).

$$\rho = \frac{\lambda}{S\mu} = \frac{0.47619}{1 \times 0.526316} = 0.904762 \qquad \text{(Operators are expected to be busy 90.5 percent of the time.)}$$

Step 3. Calculate the expected number of people waiting (L_q) and the length of the wait (W_q).

$$L_q = \frac{\rho^{\sqrt{2(S+1)}}}{1 - \rho} \times \frac{C_a^2 + C_s^2}{2} = \frac{0.904762^{\sqrt{2(1+1)}}}{1 - 0.904762} \times \frac{0.380952^2 + 1.052632^2}{2}$$

$$= 5.385596 \text{ customer} \qquad \text{(This is the number of customers that we expect to be waiting on hold.)}$$

$$W_q = \frac{L_q}{\lambda} = \frac{5.385596}{0.47619} = 11.30975 \text{ minutes}$$

On average we expect customers to wait 11 minutes and 19 seconds (0.30975 × 60) before having access to the ATM.

REVIEW AND DISCUSSION QUESTIONS

1 Cultural factors affect waiting lines. For example, fast checkout lines (e.g., 10 items or fewer) are uncommon in Japan. Why do you think this is so?

2 How many waiting lines did you encounter during your last airline flight?

3 Distinguish between a *channel* and a *phase*.

4 What is the major cost trade-off that must be made in managing waiting line situations?

5 Which assumptions are necessary to employ the formulas given for Model 1?

6 In what way might the first-come, first-served rule be unfair to the customer waiting for service in a bank or hospital?

7 Define, in a practical sense, what is meant by an *exponential service time*.

8 Would you expect the exponential distribution to be a good approximation of service times for
   a. Buying an airline ticket at the airport?
   b. Riding a merry-go-round at a carnival?
   c. Checking out of a hotel?
   d. Completing a midterm exam in your OSCM class?

9 Would you expect the Poisson distribution to be a good approximation of
   a. Runners crossing the finish line in the Boston Marathon?
   b. Arrival times of the students in your OSCM class?
   c. Arrival times of the bus to your stop at school?

PROBLEMS

1 Students arrive at the Administrative Services Office at an average of one every 15 minutes, and their requests take on average 10 minutes to be processed. The service counter is staffed by only one clerk, Judy Gumshoes, who works eight hours per day. Assume Poisson arrivals and exponential service times.
   a. What percentage of time is Judy idle?
   b. How much time, on average, does a student spend waiting in line?
   c. How long is the (waiting) line on average?
   d. What is the probability that an arriving student (just before entering the Administrative Services Office) will find at least one other student waiting in line?

2 The managers of the Administrative Services Office estimate that the time a student spends waiting in line costs them (due to goodwill loss and so on) $10 per hour. To reduce the time a student spends waiting, they know that they need to improve Judy's processing time (see Problem 1). They are currently considering the following two options:
   a. Install a computer system, with which Judy expects to be able to complete a student request 40 percent faster (from 2 minutes per request to 1 minute and 12 seconds, for example).
   b. Hire another temporary clerk, who will work at the same rate as Judy.
   If the computer costs $99.50 to operate per day, while the temporary clerk gets paid $75 per day, is Judy right to prefer the hired help? Assume Poisson arrivals and exponential service times.

3 Sharp Discounts Wholesale Club has two service desks, one at each entrance of the store. Customers arrive at each service desk at an average of one every six minutes. The service rate at each service desk is four minutes per customer.
   a. How often (what percentage of time) is each service desk idle?
   b. What is the probability that both service clerks are busy?
   c. What is the probability that both service clerks are idle?
   d. How many customers, on average, are waiting in line in front of each service desk?
   e. How much time does a customer spend at the service desk (waiting plus service time)?

4 Sharp Discounts Wholesale Club is considering consolidating its two service desks (see Problem 3) into one location, staffed by two clerks. The clerks will continue to work at the same individual speed of four minutes per customer.
   a. What is the probability of waiting in line?
   b. How many customers, on average, are waiting in line?
   c. How much time does a customer spend at the service desk (waiting plus service time)?
   d. Do you think the Sharp Discounts Wholesale Club should consolidate the service desks?

5 Burrito King (a new fast-food franchise opening up nationwide) has successfully automated burrito production for its drive-up fast-food establishments. The Burro-Master 9000 requires a constant 45 seconds to produce a batch of burritos. It has been estimated that customers will arrive at the drive-up window according to a Poisson distribution at an average of one every 50 seconds. To help determine the amount of space needed for the line at the drive-up

window, Burrito King would like to know the expected average time in the system, the average line length (in cars), and the average number of cars in the system (both in line and at the window).

6 The Bijou Theater in Hermosa Beach, California, shows vintage movies. Customers arrive at the theater line at the rate of 100 per hour. The ticket seller averages 30 seconds per customer, which includes placing validation stamps on customers' parking lot receipts and punching their frequent watcher cards. (Because of these added services, many customers don't get in until after the feature has started.)
   a. What is the average customer time in the system?
   b. What would be the effect on customer time in the system of having a second ticket taker doing nothing but validations and card punching, thereby cutting the average service time to 20 seconds?
   c. Would system waiting time be less than you found in *b* if a second window was opened with each server doing all three tasks?

7 To support National Heart Week, the Heart Association plans to install a free blood pressure testing booth in El Con Mall for the week. Previous experience indicates that, on the average, 10 persons per hour request a test. Assume arrivals are Poisson distributed from an infinite population. Blood pressure measurements can be made at a constant time of five minutes each. Assume the queue length can be infinite with FCFS discipline.
   a. What average number in line can be expected?
   b. What average number of persons can be expected to be in the system?
   c. What is the average amount of time that a person can expect to spend in line?
   d. On the average, how much time will it take to measure a person's blood pressure, including waiting time?
   e. On weekends, the arrival rate can be expected to increase to over 12 per hour. What effect will this have on the number in the waiting line?

8 A cafeteria serving line has a coffee urn from which customers serve themselves. Arrivals at the urn follow a Poisson distribution at the rate of three per minute. In serving themselves, customers take about 15 seconds, exponentially distributed.
   a. How many customers would you expect to see on the average at the coffee urn?
   b. How long would you expect it to take to get a cup of coffee?
   c. What percentage of time is the urn being used?
   d. What is the probability that three or more people are in the cafeteria?
   e. If the cafeteria installs an automatic vendor that dispenses a cup of coffee at a constant time of 15 seconds, how does this change your answers to *a* and *b*?

9 An engineering firm retains a technical specialist to assist four design engineers working on a project. The help that the specialist gives engineers ranges widely in time consumption. The specialist has some answers available in memory; others require computation, and still others require significant search time. On the average, each request for assistance takes the specialist one hour.

   The engineers require help from the specialist on the average of once each day. Because each assistance takes about an hour, each engineer can work for seven hours, on the average, without assistance. One further point: Engineers needing help do not interrupt if the specialist is already involved with another problem.

   Treat this as a finite queuing problem and answer the following questions:
   a. How many engineers, on average, are waiting for the technical specialist for help?
   b. What is the average time that an engineer has to wait for the specialist?
   c. What is the probability that an engineer will have to wait in line for the specialist?

10 L. Winston Martin (an allergist in Tucson) has an excellent system for handling his regular patients who come in just for allergy injections. Patients arrive for an injection and fill out a name slip, which is then placed in an open slot that passes into another room staffed by one or two nurses. The specific injections for a patient are prepared, and the patient is called through a speaker system into the room to receive the injection. At certain times during the day, patient load drops and only one nurse is needed to administer the injections.

   Let's focus on the simpler case of the two—namely, when there is one nurse. Also, assume that patients arrive in a Poisson fashion and the service rate of the nurse is exponentially distributed. During this slower period, patients arrive with an interarrival time of approximately three minutes. It takes the nurse an average of two minutes to prepare the patients' serum and administer the injection.
   a. What is the average number you would expect to see in Dr. Martin's facilities?
   b. How long would it take for a patient to arrive, get an injection, and leave?
   c. What is the probability that there will be three or more patients on the premises?

    d. What is the utilization of the nurse?

    e. Assume three nurses are available. Each takes an average of two minutes to prepare the patients' serum and administer the injection. What is the average total time of a patient in the system?

11 The Judy Gray Income Tax Service is analyzing its customer service operations during the month prior to the April filing deadline. On the basis of past data, it has been estimated that customers arrive according to a Poisson process with an average interarrival time of 12 minutes. The time to complete a return for a customer is exponentially distributed with a mean of 10 minutes. Based on this information, answer the following questions:

    a. If you went to Judy, how much time would you allow for getting your return done?

    b. On average, how much room should be allowed for the waiting area?

    c. If Judy stayed in the office 12 hours per day, how many hours on average, per day, would she be busy?

    d. What is the probability that the system is idle?

    e. If the arrival rate remained unchanged, but the average time in the system must be 45 minutes or less, what would need to be changed?

12 A graphics reproduction firm has four units of equipment that are automatic but occasionally become inoperative because of the need for supplies, maintenance, or repair. Each unit requires service roughly twice each hour, or, more precisely, each unit of equipment runs an average of 30 minutes before needing service. Service times vary widely, ranging from a simple service (such as pressing a restart switch or repositioning paper) to more involved equipment disassembly. The average service time, however, is five minutes.

    Equipment downtime results in a loss of $20 per hour. The one equipment attendant is paid $6 per hour.

    Using finite queuing analysis, answer the following questions:

    a. What is the average number of units in line?

    b. What is the average number of units still in operation?

    c. What is the average number of units being serviced?

    d. The firm is considering adding another attendant at the same $6 rate. Should the firm do it?

13 Benny the Barber owns a one-chair shop. At barber college, they told Benny that his customers would exhibit a Poisson arrival distribution and that he would provide an exponential service distribution. His market survey data indicate that customers arrive at a rate of two per hour. It will take Benny an average of 20 minutes to give a haircut. Based on these figures, find the following:

    a. The average number of customers waiting.

    b. The average time a customer waits.

    c. The average time a customer is in the shop.

    d. The average utilization of Benny's time.

14 Bobby the Barber is thinking about advertising in the local newspaper since he is idle 45 percent of the time. Currently, customers arrive on average every 40 minutes. What does the arrival rate need to be for Bobby to be busy 85 percent of the time?

15 Benny the Barber (see Problem 13) is considering the addition of a second chair. Customers would be selected for a haircut on a FCFS basis from those waiting. Benny has assumed that both barbers would take an average of 20 minutes to give a haircut and that business would remain unchanged with customers arriving at a rate of two per hour. Find the following information to help Benny decide if a second chair should be added:

    a. The average number of customers waiting.

    b. The average time a customer waits.

    c. The average time a customer is in the shop.

16 Customers enter the camera department of a store at the average rate of six per hour. The department is staffed by one employee, who takes an average of six minutes to serve each arrival. Assume this is a simple Poisson arrival, exponentially distributed service time situation.

    a. As a casual observer, how many people would you expect to see in the camera department (excluding the clerk)? How long would a customer expect to spend in the camera department (total time)?

    b. What is the utilization of the clerk?

    c. What is the probability that there are more than two people in the camera department (excluding the clerk)?

    d. Another clerk has been hired for the camera department who also takes an average of six minutes to serve each arrival. How long would a customer expect to spend in the department now?

17 Cathy Livingston, bartender at the Tucson Racquet Club, can serve drinks at the rate of one every 50 seconds. During a hot evening recently, the bar was particularly busy and every 55 seconds someone was at the bar asking for a drink.

    a. Assuming that everyone in the bar drank at the same rate and that Cathy served people on a first-come, first-served basis, how long would you expect to have to wait for a drink?

    b. How many people would you expect to be waiting for drinks?

    c. What is the probability that three or more people are waiting for drinks?

    d. What is the utilization of the bartender (how busy is she)?

    e. If the bartender is replaced with an automatic drink dispensing machine, how would this change your answer in part *a*?

18 An office employs several clerks who originate documents and one operator who enters the document information in a word processor. The group originates documents at a rate of 25 per hour. The operator can enter the information with average exponentially distributed time of two minutes. Assume the population is infinite, arrivals are Poisson, and queue length is infinite with FCFS discipline.

    a. Calculate the percentage utilization of the operator.

    b. Calculate the average number of documents in the system.

    c. Calculate the average time in the system.

    d. Calculate the probability of four or more documents being in the system.

    e. If another clerk were added, the document origination rate would increase to 30 per hour. What would this do to the word processor workload? Show why.

19 A study-aid desk staffed by a graduate student has been established to answer students' questions and help in working problems in your OSCM course. The desk is staffed eight hours per day. The dean wants to know how the facility is working. Statistics show that students arrive at a rate of four per hour and the distribution is approximately Poisson. Assistance time averages 10 minutes, distributed exponentially. Assume population and line length can be infinite and queue discipline is FCFS.

    a. Calculate the percentage utilization of the graduate student.

    b. Calculate the average number of students in the system.

    c. Calculate the average time in the system.

    d. Calculate the probability of four or more students being in line or being served.

    e. Before a test, the arrival of students increases to six per hour on the average. What does this do to the average length of the line?

20 At the California border inspection station, vehicles arrive at the rate of 10 per minute in a Poisson distribution. For simplicity in this problem, assume that there is only one lane and one inspector, who can inspect vehicles at the rate of 12 per minute in an exponentially distributed fashion.

    a. What is the average length of the waiting line?

    b. What is the average time that a vehicle must wait to get through the system?

    c. What is the utilization of the inspector?

    d. What is the probability that when you arrive there will be three or more vehicles ahead of you?

21 The California border inspection station (see Problem 20) is considering the addition of a second inspector. The vehicles would wait in one lane and then be directed to the first available inspector. Arrival rates would remain the same (10 per minute) and the new inspector would process vehicles at the same rate as the first inspector (12 per minute).

    a. What would be the average length of the waiting line?

    b. What would be the average time that a vehicle must wait to get through the system?

    If a second lane was added (one lane for each inspector):

    c. What would be the average length of the waiting line?

    d. What would be the average time that a vehicle must wait to get through the system?

22 During the campus Spring Fling, the bumper car amusement attraction has a problem of cars becoming disabled and in need of repair. Repair personnel can be hired at the rate of $20 per hour, but they only work as one team. Thus, if one person is hired, he or she works alone; two or three people work together on the same repair.

    One repairer can fix cars in an average time of 30 minutes. Two repairers take 20 minutes, and three take 15 minutes. While these cars are down, lost income is $40 per hour. Cars tend to break down at the rate of two per hour.

    How many repairers should be hired?

23 A toll tunnel has decided to experiment with the use of a debit card for the collection of tolls. Initially, only one lane will be used. Cars are estimated to arrive at this

experimental lane at the rate of 750 per hour. It will take exactly four seconds to verify the debit card.

   a. In how much time would you expect the customer to wait in line, pay with the debit card, and leave?

   b. How many cars would you expect to see in the system?

24   You are planning a bank. You plan for six tellers. Tellers take 15 minutes per customer with a standard deviation of 7 minutes. Customers arrive one every three minutes according to an exponential distribution (recall that the standard deviation is equal to the mean). Every customer that arrives eventually gets serviced.

   a. On average, how many customers would be waiting in line?

   b. On average, how long would a customer spend in the bank?

   c. If a customer arrived, saw the line, and decided not to get in line, that customer has _____.

   d. A customer who enters the line but decides to leave the line before getting service is said to have _____.

25   You are planning the new layout for the local branch of the Sixth Ninth Bank. You are considering separate cashier windows for the three different classes of service. Each class of service would be separate with its own cashiers and customers. Oddly enough, each class of service, while different, has exactly the same demand and service times. People for one class of service arrive every four minutes and arrival times are exponentially distributed (the standard deviation is equal to the mean). It takes seven minutes to service each customer, and the standard deviation of the service times is three minutes. You assign two cashiers to each type of service.

   a. On average, how long will each line be at each of the cashier windows?

   b. On average how long will a customer spend in the bank (assume they enter, go directly to one line, and leave as soon as service is complete).

      You decide to consolidate all the cashiers so they can handle all types of customers without increasing the service times.

   c. What will happen to the amount of time each cashier spends idle? (increase, decrease, stay the same, depends on _____)

   d. What will happen to the average amount of time a customer spends in the bank? (increase, decrease, stay the same, depends on _____)

26   A local fast-food restaurant wants to analyze its drive-through window. At this time, the only information known is the average number of customers in the system (4.00) and the average time a customer spends at the restaurant (1.176 minutes). What are the arrival rate and the service rate?

CASE: COMMUNITY HOSPITAL EVENING OPERATING ROOM

The American College of Surgeons has developed criteria for determining operating room standards in the United States. Level I and II trauma centers are required to have in-house operating room (OR) staff 24 hours per day. So a base level of a single OR team available 24 hours a day is mandatory. During normal business hours, a hospital will typically have additional OR teams available since surgery is scheduled during these times and these additional teams can be used in an emergency. An important decision, though, must be made concerning the availability of a backup team during the evening hours.

A backup team is needed during the evening hours if the probability of having two or more cases simultaneously is significant. "Significant" is difficult to judge, but for the purposes of this case assume that a backup OR team should be employed if the expected probability of two or more cases occurring simultaneously is greater than 1 percent.

A real application was recently studied by doctors at the Columbia University College of Physicians and Surgeons in Stamford, CT.[3] The doctors studied emergency OR patients that arrived after 11 P.M.

and before 7 A.M. during a one-year period. During this time period, there were 62 patients that required OR treatment. The average service time was 80.79 minutes.

In analyzing the problem, think about this as a single-channel, single-phase system with Poisson arrivals and exponential service times.

QUESTIONS

1   Calculate the average customer arrival rate and service rate per hour.

2   Calculate the probability of zero patients in the system (P0), probability of one patient (P1), and the probability of two or more patients simultaneously arriving during the night shift.

3   Using a criterion that if the probability is greater than 1 percent, a backup OR team should be employed, make a recommendation to hospital administration.

SUPER QUIZ

1 The queuing models assume that customers are served in what order?

2 Consider two identical queuing systems except for the service time distribution. In the first system the service time is random and Poisson distributed. The service time is constant in the second system. How would the waiting time differ in the two systems?

3 What is the average utilization of the servers in a system that has three servers? On average 15 customers arrive every 15 minutes. It takes a server exactly three minutes to wait on each customer.

4 What is the expected waiting time for the system described in question 3?

5 Firms that desire high service levels where customers have short wait times should target server utilization levels at no more than this percentage.

6 If a firm increases its service capacity by 10 percent, it would expect waiting times to be reduced by what percentage? Assume customer arrivals and service times are random.

1. First-come-first-serve 2. Waiting time in the first system is two times the second 3. 100% 4. Infinite 5. 70 80% 6. Greater than 10%

SELECTED BIBLIOGRAPHY

Gross, D., and C. M. Harris. *Fundamentals of Queuing Theory*. New York: Wiley, 1997.

Hillier, F. S., et al. *Queuing Tables and Graphs*. New York: Elsevier–North Holland, 1981.

Kleinrock, L., and R. Gail. *Queuing Systems: Problems and Solutions*. New York: Wiley, 1996.

Winston, W. L., and S. C. Albright. *Practical Management Science: Spreadsheet Modeling and Application*. New York: Duxbury, 2000.

FOOTNOTES

1 $n!$ is defined as $n(n - 1)(n - 2) \ldots (2)(1)$.

2 We are indebted to Gilvan Souza of the Robert H. Smith School of Business, University of Maryland, for his help with this section.

3 J. B. Tucker, J. E. Barone, J. Cecere, R. G. Blabey, and C. K. Rha, "Using Queuing Theory to Determine Operating Room Staffing Needs," *Journal of Trauma* 46, no. 1 (1999), pp. 71–79.

HEALTH CARE PROCESSES

chapter 8

A PRESCRIPTION FOR INNOVATION

THE MAYO CLINIC'S NEW SPARC LAB IS DRIVING EXPERIMENTATION AT THE FRONTIER OF HEALTH CARE. HOW? BY GETTING PHYSICIANS TO THINK MORE LIKE DESIGNERS

The first prototype kiosk looked like a grade-school project or a prank. It did not have a screen. It did not even plug in. Patients stared at a piece of paper and tried to imagine the real thing, a terminal that would allow self-service check-in for a doctor's appointment. The next iteration was less

Service

After reading this chapter you will:

1. Have a perspective on the unique operations and supply management (OSCM) challenges faced in health care.

2. Understand how selected OSCM concepts and approaches can be applied to hospitals.

3. Understand important health care terminology as it relates to OSCM decisions.

primitive, a laptop with an apparent touch screen, except that it didn't work; someone sitting beside it, using a separate keyboard, typed in the system's response like a high-tech ventriloquist. The model after that had a responsive touch screen, but the functionality was sparse. No matter. The kiosk was getting there. And that was the idea: Put the earliest version, the rough sketch, in front of patients to see what they thought. Then use the feedback to tweak and retest. Then do the whole thing over again.

The Mayo Clinic in Rochester, Minnesota, is no stranger to innovation. W. W. Mayo and his sons, still known here as Dr. Charlie and Dr. Will, founded their rural group practice in the late 1800s around

SOURCE: ADAPTED FROM CHUCK SALTER, "A PRESCRIPTION FOR INNOVATION," *FAST COMPANY* WEB SITE, DECEMBER 19, 2007.

a new concept at the time: integrated medical care, which involved various specialists working together in the same building, performing comprehensive evaluations, and administering coordinated treatment. Ever since, innovation has been a vital part of the clinic's DNA, traditionally in the research lab.

But the approach with the kiosk, rolling out unfinished ideas to patients, is something new. Last summer, Mayo opened SPARC, a clinical innovation lab that operates like a design shop and that specializes in the "patient experience." The acronym, which stands for "see, plan, act, refine, and communicate," is meant to remind participants of the design-oriented methodology so they'll continue to employ it when they return to their departments. Doctors, nurses, and other staffers do what designers do: They interview, shadow, and observe customers (in this case, patients) to uncover their needs, brainstorm with abandon, and engage in rapid prototyping—hence, the paper kiosk.

Despite its status as one of the best known and most respected medical facilities in the world, Mayo is wrestling with the same issues that designers routinely tackle: In an increasingly competitive field, how do you differentiate yourself? How do you generate fresh ideas and implement them in a timely fashion? And how do you make sure those ideas actually benefit customers?

> *A hospital is a combination care facility, hotel, restaurant, and store staffed by highly skilled professionals supported by semiskilled and low-skilled workers, using state of the art technology and employing precise discipline to perform work of zero-defect quality on a heterogeneous population, all while trying to be affordable.*
>
> *It ain't easy . . .*

Service

Health care is the most intensive of service industries in the range of service activities and the impact these activities have on the customer. Nowhere is this more evident than in the hospital, where operational excellence is central to the clinical treatment of patients, the quality of their experience, and, of course, cost. This is particularly critical in the United States, where more than $2 trillion is spent on health care each year. It's not just high cost alone—recent surveys show that more than 55 percent of all Americans said they were dissatisfied with the quality of health care. Nevertheless, numerous health care organizations, like the Mayo Clinic, are innovative and excel in their operations performance. In this chapter, we will discuss some of the unique features of hospitals and health care centers and how OSCM concepts and tools are used to achieve outstanding results in this critical service industry.

THE NATURE OF HEALTH CARE OPERATIONS

Health care operations management

Health care operations management may be defined as the design, management, and improvement of the systems that deliver health care services. Health care as a service is characterized by extensive customer contact, a wide variety of providers, and literally life or death as potential outcomes.

Hospital

The focus of our discussion of health care operations is the hospital, although everything here is also applicable to the smaller health care clinic. The standard definition of a hospital is a facility whose staff provides services relating to observation, diagnosis, and treatment to cure or lessen the suffering of patients. Observation involves studying patients and conducting tests to arrive at a diagnosis; diagnosis is the medical expert's explanation of the cause of the symptoms; and treatment is the course of action to be followed based upon the diagnosis. All of the services provided in a hospital are generally organized around at least one of these three areas.

Here are important factors that set hospitals' operations apart from other organizations:

- The key operators in the core processes are highly trained professionals (medical specialists) who generate requests for service (orders) but are also involved in delivering the service.
- The relationship between the prices that can be charged and actual performance is not as direct as in most other production environments. Quality and service measures are largely based on opinion rather than hard evidence.
- Hospitals do not have a simple line of command, but are characterized by a delicate balance of power between different interest groups (management, medical specialists, nursing staff, and referring doctors), each of them having ideas about what should be targets for operations performance.
- Production control approaches presuppose complete and explicit specifications of end product requirements and delivery requirements; in hospitals product specifications are often subjective and vague.
- Hospital care is not a commodity that can be stocked; the hospital is a resource-oriented service organization.

CLASSIFICATION OF HOSPITALS
The American Hospital Association classifies hospitals as follows:

- *General hospital/emergency room*—Provides a broad range of services for multiple conditions.
- *Specialty*—Provides services for a specific medical condition, for example, cardiology (heart conditions)
- *Psychiatric*—Provides care for behavioral and mental disorders.
- *Rehabilitation*—Provides services focused on restoring health.

As in other industries, the complexity of hospital operations has a major impact on performance. In Exhibit 8.1, we have arrayed these four types of hospitals in a product–process

Hospital Product–Process Framework   exhibit 8.1

framework matching range of health care product lines with complexity of operations. The inherent complexity of general hospitals is magnified by their need for physical size and extensive technology to handle a wide range of patient needs. Chris Hani Baragwanath Hospital is the largest hospital in the world, occupying 173 acres, with 3,200 beds and 6,760 staff members. The hospital is in the Soweto area of Johannesburg, South Africa. Specialty hospital facilities may be large as well, but they tend to have a narrower range of medical skills and technology on site. An example would be the Johns Hopkins Hospital in Baltimore, which focuses on cancer patients. Psychiatric hospitals are in a sense specialty hospitals, but because their clinical focus is on the mind rather than the body, they are generally less technology-intense than those focusing on physical illnesses. An example of a psychiatric hospital is McLean Hospital, affiliated with Harvard University. It is well known for its patient list of famous people. Rehabilitation facilities are seen as least complex because, although they use technology, the type of work done is more custodial compared to the active treatment found in other hospitals. Veterans Administration hospitals are representative of this category.

HOSPITAL LAYOUT AND CARE CHAINS

The layout sets the physical constraints on a hospital's operations. The goal of hospital layout is to move patients and resources through the units and floors to minimize wait and transport times. The layout can be determined using software models that minimize the total combined costs of travel of patients and staff. For those situations where numerical flow of patients and staff does not reveal quantitative factors, manual methods such as systematic layout planning (discussed in the layout chapter) may be more appropriate.

A general rule for the design of a hospital is to separate patient and guest traffic flows from staff flows. Use of separate elevators and dedicated resource corridors is particularly important in avoiding congestion and delays. The principal element of the overall layout of a hospital is the nursing station, which is the area support staff work from. Many nursing stations are located in the hospital to support the various patient areas. Nursing stations today tend to be more compact shapes than the elongated rectangles of the past. Compact rectangles, modified triangles, or even circles have been used in an attempt to shorten the distance between the nursing station and the patient's bed. The choice depends on such issues as the organization of the nursing program, number of beds to a nursing unit, and number of beds to a patient room. The growth of more holistic, patient-centered treatment and environments is leading to modifications in layout to include providing small medical libraries and computer terminals, so patients can research their conditions and treatments, and locating kitchens and dining areas in patient units so family members can prepare food for patients and families to eat together.

Care chain

The flow of work through a hospital is sometimes referred to as a **care chain**, consisting of the services for patients provided by various medical specialties and functions, within and across departments. Exhibit 8.2 lists typical characteristics of care chain processes for

---

exhibit 8.2   Characteristics of Processes/Care Chain in a Typical General Surgery Unit

CHARACTERISTIC OF PROCESS/ CARE CHAIN	TRAUMA PATIENTS	ONCOLOGY (E.G., TUMOR) PATIENTS	JOINT REPLACEMENT PATIENTS
Emergency or elective	Emergency	Elective	Elective
Urgency	High	Moderate	Low
Volume	High	Medium	High
Short, long, or chronic treatment	Short	Chronic	Short
Diagnostic requirements	Immediate	Ongoing	Ongoing
Consultation requirements	Limited time possible	Involved	Little
Number of specialties involved	Depends on situation	Many	Few
Bottleneck	Operating room	Operating room	Operating room
Decoupling point	After surgery	Diagnosis	Diagnosis

SOURCE: BASED ON J. VISSERS AND R. BEECH, *HEALTH OPERATIONS MANAGEMENT* (LONDON: ROUTLEDGE, 2005), P. 45.

Care Chain Diagram of Hip Replacement Surgery

exhibit 8.3

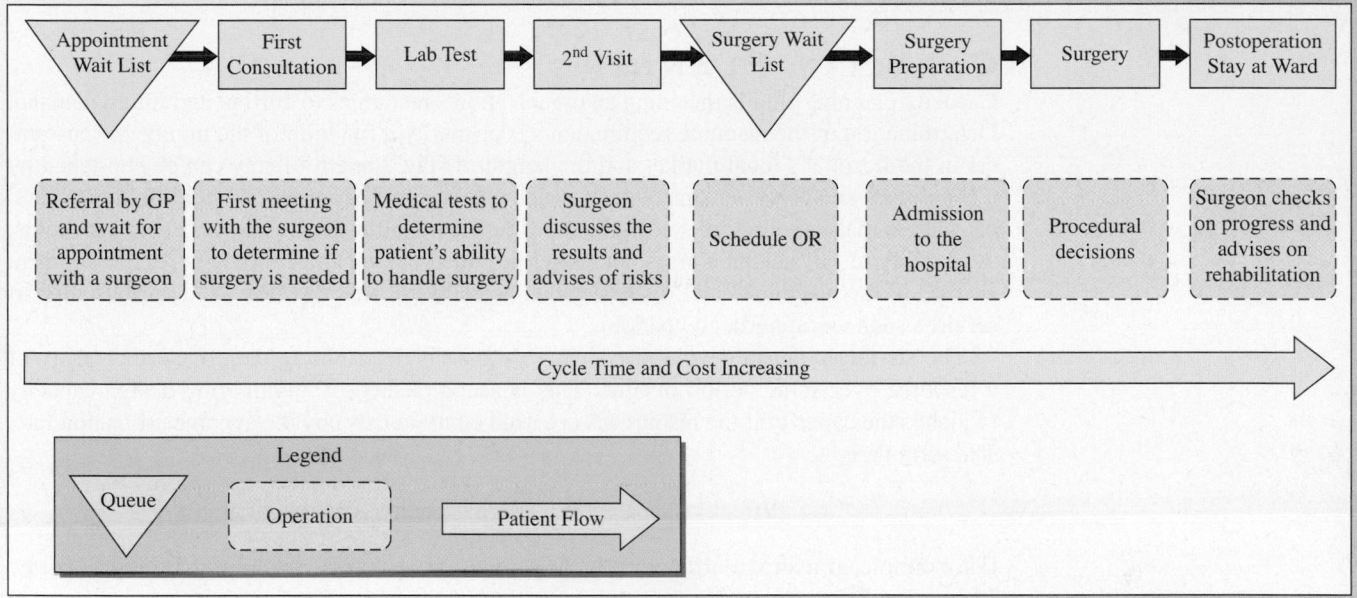

key patient groups within general surgery. A major distinction among health care processes shown in the exhibit is the extent to which access to medical treatment and resources can be scheduled efficiently. Emergency situations such as trauma must be dealt with immediately, require rapid access to medical staff, and, as a result, are inherently inefficient. Elective procedures, on the other hand, can be scheduled to achieve more efficient use of resources. The number of steps, the time of each step, and whether the care chain has a definite end affects resource use and schedule complexity. A chronic condition, for example, may lack a clearly identifiable ending. Complexity is also increased by the need for rapid diagnostics, extensive consultation, and the need to work with other specialties. Decoupling points are steps in the process where waiting takes place, either before or after the procedure is performed. For many operations, it is after diagnosis; for trauma cases, it might be after the emergency treatment and when the patient is transferred from the recovery room to a ward.

Decoupling points

A work flow diagram of a care chain is shown in Exhibit 8.3. It focuses on the contacts between the patient and the provider for surgery such as a hip replacement. The actual flow can be lengthier, as when the patient wants a second opinion, and we have left out recuperation at home. Also omitted are process flow modifications resulting from, say, the patient's medical tests indicating a particular issue like a drop in blood pressure. In this case the patient can either be processed serially by different specialties (e.g., blood pressure first and hip replacement second), in parallel (blood pressure and hip replacement at the same time with one specialty assisting the other), or as a team (both specialties present in the operating room to work at the same time).

Tracking of Work Flow Using RFID   Radio frequency identification uses electronic tags that can store, send, and receive data over wireless frequencies. They are now being used in a few of the more progressive hospitals to track the location of patients, medical staff, and physical assets as they move through the hospital. Among the benefits of using RFID for patient flow are improvement of patient check-in process and tighter links between patient and medical records. For example, RFID readers placed on doors throughout the hospital can automatically detect patients as they pass through. With this knowledge, clerks can determine where bottlenecks are likely to occur and redirect patients to other treatment areas if the process is not sequence dependent. Thus, for example, a hip replacement patient rather than waiting in the cardiology department for a cardiogram could be sent to X-ray for a required test where there is no waiting. With regard to physical assets, RFID can pinpoint the location of equipment such as gurneys, portable X-ray machines, and wheelchairs to help get them to the patient when needed. In addition, knowing where each piece of equipment is can save hours that are spent at the end of the day conducting "equipment round-ups."

CAPACITY PLANNING

Capacity planning entails matching an organization's resources to current and future demand. Determination of the resource requirements is primarily a function of the number of customers in the hospital's local market and the length of stay. Length of stay can be shortened by technologies and process management, which can increase patient throughput. In health care, capacity is measured in terms of multiple resources including beds, clinics, treatment rooms; availability of physicians, nurses, and other providers, medical technologies, and equipment such as X-ray machines; facility space such as hallways and elevators; and various support services such as cafeteria and parking.

The starting point in developing a capacity plan is determining the effective capacity of a resource over some period of time. This is accomplished by multiplying design capacity (which is the capacity if the resource is operated continuously) by the average utilization rate. The formula is

$$\text{Effective capacity} = \text{Design capacity} \times \text{Utilization}$$

For example, if average utilization is 70 percent on an X-ray machine that could operate 24 hours per day, 7 days a week, then its effective capacity per day is 16.8 hours per day (24 hours $\times$ 0.7 = 16.8 hours). It should be noted that the 70 percent utilization figure is in line with the 70 percent utilization target common to companies seeking a high level of service. The subsequent steps consist of (1) forecasting patient demand by hour, location, specialty, and so on; (2) translating this demand, adjusted by productivity estimates, into capacity requirements; (3) determining the current capacity level in terms of hours of staff, facilities, and equipment; (4) calculating the gap between demand and capacity on a per-hour basis; and (5) developing a strategy to close the gap. This can be done by several common approaches, including transferring capacity from other units, increasing capacity through overtime, subcontracting with other hospitals, and bottleneck reduction.

WORKFORCE SCHEDULING

The primary areas of importance in hospital scheduling are nurse shift scheduling and operating room scheduling. Nurses constitute the largest component of the hospital's workforce, and operating rooms (or surgical suites) are typically the largest revenue-generating center.

The nurse shift schedules can be classified as either permanent (cyclical) or flexible (discretionary). In *cyclical scheduling,* the work is usually planned for a four- to six-week period, where employees work on a fixed schedule each week over the period (for example, the conventional fixed, five 8-hour days each week). Several types of *flexible scheduling* are used, but the most popular is the flexible week, where nurses maintain 8-hour days and average 40 hours per week but can alternate between, say, 8 hours for four days and 8 hours for six days. Both cyclical and flexible schedules have their pros and cons, though the edge seems to go to flexible systems since they are better suited to handle fluctuations in demand as well as meeting desires of nurses to change from full to part time. Several personnel scheduling techniques are described in Chapter 19.

QUALITY MANAGEMENT AND PROCESS IMPROVEMENT

Ever since the work of Florence Nightingale (see box), hospitals have been seeking ways to achieve quality and process improvement. TQM approaches have been a staple for decades, and within the past few years Six Sigma and Lean concepts are being instituted in many hospitals. Hospital personnel are well suited to analytics of TQM because so much of health care involves precise measuring of patient responses to drugs and clinical procedures.

FLORENCE NIGHTINGALE, HOSPITAL QUALITY IMPROVEMENT PIONEER

Long before Deming, Crosby, and the other industrial quality gurus, Britain's Florence Nightingale was leading a quality revolution in hospitals. During the Crimean War the British

public was shocked by reports of the terrible conditions of British hospitals and Nightingale, founder of the modern profession of nursing, was sent to Scutari, Turkey, to improve them. In addition to overseeing the introduction of nurses to the hospitals, she also led the effort to improve sanitary conditions in the hospitals. Central to her approach was collecting, tabulating, interpreting, and graphically displaying data relating to process care changes on outcomes. (She is credited as being the developer of the pie chart.) For example, to quantify the overcrowding of hospitals, she compared the amount of space per patient in London hospitals, 1,600 square feet, to that of Scutari, 400 square feet. She also developed a standard statistical form to enable the collection of data for analysis and comparison. The results of these innovations were astounding: The mortality of patients decreased from 42 percent in February 1855 to 2.2 percent in June of that year. Nightingale's approach, termed *evidence-based medicine*, underlies current approaches to medical practices.

Gap Errors and Bottlenecks   Two problems that get frequent attention in quality programs are dealing with gap errors and bottlenecks. *Gap errors* are information mistakes that arise when a task is transferred or handed off between people or groups. Many professional routines, such as formal handoff procedures between shifts of nurses and physicians are designed to bridge gaps. A recent Massachusetts General Hospital study concluded that handoffs may be as significant a source of serious patient harm as are medication-related events.[1] The study reported that while 94 percent of the handoffs were conducted face-to-face, more than half of the 161 residents surveyed reported that they were rarely done in a quiet, private setting, and over a third reported frequent interruptions. One successful approach to managing handoffs is the SBAR (Situation-Background-Assessment-Recommendation) checklist technique for communicating information about a patient's condition between members of the health care team. Adapted from a program used to provide quick briefings of nuclear submariners during a change in command, SBAR is an easy-to-remember tool for framing any conversation requiring a clinician's immediate attention and action.

As discussed elsewhere in the book, a *bottleneck* is that part of the system that has the smallest capacity relative to the demand on it. Bottlenecks frequently result from individual departments optimizing their own throughput—the number of patients or procedures per hour—without considering the effects on upstream or downstream departments. If changes are made to improve parts of a system without addressing the constraint, the changes may not result in reduction of delays and waiting times for the entire system. To identify the constraint, the Institute for Healthcare Improvement's handbook *Reducing Delays and Waiting Times* recommends observing where the work is piling up or where lines are forming, and performing some simple calculations.[2] For example, Exhibit 8.4 shows the capacity of the five processes in a preoperative clinic at Beth Israel Deaconess Medical Center in Boston. (Note that nursing is the bottleneck.)

The handbook provides suggestions for eliminating bottlenecks. These are presented in Exhibit 8.5.

Service Quality   Hospitals, like other customer contact businesses, have been raising the level of their customer service to improve the patient experience. This has been shown to save money through reduction of malpractice suits, reduction in no-shows, and lower nurse

exhibit 8.4   Preop Clinical Capacity at Beth Israel Deaconess Medical Center

	ANESTHESIA	NURSING	PHLEBOTOMY	EXG	X-RAY
Total process (minutes including paperwork)	15	18	8	10	9
Estimated capacity (number of visits per day) with breaks, calls, lunch	48	36	58	42	On-call
Range of visits per day (4-day period)	27–45	23–41	22–41	11–30	7–21
Average number of visits per day (4-day period)	35	27	29	20	14

exhibit 8.5   Diagnoses and Remedies for Eliminating Bottlenecks

HOW TO MANAGE THE CONSTRAINT	DIAGNOSES (Dx's)	REMEDIES (Rx's)
Constraints should not have idle time	The doctor is in the exam room waiting to see the first patient of the day while the patient is being registered	Register the patient after the exam
If experts are the constraint, they should be doing only work for which an expert is needed	In preoperative testing, patients are backed up waiting for the nurse (the constraint in the process)	The receptionist or assistant assumes tasks that are being done by the nurse but do not require nursing skills
Put inspection in front of a constraint	On the day of the surgery, key X-rays are not available	One person coordinates and expedites all necessary information on the day of the surgery

turnover. The standard philosophy is an end-to-end customer focus. An example of this focus is Good Samaritan Hospital in Los Angeles. When patients arrive at "Good Sam" for an appointment, rather than having to sit in a waiting room they are greeted at a modern hotel-like lobby and escorted directly to the unit of the hospital where they are to be treated. During their stay, efforts are made to ensure that their comfort needs are anticipated (such as having an extra pillow in the room); and before leaving a patient, every employee is to ask, "Is there anything else I can do for you?" In addition, hospital patients can use the Red Carpet Hospitality Program, which provides conciergelike services such as ordering-in of meals from local restaurants and providing information about local accommodations and spas for families.

Supply Chain

HEALTH CARE SUPPLY CHAINS

Hospital Supply Chains   Exhibit 8.6 presents a hospital supply chain, showing the flow of three essential resources: information, funds, and goods and services. Goods and services move downstream from the manufacturer to distributors/third-party logistics providers (3PL) and retailers to the hospital warehouse to receiving to central stores, and then to nursing and patient. Cash/funds flow upstream. On a day-to-day basis, hospital supply chain management focuses on medical supplies and pharmaceutical supplies. Traditionally these activities are operated as separate organizational units. The medical-surgical supplies are complex, and are ordered from multiple vendors and from the manufacturer. For the pharmacy the vast majority of medications come directly from the distributors. Very few ship directly from the manufacturer. Current approaches involve merging of the two procurement operations within one department to reduce the number of vendors and to get better transparency.

Physican-Driven Service Chains   The widespread use of computerized physician order entry (CPOE) systems for prescriptions has led experts to propose broadening their application to include scheduling all resources needed by physicians to treat their individual patients. Called "event management," the way it works is that the admission order for a patient, for example, for a surgery procedure, triggers a series of follow-up events that are automatically entered into the information system (see Exhibit 8.7). The information system then initiates an

Health Care Supply Chain

exhibit 8.6

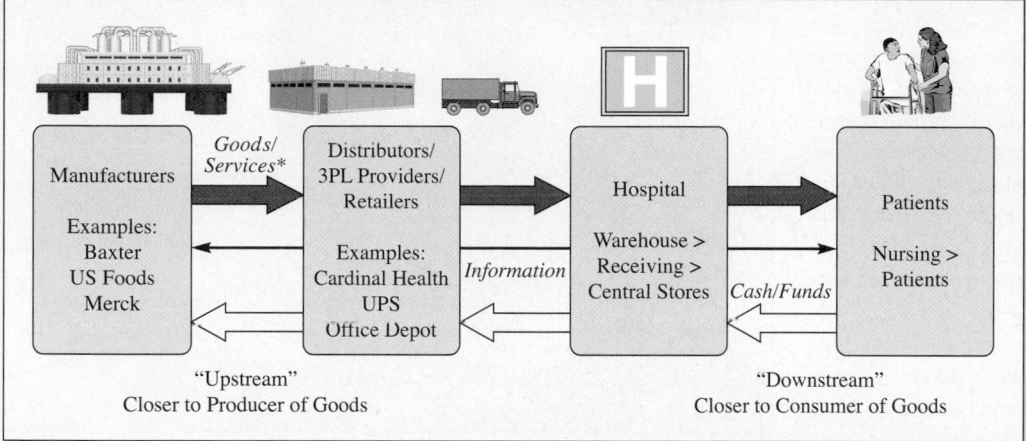

"Upstream"
Closer to Producer of Goods

"Downstream"
Closer to Consumer of Goods

*Goods include Food, medical supplies, pharmaceuticals, linens, lab supplies, equipment, and Office and other supplies.

SOURCE: J. R. LANGABEER II, *HEALTH CARE OPERATIONS MANAGEMENT* (SUDBURY, MA: JONES AND BARTLETT, 2008), P. 213.

admission date and books an operating room date, a surgical team (including an anesthesiologist and nurses), recovery room, and lab tests. These activities and processes are linked as well. For example, an electronically issued lab order for blood work is routed directly to the phlebotomist, who then draws and ships blood to the lab for analysis. Lab managers use the information to batch orders. Behind the scenes, accounting transactions are generated for billing insurance companies, recording copayments, placing purchase orders for supplies, and so on.

Supply Chain Event Management

exhibit 8.7

Supply Chain

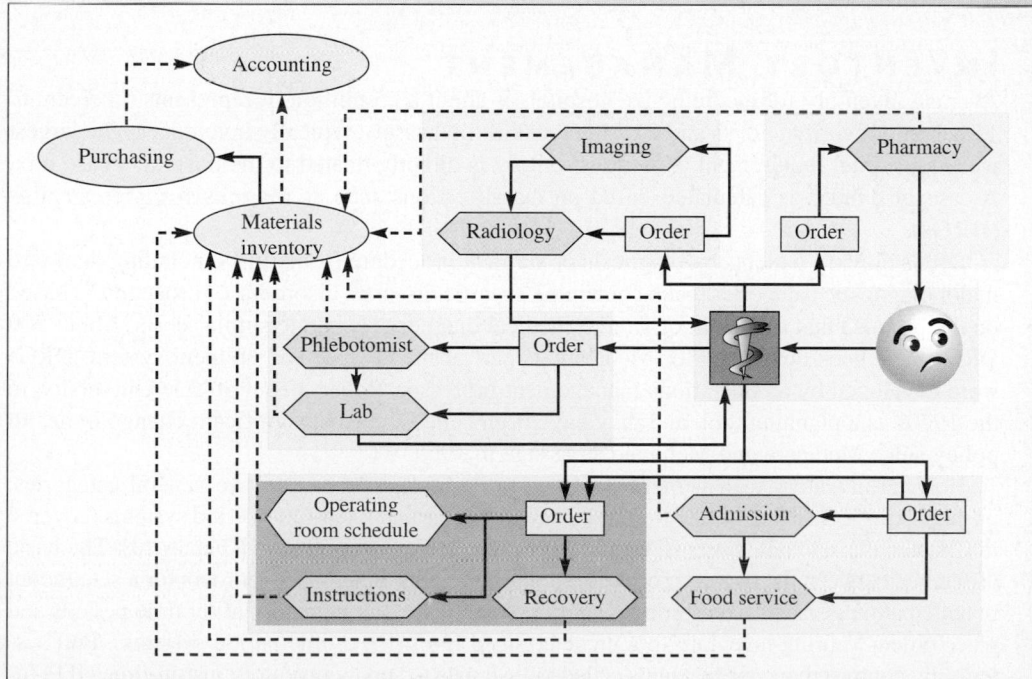

SOURCE: JOE F. SCHRIEVER, "SUPPLY CHAIN FITNESS," *APICS MAGAZINE*, JUNE 2007, P. 34.

LAHEY CLINIC: BEST PRACTICES IN ACTION

Lahey Clinic is a physician-led, nonprofit health care group in suburban Boston, with more than 500 physicians and 4,600 other personnel supporting a 327-bed hospital and a 24-hour ambulatory care center. In enhancing its supply chain operations, Lahey first moved to a stockless inventory system, which essentially replaces the hospital's bulk stockroom with inventory owned by their suppliers. In this case, a major supplier, Cardinal Health, now manages the clinic's inventory and arranges for just-in-time delivery of clinical products to stocking cabinets in the hospital's units and laboratories.

Lahey also deployed Pyxis Products' automated dispensing cabinets to control the dispensation of medications and medical supplies in a way that automates inventory management and enables usage to be tracked to employees and patients. Employees use ID numbers or fingerprints to access inventory. The system then transfers the information to the hospital's billing system and generates reports that can be used to optimize medication and supply utilization and manage costs.

Lahey also worked closely with Cardinal Health to implement an enterprisewide systems approach to supply chain

efficiency to replace its management-by-committee approach. The clinic created a new position, Director of Supply Chain Management, to help implement recommendations and drive greater compliance. This experienced supply chain administrator built a team that is able to streamline the material management information system to enable more effective use of the data generated by the Pyxis cabinets. This data is analyzed to better illustrate precisely what drives the cost structure and allows the team to improve inventory control, reduce waste, and improve workflow.

SOURCE: MIKE DUFFY, "IS SUPPLY CHAIN THE CURE FOR RISING HEALTHCARE COSTS?" *SUPPLY CHAIN MANAGEMENT REVIEW*, SEPTEMBER 2009, P. 34.

INVENTORY MANAGEMENT

Average inventory for medium-size hospitals is about $3.5 million. It represents 5 percent to 15 percent of current assets and 2 to 4 percent of total assets; typically inventory is the largest working capital requirement. Cost of inventory is directly related to the hospital's case mix. A case mix index is calculated based on classifications such as **diagnosis-related groups (DRGs)**.

Diagnosis-related groups (DRGs)

DRGs classify patients by diagnosis or surgical procedure (sometimes including age) into major diagnostic categories (each containing specific diseases, disorders, or procedures) based on the premise that treatment of similar medical diagnoses generate similar costs. About 500 DRGs have been developed for Medicare as part of the prospective payment system. DRGs were developed by an operations management professor, Robert Fetter at Yale University, in the 1970s as a planning tool, and they have been called the most significant change in health policy since Medicare and Medicaid's passage in 1965.

Hospital inventory management systems can be broken down into two general categories: push systems, consisting of fixed-order quantity systems and fixed-time-period systems (covered in Chapter 17), and pull systems, using just-in-time delivery (covered in Chapter 13). The basic difference between the two categories is that push systems either place reorders for a set amount in anticipation of need (fixed-order quantity systems) or count inventory at set time periods and place orders to bring inventory to a predetermined level (fixed-time-period systems). Pull systems, by contrast, have mechanisms called pull signals to supply inventory just-in-time (JIT) for use. Push systems make sense when a hospital owns its own inventory or buys in bulk and then breaks it down to distribute to nursing units or floors when required. JIT makes sense for expensive items such as implants, which are supplied by a partner vendor on a pull-system basis.

Mayo Clinic Performance Management and Measurement System

exhibit 8.8

PERFORMANCE CATEGORY	PERFORMANCE INDICATOR
Customer satisfaction	Rating of primary care provided Rating of subspecialty care provided
Clinical productivity and efficiency	Clinic productivity per physician per workday Outpatient visits per physician per workday
Financial	Expense per relative value unit (unit of service)
Internal operations	General examination average itinerary length in days Patient complaints per 1,000 patients Patient waiting time/access to appointments
Mutual respect and diversity	Percentage of staff from underrepresented groups Employee satisfaction survey
Social commitment	Mayo's contribution to society
External environment assessment	Board of Governors environmental scan Market share
Patient characteristics	Patient mix by geography and payer group

SOURCE: J. W. CURTRIGHT; S. C. STOLP-SMITH; AND E. S. EDELL, "STRATEGIC PERFORMANCE MANAGEMENT: DEVELOPMENT OF A PERFORMANCE MEASUREMENT SYSTEM AT THE MAYO CLINIC," *JOURNAL OF HEALTHCARE MANAGEMENT*, 45 (JANUARY/FEBRUARY 2000); P. 1.

A major distinction between health care inventory management and that of other businesses is planning safety stock. The standard calculation of safety stock is predicated on trading off the cost of carrying an additional unit of inventory with the cost of being out of stock. In a department store we can easily balance the cost of holding too many pairs of jeans with the cost (or lost profit) caused by running out of them. In hospitals such trade-offs are much trickier when faced with balancing the cost of holding, say, a unit of type A blood with the cost of running out of it. The problem with estimating the cost of a stockout in a hospital is that consequences such as prolonged patient pain or even (though rarely) a threat to the life of the patient may be an issue. For critical items, backup contingency plans such as borrowing from a nearby hospital are often developed.

PERFORMANCE MEASURES

Exhibit 8.8 lists the indicators used by the Mayo Clinic in its own performance management and measuring system at the strategic level. As can be seen, most of the performance indicators are tied to operations management.

Performance Dashboards   Current practice is to present detailed day-to-day performance measures on dashboards in three major categories: customer service, clinical operations, and key processes. A *customer service dashboard* provides such scoring information as percentage of patients who would recommend the hospital to others and rating of such items as inpatient parking, courtesy of staff, cleanliness, caring of staff, meal quality, follow-up education and instruction, and pain management, as well as an overall satisfaction. A *clinical dashboard* measures performance metrics such as mortality rate, quality improvement, readmission rate, and various procedure-specific key performance indicators. A *key process dashboard* would display, for example, percentage of transfusions having reactions, accurate performance of transfusions protocols, adverse drug reactions, medicine error severity, autopsy rate, employee exposures to blood and bodily fluids, and code response times.

TRENDS IN HEALTH CARE

Among the major trends in health care that relate to OSCM are the following.

> **Evidence-based medicine (EBM):**   EBM is the application of the scientific method to evaluate alternative treatment methods and create guidelines for similar clinical situations. Essentially, it is the development of standard methods for therapeutic interventions.

MR. ROUNDER IS ON-CALL AT HACKENSACK UNIVERSITY MEDICAL CENTER

It's the day after surgery, you're lying in bed and the nurse informs you the doctor will be in shortly. Good news—just the person you're hoping to see will be in soon. Sure enough in rolls your doctor, all 5 feet, 4 inches and 215 pounds and you can't believe your eyes. Not because the doctor is there as promised, but because your doctor is housed within a remote-controlled adult-sized robot. Does this sound a bit like science fiction? It isn't.

The sophisticated mechanical physician made its debut at Hackensack University Medical Center. As part of an initiative to improve the quality and efficiency of patient care, the medical center introduced InTouch Health's RP-6 for Remote Presence, "Mr. Rounder," dubbed affectionately by staff, as part of the services available to patients. Physician-to-patient communication is now possible regardless of whether a physician is out of town or out of the country for that matter. Garth H. Ballantyne, M.D., chief of Minimally Invasive Surgery at the medical center and Professor of Surgery at the University of Medicine and Dentistry of New Jersey (UMDNJ), is the first to "test drive" Mr. Rounder at Hackensack University Medical Center. Dr. Ballantyne is able to make his rounds off-site or from his office anytime of the day via a laptop computer connected to the Internet via broadband and a wireless network. The robot has a two-way video and 24 infrared sensors to navigate its travels. Dr. Ballantyne's image is displayed on a flat-screen computer monitor mounted on top of the robot. The screen rotates 340 degrees and pivots up and down creating personalized mechanical affectations. He views the patient and surroundings through a video camera located above the monitor allowing live interactive communication. Of course in the meantime, patients continue to be monitored by the medical center's Magnet award–winning nursing staff.

"The robot is remarkably personal. It provides virtual communication and patients really like him. It has received an enthusiastic response," said Dr. Ballantyne. "In essence, we are providing extra coverage patients might not ordinarily get. I am now able to connect and see my patients when family members are visiting. Driving the robot into the room is more personal than a phone call from my office." Mr. Rounder also provides access to electronic patient files. "I can view vital signs, CT scans, blood tests—much of the technical data needed for patient care," noted Dr. Ballantyne. As you watch Mr. Rounder humming through the halls, you get a sense he's become a familiar face around Hackensack University Medical Center as staff passing by quickly greet Dr. Ballantyne as though he's really there—physically that is!

 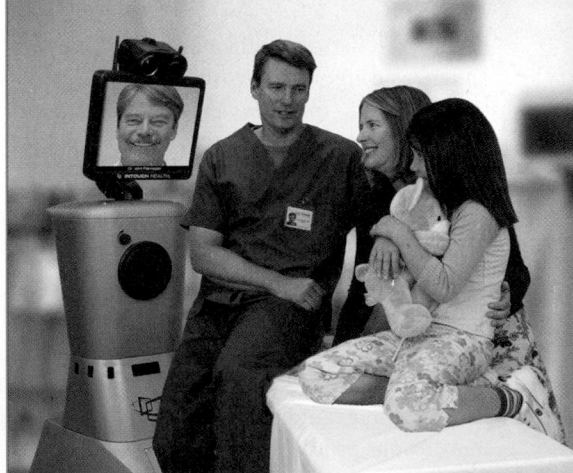

GARTH H. BALLANTYNE, M.D., CHIEF OF MINIMALLY INVASIVE SURGERY AT HACKENSACK UNIVERSITY MEDICAL CENTER AND PROFESSOR OF SURGERY AT UMDNJ, IS BUSILY MAKING THE ROUNDS WITHOUT LEAVING HIS OFFICE VIA THE INTOUCH HEALTH'S RP-6 FOR REMOTE PRESENCE ROBOT, MR. ROUNDER. THE PATIENT, VERONICA MATHIESON OF CLIFTON, CARRIES ON A LIVE CONVERSATION WITH DR. BALLANTYNE AS HIS IMAGE IS DISPLAYED ON A FLAT SCREEN COMPUTER MONITOR.

SOURCE: HACKENSACK UNIVERSITY MEDICAL CENTER PRESS RELEASE, DECEMBER 2004, http://www.intouchhealth.com/prhumc.pdf.

Integrated medical care: Developed by the Mayo Clinic, this approach has a number of philosophical as well as operational features including staff/team work with multispecialty integration, unhurried examination with time to listen to the patient, the hospital physician taking personal responsibility for directing patient care over time in a partnership with the local physician, and integrated medical records with common support services for all patients.

Electronic medical records: Digital technologies are revolutionizing the way patient records are gathered and stored. For example, emergency department doctors and nurses at Kaiser Permanente in Oakland carry flat computer tablets that can access every patient's entire medical record. These tablets also enable doctors and nurses to call up medical test records and X-rays right at the patient's bedside. Similar technologies are now within the reach of smaller medical practices with hand-held tablet PCs for medical records being sold by Walmart.

Health information exchanges (HIEs):   HIEs provide the capability to electronically move clinical information over various kinds of information systems while maintaining the meaning of the information being exchanged. For example, the Indiana Health Information Exchange (IHIE) allows physicians to track in real time those patients who are due for preventive screenings and chronic disease follow-up care.

Computer-assisted diagnosis: This approach uses expert system software programs to arrive at a diagnosis. Suppose the doctor with a child patient who has pain in the joints wants to determine its most likely cause. The expert system matches the child's symptoms with the criteria tables for each type of illness and reaches diagnostic conclusions at three different levels of certainty: definite, probable, and possible. If the diagnosis is suggested at the "possible" level, the system recommends looking for further clues to exclude or include it.

Remote diagnosis: Called *telemedicine,* it uses electronic devices for measuring blood pressure, heart rate, blood oxygen levels, and so on, for diagnosing patients who are far from the hospital. This is especially valuable in areas where few specialists are available to rapidly diagnose a patient's problem.

Robots: Robots are being used in the operating room for a range of illnesses including breast cancer and gall bladder removal. In using robots, surgeons employ a tiny camera to guide them as they manipulate the robot's instruments from a console. Benefits of robots are that their "hands" are steady and they have a wide range of motions, which can result in less pain and blood loss than with manual surgery. An interesting low-tech robotic application is Mr. Rounder, described in the nearby box.

SUMMARY

The level of sophistication in clinical treatment has enabled medical cures that were seen as impossible just a few years ago. OSCM concepts and tools have done much to facilitate clinical support activities such as scheduling, work flow management, and capacity management, but experts agree that much remains to be done to better manage hospital processes. One suggestion is for hospital administrators to create new OSCM-type positions, such as production control manager and process analyst. The production control position is similar to that of a production controller in manufacturing—monitoring the overall process flow and quickly redeploying resources to solve day-to-day logistics problems. The production analyst position performs in the role of an operations expert who oversees the hospital's end-to-end processes and recommends changes that might improve the system. A somewhat different type of position is that of the hospital concierge, who focuses on improving the patient's experience.

KEY TERMS

Health care operations management The design, management, and improvement of the systems that create and deliver health care services.

Hospital A facility whose staff provides services relating to observation, diagnosis, and treatment to cure or lessen the suffering of patients

Care chains The flow of work through a hospital consisting of the services for patients provided by various medical specialties and functions, within and across departments.

Decoupling points Stages in the process where waiting takes place, either before or after the procedure is performed.

Diagnosis-related groups (DRGs) Homogeneous units of hospital activity for planning and costing surgeries—essentially a bill of labor and materials.

REVIEW AND DISCUSSION QUESTIONS

1 Where would you place Shouldice Hospital on the product–process framework (see Chapter 4 case, "Shouldice Hospital—A Cut Above")? What are the implications of adding a specialty such as cosmetic surgery?
2 Think about your latest trip to a hospital/health care facility. How many different handoffs did you encounter? How would you rate the quality of the service relative to the patient experience and relative to that of the friends and family?
3 Some have argued that for hospitals, both medical schools and nursing schools should be considered part of the supply chain. Do you agree?
4 Hospitals are major users of poka-yoke (fail-safe) devices. Can you think of any?
5 Could a hospital or physician offer a service guarantee? Explain.
6 How does a physician-driven supply chain differ from a typical materials supply chain?
7 What could a hospital learn from benchmarking a Ritz-Carlton Hotel? Southwest Airlines? Disneyland?

CASE: VENICE FAMILY CLINIC: MANAGING PATIENT WAIT TIMES

Dr. Susan Fleishman is Medical Director of the Venice Family Clinic in Southern California (VFC). She is concerned about the long wait times of patients visiting the clinic and would like to improve operations. The situation is as follows: The patients are seen in the clinic between the hours of 9:00 A.M. and 12:00 P.M. and between 1:00 and 5:00 P.M. The clinic sees, on average, 150 patients per day. Nine physicians are usually on duty to see patients during each clinic session. They are supported by seven medical assistants who take vital signs and put patients in exam rooms. Four registration clerks are present to register patients, enroll them in federal and local aid programs, prep their medical records, and collect copayments. In addition, there are three coordinators who make follow-up appointments and arrange referrals, a security guard, a pharmacist, and two pharmacy technicians. The facility itself has a security window at the front door with a guard-controlled entry door, a large waiting area, 5 registration windows, 11 exam rooms (3 of which are used for taking vitals), and 4 coordinator's desks.

PATIENT PERSPECTIVE

Most patients make appointments (120 per day), but 30 additional patients come for prescription refills. When patients arrive, they must first pass through security. Often, there is a small wait outside at the door, but it can be fairly long early in the morning. The average wait time at security is 10 minutes, while the average processing time is 2 minutes. The security guard is present from 7 A.M. to 6 P.M. The guard at the door double-checks the appointment time and issues the patient a colored card with a number on it—either red or yellow. Red cards are reserved for patients without appointments who need only medication refills. These patients must pass through registration but do not need to see a provider. All patients then proceed to the waiting room where they wait for their color and number to be called. This wait can often be quite long, but on average takes 24 minutes.

Once patients are called by a registration clerk, their information is verified. This process can take anywhere from 1 minute up to

40 minutes if the patient is new and needs to be enrolled in several programs. On average, eight new patients come per day. Average time to complete registration is 7 minutes for returning patients and 22 minutes for new patients with an overall average registration time of 8 minutes. The patients then return to the waiting area and wait another 15 minutes to be called by a medical assistant to have their vital signs taken. This takes 6 minutes, after which they return again to the waiting area and wait 8 minutes more to be called back to a provider room. Once in a provider room, the patient waits 17 minutes on average for the provider (physician) to arrive. Providers spend approximately 20 minutes with each patient, but if the patient needs urgent labs or nursing procedures, this time can be longer. After the patient has seen the doctor, the patient's chart goes either to a coordinator or to the pharmacy if prescriptions are to be filled. On average, 50% of patients continue onto the pharmacy following their medical visit. The patient waits 25 minutes to be called by a coordinator to schedule further laboratory tests, get referrals to specialists, and make follow-up appointments, which takes an additional 7 minutes. Coordinators see patients from 9:00 A.M. until 5:30 P.M. with a one-hour break during the day. If the patient only needs a prescription, the wait is 13 minutes before the pharmacy can process the prescription and an average of 11 minutes for the prescription to be filled. Each pharmacy technician works independently and fills the prescription after consulting the pharmacist. The pharmacy is open from 9:00 A.M. to 5:30 P.M., with a lunch break from noon to 1:00.

In general, patient satisfaction with the quality of medical services at VFC remains high, but there are still complaints each day about the waiting times for these services. Waiting times are critical for these patients, as they often directly lead to lost income during the hours spent waiting.

PHYSICIAN PERSPECTIVE

Each of the staff physicians is placed on a team, A, B, or C. These groups of two or three physicians all see the same patients, helping to ensure continuity for the patients. Each patient, therefore, will see one of the team's physicians at any given visit and has a high likelihood of seeing the same doctor each time.

Each day, a specific team is assigned to a group of exam rooms. Patients placed in those rooms will see providers for that team only. Physicians arrive at 9:00 A.M. and wait for their first patients to arrive. Often, due to the lag at registration and the wait for open rooms for the medical assistants to take vitals, patients are not in the exam rooms until well after 9:30. In addition, because of the team system, one provider may have three patients waiting while another is still waiting for his or her first patient to check in at registration. The registration desk has no communication link to the physicians' area; consequently, clerks may check in three patients in a row for one team, but none for another. In addition, new patients are randomly assigned to teams regardless of who is busiest that day. Once a patient is in an exam room, the chart is placed in a rack for the physician to review prior to seeing the patient. If key lab or X-ray results are missing, the physician must call for medical records or call outside facilities and wait for the results to be faxed or called in before seeing the patient. This happens 60 to 70 percent of the time, causing a 10-minute delay per patient. These challenges often lead to inefficient use of the provider's time.

After seeing a patient, the physician will either have the patient wait in the waiting room to see the coordinator or have the patient wait in the exam room for further testing or nursing procedures. Rarely, if no follow-up or prescriptions are needed, the patient is free to leave the clinic. VFC physicians generally are extremely committed to the clinic's mission but are frustrated with their patients' long wait times, the incomplete medical records, and the disorganized patient flow through the clinic.

ADMINISTRATION PERSPECTIVE

At the start of each day, four registration clerks prepare by printing out copies of that day's scheduled appointments. Charts of patients with appointments are pulled the night before and placed within easy reach of the clerks. The four clerks work from 8:30 until 11:00 A.M. and close the registration windows until 12:30 P.M. During this time, in addition to eating lunch, the clerks pull the charts for the afternoon clinic and finish up paperwork. At 12:30, the registration windows are reopened for the afternoon clinic and patients are checked in until 4:00 P.M.

QUESTIONS

1. Draw a process flow diagram for each type of patient.
2. Calculate the capacity and utilization of each resource and identify bottlenecks.
3. Calculate the average wait and time in service for new and returning patients with appointments and those returning for a prescription refill.
4. What are your recommendations for improvement?

SOURCE: CONDENSED FROM KUMAR RAJARAM AND KAREN CONNER, VENICE FAMILY CLINIC, MANAGING PATIENT WAIT TIMES," CASE STUDY, ANDERSON SCHOOL OF MANAGEMENT, UCLA, 2008.

SUPER QUIZ

1. A hospital consists of these three basic services.
2. The location of the largest hospital in the world.
3. The most complex type of health care facility.
4. The type of schedule where workers work on a fixed schedule each week over a four- to six-week period.
5. The hospital quality pioneer who is credited as the developer of the pie chart.
6. A term used to refer to information mistakes at handoffs.
7. A checklist technique developed by submariners now used in hospitals.
8. A widely used case mix index classification scheme.
9. Use of the scientific method to develop standard methods for therapeutic interventions.
10. The two general categories of hospital inventory management systems.
11. A nickname for InTouch Health's RP-6 for Remote Presence.
12. Stage in a health care process where waiting takes place.

1. Observation, diagnosis, and treatment 2. Johannesburg, South Africa 3. General hospital/emergency room 4. Cyclical schedule 5. Florence Nightingale 6. Gap error 7. SBAR (Situation-Background-Assessment-Recommendation) 8. Diagnosis-related groups 9. Evidence-based medicine 10. Push systems and pull systems 11. Mr. Rounder 12. Decoupling point

SELECTED BIBLIOGRAPHY

Langabeer J. R., II. *Health Care Operations Management.* Sudbury, MA: Jones and Bartlett, 2008.

McLaughlin, D. B., and J. M. Hays. *Health Care Operations Management.* Chicago: Health Administration Press; Washington, DC: AUPHA Press, 2008.

Ozcan, Y. A. *Quantitative Methods in Health Care Management: Techniques and Applications.* San Francisco: Jossey-Bass, 2005.

Vissers, J., and R. Beech. *Health Operations Management.* London: Routledge, 2005.

FOOTNOTES

1. Massachusetts General Hospital News Report, "Hospital Residents Report Patient-Handoff Problems Common, Can Lead to Patient Harm," September 23, 2008.
2. T. Nolan, et al., *Reducing Delays and Waiting Times Throughout the Healthcare System* (Boston: Institute for Healthcare Improvement, 1996), pp. 36–37.

SIX-SIGMA QUALITY

chapter 9

eneral Electric (GE) has been a major promoter of Six Sigma for more than 10 years. Jack Welch, the legendary and now retired CEO, declared that "the big myth is that Six Sigma is about quality control and statistics. It is that—but it's much more. Ultimately, it drives leadership to be better by providing tools to think through tough issues. At Six Sigma's core is an idea that can turn a company inside out, focusing the organization outward on the customer." GE's commitment to quality centers on Six Sigma. Six Sigma is defined on the GE Web site as follows:

First, What is Six Sigma? First, what it is not. It is not a secret society, a slogan or a cliché. Six Sigma is a highly disciplined process that helps us focus on developing and delivering

After reading this chapter you will:

1. Understand total quality management.
2. Describe how quality is measured and be aware of the different dimensions of quality.
3. Explain the define, measure, analyze, improve, and control (DMAIC) quality improvement process.
4. Understand what ISO certification means.

near-perfect products and services. Why "Sigma"? The word is a statistical term that measures how far a given process deviates from perfection. The central idea behind Six Sigma is that if you can measure how many "defects" you have in a process, you can systematically figure out how to eliminate them and get as close to "zero defects" as possible. To achieve Six Sigma Quality, a process must produce no more than 3.4 defects per million opportunities. An "opportunity" is defined as a chance for nonconformance, or not meeting the required specifications. This means we need to be nearly flawless in executing our key processes.

At its core, Six Sigma revolves around a few key concepts.

Critical to Quality:	Attributes most important to the customer
Defect:	Failing to deliver what the customer wants
Process Capability:	What your process can deliver
Variation:	What the customer sees and feels

| Stable Operations: | Ensuring consistent, predictable processes to improve what the customer sees and feels |
| Design for Six Sigma: | Designing to meet customer needs and process capability |

In this chapter, we first review the general subject of total quality management and the quality movement. We then develop the basic features and concepts of the Six-Sigma approach to TQM. We then describe the Shingo system, which takes a unique approach to quality by focusing on preventing mistakes. This is followed by a review of ISO 9000 and 14000 standards for quality certification used by many companies throughout the world. Finally, we provide the major steps of external benchmarking for quality improvement.

TOTAL QUALITY MANAGEMENT

Total quality management

Global

Total quality management may be defined as "managing the entire organization so that it excels on all dimensions of products and services that are important to the customer." It has two fundamental operational goals:

1. Careful design of the product or service.
2. Ensuring that the organization's systems can consistently produce the design.

These two goals can only be achieved if the entire organization is oriented toward them—hence the term *total* quality management. TQM became a national concern in the United States in the 1980s primarily as a response to Japanese quality superiority in manufacturing automobiles and other durable goods such as room air conditioners. A widely cited study of Japanese and U.S. air-conditioning manufacturers showed that the best-quality American products had *higher* average defect rates than those of the poorest Japanese manufacturers.[1]

THE MALCOLM BALDRIGE NATIONAL QUALITY AWARD

The Award is given to organizations that have demonstrated outstanding quality in their products and processes. Three Awards may be given annually in each of these categories: manufacturing, service, small business, education, health care, and nonprofit.

Applicants for the Award must submit an application of 50 pages or less that details the processes and results of their activities under seven major categories: Leadership; Strategic Planning; Customer and Market Focus; Measurement, Analysis and Knowledge Management; Workforce Focus; Process Management; and Results. The applications are scored on total points out of 1,000 by the Baldrige Board of Examiners and Judges. High-scoring applications are selected for site visits and Award recipients are selected from this group. The president of the United States traditionally presents the Awards at a special ceremony in Washington, DC. A major benefit to all applicants is the feedback report prepared by Examiners that is based on their processes and practices. Many states have used the Baldrige criteria as the basis of their quality programs. A report, *Building on Baldrige: American Quality for the*

21st Century, by the private Council on Competitiveness, said, "More than any other program, the Baldrige Quality Award is responsible for making quality a national priority and disseminating best practices across the United States."

So severe was the quality shortfall in the United States that improving it throughout industry became a national priority, with the Department of Commerce establishing the Malcolm Baldrige National Quality Award in 1987 to help companies review and structure their quality programs. Also gaining major attention at this time was the requirement that suppliers demonstrate that they are measuring and documenting their quality practices according to specified criteria, called ISO standards, if they wished to compete for international contracts. We will have more to say about this later.

The philosophical leaders of the quality movement, notably Philip Crosby, W. Edwards Deming, and Joseph M. Juran—the so-called Quality Gurus—had slightly different definitions of what quality is and how to achieve it (see Exhibit 9.1), but they all had the same general message: To achieve outstanding quality requires quality leadership from senior management, a customer focus, total involvement of the workforce, and continuous improvement based upon rigorous analysis of processes. Later in the chapter, we will discuss how these precepts are applied in the latest approach to TQM—Six Sigma. We will now turn to some fundamental concepts that underlie any quality effort: quality specifications and quality costs.

Malcolm Baldrige National Quality Award

The Quality Gurus Compared

exhibit 9.1

	CROSBY	DEMING	JURAN
Definition of quality	Conformance to requirements	A predictable degree of uniformity and dependability at low cost and suited to the market	Fitness for use (satisfies customer's needs)
Degree of senior management responsibility	Responsible for quality	Responsible for 94% of quality problems	Less than 20% of quality problems are due to workers
Performance standard/ motivation	Zero defects	Quality has many "scales"; use statistics to measure performance in all areas; critical of zero defects	Avoid campaigns to do perfect work
General approach	Prevention, not inspection	Reduce variability by continuous improvement; cease mass inspection	General management approach to quality, especially human elements
Structure	14 steps to quality improvement	14 points for management	10 steps to quality improvement
Statistical process control (SPC)	Rejects statistically acceptable levels of quality (wants 100% perfect quality)	Statistical methods of quality control must be used	Recommends SPC but warns that it can lead to tool-driven approach
Improvement basis	A process, not a program; improvement goals	Continuous to reduce variation; eliminate goals without methods	Project-by-project team approach; set goals
Teamwork	Quality improvement teams; quality councils	Employee participation in decision making; break down barriers between departments	Team and quality circle approach
Costs of quality	Cost of nonconformance; quality is free	No optimum; continuous improvement	Quality is not free; there is not an optimum
Purchasing and goods received	State requirements; supplier is extension of business; most faults due to purchasers themselves	Inspection too late; sampling allows defects to enter system; statistical evidence and control charts required	Problems are complex; carry out formal surveys
Vendor rating	Yes; quality audits useless	No, critical of most systems	Yes, but help supplier improve

QUALITY SPECIFICATION AND QUALITY COSTS

Fundamental to any quality program is the determination of quality specifications and the costs of achieving (or *not* achieving) those specifications.

DEVELOPING QUALITY SPECIFICATIONS

Design quality

The quality specifications of a product or service derive from decisions and actions made relative to the quality of its design and the quality of its conformance to that design. **Design quality** refers to the inherent value of the product in the marketplace and is thus a strategic decision for the firm. The dimensions of quality are listed in Exhibit 9.2. These dimensions refer to features of the product or service that relate directly to design issues. A firm designs a product or service to address the need of a particular market.

A firm designs a product or service with certain performance characteristics and features based on what the intended market expects. Materials and manufacturing process attributes can greatly impact the reliability and durability of a product. Here the company attempts to design a product or service that can be produced or delivered at reasonable cost. The service-ability of the product may have a great impact on the cost of the product or service to the customer after the initial purchase is made. It also may impact the warranty and repair cost to the firm. Aesthetics may greatly impact the desirability of the product or service, in particular consumer products. Especially when a brand name is involved, the design often represents the next generation of an ongoing stream of products or services. Consistency in the relative performance of the product compared to the state of the art, for example, may have a great impact on how the quality of the product is perceived. This may be very important to the long-run success of the product or service.

Conformance quality

Conformance quality refers to the degree to which the product or service design specifications are met. The activities involved in achieving conformance are of a tactical, day-to-day nature. It should be evident that a product or service can have high design quality but low conformance quality, and vice versa.

Quality at the source

Quality at the source is frequently discussed in the context of conformance quality. This means that the person who does the work takes responsibility for making sure that his or her output meets specifications. Where a product is involved, achieving the quality specifications is typically the responsibility of manufacturing management; in a service firm, it is usually the responsibility of the branch operations management. Exhibit 9.3 shows two examples of

Dimensions of quality

the **dimensions of quality**. One is a laser printer that meets the pages-per-minute and print density standards; the second is a checking account transaction in a bank.

Both quality of design and quality of conformance should provide products that meet the customer's objectives for those products. This is often termed the product's *fitness for use*, and it entails identifying the dimensions of the product (or service) that the customer wants (that is, the voice of the customer) and developing a quality control program to ensure that these dimensions are met.

exhibit 9.2   The Dimensions of Design Quality

DIMENSION	MEANING
Performance	Primary product or service characteristics
Features	Added touches, bells and whistles, secondary characteristics
Reliability/durability	Consistency of performance over time, probability of failing, useful life
Serviceability	Ease of repair
Aesthetics	Sensory characteristics (sound, feel, look, and so on)
Perceived quality	Past performance and reputation

Examples of Dimensions of Quality

exhibit 9.3

| DIMENSION | MEASURES | |
	PRODUCT EXAMPLE: LASER PRINTER	SERVICE EXAMPLE: CHECKING ACCOUNT AT A BANK
Performance	Pages per minute Print density	Time to process customer requests
Features	Multiple paper trays Color capability	Automatic bill paying
Reliability/durability	Mean time between failures Estimated time to obsolescence Expected life of major components	Variability of time to process requests Keeping pace with industry trends
Serviceability	Availability of authorized repair centers Number of copies per print cartridge Modular design	Online reports Ease of getting updated information
Aesthetics	Control button layout Case style Courtesy of dealer	Appearance of bank lobby Courtesy of teller
Perceived quality	Brand name recognition Rating in *Consumer Reports*	Endorsed by community leaders

COST OF QUALITY

Although few can quarrel with the notion of prevention, management often needs hard numbers to determine how much prevention activities will cost. This issue was recognized by Joseph Juran, who wrote about it in 1951 in his *Quality Control Handbook*. Today, cost of quality (COQ) analyses are common in industry and constitute one of the primary functions of QC departments.

Cost of quality

There are a number of definitions and interpretations of the term *cost of quality*. From the purist's point of view, it means all of the costs attributable to the production of quality that is not 100 percent perfect. A less stringent definition considers only those costs that are the difference between what can be expected from excellent performance and the current costs that exist.

How significant is the cost of quality? It has been estimated at between 15 and 20 percent of every sales dollar—the cost of reworking, scrapping, repeated service, inspections, tests, warranties, and other quality-related items. Philip Crosby states that the correct cost for a well-run quality management program should be under 2.5 percent.[2]

Three basic assumptions justify an analysis of the costs of quality: (1) failures are caused, (2) prevention is cheaper, and (3) performance can be measured.

The costs of quality are generally classified into four types:

1. **Appraisal costs.** Costs of the inspection, testing, and other tasks to ensure that the product or process is acceptable.
2. **Prevention costs.** The sum of all the costs to prevent defects such as the costs to identify the cause of the defect, to implement corrective action to eliminate the cause, to train personnel, to redesign the product or system, and to purchase new equipment or make modifications.

A GOODYEAR ASSOCIATE INSPECTS A RADIAL TIRE AT THE SAO PAULO, BRAZIL, FACTORY. GOODYEAR PRACTICES BOTH VISUAL AND INTERNAL INSPECTIONS OF TIRES, EVEN PULLING SOME TIRES FROM THE PRODUCTION LINE TO BE X-RAYED.

exhibit 9.4

Quality Cost Report

	CURRENT MONTH'S COST	PERCENTAGE OF TOTAL
Prevention costs		
Quality training	$ 2,000	1.3%
Reliability consulting	10,000	6.5
Pilot production runs	5,000	3.3
Systems development	8,000	5.2
Total prevention	25,000	16.3
Appraisal costs		
Materials inspection	6,000	3.9
Supplies inspection	3,000	2.0
Reliability testing	5,000	3.3
Laboratory testing	25,000	16.3
Total appraisal	39,000	25.5
Internal failure costs		
Scrap	15,000	9.8
Repair	18,000	11.8
Rework	12,000	7.8
Downtime	6,000	3.9
Total internal failure	51,000	33.3
External failure costs		
Warranty costs	14,000	9.2
Out-of-warranty repairs and replacement	6,000	3.9
Customer complaints	3,000	2.0
Product liability	10,000	6.5
Transportation losses	5,000	3.3
Total external failure	38,000	24.9
Total quality costs	$153,000	100.0

3. **Internal failure costs.**   Costs for defects incurred within the system: scrap, rework, repair.
4. **External failure costs.**   Costs for defects that pass through the system: customer warranty replacements, loss of customers or goodwill, handling complaints, and product repair.

Exhibit 9.4 illustrates the type of report that might be submitted to show the various costs by categories. Prevention is the most important influence. A rule of thumb says that for every dollar you spend in prevention, you can save $10 in failure and appraisal costs.

Often increases in productivity occur as a by-product of efforts to reduce the cost of quality. A bank, for example, set out to improve quality and reduce the cost of quality and found that it had also boosted productivity. The bank developed this productivity measure for the loan processing area: the number of tickets processed divided by the resources required (labor cost, computer time, ticket forms). Before the quality improvement program, the productivity index was 0.2660 [2,080/($11.23 × 640 hours + $0.05 × 2,600 forms + $500 for systems costs)]. After the quality improvement project was completed, labor time fell to 546 hours and the number of forms rose to 2,100, for a change in the index to 0.3088, an increase in productivity of 16 percent.

Service

FUNCTIONS OF THE QC DEPARTMENT

Although the focus of this chapter is on corporatewide quality programs, it is useful to comment on the functions of QC departments.

The typical manufacturing QC department has a variety of functions to perform. These include testing designs for their reliability in the lab and the field; gathering performance data on products in the field and resolving quality problems in the field; planning and budgeting the QC program in the plant; and, finally, designing and overseeing quality control systems and inspection procedures, and actually carrying out inspection activities requiring special

J. D. POWER AND ASSOCIATES INITIAL QUALITY STUDY OF NEW CARS

The J. D. Power and Associates Initial Quality Study[SM] serves as the industry benchmark for new-vehicle quality measured at 90 days of ownership. The study is used extensively by manufacturers worldwide to help them design and build higher quality vehicles and by consumers to help them in their purchase decisions. Initial quality has been shown over the years to be a good predictor of long-term durability, which can significantly impact consumer purchase decisions. The study captures problems experienced by owners in two distinct categories: 1) design-related problems and 2) defects and malfunctions.

1   Exterior
    a   Design-related problems: front or sliding doors with handles that are difficult to operate.
    b   Defects/Malfunctions: front or sliding doors that are difficult to open or close, excessive wind noise, or paint imperfections—including chips or scratches at delivery.

2   The Driving Experience
    a   Design-related problem: too much play or looseness in the steering system, excessive brake dust, or foot pedals that are too close together.
    b   Defects/Malfunctions: brakes that pull noticeably, are noisy, or emit excessive brake dust.

3   Features/Controls/Displays
    a   Design-related problems: problems with the remote keyless entry system, door locks, or cruise control

systems that are difficult to use. Controls that are awkwardly located.
    b   Defects/Malfunctions: problems with remote keyless entry systems, door locks, or cruise control systems that are not working properly.

4   Audio/Entertainment/Navigation
    a   Design-related problems: audio and entertainment systems with controls that are difficult to use or awkwardly located, or hands-free communication systems that don't recognize commands.
    b   Defects/Malfunctions: CD players with loading problems or radios with poor/no reception on AM/FM stations.

5   Seats
    a   Design-related problems: forward/backward seat adjustments or memory seat controls that are difficult to understand or use.
    b   Defects/Malfunctions: forward/backward seat adjustment or memory seats that are broken or not working properly.

6   Heat, Ventilation and Air Conditioning
    a   Design-related problems: a vehicle heater that doesn't get hot fast enough or windows that fog up too often.
    b   Defects/Malfunctions: a fan/blower with excessive noise or vents that emit air with a moldy or stale smell.

7   Interior
    a   Design-related problems: a glove box or center console that is difficult to use.
    b   Defects/Malfunctions: instrument panel or dash lights that are not working or a glove box or center console that is broken or damaged.

8   Engine/Transmission
    a   Design-related problems: an engine that loses power when the AC is on or a manual transmission that is hard to operate.
    b   Defects/Malfunctions: an engine that runs and then dies/stalls or an automatic transmission that shifts at the wrong time.

SOURCE: DIRECT COMMUNICATION WITH J. D. POWER AND ASSOCIATES.

technical knowledge to accomplish. The tools of the QC department fall under the heading of statistical quality control (SQC) and consist of two main sections: acceptance sampling and process control. These topics are covered in Chapter 9A.

SIX-SIGMA QUALITY

Six Sigma refers to the philosophy and methods companies such as General Electric and Motorola use to eliminate defects in their products and processes. A defect is simply any component that does not fall within the customer's specification limits. Each step or activity in a company represents an opportunity for defects to occur, and Six-Sigma programs seek to

Six Sigma

reduce the variation in the processes that lead to these defects. Indeed, Six-Sigma advocates see variation as the enemy of quality, and much of the theory underlying Six Sigma is devoted to dealing with this problem. A process that is in Six-Sigma control will produce no more than two defects out of every billion units. Often, this is stated as four defects per million units, which is true if the process is only running somewhere within one sigma of the target specification.

One of the benefits of Six-Sigma thinking is that it allows managers to readily describe the performance of a process in terms of its variability and to compare different processes using a common metric. This metric is **defects per million opportunities (DPMO)**. This calculation requires three pieces of data:

DPMO

1. **Unit.**   The item produced or being serviced.
2. **Defect.**   Any item or event that does not meet the customer's requirements.
3. **Opportunity.**   A chance for a defect to occur.

A straightforward calculation is made using the following formula:

$$\text{DPMO} = \frac{\text{Number of defects}}{\text{Number of opportunities for error per unit} \times \text{Number of units}} \times 1{,}000{,}000$$

Service

Step by Step

EXAMPLE 9.1

The customers of a mortgage bank expect to have their mortgage applications processed within 10 days of filing. This would be called a *critical customer requirement*, or CCR, in Six-Sigma terms. Suppose all defects are counted (loans in a monthly sample taking more than 10 days to process) and it is determined that there are 150 loans in the 1,000 applications processed last month that don't meet this customer requirement. Thus, the DPMO = 150/1,000 × 1,000,000, or 150,000 loans out of every million processed that fail to meet a CCR. Put differently, it means that only 850,000 loans out of a million are approved within time expectations. Statistically, 15 percent of the loans are defective and 85 percent are correct. This is a case where all the loans processed in less than 10 days meet our criteria. Often there are upper and lower customer requirements rather than just a single upper requirement as we have here. ●

There are two aspects to Six-Sigma programs: the methodology side and the people side. We will take these up in order.

SIX-SIGMA METHODOLOGY

While Six Sigma's methods include many of the statistical tools that were employed in other quality movements, here they are employed in a systematic project-oriented fashion through the define, measure, analyze, improve, and control (**DMAIC**) cycle. The DMAIC cycle is a more detailed version of the Deming **PDCA cycle**, which consists of four steps—plan, do, check, and act—that underly **continuous improvement**. (Continuous improvement, also called **kaizen**, seeks continual improvement of machinery, materials, labor utilization, and production methods through applications of suggestions and ideas of company teams.) Like Six Sigma, it also emphasizes the scientific method, particularly hypothesis testing about the relationship between process inputs (X's) and outputs (Y's) using design of experiments (DOE) methods. The availability of modern statistical software has reduced the drudgery of analyzing and displaying data and is now part of the Six-Sigma tool kit. The overarching focus of the methodology, however, is understanding and achieving what the customer wants, since that is seen as the key to profitability of a production process. In fact, to get across this point, some use the DMAIC as an acronym for "Dumb Managers Always Ignore Customers."

DMAIC
PDCA cycle
Continuous improvement
kaizen

The standard approach to Six-Sigma projects is the DMAIC methodology developed by General Electric, described below:[3]

1. Define (D)
   - Identify customers and their priorities.
   - Identify a project suitable for Six-Sigma efforts based on business objectives as well as customer needs and feedback.
   - Identify CTQs (critical-to-quality characteristics) that the customer considers to have the most impact on quality.

2. Measure (M)
   - Determine how to measure the process and how it is performing.
   - Identify the key internal processes that influence CTQs and measure the defects currently generated relative to those processes.
3. Analyze (A)
   - Determine the most likely causes of defects.
   - Understand why defects are generated by identifying the key variables that are most likely to create process variation.
4. Improve (I)
   - Identify means to remove the causes of defects.
   - Confirm the key variables and quantify their effects on the CTQs.
   - Identify the maximum acceptance ranges of the key variables and a system for measuring deviations of the variables.
   - Modify the process to stay within an acceptable range.
5. Control (C)
   - Determine how to maintain the improvements.
   - Put tools in place to ensure that the key variables remain within the maximum acceptance ranges under the modified process.

ANALYTICAL TOOLS FOR SIX SIGMA AND CONTINUOUS IMPROVEMENT

The analytical tools of Six Sigma have been used for many years in traditional quality improvement programs. What makes their application to Six Sigma unique is the integration of these tools in a corporatewide management system. The tools common to all quality efforts, including Six Sigma, are flowcharts, run charts, Pareto charts, histograms, checksheets, cause-and-effect diagrams, and control charts. Examples of these, along with an opportunity flow diagram, are shown in Exhibit 9.5 arranged according to DMAIC categories where they commonly appear.

Flowcharts. There are many types of flow charts. The one shown in Exhibit 9.5 depicts the process steps as part of a SIPOC (supplier, input, process, output, customer) analysis. SIPOC in essence is a formalized input-output model, used in the define stage of a project.

Run charts. They depict trends in data over time, and thereby help to understand the magnitude of a problem at the define stage. Typically, they plot the median of a process.

Pareto charts. These charts help to break down a problem into the relative contributions of its components. They are based on the common empirical finding that a large percentage of problems are due to a small percentage of causes. In the example, 80 percent of customer complaints are due to late deliveries, which are 20 percent of the causes listed.

Checksheets. These are basic forms that help standardize data collection. They are used to create histograms such as shown on the Pareto chart.

Cause-and-effect diagrams. Also called *fishbone diagrams,* they show hypothesized relationships between potential causes and the problem under study. Once the C&E diagram is constructed, the analysis would proceed to find out which of the potential causes were in fact contributing to the problem.

Opportunity flow diagram. This is used to separate value-added from non-value-added steps in a process.

Control charts. These are time-sequenced charts showing plotted values of a statistic, including a centerline average and one or more control limits. It is used here to assure that changes introduced are in statistical control. See Chapter 9A for a discussion of the various types and uses of charts for process control.

Other tools that have seen extensive use in Six Sigma projects are failure mode and effect analysis (FMEA) and design of experiments (DOE).

Failure mode and effect analysis. This is a structured approach to identify, estimate, prioritize, and evaluate risk of possible failures at each stage of a process. It begins with

exhibit 9.5   Analytical Tools for Six Sigma and Continuous Improvement

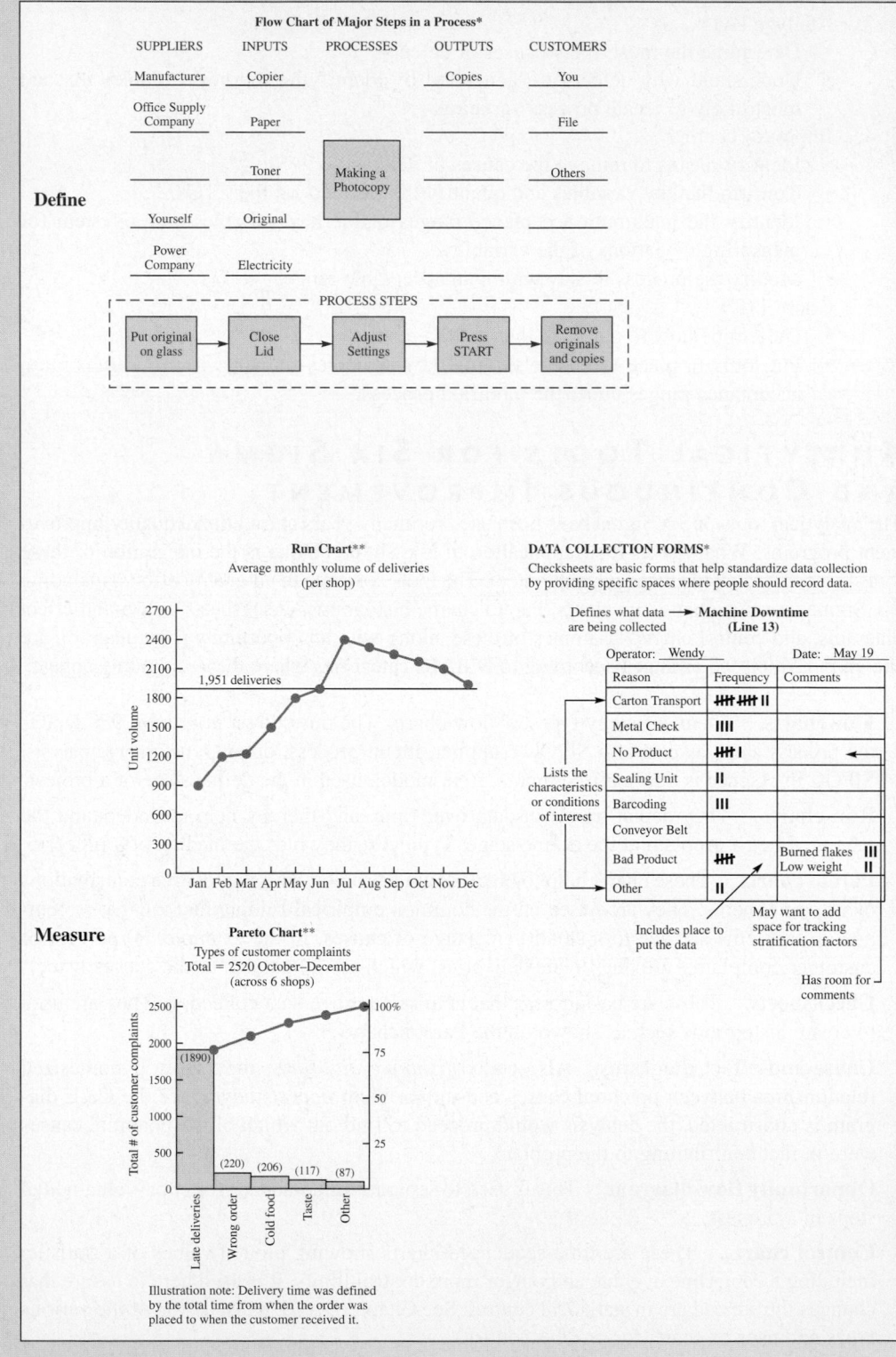

SOURCE: RATH & STRONG, RATH & STRONG'S SIX SIGMA POCKET GUIDE, 2001.
**SOURCE: RAYTHEON SIX SIGMA, THE MEMORY JOGGER™ II, 2001.*

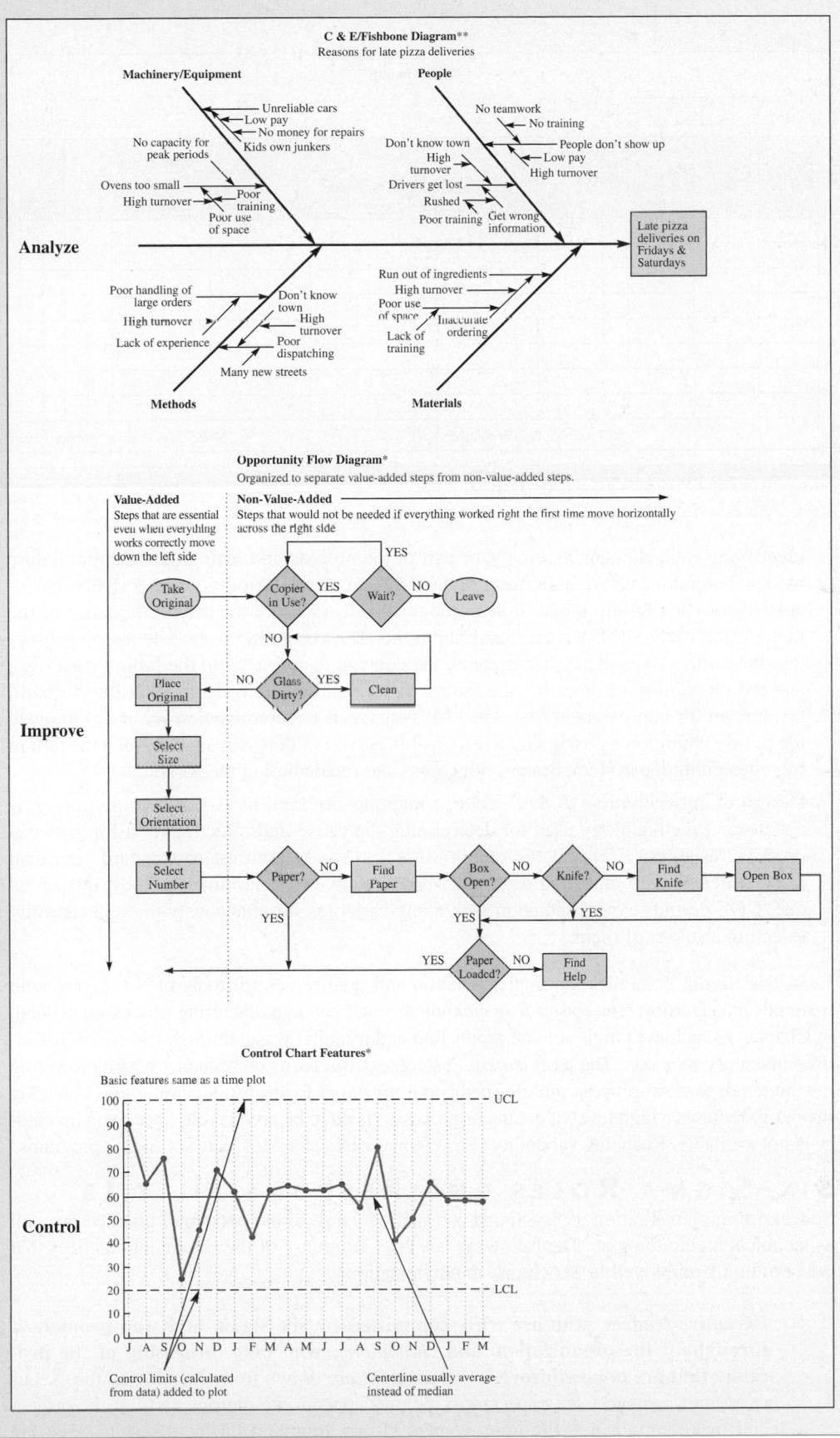

C & E/Fishbone Diagram**
Reasons for late pizza deliveries

Analyze

Machinery/Equipment
- Unreliable cars
- Low pay
- No money for repairs
- Kids own junkers
- No capacity for peak periods
- Ovens too small
- High turnover
- Poor training
- Poor use of space

People
- No teamwork
- No training
- Don't know town
- People don't show up
- High turnover
- Low pay
- High turnover
- Drivers get lost
- Rushed
- Poor training
- Get wrong information

Late pizza deliveries on Fridays & Saturdays

Methods
- Poor handling of large orders
- High turnover
- Lack of experience
- Don't know town
- High turnover
- Poor dispatching
- Many new streets

Materials
- Run out of ingredients
- High turnover
- Poor use of space
- Lack of training
- Inaccurate ordering

Opportunity Flow Diagram*
Organized to separate value-added steps from non-value-added steps.

Improve

Value-Added
Steps that are essential even when everything works correctly move down the left side

Non-Value-Added
Steps that would not be needed if everything worked right the first time move horizontally across the right side

Take Original → Copier in Use? → YES → Wait? → YES
Wait? → NO → Leave
Copier in Use? → NO
Glass Dirty? → YES → Clean
Glass Dirty? → NO → Place Original
Place Original → Select Size → Select Orientation → Select Number
Select Number → Paper? → NO → Find Paper → Box Open? → NO → Knife? → NO → Find Knife → Open Box
Knife? → YES
Box Open? → YES
Paper? → YES
Paper Loaded? → YES
Paper Loaded? → NO → Find Help

Control Chart Features*

Basic features same as a time plot

[line chart with y-axis 0 to 100, UCL at 100, LCL at 20, centerline at 60; x-axis months J A S O N D J F M A M J J A S O N D J F M]

Control limits (calculated from data) added to plot

Centerline usually average instead of median

exhibit 9.6 FMEA Form

FMEA Analysis

Project: ________________ Date: ________(original)

Team: ________________ ________(revised)

Item or Process Step	Potential Failure Mode	Potential Effects of Failure	Severity	Potential Cause(s)	Occurrence	Current Controls	Detection	RPN	Recommended Action	Responsibility and Target Date	"After" → Action Taken	Severity	Occurrence	Detection	RPN
Total Risk Priority Number:									"After" Risk Priority Number:						

SOURCE: RATH & STRONG, *RATH & STRONG'S SIX SIGMA POCKET GUIDE*: 2001, P. 31.

identifying each element, assembly, or part of the process and listing the potential failure modes, potential causes, and effects of each failure. A risk priority number (RPN) is calculated for each failure mode. It is an index used to measure the rank importance of the items listed in the FMEA chart. See Exhibit 9.6. These conditions include the probability that the failure takes place (occurrence), the damage resulting from the failure (severity), and the probability of detecting the failure in-house (detection). High RPN items should be targeted for improvement first. The FMEA suggests a recommended action to eliminate the failure condition by assigning a responsible person or department to resolve the failure by redesigning the system, design, or process and recalculating the RPN.

Design of experiments (DOE). DOE, sometimes referred to as *multivariate testing,* is a statistical methodology used for determining the cause-and-effect relationship between process variables (X's) and the output variable (Y). In contrast to standard statistical tests, which require changing each individual variable to determine the most influential one, DOE permits experimentation with many variables simultaneously through carefully selecting a subset of them.

Lean Six Sigma

Lean Six Sigma combines the implementation and quality control tools of Six Sigma with materials management concepts of *lean manufacturing*. Lean manufacturing (discussed in detail in Chapter 13) achieves high-volume production and minimal waste through the use of just-in-time inventory methods. The term *lean* in this context is a focus on reducing cost by lowering raw material, work-in-process, and finished goods inventory to an absolute minimum. Lowering inventory requires a high level of quality as processes need to be predictable since extra inventory is not available. Reducing variability is a key driver in successful lean Six-Sigma programs.

SIX-SIGMA ROLES AND RESPONSIBILITIES

Successful implementation of Six Sigma is based on using sound personnel practices as well as technical methodologies. The following is a brief summary of the personnel practices that are commonly employed in Six-Sigma implementation.

1. ***Executive leaders,* who are truly committed to Six Sigma and who promote it throughout the organization, and *champions,* who take ownership of the processes that are to be improved.** Champions are drawn from the ranks of the executives, and managers are expected to identify appropriate metrics early in the project and make certain that the improvement efforts focus on business results. (See the Breakthrough box "What Makes a Good Champion?")

BREAKTHROUGH

WHAT MAKES A GOOD CHAMPION?

At a manufacturing company implementing Six Sigma, a designated champion regularly met with his black belts. At one report-out meeting, a black belt informed him that she needed to purchase and install a table for sorting defects off-line. It would cost about $17,000, but it would provide an alternative to shutting down the entire line, which would cost far more. The controller told her to go through the normal requisition process and she'd have her table in about four months. That delay would have killed the project

right then and there: to submit the project to "business as usual" would have shown little real commitment to supporting Six Sigma. So the champion asked for the data that backed up her request, analyzed it, agreed with it, and then got immediate executive sign-off on securing a table the following week.

This is the stuff of a good champion: removing barriers and sending a clear signal that he and upper management are aligned and committed to Six Sigma. The champion does whatever it takes to support the black belts.

SOURCE: GREG BRUE, *SIX SIGMA FOR MANAGERS* (NEW YORK: MCGRAW-HILL, 2002), P. 84.

2. **Corporatewide training in Six-Sigma concepts and tools.** GE spent over a billion dollars training its professional workforce in the concepts. Now, virtually every professional in the organization is qualified in Six-Sigma techniques. To convey the need to vigorously attack problems, professionals are given martial arts titles reflecting their skills and roles: black belts, who coach or actually lead a Six-Sigma improvement team; master black belts, who receive in-depth training on statistical tools and process improvement (they perform many of the same functions as black belts but for a larger number of teams); and green belts, who are employees who have received enough Six-Sigma training to participate in a team or, in some companies, to work individually on a small-scale project directly related to their own job. Different companies use these "belts" in different combinations with sponsors and champions to guide teams.

Black belts

Master black belts

Green belts

3. **Setting of stretch objectives for improvement.**
4. **Continuous reinforcement and rewards.** At GE, before any savings from a project are declared, the black belt in charge must provide proof that the problems are fixed permanently.

THE SHINGO SYSTEM: FAIL-SAFE DESIGN

The Shingo system developed in parallel and in many ways in conflict with the statistically based approach to quality control. This system—or, to be more precise, philosophy of production management—is named after the codeveloper of the Toyota just-in-time system, Shigeo Shingo. Two aspects of the Shingo system in particular have received great attention. One is how to accomplish drastic cuts in equipment setup times by *s*ingle-*m*inute *e*xchange of *d*ie (SMED) procedures. The other, the focus of this section, is the use of source inspection and the poka-yoke system to achieve zero defects.

Shingo has argued that SQC methods do not prevent defects. Although they provide information to tell us probabilistically when a defect will occur, they are after the fact. The way to prevent defects from coming out at the end of a process is to introduce controls within the process. Central to Shingo's approach is the difference between errors and defects. Defects arise because people make errors. Even though errors are inevitable, defects can be prevented if feedback leading to corrective action takes place immediately after the errors are made. Such feedback and action require inspection, which should be done on 100 percent of the items produced. This inspection can be one of three types: successive check, self-check, and source inspection. *Successive check* inspection is performed by the next person in the process or by an objective evaluator such as a group leader. Information on defects is immediate feedback for the worker who produced the

exhibit 9.7   Poka-Yoke Example (Placing labels on parts coming down a conveyor)

Before Improvement

The operation depended on the worker's vigilance.

After Improvement

Device to ensure attachment of labels

The tape fed out by the labeler turns sharply so that the labels detach and project out from the tape. This is detected by a photoelectric tube and, if the label is not removed and applied to the product within the tact time of 20 seconds, a buzzer sounds and the conveyor stops.

Effect: Label application failures were eliminated.
Cost: ¥ 15,000 ($145)

Labeler

Label

Blank tape

Photoelectric tube

product, who then makes the repair. *Self-check* is done by the individual worker and is appropriate by itself on all but items that require sensory judgment (such as existence or severity of scratches, or correct matching of shades of paint). These require successive checks. *Source inspection* is also performed by the individual worker, except instead of checking for defects, the worker checks for the errors that will cause defects. This prevents the defects from ever occurring and, hence, requiring rework. All three types of inspection rely on controls consisting of fail-safe procedures or devices (called poka-yoke). Poka-yoke includes such things as checklists or special tooling that (1) prevents the worker from making an error that leads to a defect before starting a process or (2) gives rapid feedback of abnormalities in the process to the worker in time to correct them.

Fail-safe procedures
Poka-yoke

There are a wide variety of poka-yokes, ranging from kitting parts from a bin (to ensure that the right number of parts are used in assembly) to sophisticated detection and electronic signaling devices. An example taken from the writings of Shingo is shown in Exhibit 9.7.

There is a good deal more to say about the work of Shingo. Blasting industry's preoccupation with control charts, Shingo states they are nothing but a mirror reflecting current conditions. When a chemical plant QC manager proudly stated that it had 200 charts in a plant of 150 people, Shingo asked him if "they had a control chart for control charts."[4]

ISO 9000 AND ISO 14000

Global

ISO 9000

ISO 9000 and ISO 14000 are international standards for quality management and assurance. The standards are designed to help companies document that they are maintaining an efficient quality system. The standards were originally published in 1987 by the International Organization for Standardization (ISO), a specialized international agency recognized by affiliates in more than 160 countries. ISO 9000 has become an international reference for quality management requirements in business-to-business dealing, and ISO 14000 is primarily concerned with environmental management.

The idea behind the standards is that defects can be prevented through the planning and application of *best practices* at every stage of business—from design through manufacturing and then installation and servicing. These standards focus on identifying criteria by which any organization, regardless of whether it is manufacturing or service oriented, can ensure that product leaving its facility meets the requirements of its customers. These standards ask a company first to document and implement its systems for quality management and then to verify, by means of an audit conducted by an independent accredited third party, the compliance of those systems with the requirements of the standards.

The ISO 9000 standards are based on eight quality management principles that are defined in the ISO 9000:2000 document. These principles focus on business processes related to the following areas in the firm: (1) customer focus, (2) leadership, (3) involvement of people, (4) process approach, (5) system approach to management, (6) continual improvement, (7) factual approach to decision making, and (8) mutually beneficial supplier relationships. The ISO documents provide detailed requirements for meeting the standards and describe standard tools that are used for improving quality in the firm. These documents are intended to be generic and applicable to any organization producing products or services.

The ISO 14000 family of standards on environmental management addresses the need to be environmentally responsible. The standards define a three-pronged approach for dealing with environmental challenges. The first is the definition of more than 350 international standards for monitoring the quality of air, water, and soil. For many countries, these standards serve as the technical basis for environmental regulation. The second part of ISO 14000 is a strategic approach defining the requirements of an environmental management system that can be implemented using the monitoring tools. Finally, the environmental standard encourages the inclusion of environment aspects in product design and encourages the development of profitable environment-friendly products and services.

In addition to the generic ISO 9000 and ISO 14000 standards, many other specific standards have been defined. The following are some examples:

- QS-9000 is a quality management system developed by DaimlerChrysler, Ford, and General Motors for suppliers of production parts, materials, and services to the automotive industry.
- ISO/TS 16949, developed by the International Automotive Task Force, aligns existing American, German, French, and Italian automotive quality standards within the global automotive industry.
- ISO 14001 environmental standards are applied by automobile suppliers as a requirement from Ford and General Motors.
- ANSI/ASQ Z1.4-2003 provides methods for collecting, analyzing, and interpreting data for inspection by attributes, while Z1.9-2003 relates to inspection by variables.
- TL 9000 defines the telecommunications quality system requirements for the design, development, production, delivery, installation, and maintenance of products and services in the telecommunications industry.

The ISO standards provide accepted global guidelines for quality. Although certification is not required, many companies have found it is essential to be competitive in the global markets. Consider the situation where you need to purchase parts for your firm and several suppliers offer similar parts at similar prices. Assume that one of these firms has been ISO 9000–certified and the others have not. From whom would you purchase? There is no doubt that the ISO 9000–certified company would have the inside track in your decision making. Why? Because ISO 9000 specifies the way the supplier firm operates as well as its quality standards, delivery times, service levels, and so on.

Supply Chain

There are three forms of certification:

1. First party: A firm audits itself against ISO 9000 standards.
2. Second party: A customer audits its supplier.
3. Third party: A "qualified" national or international standards or certifying agency serves as an auditor.

The best certification of a firm is through a third party. Once passed by the third-party audit, a firm is certified and may be registered and recorded as having achieved ISO 9000 status and it becomes a part of a registry of certified companies. This third-party certification also has legal advantages in the European Community. For example, a manufacturer is liable for injury to a user of the product.

The firm, however, can free itself from any liability by showing that it has used the appropriate standards in its production process and carefully selected its suppliers as part of its purchasing requirements. For this reason, there is strong motivation to choose ISO 9000–certified suppliers.

EXTERNAL BENCHMARKING FOR QUALITY IMPROVEMENT

External benchmarking

Global

The quality improvement approaches described so far are more or less inward looking. They seek to make improvements by analyzing in detail the current practices of the company itself. **External benchmarking**, however, goes outside the organization to examine what industry competitors and excellent performers outside of the industry are doing. Benchmarking typically involves the following steps:

Identify processes needing improvement.   Identify a firm that is the world leader in performing the process. For many processes, this may be a company that is not in the same industry. Examples would be Procter & Gamble using L.L Bean as the benchmark in evaluating its order entry system, or ICL (a large British computer maker) benchmarking Marks and Spencer (a large U.K. clothing retailer) to improve its distribution system. A McKinsey study cited a firm that measured pit stops on a motor racing circuit as a benchmark for worker changes on its assembly line.[5] *Contact the managers of that company and make a personal visit to interview managers and workers.* Many companies select a team of workers from that process as part of the team of visitors.

Analyze data.   This entails looking at gaps between what your company is doing and what the benchmarking company is doing. There are two aspects of the study: one is comparing the actual processes; the other is comparing the performance of these processes according to a set of measures. The processes are often described using flowcharts and subjective evaluations of how workers relate to the process. In some cases, companies permit videotaping, although there is a tendency now for benchmarked companies to keep things under wraps for fear of giving away process secrets.

SUMMARY

How to achieve TQM is no secret any more. The challenge is to make certain that a quality program really does have a customer focus and is sufficiently agile to be able to make improvements quickly without losing sight of the real-time needs of the business. The quality system must be analyzed for its own quality. There is also a need for sustaining a quality culture over the long haul. Some companies (which will remain nameless) that gained a great reputation for quality in the 1980s and 90s simply ran out of gas in their quality efforts—their managers just couldn't sustain the level of enthusiasm necessary for quality to remain a top priority goal. As Tom Peters said, "Most Quality programs fail for one of two reasons: they have system without passion, or passion without system."[6]

KEY TERMS

Total quality management (TQM) Managing the entire organization so that it excels on all dimensions of products and services that are important to the customer.

Malcolm Baldrige National Quality Award An award established by the U.S. Department of Commerce and given annually to companies that excel in quality.

Design quality The inherent value of the product in the marketplace.

Conformance quality The degree to which the product or service design specifications are met.

Quality at the source The person who does the work is responsible for ensuring that specifications are met.

Dimensions of quality Criteria by which quality is measured.

Cost of quality Expenditures related to achieving product or service quality such as the costs of prevention, appraisal, internal failure, and external failure.

Six Sigma A statistical term to describe the quality goal of no more than four defects out of every million units. Also refers to a quality improvement philosophy and program.

DPMO (defects per million opportunities) A metric used to describe the variability of a process.

DMAIC An acronym for the **D**efine, **M**easure, **A**nalyze, **I**mprove, and **C**ontrol improvement methodology followed by companies engaging in Six-Sigma programs.

PDCA cycle Also called the "Deming cycle or wheel"; refers to the plan–do–check–act cycle of continuous improvement.

Continuous improvement The philosophy of continually seeking improvements in processes through the use of team efforts.

Kaizen Japanese term for continuous improvement.

Lean Six Sigma Combines the implementation and quality control tools of Six Sigma with the materials management concept of lean manufacturing with a focus on reducing cost by lowering inventory to an absolute minimum.

Black belts, master black belts, green belts Terms used to describe different levels of personal skills and responsibilities in Six-Sigma programs.

Fail-safe or poka-yoke procedures Simple practices that prevent errors or provide feedback in time for the worker to correct errors.

ISO 9000 Formal standards used for quality certification, developed by the International Organization for Standardization.

External benchmarking Looking outside the company to examine what excellent performers inside and outside the company's industry are doing in the way of quality.

REVIEW AND DISCUSSION QUESTIONS

1   Is the goal of Six Sigma realistic for services such as Blockbuster Video stores?
2   "If line employees are required to work on quality improvement activities, their productivity will suffer." Discuss.
3   "You don't inspect quality into a product; you have to build it in." Discuss the implications of this statement.
4   "Before you build quality in, you must think it in." How do the implications of this statement differ from those in question 3?
5   Business writer Tom Peters has suggested that in making process changes, we should "Try it, test it, and get on with it." How does this square with the DMAIC/continuous improvement philosophy?
6   Shingo told a story of a poka-yoke he developed to make sure that the operators avoided the mistake of putting fewer than the required four springs in a push-button device. The existing method involved assemblers taking individual springs from a box containing several hundred and then placing two of them behind an ON button and two more behind an OFF button. What was the poka-yoke Shingo created?
7   A typical word processing package is loaded with poka-yokes. List three. Are there any others you wish the packages had?

PROBLEMS

1   A manager states that his process is really working well. Out of 1,500 parts, 1,477 were produced free of a particular defect and passed inspection. Based upon Six-Sigma theory, how would you rate this performance, other things being equal?
2   Professor Chase is frustrated by his inability to make a good cup of coffee in the morning. Show how you would use a fishbone diagram to analyze the process he uses to make a cup of his evil brew.
3   Use the benchmarking process and as many DMAIC/CI analytical tools as you can to show how you can improve your performance in your weakest course in school.
4   Prepare a SIPOC flowchart (Exhibit 9.5) of the major steps in the process of boarding a commercial flight. Start the process with the passenger arriving curbside at your local airport.
5   Prepare an opportunity flow diagram for the same process of boarding a commercial flight.
6   The following table lists all costs of quality incurred by Sam's Surf Shop last year. What was Sam's appraisal cost for quality last year?

Annual inspection costs	$ 155,000
Annual cost of scrap materials	$ 286,000
Annual rework cost	$ 34,679
Annual cost of quality training	$ 456,000
Annual warranty cost	$1,546,000
Annual testing cost	$ 543,000

7   Below is a table of data collected over a six-month period in a local grocery store. Construct a Pareto analysis of the data and determine the percentage of total complaints represented by the two most common categories.

All Other	71
Checker	59
General	58
Service Level	55
Policy/Procedures	40
Price Marking	45
Product Quality	87
Product Request	105
Checkout Queue	33
Stock Condition	170

8   A common problem that many drivers encounter is a car that will not start. Create a fishbone diagram to assist in the diagnosis of the potential causes of this problem.

INTERNET ENRICHMENT EXERCISES

1   Visit the Baldrige Award Web site and see who won this year. What quality ideas did the winner demonstrate? What did the winner do that was particularly creative?
2   Visit the Six-Sigma Web site to see how companies are applying the concept.

CASE: HANK KOLB, DIRECTOR OF QUALITY ASSURANCE

Hank Kolb was whistling as he walked toward his office, still feeling a bit like a stranger since he had been hired four weeks before as director of quality assurance. All that week he had been away from the plant at a seminar given for quality managers of manufacturing plants by the corporate training department. He was now looking forward to digging into the quality problems at this industrial products plant employing 1,200 people.

Kolb poked his head into Mark Hamler's office, his immediate subordinate as the quality control manager, and asked him how things had gone during the past week. Hamler's muted smile and an "Oh, fine," stopped Kolb in his tracks. He didn't know Hamler very well and was unsure about pursuing this reply any further. Kolb was still uncertain of how to start building a relationship with him since Hamler had been passed over for the promotion to Kolb's job; Hamler's evaluation form had stated "superb technical knowledge; managerial skills lacking." Kolb decided to inquire a little further and asked Hamler what had happened; he replied, "Oh, just another typical quality snafu. We had a little problem on the Greasex line last week [a specialized degreasing solvent packed in a spray can for the high-technology sector]. A little high pressure was found in some cans on the second shift, but a supervisor vented them so that we could ship them out. We met our delivery schedule!" Because Kolb was still relatively unfamiliar with the plant and its products, he asked Hamler to elaborate; painfully, Hamler continued:

We've been having some trouble with the new filling equipment and some of the cans were pressurized beyond the upper specification limit.

The production rate is still 50 percent of standard, about 14 cases per shift, and we caught it halfway into the shift. Mac Evans [the inspector for that line] picked it up, tagged the cases "hold," and went on about his duties.

When he returned at the end of the shift to write up the rejects, Wayne Simmons, first-line supervisor, was by a pallet of finished goods finishing sealing up a carton of the rejected Greasex; the reject "hold" tags had been removed. He told Mac that he had heard about the high pressure from another inspector at coffee break, had come back, taken off the tags, individually turned the cans upside down and vented every one of them in the eight rejected cartons. He told Mac that production planning was really pushing for the stuff and they couldn't delay by having it sent through the rework area. He told Mac that he would get on the operator to run the equipment right next time. Mac didn't write it up but came in about three days ago to tell me about it. Oh, it happens every once in a while and I told him to make sure to check with maintenance to make sure the filling machine was adjusted; and I saw Wayne in the hall and told him that he ought to send the stuff through rework next time.

Kolb was a bit dumbfounded at this and didn't say much—he didn't know if this was a big deal or not. When he got to his office, he thought again what Morganthal, general manager, had said when he had hired him. He warned Kolb about the "lack of quality attitude" in the plant and said that Kolb "should try and do something about this." Morganthal further emphasized the quality problems in the plant: "We have to improve our quality; it's costing us a lot of money, I'm sure of it, but I can't prove it! Hank, you have my full support in this matter; you're in charge of these quality problems. This downward quality–productivity–turnover spiral has to end!"

The incident had happened a week before; the goods were probably out in the customers' hands by now, and everyone had forgotten about it (or wanted to). There seemed to be more pressing problems than this for Kolb to spend his time on, but this continued to nag him. He felt that the quality department was being treated as a joke, and he also felt that this was a personal slap from manufacturing. He didn't want to start a war with the production people, but what could he do? Kolb was troubled enough to cancel his appointments and spend the morning talking to a few people. After a long and very tactful morning, he learned the following information:

1 **From personnel.** The operator for the filling equipment had just been transferred from shipping two weeks ago. He had no formal training in this job but was being trained by Wayne, on the job, to run the equipment. When Mac had tested the high-pressure cans, the operator was nowhere to be found and had only learned of the rejected material from Wayne after the shift was over.

2 **From plant maintenance.** This particular piece of automated filling equipment had been purchased two years ago for use on another product. It had been switched to the Greasex line six months ago and maintenance completed 12 work orders during the last month for repairs or adjustments on it. The equipment had been adapted by plant maintenance for handling the lower viscosity of Greasex, which it had not originally been designed for. This included designing a special filling head. There was no scheduled preventive maintenance for this equipment and the parts for the sensitive filling head, replaced three times in the last six months, had to be made at a nearby machine shop. Nonstandard downtime was 15 percent of actual running time.

3 **From purchasing.** The plastic nozzle heads for the Greasex can, designed by a vendor for this new product on a rush order, were often found to have slight burrs on the inside rim, and this caused some trouble in fitting the top to the can. An increase in application pressure at the filling head by maintenance adjustment had solved the burr application problem or had at least forced the nozzle heads on despite burrs. Purchasing agents said that they were going to talk to the sales representative of the nozzle head supplier about this the next time he came in.

4 **From product design and packaging.** The can, designed especially for Greasex, had been contoured to allow better gripping by the user. This change, instigated by marketing research, set Greasex apart from the appearance of its competitors and was seen as significant by the designers. There had been no test of the effects of the contoured can on filling speed or filling hydrodynamics from a high-pressured filling head. Kolb had a hunch that the new design was acting as a venturi (carrier creating suction) when being filled, but the packaging designer thought that was unlikely.

5 **From the manufacturing manager.** He had heard about the problem; in fact, Simmons had made a joke about it, bragging about how he beat his production quota to the other foremen and shift supervisors. The manufacturing manager thought Simmons was one of the "best foremen we have . . . he always got his production out." His promotion papers were actually on the manufacturing manager's desk when Kolb dropped by. Simmons was being strongly considered for promotion to shift supervisor. The manufacturing manager, under pressure from Morganthal for cost improvements and reduced delivery times, sympathized with Kolb but said that the rework area would have vented with their pressure gauges what Wayne had done by hand. "But I'll speak with Wayne about the incident," he said.

6 **From marketing.** The introduction of Greasex had been rushed to market to beat competitors, and a major promotional advertising campaign was under way to increase consumer awareness. A deluge of orders was swamping the order-taking department and putting Greasex high on the back-order list. Production had to turn the stuff out; even being a little off spec was tolerable because "it would be better to have it on the shelf than not there at all. Who cares if the label is a little crooked or the stuff comes out with a little too much pressure? We need market share now in that high-tech segment."

What bothered Kolb most was the safety issue of the high pressure in the cans. He had no way of knowing how much of a hazard the high pressure was or if Simmons had vented them enough to effectively reduce the hazard. The data from the can manufacturer, which Hamler had showed him, indicated that the high pressure found by the inspector was not in the danger area. But, again, the inspector had used only a sample testing procedure to reject the eight cases. Even if he could morally accept that there was no product safety hazard, could Kolb make sure that this would never happen again?

Skipping lunch, Kolb sat in his office and thought about the morning's events. The past week's seminar had talked about the role of quality, productivity and quality, creating a new attitude, and the quality challenge; but where had they told him what to do when this happened? He had left a very good job to come here because he thought the company was serious about the importance of quality, and he wanted a challenge. Kolb had demanded and received a salary equal to the manufacturing, marketing, and R&D directors, and he was one of the direct reports to the general manager. Yet he still didn't know exactly what he should or shouldn't do, or even what he could or couldn't do under these circumstances.

QUESTIONS

1 What are the causes of the quality problems on the Greasex line? Display your answer on a fishbone diagram.

2 What general steps should Hank follow in setting up a continuous improvement program for the company? What problems will he have to overcome to make it work?

SOURCE: COPYRIGHT 1981 BY PRESIDENT AND FELLOWS OF HARVARD COLLEGE, HARVARD BUSINESS SCHOOL. CASE 681.083. THIS CASE WAS PREPARED BY FRANK S. LEONARD AS THE BASIS FOR CLASS DISCUSSION RATHER THAN TO ILLUSTRATE EITHER EFFECTIVE OR INEFFECTIVE HANDLING OF AN ADMINISTRATIVE SITUATION. REPRINTED BY PERMISSION OF THE HARVARD BUSINESS SCHOOL.

CASE: APPRECIATIVE INQUIRY—A DIFFERENT KIND OF FISHBONE

The standard cause-and-effect, or fishbone, diagram approach focuses on identifying the root cause of a problem. Finding this cause then becomes an input into developing a solution. On the other hand, improvements aren't always about finding out what went wrong; rather, they may be about identifying what was done right. This is what the AI approach is designed to do. The way it works is

exhibit 9.8   Identifying Excellence Drivers (the Hows of Excellence)

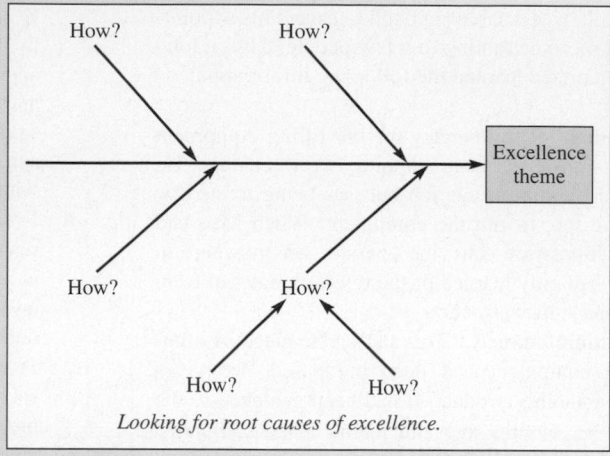

Looking for root causes of excellence.

exhibit 9.9   Root Causes of Excellence

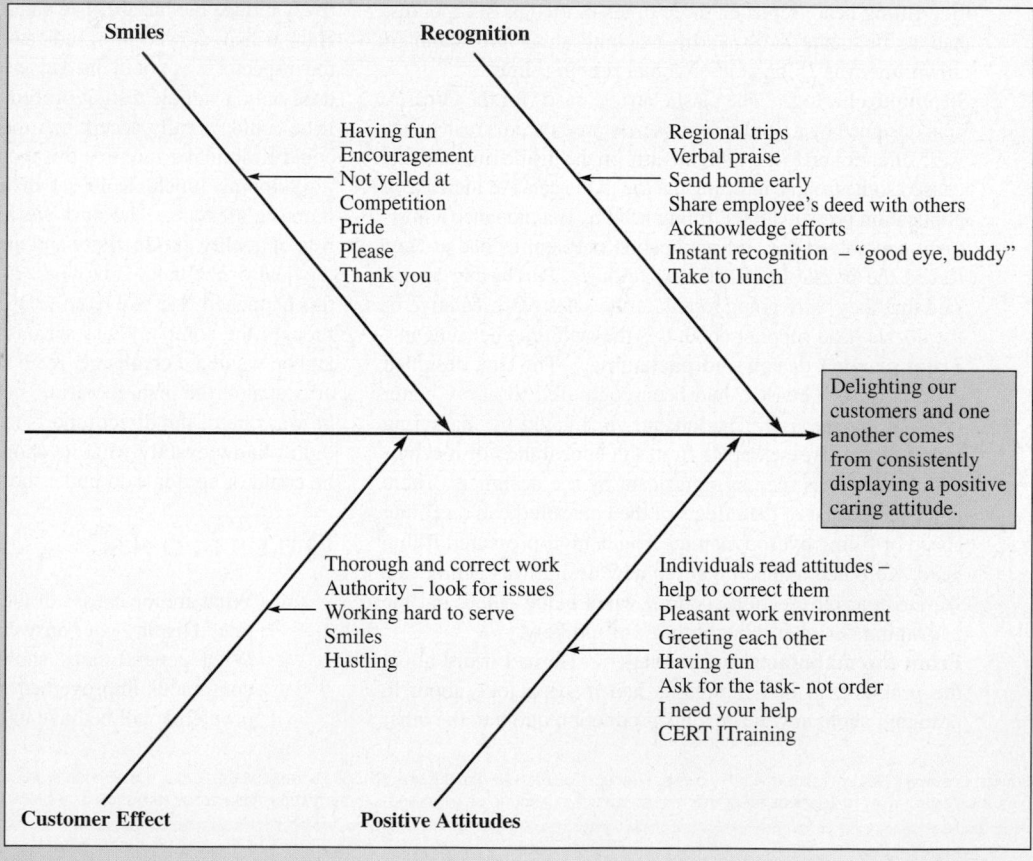

it solicits success stories from employees about how, for example, they delighted their customers. These are then put on the head of the fishbone diagram as the theme for study. (See Exhibit 9.8.) The approach then gathers the causes of success, which are entered on the fishbone as the "hows" of success. One of the particular benefits of this is that it builds on the unique capabilities of the company rather than copying approaches taken by others.

This approach has been used successfully by Direct Discount Tires executive Steve Fornier Jr., who says, "AI is a simple tool that we can use to find out what and why things are done the way they are done. It gives our employees a chance to think for themselves, find solutions, and execute at higher levels rather than being recipients of a 'do this' 'do that' kind of speech. Because they are figuring out answers for themselves, it drives the entrepreneurial spirit, promotes innovation, and eventually creates new leaders and new best practices from the front line that will continue to keep us 'The Best.' Without this new innovation, we risk becoming stagnated." (The fishbone diagram for Direct Discount Tires is shown in Exhibit 9.9.)

QUESTIONS

1 From a worker's perspective, what do you see as the major benefit of appreciative inquiry compared to standard cause-and-effect analysis?

2 As an interesting exercise, think about your favorite instructor. Develop an appreciative inquiry fishbone diagram that identifies why you feel this instructor is so outstanding.

SOURCE: WILLIAM YOUNGDAHL AND CAREN SIEHL, LECTURE NOTES, AMERICAN GRADUATE SCHOOL OF INTERNATIONAL MANAGEMENT, 2006.

SUPER QUIZ

1 This refers to the inherent value of the product in the marketplace and is a strategic decision for the firm.

2 Relates to how well a product or services meets design specifications.

3 Relates to how the customer views quality dimensions of a product or service.

4 The series of international quality standards.

5 What is the enemy of good quality?

6 A Six-Sigma process that is running at the center of its control limits would expect this defect rate.

7 The standard quality improvement methodology developed by General Electric.

1. Design quality 2. Conformance quality 3. Fitness for use 4. ISO 9000 5. Variation 6. 2 parts per billion units 7. DMAIC cycle

SELECTED BIBLIOGRAPHY

Bemowski, K., and B. Stratton, eds. *101 Good Ideas: How to Improve Just About Any Process.* Washington, DC: American Society for Quality, 1999.

Blakeslee, J. A., Jr. "Implementing the Six Sigma Solution." *Quality Progress,* July 1999, pp. 77–85.

Brue, G. *Six Sigma for Managers.* New York: McGraw-Hill, 2002.

Chowdhury, S. *Design for Six Sigma.* Chicago: Dearborn Trade Publishing, 2002.

Chowdhury, S., and K. Zimmer. *QS-9000 Pioneers—Registered Companies Share Their Strategies for Success.* Burr Ridge, IL: Richard D. Irwin, 1996.

Crosby, P. B. *Quality Is Free.* New York: McGraw-Hill, 1979 (reissue 1992).

———. *Quality Is Still Free.* New York: McGraw-Hill, 1996.

Deming, W. E. *Quality, Productivity and Competitive Position.* Cambridge, MA: MIT Center for Advanced Engineering Study, 1982.

Eckes, G. *Six Sigma Revolution: How General Electric and Others Turned Process into Profits.* New York: John Wiley & Sons, 2001.

Evans, J. R., and W. M. Lindsay. *The Management and Control of Quality.* Cincinnati: South-Western/Thomson Learning, 2002.

Feigenbaum, A. V. *Total Quality Control.* New York: McGraw-Hill, 1991.

Gitlow, H.; A. Oppenheim, and R. Oppenheim. *Quality Management: Tools and Methods for Improvement.* 2nd ed. New York: Irwin/McGraw-Hill, 1995.

Juran, J. M. *Quality Control Handbook.* 3rd ed. New York: McGraw-Hill, 1979.

Juran, J. M., and F. M. Gryna. *Quality Planning and Analysis.* 2nd ed. New York: McGraw-Hill, 1980.

Pande, P. S.; R. P. Neuman; and R. R. Cavanagh. *The Six Sigma Way.* New York: McGraw-Hill, 2000.

———. *The Six Sigma Way Team Fieldbook.* New York: McGraw-Hill, 2002.

Robinson, A. *Modern Approaches to Manufacturing Improvement: The Shingo System.* Cambridge, MA: Productivity Press, 1990.

Shingo, S. *Zero Quality Control: Source Inspection and the Poka-Yoke System.* Stamford, CT: Productivity Press, 1986.

Taormina, T. *Virtual Leadership and the ISO 9000 Imperative.* Englewood Cliffs, NJ: Prentice Hall, 1996.

Welch, J. *Jack: Straight from the Gut.* New York: Warner Business Books, 2001.

FOOTNOTES

1 D. A. Garvin, *Managing Quality* (New York: Free Press, 1988).

2 P. B. Crosby, *Quality Is Free* (New York: New American Library, 1979), p. 15.

3 S. Walleck, D. O'Halloran, and C. Leader, "Benchmarking World-Class Performance," *McKinsey Quarterly,* no. 1 (1991), p. 7.

4 A. Robinson, *Modern Approaches to Manufacturing Improvement: The Shingo System* (Cambridge, MA: Productivity Press, 1990), p. 234.

5 Walleck, O'Halloran, and Leader, "Benchmarking World-Class Performance," p. 7.

6 T. Peters, *Thriving on Chaos* (New York: Knopf, 1987), p. 74.

chapter 9A

PROCESS CAPABILITY AND SPC

After reading this chapter you will:

1. Explain what statistical quality control is.
2. Calculate the capability of a process.
3. Understand how processes are monitored with control charts.
4. Recognize acceptance sampling concepts.

This chapter on statistical process control (SPC) covers the quantitative aspects of quality management. In general, SPC is a number of different techniques designed to evaluate quality from a conformance view. That is, how well are we doing at meeting the specifications that have been set during the design of the parts or services that we are providing? Managing quality performance using SPC techniques usually involves periodic sampling of a process and analysis of these data using statistically derived performance criteria.

As you will see, SPC can be applied to both manufacturing and service processes. Here are some examples of the types of situations where SPC can be applied:

- How many paint defects are there in the finish of a car? Have we improved our painting process by installing a new sprayer?
- How long does it take to execute market orders in our Web-based trading system? Has the installation of a new server improved the service? Does the performance of the system vary over the trading day?
- How well are we able to maintain the dimensional tolerance on our three-inch ball bearing assembly? Given the variability of our process for making this ball bearing, how many defects would we expect to produce per million bearings that we make?
- How long do customers wait to be served from our drive-through window during the busy lunch period?

Service

Processes that provide goods and services usually exhibit some variation in their output. This variation can be caused by many factors, some that we can control and others that are inherent in the process. Variation caused by factors that can be clearly identified and possibly even managed is called **assignable variation**. For example, variation caused by workers not being equally trained or by improper machine adjustment is assignable variation. Variation that is inherent in the process is called **common variation**. Common variation is often referred to as *random variation* and may be the result of the type of equipment used to complete a process, for example.

Assignable variation

Common variation

As the title of this chapter implies, this material requires an understanding of very basic statistics. Recall from your study of statistics involving numbers that are normally distributed the definition of the mean and standard deviation. The mean ($\overline{X}$) is just the average value of a set of numbers. Mathematically this is

$$\overline{X} = \sum_{i=1}^{N} x_i / N \qquad \text{[9A.1]}$$

where:

x_i = Observed value

N = Total number of observed values

The standard deviation is

$$\sigma = \sqrt{\frac{\sum_{i=1}^{N}(x_i - \overline{X})^2}{N}}$$

[9A.2]

In monitoring a process using SPC, samples of the process output would be taken and sample statistics calculated. The distribution associated with the samples should exhibit the same kind of variability as the actual distribution of the process, although the actual variance of the sampling distribution would be less. This is good because it allows the quick detection of changes in the actual distribution of the process. The purpose of sampling is to find when the process has changed in some nonrandom way, so that the reason for the change can be quickly determined.

In SPC terminology, *sigma* is often used to refer to the sample standard deviation. As you will see in the examples, sigma is calculated in a few different ways, depending on the underlying theoretical distribution (i.e., a normal distribution or a Poisson distribution).

VARIATION AROUND US

It is generally accepted that as variation is reduced, quality is improved. Sometimes that knowledge is intuitive. If a train is always on time, schedules can be planned more precisely. If clothing sizes are consistent, time can be saved by ordering from a catalog. But rarely are such things thought about in terms of the value of low variability. With engineers, the knowledge is better defined. Pistons must fit cylinders, doors must fit openings, electrical components must be compatible, and boxes of cereal must have the right amount of raisins—otherwise quality will be unacceptable and customers will be dissatisfied.

However, engineers also know that it is impossible to have zero variability. For this reason, designers establish specifications that define not only the target value of something but also acceptable limits about the target. For example, if the aim value of a dimension is 10 inches, the design specifications might then be 10.00 inches $\pm$ 0.02 inch. This would tell the manufacturing department that, while it should aim for exactly 10 inches, anything between 9.98 and 10.02 inches is OK. These design limits are often referred to as the **upper and lower specification limits** or the **upper and lower tolerance limits**.

Upper and lower specification or tolerance limits

A traditional way of interpreting such a specification is that any part that falls within the allowed range is equally good, whereas any part falling outside the range is totally bad. This is illustrated in Exhibit 9A.1A. (Note that the cost is zero over the entire specification range, and then there is a quantum leap in cost once the limit is violated.)

Genichi Taguchi, a noted quality expert from Japan, has pointed out that the traditional view illustrated in Exhibit 9A.1A is nonsense for two reasons:

1. From the customer's view, there is often practically no difference between a product just inside specifications and a product just outside. Conversely, there is a far greater difference in the quality of a product that is the target and the quality of one that is near a limit.
2. As customers get more demanding, there is pressure to reduce variability. However, Exhibit 9A.1A does not reflect this logic.

Taguchi suggests that a more correct picture of the loss is shown in Exhibit 9A.1B. Notice that, in this graph, the cost is represented by a smooth curve. There are dozens of illustrations of this notion: the meshing of gears in a transmission, the speed of photographic film, the temperature in a workplace or department store. In nearly anything that can be measured, the customer sees not a sharp line, but a gradation of acceptability away from the "Aim" specification. Customers see the loss function as Exhibit 9A.1B rather than Exhibit 9A.1A.

Of course, if products are consistently scrapped when they are outside specifications, the loss curve flattens out in most cases at a value equivalent to scrap cost in the ranges outside

Views of the Cost of Variability

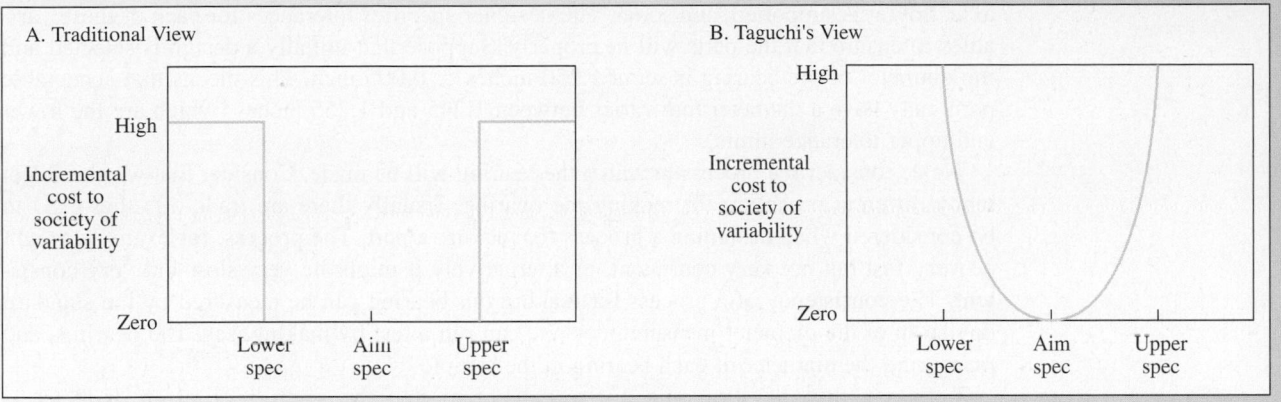

specifications. This is because such products, theoretically at least, will never be sold so there is no external cost to society. However, in many practical situations, either the process is capable of producing a very high percentage of product within specifications and 100 percent checking is not done, or if the process is not capable of producing within specifications, 100 percent checking is done and out-of-spec products can be reworked to bring them within specs. In any of these situations, the parabolic loss function is usually a reasonable assumption.

In the next two sections, we discuss two concepts—process capability and control charts. Process capability relates to how good the process is at making parts when it is running properly. Control charts are used to continuously check that the process is running properly.

PROCESS CAPABILITY

Taguchi argues that being within tolerance is not a yes/no decision, but rather a continuous function. The Motorola quality experts, on the other hand, argue that the process used to produce a good or deliver a service should be so good that the probability of generating a defect should be very, very low. Motorola made process capability and product design famous by adopting Six-Sigma limits. When we design a part, we specify that certain dimensions should be within the upper and lower specification limits.

As a simple example, assume that we are designing a bearing for a rotating shaft—say an axle for the wheel of a car. Both the bearing and the axle are subject to many variables—for example, the width of the bearing, the size of the rollers, the size of the axle, the length of the axle, how it is supported, and so on. The designer specifies tolerances for each of these variables to ensure that the parts will fit properly. Suppose that initially a design is selected and the diameter of the bearing is set at 1.250 inches ± 0.005 inch. This means that acceptable parts may have a diameter that varies between 1.245 and 1.255 inches (which are the lower and upper tolerance limits).

Next, consider the process in which the bearing will be made. Consider that we can select many different processes for making the bearing. Usually there are trade-offs that need to be considered when designing a process for making a part. The process, for example, might be very fast but not very consistent, or alternatively it might be very slow but very consistent. The consistency of a process for making our bearing can be measured by the standard deviation of the diameter measurement. We can run a test by making, say, 100 bearings and measuring the diameter of each bearing in the sample.

Let's say that, after running our test, we find that the average or mean diameter is 1.250 inches. Another way to say this is that the process is "centered" right in the middle of the upper and lower specification limits. In reality, it may be very difficult to have a perfectly centered process like our example. Let's say that the diameter values have a standard deviation or sigma equal to 0.002 inch. What this means is that our process does not make each bearing exactly the same size.

As we will see later in this chapter, normally we monitor a process using control charts such that if the process starts making bearings that are more than three standard deviations (±0.006 inch) above or below 1.250 inches, we stop the process. This means that we will produce parts that vary between 1.244 [this is 1.250 − (3 × .002)] and 1.256 [this is 1.250 + (3 × .002)] inches. The 1.244 and 1.256 are referred to as the upper and lower process limits. Be careful and do not get confused with the terminology here. The "process" limits relate to how consistent our process is for making the bearing. Our goal in managing the process is to keep it within plus or minus three standard deviations of the process mean. The "specification" limits are related to the design of the part. Recall that, from a design view, acceptable parts have a diameter between 1.245 and 1.255 inches (which are the lower and upper specification limits).

As we can see, our process limits are slightly greater than the specification limits given to us by the designer. This is not good because we will produce some parts that do not meet specifications. Companies with Six-Sigma processes insist that a process making a part be capable of operating so that the design specification limits are six standard deviations away from the process mean. For our bearing process, how small would the process standard deviation need to be for it to be Six-Sigma capable? Recall that our design specification was 1.250 inches plus or minus 0.005 inch. When you think about it, that 0.005 inch must relate to the variation in the process. By dividing 0.005 inch by 6, which equals 0.00083, we can determine our process standard deviation for a Six-Sigma process. So for our process to be Six-Sigma capable, the mean diameter produced by the process would need to be exactly 1.250 inches and the process standard deviation would need to be less than or equal to 0.00083 inch.

We can imagine that some of you are really confused at this point with the whole idea of Six Sigma. Why doesn't our company, for example, just check the diameter of each bearing and throw out the ones with a diameter less than 1.245 or greater than 1.255? This could certainly be done, and for many, many parts 100 percent testing is done. The problem is for a company that is making thousands of parts each hour, testing each critical dimension of each part made can be very expensive. For our bearing, there could easily be 10 or more additional critical dimensions in addition to the diameter. These would all need to be checked. Using a 100 percent testing approach, the company would spend more time testing than it takes to actually make the part! This is why a company uses small samples to periodically check that the process is in statistical control. We discuss exactly how this statistical sampling works later in the chapter.

We say that a process is *capable* when the mean and standard deviation of the process are operating such that the upper and lower control limits are acceptable relative to the upper and lower specification limits. Consider diagram A in Exhibit 9A.2. This represents the distribution of the bearing diameter dimension in our original process. The average or mean

Process Capability

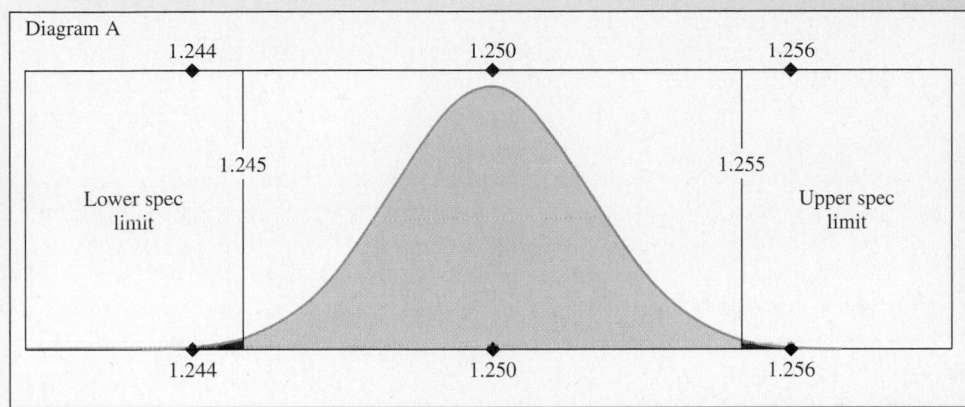

Diagram A

1.244   1.250   1.256

1.245   1.255

Lower spec limit   Upper spec limit

1.244   1.250   1.256

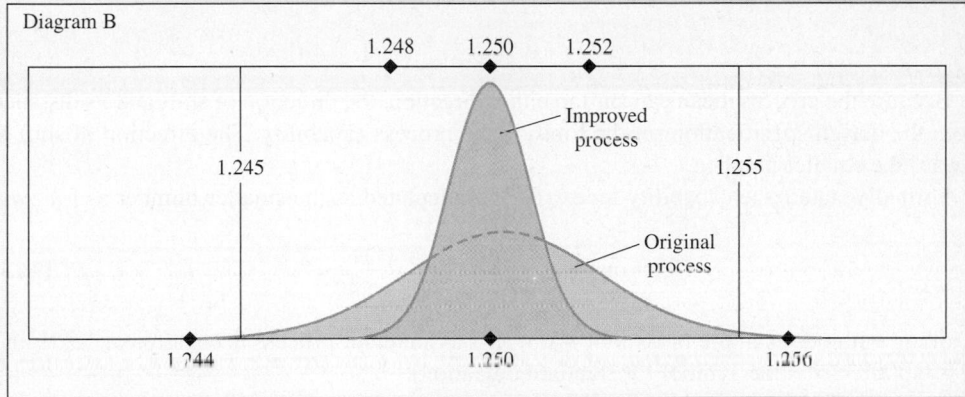

Diagram B

1.248 1.250 1.252

Improved process

1.245   1.255

Original process

1.244   1.250   1.256

value is 1.250 and the lower and upper design specifications are 1.245 and 1.255, respectively. Process control limits are plus and minus three standard deviations (1.244 and 1.256). Notice that there is a probability (the red areas) of producing defective parts.

If we can improve our process by reducing the standard deviation associated with the bearing diameter, the probability can be reduced. Diagram B in Exhibit 9A.2 shows a new process where the standard deviation has been reduced to 0.00083 (the orange area). Even though we cannot see it in the diagram, there is some probability that a defect could be produced by this new process, but that probability is very, very small.

Suppose that the central value or mean of the process shifts away from the mean. Exhibit 9A.3 shows the mean shifted one standard deviation closer to the upper specification limit. This, of course, causes a slightly higher number of expected defects, but we can see that this is still very, very good. We use the *capability index* to measure how well our process is capable of producing relative to the design tolerances. We describe how to calculate this index in the next section.

CAPABILITY INDEX (C_{pk})

The **capability index** (C_{pk}) shows how well the parts being produced fit into the range specified by the design limits. If the design limits are larger than the three sigma allowed in the process, then the mean of the process can be allowed to drift off-center before readjustment, and a high percentage of good parts will still be produced.

Referring to Exhibits 9A.2 and 9A.3, the capability index (C_{pk}) is the position of the mean and tails of the process relative to design specifications. The more off-center, the greater the chance to produce defective parts.

Capability index (C_{pk})

Excel: SPC

exhibit 9A.3   Process Capability with a Shift in the Process Mean

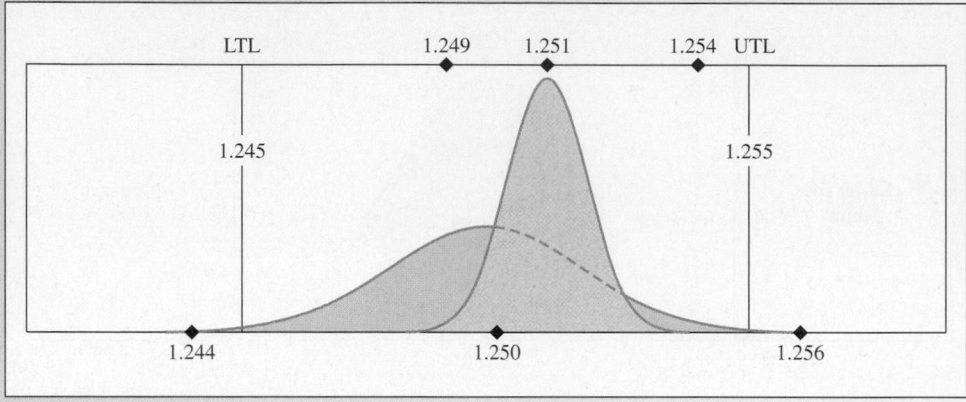

Because the process mean can shift in either direction, the direction of shift and its distance from the design specification set the limit on the process capability. The direction of shift is toward the smaller number.

Formally stated, the capability index (C_{pk}) is calculated as the smaller number as follows:

$$C_{pk} = \min\left[\frac{\overline{X} - LTL}{3\sigma} \quad \text{or} \quad \frac{UTL - \overline{X}}{3\sigma}\right] \qquad \text{[9A.3]}$$

Working with our example in Exhibit 9A.3, let's assume our process is centered at 1.251 and $\sigma = 0.00083$ (σ is the symbol for standard deviation).

$$C_{pk} = \min\left[\frac{1.251 - 1.245}{3(.00083)} \quad \text{or} \quad \frac{1.255 - 1.251}{3(.00083)}\right]$$

$$= \min\left[\frac{.006}{.00249} \quad \text{or} \quad \frac{.004}{.00249}\right]$$

$$C_{pk} = \min[2.4 \quad \text{or} \quad 1.6]$$

$C_{pk} = 1.6$, which is the smaller number.

This tells us that the process mean has shifted to the right similar to Exhibit 9A.3, but parts are still well within design limits.

At times it is useful to calculate the actual probability of producing a defect. Assuming that the process is producing with a consistent standard deviation, this is a fairly straightforward calculation, particularly when we have access to a spreadsheet. The approach to use is to calculate the probability of producing a part outside the lower and upper design limits given the mean and standard deviation of the process.

Working with our example, where the process is not centered, with a mean of 1.251 inches, $\sigma = .00083$, LTL = 1.245, and UTL = 1.255, we first need to calculate the Z score associated with the upper and lower tolerance (specification) limits. Recall from your study of statistics that the Z score is the standard deviation either to the right or to the left of zero in a probability distribution.

$$Z_{LTL} = \frac{LTL - \overline{X}}{\sigma} \qquad Z_{UTL} = \frac{UTL - \overline{X}}{\sigma}$$

For our example,

$$Z_{LTL} = \frac{1.245 - 1.251}{.00083} = -7.2289 \qquad Z_{UTL} = \frac{1.255 - 1.251}{.00083} = 4.8193$$

An easy way to get the probabilities associated with these Z values is to use the NORMSDIST function built into Excel (you also can use the table in Appendix G). The format for this function is NORMSDIST(Z), where Z is the Z value calculated above. Excel returns the following values. (We have found that you might get slightly different results from those given here, depending on the version of Excel you are using.)

$$\text{NORMSDIST}(-7.2289) = 2.43461\text{E-}13 \quad \text{and} \quad \text{NORMSDIST}(4.8193) = .99999928$$

Interpreting this information requires understanding exactly what the NORMSDIST function is providing. NORMSDIST is giving the cumulative probability to the left of the given Z value. Since $Z = -7.2289$ is the number of standard deviations associated with the lower specification limit, the fraction of parts that will be produced lower than this is 2.43461E-13. This number is in scientific notation, and that E-13 at the end means we need to move the decimal over 13 places to get the real fraction defective. So the fraction defective is .00000000000024361, which is a very small number! Similarly, we see that approximately .99999928 of our parts will be below our upper specification limit. What we are really interested in is the fraction that will be above this limit since these are the defective parts. This fraction defective above the upper spec is $1 - .99999928 = .00000082$ of our parts.

Adding these two fraction defective numbers together we get .00000082000024361. We can interpret this to mean that we only expect about .82 part per million to be defective. Clearly, this is a great process. You will discover as you work the problems at the end of the chapter that this is not always the case.

EXAMPLE 9A.1

The quality assurance manager is assessing the capability of a process that puts pressurized grease in an aerosol can. The design specifications call for an average of 60 pounds per square inch (psi) of pressure in each can with an upper tolerance limit of 65 psi and a lower tolerance limit of 55 psi. A sample is taken from production and it is found that the cans average 61 psi with a standard deviation of 2 psi. What is the capability of the process? What is the probability of producing a defect?

Step by Step

SOLUTION

Step 1—Interpret the data from the problem

$$\text{LTL} = 55 \quad \text{UTL} = 65 \quad \overline{X} = 61 \quad \sigma = 2$$

Step 2—Calculate the C_{pk}

$$C_{pk} = \min\left[\frac{\overline{X} - \text{LTL}}{3\sigma}, \frac{\text{UTL} - \overline{X}}{3\sigma}\right]$$

$$C_{pk} = \min\left[\frac{61 - 55}{3(2)}, \frac{65 - 61}{3(2)}\right]$$

$$C_{pk} = \min[1, .6667] = .6667$$

Step 3—Calculate the probability of producing a defect
Probability of a can with less than 55 psi

$$Z = \frac{X - \overline{X}}{\sigma} = \frac{55 - 61}{2} = -3$$

$$\text{NORMSDIST}(-3) = .001349898$$

Probability of a can with more than 65 psi

$$Z = \frac{X - \overline{X}}{\sigma} = \frac{65 - 61}{2} = 2$$

$$1 - \text{NORMSDIST}(2) = 1 - .977249868 = .022750132$$

Probability of a can less than 55 psi or more than 65 psi

$$\text{Probability} = .001349898 + .022750132 = .024100030$$

Or approximately 2.4 percent of the cans will be defective. ●

The following table is a quick reference for the fraction of defective units for various design limits (expressed in standard deviations). This table assumes that the standard deviation is constant and that the process is centered exactly between the design limits.

DESIGN LIMITS	DEFECTIVE PARTS	FRACTION DEFECTIVE
$\pm 1\sigma$	317 per thousand	.3173
$\pm 2\sigma$	45 per thousand	.0455
$\pm 3\sigma$	2.7 per thousand	.0027
$\pm 4\sigma$	63 per million	.000063
$\pm 5\sigma$	574 per billion	.000000574
$\pm 6\sigma$	2 per billion	.000000002

Motorola's design limit of six sigma with a shift of the process off the mean by 1.5σ ($C_{pk} = 1.5$) gives 3.4 defects per million. If the mean is exactly in the center ($C_{pk} = 2$), then 2 defects per *billion* are expected, as the table above shows.

PROCESS CONTROL PROCEDURES

Statistical process control (SPC)

Attributes

Process control is concerned with monitoring quality *while the product or service is being produced.* Typical objectives of process control plans are to provide timely information on whether currently produced items are meeting design specifications and to detect shifts in the process that signal that future products may not meet specifications. **Statistical process control (SPC)** involves testing a random sample of output from a process to determine whether the process is producing items within a preselected range.

The examples given so far have all been based on quality characteristics (or *variables*) that are measurable, such as the diameter or weight of a part. **Attributes** are quality characteristics that are classified as either conforming or not conforming to specification. Goods or services may be observed to be either good or bad, or functioning or malfunctioning. For example, a lawnmower either runs or it doesn't; it attains a certain level of torque and horsepower or it doesn't. This type of measurement is known as sampling by attributes. Alternatively, a lawnmower's torque and horsepower can be measured as an amount of deviation from a set standard. This type of measurement is known as sampling by variables. The following section describes some standard approaches to controlling processes: first an approach useful for attribute measures and then an approach for variable measures. Both of these techniques result in the construction of control charts. Exhibit 9A.4 shows some examples of how control charts can be analyzed to understand how a process is operating.

PROCESS CONTROL WITH ATTRIBUTE MEASUREMENTS: USING *p* CHARTS

Measurement by attributes means taking samples and using a single decision—the item is good or it is bad. Because it is a yes or no decision, we can use simple statistics to create a *p* chart with an upper control limit (UCL) and a lower control limit (LCL). We can draw these control limits on a graph and then plot the fraction defective of each individual sample tested. The process is assumed to be working correctly when the samples, which are taken periodically during the day, continue to stay between the control limits.

Control Chart Evidence for Investigation

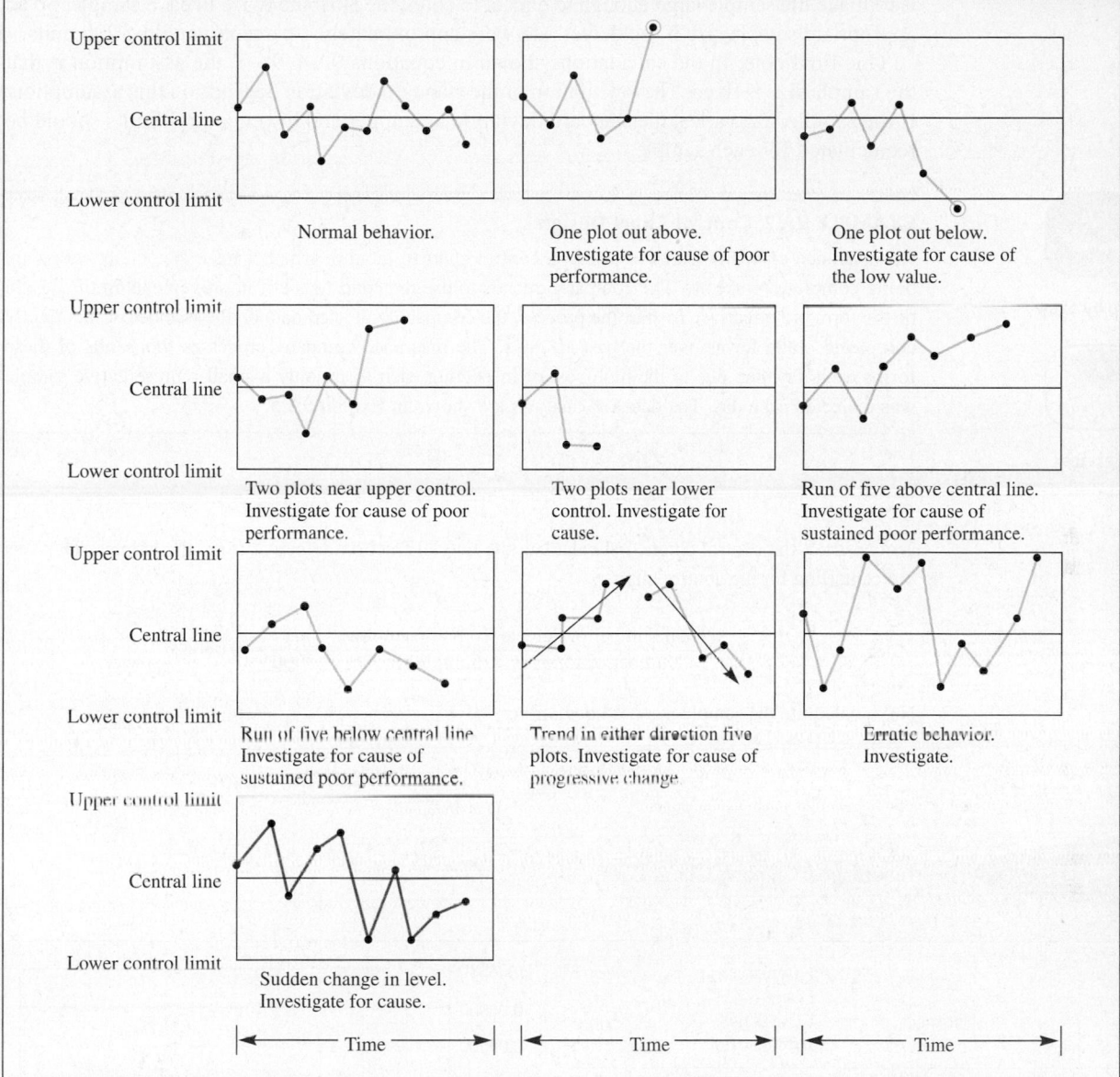

$$\bar{p} = \frac{\text{Total number of defects from all samples}}{\text{Number of samples} \times \text{Sample size}} \qquad \text{[9A.4]}$$

$$s_p = \sqrt{\frac{\bar{p}(1 - \bar{p})}{n}} \qquad \text{[9A.5]}$$

$$\text{UCL} = \bar{p} + zs_p \qquad \text{[9A.6]}$$

$$\text{LCL} = \bar{p} - zs_p \qquad \text{[9A.7]}$$

where $\bar{p}$ is the fraction defective, s_p is the standard deviation, n is the sample size, and z is the number of standard deviations for a specific confidence. Typically, $z = 3$ (99.7 percent confidence) or $z = 2.58$ (99 percent confidence) is used.

Size of the Sample   The size of the sample must be large enough to allow counting of the attribute. For example, if we know that a machine produces 1 percent defects, then a sample size of five would seldom capture a defect. A rule of thumb when setting up a p chart is to make the sample large enough to expect to count the attribute twice in each sample. So an appropriate sample size if the defect rate were approximately 1 percent would be 200 units.

One final note: In the calculations shown in equations 9A.4–9A.7, the assumption is that the sample size is fixed. The calculation of the standard deviation depends on this assumption. If the sample size varies, the standard deviation and upper and lower control limits should be recalculated for each sample.

Step by Step

Service

EXAMPLE 9A.2: Control Chart Design

An insurance company wants to design a control chart to monitor whether insurance claim forms are being completed correctly. The company intends to use the chart to see if improvements in the design of the form are effective. To start the process, the company collected data on the number of incorrectly completed claim forms over the past 10 days. The insurance company processes thousands of these forms each day, and due to the high cost of inspecting each form, only a small representative sample was collected each day. The data and analysis are shown in Exhibit 9A.5.

SOLUTION

To construct the control chart, first calculate the overall fraction defective from all samples. This sets the centerline for the control chart.

$$\bar{p} = \frac{\text{Total number of defects from all samples}}{\text{Number of samples} \times \text{Sample size}} = \frac{91}{3000} = 0.03033$$

Next, calculate the sample standard deviation:

$$s_p = \sqrt{\frac{\bar{p}(1 - \bar{p})}{n}} = \sqrt{\frac{0.03033(1 - 0.03033)}{300}} = 0.00990$$

exhibit 9A.5   Insurance Company Claim Form

SAMPLE	NUMBER INSPECTED	NUMBER OF FORMS COMPLETED INCORRECTLY	FRACTION DEFECTIVE
1	300	10	0.03333
2	300	8	0.02667
3	300	9	0.03000
4	300	13	0.04333
5	300	7	0.02333
6	300	7	0.02333
7	300	6	0.02000
8	300	11	0.03667
9	300	12	0.04000
10	300	8	0.02667
Totals	3000	91	0.03033
Sample standard deviation			0.00990

Finally, calculate the upper and lower control limits. A *z*-value of 3 gives 99.7 percent confidence that the process is within these limits.

$$UCL = \bar{p} + 3s_p = 0.03033 + 3(0.00990) = 0.06003$$

$$LCL = \bar{p} - 3s_p = 0.03033 - 3(0.00990) = 0.00063$$

The calculations in Exhibit 9A.5, including the control chart, are included in the spreadsheet SPC. ●

Excel: SPC

PROCESS CONTROL WITH ATTRIBUTE MEASUREMENTS: USING c CHARTS

In the case of the *p* chart, the item was either good or bad. There are times when the product or service can have more than one defect. For example, a board sold at a lumber yard may have multiple knotholes and, depending on the quality grade, may or may not be defective. To monitor the number of defects per unit, the *c* chart is appropriate.

The underlying distribution for the *c* chart is the Poisson, which is based on the assumption that defects occur randomly on each unit. If *c* is the number of defects for a particular unit, then $\bar{c}$ is the average number of defects per unit, and the standard deviation is $\sqrt{\bar{c}}$. For the purposes of our control chart we use the normal approximation to the Poisson distribution and construct the chart using the following control limits.

$$\bar{c} = \text{Average number of defects per unit} \qquad [9A.8]$$

$$s_p = \sqrt{\bar{c}} \qquad [9A.9]$$

$$UCL = \bar{c} + z\sqrt{\bar{c}} \qquad [9A.10]$$

$$LCL = \bar{c} - z\sqrt{\bar{c}} \quad \text{or} \quad 0 \text{ if less than } 0 \qquad [9A.11]$$

Just as with the *p* chart, typically $z = 3$ (99.7 percent confidence) or $z = 2.58$ (99 percent confidence) is used.

Example 9A.3

The owners of a lumber yard want to design a control chart to monitor the quality of 2 × 4 boards that come from their supplier. For their medium-quality boards they expect an average of four knotholes per 8 foot board. Design a control chart for use by the person receiving the boards using three-sigma (standard deviation) limits.

Step by Step

SOLUTION

For this problem, $\bar{c} = 4$, $s_p = \sqrt{\bar{c}} = 2$

$$UCL = \bar{c} + z\sqrt{\bar{c}} = 4 + 3(2) = 10$$

$$LCL = \bar{c} - z\sqrt{\bar{c}} = 4 - 3(2) = -2 \rightarrow 0 \qquad ●$$

PROCESS CONTROL WITH VARIABLE MEASUREMENTS: USING X̄ AND R CHARTS

$\bar{X}$ and *R* (range) charts are widely used in statistical process control.

In attribute sampling, we determine whether something is good or bad, fits or doesn't fit—it is a go/no-go situation. In **variables** sampling, however, we measure the actual weight, volume, number of inches, or other variable measurements, and we develop control charts to determine the acceptability or rejection of the process based on those measurements.

Variables

A FOREMAN AND TEAM COACH EXAMINE PROCESS CONTROL CHARTS AT THE FORD FIESTA ASSEMBLY LINE IN COLOGNE-NIEHL, GERMANY.

For example, in attribute sampling, we might decide that if something is over 10 pounds we will reject it and under 10 pounds we will accept it. In variable sampling, we measure a sample and may record weights of 9.8 pounds or 10.2 pounds. These values are used to create or modify control charts and to see whether they fall within the acceptable limits.

The four main issues to address in creating a control chart are the size of the samples, number of samples, frequency of samples, and control limits.

Size of Samples   For industrial applications in process control involving the measurement of variables, it is preferable to keep the sample size small. There are two main reasons. First, the sample needs to be taken within a reasonable length of time; otherwise, the process might change while the samples are taken. Second, the larger the sample, the more it costs to take.

Sample sizes of four or five units seem to be the preferred numbers. The *means* of samples of this size have an approximately normal distribution, no matter what the distribution of the parent population looks like. Sample sizes greater than five give narrower control limits and thus more sensitivity. For detecting finer variations of a process, it may be necessary, in fact, to use larger sample sizes. However, when sample sizes exceed 15 or so, using $\overline{X}$ charts with standard deviation σ would be better than using $\overline{X}$ charts with the range R as in Example 9A.4.

Number of Samples   Once the chart has been set up, each sample taken can be compared to the chart and a decision can be made about whether the process is acceptable. To set up the charts, however, prudence and statistics suggest that 25 or so samples be taken.

Frequency of Samples   How often to take a sample is a trade-off between the cost of sampling (along with the cost of the unit if it is destroyed as part of the test) and the benefit of adjusting the system. Usually, it is best to start off with frequent sampling of a process and taper off as confidence in the process builds. For example, one might start with a sample of five units every half hour and end up feeling that one sample per day is adequate.

Control Limits   Standard practice in statistical process control for variables is to set control limits three standard deviations above the mean and three standard deviations below. This means that 99.7 percent of the sample means are expected to fall within these control limits (that is, within a 99.7 percent confidence interval). Thus, if one sample mean falls outside this obviously wide band, we have strong evidence that the process is out of control.

HOW TO CONSTRUCT $\bar{X}$ AND R CHARTS

If the standard deviation of the process distribution is known, the $\bar{X}$ chart may be defined:

$$\text{UCL}_{\bar{X}} = \bar{\bar{X}} + zs_{\bar{X}} \quad \text{and} \quad \text{LCL}_{\bar{X}} = \bar{\bar{X}} - zs_{\bar{X}} \qquad \text{[9A.12]}$$

where

$S_{\bar{X}} = s/\sqrt{n} = $ Standard deviation of sample means

$s = $ Standard deviation of the process distribution

$n = $ Sample size

$\bar{\bar{X}} = $ Average of sample means or a target value set for the process

$z = $ Number of standard deviations for a specific confidence level (typically, $z = 3$)

An $\bar{X}$ chart is simply a plot of the means of the sample s that were taken from a process. $\bar{\bar{X}}$ is the average of the means.

In practice, the standard deviation of the process is not known. For this reason, an approach that uses actual sample data is commonly used. This practical approach is described in the next section.

An R chart is a plot of the range within each sample. The range is the difference between the highest and the lowest numbers in that sample. R values provide an easily calculated measure of variation used like a standard deviation. An $\bar{R}$ chart is the average of the range of each sample. More specifically defined, these are

$$\bar{X} = \frac{\sum_{i=1}^{n} X_i}{n} \qquad \text{[Same as 9A.1]}$$

where

$\bar{X} = $ Mean of the sample

$i = $ Item number

$n = $ Total number of items in the sample

$$\bar{\bar{X}} = \frac{\sum_{j=1}^{m} \bar{X}_j}{m} \qquad \text{[9A.13]}$$

where

$\bar{\bar{X}} = $ The average of the means of the samples

$j = $ Sample number

$m = $ Total number of samples

$$\bar{R} = \frac{\sum_{j=1}^{m} R_j}{m} \qquad \text{[9A.14]}$$

where

$R_j = $ Difference between the highest and lowest measurement in the sample

$\bar{R} = $ Average of the measurement differences R for all samples

E. L. Grant and R. Leavenworth computed a table (Exhibit 9A.6) that allows us to easily compute the upper and lower control limits for both the $\bar{X}$ chart and the R chart.[1] These are defined as

$$\text{Upper control limit for } \bar{X} = \bar{\bar{X}} + A_2\bar{R} \qquad \text{[9A.15]}$$

exhibit 9A.6   Factor for Determining from $\bar{R}$ the Three-Sigma Control Limits for $\bar{X}$ and R Charts

NUMBER OF OBSERVATIONS IN SUBGROUP n	FACTOR FOR $\bar{X}$ CHART A_2	FACTORS FOR R CHART	
		LOWER CONTROL LIMIT D_3	UPPER CONTROL LIMIT D_4
2	1.88	0	3.27
3	1.02	0	2.57
4	0.73	0	2.28
5	0.58	0	2.11
6	0.48	0	2.00
7	0.42	0.08	1.92
8	0.37	0.14	1.86
9	0.34	0.18	1.82
10	0.31	0.22	1.78
11	0.29	0.26	1.74
12	0.27	0.28	1.72
13	0.25	0.31	1.69
14	0.24	0.33	1.67
15	0.22	0.35	1.65
16	0.21	0.36	1.64
17	0.20	0.38	1.62
18	0.19	0.39	1.61
19	0.19	0.40	1.60
20	0.18	0.41	1.59

Upper control limit for $\bar{X} = \text{UCL}_{\bar{X}} = \bar{\bar{X}} + A_2\bar{R}$
Lower control limit for $\bar{X} = \text{LCL}_{\bar{X}} = \bar{\bar{X}} - A_2\bar{R}$
Upper control limit for $R = \text{UCL}_R = D_4\bar{R}$
Lower control limit for $R = \text{LCL}_R = D_3\bar{R}$

Note: All factors are based on the normal distribution.

Excel: SPC

$$\text{Lower control limit for } \bar{X} = \bar{\bar{X}} - A_2\bar{R} \qquad \text{[9A.16]}$$

$$\text{Upper control limit for } R = D_4\bar{R} \qquad \text{[9A.17]}$$

$$\text{Lower control limit for } R = D_3\bar{R} \qquad \text{[9A.18]}$$

Step by Step

EXAMPLE 9A.4: $\bar{X}$ and R Charts

We would like to create $\bar{X}$ and R charts for a process. Exhibit 9A.7 shows measurements for all 25 samples. The last two columns show the average of the sample $\bar{X}$ and the range R.

Values for A_2, D_3, and D_4 were obtained from Exhibit 9A.6.

$$\text{Upper control limit for } \bar{X} = \bar{\bar{X}} + A_2\bar{R} = 10.21 + 0.58(0.60) = 10.56$$

$$\text{Lower control limit for } \bar{X} = \bar{\bar{X}} - A_2\bar{R} = 10.21 - 0.58(0.60) = 9.86$$

$$\text{Upper control limit for } R = D_4\bar{R} = 2.11(0.60) = 1.27$$

$$\text{Lower control limit for } R = D_3\bar{R} = 0(0.60) = 0$$

Measurements in Samples of Five from a Process

SAMPLE NUMBER	EACH UNIT IN SAMPLE					AVERAGE $\overline{X}$	RANGE R
1	10.60	10.40	10.30	9.90	10.20	10.28	.70
2	9.98	10.25	10.05	10.23	10.33	10.17	.35
3	9.85	9.90	10.20	10.25	10.15	10.07	.40
4	10.20	10.10	10.30	9.90	9.95	10.09	.40
5	10.30	10.20	10.24	10.50	10.30	10.31	.30
6	10.10	10.30	10.20	10.30	9.90	10.16	.40
7	9.98	9.90	10.20	10.40	10.10	10.12	.50
8	10.10	10.30	10.40	10.24	10.30	10.27	.30
9	10.30	10.20	10.60	10.50	10.10	10.34	.50
10	10.30	10.40	10.50	10.10	10.20	10.30	.40
11	9.90	9.50	10.20	10.30	10.35	10.05	.85
12	10.10	10.36	10.50	9.80	9.95	10.14	.70
13	10.20	10.50	10.70	10.10	9.90	10.28	.80
14	10.20	10.60	10.50	10.30	10.40	10.40	.40
15	10.54	10.30	10.40	10.55	10.00	10.36	.55
16	10.20	10.60	10.15	10.00	10.50	10.29	.60
17	10.20	10.40	10.60	10.80	10.10	10.42	.70
18	9.90	9.50	9.90	10.50	10.00	9.96	1.00
19	10.60	10.30	10.50	9.90	9.80	10.22	.80
20	10.60	10.40	10.30	10.40	10.20	10.38	.40
21	9.90	9.60	10.50	10.10	10.60	10.14	1.00
22	9.95	10.20	10.50	10.30	10.20	10.23	.55
23	10.20	9.50	9.60	9.80	10.30	9.88	.80
24	10.30	10.60	10.30	9.90	9.80	10.18	.80
25	9.90	10.30	10.60	9.90	10.10	10.16	.70

$$\overline{\overline{X}} = 10.21$$

$$\overline{R} = 0.60$$

Excel: SPC

$\overline{X}$ Chart and R Chart

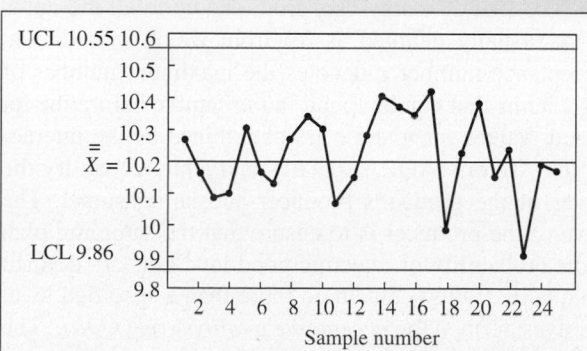

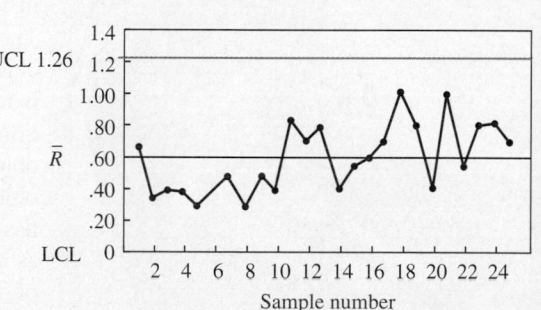

Excel: SPC

SOLUTION

Exhibit 9A.8 shows the $\overline{X}$ chart and R chart with a plot of all the sample means and ranges of the samples. All the points are well within the control limits, although sample 23 is close to the $\overline{X}$ lower control limit. ●

ACCEPTANCE SAMPLING

DESIGN OF A SINGLE SAMPLING PLAN FOR ATTRIBUTES

Acceptance sampling is performed on goods that already exist to determine what percentage of products conform to specifications. These products may be items received from another company and evaluated by the receiving department, or they may be components that have passed through a processing step and are evaluated by company personnel either in production or later in the warehousing function. Whether inspection should be done at all is addressed in the following example.

Acceptance sampling is executed through a sampling plan. In this section, we illustrate the planning procedures for a single sampling plan—that is, a plan in which the quality is determined from the evaluation of one sample. (Other plans may be developed using two or more samples. See J. M. Juran and F. M. Gryna's *Quality Planning and Analysis* for a discussion of these plans.)

Step by Step

Excel: SPC

EXAMPLE 9A.5: Costs to Justify Inspection

Total (100 percent) inspection is justified when the cost of a loss incurred by not inspecting is greater than the cost of inspection. For example, suppose a faulty item results in a $10 loss and the average percentage defective of items in the lot is 3 percent.

SOLUTION

If the average percentage of defective items in a lot is 3 percent, the expected cost of faulty items is $0.03 \times \$10$, or $0.30 each. Therefore, if the cost of inspecting each item is less than $0.30, the economic decision is to perform 100 percent inspection. Not all defective items will be removed, however, because inspectors will pass some bad items and reject some good ones.

The purpose of a sampling plan is to test the lot to either (1) find its quality or (2) ensure that the quality is what it is supposed to be. Thus, if a quality control supervisor already knows the quality (such as the 0.03 given in the example), he or she does not sample for defects. Either all of them must be inspected to remove the defects or none of them should be inspected, and the rejects pass into the process. The choice simply depends on the cost to inspect and the cost incurred by passing a reject. ●

ALUMINUM SHEETS ARE EXAMINED UNDER QUALITY CONTROL LIGHTS ON THE ALUMINUM PRODUCTION LINE AT THE ALCOA SZÉKESFEHÉRVÁR, HUNGARY, EXTRUSION PLANT.

A single sampling plan is defined by n and c, where n is the number of units in the sample and c is the acceptance number. The size of n may vary from one up to all the items in the lot (usually denoted as N) from which it is drawn. The acceptance number c denotes the maximum number of defective items that can be found in the sample before the lot is rejected. Values for n and c are determined by the interaction of four factors (AQL, α, LTPD, and β) that quantify the objectives of the product's producer and its consumer. The objective of the producer is to ensure that the sampling plan has a low probability of rejecting good lots. Lots are defined as high quality if they contain no more than a specified level of defectives, termed the *acceptable quality level (AQL)*.[2] The objective of the consumer is to ensure that the sampling plan has a low probability of accepting bad lots. Lots are defined as low quality if the percentage of defectives is greater than a specified amount, termed *lot tolerance percent defective (LTPD)*. The probability associated with rejecting a high-quality lot is denoted by the Greek letter alpha (α) and is termed the *producer's risk*. The probability associated with

Excerpt from a Sampling Plan Table for $\alpha = 0.05$, $\beta = 0.10$

c	LTPD ÷ AQL	$n \cdot$ AQL	c	LTPD ÷ AQL	$n \cdot$ AQL
0	44.890	0.052	5	3.549	2.613
1	10.946	0.355	6	3.206	3.286
2	6.509	0.818	7	2.957	3.981
3	4.890	1.366	8	2.768	4.695
4	4.057	1.970	9	2.618	5.426

accepting a low-quality lot is denoted by the letter beta (β) and is termed the *consumer's risk*. The selection of particular values for AQL, α, LTPD, and β is an economic decision based on a cost trade-off or, more typically, on company policy or contractual requirements.

There is a humorous story supposedly about Hewlett-Packard during its first dealings with Japanese vendors, who place great emphasis on high-quality production. HP had insisted on 2 percent AQL in a purchase of 100 cables. During the purchase agreement, some heated discussion took place wherein the Japanese vendor did not want this AQL specification; HP insisted that they would not budge from the 2 percent AQL. The Japanese vendor finally agreed. Later, when the box arrived, there were two packages inside. One contained 100 good cables. The other package had 2 cables with a note stating: "We have sent you 100 good cables. Since you insisted on 2 percent AQL, we have enclosed 2 defective cables in this package, though we do not understand why you want them."

The following example, using an excerpt from a standard acceptance sampling table, illustrates how the four parameters—AQL, α, LTPD, and β—are used in developing a sampling plan.

EXAMPLE 9A.6: Values of *n* and *c*

Hi-Tech Industries manufactures Z-Band radar scanners used to detect speed traps. The printed circuit boards in the scanners are purchased from an outside vendor. The vendor produces the boards to an AQL of 2 percent defectives and is willing to run a 5 percent risk (α) of having lots of this level or fewer defectives rejected. Hi-Tech considers lots of 8 percent or more defectives (LTPD) unacceptable and wants to ensure that it will accept such poor-quality lots no more than 10 percent of the time (β). A large shipment has just been delivered. What values of *n* and *c* should be selected to determine the quality of this lot?

Step by Step

SOLUTION

The parameters of the problem are AQL = 0.02, α = 0.05, LTPD = 0.08, and β = 0.10. We can use Exhibit 9A.9 to find *c* and *n*.

First, divide LTPD by AQL (0.08 ÷ 0.02 = 4). Then, find the ratio in column 2 that is equal to or just greater than that amount (4). This value is 4.057, which is associated with *c* = 4.

Finally, find the value in column 3 that is in the same row as *c* = 4 and divide that quantity by AQL to obtain *n* (1.970 ÷ 0.02 = 98.5).

The appropriate sampling plan is *c* = 4, *n* = 99. ●

OPERATING CHARACTERISTIC CURVES

While a sampling plan such as the one just described meets our requirements for the extreme values of good and bad quality, we cannot readily determine how well the plan discriminates between good and bad lots at intermediate values. For this reason, sampling plans are generally displayed graphically through the use of operating characteristic (OC) curves. These curves, which are unique for each combination of *n* and *c*, simply illustrate the probability of accepting lots with varying percentages of defectives. The procedure we have followed in

exhibit 9A.10 Operating Characteristic Curve for AQL = 0.02, $\alpha = 0.05$, LTPD = 0.08, $\beta = 0.10$

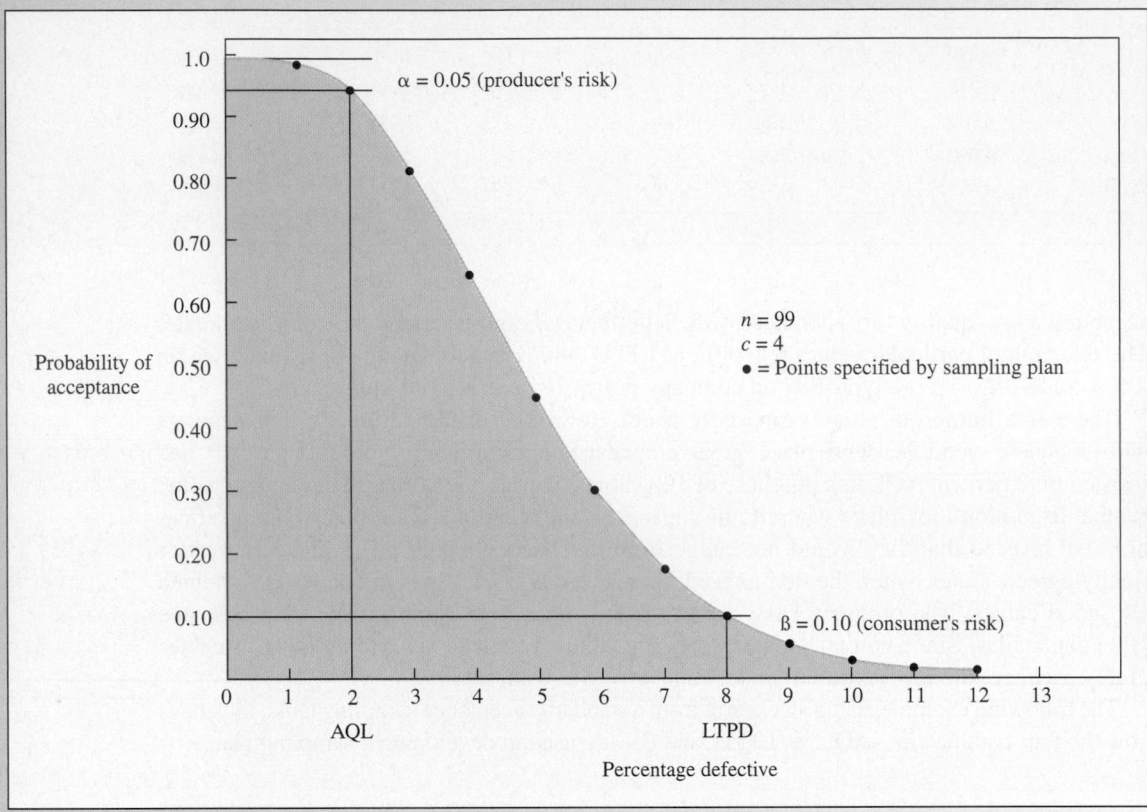

developing the plan, in fact, specifies two points on an OC curve: one point defined by AQL and $1 - \alpha$ and the other point defined by LTPD and β. Curves for common values of n and c can be computed or obtained from available tables.[3]

Shaping the OC Curve A sampling plan discriminating perfectly between good and bad lots has an infinite slope (vertical) at the selected value of AQL. In Exhibit 9A.10, any percentage defective to the left of 2 percent would always be accepted, and those to the right, always rejected. However, such a curve is possible only with complete inspection of all units and thus is not a possibility with a true sampling plan.

An OC curve should be steep in the region of most interest (between the AQL and the LTPD), which is accomplished by varying n and c. If c remains constant, increasing the sample size n causes the OC curve to be more vertical. While holding n constant, decreasing c (the maximum number of defective units) also makes the slope more vertical, moving closer to the origin.

The Effects of Lot Size The size of the lot that the sample is taken from has relatively little effect on the quality of protection. Consider, for example, that samples—all of the same size of 20 units—are taken from different lots ranging from a lot size of 200 units to a lot size of infinity. If each lot is known to have 5 percent defectives, the probability of accepting the lot based on the sample of 20 units ranges from about 0.34 to about 0.36. This means that as long as the lot size is several times the sample size, it makes little difference how large the lot is. It seems a bit difficult to accept, but statistically (on the average in the long run) whether we have a carload or box full, we'll get about the same answer. It just seems that a carload should have a larger sample size. Of course, this assumes that the lot is randomly chosen and that defects are randomly spread through the lot.

SUMMARY

Statistical quality control is a vital topic. Quality has become so important that statistical quality procedures are *expected* to be part of successful firms. Sampling plans and statistical process control are taken as given with the emphasis shifting to broader aspects (such as eliminating dockside acceptance sampling because of reliable supplier quality, and employee empowerment transforming much of the process control). World-class manufacturing companies expect people to understand the basic concepts of the material presented in this chapter.

KEY TERMS

Assignable variation Deviation in the output of a process that can be clearly identified and managed.

Common variation Deviation in the output of a process that is random and inherent in the process itself.

Upper and lower specification or tolerance limits The range of values in a measure associated with a process that are allowable given the intended use of the product or service.

Capability index (C_{pk}) The ratio of the range of values produced by a process divided by the range of values allowed by the design specification.

Statistical process control (SPC) Techniques for testing a random sample of output from a process to determine whether the process is producing items within a prescribed range.

Attributes Quality characteristics that are classified as either conforming or not conforming to specification.

Variables Quality characteristics that are measured in actual weight, volume, inches, centimeters, or other measure.

FORMULA REVIEW

Mean or average

$$\overline{X} = \sum_{i=1}^{N} x_i / N \qquad\qquad [9A.1]$$

Standard deviation

$$\sigma = \sqrt{\frac{\sum_{i=1}^{N}(x_i - \overline{X})^2}{N}} \qquad\qquad [9A.2]$$

Capability index

$$C_{pk} = \min\left[\frac{\overline{X} - \text{LTL}}{3\sigma}, \quad \frac{\text{UTL} - \overline{X}}{3\sigma}\right] \qquad\qquad [9A.3]$$

Process control charts using attribute measurements

$$\overline{p} = \frac{\text{Total number of defects from all samples}}{\text{Number of samples} \times \text{Sample size}} \qquad\qquad [9A.4]$$

$$s_p = \sqrt{\frac{\overline{p}(1 - \overline{p})}{n}} \qquad\qquad [9A.5]$$

$$\text{UCL} = \overline{p} + zs_p \qquad\qquad [9A.6]$$

$$\text{LCL} = \overline{p} - zs_p \qquad\qquad [9A.7]$$

Process control c charts

$$\overline{c} = \text{Average number of defects per unit} \qquad\qquad [9A.8]$$

$$s_p = \sqrt{\overline{c}} \qquad\qquad [9A.9]$$

$$\text{UCL} = \overline{c} + z\sqrt{\overline{c}} \qquad\qquad [9A.10]$$

$$\text{LCL} = \overline{c} - z\sqrt{\overline{c}} \quad \text{or} \quad 0 \text{ if less than } 0 \qquad\qquad [9A.11]$$

Process control $\overline{X}$ and R charts

$$\text{UCL}_{\overline{X}} = \overline{\overline{X}} + zs_{\overline{X}} \quad \text{and} \quad \text{LCL}_{\overline{X}} = \overline{\overline{X}} - zs_{\overline{X}} \qquad \text{[9A.12]}$$

$$\overline{\overline{X}} = \frac{\sum\limits_{j=1}^{m} X_j}{m} \qquad \text{[9A.13]}$$

$$\overline{R} = \frac{\sum\limits_{j=1}^{m} R_j}{m} \qquad \text{[9A.14]}$$

Upper control limit for $\overline{X} = \overline{\overline{X}} + A_2\overline{R}$ **[9A.15]**

Lower control limit for $\overline{X} = \overline{\overline{X}} - A_2\overline{R}$ **[9A.16]**

Upper control limit for $R = D_4\overline{R}$ **[9A.17]**

Lower control limit for $R = D_3\overline{R}$ **[9A.18]**

SOLVED PROBLEMS

Excel: SPC

SOLVED PROBLEM 1

Completed forms from a particular department of an insurance company were sampled daily to check the performance quality of that department. To establish a tentative norm for the department, one sample of 100 units was collected each day for 15 days, with these results:

SAMPLE	SAMPLE SIZE	NUMBER OF FORMS WITH ERRORS	SAMPLE	SAMPLE SIZE	NUMBER OF FORMS WITH ERRORS
1	100	4	9	100	4
2	100	3	10	100	2
3	100	5	11	100	7
4	100	0	12	100	2
5	100	2	13	100	1
6	100	8	14	100	3
7	100	1	15	100	1
8	100	3			

a. Develop a p chart using a 95 percent confidence interval ($1.96s_p$).
b. Plot the 15 samples collected.
c. What comments can you make about the process?

Solution

a. $\overline{p} = \dfrac{46}{15(100)} = 0.0307$

$$s_p = \sqrt{\frac{\overline{p}(1 - \overline{p})}{n}} = \sqrt{\frac{0.0307(1 - 0.0307)}{100}} = \sqrt{0.0003} = 0.017$$

$$\text{UCL} = \overline{p} + 1.96s_p = 0.031 + 1.96(0.017) = 0.064$$

$$\text{LCL} = \overline{p} - 1.96s_p = 0.031 - 1.96(0.017) = -0.00232 \text{ or zero}$$

b. The defectives are plotted below.

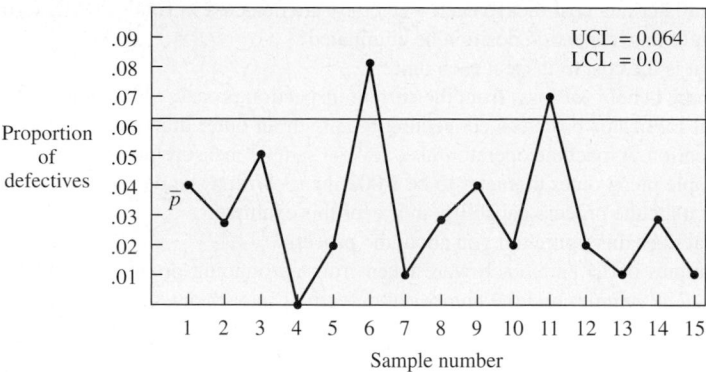

c. Of the 15 samples, 2 were out of the control limits. Because the control limits were established as 95 percent, or 1 out of 20, we would say that the process is out of control. It needs to be examined to find the cause of such widespread variation.

SOLVED PROBLEM 2

Management is trying to decide whether Part A, which is produced with a consistent 3 percent defective rate, should be inspected. If it is not inspected, the 3 percent defectives will go through a product assembly phase and have to be replaced later. If all Part A's are inspected, one-third of the defectives will be found, thus raising the quality to 2 percent defectives.

a. Should the inspection be done if the cost of inspecting is $0.01 per unit and the cost of replacing a defective in the final assembly is $4.00?

b. Suppose the cost of inspecting is $0.05 per unit rather than $0.01. Would this change your answer in *a*?

Solution

Should Part A be inspected?

0.03 defective with no inspection.

0.02 defective with inspection.

a. This problem can be solved simply by looking at the opportunity for 1 percent improvement.

Benefit = 0.01($4.00) = $0.04

Cost of inspection = $0.01

Therefore, inspect and save $0.03 per unit.

b. A cost of $0.05 per unit to inspect would be $0.01 greater than the savings, so inspection should not be performed.

REVIEW AND DISCUSSION QUESTIONS

1 The capability index allows for some drifting of the process mean. Discuss what this means in terms of product quality output.

2 Discuss the purposes of and differences between *p* charts, *c* charts and $\bar{X}$ and *R* charts.

3 In an agreement between a supplier and a customer, the supplier must ensure that all parts are within tolerance before shipment to the customer. What is the effect on the cost of quality to the customer?

4 In the situation described in Question 3, what would be the effect on the cost of quality to the supplier?

5 Discuss the trade-off between achieving a zero AQL (acceptable quality level) and a positive AQL (such as an AQL of 2 percent).

PROBLEMS

1 A company currently using an inspection process in its material receiving department is trying to install an overall cost reduction program. One possible reduction is the elimination of one inspection position. This position tests material that has a defective content on the average of 0.04. By inspecting all items, the inspector is able to remove all defects. The inspector can inspect 50 units per hour. The hourly rate including fringe benefits for this position is $9. If

the inspection position is eliminated, defects will go into product assembly and will have to be replaced later at a cost of $10 each when they are detected in final product testing.

a. Should this inspection position be eliminated?

b. What is the cost to inspect each unit?

c. Is there benefit (or loss) from the current inspection process? How much?

2 A metal fabricator produces connecting rods with an outer diameter that has a 1 ± 0.01 inch specification. A machine operator takes several sample measurements over time and determines the sample mean outer diameter to be 1.002 inches with a standard deviation of 0.003 inch.

a. Calculate the process capability index for this example.

b. What does this figure tell you about the process?

3 Ten samples of 15 parts each were taken from an ongoing process to establish a p chart for control. The samples and the number of defectives in each are shown in the following table:

SAMPLE	n	NUMBER OF DEFECTS IN SAMPLE	SAMPLE	n	NUMBER OF DEFECTS IN SAMPLE
1	15	3	6	15	2
2	15	1	7	15	0
3	15	0	8	15	3
4	15	0	9	15	1
5	15	0	10	15	0

a. Develop a p chart for 95 percent confidence (1.96 standard deviations).

b. Based on the plotted data points, what comments can you make?

4 Output from a process contains 0.02 defective unit. Defective units that go undetected into final assemblies cost $25 each to replace. An inspection process, which would detect and remove all defectives, can be established to test these units. However, the inspector, who can test 20 units per hour, is paid $8 per hour, including fringe benefits. Should an inspection station be established to test all units?

a. What is the cost to inspect each unit?

b. What is the benefit (or loss) from the inspection process?

5 There is a 3 percent error rate at a specific point in a production process. If an inspector is placed at this point, all the errors can be detected and eliminated. However, the inspector is paid $8 per hour and can inspect units in the process at the rate of 30 per hour.

If no inspector is used and defects are allowed to pass this point, there is a cost of $10 per unit to correct the defect later on.

Should an inspector be hired?

6 Resistors for electronic circuits are manufactured on a high-speed automated machine. The machine is set up to produce a large run of resistors of 1,000 ohms each.

To set up the machine and to create a control chart to be used throughout the run, 15 samples were taken with four resistors in each sample. The complete list of samples and their measured values are as follows:

SAMPLE NUMBER	READINGS (IN OHMS)			
1	1010	991	985	986
2	995	996	1009	994
3	990	1003	1015	1008
4	1015	1020	1009	998
5	1013	1019	1005	993
6	994	1001	994	1005
7	989	992	982	1020
8	1001	986	996	996
9	1006	989	1005	1007
10	992	1007	1006	979
11	996	1006	997	989
12	1019	996	991	1011
13	981	991	989	1003
14	999	993	988	984
15	1013	1002	1005	992

Develop an $\overline{X}$ chart and an R chart and plot the values. From the charts, what comments can you make about the process? (Use three-sigma control limits as in Exhibit 9A.6.)

7 In the past, Alpha Corporation has not performed incoming quality control inspections but has taken the word of its vendors. However, Alpha has been having some unsatisfactory experience recently with the quality of purchased items and wants to set up sampling plans for the receiving department to use.

For a particular component, X, Alpha has a lot tolerance percentage defective of 10 percent. Zenon Corporation, from which Alpha purchases this component, has an acceptable quality level in its production facility of 3 percent for component X. Alpha has a consumer's risk of 10 percent, and Zenon has a producer's risk of 5 percent.

a. When a shipment of Product X is received from Zenon Corporation, what sample size should the receiving department test?

b. What is the allowable number of defects in order to accept the shipment?

8 You are the newly appointed assistant administrator at a local hospital and your first project is to investigate the quality of the patient meals put out by the food-service department. You conducted a 10-day survey by submitting a simple questionnaire to the 400 patients with each meal, asking that they simply check off that the meal was either satisfactory or unsatisfactory. For simplicity in this problem, assume that the response was 1,000 returned questionnaires from the 1,200 meals each day. The results are as follows:

	NUMBER OF UNSATISFACTORY MEALS	SAMPLE SIZE
December 1	74	1,000
December 2	42	1,000
December 3	64	1,000
December 4	80	1,000
December 5	40	1,000
December 6	50	1,000
December 7	65	1,000
December 8	70	1,000
December 9	40	1,000
December 10	75	1,000
	600	10,000

a. Construct a p chart based on the questionnaire results, using a confidence interval of 95.5 percent, which is two standard deviations.

b. What comments can you make about the results of the survey?

9 Large-scale integrated (LSI) circuit chips are made in one department of an electronics firm. These chips are incorporated into analog devices that are then encased in epoxy. The yield is not particularly good for LSI manufacture, so the AQL specified by that department is 0.15 while the LTPD acceptable by the assembly department is 0.40.

a. Develop a sampling plan.

b. Explain what the sampling plan means; that is, how would you tell someone to do the test?

10 The state and local police departments are trying to analyze crime rates so they can shift their patrols from decreasing-rate areas to areas where rates are increasing. The city and county have been geographically segmented into areas containing 5,000 residences. The police recognize that not all crimes and offenses are reported: people do not want to become involved, consider the offenses too small to report, are too embarrassed to make a police report, or do not take the time, among other reasons. Every month, because of this, the police are contacting by phone a random sample of 1,000 of the 5,000 residences for data on crime. (Respondents are guaranteed anonymity.) Here are the data collected for the past 12 months for one area:

MONTH	CRIME INCIDENCE	SAMPLE SIZE	CRIME RATE
January	7	1,000	0.007
February	9	1,000	0.009
March	7	1,000	0.007
April	7	1,000	0.007

(continued)

MONTH	CRIME INCIDENCE	SAMPLE SIZE	CRIME RATE
May	7	1,000	0.007
June	9	1,000	0.009
July	7	1,000	0.007
August	10	1,000	0.010
September	8	1,000	0.008
October	11	1,000	0.011
November	10	1,000	0.010
December	8	1,000	0.008

Construct a *p* chart for 95 percent confidence (1.96) and plot each of the months. If the next three months show crime incidences in this area as

$$\text{January} = 10 \text{ (out of 1,000 sampled)}$$

$$\text{February} = 12 \text{ (out of 1,000 sampled)}$$

$$\text{March} = 11 \text{ (out of 1,000 sampled)}$$

what comments can you make regarding the crime rate?

11 Some citizens complained to city council members that there should be equal protection under the law against the occurrence of crimes. The citizens argued that this equal protection should be interpreted as indicating that high-crime areas should have more police protection than low-crime areas. Therefore, police patrols and other methods for preventing crime (such as street lighting or cleaning up abandoned areas and buildings) should be used proportionately to crime occurrence.

In a fashion similar to Problem 10, the city has been broken down into 20 geographic areas, each containing 5,000 residences. The 1,000 sampled from each area showed the following incidence of crime during the past month:

AREA	NUMBER OF CRIMES	SAMPLE SIZE	CRIME RATE
1	14	1,000	0.014
2	3	1,000	0.003
3	19	1,000	0.019
4	18	1,000	0.018
5	14	1,000	0.014
6	28	1,000	0.028
7	10	1,000	0.010
8	18	1,000	0.018
9	12	1,000	0.012
10	3	1,000	0.003
11	20	1,000	0.020
12	15	1,000	0.015
13	12	1,000	0.012
14	14	1,000	0.014
15	10	1,000	0.010
16	30	1,000	0.030
17	4	1,000	0.004
18	20	1,000	0.020
19	6	1,000	0.006
20	30	1,000	0.030
	300		

Suggest a reallocation of crime protection effort, if indicated, based on a *p* chart analysis. To be reasonably certain in your recommendation, select a 95 percent confidence level (that is, $Z = 1.96$).

12 The following table contains the measurements of the key length dimension from a fuel injector. These samples of size five were taken at one-hour intervals.

	OBSERVATIONS				
SAMPLE NUMBER	1	2	3	4	5
1	0.486	0.499	0.493	0.511	0.481
2	0.499	0.506	0.516	0.494	0.529
3	0.496	0.500	0.515	0.488	0.521
4	0.495	0.506	0.483	0.487	0.489
5	0.472	0.502	0.526	0.469	0.481
6	0.473	0.495	0.507	0.493	0.506
7	0.495	0.512	0.490	0.471	0.504
8	0.525	0.501	0.498	0.474	0.485
9	0.497	0.501	0.517	0.506	0.516
10	0.495	0.505	0.516	0.511	0.497
11	0.495	0.482	0.468	0.492	0.492
12	0.483	0.459	0.526	0.506	0.522
13	0.521	0.512	0.493	0.525	0.510
14	0.487	0.521	0.507	0.501	0.500
15	0.493	0.516	0.499	0.511	0.513
16	0.473	0.506	0.479	0.480	0.523
17	0.477	0.485	0.513	0.484	0.496
18	0.515	0.493	0.493	0.485	0.475
19	0.511	0.536	0.486	0.497	0.491
20	0.509	0.490	0.470	0.504	0.512

Construct a three-sigma $\overline{X}$ chart and R chart (use Exhibit 9A.6) for the length of the fuel injector. What can you say about this process?

13 C-Spec, Inc., is attempting to determine whether an existing machine is capable of milling an engine part that has a key specification of 4 ± 0.003 inches. After a trial run on this machine, C-Spec has determined that the machine has a sample mean of 4.001 inches with a standard deviation of 0.002 inch.

a. Calculate the C_{pk} for this machine.

b. Should C-Spec use this machine to produce this part? Why?

14 The manager of an assembly line took five samples, each with six observations, under ideal conditions to develop control limits for an X-bar chart. The mean and range of each sample is shown in the table below:

SAMPLE NUMBER	SAMPLE MEAN	SAMPLE RANGE
1	2.18	0.33
2	2.12	0.38
3	1.86	0.40
4	1.98	0.38
5	2.02	0.35

What would be the 3 standard deviation lower control limit?

15 Interpret the following control chart and determine what action, if any, is appropriate.

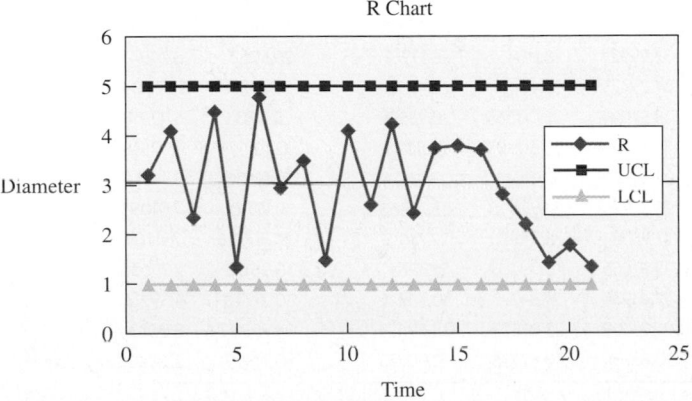

R Chart

16   Below are the X-bar and R values for five samples. If the lower control limit for the X-bar chart is 8.34, what is the sample size?

SAMPLE	$\overline{X}$ BAR	R
1	8.51	0.44
2	8.37	0.58
3	8.42	0.66
4	8.61	0.47
5	8.54	0.60

ADVANCED PROBLEM

17   Design specifications require that a key dimension on a product measure 100 ± 10 units. A process being considered for producing this product has a standard deviation of four units.
   a. What can you say (quantitatively) regarding the process capability?
   b. Suppose the process average shifts to 92. Calculate the new process capability.
   c. What can you say about the process after the shift? Approximately what percentage of the items produced will be defective?

CASE: HOT SHOT PLASTICS COMPANY

Plastic keychains are being produced in a company named Hot Shot Plastics. The plastic material is first molded and then trimmed to the required shape. The curetimes (which is the time for the plastic to cool) during the molding process affect the edge quality of the keychains produced. The aim is to achieve statistical control of the curetimes using $\overline{X}$ and R charts.

Curetime data of 25 samples, each of size four, have been taken when the process is assumed to be in control. These are shown below (note: the spreadsheet "Hot Shot Plastics.xls" has these data).

SAMPLE NO.	OBSERVATIONS				MEAN	RANGE
1	27.34667	27.50085	29.94412	28.21249	28.25103	2.59745
2	27.79695	26.15006	31.21295	31.33272	29.12317	5.18266
3	33.53255	29.32971	29.70460	31.05300	30.90497	4.20284
4	37.98409	32.26942	31.91741	29.44279	32.90343	8.54130
5	33.82722	30.32543	28.38117	33.70124	31.55877	5.44605
6	29.68356	29.56677	27.23077	34.00417	30.12132	6.77340
7	32.62640	26.32030	32.07892	36.17198	31.79940	9.85168
8	30.29575	30.52868	24.43315	26.85241	28.02750	6.09553
9	28.43856	30.48251	32.43083	30.76162	30.52838	3.99227
10	28.27790	33.94916	30.47406	28.87447	30.39390	5.67126
11	26.91885	27.66133	31.46936	29.66928	28.92971	4.55051
12	28.46547	28.29937	28.99441	31.14511	29.22609	2.84574
13	32.42677	26.10410	29.47718	37.20079	31.30221	11.09669
14	28.84273	30.51801	32.23614	30.47104	30.51698	3.39341
15	30.75136	32.99922	28.08452	26.19981	29.50873	6.79941
16	31.25754	24.29473	35.46477	28.41126	29.85708	11.17004
17	31.24921	28.57954	35.00865	31.23591	31.51833	6.42911
18	31.41554	35.80049	33.60909	27.82131	32.16161	7.97918
19	32.20230	32.02005	32.71018	29.37620	31.57718	3.33398
20	26.91603	29.77775	33.92696	33.78366	31.10110	7.01093
21	35.05322	32.93284	31.51641	27.73615	31.80966	7.31707
22	32.12483	29.32853	30.99709	31.39641	30.96172	2.79630
23	30.09172	32.43938	27.84725	30.70726	30.27140	4.59213
24	30.04835	27.23709	22.01801	28.69624	26.99992	8.03034
25	29.30273	30.83735	30.82735	31.90733	30.71869	2.60460
			Means		30.40289	5.932155

QUESTIONS

1 Prepare $\overline{X}$ and R charts using these data using the method described in the chapter.
2 Analyze the chart and comment on whether the process appears to be in control and stable.
3 Twelve additional samples of curetime data from the molding process were collected from an actual production run.

The data from these new samples are shown below. Update your control charts and compare the results with the previous data. The $\overline{X}$ and R charts are drawn with the new data using the same control limits established before. Comment on what the new charts show.

SAMPLE NO.	OBSERVATIONS				MEAN	RANGE
1	31.65830	29.78330	31.87910	33.91250	31.80830	4.12920
2	34.46430	25.18480	37.76689	39.21143	34.15686	14.02663
3	41.34268	39.54590	29.55710	32.57350	35.75480	11.78558
4	29.47310	25.37840	25.04380	24.00350	25.97470	5.46960
5	25.46710	34.85160	30.19150	31.62220	30.53310	9.38450
6	46.25184	34.71356	41.41277	44.63319	41.75284	11.53828
7	35.44750	38.83289	33.08860	31.63490	34.75097	7.19799
8	34.55143	33.86330	35.18869	42.31515	36.47964	8.45185
9	43.43549	37.36371	38.85718	39.25132	39.72693	6.07178
10	37.05298	42.47056	35.90282	38.21905	38.41135	6.56774
11	38.57292	39.06772	32.22090	33.20200	35.76589	6.84682
12	27.03050	33.63970	26.63060	42.79176	32.52314	16.16116

SUPER QUIZ

1 Variation that can be clearly identified and possibly managed.
2 Variation inherent in the process itself.
3 If a process has a capability index of 1 and is running normally (centered between the design limits), what percentage of the units would one expect to be defective?
4 An alternative to viewing an item as simply good or bad due to its falling in or out of the tolerance range.
5 Quality characteristics that are classified as either conforming or not conforming to specification.

6 Quality characteristics that are actually measured, such as the weight of an item.
7 A quality chart suitable for when an item is either good or bad.
8 A quality chart suitable for when a number of blemishes are expected on each unit, such as a spool of yarn.
9 Useful for checking quality when we periodically purchase large quantities of an item and it would be very costly to check each unit individually.
10 A chart that depicts the manufacturer's and consumer's risk associated with a sampling plan.

1. Assignable variation 2. Common variation 3. Design limits are at $\pm 3\sigma$ or 2.7 defects per thousand 4. Taguchi loss function 5. Attributes 6. Variables 7. *p*-chart 8. *c*-chart 9. Acceptance sampling 10. Operating characteristic curve

SELECTED BIBLIOGRAPHY

Evans, J. R., and W. M. Lindsay. *Managing for Quality and Performance Excellence.* 7th ed. Mason, OH: South-Western College Publications, 2007.

Juran, J. M., and F. M. Gryna. *Quality Planning and Analysis.* 2nd ed. New York: McGraw-Hill, 1980.

Rath & Strong. *Rath & Strong's Six Sigma Pocket Guide.* Rath & Strong, Inc., 2000.

Small, B. B. (with committee). *Statistical Quality Control Handbook.* Western Electric Co., Inc., 1956.

Zimmerman, S. M., and M. L. Icenogel. *Statistical Quality Control; Using Excel.* 2nd ed. Milwaukee, WI: ASQ Quality Press, 2002.

FOOTNOTES

1 E. L. Grant and R. S. Leavenworth, *Statistical Quality Control* (New York: McGraw-Hill, 1996).

2 There is some controversy surrounding AQLs. This is based on the argument that specifying some acceptable percentage of defectives is inconsistent with the philosophical goal of zero defects. In practice, even in the best QC companies, there is an acceptable quality level. The difference is that it may be stated in parts per million rather than in parts per hundred. This is the case in Motorola's Six-Sigma quality standard, which holds that no more than 3.4 defects per million parts are acceptable.

3 See, for example, H. F. Dodge and H. G. Romig, *Sampling Inspection Tables—Single and Double Sampling* (New York: John Wiley & Sons, 1959); and *Military Standard Sampling Procedures and Tables for Inspection by Attributes* (MIL-STD-105D) (Washington, DC: U.S. Government Printing Office, 1983).

chapter 10

PROJECTS

NATIONAL AERONAUTICS AND SPACE ADMINISTRATION'S CONSTELLATION PROGRAM MAY LAND MEN ON THE MOON BY 2020

It has been over 40 years since United States astronaut Neil Armstrong set foot on the Moon on July 20, 1969. Today the United States Space Exploration Policy calls "*. . . for a sustained and affordable exploration program to explore the solar system, including a return to the Moon by the end of the next decade, to establish a human presence there, and to open the path to other destinations including Mars.*"

After reading this chapter you will:

1. Explain what project management is and why it is important.
2. Identify the different ways projects can be structured.
3. Describe how projects are organized into major subprojects.
4. Understand what a project milestone is.
5. Determine the "critical path" for a project.
6. Demonstrate how to "crash," or reduce the length of, a project.

NASA's exploration activity is now in a period of transition, as the Agency works to complete the International Space Station and retire the Shuttle fleet by 2010, while developing the next generation of spacecraft to support human space flight.

To complete the goal of returning to the Moon, NASA has initiated the Constellation Program to accomplish the feat. The Constellation Program is developing and testing a set of space exploration systems that include the Orion crew exploration vehicle, the Ares I launch vehicle that is intended to propel Orion to low Earth orbit, and the Ares V, which is intended to carry a lunar lander to low Earth orbit to dock with Orion and deliver the crew and cargo to the Moon.

The implementation schedule shows the timeline for each of the major projects within the program. The Orion, Ares I, and Ares V projects

Source: NASA 2010 Budget request. http://www.nasa.gov.

Implementation Schedule

Project	Schedule by Fiscal Year		Phase Dates		
	Prior 08 09 10 11 12 13 14 15 16 17 18 19 20 21 / 22			Beg	End
Orion		Tech			
		Form		Nov-04	Feb-10
		Dev		Feb-10	Sep-15
		Ops		Oct-15	Sep-20
		Res			
Ares I Crew Launch Vehicle (under review)		Tech			
		Form		Nov-04	Dec-08
		Dev		Jan-09	Sep-15
		Ops		Oct-15	Sep-20
		Res			
Ares V Cargo Launch Vehicle (preliminary dates)		Tech			
		Form		Oct-07	Apr-13
		Dev		May-13	Apr-20
		Ops		May-20	
		Res			

Legend:
- Tech & Adv Concepts (Tech)
- Formulation (Form)
- Development (Dev)
- Operations (Ops)
- Research (Res)
- Represents a period of no activity for the Project

are each divided into major phases starting with Technology and Advanced concepts, Formulation, Development and Operations. NASA uses the techniques described in this chapter to organize the Constellation Program and to manage the projects within the program. It will be exciting to track this nearly trillion dollar program where man will once again have the opportunity to explore our galaxy for real.

> *"The high-impact project is the gem . . . the fundamental nugget . . . the fundamental atomic particle from which the new white collar world will be constructed and/or reconstructed. Projects should be, well WOW!"*
>
> —Tom Peters

Although most of the material in this chapter focuses on the technical aspects of project management (structuring project networks and calculating the critical path), as we see in the opening vignette, the management aspects are certainly equally important. Success in project management is very much an activity that requires careful control of critical resources. We spend much of the time in this book focused on the management of nonhuman resources such as machines and material; for projects, however, the key resource is often our employees' time. Human resources are often the most expensive and those people involved in the projects critical to the success of the firm are often the most valuable managers, consultants, and engineers.

At the highest levels in an organization, management often involves juggling a portfolio of projects. There are many different types of projects ranging from the development of totally new products, revisions to old products, new marketing plans, and a vast array of projects for better serving customers and reducing costs.

Most companies deal with projects individually—pushing each through the pipeline as quickly and cost-effectively as possible. Many of these same companies are very good at applying the techniques described in this chapter in a manner where the myriad of tasks are executed flawlessly, but the projects just do not deliver the expected results. Worse, what often happens is the projects consuming the most resources have the least connection to the firm's strategy.

The vital big-picture decision is what mix of projects is best for the organization. A firm should have the right mix of projects that best support a company's strategy. Projects should be selected from the following types: derivative (incremental changes such as new product

Types of Development Projects

exhibit 10.1

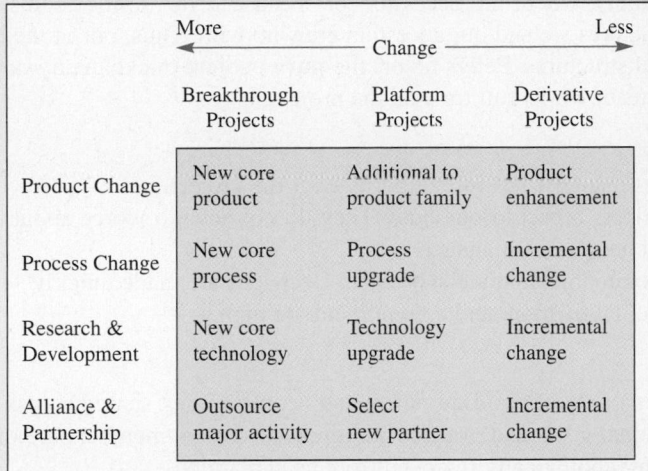

| | More ←——— Change ———→ Less | | |
	Breakthrough Projects	Platform Projects	Derivative Projects
Product Change	New core product	Additional to product family	Product enhancement
Process Change	New core process	Process upgrade	Incremental change
Research & Development	New core technology	Technology upgrade	Incremental change
Alliance & Partnership	Outsource major activity	Select new partner	Incremental change

packaging or no-frills versions), breakthrough (major changes that create entirely new markets), platform (fundamental improvements to existing products). Projects can be categorized in four major areas: product change, process change, research and development, and alliance and partnership (see Exhibit 10.1).

In this chapter we only scratch the surface in our introduction to the topic of project management. Professional project managers are individuals skilled at not only the technical aspects of calculating such things as early start and early finish time but, just as important, the people skills related to motivation. In addition, the ability to resolve conflicts as key decision points occur in the project is a critical skill. Without a doubt, leading successful projects is the best way to prove your promotability to the people who make promotion decisions. Virtually all project work is teamwork and leading a project involves leading a team. Your success at leading a project will spread quickly through the individuals on the team. As organizations flatten (through reengineering, downsizing, outsourcing), more will depend on projects and project leaders to get work done, work that previously was handled within departments.

WHAT IS PROJECT MANAGEMENT?

A **project** may be defined as a series of related jobs usually directed toward some major output and requiring a significant period of time to perform. **Project management** can be defined as planning, directing, and controlling resources (people, equipment, material) to meet the technical, cost, and time constraints of the project.

Project

Project management

Although projects are often thought to be one-time occurrences, the fact is that many projects can be repeated or transferred to other settings or products. The result will be another project output. A contractor building houses or a firm producing low-volume products such as supercomputers, locomotives, or linear accelerators can effectively consider these as projects.

STRUCTURING PROJECTS

Before the project starts, senior management must decide which of three organizational structures will be used to tie the project to the parent firm: pure project, functional project, or matrix project. We next discuss the strengths and weaknesses of the three main forms.

PURE PROJECT

Pure project

Tom Peters predicts that most of the world's work will be "brainwork," done in semipermanent networks of small project-oriented teams, each one an autonomous, entrepreneurial center of opportunity, where the necessity for speed and flexibility dooms the hierarchical management structures we and our ancestors grew up with. Thus, out of the three basic project organizational structures, Peters favors the **pure project** (nicknamed *skunkworks*), where a self-contained team works full time on the project.

ADVANTAGES
- The project manager has full authority over the project.
- Team members report to one boss. They do not have to worry about dividing loyalty with a functional-area manager.
- Lines of communication are shortened. Decisions are made quickly.
- Team pride, motivation, and commitment are high.

DISADVANTAGES
- Duplication of resources. Equipment and people are not shared across projects.
- Organizational goals and policies are ignored, as team members are often both physically and psychologically removed from headquarters.
- The organization falls behind in its knowledge of new technology due to weakened functional divisions.
- Because team members have no functional area home, they worry about life-after-project, and project termination is delayed.

FUNCTIONAL PROJECT

Functional project

At the other end of the project organization spectrum is the **functional project**, housing the project within a functional division.

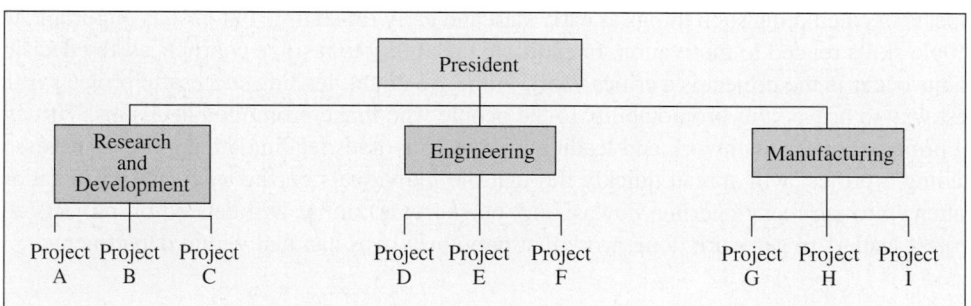

ADVANTAGES
- A team member can work on several projects.
- Technical expertise is maintained within the functional area even if individuals leave the project or organization.
- The functional area is a home after the project is completed. Functional specialists can advance vertically.
- A critical mass of specialized functional-area experts creates synergystic solutions to a project's technical problems.

DISADVANTAGES
- Aspects of the project that are not directly related to the functional area get short-changed.
- Motivation of team members is often weak.
- Needs of the client are secondary and are responded to slowly.

MATRIX PROJECT

Matrix project

The classic specialized organizational form, "the **matrix project**," attempts to blend properties of functional and pure project structures. Each project utilizes people from different functional areas. The project manager (PM) decides what tasks and when they will be

THE WORLD'S BIGGEST CONSTRUCTION PROJECTS

Think redoing your kitchen is a headache? Imagine supervising one of these megaprojects.

SOUTH-TO-NORTH WATER TRANSFER PROJECT, CHINA

Who's building it: the Chinese government.
Budget: $62 billion (445 billion yuan).
Estimated completion date: 2050.
What it takes: 400,000 relocated citizens and a very thirsty northern China. Economic development in the North China Plain is booming, but its water supplies are falling short, far short. Desperate farming communities are digging wells as deep as 600 feet to find clean water, but the Chinese government has much more digging in mind. Drawing on an unimplemented proposal from Mao himself, the Communist Party has decided to divert water from the Yangtze—a southern river known for its rising tides—to the dry rivers of the north. If it is completed, 12 trillion gallons of water will flow northward yearly through three man-made channels whose combined construction is expected to displace almost 400,000 people. Construction is well under way for the east and central canals, but environmental concerns have kept the western route at the planning stage. The project's $62 billion price tag also makes the South-to-North project by far the most expensive construction project ever in China. But having finished the Three Gorges Dam—a $25 billion project that has forced the relocation of more than 1 million people—China is no stranger to pricey megaprojects.

PANAMA CANAL EXPANSION

Who's building it: the Panamanian government.
Budget: $5.2 billion.
Estimated completion date: 2014.
What it takes: 123 million cubic meters of excavated material and 3,000 ships that just don't fit. Once a marvel of engineering, today's Panama Canal is too narrow to fit 92 percent of the world's shipping fleet through its passage. More than a quarter of the goods that are transported through its locks are carried on Panamax-size vessels—ships that are the maximum size that can fit through the canal. But in a project that broke ground—or canal bed—in the fall of 2007, the Panama Canal will soon be equipped with the world's biggest locks, capable of handling most shipping vessels that are over Panamax size. Also, by adding a wider, deeper, and longer third lock lane to the existing two, the project will more than double the canal's current effective capacity of 15,000 transits per year.

CRYSTAL ISLAND, MOSCOW

Who's building it: Shalva Chigirinsky, oil and real estate mogul.
Budget: $4 billion (98 billion rubles).
Estimated completion date: 2014.
What it takes: 27 million square feet of floor space in the middle of the Moscow River and an eye for the extreme. In a city booming with petro-wealth projects, Crystal Island—designed to be the largest building in the world—is sure to grab most of the attention. Planned as a "city in microcosm," this tentlike structure of steel and glass will, if completed, stand at almost 1,500 feet and house 900 apartments, 3,000 hotel rooms, shopping spaces, offices, an international school for 500 students, a major sports complex, an IMAX theater, and a system of solar panels, wind turbines, and naturally insulating winter gardens designed for energy efficiency. Throw in a few onion domes, and Crystal Island could replace Moscow altogether. Filling one of the few large-scale sites left near the city's center, Crystal Island will sit on the Nagatinskaya, a large peninsula that juts into the Moscow River, less than 5 miles from the Kremlin.

SOURCE: http://www.foreignpolicy.com/

performed, but the functional managers control which people and technologies are used. If the matrix form is chosen, different projects (rows of the matrix) borrow resources from functional areas (columns). Senior management must then decide whether a weak, balanced, or strong form of a matrix is to be used. This establishes whether project managers have little, equal, or more authority than the functional managers with whom they negotiate for resources.

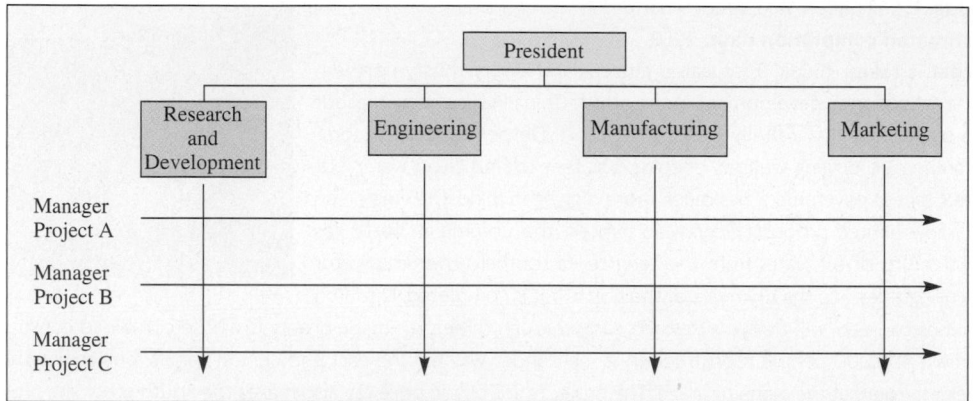

ADVANTAGES

- Communication between functional divisions is enhanced.
- A project manager is held responsible for successful completion of the project.
- Duplication of resources is minimized.
- Team members have a functional "home" after project completion, so they are less worried about life-after-project than if they were a pure project organization.
- Policies of the parent organization are followed. This increases support for the project.

DISADVANTAGES

- There are two bosses. Often the functional manager will be listened to before the project manager. After all, who can promote you or give you a raise?
- It is doomed to failure unless the PM has strong negotiating skills.
- Suboptimization is a danger, as PMs hoard resources for their own project, thus harming other projects.

Note that regardless of which of the three major organizational forms is used, the project manager is the primary contact point with the customer. Communication and flexibility are greatly enhanced because one person is responsible for successful completion of the project.

WORK BREAKDOWN STRUCTURE

A project starts out as a *statement of work* (SOW). The SOW may be a written description of the objectives to be achieved, with a brief statement of the work to be done and a proposed schedule specifying the start and completion dates. It also could contain performance measures in terms of budget and completion steps (milestones) and the written reports to be supplied.

A *task* is a further subdivision of a project. It is usually not longer than several months in duration and is performed by one group or organization. A *subtask* may be used if needed to further subdivide the project into more meaningful pieces.

A *work package* is a group of activities combined to be assignable to a single organizational unit. It still falls into the format of all project management; the package provides a description of what is to be done, when it is to be started and completed, the budget, measures of performance, and specific events to be reached at points in time. These specific events are called **project milestones**. Typical milestones might be the completion of the design, the production of a prototype, the completed testing of the prototype, and the approval of a pilot run.

Project milestone

The **work breakdown structure** (WBS) defines the hierarchy of project tasks, subtasks, and work packages. Completion of one or more work packages results in the completion of a subtask; completion of one or more subtasks results in the completion of a task; and finally, the completion of all tasks is required to complete the project. A representation of this structure is shown in Exhibit 10.2.

Work breakdown structure

Exhibit 10.3 shows the WBS for an optical scanner project. The WBS is important in organizing a project because it breaks the project down into manageable pieces. The number

An Example of a Work Breakdown Structure   **exhibit 10.2**

Work Breakdown Structure, Large Optical Scanner Design   **exhibit 10.3**

Level						
1	2	3	4			
x				1		Optical simulator design
	x			1.1		Optical design
		x		1.1.1		Telescope design/fab
		x		1.1.2		Telescope/simulator optical interface
		x		1.1.3		Simulator zoom system design
		x		1.1.4		Ancillary simulator optical component specification
	x			1.2		System performance analysis
		x		1.2.1		Overall system firmware and software control
			x	1.2.1.1		Logic flow diagram generation and analysis
			x	1.2.1.2		Basic control algorithm design
		x		1.2.2		Far beam analyzer
		x		1.2.3		System inter- and intra-alignment method design
		x		1.2.4		Data recording and reduction requirements
	x			1.3		System integration
	x			1.4		Cost analysis
		x		1.4.1		Cost/system schedule analysis
		x		1.4.2		Cost/system performance analysis
	x			1.5		Management
		x		1.5.1		System design/engineering management
		x		1.5.2		Program management
	x			1.6		Long lead item procurement
		x		1.6.1		Large optics
		x		1.6.2		Target components
		x		1.6.3		Detectors

of levels will vary depending on the project. How much detail or how many levels to use depends on the following:

- The level at which a single individual or organization can be assigned responsibility and accountability for accomplishing the work package.
- The level at which budget and cost data will be collected during the project.

There is not a single correct WBS for any project, and two different project teams might develop different WBSs for the same project. Some experts have referred to project management as an art rather than a science, because there are so many different ways that a project can be approached. Finding the correct way to organize a project depends on experience with the particular task.

Activities

Activities are defined within the context of the work breakdown structure and are pieces of work that consume time. Activities do not necessarily require the expenditure of effort by people, although they often do. For example, waiting for paint to dry may be an activity in a project. Activities are identified as part of the WBS. From our sample project in Exhibit 10.3, activities would include telescope design and fabrication (1.1.1), telescope/simulator optical interface (1.1.2), and data recording (1.2.4). Activities need to be defined in such a way that when they are all completed, the project is done.

PROJECT CONTROL CHARTS

The U.S. Department of Defense (one of the earliest large users of project management) has published a variety of helpful standard forms. Many are used directly or have been modified by firms engaged in project management. Computer programs are available to quickly generate the charts described in this section. Charts are useful because their visual presentation is easily understood. Exhibit 10.4 shows a sample of the available charts.

Gantt chart

Exhibit 10.4A is a sample Gantt chart, sometimes referred to as a *bar chart,* showing both the amount of time involved and the sequence in which activities can be performed. The chart is named after Henry L. Gantt, who won a presidential citation for his application of this type of chart to shipbuilding during World War I. In the example in Exhibit 10.4A, "long lead procurement" and "manufacturing schedules" are independent activities and can occur simultaneously. All other activities must be done in the sequence from top to bottom. Exhibit 10.4B graphs the amounts of money spent on labor, material, and overhead. Its value is its clarity in identifying sources and amounts of cost.

Exhibit 10.4C shows the percentage of the project's labor hours that comes from the various areas of manufacturing, finance, and so on. These labor hours are related to the proportion of the project's total labor cost. For example, manufacturing is responsible for 50 percent of the project's labor hours, but this 50 percent has been allocated just 40 percent of the total labor dollars charged.

The top half of Exhibit 10.4D shows the degree of completion of these projects. The dashed vertical line signifies today. Project 1, therefore, is already late because it still has work to be done. Project 2 is not being worked on temporarily, so there is a space before the projected work. Project 3 continues to be worked on without interruption. The bottom of Exhibit 10.4D compares actual total costs and projected costs. As we see, two cost overruns occurred, and the current cumulative costs are over projected cumulative costs.

Exhibit 10.4E is a milestone chart. The three milestones mark specific points in the project where checks can be made to see if the project is on time and where it should be. The best place to locate milestones is at the completion of a major activity. In this exhibit, the major activities completed were "purchase order release," "invoices received," and "material received."

Other standard reports can be used for a more detailed presentation comparing cost to progress (such as cost schedule status report—CSSR) or reports providing the basis for partial payment (such as the earned value report, which we discuss next).

Sample of Graphic Project Reports

exhibit 10.4

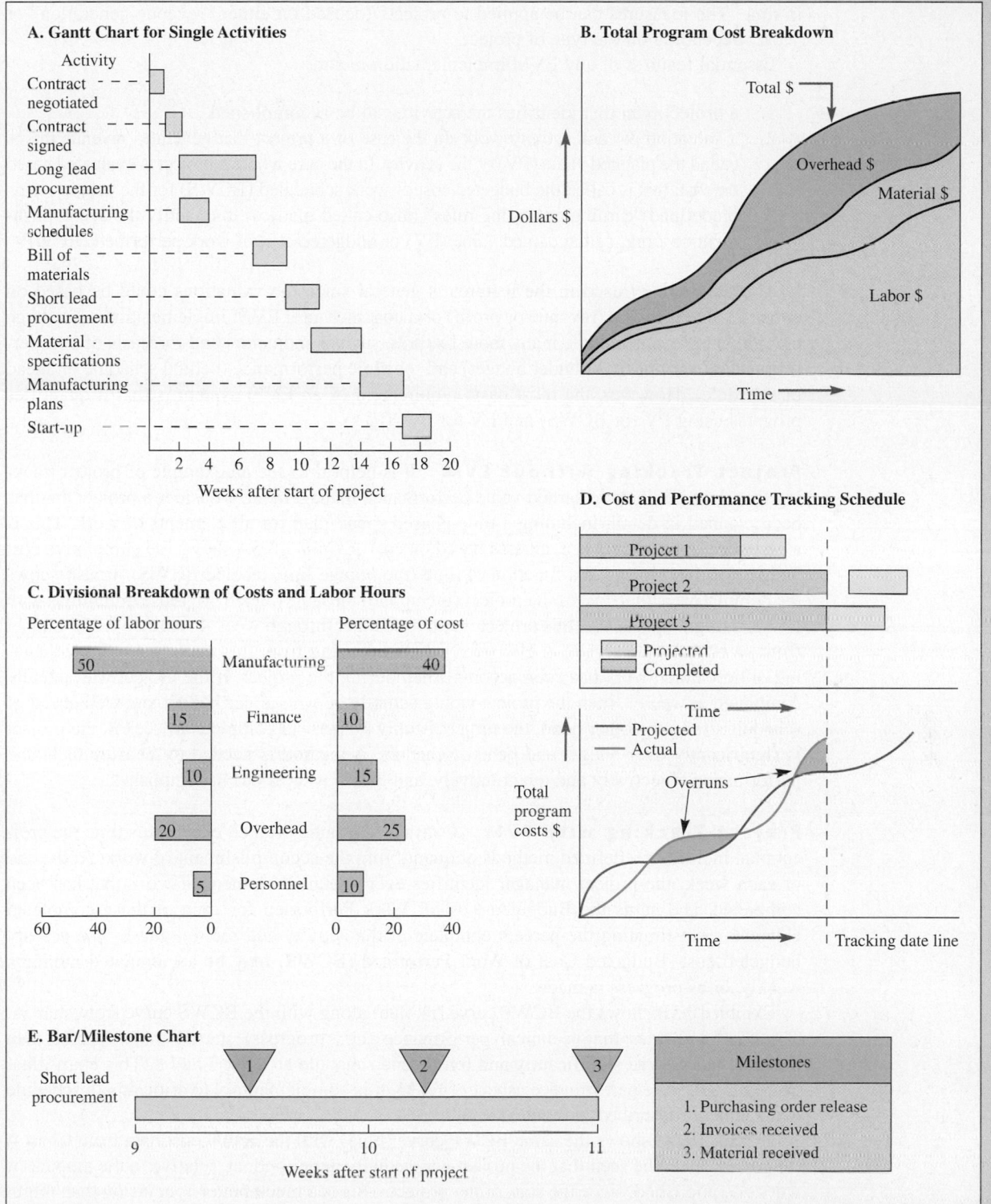

A. Gantt Chart for Single Activities

Activity
- Contract negotiated
- Contract signed
- Long lead procurement
- Manufacturing schedules
- Bill of materials
- Short lead procurement
- Material specifications
- Manufacturing plans
- Start-up

2 4 6 8 10 12 14 16 18 20
Weeks after start of project

B. Total Program Cost Breakdown

Total $
Overhead $
Material $
Labor $
Dollars $
Time →

C. Divisional Breakdown of Costs and Labor Hours

Percentage of labor hours		Percentage of cost
50	Manufacturing	40
15	Finance	10
10	Engineering	15
20	Overhead	25
5	Personnel	10

60 40 20 0   0 20 40

D. Cost and Performance Tracking Schedule

Project 1
Project 2
Project 3
- Projected
- Completed

Time →
Projected
Actual
Overruns
Total program costs $
Time →   Tracking date line

E. Bar/Milestone Chart

Short lead procurement

1   2   3

9   10   11
Weeks after start of project

Milestones
1. Purchasing order release
2. Invoices received
3. Material received

EARNED VALUE MANAGEMENT (EVM)

EVM is a technique for measuring project progress in an objective manner. EVM has the ability to combine measurements of scope, schedule, and cost in a project. When properly applied, EVM provides a method for evaluating the relative success of a project at a point in time. The measures can be applied to projects focused on either "revenue generation" or "cost" depending on the type of project.

Essential features of any EVM implementation include

1. a project plan that identifies the activities to be accomplished,
2. a valuation of each activity work. In the case of a project that generates revenue this is called the planned value (PV) of the activity. In the case where a project is evaluated based on cost, this is called the budgeted cost of work scheduled (BCWS) for the activity, and
3. predefined "earning or costing rules" (also called metrics) to quantify the accomplishment of work, called earned value (EV) or budgeted cost of work performed (BCWP).

The terminology used in the features is general since the valuations could be based on either a value measure (revenue or profit) or a cost measure. EVM implementations for large or complex projects include many more features, such as indicators and forecasts of cost performance (over budget or under budget) and schedule performance (behind schedule or ahead of schedule). However, the most basic requirement of an EVM system is that it quantifies progress using PV (or BCWS) and EV (or BCWP).

Project Tracking without EVM   It is helpful to see an example of project tracking that does not include earned value performance management. Consider a project that has been planned in detail, including a time-phased spend plan for all elements of work. This is a case where the project is evaluated based on cost. Exhibit 10.5A shows the cumulative cost budget for this project as a function of time (the orange line, labeled BCWS). It also shows the cumulative actual cost of the project (green line) through week 8. To those unfamiliar with EVM, it might appear that this project was over budget through week 4 and then under budget from week 6 through week 8. However, what is missing from this chart is any understanding of how much work has been accomplished during the project. If the project was actually completed at week 8, then the project would actually be well under budget and well ahead of schedule. If, on the other hand, the project is only 10 percent complete at week 8, the project is significantly over budget and behind schedule. A method is needed to measure technical performance objectively and quantitatively, and that is what EVM accomplishes.

Project Tracking with EVM   Consider the same project, except this time the project plan includes predefined methods of quantifying the accomplishment of work. At the end of each week, the project manager identifies every detailed element of work that has been completed, and sums the Budgeted Cost of Work Performed for each of these completed elements by estimating the percent complete of the activity and multiplying by the activity budgeted cost. Budgeted Cost of Work Performed (BCWP) may be accumulated monthly, weekly, or as progress is made.

Exhibit 10.5B shows the BCWP curve (in blue) along with the BCWS curve from chart A. The chart indicates that technical performance (i.e., progress) started more rapidly than planned, but slowed significantly and fell behind schedule at week 7 and 8. This chart illustrates the schedule performance aspect of EVM. It is complementary to critical path schedule management (described in the next section).

Exhibit 10.5C shows the same BCWP curve (blue) with the actual cost data from Chart A (in green). It can be seen that the project was actually under budget, relative to the amount of work accomplished, since the start of the project. This is a much better conclusion than might be derived from Chart A.

Exhibit 10.5D shows all three curves together—which is a typical EVM line chart. The best way to read these three-line charts is to identify the BCWS curve first, then compare it to BCWP (for schedule performance) and AC (for cost performance). It can be seen from this illustration that a true understanding of cost performance and schedule performance *relies first on measuring technical performance objectively*. This is the *foundational principle* of EVM.

Earned Value Management Charts

exhibit 10.5

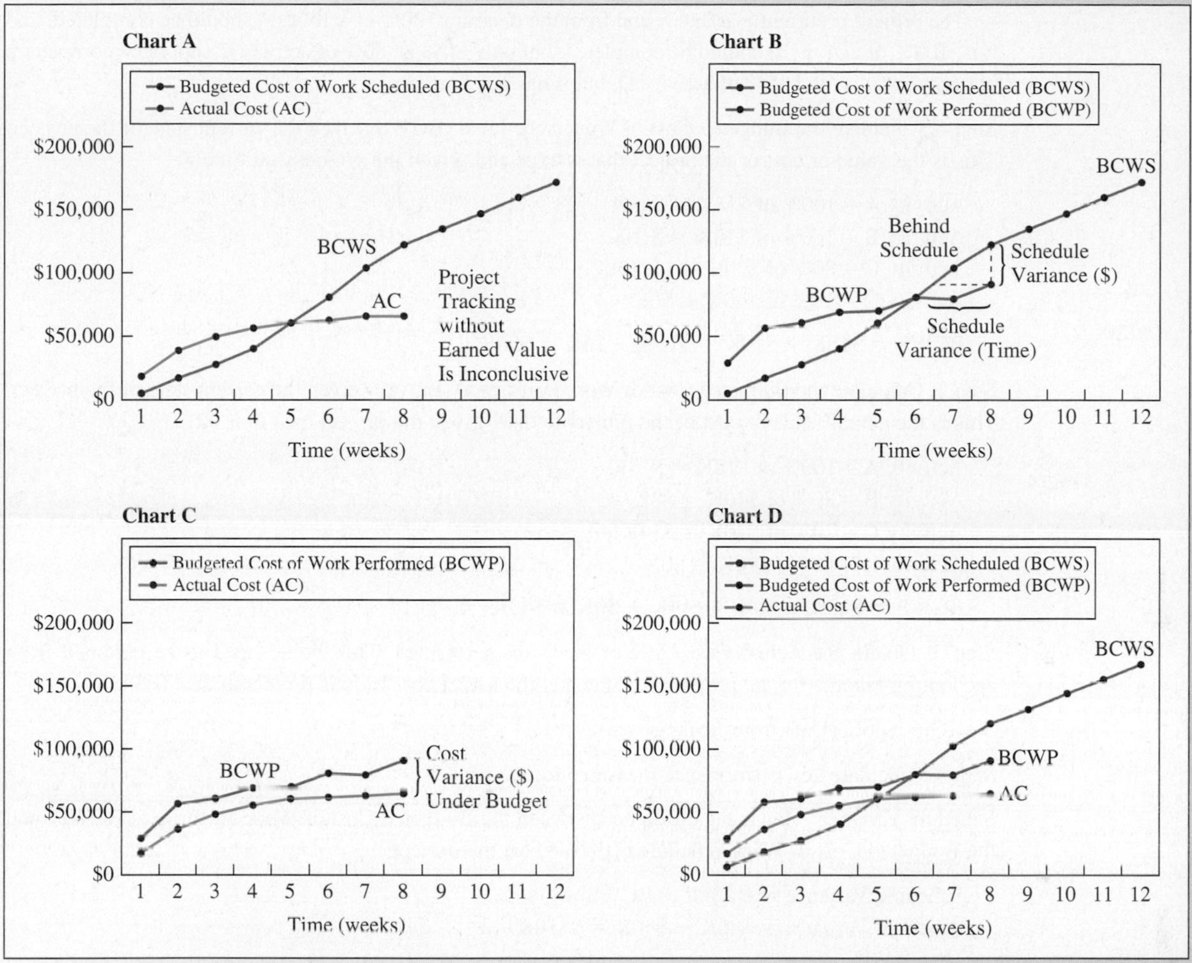

Chart A

Budgeted Cost of Work Scheduled (BCWS)
Actual Cost (AC)

BCWS

AC

Project
Tracking
without
Earned Value
Is Inconclusive

Time (weeks)

Chart B

Budgeted Cost of Work Scheduled (BCWS)
Budgeted Cost of Work Performed (BCWP)

BCWS

Behind
Schedule

Schedule
Variance ($)

BCWP

Schedule
Variance (Time)

Time (weeks)

Chart C

Budgeted Cost of Work Performed (BCWP)
Actual Cost (AC)

BCWP

Cost
Variance ($)
Under Budget

AC

Time (weeks)

Chart D

Budgeted Cost of Work Scheduled (BCWS)
Budgeted Cost of Work Performed (BCWP)
Actual Cost (AC)

BCWS

BCWP

AC

Time (weeks)

EXAMPLE 10.1: Earned Value Management

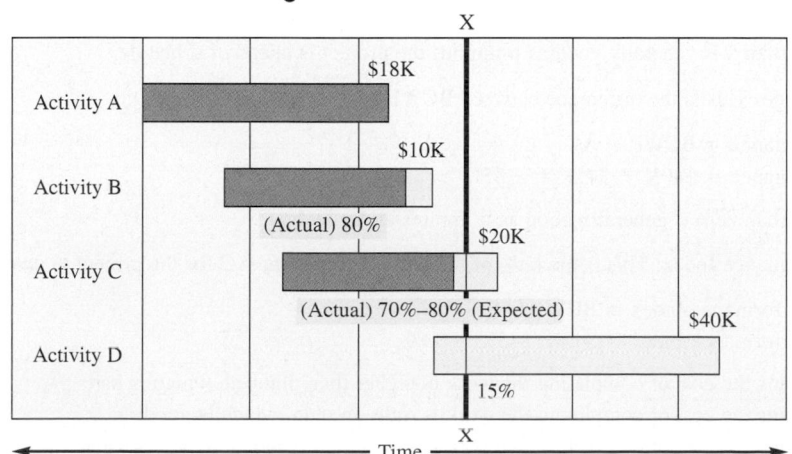

Step by Step

The figure above illustrates how to determine the Budgeted Cost of Work Scheduled by summing the dollar values (in $1,000s of the work scheduled for accomplishment at the end of period X. The Budgeted Cost of Work Performed is determined by summing the earned value for the work actually accomplished, shown in red shading.

SOLUTION

From the diagram the budgeted cost of all the project work is the following: Activity A − $18K, B − $10K, C − $20K, D − $40K. This is the cost of each activity when they are 100% completed.

The project is currently at day X and from the diagram 100% of activity A should be completed, and it is; 100% of activity B should be completed, but only 80% is; 80% of activity C should be completed, but only 70% is; and 15% of activity D, but it has not started.

Step 1: Calculate the Budgeted Cost of Work Scheduled (BCWS) given the current state of the project. This is the value or cost of the project that is expected, given the project is at time X:

Activity A − 100% of $18K = $18K
Activity B − 100% of $10K = $10K
Activity C − 80% of $20K = $16K
Activity D − 15% of $40K = $6K

BCWS = $18K + $10K + $16K + $6K = $50K

Step 2: Calculate the Budgeted Cost of Work Performed (BCWP) given the current state of the project. This is the actual value or cost of the project to date, given the project is at time X:

Activity A − 100% of $18K = $18K
Activity B − 80% of $10K = $8K
Activity C − 70% of $20K = $14K
Activity D − 0% of $40K = $0

BCWP = $18K + $8K + $14K + $0K = $40K

Step 3: Obtain the Actual Cost (AC) of the work performed. This would need to be obtained from accounting records for the project. Assume that the actual cost for this project to date is $45K.

AC = $45K (Data from Acct. System)

Step 4: Calculate key performance measures for the project:

Schedule Variance: This is the difference between the Budgeted Cost of Work Performed (BCWP) and the Budgeted Cost of Work Scheduled (BCWS) for the project:

Schedule Variance = BCWP − BCWS
Schedule Variance = $40K − $50K = 2$10K

Greater than 0 is generally good as it implies the project is ahead of schedule.

Schedule Performance Index: This is the ratio of the BCWP versus the BCWS for the project:

Schedule Performance Index = BCWP/BCWS
Schedule Performance Index = $40K/$50K = 0.8

Greater than 1 is generally good as it implies the project is ahead of schedule.

Cost Variance: This is the difference between BCWP and the Actual Cost (AC):

Cost Variance = BCWP − AC
Cost Variance = $40K − $45K = −$5K

Greater than zero is generally good as it implies under budget.

Cost Performance Index: This is the ratio of the BCWP versus the AC for the project to date:

Cost Performance Index = BCWP/AC
Cost Performance Index = $40K/$45K = 0.89

< 1 means the cost of completing the work is higher than planned, which is bad;
= 1 means the cost of completing the work is right on plan, which is good;
> 1 means the cost of completing the work is lower than planned, which is usually good.

That means the project is spending about $1.13 for every $1.00 of budgeted work accomplished. This is not very good as the project is over budget and tasks are not being completed on time or on budget. A Schedule Performance Index and a Cost Performance Index greater than one are desirable. ●

NETWORK-PLANNING MODELS

The two best-known network-planning models were developed in the 1950s. The Critical Path Method (CPM) was developed for scheduling maintenance shutdowns at chemical processing plants owned by Du Pont. Since maintenance projects are performed often in this industry, reasonably accurate time estimates for activities are available. CPM is based on the assumptions that project activity times can be estimated accurately and that they do not vary. The Program Evaluation and Review Technique (PERT) was developed for the U.S. Navy's Polaris missile project. This was a massive project involving over 3,000 contractors. Because most of the activities had never been done before, PERT was developed to handle uncertain time estimates. As years passed, features that distinguished CPM from PERT have diminished, so in our treatment here we just use the term CPM.

NEW ZEALAND'S TE APITI WIND FARM PROJECT CONSTRUCTED THE LARGEST WIND FARM IN THE SOUTHERN HEMISPHERE, WITHIN ONE YEAR FROM COMMISSION TO COMPLETION, ON-TIME AND WITHIN BUDGET. EMPLOYING EFFECTIVE PROJECT MANAGEMENT AND USING THE CORRECT TOOLS AND TECHNIQUES, THE MERIDIAN ENERGY COMPANY PROVIDED A VIABLE OPTION FOR RENEWABLE ENERGY IN NEW ZEALAND, AND ACTS AS BENCHMARK FOR LATER WIND FARM PROJECTS.

In a sense, the CPM techniques illustrated here owe their development to the widely used predecessor, the Gantt chart. Although the Gantt chart is able to relate activities to time in a usable fashion for small projects, the interrelationship of activities, when displayed in this form, becomes extremely difficult to visualize and to work with for projects that include more than 25 activities. Also, the Gantt chart provides no direct procedure for determining more than 25 activities, nor does the Gantt chart provide any direct procedure for determining the critical path, which is of great practical value to identify.

The **critical path** of activities in a project is the sequence of activities that form the longest chain in terms of their time to complete. If any one of the activities in the critical path is delayed, then the entire project is delayed. It is possible and it often happens that there are multiple paths of the same length through the network so there are multiple critical paths. Determining scheduling information about each activity in the project is the major goal of CPM techniques. The techniques calculate when an activity must start and end, together with whether the activity is part of the critical path.

Critical path

CRITICAL PATH METHOD (CPM)

Here is a procedure for scheduling a project. In this case, a single time estimate is used because we are assuming that the activity times are known. A very simple project will be scheduled to demonstrate the basic approach.

Consider that you have a group assignment that requires a decision on whether you should invest in a company. Your instructor has suggested that you perform the analysis in the following four steps:

A Select a company.

B Obtain the company's annual report and perform a ratio analysis.

C Collect technical stock price data and construct charts.

D Individually review the data and make a team decision on whether to buy the stock.

Your group of four people decides that the project can be divided into four activities as suggested by the instructor. You decide that all the team members should be involved in selecting the company and that it should take one week to complete this activity. You will meet at the end of the week to decide what company the group will consider. During this meeting you will divide your group: two people will be responsible for the annual report and ratio analysis, and the other two will collect the technical data and construct the charts. Your group expects to take two weeks to get the annual report and perform the ratio analysis, and a week to collect the stock price data and generate the charts. You agree that the two groups can work independently. Finally, you agree to meet as a team to make the purchase decision. Before you meet, you want to allow one week for each team member to review all the data.

This is a simple project, but it will serve to demonstrate the approach. The following are the appropriate steps.

1. **Identify each activity to be done in the project and estimate how long it will take to complete each activity.** This is simple, given the information from your instructor. We identify the activities as follows: A(1), B(2), C(1), D(1). The number is the expected duration of the activity.

2. **Determine the required sequence of activities and construct a network reflecting the precedence relationships.** An easy way to do this is to first identify the **immediate predecessors** associated with an activity. The immediate predecessors are the activities that need to be completed immediately before an activity. Activity A needs to be completed before activities B and C can start. B and C need to be completed before D can start. The following table reflects what we know so far:

Immediate predecessors

ACTIVITY	DESIGNATION	IMMEDIATE PREDECESSORS	TIME (WEEKS)
Select company	A	None	1
Obtain annual report and perform ratio analysis	B	A	2
Collect stock price data and perform technical analysis	C	A	1
Review data and make a decision	D	B and C	1

Here is a diagram that depicts these precedence relationships:

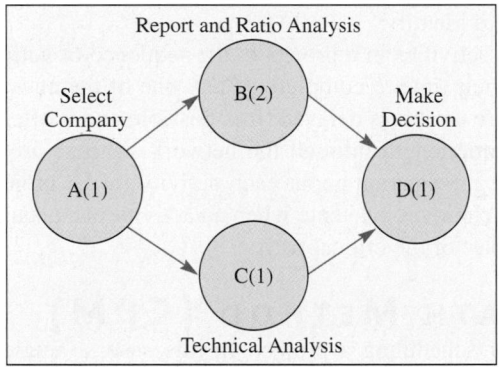

3. **Determine the critical path.** Consider each sequence of activities that runs from the beginning to the end of the project. For our simple project there are two paths: A–B–D and A–C–D. The critical path is the path where the sum of the activity times is the longest. A–B–D has a duration of four weeks and A–C–D, a duration of three weeks. The critical path, therefore, is A–B–D. If any activity along the critical path is delayed, then the entire project will be delayed.

4. **Determine the early start/finish and late start/finish schedule.** To schedule the project, find when each activity needs to start and when it needs to finish. For some activities in a project there may be some leeway in when an activity can start and finish. This is called the **slack time** in an activity. For each activity in the project, we calculate four points in time: the early start, early finish, late start, and late finish times. The early start and early finish are the earliest times that the activity can start and be finished. Similarly, the late start and late finish are the latest times the activities can start and finish. The difference between the late start time and early start time is the slack time. To help keep all of this straight, we place these numbers in special places around the nodes that represent each activity in our network diagram, as shown here.

Slack time

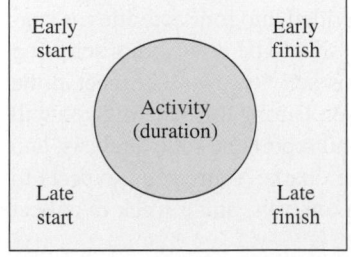

To calculate numbers, start from the beginning of the network and work to the end, calculating the early start and early finish numbers. Start counting with the current period, designated as period 0. Activity A has an early start of 0 and an early finish of 1. Activity B's early start is A's early finish, or 1. Similarly, C's early start is 1. The early finish for B is 3, and the early finish for C is 2. Now consider activity D. D cannot start until both B and C are done. Because B cannot be done until 3, D cannot start until that time. The early start for D, therefore, is 3, and the early finish is 4. Our diagram now looks like this.

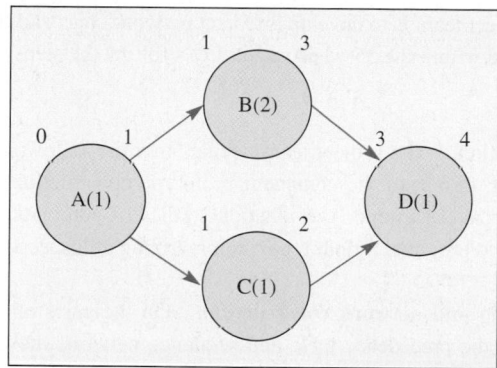

To calculate the late finish and late start times, start from the end of the network and work toward the front. Consider activity D. The earliest that it can be done is at time 4; and if we do not want to delay the completion of the project, the late finish needs to be set to 4. With a duration of 1, the latest that D can start is 3. Now consider activity C. C must be done by time 3 so that D can start, so C's late finish time is 3 and its late start time is 2. Notice the difference between the early and late start and finish times: This activity has one week of slack time. Activity B must be done by time 3 so that D can start, so its late finish time is 3 and late start time is 1. There is no slack in B. Finally, activity A must be done so that B and C can start. Because B must start earlier than C, and A must get done in time for B to start, the late finish time for A is 1. Finally, the late start time for A is 0. Notice there is no slack in activities A, B, and D. The final network looks like this. (Hopefully the stock your investment team has chosen is a winner!)

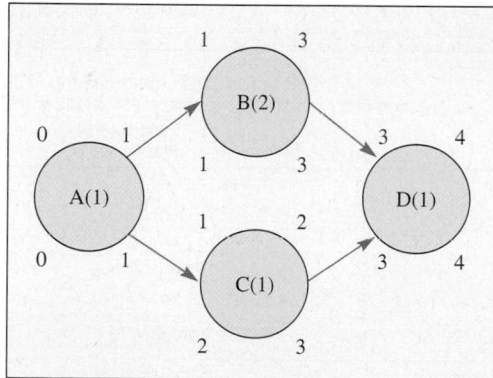

EXAMPLE 10.2: Critical Path Method

Many firms that have tried to enter the notebook computer market have failed. Suppose your firm believes that there is a big demand in this market because existing products have not been designed correctly. They are too heavy, too large, or too small to have standard-size keyboards. Your intended computer will be small enough to carry inside a jacket pocket if need be. The ideal size will be no larger than 5 inches × 9½ inches × 1 inch with a folding keyboard. It should weigh no more than 15 ounces and have an LCD display, a micro disk drive, and a wireless connection. This should appeal to traveling businesspeople, but it could have a much wider market, including students. It should be priced in the $175–$200 range.

Excel: Project Management

Step by Step

The project, then, is to design, develop, and produce a prototype of this small computer. In the rapidly changing computer industry, it is crucial to hit the market with a product of this sort in less than a year. Therefore, the project team has been allowed approximately eight months (35 weeks) to produce the prototype.

SOLUTION

The first charge of the project team is to develop a project network chart and determine if the prototype computer can be completed within the 35-week target. Let's follow the steps in the development of the network.

1. **Activity identification.** The project team decides that the following activities are the major components of the project: design of the computer, prototype construction, prototype testing, methods specification (summarized in a report), evaluation studies of automatic assembly equipment, an assembly equipment study report, and a final report summarizing all aspects of the design, equipment, and methods.

2. **Activity sequencing and network construction.** On the basis of discussion with staff, the project manager develops the precedence table and sequence network shown in Exhibit 10.6. When constructing a network, take care to ensure that the activities are in the proper order and that the logic of their relationships is maintained. For example, it would be illogical to have a situation where Event A precedes Event B, B precedes C, and C precedes A.

3. **Determine the critical path.** The critical path is the longest sequence of connected activities through the network and is defined as the path with zero slack time. This network has four different paths: A–C–F–G, A–C–E–G, A–B–D–F–G, and A–B–D–E–G. The lengths of these paths are 38, 35, 38, and 35 weeks. Note that this project has two different critical paths; this might indicate that this would be a fairly difficult project to manage. Calculating the early start and late start schedules gives additional insight into how difficult this project might be to complete on time. ●

---

exhibit 10.6   CPM Network for Computer Design Project

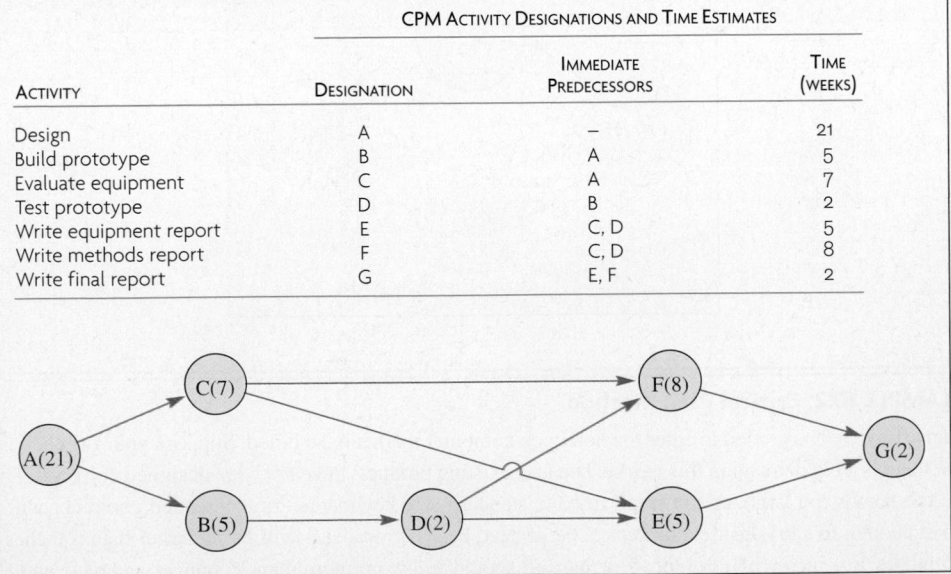

CPM ACTIVITY DESIGNATIONS AND TIME ESTIMATES

ACTIVITY	DESIGNATION	IMMEDIATE PREDECESSORS	TIME (WEEKS)
Design	A	–	21
Build prototype	B	A	5
Evaluate equipment	C	A	7
Test prototype	D	B	2
Write equipment report	E	C, D	5
Write methods report	F	C, D	8
Write final report	G	E, F	2

CPM Network for Computer Design Project

exhibit 10.7

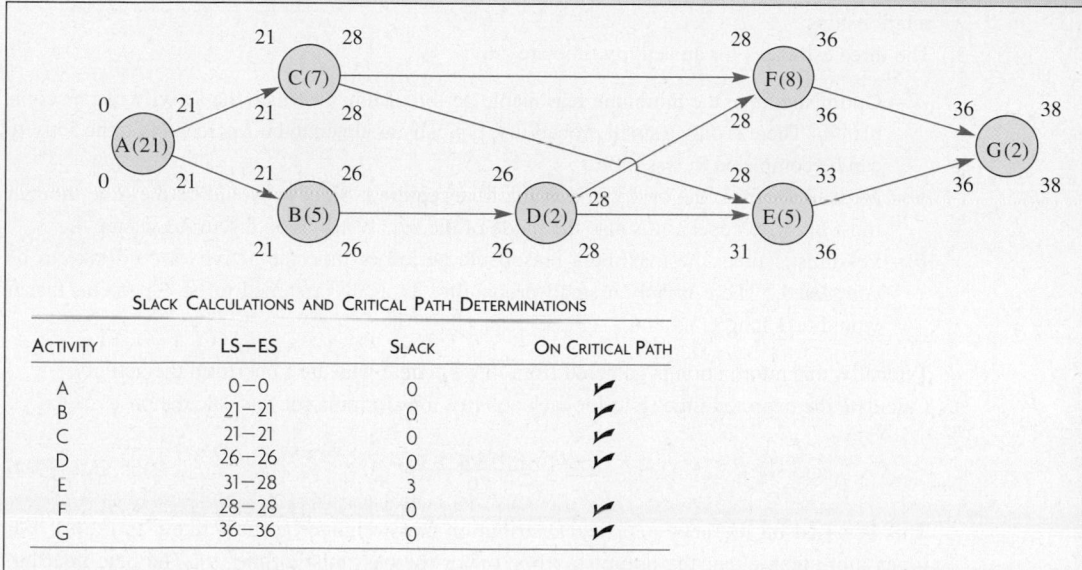

		SLACK CALCULATIONS AND CRITICAL PATH DETERMINATIONS	
ACTIVITY	LS−ES	SLACK	ON CRITICAL PATH
A	0−0	0	✔
B	21−21	0	✔
C	21−21	0	✔
D	26−26	0	✔
E	31−28	3	
F	28−28	0	✔
G	36−36	0	✔

Early Start and Late Start Schedules An early start schedule is one that lists all of the activities by their early start times. For activities not on the critical path, there is slack time between the completion of each activity and the start of the next activity. The early start schedule completes the project and all its activities as soon as possible.

Early start schedule

A late start schedule lists the activities to start as late as possible without delaying the completion date of the project. One motivation for using a late start schedule is that savings are realized by postponing purchases of materials, the use of labor, and other costs until necessary. These calculations are shown in Exhibit 10.7. From this we see that the only activity that has slack is activity E. This certainly would be a fairly difficult project to complete on time.

Late start schedule

CPM WITH THREE ACTIVITY TIME ESTIMATES

If a single estimate of the time required to complete an activity is not reliable, the best procedure is to use three time estimates. These three times not only allow us to estimate the activity time but also let us obtain a probability estimate for completion time for the entire network. Briefly, the procedure is as follows: The estimated activity time is calculated using a weighted average of a minimum, maximum, and most likely time estimate. The expected completion time of the network is computed using the procedure described above. Using estimates of variability for the activities on the critical path, the probability of completing the project by particular times can be estimated. (Note that the probability calculations are a distinguishing feature of the classic PERT approach.)

EXAMPLE 10.3: Three Time Estimates

We use the same information as in Example 10.2 with the exception that activities have three time estimates.

Step by Step

SOLUTION

1. Identify each activity to be done in the project.
2. Determine the sequence of activities and construct a network reflecting the precedence relationships.
3. The three estimates for an activity time are

   a = Optimistic time: the minimum reasonable period of time in which the activity can be completed. (There is only a small probability, typically assumed to be 1 percent, that the activity can be completed in less time.)

   m = Most likely time: the best guess of the time required. Since m would be the time thought most likely to appear, it is also the mode of the beta distribution discussed in step 4.

   b = Pessimistic time: the maximum reasonable period of time the activity would take to be completed. (There is only a small probability, typically assumed to be 1 percent, that it would take longer.)

   Typically, this information is gathered from those people who are to perform the activity.
4. Calculate the expected time (ET) for each activity. The formula for this calculation is

$$ET = \frac{a + 4m + b}{6} \qquad [10.1]$$

   This is based on the beta statistical distribution and weights the most likely time (m) four times more than either the optimistic time (a) or the pessimistic time (b). The beta distribution is extremely flexible. It can take on the variety of forms that typically arise; it has finite end points (which limit the possible activity times to the area between a and b); and, in the simplified version, it permits straightforward computation of the activity mean and standard deviation.
5. Determine the critical path. Using the expected times, a critical path is calculated in the same way as the single time case.
6. Calculate the variances (σ^2) of the activity times. Specifically, this is the variance, σ^2, associated with each ET and is computed as follows:

$$\sigma^2 = \left(\frac{b - a}{6}\right)^2 \qquad [10.2]$$

   As you can see, the variance is the square of one-sixth the difference between the two extreme time estimates. Of course, the greater this difference, the larger the variance.
7. Determine the probability of completing the project on a given date, based on the application of the standard normal distribution. A valuable feature of using three time estimates is that it enables the analyst to assess the effect of uncertainty on project completion time. (If you are not familiar with this type of analysis, see the box titled "Probability Analysis.") The mechanics of deriving this probability are as follows:

   a. Sum the variance values associated with each activity on the critical path.

   b. Substitute this figure, along with the project due date and the project expected completion time, into the Z transformation formula. This formula is

$$Z = \frac{D - T_{\mathrm{E}}}{\sqrt{\Sigma\, \sigma^2_{cp}}} \qquad [10.3]$$

   where

$$D = \text{Desired completion date for the project}$$

$$T_{\mathrm{E}} = \text{Expected completion time for the project}$$

$$\Sigma\, \sigma^2_{cp} = \text{Sum of the variances along the critical path}$$

   c. Calculate the value of Z, which is the number of standard deviations (of a standard normal distribution) that the project due date is from the expected completion time.

   d. Using the value of Z, find the probability of meeting the project due date (using a table of normal probabilities such as Appendix G). The *expected completion time* is the starting time plus the sum of the activity times on the critical path.

Activity Expected Times and Variances

exhibit 10.8

ACTIVITY	ACTIVITY DESIGNATION	TIME ESTIMATES			EXPECTED TIMES (ET) $\dfrac{a + 4m + b}{6}$	ACTIVITY VARIANCES (σ^2) $\left(\dfrac{b - a}{6}\right)^2$
		a	m	b		
Design	A	10	22	28	21	9
Build prototype	B	4	4	10	5	1
Evaluate equipment	C	4	6	14	7	$2\frac{7}{9}$
Test prototype	D	1	2	3	2	$\frac{1}{9}$
Write report	E	1	5	9	5	$1\frac{7}{9}$
Write methods report	F	7	8	9	8	$\frac{1}{9}$
Write final report	G	2	2	2	2	0

Excel: Project Management

Following the steps just outlined, we developed Exhibit 10.8 showing expected times and variances. The project network was created the same as we did previously. The only difference is that the activity times are weighted averages. We determine the critical path as before, using these values as if they were single numbers. The difference between the single time estimate and the three times (optimistic, most likely, and pessimistic) is in computing probabilities of completion. Exhibit 10.9 shows the network and critical path.

PROBABILITY ANALYSIS

The three-time-estimate approach introduces the ability to consider the probability that a project will be completed within a particular amount of time. The assumption needed to make this probability estimate is that the activity duration times are independent random variables. If this is true, the central limit theorem can be used to find the mean and the variance of the sequence of activities that form the critical path. The central limit theorem says that the sum of a group of independent, identically distributed random variables approaches a normal distribution as the number of random variables increases. In the case of project management problems, the random variables are the actual times for the activities in the project. (Recall that the time for each activity is assumed to

be independent of other activities, and to follow a beta statistical distribution.) For this the expected time to complete the critical path activities is the sum of the activity times.

Likewise, because of the assumption of activity time independence, the sum of the variances of the activities along the critical path is the variance of the expected time to complete the path. Recall that the standard deviation is equal to the square root of the variance.

To determine the actual probability of completing the critical path activities within a certain amount of time, we need to find where on our probability distribution the time falls. Appendix G shows the areas of the cumulative standard normal distribution for different values of Z. Z measures the number of standard deviations either to the right or to the left of zero in the distribution. The values correspond to the cumulative probability associated with each value of Z. For example, the first value in the table, -4.00, has a $G(z)$ equal to .00003. This means that the probability associated with a Z value of -4.0 is only .003 percent. Similarly, a Z value of 1.50 has a $G(z)$ equal to .93319 or 93.319 percent. The Z values are calculated using equation (10.3) given in Step 7b of the "Three Time Estimates" example solution. These cumulative probabilities also can be obtained by using the NORMSDIST (Z) function built into Microsoft Excel.

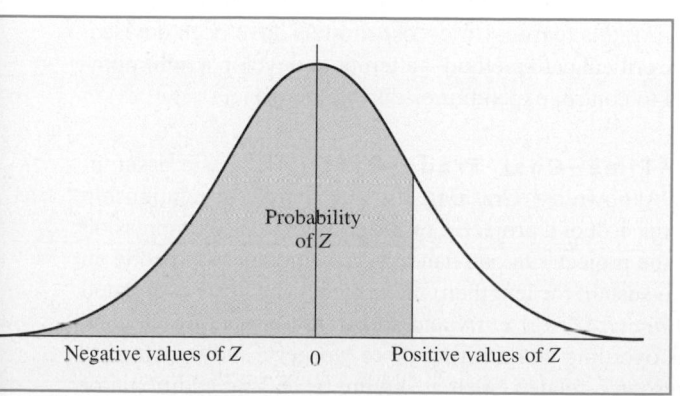

exhibit 10.9   Computer Design Project with Three Time Estimates

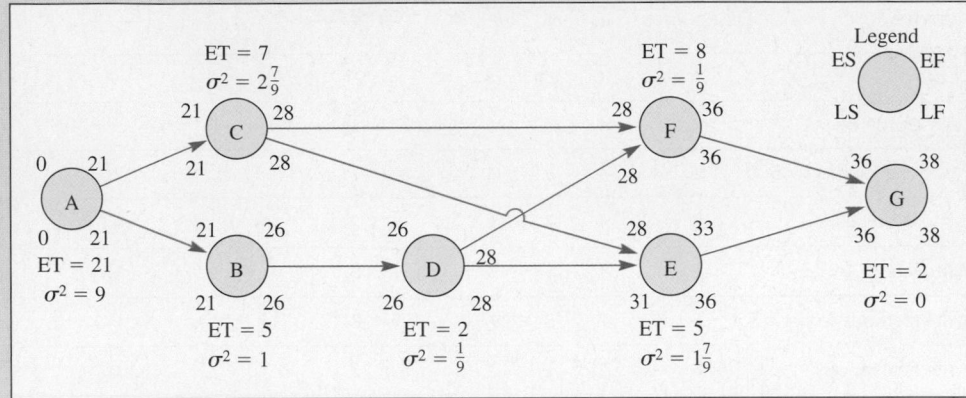

Because there are two critical paths in the network, we must decide which variances to use in arriving at the probability of meeting the project due date. A conservative approach dictates using the path with the largest total variance to focus management's attention on the activities most likely to exhibit broad variations. On this basis, the variances associated with activities A, C, F, and G would be used to find the probability of completion. Thus $\Sigma\sigma_{cp}^2 = 9 + 2\frac{7}{9} + \frac{1}{9} + 0 = 11.89$. Suppose management asks for the probability of completing the project in 35 weeks. D, then, is 35. The expected completion time was found to be 38. Substituting into the Z equation and solving, we obtain

$$Z = \frac{D - T_E}{\sqrt{\Sigma\sigma_{cp}^2}} = \frac{35 - 38}{\sqrt{11.89}} = -0.87$$

Looking at Appendix G, we see that a Z value of -0.87 yields a probability of 0.1922, which means that the project manager has only about a 19 percent chance of completing the project in 35 weeks. Note that this probability is really the probability of completing the critical path A–C–F–G. Because there is another critical path and other paths that might become critical, the probability of completing the project in 35 weeks is actually less than 0.19. ●

TIME–COST MODELS AND PROJECT CRASHING

Time–cost models

In practice, project managers are as much concerned with the cost to complete a project as with the time to complete the project. For this reason, time–cost models have been devised. These models—extensions of the basic critical path method—attempt to develop a minimum-cost schedule for an entire project and to control expenditures during the project.

Minimum-Cost Scheduling (Time–Cost Trade-Off)   The basic assumption in minimum-cost scheduling, also known as "Crashing," is that there is a relationship between activity completion time and the cost of a project. Crashing refers to the compression or shortening of the time to complete the project. On one hand, it costs money to expedite an activity; on the other, it costs money to sustain (or lengthen) the project. The costs associated with expediting activities are termed *activity direct costs* and add to the project direct cost. Some may be worker-related, such as overtime work, hiring more workers, and transferring workers from other jobs; others are resource-related, such as buying or leasing additional or more efficient equipment and drawing on additional support facilities.

reduce each of the activities by a single day. For example, for activity A, it normally costs $6 to complete in two days. It could be completed in one day at a cost of $10, a $4 increase. So we indicate the cost to expedite activity A by one day is $4. For activity B, it normally costs $9 to complete in five days. It could be completed in two days at a cost of $18. Our cost to reduce B by three days is $9, or $3 per day. For C, it normally costs $5 to complete in three days. It could be completed in one day at a cost of $9; a two-day reduction would cost $4 ($2 per day). The least expensive alternative for a one-day reduction in time is to expedite activity D at a cost of $2. Total cost for the network goes up to $28 and the project completion time is reduced to nine days.

Our next iteration starts in line three, where the goal is to reduce the project completion time to eight days. The nine-day critical path is A–B–D. We could shorten activity A by one day, B by three days, and D by one day (note D has already been reduced from three to two days). Cost to reduce each activity by one day is the same as in line two. Again, the least expensive activity to reduce is D. Reducing activity D from two to one day results in the total cost for all activities in the network going up to $30 and the project completion time coming down to eight days.

Line four is similar to line three, but now only A and B are on the critical path and can be reduced. B is reduced, which takes our cost up $3 to $33 and reduces the project completion time to seven days.

In line five (actually our fifth iteration in solving the problem), activities A, B, C, and D are all critical. D cannot be reduced, so our only options are activities A, B, and C. Note that B and C are in parallel, so it does not help to reduce B without reducing C. Our options are to reduce A alone at a cost of $4 or B and C together at a cost of $5 ($3 for B and $2 for C), so we reduce A in this iteration.

In line six, we take the B and C option that was considered in line five. Finally, in line seven, our only option is to reduce activity B. Since B and C are in parallel and we cannot reduce C, there is no value in reducing B alone. We can reduce the project completion time no further.

5. **Plot project direct, indirect, and total-cost curves and find the minimum-cost schedule.** Exhibit 10.13 shows the indirect cost plotted as a constant $10 per day for up to eight days and increasing $5 per day thereafter. The direct costs are plotted from Exhibit 10.12, and the total project cost is shown as the total of the two costs.

Summing the values for direct and indirect costs for each day yields the project total cost curve. As you can see, this curve is at its minimum with an eight-day schedule, which costs $40 ($30 direct + $10 indirect).

Plot of Costs and Minimum-Cost Schedule   **exhibit 10.13**

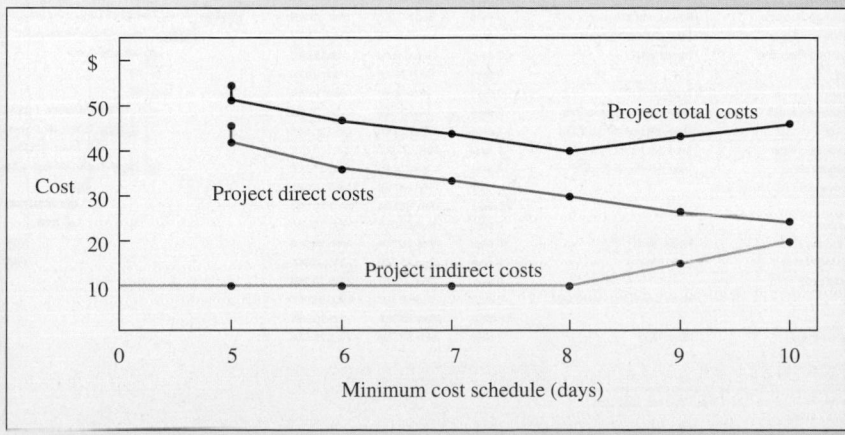

MANAGING RESOURCES

In addition to scheduling each task, we must assign resources. Modern software quickly highlights overallocations—situations in which allocations exceed resources.

To resolve overallocations manually, you can either add resources or reschedule. Moving a task within its slack can free up resources.

Mid- to high-level project management information systems (PMIS) software can resolve overallocations through a "leveling" feature. Several rules of thumb can be used. You can specify that low-priority tasks should be delayed until higher-priority ones are complete, or that the project should end before or after the original deadline.

PROJECT MANAGEMENT INFORMATION SYSTEMS

Interest in the techniques and concepts of project management has exploded in the past 10 years. This has resulted in a parallel increase in project management software offerings. Now there are over 100 companies offering project management software. For the most up-to-date information about software available, check out the Web site of the Project Management Institute (www.pmi.org). Two of the leading companies are Microsoft, with Microsoft Project, and Primavera, with Primavera Project Planner. The following is a brief review of these two programs:

The Microsoft Project program comes with an excellent online tutorial, which is one reason for its overwhelming popularity with project managers tracking midsized projects. This package is compatible with the Microsoft Office Suite, which opens all the communications and Internet integration capability that Microsoft offers. The program includes features for scheduling, allocating, and leveling resources, as well as controlling costs and producing presentation-quality graphics and reports.

Finally, for managing very large projects or programs having several projects, Primavera Project Planner is often the choice. Primavera was the first major vendor of this type of software and has possibly the most sophisticated capability.

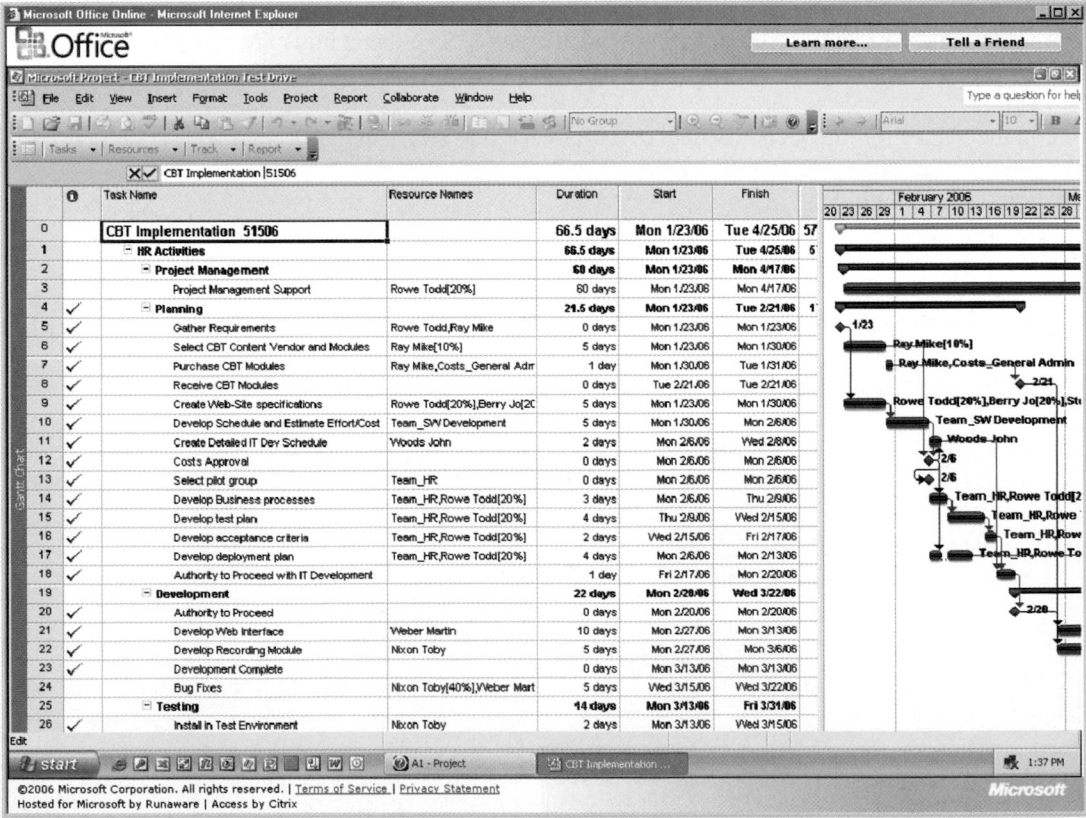

TRACKING PROGRESS

The real action starts after the project gets under way. Actual progress will differ from your original, or baseline, planned progress. Software can hold several different baseline plans, so you can compare monthly snapshots.

A *tracking Gantt chart* superimposes the current schedule onto a baseline plan so deviations are easily noticed. If you prefer, a spreadsheet view of the same information could be output. Deviations between planned start/finish and newly scheduled start/finish also appear, and a "slipping filter" can be applied to highlight or output only those tasks that are scheduled to finish at a later date than the planned baseline.

Management by exception also can be applied to find deviations between budgeted costs and actual costs. (See the box titled "Project Management Information Systems.")

SUMMARY

This chapter provides a description of the basics of managing projects. The chapter first describes how the people involved with a project are organized from a management viewpoint. The scope of the project will help define the organization. This organization spans the use of a dedicated team to a largely undedicated matrix structure. Next, the chapter considers how project activities are organized into subprojects by using the work breakdown structure. Following this, the technical details of calculating the shortest time it should take to complete a project are covered. Finally, the chapter considers how projects can be shortened through the use of "crashing" concepts.

KEY TERMS

Project A series of related jobs usually directed toward some major output and requiring a significant period of time to perform.

Project management Planning, directing, and controlling resources (people, equipment, material) to meet the technical, cost, and time constraints of a project.

Pure project A structure for organizing a project where a self-contained team works full time on the project.

Functional project A structure where team members are assigned from the functional units of the organization. The team members remain a part of their functional units and typically are not dedicated to the project.

Matrix project A structure that blends the functional and pure project structures. Each project uses people from different functional areas. A dedicated project manager decides what tasks need to be performed and when, but the functional managers control which people to use.

Project milestone A specific event in a project.

Work breakdown structure The hierarchy of project tasks, subtasks, and work packages.

Activities Pieces of work within a project that consume time. The completion of all the activities of a project marks the end of the project.

Gantt chart Shows in a graphic manner the amount of time involved and the sequence in which activities can be performed. Often referred to as a *bar chart*.

Earned value management Technique that combines measures of scope, schedule, and cost for evaluating project progress.

Critical path The sequence of activities in a project that forms the longest chain in terms of their time to complete. This path contains zero slack time. It is possible for there to be multiple critical paths in a project. Techniques used to find the critical path are called CPM or Critical Path Method techniques.

Immediate predecessor Activity that needs to be completed immediately before another activity.

Slack time The time that an activity can be delayed; the difference between the late and early start times of an activity.

Early start schedule A project schedule that lists all activities by their early start times.

Late start schedule A project schedule that lists all activities by their late start times. This schedule may create savings by postponing purchases of material and other costs associated with the project.

Time–cost models Extension of the critical path models that considers the trade off between the time required to complete an activity and cost. This is often referred to as "crashing" the project.

FORMULA REVIEW

Expected Time

$$ET = \frac{a + 4m + b}{6}$$

[10.1]

Variance (σ^2) of the activity times

$$\sigma^2 = \left(\frac{b - a}{6}\right)^2$$

[10.2]

Z transformation formula

$$Z = \frac{D - T_E}{\sqrt{\Sigma\sigma^2_{cp}}}$$

[10.3]

SOLVED PROBLEMS

SOLVED PROBLEM 1

You have been asked to calculate the Cost Performance Index for a project using Earned Value Management techniques. It is currently day 20 of the project and the following summarizes the current status of the project:

Activity	Expected Cost	Activity Duration	Expected Start Date	Expected Completion Date	Expected % Complete	Actual % Complete	Actual Cost to Date
Startup	$100,000	10 days	0	10	100%	100%	$105,000
Construction	$325,000	14 days	8	22	12/14 = 85.7%	90%	$280,000
Finishing	$50,000	12 days	18	30	2/12 = 16.7%	25%	$2,500

Calculate the Schedule Variance, Schedule Performance Index, and the Cost Performance Index for the project.

Solution

Step 1: Calculate budgeted cost of the work scheduled to date:

Startup is 100% complete and we are beyond the expected completion date, so budgeted cost is $100,000 for this activity.

Would expect Construction to be 85.7% complete and cost $278,200 to date.
Would expect Finishing to be 16.7% complete at a cost of $8,333 to date.

Budgeted cost of work scheduled = $100,000 + 278,200 + 8,333 = $386,533

Step 2: Calculate the budgeted cost of the work performed to date:

Startup is 100% complete, so budgeted cost is $100,000.
Construction is actually only 90% complete, so budget cost for this much of the activity is (325,000 × .9) = $292,500.

Finishing is now 25% complete, so budgeted cost is $(50,000 \times .25) = \$12,500$.

Budgeted cost of work performed $= 100,000 + 292,500 + 12,500 = \$405,000$

Step 3: Actual cost of the project to date is $105,000 + 280,000 + 2,500 = \$387,500$.

Step 4: Calculate performance measures:

Schedule variance $= \$405,000 - \$386,533 = \$18,467$
Schedule Performance Index $= \$405,000/\$386,533 = 1.047$
Cost Performance Index $= \$405,000/\$387,500 = 1.045$

The project looks good since it is both ahead of schedule and ahead of budgeted cost.

SOLVED PROBLEM 2

A project has been defined to contain the following list of activities, along with their required times for completion:

ACTIVITY	TIME (DAYS)	IMMEDIATE PREDECESSORS
A	1	—
B	4	A
C	3	A
D	7	A
E	6	B
F	2	C, D
G	7	E, F
H	9	()
I	4	G, H

**Excel:
PM_Solved
Problems**

  a. Draw the critical path diagram.
  b. Show the early start, early finish, late start, and late finish times.
  c. Show the critical path.
  d. What would happen if activity F was revised to take four days instead of two?

Solution

The answers to *a*, *b*, and *c* are shown in the following diagram.

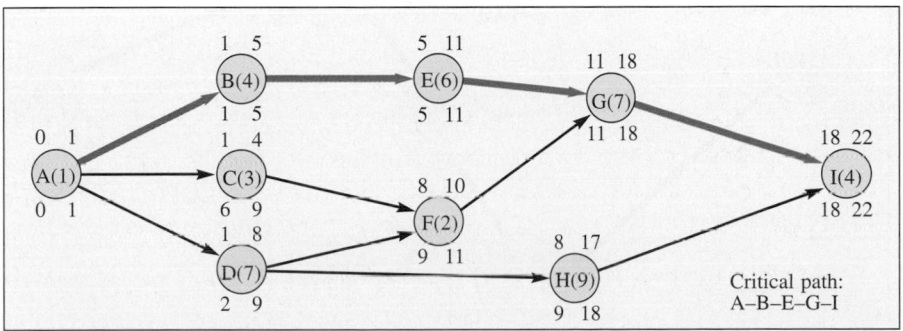

  d. New critical path: A–D–F–G–I. Time of completion is 23 days.

SOLVED PROBLEM 3

A project has been defined to contain the following activities, along with their time estimates for completion:

**Excel:
PM_Solved
Problems**

	TIME ESTIMATES (WK)			IMMEDIATE
ACTIVITY	a	m	b	PREDECESSOR
A	1	4	7	—
B	2	6	7	A
C	3	4	6	A, D
D	6	12	14	A
E	3	6	12	D
F	6	8	16	B, C
G	1	5	6	E, F

a. Calculate the expected time and the variance for each activity.
b. Draw the critical path diagram.
c. Show the early start, early finish times and late start, late finish times.
d. Show the critical path.
e. What is the probability that the project can be completed in 34 weeks?

Solution

a.

ACTIVITY	EXPECTED TIME $\dfrac{a + 4m + b}{6}$	ACTIVITY VARIANCE $\left(\dfrac{b - a}{6}\right)^2$
A	4.00	1
B	5.50	$\frac{25}{36}$
C	4.17	$\frac{1}{4}$
D	11.33	$1\frac{7}{9}$
E	6.50	$2\frac{1}{4}$
F	9.00	$2\frac{7}{9}$
G	4.50	$\frac{25}{36}$

b.

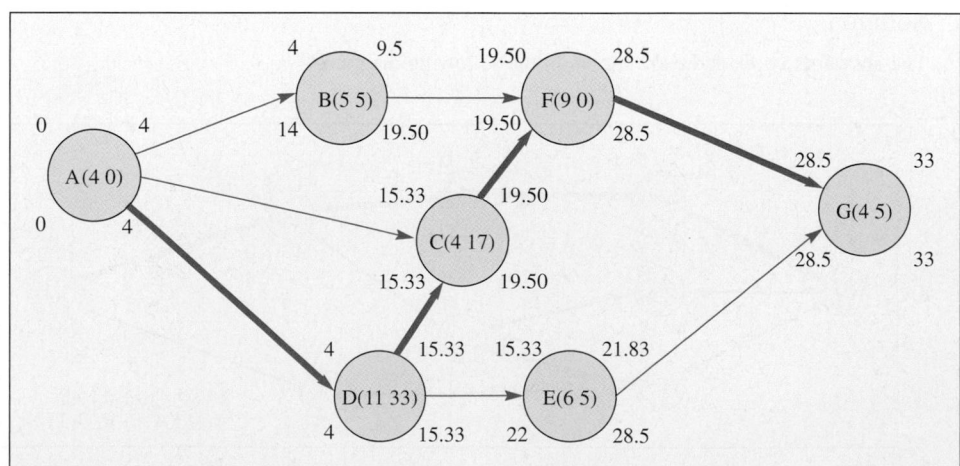

c. Shown on diagram.
d. Shown on diagram.

e. $Z = \dfrac{D - T_E}{\sqrt{\Sigma\sigma_{cp}^2}} = -\dfrac{34 - 33}{\sqrt{1 + 1\frac{7}{9} + \frac{1}{4} + 2\frac{7}{9} + \frac{25}{36}}} = \dfrac{1}{2.5495} = .3922$

Look up that value in Appendix G and we see that there is about a 65 percent chance of completing the project by that date.

SOLVED PROBLEM 4

Here are the precedence requirements, normal and crash activity times, and normal and crash costs for a construction project:

		REQUIRED TIME (WEEKS)		COST	
ACTIVITY	PRECEDING ACTIVITIES	NORMAL	CRASH	NORMAL	CRASH
A	—	4	2	$10,000	$11,000
B	A	3	2	6,000	9,000
C	A	2	1	4,000	6,000
D	B	5	3	14,000	18,000
E	B, C	1	1	9,000	9,000
F	C	3	2	7,000	8,000
G	E, F	4	2	13,000	25,000
H	D, E	4	1	11,000	18,000
I	H, G	6	5	20,000	29,000

a. What are the critical path and the estimated completion time?

b. To shorten the project by three weeks, which tasks would be shortened and what would the final total project cost be?

Solution

The construction project network is shown below:

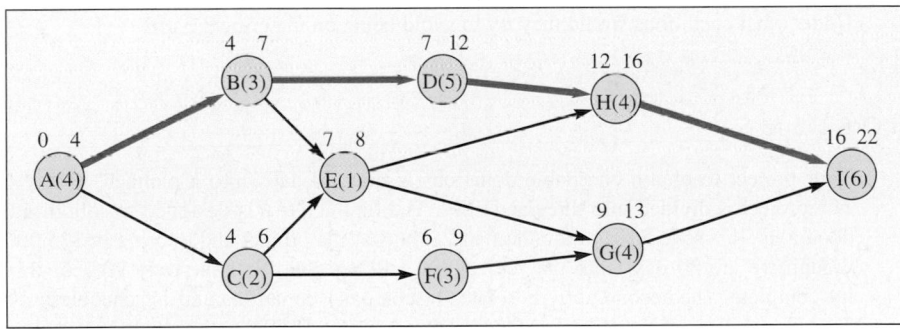

a. Critical path A–B–D–H–I.
   Normal completion time is 22 weeks.

b.

ACTIVITY	CRASH COST	NORMAL COST	NORMAL TIME	CRASH TIME	COST PER WEEK	WEEKS
A	$11,000	$10,000	4	2	$ 500	2
B	9,000	6,000	3	2	3,000	1
C	6,000	4,000	2	1	2,000	1
D	18,000	14,000	5	3	2,000	2
E	9,000	9,000	1	1		0
F	8,000	7,000	3	2	1,000	1
G	25,000	13,000	4	2	6,000	2
H	18,000	11,000	4	1	2,333	3
I	29,000	20,000	6	5	9,000	1

(1) 1st week: CP = A–B–D–H–I. Cheapest is A at $500. Critical path stays the same.
(2) 2nd week: A is still the cheapest at $500. Critical path stays the same.
(3) 3rd week: Because A is no longer available, the choices are B (at $3,000), D (at $2,000), H (at $2,333), or I (at $9,000). Therefore, choose D at $2,000.

Total project cost shortened three weeks is

A	$ 11,000
B	6,000
C	4,000
D	16,000
E	9,000
F	7,000
G	13,000
H	11,000
I	20,000
	$97,000

REVIEW AND DISCUSSION QUESTIONS

1   What was the most complex project that you have been involved in? Give examples of the following as they pertain to the project: the work breakdown structure, tasks, subtasks, and work package. Were you on the critical path? Did it have a good project manager?
2   What are some reasons project scheduling is not done well?
3   Discuss the graphic presentations in Exhibit 10.4. Are there any other graphic outputs you would like to see if you were project manager?
4   Which characteristics must a project have for critical path scheduling to be applicable? What types of projects have been subjected to critical path analysis?
5   What are the underlying assumptions of minimum-cost scheduling? Are they equally realistic?
6   "Project control should always focus on the critical path." Comment.
7   Why would subcontractors for a government project want their activities on the critical path? Under what conditions would they try to avoid being on the critical path?

PROBLEMS

1   Your project to obtain charitable donations is now 30 days into a planned 40-day project. The project is divided into three activities. The first activity is designed to solicit individual donations. It is scheduled to run the first 25 days of the project and to bring in $25,000. Even though we are 30 days into the project, we still see that we have only 90% of this activity complete. The second activity relates to company donations and is scheduled to run for 30 days starting on day 5 and extending through day 35. We estimate that even though we should have (25/30) 83% of this activity complete, it is actually only 50% complete. This part of the project was scheduled to bring in $150,000 in donations. The final activity is for matching funds. This activity is scheduled to run the last 10 days of the project and has not started. It is scheduled to bring in an additional $50,000. So far $175,000 has actually been brought in on the project.

   Calculate the schedule variance, schedule performance index, and cost (actually value in this case) performance index. How is the project going? Hint: Note that this problem is different since revenue rather than cost is the relevant measure. Use care in how the measures are interpreted.

2   A project to build a new bridge seems to be going very well since the project is well ahead of schedule and costs seem to be running very low. A major milestone has been reached where the first two activities have been totally completed and the third activity is 60% complete. The planners were only expecting to be 50% through the third activity at this time. The first activity involves prepping the site for the bridge. It was expected that this would cost $1,420,000 and it was done for only $1,300,000. The second activity was the pouring of concrete for the bridge. This was expected to cost $10,500,000 but was actually done for

$9,000,000. The third and final activity is the actual construction of the bridge superstructure. This was expected to cost a total of $8,500,000. To date they have spent $5,000,000 on the superstructure.

Calculate the schedule variance, schedule performance index, and the cost index for the project to date. How is the project going?

3   The following activities are part of a project to be scheduled using CPM:

ACTIVITY	IMMEDIATE PREDECESSOR	TIME (WEEKS)
A	——	6
B	A	3
C	A	7
D	C	2
E	B, D	4
F	D	3
G	E, F	7

a. Draw the network.
b. What is the critical path?
c. How many weeks will it take to complete the project?
d. How much slack does activity B have?

4   Schedule the following activities using CPM:

ACTIVITY	IMMEDIATE PREDECESSOR	TIME (WEEKS)
A	——	1
B	A	4
C	A	3
D	B	2
E	C, D	5
F	D	2
G	F	2
H	E, G	3

a. Draw the network.
b. What is the critical path?
c. How many weeks will it take to complete the project?
d. Which activities have slack, and how much?

5   The R&D department is planning to bid on a large project for the development of a new communication system for commercial planes. The accompanying table shows the activities, times, and sequences required:

ACTIVITY	IMMEDIATE PREDECESSOR	TIME (WEEKS)
A	—	3
B	A	2
C	A	4
D	A	4
E	B	6
F	C, D	6
G	D, F	2
H	D	3
I	E, G, H	3

a. Draw the network diagram.
b. What is the critical path?
c. Suppose you want to shorten the completion time as much as possible, and you have the option of shortening any or all of B, C, D, and G each one week. Which would you shorten?
d. What is the new critical path and earliest completion time?

6   The following represents a project that should be scheduled using CPM:

		TIMES (DAYS)		
ACTIVITY	IMMEDIATE PREDECESSORS	*a*	*m*	*b*
A	—	1	3	5
B	—	1	2	3
C	A	1	2	3
D	A	2	3	4
E	B	3	4	11
F	C, D	3	4	5
G	D, E	1	4	6
H	F, G	2	4	5

   a. Draw the network.
   b. What is the critical path?
   c. What is the expected project completion time?
   d. What is the probability of completing this project within 16 days?

7   There is an 82% chance the project below can be completed in *X* weeks or less. What is *X*?

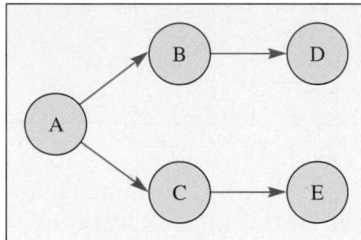

ACTIVITY	MOST OPTIMISTIC	MOST LIKELY	MOST PESSIMISTIC
A	2	5	11
B	3	3	3
C	1	3	5
D	6	8	10
E	4	7	10

8   The following table represents a plan for a project:

		TIMES (DAYS)		
JOB NO.	PREDECESSOR JOB(S)	*a*	*m*	*b*
1	—	2	3	4
2	1	1	2	3
3	1	4	5	12
4	1	3	4	11
5	2	1	3	5
6	3	1	2	3
7	4	1	8	9
8	5, 6	2	4	6
9	8	2	4	12
10	7	3	4	5
11	9, 10	5	7	8

   a. Construct the appropriate network diagram.
   b. Indicate the critical path.
   c. What is the expected completion time for the project?
   d. You can accomplish any one of the following at an additional cost of $1,500:
       (1) Reduce job 5 by two days.
       (2) Reduce job 3 by two days.
       (3) Reduce job 7 by two days.
       If you will save $1,000 for each day that the earliest completion time is reduced, which action, if any, would you choose?
   e. What is the probability that the project will take more than 30 days to complete?

9   A construction project is broken down into the following 10 activities:

ACTIVITY	IMMEDIATE PREDECESSOR	TIME (WEEKS)
1	—	4
2	1	2
3	1	4
4	1	3
5	2, 3	5
6	3	6
7	4	2
8	5	3
9	6, 7	5
10	8, 9	7

a. Draw the network diagram.

b. Find the critical path.

c. If activities 1 and 10 cannot be shortened, but activities 2 through 9 can be shortened to a minimum of one week each at a cost of $10,000 per week, which activities would you shorten to cut the project by four weeks?

10   Here is a CPM network with activity times in weeks:

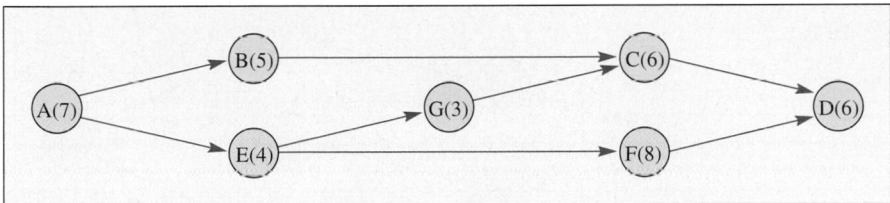

a. Determine the critical path.

b. How many weeks will the project take to complete?

c. Suppose F could be shortened by two weeks and B by one week. How would this affect the completion date?

11   Here is a network with the activity times shown in days:

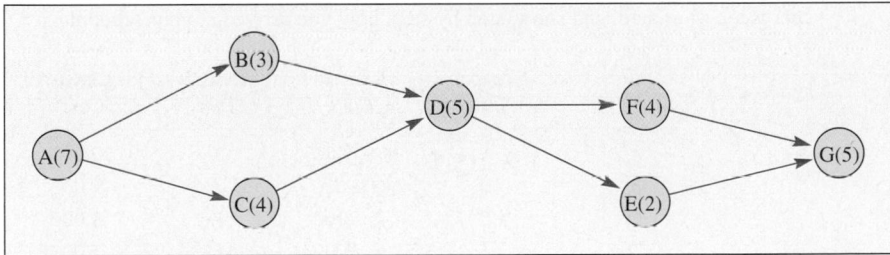

a. Find the critical path.

b. The following table shows the normal times and the crash times, along with the associated costs for each activity.

ACTIVITY	NORMAL TIME	CRASH TIME	NORMAL COST	CRASH COST
A	7	6	$7,000	$ 8,000
B	3	2	5,000	7,000
C	4	3	9,000	10,200
D	5	4	3,000	4,500
E	2	1	2,000	3,000
F	4	2	4,000	7,000
G	5	4	5,000	8,000

If the project is to be shortened by four days, show which activities, in order of reduction, would be shortened and the resulting cost.

12   The home office billing department of a chain of department stores prepares monthly inventory reports for use by the stores' purchasing agents. Given the following information, use the critical path method to determine:
a. How long the total process will take.
b. Which jobs can be delayed without delaying the early start of any subsequent activity.

	JOB AND DESCRIPTION	IMMEDIATE PREDECESSORS	TIME (HOURS)
a	Start	—	0
b	Get computer printouts of customer purchases	a	10
c	Get stock records for the month	a	20
d	Reconcile purchase printouts and stock records	b, c	30
e	Total stock records by department	b, c	20
f	Determine reorder quantities for coming period	e	40
g	Prepare stock reports for purchasing agents	d, f	20
h	Finish	g	0

13   For the network shown:

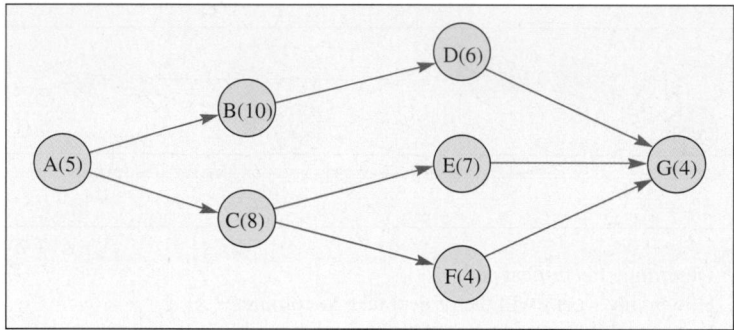

a. Determine the critical path and the early completion time in weeks for the project.
b. For the data shown, reduce the project completion time by three weeks. Assume a linear cost per week shortened, and show, step by step, how you arrived at your schedule.

ACTIVITY	NORMAL TIME	NORMAL COST	CRASH TIME	CRASH COST
A	5	$ 7,000	3	$13,000
B	10	12,000	7	18,000
C	8	5,000	7	7,000
D	6	4,000	5	5,000
E	7	3,000	6	6,000
F	4	6,000	3	7,000
G	4	7,000	3	9,000

14   The following CPM network has estimates of the normal time in weeks listed for the activities:

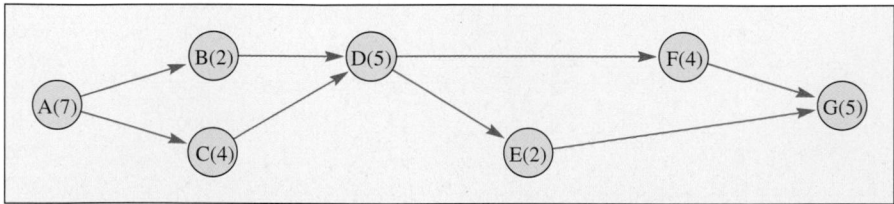

a. Identify the critical path.
b. What is the length of time to complete the project?

c. Which activities have slack, and how much?

d. Here is a table of normal and crash times and costs. Which activities would you shorten to cut two weeks from the schedule in a rational fashion? What would be the incremental cost? Is the critical path changed?

ACTIVITY	NORMAL TIME	CRASH TIME	NORMAL COST	CRASH COST
A	7	6	$7,000	$ 8,000
B	2	1	5,000	7,000
C	4	3	9,000	10,200
D	5	4	3,000	4,500
E	2	1	2,000	3,000
F	4	2	4,000	7,000
G	5	4	5,000	8,000

15 Bragg's Bakery is building a new automated bakery in downtown Sandusky. Here are the activities that need to be completed to get the new bakery built and the equipment installed.

ACTIVITY	PREDECESSOR	NORMAL TIME (WEEKS)	CRASH TIME (WEEKS)	EXPEDITING COST/WEEK
A	—	9	6	$3,000
B	A	8	5	$3,500
C	A	15	10	$4,000
D	B, C	5	3	$2,000
E	C	10	6	$2,500
F	D, E	2	1	$5,000

a. Draw the project diagram.

b. What is the normal project length?

c. What is the project length if all activities are crashed to their minimum?

d. Bragg's loses $3,500 in profit per week for every week the bakery is not completed. How many weeks will the project take if we are willing to pay crashing cost as long as it is less than $3,500?

ADVANCED PROBLEM

16 Assume the network and data that follow:

ACTIVITY	NORMAL TIME (WEEKS)	NORMAL COST	CRASH TIME (WEEKS)	CRASH COST	IMMEDIATE PREDECESSORS
A	2	$50	1	$70	—
B	4	80	2	160	A
C	8	70	4	110	A
D	6	60	5	80	A
E	7	100	6	130	B
F	4	40	3	100	D
G	5	100	4	150	C, E, F

a. Construct the network diagram.

b. Indicate the critical path when normal activity times are used.

c. Compute the minimum total direct cost for each project duration based on the cost associated with each activity. Consider durations of 13, 14, 15, 16, 17, and 18 weeks.

d. If the indirect costs for each project duration are $400 (18 weeks), $350 (17 weeks), $300 (16 weeks), $250 (15 weeks), $200 (14 weeks), and $150 (13 weeks), what is the total project cost for each duration? Indicate the minimum total project cost duration.

CASE: CELL PHONE DESIGN PROJECT

You work for Motorola in its global cell phone group. You have been made project manager for the design of a new cell phone model. Your supervisors have already scoped the project so you have a list showing the work breakdown structure and this includes major project activities. You must plan the project schedule and calculate project duration and project costs. Your boss wants the schedule and costs on his desk tomorrow morning!

You have been given the information in Exhibit 10.14. It includes all the activities required in the project and the duration of each activity. Also, dependencies between the activities have been identified. Remember that the preceding activity must be fully completed before work on the following activity can be started.

Your project is divided into five major tasks. Task P involves developing specifications for the new cell phone. Here decisions related to such things as battery life, size of the phone, and features need to be determined. These details are based on how a customer uses the cell phone. These user specifications are redefined in

terms that have meaning to the subcontractors that will actually make the new cell phone in Task S, supplier specifications. These involve engineering details for how the product will perform. The individual components that make up the product are the focus of Task D. Task I brings all the components together and a working prototype is built and tested. Finally in Task V, vendors are selected and contracts are negotiated.

1 Draw a project network that includes all the activities.
2 Calculate the start and finish times for each activity and determine the minimum number of weeks for completing the project. Find the critical set of activities for the project.
3 Identify slack in the activities not on the project critical path.
4 Your boss would like you to suggest changes that could be made to the project that would significantly shorten it. What would you suggest?

---

exhibit 10.14   Work Breakdown Structure and Activities for the Cell Phone Design Project

**Excel:
Cell_Phone
Design**

MAJOR PROJECT TASKS/ACTIVITIES	ACTIVITY IDENTIFICATION	DEPENDENCY	DURATION (WEEKS)
Product specifications (P)			
Overall product specifications	P1	—	4
Hardware specifications	P2	P1	5
Software specifications	P3	P1	5
Market research	P4	P2, P3	2
Supplier specifications (S)			
Hardware	S1	P2	5
Software	S2	P3	6
Market research	S3	P4	1
Product design (D)			
Circuits	D1	S1, D7	8
Battery	D2	S1	1
Display	D3	S1	2
Outer cover	D4	S3	4
User interface	D5	S2	4
Camera	D6	S1, S2, S3	1
Functionality	D7	D5, D6	4
Product integration (I)			
Hardware	I1	D1, D2, D3, D4, D6	3
Software	I2	D7	5
Prototype testing	I3	I1, I2	5
Subcontracting (V)			
Vendor selection	V1	D7	10
Contract negotiation	V2	I3, V1	2

CASE: THE CAMPUS WEDDING (A)

On March 31 of last year, Mary Jackson burst into the family living room and announced that she and Larry Adams (her college boyfriend) were going to be married. After recovering from the shock, her mother hugged her and asked, "When?" The following conversation resulted:

Mary: April 22.

Mother: What!

Father: The Adams–Jackson wedding will be the social hit of the year. Why so soon?

Mary: Because on April 22 the cherry blossoms on campus are always in full bloom! The wedding pictures will be beautiful.

Mother: But honey, we can't possibly finish all the things that need to be done by then. Remember all the details that were involved in your sister's wedding? Even if we start tomorrow, it takes a day to reserve the church and reception hall, and they need at least 17 days' notice. That has to be done before we can start decorating the church, which takes three days. An extra $100 contribution on Sunday would probably cut that 17-day notice to 10 days, though.

Father: Ugh!

Mary: I want Jane Summers to be my maid of honor.

Father: But she's in the Peace Corps, in Guatemala, isn't she? It would take her 10 days to get ready and drive up here.

Mary: But we could fly her up in two days, and it would cost only $500. She would have to be here in time to have her dress fitted.

Father: Ugh!

Mother: And catering! It takes two days to choose the cake and table decorations, and Jack's Catering wants at least 10 days' notice prior to the rehearsal dinner (the night before the wedding).

Mary: Can I wear your wedding dress, Mom?

Mother: Well, we'd have to replace some lace, but you could wear it, yes. We could order the lace from New York when we order the material for the bridesmaids' dresses. It takes eight days to order and receive the material. The pattern needs to be chosen first, and that would take three days.

Father: We could get the material here in five days if we paid an extra $25 to airfreight it.

Mary: I want Mrs. Watson to work on the dresses.

Father: But she charges $120 a day!

Mother: If we did all the sewing, we could finish the dresses in 11 days. If Mrs. Watson helped, we could cut that down to six days, at a cost of $120 for each day less than 11 days.

Mary: I don't want anyone but her.

Mother: It would take another two days to do the final fitting. It normally takes two days to clean and press the dresses, but that new cleaner downtown could do them in one day if we pay the $30 charge for express service.

Father: Everything should be completed by rehearsal night, and that's only 21 days from now. I bet that will be a busy day.

Mother: We've forgotten something. The invitations.

Father: We should order the invitations from Bob's Printing Shop, and that usually takes 12 days. I'll bet he would do it in five days if we slipped him an extra $35.

Mother: It would take us three days to choose the invitation style before we could order them, and we want the envelopes printed with our return address.

Mary: Oh! That will be elegant.

Mother: The invitations should go out at least 10 days before the wedding. If we let them go any later, some of the relatives would get theirs too late to come, and that would make them mad. I'll bet that if we didn't get them out until eight days before the wedding, Aunt Ethel couldn't make it, and she would reduce her wedding gift by $200.

Father: Ugh!

Mother: We'll have to take them to the post office to mail them, and that takes a day. Addressing would take four days unless we hired some part-time help, and we can't start until the printer is finished. If we hired someone, we could probably save two days by spending $25 for each day saved.

Mary: We need to get gifts to give to the bridesmaids at the rehearsal dinner. I can spend a day and do that.

Mother: Before we can even start to write out those invitations, we need a guest list. Heavens, that will take four days to get in order, and only I can understand our address file.

Mary: Oh, Mother, I'm so excited. We can start each of the relatives on a different job.

Mother: Honey, I don't see how we can do it. Why, we've got to choose the invitations and patterns and reserve the church and . . .

Father: Why don't you just take $1,500 and elope. Your sister's wedding cost me $1,200, and she didn't have to fly people up from Guatemala, hire extra people, use airfreight, or anything like that.

QUESTIONS

1 Given the activities and precedence relationships described in the (A) case, develop a network diagram for the wedding plans.
2 Identify the paths. Which are critical?
3 What is the minimum-cost plan that meets the April 22 date?

CASE: THE CAMPUS WEDDING (B)

Several complications arose during the course of trying to meet the deadline of April 21 for the Adams–Jackson wedding rehearsal. Because Mary Jackson was adamant about having the wedding on April 22 (as was Larry Adams, because he wanted her to be happy), the implications of each of these complications had to be assessed.

1   On April 1 the chairman of the Vestry Committee at the church was left unimpressed by the added donation and said he wouldn't reduce the notice period from 17 to 10 days.

2   A call to Guatemala revealed that the potential bridesmaid had several commitments and could not possibly leave the country until April 10.

3   Mother came down with the four-day flu just as she started on the guest list.

4   The lace and dress materials were lost in transit. Notice of the loss was delivered to the Jackson home early on April 10.

5   There was a small fire at the caterer's shop on April 8. It was estimated that the shop would be closed two or three days for repairs.

Mary Jackson's father, in particular, was concerned about expenses and kept offering $1,500 to Mary and Larry for them to elope.

QUESTION

1   Given your answers to the (A) case, describe the effects on the wedding plans of each incident noted in the (B) case.

SOURCE: ADAPTED FROM A CASE ORIGINALLY WRITTEN BY PROFESSOR D. C. WHYBANK, UNIVERSITY OF NORTH CAROLINA, CHAPEL HILL, NORTH CAROLINA.

SUPER QUIZ

1   A project structured where a self-contained team works full time on the project.

2   Specific events that upon completion mark important progress toward completing a project.

3   This defines the hierarchy of project tasks, subtasks, and work packages.

4   Pieces of work in a project that consume time to complete.

5   A chart that shows both the time and sequence for completing the activities in a project.

6   Activities that in sequence form the longest chain in a project.

7   The difference between the late and early start time for an activity.

8   When activities are scheduled with probabilistic task times.

9   The procedure used to reduce project completion time by trading off time versus cost.

10   A key assumption related to the resources needed to complete activities when using the critical path method.

1. Pure project or skunkworks 2. Milestones 3. Work breakdown structure 4. Activities 5. Gantt chart 6. Critical path(s) 7. Slack 8. The Program Evaluation and Review Technique (PERT) 9. Crashing 10. Resources are always available

SELECTED BIBLIOGRAPHY

Gray, C. *Agile Project Management: How to Succeed in the Face of Changing Project Requirements.* New York: American Management Association, 2004.

Gray, C. F., and E. W. Larson. *Project Management: The Managerial Process.* New York: Irwin/McGraw-Hill, 2002.

Kerzner, H. *Project Management: A Systems Approach to Planning, Scheduling, and Controlling.* 8th ed. New York: Wiley, 2002.

Lewis, James P. *The Project Manager's Desk Reference.* New York: McGraw-Hill Professional Publishing, 1999.

section 3

SUPPLY CHAIN PROCESSES

THE GREEN SUPPLY CHAIN

An important part of sustainability initiatives at global organizations is the close examination of their supply chain environmental footprint. The term *environmental footprint* relates to the impact that running the supply chain has on the environment. It is essential that companies orchestrate greening efforts across all supply chain processes, starting with product development, sourcing, manufacturing, packaging, transportation, demand fulfillment, and end-of-life management.

Managing logistics, which are transportation-related processes, is probably one of the more discussed greening efforts in supply chain management. There is a direct relationship between transportation efficiency and transportation costs. Minimizing miles traveled, using more efficient means for moving goods, and improving capacity utilization through consolidation of shipments reduces energy consumption and transportation costs, while at the same time reducing carbon emissions.

Supply Chain

chapter 11

GLOBAL SOURCING AND PROCUREMENT

THE WORLD IS FLAT

FLATTENER 5: OUTSOURCING
FLATTENER 6: OFFSHORING

Global

After reading the chapter you will:

1. Understand how important sourcing decisions go beyond simple material purchasing decisions.

2. Demonstrate the "bullwhip effect" and how it is important to synchronize the flow of material between supply chain partners.

3. Describe how characteristics of supply and demand have an impact on structuring supply chains.

4. Know the reason for outsourcing capabilities.

5. Illustrate what "green" sourcing is.

6. Analyze the total cost of ownership.

7. Calculate inventory turnover and days of supply.

The owner of a fuel pump factory in Beijing posted the following African proverb, translated into Mandarin, on his factory floor:

Every morning in Africa, a gazelle wakes up.
It knows it must run faster than the fastest lion or it will be killed.
Every morning a lion wakes up.
It knows it must outrun the slowest gazelle or it will starve to death.
It doesn't matter whether you are a lion or a gazelle.
When the sun comes up, you better start running.

The opening of China to the rest of the world started on December 11, 2001, when that country formally joined the World Trade Organization (WTO). Ever since China joined the WTO, both it and the rest of the world have had to run faster

and faster. This is because China's membership in the WTO gave a huge boost to another form of collaboration: offshoring. Offshoring, which has been around for decades, is different from outsourcing. Outsourcing means taking some specific but limited function that your company was doing in-house—such as research, call centers, or accounts receivable—and having another company perform the exact same function for you and then reintegrating its work back into your overall operation. Offshoring, by contrast, is when a company takes one of its factories that is operating in Canton, Ohio, and moves the whole factory offshore to Canton, China. There, it produces the very same product

ADAPTED FROM: THOMAS L. FRIEDMAN, *THE WORLD IS FLAT* [UPDATED AND EXPANDED], NEW YORK: FARRAR, STRAUS AND GIROUX, 2006, P. 136.

in the very same way, only with cheaper labor, lower taxes, subsidized energy, and lower health-care costs. Just as Y2K took India and the world to a whole new level of outsourcing, China's joining the WTO took Beijing and the world to a whole new level of offshoring, with more companies shifting production offshore and then integrating it into the global supply chain.

STRATEGIC SOURCING

Strategic sourcing

**Supply
Chain**

Strategic sourcing is the development and management of global supplier relationships to acquire goods and services in a way that aids in achieving the immediate needs of the business. In the past the term *sourcing* was just another term for purchasing, a corporate function that financially was important but strategically was not the center of attention. Today, as a result of globalization and inexpensive communications technology, the basis for competition is changing. A firm is no longer constrained by the capabilities it owns; what matters is its ability to make the most of capabilities available globally, whether they are owned by the firm or not. Outsourcing is so sophisticated that even core functions such as engineering, research and development, manufacturing, information technology, and marketing can be moved outside the firm.

Sourcing activities can vary greatly and depend on the item being purchased. Exhibit 11.1 maps different processes for sourcing or purchasing an item. The term *sourcing* implies a more complex process suitable for products that are strategically important. Purchasing processes that span from a simple "spot" or one-time purchase to a long-term strategic alliance are depicted on the diagram. The diagram positions a purchasing process according to the specificity of the item, contract duration, and intensity of transaction costs.

Specificity refers to how common the item is and, in a relative sense, how many substitutes might be available. For example, blank DVD disks are commonly available from many different vendors and would have low specificity. A custom-made envelope that is padded and specially shaped to contain a specific item that is to be shipped would be an example of a high specificity item.

Commonly available products can be purchased using a relatively simple process. For low volume and inexpensive items purchased during the regular routine of work, a firm may order

exhibit 11.1   The Sourcing/Purchasing Design Matrix

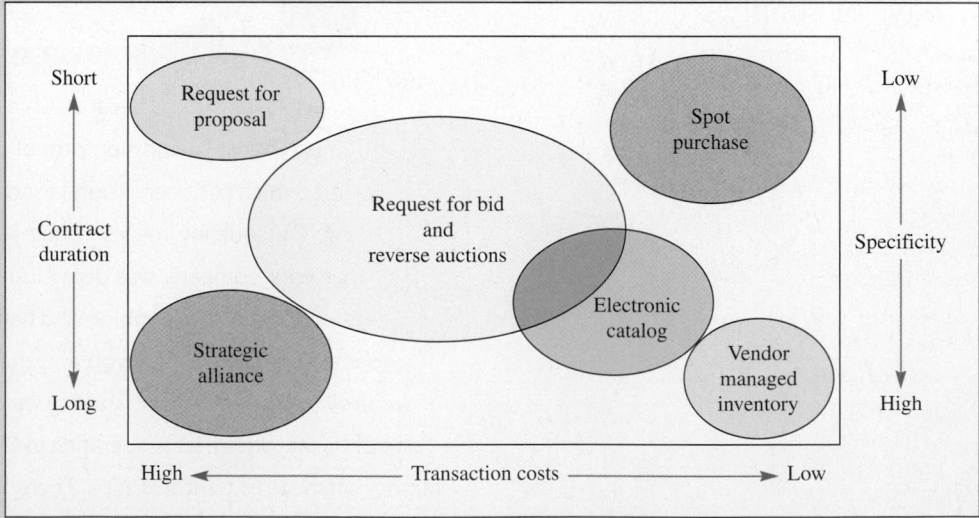

from an online catalog. Often, these online catalogs are customized for a customer. Special user identifications can be set up to authorize customer-employees to purchase certain groups of items within spending limits. Other items require a more complex process.

A request for proposal (RFP) is commonly used for purchasing items that are more complex or expensive and where there may be a number of potential vendors. A detailed information packet describing what is to be purchased is prepared and distributed to potential vendors. The vendor then responds with a detailed proposal of how the company intends to meet the terms of the RFP. A request for bid or reverse auction is similar in terms of the information packet needed. A major difference is how the bid price is negotiated. In the RFP, the bid is included in the proposal, whereas in a request for bid or reverse auction, vendors actually bid on the item in real time and often using Internet software.

Vendor managed inventory is when the supplier takes full responsibility to manage an item or group of items for the customer. In this case the supplier is given the freedom to

Vendor managed inventory

replenish the item as the supplier sees fit. Typically, there are some constraints related to the maximum that the customer is willing to carry, required service levels, and other billing transaction processes. Selecting the proper process depends on minimizing the balance between the supplier's delivered costs of the item over a period of time; say a year, and the customer's costs of managing the inventory. This is discussed later in the chapter in the context of the "total cost of ownership" for a purchased item.

THE BULLWHIP EFFECT

Marshall Fisher argues that in many cases there are adversarial relations between supply chain partners as well as dysfunctional industry practices such as a reliance on price promotions.[1] Consider the common food industry practice of offering price promotions every January on a product. Retailers respond to the price cut by stocking up, in some cases buying a year's supply—a practice the industry calls *forward buying*. Nobody wins in the deal. Retailers have to pay to carry the year's supply, and the shipment bulge adds cost throughout the supplier's system. For example, the supplier plants must go on overtime starting in October to meet the bulge. Even the vendors that supply the manufacturing plants are affected because they must quickly react to the large surge in raw material requirements.

The impact of these types of practices has been studied at companies such as Procter & Gamble. Exhibit 11.2 shows typical order patterns faced by each node in a supply chain that consists of a manufacturer, a distributor, a wholesaler, and a retailer. In this case, the demand is for disposable baby diapers. The retailer's orders to the wholesaler display greater variability than the end-consumer sales; the wholesaler's orders to the manufacturer show even more oscillations; and, finally, the manufacturer's orders to its suppliers are the most volatile. This phenomenon of variability magnification as we move from the customer to the producer in the supply chain is often referred to as the **bullwhip effect**. The effect indicates a lack of synchronization among supply chain members. Even a slight change in consumer sales ripples backward in the form of magnified oscillations upstream, resembling the result of a flick of a bullwhip handle. Because the supply patterns do not match the demand patterns, inventory accumulates at various stages, and shortages and delays occur at others. This bullwhip effect has been observed by many firms in numerous industries, including Campbell Soup and Procter & Gamble in consumer products; Hewlett-Packard, IBM, and Motorola in electronics; General Motors in automobiles; and Eli Lilly in pharmaceuticals.

Bullwhip effect

Campbell Soup has a program called *continuous replenishment* that typifies what many manufacturers are doing to smooth the flow of materials through their supply chain. Here is how the program works. Campbell establishes electronic data interchange (EDI) links with retailers and offers an "everyday low price" that eliminates discounts. Every morning, retailers electronically inform the company of their demand for all Campbell products and of the level of inventories in their distribution centers. Campbell uses that information to forecast demand and to determine which products require replenishment based on upper and lower inventory limits previously established with each supplier. Trucks leave the Campbell

exhibit 11.2   Increasing Variability of Orders up the Supply Chain

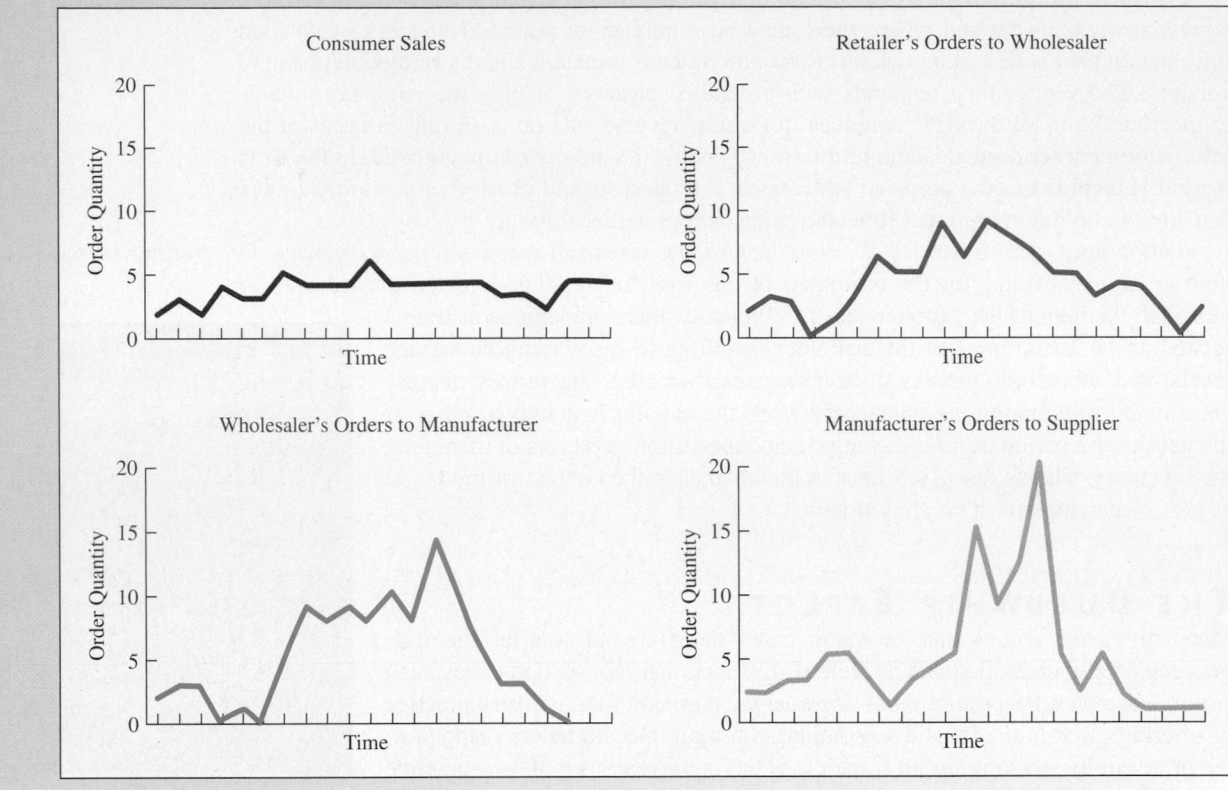

Supply Chain

shipping plant that afternoon and arrive at the retailers' distribution centers with the required replenishments the same day. Using this system, Campbell can cut the retailers' inventories, which under the old system averaged four weeks of supply, to about two weeks of supply.

This solves some problems for Campbell Soup, but what are the advantages for the retailer? Most retailers figure that the cost to carry the inventory of a given product for a year equals at least 25 percent of what they paid for the product. A two-week inventory reduction represents

a cost savings equal to nearly 1 percent of sales. The average retailer's profits equal about 2 percent of sales, so this saving is enough to increase profits by 50 percent. Because the retailer makes more money on Campbell products delivered through continuous replenishment, it has an incentive to carry a broader line of them and to give them more shelf space. Campbell Soup found that after it introduced the program, sales of its products grew twice as fast through participating retailers as they did through other retailers.

Fisher has developed a framework to help managers understand the nature of demand for their products and then devise the supply chain that can best satisfy that demand. Many aspects of a product's demand are important—for example, product life cycle, demand predictability, product variety, and market standards for lead times and service. Fisher has found that products can be categorized as either primarily functional or primarily innovative. Because each category requires a distinct kind of supply chain, the root cause of supply chain problems is a mismatch between the type of product and type of supply chain.

Functional products include the staples that people buy in a wide range of retail outlets, such as grocery stores and gas stations. Because such products satisfy basic needs, which do not change much over time, they have stable, predictable demand and long life cycles. But their stability invites competition, which often leads to low profit margins. Specific criteria suggested by Fisher for identifying functional products include the following: product life cycle of more than two years, contribution margin of 5 to 20 percent, only 10 to 20 product variations, an average forecast error at time of production of only 10 percent, and a lead time for make-to-order products of from six months to one year.

Functional products

To avoid low margins, many companies introduce innovations in fashion or technology to give customers an additional reason to buy their products. Fashionable clothes and personal computers are good examples. Although innovation can enable a company to achieve higher profit margins, the very newness of the innovative products makes demand for them unpredictable. These **innovative products** typically have a life cycle of just a few months. Imitators quickly erode the competitive advantage that innovative products enjoy, and companies are forced to introduce a steady stream of newer innovations. The short life cycles and the great variety typical of these products further increase unpredictability. Exhibit 11.3 summarizes the differences between functional and innovative products.

Innovative products

Hau Lee expands on Fisher's ideas by focusing on the "supply" side of the supply chain.[2] While Fisher has captured important demand characteristics, Lee points out that there are uncertainties revolving around the supply side that are equally important drivers for the right supply chain strategy.

Lee defines a *stable supply process* as one where the manufacturing process and the underlying technology are mature and the supply base is well established. In contrast, an *evolving supply process* is where the manufacturing process and the underlying technology are still under early development and are rapidly changing. As a result the supply base may be limited in both size and experience. In a stable supply process, manufacturing complexity tends to be low or manageable. Stable manufacturing processes tend to be highly automated, and long-term supply contracts are prevalent. In an evolving supply process, the manufacturing process requires a lot of fine-tuning and is often subject to breakdowns and uncertain yields. The supply base may not be reliable, as the suppliers themselves are going through process innovations. Exhibit 11.3 summarizes some of the differences between stable and evolving supply processes.

Lee argues that while functional products tend to have a more mature and stable supply process, that is not always the case. For example, the annual demand for electricity and other utility products in a locality tend to be stable and predictable, but the supply of hydroelectric power, which relies on rainfall in a region, can be erratic year by year. Some food products

Demand and Supply Uncertainty Characteristics

exhibit 11.3

DEMAND CHARACTERISTICS		SUPPLY CHARACTERISTICS	
FUNCTIONAL	INNOVATIVE	STABLE	EVOLVING
Low demand uncertainty	High demand uncertainty	Less breakdowns	Vulnerable to breakdowns
More predictable demand	Difficult to forecast	Stable and higher yields	Variable and lower yields
Long product life	Short selling season	Fewer quality problems	Potential quality problems
Low inventory cost	High inventory cost	More supply sources	Limited supply sources
Low profit margin	High profit margin	Reliable suppliers	Unreliable suppliers
Low product variety	High product variety	Fewer process changes	More process changes
Higher volume	Low volume	Fewer capacity constraints	Potential capacity constrained
Low stockout cost	High stockout cost	Easier to change over	Difficult to change over
Low obsolescence	High obsolescence	Dependable lead times	Variable lead time

exhibit 11.4   Hau Lee's Uncertainty Framework—Examples and Types of Supply Chain Needed

		DEMAND UNCERTAINTY	
		LOW (FUNCTIONAL PRODUCTS)	HIGH (INNOVATIVE PRODUCTS)
SUPPLY UNCERTAINTY	Low (Stable Process)	Grocery, basic apparel, food, oil and gas Efficient supply chain	Fashion apparel, computers, popular music Responsive supply chain
	High (Evolving Process)	Hydroelectric power, some food produce Risk-hedging supply chain	Telecom, high-end computers, semiconductor Agile supply chain

also have a very stable demand, but the supply (both quantity and quality) of the products depends on yearly weather conditions. Similarly, there are also innovative products with a stable supply process. Fashion apparel products have a short selling season and their demand is highly unpredictable. However, the supply process is very stable, with a reliable supply base and a mature manufacturing process technology. Exhibit 11.4 gives some examples of products that have different demand and supply uncertainties.

According to Lee, it is more challenging to operate a supply chain that is in the right column of Exhibit 11.4 than in the left column, and similarly it is more challenging to operate a supply chain that is in the lower row of Exhibit 11.4 than in the upper row. Before setting up a supply chain strategy, it is necessary to understand the sources of the underlying uncertainties and explore ways to reduce these uncertainties. If the uncertainty characteristics of the product can be moved from the right column to the left or from the lower row to the upper; then the supply chain performance will improve.

Lee characterizes four types of supply chain strategies as shown in Exhibit 11.4. Information technologies play an important role in shaping such strategies.

Supply Chain

- **Efficient supply chains.** These are supply chains that utilize strategies aimed at creating the highest cost efficiency. For such efficiencies to be achieved, non-value-added activities should be eliminated, scale economies should be pursued, optimization techniques should be deployed to get the best capacity utilization in production and distribution, and information linkages should be established to ensure the most efficient, accurate, and cost-effective transmission of information across the supply chain.

- **Risk-hedging supply chains.** These are supply chains that utilize strategies aimed at pooling and sharing resources in a supply chain so that the risks in supply disruption can be shared. A single entity in a supply chain can be vulnerable to supply disruptions, but if there is more than one supply source or if alternative supply resources are available, then the risk of disruption is reduced. A company may, for example, increase the safety stock of its key component to hedge against the risk of supply disruption, and by sharing the safety stock with other companies that also need this key component, the cost of maintaining this safety stock can be shared. This type of strategy is common in retailing, where different retail stores or dealerships share inventory. Information technology is important for the success of these strategies since real-time information on inventory and demand allows the most cost-effective management and transshipment of goods between partners sharing the inventory.

- **Responsive supply chains.** These are supply chains that utilize strategies aimed at being responsive and flexible to the changing and diverse needs of the customers. To be responsive, companies use build-to-order and mass customization processes as a means to meet the specific requirements of customers.

- **Agile supply chains.** These are supply chains that utilize strategies aimed at being responsive and flexible to customer needs, while the risks of supply shortages or disruptions are hedged by pooling inventory and other capacity resources. These supply chains essentially have strategies in place that combine the strengths of "hedged" and "responsive" supply chains. They are agile because they have the ability to be responsive to the changing, diverse, and unpredictable demands of customers on the front end, while minimizing the back-end risks of supply disruptions.

Demand and supply uncertainty is a good framework for understanding supply chain strategy. Innovative products with unpredictable demand and an evolving supply process face a major challenge. Because of shorter and shorter product life cycles, the pressure for dynamically adjusting and adopting a company's supply chain strategy is great. In the following we explore the concepts of outsourcing, green sourcing, and total cost of ownership. These are important tools for coping with demand and supply uncertainty.

OUTSOURCING

Outsourcing is the act of moving some of a firm's internal activities and decision responsibility to outside providers. The terms of the agreement are established in a contract. Outsourcing goes beyond the more common purchasing and consulting contracts because not only are the activities transferred, but resources that make the activities occur, including people, facilities, equipment, technology, and other assets, are also transferred. The responsibilities for making decisions over certain elements of the activities are also transferred as well. Taking complete responsibility for this is a specialty of contract manufacturers such as Flextronics.[3]

Outsourcing

The reasons why a company decides to outsource can vary greatly. Exhibit 11.5 lists examples of reasons to outsource and the accompanying benefits. Outsourcing allows a firm to focus on activities that represent its core competencies. Thus, the company can create a competitive advantage while reducing cost. An entire function may be outsourced, or some elements of an activity may be outsourced, with the rest kept in-house. For example, some of the elements of information technology may be strategic, some may be critical, and some may be performed less expensively by a third party. Identifying a function as a potential outsourcing target, and then breaking that function into its components, allows decision makers to determine which activities are strategic or critical and should remain in-house and which can be outsourced like commodities. As an example, outsourcing the logistics function will be discussed.

Reasons to Outsource and the Resulting Benefits

exhibit 11.5

FINANCIALLY DRIVEN REASONS

Improve return on assets by reducing inventory and selling unnecessary assets.
Generate cash by selling low-return entities.
Gain access to new markets, particularly in developing countries.
Reduce costs through a lower cost structure.
Turn fixed costs into variable costs.

IMPROVEMENT-DRIVEN REASONS

Improve quality and productivity.
Shorten cycle time.
Obtain expertise, skills, and technologies that are not otherwise available.
Improve risk management.
Improve credibility and image by associating with superior providers.

ORGANIZATIONALLY DRIVEN REASONS

Improve effectiveness by focusing on what the firm does best.
Increase flexibility to meet changing demand for products and services.
Increase product and service value by improving response to customer needs.

Logistics

There has been dramatic growth in outsourcing in the logistics area. Logistics is a term that refers to the management functions that support the complete cycle of material flow: from the purchase and internal control of production materials; to the planning and control of work-in-process; to the purchasing, shipping, and distribution of the finished product. The emphasis on lean inventory means there is less room for error in deliveries. Trucking companies such as Ryder have started adding the logistics aspect to their businesses—changing from merely moving goods from point A to point B, to managing all or part of all shipments over a longer period, typically three years, and replacing the shipper's employees with their own. Logistics companies now have complex computer tracking technology that reduces the risk in transportation and allows the logistics company to add more value to the firm than it could if the function were performed in-house. Third-party logistics providers track freight using electronic data interchange technology and a satellite system to tell customers exactly where its drivers are and when deliveries will be made. Such technology is critical in some environments where the delivery window may be only 30 minutes long.

Federal Express has one of the most advanced systems available for tracking items being sent through its services. The system is available to all customers over the Internet. It tells the exact status of each item currently being carried by the company. Information on the exact time a package is picked up, when it is transferred between hubs in the company's network, and when it is delivered is available on the system. You can access this system at the FedEx Web site (www.fedex.com). Select your country on the initial screen and then select "Track Shipments" in the Track box in the lower part of the page. Of course, you will need the actual tracking number for an item currently in the system to get information. Federal Express has integrated its tracking system with many of its customers' in-house information systems.

Another example of innovative outsourcing in logistics involves Hewlett-Packard. Hewlett-Packard turned over its inbound raw materials warehousing in Vancouver, Washington, to Roadway Logistics. Roadway's 140 employees operate the warehouse 24 hours a day, seven days a week, coordinating the delivery of parts to the warehouse and managing storage. Hewlett-Packard's 250 employees were transferred to other company activities. Hewlett-Packard reports savings of 10 percent in warehousing operating costs.

One of the drawbacks to outsourcing is the layoffs that often result. Even in cases where the outsourcing partner hires former employees, they are often hired back at lower wages with fewer benefits. Outsourcing is perceived by many unions as an effort to circumvent union contracts.

In theory, outsourcing is a no-brainer. Companies can unload noncore activities, shed balance sheet assets, and boost their return on capital by using third-party service providers. But in reality, things are more complicated. "It's really hard to figure out what's core and what's noncore today," says Jane Linder, senior research fellow and associate director of Accenture's Institute for Strategic Change in Cambridge, Massachusetts. "When you take another look tomorrow, things may have changed. On September 9, 2001, airport security workers were noncore; on September 12, 2001, they were core to the federal government's ability to provide security to the nation. It happens every day in companies as well."[4]

Exhibit 11.6 is a useful framework to help managers make appropriate choices for the structure of supplier relationships. The decision goes beyond the notion that "core competencies" should be maintained under the direct control of management of the firm and that other activities should be outsourced. In this framework, a continuum that ranges from vertical integration to arm's-length relationships forms the basis for the decision.

An activity can be evaluated using the following characteristics: required coordination, strategic control, and intellectual property. Required coordination refers to how difficult it is to ensure that the activity will integrate well with the overall process. Uncertain activities that require much back-and-forth exchange of information

DHL SMARTTRUCKS USE A TYPE OF ROUTE PLANNING SOFTWARE WHICH NAVIGATES AWAY FROM INNER CITY TRAFFIC JAMS AND CALCULATES THE BEST ROUTE TO DELIVER PACKAGES. THIS REDUCES TIME AND COSTS BUT ALSO FUEL CONSUMPTION AND CO_2 EMISSIONS. TRANSPORTED MAIL ITEMS USE RADIO FREQUENCY IDENTIFICATION (RFID) SMART TAGS ATTACHED TO THEM TO MONITOR VEHICLE LOADS.

A Framework for Structuring Supplier Relationships   **exhibit 11.6**

	VERTICAL INTEGRATION (DO NOT OUTSOURCE)	ARM'S-LENGTH RELATIONSHIPS (OUTSOURCE)
Coordination	"Messy" interfaces; adjacent tasks involve a high degree of mutual adaptation, exchange of implicit knowledge, and learning-by-doing. Requisite information is highly particular to the task.	Standardized interfaces between adjacent tasks; requisite information is highly codified and standardized (prices, quantities, delivery schedules, etc.).
Strategic control	Very high: significant investments in highly durable relationship-specific assets needed for optimal execution of tasks. Investments cannot be recovered if relationship terminates: • Co-location of specialized facilities • Investment in brand equity • Large proprietary learning curves • Long-term investments in specialized R&D programs	Very low: assets applicable to businesses with a large number of other potential customers or suppliers.
Intellectual property	Unclear or weak intellectual property protection Easy-to-imitate technology "Messy" interfaces between different technological components	Strong intellectual property protection Difficult-to-imitate technology "Clean" boundaries between different techno logical components

SOURCE: ROBERT HAYES, GARY PISANO, DAVID UPTON, AND STEVEN WHEELWRIGHT, *OPERATIONS STRATEGY AND TECHNOLOGY: PURSUING THE COMPETITIVE EDGE* (NEW YORK: JOHN WILEY & SONS, 2005), P. 137. COPYRIGHT © 2005 JOHN WILEY & SONS. REPRINTED BY PERMISSION.

should not be outsourced whereas activities that are well understood and highly standardized can easily move to business partners who specialize in the activity. Strategic control refers to the degree of loss that would be incurred if the relationship with the partner were severed. There could be many types of losses that would be important to consider including specialized facilities, knowledge of major customer relationships, and investment in research and development. A final consideration is the potential loss of intellectual property through the partnership.

Intel is an excellent example of a company that recognized the importance of this type of decision framework in the mid-1980s. During the early 1980s, Intel found itself being squeezed out of the market for the memory chips that it had invented by Japanese competitors such as Hitachi, Fujitsu, and NEC. These companies had developed stronger capabilities to develop and rapidly scale up complex semiconductor manufacturing processes. It was clear by 1985 that a major Intel competency was its ability to design complex integrated circuits, not in manufacturing or developing processes for more standardized chips. As a result, faced with growing financial losses, Intel was forced to exit the memory chip market.

Learning a lesson from the memory market, Intel shifted its focus to the microprocessor market, a device that it had invented in the late 1960s. To keep from repeating the mistake with memory chips, Intel felt it was essential to develop strong capabilities in process development and manufacturing. A pure "core competency" strategy would have suggested that Intel focus on the design of microprocessors and use outside partners to manufacture them. Given the close connection between semiconductor product development and process development, however, relying on outside parties for manufacturing would likely have created costs in terms of longer development lead times. Over the late 1980s Intel invested heavily in building world-class capabilities in process development and manufacturing. These capabilities are one of the chief reasons it has been able to maintain approximately 90 percent of the personal computer microprocessor market, despite the ability of competitors like AMD to "clone" Intel designs relatively quickly. Expanding its capabilities beyond its original core capability of product design has been a critical ingredient in Intel's sustained success.

Good advice is to keep control of—or acquire—activities that are true competitive differentiators or have the potential to yield a competitive advantage, and to outsource the rest. It is important to make a distinction between "core" and "strategic" activities. Core activities are key to the business but do not confer a competitive advantage, such as a bank's information technology operations. Strategic activities are a key source of competitive advantage.

Global

CAPABILITY SOURCING AT 7-ELEVEN

The term *capability sourcing* was coined to refer to the way companies focus on the things they do best and outsource other functions to key partners. The idea is that owning capabilities may not be as important as having control of those capabilities. This allows many additional capabilities to be outsourced. Companies are under intense pressure to improve revenue and margins because of increased competition. An area where this has been particularly intense is the convenience store industry, where 7-Eleven is a major player.

Before 1991, 7-Eleven was one of the most vertically integrated convenience store chains. When it is vertically integrated, a firm controls most of the activities in its supply chain. In the case of 7-Eleven, the firm owned its own distribution network, which delivered gasoline to each store, made its own candy and ice, and required the managers to handle store maintenance, credit card processing, store payroll, and even the in-store information technology (IT) system. For a while 7-Eleven even owned the cows that produced the milk sold in the stores. It was difficult for 7-Eleven to manage costs in this diverse set of functions.

At that time 7-Eleven had a Japanese branch that was very successful but was based on a totally different integration model. Rather than using a company-owned and vertically integrated model, the Japanese stores had partnerships with suppliers that carried out many of the day-to-day functions. Those suppliers specialized in each area, enhancing quality and improv-

ing service while reducing cost. The Japanese model involved outsourcing everything possible without jeopardizing the business by giving competitors critical information. A simple rule said that if a partner could provide a capability more effectively than 7-Eleven could itself, that capability should be outsourced. In the United States the company eventually outsourced activities such as human resources, finance, information technology, logistics, distribution, product development, and packaging. 7-Eleven still maintains control of all vital information and handles all merchandising, pricing, positioning, promotion of gasoline, and ready-to-eat food.

The following chart shows how 7-Eleven has structured key partnerships:

ACTIVITY	OUTSOURCING STRATEGY
Gasoline	Outsourced distribution of fuel products. Maintains control over pricing and promotion. These are activities that can differentiate its stores.
Snack foods	Frito-Lay distributes its products directly to the stores. 7-Eleven makes critical decisions about order quantities and shelf placement. 7-Eleven mines extensive data on local customer purchase patterns to make these decisions at each store.
Prepared foods	Joint venture with E.A. Sween: Combined Distribution Centers (CDC), a direct-store delivery operation that supplies 7-Eleven stores with sandwiches and other fresh goods two times a day.
Specialty products	Many are developed specially for 7-Eleven customers. For example, 7-Eleven worked with Hershey to develop an edible straw used with the popular Twizzler treat. Worked with Anheuser-Bush on special NASCAR and Major League Baseball promotions.
Data analysis	7-Eleven relies on an outside vendor, IRI, to maintain and format purchasing data while keeping the data proprietary. Only 7-Eleven can see the actual mix of products its customers purchase at each location.
New capabilities	American Express supplies automated teller machines. Western Union handles money wire transfers. CashWorks furnishes check-cashing capabilities. Electronic Data Systems (EDS) maintains network functions.

Because the competitive environment can change rapidly, companies need to monitor the situation constantly and adjust accordingly. As an example, Coca-Cola, which decided to stay out of the bottling business in the early 1900s, partnered instead with independent bottlers and quickly built market share. The company reversed itself in the 1980s when bottling became a key competitive element in the industry.

GREEN SOURCING

Being environmentally responsible has become a business imperative and many firms are looking to their supply chains to deliver "green" results. A significant area of focus relates to how a firm works with suppliers where the opportunity to save money and benefit the environment might not be a strict trade-off proposition. Financial results can often be improved through both cost reductions and boosting revenues.

Deloitte (www.deloitte.com) has developed a green strategic sourcing process that can be used with conventional sourcing techniques to enhance sourcing savings by taking advantage of environmental factors. Before looking at this six-step process, it is worth considering the long-term benefits of this type of approach. Green sourcing is not just about finding new environmentally friendly technologies or increasing the use of recyclable materials. It can also help drive cost reductions in a variety of ways including product content substitution, waste reduction, and lower usage.

A comprehensive green sourcing effort should assess how a company uses items that are purchased internally, in its own operations, or in its products and services. As costs of commodity items like steel, electricity, and fossil fuels continue to increase, properly designed green sourcing efforts should find ways to significantly reduce and possibly eliminate the need for these types of commodities. As an example, consider retrofitting internal lighting in a large office building to a modern energy efficient technology. Electricity cost savings of 10 to 12 percent per square foot can easily translate into millions of dollars in associated electricity cost savings.

Another important cost area in green sourcing is waste reduction opportunities. This includes everything from energy and water to packaging and transportation. A great example of this is the redesigned milk jug introduced recently by leading grocery retailers. Using the new jug, with more rectangular dimensions and a square base, cuts the associated water consumption of the jugs by 60 to 70 percent compared to earlier jug designs because the new design does not require the use of milk crates. Milk crates typically become filthy during use due to spillage and other natural factors; thus, they are usually hosed down before reuse, consuming thousands of gallons of water. The new design also reduces fuel costs. Since crates are no longer used, they also do not have to be transported back to the dairy plant or farm distribution point for future shipments. Furthermore, the new jugs have the unexpected benefit of fitting better in modern home refrigerator doors and allow retailers to fit more of them in their in-store coolers. Breakthrough results like the new milk jug can result from comprehensive partnerships between users and their suppliers working to find innovative solutions.

A recent supply chain survey by Florida International University (see business.fiu.edu/greensupplychain) revealed that working with suppliers can result in opportunities that improve revenue. They can be the opportunity to turn waste products into sources of revenue. For example, a leading beverage manufacturer operates a recycling subsidiary that sources used aluminum cans from a large number of suppliers. The subsidiary actually processes more aluminum cans than are used in the company's own products, consequently developing a strong secondary revenue stream for the company.

In other cases, green sourcing can help establish entirely new lines of business to serve environmentally conscious customers. In the cleaning products aisle of a supermarket shoppers will find numerous options of "green" cleaning products from a variety of consumer products companies. These products typically use natural ingredients in lieu of chemicals, and many are in concentrated amounts to reduce overall packaging costs.

Green sourcing can also be essential for companies interested in winning high-profile deals. Being green can be the "order winner" for selection when many sourcing options are available. For example, the organizers of the 2008 U.S. Democratic National Convention (DNC) stipulated very stringent green procurement regulations for the convention's food suppliers. Suppliers that could source food from local and organic farms won the majority of the DNC's business.

exhibit 11.7   Six-Step Process for Green Sourcing

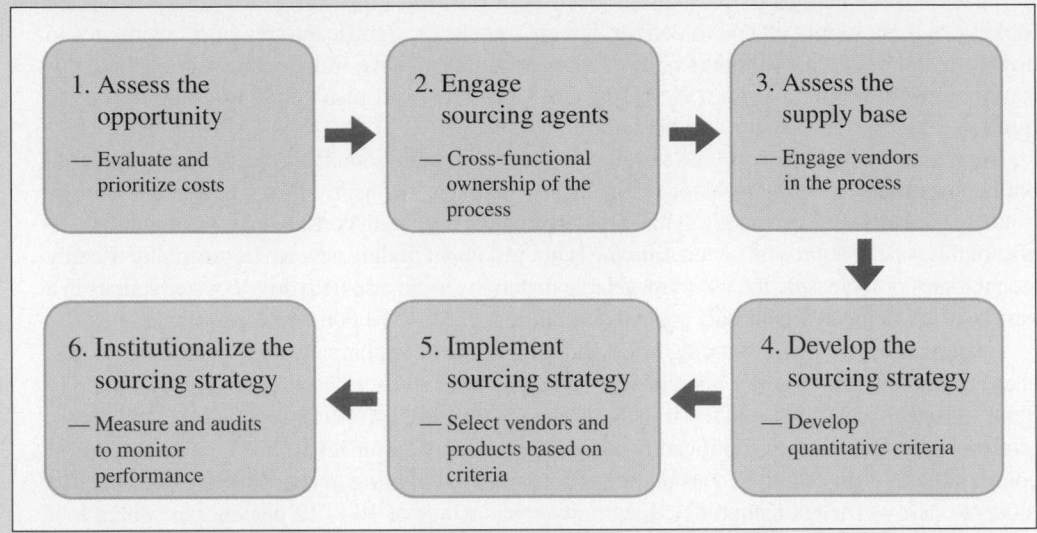

SOURCE: ADAPTED FROM www.deloite.com.

Logistics suppliers could find business opportunities coming directly to them as a result of the green trend. A large automobile manufacturer completed a project to green its logistics/distribution network. The automaker analyzed the shipping carriers, locations, and overall efficiency of its distribution network for both parts and finished automobiles. By increasing the use of rail transportation for parts, consolidating shipments in fewer ports, and partnering with its logistics providers to increase fuel efficiency for both marine and road transportation, the company reduced its overall distribution-related carbon dioxide emissions by several thousand tons per year.

The following is an outline of a six-step process (see Exhibit 11.7) designed to transform a traditional process to a green sourcing process:

Supply Chain

1. **Assess the opportunity.**   For a given category of expense, all relevant costs need to be taken into account. The five most common areas include electricity and other energy costs; disposal and recycling; packaging; commodity substitution (alternative materials to replace materials such as steel or plastic); and water (or other related resources). These costs are identified and incorporated into an analysis of total cost (sometimes referred to as "spend" cost analysis) at this step. From this analysis it is possible to prioritize the different costs based on the highest potential savings and criticality to the organization. This is important to directing effort to where it will likely have the most impact on the firm's financial position and cost reduction goals.

2. **Engage internal supply chain sourcing agents.**   Internal sourcing agents are those within the firm that purchase items and have direct knowledge of business requirements, product specifications, and other internal perspectives inherent in the supply chain. These individuals and groups need to be "on-board" and partners in the improvement process to help set realistic green goals. The goal of generating no waste, for example, becomes a cross-functional supply chain effort that relies heavily on finding and developing the right suppliers. These internal managers need to identify the most significant opportunities. They can develop a robust baseline model of what should be possible for reducing current and ongoing costs. In the case of procuring new equipment, for example, the baseline model would include not just the initial price of the equipment as in traditional sourcing, but also energy, disposal, recycling, and maintenance costs.

3. **Assess the supply base.**   A sustainable sourcing process requires engaging new and existing vendors. As in traditional sourcing, the firm needs to understand vendor capabilities, constraints, and product offering. The green process needs to be augmented

with formal requirements that relate to green opportunities, including possible commodity substitutions and new manufacturing processes. These requirements need to be incorporated in vendor bid documents or the request for proposals (RFPs).

A good example is concrete that uses fly ash, a by-product from coal-fired power plants. Fly ash can be substituted for Portland cement in ready-mix concrete or in concrete block to produce a stronger and lighter product with reduced water consumption. Fly ash substitution helped a company reduce its exposure to volatile and rapidly increasing prices for cement. At the same time, the reduced weight of the block lowered transportation costs to the company's new facilities. The company was also able to establish a specification incorporating fly ash for all new construction sites to follow. Finally, the substitution also helped the power plant, by providing a new market for the fly ash, which previously had to be discarded.

4. **Develop the sourcing strategy.** The main goal of this step is to develop quantitative and qualitative criteria that will be used to evaluate the sourcing process. These are needed to properly analyze associated costs and benefits. These criteria need to be clearly articulated in bid documents and RFP when working with potential suppliers so that their proposals will address relevant goals related to sustainability.

5. **Implement the sourcing strategy.** The evaluation criteria developed in step 4 should help in the selection of vendors and products for each business requirement. The evaluation process should consider initial cost and the total cost of ownership for the items in the bid. So, for example, energy-efficient equipment that is proposed with a higher initial cost may, over its productive life, actually result in a lower total cost due to energy savings and a related lower carbon footprint. Relevant green opportunities such as energy efficiency and waste reduction need to be modeled and then incorporated into the sourcing analysis to make it as comprehensive as possible and to facilitate an effective vendor selection process that supports the firm's needs.

6. **Institutionalize the sourcing strategy.** Once the vendor is selected and contracts finalized, the procurement process begins. Here the sourcing and procurement department needs to define a set of metrics against which the supplier will be measured for the contract's duration. These metrics should be based on performance, delivery, compliance with pricing guidelines, and similar factors. It is vital that metrics that relate to the company's sustainability goals are considered as well. Periodic audits may also need to be incorporated in the process to directly observe practices that relate to these metrics to ensure honest reporting of data.

A key aspect of green sourcing, compared to a traditional process, is the expanded view of the sourcing decision. This expanded view requires the incorporation of new criteria for evaluating alternatives. Further, it requires a wider range of internal integration such as designers, engineers, and marketers. Finally, visualizing and capturing the green sourcing savings often involves greater complexity and longer payback periods compared to a traditional process.

FLY ASH IS GENERALLY STORED AT COAL POWER PLANTS OR PLACED IN LANDFILLS AS SHOWN HERE. ABOUT 43 PERCENT IS RECYCLED REDUCING THE HARMFUL IMPACT ON THE ENVIRONMENT FROM LANDFILLS.

TOTAL COST OF OWNERSHIP

The **total cost of ownership** (TCO) is an estimate of the cost of an item that includes all the costs related to the procurement and use of an item, including any related costs in disposing of the item after it is no longer useful. The concept can be applied to a company's internal costs or it can be viewed more broadly to consider costs throughout the supply chain. To fully appreciate the cost of purchasing an item from a particular vendor, an approach that captures the costs of the activities associated with purchasing and actually using the item should be considered. Depending on the complexity of the purchasing process, activities such as pre-bid conferences, visits by potential suppliers, and even visits to potential suppliers can significantly impact the total cost of the item.

Total cost of ownership

exhibit 11.8   Total Cost of Ownership

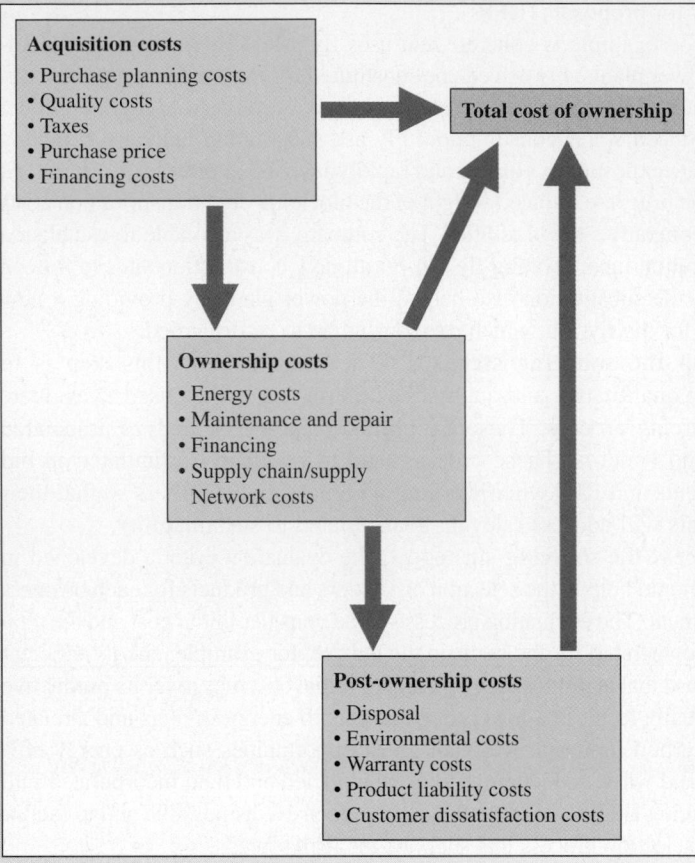

A TCO analysis is highly dependent on the actual situation, although, in general, the costs outlined in Exhibit 11.8 should be considered. The costs can be categorized into three broad areas: acquisition costs, ownership costs, and post-ownership costs.[5] Acquisition costs are the initial costs associated with the purchase of materials, products, and services. They are not long-term costs of ownership but represent an immediate cash outflow. Acquisition costs include the prepurchase costs associated with preparing documents to distribute to potential suppliers, identifying suppliers and evaluating suppliers, and other costs associated with procuring the item. The actual purchase prices, including taxes and transportation costs, are also included.

Ownership costs are incurred after the initial purchase and are associated with the ongoing use of the product or material. Examples of costs that are quantifiable include energy usage, scheduled maintenance, repair, and financing (leasing situation). There can also be qualitative costs such as aesthetic factors (e.g., the item is psychologically pleasing to the eye), and ergonomic factors (e.g., productivity improvement or reducing fatigue). These ownership costs can often exceed the initial purchase price and have an impact on cash flow, profitability, and even employee morale and productivity.

Major costs associated with post-ownership include salvage value and disposal costs. For many purchases, there are established markets that provide data to help estimate reasonable future values, such as the *Kelley Blue Book* for used automobiles. Other areas that can be included are the long-term environment impact (particularly when the firm has sustainability goals), warranty and product liabilities, and the negative marketing impact of low customer satisfaction with the item.

Overemphasis on acquisition cost or purchase price frequently results in failure to address other significant ownership and post-ownership costs. TCO is a philosophy for understanding all relevant costs of doing business with a particular supplier for a good or service. It is not only

Analysis of the Purchase of an Office Copier

exhibit 11.9

YEAR	Now	1	2	3	4	5	6
Cost of copier including installation	−$120,000						
Manufacturer required overhaul				$−9,000			
Cash inflows from using the machine		$ 40,000	$ 40,000	$ 40,000	$ 40,000	$ 40,000	$ 40,000
Supplies needed to use the machine		$−7,000	$−7,000	$−7,000	$−7,000	$−7,000	$−7,000
Salvage value							$ 7,500
Total of annual streams	−$120,000	$ 33,000	$ 33,000	$ 24,000	$ 33,000	$ 33,000	$ 40,500
Discount factor $(1 + .2)^{-\text{Year}}$	1.000	0.833	0.694	0.579	0.482	0.402	0.335
Present value − yearly	−$120,000	$ 27,500	$ 22,917	$ 13,889	$ 15,914	$ 13,262	$ 13,563
Present value	$−12,955						

Discount factor = 20%.
Note: These calculations were done using the full precision of a spreadsheet.

relevant for a business that wants to reduce its cost of doing business but also for a firm that aims to design products or services that provide the lowest total cost of ownership to customers. For example, some automobile manufacturers have extended the tune-up interval on many models to 100,000 miles, thereby reducing vehicle operating cost for car owners. Viewing TCO in this way can lead to an increased value of the product to existing and potential customers.

These costs can be estimated as cash inflows (the sale of used equipment, etc.) or outflows (purchase prices, demolition of an obsolete facility, etc.). The following example shows how this analysis can be organized using a spreadsheet. Keep in mind that the costs considered need to be adapted to the decision being made. Costs that do not vary based on the decision need not be considered, but relevant costs that vary depending on the decision should be included in the analysis.

EXAMPLE 11.1: Total Cost of Ownership Analysis

Consider the analysis of the purchase of a copy machine that might be used in a copy center. The machine has an initial cost of $120,000 and is expected to generate income of $40,000 per year.[6] Supplies are expected to be $7,000 per year and the machine needs to be overhauled during year 3 at a cost of $9,000. It has a salvage value of $7,500 when we plan to sell it at year 6.

Step by Step

SOLUTION

Laying these costs out over time can lead to the use of net present value analysis to evaluate the decision. Consider Exhibit 11.9. Are the present values of each yearly stream discounted to now? (See Appendix E for a present value table.) As we can see, the present value in this analysis shows that the present value cost of the copier is $12,955. ●

TCO actually draws on many areas for a thorough analysis. These include finance (net present value), accounting (product pricing and costing), operations management (reliability, quality, need and inventory planning), marketing (demand), and information technology (systems integration). It is probably best to approach this using a cross-functional team representing the key functional areas.

MEASURING SOURCING PERFORMANCE

One view of sourcing is centered on the inventories that are positioned in the system. Exhibit 11.10 shows how hamburger meat and potatoes are stored in various locations in a typical fast-food restaurant chain. Here we see the steps that the beef and potatoes move

exhibit 11.10   Inventory in the Supply Chain—Fast-Food Restaurant

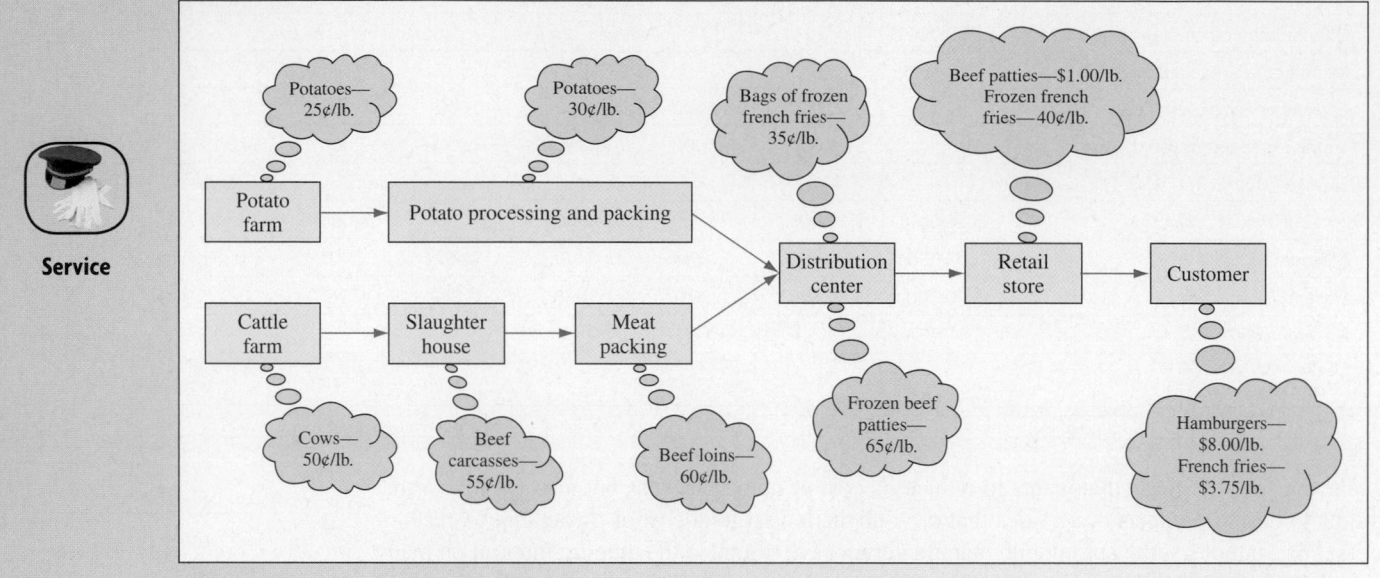

Service

**Tutorials:
Strategic
Sourcing**

through on their way to the local retail store and then to the customer. At each step inventory is carried, and this inventory has a particular cost to the company. Inventory serves as a buffer, thus allowing each stage to operate independently of the others. For example, the distribution center inventory allows the system that supplies the retail stores to operate independently of the meat and potato packing operations. Because the inventory at each stage ties up money, it is important that the operations at each stage are synchronized to minimize the size of these buffer inventories. The efficiency of the supply chain can be measured based on the size of the inventory investment in the supply chain. The inventory investment is measured relative to the total cost of the goods that are provided through the supply chain.

Two common measures to evaluate supply chain efficiency are *inventory turnover* and *weeks of supply*. These essentially measure the same thing and mathematically are the inverse of one another. **Inventory turnover** is calculated as follows:

Inventory turnover

$$\text{Inventory turnover} = \frac{\text{Cost of goods sold}}{\text{Average aggregate inventory value}} \qquad [11.1]$$

Cost of goods sold

Average aggregate inventory value

The cost of goods sold is the annual cost for a company to produce the goods or services provided to customers; it is sometimes referred to as the *cost of revenue*. This does not include the selling and administrative expenses of the company. The average aggregate inventory value is the total value of all items held in inventory for the firm valued at cost. It includes the raw material, work-in-process, finished goods, and distribution inventory considered owned by the company.

Good inventory turnover values vary by industry and the type of products being handled. At one extreme, a grocery store chain may turn inventory over 100 times per year. Values of six to seven are typical for manufacturing firms.

Weeks of supply

In many situations, particularly when distribution inventory is dominant, weeks of supply is the preferred measure. This is a measure of how many weeks' worth of inventory is in the system at a particular point in time. The calculation is as follows:

$$\text{Weeks of supply} = \left(\frac{\text{Average aggregate inventory value}}{\text{Cost of goods sold}} \right) \times 52 \text{ weeks} \qquad [11.2]$$

When company financial reports cite inventory turnover and weeks of supply, we can assume that the measures are being calculated firmwide. This type of calculation is shown in the example that follows using Dell Computer data. These calculations, though, can be done on individual entities within the organization. For example, we might be interested in the production raw materials inventory turnover or the weeks of supply associated with the warehousing operation of a firm. In these cases, the cost would be that associated with the total amount of inventory that runs through the specific inventory. In some very-low-inventory operations, days or even hours are a better unit of time for measuring supply.

A firm considers inventory an investment because the intent is for it to be used in the future. Inventory ties up funds that could be used for other purposes, and a firm may have to borrow money to finance the inventory investment. The objective is to have the proper amount of inventory and to have it in the correct locations in the supply chain. Determining the correct amount of inventory to have in each position requires a thorough analysis of the supply chain coupled with the competitive priorities that define the market for the company's products.

EXAMPLE 11.2: Inventory Turnover Calculation

Dell Computer reported the following information in its 2005 annual report (all dollar amounts are expressed in millions):

Step by Step

Net revenue (fiscal year 2005)	$49,205
Cost of revenue (fiscal year 2005)	$40,190
Production materials on hand (28 January 2005)	$ 228
Work-in-process and finished goods on hand (28 January 2005)	$ 231
Days of supply in inventory	4 days

The cost of revenue corresponds to what we call cost of goods sold. One might think that U.S. companies, at least, would use a common accounting terminology, but this is not true. The inventory turnover calculation is

$$\text{Inventory turnover} = \frac{40,190}{228 + 231} = 87.56 \text{ turns per year}$$

This is amazing performance for a high-tech company, but it explains much of why the company is such a financial success.

The corresponding weeks of supply calculation is

$$\text{Weeks of supply} = \left(\frac{228 + 231}{40,190}\right) \times 52 = .59 \text{ week} \bullet$$

SUMMARY

Strategic sourcing is important in business today. Outsourcing is an important way to reduce cost while improving the strategic focus of a firm. Many companies have enjoyed significant success as a result of the unique ways in which they work with their suppliers. Many firms have adopted sourcing strategies that incorporate criteria that consider sustainable goals related to the environment and people.

Measures of sourcing efficiency are inventory turnover and weeks of supply. Efficient processes should be used for functional products, and responsive processes for innovative products. This alignment of sourcing strategy and product demand characteristics is extremely important to the operational success of a company.

Companies that face diverse sourcing, production, and distribution decisions need to weigh the costs associated with materials, transportation, production, warehousing, and distribution to develop a comprehensive network designed to minimize costs and preserve the environments.

KEY TERMS

Strategic sourcing The development and management of supplier relationships to acquire goods and services in a way that aids in achieving the immediate needs of a business.

Vendor managed inventory When a customer allows the supplier to manage an item or group of items.

Bullwhip effect The variability in demand is magnified as we move from the customer to the producer in the supply chain.

Functional products Staples that people buy in a wide range of retail outlets, such as grocery stores and gas stations.

Innovative products Products such as fashionable clothes and personal computers that typically have a life cycle of just a few months.

Outsourcing Moving some of a firm's internal activities and decision responsibility to outside providers.

Logistics Management functions that support the complete cycle of material flow: from the purchase and internal control of production materials; to the planning and control of work-in-process; to the purchasing, shipping, and distribution of the finished product.

Total cost of ownership (TCO) Estimate of the cost of an item that includes all the costs related to the procurement and use of the item including disposing of the item after its useful life.

Inventory turnover and weeks of supply Measures of supply chain efficiency that are mathematically the inverse of one another.

Cost of goods sold The annual cost for a company to produce the goods or services provided to customers.

Average aggregate inventory value The total value of all items held in inventory for the firm, valued at cost.

Weeks of supply A measure of how many weeks' worth of inventory is in the system at a particular point in time.

FORMULA REVIEW

$$\text{Inventory turnover} = \frac{\text{Cost of goods sold}}{\text{Average aggregate inventory value}} \qquad [11.1]$$

$$\text{Weeks of supply} = \left(\frac{\text{Average aggregate inventory value}}{\text{Cost of goods sold}}\right) \times 52 \text{ weeks} \qquad [11.2]$$

REVIEW AND DISCUSSION QUESTIONS

1 What recent changes have caused supply chain management to gain importance?
2 With so much productive capacity and room for expansion in the United States, why would a company based in the United States choose to purchase items from a foreign firm? Discuss the pros and cons.
3 Describe the differences between functional and innovative products.
4 What are characteristics of efficient, responsive, risk-hedging, and agile supply chains? Can a supply chain be both efficient and responsive? Risk-hedging and agile? Why or why not?
5 As a supplier, which factors about a buyer (your potential customer) would you consider to be important in setting up a long-term relationship?
6 Describe how outsourcing works. Why would a firm want to outsource?

PROBLEMS

1 One of your Taiwanese suppliers has bid on a new line of molded plastic parts that is currently being assembled at your plant. The supplier has bid $0.10 per part, given a forecasted demand of 200,000 parts in year 1; 300,000 in year 2; and 500,000 in year 3. Shipping and handling of parts from the supplier's factory is estimated at $0.01 per unit. Additional inventory handling charges should amount to $0.005 per unit. Finally, administrative costs are estimated at $20 per month.

   Although your plant is able to continue producing the part, the plant would need to invest in another molding machine, which would cost $10,000. Direct materials can be purchased for $0.05 per unit. Direct labor is estimated at $0.03 per unit plus a 50 percent surcharge for benefits; indirect labor is estimated at $0.011 per unit plus 50 percent benefits. Up-front engineering and design costs will amount to $30,000. Finally, management has insisted that overhead be allocated if the parts are made in-house at a rate of 100 percent of direct labor cost. The firm uses a cost of capital of 15 percent per year.

   What should you do, continue to produce in-house or accept the bid from your Taiwanese supplier?

2 Your company assembles five different models of a motor scooter that is sold in specialty stores in the United States. The company uses the same engine for all five models. You have been given the assignment of choosing a supplier for these engines for the coming year. Due to the size of your warehouse and other administrative restrictions, you must order the engines in lot sizes of 1,000 each. Because of the unique characteristics of the engine, special tooling is needed during the manufacturing process, for which you agree to reimburse the supplier. Your assistant has obtained quotes from two reliable engine suppliers and you need to decide which to use. The following data have been collected:

Requirements (annual forecast)	12,000 units
Weight per engine	22 pounds
Order processing cost	$125 per order
Inventory carry cost	20 percent of the average value of inventory per year

Note: Assume that half of lot size is in inventory on average (1,000/2 = 500 units).

Two qualified suppliers have submitted the following quotations:

UNIT PRICE	SUPPLIER 1	SUPPLIER 2
1 to 999 units/order	$ 510.00	$505.00
1,000 to 2,999 units/order	500.00	498.00
3,000 + units/order	490.00	488.00
Tooling costs	$22,000	$20,000
Distance	125 miles	100 miles

Your assistant has obtained the following freight rates from your carrier:

| Truckload (40,000 each load): | $0.80 per ton-mile |
| Less-than-truckload: | $1.20 per ton-mile |

Note: Per ton-mile = 2,000 lbs. per mile

a. Perform a total cost of ownership analysis and select a supplier.

b. If you could move the lot size up to ship in truckload quantities, would your supplier selection change?

3 The McDonald's fast-food restaurant on campus sells an average of 4,000 quarter-pound hamburgers each week. Hamburger patties are resupplied twice a week, and on average the store has 350 pounds of hamburger in stock. Assume that the hamburger costs $1.00 a pound. What is the inventory turnover for the hamburger patties? On average, how many days of supply are on hand?

4 The U.S. Airfilter company has hired you as a supply chain consultant. The company makes air filters for residential heating and air-conditioning systems. These filters are made in a single plant located in Louisville, Kentucky, in the United States. They are distributed to retailers through wholesale centers in 100 locations in the United States, Canada, and Europe. You have collected the following data relating to the value of inventory in the U.S. Airfilter supply chain:

	QUARTER 1 (JANUARY THROUGH MARCH)	QUARTER 2 (APRIL THROUGH JUNE)	QUARTER 3 (JULY THROUGH SEPTEMBER)	QUARTER 4 (OCTOBER THROUGH DECEMBER)
Sales (Total Quarter):				
United States	300	350	405	375
Canada	75	60	75	70
Europe	30	33	20	15
Cost of goods sold (total quarter)	280	295	340	350
Raw materials at the Louisville plant (end-of-quarter)	50	40	55	60
Work-in-process and finished goods at the Louisville plant (end-of-quarter)	100	105	120	150
Distribution center inventory (end-of-quarter):				
United States	25	27	23	30
Canada	10	11	15	16
Europe	5	4	5	5

All amounts in millions of U.S. dollars

Excel: U.S. Airfilter

a. What is the average inventory turnover for the firm?
b. If you were given the assignment to increase inventory turnover, what would you focus on? Why?
c. The company reported that it used $500M worth of raw material during the year. On average, how many weeks of supply of raw material are on hand at the factory?

CASE: PEPE JEANS

Pepe began to produce and sell denim jeans in the early 1970s in the United Kingdom and has achieved enormous growth. Pepe's success was the result of a unique approach in a product market dominated by strong brands and limited variety. Pepe presented a range of jeans styles that offered a better fit than traditional five-pocket Western jeans (such as those made by Levi Strauss in the United States)—particularly for female customers. The Pepe range of basic styles is modified each season, but each style keeps its identity with a slightly whimsical name featured prominently on the jeans and on the point-of-sale material. Variations such as modified washes, leather trim, and even designer wear marks are applied to respond to changing fashion trends. To learn more about Pepe and its products, visit its Web site at http://www.pepejeans.com.

Pepe's brand strength is such that the company can demand a retail price that averages about £45 (£1 = $1.8) for its standard products. A high percentage of Pepe sales are through about 1,500 independent outlets throughout the United Kingdom. The company maintains contact with its independent retailers via a group of approximately 10 agents, who are self-employed and work exclusively for Pepe. Each agent is responsible for retailers in a particular area of the country.

Pepe is convinced that a good relationship with the independent retailers is vital to its success. The agent meets with each independent retailer three to four times each year in order to present the new collections and to take sales orders. Because the number of accounts for each agent is so large, contact is often achieved by holding a presentation in a hotel for several retailers. Agents take orders from retailers for six-month delivery. After Pepe receives an order, the retailer has only one week in which to cancel because of the need to place immediate firm orders in Hong Kong to meet the delivery date. The company has had a long-standing policy of not holding any inventory of jeans in the United Kingdom.

After an order is taken and confirmed, the rest of the process up to delivery is administered from the Pepe office in Willesden. The status of orders can be checked from a Web site maintained by Pepe. The actual orders are sent to a sourcing agent in Hong Kong who arranges for manufacturing the jeans. The sourcing agent handles all the details associated with materials, fabrication, and shipping the completed jeans to the retailer. Pepe has an outstanding team of young in-house designers who are responsible for developing new styles and the accompanying point-of-sale material. Jeans are made to specifications provided by this team. The team works closely with the Hong Kong sourcing agent to ensure that the jeans are made properly and that the material used is of the highest quality.

A recent survey of the independent retailers indicated some growing problems. The independents praised the fit, quality, and variety of Pepe's jeans, although many thought that they had become much less of a trendsetter than in their early days. It was felt that Pepe's variety of styles and quality were the company's key advantage over the competition. However, the independents were unhappy with Pepe's requirements to place firm orders six months in advance with no possibility of amendment, cancellation, or repeat ordering. Some claimed that the inflexible order system forced them to order less, resulting in stockouts of particular sizes and styles. The retailers estimated that Pepe's sales would increase by about 10 percent with a more flexible ordering system.

The retailers expected to have some slow-moving inventory, but the six-month order lead time made it difficult to accurately order and worsened the problem. Because the fashion market was so impulsive, the current favorites were often not in vogue six months in the future. On the other hand, when demand exceeded expectations, it took a long time to fill the gap. What the retailers wanted was some method of limited returns, exchange, or reordering to overcome the worst of these problems. Pepe was feeling some pressure to respond to these complaints because some of Pepe's smaller competitors offered delivery in only a few days.

Pepe has enjoyed considerable financial success with its current business model. Sales last year were approximately £200M. Cost of sales was approximately 40 percent, operating expenses 28 percent, and profit before taxes nearly 32 percent of sales. The company has no long-term debt and has a very healthy cash position.

Pepe was feeling considerable pressure and felt that a change was going to be needed soon. In evaluating alternatives the company found that the easiest would be to work with the Hong Kong sourcing agent to reduce the lead time associated with orders. The agent agreed that the lead time could be shortened, possibly to as little as six weeks, but costs would increase significantly. Currently, the agent collects orders over a period of time and about every two weeks puts these orders out on bid to about 1,000 potential suppliers. The sourcing agent estimated that costs might go up 30 percent if the lead time were shortened to six weeks. Even with the significant increase in cost, consistent delivery schedules would be difficult to keep.

The sourcing agent suggested that Pepe consider building a finishing operation in the United Kingdom. The agent indicated that a major retail chain in the United States had moved to this type of structure with considerable success. Basically, all the finishing operation did for the U.S. retail chain was apply different washes to the jeans to give them different "worn" looks. The U.S. operation also took orders for the retail stores and shipped the orders. The U.S. firm found that it could give two-day response time to the retail stores.

The sourcing agent indicated that costs for the basic jeans (jeans where the wash has not been applied) could probably be reduced by 10 percent because the volumes would be higher. In addition, lead time for the basic jeans could be reduced to approximately three months because the finishing step would be eliminated and the orders would be larger.

The Pepe designers found this an interesting idea, so they visited the U.S. operation to see how the system worked. They found that they would have to keep about six weeks' supply of basic jeans on hand in the United Kingdom and that they would have to invest in about £1,000,000 worth of equipment. They estimated that it would cost about £500,000 to operate the facility each year. They could locate the facility in the basement of the current Willesden office building, and the renovations would cost about £300,000.

QUESTIONS

1 Acting as an outside consultant, what would you recommend that Pepe do? Given the data in the case, perform a financial analysis to evaluate the alternatives that you have identified. (Assume that the new inventory could be valued at six weeks' worth of the yearly cost of sales. Use a 30 percent inventory carrying cost rate.) Calculate a payback period for each alternative.

2 Are there other alternatives that Pepe should consider?

SOURCE: THE IDEA FOR THIS CASE CAME FROM A CASE TITLED "PEPE JEANS" WRITTEN BY D. BRAMLEY AND C. JOHN OF THE LONDON BUSINESS SCHOOL. PEPE JEANS IS A REAL COMPANY, BUT THE DATA GIVEN IN THE CASE DO NOT REPRESENT ACTUAL COMPANY DATA.

SUPER QUIZ

1 Refers to how common an item is or how many substitutes might be available.

2 When a customer allows the supplier to manage an item or group of items.

3 A phenomenon characterized by increased variation in ordering as we move from the customer to the manufacturer in the supply chain.

4 Products that satisfy basic needs and do not change much over time.

5 Products with short life cycles and typically high profit margins.

6 A supply chain that must deal with high levels of both supply and demand uncertainty.

7 In order to cope with high levels of supply uncertainty a firm would use this strategy to reduce risk.

8 Used to describe functions related to the flow of material in a supply chain.

9 When a firm works with suppliers to look for opportunities to save money and benefit the environment.

10 Refers to an estimate of the cost of an item that includes all costs related to the procurement and use of an item, including the costs of disposing after its useful life.

1. Specificity 2. Vendor managed inventory 3. Bullwhip effect 4. Functional products 5. Innovative products 6. Agile supply chain 7. Multiple sources of supply (pooling) 8. Logistics 9. Green sourcing 10. Total cost of ownership.

SELECTED BIBLIOGRAPHY

Bowersox, D. J.; D. J. Closs; and M. B. Cooper. *Supply Chain and Logistics Management.* New York: Irwin/McGraw-Hill, 2002.

Burt, D. N.; D. W. Dobler; and S. L. Starling. *World Class Supply Management*[SM]*: The Key to Supply Chain Management.* 7th ed. New York: McGraw-Hill/Irwin, 2003.

Chopra, S., and P. Meindl. *Supply Chain Management: Strategy, Planning, and Operations.* 2nd ed. Upper Saddle River, NJ: Prentice Hall, 2003.

Greaver II, M. F. *Strategic Outsourcing: A Structured Approach to Outsourcing Decisions and Initiatives.* New York: American Management Association, 1999.

Hayes, R.; G. Pisano; D. Upton; and S. Wheelwright. *Operations Strategy and Technology: Pursuing the Competitive Edge.* New York: John Wiley & Sons, 2005.

Simchi-Levi, D.; P. Kaminski; and E. Simchi-Levi. *Supply Chain Management.* 2nd ed. New York: McGraw-Hill, 2003.

Vollmann, T.; W. L. Berry; D. C. Whybark; and F. R. Jacobs. *Manufacturing Planning and Control Systems for Supply Chain Management: The Definitive Guide for Professionals.* New York: McGraw-Hill/Irwin, 2004.

FOOTNOTES

1 M. L. Fisher, "What Is the Right Supply Chain for Your Product?" *Harvard Business Review,* March–April 1997, pp. 105–16.

2 Hau L. Lee, "Aligning Supply Chain Strategies with Product Uncertainties," *California Management Review* 44, no. 3 (Spring 2002), pp. 105–19. Copyright © 2002 by the Regents of the University of California. By permission of the Regents.

3 "Have Factory Will Travel," *The Economist,* February 12–18, 2000, pp. 61–62.

4 Adapted from Martha Craumer, "How to Think Strategically about Outsourcing," *Harvard Management Update,* May 2002, p. 4.

5 See David Burt et al., *Supply Management,* 8th ed. (McGraw-Hill/Irwin, 2010), pp. 306–10.

6 Example is from Burt et al., *Supply Management,* p. 311.

chapter 12

LOCATION, LOGISTICS, AND DISTRIBUTION

FEDEX: A LEADING GLOBAL LOGISTICS COMPANY

FedEx provides a host of logistics solutions to its customers. Those services are segmented on the basis of types of customer needs, ranging from turnkey distribution centers to full-scale logistics services that incorporate expedited delivery. Following are some of the major services provided to the business customer:

Service

Supply Chain

Global

FedEx Distribution Centers: These centers provide turnkey warehousing services to businesses, using a network of warehouses in the United States and abroad. This service is targeted particularly at time-critical businesses. Goods stored in these centers are continuously available for 24-hour deliveries.

After reading the chapter you will:

1. Describe what a third-party logistics provider is.

2. Assess the major issues that need to be considered in locating a plant or warehouse facility.

3. Set up the transportation model to analyze location problems and use Excel Solver to find solutions to these models.

4. Understand the centroid method for locating entities such as cell phone communication towers.

5. Know how a factor-rating system can be used to narrow potential location sites.

FedEx Returns Management: FedEx Return solutions are designed to streamline the return area of a company's supply chain. These process-intelligent tools give customers services that offer pickup, delivery, and online status tracking for items that need to be returned.

Other Value-Added Services: FedEx offers many other value-added services to its customers. One example is a merge-in-transit service offered to many customers that require rapid delivery. For example, under the merge-in-transit program, for a shipper of computers, FedEx could store peripheral products such as monitors and printers in its Memphis air hub and match those products up with the computer en route to a customer.

LOGISTICS

Supply Chain

Global

Logistics

International logistics

Third-party logistics company

A major issue in designing a great supply chain for manufactured goods is determining the way those items are moved from the manufacturing plant to the customer. For consumer products this often involves moving product from the manufacturing plant to a warehouse and then to a retail store. You probably do not think about this often, but consider all those items with "Made in China" on the label. That sweatshirt probably has made a trip longer than you may ever make. If you live in Chicago in the United States and the sweatshirt is made in the Fujian region of China, that sweatshirt traveled over 6,600 miles, or 10,600 kilometers, nearly halfway around the world, to get to the retail store where you bought it. To keep the price of the sweatshirt down, that trip must be made as efficiently as possible. There is no telling how that sweatshirt made the trip. It might have been flown in an airplane or might have traveled in a combination of vehicles, possibly going by truck part of the way and by boat or plane the rest. Logistics is about this movement of goods through the supply chain.

The Association for Operations Management defines **logistics** as "the art and science of obtaining, producing, and distributing material and product in the proper place and in proper quantities." This is a fairly broad definition, and this chapter will focus on how to analyze where we locate warehouses and plants and how to evaluate the movement of materials to and from those locations. The term **international logistics** refers to managing these functions when the movement is on a global scale. Clearly, if the China-made sweatshirt is sold in the United States or Europe, this involves international logistics.

There are companies that specialize in logistics, such as United Parcel Service (UPS), Federal Express (FedEx), and DHL. These global companies are in the business of moving everything from flowers to industrial equipment. Today a manufacturing company most often will contract with one of those companies to handle many of its logistics functions. In this case, those transportation companies often are called a **third-party logistics company**. The most basic function would be simply moving the goods from one place to another. The logistics company also may provide additional services such as warehouse management, inventory control, and other customer service functions.

Logistics is big business, accounting for 8 to 9 percent of the U.S. gross domestic product, and growing. Today's modern, efficient warehouse and distribution centers are the heart of logistics. These centers are carefully managed and efficiently operated to ensure the secure storage and quick flow of goods, services, and related information from the point of origin to the point of consumption.

DECISIONS RELATED TO LOGISTICS

The problem of deciding how best to transport goods from plants to customers is a complex one that affects the cost of a product. Major trade-offs related to the cost of transporting the product, speed of delivery, and flexibility to react to changes are involved. Information systems play a major role in coordinating activities and include activities such as allocating resources, managing inventory levels, scheduling, and order tracking. A full discussion of these systems is beyond the scope of this book, but we cover basic inventory control and scheduling in later chapters.

A key decision area is deciding how material will be transported. The Logistics-System Design Matrix shown in Exhibit 12.1 depicts the basic alternatives. There are six widely recognized modes of transportation: highway (trucks), water (ships), air (aircraft), rail (trains), pipelines, and hand delivery. Each mode is uniquely suited to handle certain types of products, as described next:

- **Highway (truck).** Actually, few products are moved without some highway transportation. The highway offers great flexibility for moving goods to virtually any location not separated by water. Size of the product, weight, and liquid or bulk can all be accommodated with this mode.
- **Water (ship).** Very high capacity and very low cost, but transit times are slow, and large areas of the world are not directly accessible to water carriers. This mode is especially useful for bulk items such as oil, coal, and chemical products.
- **Air.** Fast but expensive. Small, light, expensive items are most appropriate for this mode of transportation.

Logistics-System Design Matrix: Framework Describing Logistics Processes   **exhibit 12.1**

- **Rail (trains).** This is a fairly low-cost alternative, but transit times can be long and may be subject to variability. The suitability of rail can vary depending on the rail infrastructure. The European infrastructure is highly developed, making this an attractive alternative compared to trucks, while in the United States, the infrastructure has declined over the last 50 years, making it less attractive.
- **Pipelines.** This is highly specialized and limited to liquids, gases, and solids in slurry forms. No packaging is needed and the costs per mile are low. The initial cost to build a pipeline is very high.
- **Hand Delivery.** This is the last step in many supply chains. Getting the product in the customer's hand is a relatively slow and costly activity due to the high labor content.

Few companies use a single mode of transportation. Multimodal solutions are the norm, and finding the correct multimode strategies can be a significant problem. The problem of coordination and scheduling the carriers requires comprehensive information systems capable of tracking goods through the system. Standardized containers often are used so that a product can be transferred efficiently from a truck to an airplane or ship.

CROSS-DOCKING

Cross-docking

Special consolidation warehouses are used when shipments from various sources are pulled together and combined into larger shipments with a common destination. This improves the efficiency of the entire system. Cross-docking is an approach used in these consolidation warehouses, where, instead of larger shipments, large shipments are broken down into small shipments for local delivery in an area. This often can be done in a coordinated manner so that the goods never are stored in inventory.

Retailers receive shipments from many suppliers in their regional warehouses and immediately sort those shipments for delivery to individual stores by using cross-docking systems coordinated by computerized control systems. This results in a minimal amount of inventory being carried in the warehouses.

Hub-and-spoke systems

Hub-and-spoke systems combine the idea of consolidation and that of cross-docking. Here the warehouse is referred to as a "hub" and its sole purpose is sorting goods. Incoming goods are sorted immediately to consolidation areas, where each area is designated for shipment to a specific location. Hubs are located in strategic locations near the geographic center of the region they are to serve to minimize the distance a good must travel.

Designing a system is an interesting and complex task. The following section focuses on the plant and warehouse location problem as representative of the types of logistics decisions that need to be made. Logistics is a broad topic, and its elements evolve as the value-added services provided by major logistics vendors expand. Having the proper network design is fundamental to efficiency in the industry.

ISSUES IN FACILITY LOCATION

Global

The problem of facility location is faced by both new and existing businesses, and its solution is critical to a company's eventual success. An important element in designing a company's supply chain is the location of its facilities. For instance, 3M has moved a significant part of its corporate activity, including R&D, to the more temperate climate of Austin, Texas. Toys "Я" Us has opened a location in Japan as a part of its global strategy. Disney chose Paris, France, for its European theme park, and BMW assembles the Z3 sports car in South Carolina. Manufacturing and service companies' location decisions are guided by a variety of criteria defined by competitive imperatives. Criteria that influence manufacturing plant and warehouse location planning are discussed next.

Proximity to Customers   Japan's NTN Driveshafts Inc. built a major plant in Columbus, Indiana, to be closer to major automobile manufacturing plants in the United States—

whose buyers want their goods delivered yesterday. Such proximity also helps ensure that customer needs are incorporated into products being developed and built.

Business Climate A favorable business climate can include the presence of similar-sized businesses, the presence of companies in the same industry, and, in the case of international locations, the presence of other foreign companies. Probusiness government legislation and local government intervention to facilitate businesses locating in an area via subsidies, tax abatements, and other support are also factors.

Total Costs The objective is to select a site with the lowest total cost. This includes regional costs, inbound distribution costs, and outbound distribution costs. Land, construction, labor, taxes, and energy costs make up the regional costs. Additional hidden costs are difficult to measure. These involve (1) excessive moving of preproduction material between locations before final delivery to the customers and (2) loss of customer responsiveness arising from locating away from the main customer base.

Infrastructure Adequate road, rail, air, and sea transportation is vital. Energy and telecommunications requirements also must be met. In addition, the local government's willingness to invest in upgrading infrastructure to the levels required may be an incentive to select a specific location.

Quality of Labor The educational and skill levels of the labor pool must match the company's needs. Even more important are the willingness and ability to learn.

Suppliers A high-quality and competitive supplier base makes a given location suitable. The proximity of important suppliers' plants also supports lean production methods.

Other Facilities The location of other plants or distribution centers of the same company may influence a new facility's location in the network. Issues of product mix and capacity are strongly interconnected to the location decision in this context.

Free Trade Zones A foreign trade zone or a free trade zone is typically a closed facility (under the supervision of the customs department) into which foreign goods can be brought without being subject to the normal customs requirements. There are about 260 such free trade zones in the United States today. Such specialized locations also exist in other countries. Manufacturers in free trade zones can use imported components in the final product and delay payment of customs duties until the product is shipped into the host country.

Political Risk The fast-changing geopolitical scenes in numerous nations present exciting, challenging opportunities. But the extended phase of transformation that many countries are undergoing makes the decision to locate in those areas extremely difficult. Political risks in both the country of location and the host country influence location decisions.

Government Barriers Barriers to enter and locate in many countries are being removed today through legislation. Yet many nonlegislative and cultural barriers should be considered in location planning.

Trading Blocs The Central America Free Trade Agreement (CAFTA) is one of the new trading blocs in our hemisphere. Such agreements influence location decisions, both within and outside trading bloc countries. Firms typically locate, or relocate, within a bloc to take advantage of new market opportunities or lower total costs afforded by the trading agreement. Other companies (those outside the trading bloc countries) decide on locations within the bloc so as not to be disqualified from competing in the new market. Examples

Free trade zone

Global

Trading blocs

CONVENIENCE DRIVES HONDA DECISION

When Honda announced that it would build its sixth assembly plant in Greensburg, Indiana, the *Chicago Tribune* said the decision was based on "Location, location, location." Indiana had it. Illinois and Ohio did not. Honda invested $550 million to build the operation which now employs 1,000 workers in this "flex plant" capable of producing multiple models. In May of 2009, the plant produced its first Civic GX, the only natural gas vehicle built by a major automaker in the U.S.

While Indiana promised Honda $141.5 million in incentives to locate in Greensburg, Larry Jutte, a company executive, rejected the idea that handouts were a factor. "It wasn't a matter of incentives offered; that was never a consideration. It was a matter of logistics, the human factor, the infrastructure, and the location." He said the decision was based on being in close proximity to suppliers of parts, particularly the source of four-cylinder engines from Honda's operation in Anna, Ohio. The 1,700-acre Greensburg site is near I-74 and about 50 miles southwest of Indianapolis, and will be built with expansion as a possibility. Altogether, so far, Honda has invested $9 billion locating facilities in North America.

An interesting sidelight is that this plant will now be close to the Indy 500. "For more than 50 years, racing has been a key part of the Honda culture, and we use racing to help train our engineers," said Koichi Kondo, president and CEO of American Honda. "Last month the winning car at the Indy 500 was powered by a Honda engine. In fact all 33 cars in the race were powered by Honda engines." Amazingly, since Honda became the sole supplier of engines for the Indy 500 in 2006 and through the 2009 race, there have been no engine failures. Kondo said Honda and Indiana are beginning a long race together.

SOURCES: "CONVENIENCE DRIVES INDIANA TO VICTORY," *CHICAGO TRIBUNE*—BUSINESS, JUNE 29, 2006; http://blogs.edmunds.com/; http://corporate .honda.com/press; MOTOR SPORT FORUM, MAY 9, 2009.

include the location of various Japanese auto manufacturing plants in Europe before 1992 as well as recent moves by many communications and financial services companies into Mexico in a post-NAFTA environment.

Environmental Regulation   The environmental regulations that impact a certain industry in a given location should be included in the location decision. Besides measurable cost implications, these regulations influence the relationship with the local community.

Host Community   The host community's interest in having the plant in its midst is a necessary part of the evaluation process. Local educational facilities and the broader issue of quality of life are also important.

Global

Competitive Advantage   An important decision for multinational companies is the nation in which to locate the home base for each distinct business. Porter suggests that a company can have different home bases for distinct businesses or segments. Competitive advantage is created at a home base where strategy is set, the core product and process technology are created, and a critical mass of production takes place. So a company should move its home base to a country that stimulates innovation and provides the best environment for global competitiveness.[1] This concept can also be applied to domestic companies seeking to gain sustainable competitive advantage. It partly explains the southeastern states' recent emergence as the preferred corporate destination within the United States (that is, their business climate fosters innovation and low-cost production).

PLANT LOCATION METHODS

As we will see, many techniques are available for identifying potential sites for plants or other types of facilities. The process required to narrow the decision down to a particular area can vary significantly depending on the type of business and the competitive pressures that must be considered. As we have discussed, often many different criteria need to be considered when selecting from the set of feasible sites.

In this section, we sample three different types of techniques that have proven to be very useful to many companies. The first is the *factor-rating system* that allows us to consider many different types of criteria using simple point-rating scales. Next, we consider the *transportation method* of linear programming, a powerful technique for estimating the cost of using a network of plants and warehouses. Following this, we consider the *centroid method*, a technique often used by communications companies (cell phone providers) to locate their transmission towers. Finally, later in the chapter we consider how service firms such as McDonald's and State Farm Insurance use statistical techniques to find desirable locations for their facilities.

FACTOR-RATING SYSTEMS

Factor-rating systems are perhaps the most widely used of the general location techniques because they provide a mechanism to combine diverse factors in an easy-to-understand format.

Factor-rating systems

By way of example, a refinery assigned the following range of point values to major factors affecting a set of possible sites:

	RANGE
Fuels in region	0 to 330
Power availability and reliability	0 to 200
Labor climate	0 to 100
Living conditions	0 to 100
Transportation	0 to 50
Water supply	0 to 10
Climate	0 to 50
Supplies	0 to 60
Tax policies and laws	0 to 20

Each site was then rated against each factor, and a point value was selected from its assigned range. The sums of assigned points for each site were then compared. The site with the most points was selected.

A major problem with simple point-rating schemes is that they do not account for the wide range of costs that may occur within each factor. For example, there may be only a few hundred dollars' difference between the best and worst locations on one factor and several thousands of dollars' difference between the best and the worst on another. The first factor may have the most points available to it but provide little help in making the location decision; the second may have few points available but potentially show a real difference in the value of locations. To deal with this problem, it has been suggested that points possible for each factor be derived using a weighting scale based on standard deviations of costs rather than simply total cost amounts. In this way, relative costs can be considered.

TRANSPORTATION METHOD OF LINEAR PROGRAMMING

The **transportation method** is a special linear programming method. (Note that linear programming is developed in detail in Appendix A.) It gets its name from its application to problems involving transporting products from several sources to several destinations. The

Transportation method

exhibit 12.2   Data for U.S. Pharmaceutical Transportation Problem

					SHIPPING COSTS PER CASE (IN DOLLARS)			
FACTORY	SUPPLY	WAREHOUSE	DEMAND	FROM	To COLUMBUS	To ST. LOUIS	To DENVER	To LOS ANGELES
Indianapolis	15	Columbus	10	Indianapolis	$25	$35	$36	$60
Phoenix	6	St. Louis	12	Phoenix	55	30	25	25
New York	14	Denver	15	New York	40	50	80	90
Atlanta	11	Los Angeles	9	Atlanta	30	40	66	75

exhibit 12.3   Transportation Matrix for U.S. Pharmaceutical Problem

From \ To	Columbus	St. Louis	Denver	Los Angeles	Factory supply
Indianapolis	25	35	36	60	15
Phoenix	55	30	25	25	6
New York	40	50	80	90	14
Atlanta	30	40	66	75	11
Destination requirements	10	12	15	9	46 / 46

two common objectives of such problems are either (1) minimize the cost of shipping *n* units to *m* destinations or (2) maximize the profit of shipping *n* units to *m* destinations.

Step by Step

Tutorial: Transportation Method Solver

EXAMPLE 12.1: U.S. Pharmaceutical Company

Suppose the U.S. Pharmaceutical Company has four factories supplying the warehouses of four major customers and its management wants to determine the minimum-cost shipping schedule for its monthly output to these customers. Factory supply, warehouse demands, and shipping costs per case for these drugs are shown in Exhibit 12.2.

The transportation matrix for this example appears in Exhibit 12.3, where supply availability at each factory is shown in the far right column and the warehouse demands are shown in the bottom row. The shipping costs are shown in the small boxes within the cells. For example, the cost to ship one unit from the Indianapolis factory to the customer warehouse in Columbus is $25. The actual flows would be shown in the cells intersecting the factory rows and warehouse columns.

SOLUTION

This problem can be solved by using Microsoft Excel's Solver function. If you are not familiar with the Solver, you should study Appendix A, "Linear Programming Using the Excel Solver." Exhibit 12.4 shows how the problem can be set up in the spreadsheet. Cells B6 through E6 contain the requirement for each customer warehouse. Cells F2 through F5 contain the amount that can be supplied from each plant. Cells B2 through E5 are the cost of shipping one unit for each potential plant and warehouse combination.

Excel Screen Showing the U.S. Pharmaceutical Problem

exhibit 12.4

**Excel:
US Pharmaceutical**

Microsoft Excel - US Pharmaceutical.xls

File Edit View Insert Format Tools Data Window Help

F20   =   =SUM(B16:E19)

	A	B	C	D	E	F
1	**From/To**	Columbus	St. Louis	Denver	Los Angeles	**Factory Supply**
2	Indianapolis	25	35	36	60	15
3	Phoenix	55	30	25	25	6
4	New York	40	50	80	90	14
5	Atlanta	30	40	66	75	11
6	**Requirements**	10	12	15	9	
7						
8	**Candidate Solution**					**Total Shipped**
9	Indianapolis	0	0	15	0	15
10	Phoenix	0	0	0	6	6
11	New York	10	4	0	0	14
12	Atlanta	0	8	0	3	11
13	**Total Supplied**	10	12	15	9	
14						
15	**Cost Calculations**					
16	Indianapolis	0	0	540	0	
17	Phoenix	0	0	0	150	
18	New York	400	200	0	0	
19	Atlanta	0	320	0	225	
20					**Total Cost**	$1,835
21						
22						

US Pharmaceutical

Ready   NUM

**Tutorial:
Intro to Solver**

Cells for the solution of the problem are B9 through E12. These cells can initially be left blank when setting up the spreadsheet. Column cells F9 through F12 are the sum of each row, indicating how much is actually being shipped from each factory in the candidate solution. Similarly, row cells B13 through E13 are sums of the amount being shipped to each customer in the candidate solution. The Excel Sum function can be used to calculate these values.

The cost of the candidate solution is calculated in cells B16 through E19. Multiplying the amount shipped in the candidate solution by the cost per unit of shipping over that particular route makes this calculation. For example, multiplying B2 by B9 in cell B16 gives the cost of shipping between Indianapolis and Columbus for the candidate solution. The total cost shown in cell F20 is the sum of all these individual costs.

To solve the problem, the Excel Solver application needs to be accessed. The Solver is found by selecting Tools and then Solver from the Excel menu. A screen similar to what is shown below should appear. If you cannot find Solver at that location, the required add-in might not have been added when Excel was initially installed on your computer. Solver can easily be added if you have your original Excel installation disk.

Solver parameters now need to be set. First set the target cell. This is the cell where the total cost associated with the solution is calculated. In our sample problem, this is cell F20. Next we need to indicate that we are minimizing this cell. Selecting the "Min" button does this. The location of our solution is indicated in the "Changing Cells." These cells are B9 through E12 in our example.

Next we need to indicate the constraints for our problem. For our transportation problem we need to be sure that customer demand is met and that we do not exceed the capacity of our manufacturing plants. To ensure that demand is met, click on "Add" and highlight the range of cells where we have calculated the total amount being shipped to each customer. This range is B13 to E13 in our example. Next select "=" indicating that we want the amount shipped to equal demand. Finally, on the right side enter the range of cells where the actual customer demand is stated in our spreadsheet. This range is B6 to E6 in our example.

The second set of constraints that ensures that the capacity of our manufacturing plants is not exceeded is entered similarly. The range of cells that indicated how much is being shipped from each factory is F9 to F12. These values need to be less than or equal to ($<=$) the capacity of each factory,

**Tutorials:
Intro to Solver**

which is in cells F2 to F5. To set up the Solver, a few options need to be set as well. Click on the "Options" button and the following screen should appear:

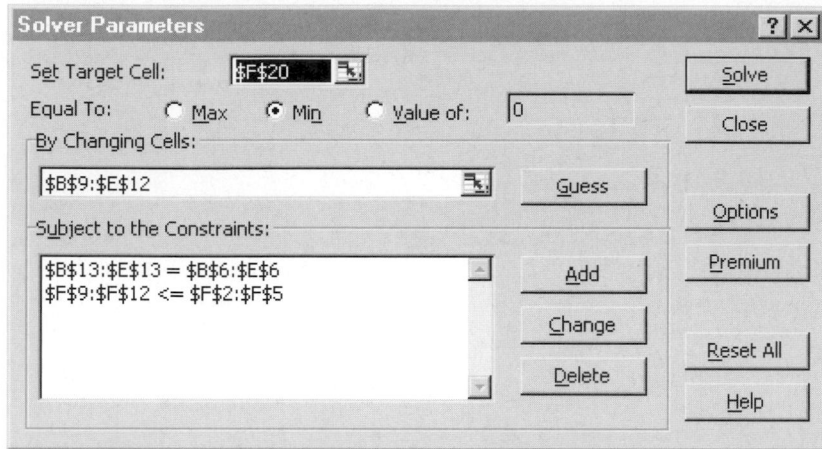

Excel® Screen shots from Microsoft® Excel © 2007 Microsoft Corporation.

Two options need to be set for solving transportation problems. First we need "Assume Linear Model." This tells the Solver that there are no nonlinear calculations in our spreadsheet. This is important because the Solver can use a very efficient algorithm to calculate the optimal solution to this problem if this condition exists. Next the "Assume Non-Negative" box needs to be checked. This tells

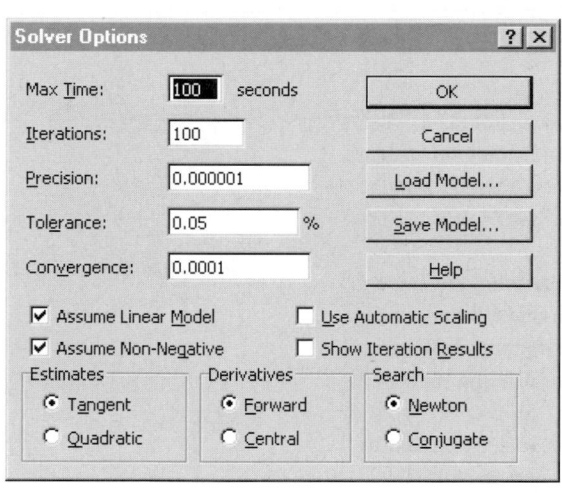

Solver that the values in our solution need to be greater than or equal to zero. In transportation problems, shipping negative quantities does not make any sense. Click "OK" to return to the main Solver box, and then click "Solve" to actually solve the problem. Solver will notify you that it found a solution. Indicate that you want that solution saved. Finally, click OK to go back to the main spreadsheet. The solution should be in cells B9 to E12.

The transportation method can be used to solve many different types of problems if it is applied innovatively. For example, it can be used to test the cost impact of different candidate locations on the entire production–distribution network. To do this we might add a new row that contains the unit shipping cost from a factory in a new location, say, Dallas, to the existing set of customer warehouses, along with the total amount it could supply. We could then solve this particular matrix for minimum total cost. Next we would replace the factory located in Dallas in the same row of the matrix with a factory at a different location, Houston, and again solve for minimum total cost. Assuming the factories in Dallas and Houston would be identical in other important respects, the location resulting in the lowest total cost for the network would be selected.

For additional information about using the Solver, see Appendix A, "Linear Programming Using the Excel Solver." ●

CENTROID METHOD

Centroid method

The **centroid method** is a technique for locating single facilities that considers the existing facilities, the distances between them, and the volumes of goods to be shipped. The technique is often used to locate intermediate or distribution warehouses. In its simplest form, this method assumes that inbound and outbound transportation costs are equal, and it does not include special shipping costs for less than full loads.

Another major application of the centroid method today is the location of communication towers in urban areas. Examples include radio, TV, and cell phone towers. In this application the goal is to find sites that are near clusters of customers, thus ensuring clear radio signals.

The centroid method begins by placing the existing locations on a coordinate grid system. Coordinates are usually based on longitude and latitude measures due to the rapid adoption of GPS systems for mapping locations. To keep it simple for our examples, we use arbitrary *X, Y* coordinates. Exhibit 12.5 shows an example of a grid layout.

Grid Map for Centroid Example

exhibit 12.5

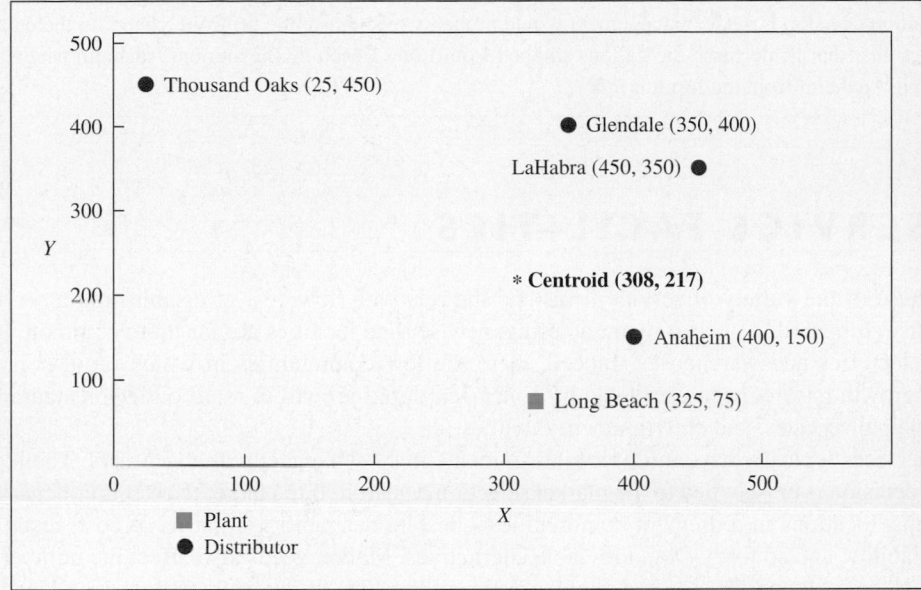

**Excel:
Centroid_method**

LOCATIONS	GALLONS OF GASOLINE PER MONTH (000,000)
Long Beach	1,500
Anaheim	250
LaHabra	450
Glendale	350
Thousand Oaks	450

The centroid is found by calculating the X and Y coordinates that result in the minimal transportation cost. We use the formulas

$$C_x = \frac{\Sigma d_{ix} V_i}{\Sigma V_i} \qquad C_y = \frac{\Sigma d_{iy} V_i}{\Sigma V_i}$$

[12.1]

where

C_x = X coordinate of the centroid

C_y = Y coordinate of the centroid

d_{ix} = X coordinate of the *i*th location

d_{iy} = Y coordinate of the *i*th location

V_i = Volume of goods moved to or from the *i*th location

EXAMPLE 12.2: HiOctane Refining Company

The HiOctane Refining Company needs to locate an intermediate holding facility between its refining plant in Long Beach and its major distributors. Exhibit 12.5 shows the coordinate map and the amount of gasoline shipped to or from the plant and distributors.

In this example, for the Long Beach location (the first location), $d_{1x} = 325$, $d_{1y} = 75$, and $V_1 = 1,500$.

Step by Step

SOLUTION

Using the information in Exhibit 12.5, we can calculate the coordinates of the centroid:

$$C_x = \frac{(325 \times 1,500) + (400 \times 250) + (450 \times 450) + (350 \times 350) + (25 \times 450)}{1,500 + 250 + 450 + 350 + 450}$$

$$= \frac{923,750}{3,000} = 307.9$$

$$C_y = \frac{(75 \times 1,500) + (150 \times 250) + (350 \times 450) + (400 \times 350) + (450 \times 450)}{1,500 + 250 + 450 + 350 + 450}$$

$$= \frac{650,000}{3,000} = 216.7$$

This gives management the *X* and *Y* coordinates of approximately 308 and 217, respectively, and provides an initial starting point to search for a new site. By examining the location of the calculated centroid on the grid map, we can see that it might be more cost-efficient to ship directly between the Long Beach plant and the Anaheim distributor than to ship via a warehouse near the centroid. Before a location decision is made, management would probably recalculate the centroid, changing the data to reflect this (that is, decrease the gallons shipped from Long Beach by the amount Anaheim needs and remove Anaheim from the formula). ●

LOCATING SERVICE FACILITIES

Service

Because of the variety of service firms and the relatively low cost of establishing a service facility compared to one for manufacturing, new service facilities are far more common than new factories and warehouses. Indeed, there are few communities in which rapid population growth has not been paralleled by concurrent rapid growth in retail outlets, restaurants, municipal services, and entertainment facilities.

Services typically have multiple sites to maintain close contact with customers. The location decision is closely tied to the market selection decision. If the target market is college-age groups, locations in retirement communities—despite desirability in terms of cost, resource availability, and so forth—are not viable alternatives. Market needs also affect the number of sites to be built and the size and characteristics of the sites. Whereas manufacturing location decisions are often made by minimizing costs, many service location decision techniques maximize the profit potential of various sites. Next we present a multiple regression model that can be used to help select good sites.

Step by Step

EXAMPLE 12.3: Screening Hotel Location Sites

Selecting good sites is crucial to a hotel chain's success. Of the four major marketing considerations (price, product, promotion, and location), location and product have been shown to be most important for multisite firms. As a result, hotel chain owners who can pick good sites quickly have a distinct competitive advantage.

Exhibit 12.6 shows the initial list of variables included in a study to help a hotel chain screen potential locations for its new hotels. Data were collected on 57 existing sites. Analysis of the data identified the variables that correlated with operating profit in two years. (See Exhibit 12.7.)

SOLUTION

A *regression model* (see Chapter 15) was constructed. Its final form was

$$\text{Profitability} = 39.05 - 5.41 \times \text{State population per inn (1,000)}$$
$$+ 5.86 \times \text{Price of the inn}$$
$$- 3.91 \times \text{Square root of the median income of the area (1,000)}$$
$$+ 1.75 \times \text{College students within four miles}$$

The model shows that profitability is affected by market penetration, positively affected by price, negatively affected by higher incomes (the inns do better in lower-median-income areas), and positively affected by colleges nearby.

The hotel chain implemented the model on a spreadsheet and routinely uses the spreadsheet to screen potential real estate acquisitions. The founder and president of the hotel chain has accepted the model's validity and no longer feels obligated to personally select the sites.

This example shows that a specific model can be obtained from the requirements of service organizations and used to identify the most important features in site selection. ●

Independent Variables Collected for the Initial Model-Building Stage

exhibit 12.6

CATEGORY	NAME	DESCRIPTION
Competitive	INNRATE	Inn price
	PRICE	Room rate for the inn
	RATE	Average competitive room rate
	RMS 1	Hotel rooms within 1 mile
	RMSTOTAL	Hotel rooms within 3 miles
	ROOMSINN	Inn rooms
Demand generators	CIVILIAN	Civilian personnel on base
	COLLEGE	College enrollment
	HOSP1	Hospital beds within 1 mile
	HOSPTOTL	Hospital beds within 4 miles
	HVYIND	Heavy industrial employment
	LGTIND	Light industrial acreage
	MALLS	Shopping mall square footage
	MILBLKD	Military base blocked
	MILITARY	Military personnel
	MILTOT	MILITARY+CIVILIAN
	OFC1	Office space within 1 mile
	OFCTOTAL	Office space within 4 miles
	OFCCBD	Office space in central business district
	PASSENGR	Airport passengers enplaned
	RETAIL	Scale ranking of retail activity
	TOURISTS	Annual tourists
	TRAFFIC	Traffic count
	VAN	Airport van
Demographic	EMPLYPCT	Unemployment percentage
	INCOME	Average family income
	POPULACE	Residential population
Market awareness	AGE	Years inn has been open
	NEAREST	Distance to nearest inn
	STATE	State population per inn
	URBAN	Urban population per inn
Physical	ACCESS	Accessibility
	ARTERY	Major traffic artery
	DISTCBD	Distance to central business district
	SIGNVIS	Sign visibility

A Summary of the Variables That Correlated with Operating Margin

exhibit 12.7

VARIABLE	YEAR 1	YEAR 2
ACCESS	.20	
AGE	.29	.49
COLLEGE		.25
DISTCBD		−.22
EMPLYPCT	−.22	−.22
INCOME		−.23
MILTOT		.22
NEAREST	−.51	
OFCCBD	.30	
POPULACE	.30	.35
PRICE	.38	.58
RATE		.27
STATE	−.32	−.33
SIGNVIS	.25	
TRAFFIC	.32	
URBAN	−.22	−.26

SUMMARY

In this chapter the focus was on locating the manufacturing and distribution sites in the supply chain. Certainly, the term *logistics* is more comprehensive in scope and includes not only the design issues addressed in this chapter, but also the more comprehensive problem involved with moving goods through the supply chain.

In the chapter we covered common techniques for designing the supply chain. Linear programming and in particular the transportation method is a useful way to structure these logistics design problems. The problems can be easily solved using the Excel Solver, and how to do this is covered in the chapter. Dramatic changes in the global business environment have placed a premium on making decisions relating to how products will be sourced and delivered. These decisions need to be made quickly and must be based on the actual costs involved. Cost modeling using spreadsheets when combined with optimization is a powerful tool for analysis of these problems.

The chapter also briefly looked at locating service facilities such as restaurants and retail stores by using regression analysis. These problems are challenging and spreadsheet modeling is again an important analysis tool.

KEY TERMS

Logistics (1) In an industrial context, the art and science of obtaining, producing, and distributing material and product in the proper place and in the proper quantities. (2) In a military sense (where it has greater usage), its meaning also can include the movement of personnel.

International logistics All functions concerned with the movement of materials and finished goods on a global scale.

Third-party logistics company A company that manages all or part of another company's product delivery operations.

Cross-docking An approach used in consolidation warehouses where rather than making larger shipments, large shipments are broken down into small shipments for local delivery in an area.

Hub-and-spoke systems Systems that combine the idea of consolidation and that of cross-docking.

Free trade zone A closed facility (under the supervision of government customs officials) into which foreign goods can be

brought without being subject to the payment of normal import duties.

Trading bloc A group of countries that agree on a set of special arrangements governing the trading of goods between member countries. Companies may locate in places affected by the agreement to take advantage of new market opportunities.

Factor-rating system An approach for selecting a facility location by combining a diverse set of factors. Point scales are developed for each criterion. Each potential site is then evaluated on each criterion and the points are combined to calculate a rating for the site.

Transportation method A special linear programming method that is useful for solving problems involving transporting products from several sources to several destinations.

Centroid method A technique for locating single facilities that considers the existing facilities, the distances between them, and the volumes of goods to be shipped.

FORMULA REVIEW

Centroid

$$C_x = \frac{\Sigma d_{ix} V_i}{\Sigma V_i} \qquad C_y = \frac{\Sigma d_{iy} V_i}{\Sigma V_i}$$ [12.1]

SOLVED PROBLEM

Cool Air, a manufacturer of automotive air conditioners, currently produces its XB-300 line at three different locations: Plant A, Plant B, and Plant C. Recently management decided to build all compressors, a major product component, in a separate dedicated facility, Plant D.

Plant Location Matrix

exhibit 12.8

| | COMPRESSORS REQUIRED |
PLANT	PER YEAR
A	6,000
B	8,200
C	7,000

**Excel:
Centroid_method**

Plot showing:
Plant C (275, 380)
Plant B (100, 300)
Plant A (150, 75)
with Y axis (100–400) and X axis (100–400)

Using the centroid method and the information displayed in Exhibit 12.8, determine the best location for Plant D. Assume a linear relationship between volumes shipped and shipping costs (no premium charges).

Solution

$$d_{1x} = 150 \quad d_{1y} = 75 \quad V_1 = 6,000$$
$$d_{2x} = 100 \quad d_{2y} = 300 \quad V_2 = 8,200$$
$$d_{3x} = 275 \quad d_{3y} = 380 \quad V_3 = 7,000$$

$$C_x = \frac{\Sigma d_{ix} V_i}{\Sigma V_i} = \frac{(150 \times 6,000) + (100 \times 8,200) + (275 \times 7,000)}{6,000 + 8,200 + 7,000} = 172$$

$$C_y = \frac{\Sigma d_{iy} V_i}{\Sigma V_i} = \frac{(75 \times 6,000) + (300 \times 8,200) + (380 \times 7,000)}{21,200} = 262.7$$

Plant D$[C_x, C_y]$ = D[172, 263]

REVIEW AND DISCUSSION QUESTIONS

1   What motivations typically cause firms to initiate a facilities location or relocation project?
2   List five major reasons why a new electronic components manufacturing firm should move into your city or town.
3   How do facility location decisions differ for service facilities and manufacturing plants?
4   What are the pros and cons of relocating a small or midsized manufacturing firm (that makes mature products) from the United States to Mexico in the post-NAFTA environment?
5   If you could locate your new software development company anywhere in the world, which place would you choose, and why?

PROBLEMS

1   Refer to the information given in the solved problem. Suppose management decides to shift 2,000 units of production from Plant B to Plant A. Does this change the proposed location of Plant D, the compressor production facility? If so, where should Plant D be located?

2   A small manufacturing facility is being planned that will feed parts to three heavy manufacturing facilities. The locations of the current plants with their coordinates and volume requirements are given in the following table:

PLANT LOCATION	COORDINATES (x, y)	VOLUME (PARTS PER YEAR)
Peoria	300, 320	4,000
Decatur	375, 470	6,000
Joliet	470, 180	3,000

Use the centroid method to determine the best location for this new facility.

3   Bindley Corporation has a one-year contract to supply motors for all washing machines produced by Rinso Ltd. Rinso manufactures the washers at four locations around the country: New York, Fort Worth, San Diego, and Minneapolis. Plans call for the following numbers of washing machines to be produced at each location:

New York	50,000
Fort Worth	70,000
San Diego	60,000
Minneapolis	80,000

Bindley has three plants that can produce the motors. The plants and production capacities are

Boulder	100,000
Macon	100,000
Gary	150,000

Due to varying production and transportation costs, the profit Bindley earns on each 1,000 units depends on where they were produced and where they were shipped. The following table gives the accounting department estimates of the dollar profit per unit. (Shipment will be made in lots of 1,000.)

	SHIPPED TO			
PRODUCED AT	NEW YORK	FORT WORTH	SAN DIEGO	MINNEAPOLIS
Boulder	7	11	8	13
Macon	20	17	12	10
Gary	8	18	13	16

Given profit maximization as a criterion, Bindley would like to determine how many motors should be produced at each plant and how many motors should be shipped from each plant to each destination.

a. Develop a transportation grid for this problem.

b. Find the optimal solution using Microsoft Excel.

4   Rent'R Cars is a multisite car rental company in the city. It is trying out a new "return the car to the location most convenient for you" policy to improve customer service. But this means that the company has to constantly move cars around the city to maintain required levels of vehicle availability. The supply and demand for economy cars, and the total cost of moving these vehicles between sites, are shown below.

From \ To	D	E	F	G	Supply
A	$9	$8	$6	$5	50
B	9	8	8	0	40
C	5	3	3	10	75
Demand	50	60	25	30	165 / 165

a. Find the solution that minimizes moving costs using Microsoft Excel.

b. What would you have to do to the costs to assure that *A* always sends a car to *D* as part of the optimal solution?

5   A local manufacturer of wire harnesses is considering merging its three production facilities located in the same county into one new facility. Using the centroid method, determine the best location for the new facility. It is fair to assume a linear relationship between amount shipped and shipping costs.

The plan matrix is shown below with coordinates:

LOCATION	COORDINATES	UNITS PER YEAR
Jasper	150, 100	6500
Huntingburg	100, 400	7500
Celestine	300, 350	8000

6   Whirlpool Appliances produces refrigerators in Los Angeles and Detroit and supplies refrigerators to customers in Houston and Tampa. The costs of shipping a refrigerator between various points are listed below. Los Angeles can produce up to 2,900 units and Detroit up to 2,000. Determine how to best use your Los Angeles and Detroit capacity to minimize shipping costs.

UNIT SHIPPING COSTS

FROM/TO	LA	DETROIT	ATLANTA	HOUSTON	TAMPA
LA		$140	$100	$90	$225
Detroit	$145		$111	$110	$119
Atlanta	$105	$115		$113	$78
Houston	$89	$109	$121		
Tampa	$210	$117	$82		

7   The Peoples Credit Union has two check processing sites. Site 1 can process 10,000 checks per day, and site 2 can process 6000 checks per day. The credit union processes three types of checks: business, salary and personal. The processing cost per check depends on the site, as listed below. Each day 5000 checks of each type must be processed. Determine how to minimize the daily cost of processing checks using Excel.

	BUSINESS	SALARY	PERSONAL
Site 1	$0.05	$0.04	$0.02
Site 2	$0.03	$0.04	$0.05

8   Moving resources efficiently from supplier to consumer is a challenging problem that can be solved using OR techniques. The figure below shows a map of blue factories that supply food to orange towns. The numbers below the factories and towns indicate how much food (in kg) each supplies and demands, respectively. Any factory can supply any amount of food to one or several towns. A new factory is being built that can supply 1,000 kg of food but the location of the factory has not yet been determined. The distance between adjacent cells on the map is 1 km. The cost to transport 1 kg of food 1 km is $10.

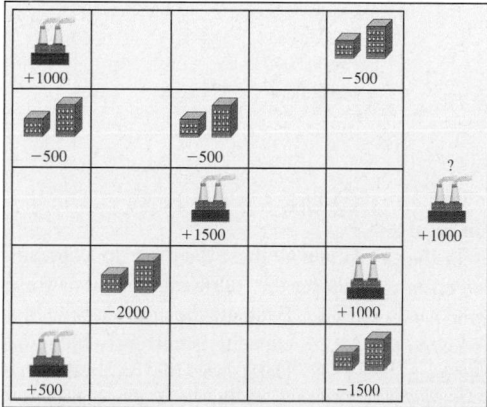

If the new factory is optimally located, what is the total transportation cost to satisfy the demand of all towns? The new factory cannot occupy a cell that already contains an existing factory or town.

SOURCE: THIS PROBLEM TAKEN FROM JOHN TOCZEK, *ORMS TODAY*, FEBRUARY 2009, P. 16.

CASE: APPLICHEM—THE TRANSPORTATION PROBLEM

Applichem management is faced with the difficult problem of allocating to its customers the capacity of manufacturing plants that are located around the world. Management has long recognized that the manufacturing plants differ greatly in efficiency but has had little success in improving the operations of the inefficient plants. At this time, management has decided to focus on how best to use the capacity of its plants given the differences in manufacturing costs that currently exist. They recognize that this study may result in the significant reduction of output or possibly the shutting down of one or more of the existing plants.

Applichem makes a product called Release-ease. Plastics molding manufacturers use this chemical product. Plastic parts are made by injecting hot plastic into a mold made in the shape of the part. After the plastic has sufficiently cooled, the fresh part is removed from the mold and the mold is then reused to make subsequent parts. Release-ease is a dry powder, applied as part of the manufacturing process, that makes it easy to remove the part from the mold.

Applichem has made the product since the early 1950s, and demand has been consistent over time. A recent study by Applichem's market research team has indicated that demand for Release-ease should be fairly steady for the next five years. Although Applichem does have some competition, particularly in the European markets, management feels that as long as they can provide a quality product at a competitive cost, customers should stick with Applichem. Release-ease sells at an average price of $1.00 per pound.

The company owns plants capable of making Release-ease in the following cities: Gary, Indiana; Windsor, Ontario, Canada; Frankfurt, Germany; Mexico City, Mexico; Caracas, Venezuela; and Osaka, Japan. Although the plants are focused on meeting demand for the immediate surrounding regions, there is considerable exporting and importing of product for various reasons. The following table contains data on how demand has been met during the past year:

PRODUCT MADE AND SHIPPED DURING PAST YEAR (× 100,000 POUNDS)

FROM/TO	MEXICO	CANADA	VENEZUELA	EUROPE	UNITED STATES	JAPAN
Mexico City	3.0		6.3			7.9
Windsor, Ontario		2.6				
Caracas			4.1			
Frankfurt			5.6	20.0	12.4	
Gary					14.0	
Osaka						4.0

Differences in the technologies used in the plants and in local raw material and labor costs created significant differences in the cost to produce Release-ease in the various locations. These costs may change dramatically due to currency valuation and labor law changes in some of the countries. This is especially true in Mexico and Venezuela. The capacity of each plant also differs at each location, and management has no interest in increasing capacity anywhere at this time. The following table gives details on the costs to produce and capacity of each plant:

PLANT PRODUCTION COSTS AND CAPACITY

PLANT	PRODUCTION COST (PER 1,000 LBS)	PLANT CAPACITY (× 100,000 LBS)
Mexico City	95.01	22.0
Windsor, Ontario	97.35	3.7
Caracas	116.34	4.5
Frankfurt	76.69	47.0
Gary	102.93	18.5
Osaka	153.80	5.0

In considering how best to use the capacity of its plants, Applichem management needs to consider the cost of shipping product from one customer region to another. Applichem now commonly ships product in bulk around the world, but it is expensive. The costs involved are not only the transportation costs but also import duties that are assessed by customs in some countries. Applichem is committed to meeting demand, though, and sometimes this is done even though profit might not be made on all orders.

The following table details the demand in each country, the cost to transport product from each plant to each country, and the current import duty rate levied by each country. (These percentages do not reflect current duties.) Import duty is calculated on the approximate production plus transportation cost of product brought into the country. (For example, if the production and shipping cost for 1,000 pounds of Release-ease shipped into Venezuela were $100, the import duty would be $100 × .5 = $50.)

TRANSPORTATION COST (PER 1,000 LBS), IMPORT DUTIES, AND DEMANDS FOR RELEASE-EASE

PLANT/COUNTRY	MEXICO	CANADA	VENEZUELA	EUROPE	UNITED STATES	JAPAN
Mexico City	0	11.40	7.00	11.00	11.00	14.00
Windsor, Ontario	11.00	0	9.00	11.50	6.00	13.00
Caracas	7.00	10.00	0	13.00	10.40	14.30
Frankfurt	10.00	11.50	12.50	0	11.20	13.30
Gary	10.00	6.00	11.00	10.00	0	12.50
Osaka	14.00	13.00	12.50	14.20	13.00	0
Total demand (×100,000 lbs)	3.0	2.60	16.0	20.0	26.4	11.9
Import duty	0.0%	0.0%	50.0%	9.5%	4.5%	6.0%

QUESTIONS

Given all these data, set up a spreadsheet (Applichem is a start) and answer the following questions for management:

1. Evaluate the cost associated with the way Applichem's plant capacity is currently being used.
2. Determine the optimal use of Applichem's plant capacity using the Solver in Excel.
3. What would you recommend that Applichem management do? Why?

Excel: Applich

SOURCE: THIS CASE IS ROUGHLY BASED ON DATA CONTAINED IN "APPLICHEM (A)," HARVARD BUSINESS SCHOOL, 9-685-051.

SUPER QUIZ

1 This is the art and science of obtaining, producing, and distributing material and product in the proper place and quantities.
2 A company that is hired to handle logistics functions.
3 A mode of transportation that is the most flexible relative to cost, volume, and speed of delivery.
4 When large shipments are broken down directly into smaller shipments for local delivery.
5 Sorting goods is the main purpose of this type of warehouse.
6 A place where foreign goods can be brought into the United States without being subject to normal customs requirements.

7 The main cost criterion used when a transportation model is used for analyzing a logistics network.
8 The Microsoft Excel function used to solve the transportation model.
9 For the transportation model to be able to find a feasible solution, this must always be greater than or equal to demand.
10 The "changing cells" in a transportation model represent this.
11 This is a method that locates facilities relative to an X, Y grid.
12 A technique that is useful for screening potential locations for services.

1. Logistics 2. Third-party logistics company 3. Highway 4. Cross-docking 5. Hub 6. Free trade zone
7. Cost of shipping 8. Solver 9. Total capacity 10. Allocation of demand to a plant or warehouse
11. Centroid method 12. Regression analysis

SELECTED BIBLIOGRAPHY

Ballou, R. H. *Business Logistics Management.* 4th ed. Upper Saddle River, NJ: Prentice Hall, 1998.

Drezner, Z., and H. Hamacher. *Facility Location: Applications and Theory.* Berlin: Springer Verlag, 2002.

Klamroth, K. *Single Facility Location Problems with Barriers.* Berlin: Springer-Verlag Telos, 2002.

FOOTNOTE

1 M. E. Porter, "The Competitive Advantage of Nation," *Harvard Business Review,* March–April 1990.

chapter 13

LEAN AND SUSTAINABLE SUPPLY CHAINS

GREEN IS THE NEW BLACK[1]

SURVEY SUGGESTS THAT ENVIRO-CONSCIOUS MANUFACTURERS ARE THE BEST RISK FOR INVESTORS

Many manufacturers still have a long way to go to address the risks and opportunities posed by the push toward more environment-friendly production processes, according to a new study conducted by RiskMetrics Group, a provider of risk management services. Those risks include higher energy costs due to tighter

After reading this chapter you will:

1. Describe how Green and Lean can complement each other.
2. Explain how a production pull system works.
3. Understand Toyota Production System concepts.
4. Summarize important attributes of a lean supply chain.
5. Analyze a supply chain process using value stream mapping.
6. Know the principles of supply chain design.

greenhouse gas (GHG) emissions standards, and the opportunities include growing global demand for more energy-efficient products.

The report ranks large manufacturers and other companies on their effectiveness in such areas as reducing GHG emissions, introducing energy-efficient projects, expanding renewable energy purchases, and integrating climate factors into product designs. However, perhaps reflecting

Top Ten Green
Manufacturers

1. IBM Corp.
2. Dell Inc.
3. Intel
4. Johnson & Johnson
5. Nike
6. Applied Materials
7. Coca-Cola
8. Sun Microsystems
9. Hewlett-Packard
10. Molson Coors

SOURCE: RISKMETRICS GROUP

**Supply
Chain**

the skepticism many people still have as to exactly what role, if any, manufacturing plays in global warming, many companies are largely ignoring climate change, particularly at the board and CEO level.

According to the report, which was sponsored by the Ceres Investor coalition, only 17 percent of the respondent companies say their boards receive climate-specific updates from management; 11 percent of the CEOs have taken leadership roles on climate change initiatives. The survey indicates that none of the companies have linked executive compensation directly to climate-related performance.

The survey indicates that green strategies that save energy and fight global warming have broad consumer appeal and political support. Companies that seize the initiative can gain market share, build investor confidence, and insulate themselves against future energy shocks and climate change regulations. It's simply smart business to employ these governance practices today.

The highest ranking green manufacturers in the study tend to be high-tech, with IBM leading the way, followed by Dell, Intel, Johnson & Johnson and Nike (see chart, "Top Ten Green Manufacturers"). High-tech companies were noteworthy for their product and service innovation, when it comes to making their operations, data centers, and product lines more energy efficient. IBM's energy conservation programs, for instance, helped save the company nearly $20 million last year.

Among other suggestions, the report recommends that companies raise supply chain awareness by including supply chain greenhouse gas emissions—those emissions that result from raw material extraction, production, transport, and packaging—in emissions inventories, as well as setting emission standards for suppliers.

LEAN PRODUCTION

Lean production

**Supply
Chain**

Global

Customer value

The most significant operations and supply management approach of the past 50 years is **lean production**. In the context of supply chains, lean production refers to a focus on eliminating as much waste as possible. Moves that are not needed, unnecessary processing steps, and excess inventory in the supply chain are targets for improvement during the *learning* process. Some consultants in industry have coined the phrase *value chain* to refer to a process that identifies each step in the supply chain that delivers products and services to customers, emphasizes those that create value, and removes those that do not create value. Lean production may be one of the best tools for implementing green strategies in manufacturing and service processes.

The basis of lean thinking came from the just-in-time (JIT) production concepts pioneered in Japan at Toyota. Even though JIT gained worldwide prominence in the 1970s, some of its philosophy can be traced to the early 1900s in the United States. Henry Ford used JIT concepts as he streamlined his moving assembly lines to make automobiles. For example, to eliminate waste, he used the bottom of the packing crates for car seats as the floor board of the car. Although elements of JIT were being used by Japanese industry as early as the 1930s, it was not fully refined until the 1970s when Tai-ichi Ohno of Toyota Motors used JIT to take Toyota's cars to the forefront of delivery time and quality.

Customer value, in the context of lean production, is defined as something for which the customer is willing to pay. Value-adding activities transform materials and information into something the customer wants. Non-value-adding activities consume resources and do not directly contribute to the end result desired by the customer. Waste, therefore, is defined   **Waste** as anything that does not add value from the customer's perspective. Examples of process wastes are defective products, overproduction, inventories, excess motion, processing steps, transportation, and waiting.

Lean concepts also apply to service industries. Consider the nonmanufacturing example of a flight to the Bahamas.[2] The value-adding part of that process is the flight itself. The non-value-added parts of that process are driving to the airport, parking, walking to the terminal, checking-in, waiting in line at check-in, walking to the security check, and so on. Many times the non-value-added time far exceeds the value-added time in this type of process. Where should improvement efforts be focused—on the non-value-added steps or on making the plane fly faster?

Understanding the difference between value and waste and value-added and non-value-added processes is critical to understanding lean production. Sometimes it is not easy to discern the difference when looking at the entire supply chain. The best way is to look at the individual components and apply lean thinking to each one. Then determine how to link the processes to reduce waste.

This chapter starts by reviewing the evolution of lean concepts from Japan and Toyota. We then expand this view to encompass a complete supply chain. The remainder of the chapter is devoted to value stream mapping, a tool that can be used to drive out waste and improve the efficiency of the supply chain.

LEAN LOGIC

Lean production is an integrated set of activities designed to achieve production using minimal inventories of raw materials, work-in-process, and finished goods. Parts arrive at the next workstation "just-in-time" and are completed and move through the process quickly. Lean is also based on the logic that nothing will be produced until it is needed. Exhibit 13.1 illustrates the process. Production need is created by actual demand for the product. When an item is sold, in theory, the market pulls a replacement from the last position in the system—final assembly in this case. This triggers an order to the factory production line, where a worker then pulls another unit from an upstream station in the flow to replace the unit taken. This upstream station then pulls from the next station further upstream and so on back to the release of raw materials. To enable this pull process to work smoothly, lean production demands high levels of quality at each stage of the process, strong vendor relations, and a fairly predictable demand for the end product.

Lean Production Pull System

e x h i b i t   13.1

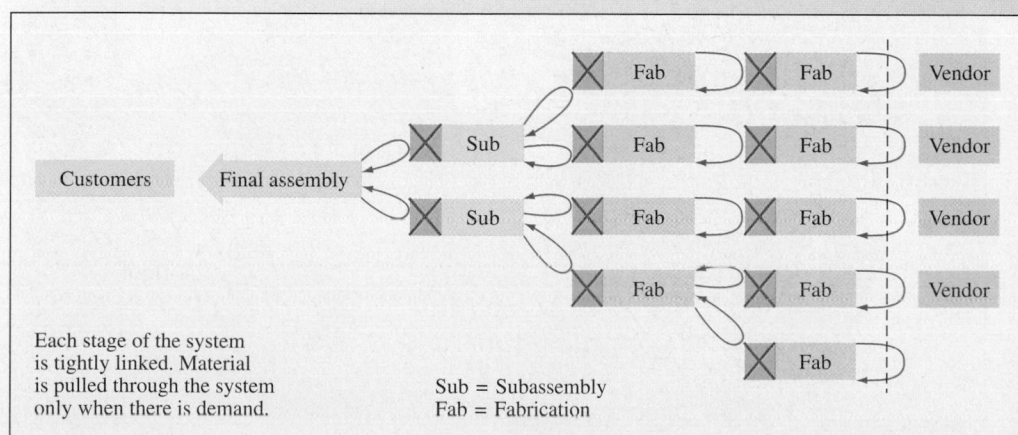

Customers ← Final assembly

Each stage of the system is tightly linked. Material is pulled through the system only when there is demand.

Sub = Subassembly
Fab = Fabrication

THE TOYOTA PRODUCTION SYSTEM

In this section we examine the philosophy and elements of lean production developed in Japan and embodied in the Toyota Production System—the benchmark for lean manufacturing. The Toyota Production System was developed to improve quality and productivity and is predicated upon two philosophies that are central to the Japanese culture: elimination of waste and respect for people.[3]

Global

ELIMINATION OF WASTE

Waste, as defined by Toyota's past president, Fujio Cho, is "anything other than the minimum amount of equipment, materials, parts, and workers (working time) which are absolutely essential to production." An expanded lean definition advanced by Fujio Cho identifies seven prominent types of waste to be eliminated from the supply chain: (1) waste from overproduction, (2) waste of waiting time, (3) transportation waste, (4) inventory waste, (5) processing waste, (6) waste of motion, and (7) waste from product defects.[4]

Global

RESPECT FOR PEOPLE

Respect for people is a key to the Toyota Production System. Toyota has traditionally strived to ensure lifetime employment for permanent positions and to maintain level payrolls even when business conditions deteriorate. Permanent workers (about one-third of the total workforce of Japan) have job security and tend to be more flexible, remain with a company, and do all they can to help a firm achieve its goals. (Global recessions have caused many Japanese companies to move away from this ideal.)

Company unions at Toyota as well as elsewhere in Japan exist to foster a cooperative relationship with management. All employees receive two bonuses a year in good times. Employees know that if the company performs well, they will get a bonus. This encourages workers to improve productivity. Management views workers as assets, not as human machines. Automation and robotics are used extensively to perform dull or routine jobs so employees are free to focus on important improvement tasks.

Toyota relies heavily on subcontractor networks. Indeed, more than 90 percent of all Japanese companies are part of the supplier network of small firms. Some suppliers are

TOYOTA'S DESIGN TEAM AT THEIR CALTY DESIGN RESEARCH FACILITIES IN CALIFORNIA. FROM CONCEPT TO COMPETITION VEHICLES, EACH TEAM MEMBER IS CONSIDERED AS IMPORTANT AS THE VEHICLES THEY DESIGN. CALTY PROVIDES DESIGN SOLUTIONS FOR TOYOTA, LEXUS AND SCION PRODUCT DEVELOPMENT.

specialists in a narrow field, usually serving multiple customers. Firms have long-term partnerships with their suppliers and customers. Suppliers consider themselves part of a customer's family.

A study by Christer Karlsson of the Stockholm School of Economics points out that the lean ideas found here are not universally used in all manufacturing companies in Japan. Rather, they are applied situationally and where appropriate. However, the fundamental ideas of elimination of waste and respect for workers are still foundations of the exceptional productivity of most Japanese manufacturing companies.[5]

LEAN SUPPLY CHAINS

The focus of the Toyota Production System is on elimination of waste and respect for people. The goals align well with the sustainability goals of profit, planet, and people discussed in Chapters 1, 2, and 11 of this book. As the concepts have evolved and become applied to the supply chain, the goal of maximizing customer value has been added. Customer value when considered in the context of the entire supply chain should center on the perspective of the end customer with the goal being to maximize what the customer is willing to pay for a firm's goods or services. The **value stream** consists of the value-adding and non-value-adding activities required to design, order, and provide a product or service from concept to launch, order to delivery, and raw materials to customers. Exhibit 13.2 is a map that depicts the flow of an item through a supply chain. This all-inclusive view of the system is a significant expansion of the scope of application of the lean concepts pioneered by Toyota. When applied to supply chains, **waste reduction** relates to the optimization of the value-adding activities and the elimination of non-value-adding activities that are part of the value stream.

Supply Chain

Value stream

Waste reduction

In the following we discuss the different components of a supply chain and what would be expected using a lean focus:

Lean Suppliers Lean suppliers are able to respond to changes. Their prices are generally lower due to the efficiencies of lean processes, and their quality has improved to the point that incoming inspection at the next link is not needed. Lean suppliers deliver on time and their culture is one of continuous improvement. To develop lean suppliers, organizations should include them in their value stream planning. This will help them fix problems and share savings.

Lean Procurement A key to lean procurement is automation. The term *e-procurement* relates to automatic transaction, sourcing, bidding, and auctions using Web-based applications, and the use of software that removes human interaction and integrates with the financial reporting of the firm. The key to lean procurement is visibility. Suppliers must be able to "see" into the customers' operations and customers must be able

POST LOGISTICS IN AUSTRALIA DISTRIBUTES THE SPEEDO SWIMWEAR BRAND. THREE LEVELS OF STORAGE ARE CONNECTED BY A SPIRAL CONVEYOR LINKED TO A "SMART" HORIZONTAL CONVEYOR SYSTEM THAT INTERCONNECTS PICKING ZONES ON EACH OF THE THREE LEVELS AND CARRIES THROUGH TO A SIX-LANE PACKING AND DISTRIBUTION AREA.

exhibit 13.2   ACME Fulfillment Stream Current State: SKU 918

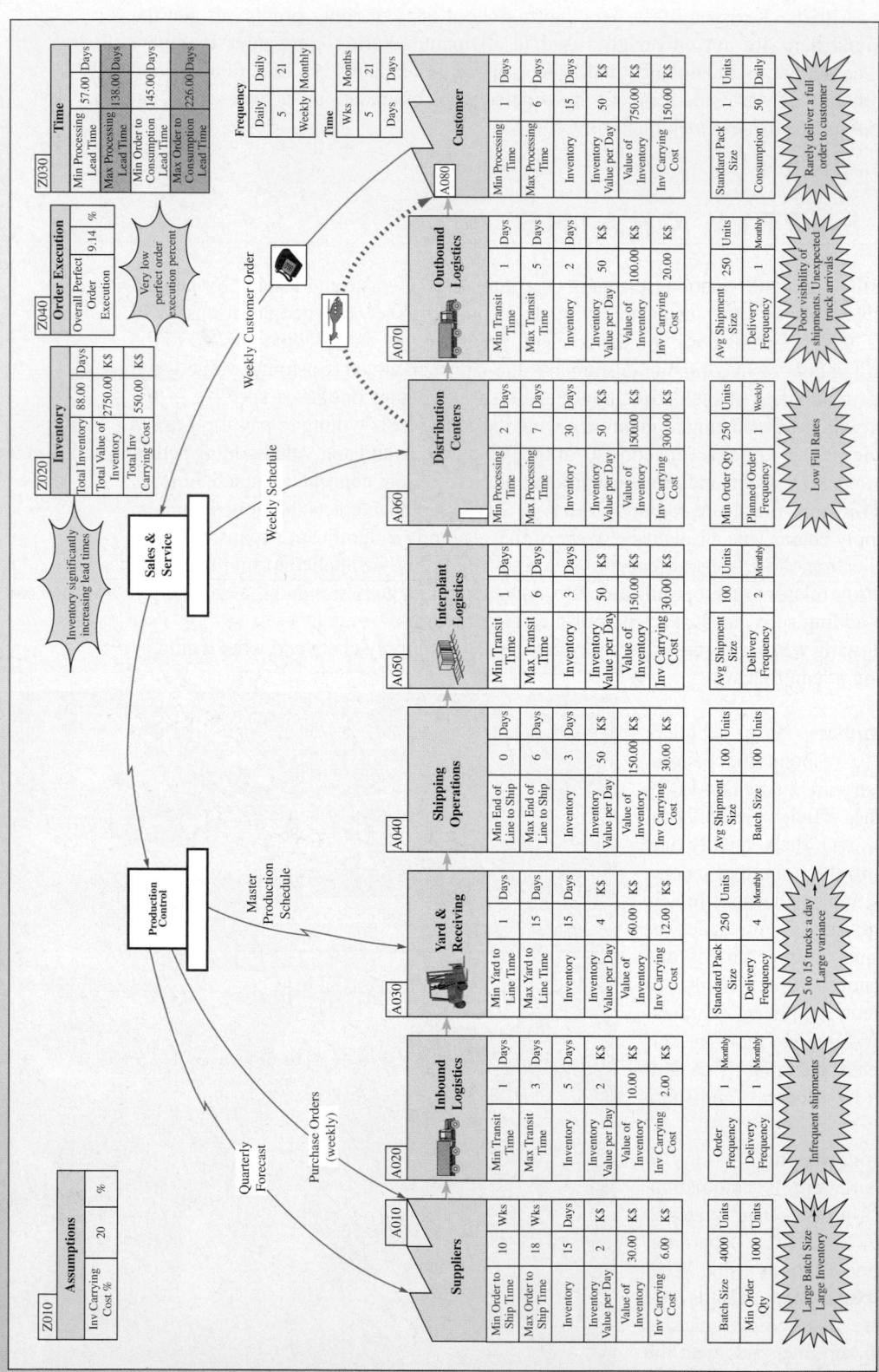

to "see" into their suppliers' operations. The overlap of these processes needs to be optimized to maximize value from the end customer perspective.

Lean Manufacturing   Lean manufacturing systems produce what customers want, in the quantity they want, when they want it, and with minimum resources. Applying lean concepts in manufacturing typically presents the greatest opportunities for cost reduction and quality improvement.

Lean Warehousing   This relates to eliminating non-value-added steps and waste in product storage processes. Typical functions include the following: receiving of material; put-away/storing; replenishment of inventory; picking inventory; packing for shipment; and shipping. Waste can be found in many warehousing processes, including shipping defects, which create returns; overproduction or overshipment of products; excess inventory, which requires extra space and reduces ware-

VOICE-DIRECTED ORDER FULFILLMENT ALLOWS WORKERS HANDS-FREE OPERATION FOR FASTER, SAFER, AND MORE ACCURATE INVENTORY PICKING. IT ALSO SUPPORTS THE USE OF MULTIPLE LANGUAGES.

house efficiency; excess motion and handling; waiting for parts; and inadequate information systems.

Lean Logistics   Lean concepts can be applied to the functions associated with the movement of material through the system. Some of the key areas include optimized mode selection and pooling orders; combined multistop truckloads; optimized routing; cross docking; import/export transportation processes; and backhaul minimization. Just as with the other areas, these logistics functions need to be optimized by eliminating non-value-adding activities while improving the value-adding activities.

Lean Customers   Lean customers have a great understanding of their business needs and specify meaningful requirements. They value speed and flexibility and expect high levels of delivery performance. Lean customers are interested in establishing effective partnerships with their suppliers. Lean customers expect value from the products they purchase and provide value to their customers.

The benefits of a lean supply chain primarily are in the improved responsiveness to the customer. As business conditions change, the supply chain adapts to dynamic needs. The ideal is a culture of rapid change with a bias for change when it is needed. The reduced inventory inherent in a lean supply chain reduces obsolescence and reduces flow time through the value-added processes. The reduced cost along with improved customer service affords the firms using a lean supply chain a significant competitive advantage in the global marketplace.

VALUE STREAM MAPPING

Value stream mapping (VSM) is a special type of flowcharting tool that is valuable for the development of lean processes. The technique is used to visualize product flows through various processing steps. The tool also illustrates information flows that result from the process as well as information used to control flow through the process. The aim of this section is to provide a brief introduction to VSM and to illustrate its use with an example.

Value stream mapping

To create a lean process, one needs to have a full understanding of the business, including production processes, material flows, and information flows. In this section we discuss this in the context of a production process where a product is being made. VSM is not limited to this context and can be readily applied to service, logistics, distribution, or virtually any type of process.

exhibit 13.3   Manufacturing Process Map

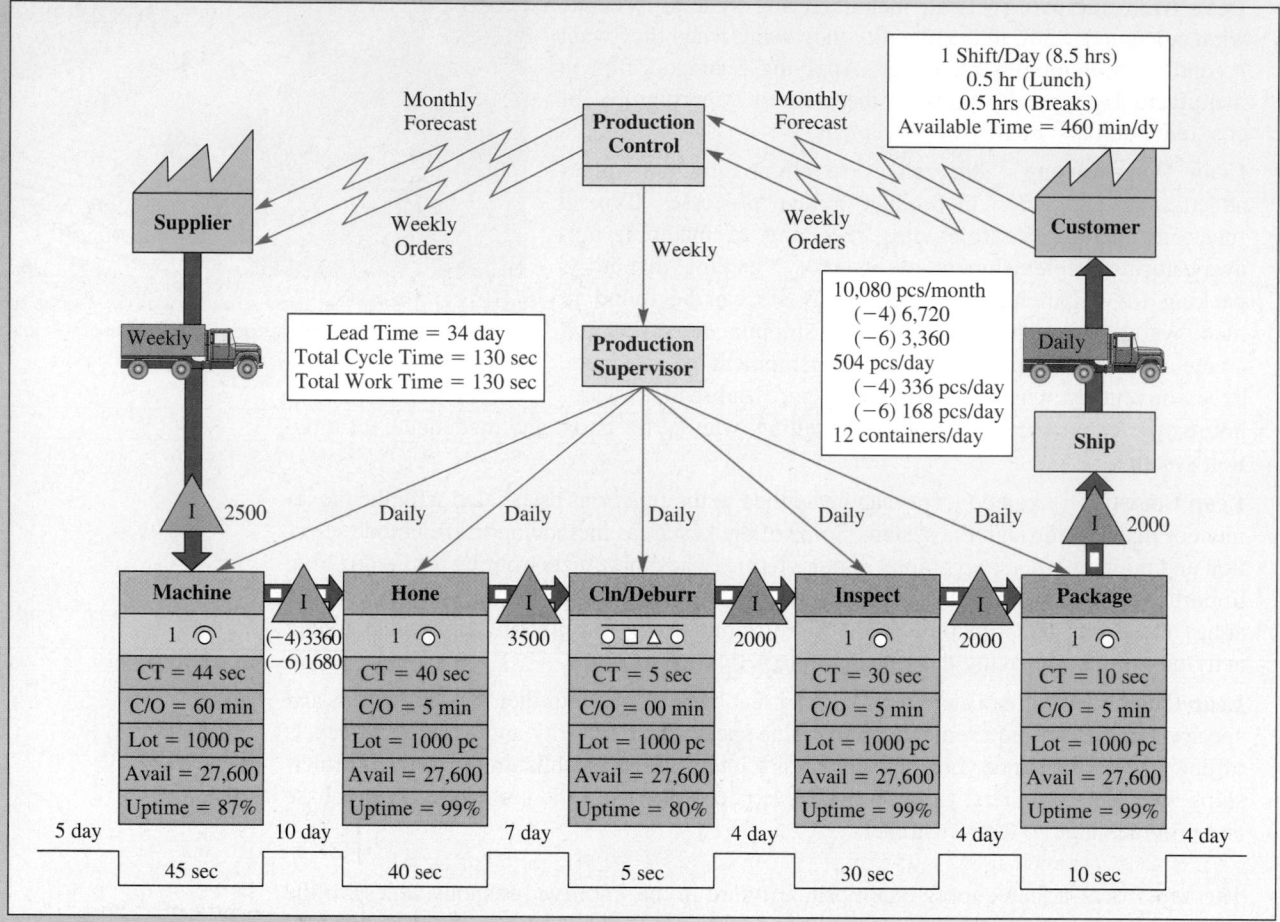

In the context of a production process such as a manufacturing plant, the technique is used to identify all of the value-adding as well as non-value-adding processes that materials are subjected to within a plant, from raw material coming into the plant through delivery to the customer. Exhibit 13.3 is a sample map that depicts a production process. With this map, identification of wasteful processes and flows can be made so that they can be modified or eliminated, and the manufacturing system can be made more productive.

Details explaining the symbols will be discussed later in the section but here it is useful to discuss what the information in the map depicted in Exhibit 13.3 actually means.[6] Starting from the left, we see that material is supplied on a weekly basis and deposited in a raw material inventory indicated by the triangle. The average level for this inventory is 2,500 units. This material is run through a five-step process consisting of machining, honing, cleaning, inspection, and packaging. The machining, honing, inspection, and packaging process all use a single operator. Under each of these process symbols is the activity cycle time (CT), changeover time (C/O time to switch from one type of item to another), lot size, available number of seconds per day, and percent uptime. The cleaning/duburring activity is a multistep process where items are handled on a first-come-first-served basis. Between each process are inventory buffers with the average inventory in these buffers depicted in the exhibit.

Information flows are shown on the map. In Exhibit 13.3 we see that production control issues monthly demand forecasts, weekly orders to the supplier, and a weekly production

exhibit 13.4

Value Stream Mapping Symbols

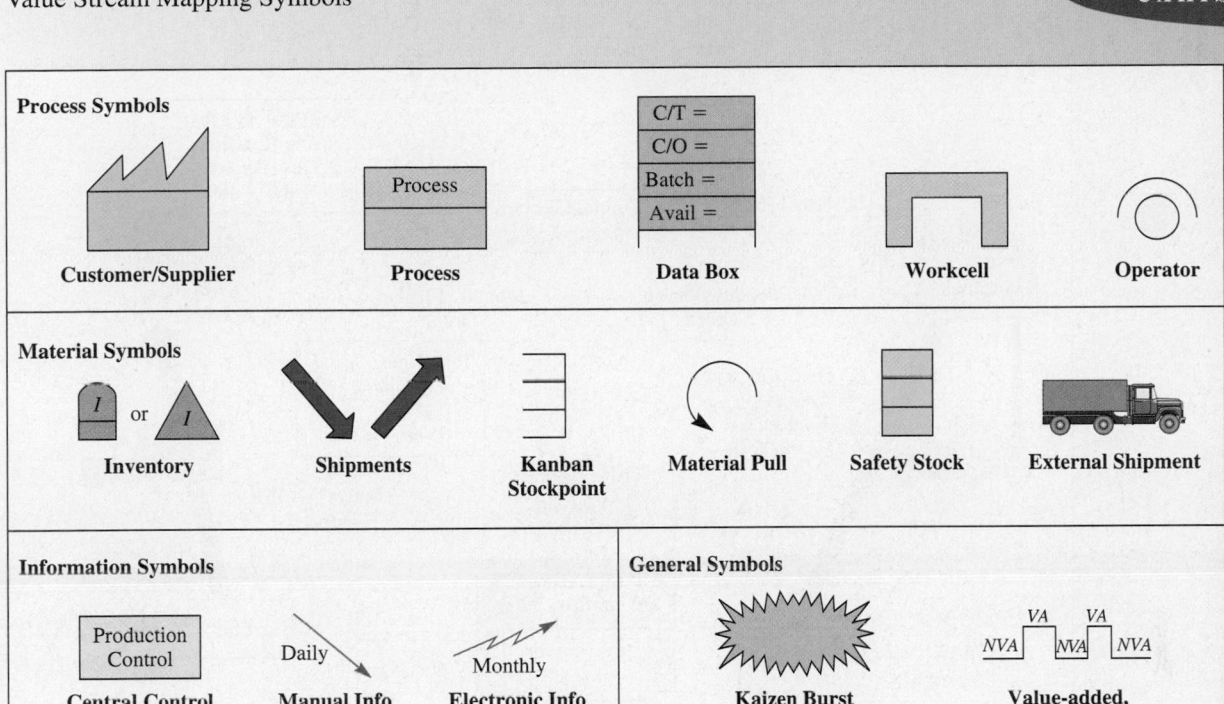

schedule that is managed by the supervisor on a daily basis. Monthly forecasts are provided by customers, and they place their orders on a weekly basis. The time line at the bottom shows the processing time for each production activity (in seconds) together with the average inventory wait time. Adding these times together gives an estimate of the lead time through the entire system.

VSM symbols are generally standardized but there are many variations. Several common symbols are depicted in Exhibit 13.4. These are categorized as process, material, information, and general symbols.

Value stream mapping is a two-part process—first depicting the "current state" of the process, and second a possible "future state." Exhibit 13.5 depicts another map of the same process with suggested improvements. The map has been annotated using Kaizen bursts that suggest the areas for improvement. **Kaizen** is the Japanese philosophy that focuses on continuous improvement. In this exhibit we see a totally redesigned process where the individual production operations have been combined into a workcell operated by three employees. In addition, rather than "pushing" material through the system based on weekly schedules generated by production control, the entire process is converted to a pull system that is operated directly in response to customer demand. Note that the lead time in the new system is only 5 days, compared to the 34-day lead time with the old system.

Kaizen

To study another example using value stream mapping (VSM), consider Solved Problem 1 at the end of the chapter. VSM is a great visual way to analyze an existing system and to find areas where waste can be eliminated. Value stream maps are simple to draw and it is possible to construct the maps totally using paper and pencil. These maps can, however, be more easily constructed using standard office software or graphics packages. Additionally, dedicated VSM software is available from Strategos (**www.strategosinc.com**) and System2win (**www.Systems2win.com**).

exhibit 13.5   Analysis Showing Potential Areas for Improving a Process

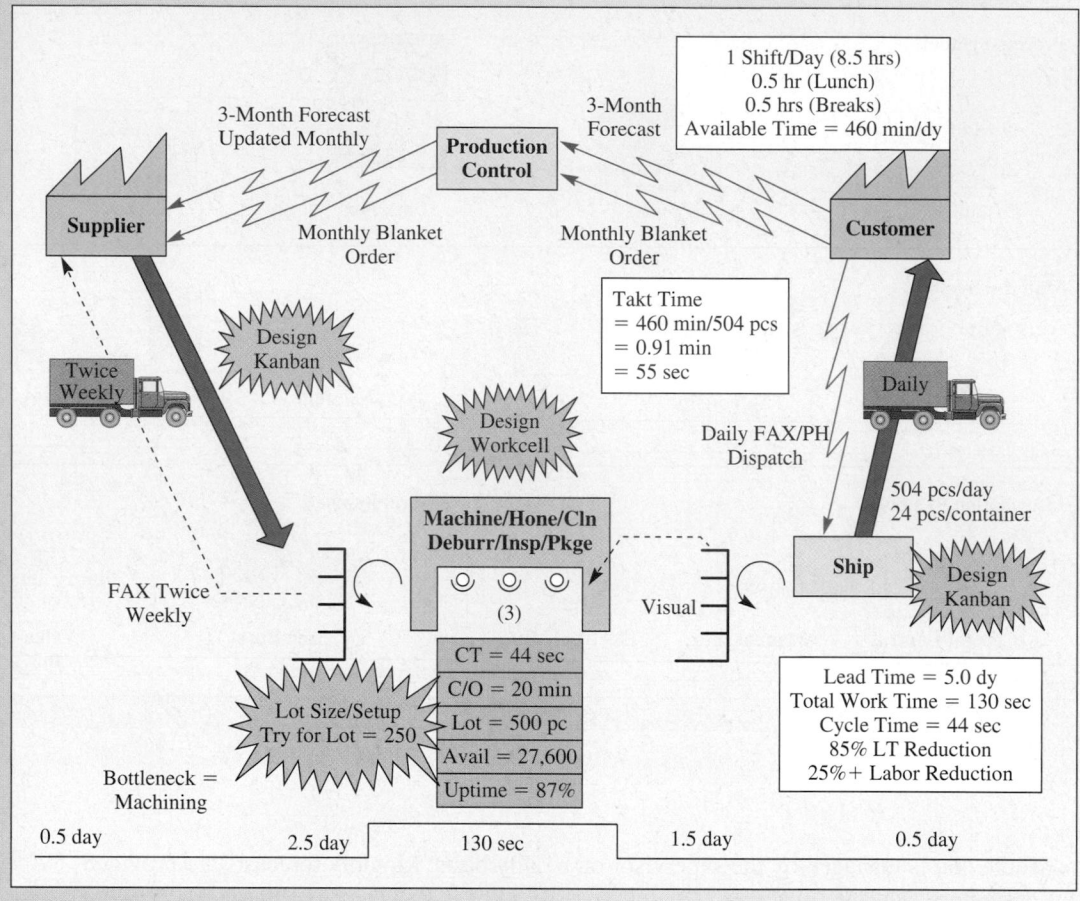

LEAN SUPPLY CHAIN DESIGN PRINCIPLES

Supply Chain

Value stream mapping is a great way to analyze existing processes. Looking for ways to improve supply chain processes should be based on ideas that have been proven over time. In the following we review a set of key principles which can guide the design of lean supply chains. We divide our design principles into three major categories. The first two sets of principles relate to internal production processes. These are the processes that actually create the goods and services within a firm. The third category applies lean concepts to the entire supply chain. These principles include:

1. Lean Layouts
   a. Group technology
   b. Quality at the source
   c. JIT production
2. Lean Production Schedules
   a. Uniform plant loading
   b. Kanban production control system
   c. Determination of number of Kanbans needed
   d. Minimized setup times
3. Lean supply chains
   a. Specialized plants
   b. Work with suppliers
   c. Building a lean supply chain

LEAN LAYOUTS

Lean requires the plant layout to be designed to ensure balanced work flow with a minimum of work-in-process inventory. Each workstation is part of a production line, whether or not a physical line actually exists. Capacity is balanced using the same logic for an assembly line, and operations are linked through a pull system. In addition, the system designer must visualize how all aspects of the internal and external logistics system tie to the layout.

Preventive maintenance is emphasized to ensure that flows are not interrupted by downtime or malfunctioning equipment. Preventive maintenance involves periodic inspection and repair designed to keep a machine reliable. Operators perform much of the maintenance because they are most familiar with their machines and because machines are easier to repair, as lean operations favor several simple machines rather than one large complex one.

Preventive maintenance

Group Technology   Group technology (GT) is a philosophy in which similar parts are grouped into families, and the processes required to make the parts are arranged in a manufacturing cell. Instead of transferring jobs from one specialized department to another, GT considers all operations required to make a part and groups those machines together. Exhibit 13.6 illustrates the difference between the clusters of different machines grouped into cells versus departmental layouts. The group technology cells eliminate movement and queue (waiting) time between operations, reduce inventory, and reduce the number of employees required. Workers, however, must be flexible to run several machines and processes. Due to their advanced skill level, these workers have increased job security.

Group technology

Quality at the Source   Quality at the source means do it right the first time and, when something goes wrong, stop the process or assembly line immediately. Factory workers become their own inspectors, personally responsible for the quality of their output. Workers concentrate on one part of the job at a time so quality problems are uncovered. If the pace is too fast, if the worker finds a quality problem, or if a safety issue is discovered, the worker is obligated to push a button to stop the line and turn on a visual signal. People from other areas respond to the alarm and the problem. Workers are empowered to do their own maintenance and housekeeping until the problem is fixed.

Quality at the source

JIT Production   JIT (just-in-time) means producing what is needed when needed and no more. Anything over the minimum amount necessary is viewed as waste, because effort

Group Technology versus Departmental Specialty   **exhibit 13.6**

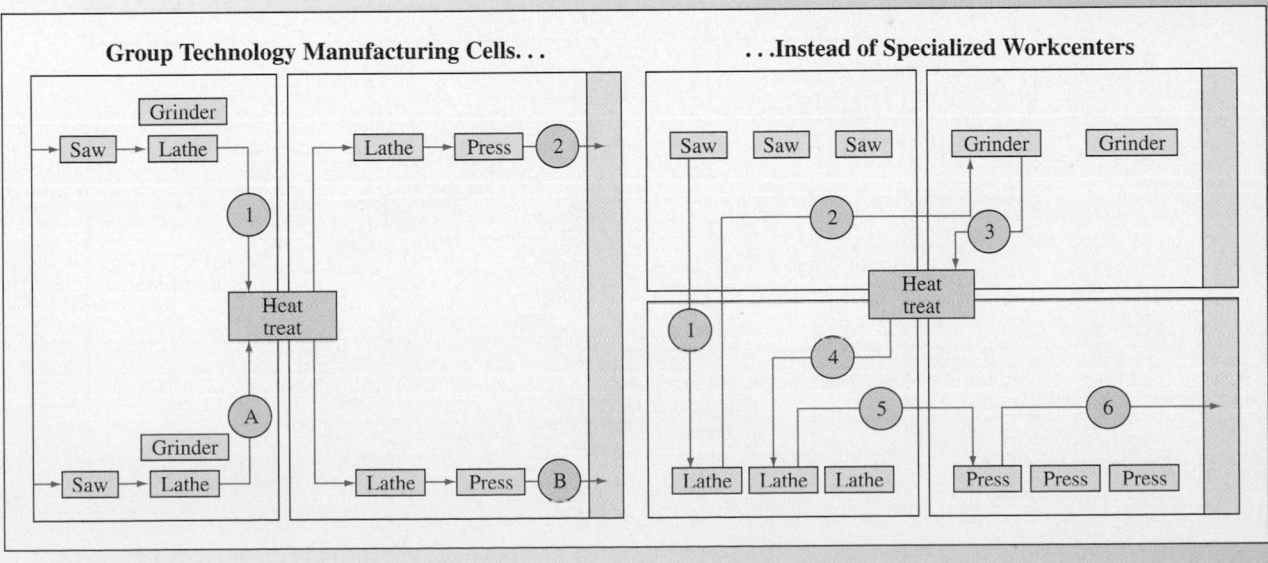

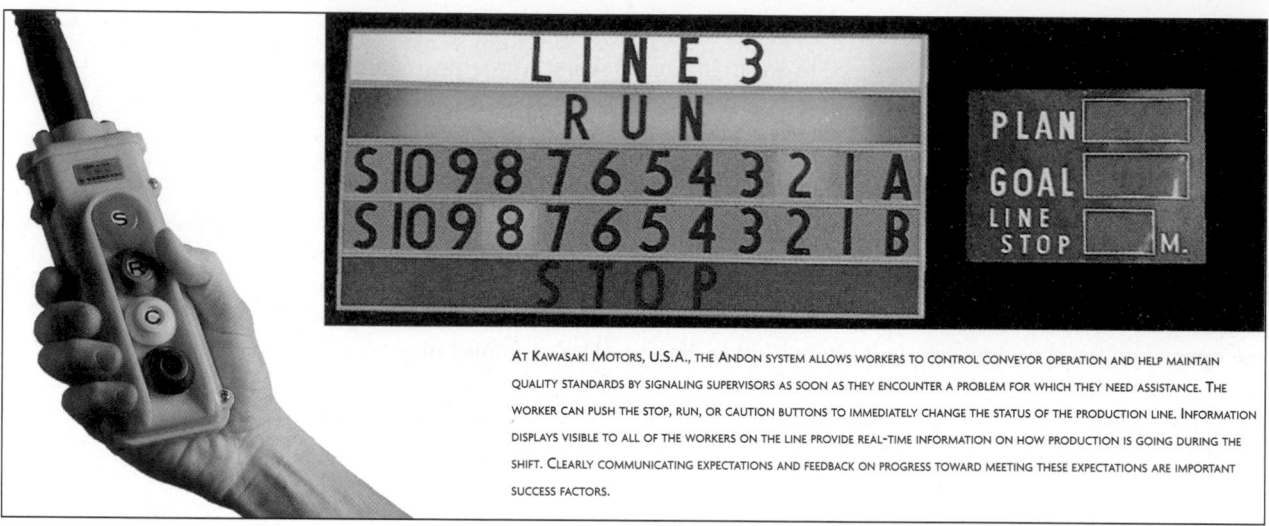

At Kawasaki Motors, U.S.A., the Andon system allows workers to control conveyor operation and help maintain quality standards by signaling supervisors as soon as they encounter a problem for which they need assistance. The worker can push the stop, run, or caution buttons to immediately change the status of the production line. Information displays visible to all of the workers on the line provide real-time information on how production is going during the shift. Clearly communicating expectations and feedback on progress toward meeting these expectations are important success factors.

and material expended for something not needed now cannot be utilized now. This is in contrast to relying on extra material just in case something goes wrong.

JIT is typically applied to repetitive manufacturing, which is when the same or similar items are made one after another. JIT does not require large volumes and can be applied to any repetitive segments of a business regardless of where they appear. Under JIT the ideal lot size or production batch is one. Although workstations may be geographically dispersed, it is important to minimize transit time and keep transfer quantities small—typically one-tenth of a day's production. Vendors even ship several times a day to their customers to keep lot sizes small and inventory low. The goal is to drive all inventory queues to zero, thus minimizing inventory investment and shortening lead times.

When inventory levels are low, quality problems become very visible. Exhibit 13.7 illustrates this idea. If the water in a pond represents inventory, the rocks represent problems that could occur in a firm. A high level of water hides the problems (rocks). Management assumes everything is fine, but as the water level drops in an economic downturn, problems are presented. If you deliberately force the water level down (particularly in good economic times), you can expose and correct problems before they cause worse problems. JIT manufacturing exposes problems otherwise hidden by excess inventories and staff.

exhibit 13.7   Inventory Hides Problems

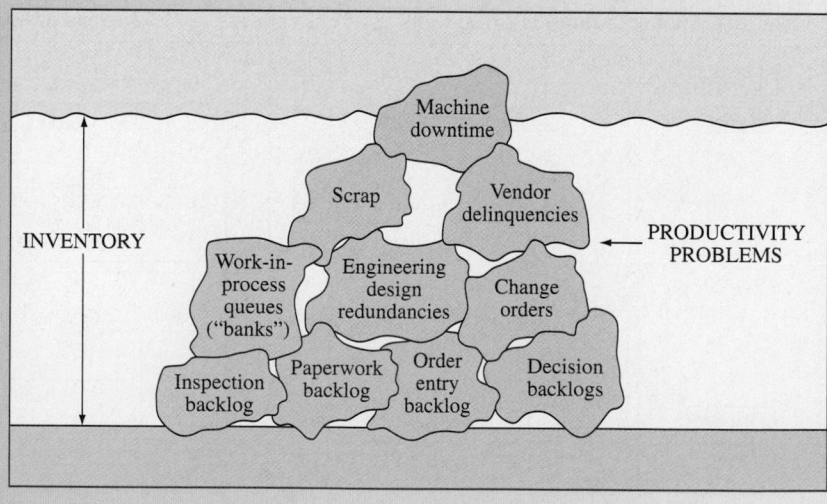

LEAN PRODUCTION SCHEDULES

As noted earlier, lean production requires a stable schedule over a lengthy time horizon. This is accomplished by level scheduling, freeze windows, and underutilization of capacity. A level schedule is one that requires material to be pulled into final assembly in a pattern uniform enough to allow the various elements of production to respond to pull signals. It does not necessarily mean that the usage of every part on an assembly line is identified hour by hour for days on end; it does mean that a given production system equipped with flexible setups and a fixed amount of material in the pipelines can respond.[7]

Level schedule

The term freeze window refers to that period of time during which the schedule is fixed and no further changes are possible. An added benefit of the stable schedule is seen in how parts and components are accounted for in a pull system. Here, the concept of backflush is used where the parts that go into each unit of the product are periodically removed from inventory and accounted for based on the number of units produced. This eliminates much of the shop-floor data collection activity, which is required if each part must be tracked and accounted for during production.

Freeze window

Backflush

Underutilization and overutilization of capacity are controversial features of lean production. Conventional approaches use safety stocks and early deliveries as a hedge against production problems like poor quality, machine failures, and unanticipated bottlenecks in traditional manufacturing. Under lean production, excess labor, machines, and overtime provide the hedge. The excess capacity in labor and equipment that results is much cheaper than carrying excess inventory. When demand is greater than expected, overtime must be used. Often part-time labor is used when additional capacity is needed. During idle periods, personnel can be put to work on other activities such as special projects, work group activities, and workstation housekeeping.

Uniform Plant Loading   Smoothing the production flow to dampen the reaction waves that normally occur in response to schedule variations is called uniform plant loading. When a change is made in a final assembly, the changes are magnified throughout the line and the supply chain. The only way to eliminate the problem is to make adjustments as small as possible by setting a firm monthly production plan for which the output rate is frozen.

Uniform plant loading

Toyota found it could do this by building the same mix of products every day in small quantities. Thus, a total mix is always available to respond to variations in demand. A Toyota example is shown in Exhibit 13.8. Monthly car style quantities are reduced to daily quantities (assuming a 20-day month) in order to compute a model *cycle time* (defined here as the time between two identical units being completed on the line). The cycle time figure is used to adjust resources to produce the precise quantity needed. The speed of equipment or of the production line is adjusted so only the needed quantity is produced each day. JIT strives to produce on schedule, on cost, and on quality.

Kanban Production Control Systems   A kanban control system uses a signaling device to regulate JIT flows. Kanban means "sign" or "instruction card" in Japanese. In a paperless control system, containers can be used instead of cards. The cards or containers

Kanban

Toyota Example of Mixed-Model Production Cycle in a Japanese Assembly Plant

exhibit 13.8

MODEL	MONTHLY QUANTITY	DAILY QUANTITY	MODEL CYCLE TIME (MINUTES)
Sedan	5,000	250	2
Hardtop	2,500	125	4
Wagon	2,500	125	4

SEQUENCE: SEDAN, HARDTOP, SEDAN, WAGON, SEDAN, HARDTOP, SEDAN, WAGON, AND SO ON (ONE MINUTE APART)

exhibit 13.9   Flow of Two Kanbans

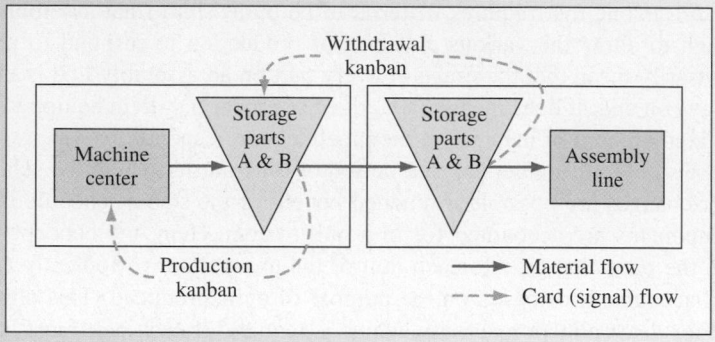

Kanban pull system

make up the **kanban pull system**. The authority to produce or supply additional parts comes from downstream operations. Consider Exhibit 13.9, where we show an assembly line that is supplied with parts by a machine center. The machine center makes two parts, A and B. These two parts are stored in containers that are located next to the assembly line and next to the machine center. Each container next to the assembly line has a withdrawal kanban, and each container next to the machine center has a production kanban. This is often referred to as a two-card kanban system.

When the assembly line takes the first part A from a full container, a worker takes the withdrawal kanban from the container, and takes the card to the machine center storage area. In the machine center area, the worker finds a container of part A, removes the production kanban, and replaces it with the withdrawal kanban. Placement of this card on the container authorizes the movement of the container to the assembly line. The freed production kanban is placed on a rack by the machine center, which authorizes the production of another lot of material. A similar process is followed for part B. The cards on the rack become the dispatch list for the machine center. Cards are not the only way to signal the need for production of a part; other visual methods are possible, as shown in Exhibit 13.10.

exhibit 13.10   Diagram of Outbound Stockpoint with Warning Signal Marker

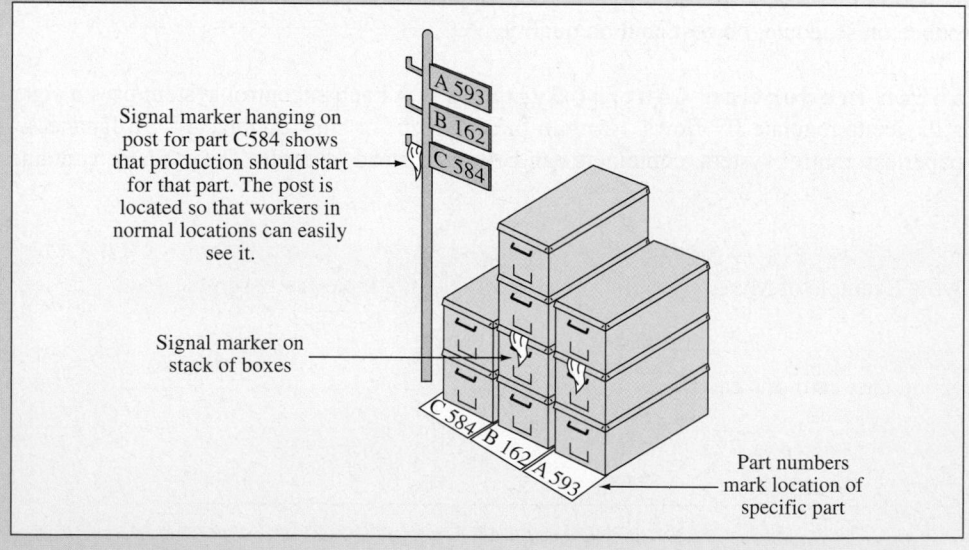

The following are some other possible approaches:

Kanban squares.   Some companies use marked spaces on the floor or on a table to identify where material should be stored. When the square is empty, the supplying operations are authorized to produce; when the square is full, no parts are needed.

Container system.   Sometimes the container itself can be used as a signal device. In this case, an empty container on the factory floor visually signals the need to fill it. The amount of inventory is adjusted by simply adding or removing containers.

Colored golf balls.   At a Kawasaki engine plant, when a part used in a subassembly is down to its queue limit, the assembler rolls a colored golf ball down a pipe to the replenishment machine center. This tells the operator which part to make next. Many variations have been developed on this approach.

The kanban pull approach can be used not only within a manufacturing facility but also between manufacturing facilities (pulling engines and transmissions into an automobile assembly operation, for example) and between manufacturers and external suppliers.

Supply Chain

Determining the Number of Kanbans Needed   Setting up a kanban control system requires determination of the number of kanban cards (or containers) needed. In a two-card system, we are finding the number of sets of withdrawal and production cards. The kanban cards represent the number of containers of material that flow back and forth between the supplier and the user areas. Each container represents the minimum production lot size to be supplied. The number of containers, therefore, directly controls the amount of work-in-process inventory in the system.

Accurately estimating the lead time needed to produce a container of parts is the key to determining the number of containers. This lead time is a function of the processing time for the container, any waiting time during the production process, and the time required to transport the material to the user. Enough kanbans are needed to cover the expected demand during this lead time plus some additional amount for safety stock. The number of kanban card sets is

$$k = \frac{\text{Expected demand during lead time} + \text{Safety stock}}{\text{Size of the container}}$$

$$= \frac{DL(1 + S)}{C} \qquad \text{[13.1]}$$

where

k = Number of kanban card sets

D = Average number of units demanded per period (lead time and demand must be expressed in the same time units)

L = Lead time to replenish an order (expressed in the same units as demand)

S = Safety stock expressed as a percentage of demand during the lead time (This can be based on a service level and variance as shown in Chapter 17.)

C = Container size

Observe that a kanban system does not produce zero inventory; rather, it controls the amount of material that can be in process at a time—the number of containers of each item. The kanban system can be easily adjusted to fit the current way the system is operating, because card sets can be easily added or removed from the system. If the workers find that they are not able to consistently replenish the item on time, an additional container of material, with the accompanying kanban cards, can be added. If it is found that excess containers of material accumulate, card sets can be easily removed, thus reducing the amount of inventory.

EXAMPLE 13.1: Determining the Number of Kanban Card Sets

Arvin Automotive, a company that makes muffler assemblies for the Big Three, is committed to the use of kanban to pull material through its manufacturing cells. Arvin has designed each cell to fabricate a specific family of muffler products. Fabricating a muffler assembly involves cutting and bending pieces

Step by Step

of pipe that are welded to a muffler and a catalytic converter. The mufflers and catalytic converters are pulled into the cell based on current demand. The catalytic converters are made in a specialized cell.

Catalytic converters are made in batches of 10 units and are moved in special hand carts to the fabrication cells. The catalytic converter cell is designed so that different types of catalytic converters can be made with virtually no setup loss. The cell can respond to an order for a batch of catalytic converters in approximately four hours. Because the catalytic converter cell is right next to the muffler assembly fabrication cell, transportation time is virtually zero.

The muffler assembly fabrication cell averages approximately eight assemblies per hour. Each assembly uses the same catalytic converter. Due to some variability in the process, management has decided to have safety stock equivalent to 10 percent of the needed inventory.

How many kanban sets are needed to manage the replenishment of the catalytic converters?

SOLUTION

In this case, the lead time for replenishment of the converters (L) is four hours. The demand (D) for the catalytic converters is eight per hour. Safety stock (S) is 10 percent of the expected demand, and the container size (C) is 10 units.

$$k = \frac{8 \times 4(1 + .1)}{10} = \frac{35.2}{10} = 3.52$$

In this case, we would need four kanban card sets, and we would have four containers of converters in the system. In all cases, when we calculate k, we will round the number up because we always need to work with full containers of parts. ●

Minimized Setup Times   The reductions in setup and changeover times are necessary to achieve a smooth flow. Exhibit 13.11 shows the relationship between lot size and setup costs. Under a traditional approach, setup cost is treated as a constant, and the optimal order quantity is shown as six. Under the kanban approach, setup cost is significantly reduced and

exhibit 13.11   Relationship between Lot Size and Setup Cost

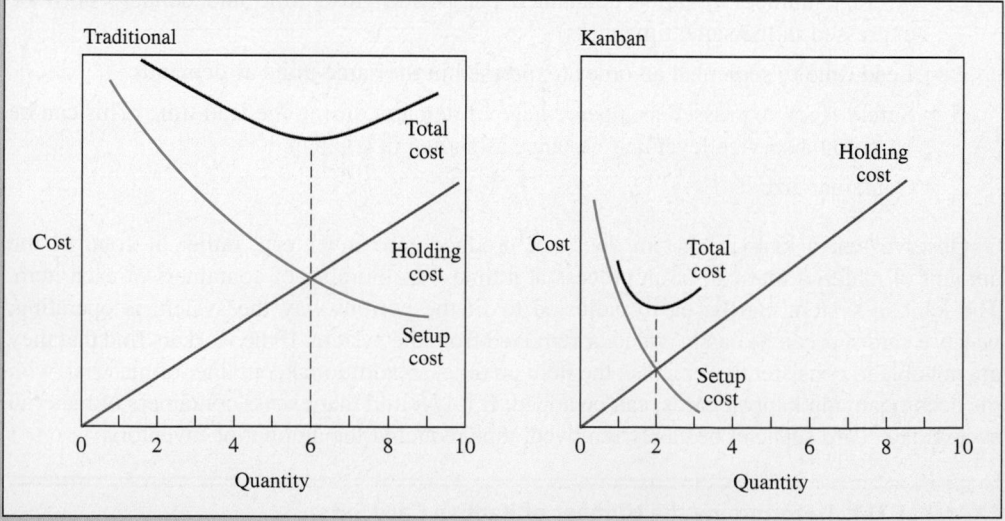

Definitions: *Holding* cost includes the costs of storing inventory and the cost of money tied up in inventory. Setup cost includes the wage costs attributable to workers making the setup, and various administrative and supplies costs. (These are defined in total in Chapter 17, "Inventory Control.")

the corresponding optimal order quantity is reduced. In the exhibit, the order quantity has been reduced from six to two under lean methods by employing setup-time–saving procedures. This organization will ultimately strive for a lot size of one.

In a widely cited example from the late 1970s, Toyota teams of press operators producing car hoods and fenders were able to change an 800-ton press in 10 minutes, compared with the average of six hours for U.S. workers and four hours for German workers. (Now, however, such speed is common in most U.S. auto plants.) To achieve such setup time reduction, setups are divided into internal and external activities. Internal setups must be done while a machine is stopped. External setups can be done while the machine is running. Other time-saving devices such as duplicate tool holders also are used to speed setups.

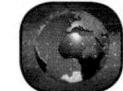

Global

LEAN SUPPLY CHAINS

Building a lean supply chain involves taking a systems approach to integrating the partners. Supply must be coordinated with the need of the production facilities and production must be tied directly to the demand of the customers for products. The importance of speed and steady, consistent flow that is responsive to actual customer demand cannot be overemphasized. Concepts that relate to lean network design are discussed next.

Supply Chain

Specialized Plants   Small specialized plants rather than large vertically integrated manufacturing facilities are important. Large operations and their inherent bureaucracies are difficult to manage and not in line with the lean philosophy. Plants designed for one purpose can be constructed and operated more economically. These plants need to be linked so they can be synchronized to one another and to the actual need of the market. Speed and quick response to changes are keys to the success of a lean supply chain.

Work with Suppliers   Just as customers and employees are key components of lean systems, suppliers are also important to the process. If a firm shares its projected usage requirements with its vendors, they have a long-run picture of the demands that will be placed on their production and distribution systems. Some vendors are linked online with a customer to share production scheduling and input needs data. This permits them to develop level production systems. Confidence in the supplier or vendor's delivery commitment allows reductions of buffer inventories. Maintaining stock at a lean level requires frequent deliveries during the day. Some suppliers even deliver directly to a location on the production line and not at a receiving dock. When vendors adopt quality practices, incoming receiving inspections of their products can be bypassed.

Building a Lean Supply Chain   As we discussed in Chapter 11, a supply chain is the sum total of organizations involved—from raw materials firms through tiers of suppliers to original equipment manufacturers, onward to the ultimate distribution and delivery of the finished product to the customer. Womack and Jones, in their seminal work *Lean Thinking,* provide the following guidelines for implementing a lean supply chain:[8]

- Value must be defined jointly for each product family along with a target cost based on the customer's perception of value.
- All firms along the value stream must make an adequate return on their investments related to the value stream.
- The firms must work together to identify and eliminate *muda* (waste) to the point where the overall target cost and return-on-investment targets of each firm are met.
- When cost targets are met, the firms along the stream will immediately conduct new analyses to identify remaining *muda* and set new targets.
- Every participating firm has the right to examine every activity in every firm relevant to the value stream as part of the joint search for waste.

To summarize: To be lean, everyone's got to be on the same page!

LEAN SERVICES

Service

Global

Many lean techniques have been successfully applied by service firms. Just as in manufacturing, the suitability of each technique and the corresponding work steps depend on the characteristics of the firm's markets, production and equipment technology, skill sets, and corporate culture. Service firms are not different in this respect. Here are 10 of the more successful techniques applied to service companies:

1. **Organize Problem-Solving Groups**   Honeywell is extending its use of quality teams from manufacturing into its service operations. Other corporations as diverse as First Bank/Dallas, Standard Meat Company, and Miller Brewing Company are using similar approaches to improve service. British Airways used quality teams as a fundamental part of its strategy to implement new service practices.

2. **Upgrade Housekeeping**   Good housekeeping means more than winning the clean broom award. It means that only the necessary items are kept in a work area, that there is a place for everything, and that everything is clean and in a constant state of readiness. The employees clean their own areas.

   Service organizations such as McDonald's, Disneyland, and Speedi-Lube have recognized the critical nature of housekeeping. Their dedication to housekeeping has meant that service processes work better, the attitude of continuous improvement is easier to develop, and customers perceive that they are receiving better service.

3. **Upgrade Quality**   The only cost-effective way to improve quality is to develop reliable process capabilities. Process quality is quality at the source—it guarantees first-time production of consistent and uniform products and services.

   McDonald's is famous for building quality into its service delivery process. It literally "industrialized" the service delivery system so that part-time, casual workers could provide the same eating experience anywhere in the world. Quality doesn't mean producing the best; it means consistently producing products and services that give the customers their money's worth.

4. **Clarify Process Flows**   Clarification of flows, based on JIT themes, can dramatically improve the process performance. Here are three examples.

   First, Federal Express Corporation changed air flight patterns from origin-to-destination to origin-to-hub, where the freight is transferred to an outbound plane heading for the destination. This revolutionized the air transport industry. Second, the order-entry department of a manufacturing firm converted from functional subdepartments to customer-centered work groups and reduced the order processing lead time from eight to two days. Finally, Supermaids sends in a team of house cleaners, each with a specific responsibility, to clean a part of each house quickly with parallel processes. Changes in process flows can literally revolutionize service industries.

5. **Revise Equipment and Process Technologies**   Revising technologies involves evaluation of the equipment and processes for their ability to meet the process requirements, to process consistently within tolerance, and to fit the scale and capacity of the work group.

   Speedi-Lube converted the standard service station concept to a specialized lubrication and inspection center by changing the service bays from drive-in to drive-through and by eliminating the hoists and instead building pits under the cars where employees have full access to the lubrication areas on the vehicle.

   A hospital reduced operating room setup time so that it had the flexibility to perform a wider range of operations without reducing the operating room availability.

6. **Level the Facility Load**   Service firms synchronize production with demand. They have developed unique approaches to leveling demand so they can avoid making customers wait for service. McDonald's offers a special breakfast menu in the morning. Retail stores use take-a-number systems. The post office charges more for next-day delivery. These are all examples of the service approach for creating uniform facility loads.

7. **Eliminate Unnecessary Activities** A step that does not add value is a candidate for elimination. A step that does add value may be a candidate for reengineering to improve the process consistency or to reduce the time to perform the tasks.

   A hospital discovered that significant time was spent during an operation waiting for an instrument that was not available when the operation began. It developed a checklist of instruments required for each category of operation. Speedi-Lube eliminated steps, but also added steps that did not improve the lubrication process but did make customers feel more assured about the work being performed.

8. **Reorganize Physical Configuration** Work area configurations frequently require reorganization during a lean implementation. Often manufacturers accomplish this by setting up manufacturing cells to produce items in small lots, synchronous to demand. These cells amount to microfactories inside the plant.

   Most service firms are far behind manufacturers in this area. However, a few interesting examples do come out of the service sector. Some hospitals—instead of routing patients all over the building for tests, exams, X-rays, and injections—are reorganizing their services into work groups based on the type of problem. Teams that treat only trauma are common, but other work groups have been formed to treat less immediate conditions like hernias. These amount to microclinics within the hospital facility.

9. **Introduce Demand-Pull Scheduling** Due to the nature of service production and consumption, demand-pull (customer-driven) scheduling is necessary for operating a service business. Moreover, many service firms are separating their operations into "back room" and "customer contact" facilities. This approach creates new problems in coordinating schedules between the facilities. The original Wendy's restaurants were set up so cooks could see cars enter the parking lot. They put a preestablished number of hamburger patties on the grill for each car. This pull system was designed to have a fresh patty on the grill before the customer even placed an order.

10. **Develop Supplier Networks** The term *supplier networks* in the lean context refers to the cooperative association of suppliers and customers working over the long term for mutual benefit. Service firms have not emphasized supplier networks for materials because the service costs are often predominantly labor. Notable exceptions include service organizations like McDonald's, one of the biggest food products purchasers in the world, which has been developing lean practices. Manpower and other employment agencies have established lean-type relationships with a temporary employment service and a trade school to develop a reliable source of trained assemblers.

SUMMARY

Lean production has proven its value to thousands of companies throughout the world. The idea behind *lean* is achieving high volume with minimal inventory. Toyota pioneered the ideas associated with *lean production* with the Toyota Production System. Lean concepts are best applied in environments where the same products are produced over and over at relatively high volume. Value stream mapping is a useful tool for visualizing supply chains and for applying lean concepts.

KEY TERMS

Lean production Integrated activities designed to achieve high-volume, high-quality production using minimal inventories of raw materials, work-in-process, and finished goods.

Customer value In the context of lean, something for which the customer is willing to pay.

Waste Something that does not add value from the customer's perspective.

Value stream These are the value-adding and non-value-adding activities required to design, order, and provide a product from concept to launch, order to delivery, and raw materials to customers.

Waste reduction The optimization of value-adding activities and elimination of non-value-adding activities that are part of the value stream.

Value stream mapping A graphical way to analyze where value is or is not being added as material flows through a process.

Kaizen Japanese philosophy that focuses on continuous improvement.

Preventive maintenance Periodic inspection and repair designed to keep equipment reliable.

Group technology A philosophy in which similar parts are grouped into families, and the processes required to make the parts are arranged in a specialized work cell.

Quality at the source Philosophy of making factory workers personally responsible for the quality of their output. Workers are expected to make the part correctly the first time and to stop the process immediately if there is a problem.

Level schedule A schedule that pulls material into final assembly at a constant rate.

Freeze window The period of time during which the schedule is fixed and no further changes are possible.

Backflush Calculating how many of each part were used in production and using these calculations to adjust actual on-hand inventory balances. This eliminates the need to actually track each part used in production.

Uniform plant loading Smoothing the production flow to dampen schedule variation.

Kanban and the kanban pull system An inventory or production control system that uses a signaling device to regulate flows.

FORMULA REVIEW

Determining the number of kanbans

$$k = \frac{DL(1 + S)}{C}$$

[13.1]

SOLVED PROBLEMS

SOLVED PROBLEM 1

Value Stream Mapping Example: Bolt Manufacturing[9]

A simple example will illustrate the use of value stream mapping. Exhibit 13.12 depicts a bolt manufacturing operation that ships 7,500 bolts per week. The current state map provides cycle time and setup time information for each of the 15 processes used, and it provides inventory levels at each location. The map also depicts information flow between the steel supplier, the bolt customer, and management via production scheduling. The total value-added time, denoted as processing time, is obtained by summing all of the individual value-added contributions at each processing step on the time line. For the example, it equals 28.88 seconds. At each inventory location, lead time is calculated by dividing inventory level by daily production demand, which is 1,500 bolts. Summing all of the lead time produces an overall production lead time of 66.1 days, which is the entire time it takes an individual bolt to make its way through the plant.

There are several possibilities to optimize the current production scenario. Exhibit 13.13 provides a few of these, shown as Kaizen bursts, including eliminating several processing steps, modifying some of the existing processes, and reducing travel distances between processes. Exhibit 13.14, the future state map, illustrates the incorporation of these modifications. As shown, the changes reduce production lead time to 50.89 days, which is a 23 percent reduction. The production scenario could be enhanced even more if pull systems were incorporated at various locations.

SOLVED PROBLEM 2

A local hospital wants to set up a kanban system to manage its supply of blood with the regional blood bank. The regional blood bank delivers blood to the hospital each day with a one-day order lead time (an order placed by 6 P.M. today will be delivered tomorrow afternoon). Internally, the hospital purchasing group places orders for blood each day at 5 P.M. Blood is measured by the pint and is shipped in containers that contain six pints. For a particular blood type, the hospital uses an average of 12 pints per day. Due to the critical nature of a blood shortage, the hospital wants to carry a safety stock of two days' expected supply. How many kanban card sets should the hospital prepare?

exhibit 13.12   Current State Map for Bolt Manufacturing Example

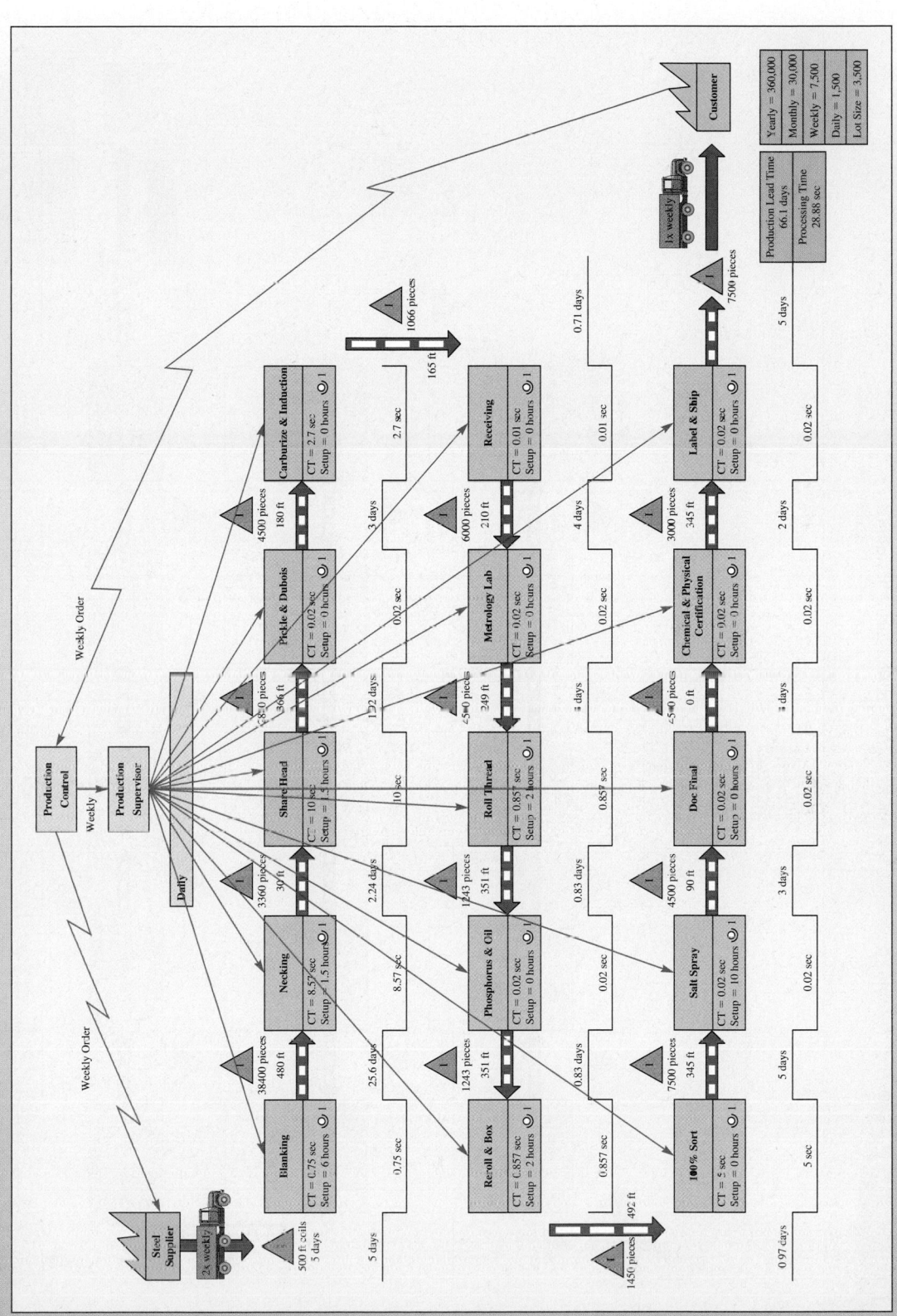

exhibit 13.13   Potential Process Changes for Bolt Manufacturing Example

exhibit 13.14   Future State Map for Bolt Manufacturing Example

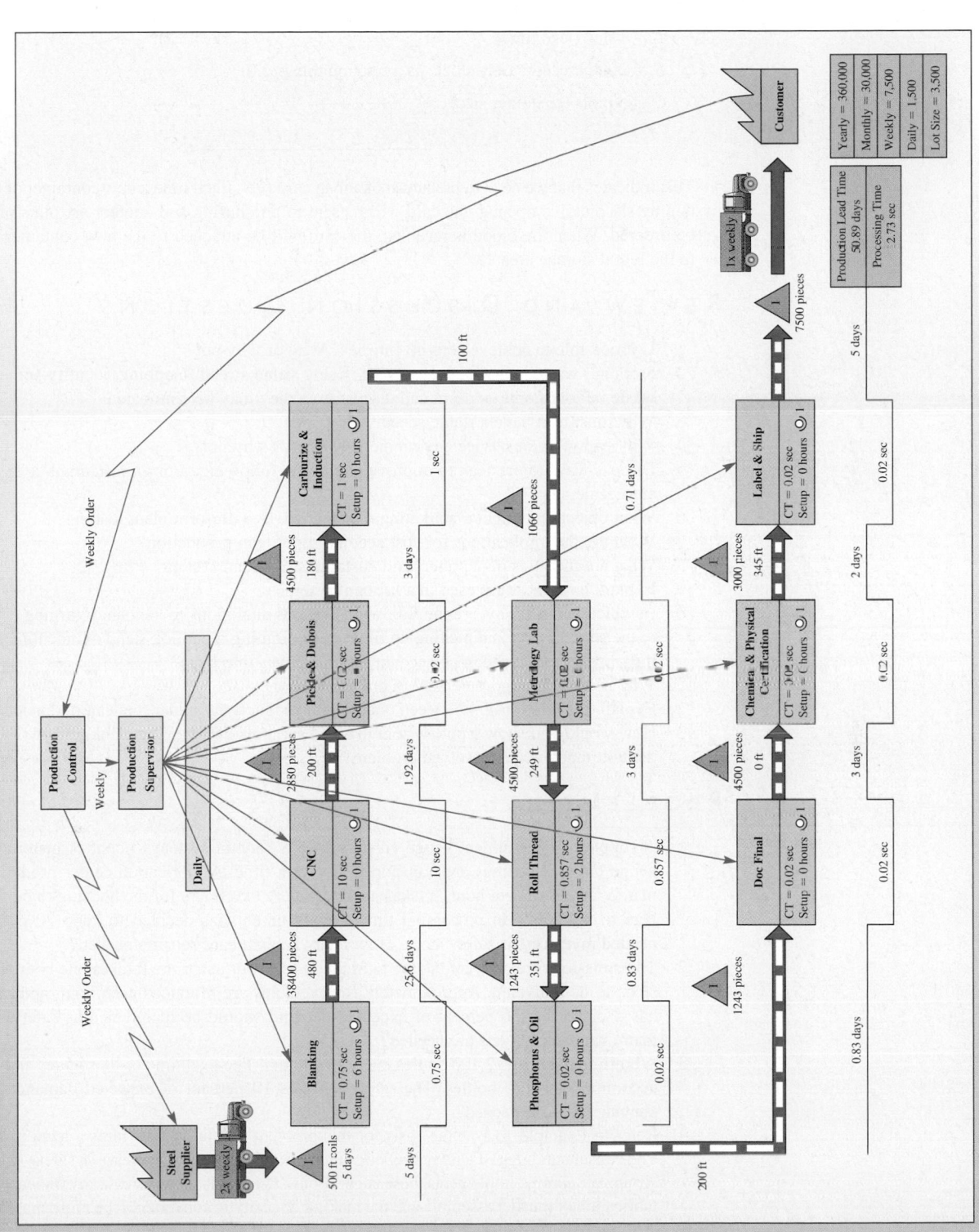

Solution

This problem is typical of how a real application might look. Using the data given, the variables for this problem are as follows:

$D = 12$ pints per day (average demand)

$L = 1$ day (lead time)

$S = 200$ percent (safety stock, as a fraction this is 2.0)

$C = 6$ pints (container size)

$$k = \frac{DL(1 + S)}{C} = \frac{12(1 + 2)}{6} = 6$$

This indicates that we need to prepare six kanban card sets. Each time a new container of blood (containing six pints) is opened, the card will be sent to purchasing and another six pints of blood will be ordered. When the blood is received, the card will be attached to the new container and moved to the blood storage area.

REVIEW AND DISCUSSION QUESTIONS

1. Is it possible to achieve zero inventories? Why or why not?
2. Stopping waste is a vital part of lean. Using value stream mapping, identify some sources of waste in your home or dorm and discuss how they may be eliminated.
3. Why must lean have a stable schedule?
4. Will lean work in service environments? Why or why not?
5. Discuss ways to use lean to improve one of the following: a pizza restaurant, a hospital, or an auto dealership.
6. What objections might a marketing manager have to uniform plant loading?
7. What are the implications for cost accounting of lean production?
8. What are the roles of suppliers and customers in a lean system?
9. Explain how cards are used in a kanban system.
10. In which ways, if any, are the following systems analogous to kanban: returning empty bottles to the supermarket and picking up filled ones; running a hot dog stand at lunchtime; withdrawing money from a checking account; raking leaves into bags?
11. Why is lean hard to implement in practice?
12. Explain the relationship between quality and productivity under the lean philosophy.
13. How would you show a pull system in VSM symbols between the blanking and CNC stages of the bolt manufacturing solved problem?

PROBLEMS

1. A supplier of instrument gauge clusters uses a kanban system to control material flow. The gauge cluster housings are transported five at a time. A fabrication center produces approximately 10 gauges per hour. It takes approximately two hours for the housing to be replenished. Due to variations in processing times, management has decided to keep 20 percent of the needed inventory as safety stock. How many kanban card sets are needed?
2. Transmissions are delivered to the fabrication line four at a time. It takes one hour for transmissions to be delivered. Approximately four vehicles are produced each hour, and management has decided that 50 percent of expected demand should be maintained as safety stock. How many kanban card sets are needed?
3. A bottling plant fills 2,400 bottles every two hours. The lead time is 40 minutes and a container accommodates 120 bottles. The safety stock is 10 percent of expected demand. How many kanban cards are needed?
4. Refer to Example 13.1 as the basis for this problem. Arvin Meritor hires a team of consultants. The consultants suggest a partial robotic automation as well as an increase in safety stock to 0.125. Arvin Automotive implements these suggestions. The result is an increase in efficiency in both the fabrication of muffler assembly and the making of catalytic converters. The muffler assembly fabrication cell now averages 16 assemblies per hour and the lead time has been decreased to two hours' response time for a batch of 10 catalytic converters. How many kanban cards are now needed?
5. Arvin Meritor is so pleased with the outcome from previous suggestions that the consultants are invited back for more work. The consultants now suggest a more complete robotic automation of the making of muffler assemblies and also a reduction in container size to eight per container. Arvin Meritor implements these suggestions and the result is that the muffler assembly

fabrication cell now averages approximately 32 assemblies per hour, and the catalytic converter assembly cell can now respond to an order for a batch of catalytic converters in one hour. The safety stock remains at 0.125. How many kanban cards are needed?

6   A manufacturer of high-end leather bracelets uses a kanban system to control material flow. The bracelets are transported in sets of 12. A cutting operation, on average, produces approximately 200 bracelets per hour. It takes one hour for the sets of collars to be replenished. Due to variations in processing times due to the size and length of the bracelets, it has been decided to keep 25 percent of the needed inventory as safety stock. How many kanban card sets are needed?

7   Suppose a switch assembly is assembled in batches of 4 units from an "upstream" assembly area and delivered in a special container to a "downstream" control-panel assembly operation. The control-panel assembly area requires 5 switch assemblies per hour. The switch assembly area can produce a container of switch assemblies in 2 hours and safety stock has been set at 10 percent of needed inventory.

CASE: QUALITY PARTS COMPANY

Quality Parts Company supplies gizmos for a computer manufacturer located a few miles away. The company produces two different models of gizmos in production runs ranging from 100 to 300 units.

The production flow of models X and Y is shown in Exhibit 13.15. Model Z requires milling as its first step, but otherwise follows the same flow pattern as X and Y. Skids can hold up to 20 gizmos at a time. Approximate times per unit by operation number and equipment setup times are shown in Exhibit 13.16.

Demand for gizmos from the computer company ranges between 125 and 175 per month, equally divided among X, Y, and Z. Subassembly builds up inventory early in the month to make certain that a buffer stock is always available. Raw materials and purchased parts for subassemblies each constitute 40 percent of the manufacturing cost of a gizmo. Both categories of parts are multiple-sourced from about 80 vendors and are delivered at random times. (Gizmos have 40 different part numbers.)

Scrap rates are about 10 percent at each operation, inventory turns twice yearly, employees are paid on a day rate, employee turnover is 25 percent per year, and net profit from operations is steady at 5 percent per year. Maintenance is performed as needed.

The manager of Quality Parts Company has been contemplating installing an automated ordering system to help control inventories and to "keep the skids filled." (She feels that two days

of work in front of a workstation motivates the worker to produce at top speed.) She is also planning to add three inspectors to clean up the quality problem. Further, she is thinking about setting up a rework line to speed repairs. Although she is pleased with the high utilization of most of her equipment and labor, she is concerned about the idle time of the milling machine. Finally, she has asked the industrial engineering department to look into high-rise shelving to store parts coming off machine 4.

QUESTIONS

1   Which of the changes being considered by the manager of Quality Parts Company are counter to the lean philosophy?

2   Make recommendations for lean improvements in such areas as scheduling, layout, kanban, task groupings, and inventory. Use quantitative data as much as possible; state necessary assumptions.

3   Sketch the operation of a pull system for running Quality Parts Company's current system.

4   Outline a plan for introducing lean at Quality Parts Company.

CASE: VALUE STREAM MAPPING

Value stream mapping involves first developing a baseline map of the current situation of a company's external and/or internal operations and then, applying lean concepts, developing a future state map that shows improved operations. Exhibit 13.17, for example, shows the current state with a production lead time of 4.5 days. This system is a batch/push system (indicated by striped arrows) resulting in long delays and inventory buildups. Exhibit 13.18 shows the future state map with production lead time of 0.25 day. This was accomplished by moving to a continuous-flow pull system and attacking the seven wastes. Value stream mapping uses a number of special icons and display format of boxes and flows. For a more complete discussion of the methodology, see Jared Lovelle.[10]

QUESTIONS

1   Eliminating the queue of work dramatically quickens the time it takes a part to flow through the system. What are the disadvantages of removing those queues?

2   How do you think the machine operators would react to the change?

3   What would you do to ensure that the operators were kept busy?

exhibit 13.15

Gizmo Production Flow

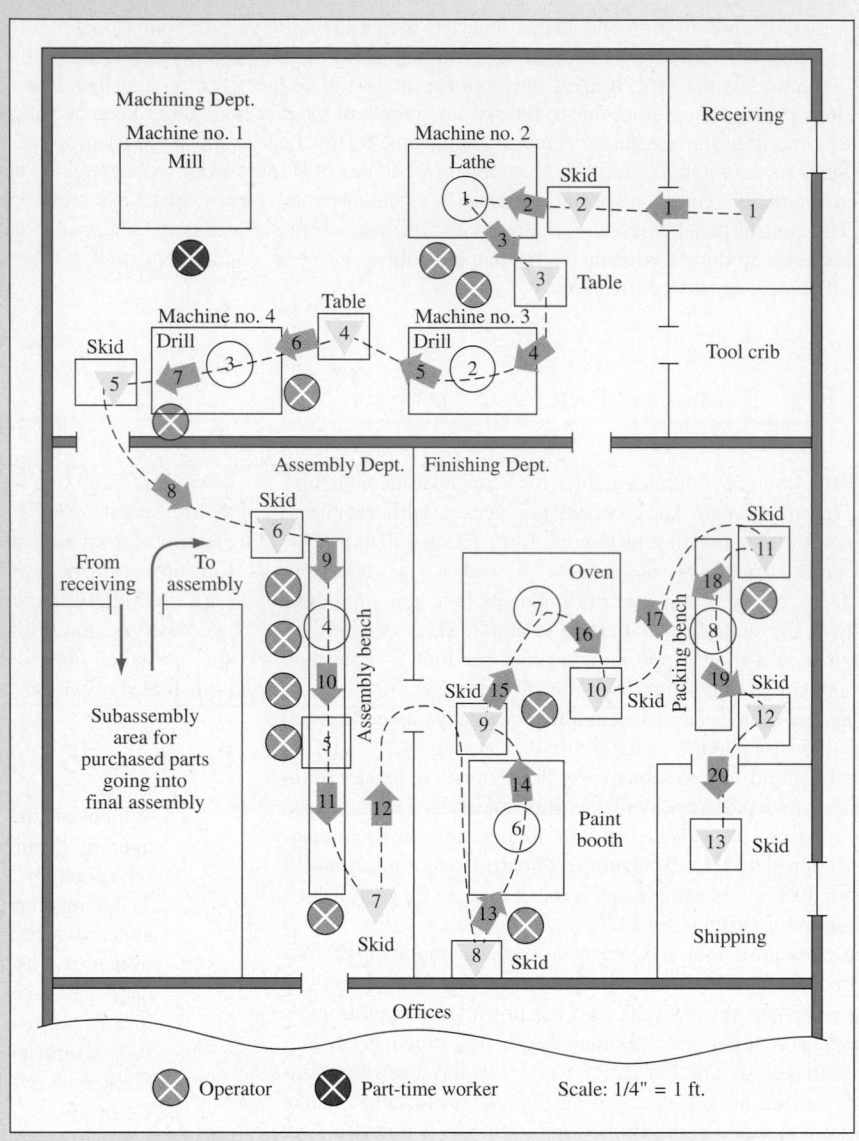

exhibit 13.16

Operations and Setup Time

OPERATION NUMBER AND NAME	OPERATION TIME (MINUTES)	SETUP TIME (MINUTES)
Milling for Model Z	20	60
1 Lathe	50	30
2 Mod. 14 drill	15	5
3 Mod. 14 drill	40	5
4 Assembly step 1	50	
Assembly step 2	45	
Assembly step 3	50	
5 Inspection	30	
6 Paint	30	20
7 Oven	50	
8 Packing	5	

Map of the Current State

exhibit 13.17

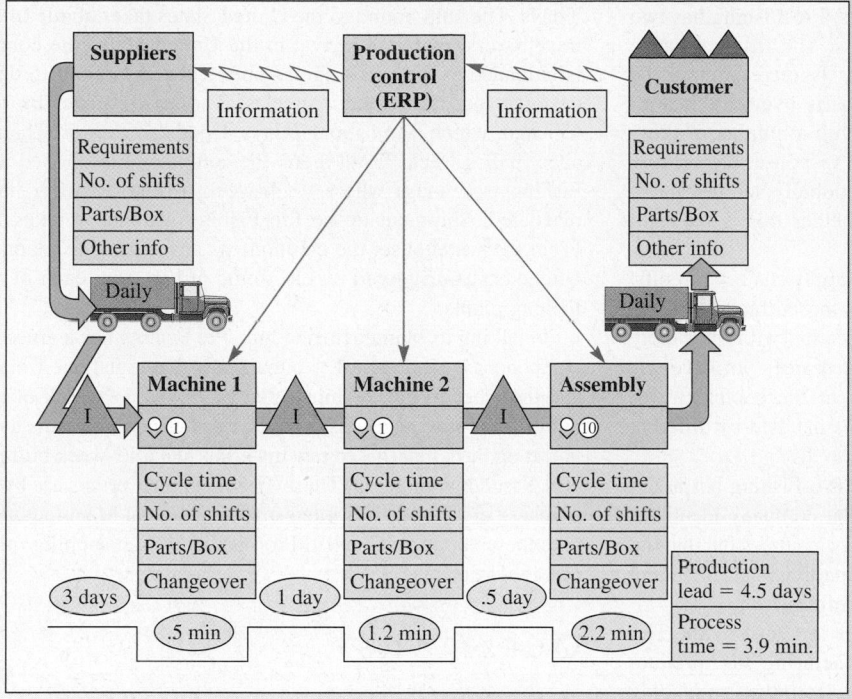

SOURCE: JARED LOVELLE, "MAPPING THE VALUE STREAM," *IIE SOLUTIONS* 33, NO. 2 (FEBRUARY 2001), P. 32.

Map of the Future State

exhibit 13.18

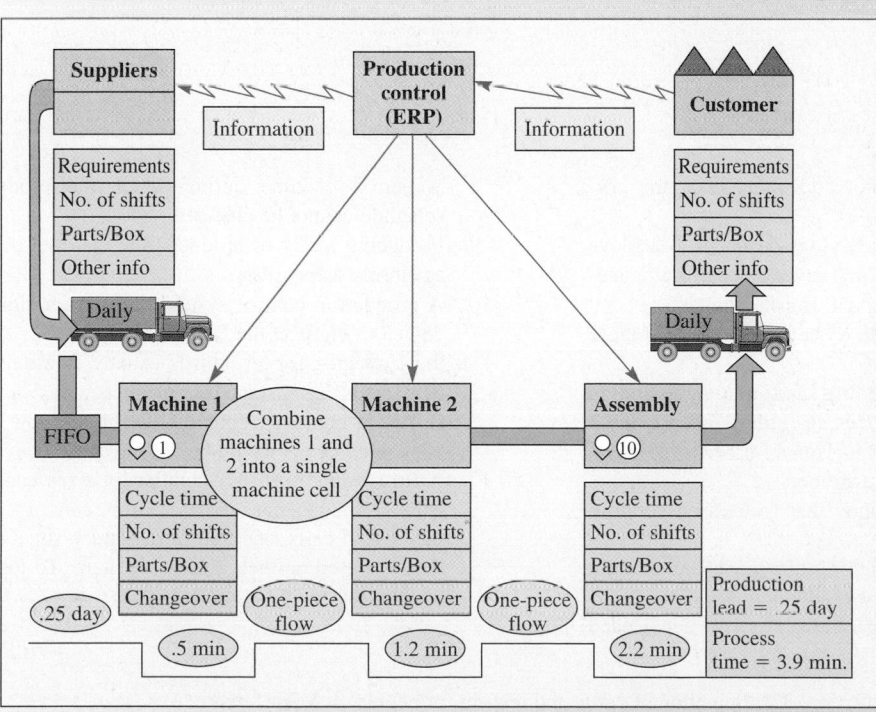

SOURCE: JARED LOVELLE, "MAPPING THE VALUE STREAM," *IIE SOLUTIONS* 33, NO. 2 (FEBRUARY 2001), P. 30.

CASE: PRO FISHING BOATS—A VALUE STREAM MAPPING EXERCISE

A fishing boat manufacturer, Pro Fishing Boats, is having many problems with critical globally sourced parts. Pro Fishing has two manufacturing facilities in the United States. The firm's reliance on efficient global supply chain operations is increasing as the manufacturer is sourcing more and more parts overseas, including critical components. Recent problems with a number of these critical parts have caused line shutdowns. In response, Pro Fishing has *mandated* a six-week inventory on all globally sourced parts. Management has asked you to evaluate whether this is the right decision.

First, you must understand Pro Fishing's supply chain. Currently, there is very little visibility (knowledge of the current status) of inventory in the supply chain and communication with the supply base is minimal. In fact, the boat manufacturer does not have *any* visibility past the Tier I suppliers. Adding to the complexity of this problem, each part of the supply chain is handled by different departments within the company.

In order to understand the supply chain, Pro Fishing has asked you to map their supply chain. To do so, the company identified a critical component to follow in the supply chain. After having the opportunity to interview supply chain participants, including suppliers, you have collected the following information.

The component is manufactured overseas in China by the Tier I supplier, Manufacturing Inc. The Manufacturing Inc. production schedule is based on orders sent via fax from the Pro Fishing warehouse. The supplier operates on a 90-60-30 day forecast along with a weekly order. Upon completion of the component, Manufacturing Inc. sends the component via truck to the Shanghai Port where it is loaded onto a ship heading to the United States. Loading at the port takes 1 week and truck transport takes 3 days. Manufacturing Inc. holds a 9-week finished goods buffer

inventory. Manufacturing time for each component is only about 3 days. The ship bound to the United States takes about 14 days to travel overseas. Upon arrival in the United States the component is unloaded at the Los Angeles port. This takes about 5 days and customs inspects in Los Angeles. The goods travel by train to Chicago, which takes about 7 days. Goods are held in Chicago for about half a week. From there, the component is trucked to a Pro Fishing warehouse where the 6-week inventory buffer has been mandated. Shipment to the Pro Fishing warehouse takes 2 days. From the warehouse, the components are trucked to plants in the United States triggered by electronic orders from each of the Pro Fishing plants.

In talking to Manufacturing Inc., Pro Fishing has learned that its component is made up of two main raw materials: one from China and the other from the United States. To avoid the risk of running out of these raw materials, Manufacturing Inc. maintains a 4-week buffer on the China-based raw materials and a 12-week buffer in the U.S. based raw material. These Tier II supplier orders are by formal purchase order only. It is interesting to note that Manufacturing Inc. uses these suppliers to fulfill Pro Fishing's strict supplier qualification requirements.

QUESTIONS

1. Create a value stream map (VSM) of this supply chain. What other information is needed?
2. Where is there risk for supply chain disruptions or stoppages to the flow of materials?
3. Where do opportunities reside in improving supply chain operations and how has VSM helped to reveal these?

SUPER QUIZ

1. Anything that does not add value from the customer's perspective.
2. An integrated set of activities designed to achieve production using minimal inventories of raw materials, work-in-process, and finished goods.
3. The Toyota Production System is founded in these two philosophies.
4. The set of value-adding and non-value-adding activities required to design, order, and provide a product from concept to launch, order to delivery, and raw materials to customers.
5. The Japanese philosophy that focuses on continuous improvement.
6. A philosophy in which similar parts are brought together in families for production purposes.
7. Means only producing what is needed when needed and no more.

8. A period of time during which the production schedule cannot be changed.
9. Producing a mix of products that matches demand as closely as possible.
10. A production control system that uses a signaling device to regulate the flow of material.
11. If the lead time for an item is exactly five days, the demand is a constant four units per day, and the shipment container contains two units, how many kanban card sets would be needed?
12. A firm wants to justify smaller lot sizes economically. Management knows that it cannot change the cost to carry one unit in inventory since this is largely based on the value of the item. To justify a smaller lot size what must they do?

1. Waste 2. Lean production 3. Elimination of waste and respect for people 4. Value stream 5. Kaizen
6. Group technology 7. JIT (just-in-time) production 8. Freeze window 9. Uniform plant loading
10. Kanban 11. 10 card sets 12. Reduce setup cost

SELECTED BIBLIOGRAPHY

Allen, M. "Picture-Perfect Manufacturing [Using Value Stream Mapping]." *Modern Machine Shop Magazine Online,* August 2004.

George, M. L. *Lean Six Sigma.* New York: McGraw-Hill, 2002.

Gross, J. M., and K. R. McInnis. *Kanban Made Simple: Demystifying and Applying Toyota's Legendary Manufacturing Process.* New York: AMACOM, 2003.

Monden, Y. *Toyota Production System: An Integrated Approach to Just-in-Time.* Atlanta, GA: Institute of Industrial Engineers, 1998.

Phelps, T.; M. Smith; and T. Hoenes. "Building a Lean Supply Chain." *Manufacturing Engineering* 132, no. 5 (May 2004), pp. 107–13.

Womack, J. P., and D. T. Jones. *Lean Thinking: Banish Waste and Create Wealth in Your Corporation.* New York: Simon & Schuster, 1996.

Womack, J. P.; D. T. Jones; and D. Roos. *The Machine That Changed the World.* New York: R. A. Rawston Associates, 1990.

FOOTNOTES

1 Adapted from D. Blanchard, *Green Is the New Black,* March 1, 2009, IndustryWeek.com.

2 Adapted from B. Tompkins, *Lean Thinking for the Supply Chain,* from www.tompkinsinc.com.

3 K. A. Wantuck, *The Japanese Approach to Productivity* (Southfield, MI: Bendix Corporation, 1983).

4 K. Suzaki, *The New Manufacturing Challenge: Techniques for Continuous Improvement* (New York: Free Press, 1987), pp. 7–25.

5 C. Karlsson, *Japanese Production Management in Sunrise or Sunset* (Stockholm, Sweden: Stockholm School of Economics, EFI/ The Economic Research Institute. 1999).

6 This was adapted from material from Strategos Consultants. See www.strategosinc.com.

7 R. H. Hall, *Zero Inventories* (Homewood, IL: Dow Jones-Irwin, 1983), p. 64.

8 J. P. Womack and D. T. Jones, *Lean Thinking* (New York: Simon & Schuster, 1996), p. 277.

9 K. A. Rosentrater and R. Balamuralikrishna, *Value Stream Mapping—A Tool for Engineering and Technology Education and Practice.* ASEE Illinois-Indiana Sectional Conference, Fort Wayne, IN. American Society for Engineering Education. Presented April 1, 2006.

10 J. Lovelle, "Mapping the Value Stream," *IIE Solutions* 33, no. 2 (February 2001), pp. 26–33.

OPERATIONS CONSULTING AND REENGINEERING

After reading this chapter you will:

1. Know the scope of operations consulting.
2. Understand how consulting firms make money.
3. Have a framework for the operations consulting process.
4. Describe the basic tools that operations consultants use.
5. Be introduced to business process reengineering and the principles of reengineering.

PITTIGLIO RABIN TODD & McGRATH (PRTM)—A LEADING OPERATIONS CONSULTING COMPANY

Good business strategy plots changes in where a company is going. A winning operational strategy translates that direction into operational reality, creating strategic competitive advantage in the process. PRTM is a leading company specializing in finding ways to structure business operations to create breakout results in top-line growth, earnings, and valuation.

Today's operational CEOs realize that brilliant business strategies and operational strategies are interconnected. Business strategies drive the need for new operational capabilities, and evolving operational capabilities shape the future business strategies. PRTM Consultants focus on six essential ingredients of operational strategy:

- **Transform market forces into operational advantage.** This is the kind of insight that Black & Decker used to turn a regulatory requirement for double-insulated power tools into a new modular product platform that redefined cost and performance in category after category. The same type of insight helped Progressive Insurance transform automobile claims from an unproductive part of its cost structure into a far more economical and valued source of competitive advantage.

- **Do one thing extraordinarily well.** Consider the case of Apple iTunes. Its gigantic share of the digital music player market is fueled by Apple's relentless pursuit of ease of use as a basis of competition. Companies like Walmart are all about cost leadership, attaining the lowest end-to-end operational cost, and the highest productivity.

- **Think end-to-end, continuous, real-time, and horizontally.** Every organization has a set of core operational domains that make up its operational model. For most, these comprise some combination of the product development chain, the supply chain, and the customer chain. Operational strategy configures these operational domains to deliver against business strategy, and create advantage in their own right.

SOURCE: ADAPTED FROM A STATEMENT BY TOM GODWARD AND MARK DECK, PARTNERS IN PRTM'S WORLDWIDE OPERATIONAL STRATEGY PRACTICE, www.prtm.com.

- **Think and execute globally.**   Due to global markets for products and global availability of supply many companies need to consider strategies that best position the firm to compete in this domain. Global opportunities are often the key driver to changes to both business and operational strategies.

- **Drive innovation in your operations and business model.**   Peter Drucker defined innovation as change that creates a new dimension of performance. He also stated that a key accountability of the CEO is innovation. Too often innovation is perceived to be a technical or product-oriented activity. The reality is that operational innovation is creating the commanding leaders today.

- **Execute relentlessly.**   A complete operational strategy requires a commitment to execution. Companies with commanding leads in their markets execute relentlessly, informed by their global marketplace insight, aligned to a singular competitive focus, emboldened by a clear innovation intent, and guided by a sound operational model aligned with business strategy and business economics.

In the 21st century, companies that make all aspects of their operations a source of strategic innovation will dominate their markets, delivering unparalleled revenue growth, earnings performance, and shareholder return.

Operations consulting has become one of the major areas of employment for business school graduates. The above page from the PRTM Web site nicely summarizes the importance of operations on bottom-line performance. In this chapter, we discuss how one goes about consulting for operations, as well as the nature of the consulting business in general. We also survey the tools and techniques used in operations consulting and provide an overview of business process reengineering since much OSCM consulting entails this activity.

WHAT IS OPERATIONS CONSULTING?

Operations consulting

Operations consulting deals with assisting clients in developing operations strategies and improving production processes. In strategy development, the focus is on analyzing the capabilities of operations in light of the firm's competitive strategy. By way of example, Treacy and Wiersema suggest that market leadership can be attained in one of three ways: through product leadership, through operational excellence, or through customer intimacy.[1] Each of these strategies may well call for different operations capabilities and focus. The operations consultant must be able to assist management in understanding these differences and be able to define the most effective combination of technology and systems to execute the strategy. In process improvement, the focus is on employing analytical tools and methods to help operating managers enhance performance of their departments. Deloitte & Touche Consulting lists the actions to improve processes as follows: refine/revise processes, revise activities, reconfigure flows, revise policies/procedures, change outputs, and realign structure. We say more about both strategy issues and tools later. Regardless of where one focuses, *an effective job of operations consulting results in an alignment between strategy and process dimensions that enhances the business performance of the client.*

THE MANAGEMENT CONSULTING INDUSTRY

The management consulting industry can be categorized in three ways: by size, by specialization, and by in-house and external consultants. Most consulting firms are small, generating less than $1 million in annual revenue.[2] Relative to specialization, although all large firms provide a variety of services, they also may specialize by function, such as operations management, or by industry, such as manufacturing. Most large consulting companies are built on information technology (IT) and accounting work. The third basis for segmentation, in-house versus external, refers to whether a company maintains its own consulting organization or buys consulting services from the outside. Collis observes that internal consulting arms are common in large companies and are often affiliated with planning departments.[3]

Consulting firms are also frequently characterized according to whether their primary skill is in strategic planning or in tactical analysis and implementation. McKinsey & Company and the Boston Consulting Group are standard examples of strategy-type companies, whereas Gemini Consulting and A. T. Kearney focus rather extensively on tactical and implementation projects. The big accounting firms and Accenture are known for providing a wide range of services. The major new players in the consulting business are the large information technology firms such as Infosys Technology, Computer Sciences Corporation (CSC), Electronic Data Systems (EDS), and IBM. Consultancies are faced with problems similar to those of their clients: the need to provide a global presence, the need to computerize to coordinate activities, and the need to continually recruit and train their workers. This has led consultancies to make the hard choice of being very large or being a boutique firm. Being in the middle creates problems of lack of scale economies on the one hand and lack of focus and flexibility on the other.

The hierarchy of the typical consulting firm can be viewed as a pyramid. At the top of the pyramid are the partners or seniors, whose primary function is sales and client relations. In the middle are managers, who manage consulting projects or "engagements." At the bottom are juniors, who carry out the consulting work as part of a consulting team. There are gradations in rank within each of these categories (such as senior partners). The three categories are frequently referred to colloquially as the **"finders"** (of new business), the **"minders"** (or managers) of the project teams, and the **"grinders"** (the consultants who do the work). Consulting firms typically work in project teams, selected according to client needs and the preferences of the project managers and the first-line consultants themselves. Getting oneself assigned to interesting, high-visibility projects with good co-workers is an important career strategy of most junior consultants. Being in demand for team membership and obtaining quality consulting experiences are critical for achieving long-term success with a consulting firm (or being attractive to another firm within or outside of consulting).

"Finders"
"Minders"
"Grinders"

ECONOMICS OF CONSULTING FIRMS

The economics of consulting firms have been written about extensively by David H. Maister. In his classic article "Balancing the Professional Service Firm," he draws the analogy of the consulting firm as a job shop, where the right kinds of "machines" (professional staff) must be correctly allocated to the right kinds of jobs (consulting projects).[4] As in any job shop, the degree of job customization and attendant complexity is critical. The most complex projects, which Maister calls *brain surgery* projects, require innovation and creativity. Next come *gray hair* projects, which require a great deal of experience but little in the way of innovation. A third type of project is the *procedures* project, where the general nature of the problem is well known and the activities necessary to complete it are similar to those performed on other projects.

Because consulting firms are typically partnerships, the goal is to maximize profits for the partners. This, in turn, is achieved by leveraging the skills of the partners through the effective use of midlevel and junior consultants. This is often presented as a ratio of partners to midlevel to junior consultants for the average project. (See Exhibit 13A.1 for a numerical example of how profitability is calculated for a hypothetical consulting firm, Guru Associates.) Because most consulting firms are engaged in multiple projects simultaneously, the percentage of billable employee hours assigned to all projects (target utilization) will be less than 100 percent. A practice that specializes in cutting-edge, high-client risk (brain surgery) work must be staffed with a high partner-to-junior ratio because lower-level people

exhibit 13A.1   The Economics of Guru Associates

LEVEL	No.	TARGET UTILIZATION	TARGET BILLABLE HOURS @ 2,000 HOURS PER PERSON PER YEAR	BILLING RATE	FEES	SALARY PER INDIVIDUAL	TOTAL SALARIES
Partner (senior)	4	75%	6,000	$200	$1,200,000	(see calculations below)	
Middle	8	75%	12,000	$100	$1,200,000	$75,000	$600,000
Junior	20	90%	36,000	$ 50	$1,800,000	$32,000	$640,000
Totals					$4,200,000		$1,240,000

Fees	$4,200,000
Salaries	(1,240,000)
Contributions	$2,960,000
Overhead*	$1,280,000
Partner profits	$1,680,000
Per partner	$ 420,000

*Assume overhead costs of $40,000 per professional.

SOURCE: D. H. MAISTER, *MANAGING THE PROFESSIONAL SERVICE FIRM* (NEW YORK: THE FREE PRESS, 1993), P. 11.

will not be able to deliver the quality of services required. In contrast, practices that deal with more procedural, low-risk work will be inefficient if they do not have a lower ratio of partners to juniors because high-priced staff should not be doing low-value tasks.

The most common method for improving efficiency is the use of uniform approaches to each aspect of a consulting job. Accenture, the company most famous for this approach, sends its new consultants through a boot camp at its St. Charles, Illinois, training facility. At this boot camp, it provides highly refined, standardized methods for such common operations work as systems design, process reengineering, and continuous improvement, and for the project management and reporting procedures by which such work is carried out. Of course, other large consulting firms have their own training methods and step-by-step procedures for selling, designing, and executing consulting projects.

WHEN OPERATIONS CONSULTING IS NEEDED

The following are some of the major strategic and tactical areas where companies typically seek operations consulting. Looking first at manufacturing consulting areas (grouped under what could be called *the 5 Ps of production*), we have

- *Plant:* Adding and locating new plants; expanding, contracting, or refocusing existing facilities.
- *People:* Quality improvement, setting/revising work standards, learning curve analysis.
- *Parts:* Make or buy decisions, vendor selection decisions.
- *Processes:* Technology evaluation, process improvement, reengineering.
- *Planning and control systems:* Supply chain management, ERP, MRP, shop-floor control, warehousing, distribution.

Obviously, many of these issues are interrelated, calling for systemwide solutions. Examples of common themes reflecting this are developing manufacturing strategy; designing and implementing JIT systems; implementing MRP or proprietary ERP software such as SAP; and systems integration involving client–server technology. Typical questions addressed are "How can the client cut lead times? How can inventory be reduced? How can better control be maintained over the shop floor?" Among the hot areas of manufacturing strategy consulting are sustainability; outsourcing; supply chain management; and global manufacturing networks. At the tactical level, there is a huge market for consulting in E-operations, product development, ISO 9000 quality certification, and designing and implementing decentralized production control systems.

Turning to services, while consulting firms in manufacturing may have broad specialties in process industries on the one hand and assembly or discrete product manufacture on the other, service operations consulting typically has a strong industry or sector focus. A common consulting portfolio of specialties in services (and areas of consulting need) would include the following:

Financial services (staffing, automation, quality studies).

Health care (staffing, billing, office procedures, phone answering, layout).

Transportation (route scheduling and shipping logistics for goods haulers, reservation systems, and baggage handling for airlines).

Hospitality (reservations, staffing, cost containment, quality programs).

For both manufacturing and service industries, the current hot area for consultants as well as in-house teams is Lean Six Sigma. The reason is companies have reached their limit on how much can be done by downsizing and are thus focusing on rigorously measuring and perfecting various processes. Pharmaceutical companies, large retailers, and food companies are examples of industries with heavy demand for consultants who specialize in such programs.[5]

OPERATIONS CONSULTING FIRMS SUCH AS KEVIN KENNEDY AND ASSOCIATES INC. HELP COMPANIES FOCUS ON THE STRATEGIC OR TACTICAL LEVEL OF DECISIONS.

Service

WHEN ARE OPERATIONS CONSULTANTS NEEDED?

Companies typically seek out operations consultants when they are faced with major investment decisions or when they believe that they are not getting maximum effectiveness from their productive capacity. As an example of the first type of situation, consider the following:

A national pie restaurant chain retained consultants to determine if a major addition to its freezer storage capacity was needed at its pie-making plant. Its lease had run out on a nearby freezer warehouse, so the firm had to make a decision rather quickly. The pie plant manager wanted a $500,000 increase in capacity. After analysis of the demand for various types of pies, the distribution system, and the contractual arrangement with the shipper, the consultant concluded that management could avoid all but a $30,000 investment in capacity if they did the following: Run a mixed-model production schedule for pies according to a forecast for each of 10 kinds of pies (for example, 20 percent strawberry, 30 percent cherry, 30 percent apple, and 20 percent other pies each two-day pie production cycle). To do this, more timely information about pie demand at each of the chain restaurants had to be obtained. This in turn required that information links for pie requirements go directly to the factory. (Previously the distributor bought the pies and resold them to the restaurants.) Finally, the company renegotiated pickup times from the pie plant to enable just-in-time delivery at the restaurants. The company was in a much stronger bargaining situation than it had been five years previously, and the distributor was willing to make reasonable adjustments.

The lesson from this is that few investment decisions in operations are all or nothing, and good solutions can be obtained by simply applying standard OSCM concepts of production planning, forecasting, and scheduling. The solution recognized that the problem must be viewed at a systemwide level to see how better planning and distribution could substitute for brick-and-mortar capacity.

THE OPERATIONS CONSULTING PROCESS

The broad steps in the operations consulting process (see Exhibit 13.A2) are roughly the same as for any type of management consulting. The major differences exist in the nature of the problem to be analyzed and the kinds of analytical methods to be employed. Like general management consulting, operations consulting may focus on the strategic level or tactical level, and the process itself generally requires extensive interviewing of employees, managers, and, frequently, customers. If there is one large difference, it is that operations consulting leads to changes in physical or information processes whose results are measurable immediately. General management consulting usually calls for changes in attitudes and culture, which take longer to yield measurable results. The roles in which consultants find themselves range from an *expert,* to a *pair of hands*, to a *collaborative or process consultant*. Generally, the collaborative or process consultation role is most effective in operations management consulting projects. Some consulting firms now provide the expert role online.

The steps in a typical operations consulting process are summarized in Exhibit 13A.2. A book by Ethan M. Rasiel on the McKinsey & Company approach offers some practical guidelines for conducting consulting projects:[6]

- Be careful what you promise in structuring an engagement. *Underpromise and overdeliver* is a good maxim.
- Get the team mix right. You can't just throw four random people at a problem and expect them to solve it. Think about what sorts of skills and personalities work best for the project at hand, and choose your teammates accordingly.
- The 80–20 rule is a management truth. Eighty percent of sales come from 20 percent of the sales force; 80 percent of your time is taken up with 20 percent of your job; and so on.

exhibit 13A.2   Stages in the Operations Consulting Process

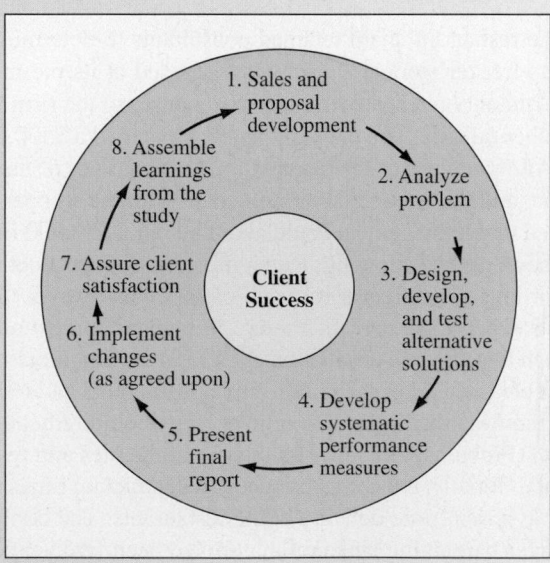

- Don't boil the ocean. Don't try to analyze everything—be selective in what you investigate.
- Use the elevator test. If you know your solution so well that you can explain it clearly and precisely to your client in a 30-second elevator ride, you are doing well enough to sell it to the client.
- Pluck the low-hanging fruit. If you can make an immediate improvement even though you are in the middle of a project, do it. It boosts morale and gives credibility to your analysis.
- Make a chart every day. Commit your learning to paper; it will help push your thinking and assure that you won't forget it.
- Hit singles. You can't do everything, so don't try. It's better to get to first base consistently than to try to hit a home run and strike out 9 times out of 10.
- Don't accept "I have no idea." Clients and their staff always know something, so probe them for some educated guesses.
- Engage the client in the process. If the client doesn't support you, the project will stall. Keep your clients engaged by keeping them involved.
- Get buy-in throughout the organization. If your solution is to have lasting impact on your client, you have to get support for it throughout the organization.
- Be rigorous about implementation. Making change happen takes a lot of work. Be rigorous and thorough. Make sure someone takes responsibility for getting the job done.

OPERATIONS CONSULTING TOOL KIT

Operations consulting tools can be categorized as tools for *problem definition, data gathering, data analysis and solution development, cost impact and payoff analysis,* and *implementation.* These—along with some tools from strategic management, marketing, and information systems that are commonly used in OSCM consulting—are noted in Exhibit 13A.3 and are described next. (Note that several of these tools are used in more than one stage of a project.)

PROBLEM DEFINITION TOOLS

Issue Trees   Issue trees are used by McKinsey to structure or map the key problems to be investigated and provide a working initial hypothesis as to the likely solution to these problems. As can be seen in Exhibit 13A.4, a tree starts with the general problem (increase widget sales) and then goes level by level until potential sources of the problem are identified. Once the tree is laid out, the relationships it proposes and possible solutions are debated, and the project plan is then specified.

Customer Surveys   Frequently OSCM consultants are called in to address problems identified by customer surveys performed by marketing consultants or marketing staff. Often, however, these are out of date or are in a form that does not separate process issues from advertising or other marketing concerns. Even if the surveys are in good form, calling customers and soliciting their experience with the company is a good way to get a feel for process performance. A key use of customer surveys is *customer loyalty analysis,* although in reality customers are not so much "loyal" (your dog, Spot, is loyal) as "earned" through effective performance. Nevertheless, the term *loyalty* captures the flavor of how well an organization is performing according to three critical market measures: customer retention, share of wallet, and price sensitivity relative to competitors. Having such information available helps the OSCM consultant drill down into the organization to find what operational factors are directly linked to customer retention. Although loyalty studies are usually performed by marketing groups, OSCM consultants should be aware of their importance.

Operations Consulting Tool Kit

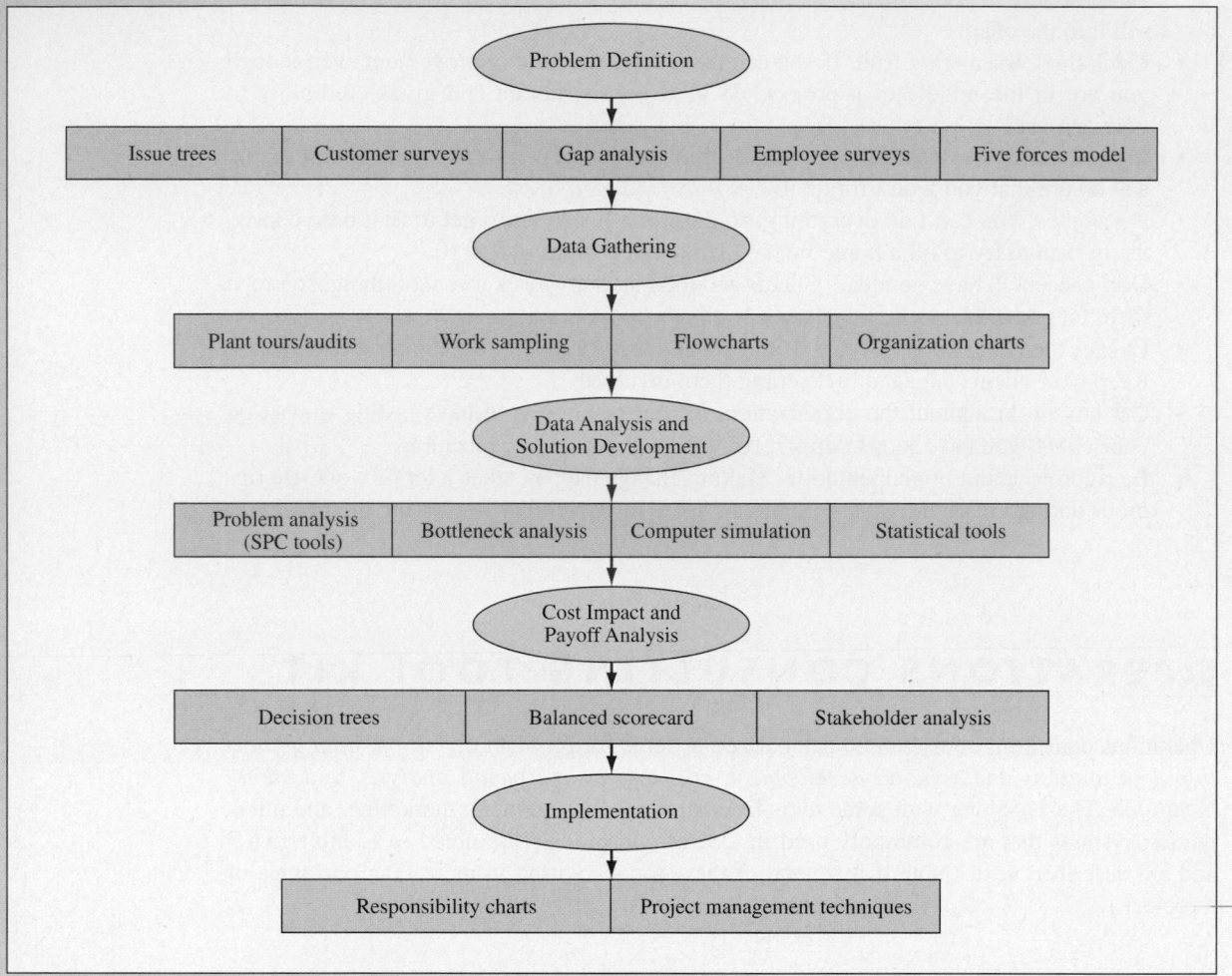

Gap Analysis   Gap analysis is used to assess the client's performance relative to the expectations of its customers, or relative to the performance of its competitors. An example is shown in Exhibit 13A.5.

Another form of gap analysis is benchmarking particular client company processes against exemplars in the process and measuring the differences. For example, if one is interested in billing process accuracy and problem resolution, American Express would be the benchmark; for timeliness and efficiency in railway transportation, Japanese Railways; for order entry in catalog sales, it would be L. L. Bean.

Employee Surveys   Such surveys range from employee satisfaction surveys to suggestion surveys. A key point to remember is if the consultant requests employee suggestions, such information must be carefully evaluated and acted upon by management. A few years ago, Singapore Airlines distributed a questionnaire to its flight personnel, but made the mistake of not following through to address their concerns. As a result, the employees were more critical of the company than if the survey had not been taken, and to this day the company does not use this form of evaluation.

Five Forces Model   This is one of the better-known approaches to evaluating a company's competitive position in light of the structure of its industry. The five forces are buyer

Issue Tree for Acme Widgets

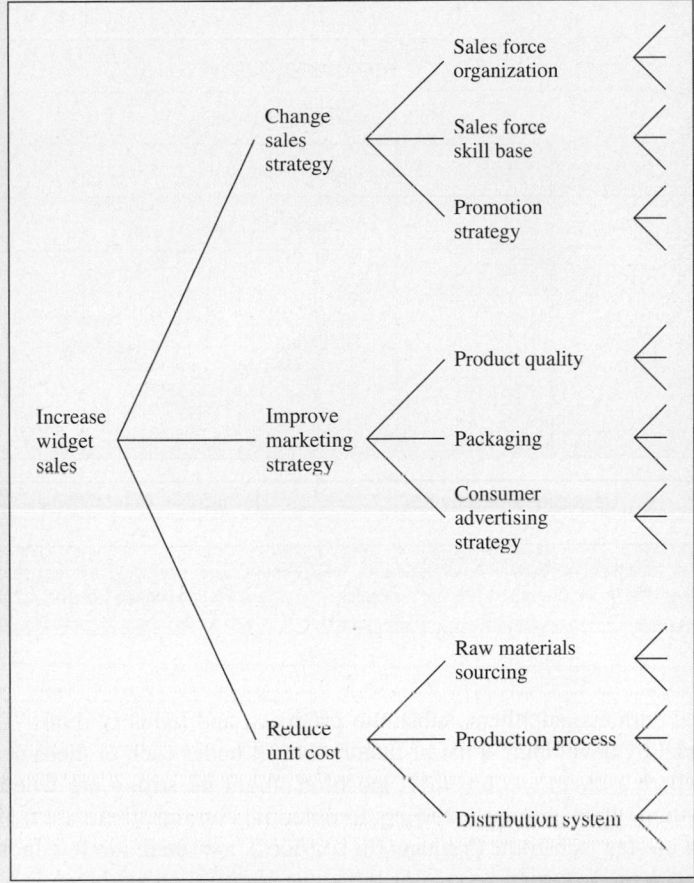

SOURCE: E. M. RASIEL, *THE MCKINSEY WAY* (NEW YORK, MCGRAW-HILL, 1998), P. 12. USED WITH PERMISSION.

Gap Analysis

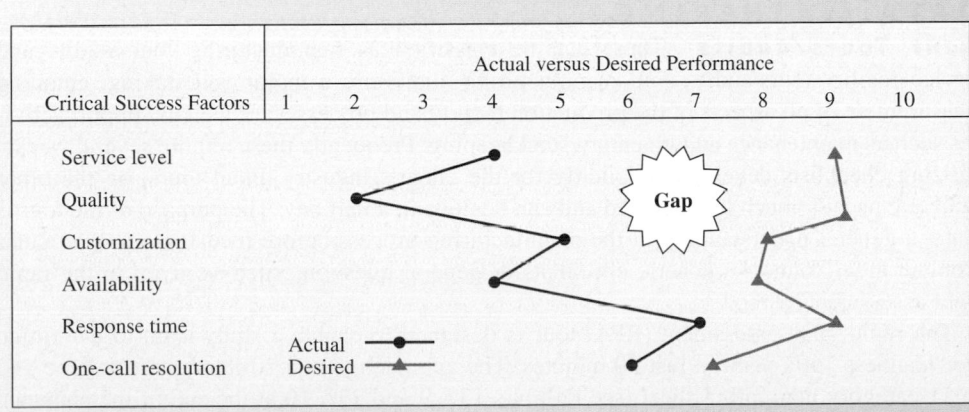

SOURCE: DELOITTE & TOUCHE CONSULTING GROUP.

exhibit 13A.6   Value Chain

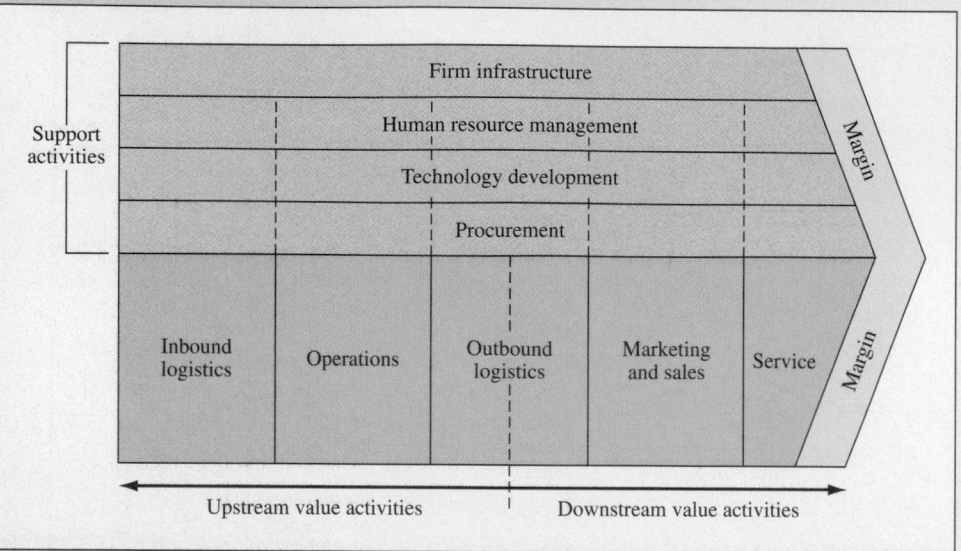

power, potential entrants, suppliers, substitute products, and industry rivals. The consultant applies the model by developing a list of factors that fit under each of these headings. Some examples of where a client's competitive position might be strong are when buyers have limited information, there are major barriers to potential entrants, there are many alternative suppliers, there are few substitute products (or services), and there are few industry rivals.

Often used with the five forces model is the *value chain,* such as shown in Exhibit 13A.6. The value chain provides a structure to capture the linkage of organizational activities that create value for the customer and profit for the firm. It is particularly useful to get across the notion that operations and the other activities must work cross-functionally for optimal organizational performance (and avoid the dreaded "functional silo" syndrome).

A tool similar to the five forces model is *SWOT analysis.* This is a somewhat more general method of evaluating an organization and has the advantage of being easy to remember: *S*trengths of the client, *W*eaknesses of the client, *O*pportunities for the client in the industry, and *T*hreats from competitors or the economic and market environment.

DATA GATHERING

Plant Tours/Audits   These can be classified as manufacturing tours/audits and service facility tours/audits. Full manufacturing audits are a major undertaking, entailing measurement of all aspects of the production facility and processes, as well as support activities such as maintenance and inventory stockkeeping. Frequently these require several weeks, utilizing checklists developed explicitly for the client's industry. Plant tours, on the other hand, are usually much less detailed and can be done in a half day. The purpose of the tour is to get a general understanding of the manufacturing process before focusing on a particular problem area. Tours use generic checklists or general questions such as given in the rapid plant assessment method.[7]

The rapid plant assessment (RPA) tour is designed to enable a study team to determine the "leanness" of a plant in just 30 minutes. The approach uses a 20-item questionnaire and an 11-category item rating sheet (see Exhibits 13A.9 and 13A.10 at the end of the chapter). During the tour, team members talk with workers and managers and look for evidence of best practices. RPA's developer, R. Eugene Goodson, suggests that each member of the team focus

BREAKTHROUGH

RAPID PLANT ASSESSMENT

1 **Customer satisfaction.** A customer-oriented workforce will take pride in satisfying both external and internal customers. The extent of this orientation should be apparent even in a brief plant tour. For example, when asked about the next step in the process, customer-aware employees will respond by giving a person's name or product, rather than saying that they just put it on the pallet and it's moved later. Cordiality to the touring group and posted quality and customer satisfaction ratings are other signs of a customer-oriented workforce. (Questions 1, 2, and 20 on the RPA questionnaire relate to this measure. This questionnaire is included at the end of this chapter.)

2 **Safety, environment, cleanliness, and order.** The physical environment of a plant is important to operating effectiveness. Cleanliness, low noise levels, good lighting, and air quality are obvious things to look for. Labeling and tracking of all inventory items, not just expensive ones, should be in evidence. (Not having the required nuts and bolts can be as disruptive to production as lacking a major component.) (Questions 3–5 and 20.)

3 **Visual management system.** Production management tools such as work instructions, kanban schedules, and quality and productivity charts should be easily visible. Posted workflow diagrams linking each stage of a process (such as found in chemical plants) are particularly effective visual cues. (Questions 2, 4, 6–10, and 20.)

The next three categories are intertwined. Rating a plant quickly on these three is straightforward from obvious visual clues.

4 **Scheduling system.** Scheduling involves pacing of the workflow. Goodson suggests that there should be a single "pacing process" for each product line and its suppliers. This process, usually at the end of the line, controls speed and production for all the upstream activities, much as a pace car sets the speed at a racetrack. Demand for product at each work center is triggered by demand at the next. This keeps inventory from building up, improves quality, and reduces downtime because production lines aren't kept waiting for parts. This is usually not the case in plants that use a central scheduling system; in these plants, production orders come from a central computer, not from the production area or line that uses the part. Other things to look for: visual and verbal communication among operators on the same line; inventory buildup at one work center indicating lack of coordination. (Questions 11 and 20.)

5 **Use of space, movement of materials, and product line flow.** Good indicators of efficient space utilization are minimum material movement over short distances, use of efficient containers; materials stored at the point of use, not in separate inventory storage areas; tooling kept near the machines; and product flow layout rather than process layout. (Questions 7, 12, 13, and 20.)

6 **Levels of inventory and work in process.** Counting the number of items coming off a line provides a quick gauge of how much inventory is required. If a line produces 60 units an hour, then an inventory of two or three times that amount sitting by the machine is a sign of scheduling problems. (Questions 7, 11, and 20.)

7 **Teamwork and motivation.** Discussions with workers and visible indicators of teamwork such as names of teams over a work area and productivity award banners are quick ways of determining how the workforce feels about their jobs, the company, and their co-workers. (Questions 6, 9, 14, 15, and 20.)

8 **Condition and maintenance of equipment and tools.** Purchase dates and equipment costs should be stenciled on the side of machinery, and maintenance records should be posted nearby. Asking people on the factory floor how things are working and whether they are involved in purchasing tools and equipment is also indicative of the extent to which workers are encouraged to address these issues. (Questions 16 and 20.)

9 **Management of complexity and variability.** This depends greatly on the type of industry. Obviously, industries with narrow product lines have less difficulty handling complexity and variability. Indicators to watch for in general are the number of people manually recording data and the number of keyboards available for data entry. (Questions 8, 17, and 20.)

10 **Supply chain integration.** It is generally desirable to work closely with a relatively small number of dedicated and supportive suppliers. A rough estimate of the number of suppliers can be ascertained by looking at container labels to see what supplier names appear on containers. Containers that appear to be designed and labeled specifically for customized parts shipped to a plant indicate the extent to which a strong supplier partnership exists. A sign of poor supply chain integration is lots of paperwork on the receiving dock. This indicates lack of a smooth pull system where plants pull the materials from their suppliers as if it was just another link in the pull system for each product line. (Questions 18 and 20.)

11 **Commitment to quality.** Attention to quality is evidenced in many ways, including posting of quality awards, quality scorecards, and quality goal statements. One that we found to be particularly interesting was a door panel hung on a wall at the Toyota plant in Paramount, California, which had a large circle painted around a nonexistent scratch with the inscription: "An acceptable paint scratch." Asking what people do with scrap also sheds light on quality practices. Quality is reflected in many of the other plant activities such as product development and start-ups. (Questions 15, 17, 19, and 20.)

SOURCE: MODIFIED FROM R. EUGENE GOODSON, "READ A PLANT—FAST," *HARVARD BUSINESS REVIEW* 80, NO. 5 (MAY 2002), PP. 105–13. COPYRIGHT © 2002 BY THE HARVARD BUSINESS SCHOOL PUBLISHING CORPORATION. ALL RIGHTS RESERVED.

on a few categories and not take notes since this interferes with conversations with the workers and picking up visual cues. At the end of the tour, members discuss their impressions and fill out the work sheets. The categories are key to the tour. Their features are summarized in the Breakthrough box, "Rapid Plant Assessment."

Goodson reports that based upon tours of 150 companies, the typical scores for the sum of the ratings of the 11 categories, 11 points possible for each category, range between 30 and 90, with an average of 55. Categories 4, 5, and 6 (scheduling, space and materials flow, and inventory) in the rating sheet consistently receive the lowest ratings. The reason for this, according to Goodson, is that few plants have an obvious strategy for how they move materials, resulting in inefficient use of space and equipment. One of the major strengths of the RPA method is that it tends to give very consistent results among raters, since it is very hard to "fake leanness." As Goodson says, "if an operation looks good to a trained eye, it usually is."

Complete service facility audits are also a major undertaking, but they differ from manufacturing audits in that, when properly done, they focus on the customer's experience as much as on the utilization of resources. Typical questions in a service audit address time to get service, the cleanliness of the facility, staff sizing, and customer satisfaction. A service facility tour or walk-through can often be done as a mystery shopper, where the consultant actually partakes of the service and records his or her experiences.

Service

Work Sampling   Work sampling entails random sampling observations of work activities, designed to give a statistically valid picture of how time is spent by a worker or the utilization of equipment. Diary studies are another way to collect activity data. These are used by consultants to get an understanding of specific tasks being performed by the workforce. In these, the employee simply writes down the activities he or she performs during the week as they occur. This avoids the problem of having analysts look over a worker's shoulder to gather data. Examples of where these studies are used include library front desks, nursing, and knowledge work.

Service

Flowcharts   Flowcharts can be used in both manufacturing and services to track materials, information, and people flows. Workflow software such as Optima! and BPR Capture are widely used for process analysis. In addition to providing capabilities for defining a process, most workflow software provides four other basic functions: work assignment and routing, scheduling, work list management, and automatic status and process metrics. Flowcharts used in services—service blueprints—are basically the same thing, but add the important distinction of the line of visibility to clearly differentiate activities that take place with the customer versus those that are behind the scenes. In our opinion, the service blueprint is not used to its full potential by consulting firms, perhaps because relatively few consultants are exposed to them in their training.

Organization Charts   Organization charts are often subject to change, so care must be taken to see who really reports to whom. Some companies are loath to share organization charts externally. Several years ago, a senior manager from a large electronics firm told us that a detailed organization chart gives free information to the competition.

DATA ANALYSIS AND SOLUTION DEVELOPMENT

Problem Analysis (SPC Tools)   Pareto analysis, fishbone diagrams, run charts, scatter diagrams, and control charts are fundamental tools in virtually every continuous improvement project. *Pareto analysis* is applied to inventory management under the heading of ABC analysis. Such ABC analysis is still the standard starting point of production control consultants when examining inventory management problems. *Fishbone diagrams* (or cause-and-effect diagrams) are a great way to organize one's first cut at a consulting problem (and they make a great impression when used to analyze, for example, a case study as part of the employment selection process for a consulting firm). *Run charts, scatter diagrams,* and *control charts* are tools that one is simply expected to know when doing operations consulting.

Bottleneck Analysis   Resource bottlenecks appear in most OSCM consulting projects. In such cases, the consultant has to specify how available capacity is related to required capacity for some product or service in order to identify and eliminate the bottleneck. This isn't always evident, and abstracting the relationships calls for the same kind of logical analysis used in the classic "word problems" you loved in high school algebra.

Computer Simulation   Computer simulation analysis has become a very common tool in OSCM consulting. The most common general-purpose simulation packages are Extend and Crystal Ball. SimFactory and ProModel (for manufacturing systems), MedModel (hospital simulation), and Service Model are examples of specialized packages. For smaller and less complex simulation, consultants often use Excel. Chapter 19A introduces the topic of simulation in this book.

A growing interest in simulation is in the analysis of "system dynamics." System dynamics is a language that helps us see the patterns that underlie complex situations. These complex situations are modeled using causal loop diagrams that are useful when factors either enhance or degrade system performance. Causal loops are of two types: reinforcing loops and balancing loops. *Reinforcing loops* are positive feedback loops driving positive values in criteria important to the system. *Balancing loops* reflect the mechanisms that counter reinforcing loops, thereby driving the system toward equilibrium. By way of example, with reference to Exhibit 13A.7, suppose you have a quality goal that is reflected in a quality standard. The reinforcing loop (R) indicates that the standard, if left unmodified, would yield an ever-increasing (or decreasing) level of actual quality. In reality, what happens is that the balancing loop (B) comes into play. Effective time required to meet the standard determines time pressure (on the workers), which, in turn, modifies the actual quality achieved and ultimately achievement of the quality standard itself. An obvious use of the system shown here would be to hypothesize the consequences of raising the quality goal, or raising or lowering the values of the other variables in the system. In addition to its use in problem analysis, causal loop analysis simulations are often used by consultants to help client companies become more effective learning organizations.[8]

Statistical Tools   *Correlation analysis* and *regression analysis* are expected skills for consulting in OSCM. The good news is that these types of analyses are easily performed with spreadsheets. *Hypothesis testing* is mentioned frequently in the consulting firm methodology manuals, and one should certainly be able to perform Chi-square and *t*-tests in analyzing data.

exhibit 13A.7   Causal Loop Analysis

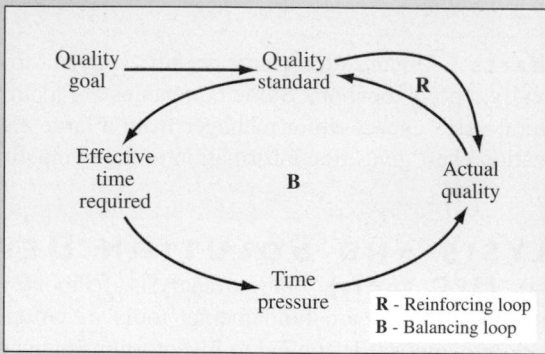

Two other widely used tools that use statistical analysis are *queuing theory* and *forecasting*. Consultants frequently use queuing theory to investigate how many service channels are needed to handle customers in person or on the phone. Forecasting problems likewise arise continually in OSCM consulting (such as forecasting the incoming calls to a call center).

A newly emerging tool (not shown on our exhibit) is *data envelopment analysis*. DEA is a linear programming technique used to measure the relative performance of branches of multisite service organizations such as banks, franchise outlets, and public agencies. A DEA model compares each branch with all other branches and computes an efficiency rating based on the ratio of resource inputs to product or service outputs. The key feature of the approach is that it permits using multiple inputs such as materials and labor hours, and multiple outputs such as products sold and repeat customers, to get an efficiency ratio. This feature provides a more comprehensive and reliable measure of efficiency than a set of operating ratios or profit measures.

COST IMPACT AND PAYOFF ANALYSIS

Decision Trees   Decision trees represent a fundamental tool from the broad area of risk analysis. They are widely used in examining plant and equipment investments and R&D projects. Decision trees are built into various software packages such as TreeAge (**www.treeage.com**).

Stakeholder Analysis   Most consulting projects impact in some way each of five types of stakeholders: customers, stockholders, employees, suppliers, and the community. The importance of considering the interest of all stakeholders is reflected in the mission statements of virtually all major corporations and, as such, provides guidance for consultants in formulating their recommendations.

Balanced Scorecard   In an attempt to reflect the particular needs of each stakeholder group in a performance measurement system, accountants have developed what is termed a *balanced scorecard*. (Balance refers to the fact that the scorecard looks at more than just the bottom line or one or two other performance measures.) Atkinson et al. note how the Bank of Montreal has used the balanced scorecard notion in setting specific goals and measures for customer service, employee relations, return to owners, and community relations. A key feature of the system is that it is tailored to what senior management and branch-level management can control.[9]

Process Dashboards   In contrast to the balanced scorecard, which focuses on organizationwide performance data, process dashboards are designed to provide summary performance updates for specific processes. Dashboards consist of a selection of performance metrics presented in graphical form with color-coding of trend lines, alarms

Dashboard for Suppliers

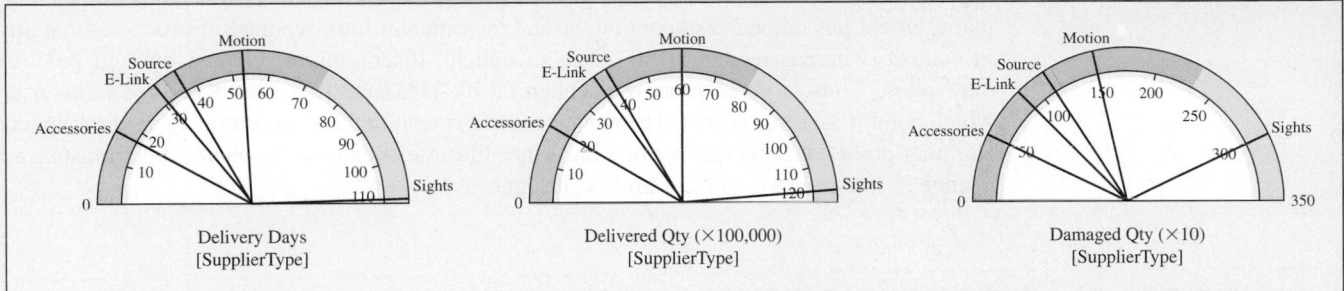

in the form of exclamation marks, and so forth, to show when key indicators are nearing a problem level. For example, three different dials on a dashboard for suppliers are shown in Exhibit 13A.8.

IMPLEMENTATION

Responsibility Charts   A responsibility chart is used in planning the task responsibilities for a project. It usually takes the form of a matrix with tasks listed across the top and project team members down the side. The goal is to make sure that a checkmark exists in each cell to assure that a person is assigned to each task.

Project Management Techniques   Consulting firms use the project management techniques of CPM/PERT and Gantt charts to plan and monitor the entire portfolio of consulting engagements of the firm, as well as individual consulting projects. Microsoft Project and Primavera Project Planner are examples of commonly used software to automate such tools. Evolve Software has developed a software suite for professional service firms, modeled on ERP for manufacturing, that allows management to integrate opportunity management (the selling process), resource management, and delivery management. It should be emphasized that these planning tools are very much secondary to the people management skills needed to successfully execute a consulting project. This admonition is likewise true for all of the tools we have discussed in this section.

BUSINESS PROCESS REENGINEERING (BPR)

Michael Hammer, the management expert who initiated the reengineering movement, defines reengineering as "the fundamental rethinking and radical redesign of business processes to achieve dramatic improvements in critical, contemporary measures of performance, such as cost, quality, service, and speed."[10] It uses many of the tools just discussed to achieve these goals.

Reengineering

The concept of reengineering has been around for nearly two decades and was implemented in a piecemeal fashion in organizations. Production organizations have been in the vanguard without knowing it. They have undertaken reengineering by implementing concurrent engineering, lean production, cellular manufacturing, group technology, and pull type production systems. These represent fundamental rethinking of the manufacturing process.

Reengineering is often compared to total quality management (TQM), a topic covered in Chapter 9. Some people have said that the two are, in fact, the same, whereas others have even argued that they are incompatible. Michael Hammer says that the two concepts are compatible and actually complement one another. Both concepts are centered on a customer focus. The concepts of teamwork, worker participation and empowerment, cross-functionality, process analysis and measurement, supplier involvement, and benchmarking are significant contributions from quality management. In addition, the need for a "total" view of the organization has been reemphasized by quality management in an era of extensive functionalization of business. Quality management has also influenced company culture and values by exposing organizations to the need for change. The basic difference between the two is that quality management has emphasized continuous and incremental improvement of processes that are in control, whereas reengineering is about radical, discontinuous change through process innovation. Thus, a given process is enhanced by TQM until its useful lifetime is over, at which point it is reengineered. Then enhancement is resumed and the entire cycle starts again. Hammer points out that this is not a once-in-a-lifetime endeavor. As business circumstances change in major ways, so must process designs.

PRINCIPLES OF REENGINEERING

Reengineering is about achieving a significant improvement in processes so that contemporary customer requirements of quality, speed, innovation, customization, and service are met. Hammer has proposed seven principles or rules for reengineering and integration.[11]

Rule 1. Organize around Outcomes, Not Tasks   Several specialized tasks previously performed by different people should be combined into a single job. This could be performed by an individual "case worker" or by a "case team." The new job created should involve all the steps in a process that creates a well-defined outcome. Organizing around outcomes eliminates the need for handoffs, resulting in greater speed, productivity, and customer responsiveness. It also provides a single knowledgeable point of contact for the customer.

Rule 2. Have Those Who Use the Output of the Process Perform the Process   In other words, work should be carried out where it makes the most sense to do it. This results in people closest to the process actually performing the work, which shifts work across traditional intra- and interorganizational boundaries. For instance, employees can make some of their own purchases without going through purchasing, customers can perform simple repairs themselves, and suppliers can be asked to manage parts inventory. Relocating work in this fashion eliminates the need to coordinate the performers and users of a process.

Rule 3. Merge Information-Processing Work into the Real Work That Produces the Information   This means that people who collect information should also be responsible for processing it. It minimizes the need for another group to reconcile and process that information, and greatly reduces errors by cutting the number of external contact points for a process. A typical accounts payable department that reconciles purchase orders, receiving notices, and supplier invoices is a case in point. By eliminating the need for invoices by processing orders and receiving information online, much of the work done in the traditional accounts payable function becomes unnecessary.

Rule 4. Treat Geographically Dispersed Resources as Though They Were Centralized   Information technology now makes the concept of hybrid centralized/decentralized operations a reality. It facilitates the parallel processing of work by separate organizational units that perform the same job, while improving the company's overall control. For instance, centralized databases and telecommunication networks now allow companies to link with separate units or individual field personnel, providing them with economies of scale while maintaining their individual flexibility and responsiveness to customers.

Rule 5. Link Parallel Activities Instead of Integrating Their Results
The concept of integrating only the outcomes of parallel activities that must eventually come together is the primary cause for rework, high costs, and delays in the final outcome of the overall process. Such parallel activities should be linked continually and coordinated during the process.

TEXAS INSTRUMENTS' REENGINEERING STAFF, THE STRATEGIC SERVICES GROUP, HAS ONGOING PROJECTS IN HUMAN RESOURCES, SUPPLY CHAIN IMPROVEMENT, AND PRODUCT AND STRATEGY DESIGN. MEMBERS OF THE GROUP ACT AS BUSINESS ADVOCATES TO LOOK FOR PROCESS IMPROVEMENT OPPORTUNITIES.

Rule 6. Put the Decision Point Where the Work Is Performed, and Build Control into the Process   Decision making should be made part of the work performed. This is possible today with a more educated and knowledgeable workforce plus decision-aiding technology. Controls are now made part of the process. The vertical compression that results produces flatter, more responsive organizations.

Rule 7. Capture Information Once—at the Source   Information should be collected and captured in the company's online information system only once—at the source where it was created. This approach avoids erroneous data entries and costly reentries.

GUIDELINES FOR IMPLEMENTATION

The principles of business process reengineering just enumerated are based on a common platform of the innovative use of information technology. But creating a new process and sustaining the improvement requires more than a creative application of information technology. A detailed study of reengineering applications in 765 hospitals yielded the following three managerial guidelines that apply to almost every organization contemplating reengineering:

1. **Codification of reengineering.**   Organizationwide change programs such as reengineering are complex processes whose implementation may be separated by space and time. Middle managers are often left to implement significant portions of reengineering proposals. Codifying provides guidance and direction for consistent, efficient implementation.
2. **Clear goals and consistent feedback.**   Goals and expectations must be clearly established, preapplication baseline data gathered, and the results monitored and fed back to employees. Without clear feedback, employees often became dissatisfied and their perceptions of reengineering success can be quite different from actual outcomes. For example, the hospital researchers found that at 10 hospitals they studied in depth, most employees in four of them felt that the reengineering program had done little to change costs, even though their costs had actually dropped 2 to 12 percent relative to their competitors'. On the other hand, four hospitals in which most felt that

reengineering had lowered costs actually experienced an increase in relative costs and a deterioration of their cost position.

3. **High executive involvement in clinical changes.**   A high level of involvement by the chief executive officer in major process changes (clinical changes in hospitals) improves reengineering outcomes. Bogue et al. found that CEOs in unsuccessful applications tended to be more involved in reductions of managers and employees and less engaged in activities surrounding clinical changes.[12]

SUMMARY

Consulting opportunities abound for individuals with OSCM skills. This is true not only for the major consulting firms but also for the smaller niche firms, particularly those with capabilities in supply chain management and Internet applications. The profitability to partners of a consulting firm depends on their ability to effectively leverage their time with that of their junior consultants. For beginning consultants, the goal is to get involved in high-visibility projects where they can demonstrate their skills and increase their skill sets. Companies such as Accenture and McKinsey & Company have developed special approaches to consulting that are part art and part procedure. Much of the success of a consulting engagement depends on the people-handling skills of the consultants and their ability to make their work visible. This is especially true for reengineering, where changing not just practices and procedures but also work cultures is often necessary if the reengineering is to succeed.

KEY TERMS

Operations consulting Assisting clients in developing operations strategies and improving production processes.

"Finders" Partners or senior consultants whose primary function is sales and client relations.

"Minders" Managers of a consulting firm whose primary function is managing consulting projects.

"Grinders" Junior consultants whose primary function is to do the work.

Reengineering (or business process reengineering) The fundamental rethinking and radical redesign of business processes to achieve dramatic improvements in cost, quality, service, and speed.

REVIEW AND DISCUSSION QUESTIONS

1   Check the Web sites of the consulting companies listed in the chapter. Which ones impressed you most as a potential client and as a potential employee?
Boston Consulting Group (www.bcg.com)
Deloitte Touche Tohmatsu (www.deloitte.com)
McKinsey & Co. (www.McKinsey.com)
2   What does it take to be a good consultant? Is this the career for you?
3   Think about the registration process at your university. Develop a flowchart to understand it. How would you radically redesign this process?
4   Have you driven any car lately? Try not to think of the insurance claim settlement process while you drive! How would you reengineer your insurance company's claim process?
5   Identify the typical processes in manufacturing firms. Discuss how the new product development process interacts with the traditional functions in the firm.
6   In discussing characteristics of efficient plants, Goodson, developer of rapid plant assessments (see the Breakthrough box), suggests that numerous forklifts are a sign of poor space utilization. What do you think is behind this observation?

PROBLEMS

1   You have been asked to bid on a consulting job to increase the profitability of a golf course company. It owns three courses in Cleveland, Ohio. Prepare a proposal to find out why other companies are more profitable and what to do about it.
2   Work with two other students to develop a two-page prospectus describing the particular features of an OSCM consulting practice you would start after graduation. (Hint: Identify a target market and unique skills your team possesses that fit that market.)

3   Sketch a typical materials procurement process that exists in functional organizations. Using reengineering principles, challenge the status quo and redesign this process.

4   An equipment manufacturer has the following steps in its order entry process:

a. Take the order and fax it to order entry.

b. Enter the order into the system (10 percent unclear or incorrect).

c. Check stock availability (stock not available for 15 percent of orders).

d. Check customer credit (10 percent of orders have credit questions).

e. Send bill of materials to warehouse.

The order receipt to warehouse cycle time is typically 48 hours; 80 percent of the orders are handled without error; and order-handling costs are 6 percent of order revenue. Should you reengineer this process or is continuous improvement the appropriate approach? If you choose to reengineer, how would you go about it?

5   Rapid plant assessment (RPA) leanness exercise: Form a team of four to five people and take a 30-minute tour of a plant or service business. At the conclusion of the tour, rate the leanness of the operation using the RPA questionnaire and rating sheet given in Exhibits 13A.9 and 13A.10. (According to the questionnaire's developer, the average number of yeses for over 400 plant tours was seven, and the standard deviation was 2.) In class, discuss those areas where leanness is generally lacking across all companies visited.

6   Advanced analysis:

a. Use the results from filling out the leanness questionnaire and your team's observations to develop a consensus score for each item in the RPA rating sheet. (There are many quantifiable factors by which to assess performance in the rating sheet's 11 categories. They are presented on Goodson's Web site: www.bus.umich.edu/rpa.)

b. Prioritize targets of opportunity for management.

c. Develop a two-page action plan that you would present to management to help them make improvements.

RPA Questionnaire

exhibit 13A.9

The total number of yeses on this questionnaire is an indicator of a plant's leanness: the more yeses, the leaner the plant. Each question should be answered yes only if the plant obviously adheres to the principle implied by the question. In case of doubt, answer no.

		YES	NO
1	Are visitors welcomed and given information about plant layout, workforce, customers, and products?	○	○
2	Are ratings for customer satisfaction and product quality displayed?	○	○
3	Is the facility safe, clean, orderly, and well lit? Is the air quality good, and are noise levels low?	○	○
4	Does a visual labeling system identify and locate inventory, tools, processes, and flow?	○	○
5	Does everything have its own place, and is everything stored in its place?	○	○
6	Are up-to-date operational goals and performance measures for those goals prominently posted?	○	○
7	Are production materials brought to and stored at line side rather than in separate inventory storage areas?	○	○
8	Are work instructions and product quality specifications visible at all work areas?	○	○
9	Are updated charts on productivity, quality, safety, and problem solving visible for all teams?	○	○
10	Can the current state of the operation be viewed from a central control room, on a status board, or on a computer display?	○	○
11	Are production lines scheduled off a single pacing process, with appropriate inventory levels at each stage?	○	○
12	Is material moved only once and as short a distance as possible? Is material moved efficiently in appropriate containers?	○	○
13	Is the plant laid out in continuous product line flows rather than in "shops"?	○	○
14	Are work teams trained, empowered, and involved in problem solving and ongoing improvements?	○	○
15	Do employees appear committed to continuous improvement?	○	○
16	Is a timetable posted for equipment preventive maintenance and ongoing improvement of tools and processes?	○	○
17	Is there an effective project-management process, with cost and timing goals, for new product start-ups?	○	○
18	Is a supplier certification process—with measures for quality, delivery, and cost performance—displayed?	○	○
19	Have key product characteristics been identified, and are fail-safe methods used to forestall propagation of defects?	○	○
20	Would you buy the products this operation produces?	○	○

Total number of yeses ____

exhibit 13A.10 Rating Sheet

Rating Leanness

Plant: ____________

Tour date: ____________

Rated by: ____________

RPA Rating Sheet

Team members use the RPA rating sheet to assess a plant in 11 categories on a scale from "poor" (1) to "excellent" (9) to "best in class" (11). The total score for all categories will fall between 11 (poor in all categories) and 121 (the best in the world in all categories), with an average score of 55. Factors to consider to rate a plant in each category are described in Chapter 13A. A more detailed list of evaluative factors appears on the Web at www.bus.umich.edu/rpa. The rating sheet also guides team members to questions in the RPA questionnaire (Exhibit 13A.9) that relate specifically to each category.

When plants are rated every year, the ratings for most tend to improve. Ratings are usually shared with plants, and motivated managers first improve their plants in the categories that receive the lowest ratings.

		Ratings						
Categories	Related Questions in RPA Questionnaire	Poor (1)	Below Average (3)	Average (5)	Above Average (7)	Excellent (9)	Best in Class (11)	Category Score
1 Customer satisfaction	1, 2, 20							
2 Safety, environment, cleanliness, and order	3–5, 20							
3 Visual management system	2, 4, 6–10, 20							
4 Scheduling system	11, 20							
5 Use of space, movement of materials, and product line flow	7, 12, 13, 20							
6 Levels of inventory and work in process	7, 11, 20							
7 Teamwork and motivation	6, 9, 14, 15, 20							
8 Condition and maintenance of equipment and tools	16, 20							
9 Management of complexity and variability	8, 17, 20							
10 Supply chain integration	18, 20							
11 Commitment to quality	15, 17, 19, 20							
							Total score for 11 categories (*max* = 121)	______

SOURCE: R. EUGENE GOODSON, "READ A PLANT—FAST," *HARVARD BUSINESS REVIEW* 80, NO. 5 (MAY 2002), P. 108.

SUPER QUIZ

1 Name the three categories of consultants.
2 This type of project requires a great deal of experience but little innovation.
3 Accenture is well known for this type of approach to training consultants.
4 Target utilization is usually highest for which level of consultant?
5 McKinsey uses these to structure or map the key problems to be investigated.

6 These are the five forces of the five forces model.
7 Gap analysis measures the difference between these two factors.
8 Rapid plant assessment is used to measure this variable.
9 An accounting approach to reflect the needs of each stakeholder is called this.
10 In contrast to TQM, this approach seeks radical change through innovation.

1. Finders, minders, and grinders 2. Gray hair 3. Uniform approaches 4. Junior level 5. Issue trees 6. Buyer power, potential entrants, suppliers, substitute products, and industry rivals 7. Actual and desired performance 8. Leanness of a plant 9. Balanced scorecard 10. Business process reengineering

SELECTED BIBLIOGRAPHY

Chase, R., and K. R. Kumar. "Operations Management Consulting." In L. E. Greiner and F. Poulfelt, *The Contemporary Consultant: Handbook of Management Consulting.* Mason, OH: Thompson South-Western, 2005, pp. 115–32.

Deimler, M. S. *The Boston Consulting Group on Strategy: Classic Concepts and New Perspectives.* 2nd ed. New York: Wiley, 2006.

George, M. L. *Lean Six Sigma: Combining Six Sigma Quality with Lean Speed.* New York: McGraw-Hill, 2002.

Goodson, R. F. "Read a Plant—Fast." *Harvard Business Review* 80, no. 5 (May 2002), pp. 105–13.

Greiner, L. E., and F. Poulfelt, eds. *The Contemporary Consultant: Handbook of Management Consulting: Insights from World Experts.* Mason, OH: Thomson, South-Western, 2005.

Hammer, M., and J. Champy. *Reengineering the Corporation: A Manifesto for Business Revolution.* New York: Harper Business, 1993.

Hoovers.com Consulting Industry Financials Web site, 2009.

Maister, D. H. *Managing the Professional Service Firm.* New York: The Free Press, 1993.

Rasiel, E. M. *The McKinsey Way: Using the Techniques of the World's Top Strategic Consultants to Help You and Your Business.* New York: McGraw-Hill, 1998.

FOOTNOTES

1 M. Treacy and F. Wiersema, "Value Disciplines," *12Manage.com,* 2009.

2 Hoovers.com Consulting Industry Financials Web site, September 10, 2009.

3 D. J. Collis, "The Management Consulting Industry," *Internet Class Notes,* Harvard Business School, 1996.

4 D. H. Maister, "Balancing the Professional Service Firm," *Sloan Management Review* 24, no. 1 (Fall 1982), pp. 15–29.

5 "The Six Sigma Black Belts Are Back," *BusinessWeek,* September 21, 2009, pp. 64–65.

6 E. M. Rasiel, *The McKinsey Way: Using the Techniques of the World's Top Strategic Consultants to Help You and Your Business* (New York: McGraw-Hill, 1998).

7 R. E. Goodson, "Read a Plant—Fast," *Harvard Business Review* 80, no. 5 (May 2002), pp. 105–13.

8 See J. D. Sterman, "System Dynamics Modeling: Tools for Learning in a Complex World," *California Management Review* 43, no. 4 (Summer 2002), pp. 8–26.

9 A. Atkinson, R. Banker, R. Kaplan, and M. Young, *Management Accounting,* 3rd ed. (Englewood Cliffs, NJ: Prentice Hall, 2001), p. 46.

10 M. Hammer and J. Champy, *Reengineering the Corporation: A Manifesto for Business Revolution* (New York: Harper Business, 1993), p. 30.

11 M. Hammer, "Reengineering Work: Don't Automate, Obliterate," *Harvard Business Review* 90, no. 4 (July–August 1990), pp. 104–12.

12 E. M. Bogue, M. J. Schwartz, and S. L. Watson, "The Effects of Reengineering: Fad or Competitive Factor?" *Journal of Healthcare Management* 44, no. 6 (November–December 1999), pp. 456–76.

section 4

SUPPLY AND DEMAND PLANNING

IN RUNNING A BUSINESS, COMPUTERS CAN DO MORE THAN JUST WORD PROCESSING AND E-MAIL

Running a business requires a great planning system. What do we expect to sell in the future? How many people should we hire to handle the Christmas rush? How much inventory do we need? What should we make today? This section discusses various approaches used to answer these questions. The use of comprehensive software packages is common practice, but it is important to understand the basic planning concepts that underlie them so that the right software can be purchased and configured correctly. Moreover, given this basic understanding a spreadsheet can be created for simple production planning situations.

ENTERPRISE RESOURCE PLANNING SYSTEMS

chapter 14

INFORMATION CRISIS— THE MISSING DESK

"Okay, Jerry, what's up?"

"I'll tell you what's up! $20,000 is what's up. We've lost the desk for that lawyer in Atlanta. You remember, the one that was supposed to ship a couple of weeks ago. He called me yesterday and said enough is enough. He reminded me of all the delays we had since he first placed the order. I reminded him of all the changes he wanted made. He reminded me that the last notice he got after the final change was that the desk would be there no later than last week. Well, he didn't believe us, so he postponed some big cocktail party until this week so the desk would be there. I stopped reminding him of stuff and said I'd find out what was going on." Jerry was not happy.

"What did you find out?"

"Nothing. I went out in the shop yesterday evening and couldn't find the thing. I tried to call you at home but I guess you didn't get enough vacation."

"Wait a minute, going over to the in-laws to swap the pictures of sand we each took at the beach isn't exactly an extended vacation. How the heck can we lose a lawyer's desk?" Billy was not happy.

"I don't know, and neither did the two guys I talked to from the shop. They said it was still sitting there yesterday. What is going on anyway?" asked Jerry.

"Well, I remember now. There was a delay because of the last minute change in some of the hardware that the guy wanted. Remember, we found out the vendor couldn't ship that until last week, and then we needed some time to make sure the finish was okay. When we ran the MRP system to check the schedules, I learned that the desk wouldn't ship until late last week, but it didn't go. It must have gone yesterday, late. I'll check and let you know."

Back in his office, Billy pulled up the record for the desk and found the order was closed out. He went back to the history file and learned that it indeed had been shipped late yesterday and was off the production books. Why the sales people didn't know it had shipped was

SOURCE: F. R. JACOBS AND D. C. WHYBARK, *WHY ERP? A PRIMER ON SAP IMPLEMENTATION* (NEW YORK: IRWIN/MCGRAW-HILL, 2000), PP. 10–11.

After reading this chapter you will:

1. Understand the scope of enterprise resource planning (ERP) systems.

2. Recognize the client/server structure of ERP systems.

3. Relate the value of integrated information in a complex firm.

4. Identify the challenges associated with implementing ERP systems.

a mystery to him. He called the trucking company and asked them where the shipment was. Expecting to be told they would check and call back, he was pleasantly surprised to be told immediately that the shipment was picked up late yesterday, it had gone to Raleigh where another Atlanta-bound shipment was picked up, and the truck was now on the outer beltway of Atlanta. The clerk apologized and said that it might be midday before the delivery could be made. They had to drop off the other shipment first. Finally, the clerk took Billy's number and said he would call if there was any delay in getting the shipment to the customer by noon.

"Why can't we do that?" wondered Billy.

He called Jerry and told him to tell the lawyer to go ahead with his party. Then he asked why the shipment never got picked up in the sales system. Jerry replied, "It looks like it never got entered yesterday. It's probably still on someone's desk. I'll check and see, but I'm really more worried about our not knowing of the delay two weeks ago when you did."

"I wonder if this is a problem that comes from lack of integration," mused Billy as he set about learning about how many forecasts the company had for next month.

Enterprise resource planning (ERP)

The missing desk tale depicts a typical situation in a company where information is not integrated. An **enterprise resource planning (ERP)** system, when implemented correctly, links all the areas of the business. Manufacturing knows about new orders as soon as they are entered in the system. Sales knows the exact status of a customer order. Purchasing knows what manufacturing needs to the minute, and the accounting system is updated as all the relevant transactions occur. The potential benefits are huge. Savings in the redundant posting of information alone can save a company millions of dollars a year. The real value, though, is in the new ways that a company can do business. Many redundant jobs can simply be eliminated. The time taken to do the remaining jobs can be reduced significantly due to the quick availability of information. With a well-designed ERP system, new ways to run the business are possible. Of course, this is not without cost. ERP systems are complex and expensive and may require major changes in processes.

The purpose of this chapter is to provide an overview of what an ERP system is and why it can benefit a company. The current ERP vendors have set new standards in information integration. In this chapter, we focus on a company called SAP AG and its flagship product, R/3. Our intent is not to endorse the SAP product as the only software product that a firm should consider; rather, this is a good benchmark for comparing other competing products.

Exhibit 14.1 lists the major developers of ERP software. In a sense, it can be argued that SAP AG was in the right place at the right time.

In the early 1990s, many large companies realized that it was time to update their existing information systems to take advantage of new technologies. Programs written in programming languages such as COBOL, PL1, RPG, and assembler were becoming increasingly expensive to maintain. Further, the mainframe computer technology was not cost-effective compared to the ever more powerful and inexpensive microprocessor-based computers. Change was inevitable, and SAP offered a comprehensive solution.

Major Developers of Enterprise Resource Planning Software

exhibit 14.1

VENDOR	SPECIAL SOFTWARE FEATURES	WEB SITE
INFOR/SSA Global	Comprehensive selection of software for discrete and process manufacturing	http://ssaglobal.com/solutions/erp
i2 Technologies	Forecasting; flow manufacturing	http://www.i2.com
JDA	Supply and demand—chain industry—specialized suite	http://www.jda.com/solutions
Oracle	Comprehensive system; major database vendor	http://www.oracle.com
SAP	Integrated client/server system	http://www.sap.com
SCLogix	Optimization of logistics function	http://www.sclogix.com

Three-Tier Client/Server Configuration

exhibit 14.2

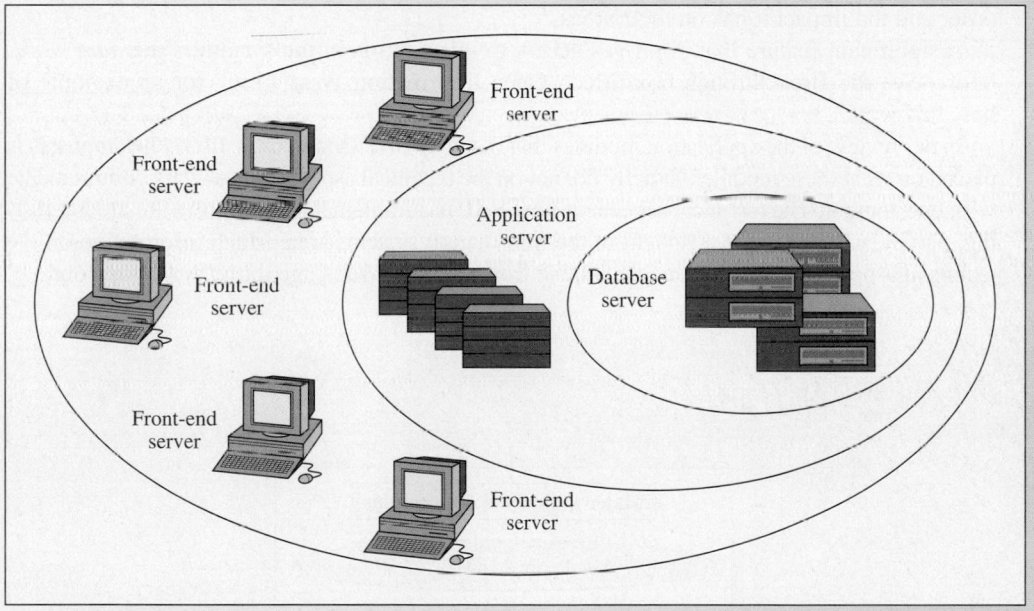

SAP

SAP AG, a German firm, is the world leader in providing ERP software. Its flagship product is known as R/3. The software is designed to operate in a three-tier client/server configuration. As shown in Exhibit 14.2, the core of the system is a high-speed network of database servers. These database servers are special computers designed to efficiently handle a large database of information. The applications, which consist of the software modules discussed in the next section, can be run on separate computers. The applications are networked around the database cluster and have independent access to it. Users communicate with the applications through the front-end servers.

The applications are fully integrated so that data are shared between all applications. If, for example, an employee posts a shipping transaction in the Sales and Distribution module, the

Global

transaction is immediately seen by Accounts Payable in the Financial Accounting module and by Inventory Management in the Materials Management module. The Manufacturing and Logistics module has applications that support virtually all of the topics discussed in this book.

Much of the success of the product is due to the comprehensive coverage of business applications. In a sense, SAP has changed the face of information technology. We now have the enterprisewide integrated system we only dreamed of a few years ago. Companies can consider the automation of their basic business processes as if it were a utility like electricity or water: Hook it up and get back to the real, challenging business at hand.

Of course, it is not really this simple. The problem is that many of the applications do not line up with the way a company operates. The SAP consultants argue that the modules are designed around industry "best practices." But this, in many cases, means that a firm wishing to use SAP needs to change its practices to those implemented by the SAP programmers.

SAP APPLICATION MODULES

The software is built around a comprehensive set of application modules that can be used either alone or in combination. Exhibit 14.3 shows the major modules SAP offers. The modules can be used to support processes that span different functional areas in the firm. Because the modules are integrated and use a common database, transactions processed in one area immediately update all other areas. For example, if an order is received from a customer via the Internet, accounting, production scheduling, and purchasing immediately know about the order and the impact it has on their areas.

A significant feature that improves access to information in the system is the *data warehouse*. See the Breakthrough box titled "Open Information Warehouse" for an example of how this works.

In our review of the application modules that make up SAP (see Exhibit 14.3), the emphasis is placed on what these modules actually do, not on the technical aspects of how they communicate with one another. The technical aspects of how SAP has implemented this software are interesting, particularly if you are a student in the information systems area. Much information on the technical aspects of the software is available from the SAP Web page (http://www.sap.com).

exhibit 14.3   SAP Enterprise Applications

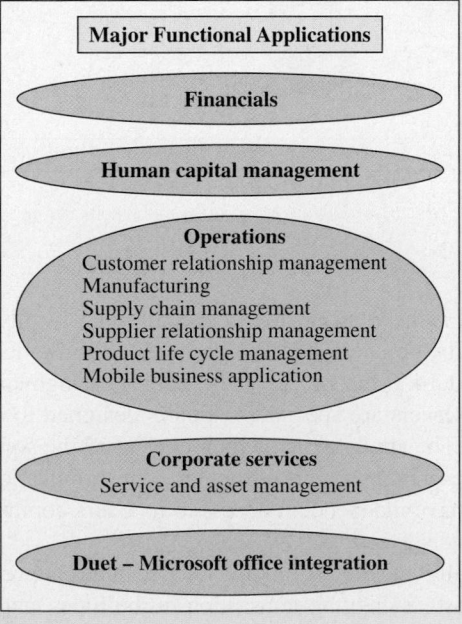

Major Functional Applications

Financials

Human capital management

Operations
Customer relationship management
Manufacturing
Supply chain management
Supplier relationship management
Product life cycle management
Mobile business application

Corporate services
Service and asset management

Duet – Microsoft office integration

B R E A K T H R O U G H

OPEN INFORMATION WAREHOUSE

Any modern database will let you easily formulate an SQL query like "What sales did my company have in Italy in 1997?" A report generated in response to such a query could look like this:

REGION	Q1	Q2	Q3	Q4	TOTAL
Umbria	1000	1200	800	2000	5000
Toscana	2000	2600	1600	2800	9000
Calabria	400	300	150	450	1300
Total	3400	4100	2550	5250	15300

But things get more complex if, for instance, we then want to use this answer as the basis for *drilling down* to look at the sales for different quarters and sales representatives in the various regions. Drilling down means descending through an existing hierarchy to bring out more and more detail.

In the following example, we drill down through the sales hierarchy (sales representatives in Toscana). Signore Corleone's sales do not appear to have been affected by the holiday season in the third quarter.

SALES	Q1	Q2	Q3	Q4	TOTAL
S. Paolo	500	600	300	500	1900
S. Vialli	700	600	200	700	2200
S. Ferrari	600	700	400	700	2400
S. Corleone	200	700	700	900	2500
Total	2000	2600	1600	2800	9000

At this point, you can switch to another dimension—for instance, from sales representative to product sold. This is often referred to as *slice and dice.*

PRODUCT	Q1	Q2	Q3	Q4	TOTAL
X-11	2000	2500	1500	3550	9550
Z-12	1400	1600	1050	1700	5750
Total	3400	4100	2550	5250	15300

From the standpoint of a data analyst, it can now be useful to check sales of particular products in each region. SAP allows the end user to do this easily using the data warehouse approach implemented within the system.

SOURCE: THIS EXAMPLE WAS TAKEN FROM C. HEINRICH AND M. HOFMANN, "DECISION SUPPORT FROM THE SAP OPEN INFORMATION WAREHOUSE," SAP WEB SITE, http://www.sap.com.

SAP Applications are built around scenarios that are likely to occur in a business. For example, one of the scenarios covered in the Customer Relationship Management Suite is that of a salesperson who travels around to customers and takes orders on a recurring basis. Keeping track of these visits, trends in the customers' orders, and expectations for the future is supported with an application in the suite. Further, support for placing the orders using a mobile device such as a Palm or BlackBerry is provided using the Mobile Business Application. Literally 1,000 different scenarios are supported by the software. Customers need to pick the applications that best fit their needs. SAP is developing new applications for different scenarios on an ongoing basis so that their software is applicable to a broader group of customers.

The core or basic ERP applications are the "Financials," "Human Capital Management," "Operations," and "Corporate Services," which are applicable to many large companies. In the following, we briefly describe the functionality of these applications. SAP indicates that modules are updated twice a year, based upon changes in business practices, technological advances, and the requirements of their customers.

FINANCIALS

The financial application provides the functionality to run the financial accounts for the company. The application is divided into three areas. The financial and management accounting module includes general ledger, accounts payable, accounts receivable, and capital investments. Also included are procedures for closing the books for the month and year and preparing financial statements, including the balance sheet. The second area is corporate governance, which is the internal control and audit functions needed to adhere to corporate governance standards, documentation of internal controls, and audits that comply with current requirements. The third area is financial supply chain management, designed to handle the money flow related to supply chain activities. This includes customer and supplier credit management, in-house banking, cash flow management, and bank-relationship management.

HUMAN CAPITAL MANAGEMENT

The applications in this segment contain the full set of capabilities needed to manage, schedule, pay, and hire the people who make a company run. It includes payroll, benefits administration, application data administration, personnel development planning, workforce planning, schedule and shift planning, time management, and travel expense accounting. The "talent management" functions are designed to help align employee goals with corporate goals by maximizing the impact of training by helping match employees to sponsored programs. Integrated goal setting and tracking are included in the application. "Workforce deployment" applications are to aid in deploying the right people with the right skills to positions in the firm. Managing project teams, monitoring the progress of projects, and tracking time are supported by the application.

OPERATIONS

Supply Chain

The operations segment is complex and includes many applications. The basic "procurement and logistics" applications include material management, plant maintenance, quality management, and production planning and control. Materials management covers all tasks within the supply chain, including purchasing, vendor evaluation, invoice verification, and material use planning. It also includes inventory and warehouse management.

Plant maintenance supports the activities associated with planning and performing repairs and preventive maintenance. Completion and cost reports are available. Maintenance activities can be managed and measured.

The quality management capability plans and implements procedures for inspection and quality assurance and is built around the ISO 9001 specifications. It is integrated with the procurement and production processes so that the user can identify inspection points both for incoming materials and for products during the manufacturing process.

Production planning and control supports both discrete and process manufacturing processes. Repetitive and configure-to-order approaches are provided. This set of modules supports all phases of manufacturing, providing capacity leveling and requirements planning, material requirements planning, product costing, bills of material processing, and engineering change management.

Sales and distribution are also applications included here. Sales order management, configuration management, distribution export control, and shipping and transportation management are handled in these applications. These applications, like the others, can be implemented globally, allowing the user to manage the sales process worldwide. For example, an order may be received in Hong Kong. If the products are not available locally, they may

be internally procured from warehouses in other parts of the world and shipped to arrive together at the Hong Kong customer's site.

In sales and distribution, products or services are sold to customers. In implementing the module (as in other modules), the company structure must be represented in the system so that, for example, SAP knows where and when to recognize revenue. It is possible to represent the structure of the firm from the point of view of accounting, materials management, or sales and distribution. These structures also can be combined.

When a sales order is entered, it automatically includes the correct information on pricing, promotions, availability, and shipping options. Batch order processing is available for specialized industries such as food, pharmaceutical, or chemical. Users can reserve inventory for specific customers, request production of subassemblies, or enter orders that are assemble-to-order, build-to-order, or engineer-to-order as well as special customized orders. Exhibit 14.4 depicts the complex data linkages between modules needed to integrate information managed by the system.

Logistics Integration Overview

exhibit 14.4

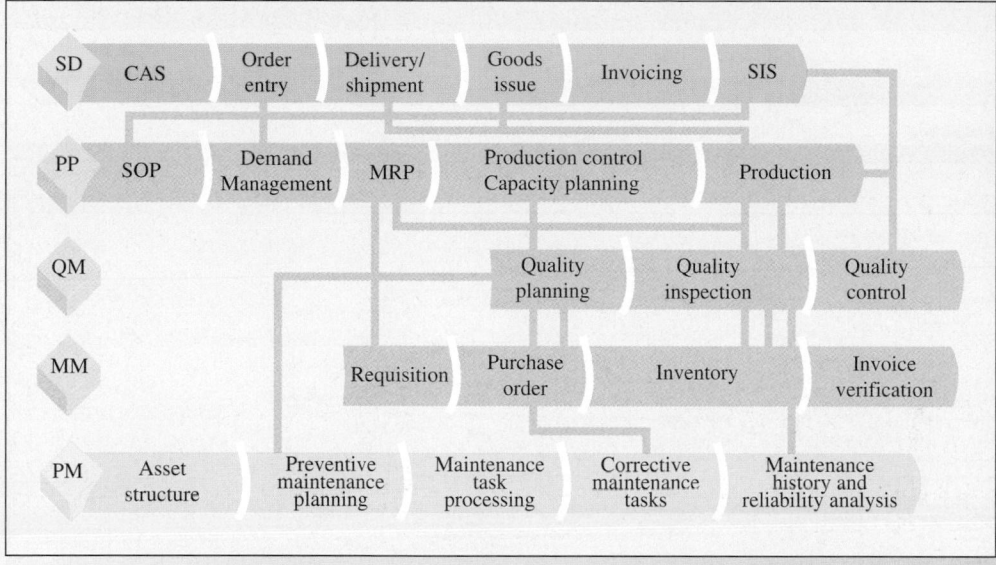

CORPORATE SERVICES

The corporate services applications are designed to manage both centralized and decentralized services. This includes managing the firm's real estate portfolio, including property acquisition and disposal, property management, building operations and maintenance, and investment reporting. Another major aspect of the corporate services is travel management. This supports all aspects of travel, including travel requests and approvals through planning and reservation management.

Service

The modules included with the system are built on what SAP considers best practices. SAP has a research and development group that continually looks for better ways to carry out a particular process or subprocess. System upgrades are designed to reflect the newest best practices.

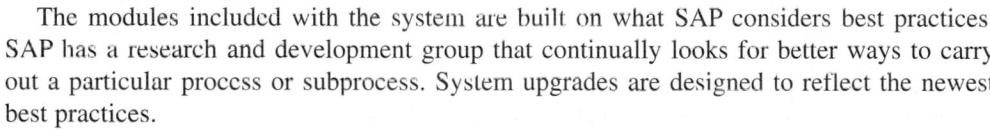

MYSAP.COM AND SAP NETWEAVER—INTEGRATED E-BUSINESS APPLICATIONS

SAP's strategy is to build a set of business software solutions around the applications. Each of these solutions is designed for a specific purpose. The solutions can all be implemented using an Internet interface. SAP offers mySAP versions of the applications preprogrammed to work over the Internet, thus making it possible for users to have the full functionality of the SAP software without requiring the deployment of any special software to the users. The user only needs a functioning Web browser to use the system. To further simplify implementation, a company can even totally outsource the running of the SAP software by using a provider specialized in serving SAP over the Internet.

The term **cloud computing** is used to refer to delivering hosted services over the Internet. A cloud service has three distinct characteristics that differentiate it from traditional hosting. It is sold on demand, typically by the minute or the hour; it is elastic—a user can have as much or as little of a service as they want at any given time; and the service is fully managed by the provider (the customer needs nothing but a personal computer and Internet access). The use of this type of service can significantly reduce cost of ERP to small and medium-sized businesses.

Cloud computing

exhibit 14.5   SAP NetWeaver

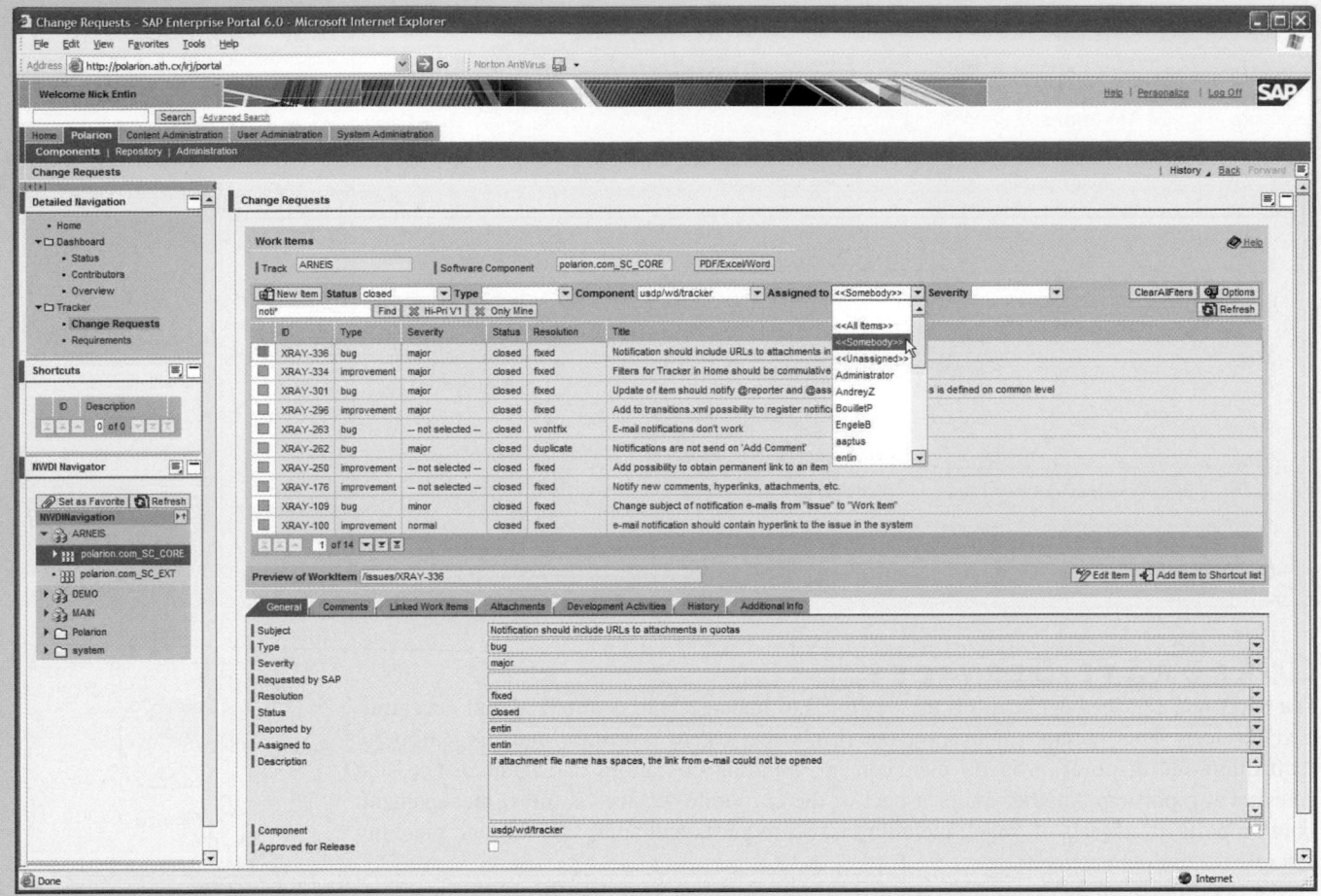

In many cases, users may want to build their own Internet applications on top of those provided by SAP. This can be done by using a product known as NetWeaver. Exhibit 14.5 shows a NetWeaver application that manages change requests. Using NetWeaver, users within a firm and third-party vendors can offer an unlimited variety of specialized applications to meet needs. Many of the NetWeaver applications are designed to provide supplier and customer need for data that is maintained by the ERP system. In addition, ERP applications that need special information from those outside the company can be programmed using NetWeaver.

To illustrate how the topics covered in the chapters in this section of the book are implemented by SAP, we focus on the Supply Chain Management (SCM) product. SAP, just as we have organized the topics in these chapters, organizes its software into planning scenarios that represent the basic needs of the organization. Within SCM, the planning scenarios are called "collaborative demand planning," "sales and operations planning," and "collaborative supply and distribution planning."

SCM Demand Planning is basically a toolkit of statistical forecasting techniques and planning features that helps the user create accurate estimates of future requirements. These techniques are the topic of Chapter 15, "Demand Management and Forecasting." The software gives visibility to all levels of detail using the data warehouse technology described in the earlier Breakthrough box. The software includes time series techniques such as exponential smoothing complete with trend and seasonal indexes. Causal analyses where factors such as price, number of stores, or demographics are considered are included in the tools. SAP also offers a set of collaborative planning tools implemented through Internet forms as part of the package. Collaborative forecasting is a topic discussed in Chapter 15 together with the time series and causal techniques.

Sales and Operations Planning is the entire process of integrating sales and marketing plans with plans for producing products and delivering services. In Chapter 16 we cover this topic and show a technique for bringing the demand and operations information together in a spreadsheet format. SAP uses the "Supply Chain Cockpit," which consists of a graphical instrument panel that is configured to allow the user to view and manage key elements of the supply chain.

A key element of SAP's Sales and Operations Planning is the Advanced Planner and Optimizer (APO) functions that are available. APO is a library of advanced, highly configurable planning and optimization algorithms to provide task-specific, industry-specific, and even company-specific optimization. In the case of this book, we built custom spreadsheets for each planning problem and then used the Microsoft Excel® Solver to aid in finding solutions to these problems. Our approach works well for smaller problems like those we cover in the book. Large applications, as would be encountered in a real firm, require more powerful techniques. APO is the software that SAP uses to formulate and solve these problems. SAP also supports the exporting of data to Microsoft Excel, allowing user-developed applications to be used.

The final element of SCM is the collaborative supply and distribution planning functions. These functions allow the user to create plans for purchasing, manufacturing, distributing inventory, and transporting material. The software supports different types of strategies such as make to stock, make to order, and assemble to order. Being an integrated system, SAP gives a real-time view of plans. When plans change and when actual transactions are executed, the impact on the system is immediately known. Actual planning is supported by a simulation mode where what-if scenarios can be quickly run. In the book, simulation is covered in Chapter 19A. In addition, techniques from the APO library also can be used to optimize certain decisions.

In this book, we cover the details related to these functions in Chapters 17 and 18. Planning safety stock is discussed in Chapter 17 together with the logic for targeting inventory levels throughout the supply chain. SAP implements the logic on an item and individual location basis using the same logic as described in the book. The special case of manufacturing inventory is covered in Chapter 18. The book describes material requirements planning logic in detail through relatively simple examples. In SAP this logic is implemented in a manner that can support the simultaneous planning of thousands of items.

IMPLEMENTING ERP SYSTEMS

SAP has some strong competition. Companies such as Oracle, i2 Technologies, and PeopleSoft (now owned by Oracle) have aggressively gone after the market. SAP, though, is the market leader with over 100,000 sites and over 12,000,000 users worldwide. Implementation of ERP is costly, with the actual cost of the software typically one-third or less of the total cost. Large companies such as Chevron Corp. and Bristol-Myers Squibb typically earmark $250 million or more to implement an ERP system.

Implementing these systems does not always work out. A survey conducted by the Harvard Business School revealed that a large percentage of executives had negative feelings toward ERP software.[1] In particular, they felt that (1) ERP technology could not support their businesses, (2) their organizations could not make changes needed to extract benefits from the new systems, and (3) ERP implementation might actually damage their businesses. The same survey indicated that many companies implementing ERP had overrun cost and schedule targets and had not achieved the benefits sought.

Despite the reservations about ERP, most companies surveyed by Harvard were going ahead with ERP initiatives. The most popular reasons cited included a desire to standardize and improve processes, to improve systems integration, and to improve information quality. Even though there is evidence of many problems with implementing ERP systems, firms continue in their ERP efforts because of the opportunity for substantial reward. SAP is now targeting small and medium-size firms with its SAP Business One product described in the Breakthrough box.

BREAKTHROUGH

SAP BUSINESS ONE

SAP has a special version of its software for small and medium-size firms. SAP Business One provides features and functions for operational analysis to help optimize total customer satisfaction. The offering includes features that support the following business activities:

- **Procurement monitoring.** Monitor purchasing operations and provide a detailed analysis of purchasing activities and procurement processes.
- **Inventory and warehouse management.** Assess your organization's actual stock situation based on quantity- and value-based criteria. Analyze warehouse activities such as the physical flow of materials and workloads.
- **Manufacturing reporting.** Provide various standard reports and analyses detailing production-related information.
- **Order fulfillment analysis.** Evaluate and improve order fulfillment using key performance indicators (KPIs) for transportation and order management, strategic performance measurements or the distribution statistics needed for supply chain optimization, and operative performance measurements that capture the day-to-day information used for process optimization.

- **Customer service analysis.** Monitor financial trends, costs, and revenues per customer, as well as service contracts and operations. The solution also supports installed-base analysis and provides both customer analytics and warranty analytics.
- **Program and project management.** Monitor and control project data, evaluate projects, and enable design-to-cost engineering to optimize product costs.
- **Quality management.** Plan, collect, settle, and evaluate quality-related costs. The solution includes quality management features that provide data to determine standard or user-defined quality scores.
- **Enterprise asset management.** Perform strategic evaluations, including mean time to repair (MTTR) and mean time between repair (MTBR) analyses.
- **Sales planning.** Set sales targets by using multiple dimensions and key figures, integrate and consolidate sales planning with marketing or service plans, and optimize your supply chain through offline account planning. The solution enables territory management according to regions, product lines, or other variables, as well as opportunity planning and analysis and partner planning.
- **Sales analysis.** Provide your sales organizations with an accurate overview of current sales performance and an overview of sales force effectiveness.

SUMMARY

The reason for including this chapter at this point in the book is so you can see that the techniques described in this section are now commonly available and widely implemented in companies. In the following sections, we discuss such forecasting tools as moving averages and exponential smoothing, inventory control tools such as material requirements planning, and scheduling using earliest due-date logic. All of these techniques are included in the leading ERP packages. One might think that there is no need to learn how these techniques actually work; all that needs to be done is fire up the ERP system and let it make all the decisions. If it were that simple, we would all be out of work.

In reality, there are many ways to implement these different techniques, and different techniques are applicable to different types of firms. SAP, for example, has three ways that forecasts can be calculated (discussed in Chapter 15) and five different lot-sizing rules for batch production (discussed in Chapter 18). So many different decisions need to be made to properly use any system.

To select from the many ERP systems that are available, one needs to evaluate the strengths and weaknesses of each offering. i2 Technologies has a very strong forecasting capability and is known for flow manufacturing scheduling. In Chapter 15 the different types of forecasting systems are discussed in some depth, giving you the ability to evaluate whether the unique characteristics of the i2 offering match what is needed by your firm. Similarly, in Chapter 18, all the different lot-sizing rules are studied, and the flow manufacturing concept is compared to traditional material requirements planning (MRP). Given this information, you can evaluate whether i2 would be good for your company.

In our writing this chapter, one temptation was to include an extensive comparison of the various ERP systems available. (A great source of the most current information is the Operations Management Center at http://www.mhhe.com/omc/index.html). The problem with doing this and publishing it in a textbook is that by the time the book is printed, the comparison would be out of date. Business software technology is moving at an amazing rate. Every day a new package becomes available with some slick trick that supposedly makes it better than the rest. To make matters worse, each vendor likes to tag names to things to give the appearance of something new. In reality, there are not many new ideas; conventional techniques are typically repackaged in new ways. Sometimes more efficient ways to implement these techniques are developed. Understanding the conventional approaches is an important first step to being able to keep up with this rapidly expanding area of software technology.

KEY TERM

Enterprise resource planning (ERP) A computer system that integrates application programs in accounting, sales, manufacturing, and the other functions in a firm. This integration is accomplished through a database shared by all the application programs.

Cloud computing A term that refers to delivering hosted ERP services over the Internet. This can significantly reduce the cost of ERP.

REVIEW AND DISCUSSION QUESTIONS

1   What key technological features of SAP set it apart from conventional business accounting/planning/control software?
2   SAP allows the human resources, financial accounting, and manufacturing and logistics modules to be implemented separately. How would this change impact the implementation process?
3   Many companies take customer orders via Web sites. Put yourself in the place of the person at Ford Motor Company considering this approach to taking customer orders for the Ford Explorer sport utility vehicle. What information would you need to collect from the customer? What information would you give the customer regarding the order? How would the information be used within Ford Motor Company? What major problems would you anticipate need solving prior to implementing the system? If this project is successful—that is, customers find ordering their Explorer over the Web preferable to negotiating with a dealer—what are the long-term implications to Ford Motor Company?

SUPER QUIZ

1   A computer system that links all areas of a company using an integrated set of application programs and a common database.
2   This is the term used to describe a three-tier system where the database, application, and user programs are potentially run on different computer.
3   The application programs are designed in accordance with industry norms or _____.
4   True/False: Implementing an ERP system is a simple exercise that involves loading software on a computer.
5   A term used for delivering ERP services on demand over the Internet.

1. Enterprise resource planning (ERP) system 2. Client–server configuration 3. Best practices 4. False 5. Cloud computing

SELECTED BIBLIOGRAPHY

Bendoly, E., and F. R. Jacobs. *Strategic ERP: Extension and Use.* Palo Alto, CA: Stanford Business Books, 2005.

Curran, T.; G. Keller; and A. Ladd. *Business Blueprint: Understanding SAP's R/3 Reference Model.* Upper Saddle River, NJ: Prentice Hall, 1998.

Davenport, T. H. "Putting the Enterprise into the System." *Harvard Business Review,* July–August 1998.

Hernández, J. A. *The SAP R/3 Handbook.* New York: McGraw-Hill, 1997.

Jacobs, F. R., and F. C. Weston Jr. "Enterprise Resource Planning (ERP)—A Brief History." *Journal of Operations Management* 25 (2007), pp. 357–63.

Jacobs, F. R., and D. C. Whybark. *Why ERP? A Primer on SAP Implementation.* New York: Irwin/McGraw-Hill, 2000.

Madu, C. *ERP and Supply Chain Management.* Fairfield, CT: Chi Publishers, 2005.

Monk, E., and B. Wagher. *Concepts in Enterprise Resource Planning.* 2nd ed. Boston: Course Technology, 2005.

Norris, G. *E-Business and ERP: Transforming the Enterprise.* New York: Wiley, 2000.

Wallace, T. F., and M. H. Kremzar. *ERP: Making It Happen: The Implementers' Guide to Success with Enterprise Resource Planning.* New York: Wiley, 2001.

FOOTNOTE

1 C. X. Escalle and M. Cotteleer, "Enterprise Resource Planning (ERP)," 9-699-020, Harvard Business School, February 11, 1999, p. 3.

DEMAND MANAGEMENT AND FORECASTING

chapter 15

WALMART'S DATA WAREHOUSE

Walmart's size and power in the retail industry is having a huge influence in the database industry. Walmart manages one of the world's largest data warehouses with more than 35 terabytes of data. A terabyte is equal to 1,024 gigabytes or a trillion bytes. Your computer is probably 500–750 gigabytes. Walmart's formula for success—getting the right product on the appropriate shelf at the lowest price—owes much to the company's multimillion-dollar investment in data warehousing. Walmart has more detail than most of its competitors on what's going on by product, by store, and by day.

The systems track point of sale data at each store, inventory levels by store, products in transit, market statis-

tics, customer demographics, finance, product returns, and supplier performance. The data are used for three broad areas of decision support: analyzing trends, managing inventory, and understanding customers. What emerges are "personality traits" for each of Walmart's 3,000 or so outlets, which Walmart managers use to determine product mix and presentation for each store.

Data mining is next. Walmart has developed a demand-forecasting application that looks at individual items for individual stores to decide the seasonal sales profile of each item. The system keeps a year's worth of data on the sales of 100,000 products and predicts which items will be needed in each store.

After reading this chapter you will:

1. Understand the role of forecasting as a basis for supply chain planning.

2. Compare the differences between independent and dependent demand.

3. Identify the basic components of independent demand: average, trend, seasonal, and random variation.

4. Describe the common qualitative forecasting techniques such as the Delphi method and Collaborative Forecasting.

5. Show how to make a time series forecast using regression, moving averages, and exponential smoothing.

6. Use decomposition to forecast when trend and seasonality is present.

Walmart is now doing market-basket analysis. Data are collected on items that make up a shopper's total purchase so that the company can analyze relationships and patterns in customer purchases. The data warehouse is made available over the Web to its store managers and suppliers.

Forecasts are vital to every business organization and for every significant management decision. Forecasting is the basis of corporate long-run planning. In the functional areas of finance and accounting, forecasts provide the basis for budgetary planning and cost control. Marketing relies on sales forecasting to plan new products, compensate sales personnel, and make other key decisions. Production and operations personnel use forecasts to make periodic decisions involving supplier selection, process selection, capacity planning, and facility layout, as well as for continual decisions about purchasing, production planning, scheduling, and inventory.

In considering what forecasting approach to use it is important to consider the purpose of the forecast. Some forecasts are for very high-level demand analysis. What do we expect the demand to be for a group of products over the next year, for example? Some forecasts are used to help set the strategy of how, in an aggregate sense, we will meet demand. We will call these **strategic forecasts**. Relative to the material in the book, strategic forecasts are most appropriate when making decisions related to overall strategy (Chapter 2), capacity (Chapter 4), production process design (Chapter 6), service process design (Chapter 7), sourcing (Chapter 11), location and distribution design (Chapter 12), and in sales and operations planning (Chapter 16). These all involve relatively long-term decisions that relate to how demand will be met strategically.

Forecasts are also needed for how a firm operates processes on a day-to-day basis. For example, when should the inventory for an item be replenished, or how much production should we schedule for an item next week? These are **tactical forecasts** where the goal is to estimate demand in the relative short term, a few weeks or months. These forecasts are important to ensure that in the short term we are able to meet customer lead time expectations and other criteria related to the availability of our products and services.

In Chapter 6, the concept of decoupling points was discussed. These are points within the supply chain where inventory is positioned to allow processes or entities in the supply chain to operate independently. For example, if a product is stocked at a retailer, the customer pulls

Strategic forecasts

Tactical forecasts

Supply Chain

the item from the shelf and the manufacturer never sees a customer order. Inventory acts as a buffer to separate the customer from the manufacturing process. Selection of decoupling points is a strategic decision that determines customer lead times and can greatly impact inventory investment. The closer this point is to the customer, the quicker the customer can be served. Typically, a trade-off is involved where quicker response to customer demand comes at the expense of greater inventory investment, because finished goods inventory is more expensive than raw material inventory.

Forecasting is needed at these decoupling points to set appropriate inventory levels for these buffers. The actual setting of these levels is the topic of Chapter 17, Inventory Control, but an essential input into those decisions is a forecast of expected demand and the expected error associated with that demand. If, for example, we are able to forecast demand very accurately, then inventory levels can be set precisely to expected customer demand. On the other hand, if predicting short-term demand is difficult, then extra inventory to cover this uncertainty will be needed.

The same is true relative to service settings where inventory is not used to buffer demand. Here capacity availability relative to expected demand is the issue. If we can predict demand in a service setting very accurately, then tactically all we need to do is ensure that we have the appropriate capacity in the short term. When demand is not predictable then excess capacity may be needed if servicing customers quickly is important.

Service

Bear in mind that a perfect forecast is virtually impossible. Too many factors in the business environment cannot be predicted with certainty. Therefore, rather than search for the perfect forecast, it is far more important to establish the practice of continual review of forecasts and to learn to live with inaccurate forecasts. This is not to say that we should not try to improve the forecasting model or methodology or even to try to influence demand in a way that reduces demand uncertainty. When forecasting, a good strategy is to use two or three methods and look at them for the commonsense view. Will expected changes in the general economy affect the forecast? Are changes in our customers' behaviors that will impact demand not being captured by our current approaches? In this chapter we look at both *qualitative* techniques that use managerial judgment and also *quantitative* techniques that rely on mathematical models. In our view, combining these techniques is essential to a good forecasting process that is appropriate to the decisions being made.

DEMAND MANAGEMENT

The purpose of demand management is to coordinate and control all sources of demand so the supply chain can be run efficiently and the product delivered on time.

Where does demand for a firm's product or service come from, and what can a firm do to manage it? There are two basic sources of demand: dependent demand and independent demand. **Dependent demand** is the demand for a product or service caused by the demand for other products or services. For example, if a firm sells 1,000 tricycles, then 1,000 front wheels and 2,000 rear wheels are needed. This type of internal demand needs no forecast, just a tabulation. As to how many tricycles the firm might sell, this is called **independent demand** because its demand cannot be derived directly from that of other products.[1] We discuss dependence and independence more fully in Chapters 17 and 18.

Dependent demand

Independent demand

There is not much a firm can do about dependent demand. It must be met (although the product or service can be purchased rather than produced internally). But there is a lot a firm can do about independent demand—if it wants to. The firm can:

1. **Take an active role to influence demand.**   The firm can apply pressure on its sales force, it can offer incentives both to customers and to its own personnel, it can wage campaigns to sell products, and it can cut prices. These actions can increase demand. Conversely, demand can be decreased through price increases or reduced sales efforts.

2. **Take a passive role and simply respond to demand.**   There are several reasons a firm may not try to change demand but simply accept what happens. If a firm is running at full capacity, it may not want to do anything about demand. Other reasons are a firm may be powerless to change demand because of the expense to advertise; the market may be fixed in size and static; or demand is beyond its control (such as in the case of sole supplier). There are other competitive, legal, environmental, ethical, and moral reasons that market demand is passively accepted.

A great deal of coordination is required to manage these dependent, independent, active, and passive demands. These demands originate both internally and externally in the form of new product sales from marketing, repair parts for previously sold products from product service, restocking from the factory warehouses, and supply items for manufacturing. In this chapter, our primary interest is in forecasting for independent items.

TYPES OF FORECASTING

Forecasting can be classified into four basic types: *qualitative, time series analysis, causal relationships,* and *simulation.*

Time series analysis

Qualitative techniques are subjective or judgmental and are based on estimates and opinions. Time series analysis, the primary focus of this chapter, is based on the idea that data relating to past demand can be used to predict future demand. Past data may include several components, such as trend, seasonal, or cyclical influences, and are described in the following section. Causal forecasting, which we discuss using the linear regression technique, assumes that demand is related to some underlying factor or factors in the environment. Simulation models allow the forecaster to run through a range of assumptions about the condition of the forecast. In this chapter we focus on qualitative and time series techniques since these are most often used in supply chain planning and control.

COMPONENTS OF DEMAND

In most cases, demand for products or services can be broken down into six components: average demand for the period, a trend, seasonal element, cyclical elements, random variation, and autocorrelation. Exhibit 15.1 illustrates a demand over a four-year period, showing the average, trend, and seasonal components and randomness around the smoothed demand curve.

exhibit 15.1   Historical Product Demand Consisting of a Growth Trend and Seasonal Demand

**Excel:
Components of
Demand**

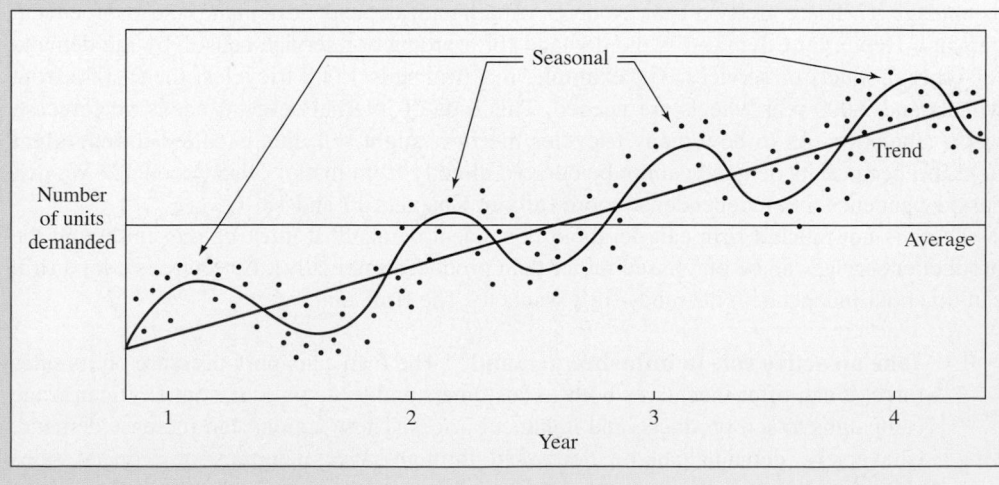

Cyclical factors are more difficult to determine because the time span may be unknown or the cause of the cycle may not be considered. Cyclical influence on demand may come from such occurrences as political elections, war, economic conditions, or sociological pressures.

Random variations are caused by chance events. Statistically, when all the known causes for demand (average, trend, seasonal, cyclical, and autocorrelative) are subtracted from total demand, what remains is the unexplained portion of demand. If we cannot identify the cause of this remainder, it is assumed to be purely random chance.

Autocorrelation denotes the persistence of occurrence. More specifically, the value expected at any point is highly correlated with its own past values. In waiting line theory, the length of a waiting line is highly autocorrelated. That is, if a line is relatively long at one time, then shortly after that time, we would expect the line still to be long.

When demand is random, it may vary widely from one week to another. Where high autocorrelation exists, demand is not expected to change very much from one week to the next.

Trend lines are the usual starting point in developing a forecast. These trend lines are then adjusted for seasonal effects, cyclical elements, and any other expected events that may influence the final forecast. Exhibit 15.2 shows four of the most common types of trends. A linear trend is obviously a straight continuous relationship. An S-curve is typical of a product growth and maturity cycle. The most important point in the S-curve is where the trend changes from slow growth to fast growth, or from fast to slow. An asymptotic trend starts with the highest

Common Types of Trends

exhibit 15.2

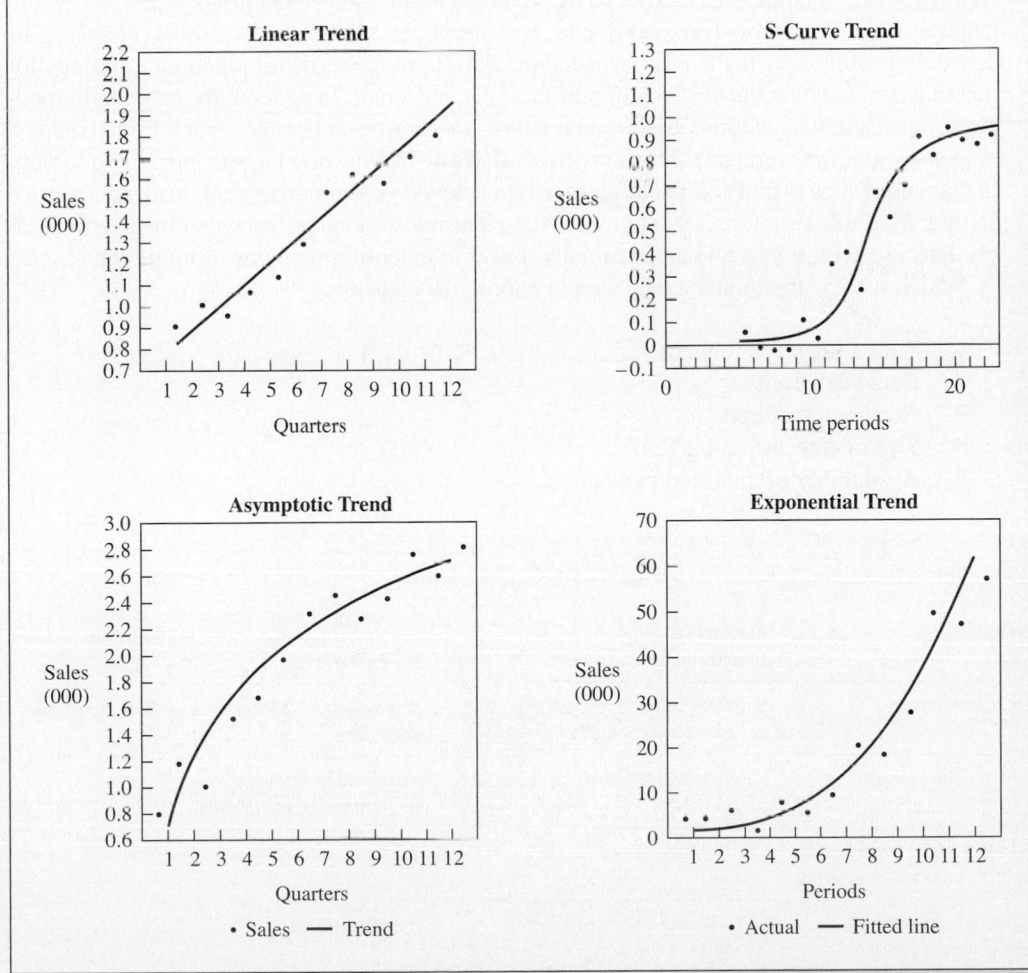

demand growth at the beginning but then tapers off. Such a curve could happen when a firm enters an existing market with the objective of saturating and capturing a large share of the market. An exponential curve is common in products with explosive growth. The exponential trend suggests that sales will continue to increase—an assumption that may not be safe to make.

A widely used forecasting method plots data and then searches for the curve pattern (such as linear, S-curve, asymptotic, or exponential) that fits best. The attractiveness of this method is that because the mathematics for the curve are known, solving for values for future time periods is easy.

Sometimes our data do not seem to fit any standard curve. This may be due to several causes essentially beating the data from several directions at the same time. For these cases, a simplistic but often effective forecast can be obtained by simply plotting data.

TIME SERIES ANALYSIS

Time series forecasting models try to predict the future based on past data. For example, sales figures collected for the past six weeks can be used to forecast sales for the seventh week. Quarterly sales figures collected for the past several years can be used to forecast future quarters. Even though both examples contain sales, different forecasting time series models would likely be used.

Exhibit 15.3 shows the time series models discussed in the chapter and some of their characteristics. Terms such as *short, medium,* and *long* are relative to the context in which they are used. However, in business forecasting *short term* usually refers to under three months; *medium term,* three months to two years; and *long term,* greater than two years. We would generally use short-term forecasts for tactical decisions such as replenishing inventory or scheduling employees in the near term and medium-term forecasts for planning a strategy for meeting demand over the next six months to a year and a half. In general, the short-term models compensate for random variation and adjust for short-term changes (such as consumers' responses to a new product). They are especially good for measuring the current variability in demand, which is useful for setting safety stock levels or estimating peak loads in a service setting. Medium-term forecasts are useful for capturing seasonal effects, and long-term models detect general trends and are especially useful in indentifying major turning points.

Which forecasting model a firm should choose depends on:

1. Time horizon to forecast.
2. Data availability.
3. Accuracy required.
4. Size of forecasting budget.
5. Availability of qualified personnel.

exhibit 15.3   A Guide to Selecting an Appropriate Forecasting Method

FORECASTING METHOD	AMOUNT OF HISTORICAL DATA	DATA PATTERN	FORECAST HORIZON
Linear regression	10 to 20 observations for seasonally at least 5 observations per season	Stationary, trend, and seasonality	Short to medium
Simple moving average	6 to 12 months, weekly data are often used	Data should be stationary (i.e., no trend or seasonality)	Short
Weighted moving average and simple exponential smoothing	5 to 10 observations needed to start	Data should be stationary	Short
Exponential smoothing with trend	5 to 10 observations needed to start	Stationary and trend	Short

In selecting a forecasting model, there are other issues such as the firm's degree of flexibility. (The greater the ability to react quickly to changes, the less accurate the forecast needs to be.) Another item is the consequence of a bad forecast. If a large capital investment decision is to be based on a forecast, it should be a good forecast.

LINEAR REGRESSION ANALYSIS

Regression can be defined as a functional relationship between two or more correlated variables. It is used to predict one variable given the other. The relationship is usually developed from observed data. The data should be plotted first to see if they appear linear or if at least parts of the data are linear. *Linear regression* refers to the special class of regression where the relationship between variables forms a straight line.

The linear regression line is of the form $Y = a + bX$, where Y is the value of the dependent variable that we are solving for, a is the Y intercept, b is the slope, and X is the independent variable. (In time series analysis, X is units of time.)

Linear regression is useful for long-term forecasting of major occurrences and aggregate planning. For example, linear regression would be very useful to forecast demands for product families. Even though demand for individual products within a family may vary widely during a time period, demand for the total product family is surprisingly smooth.

The major restriction in using **linear regression forecasting** is, as the name implies, that past data and future projections are assumed to fall about a straight line. Although this does limit its application, sometimes, if we use a shorter period of time, linear regression analysis can still be used. For example, short segments of the longer period may be approximately linear.

Linear regression forecasting

Linear regression is used both for time series forecasting and for causal relationship forecasting. When the dependent variable (usually the vertical axis on a graph) changes as a result of time (plotted as the horizontal axis), it is time series analysis. If one variable changes because of the change in another variable, this is a causal relationship (such as the number of deaths from lung cancer increasing with the number of people who smoke).

We use the following example to demonstrate linear least squares regression analysis.

EXAMPLE 15.1: Least Squares Method

A firm's sales for a product line during the 12 quarters of the past three years were as follows:

QUARTER	SALES	QUARTER	SALES
1	600	7	2,600
2	1,550	8	2,900
3	1,500	9	3,800
4	1,500	10	4,500
5	2,400	11	4,000
6	3,100	12	4,900

Step by Step

The firm wants to forecast each quarter of the fourth year—that is, quarters 13, 14, 15, and 16.

SOLUTION

The least squares equation for linear regression is

$$Y = a + bx \qquad\qquad [15.1]$$

where

Y = Dependent variable computed by the equation
y = The actual dependent variable data point (used below)
a = Y intercept
b = Slope of the line
x = Time period

exhibit 15.4   Least Squares Regression Line

**Excel:
Forecasting**

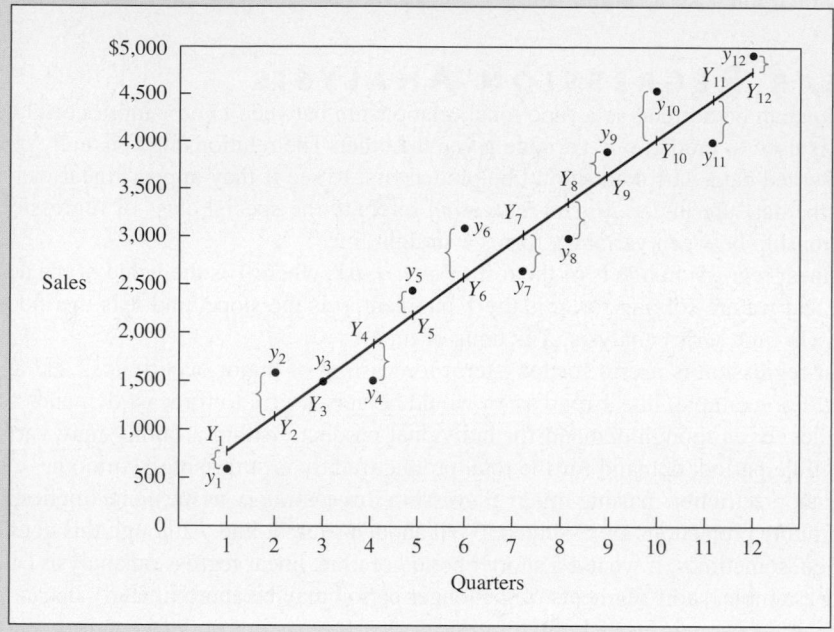

The least squares method tries to fit the line to the data *that minimizes the sum of the squares of the vertical distance* between each data point and its corresponding point on the line. If a straight line is drawn through the general area of the points, the difference between the point and the line is $y - Y$. Exhibit 15.4 shows these differences. The sum of the squares of the differences between the plotted data points and the line points is

$$(y_1 - Y_1)^2 + (y_2 - Y_2)^2 + \cdots + (y_{12} - Y_{12})^2$$

The best line to use is the one that minimizes this total.

As before, the straight line equation is

$$Y = a + bx$$

Previously we determined a and b from the graph. In the least squares method, the equations for a and b are

$$a = \bar{y} - b\bar{x} \qquad\qquad\qquad \textbf{[15.2]}$$

$$b = \frac{\sum xy - n\bar{x} \cdot \bar{y}}{\sum x^2 - n\bar{x}^2} \qquad\qquad \textbf{[15.3]}$$

where

$a = Y$ intercept
$b =$ Slope of the line
$\bar{y} =$ Average of all ys
$\bar{x} =$ Average of all xs
$x = x$ value at each data point
$y = y$ value at each data point
$n =$ Number of data points
$Y =$ Value of the dependent variable computed with the regression equation

Least Squares Regression Analysis

exhibit 15.5

(1) x	(2) y	(3) xy	(4) x^2	(5) y^2	(6) Y
1	600	600	1	360,000	801.3
2	1,550	3,100	4	2,402,500	1,160.9
3	1,500	4,500	9	2,250,000	1,520.5
4	1,500	6,000	16	2,250,000	1,880.1
5	2,400	12,000	25	5,760,000	2,239.7
6	3,100	18,600	36	9,610,000	2,599.4
7	2,600	18,200	49	6,760,000	2,959.0
8	2,900	23,200	64	8,410,000	3,318.6
9	3,800	34,200	81	14,440,000	3,678.2
10	4,500	45,000	100	20,250,000	4,037.8
11	4,000	44,000	121	16,000,000	4,397.4
12	4,900	58,800	144	24,010,000	4,757.1
78	33,350	268,200	650	112,502,500	

$\bar{x} = 6.5$ $b - 359.6153$
$\bar{y} = 2,779.17$ $a = 441.6666$
Therefore, $Y = 441.66 + 359.6x$
    $S_{yx} - 363.9$

**Excel:
Forecasting**

Exhibit 15.5 shows these computations carried out for the 12 data points in the problem. Note that the final equation for Y shows an intercept of 441.6 and a slope of 359.6. The slope shows that for every unit change in X, Y changes by 359.6.

Strictly based on the equation, forecasts for periods 13 through 16 would be

$$Y_{13} = 441.6 + 359.6(13) = 5,116.4$$
$$Y_{14} = 441.6 + 359.6(14) = 5,476.0$$
$$Y_{15} = 441.6 + 359.6(15) = 5,835.6$$
$$Y_{16} = 441.6 + 359.6(16) = 6,195.2$$

The standard error of estimate, or how well the line fits the data, is[2]

$$S_{yx} = \sqrt{\frac{\sum_{i=1}^{n}(y_i - Y_i)^2}{n - 2}}$$ [15.4]

The standard error of estimate is computed from the second and last columns of Exhibit 15.5:

$$S_{yx} = \sqrt{\frac{(600 - 801.3)^2 + (1,550 - 1,160.9)^2 + (1,500 - 1,520.5)^2 + \cdots + (4,900 - 4,757.1)^2}{10}}$$

$$= 363.9$$

Microsoft Excel has a very powerful regression tool designed to perform these calculations. To use the tool, a table is needed that contains data relevant to the problem (see Exhibit 15.6). The tool is part of the Data Analysis ToolPak that is accessed from the Tools menu (or Data tab in Excel 2007) (you may need to add this to your Tools options by using the Add-In option under Tools).

To use the tool, first input the data in two columns in your spreadsheet, then access the Regression option from the Tools → Data Analysis menu. Next, specify the Y Range, which is B2:B13, and the X Range, which is A2:A13 in our example. Finally, an Output Range is specified. This is where you would like the results of the regression analysis placed in your spreadsheet. In the example, A16 is

exhibit 15.6   Excel Regression Tool

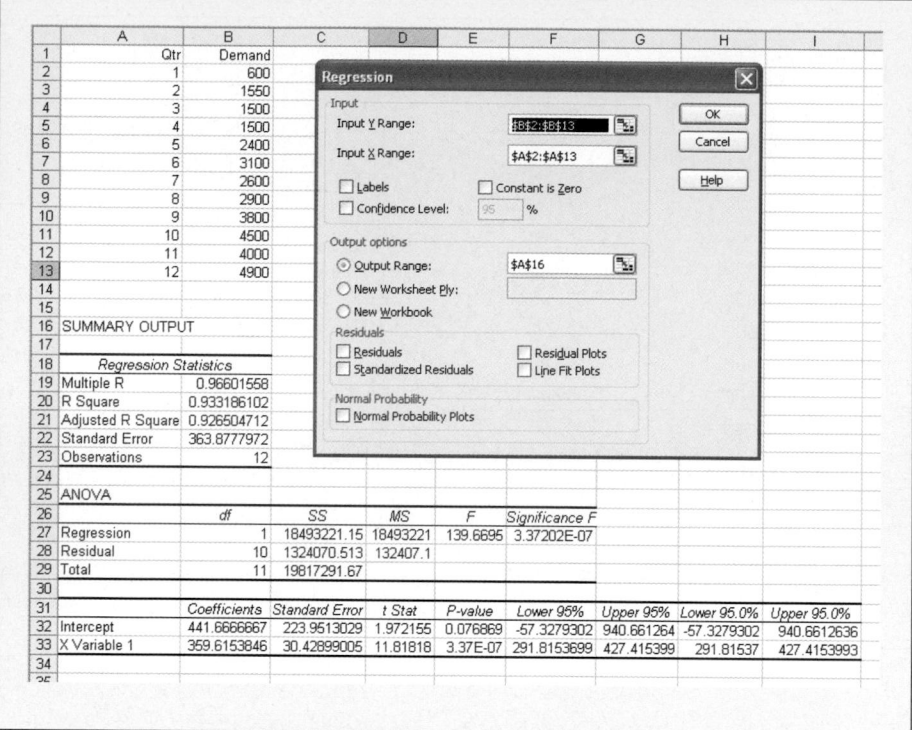

entered. Some of the information provided goes beyond what we have covered, but what you are looking for is the Intercept and X Variable coefficients that correspond to the intercept and slope values in the linear equation. These are in rows 32 and 33 in Exhibit 15.6. ●

We discuss the possible existence of seasonal components in the next section on decomposition of a time series.

DECOMPOSITION OF A TIME SERIES

A *time series* can be defined as chronologically ordered data that may contain one or more components of demand: trend, seasonal, cyclical, autocorrelation, and random. *Decomposition* of a time series means identifying and separating the time series data into these components. In practice, it is relatively easy to identify the trend (even without mathematical analysis, it is usually easy to plot and see the direction of movement) and the seasonal component (by comparing the same period year to year). It is considerably more difficult to identify the cycles (these may be many months or years long), autocorrelation, and random components. (The forecaster usually calls random anything left over that cannot be identified as another component.)

When demand contains both seasonal and trend effects at the same time, the question is how they relate to each other. In this description, we examine two types of seasonal variation: *additive* and *multiplicative*.

Additive Seasonal Variation   Additive seasonal variation simply assumes that the seasonal amount is a constant no matter what the trend or average amount is.

$$\text{Forecast including trend and seasonal} = \text{Trend} + \text{Seasonal}$$

Exhibit 15.7A shows an example of increasing trend with constant seasonal amounts.

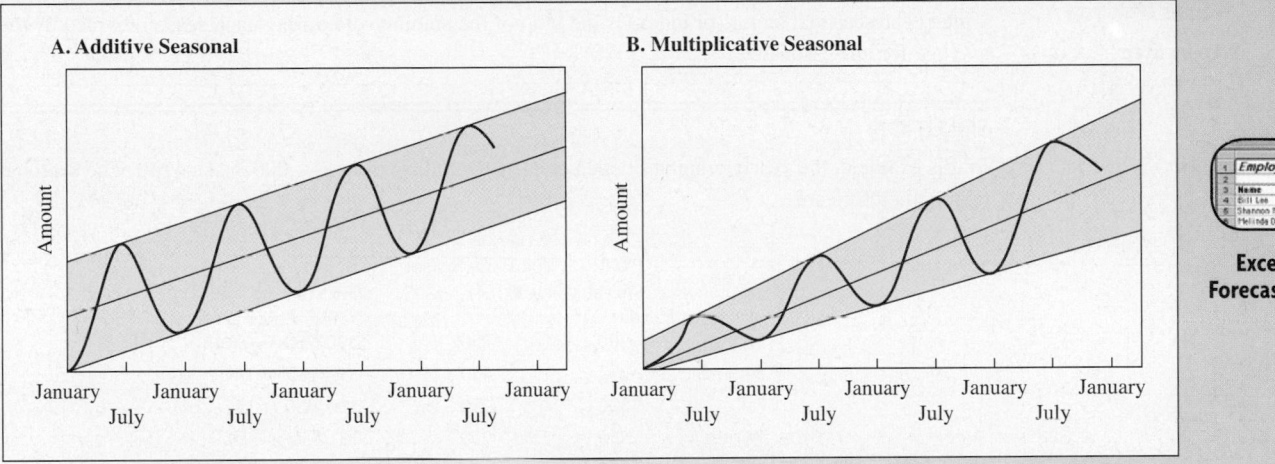

Additive and Multiplicative Seasonal Variation Superimposed on Changing Trend

exhibit 15.7

A. Additive Seasonal

B. Multiplicative Seasonal

Excel:
Forecasting

Multiplicative Seasonal Variation   In multiplicative seasonal variation, the trend is multiplied by the seasonal factors.

$$\text{Forecast including trend and seasonal} = \text{Trend} \times \text{Seasonal factor}$$

Exhibit 15.7B shows the seasonal variation increasing as the trend increases because its size depends on the trend.

The multiplicative seasonal variation is the usual experience. Essentially, this says that the larger the basic amount projected, the larger the variation around this that we can expect.

Seasonal Factor (or Index)   A seasonal factor is the amount of correction needed in a time series to adjust for the season of the year.

We usually associate *seasonal* with a period of the year characterized by some particular activity. We use the word *cyclical* to indicate other than annual recurrent periods of repetitive activity.

The following examples show how seasonal indexes are determined and used to forecast (1) a simple calculation based on past seasonal data and (2) the trend and seasonal index from a hand-fit regression line. We follow this with a more formal procedure for the decomposition of data and forecasting using least squares regression.

COMPANIES SUCH AS TORO MANUFACTURE LAWNMOWERS AND SNOW BLOWERS TO MATCH SEASONAL DEMAND. USING THE SAME EQUIPMENT AND ASSEMBLY LINES PROVIDES BETTER CAPACITY UTILIZATION, WORKFORCE STABILITY, PRODUCTIVITY, AND REVENUE.

Step by Step

EXAMPLE 15.2: Simple Proportion

Assume that in past years, a firm sold an average of 1,000 units of a particular product line each year. On the average, 200 units were sold in the spring, 350 in the summer, 300 in the fall, and 150 in the winter. The seasonal factor (or index) is the ratio of the amount sold during each season divided by the average for all seasons.

SOLUTION

In this example, the yearly amount divided equally over all seasons is $1,000 \div 4 = 250$. The seasonal factors therefore are

	PAST SALES	AVERAGE SALES FOR EACH SEASON (1,000/4)	SEASONAL FACTOR
Spring	200	250	200/250 = 0.8
Summer	350	250	350/250 = 1.4
Fall	300	250	300/250 = 1.2
Winter	150	250	150/250 = 0.6
Total	1,000		

Using these factors, if we expected demand for next year to be 1,100 units, we would forecast the demand to occur as

	EXPECTED DEMAND FOR NEXT YEAR	AVERAGE SALES FOR EACH SEASON (1,100/4)		SEASONAL FACTOR		NEXT YEAR'S SEASONAL FORECAST
Spring		275	×	0.8	=	220
Summer		275	×	1.4	=	385
Fall		275	×	1.2	=	330
Winter		275	×	0.6	=	165
Total	1,100					

The seasonal factor may be periodically updated as new data are available. The following example shows the seasonal factor and multiplicative seasonal variation.

Step by Step

EXAMPLE 15.3: Computing Trend and Seasonal Factor from a Hand-Fit Straight Line

Here we must compute the trend as well as the seasonal factors.

SOLUTION

We solve this problem by simply hand fitting a straight line through the data points and measuring the trend and intercept from the graph. Assume the history of data is

QUARTER	AMOUNT	QUARTER	AMOUNT
I–2008	300	I–2009	520
II–2008	200	II–2009	420
III–2008	220	III–2009	400
IV–2008	530	IV–2009	700

First, we plot as in Exhibit 15.8 and then visually fit a straight line through the data. (Naturally, this line and the resulting equation are subject to variation. We show how to do this using regression in the next section.) The equation for the line is

$$\text{Trend}_t = 170 + 55t$$

Our equation was derived from the intercept 170 plus a rise of $(610 - 170) \div 8$ periods. Next we can derive a seasonal index by comparing the actual data with the trend line as in Exhibit 15.8. The seasonal factor was developed by averaging the same quarters in each year.

Computing a Seasonal Factor from the Actual Data and Trend Line

exhibit 15.8

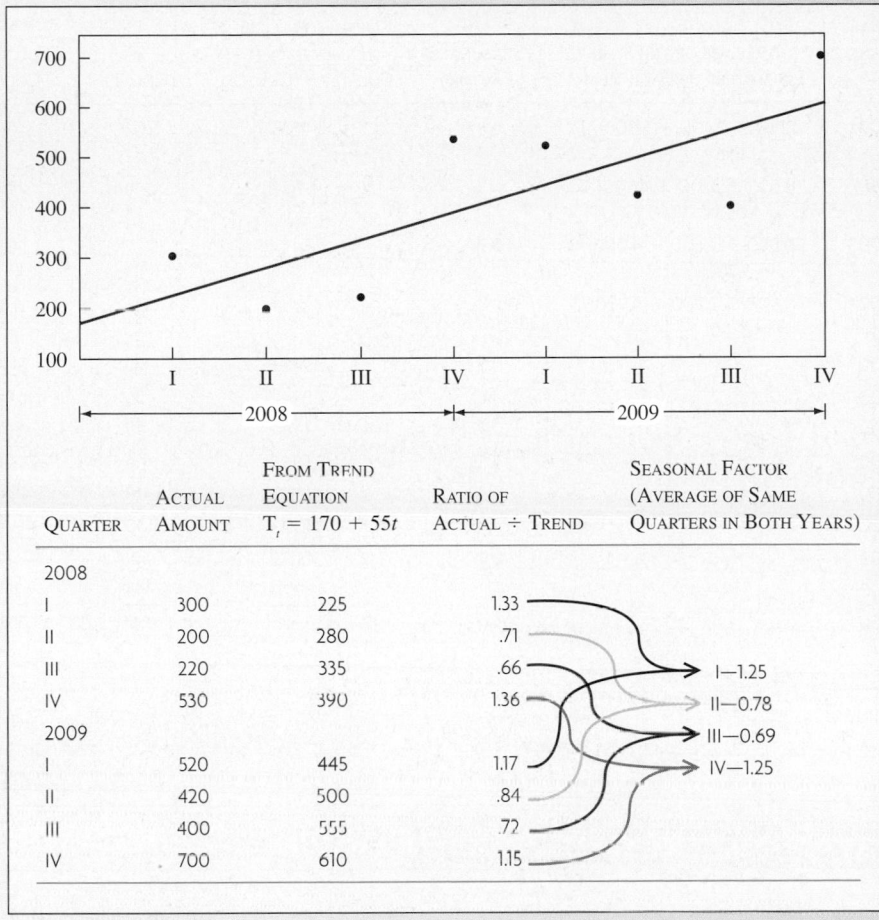

Excel: Forecasting

We can compute the 2010 forecast including trend and seasonal factors (FITS) as follows:

$$FITS_t = Trend \times Seasonal$$
$$I—2010\ FITS_9 = [170 + 55(9)]1.25 = 831$$
$$II—2010\ FITS_{10} = [170 + 55(10)]0.78 = 562$$
$$III—2010\ FITS_{11} = [170 + 55(11)]0.69 = 535$$
$$IV—2010\ FITS_{12} = [170 + 55(12)]1.25 = 1,038 \bullet$$

Decomposition Using Least Squares Regression   Decomposition of a time series means finding the series' basic components of trend, seasonal, and cyclical. Indexes are calculated for seasons and cycles. The forecasting procedure then reverses the process by projecting the trend and adjusting it by the seasonal and cyclical indexes, which were determined in the decomposition process. More formally, the process is:

1. Decompose the time series into its components.
   a. Find seasonal component.
   b. Deseasonalize the demand.
   c. Find trend component.
2. Forecast future values of each component.
   a. Project trend component into the future.
   b. Multiply trend component by seasonal component.

exhibit 15.9   Deseasonalized Demand

(1) PERIOD (x)	(2) QUARTER	(3) ACTUAL DEMAND (y)	(4) AVERAGE OF THE SAME QUARTERS OF EACH YEAR	(5) SEASONAL FACTOR	(6) DESEASONALIZED DEMAND (yd) COL. (3) ÷ COL. (5)	(7) x^2 (COL. 1)^2	(8) $x \times yd$ COL. (1) × COL. (6)
1	I	600	(600 + 2,400 + 3,800)/3 = 2,266.7	0.82	735.7	1	735.7
2	II	1,550	(1,550 + 3,100 + 4,500)/3 = 3,050	1.10	1,412.4	4	2,824.7
3	III	1,500	(1,500 + 2,600 + 4,000)/3 = 2,700	0.97	1,544.0	9	4,631.9
4	IV	1,500	(1,500 + 2,900 + 4,900)/3 = 3,100	1.12	1,344.8	16	5,379.0
5	I	2,400		0.82	2,942.6	25	14,713.2
6	II	3,100		1.10	2,824.7	36	16,948.4
7	III	2,600		0.97	2,676.2	49	18,733.6
8	IV	2,900		1.12	2,599.9	64	20,798.9
9	I	3,800		0.82	4,659.2	81	41,932.7
10	II	4,500		1.10	4,100.4	100	41,004.1
11	III	4,000		0.97	4,117.3	121	45,290.1
12	IV	4,900		1.12	4,392.9	144	52,714.5
78		33,350		12.03	33,350.1*	650	265,706.9

$$\bar{x} = \frac{78}{12} = 6.5 \qquad b = \frac{\sum xy_d - n\bar{x}\bar{y}_d}{\sum \bar{x}^2 - n\bar{x}^2} = \frac{265,706.9 - 12(6.5)2,779.2}{650 - 12(6.5)^2} = 342.2$$

$$\bar{y}_d = 33,350/12 = 2,779.2 \qquad a = \bar{y}_d - b\bar{x} = 2,779.2 - 342.2(6.5) = 554.9$$

Therefore, $Y = a + bx = 554.9 + 342.2x$

*COLUMN 3 AND COLUMN 6 TOTALS SHOULD BE EQUAL AT 33,350. DIFFERENCES ARE DUE TO ROUNDING. COLUMN 5 WAS ROUNDED TO TWO DECIMAL PLACES.

Note that the random component is not included in this list. We implicitly remove the random component from the time series when we average as in step 1. It is pointless to attempt a projection of the random component in step 2 unless we have information about some unusual event, such as a major labor dispute, that could adversely affect product demand (and this would not really be random).

Exhibit 15.9 shows the decomposition of a time series using least squares regression and the same basic data we used in our first regression example. Each data point corresponds to using a single three-month quarter of the three-year (12-quarter) period. Our objective is to forecast demand for the four quarters of the fourth year.

Step 1. Determine the seasonal factor (or index).   Exhibit 15.9 summarizes the calculations needed. Column 4 develops an average for the same quarters in the three-year period. For example, the first quarters of the three years are added together and divided by 3. A seasonal factor is then derived by dividing that average by the general average for all 12 quarters $\left(\frac{33,350}{12}, \text{ or } 2,779\right)$. For example, this first quarter seasonal factor is $\frac{2,266.7}{2,779} =$ 0.82. These are entered in column 5. Note that the seasonal factors are identical for similar quarters in each year.

Step 2. Deseasonalize the original data.   To remove the seasonal effect on the data, we divide the original data by the seasonal factor. This step is called the deseasonalization of demand and is shown in column 6 of Exhibit 15.9.

Straight Line Graph of Deseasonalized Equation

exhibit 15.10

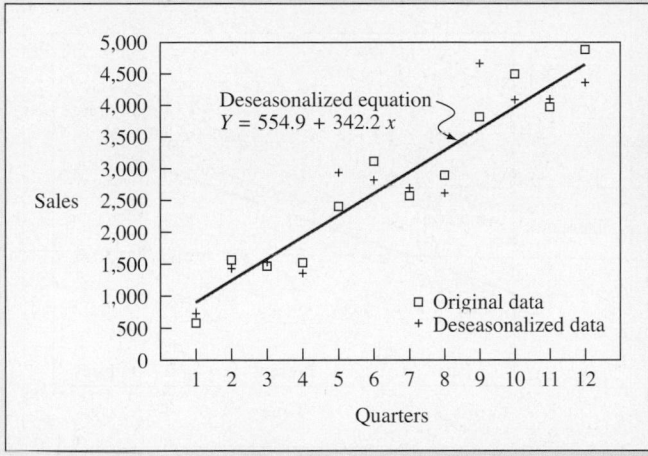

**Excel:
Forecasting**

Step 3. Develop a least squares regression line for the deseasonalized data. The purpose here is to develop an equation for the trend line Y, which we then modify with the seasonal factor. The procedure is the same as we used before:

$$Y = a + bx$$

where

y_d = Deseasonalized demand (see Exhibit 15.9)

x $-$ Quarter

Y = Demand computed using the regression equation $Y = a + bx$

a = Y intercept

b = Slope of the line

The least squares calculations using columns 1, 7, and 8 of Exhibit 15.9 are shown in the lower section of the exhibit. The final deseasonalized equation for our data is $Y = 554.9 + 342.2x$. This straight line is shown in Exhibit 15.10.

Step 4. Project the regression line through the period to be forecast. Our purpose is to forecast periods 13 through 16. We start by solving the equation for Y at each of these periods (shown in step 5, column 3).

Step 5. Create the final forecast by adjusting the regression line by the seasonal factor. Recall that the Y equation has been deseasonalized. We now reverse the procedure by multiplying the quarterly data we derived by the seasonal factor for that quarter:

PERIOD	QUARTER	Y FROM REGRESSION LINE	SEASONAL FACTOR	FORECAST ($Y \times$ SEASONAL FACTOR)
13	1	5,003.5	0.82	4,102.87
14	2	5,345.7	1.10	5,880.27
15	3	5,687.9	0.97	5,517.26
16	4	6,030.1	1.12	6,753.71

Our forecast is now complete. The procedure is generally the same as what we did in the hand-fit previous example. In the present example, however, we followed a more formal procedure and computed the least squares regression line as well.

exhibit 15.11   Prediction Intervals for Linear Trend

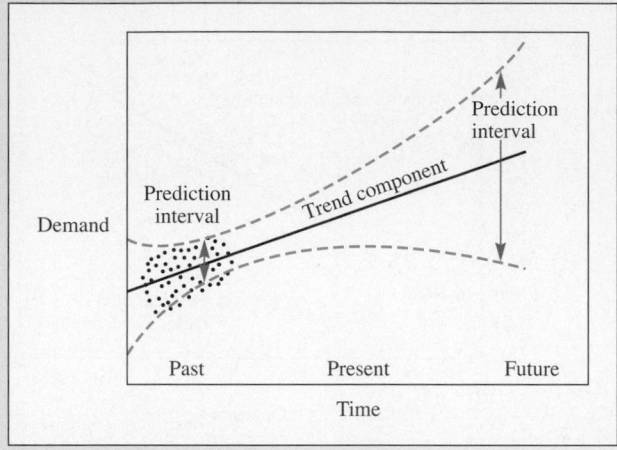

Error Range   When a straight line is fitted through data points and then used for forecasting, errors can come from two sources. First, there are the usual errors similar to the standard deviation of any set of data. Second, there are errors that arise because the line is wrong. Exhibit 15.11 shows this error range. Instead of developing the statistics here, we will briefly show why the range broadens. First, visualize that one line is drawn that has some error such that it slants too steeply upward. Standard errors are then calculated for this line. Now visualize another line that slants too steeply downward. It also has a standard error. The total error range, for this analysis, consists of errors resulting from both lines as well as all other possible lines. We included this exhibit to show how the error range widens as we go further into the future.

SIMPLE MOVING AVERAGE

When demand for a product is neither growing nor declining rapidly, and if it does not have seasonal characteristics, a moving average can be useful in removing the random fluctuations for forecasting. Although *moving averages* are frequently centered, it is more convenient to use past data to predict the following period directly. To illustrate, a centered five-month average of January, February, March, April, and May gives an average centered on March. However, all five months of data must already exist. If our objective is to forecast for June, we must project our moving average—by some means—from March to June. If the average is not centered but is at the forward end, we can forecast more easily, though we may lose some accuracy. Thus, if we want to forecast June with a five-month moving average, we can take the average of January, February, March, April, and May. When June passes, the forecast for July would be the average of February, March, April, May, and June. This is how Exhibit 15.12 was computed.

Although it is important to select the best period for the moving average, there are several conflicting effects of different period lengths. The longer the moving average period, the more the random elements are smoothed (which may be desirable in many cases). But if there is a trend in the data—either increasing or decreasing—the moving average has the adverse characteristic of lagging the trend. Therefore, while a shorter time span produces more oscillation, there is a closer following of the trend. Conversely, a longer time span gives a smoother response but lags the trend.

The formula for a simple moving average is

$$F_t = \frac{A_{t-1} + A_{t-2} + A_{t-3} + \cdots + A_{t-n}}{n}$$

[15.5]

where

F_t = Forecast for the coming period
n = Number of periods to be averaged

Forecast Demand Based on a Three- and a Nine-Week Simple Moving Average

exhibit 15.12

Week	Demand	3 Week	9 Week	Week	Demand	3 Week	9 Week
1	800			16	1,700	2,200	1,811
2	1,400			17	1,800	2,000	1,800
3	1,000			18	2,200	1,833	1,811
4	1,500	1,067		19	1,900	1,900	1,911
5	1,500	1,300		20	2,400	1,967	1,933
6	1,300	1,333		21	2,400	2,167	2,011
7	1,800	1,433		22	2,600	2,233	2,111
8	1,700	1,533		23	2,000	2,467	2,144
9	1,300	1,600		24	2,500	2,333	2,111
10	1,700	1,600	1,367	25	2,600	2,367	2,167
11	1,700	1,567	1,467	26	2,200	2,367	2,267
12	1,500	1,567	1,500	27	2,200	2,433	2,311
13	2,300	1,633	1,556	28	2,500	2,333	2,311
14	2,300	1,833	1,644	29	2,400	2,300	2,378
15	2,000	2,033	1,733	30	2,100	2,367	2,378

**Excel:
Forecasting**

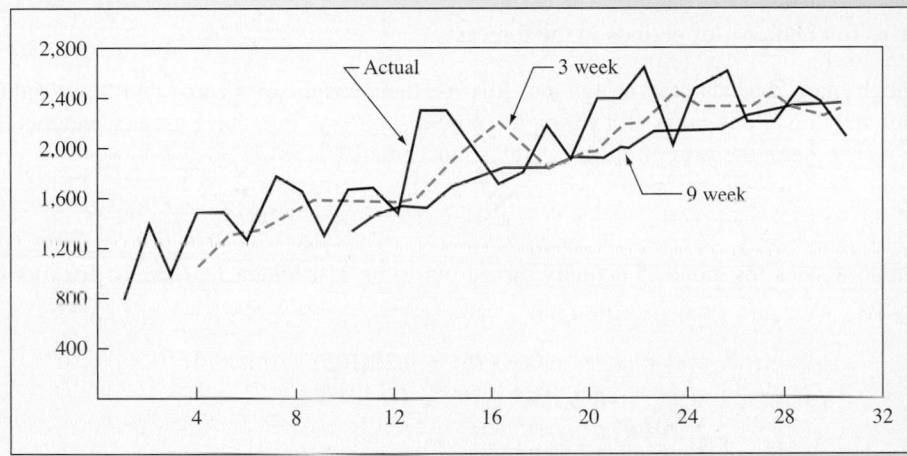

A_{t-1} = Actual occurrence in the past period

A_{t-2}, A_{t-3}, and A_{t-n} = Actual occurrences two periods ago, three periods ago, and so on up to n periods ago

A plot of the data in Exhibit 15.12, shows the effects of various lengths of the period of a moving average. We see that the growth trend levels off at about the 23rd week. The three-week moving average responds better in following this change than the nine-week average, although overall, the nine-week average is smoother.

The main disadvantage in calculating a moving average is that all individual elements must be carried as data because a new forecast period involves adding new data and dropping the earliest data. For a three- or six-period moving average, this is not too severe. But plotting a 60-day moving average for the usage of each of 20,000 items in inventory would involve a significant amount of data.

WEIGHTED MOVING AVERAGE

Whereas the simple moving average gives equal weight to each component of the moving average database, a weighted moving average allows any weights to be placed on each element, providing, of course, that the sum of all weights equals 1. For example, a department store may find that in a four-month period, the best forecast is derived by using 40 percent of the actual sales for the most recent month, 30 percent of two months ago, 20 percent of three months ago, and 10 percent of four months ago. If actual sales experience was

MONTH 1	MONTH 2	MONTH 3	MONTH 4	MONTH 5
100	90	105	95	?

the forecast for month 5 would be

$$F_5 = 0.40(95) + 0.30(105) + 0.20(90) + 0.10(100)$$
$$= 38 + 31.5 + 18 + 10$$
$$= 97.5$$

The formula for a weighted moving average is

$$F_t = w_1 A_{t-1} + w_2 A_{t-2} + \cdots + wn A_{t-n} \qquad [15.6]$$

where

w_1 = Weight to be given to the actual occurrence for the period $t - 1$
w_2 = Weight to be given to the actual occurrence for the period $t - 2$
w_n = Weight to be given to the actual occurrence for the period $t - n$
n = Total number of periods in the forecast

Although many periods may be ignored (that is, their weights are zero) and the weighting scheme may be in any order (for example, more distant data may have greater weights than more recent data), the sum of all the weights must equal 1.

$$\sum_{i=1}^{n} w_i = 1$$

Suppose sales for month 5 actually turned out to be 110. Then the forecast for month 6 would be

$$F_6 = 0.40(110) + 0.30(95) + 0.20(105) + 0.10(90)$$
$$= 44 + 28.5 + 21 + 9$$
$$= 102.5$$

Choosing Weights   Experience and trial and error are the simplest ways to choose weights. As a general rule, the most recent past is the most important indicator of what to expect in the future, and, therefore, it should get higher weighting. The past month's revenue or plant capacity, for example, would be a better estimate for the coming month than the revenue or plant capacity of several months ago.

However, if the data are seasonal, for example, weights should be established accordingly. Bathing suit sales in July of last year should be weighted more heavily than bathing suit sales in December (in the Northern Hemisphere).

The weighted moving average has a definite advantage over the simple moving average in being able to vary the effects of past data. However, it is more inconvenient and costly to use than the exponential smoothing method, which we examine next.

EXPONENTIAL SMOOTHING

In the previous methods of forecasting (simple and weighted moving averages), the major drawback is the need to continually carry a large amount of historical data. (This is also true for regression analysis techniques, which we soon will cover.) As each new piece of data is added in these methods, the oldest observation is dropped, and the new forecast is calculated. In many applications (perhaps in most), the most recent occurrences are more indicative of the future than those in the more distant past. If this premise is valid—that the importance of data diminishes as the past becomes more distant—then **exponential smoothing** may be the most logical and easiest method to use.

Exponential smoothing

The reason this is called exponential smoothing is that each increment in the past is decreased by $(1 - \alpha)$. If α is 0.05, for example, weights for various periods would be as follows (α is defined below):

	WEIGHTING AT $\alpha = 0.05$
Most recent weighting $= \alpha(1 - \alpha)^0$	0.0500
Data one time period older $= \alpha(1 - \alpha)^1$	0.0475
Data two time periods older $= \alpha(1 - \alpha)^2$	0.0451
Data three time periods older $= \alpha(1 - \alpha)^3$	0.0429

Therefore, the exponents 0, 1, 2, 3, . . . , give it its name.

Exponential smoothing is the most used of all forecasting techniques. It is an integral part of virtually all computerized forecasting programs, and it is widely used in ordering inventory in retail firms, wholesale companies, and service agencies.

Exponential smoothing techniques have become well accepted for six major reasons:

1. Exponential models are surprisingly accurate.
2. Formulating an exponential model is relatively easy.
3. The user can understand how the model works.
4. Little computation is required to use the model.
5. Computer storage requirements are small because of the limited use of historical data.
6. Tests for accuracy as to how well the model is performing are easy to compute.

In the exponential smoothing method, only three pieces of data are needed to forecast the future: the most recent forecast, the actual demand that occurred for that forecast period, and a **smoothing constant alpha (α)**. This smoothing constant determines the level of smoothing and the speed of reaction to differences between forecasts and actual occurrences. The value for the constant is determined both by the nature of the product and by the manager's sense of what constitutes a good response rate. For example, if a firm produced a standard item with relatively stable demand, the reaction rate to differences between actual and forecast demand would tend to be small, perhaps just 5 or 10 percentage points. However, if the firm were experiencing growth, it would be desirable to have a higher reaction rate, perhaps 15 to 30 percentage points, to give greater importance to recent growth experience. The more rapid the growth, the higher the reaction rate should be. Sometimes users of the simple moving average switch to exponential smoothing but like to keep the forecasts about the same as the simple moving average. In this case, α is approximated by $2 \div (n + 1)$, where n is the number of time periods.

Smoothing constant alpha (α)

The equation for a single exponential smoothing forecast is simply

$$F_t = F_{t-1} + \alpha(A_{t-1} - F_{t-1}) \qquad [15.7]$$

where

F_t = The exponentially smoothed forecast for period t
F_{t-1} = The exponentially smoothed forecast made for the prior period
A_{t-1} = The actual demand in the prior period
α = The desired response rate, or smoothing constant

This equation states that the new forecast is equal to the old forecast plus a portion of the error (the difference between the previous forecast and what actually occurred).[3]

To demonstrate the method, assume that the long-run demand for the product under study is relatively stable and a smoothing constant (α) of 0.05 is considered appropriate. If the exponential method were used as a continuing policy, a forecast would have been made for last month.[4] Assume that last month's forecast (F_{t-1}) was 1,050 units. If 1,000 actually were demanded, rather than 1,050, the forecast for this month would be

$$F_t = F_{t-1} + \alpha(A_{t-1} - F_{t-1})$$
$$= 1{,}050 + 0.05(1{,}000 - 1{,}050)$$
$$= 1{,}050 + 0.05(-50)$$
$$= 1{,}047.5 \text{ units}$$

exhibit 15.13

Exponential Forecasts versus Actual Demand for Units of a Product over Time Showing the Forecast Lag

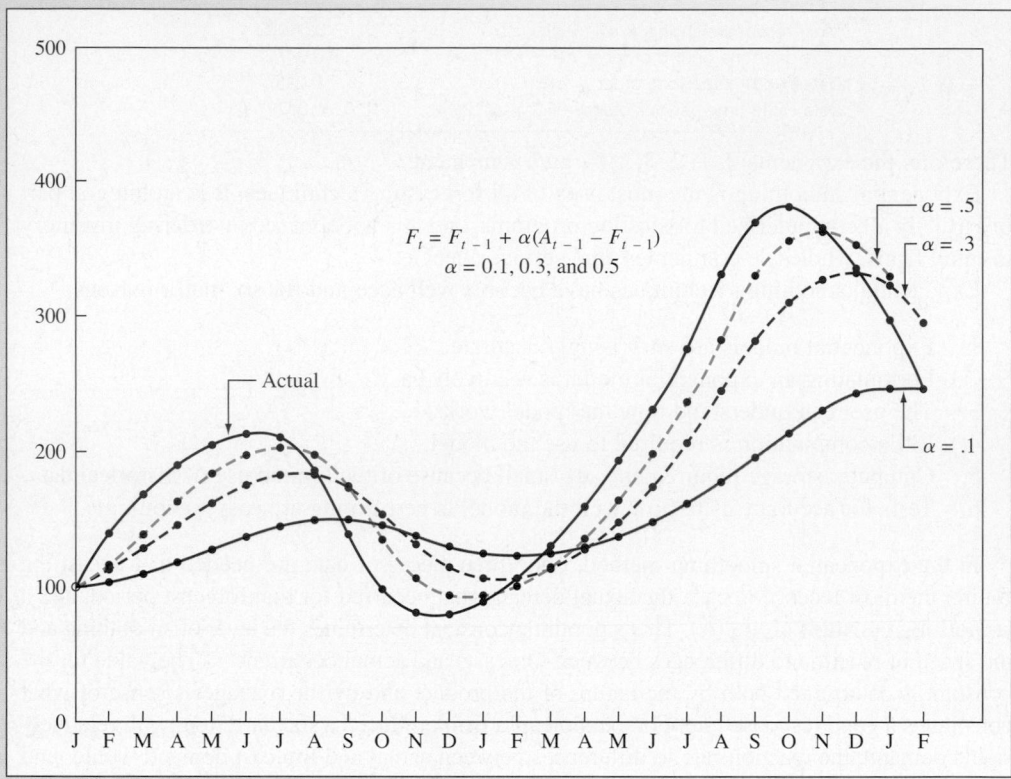

Because the smoothing coefficient is small, the reaction of the new forecast to an error of 50 units is to decrease the next month's forecast by only $2\frac{1}{2}$ units.

Single exponential smoothing has the shortcoming of lagging changes in demand. Exhibit 15.13 presents actual data plotted as a smooth curve to show the lagging effects of the exponential forecasts. The forecast lags during an increase or decrease but overshoots when a change in direction occurs. Note that the higher the value of alpha, the more closely the forecast follows the actual. To more closely track actual demand, a trend factor may be added. Adjusting the value of alpha also helps. This is termed *adaptive forecasting*. Both trend effects and adaptive forecasting are briefly explained in following sections.

Trend Effects in Exponential Smoothing   Remember that an upward or downward trend in data collected over a sequence of time periods causes the exponential forecast to always lag behind (be above or below) the actual occurrence. Exponentially smoothed forecasts can be corrected somewhat by adding in a trend adjustment. To correct the trend, we need two smoothing constants. Besides the smoothing constant α, the trend equation also uses a **smoothing constant delta (δ)**. The delta reduces the impact of the error that occurs between the actual and the forecast. If both alpha and delta are not included, the trend overreacts to errors.

Smoothing constant delta (δ)

To get the trend equation going, the first time it is used the trend value must be entered manually. This initial trend value can be an educated guess or a computation based on observed past data.

The equation to compute the forecast including trend (FIT) is

$$\text{FIT}_t = F_t + T_t \qquad\qquad [15.8]$$
$$F_t = \text{FIT}_{t-1} + \alpha(A_{t-1} - \text{FIT}_{t-1}) \qquad\qquad [15.9]$$
$$T_t = T_{t-1} + \delta(F_t - \text{FIT}_{t-1}) \qquad\qquad [15.10]$$

where

F_t = The exponentially smoothed forecast for period t

T_t = The exponentially smoothed trend for period t

FIT_t = The forecast including trend for period t

FIT_{t-1} = The forecast including trend made for the prior period

A_{t-1} = The actual demand for the prior period

α = Smoothing constant

δ = Smoothing constant

Step by Step

EXAMPLE 15.4: Forecast Including Trend

Assume an initial starting F_t of 100 units, a trend of 10 units, an alpha of 0.20, and a delta of 0.30. If actual demand turned out to be 115 rather than the forecast 100, calculate the forecast for the next period.

SOLUTION

Adding the starting forecast and the trend, we have

$$FIT_{t-1} = F_{t-1} + T_{t-1} = 100 + 10 = 110$$

The actual A_{t-1} is given as 115. Therefore,

$$F_t = FIT_{t-1} + \alpha(A_{t-1} - FIT_{t-1})$$
$$= 110 + 0.2(115 - 110) = 111.0$$
$$T_t = T_{t-1} + \delta(F_t - FIT_{t-1})$$
$$= 10 + 0.3(111 - 110) = 10.3$$
$$FIT_t = F_t + T_t = 111.0 + 10.3 = 121.3$$

If, instead of 121.3, the actual turned out to be 120, the sequence would be repeated and the forecast for the next period would be

$$F_{t+1} = 121.3 + 0.2(120 - 121.3) = 121.04$$
$$T_{t+1} = 10.3 + 0.3(121.04 - 121.3) = 10.22$$
$$FIT_{t+1} = 121.04 + 10.22 = 131.26 \ \bullet$$

Choosing the Appropriate Value for Alpha   Exponential smoothing requires that the smoothing constant alpha (α) be given a value between 0 and 1. If the real demand is stable (such as demand for electricity or food), we would like a small alpha to lessen the effects of short-term or random changes. If the real demand is rapidly increasing or decreasing (such as in fashion items or new small appliances), we would like a large alpha to try to keep up with the change. It would be ideal if we could predict which alpha we should use. Unfortunately, two things work against us. First, it would take some passage of time to determine the alpha that would best fit our actual data. This would be tedious to follow and revise. Second, because demands do change, the alpha we pick this week may need to be revised soon. Therefore, we need some automatic method to track and change our alpha values.

There are two approaches to controlling the value of alpha. One uses various values of alpha. The other uses a tracking signal.

1. **Two or more predetermined values of alpha.**   The amount of error between the forecast and the actual demand is measured. Depending on the degree of error, different values of alpha are used. If the error is large, alpha is 0.8; if the error is small, alpha is 0.2.

2. **Computed values for alpha.**   A tracking alpha computes whether the forecast is keeping pace with genuine upward or downward changes in demand (as opposed to random changes). In this application, the tracking alpha is defined as the exponentially smoothed actual error divided by the exponentially smoothed absolute error. Alpha changes from period to period within the possible range of 0 to 1.

FORECAST ERRORS

In using the word *error,* we are referring to the difference between the forecast value and what actually occurred. In statistics, these errors are called *residuals.* As long as the forecast value is within the confidence limits, as we discuss later in "Measurement of Error," this is not really an error. But common usage refers to the difference as an error.

Demand for a product is generated through the interaction of a number of factors too complex to describe accurately in a model. Therefore, all forecasts certainly contain some error. In discussing forecast errors, it is convenient to distinguish between *sources of error* and the *measurement of error.*

SOURCES OF ERROR

Errors can come from a variety of sources. One common source that many forecasters are unaware of is projecting past trends into the future. For example, when we talk about statistical errors in regression analysis, we are referring to the deviations of observations from our regression line. It is common to attach a confidence band (that is, statistical control limits) to the regression line to reduce the unexplained error. But when we then use this regression line as a forecasting device by projecting it into the future, the error may not be correctly defined by the projected confidence band. This is because the confidence interval is based on past data; it may not hold for projected data points and therefore cannot be used with the same confidence. In fact, experience has shown that the actual errors tend to be greater than those predicted from forecast models.

Errors can be classified as bias or random. *Bias errors* occur when a consistent mistake is made. Sources of bias include the failure to include the right variables; the use of the wrong relationships among variables; employing of the wrong trend line; a mistaken shift in the seasonal demand from where it normally occurs; and the existence of some undetected secular trend. *Random errors* can be defined as those that cannot be explained by the forecast model being used.

MEASUREMENT OF ERROR

Several common terms used to describe the degree of error are *standard error, mean squared error* (or *variance*), and *mean absolute deviation.* In addition, tracking signals may be used to indicate any positive or negative bias in the forecast.

Standard error is discussed in the section on linear regression in this chapter. Because the standard error is the square root of a function, it is often more convenient to use the function itself. This is called the mean square error or variance.

Mean absolute deviation (MAD)

The mean absolute deviation (MAD) was in vogue in the past but subsequently was ignored in favor of standard deviation and standard error measures. In recent years, MAD has made a comeback because of its simplicity and usefulness in obtaining tracking signals. MAD is the average error in the forecasts, using absolute values. It is valuable because MAD, like the standard deviation, measures the dispersion of some observed value from some expected value.

MAD is computed using the differences between the actual demand and the forecast demand without regard to sign. It equals the sum of the absolute deviations divided by the number of data points, or, stated in equation form,

$$\text{MAD} = \frac{\sum_{i=1}^{n} |A_t - F_t|}{n}$$

[15.11]

where

t = Period number

A = Actual demand for the period

F = Forecast demand for the period

n = Total number of periods

$| \ |$ = A symbol used to indicate the absolute value disregarding positive and negative signs

When the errors that occur in the forecast are normally distributed (the usual case), the mean absolute deviation relates to the standard deviation as

$$1 \text{ standard deviation} = \sqrt{\frac{\pi}{2}} \times \text{MAD, or approximately 1.25 MAD}$$

Conversely,

$$1 \text{ MAD} = 0.8 \text{ standard deviation}$$

The standard deviation is the larger measure. If the MAD of a set of points was found to be 60 units, then the standard deviation would be 75 units. In the usual statistical manner, if control limits were set at plus or minus 3 standard deviations (or ±63.75 MADs), then 99.7 percent of the points would fall within these limits.

An additional measure of error that is often useful is the **mean absolute percent error (MAPE)**. This measure gauges the error relative to the average demand. For example, if the MAD is 10 units and average demand is 20 units, the error is large and significant, but relatively insignificant on an average demand of 1,000 units. MAPE is calculated by taking the MAD and dividing by the average demand,

Mean absolute percent error (MAPE)

$$\text{MAPE} = \frac{\text{MAD}}{\text{Average demand}} \qquad \text{[15.12]}$$

This is a useful measure because it is an estimate of how much error to expect with a forecast. So if the MAD were 10 and average demand 20, the MAPE would be 50 percent $\left(\frac{10}{20} = 50\right)$. In the case of an average demand of 1,000 units, the MAPE would be only 1 percent $\left(\frac{10}{1,000} = 1\right)$.

A **tracking signal** is a measurement that indicates whether the forecast average is keeping pace with any genuine upward or downward changes in demand. As used in forecasting, the tracking signal is the *number* of mean absolute deviations that the forecast value is above or below the actual occurrence. Exhibit 15.14 shows a normal distribution with a mean of 0 and a MAD equal to 1. Thus, if we compute the tracking signal and find it equal to minus 2, we can see that the forecast model is providing forecasts that are quite a bit above the mean of the actual occurrences.

Tracking signal

A Normal Distribution with Mean = 0 and MAD = 1

exhibit 15.14

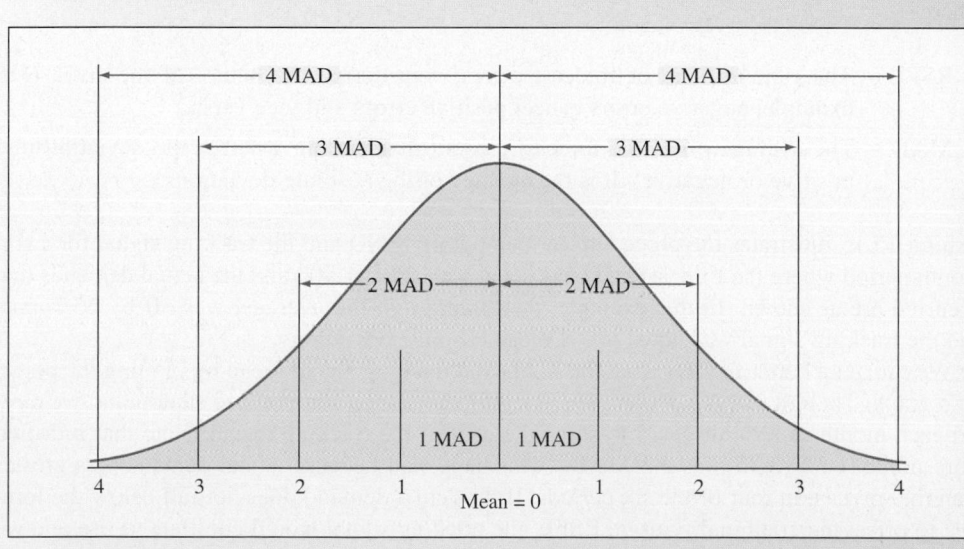

exhibit 15.15

Computing the Mean Absolute Deviation (MAD), the Running Sum of Forecast Errors (RSFE), and the Tracking Signal (TS) from Forecast and Actual Data

Excel:
Forecasting

MONTH	DEMAND FORECAST	ACTUAL	DEVIATION	RSFE	ABS. DEV.	SUM OF ABS. DEV.	MAD*	$TS = \frac{RSFE^{\dagger}}{MAD}$
1	1,000	950	−50	−50	50	50	50	−1
2	1,000	1,070	+70	+20	70	120	60	.33
3	1,000	1,100	+100	+120	100	220	73.3	1.64
4	1,000	960	−40	+80	40	260	65	1.2
5	1,000	1,090	+90	+170	90	350	70	2.4
6	1,000	1,050	+50	+220	50	400	66.7	3.3

*For month 6, MAD = 400 ÷ 6 = 66.7.

†For month 6, $TS = \frac{RSFE}{MAD} = \frac{220}{66.7} = 3.3$ MADs.

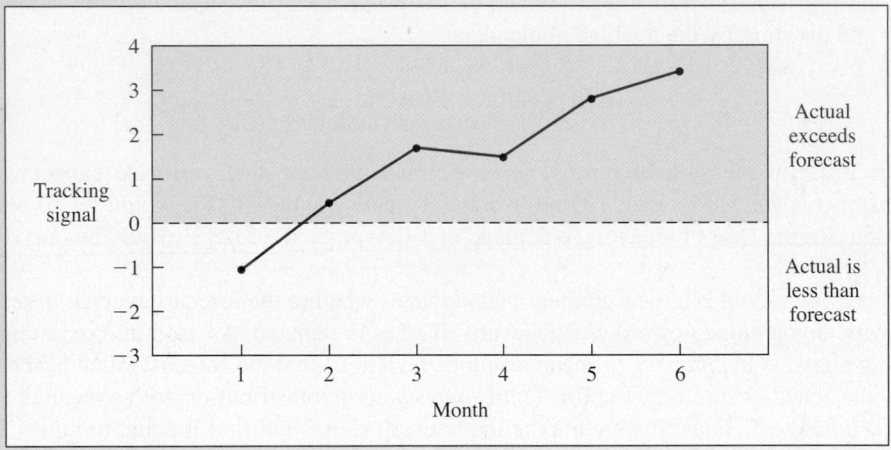

A tracking signal (TS) can be calculated using the arithmetic sum of forecast deviations divided by the mean absolute deviation:

$$TS = \frac{RSFE}{MAD}$$

[15.13]

where

RSFE = The running sum of forecast errors, considering the nature of the error. (For example, negative errors cancel positive errors and vice versa.)

MAD = The average of all the forecast errors (disregarding whether the deviations are positive or negative). It is the average of the absolute deviations.

Exhibit 15.15 illustrates the procedure for computing MAD and the tracking signal for a six-month period where the forecast had been set at a constant 1,000 and the actual demands that occurred are as shown. In this example, the forecast, on the average, was off by 66.7 units and the tracking signal was equal to 3.3 mean absolute deviations.

We can get a better feel for what the MAD and tracking signal mean by plotting the points on a graph. Though this is not completely legitimate from a sample-size standpoint, we plotted each month in Exhibit 15.15 to show the drift of the tracking signal. Note that it drifted from minus 1 MAD to plus 3.3 MADs. This happened because actual demand was greater than the forecast in four of the six periods. If the actual demand does not fall below the forecast to offset the continual positive RSFE, the tracking signal would continue to rise and we would conclude that assuming a demand of 1,000 is a bad forecast.

CAUSAL RELATIONSHIP FORECASTING

Causal relationship forecasting uses independent variables other than time to predict future demand. To be of value for the purpose of forecasting, any independent variable must be a leading indicator. For example, we can expect that an extended period of rain will increase sales of umbrellas and raincoats. The rain causes the sale of rain gear. This is a **causal relationship**, where one occurrence causes another. If the causing element is known far enough in advance, it can be used as a basis for forecasting.

Causal relationship

The first step in causal relationship forecasting is to find those occurrences that are really the causes. Often leading indicators are not causal relationships, but in some indirect way, they may suggest that some other things might happen. Other noncausal relationships just seem to exist as a coincidence. The following shows one example of a forecast using a causal relationship.

EXAMPLE 15.5: Forecasting Using a Causal Relationship

The Carpet City Store in Carpenteria has kept records of its sales (in square yards) each year, along with the number of permits for new houses in its area.

Step by Step

	NUMBER OF HOUSING STARTS	
YEAR	PERMITS	SALES (IN SQ. YDS.)
1999	18	13,000
2000	15	12,000
2001	12	11,000
2002	10	10,000
2003	20	14,000
2004	28	16,000
2005	35	19,000
2006	30	17,000
2007	20	13,000

Carpet City's operations manager believes forecasting sales is possible if housing starts are known for that year. First, the data are plotted in Exhibit 15.16, with

x = Number of housing start permits
y = Sales of carpeting

Causal Relationship: Sales to Housing Starts

exhibit 15.16

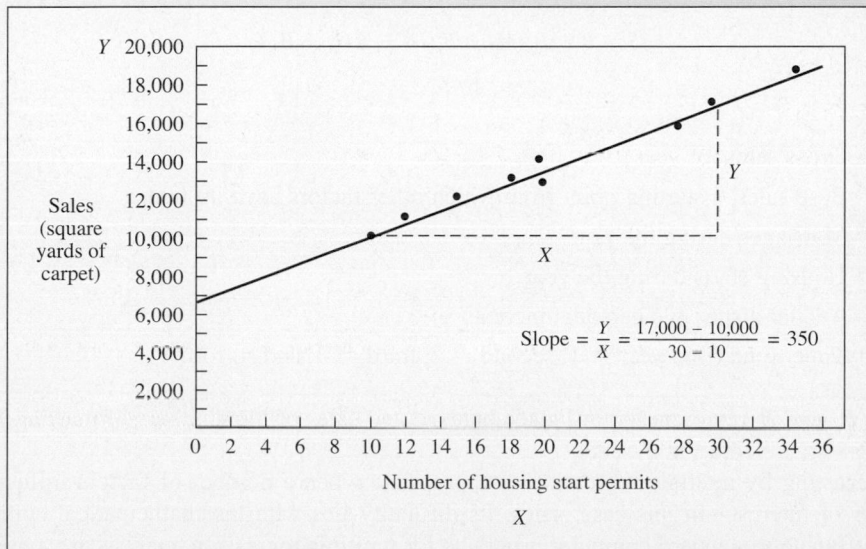

$$\text{Slope} = \frac{Y}{X} = \frac{17,000 - 10,000}{30 - 10} = 350$$

Excel: Forecasting

Because the points appear to be in a straight line, the manager decides to use the linear relationship $Y = \alpha + bx$. We solve this problem by hand fitting a line. We also could solve for this equation using least squares regression as we did earlier.

SOLUTION

Projecting the hand-fit line causes it to intercept the Y axis at about 7,000 yards. This could be interpreted as the demand when no new houses are built, that is, probably as replacement for old carpeting. To estimate the slope, two points are selected, such as

YEAR	x	y
2005	10	10,000
2009	30	17,000

From algebra the slope is calculated as

$$b = \frac{y(2009) - y(2005)}{x(2009) - x(2005)} = \frac{17,000 - 10,000}{30 - 10} = \frac{7,000}{20} = 350$$

The manager interprets the slope as the average number of square yards of carpet sold for each new house built in the area. The forecasting equation is therefore

$$Y = 7,000 + 350x$$

Now suppose that there are 25 permits for houses to be built in 2010. The 2010 sales forecast would therefore be

$$7,000 + 350(25) = 15,750 \text{ square yards}$$

In this problem, the lag between filing the permit with the appropriate agency and the new homeowner coming to Carpet City to buy carpet makes a causal relationship feasible for forecasting. ●

MULTIPLE REGRESSION ANALYSIS

Another forecasting method is multiple regression analysis, in which a number of variables are considered, together with the effects of each on the item of interest. For example, in the home furnishings field, the effects of the number of marriages, housing starts, disposable income, and the trend can be expressed in a multiple regression equation as

$$S = B + B_m(M) + B_h(H) + B_i(I) + B_t(T)$$

where

> S = Gross sales for year
> B = Base sales, a starting point from which other factors have influence
> M = Marriages during the year
> H = Housing starts during the year
> I = Annual disposable personal income
> T = Time trend (first year = 1, second = 2, third = 3, and so forth)

B_m, B_h, B_i, and B_t represent the influence on expected sales of the numbers of marriages and housing starts, income, and trend.

Forecasting by multiple regression is appropriate when a number of factors influence a variable of interest—in this case, sales. Its difficulty lies with the mathematical computation. Fortunately, standard computer programs for multiple regression analysis are available, relieving the need for tedious manual calculation.

Microsoft Excel supports the time series analysis techniques described in this section. These functions are available under the Data Analysis tools for exponential smoothing, moving averages, and regression.

QUALITATIVE TECHNIQUES IN FORECASTING

Qualitative forecasting techniques generally take advantage of the knowledge of experts and require much judgment. These techniques typically involve processes that are well defined to those participating in the forecasting exercise. For example, in the case of forecasting the demand for new fashions merchandise in a retail store, the firm can include a combination of typical customers to express preferences and store managers who understand product mix and store volumes, where they view the merchandise and run through a series of exercises designed to bring the group to a consensus estimate. The point is that these are not wild guesses as to the expected demand but rather involve a well-thought-out and structured decision-making approach.

Service

These techniques are most useful when the product is new or there is little experience with selling into a new region. Here such information as knowledge of similar products, the habits of customers in the area, and how the product will be advertised and introduced may be important to estimate demand successfully. In some cases it may even be useful to consider industry data and the experience of competing firms in making estimates of expected demand.

The following are samples of qualitative forecasting techniques.

MARKET RESEARCH

Firms often hire outside companies that specialize in *market research* to conduct this type of forecasting. You may have been involved in market surveys through a marketing class. Certainly you have not escaped e-mails asking you about product preferences, your income, habits, and so on.

Market research is used mostly for product research in the sense of looking for new product ideas, likes and dislikes about existing products, which competitive products within a particular class are preferred, and so on. Again, the data collection methods are primarily surveys and interviews.

PANEL CONSENSUS

In a *panel consensus,* the idea that two heads are better than one is extrapolated to the idea that a panel of people from a variety of positions can develop a more reliable forecast than a narrower group. Panel forecasts are developed through open meetings with free exchange of ideas from all levels of management and individuals. The difficulty with this open style is that lower employee levels are intimidated by higher levels of management. For example, a salesperson in a particular product line may have a good estimate of future product demand but may not speak up to refute a much different estimate given by the vice president of marketing. The Delphi technique (which we discuss shortly) was developed to try to correct this impairment to free exchange.

When decisions in forecasting are at a broader, higher level (as when introducing a new product line or concerning strategic product decisions such as new marketing areas), the term *executive judgment* is generally used. The term is self-explanatory: a higher level of management is involved.

A NUMBER OF FIRMS, INCLUDING THE GILMORE RESEARCH GROUP, NOW OFFER MARKETERS SOFTWARE OR DATABASES TO HELP THEM MORE ACCURATELY FORECAST SALES FOR SPECIFIC MARKET AREAS, PRODUCTS, OR SEGMENTS.

HISTORICAL ANALOGY

In trying to forecast demand for a new product, an ideal situation would be where an existing product or generic product could be used as a model. There are many ways to classify such analogies—for example, complementary products, substitutable or competitive products, and products as a function of income. Again, you have surely gotten a deluge of mail advertising products in a category similar to a product purchased via catalog, the Internet, or mail order. If you buy a DVD through the mail, you will receive more mail about new DVDs and DVD players. A causal relationship would be that demand for compact discs is caused by demand for DVD players. An analogy would be forecasting the demand for digital videodisc players by analyzing the historical demand for VCRs. The products are in the same general category of electronics and may be bought by consumers at similar rates. A simpler example would be toasters and coffee pots. A firm that already produces toasters and wants to produce coffee pots could use the toaster history as a likely growth model.

DELPHI METHOD

As we mentioned under panel consensus, a statement or opinion of a higher-level person will likely be weighted more than that of a lower-level person. The worst case is where lower-level people feel threatened and do not contribute their true beliefs. To prevent this problem, the *Delphi method* conceals the identity of the individuals participating in the study. Everyone has the same weight. Procedurally, a moderator creates a questionnaire and distributes it to participants. Their responses are summed and given back to the entire group along with a new set of questions.

The step-by-step procedure for the Delphi method is:

1. Choose the experts to participate. There should be a variety of knowledgeable people in different areas.
2. Through a questionnaire (or e-mail), obtain forecasts (and any premises or qualifications for the forecasts) from all participants.
3. Summarize the results and redistribute them to the participants along with appropriate new questions.
4. Summarize again, refining forecasts and conditions, and again develop new questions.
5. Repeat step 4 if necessary. Distribute the final results to all participants.

The Delphi technique can usually achieve satisfactory results in three rounds. The time required is a function of the number of participants, how much work is involved for them to develop their forecasts, and their speed in responding.

WEB-BASED FORECASTING: COLLABORATIVE PLANNING, FORECASTING, AND REPLENISHMENT (CPFR)[5]

Collaborative Planning, Forecasting, and Replenishment (CPFR)

Supply Chain

Collaborative Planning, Forecasting, and Replenishment (CPFR) is a Web-based tool used to coordinate demand forecasting, production and purchase planning, and inventory replenishment between supply chain trading partners. CPFR is being used as a means of integrating all members of an *n*-tier supply chain, including manufacturers, distributors, and retailers. As depicted in Exhibit 15.17, the ideal point of collaboration utilizing CPFR is the retail-level demand forecast, which is successively used to synchronize forecasts, production, and replenishment plans upstream through the supply chain.

Although the methodology is applicable to any industry, CPFR applications to date have largely focused on the food, apparel, and general merchandise industries. The potential benefits of sharing information for enhanced planning visibility in any supply chain are enormous. Various estimates for cost savings attributable to improved supply chain coordination have been proposed, including $30 billion annually in the food industry alone.[6]

n-Tier Supply Chain with Retail Activities

exhibit 15.17

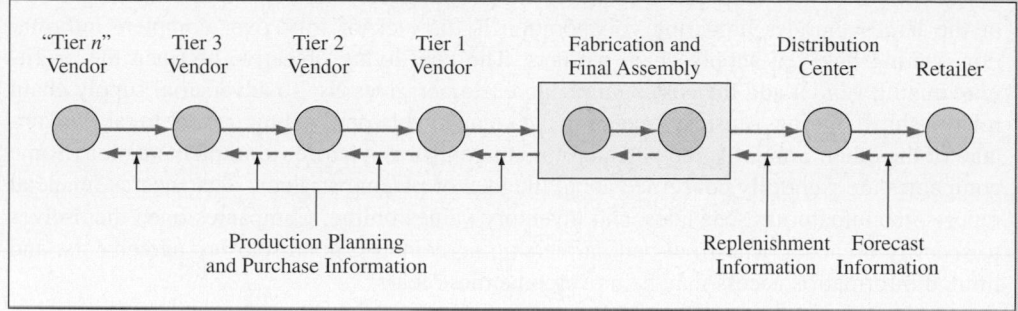

Supply Chain

CPFR's objective is to exchange selected internal information on a shared Web server in order to provide for reliable, longer-term future views of demand in the supply chain. CPFR uses a cyclic and iterative approach to derive consensus supply chain forecasts. It consists of the following five steps:

Step 1. Creation of a front-end partnership agreement. This agreement specifies (1) objectives (e.g., inventory reductions, lost sale elimination, lower product obsolescence) to be gained through collaboration, (2) resource requirements (e.g., hardware, software, performance metrics) necessary for the collaboration, and (3) expectations of confidentiality concerning the prerequisite trust necessary to share sensitive company information, which represents a major implementation obstacle.

Step 2. Joint business planning. Typically partners create partnership strategies, design a joint calendar identifying the sequence and frequency of planning activities to follow that affect product flows, and specify exception criteria for handling planning variances between the trading partners' demand forecasts.

Step 3. Development of demand forecasts. Forecast development may follow pre-existing company procedures. Retailers should play a critical role as shared *point-of-sale* (POS) data permit the development of more accurate and timely expectations (compared with extrapolated warehouse withdrawals or aggregate store orders) for both retailers and vendors. Given the frequency of forecast generation and the potential for vast numbers of items requiring forecast preparation, a simple forecast procedure such as a moving average is commonly used within CPFR. Simple techniques are easily used in conjunction with expert knowledge of promotional or pricing events to modify forecast values accordingly.

Step 4. Sharing forecasts. Retailer (order forecasts) and vendor (sales forecasts) then electronically post their latest forecasts for a list of products on a shared, dedicated server. The server examines pairs of corresponding forecasts and issues an exception notice for any forecast pair where the difference exceeds a preestablished safety margin (e.g., 5 percent). If the safety margin is exceeded, planners from both firms may collaborate electronically to derive a consensus forecast.

Step 5. Inventory replenishment. Once the corresponding forecasts are in agreement, the order forecast becomes an actual order, which commences the replenishment process. Each of these steps is then repeated iteratively in a continuous cycle, at varying times, by individual products and the calendar of events established between trading partners. For example, partners may review the front-end partnership agreement annually, evaluate the joint business plans quarterly, develop forecasts weekly to monthly, and replenish daily.

The early exchange of information between trading partners provides for reliable, longer-term future views of demand in the supply chain. The forward visibility based upon information sharing leads to a variety of benefits within supply chain partnerships.

As with most new corporate initiatives, there is skepticism and resistance to change. One of the largest hurdles hindering collaboration is the lack of trust over complete information sharing between supply chain partners. The conflicting objective between the profit-maximizing vendor and the cost-minimizing customer gives rise to adversarial supply chain relationships. Sharing sensitive operating data may enable one trading partner to take advantage of the other. Similarly, the potential loss of control is a barrier to implementation. Some companies are rightfully concerned about the idea of placing strategic data such as financial reports, manufacturing schedules, and inventory values online. Companies open themselves to security breaches. The front-end partnership agreements, nondisclosure agreements, and limited information access may help overcome these fears.

SUMMARY

Developing a forecasting system is not easy. However, it must be done because forecasting is fundamental to any planning effort. In the short run, a forecast is needed to predict the requirements for materials, products, services, or other resources to respond to changes in demand. Forecasts permit adjusting schedules and varying labor and materials. In the long run, forecasting is required as a basis for strategic changes, such as developing new markets, developing new products or services, and expanding or creating new facilities.

For medium and long-term strategic forecasts that lead to heavy financial commitments, great care should be taken to derive the forecast. Several approaches should be used. Regression analysis or multiple regression analysis are best suited for these problems. These provide a basis for discussion. Economic factors, product trends, growth factors, and competition, as well as myriad other possible variables, need to be considered and the forecast adjusted to reflect the influence of each.

Short- and intermediate-term forecasting (such as required for inventory control as well as staffing and material scheduling) may be satisfied with simpler models, such as exponential smoothing with perhaps an adaptive feature or a seasonal index. In these applications, thousands of items are usually being forecast. The forecasting routine should therefore be simple and run quickly on a computer. The routines also should detect and respond rapidly to definite short-term changes in demand while at the same time ignoring the occasional spurious demands. Exponential smoothing, when monitored by management to control the value of alpha, is an effective technique.

Web-based collaborative forecasting systems that use combinations of the forecasting methods will be the wave of the future in many industries. Information sharing between trading partners with direct links into each firm's ERP system ensures rapid and error-free information, at very low cost.

In summary, forecasting is tough. A perfect forecast is like a hole in one in golf: great to get but we should be satisfied just to get close to the cup—or, to push the analogy, just to land on the green. The ideal philosophy is to create the best forecast that you reasonably can and then hedge by maintaining flexibility in the system to account for the inevitable forecast error.

KEY TERMS

Strategic forecasts Medium and long-term forecasts that are used to make decisions related to design and plans for meeting demand.

Tactical forecasts Short-term forecasts used as input for making day-to-day decisions related to meeting demand.

Dependent demand Requirements for a product or service caused by the demand for other products or services. This type of internal demand does not need a forecast, but can be calculated based on the demand for the other products or services.

Independent demand Demand that cannot be directly derived from the demand for other products.

Time series analysis A type of forecast in which data relating to past demand are used to predict future demand.

Linear regression forecasting A forecasting technique that assumes that past data and future projections fall around a straight line.

Exponential smoothing A time series forecasting technique in which each increment of past demand data is decreased by $(1 - \alpha)$.

Smoothing constant alpha (α) The parameter in the exponential smoothing equation that controls the speed of reaction to differences between forecasts and actual demand.

Smoothing constant delta (δ) An additional parameter used in an exponential smoothing equation that includes an adjustment for trend.

Mean absolute deviation (MAD) The average forecast error using absolute values of the error of each past forecast.

Mean absolute percent error (MAPE) The mean absolute deviation divided by the average demand. The average error expressed as a percentage of demand.

Tracking signal A measure that indicates whether the forecast average is keeping pace with any genuine upward or downward changes in demand.

Causal relationship A situation in which one event causes another. If the event is far enough in the future, it can be used as a basis for forecasting.

Collaborative Planning, Forecasting, and Replenishment (CPFR) An Internet tool to coordinate forecasting, production, and purchasing in a firm's supply chain.

FORMULA REVIEW

Least squares regression

$$Y = a + bx \qquad \text{[15.1]}$$

$$a = \bar{y} - b\bar{x} \qquad \text{[15.2]}$$

$$b = \frac{\Sigma xy - n\bar{x} \cdot \bar{y}}{\Sigma x^2 - n\bar{x}^2} \qquad \text{[15.3]}$$

Standard error of estimate

$$S_{yx} = \sqrt{\frac{\sum_{i=1}^{n}(y_i - Y_i)^2}{n - 2}} \qquad \text{[15.4]}$$

Simple moving average

$$F_t = \frac{A_{t-1} + A_{t-2} + A_{t-3} + \cdots + A_{t-n}}{n} \qquad \text{[15.5]}$$

Weighted moving average

$$F_t = w_1 A_{t-1} + w_2 A_{t-2} + \cdots + w_n A_{t-n} \qquad \text{[15.6]}$$

Single exponential smoothing

$$F_t = F_{t-1} + \alpha(A_{t-1} - F_{t-1}) \qquad \text{[15.7]}$$

Exponential smoothing with trend

$$\text{FIT}_t = F_t + T_t \qquad \text{[15.8]}$$

$$F_t = \text{FIT}_{t-1} + \alpha(A_{t-1} - \text{FIT}_{t-1}) \qquad \text{[15.9]}$$

$$T_t = T_{t-1} + \delta(F_t - \text{FIT}_{t-1}) \qquad \text{[15.10]}$$

Mean absolute deviation

$$\text{MAD} = \frac{\sum_{i=1}^{n}|A_t - F_t|}{n} \qquad \text{[15.11]}$$

Mean absolute percent error

$$\text{MAPE} = \frac{\text{MAD}}{\text{Average demand}} \qquad \text{[15.12]}$$

Tracking signal

$$TS = \frac{RSFE}{MAD}$$

[15.13]

SOLVED PROBLEMS

SOLVED PROBLEM 1

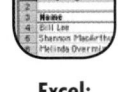

**Excel:
Forecasting**

Here are quarterly data for the past two years. From these data, prepare a forecast for the upcoming year using decomposition.

PERIOD	ACTUAL	PERIOD	ACTUAL
1	300	5	416
2	540	6	760
3	885	7	1191
4	580	8	760

Solution

(Note that the values you obtain may be slightly different due to rounding. The values given here were obtained using an Excel spreadsheet.)

(1) PERIOD x	(2) ACTUAL y	(3) PERIOD AVERAGE	(4) SEASONAL FACTOR	(5) DESEASONALIZED DEMAND
1	300	358	0.527	568.99
2	540	650	0.957	564.09
3	885	1,038	1.529	578.92
4	580	670	0.987	587.79
5	416		0.527	789.01
6	760		0.957	793.91
7	1,191		1.529	779.08
8	760		0.987	770.21
Total	5,432	2,716	8.0	
Average	679	679	1	

Column 3 is seasonal average. For example, the first-quarter average is

$$\frac{300 + 416}{2} = 358$$

Column 4 is the quarter average (column 3) divided by the overall average (679). Column 5 is the actual data divided by the seasonal index. To determine x^2 and xy, we can construct a table as follows:

PERIOD x	DESEASONALIZED DEMAND (y_d)	x^2	xy
1	568.99	1	569.0
2	564.09	4	1128.2
3	578.92	9	1736.7
4	587.79	16	2351.2
5	789.01	25	3945.0
6	793.91	36	4763.4
7	779.08	49	5453.6
8	770.21	64	6161.7
Sums	36	5,432	204	26,108.8
Average	4.5	679		

Now we calculate regression results for deseasonalized data.

$$b = \frac{(26108) - (8)(4.5)(679)}{(204) - (8)(4.5)^2} = 39.64$$

$$a = \bar{Y} - b\bar{x}$$

$$a = 679 - 39.64(4.5) = 500.6$$

Therefore, the deseasonalized regression results are

$$Y = 500.6 + 39.64x$$

PERIOD	TREND FORECAST		SEASONAL FACTOR		FINAL FORECAST
9	857.4	×	0.527	=	452.0
10	897.0	×	0.957	=	858.7
11	936.7	×	1.529	=	1431.9
12	976.3	×	0.987	=	963.4

SOLVED PROBLEM 2

Sunrise Baking Company markets doughnuts through a chain of food stores. It has been experiencing over- and underproduction because of forecasting errors. The following data are its demand in dozens of doughnuts for the past four weeks. Doughnuts are made for the following day; for example, Sunday's doughnut production is for Monday's sales, Monday's production is for Tuesday's sales, and so forth. The bakery is closed Saturday, so Friday's production must satisfy demand for both Saturday and Sunday.

Excel: Forecasting

	4 WEEKS AGO	3 WEEKS AGO	2 WEEKS AGO	LAST WEEK
Monday	2,200	2,400	2,300	2,400
Tuesday	2,000	2,100	2,200	2,200
Wednesday	2,300	2,400	2,300	2,500
Thursday	1,800	1,900	1,800	2,000
Friday	1,900	1,800	2,100	2,000
Saturday				
Sunday	2,800	2,700	3,000	2,900

Make a forecast for this week on the following basis:
a. Daily, using a simple four-week moving average.
b. Daily, using a weighted average of 0.40, 0.30, 0.20, and 0.10 for the past four weeks.
c. Sunrise is also planning its purchases of ingredients for bread production. If bread demand had been forecast for last week at 22,000 loaves and only 21,000 loaves were actually demanded, what would Sunrise's forecast be for this week using exponential smoothing with $\alpha = 0.10$?
d. Suppose, with the forecast made in *c*, this week's demand actually turns out to be 22,500. What would the new forecast be for the next week?

Solution

a. Simple moving average, four-week.

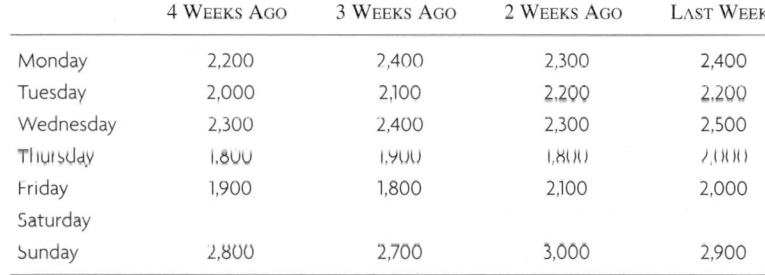

Monday $\dfrac{2,400 + 2,300 + 2,400 + 2,200}{4} = \dfrac{9,300}{4} = 2,325$ doz.

Tuesday $= \dfrac{8,500}{4} = 2,125$ doz.

Wednesday $= \dfrac{9,500}{4} = 2,375$ doz.

Thursday $= \dfrac{7,500}{4} = 1,875$ doz.

Friday $= \dfrac{7,800}{4} = 1,950$ doz.

Saturday and Sunday $= \dfrac{11,400}{4} = 2,850$ doz.

b. Weighted average with weights of .40, .30, .20, and .10.

	(.10)		(.20)		(.30)		(.40)		
Monday	220	+	480	+	690	+	960	=	2,350
Tuesday	200	+	420	+	660	+	880	=	2,160
Wednesday	230	+	480	+	690	+	1,000	=	2,400
Thursday	180	+	380	+	540	+	800	=	1,900
Friday	190	+	360	+	630	+	800	=	1,980
Saturday and Sunday	280	+	540	+	900	+	1,160	=	2,880
	1,300	+	2,660	+	4,110	+	5,600	=	13,670

c. Exponentially smoothed forecast for bread demand

$$F_t = F_{t-1} + \alpha(A_{t-1} - F_{t-1})$$
$$= 22,000 + 0.10(21,000 - 22,000)$$
$$= 22,000 - 100 = 21,900 \text{ loaves}$$

d. Exponentially smoothed forecast

$$F_{t+1} = 21,900 + .10(22,500 - 21,900)$$
$$= 21,900 + .10(600) = 21,960 \text{ loaves}$$

SOLVED PROBLEM 3

Here are the actual demands for a product for the past six quarters. Using focus forecasting rules 1 through 5, find the best rule to use in predicting the third quarter of this year.

	QUARTER			
	I	II	III	IV
Last year	1,200	700	900	1,100
This year	1,400	1,000		

Solution

Rule 1: Next three months' demand = Last three months' demand.

Testing this on the last three months, $F_{II} = A_1$; therefore, $F_{II} = 1,400$.
Actual demand was 1,000, so $\frac{1,000}{1,400} = 71.4\%$.

Rule 2: This quarter's demand equals demand in the same quarter last year.
The forecast for the second quarter this year will therefore be 700, the amount for that quarter last year.

Actual demand was 1,000, and $\frac{1,000}{700} = 142.9\%$.

Rule 3: 10 percent more than last quarter.

$$F_{II} = 1,400 \times 1.10 = 1,540$$
Actual was 1,000, and $\frac{1,000}{1,540} = 64.9\%$.

Rule 4: 50 percent more than same quarter last year.

$$F_{II} = 700 \times 1.50 = 1,050$$
Actual was 1,000, and $\frac{1,000}{1,050} = 95.2\%$.

Rule 5: Same rate of increase or decrease as last three months.

$$\frac{1,400}{1,200} = 1.167$$

$$F_{II} = 700 \times 1.167 = 816.7$$

Actual was 1,000, so $\frac{1,000}{816.7} = 122.4\%$.

Rule 4 was the closest in predicting the recent quarter—95.2 percent, or just 4.8 percent under. Using this rule (50 percent more than the same quarter last year), we would forecast the third quarter this year as 50 percent more than the third quarter last year, or

$$\text{This year } F_{III} = 1.50\, A_{III} \quad \text{(last year)}$$
$$F_{III} = 1.50(900) = 1,350 \text{ units}$$

SOLVED PROBLEM 4

Excel: Forecasting

A specific forecasting model was used to forecast demand for a product. The forecasts and the corresponding demand that subsequently occurred are shown below. Use the MAD and tracking signal technique to evaluate the accuracy of the forecasting model.

	ACTUAL	FORECAST
October	700	660
November	760	840
December	780	750
January	790	835
February	850	910
March	950	890

Solution

Evaluate the forecasting model using MAD and tracking signal.

	ACTUAL DEMAND	FORECAST DEMAND	ACTUAL DEVIATION	CUMULATIVE DEVIATION (RSFE)	ABSOLUTE DEVIATION
October	700	660	40	40	40
November	760	840	−80	−40	80
December	780	750	30	−10	30
January	790	835	−45	−55	45
February	850	910	−60	−115	60
March	950	890	60	−55	60
					Total dev. = 315

$$\text{MAD} = \frac{315}{6} = 52.5$$
$$\text{Tracking signal} = \frac{-55}{52.5} = -1.05$$

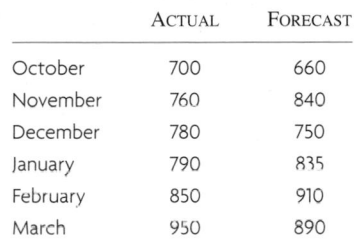

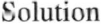

−1.05

There is not enough evidence to reject the forecasting model, so we accept its recommendations.

REVIEW AND DISCUSSION QUESTIONS

1   Examine Exhibit 15.3 and suggest which model you might use for (*a*) bathing suit demand, (*b*) demand for new houses, (*c*) electrical power usage, (*d*) new plant expansion plans.

2   What is the logic in the least squares method of linear regression analysis?

3   Explain the procedure to create a forecast using the decomposition method of least squares regression.

4   Give some very simple rules you might use to manage demand for a firm's product. (An example is "limited to stock on hand.")

5   What strategies are used by supermarkets, airlines, hospitals, banks, and cereal manufacturers to influence demand?

6   All forecasting methods using exponential smoothing, adaptive smoothing, and exponential smoothing including trend require starting values to get the equations going. How would you select the starting value for, say, F_{t-1}?

7   From the choice of simple moving average, weighted moving average, exponential smoothing, and linear regression analysis, which forecasting technique would you consider the most accurate? Why?

8   Give some examples that have a multiplicative seasonal trend relationship.

9   What is the main disadvantage of daily forecasting using regression analysis?

10   What are the main problems with using adaptive exponential smoothing in forecasting?

11   How is a seasonal index computed from a regression line analysis?

12   Discuss the basic differences between the mean absolute deviation and the standard deviation.

13   What implications do forecast errors have for the search for ultrasophisticated statistical forecasting models?

14   Causal relationships are potentially useful for which component of a time series?

PROBLEMS

1   Demand for stereo headphones and MP3 players for joggers has caused Nina Industries to grow almost 50 percent over the past year. The number of joggers continues to expand, so Nina expects demand for headsets to also expand, because, as yet, no safety laws have been passed to prevent joggers from wearing them. Demand for the stereo units for last year was as follows:

MONTH	DEMAND (UNITS)	MONTH	DEMAND (UNITS)
January	4,200	July	5,300
February	4,300	August	4,900
March	4,000	September	5,400
April	4,400	October	5,700
May	5,000	November	6,300
June	4,700	December	6,000

a.   Using least squares regression analysis, what would you estimate demand to be for each month next year? Using a spreadsheet, follow the general format in Exhibit 15.5. Compare your results to those obtained by using the forecast spreadsheet function.

b.   To be reasonably confident of meeting demand, Nina decides to use three standard errors of estimate for safety. How many additional units should be held to meet this level of confidence?

2   Historical demand for a product is

	DEMAND
January	12
February	11
March	15
April	12
May	16
June	15

a. Using a weighted moving average with weights of 0.60, 0.30, and 0.10, find the July forecast.

b. Using a simple three-month moving average, find the July forecast.

c. Using single exponential smoothing with $\alpha = 0.2$ and a June forecast $= 13$, find the July forecast. Make whatever assumptions you wish.

d. Using simple linear regression analysis, calculate the regression equation for the preceding demand data.

e. Using the regression equation in *d*, calculate the forecast for July.

3   The following tabulations are actual sales of units for six months and a starting forecast in January.

a. Calculate forecasts for the remaining five months using simple exponential smoothing with $\alpha = 0.2$.

b. Calculate MAD for the forecasts.

	ACTUAL	FORECAST
January	100	80
February	94	
March	106	
April	80	
May	68	
June	94	

4   Zeus Computer Chips, Inc., used to have major contracts to produce the Centrino-type chips. The market has been declining during the past three years because of the dual-core chips, which it cannot produce, so Zeus has the unpleasant task of forecasting next year. The task is unpleasant because the firm has not been able to find replacement chips for its product lines. Here is demand over the past 12 quarters:

2007		2008		2009	
I	4,800	I	3,500	I	3,200
II	3,500	II	2,700	II	2,100
III	4,300	III	3,500	III	2,700
IV	3,000	IV	2,400	IV	1,700

Use the decomposition technique to forecast the four quarters of 2010.

5   Sales data for two years are as follows. Data are aggregated with two months of sales in each "period."

MONTHS	SALES	MONTHS	SALES
January–February	109	January–February	115
March–April	104	March–April	112
May–June	150	May–June	159
July–August	170	July–August	182
September–October	120	September–October	126
November–December	100	November–December	106

a. Plot the data.

b. Fit a simple linear regression model to the sales data.

c. In addition to the regression model, determine multiplicative seasonal index factors. A full cycle is assumed to be a full year.

d. Using the results from parts *b* and *c*, prepare a forecast for the next year.

6   The tracking signals computed using past demand history for three different products are as follows. Each product used the same forecasting technique.

	TS 1	TS 2	TS 3
1	−2.70	1.54	0.10
2	−2.32	−0.64	0.43
3	−1.70	2.05	1.08
4	−1.10	2.58	1.74
5	−0.87	−0.95	1.94
6	−0.05	−1.23	2.24
7	0.10	0.75	2.96
8	0.40	−1.59	3.02
9	1.50	0.47	3.54
10	2.20	2.74	3.75

Discuss the tracking signals for each and what the implications are.

7   The following table shows the past two years of quarterly sales information. Assume that there are both trend and seasonal factors and that the seasonal cycle is one year. Use time series decomposition to forecast quarterly sales for the next year.

QUARTER	SALES	QUARTER	SALES
1	160	5	215
2	195	6	240
3	150	7	205
4	140	8	190

8   Tucson Machinery, Inc., manufactures numerically controlled machines, which sell for an average price of $0.5 million each. Sales for these NCMs for the past two years were as follows:

QUARTER	QUANTITY (UNITS)	QUARTER	QUANTITY (UNITS)
2008		2009	
I	12	I	16
II	18	II	24
III	26	III	28
IV	16	IV	18

a. Hand fit a line (or do a regression using Excel).
b. Find the trend and seasonal factors.
c. Forecast sales for 2010.

9   Not all the items in your office supply store are evenly distributed as far as demand is concerned, so you decide to forecast demand to help plan your stock. Past data for legal-sized yellow tablets for the month of August are

Week 1	300	Week 3	600
Week 2	400	Week 4	700

a. Using a three-week moving average, what would you forecast the next week to be?
b. Using exponential smoothing with $\alpha = 0.20$, if the exponential forecast for week 3 was estimated as the average of the first two weeks [(300 + 400)/2 = 350], what would you forecast week 5 to be?

10   Given the following history, use focus forecasting to forecast the third quarter of this year. Use three focus forecasting strategies.

	JAN	FEB	MAR	APR	MAY	JUN	JUL	AUG	SEP	OCT	NOV	DEC
Last year	100	125	135	175	185	200	150	140	130	200	225	250
This year	125	135	135	190	200	190						

11   Here are the actual tabulated demands for an item for a nine-month period (January through September). Your supervisor wants to test two forecasting methods to see which method was better over this period.

Month	Actual	Month	Actual
January	110	June	180
February	130	July	140
March	150	August	130
April	170	September	140
May	160		

a. Forecast April through September using a three-month moving average.
b. Use simple exponential smoothing with an alpha of .3 to estimate April through September.
c. Use MAD to decide which method produced the better forecast over the six-month period.

12 A particular forecasting model was used to forecast a six-month period. Here are the forecasts and actual demands that resulted:

	Forecast	Actual
April	250	200
May	325	250
June	400	325
July	350	300
August	375	325
September	450	400

Find the tracking signal and state whether you think the model being used is giving acceptable answers.

13 Harlen Industries has a simple forecasting model: Take the actual demand for the same month last year and divide that by the number of fractional weeks in that month. This gives the average weekly demand for that month. This weekly average is used as the weekly forecast for the same month this year. This technique was used to forecast eight weeks for this year, which are shown below along with the actual demand that occurred.

Week	Forecast Demand	Actual Demand	Week	Forecast Demand	Actual Demand
1	140	137	5	140	180
2	140	133	6	150	170
3	140	150	7	150	185
4	140	160	8	150	205

a. Compute the MAD of forecast errors.
b. Using the RSFE, compute the tracking signal.
c. Based on your answers to a and b, comment on Harlen's method of forecasting.

14 The following table contains the demand from the last 10 months:

Month	Actual Demand	Month	Actual Demand
1	31	6	36
2	34	7	38
3	33	8	40
4	35	9	40
5	37	10	41

a. Calculate the single exponential smoothing forecast for these data using an α of .30 and an initial forecast (F_1) of 31.
b. Calculate the exponential smoothing with trend forecast for these data using an α of .30, a δ of .30, an initial trend forecast (T_1) of 1, and an initial exponentially smoothed forecast (F_1) of 30.
c. Calculate the mean absolute deviation (MAD) for each forecast. Which is best?

15 In this problem, you are to test the validity of your forecasting model. Here are the forecasts for a model you have been using and the actual demands that occurred:

WEEK	FORECAST	ACTUAL
1	800	900
2	850	1,000
3	950	1,050
4	950	900
5	1,000	900
6	975	1,100

Use the method stated in the text to compute the MAD and tracking signal. Then decide whether the forecasting model you have been using is giving reasonable results.

16 Assume that your stock of sales merchandise is maintained based on the forecast demand. If the distributor's sales personnel call on the first day of each month, compute your forecast sales by each of the three methods requested here.

	ACTUAL
June	140
July	180
August	170

a. Using a simple three-month moving average, what is the forecast for September?
b. Using a weighted moving average, what is the forecast for September with weights of .20, .30, and .50 for June, July, and August, respectively?
c. Using single exponential smoothing and assuming that the forecast for June had been 130, forecast sales for September with a smoothing constant alpha of .30.

17 Historical demand for a product is as follows:

	DEMAND
April	60
May	55
June	75
July	60
August	80
September	75

a. Using a simple four-month moving average, calculate a forecast for October.
b. Using single exponential smoothing with $\alpha = 0.2$ and a September forecast $= 65$, calculate a forecast for October.
c. Using simple linear regression, calculate the trend line for the historical data. Say the X axis is April $= 1$, May $= 2$, and so on, while the Y axis is demand.
d. Calculate a forecast for October.

18 Sales by quarter for last year and the first three quarters of this year were as follows:

	QUARTER			
	I	II	III	IV
Last year	23,000	27,000	18,000	9,000
This year	19,000	24,000	15,000	

Using the focus forecasting procedure described in the text, forecast expected sales for the fourth quarter of this year.

19 The following table shows predicted product demand using your particular forecasting method along with the actual demand that occurred:

FORECAST	ACTUAL
1,500	1,550
1,400	1,500
1,700	1,600
1,750	1,650
1,800	1,700

   a. Compute the tracking signal using the mean absolute deviation and running sum of forecast errors.

   b. Discuss whether your forecasting method is giving good predictions.

20 Your manager is trying to determine what forecasting method to use. Based upon the following historical data, calculate the following forecast and specify what procedure you would utilize.

MONTH	ACTUAL DEMAND	MONTH	ACTUAL DEMAND
1	62	7	76
2	65	8	78
3	67	9	78
4	68	10	80
5	71	11	84
6	73	12	85

   a. Calculate the simple three-month moving average forecast for periods 4–12.

   b. Calculate the weighted three-month moving average using weights of 0.50, 0.30, and 0.20 for periods 4–12.

   c. Calculate the single exponential smoothing forecast for periods 2–12 using an initial forecast (F_1) of 61 and an α of 0.30.

   d. Calculate the exponential smoothing with trend component forecast for periods 2–12 using an initial trend forecast (T_1) of 1.8, an initial exponential smoothing forecast (F_1) of 60, an α of 0.30, and a δ of 0.30.

   e. Calculate the mean absolute deviation (MAD) for the forecasts made by each technique in periods 4–12. Which forecasting method do you prefer?

21 Use regression analysis on deseasonalized demand to forecast demand in summer 2010, given the following historical demand data:

YEAR	SEASON	ACTUAL DEMAND
2008	Spring	205
	Summer	140
	Fall	375
	Winter	575
2009	Spring	475
	Summer	275
	Fall	685
	Winter	965

22 Here are the data for the past 21 months for actual sales of a particular product:

	2008	2009
January	300	275
February	400	375
March	425	350
April	450	425
May	400	400
June	460	350
July	400	350
August	300	275
September	375	350
October	500	
November	550	
December	500	

Develop a forecast for the fourth quarter using three different focus forecasting rules. (Note that to correctly use this procedure, the rules are first tested on the third quarter; the best-performing one is used to forecast the fourth quarter.) Do the problem using quarters, as opposed to forecasting separate months.

23 Actual demand for a product for the past three months was

Three months ago	400 units
Two months ago	350 units
Last month	325 units

a. Using a simple three-month moving average, make a forecast for this month.

b. If 300 units were actually demanded this month, what would your forecast be for next month?

c. Using simple exponential smoothing, what would your forecast be for this month if the exponentially smoothed forecast for three months ago was 450 units and the smoothing constant was 0.20?

24 After using your forecasting model for six months, you decide to test it using MAD and a tracking signal. Here are the forecast and actual demands for the six-month period:

PERIOD	FORECAST	ACTUAL
May	450	500
June	500	550
July	550	400
August	600	500
September	650	675
October	700	600

a. Find the tracking signal.

b. Decide whether your forecasting routine is acceptable.

25 Here are earnings per share for two companies by quarter from the first quarter of 2006 through the second quarter of 2009. Forecast earnings per share for the rest of 2009 and 2010. Use exponential smoothing to forecast the third period of 2009, and the time series decomposition method to forecast the last two quarters of 2009 and all four quarters of 2010. (It is much easier to solve this problem on a computer spreadsheet so you can see what is happening.)

EARNINGS PER SHARE

	QUARTER	COMPANY A	COMPANY B
2006	I	$1.67	$0.17
	II	2.35	0.24
	III	1.11	0.26
	IV	1.15	0.34
2007	I	1.56	0.25
	II	2.04	0.37
	III	1.14	0.36
	IV	0.38	0.44
2008	I	0.29	0.33
	II	−0.18 (loss)	0.40
	III	−0.97 (loss)	0.41
	IV	0.20	0.47
2009	I	−1.54 (loss)	0.30
	II	0.38	0.47

a. For the exponential smoothing method, choose the first quarter of 2006 as the beginning forecast. Make two forecasts, one with $\alpha = 0.10$ and one with $\alpha = 0.30$.

b. Using the MAD method of testing the forecasting model's performance, plus actual data from 2006 through the second quarter of 2009, how well did the model perform?

c. Using the decomposition of a time series method of forecasting, forecast earnings per share for the last two quarters of 2009 and all four quarters of 2010. Is there a seasonal factor in the earnings?

d. Using your forecasts, comment on each company.

26 The following are sales revenues for a large utility company for 1999 through 2009. Forecast revenue for 2010 through 2013. Use your own judgment, intuition, or common sense concerning which model or method to use, as well as the period of data to include.

	REVENUE (MILLIONS)		REVENUE (MILLIONS)
1999	$4,865.9	2005	$5,094.4
2000	5,067.4	2006	5,108.8
2001	5,515.6	2007	5,550.6
2002	5,728.8	2008	5,738.9
2003	5,497.7	2009	5,860.0
2004	5,197.7		

27 Mark Price, the new productions manager for Speakers and Company, needs to find out which variable most affects the demand for the company's line of stereo speakers. He is uncertain whether the unit price of the product or the effects of increased marketing are the main drivers in sales and wants to use regression analysis to figure out which factor drives more demand for its particular market. Pertinent information was collected by an extensive marketing project that lasted over the past 10 years and was reduced to the data that follow:

YEAR	SALES/UNIT (THOUSANDS)	PRICE/UNIT	ADVERTISING ($000)
1998	400	280	600
1999	700	215	835
2000	900	211	1,100
2001	1,300	210	1,400
2002	1,150	215	1,200
2003	1,200	200	1,300
2004	900	225	900
2005	1,100	207	1,100
2006	980	220	700
2007	1,234	211	900
2008	925	227	700
2009	800	245	690

a. Perform a regression analysis based on these data using Excel. Answer the following questions based on your results.
b. Which variable, price or advertising, has a larger effect on sales and how do you know?
c. Predict average yearly speaker sales for Speakers and Company based on the regression results if the price was $300 per unit and the amount spent on advertising (in thousands) was $900.

28 Assume an initial starting F_t of 300 units, a trend of eight units, an alpha of 0.30, and a delta of 0.40. If actual demand turned out to be 288, calculate the forecast for the next period.

29 The following table contains the number of complaints received in a department store for the first six months of operation.

MONTH	COMPLAINTS	MONTH	COMPLAINTS
January	36	April	90
February	45	May	108
March	81	June	144

If a three-month moving average is used to smooth this series, what would have been the forecast for May?

30 The number of cases of merlot wine sold by the Connor Owen winery in an eight-year period is as follows:

YEAR	CASES OF MERLOT WINE	YEAR	CASES OF MERLOT WINE
2002	270	2006	358
2003	356	2007	500
2004	398	2008	410
2005	456	2009	376

Using an exponential smoothing model with an alpha value of 0.20, estimate the smoothed value calculated as of the end of 2009. Use the average demand for 2002 through 2004 as your initial forecast, then smooth the forecast forward to 2009.

CASE: ALTAVOX ELECTRONICS

Altavox is a manufacturer and distributor of many different electronic instruments and devices, including digital/analog multimeters, function generators, oscilloscopes, frequency counters, and other test and measuring equipment. Altavox sells a line of test meters that are popular with professional electricians. The model VC202 is sold through five distributors to retail stores in the United States. These distributors are located in Atlanta, Boston, Chicago, Dallas, and Los Angeles and have been selected to serve different regions in the country.

The model VC202 has been a steady seller over the years due to its reliability and rugged construction. Altavox does not consider this a seasonal product, but there is some variability in demand. Demand for the product over the past 13 weeks is shown in the following table.

These data are contained in an Excel spreadsheet *Altavox Data*. The demand in the regions varies between a high of 40 units on average per week in Atlanta and 48 units in Dallas. This quarter's data are pretty close to the demand last quarter.

Management would like you to experiment with some forecasting models to determine what should be used in a new system being implemented. The new system is programmed to use one of two models: simple moving average or exponential smoothing.

WEEK	1	2	3	4	5	6	7	8	9	10	11	12	13	AVERAGE
Atlanta	33	45	37	38	55	30	18	58	47	37	23	55	40	40
Boston	26	35	41	40	46	48	55	18	62	44	30	45	50	42
Chicago	44	34	22	55	48	72	62	28	27	95	35	45	47	47
Dallas	27	42	35	40	51	64	70	65	55	43	38	47	42	48
LA	32	43	54	40	46	74	40	35	45	38	48	56	50	46
Total	162	199	189	213	246	288	245	204	236	257	174	248	229	222

**Excel:
Altavox Data**

QUESTIONS

1 Consider using a simple moving average model. Experiment with models using five weeks' and three weeks' past data. The past data in each region is given below (week −1 is the week before week 1 in the table, −2 is two weeks before week 1, etc.). Evaluate the forecasts that would have been made over the 13 weeks for each distributor using the mean absolute deviation, mean absolute percent error, and tracking signal as criteria.

WEEK	−5	−4	−3	−2	−1
Atlanta	45	38	30	58	37
Boston	62	18	48	40	35
Chicago	62	22	72	44	48
Dallas	42	35	40	64	43
LA	43	40	54	46	35
Total	254	153	244	252	198

2 Next, consider using a simple exponential smoothing model. In your analysis, test two alpha values, .2 and .4. Use the same criteria for evaluating the model as in question 1. Assume that the initial previous forecast for the model using an alpha value of .2 is the past three-week average. For the model using an alpha of .4, assume that the previous forecast is the past five-week average.

3 Altavox is considering a new option for distributing the model VC202 where, instead of using five distributors, only a single distributor would be used. Evaluate this option by analyzing how accurate the forecast would be based on the demand aggregated across all regions. Use the model that you think is best from your analysis of questions 1 and 2. What are the advantages and disadvantages of aggregating demand from a forecasting view? Are there other things that should be considered when going from multiple distributors to a single distributor?

SUPER QUIZ

1 This is a type of forecast used to make long-term decisions such as where to locate a warehouse or how many employees to have in a plant next year.
2 This is the type of demand that is most appropriate for using forecasting models.
3 This is a term used for actually influencing the sale of a product or service.
4 These are the six major components of demand.
5 This type of analysis is most appropriate when the past is a good predictor of the future.
6 This is identifying and separating time series data into components of demand.
7 If the demand in the current week was 102 units and we had forecast it to be 125, what would be next week's forecast using an exponential smoothing model with an alpha of 0.3?
8 Assume that you are using exponential smoothing with an adjustment for trend. Demand is increasing

at a very steady rate of about five units per week. Would you expect your alpha and delta parameters to be closer to one or zero?
9 Your forecast is, on average, incorrect by about 10 percent. The average demand is 130 units. What is the MAD?
10 If the tracking signal for your forecast were consistently positive, you could then say this about your forecasting technique.
11 What would you suggest to improve the forecast described in question 10?
12 You know that sales are greatly influenced by the amount your firm advertises in the local paper. What forecasting technique would you suggest trying?
13 What forecasting tool is most appropriate when closely working with customers dependent on your products?

1. Strategic forecast 2. Independent demand 3. Demand management 4. Average demand for the period, trend, seasonal elements, cyclical elements, random variation, and autocorrelation 5. Time series analysis 6. Decomposition 7. 118 units 8. Zero 9. 13 10. Bias, consistently too low 11. Add a trend component 12. Causal relationship forecasting (using regression) 13. Collaborative Planning, Forecasting, and Replenishment (CPFR)

SELECTED BIBLIOGRAPHY

Diebold, F. X. *Elements of Forecasting.* 4th ed. Mason, OH: South-Western College Publishing, 2006.

Hanke, J. E.; A. G. Reitsch; and D. W. Wichern. *Business Forecasting.* 8th ed. Upper Saddle River, NJ : Prentice Hall, 2004.

Makridakis, S; S. C. Wheelwright; and R. J. Hyndman. *Forecasting: Methods for Management.* New York: John Wiley & Sons, 1998.

FOOTNOTES

1 In addition to dependent and independent demands, other relationships include complementary products and causal relationships where demand for one causes the demand for another.
2 An equation for the standard error that is often easier to compute is $S_{yx} = \sqrt{\dfrac{\Sigma y^2 - a\Sigma y - b\Sigma xy}{n-2}}$.
3 Some writers prefer to call F_t a smoothed average.
4 When exponential smoothing is first introduced, the initial forecast or starting point may be obtained by using a simple estimate or an average of preceding periods such as the average of the first two or three periods.
5 Special thanks to Gene Fliedner for help with this section. Gene Fliedner, "Hierarchical Forecasting: Issues and Use Guidelines," *Industrial Management & Data Systems* 101, no. 1 (2001), pp. 5–12.
6 Marshall L. Fisher, "What Is the Right Supply Chain for Your Product?" *Harvard Business Review*, March–April 1997, pp. 105–16.

SALES AND OPERATIONS PLANNING

et's eavesdrop on an executive staff meeting at the Acme Widget Company. The participants are not happy campers.

President: This shortage situation is terrible. When will we ever get our act together? Whenever business gets good, we run out of product and our customer service is lousy.

VP Operations: I'll tell you when. When we start to get some decent forecasts from the Sales Department . . .

After reading the chapter you will:

1. Understand what sales and operations planning is and how it coordinates manufacturing, logistics, service, and marketing plans.

2. Construct aggregate plans that employ different strategies for meeting demand.

3. Describe what yield management is and why it is an important strategy for leveling demand.

VP Sales (interrupting): Wait a minute. We forecasted this upturn.

VP Operations: . . . in time to do something about it. Yeah, we got the revised forecast—four days after the start of the month. By then it was too late.

VP Sales: I could have told you months ago. All you had to do was ask.

SOURCE: ADAPTED FROM THOMAS F. WALLACE, *SALES AND OPERATIONS PLANNING: THE HOW-TO HANDBOOK* (CINCINNATI, OH: T. F. WALLACE & CO., 2000), P. 3. COPYRIGHT © 2000 THOMAS WALLACE. USED WITH PERMISSION.

VP Finance: I'd like to be in on those conversations. We've been burned more than once by building inventories for a business upturn that doesn't happen. Then we get stuck with tons of inventory and run out of cash.

And the beat goes on. Back orders, dissatisfied customers, high inventories, late shipments, finger-pointing, cash-flow problems, demand and supply out of balance, missing the business plan. This is the norm in many companies.

It does not, however, have to be that way. Today many companies are using a business process called sales and operations planning (S&OP) to help avoid such problems. To learn what it is, and how to make it work, read on.

Aggregate operations plan

In this chapter, we focus on the **aggregate operations plan**, which translates annual and quarterly business plans into broad labor and output plans for the intermediate term (3 to 18 months). The objective of the aggregate operations plan is to minimize the cost of resources required to meet demand over that period.

WHAT IS SALES AND OPERATIONS PLANNING?

Sales and operations planning is a process that helps firms provide better customer service, lower inventory, shorten customer lead times, stabilize production rates, and give top management a handle on the business. The process is designed to coordinate activities in the field with the manufacturing and service functions that are required to meet demand over time. Depending on the situation, activities in the field may include the supply of warehouse distribution centers, retail sales outlets, or direct sales channels. The process is designed to help a company get demand and supply in balance and keep them in balance over time. The process requires teamwork among sales, distribution and logistics, operations, finance, and product development.

The sales and operations planning process consists of a series of meetings, finishing with a high-level meeting where key intermediate-term decisions are made. The end goal is an agreement between various departments on the best course of action to achieve the optimal balance between supply and demand. The idea is to put the operational plan in line with the business plan.

This balance must occur at an aggregate level and also at the detailed individual product level. By *aggregate* we mean at the level of major groups of products. Over time, we need to ensure that we have enough total capacity. Since demand is often quite dynamic, it is important that we monitor our expected needs 3 to 18 months or further in the future. When planning this far into the future, it is difficult to know exactly how many of a particular product we will need, but we should be able to know how a larger group of similar products should sell. The term *aggregate* refers to this group of products. Given that we have enough aggregate capacity, our individual product schedulers, working within aggregate capacity constraints, can handle the daily and weekly launching of individual product orders to meet short-term demand.

OVERVIEW OF SALES AND OPERATIONS PLANNING ACTIVITIES

Sales and operations planning

Exhibit 16.1 positions sales and operations planning relative to other major operations planning activities. The term **sales and operations planning** was coined by companies to refer to the process that helps firms keep demand and supply in balance. In operations management this process traditionally was called *aggregate planning*. The new terminology is meant to capture the importance of cross-functional work. Typically, this activity requires an integrated effort with cooperation from sales, distribution and logistics, operations, finance, and product development.

Within sales and operations planning, marketing develops a sales plan that extends through the next 3 to 18 months. This sales plan typically is stated in units of aggregate product

Overview of Major Operations and Supply Planning Activities

exhibit 16.1

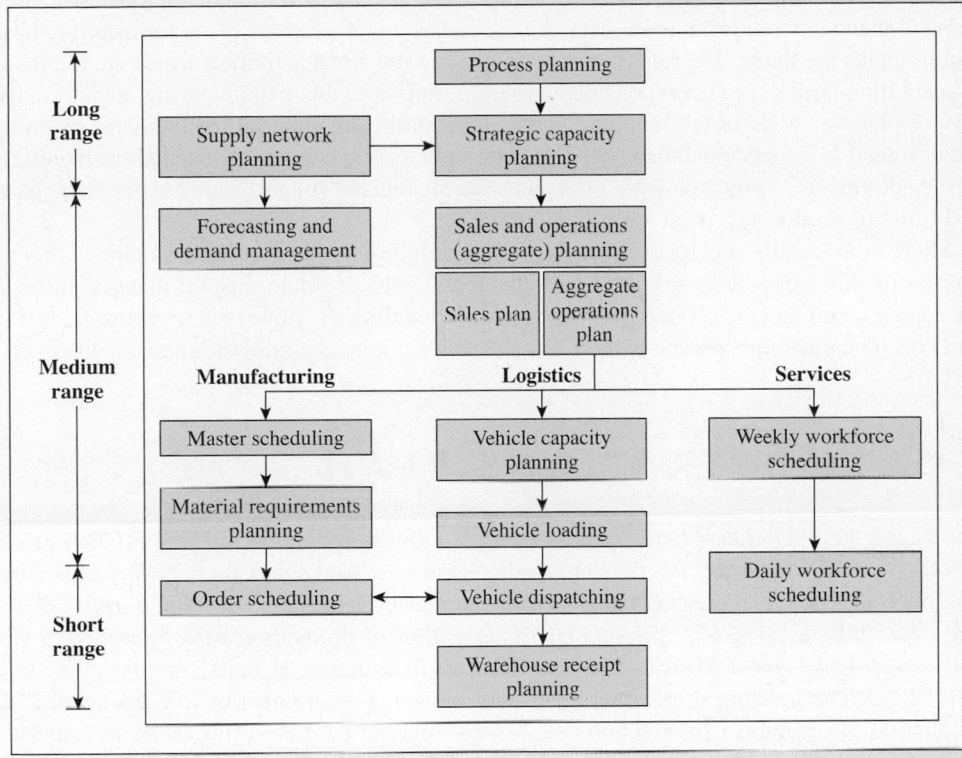

groups and often is tied into sales incentive programs and other marketing activities. The operations side develops an operations plan as an output of the process, which is discussed in depth in this chapter. By focusing on aggregate product and sales volumes, the marketing and operations functions are able to develop plans for the way demand will be met. This is a particularly difficult task when demand changes significantly changes over time as a result of market trends or other factors.

Aggregation on the supply side is done by product families, and on the demand side it is done by groups of customers. Individual product production schedules and matching customer orders can be handled more readily as a result of the sales and operations planning process. Typically, sales and operations planning occurs on a monthly cycle. Sales and operations planning links a company's strategic plans and business plan to its detailed operations and supply processes. These detailed processes include manufacturing, logistics, and service activities, as shown in Exhibit 16.1.

In Exhibit 16.1 the time dimension is shown as long, intermediate, and short range. **Long-range planning** generally is done annually, focusing on a horizon greater than one year. **Intermediate-range planning** usually covers a period from 3 to 18 months, with time increments that are weekly, monthly, or sometimes quarterly. **Short-range planning** covers a period from one day to six months, with daily or weekly time increments.

Long-range planning activities are done in two major areas. The first is the design of the manufacturing and service processes that produce the products of the firm, and the second is the design of the logistics activities that deliver products to the customer. Process planning deals with determining the specific technologies and procedures required to produce a product or service. Strategic capacity planning deals with determining the long-term capabilities (such as size and scope) of the production systems. Similarly, from a logistics point of view, supply network planning determines how the product will be distributed to the customer on the outbound side, with decisions relating to the location of warehouses and the types of transportation systems to

Long-range planning
Intermediate-range planning
Short-range planning

**Supply
Chain**

be used. On the inbound side, supply network planning involves decisions relating to outsourcing production, selection of parts and component suppliers, and related decisions.

Intermediate-term activities include forecasting and demand management and sales and operations planning. The determination of expected demand is the focus of forecasting and demand management. From these data, detailed sales and operations plans for meeting these requirements are made. The sales plans are inputs to sales force activities, which are the focus of marketing books. The operations plan provides input into the manufacturing, logistics, and service planning activities of the firm. Master scheduling and material requirements planning are designed to generate detailed schedules that indicate when parts are needed for manufacturing activities. Coordinated with these plans are the logistics plans needed to move the parts and finished products through the supply chain.

Short-term details are focused mostly on scheduling production and shipment orders. These orders need to be coordinated with the actual vehicles that transport material through the supply chain. On the service side, short-term scheduling of employees is needed to ensure that adequate customer service is provided and fair worker schedules are maintained.

Service

THE AGGREGATE OPERATIONS PLAN

The aggregate operations plan is concerned with setting production rates by product group or other broad categories for the intermediate term (3 to 18 months). Note again from Exhibit 16.1 that the aggregate plan precedes the master schedule. *The main purpose of the aggregate plan is to specify the optimal combination of production rate, workforce level, and inventory on hand.* **Production rate** refers to the number of units completed per unit of time (such as per hour or per day). **Workforce level** is the number of workers needed for production (production = production rate × workforce level). **Inventory on hand** is unused inventory carried over from the previous period.

- Production rate
- Workforce level
- Inventory on hand

Here is a formal statement of the aggregate planning problem: Given the demand forecast F_t for each period t in the planning horizon that extends over T periods, determine the production level P_t, inventory level I_t, and workforce level W_t for periods $t = 1, 2, \ldots, T$ that minimize the relevant costs over the planning horizon.

The form of the aggregate plan varies from company to company. In some firms, it is a formalized report containing planning objectives and the planning premises on which it is based. In other companies, particularly smaller ones, the owner may make simple calculations of workforce needs that reflect a general staffing strategy.

The process by which the plan itself is derived also varies. One common approach is to derive it from the corporate annual plan, as shown in Exhibit 16.1. A typical corporate plan contains a section on manufacturing that specifies how many units in each major product line need to be produced over the next 12 months to meet the sales forecast. The planner takes this information and attempts to determine how best to meet these requirements with available resources. Alternatively, some organizations combine output requirements into equivalent units and use this as the basis for the aggregate plan. For example, a division of General Motors may be asked to produce a certain number of cars of all types at a particular facility. The production planner would then take the average labor hours required for all models as a basis for the overall aggregate plan. Refinements to this plan, specifically model types to be produced, would be reflected in shorter-term production plans.

Another approach is to develop the aggregate plan by simulating various master production schedules and calculating corresponding capacity requirements to see if adequate labor and equipment exist at each work center. If capacity is inadequate, additional requirements for overtime, subcontracting, extra workers, and so forth are specified for each product line and combined into a rough-cut plan. This plan is then modified by cut-and-try or mathematical methods to derive a final and (one hopes) lower-cost plan.

PRODUCTION PLANNING ENVIRONMENT

Exhibit 16.2 illustrates the internal and external factors that constitute the production planning environment. In general, the external environment is outside the production planner's

Required Inputs to the Production Planning Systems

exhibit 16.2

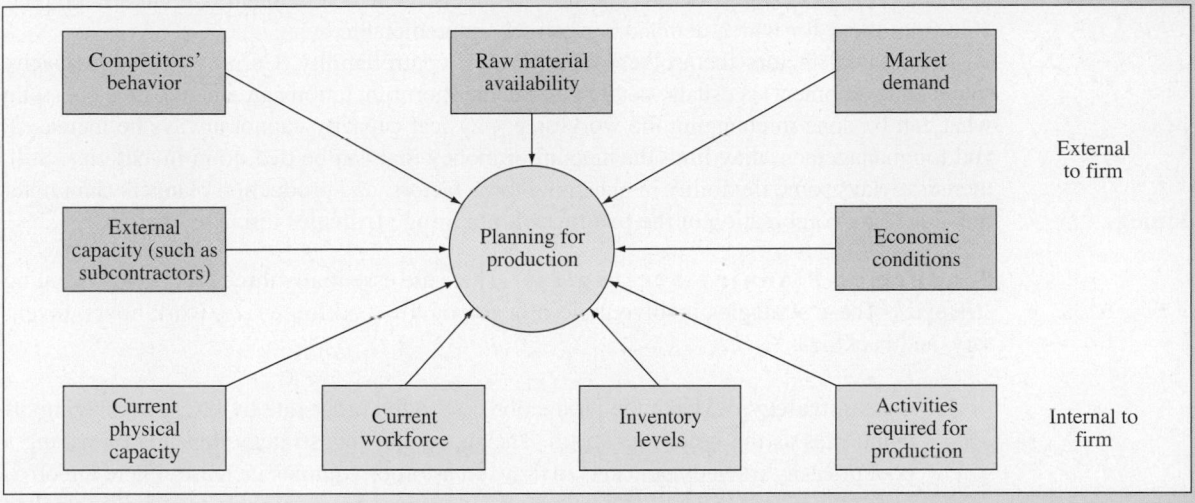

Competitors' behavior

Raw material availability

Market demand

External capacity (such as subcontractors)

Planning for production

Economic conditions

External to firm

Current physical capacity

Current workforce

Inventory levels

Activities required for production

Internal to firm

direct control, but in some firms, demand for the product can be managed. Through close cooperation between marketing and operations, promotional activities and price cutting can be used to build demand during slow periods. Conversely, when demand is strong, promotional activities can be curtailed and prices raised to maximize the revenues from those products or services that the firm has the capacity to provide. The current practices in managing demand will be discussed later in the section titled "Yield Management."

Complementary products may work for firms facing cyclical demand fluctuations. For instance, lawnmower manufacturers will have strong demand for spring and summer, but weak demand during fall and winter. Demands on the production system can be smoothed out by producing a complementary product with high demand during fall and winter, and low demand during spring and summer (for instance, snowmobiles, snowblowers, or leafblowers). With services, cycles are more often measured in hours than months. Restaurants with strong demand during lunch and dinner will often add a breakfast menu to increase demand during the morning hours.

But even so, there are limits to how much demand can be controlled. Ultimately, the production planner must live with the sales projections and orders promised by the marketing function, leaving the internal factors as variables that can be manipulated in deriving a

Service

WATER SKIS AND SNOW SKIS ARE GREAT EXAMPLES OF COMPLEMENTARY PRODUCTS.

production plan. A new approach to facilitate managing these internal factors is termed *accurate response*. This entails refined measurement of historical demand patterns blended with expert judgment to determine when to begin production of particular items. The key element of the approach is clearly identifying those products for which demand is relatively predictable from those for which demand is relatively unpredictable.[1]

The internal factors themselves differ in their controllability. Current physical capacity (plant and equipment) is usually nearly fixed in the short run; union agreements often constrain what can be done in changing the workforce; physical capacity cannot always be increased; and top management may limit the amount of money that can be tied up in inventories. Still, there is always some flexibility in managing these factors, and production planners can implement one or a combination of the **production planning strategies** discussed here.

Production planning strategies

Production Planning Strategies   There are essentially three production planning strategies. These strategies involve trade-offs among the workforce size, work hours, inventory, and backlogs.

1. **Chase strategy.**   Match the production rate to the order rate by hiring and laying off employees as the order rate varies. The success of this strategy depends on having a pool of easily trained applicants to draw on as order volumes increase. There are obvious motivational impacts. When order backlogs are low, employees may feel compelled to slow down out of fear of being laid off as soon as existing orders are completed.
2. **Stable workforce—variable work hours.**   Vary the output by varying the number of hours worked through flexible work schedules or overtime. By varying the number of work hours, you can match production quantities to orders. This strategy provides workforce continuity and avoids many of the emotional and tangible costs of hiring and firing associated with the chase strategy.
3. **Level strategy.**   Maintain a stable workforce working at a constant output rate. Shortages and surpluses are absorbed by fluctuating inventory levels, order backlogs, and lost sales. Employees benefit from stable work hours at the costs of potentially decreased customer service levels and increased inventory costs. Another concern is the possibility of inventoried products becoming obsolete.

Pure strategy
Mixed strategy

When just one of these variables is used to absorb demand fluctuations, it is termed a **pure strategy**; two or more used in combination constitute a **mixed strategy**. As you might suspect, mixed strategies are more widely applied in industry.

Subcontracting   In addition to these strategies, managers also may choose to subcontract some portion of production. This strategy is similar to the chase strategy, but hiring and laying off are translated into subcontracting and not subcontracting. Some level of subcontracting can be desirable to accommodate demand fluctuations. However, unless the relationship with the supplier is particularly strong, a manufacturer can lose some control over schedule and quality.

Relevant Costs

Four costs are relevant to the aggregate production plan. These relate to the production cost itself as well as the cost to hold inventory and to have unfilled orders. More specifically, these are

1. **Basic production costs.**   These are the fixed and variable costs incurred in producing a given product type in a given time period. Included are direct and indirect labor costs and regular as well as overtime compensation.
2. **Costs associated with changes in the production rate.**   Typical costs in this category are those involved in hiring, training, and laying off personnel. Hiring temporary help is a way of avoiding these costs.
3. **Inventory holding costs.**   A major component is the cost of capital tied up in inventory. Other components are storing, insurance, taxes, spoilage, and obsolescence.
4. **Backordering costs.**   Usually these are very hard to measure and include costs of expediting, loss of customer goodwill, and loss of sales revenues resulting from backordering.

IT'S ALL IN THE PLANNING

You're sitting anxiously in the suddenly assembled general manager's staff meeting. Voices are nervously subdued. The rumor mill is in high gear about another initiative-of-the-month about to be loosed among the leery survivors of the last purge. The meeting begins. Amid the tricolor visuals and 3D spreadsheets, the same old message is skeptically received by managers scrambling for politically correct responses in an endless game of shoot the messenger.

This is a familiar scene in corporations around the world. But interestingly, firms such as Finisar Corporation have learned how to manage the process of successfully matching supply and demand. Finisar has developed a new semiconductor laser used in computing, networking, and sensing applications. Forecasting and managing production capacity is a unique challenge for companies with a stream of new and innovative products coming to market. Using a monthly sales and operations planning process, Finisar has been able to improve their short- and long-term forecasting accuracy from 60 percent to

consistently hitting 95 percent or better. The specific steps within their plan focus the executive team on (1) the demand opportunities for current and new products and (2) the constraints on the organization's ability to produce product to meet this demand. The plan, developed in a monthly sales and operations planning executive meeting, ensures that demand is synchronized with supply, so customers get the product they want, when they want it, while inventory and costs are kept to a minimum.

Finisar managers indicated that a critical step was getting the general manager to champion the process. The second step was achieving a complete understanding of required behavior from the team, including committing to a balanced and synchronized demand/supply plan, being accountable for meeting the performance standards, having open and honest communication, not promising what cannot be delivered, and making the decisions needed to address the identified opportunities and constraints.

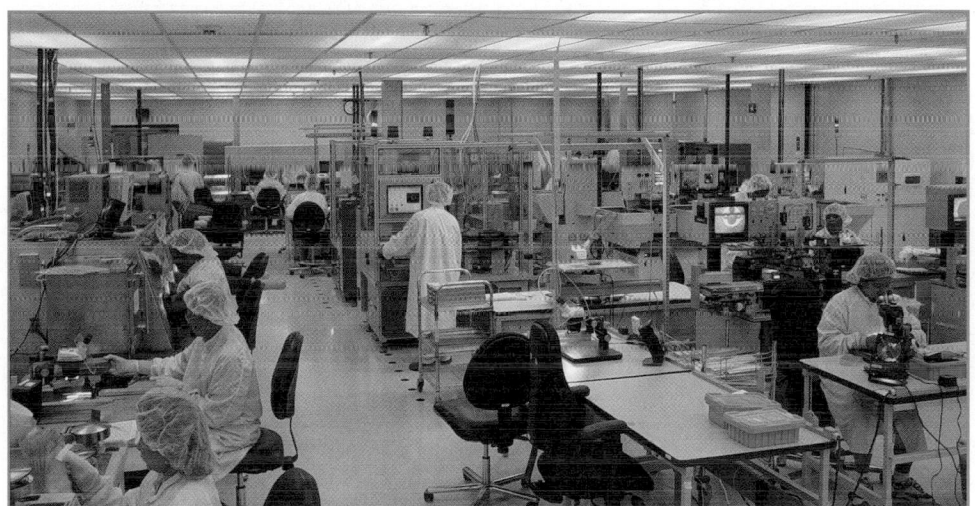

SOURCE: ADAPTED FROM http://www.themanufacturer.com.

Budgets   To receive funding, operations managers are generally required to submit annual, and sometimes quarterly, budget requests. The aggregate plan is key to the success of the budgeting process. Recall that the goal of the aggregate plan is to minimize the total production-related costs over the planning horizon by determining the optimal combination of workforce levels and inventory levels. Thus, the aggregate plan provides justification for the requested budget amount. Accurate medium-range planning increases the likelihood of (1) receiving the requested budget and (2) operating within the limits of the budget.

In the next section we provide an example of medium-range planning in a manufacturing setting. This example illustrates the trade-offs associated with different production planning strategies.[2]

AGGREGATE PLANNING TECHNIQUES

Companies commonly use simple cut-and-try charting and graphic methods to develop aggregate plans. A cut-and-try approach involves costing out various production planning alternatives and selecting the one that is best. Elaborate spreadsheets are developed to facilitate the decision process. Sophisticated approaches involving linear programming and simulation are often incorporated into these spreadsheets. In the following, we demonstrate a spreadsheet approach to evaluate four strategies for meeting demand for the JC Company. Later we discuss more sophisticated approaches using linear programming (see Appendix A).

A CUT-AND-TRY EXAMPLE: THE JC COMPANY

Service

A firm with pronounced seasonal variation normally plans production for a full year to capture the extremes in demand during the busiest and slowest months. But we can illustrate the general principles involved with a shorter horizon. Suppose we wish to set up a production plan for the JC Company for the next six months. We are given the following information:

DEMAND AND WORKING DAYS

	JANUARY	FEBRUARY	MARCH	APRIL	MAY	JUNE	TOTALS
Demand forecast	1,800	1,500	1,100	900	1,100	1,600	8,000
Number of working days	22	19	21	21	22	20	125

COSTS

Materials	$100.00/unit
Inventory holding cost	$1.50/unit/month
Marginal cost of stockout	$5.00/unit/month
Marginal cost of subcontracting	$20.00/unit ($120 subcontracting cost less $100 material savings)
Hiring and training cost	$200.00/worker
Layoff cost	$250.00/worker
Labor hours required	5/unit
Straight-time cost (first eight hours each day)	$4.00/hour
Overtime cost (time and a half)	$6.00/hour

INVENTORY

Beginning inventory	400 units
Safety stock	25% of month demand

In solving this problem, we can exclude the material costs. We could have included this $100 cost in all our calculations, but if we assume that a $100 cost is common to each demanded unit, then we need only concern ourselves with the marginal costs. Because the subcontracting cost is $120, our true cost for subcontracting is just $20 because we save the materials.

Note that many costs are expressed in a different form than typically found in the accounting records of a firm. Therefore, do not expect to obtain all these costs directly from such records, but obtain them indirectly from management personnel, who can help interpret the data.

Inventory at the beginning of the first period is 400 units. Because the demand forecast is imperfect, the JC Company has determined that a *safety stock* (buffer inventory) should be established to reduce the likelihood of stockouts. For this example, assume the safety stock should be one-quarter of the demand forecast. (Chapter 17 covers this topic in depth.)

Before investigation of alternative production plans, it is often useful to convert demand forecasts into *production requirements,* which take into account the safety stock estimates. In Exhibit 16.3, note that these requirements implicitly assume that the safety stock is never actually used, so that the ending inventory each month equals the safety stock for that month. For example, the January safety stock of 450 (25 percent of January demand of 1,800) becomes the inventory at the end of January. The production requirement for January is demand plus safety stock minus beginning inventory (1,800 + 450 − 400 = 1,850).

Aggregate Production Planning Requirements

exhibit 16.3

	JANUARY	FEBRUARY	MARCH	APRIL	MAY	JUNE
Beginning inventory	400	450	375	275	225	275
Demand forecast	1,800	1,500	1,100	900	1,100	1,600
Safety stock (.25 × Demand forecast)	450	375	275	225	275	400
Production requirement (Demand forecast + Safety stock − Beginning inventory)	1,850	1,425	1,000	850	1,150	1,725
Ending inventory (Beginning inventory + Production requirement − Demand forecast)	450	375	275	225	275	400

**Excel:
Aggregate
Planning**

Now we must formulate alternative production plans for the JC Company. Using a spreadsheet, we investigate four different plans with the objective of finding the one with the lowest total cost.

Plan 1. Produce to exact monthly production requirements using a regular eight-hour day by varying workforce size.

Plan 2. Produce to meet expected average demand over the next six months by maintaining a constant workforce. This constant number of workers is calculated by finding the average number of workers required each day over the horizon. Take the total production requirements and multiply by the time required for each unit. Then divide by the total time that one person works over the horizon [(8,000 units × 5 hours per unit) ÷ (125 days × 8 hours per day) = 40 workers]. Inventory is allowed to accumulate, with shortages filled from next month's production by backordering. Negative beginning inventory balances indicate that demand is backordered. In some cases, sales may be lost if demand is not met. The lost sales can be shown with a negative ending inventory balance followed by a zero beginning inventory balance in the next period. Notice that in this plan we use our safety stock in January, February, March, and June to meet expected demand.

Plan 3. Produce to meet the minimum expected demand (April) using a constant workforce on regular time. Subcontract to meet additional output requirements. The number of workers is calculated by locating the minimum monthly production requirement and determining how many workers would be needed for that month [(850 units × 5 hours per unit) ÷ (21 days × 8 hours per day) = 25 workers] and subcontracting any monthly difference between requirements and production.

Plan 4. Produce to meet expected demand for all but the first two months using a constant workforce on regular time. Use overtime to meet additional output requirements. The number of workers is more difficult to compute for this plan, but the goal is to finish June with an ending inventory as close as possible to the June safety stock. By trial and error it can be shown that a constant workforce of 38 workers is the closest approximation.

The next step is to calculate the cost of each plan. This requires the series of simple calculations shown in Exhibit 16.4. Note that the headings in each row are different for each plan because each is a different problem requiring its own data and calculations.

The final step is to tabulate and graph each plan and compare their costs. From Exhibit 16.5 we can see that using subcontractors resulted in the lowest cost (Plan 3). Exhibit 16.6 shows the effects of the four plans. This is a cumulative graph illustrating the expected results on the total production requirement.

Note that we have made one other assumption in this example: The plan can start with any number of workers with no hiring or layoff cost. This usually is the case because an aggregate plan draws on existing personnel, and we can start the plan that way. However, in an actual application, the availability of existing personnel transferable from other areas of the firm may change the assumptions.

exhibit 16.4   Costs of Four Production Plans

**Excel:
Aggregate
Planning**

Production Plan 1: Exact Production; Vary Workforce

	January	February	March	April	May	June	Total
Production requirement (from Exhibit 16.3)	1,850	1,425	1,000	850	1,150	1,725	
Production hours required (Production requirement × 5 hr./unit)	9,250	7,125	5,000	4,250	5,750	8,625	
Working days per month	22	19	21	21	22	20	
Hours per month per worker (Working days × 8 hrs./day)	176	152	168	168	176	160	
Workers required (Production hours required/Hours per month per worker)	53	47	30	25	33	54	
New workers hired (assuming opening workforce equal to first month's requirement of 53 workers)	0	0	0	0	8	21	
Hiring cost (New workers hired × $200)	$0	$0	$0	$0	$1,600	$4,200	$5,800
Workers laid off	0	6	17	5	0	0	
Layoff cost (Workers laid off × $250)	$0	$1,500	$4,250	$1,250	$0	$0	$7,000
Straight-time cost (Production hours required × $4)	$37,000	$28,500	$20,000	$17,000	$23,000	$34,500	$160,000
						Total cost	$172,800

Production Plan 2: Constant Workforce; Vary Inventory and Stockout

	January	February	March	April	May	June	Total
Beginning inventory	400	8	−276	−32	412	720	
Working days per month	22	19	21	21	22	20	
Production hours available (Working days per month × 8 hr./day × 40 workers)*	7,040	6,080	6,720	6,720	7,040	6,400	
Actual production (Production hours available/5 hr./unit)	1,408	1,216	1,344	1,344	1,408	1,280	
Demand forecast (from Exhibit 16.3)	1,800	1,500	1,100	900	1,100	1,600	
Ending inventory (Beginning inventory + Actual production − Demand forecast)	8	−276	−32	412	720	400	
Shortage cost (Units short × $5)	$0	$1,380	$160	$0	$0	$0	$1,540
Safety stock (from Exhibit 16.3)	450	375	275	225	275	400	
Units excess (Ending inventory − Safety stock) only if positive amount	0	0	0	187	445	0	
Inventory cost (Units excess × $1.50)	$0	$0	$0	$281	$668	$0	$948
Straight-time cost (Production hours available × $4)	$28,160	$24,320	$26,880	$26,880	$28,160	$25,600	$160,000
						Total cost	$162,488

*(Sum of production requirement in Exhibit 16.3 × 5 hr./unit)/(Sum of production hours available × 8 hr./day) = (8,000 × 5)/(125 × 8) = 40.

Plan 1 is the "S" curve when we chase demand by varying workforce. Plan 2 has the highest average production rate (the line representing cumulative demand has the greatest slope). Using subcontracting in Plan 3 results in it having the lowest production rate. Limits on the amount of overtime available results in Plan 4 being similar to Plan 2.

Each of these four plans focused on one particular cost, and the first three were simple pure strategies. Obviously, there are many other feasible plans, some of which would use a combination of workforce changes, overtime, and subcontracting. The problems at the end of this chapter include examples of such mixed strategies. In practice, the final plan chosen

PRODUCTION PLAN 3: CONSTANT LOW WORKFORCE; SUBCONTRACT							
	JANUARY	FEBRUARY	MARCH	APRIL	MAY	JUNE	TOTAL
Production requirement (from Exhibit 16.3)	1,850	1,425	1,000	850	1,150	1,725	
Working days per month	22	19	21	21	22	20	
Production hours available (Working days × 8 hrs./day × 25 workers)*	4,400	3,800	4,200	4,200	4,400	4,000	
Actual production (Production hours available/5 hr. per unit)	880	760	840	840	880	800	
Units subcontracted (Production requirement − Actual production)	970	665	160	10	270	925	
Subcontracting cost (Units subcontracted × $20)	$19,400	$13,300	$3,200	$200	$5,400	$18,500	$60,000
Straight-time cost (Production hours available × $4)	$17,600	$15,200	$16,800	$16,800	$17,600	$16,000	$100,000
						Total cost	$160,000

*MINIMUM PRODUCTION REQUIREMENT. IN THIS EXAMPLE, APRIL IS MINIMUM OF 850 UNITS. NUMBER OF WORKERS REQUIRED FOR APRIL IS $(850 \times 5)/(21 \times 8) = 25$.

PRODUCTION PLAN 4: CONSTANT WORKFORCE; OVERTIME							
	JANUARY	FEBRUARY	MARCH	APRIL	MAY	JUNE	TOTAL
Beginning inventory	400	0	0	177	554	792	
Working days per month	22	19	21	21	22	20	
Production hours available (Working days × 8 hr./day × 38 workers)*	6,688	5,776	6,384	6,384	6,688	6,080	
Regular shift production (Production hours available/5 hrs. per unit)	1,338	1,155	1,277	1,277	1,338	1,216	
Demand forecast (from Exhibit 16.3)	1,800	1,500	1,100	900	1,100	1,600	
Units available before overtime (Beginning Inventory + Regular shift production − Demand forecast). This number has been rounded to the nearest integer.	−62	−345	177	554	792	408	
Units overtime	62	375	0	0	0	0	
Overtime cost (Units overtime × 5 hr./unit × $6/hr.)	$1,860	$10,350	$0	$0	$0	$0	$12,210
Safety stock (from Exhibit 16.3)	450	375	275	225	275	400	
Units excess (Units available before overtime − Safety stock) only if positive amount	0	0	0	329	517	8	
Inventory cost (Units excessive × $1.50)	$0	$0	$0	$494	$776	$12	$1,281
Straight-time cost (Production hours available × $4)	$26,752	$23,104	$25,536	$25,536	$26,752	$24,320	$152,000
						Total cost	$165,491

*Workers determined by trial and error. See text for explanation.

would come from searching a variety of alternatives and future projections beyond the six-month planning horizon we have used.

Keep in mind that the cut-and-try approach does not guarantee finding the minimum-cost solution. However, spreadsheet programs, such as Microsoft Excel, can perform cut-and-try cost estimates in seconds and have elevated this kind of what-if analysis to a fine art. More sophisticated programs can generate much better solutions without the user having to intercede, as in the cut-and-try method.

exhibit 16.5

Comparison of Four Plans

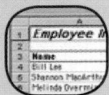

Excel:
Aggregate
Planning

COSTS	PLAN 1: EXACT PRODUCTION; VARY WORKFORCE	PLAN 2: CONSTANT WORKFORCE; VARY INVENTORY AND STOCKOUT	PLAN 3: CONSTANT LOW WORKFORCE; SUBCONTRACT	PLAN 4: CONSTANT WORKFORCE; OVERTIME
Hiring	$ 5,800	$ 0	$ 0	$ 0
Layoff	7,000	0	0	0
Excess inventory	0	948	0	1,281
Shortage	0	1,540	0	0
Subcontract	0	0	60,000	0
Overtime	0	0	0	12,210
Straight time	160,000	160,000	100,000	152,000
	$172,800	$162,488	$160,000	$165,491

exhibit 16.6

Four Plans for Satisfying a Production Requirement over the Number of Production Days Available

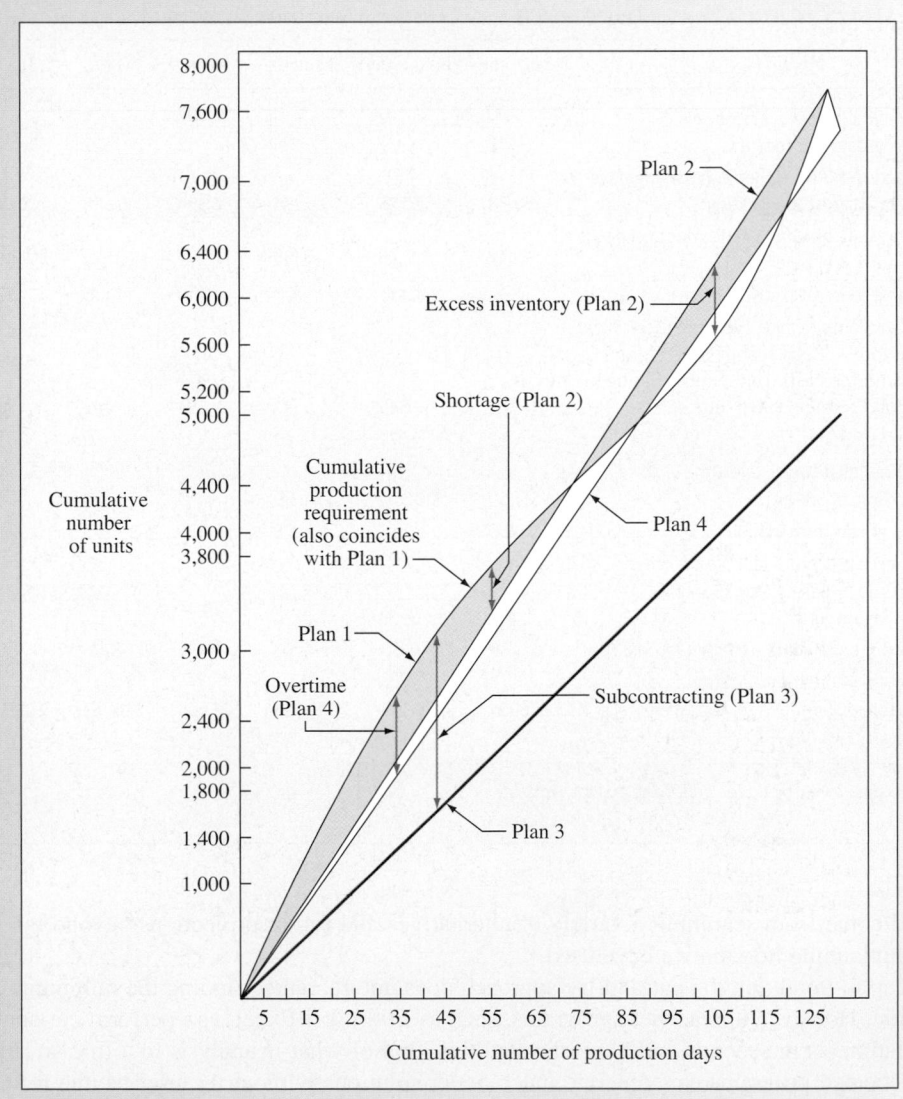

AGGREGATE PLANNING APPLIED TO SERVICES: TUCSON PARKS AND RECREATION DEPARTMENT

Charting and graphic techniques are also useful for aggregate planning in service applications. The following example shows how a city's parks and recreation department could use the alternatives of full-time employees, part-time employees, and subcontracting to meet its commitment to provide a service to the city.

Service

Tucson Parks and Recreation Department has an operation and maintenance budget of $9,760,000. The department is responsible for developing and maintaining open space, all public recreational programs, adult sports leagues, golf courses, tennis courts, pools, and so forth. There are 336 full-time-equivalent employees (FTEs). Of these, 216 are full-time permanent personnel who provide the administration and year-round maintenance to all areas. The remaining 120 FTE positions arc staffed with part-timers; about three-quarters of them are used during the summer, and the remaining quarter in the fall, winter, and spring seasons. The three-fourths (or 90 FTE positions) show up as approximately 800 part-time summer jobs: lifeguards, baseball umpires, and instructors in summer programs for children. Eight hundred part-time jobs came from 90 FTEs because many last only for a month or two, while the FTEs are a year long.

Currently, the only parks and recreation work subcontracted amounts to less than $100,000. This is for the golf and tennis pros and for grounds maintenance at the libraries and veterans' cemetery.

Because of the nature of city employment, the probable bad public image, and civil service rules, the option to hire and fire full-time help daily or weekly to meet seasonal demand is out of the question. However, temporary part-time help is authorized and traditional. Also, it is virtually impossible to have regular (full-time) staff for all the summer jobs. During the summer months, the approximately 800 part-time employees are staffing many programs that occur simultaneously, prohibiting level scheduling over a normal 40-hour week. A wider variety of skills are required (such as umpires, coaches, lifeguards, and teachers of ceramics, guitar, karate, belly dancing, and yoga) than can be expected from full-time employees.

Three options are open to the department in its aggregate planning:

1. The present method, which is to maintain a medium-level full-time staff and schedule work during off-seasons (such as rebuilding baseball fields during the winter months) and to use part-time help during peak demands.
2. Maintain a lower level of staff over the year and subcontract all additional work presently done by full-time staff (still using part-time help).
3. Maintain an administrative staff only and subcontract all work, including part-time help. (This would entail contracts to landscaping firms and pool maintenance companies as well as to newly created private firms to employ and supply part-time help.)

The common unit of measure of work across all areas is full-time equivalent jobs or employees. For example, assume in the same week that 30 lifeguards worked 20 hours each, 40 instructors worked 15 hours each, and 35 baseball umpires worked 10 hours each. This is equivalent to $(30 \times 20) + (40 \times 15) + (35 \times 10) = 1{,}550 \div 40 = 38.75$ FTE positions for that week. Although a considerable amount of workload can be shifted to off-season, most of the work must be done when required.

Full-time employees consist of three groups: (1) the skeleton group of key department personnel coordinating with the city, setting policy, determining budgets, measuring performance, and so forth; (2) the administrative group of supervisory and office personnel who are responsible for or whose jobs are directly linked to the direct-labor workers; and (3) the direct-labor workforce of 116 full-time positions. These workers physically maintain the department's areas of responsibility, such as cleaning up, mowing golf greens and ballfields, trimming trees, and watering grass.

Cost information needed to determine the best alternative strategy is

Full-time direct-labor employees	
Average wage rate	$4.45 per hour
Fringe benefits	17% of wage rate
Administrative costs	20% of wage rate
Part-time employees	
Average wage rate	$4.03 per hour
Fringe benefits	11% of wage rate
Administrative costs	25% of wage rate
Subcontracting all full-time jobs	$1.6 million
Subcontracting all part-time jobs	$1.85 million

June and July are the peak demand seasons in Tucson. Exhibit 16.7 shows the high requirements for June and July personnel. The part-time help reaches 576 FTE positions (although, in actual numbers, this is approximately 800 different employees). After a low fall and winter staffing level, the demand shown as "full-time direct" reaches 130 in March (when grounds are reseeded and fertilized) and then increases to a high of 325 in July. The present method levels this uneven demand over the year to an average of 116 full-time year-round employees by early scheduling of work. As previously mentioned, no attempt is made to hire and lay off full-time workers to meet this uneven demand.

exhibit 16.7

Actual Demand Requirement for Full-Time Direct Employees and Full-Time Equivalent (FTE) Part-Time Employees

**Excel:
Aggregate
Planning**

	JAN.	FEB.	MAR.	APR.	MAY	JUNE	JULY	AUG.	SEPT.	OCT.	NOV.	DEC.	TOTAL
Days	22	20	21	22	21	20	21	21	21	23	18	22	252
Full-time employees	66	28	130	90	195	290	325	92	45	32	29	60	
Full-time days*	1,452	560	2,730	1,980	4,095	5,800	6,825	1,932	945	736	522	1,320	28,897
Full-time equivalent part-time employees	41	75	72	68	72	302	576	72	0	68	84	27	
FTE days	902	1,500	1,512	1,496	1,512	6,040	12,096	1,512	0	1,564	1,512	594	30,240

*FULL-TIME DAYS ARE DERIVED BY MULTIPLYING THE NUMBER OF DAYS IN EACH MONTH BY THE NUMBER OF WORKERS.

Monthly Requirement for Full-Time Direct-Labor Employees (Other Than Key Personnel) and Full-Time Equivalent Part-Time Employees

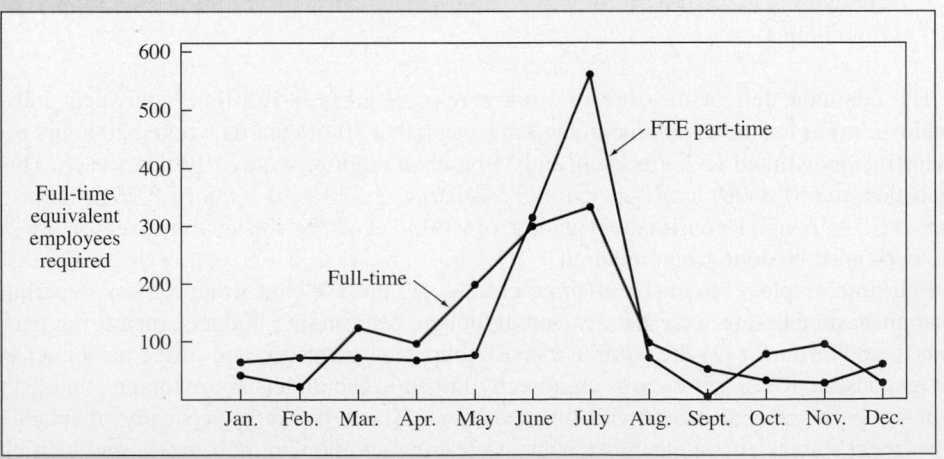

Three Possible Plans for the Parks and Recreation Department

exhibit 16.8

Alternative 1: Maintain 116 full-time regular direct workers. Schedule work during off-seasons to level workload throughout the year. Continue to use 120 full-time equivalent (FTE) part-time employees to meet high demand periods.

COSTS	DAYS PER YEAR (EXHIBIT 16.7)	HOURS (EMPLOYEES × DAYS × 8 HOURS)	WAGES (FULL-TIME, $4.45; PART-TIME, $4.03)	FRINGE BENEFITS (FULL-TIME, 17%; PART-TIME, 11%)	ADMINISTRATIVE COST (FULL-TIME, 20%; PART-TIME, 25%)
116 full-time regular employees	252	233,856	$1,040,659	$176,912	$208,132
120 part-time employees	252	241,920	974,938	107,243	243,735
Total cost = $2,751,619			$2,015,597	$284,155	$451,867

Alternative 2: Maintain 50 full-time regular direct workers and the present 120 FTE part-time employees. Subcontract jobs releasing 66 full-time regular employees. Subcontract cost, $1,100,000.

COST	DAYS PER YEAR (EXHIBIT 16.7)	HOURS (EMPLOYEES × DAYS × 8 HOURS)	WAGES (FULL-TIME, $4.45; PART-TIME, $4.03)	FRINGE BENEFITS (FULL-TIME, 17%; PART-TIME, 11%)	ADMINISTRATIVE COST (FULL-TIME, 20%; PART-TIME, 25%)	SUBCONTRACT COST
50 full-time employees	252	100,800	$ 448,560	$ 76,255	$ 89,712	
120 FTE part-time employees	252	241,920	974,938	107,243	243,735	
Subcontracting cost						$1,100,000
Total cost = $3,040,443			$1,423,498	$183,498	$333,447	$1,100,000

Alternative 3: Subcontract all jobs previously performed by 116 full-time regular employees. Subcontract cost $1,600,000. Subcontract all jobs previously performed by 120 FTE part-time employees. Subcontract cost $1,850,000.

COST	SUBCONTRACT COST
0 full-time employees	
0 part-time employees	
Subcontract full-time jobs	$1,600,000
Subcontract part-time jobs	1,850,000
Total cost	$3,450,000

Excel: Aggregate Planning

Exhibit 16.8 shows the cost calculations for all three alternatives and compares the total costs for each alternative. From this analysis, it appears that the department is already using the lowest-cost alternative (Alternative 1).

LEVEL SCHEDULING

In this chapter we looked at four primary strategies for production planning: vary workforce size to meet demand, work overtime and part-time, vary inventory through excesses and shortages, and subcontract.

A level schedule holds production constant over a period of time. It is something of a combination of the strategies we have mentioned here. For each period, it keeps the workforce constant and inventory low, and depends on demand to pull products through. Level production has a number of advantages, which makes it the backbone of JIT production:

1. The entire system can be planned to minimize inventory and work-in-process.
2. Product modifications are up-to-date because of the low amount of work-in-process.

3. There is a smooth flow throughout the production system.
4. Purchased items from vendors can be delivered when needed and, in fact, often directly to the production line.

Global

Toyota Motor Corporation, for example, creates a yearly production plan that shows the total number of cars to be made and sold. The aggregate production plan creates the system requirements to produce this total number with a level schedule. The secret to success in the Japanese level schedule is *production smoothing*. The aggregate plan is translated into monthly and daily schedules that *sequence* products through the production system. The procedure is essentially this: Two months in advance, the car types and quantities needed are established. This is converted to a detailed plan one month ahead. These quantities are given to subcontractors and vendors so that they can plan on meeting Toyota's needs. The monthly needs of various car types are then translated into daily schedules. For example, if 8,000 units of car type A are needed in one month, along with 6,000 type B, 4,000 type C, and 2,000 type D, and if we assume the line operates 20 days per month, then this would be translated to a daily output of 400, 300, 200, and 100, respectively. Further, this would be sequenced as four units of A, three of B, two of C, and one of D each 9.6 minutes of a two-shift day (960 minutes).

Each worker operates a number of machines, producing a sequence of products. To use this level scheduling technique,

1. Production should be repetitive (assembly-line format).
2. The system must contain excess capacity.
3. Output of the system must be fixed for a period of time (preferably a month).
4. There must be a smooth relationship among purchasing, marketing, and production.
5. The cost of carrying inventory must be high.
6. Equipment costs must be low.
7. The workforce must be multiskilled.

For more about level scheduling, see lean production schedules in Chapter 13. Also see the discussion on mixed-model line balancing in Chapter 6.

YIELD MANAGEMENT

Yield management

Service

Why is it that the guy sitting next to you on the plane paid half the price you paid for your ticket? Why was a hotel room you booked more expensive when you booked it six months in advance than when you checked in without a reservation (or vice versa)? The answers lie in the practice known as yield management. Yield management can be defined as the process of allocating the right type of capacity to the right type of customer at the right price and time to maximize revenue or yield. Yield management can be a powerful approach to making demand more predictable, which is important to aggregate planning.

Yield management has existed as long as there has been limited capacity for serving customers. However, its widespread scientific application began with American Airlines' computerized reservation system (SABRE), introduced in the mid-1980s. The system allowed the airline to change ticket prices on any routes instantaneously as a function of forecast demand. Peoples' Express, a no-frills, low-cost competitor airline, was one of the most famous victims of American's yield management system. Basically, the system enabled hour-by-hour updating on competing routes so that American could match or better prices wherever Peoples' Express was flying. The president of Peoples' Express realized that the game was lost when his mother flew on American to Peoples' hub for a lower price than Peoples' could offer!

From an operational perspective, yield management is most effective when

1. Demand can be segmented by customer.
2. Fixed costs are high and variable costs are low.
3. Inventory is perishable.

4. Product can be sold in advance.
5. Demand is highly variable.

Hotels illustrate these five characteristics well. They offer one set of rates during the week for the business traveler and another set during the weekend for the vacationer. The variable costs associated with a room (such as cleaning) are low in comparison to the cost of adding rooms to the property. Available rooms cannot be transferred from night to night, and blocks of rooms can be sold to conventions or tours. Finally, potential guests may cut short their stay or not show up at all.

Most organizations (such as airlines, rental car agencies, cruise lines, and hotels) manage yield by establishing decision rules for opening or closing rate classes as a function of expected demand and available supply. The methodologies for doing this can be quite sophisticated. A common approach is to forecast demand over the planning horizon and then use marginal analysis to determine the rates that will be charged if demand is forecast as being above or below set control limits around the forecast mean.

OPERATING YIELD MANAGEMENT SYSTEMS

A number of interesting issues arise in managing yield. One is that pricing structures must appear logical to the customer and justify the different prices. Such justification, commonly called *rate fences,* may have either a physical basis (such as a room with a view) or a nonphysical basis (like unrestricted access to the Internet). Pricing also should relate to addressing specific capacity problems. If capacity is sufficient for peak demand, price reductions stimulating off-peak demand should be the focus. If capacity is insufficient, offering deals to customers who arrive during nonpeak periods (or creating alternative service locations) may enhance revenue generation.

A second issue is handling variability in arrival or starting times, duration, and time between customers. This entails employing maximally accurate forecasting methods (the greater the accuracy in forecasting demand, the more likely yield management will succeed); coordinated policies on overbooking, deposits, and no-show or cancellation penalties; and well-designed service processes that are reliable and consistent.

THE HOTEL WITH FREE INTERNET ACCESS IS AN EXAMPLE OF A NON-PHYSICAL RATE FENCE.

A third issue relates to managing the service process. Some strategies include scheduling additional personnel to meet peak demand; increasing customer self service; creating adjustable capacity; utilizing idle capacity for complementary services; and cross-training employees to create reserves for peak periods.

Service

The fourth and perhaps most critical issue is training workers and managers to work in an environment where overbooking and price changes are standard occurrences that directly impact the customer. Companies have developed creative ways of mollifying overbooked customers. A golf course company offers $100 putters to players who have been overbooked at a popular tee time. Airlines, of course, frequently give overbooked passengers free tickets for other flights.

The essence of yield management is the ability to manage demand. Kimes and Chase suggest that two strategic levers can be used to accomplish this goal: pricing and duration control.[3] If these two levers are thought of in matrix form (see Exhibit 16.9) with price being either fixed or variable and duration being either predictable or unpredictable, then firms located in the variable price/predictable duration quadrant have practiced traditional applications of yield management. This type of matrix provides a framework for a firm to identify its position and the necessary actions to manage yield. For example, an action controlling duration would be to convert the service offering from an event of indeterminate time to an offering that is time-based. This improves reservation planning and hence allocation of resources. An example would be having diners reserve a fixed block of time for dining at a restaurant (e.g., 7–8 P.M.) rather than an open-ended table reservation for 7 P.M.

| exhibit 16.9 | Price/Service Duration Matrix: Positioning of Selected Service Industries |

		PRICE	
		FIXED	VARIABLE
DURATION	PREDICTABLE	Movies Stadiums/arenas Convention centers	Hotels Airlines Rental cars Cruise lines
	UNPREDICTABLE	Restaurants Golf courses Internet service providers	Continuing care hospitals

SOURCE: S. KIMES AND R. B. CHASE, "THE STRATEGIC LEVERS OF YIELD MANAGEMENT," *JOURNAL OF SERVICE RESEARCH* 1, NO. 2 (1998), PP. 298–308. COPYRIGHT © 1998 BY SAGE PUBLISHERS. USED BY PERMISSION OF SAGE PUBLICATIONS, INC.

SUMMARY

Sales and operations planning and the aggregate plan translate corporate strategic and capacity plans into broad categories of workforce size, inventory quantity, and production levels.

Demand variations are a fact of life, so the planning system must include sufficient flexibility to cope with such variations. Flexibility can be achieved by developing alternative sources of supply, cross-training workers to handle a wide variety of orders, and engaging in more frequent replanning during high-demand periods.

Decision rules for production planning should be adhered to once they have been selected. However, they should be carefully analyzed prior to implementation by checks such as simulation of historical data to see what really would have happened if the decision rules had operated in the past.

Yield management is an important tool that can be used to shape demand patterns so a firm can operate more efficiently.

KEY TERMS

Aggregate operations plan Translating annual and quarterly business plans into labor and production output plans for the intermediate term. The objective is to minimize the cost of resources required to meet demand.

Sales and operations planning A term that refers to the process that helps companies keep demand and supply in balance. The terminology is meant to capture the importance of cross-functional work.

Long-range planning Activity typically done annually and focusing on a horizon of a year or more.

Intermediate-range planning Activity that usually covers a period from 3 to 18 months with weekly, monthly, or quarterly time increments.

Short-range planning Planning that covers a period less than six months with either daily or weekly increments of time.

Production rate The number of units completed per unit of time.

Workforce level The number of production workers needed each period.

Inventory on hand Unused inventory carried from a previous period.

Production planning strategies Plans that involve trade-offs among workforce size, work hours, inventory, and backlogs.

Pure strategy A plan that uses just one of the options available for meeting demand. Typical options include chasing demand, using a stable workforce with overtime or part-time work, and constant production with shortages and overages absorbed by inventory.

Mixed strategy A plan that combines options available for meeting demand.

Yield management Allocating the right type of capacity to the right type of customer at the right price and time to maximize revenue or yield.

SOLVED PROBLEM

Jason Enterprises (JE) produces video telephones for the home market. Quality is not quite as good as it could be at this point, but the selling price is low and Jason can study market response while spending more time on R&D.

At this stage, however, JE needs to develop an aggregate production plan for the six months from January through June. You have been commissioned to create the plan. The following information should help:

Excel: Aggregate Planning Solved Problem

DEMAND AND WORKING DAYS

	JANUARY	FEBRUARY	MARCH	APRIL	MAY	JUNE	TOTALS
Demand forecast	500	600	650	800	900	800	4,250
Number of working days	22	19	21	21	22	20	125

COSTS

Materials	$100.00/unit
Inventory holding cost	$10.00/unit/month
Marginal cost of stockout	$20.00/unit/month
Marginal cost of subcontracting	$100.00/unit ($200 subcontracting cost less $100 material savings)
Hiring and training cost	$50.00/worker
Layoff cost	$100.00/worker
Labor hours required	4/unit
Straight-time cost (first eight hours each day)	$12.50/hour
Overtime cost (time and a half)	$18.75/hour

INVENTORY

Beginning inventory	200 units
Safety stock required	0% of month demand

What is the cost of each of the following production strategies?

a. Produce exactly to meet demand; vary workforce (assuming opening workforce equal to first month's requirements).

b. Constant workforce; vary inventory and allow shortages only (assuming a starting workforce of 10).

c. Constant workforce of 10; use subcontracting.

Solution

AGGREGATE PRODUCTION PLANNING REQUIREMENTS

	JANUARY	FEBRUARY	MARCH	APRIL	MAY	JUNE	TOTAL
Beginning inventory	200	0	0	0	0	0	
Demand forecast	500	600	650	800	900	800	
Safety stock (0.0 × Demand forecast)	0	0	0	0	0	0	
Production requirement (Demand forecast + Safety stock − Beginning inventory)	300	600	650	800	900	800	
Ending inventory (Beginning inventory + Production requirement − Demand forecast)	0	0	0	0	0	0	

(continued)

PRODUCTION PLAN 1: EXACT PRODUCTION; VARY WORKFORCE

	JANUARY	FEBRUARY	MARCH	APRIL	MAY	JUNE	TOTAL
Production requirement	300	600	650	800	900	800	
Production hours required (Production requirement × 4 hr./unit)	1,200	2,400	2,600	3,200	3,600	3,200	
Working days per month	22	19	21	21	22	20	
Hours per month per worker (Working days × 8 hrs./day)	176	152	168	168	176	160	
Workers required (Production hours required/Hours per month per worker)	7	16	15	19	20	20	
New workers hired (assuming opening workforce equal to first month's requirement of 7 workers)	0	9	0	4	1	0	
Hiring cost (New workers hired × $50)	$0	$450	$0	$200	$50	$0	$700
Workers laid off	0	0	1	0	0	0	
Layoff cost (Workers laid off × $100)	$0	$0	$100	$0	$0	$0	$100
Straight-time cost (Production hours required × $12.50)	$15,000	$30,000	$32,500	$40,000	$45,000	$40,000	$202,500

Total cost $203,300

PRODUCTION PLAN 2: CONSTANT WORKFORCE; VARY INVENTORY AND STOCKOUT

	JANUARY	FEBRUARY	MARCH	APRIL	MAY	JUNE	TOTAL
Beginning inventory	200	140	−80	−310	−690	−1150	
Working days per month	22	19	21	21	22	20	
Production hours available (Working days per month × 8 hr./day × 10 workers)*	1,760	1,520	1,680	1,680	1,760	1,600	
Actual production (Production hours available/4 hr./unit)	440	380	420	420	440	400	
Demand forecast	500	600	650	800	900	800	
Ending inventory (Beginning inventory + Actual production − Demand forecast)	140	−80	−310	−690	−1150	−1550	
Shortage cost (Units short × $20)	$0	$1,600	$6,200	$13,800	$23,000	$31,000	$75,600
Safety stock	0	0	0	0	0	0	
Units excess (Ending inventory − Safety stock; only if positive amount)	140	0	0	0	0	0	
Inventory cost (Units excess × $10)	$1,400	$0	$0	$0	$0	$0	$1,400
Straight-time cost (Production hours available × $12.50)	$22,000	$19,000	$21,000	$21,000	$22,000	$20,000	$125,000

Total cost $202,000

*Assume a constant workforce of 10.

PRODUCTION PLAN 3: CONSTANT WORKFORCE; SUBCONTRACT

	JANUARY	FEBRUARY	MARCH	APRIL	MAY	JUNE	TOTAL
Production requirement	300	460[†]	650	800	900	800	
Working days per month	22	19	21	21	22	20	
Production hours available (Working days × 8 hrs./ day × 10 workers)*	1,760	1,520	1,680	1,680	1,760	1,600	
Actual production (Production hours available/4 hr. per unit)	440	380	420	420	440	400	
Units subcontracted (Production requirements − Actual production)	0	80	230	380	460	400	
Subcontracting cost (Units subcontracted × $100)	$0	$8,000	$23,000	$38,000	$46,000	$40,000	$155,000
Straight-time cost (Production hours available × $12.50)	$22,000	$19,000	$21,000	$21,000	$22,000	$20,000	$125,000

Total cost $280,000

*Assume a constant workforce of 10.
[†]600 − 140 units of beginning inventory in February.

SUMMARY

PLAN DESCRIPTION	HIRING	LAYOFF	SUBCONTRACT	STRAIGHT TIME	SHORTAGE	EXCESS INVEN-TORY	TOTAL COST
1. Exact production; vary workforce	$700	$100		$202,500			$203,300
2. Constant workforce; vary inventory and shortages				$125,000	$75,600	$1,400	$202,000
3. Constant workforce; subcontract			$155,000	$125,000			$280,000

REVIEW AND DISCUSSION QUESTIONS

1 What are the major differences between aggregate planning in manufacturing and aggregate planning in services?
2 What are the basic controllable variables of a production planning problem? What are the four major costs?
3 Distinguish between pure and mixed strategies in production planning.
4 Define level scheduling. How does it differ from the pure strategies in production planning?
5 How does forecast accuracy relate, in general, to the practical application of the aggregate planning models discussed in the chapter?
6 In which way does the time horizon chosen for an aggregate plan determine whether it is the best plan for the firm?
7 Review the opening vignette. How does sales and operations planning help resolve product shortage problems?
8 How would you apply yield management concepts to a barbershop? A soft drink vending machine?

PROBLEMS

1 For the solved problem, devise the least costly plan you can. You may choose your starting workforce level.
2 Develop a production plan and calculate the annual cost for a firm whose demand forecast is fall, 10,000; winter, 8,000; spring, 7,000; summer, 12,000. Inventory at the beginning of fall is 500 units. At the beginning of fall you currently have 30 workers, but you plan to hire temporary workers at the beginning of summer and lay them off at the end of the summer. In

addition, you have negotiated with the union an option to use the regular workforce on overtime during winter or spring if overtime is necessary to prevent stockouts at the end of those quarters. Overtime is *not* available during the fall. Relevant costs are: hiring, $100 for each temp; layoff, $200 for each worker laid off; inventory holding, $5 per unit-quarter; backorder, $10 per unit; straight time, $5 per hour; overtime, $8 per hour. Assume that the productivity is 0.5 unit per worker hour, with eight hours per day and 60 days per season.

3   Plan production for a four-month period: February through May. For February and March, you should produce to exact demand forecast. For April and May, you should use overtime and inventory with a stable workforce; *stable* means that the number of workers needed for March will be held constant through May. However, government constraints put a maximum of 5,000 hours of overtime labor per month in April and May (zero overtime in February and March). If demand exceeds supply, then backorders occur. There are 100 workers on January 31. You are given the following demand forecast: February, 80,000; March, 64,000; April, 100,000; May, 40,000. Productivity is four units per worker hour, eight hours per day, 20 days per month. Assume zero inventory on February 1. Costs are hiring, $50 per new worker; layoff, $70 per worker laid off; inventory holding, $10 per unit-month; straight-time labor, $10 per hour; overtime, $15 per hour; backorder, $20 per unit. Find the total cost of this plan.

4   Plan production for the next year. The demand forecast is spring, 20,000; summer, 10,000; fall, 15,000; winter, 18,000. At the beginning of spring you have 70 workers and 1,000 units in inventory. The union contract specifies that you may lay off workers only once a year, at the beginning of summer. Also, you may hire new workers only at the end of summer to begin regular work in the fall. The number of workers laid off at the beginning of summer and the number hired at the end of summer should result in planned production levels for summer and fall that equal the demand forecasts for summer and fall, respectively. If demand exceeds supply, use overtime in spring only, which means that backorders could occur in winter. You are given these costs: hiring, $100 per new worker; layoff, $200 per worker laid off; holding, $20 per unit-quarter; backorder cost, $8 per unit; straight-time labor, $10 per hour; overtime, $15 per hour. Productivity is 0.5 unit per worker hour, eight hours per day, 50 days per quarter. Find the total cost.

5   DAT, Inc., needs to develop an aggregate plan for its product line. Relevant data are

Production time	1 hour per unit	Beginning inventory	500 units
Average labor cost	$10 per hour	Safety stock	One-half month
Workweek	5 days, 8 hours each day	Shortage cost	$20 per unit per month
Days per month	Assume 20 work days per month	Carrying cost	$5 per unit per month

The forecast for next year is

JAN.	FEB.	MAR.	APR.	MAY	JUNE	JULY	AUG.	SEPT.	OCT.	NOV.	DEC.
2,500	3,000	4,000	3,500	3,500	3,000	3,000	4,000	4,000	4,000	3,000	3,000

Management prefers to keep a constant workforce and production level, absorbing variations in demand through inventory excesses and shortages. Demand not met is carried over to the following month.

Develop an aggregate plan that will meet the demand and other conditions of the problem. Do not try to find the optimum; just find a good solution and state the procedure you might use to test for a better solution. Make any necessary assumptions.

6   Old Pueblo Engineering Contractors creates six-month "rolling" schedules, which are recomputed monthly. For competitive reasons (it would need to divulge proprietary design criteria, methods, and so on), Old Pueblo does not subcontract. Therefore, its only options to meet customer requirements are (1) work on regular time; (2) work on overtime, which is limited to 30 percent of regular time; (3) do customers' work early, which would cost an additional $5 per hour per month; and (4) perform customers' work late, which would cost an additional $10 per hour per month penalty, as provided by their contract.

Old Pueblo has 25 engineers on its staff at an hourly rate of $30. The overtime rate is $45. Customers' hourly requirements for the six months from January to June are

JANUARY	FEBRUARY	MARCH	APRIL	MAY	JUNE
5,000	4,000	6,000	6,000	5,000	4,000

Develop an aggregate plan using a spreadsheet. Assume 20 working days in each month.

7 Alan Industries is expanding its product line to include new models: Model A, Model B, and Model C. These are to be produced on the same production equipment, and the objective is to meet the demands for the three products using overtime where necessary. The demand forecast for the next four months, in required hours, is

PRODUCT	APRIL	MAY	JUNE	JULY
Model A	800	600	800	1,200
Model B	600	700	900	1,100
Model C	700	500	700	850

Because the products deteriorate rapidly, there is a high loss in quality and, consequently, a high carryover cost into subsequent periods. Each hour's production carried into future months costs $3 per production hour of Model A, $4 for Model B, and $5 for Model C.

Production can take place during either regular working hours or overtime. Regular time is paid at $4 when working on Model A, $5 for Model B, and $6 for Model C. Overtime premium is 50 percent.

The available production capacity for regular time and overtime is

	APRIL	MAY	JUNE	JULY
Regular time	1,500	1,300	1,800	1,700
Overtime	$700	650	900	850

a. Set up the problem in matrix form and show appropriate costs.

b. Show a feasible solution.

8 Shoney Video Concepts produces a line of videodisc players to be linked to personal computers for video games. With such a computer/video link, the game becomes a very realistic experience. In a simple driving game where the joystick steers the vehicle, for example, rather than seeing computer graphics on the screen, the player is actually viewing a segment of a videodisc shot from a real moving vehicle. Depending on the action of the player (hitting a guard rail, for example), the disc moves virtually instantaneously to that segment and the player becomes part of an actual accident of real vehicles (staged, of course).

Shoney is trying to determine a production plan for the next 12 months. The main criterion for this plan is that the employment level is to be held constant over the period. Shoney is continuing in its R&D efforts to develop new applications and prefers not to cause any adverse feeling with the local workforce. For the same reason, all employees should put in full work-weeks, even if this is not the lowest-cost alternative. The forecast for the next 12 months is

MONTH	FORECAST DEMAND	MONTH	FORECAST DEMAND
January	600	July	200
February	800	August	200
March	900	September	300
April	600	October	700
May	400	November	800
June	300	December	900

Manufacturing cost is $200 per set, equally divided between materials and labor. Inventory storage cost is $5 per month. A shortage of sets results in lost sales and is estimated to cost an overall $20 per unit short.

The inventory on hand at the beginning of the planning period is 200 units. Ten labor hours are required per videodisc player. The workday is eight hours.

Develop an aggregate production schedule for the year using a constant workforce. For simplicity, assume 22 working days each month except July, when the plant closes down for three weeks' vacation (leaving seven working days). Assume that total production capacity is greater than or equal to total demand.

9 Develop a production schedule to produce the exact production requirements by varying the workforce size for the following problem. Use the example in the chapter as a guide (Plan 1).

The monthly forecasts for Product X for January, February, and March are 1,000, 1,500, and 1,200, respectively. Safety stock policy recommends that half of the forecast for that month be defined as safety stock. There are 22 working days in January, 19 in February, and 21 in March. Beginning inventory is 500 units.

Manufacturing cost is $200 per unit, storage cost is $3 per unit per month, standard pay rate is $6 per hour, overtime rate is $9 per hour, cost of stockout is $10 per unit per month, marginal cost of subcontracting is $10 per unit, hiring and training cost is $200 per worker, layoff cost is $300 per worker, and worker productivity is 0.1 unit per hour. Assume that you start off with 50 workers and that they work 8 hours per day.

10   Helter Industries, a company that produces a line of women's bathing suits, hires temporaries to help produce its summer product demand. For the current four-month rolling schedule, there are three temps on staff and 12 full-time employees. The temps can be hired when needed and can be used as needed, whereas the full-time employees must be paid whether they are needed or not. Each full-time employee can produce 205 suits, while each part-time employee can produce 165 suits per month.

Demand for bathing suits for the next four months is as follows:

MAY	JUNE	JULY	AUGUST
3,200	2,800	3,100	3,000

Beginning inventory in May is 403 complete (a complete two-piece includes both top and bottom) bathing suits. Bathing suits cost $40 to produce and carrying cost is 24 percent per year. Develop an aggregate plan using a spreadsheet.

CASE: BRADFORD MANUFACTURING—PLANNING PLANT PRODUCTION

Excel: Bradford Manufacturing

THE SITUATION

You are the operations manager for a manufacturing plant that produces pudding food products. One of your important responsibilities is to prepare an aggregate plan for the plant. This plan is an important input into the annual budget process. The plan provides information on production rates, manufacturing labor requirements, and projected finished goods inventory levels for the next year.

You make those little boxes of pudding mix on packaging lines in your plant. A packaging line has a number of machines that are linked by conveyors. At the start of the line the pudding is mixed; it is then placed in small packets. These packets are inserted into the small pudding boxes, which are collected and placed in cases that hold 48 boxes of pudding. Finally, 160 cases are collected and put on a pallet. The pallets are staged in a shipping area from which they are sent to four distribution centers. Over the years, the technology of the packaging lines has improved so that all the different flavors can be made in relatively small batches with no setup time to switch between flavors. The plant has 15 of these lines, but currently only 10 are being used. Six employees are required to run each line.

The demand for this product fluctuates from month to month. In addition, there is a seasonal component, with peak sales before Thanksgiving, Christmas, and Easter each year. To complicate matters, at the end of the first quarter of each year the marketing group runs a promotion in which special deals are made for large purchases. Business is going well, and the company has been experiencing a general increase in sales.

The plant sends product to four large distribution warehouses strategically located in the United States. Trucks move product daily. The amounts shipped are based on maintaining target inventory levels at the warehouses. These targets are calculated based on anticipated weeks of supply at each warehouse. Current targets are set at two weeks of supply.

In the past, the company has had a policy of producing very close to what it expects sales to be because of limited capacity for storing finished goods. Production capacity has been adequate to support this policy.

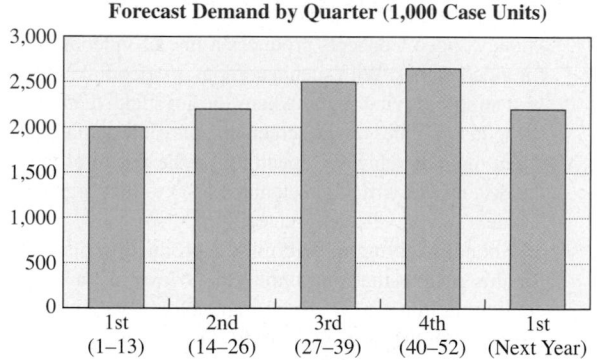

Forecast Demand by Quarter (1,000 Case Units)

A sales forecast for next year has been prepared by the marketing department. The forecast is based on quarterly sales quotas, which are used to set up an incentive program for the salespeople. Sales are mainly to the large U.S. retail grocers. The pudding is shipped to the grocers from the distribution warehouses based on orders taken by the salespeople.

Your immediate task is to prepare an aggregate plan for the coming year. The technical and economic factors that must be considered in this plan are shown next.

TECHNICAL AND ECONOMIC INFORMATION

1   Currently the plant is running 10 lines with no overtime. Each line requires six people to run. For planning purposes, the lines are run for 7.5 hours each normal shift. Employees, though, are paid for eight hours' work. It is possible to run up to two hours of overtime each day, but it must be scheduled for a week at a time, and all the lines must run overtime when it is scheduled. Workers are paid $20.00/hour during a regular shift and $30.00/hour on overtime. The standard production rate for each line is 450 cases/hour.

2   The marketing forecast for demand is as follows: Q1—2,000; Q2—2,200; Q3—2,500; Q4—2,650; and Q1 (next year)—

2,200. These numbers are in 1,000-case units. Each number represents a 13-week forecast.

3   Management has instructed manufacturing to maintain a two-week supply of pudding inventory in the warehouses. The two-week supply should be based on future expected sales. The following are ending inventory target levels for each quarter: Q1—338; Q2—385; Q3—408; Q4—338.

4   Inventory carrying cost is estimated by accounting to be $1.00 per case per year. This means that if a case of pudding is held in inventory for an entire year, the cost to just carry that case in inventory is $1.00. If a case is carried for only one week, the cost is $1.00/52, or $.01923. The cost is proportional to the time carried in inventory. There are 200,000 cases in inventory at the beginning of Q1 (this is 200 cases in the 1,000-case units that the forecast is given in).

5   If a stockout occurs, the item is backordered and shipped at a later date. The cost when a backorder occurs is $2.40 per case due to the loss of goodwill and the high cost of emergency shipping.

6   The human resource group estimates that it costs $5,000 to hire and train a new production employee. It costs $3,000 to lay off a production worker.

QUESTIONS

1   Prepare an aggregate plan for the coming year, assuming that the sales forecast is perfect. Use the spreadsheet "Bradford Manufacturing." In the spreadsheet an area has been designated for your aggregate plan solution. Supply the number of packaging lines to run and the number of overtime hours for each quarter. You will need to set up the cost calculations in the spreadsheet.

You may want to try using the Excel Solver to find a solution. Remember that your final solution needs an integer number of lines and an integer number of overtime hours for each quarter. (Solutions that require 8.9134 lines and 1.256 hours of overtime are not feasible.)

2   Review your solution carefully and be prepared to defend it. Bring a printout of your solution to class.

SUPER QUIZ

1   Term for the process a firm uses to balance supply and demand.

2   In aggregate planning, these are the three general operations–related variables that can be varied.

3   A strategy where the production rate is set to match expected demand.

4   When overtime is used to meet demand and avoid the costs associated with hiring and firing.

5   A strategy that uses inventory and backorders as part of the strategy to meet demand.

6   Sometimes a firm may choose to have all or part of the work done by an outside vendor. This is the term used for the approach.

7   If expected demand during the next four quarters were 150, 125, 100, 75 thousand units and each worker can produce 1,000 units per quarter; how many workers should be used if a level strategy were being employed?

8   Given the data from question 7, how many workers would be needed for a chase strategy?

9   In a service setting, what general operations–related variable is not available compared to a production setting?

10 The practice of allocating capacity and manipulating demand to make it more predictable.

1. Sales and operations planning 2. Production rate, workforce level, inventory 3. Chase 4. Stable workforce—variable work hours 5. Level strategy 6. Subcontracting 7. 113 8. 150, 125, 100, 75 9. Inventory 10. Yield management

SELECTED BIBLIOGRAPHY

Brandimarte, P., and A. Villa (eds.). *Modeling Manufacturing Systems: From Aggregate Planning to Real-Time Control.* New York: Springer, 1999.

Fisher, M. L.; J. H. Hammond; W. R. Obermeyer; and A. Raman. "Making Supply Meet Demand in an Uncertain World." *Harvard Business Review* 72, no. 3 (May–June 1994), pp. 83–93.

Narasimhan, S.; D. W. McLeavey; and P. J. Billington. *Production Planning and Inventory Control.* Englewood Cliffs, NJ: Prentice Hall, 1995.

Silver, E. A.; D. F. Pyke; and R. Peterson. *Inventory Management and Production Planning and Scheduling.* New York: Wiley, 1998.

Vollmann, T. E.; W. L. Berry; D. C. Whybark; and F. R. Jacobs. *Manufacturing Planning and Control for Supply Chain Management.* 5th ed. New York: Irwin/McGraw-Hill, 2004.

Wallace, T. F. *Sales and Operations Planning: The How-To Handbook.* Cincinnati, OH: T. F. Wallace & Company, 2000.

FOOTNOTES

1   M. L. Fisher, J. H. Hammond, W. R. Obermeyer, and A. Raman, "Making Supply Meet Demand in an Uncertain World," *Harvard Business Review* 72, no. 3 (May–June 1994), p. 84.

2   For an interesting application of aggregate planning in nonprofit humanitarian organizations, see C. Sheu and J. G. Wacker, "A Planning and Control Framework for Nonprofit Humanitarian Organizations," *International Journal of Operations and Production Management* 14, no. 4 (1994), pp. 64–77.

3   S. Kimes and R. B. Chase, "The Strategic Levers of Yield Management," *Journal of Service Research* 1, no. 2 (1998), pp. 298–308.

INVENTORY CONTROL

chapter 17

Supply Chain

After reading the chapter you will:

1. Explain the different purposes for keeping inventory.

2. Understand that the type of inventory system logic that is appropriate for an item depends on the type of demand for that item.

3. Calculate the appropriate order size when a one-time purchase must be made.

4. Describe what the economic order quantity is and how to calculate it.

5. Summarize fixed–order quantity and fixed–time period models, including ways to determine safety stock when there is variability in demand.

6. Discuss why inventory turn is directly related to order quantity and safety stock.

Global

DIRECT TO STORE—THE UPS VISION

Logistics visionaries have talked for years about eliminating— or, at least, drastically reducing—the role of inventory in modern supply chains. The most efficient, slack-free supply chains, after all, wouldn't require any inventory buffer, because supply and demand would be in perfect sync. This vision certainly has its appeal: The death of inventory would mean dramatically reduced logistics costs and simplified fulfillment.

There's no need to write a eulogy for inventory just yet. Most companies haven't honed their networks and technolo-

gies well enough to eliminate the need for at least minimal inventory. Logistics managers have to perform a daily, delicate balancing act, balancing

- Transportation costs against fulfillment speed
- Inventory costs against the cost of stock-outs
- Customer satisfaction against cost to serve
- New capabilities against profitability

What's more, two accelerating business trends are making it even harder to synchronize supply chains.

First, global sourcing is forcing supply chains to stretch farther across borders. The goods people consume are increasingly made in some other part of the world, particularly in Asia. This acceleration in global sourcing changes the logistics equation. When goods cross borders, considerations such as fulfillment speed (these are the activities performed once an order is received) and inventory costs get more complicated. Second, powerful retailers and other end customers with clout are starting to push value-added supply chain responsibilities further up the supply chain. More customers are asking manufacturers or third-party logistics providers to label and prepare individual items so the products are ready to go directly to store shelves. With added responsibilities, of course, come added costs. Upstream suppliers are always looking for ways to squeeze more costs out of other areas of the supply chain, such as transportation and distribution.

THE UPS DIRECT APPROACH

A growing number of companies are overcoming these barriers by taking a more direct approach to global fulfillment. This direct-to-store approach—also known as distribution center bypass or direct distribution—keeps inventory moving from manufacturer to end customer by eliminating stops at warehouses along the way. Because companies can shrink the fulfillment cycle and eliminate inventory costs, direct-to-store can offer a good balance between fulfillment speed and logistics costs.

What accounts for the emergence of the direct-to-store model?

Global sourcing and the upstream migration of value-added logistics services are certainly primary drivers. But other pieces of the puzzle have fallen into place in recent years to make direct-to-store shipments feasible.

Internet-enabled electronic links between supply chain partners have allowed better coordination and collaboration among the various supply chain segments. Meanwhile, at the front of the supply chain, increasingly sophisticated point-of-sale systems can capture product demand patterns. This information can then be fed up the supply chain to manufacturers and components suppliers. More accurate sales-forecasting tools take some of the guesswork out of production and reduce the need for large inventory safety stocks. Tracking and tracing tools are also available to follow orders across borders and through the hands of different supply partners.

In short, companies no longer need as much inventory gathering dust in warehouses because they can better synchronize production and distribution with demand. Direct-to-store lets them keep inventory in motion—across borders and around the world.

See United Parcel Service of America (UPS) Supply Chain Solutions for more information about these types of services: www.ups.com.

You should visualize inventory as stacks of money sitting on forklifts, on shelves, and in trucks and planes while in transit. That's what inventory is—money. For many businesses, inventory is the largest asset on the balance sheet at any given time, even though it is often not very liquid. It is a good idea to try to get your inventory down as far as possible.

A few years ago, Heineken, the Netherlands beer company, figured it could save a whole bunch of money on inventory-in-transit if it could just shorten the forecasting lead time. Management expected two things to happen. First, they expected to reduce the need for inventory in the pipeline, therefore cutting down the amount of money devoted to inventory itself. Second, they figured that with a shorter forecasting time, forecasts would be more accurate, reducing emergencies and waste. The Heineken system, called HOPS, cut overall inventory in the system from 16 to 18 weeks to 4 to 6 weeks—a huge

Global

drop in time, and a big gain in cash. Forecasts were more accurate, and there was another benefit, too.

Heineken found that its salespeople were suddenly more productive. That is because they were not dealing with all those calls where they had to check on inventory or solve bad forecasting problems, or change orders that were already in process. Instead, they could concentrate on good customer service and helping distributors do better. It was a "win" all the way around.

The key here involves doing things that decrease your inventory order cycle time and increase the accuracy of your forecast. Look for ways to use automated systems and electronic communication to substitute the rapid movement of electrons for the cumbersome movement of masses of atoms.

The economic benefit from inventory reduction is evident from the following statistics: The average cost of inventory in the United States is 30 to 35 percent of its value. For example, a firm that carries an inventory of $20 million accrues costs of more than $6 million per year mainly through obsolescence, insurance, and last opportunity. If the amount of inventory could be reduced to $10 million, for instance, the firm would save over $3 million, which goes directly to the bottom line. That is, the savings from reduced inventory results in increased profit.

This chapter and Chapter 18 present techniques designed to manage inventory in different supply chain settings. In this chapter, the focus is on settings where the desire is to maintain a stock of inventory that can be delivered to customers on demand. Recall in Chapter 6 the concept of *customer order decoupling point,* which is a point where inventory is positioned to allow processes or entities in the supply chain to operate independently. For example, if a product is stocked at a retailer, the customer pulls the item from the shelf and the manufacturer never sees a customer order. In this case, inventory acts as a buffer to separate the customer from the manufacturing process. Selection of decoupling points is a strategic decision that determines customer lead times and can greatly impact inventory investment. The closer this point is to the customer, the quicker the customer can be served.

Supply Chain

The techniques described in this chapter are suited for managing the inventory at these decoupling points. Typically, there is a trade-off where quicker response to customer demand comes at the expense of greater inventory investment. This is because finished goods inventory is more expensive than raw material inventory. In practice, the idea of a single decoupling point in a supply chain is unrealistic. There may actually be multiple points where buffering takes place.

Good examples of where the models described in this chapter are used include retail stores, grocery stores, wholesale distributors, hospital suppliers, and suppliers of repair parts needed to fix or maintain equipment quickly. Situations in which it is necessary to have the item "in-stock" are ideal candidates for the models described in this chapter. A distinction that needs to be made with the models included in this chapter is whether this is a one-time purchase, for example, for a seasonal item or for use at a special event, or whether the item will be stocked on an ongoing basis.

Service

Exhibit 17.1 depicts different types of supply chain inventories that would exist in a make-to-stock environment, typical of items directed at the consumer. In the upper echelons of the supply chain, which are supply points closer to the customer, stock usually is kept so that an item can be delivered quickly when a customer need occurs. Of course, there are many exceptions, but in general this is the case. The raw materials and manufacturing plant inventory held in the lower echelon potentially can be managed in a special way to take advantage of the planning and synchronization that are needed to efficiently operate this part of the supply chain. In this case, the models in this chapter are most appropriate for the upper echelon inventories (retail and warehouse), and the lower echelon should use the Material Requirements Planning (MRP) technique described in Chapter 18. The applicability of these models could be different for other environments such as when we produce directly to customer order as in the case of an aircraft manufacturer.

Supply Chain

The techniques described here are most appropriate when demand is difficult to predict with great precision. In these models, we characterize demand by using a probability

exhibit 17.1   Supply Chain Inventories—Make-to-Stock Environment

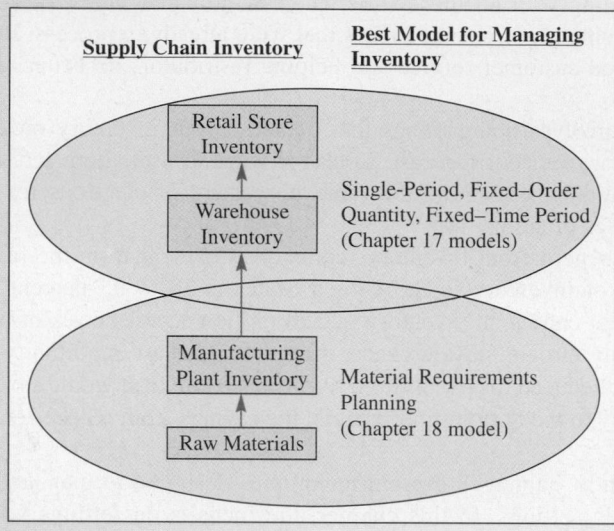

distribution and maintain stock so that the risk associated with stock out is managed. For these applications, the following three models are discussed:

1. **The single-period model.**   This is used when we are making a one-time purchase of an item. An example might be purchasing T-shirts to sell at a one-time sporting event.
2. **Fixed–order quantity model.**   This is used when we want to maintain an item "in-stock," and when we resupply the item, a certain number of units must be ordered each time. Inventory for the item is monitored until it gets down to a level where the risk of stocking out is great enough that we are compelled to order.
3. **Fixed–time period model.**   This is similar to the fixed–order quantity model; it is used when the item should be in-stock and ready to use. In this case, rather than monitoring the inventory level and ordering when the level gets down to a critical quantity, the item is ordered at certain intervals of time, for example, every Friday morning. This is often convenient when a group of items is ordered together. An example is the delivery of different types of bread to a grocery store. The bakery supplier may have 10 or more products stocked in a store, and rather than delivering each product individually at different times, it is much more efficient to deliver all 10 together at the same time and on the same schedule.

In this chapter, we want to show not only the mathematics associated with great inventory control but also the "art" of managing inventory. Ensuring accuracy in inventory records is essential to running an efficient inventory control process. Techniques such as ABC analysis and cycle counting are essential to the actual management of the system since they focus attention on the high-value items and ensure the quality of the transactions that affect the tracking of inventory levels.

DEFINITION OF INVENTORY

Inventory

Inventory is the stock of any item or resource used in an organization. An *inventory system* is the set of policies and controls that monitor levels of inventory and determine what levels should be maintained, when stock should be replenished, and how large orders should be.

By convention, *manufacturing inventory* generally refers to items that contribute to or become part of a firm's product output. Manufacturing inventory is typically classified into *raw materials, finished products, component parts, supplies,* and *work-in-process.* In services, *inventory* generally refers to the tangible goods to be sold and the supplies necessary to administer the service.

The basic purpose of inventory analysis in manufacturing and stockkeeping services is to specify (1) when items should be ordered and (2) how large the order should be. Many firms are tending to enter into longer-term relationships with vendors to supply their needs for perhaps the entire year. This changes the "when" and "how many to order" to "when" and "how many to deliver."

PURPOSES OF INVENTORY

All firms (including JIT operations) keep a supply of inventory for the following reasons:

1. **To maintain independence of operations.**   A supply of materials at a work center allows that center flexibility in operations. For example, because there are costs for making each new production setup, this inventory allows management to reduce the number of setups.

    Independence of workstations is desirable on assembly lines as well. The time needed to do identical operations will naturally vary from one unit to the next. Therefore, it is desirable to have a cushion of several parts within the workstation so that shorter performance times can compensate for longer performance times. This way the average output can be fairly stable.

2. **To meet variation in product demand.**   If the demand for the product is known precisely, it may be possible (though not necessarily economical) to produce the product to exactly meet the demand. Usually, however, demand is not completely known, and a safety or buffer stock must be maintained to absorb variation.

3. **To allow flexibility in production scheduling.**   A stock of inventory relieves the pressure on the production system to get the goods out. This causes longer lead times, which permit production planning for smoother flow and lower-cost operation through larger lot-size production. High setup costs, for example, favor producing a larger number of units once the setup has been made.

4. **To provide a safeguard for variation in raw material delivery time.**   When material is ordered from a vendor, delays can occur for a variety of reasons: a normal variation in shipping time, a shortage of material at the vendor's plant causing backlogs, an unexpected strike at the vendor's plant or at one of the shipping companies, a lost order, or a shipment of incorrect or defective material.

5. **To take advantage of economic purchase order size.**   There are costs to place an order: labor, phone calls, typing, postage, and so on. Therefore, the larger each order is, the fewer the orders that need to be written. Also, shipping costs favor larger orders—the larger the shipment, the lower the per-unit cost.

For each of the preceding reasons (especially for items 3, 4, and 5), be aware that inventory is costly and large amounts are generally undesirable. Long cycle times are caused by large amounts of inventory and are undesirable as well.

INVENTORY COSTS

In making any decision that affects inventory size, the following costs must be considered.

1. **Holding (or carrying) costs.**   This broad category includes the costs for storage facilities, handling, insurance, pilferage, breakage, obsolescence, depreciation, taxes,

and the opportunity cost of capital. Obviously, high holding costs tend to favor low inventory levels and frequent replenishment.

2. **Setup (or production change) costs.**   To make each different product involves obtaining the necessary materials, arranging specific equipment setups, filling out the required papers, appropriately charging time and materials, and moving out the previous stock of material.

   If there were no costs or loss of time in changing from one product to another, many small lots would be produced. This would reduce inventory levels, with a resulting savings in cost. One challenge today is to try to reduce these setup costs to permit smaller lot sizes. (This is the goal of a JIT system.)

3. **Ordering costs.**   These costs refer to the managerial and clerical costs to prepare the purchase or production order. Ordering costs include all the details, such as counting items and calculating order quantities. The costs associated with maintaining the system needed to track orders are also included in ordering costs.

4. **Shortage costs.**   When the stock of an item is depleted, an order for that item must either wait until the stock is replenished or be canceled. There is a trade-off between carrying stock to satisfy demand and the costs resulting from stockout. This balance is sometimes difficult to obtain, because it may not be possible to estimate lost profits, the effects of lost customers, or lateness penalties. Frequently, the assumed shortage cost is little more than a guess, although it is usually possible to specify a range of such costs.

Establishing the correct quantity to order from vendors or the size of lots submitted to the firm's production facilities involves a search for the minimum total cost resulting from the combined effects of four individual costs: holding costs, setup costs, ordering costs, and shortage costs. Of course, the timing of these orders is a critical factor that may impact inventory cost.

TOYOTA PRIUSES AND OTHER VEHICLES CLAD IN PROTECTIVE COVERING AWAIT SHIPMENT TO U.S. DEALERS AT THE LONG BEACH, CA, PORT. IN 2008 THE VALUE OF THE COMPANY'S INVENTORY TOTALED ABOUT ¥1.83 TRILLION AND THE COST OF GOODS SOLD WAS ¥21.5 TRILLION. SO TOYOTA'S INVENTORY TURNED OVER ABOUT 11.7 TIMES PER YEAR, OR ROUGHLY 31 DAYS OF INVENTORY ON HAND.

Global

INDEPENDENT VERSUS DEPENDENT DEMAND

In inventory management, it is important to understand the trade-offs involved in using different types of inventory control logic. Exhibit 17.2 is a framework that shows how characteristics of demand, transaction cost, and the risk of obsolete inventory map into different types of systems. The systems in the upper left of the exhibit are described in this chapter, and those in the lower right in Chapter 18.

Transaction cost is dependent on the level of integration and automation incorporated in the system. Manual systems such as simple *two-bin* logic depend on human posting of the transactions to replenish inventory, which is relatively expensive compared to using a computer to automatically detect when an item needs to be ordered. Integration relates to how connected systems are. For example, it is common for orders for material to be automatically transferred to suppliers electronically and for these orders to be automatically captured by the supplier inventory control system. This type of integration greatly reduces transaction cost.

The risk of obsolescence is also an important consideration. If an item is used infrequently or only for a specific purpose, there is considerable risk in using inventory control logic that does not track the specific source of demand for the item. Further, items that are sensitive to technical obsolescence, such as computer memory chips, and processors, need to be managed carefully based on actual need to reduce the risk of getting stuck with inventory that is outdated.

An important characteristic of demand relates to whether demand is derived from an end item or is related to the item itself. We use the terms independent and dependent demand to describe this characteristic. Briefly, the distinction between independent and dependent demand is this. In independent demand, the demands for various items are unrelated to each other. For example, a workstation may produce many parts that are unrelated but meet some external demand requirement. In dependent demand, the need for any one item is a direct result of the need for some other item, usually a higher-level item of which it is part.

Independent and dependent demand

In concept, dependent demand is a relatively straightforward computational problem. Needed quantities of a dependent-demand item are simply computed, based on the number needed in each higher-level item in which it is used. For example, if an automobile company plans on producing 500 cars per day, then obviously it will need 2,000 wheels and tires (plus spares). The number of wheels and tires needed is *dependent* on the production levels and

Inventory Control-System Design Matrix: Framework Describing Inventory Control Logic   **exhibit 17.2**

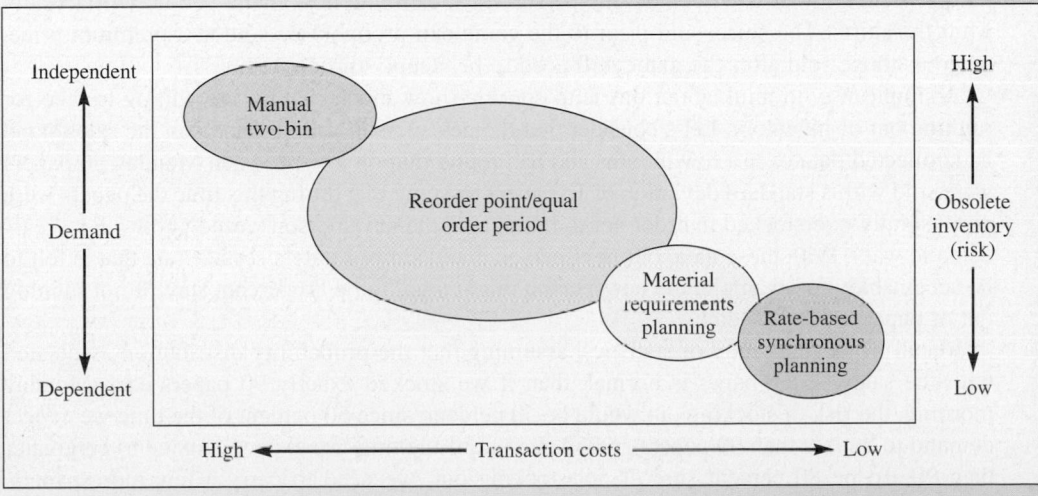

is not derived separately. The demand for cars, on the other hand, is *independent*—it comes from many sources external to the automobile firm and is not a part of other products; it is unrelated to the demand for other products.

To determine the quantities of independent items that must be produced, firms usually turn to their sales and market research departments. They use a variety of techniques, including customer surveys, forecasting techniques, and economic and sociological trends, as we discussed in Chapter 11 on forecasting. Because independent demand is uncertain, extra units must be carried in inventory. This chapter presents models to determine how many units need to be ordered, and how many extra units should be carried to reduce the risk of stocking out.

INVENTORY SYSTEMS

**Tutorial:
Inventory**

An inventory system provides the organizational structure and the operating policies for maintaining and controlling goods to be stocked. The system is responsible for ordering and receipt of goods: timing the order placement and keeping track of what has been ordered, how much, and from whom. The system also must follow up to answer such questions as, Has the supplier received the order? Has it been shipped? Are the dates correct? Are the procedures established for reordering or returning undesirable merchandise?

This section divides systems into single-period systems and multiple-period systems. The classification is based on whether the decision is just a one-time purchasing decision where the purchase is designed to cover a fixed period of time and the item will not be reordered, or the decision involves an item that will be purchased periodically where inventory should be kept in stock to be used on demand. We begin with a look at the one-time purchasing decision and the single-period inventory model.

Service

A SINGLE-PERIOD INVENTORY MODEL

Certainly, an easy example to think about is the classic single-period "newsperson" problem. For example, consider the problem that the newsperson has in deciding how many newspapers to put in the sales stand outside a hotel lobby each morning. If the person does not put enough papers in the stand, some customers will not be able to purchase a paper and the newsperson will lose the profit associated with these sales. On the other hand, if too many papers are placed in the stand, the newsperson will have paid for papers that were not sold during the day, lowering profit for the day.

Actually, this is a very common type of problem. Consider the person selling T-shirts promoting a championship basketball or football game. This is especially difficult, since the person must wait to learn what teams will be playing. The shirts can then be printed with the proper team logos. Of course, the person must estimate how many people will actually want the shirts. The shirts sold prior to the game can probably be sold at a premium price, whereas those sold after the game will need to be steeply discounted.

A simple way to think about this is to consider how much risk we are willing to take for running out of inventory. Let's consider that the newsperson selling papers in the sales stand had collected data over a few months and had found that on average each Monday 90 papers were sold with a standard deviation of 10 papers (assume that during this time the papers were purposefully overstocked in order not to run out, so the newsperson would know what "real" demand was). With these data, our newsperson could simply state a service rate that is felt to be acceptable. For example, the newsperson might want to be 80 percent sure of not running out of papers each Monday.

Recall from your study of statistics, assuming that the probability distribution associated with the sales of the paper is normal, then if we stocked exactly 90 papers each Monday morning, the risk of stocking out would be 50 percent, since 50 percent of the time we expect demand to be less than 90 papers and 50 percent of the time we expect demand to be greater than 90. To be 80 percent sure of not stocking out, we need to carry a few more papers. From the "cumulative standard normal distribution" table given in Appendix G, we see that we need approximately 0.85 standard deviation of extra papers to be 80 percent sure of not stocking out. A quick way to find the exact number of standard deviations needed for a given probability of stocking out is with the NORMSINV(probability) function in Microsoft Excel (NORMSINV(0.8) = 0.84162). Given our result from Excel, which is more accurate than what we can get from the tables, the number of extra papers would be 0.84162 × 10 = 8.416, or 9 papers (there is no way to sell 0.4 paper!).

To make this more useful, it would be good to actually consider the potential profit and loss associated with stocking either too many or too few papers on the stand. Let's say that our newspaper person pays $0.20 for each paper and sells the papers for $0.50. In this case the marginal cost associated with underestimating demand is $0.30, the lost profit. Similarly, the marginal cost of overestimating demand is $0.20, the cost of buying too many papers. The optimal stocking level, using marginal analysis, occurs at the point where the expected benefits derived from carrying the next unit are less than the expected costs for that unit. Keep in mind that the specific benefits and costs depend on the problem.

In symbolic terms, define

$$C_o = \text{Cost per unit of demand overestimated}$$
$$C_u = \text{Cost per unit of demand underestimated}$$

By introducing probabilities, the expected marginal cost equation becomes

$$P(C_o) \le (1 - P)C_u$$

where P is the probability that the unit will not be sold and $1 - P$ is the probability of it being sold, because one or the other must occur. (The unit is sold or is not sold.)[1]

Then, solving for P, we obtain

$$P \le \frac{C_u}{C_o + C_u} \qquad [17.1]$$

This equation states that we should continue to increase the size of the order so long as the probability of selling what we order is equal to or less than the ratio $C_u/(C_o + C_u)$.

Returning to our newspaper problem, our cost of overestimating demand (C_o) is $0.20 per paper and the cost of underestimating demand (C_u) is $0.30. The probability therefore is $0.3/(0.2 + 0.3) = 0.6$. Now, we need to find the point on our demand distribution that corresponds to the cumulative probability of 0.6. Using the NORMSINV function to get the number of standard deviations (commonly referred to as the Z-score) of extra newspapers to carry, we get 0.253, which means that we should stock 0.253(10) = 2.53 or 3 extra papers. The total number of papers for the stand each Monday morning, therefore, should be 93 papers.

This model is very useful and, as we will see in our solved sample problem, can even be used for many service sector problems, such as the number of seats to book on a full airline flight or the number of reservations to book on a full night at a hotel.

EXAMPLE 17.1: Hotel Reservations

A hotel near the university always fills up on the evening before football games. History has shown that when the hotel is fully booked, the number of last-minute cancellations has a mean of 5 and standard deviation of 3. The average room rate is $80. When the hotel is overbooked, policy is to find a room in a nearby hotel and to pay for the room for the customer. This usually costs the hotel approximately $200 since rooms booked on such late notice are expensive. How many rooms should the hotel overbook?

Step by Step

Service

SOLUTION

The cost of underestimating the number of cancellations is $80 and the cost of overestimating cancellations is $200.

$$P \le \frac{C_u}{C_o + C_u} = \frac{\$80}{\$200 + \$80} = 0.2857$$

Using NORMSINV(.2857) from Excel gives a Z-score of −0.56599. The negative value indicates that we should overbook by a value less than the average of 5. The actual value should be −0.56599(3) = −1.69797, or 2 reservations less than 5. The hotel should overbook three reservations on the evening prior to a football game.

Another common method for analyzing this type of problem is with a discrete probability distribution found using actual data and marginal analysis. For our hotel, consider that we have collected data and our distribution of no-shows is as follows:

NUMBER OF NO-SHOWS	PROBABILITY	CUMULATIVE PROBABILITY
0	0.05	0.05
1	0.08	0.13
2	0.10	0.23
3	0.15	0.38
4	0.20	0.58
5	0.15	0.73
6	0.11	0.84
7	0.06	0.90
8	0.05	0.95
9	0.04	0.99
10	0.01	1.00

Using these data, a table showing the impact of overbooking is created. Total expected cost of each overbooking option is then calculated by multiplying each possible outcome by its probability and summing the weighted costs. The best overbooking strategy is the one with minimum cost.

Excel: Inventory Control

No-Shows	Probability	\multicolumn{11}{c}{NUMBER OF RESERVATIONS OVERBOOKED}
		0	1	2	3	4	5	6	7	8	9	10
0	0.05	0	200	400	600	800	1,000	1,200	1,400	1,600	1,800	2,000
1	0.08	80	0	200	400	600	800	1,000	1,200	1,400	1,600	1,800
2	0.1	160	80	0	200	400	600	800	1,000	1,200	1,400	1,600
3	0.15	240	160	80	0	200	400	600	800	1,000	1,200	1,400
4	0.2	320	240	160	80	0	200	400	600	800	1,000	1,200
5	0.15	400	320	240	160	80	0	200	400	600	800	1,000
6	0.11	480	400	320	240	160	80	0	200	400	600	800
7	0.06	560	480	400	320	240	160	80	0	200	400	600
8	0.05	640	560	480	400	320	240	160	80	0	200	400
9	0.04	720	640	560	480	400	320	240	160	80	0	200
10	0.01	800	720	640	560	480	400	320	240	160	80	0
Total cost		337.6	271.6	228	212.4	238.8	321.2	445.6	600.8	772.8	958.8	1,156

From the table, the minimum total cost is when three extra reservations are taken. This approach using discrete probability is useful when valid historic data are available. ●

Single-period inventory models are useful for a wide variety of service and manufacturing applications. Consider the following:

Service

1. **Overbooking of airline flights.**   It is common for customers to cancel flight reservations for a variety of reasons. Here the cost of underestimating the number of cancellations is the revenue lost due to an empty seat on a flight. The cost of overestimating cancellations is the awards, such as free flights or cash payments, that are given to customers unable to board the flight.

2. **Ordering of fashion items.**   A problem for a retailer selling fashion items is that often only a single order can be placed for the entire season. This is often caused by long lead times and limited life of the merchandise. The cost of underestimating demand is the lost profit due to sales not made. The cost of overestimating demand is the cost that results when it is discounted.

3. **Any type of one-time order.**   Two examples are ordering T-shirts for a sporting event and printing maps that become obsolete after a certain period of time.

MULTIPERIOD INVENTORY SYSTEMS

There are two general types of multiperiod inventory systems: **fixed–order quantity models** (also called the *economic order quantity*, EOQ, and **Q-model**) and **fixed–time period models** (also referred to variously as the *periodic* system, *periodic review* system, *fixed-order interval* system, and **P-model**). Multiperiod inventory systems are designed to ensure that an item will be available on an ongoing basis throughout the year. Usually the item will be ordered multiple times throughout the year where the logic in the system dictates the actual quantity ordered and the timing of the order.

Fixed–order quantity models (Q-model)

Fixed–time period models (P-model)

The basic distinction is that fixed–order quantity models are "event triggered" and fixed–time period models are "time triggered." That is, a fixed–order quantity model initiates an order when the event of reaching a specified reorder level occurs. This event may take place at any time, depending on the demand for the items considered. In contrast, the fixed–time period model is limited to placing orders at the end of a predetermined time period; only the passage of time triggers the model.

To use the fixed–order quantity model (which places an order when the remaining inventory drops to a predetermined order point, R), the inventory remaining must be continually monitored. Thus, the fixed–order quantity model is a *perpetual* system, which requires that every time a withdrawal from inventory or an addition to inventory is made, records must be updated to reflect whether the reorder point has been reached. In a fixed–time period model, counting takes place only at the review period. (We will discuss some variations of systems that combine features of both.)

Some additional differences tend to influence the choice of systems (also see Exhibit 17.3):

- The fixed–time period model has a larger average inventory because it must also protect against stockout during the review period, T; the fixed–order quantity model has no review period.
- The fixed–order quantity model favors more expensive items because average inventory is lower.

Tutorial: Inventory

Fixed–Order Quantity and Fixed–Time Period Differences

exhibit 17.3

FEATURE	Q-MODEL FIXED–ORDER QUANTITY MODEL	P-MODEL FIXED–TIME PERIOD MODEL
Order quantity	Q—constant (the same amount ordered each time)	q—variable (varies each time order is placed)
When to place order	R—when inventory position drops to the reorder level	T—when the review period arrives
Recordkeeping	Each time a withdrawal or addition is made	Counted only at review period
Size of inventory	Less than fixed–time period model	Larger than fixed–order quantity model
Time to maintain	Higher due to perpetual recordkeeping	
Type of items	Higher-priced, critical, or important items	

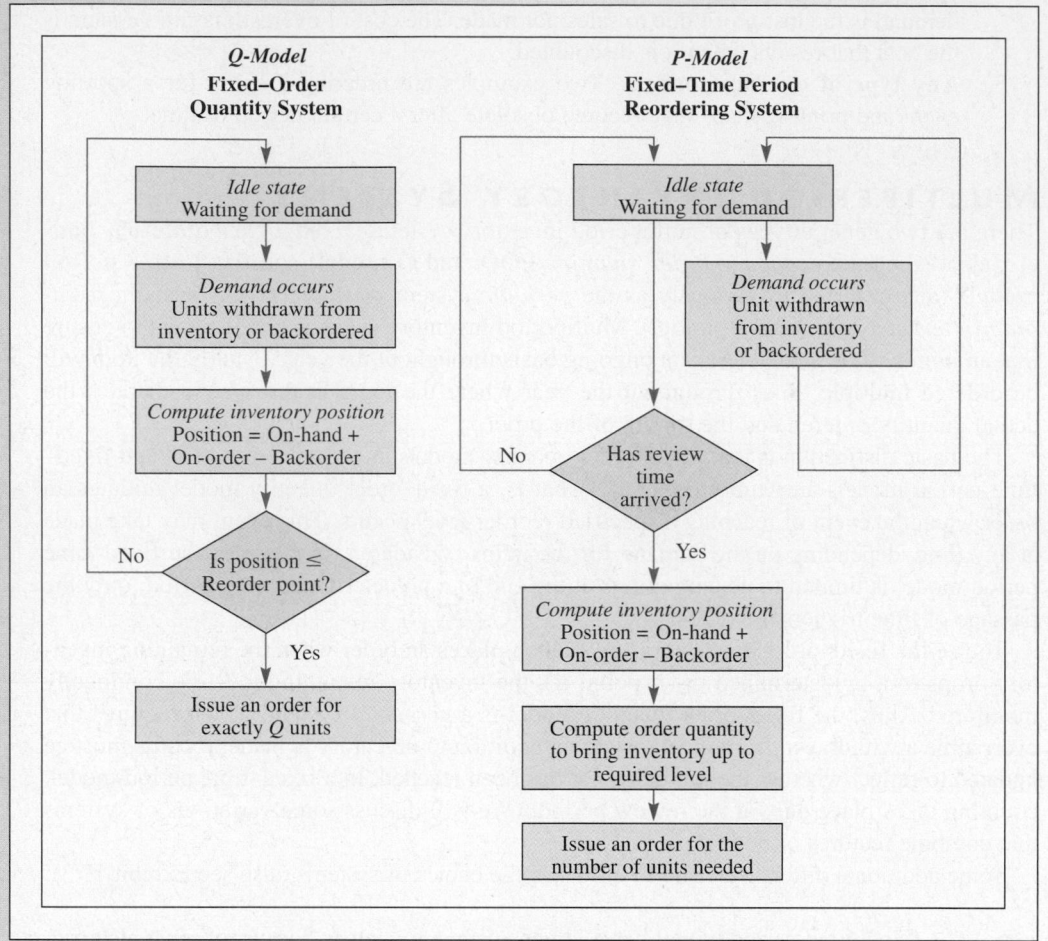

- The fixed–order quantity model is more appropriate for important items such as critical repair parts because there is closer monitoring and therefore quicker response to potential stockout.
- The fixed–order quantity model requires more time to maintain because every addition or withdrawal is logged.

Exhibit 17.4 shows what occurs when each of the two models is put into use and becomes an operating system. As we can see, the fixed–order quantity system focuses on order quantities and reorder points. Procedurally, each time a unit is taken out of stock, the withdrawal is logged and the amount remaining in inventory is immediately compared to the reorder point. If it has dropped to this point, an order for Q items is placed. If it has not, the system remains in an idle state until the next withdrawal.

In the fixed–time period system, a decision to place an order is made after the stock has been counted or reviewed. Whether an order is actually placed depends on the inventory position at that time.

FIXED–ORDER QUANTITY MODELS

Fixed–order quantity models attempt to determine the specific point, R, at which an order will be placed and the size of that order, Q. The order point, R, is always a specified number of units. An order of size Q is placed when the inventory available (currently in stock and on

Basic Fixed–Order Quantity Model

exhibit 17.5

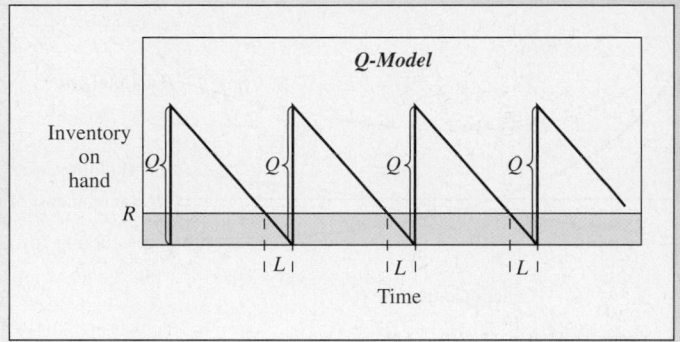

**Excel:
Inventory
Control**

order) reaches the point R. **Inventory position** is defined as the on-hand plus on-order minus backordered quantities. The solution to a fixed–order quantity model may stipulate something like this: When the inventory position drops to 36, place an order for 57 more units.

Inventory position

The simplest models in this category occur when all aspects of the situation are known with certainty. If the annual demand for a product is 1,000 units, it is precisely 1,000—not 1,000 plus or minus 10 percent. The same is true for setup costs and holding costs. Although the assumption of complete certainty is rarely valid, it provides a good basis for our coverage of inventory models.

Exhibit 17.5 and the discussion about deriving the optimal order quantity are based on the following characteristics of the model. These assumptions are unrealistic, but they represent a starting point and allow us to use a simple example.

- Demand for the product is constant and uniform throughout the period.
- Lead time (time from ordering to receipt) is constant.
- Price per unit of product is constant.
- Inventory holding cost is based on average inventory.
- Ordering or setup costs are constant.
- All demands for the product will be satisfied. (No backorders are allowed.)

The "sawtooth effect" relating Q and R in Exhibit 17.5 shows that when the inventory position drops to point R, a reorder is placed. This order is received at the end of time period L, which does not vary in this model.

In constructing any inventory model, the first step is to develop a functional relationship between the variables of interest and the measure of effectiveness. In this case, because we are concerned with cost, the following equation pertains:

$$\begin{matrix} \text{Total} \\ \text{annual cost} \end{matrix} = \begin{matrix} \text{Annual} \\ \text{purchase cost} \end{matrix} + \begin{matrix} \text{Annual} \\ \text{ordering cost} \end{matrix} + \begin{matrix} \text{Annual} \\ \text{holding cost} \end{matrix}$$

or

$$TC = DC + \frac{D}{Q}S + \frac{Q}{2}H \qquad\qquad \text{[17.2]}$$

where

TC = Total annual cost

D = Demand (annual)

C = Cost per unit

Q = Quantity to be ordered (the optimal amount is termed the *economic order quantity*—EOQ—or Q_{opt})

S = Setup cost or cost of placing an order

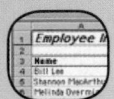

exhibit 17.6   Annual Product Costs, Based on Size of the Order

Excel:
Inventory
Control

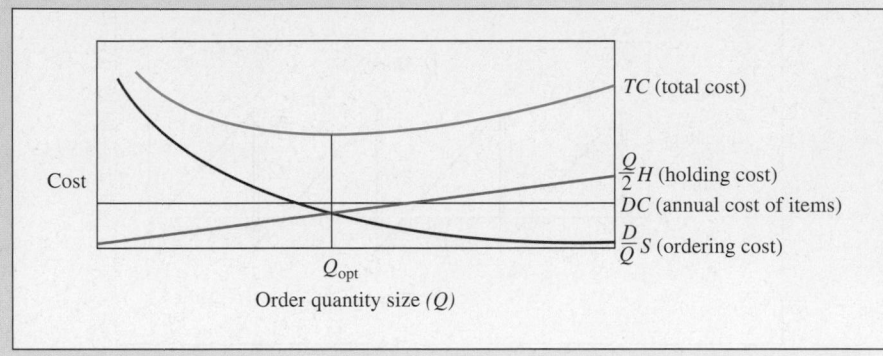

H = Annual holding and storage cost per unit of average inventory (often holding cost is taken as a percentage of the cost of the item, such as $H = iC$, where i is the percent carrying cost)

On the right side of the equation, DC is the annual purchase cost for the units; $(D/Q)S$ is the annual ordering cost (the actual number of orders placed, D/Q, times the cost of each order, S); and $(Q/2)H$ is the annual holding cost (the average inventory, $Q/2$, times the cost per unit for holding and storage, H). These cost relationships are graphed in Exhibit 17.6.

The second step in model development is to find that order quantity Q_{opt} at which total cost is a minimum. In Exhibit 17.5, the total cost is minimal at the point where the slope of the curve is zero. Using calculus, we take the derivative of total cost with respect to Q and set this equal to zero. For the basic model considered here, the calculations are

$$TC = DC + \frac{D}{Q}S + \frac{Q}{2}H$$

$$\frac{dTC}{dQ} = 0 + \left(\frac{-DS}{Q^2}\right) + \frac{H}{2} = 0$$

$$Q_{opt} = \sqrt{\frac{2DS}{H}} \qquad \text{[17.3]}$$

Because this simple model assumes constant demand and lead time, neither safety stock nor stockout cost is necessary, and the reorder point, R, is simply

$$R = \bar{d}L \qquad \text{[17.4]}$$

where

$\bar{d}$ = Average daily demand (constant)

L = Lead time in days (constant)

Excel:
Inventory
Control

Step by Step

EXAMPLE 17.2: Economic Order Quantity and Reorder Point

Find the economic order quantity and the reorder point, given

Annual demand (D) = 1,000 units
Average daily demand ($\bar{d}$) = 1,000/365
Ordering cost (S) = $5 per order
Holding cost (H) = $1.25 per unit per year
Lead time (L) = 5 days
Cost per unit (C) = $12.50

What quantity should be ordered?

SOLUTION

The optimal order quantity is

$$Q_{opt} = \sqrt{\frac{2DS}{H}} = \sqrt{\frac{2(1,000)5}{1.25}} = \sqrt{8,000} = 89.4 \text{ units}$$

The reorder point is

$$R = \bar{d}L = \frac{1,000}{365}(5) = 13.7 \text{ units}$$

Rounding to the nearest unit, the inventory policy is as follows: When the inventory position drops to 14, place an order for 89 more.

The total annual cost will be

$$TC = DC + \frac{D}{Q}S + \frac{Q}{2}H$$

$$= 1,000(12.50) + \frac{1,000}{89}(5) + \frac{89}{2}(1.25)$$

$$= \$12,611.81$$

Note that in this example, the purchase cost of the units was not required to determine the order quantity and the reorder point because the cost was constant and unrelated to order size. ●

ESTABLISHING SAFETY STOCK LEVELS

The previous model assumed that demand was constant and known. In the majority of cases, though, demand is not constant but varies from day to day. Safety stock must therefore be maintained to provide some level of protection against stockouts. Safety stock can be defined as the amount of inventory carried in addition to the expected demand. In a normal distribution, this would be the mean. For example, if our average monthly demand is 100 units and we expect next month to be the same, if we carry 120 units, then we have 20 units of safety stock.

Safety stock can be determined based on many different criteria. Frequently a company simply states that a certain number of weeks of supply must be kept in safety stock. It is better, though, to use an approach that captures the variability in demand. For example, an objective may be something like "set the safety stock level so that there will only be a 5 percent chance of stocking out if demand exceeds 300 units." We call this approach to setting safety stock the probability approach.

Safety stock

NETFLIX IS THE WORLD'S LARGEST ONLINE MOVIE RENTAL SERVICE, PROVIDING ACCESS TO MORE THAN 100,000 DVD TITLES PLUS A GROWING LIBRARY OF OVER 12,000 MOVIES AVAILABLE FOR INSTANT WATCHING ON PC OR MAC. ON AVERAGE, NETFLIX SHIPS 1.9 MILLION DVDS TO CUSTOMERS EACH DAY FROM 58 DISTRIBUTION CENTERS.

The Probability Approach   Using the probability criterion to determine safety stock is pretty simple. With the models described in this chapter, we assume that the demand over a period of time is normally distributed with a mean and a standard deviation. *Again, remember that this approach considers only the probability of running out of stock, not how many units we are short.* To determine the probability of stocking out over the time period, we can simply plot a normal distribution for the expected demand and note where the amount we have on hand lies on the curve.

Let's take a few simple examples to illustrate this. Say we expect demand to be 100 units over the next month, and we know that the standard deviation is 20 units. If we go into the month with just 100 units, we know that our probability of stocking out is 50 percent. Half of the months we would expect demand to be greater than 100 units; half of the months we would expect it to be less than 100 units. Taking this further, if we ordered a month's worth of inventory of 100 units at a time and received it at the beginning of the month, over the long run we would expect to run out of inventory in six months of the year.

If running out this often was not acceptable, we would want to carry extra inventory to reduce this risk of stocking out. One idea might be to carry an extra 20 units of inventory for the item. In this case, we would still order a month's worth of inventory at a time, but we would schedule delivery to arrive when we still have 20 units remaining in inventory. This would give us that little cushion of safety stock to reduce the probability of stocking out. If the standard deviation associated with our demand was 20 units, we would then be carrying one standard deviation worth of safety stock. Looking at the cumulative standard normal distribution (Appendix G), and moving one standard deviation to the right of the mean, gives a probability of 0.8413. So approximately 84 percent of the time we would not expect to stock out, and 16 percent of the time we would. Now if we order every month, we would expect to stock out approximately two months per year ($0.16 \times 12 = 1.92$). For those using Excel, given a z value, the probability can be obtained with the NORMSDIST function.

Companies using this approach generally set the probability of not stocking out at 95 percent. This means we would carry about 1.64 standard deviations of safety stock, or 33 units ($1.64 \times 20 = 32.8$) for our example. Once again, keep in mind that this does not mean that we would order 33 units extra each month. Rather, it means that we would still order a month's worth each time, but we would schedule the receipt so that we could expect to have 33 units in inventory when the order arrives. In this case, we would expect to stock out approximately 0.6 month per year, or that stockouts would occur in 1 of every 20 months.

FIXED–ORDER QUANTITY MODEL WITH SAFETY STOCK

A fixed–order quantity system perpetually monitors the inventory level and places a new order when stock reaches some level, R. The danger of stockout in this model occurs only during the lead time, between the time an order is placed and the time it is received. As shown in Exhibit 17.7, an order is placed when the inventory position drops to the reorder point, R. During this lead time L, a range of demands is possible. This range is determined either from an analysis of past demand data or from an estimate (if past data are not available).

The amount of safety stock depends on the service level desired, as previously discussed. The quantity to be ordered, Q, is calculated in the usual way considering the demand, shortage cost, ordering cost, holding cost, and so forth. A fixed–order quantity model can be used to compute Q, such as the simple Q_{opt} model previously discussed. The reorder point is then set to cover the expected demand during the lead time plus a safety stock determined by the desired service level. Thus, *the key difference between a fixed–order quantity model where demand is known and one where demand is uncertain is in computing the reorder point. The order quantity is the same in both cases.* The uncertainty element is taken into account in the safety stock.

exhibit 17.7   Fixed–Order Quantity Model

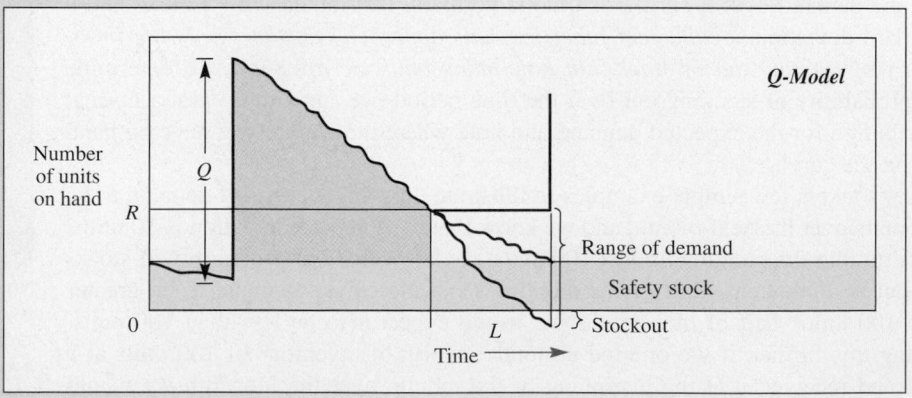

The reorder point is

$$R = \bar{d}L + z\sigma_L \qquad\qquad [17.5]$$

where

R = Reorder point in units

$\bar{d}$ = Average daily demand

L = Lead time in days (time between placing an order and receiving the items)

z = Number of standard deviations for a specified service probability

σ_L = Standard deviation of usage during lead time

The term $z\sigma_L$ is the amount of safety stock. Note that if safety stock is positive, the effect is to place a reorder sooner. That is, R without safety stock is simply the average demand during the lead time. If lead time usage was expected to be 20, for example, and safety stock was computed to be 5 units, then the order would be placed sooner, when 25 units remained. The greater the safety stock, the sooner the order is placed.

Computing $\bar{d}$, σ_L, and z Demand during the replenishment lead time is really an estimate or forecast of expected use of inventory from the time an order is placed to when it is received. It may be a single number (for example, if the lead time is a month, the demand may be taken as the previous year's demand divided by 12), or it may be a summation of expected demands over the lead time (such as the sum of daily demands over a 30-day lead time). For the daily demand situation, d can be a forecast demand using any of the models in Chapter 15 on forecasting. For example, if a 30-day period was used to calculate d, then a simple average would be

$$\bar{d} = \frac{\sum_{i=1}^{n} d_i}{n} \qquad\qquad [17.6]$$

$$= \frac{\sum_{i=1}^{30} d_i}{30}$$

where n is the number of days.

The standard deviation of the daily demand is

$$\sigma_d = \sqrt{\frac{\sum_{i=1}^{n} (d_i - \bar{d})^2}{n}} \qquad\qquad [17.7]$$

$$= \sqrt{\frac{\sum_{i=1}^{30} (d_i - \bar{d})^2}{30}}$$

Because σ_d refers to one day, if lead time extends over several days, we can use the statistical premise that the standard deviation of a series of independent occurrences is equal to the square root of the sum of the variances. That is, in general,

$$\sigma_L = \sqrt{\sigma_1^2 + \sigma_2^2 + \cdots + \sigma_L^2} \qquad\qquad [17.8]$$

For example, suppose we computed the standard deviation of demand to be 10 units per day. If our lead time to get an order is five days, the standard deviation for the five-day period, assuming each day can be considered independent, is

$$\sigma_5 = \sqrt{(10)^2 + (10)^2 + (10)^2 + (10)^2 + (10)^2} = 22.36$$

Next we need to find z, the number of standard deviations of safety stock.

Suppose we wanted our probability of not stocking out during the lead time to be 0.95. The z value associated with a 95 percent probability of not stocking out is 1.64 (see Appendix G or use the Excel NORMSINV function). Given this, safety stock is calculated as follows:

$$SS = z\sigma_L \qquad \text{[17.9]}$$
$$= 1.64 \times 22.36$$
$$= 36.67$$

We now compare two examples. The difference between them is that in the first, the variation in demand is stated in terms of standard deviation over the entire lead time, while in the second, it is stated in terms of standard deviation per day.

EXAMPLE 17.3: Reorder Point

Step by Step

Consider an economic order quantity case where annual demand $D = 1,000$ units, economic order quantity $Q = 200$ units, the desired probability of not stocking out $P = 0.95$, the standard deviation of demand during lead time $\sigma_L = 25$ units, and lead time $L = 15$ days. Determine the reorder point. Assume that demand is over a 250-workday year.

SOLUTION

In our example, $\bar{d} = \dfrac{1000}{250} = 4$, and lead time is 15 days. We use the equation

$$R = \bar{d}L + z\sigma_L$$
$$= 4(15) + z(25)$$

In this case z is 1.64.

Completing the solution for R, we have

$$R = 4(15) + 1.64(25) = 60 + 41 = 101 \text{ units}$$

This says that when the stock on hand gets down to 101 units, order 200 more. ●

EXAMPLE 17.4: Order Quantity and Reorder Point

Step by Step

Excel: Inventory Control

Daily demand for a certain product is normally distributed with a mean of 60 and standard deviation of 7. The source of supply is reliable and maintains a constant lead time of six days. The cost of placing the order is $10 and annual holding costs are $0.50 per unit. There are no stockout costs, and unfilled orders are filled as soon as the order arrives. Assume sales occur over the entire 365 days of the year. Find the order quantity and reorder point to satisfy a 95 percent probability of not stocking out during the lead time.

SOLUTION

In this problem we need to calculate the order quantity Q as well as the reorder point R.

$$\bar{d} = 60 \qquad S = \$10$$
$$\sigma_d = 7 \qquad H = \$0.50$$
$$D = 60(365) \qquad L = 6$$

The optimal order quantity is

$$Q_{\text{opt}} = \sqrt{\frac{2DS}{H}} = \sqrt{\frac{2(60)365(10)}{0.50}} = \sqrt{876,000} = 936 \text{ units}$$

To compute the reorder point, we need to calculate the amount of product used during the lead time and add this to the safety stock.

The standard deviation of demand during the lead time of six days is calculated from the variance of the individual days. Because each day's demand is independent[2]

$$\sigma_L = \sqrt{\sum_{i=1}^{L} \sigma_d^2} = \sqrt{6(7)^2} = 17.15$$

Once again, z is 1.64.

$$R = \bar{d}L + z\sigma_L = 60(6) + 1.64(17.15) = 388 \text{ units}$$

To summarize the policy derived in this example, an order for 936 units is placed whenever the number of units remaining in inventory drops to 388. ●

FIXED–TIME PERIOD MODELS

In a fixed–time period system, inventory is counted only at particular times, such as every week or every month. Counting inventory and placing orders periodically is desirable in situations such as when vendors make routine visits to customers and take orders for their complete line of products, or when buyers want to combine orders to save transportation costs. Other firms operate on a fixed time period to facilitate planning their inventory count; for example, Distributor X calls every two weeks and employees know that all Distributor X's product must be counted.

Fixed–time period models generate order quantities that vary from period to period, depending on the usage rates. These generally require a higher level of safety stock than a fixed–order quantity system. The fixed–order quantity system assumes continual tracking of inventory on hand, with an order immediately placed when the reorder point is reached. In contrast, the standard fixed–time period models assume that inventory is counted only at the time specified for review. It is possible that some large demand will draw the stock down to zero right after an order is placed. This condition could go unnoticed until the next review period. Then the new order, when placed, still takes time to arrive. Thus, it is possible to be out of stock throughout the entire review period, T, and order lead time, L. Safety stock, therefore, must protect against stockouts during the review period itself as well as during the lead time from order placement to order receipt.

FIXED–TIME PERIOD MODEL WITH SAFETY STOCK

In a fixed–time period system, reorders are placed at the time of review (T), and the safety stock that must be reordered is

$$\text{Safety stock} = z\sigma_{T+L} \qquad \text{[17.10]}$$

Exhibit 17.8 shows a fixed–time period system with a review cycle of T and a constant lead time of L. In this case, demand is randomly distributed about a mean d. The quantity to order, q, is

$$\begin{array}{ccccccc} \text{Order} \\ \text{quantity} \end{array} = \begin{array}{c} \text{Average demand} \\ \text{over the} \\ \text{vulnerable period} \end{array} + \begin{array}{c} \text{Safety} \\ \text{stock} \end{array} - \begin{array}{c} \text{Inventory currently} \\ \text{on hand (plus on} \\ \text{order, if any)} \end{array} \qquad \text{[17.11]}$$

$$q = \bar{d}(T+L) + z\sigma_{T+L} - I$$

Tutorials

where

q = Quantity to be ordered

T = The number of days between reviews

exhibit 17.8   Fixed–Time Period Inventory Model

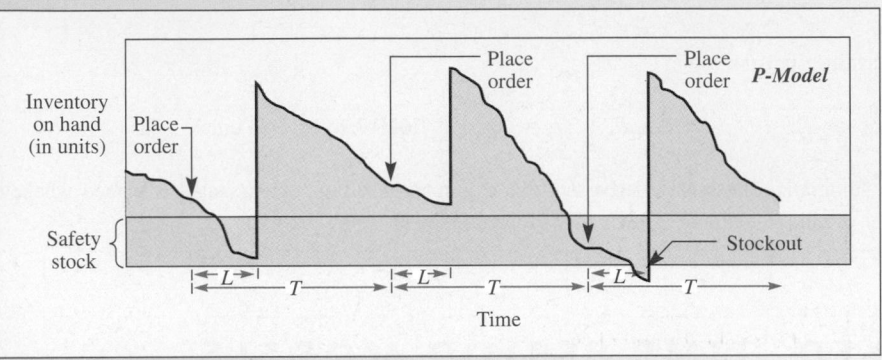

L = Lead time in days (time between placing an order and receiving it)

$\bar{d}$ = Forecast average daily demand

z = Number of standard deviations for a specified service probability

σ_{T+L} = Standard deviation of demand over the review and lead time

I = Current inventory level (includes items on order)

Note: The demand, lead time, review period, and so forth can be any time units such as days, weeks, or years so long as they are consistent throughout the equation.

In this model, demand ($\bar{d}$) can be forecast and revised each review period if desired or the yearly average may be used if appropriate. We assume that demand is normally distributed.

The value of z is dependent on the probability of stocking out and can be found using Appendix G or by using the Excel NORMSINV function.

EXAMPLE 17.5: Quantity to Order

Step by Step

**Excel:
Inventory
Control**

Daily demand for a product is 10 units with a standard deviation of 3 units. The review period is 30 days, and lead time is 14 days. Management has set a policy of satisfying 98 percent of demand from items in stock. At the beginning of this review period, there are 150 units in inventory.

How many units should be ordered?

SOLUTION

The quantity to order is

$$q = \bar{d}(T + L) + z\sigma_{T+L} - I$$
$$= 10(30 + 14) + z\sigma_{T+L} - 150$$

Before we can complete the solution, we need to find σ_{T+L} and z. To find σ_{T+L}, we use the notion, as before, that the standard deviation of a sequence of independent random variables equals the square root of the sum of the variances. Therefore, the standard deviation during the period $T + L$ is the square root of the sum of the variances for each day:

$$\sigma_{T+L} = \sqrt{\sum_{i=1}^{T+L} \sigma_d^2}$$ [17.12]

Because each day is independent and σ_d is constant,

$$\sigma_{T+L} = \sqrt{(T + L)\sigma_d^2} = \sqrt{(30 + 14)(3)^2} = 19.90$$

The z value for $P = 0.98$ is 2.05.

The quantity to order, then, is

$$q = \bar{d}(T + L) + z\sigma_{T+L} - I = 10(30 + 14) + 2.05(19.90) - 150 = 331 \text{ units}$$

To ensure a 98 percent probability of not stocking out, order 331 units at this review period. ●

INVENTORY CONTROL AND SUPPLY CHAIN MANAGEMENT

Supply Chain

It is important for managers to realize that how they run items using inventory control logic relates directly to the financial performance of the firm. A key measure that relates to company performance is inventory turn. Recall that inventory turn is calculated as follows:

$$\text{Inventory turn} = \frac{\text{Cost of goods sold}}{\text{Average inventory value}}$$

So what is the relationship between how we manage an item and the inventory turn for that item? Here, let us simplify things and consider just the inventory turn for an individual item or a group of items. First, if we look at the numerator, the cost of goods sold for an individual item relates directly to the expected yearly demand (D) for the item. Given a cost per unit (C) for the item, the cost of goods sold is just D times C. Recall this is the same as what was used in our EOQ equation. Next, consider average inventory value. Recall from EOQ that the average inventory is $Q/2$, which is true if we assume that demand is constant. When we bring uncertainty into the equation, safety stock is needed to manage the risk created by demand variability. The fixed–order quantity model and fixed–time period model both have equations for calculating the safety stock required for a given probability of stocking out. In both models, we assume that when going through an order cycle, half the time we need to use the safety stock and half the time we do not. So on average, we expect the safety stock (SS) to be on hand. Given this, the average inventory is equal to the following:

$$\text{Average inventory value} = (Q/2 + SS)C \qquad \text{[17.13]}$$

The inventory turn for an individual item then is

$$\text{Inventory turn} = \frac{DC}{(Q/2 + SS)C} = \frac{D}{Q/2 + SS} \qquad \text{[17.14]}$$

EXAMPLE 17.6: Average Inventory Calculation—Fixed–Order Quantity Model

Suppose the following item is being managed using a fixed–order quantity model with safety stock.

Step by Step

Annual demand (D) = 1,000 units
Order quantity (Q) = 300 units
Safety stock (SS) = 40 units

What are the average inventory level and inventory turn for the item?

SOLUTION

$$\text{Average inventory} = Q/2 + SS = 300/2 + 40 = 190 \text{ units}$$

$$\text{Inventory turn} = \frac{D}{Q/2 + SS} = \frac{1,000}{190} = 5.263 \text{ turns per year} ●$$

Step by Step

EXAMPLE 17.7: Average Inventory Calculation—Fixed–Time Period Model

Consider the following item that is being managed using a fixed–time period model with safety stock.

$$\text{Weekly demand } (d) = 50 \text{ units}$$
$$\text{Review cycle } (T) = 3 \text{ weeks}$$
$$\text{Safety stock } (SS) = 30 \text{ units}$$

What are the average inventory level and inventory turn for the item?

SOLUTION

Here we need to determine how many units we expect to order each cycle. If we assume that demand is fairly steady, then we would expect to order the number of units that we expect demand to be during the review cycle. This expected demand is equal to dT if we assume that there is no trend or seasonality in the demand pattern.

$$\text{Average inventory} = dT/2 + SS = 50(3)/2 + 30 = 105 \text{ units}$$

$$\text{Inventory turn} = \frac{52d}{dT/2 + SS} = \frac{52(50)}{105} = 24.8 \text{ turns per year}$$

assuming there are 52 weeks in the year. ●

PRICE-BREAK MODELS

Price-break models deal with the fact that, generally, the selling price of an item varies with the order size. This is a discrete or step change rather than a per-unit change. For example, wood screws may cost $0.02 each for 1 to 99 screws, $1.60 per 100, and $13.50 per 1,000. To determine the optimal quantity of any item to order, we simply solve for the economic order quantity for each price and at the point of price change. But not all of the economic order quantities determined by the formula are feasible. In the wood screw example, the Q_{opt} formula might tell us that the optimal decision at the price of 1.6 cents is to order 75 screws. This would be impossible, however, because 75 screws would cost 2 cents each.

In general, to find the lowest-cost order quantity, we need to calculate the economic order quantity for each possible price and check to see whether the quantity is feasible. It is possible that the economic order quantity that is calculated is either higher or lower than the range to which the price corresponds. Any feasible quantity is a potential candidate order quantity. We also need to calculate the cost at each of the price-break quantities, since we know that price is feasible at these points and the total cost may be lowest at one of these values.

The calculations can be simplified a little if holding cost is based on a percentage of unit price (they will be in all the examples and problems given in this book). In this case, we only need to look at a subset of the price-break quantities. The following two-step procedure can be used:

Step 1. Sort the prices from lowest to highest and then, beginning with the lowest price, calculate the economic order quantity for each price level until a feasible economic order quantity is found. By feasible, we mean that the price is in the correct corresponding range.

Step 2. If the first feasible economic order quantity is for the lowest price, this quantity is best and you are finished. Otherwise, calculate the total cost for the first feasible economic order quantity (you did these from lowest to highest price) and also calculate the total cost at each price break lower than the price associated with the first feasible economic order quantity. This is the lowest order quantity at which you can take advantage of the price break. The optimal Q is the one with the lowest cost.

Curves for Three Separate Order Quantity Models in a Three-Price-Break Situation (red line depicts feasible range of purchases)

exhibit 17.9

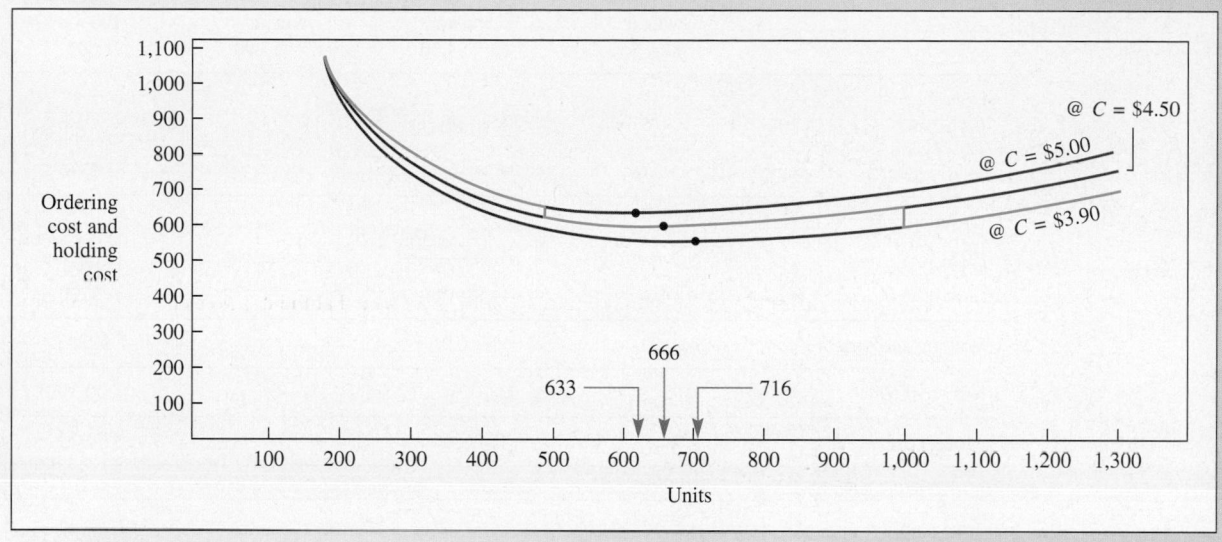

Looking at Exhibit 17.9, we see that order quantities are solved from right to left, or from the lowest unit price to the highest, until a valid Q is obtained. Then the order quantity at each *price break* above this Q is used to find which order quantity has the least cost—the computed Q or the Q at one of the price breaks.

EXAMPLE 17.8: Price Break

Consider the following case, where

D = 10,000 units (annual demand)
S = $20 to place each order
i = 20 percent of cost (annual carrying cost, storage, interest, obsolescence, etc.)
C = Cost per unit (according to the order size; orders of 0 to 499 units, $5.00 per unit; 500 to 999, $4.50 per unit; 1,000 and up, $3.90 per unit)

What quantity should be ordered?

Step by Step

SOLUTION

The appropriate equations from the basic fixed-order quantity case are

$$TC = DC + \frac{D}{Q}S + \frac{Q}{2}iC$$

and

$$Q = \sqrt{\frac{2DS}{iC}}$$ [17.15]

Solving for the economic order size, we obtain

@ C = $3.90,	Q = 716	Not feasible
@ C = $4.50,	Q = 667	Feasible, cost = $45,600
Check Q = 1,000,	Cost = $39,590	Optimal solution

In Exhibit 17.10, which displays the cost relationship and order quantity range, note that most of the order quantity–cost relationships lie outside the feasible range and that only a single, continuous

exhibit 17.10   Relevant Costs in a Three-Price-Break Model

	$Q = 633$ WHERE $C = \$5$	$Q = 667$ WHERE $C = \$4.50$	$Q = 716$ WHERE $C = \$3.90$	PRICE BREAK 1,000
Holding cost $\left(\frac{Q}{2}iC\right)$		$\frac{667}{2}(0.20)4.50$ $= \$300.15$		$\frac{1,000}{2}(0.20)3.90$ $= \$390$
Ordering cost $\left(\frac{D}{Q}S\right)$	Not feasible	$\frac{10,000(20)}{667}$ $= \$299.85$	Not feasible	$\frac{10,000(20)}{1,000}$ $= \$200$
Holding and ordering cost		$600.00		$590
Item cost (DC)		10,000(4.50)		10,000(3.90)
Total cost		$45,600		$39,590

range results. This should be readily apparent because, for example, the first order quantity specifies buying 633 units at $5.00 per unit. However, if 633 units are ordered, the price is $4.50, not $5.00. The same holds true for the third order quantity, which specifies an order of 716 units at $3.90 each. This $3.90 price is not available on orders of fewer than 1,000 units.

Exhibit 17.10 itemizes the total costs at the economic order quantities and at the price breaks. The optimal order quantity is shown to be 1,000 units. ●

One practical consideration in price-break problems is that the price reduction from volume purchases frequently makes it seemingly economical to order amounts larger than the Q_{opt}. Thus, when applying the model, we must be particularly careful to obtain a valid estimate of product obsolescence and warehousing costs.

ABC INVENTORY PLANNING

Maintaining inventory through counting, placing orders, receiving stock, and so on, takes personnel time and costs money. When there are limits on these resources, the logical move is to try to use the available resources to control inventory in the best way. In other words, focus on the most important items in inventory.

In the nineteenth century Vilfredo Pareto, in a study of the distribution of wealth in Milan, found that 20 percent of the people controlled 80 percent of the wealth. This logic of the few having the greatest importance and the many having little importance has been broadened to include many situations and is termed the *Pareto principle*.[3] This is true in our everyday lives (most of our decisions are relatively unimportant, but a few shape our future) and is certainly true in inventory systems (where a few items account for the bulk of our investment).

Any inventory system must specify when an order is to be placed for an item and how many units to order. Most inventory control situations involve so many items that it is not practical to model and give thorough treatment to each item. To get around this problem, the ABC classification scheme divides inventory items into three groupings: high dollar volume (A), moderate dollar volume (B), and low dollar volume (C). Dollar volume is a measure of importance; an item low in cost but high in volume can be more important than a high-cost item with low volume.

ABC CLASSIFICATION

If the annual usage of items in inventory is listed according to dollar volume, generally, the list shows that a small number of items account for a large dollar volume and that a large number of items account for a small dollar volume. Exhibit 17.11A illustrates the relationship.

The ABC approach divides this list into three groupings by value: A items constitute roughly the top 15 percent of the items, B items the next 35 percent, and C items the last 50 percent. From observation, it appears that the list in Exhibit 17.11A can be meaningfully grouped with A including 20 percent (2 of the 10), B including 30 percent, and C including 50 percent. These points show clear delineations between sections. The result of this segmentation is shown in Exhibit 17.11B and plotted in Exhibit 17.11C.

Segmentation may not always occur so neatly. The objective, though, is to try to separate the important from the unimportant. Where the lines actually break depends on the particular inventory under question and on how much personnel time is available. (With more time, a firm could define larger A or B categories.)

The purpose of classifying items into groups is to establish the appropriate degree of control over each item. On a periodic basis, for example, class A items may be more clearly controlled with weekly ordering, B items may be ordered biweekly, and C items may be ordered monthly or bimonthly. Note that the unit cost of items is not related to their classification.

---

exhibit 17.11

A. Annual Usage of Inventory by Value

ITEM NUMBER	ANNUAL DOLLAR USAGE	PERCENTAGE OF TOTAL VALUE
22	$ 95,000	40.69%
68	75,000	32.13
27	25,000	10.71
03	15,000	6.43
82	13,000	5.57
54	7,500	3.21
36	1,500	0.64
19	800	0.34
23	425	0.18
41	225	0.10
	$233,450	100.0%

B. ABC Grouping of Inventory Items

CLASSIFICATION	ITEM NUMBER	ANNUAL DOLLAR USAGE	PERCENTAGE OF TOTAL
A	22, 68	$170,000	72.9%
B	27, 03, 82	53,000	22.7
C	54, 36, 19, 23, 41	10,450	4.4
		$233,450	100.0%

C. ABC Inventory Classification (inventory value for each group versus the group's portion of the total list)

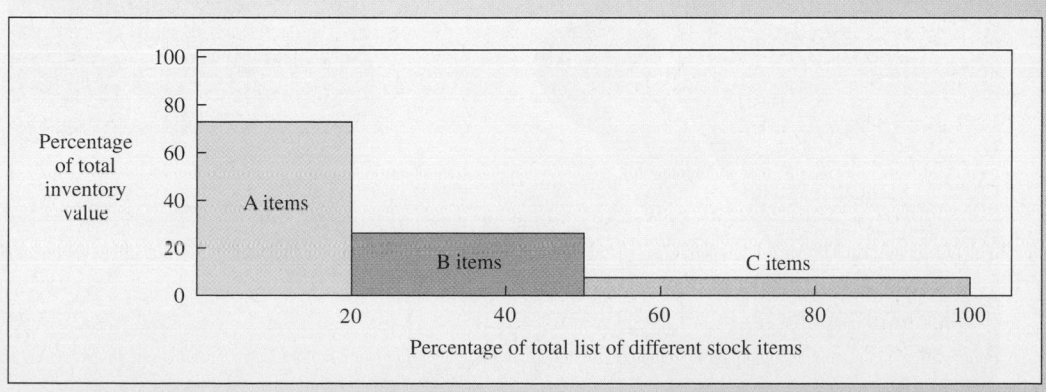

An A item may have a high dollar volume through a combination of either low cost and high usage or high cost and low usage. Similarly, C items may have a low dollar volume because of either low demand or low cost. In an automobile service station, gasoline would be an A item with daily or weekly replenishment; tires, batteries, oil, grease, and transmission fluid may be B items and ordered every two to four weeks; and C items would consist of valve stems, windshield wiper blades, radiator caps, hoses, fan belts, oil and gas additives, car wax, and so forth. C items may be ordered every two or three months or even be allowed to run out before reordering because the penalty for stockout is not serious.

Sometimes an item may be critical to a system if its absence creates a sizable loss. In this case, regardless of the item's classification, sufficiently large stocks should be kept on hand to prevent runout. One way to ensure closer control is to designate this item an A or a B, forcing it into the category even if its dollar volume does not warrant such inclusion.

INVENTORY ACCURACY AND CYCLE COUNTING

Inventory records usually differ from the actual physical count; inventory accuracy refers to how well the two agree. Companies such as Walmart understand the importance of inventory accuracy and expend considerable effort ensuring it. The question is, How much error is acceptable? If the record shows a balance of 683 of part X and an actual count shows 652, is this within reason? Suppose the actual count shows 750, an excess of 67 over the record; is this any better?

Every production system must have agreement, within some specified range, between what the record says is in inventory and what actually is in inventory. There are many reasons why records and inventory may not agree. For example, an open stockroom area allows items to be removed for both legitimate and unauthorized purposes. The legitimate removal may have been done in a hurry and simply not recorded. Sometimes parts are misplaced, turning up months later. Parts are often stored in several locations, but records may be lost or the location recorded incorrectly. Sometimes stock replenishment orders are recorded as received, when in fact they never were. Occasionally, a group of parts is recorded as removed

A SALES CLERK AT TOKYO'S MITSUKOSHI DEPARTMENT STORE READS AN RFID TAG ON JEANS TO CHECK STOCK. MITSUKOSHI AND JAPAN'S ELECTRONIC GIANT FUJITSU PARTNERED TO USE RFID TO IMPROVE STOCK CONTROL AND CUSTOMER SERVICE.

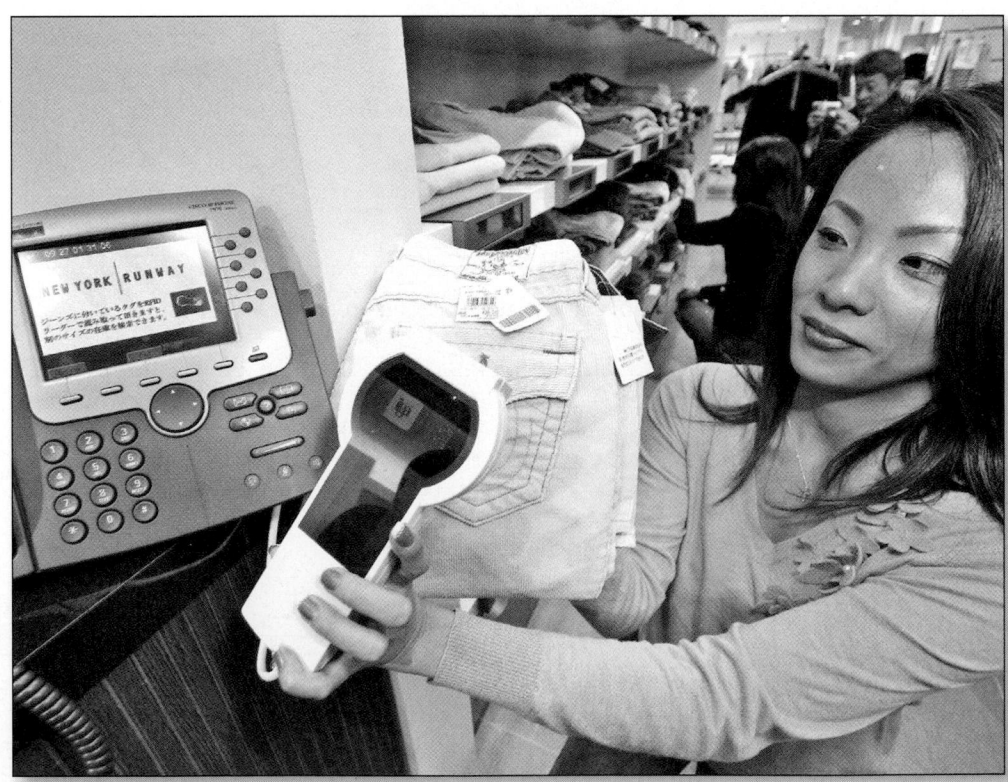

from inventory, but the customer order is canceled and the parts are replaced in inventory without canceling the record. To keep the production system flowing smoothly without parts shortages and efficiently without excess balances, records must be accurate.

How can a firm keep accurate, up-to-date records? Using bar codes and RFID tags is important to minimizing errors caused by inputting wrong numbers in the system. It is also important to keep the storeroom locked. If only storeroom personnel have access, and one of their measures of performance for personnel evaluation and merit increases is record accuracy, there is a strong motivation to comply. Every location of inventory storage, whether in a locked storeroom or on the production floor, should have a recordkeeping mechanism. A second way is to convey the importance of accurate records to all personnel and depend on them to assist in this effort. (This all boils down to this: Put a fence that goes all the way to the ceiling around the storage area so that workers cannot climb over to get parts; put a lock on the gate and give one person the key. Nobody can pull parts without having the transaction authorized and recorded.)

Another way to ensure accuracy is to count inventory frequently and match this against records. A widely used method is called *cycle counting*.

Cycle counting is a physical inventory-taking technique in which inventory is counted frequently rather than once or twice a year. The key to effective cycle counting and, therefore, to accurate records lies in deciding which items are to be counted, when, and by whom.

Cycle counting

Virtually all inventory systems these days are computerized. The computer can be programmed to produce a cycle count notice in the following cases:

1. When the record shows a low or zero balance on hand. (It is easier to count fewer items.)
2. When the record shows a positive balance but a backorder was written (indicating a discrepancy).
3. After some specified level of activity.
4. To signal a review based on the importance of the item (as in the ABC system) such as in the following table:

ANNUAL DOLLAR USAGE	REVIEW PERIOD
$10,000 or more	30 days or less
$3,000–$10,000	45 days or less
$250–$3,000	90 days or less
Less than $250	180 days or less

The easiest time for stock to be counted is when there is no activity in the stockroom or on the production floor. This means on the weekends or during the second or third shift, when the facility is less busy. If this is not possible, more careful logging and separation of items are required to count inventory while production is going on and transactions are occurring.

The counting cycle depends on the available personnel. Some firms schedule regular stockroom personnel to do the counting during lulls in the regular working day. Other companies hire private firms that come in and count inventory. Still other firms use full-time cycle counters who do nothing but count inventory and resolve differences with the records. Although this last method sounds expensive, many firms believe that it is actually less costly than the usual hectic annual inventory count generally performed during the two- or three-week annual vacation shutdown.

The question of how much error is tolerable between physical inventory and records has been much debated. Some firms strive for 100 percent accuracy, whereas others accept 1, 2, or 3 percent error. The accuracy level often recommended by experts is ± 0.2 percent for A items, ± 1 percent for B items, and ± 5 percent for C items. Regardless of the specific accuracy decided on, the important point is that the level be dependable so that safety stocks may be provided as a cushion. Accuracy is important for a smooth production process so that customer orders can be processed as scheduled and not held up because of unavailable parts.

SUMMARY

This chapter introduced the two main classes of demand: (1) independent demand, referring to the external demand for a firm's end product, and (2) dependent demand, usually referring—within the firm—to the demand for items created because of the demand for more complex items of which they are a part. Most industries have items in both classes. In manufacturing, for example, independent demand is common for finished products, service and repair parts, and operating supplies; and dependent demand is common for those parts and materials needed to produce the end product. In wholesale and retail sales of consumer goods, most demand is independent—each item is an end item, with the wholesaler or retailer doing no further assembly or fabrication.

Independent demand, the focus of this chapter, is based on statistics. In the fixed–order quantity and fixed–time period models, the influence of service level was shown on safety stock and reorder point determinations. One special-purpose model—the single-period model—was also presented.

To distinguish among item categories for analysis and control, the ABC method was offered. The importance of inventory accuracy was also noted, and cycle counting was described.

In this chapter, we also pointed out that inventory reduction requires a knowledge of the operating system. It is not simply a case of selecting an inventory model off the shelf and plugging in some numbers. In the first place, a model might not even be appropriate. In the second case, the numbers might be full of errors or even based on erroneous data. Determining order quantities is often referred to as a trade-off problem; that is, trading off holding costs for setup costs. Note that companies really want to reduce both.

The simple fact is that firms have very large investments in inventory, and the cost to carry this inventory runs from 25 to 35 percent of the inventory's worth annually. Therefore, a major goal of most firms today is to reduce inventory.

A caution is in order, though. The formulas in this chapter try to minimize cost. Bear in mind that a firm's objective should be something like "making money"—so be sure that reducing inventory cost does, in fact, support this. Usually, correctly reducing inventory lowers cost, improves quality and performance, and enhances profit.

KEY TERMS

Inventory The stock of any item or resource used in an organization.

Independent demand The demands for various items are unrelated to each other.

Dependent demand The need for any one item is a direct result of the need for some other item, usually an item of which it is a part.

Fixed–order quantity model (or Q-model) An inventory control model where the amount requisitioned is fixed and the actual ordering is triggered by inventory dropping to a specified level of inventory.

Fixed–time period model (or P-model) An inventory control model that specifies inventory is ordered at the end of a predetermined time period. The interval of time between orders is fixed and the order quantity varies.

Inventory position The amount on-hand plus on-order minus back-ordered quantities. In the case where inventory has been allocated for special purposes, the inventory position is reduced by these allocated amounts.

Safety stock The amount of inventory carried in addition to the expected demand.

Cycle counting A physical inventory-taking technique in which inventory is counted on a frequent basis rather than once or twice a year.

FORMULA REVIEW

Single-period model. Cumulative probability of not selling the last unit. Ratio of marginal cost of underestimating demand and marginal cost of overestimating demand.

$$P \leq \frac{C_u}{C_o + C_u}$$

[17.1]

Q-model. Total annual cost for an order *Q*, a per-unit cost *C*, setup cost *S*, and per-unit holding cost *H*.

$$TC = DC + \frac{D}{Q}S + \frac{Q}{2}H$$ [17.2]

Q-model. Optimal (or economic) order quantity.

$$Q_{opt} = \sqrt{\frac{2DS}{H}}$$ [17.3]

Q-model. Reorder point *R* based on average daily demand $\bar{d}$ and lead time *L* in days.

$$R = \bar{d}L$$ [17.4]

Q-model. Reorder point providing a safety stock of $z\sigma_L$.

$$R = \bar{d}L + z\sigma_L$$ [17.5]

Average daily demand over a period of *n* days.

$$\bar{d} = \frac{\sum_{i=1}^{n} d_i}{n}$$ [17.6]

Standard deviation of demand over a period of *n* days.

$$\sigma_d = \sqrt{\frac{\sum_{i=1}^{n}(d_i - \bar{d})^2}{n}}$$ [17.7]

Standard deviation of a series of independent demands.

$$\sigma_L = \sqrt{\sigma_1^2 + \sigma_2^2 + \cdots + \sigma_L^2}$$ [17.8]

Q-model. Safety stock calculation.

$$SS = z\sigma_L$$ [17.9]

P-model. Safety stock calculation.

$$SS = z\sigma_{T+L}$$ [17.10]

P-model. Optimal order quantity in a fixed-period system with a review period of *T* days and lead time of *L* days.

$$q = \bar{d}(T + L) + z\sigma_{T+L} - I$$ [17.11]

P-model. Standard deviation of a series of independent demands over the review period *T* and lead time *L*.

$$\sigma_{T+L} = \sqrt{\sum_{i=1}^{T+L} \sigma_d^2}$$ [17.12]

Average inventory.

$$\text{Average inventory value} = (Q/2 + SS)C$$ [17.13]

Inventory turn.

$$\text{Inventory turn} = \frac{DC}{(Q/2 + SS)C} = \frac{D}{Q/2 + SS}$$ [17.14]

Economic order quantity (with carrying cost percentage).

$$Q = \sqrt{\frac{2DS}{iC}}$$ [17.15]

SOLVED PROBLEMS

SOLVED PROBLEM 1

A product is priced to sell at $100 per unit, and its cost is constant at $70 per unit. Each unsold unit has a salvage value of $20. Demand is expected to range between 35 and 40 units for the period; 35 definitely can be sold and no units over 40 will be sold. The demand probabilities and the associated cumulative probability distribution (P) for this situation are shown below.

**Excel:
Inventory
Control**

NUMBER OF UNITS DEMANDED	PROBABILITY OF THIS DEMAND	CUMULATIVE PROBABILITY
35	0.10	0.10
36	0.15	0.25
37	0.25	0.50
38	0.25	0.75
39	0.15	0.90
40	0.10	1.00

How many units should be ordered?

Solution

The cost of underestimating demand is the loss of profit, or C_u = $100 − $70 = $30 per unit. The cost of overestimating demand is the loss incurred when the unit must be sold at salvage value, C_o = $70 − $20 = $50.

The optimal probability of not being sold is

$$P \le \frac{C_u}{C_o + C_u} = \frac{30}{50 + 30} = 0.375$$

From the distribution data above, this corresponds to the 37th unit.

The following is a full marginal analysis for the problem. Note that the minimum cost is when 37 units are purchased.

		NUMBER OF UNITS PURCHASED					
UNITS DEMANDED	PROBABILITY	35	36	37	38	39	40
35	0.1	0	50	100	150	200	250
36	0.15	30	0	50	100	150	200
37	0.25	60	30	0	50	100	150
38	0.25	90	60	30	0	50	100
39	0.15	120	90	60	30	0	50
40	0.1	150	120	90	60	30	0
Total cost		75	53	43	53	83	125

SOLVED PROBLEM 2

Items purchased from a vendor cost $20 each, and the forecast for next year's demand is 1,000 units. If it costs $5 every time an order is placed for more units and the storage cost is $4 per unit per year, what quantity should be ordered each time?
a. What is the total ordering cost for a year?
b. What is the total storage cost for a year?

Solution

The quantity to be ordered each time is

$$Q = \sqrt{\frac{2DS}{H}} = \sqrt{\frac{2(1,000)5}{4}} = 50 \text{ units}$$

a. The total ordering cost for a year is

$$\frac{D}{Q}S = \frac{1,000}{50}(\$5) = \$100$$

b. The storage cost for a year is

$$\frac{Q}{2}H = \frac{50}{2}(\$4) = \$100$$

SOLVED PROBLEM 3

Daily demand for a product is 120 units, with a standard deviation of 30 units. The review period is 14 days and the lead time is 7 days. At the time of review, 130 units are in stock. If only a 1 percent risk of stocking out is acceptable, how many units should be ordered?

Solution

$$\sigma_{T+L} = \sqrt{(14 + 7)(30)^2} = \sqrt{18,900} = 137.5$$
$$z = 2.33$$
$$q = \bar{d}(T + L) + z\sigma_{T+L} - I$$
$$= 120(14 + 7) + 2.33(137.5) - 130$$
$$= 2,710 \text{ units}$$

**Excel:
Inventory
Control**

SOLVED PROBLEM 4

A company currently has 200 units of a product on hand that it orders every two weeks when the salesperson visits the premises. Demand for the product averages 20 units per day with a standard deviation of 5 units. Lead time for the product to arrive is seven days. Management has a goal of a 95 percent probability of not stocking out for this product.

The salesperson is due to come in late this afternoon when 180 units are left in stock (assuming that 20 are sold today). How many units should be ordered?

Solution

Given $I = 180, T = 14, L = 7, d - 20$

$$\sigma_{T+L} = \sqrt{21(5)^2} = 23$$
$$z = 1.64$$
$$q = \bar{d}(T + L) + z\sigma_{T+L} - I$$
$$= 20(14 + 7) + 1.64(23) - 180$$
$$q = 278 \text{ units}$$

**Excel:
Inventory
Control**

REVIEW AND DISCUSSION QUESTIONS

1 Distinguish between dependent and independent demand in a McDonald's restaurant, in an integrated manufacturer of personal copiers, and in a pharmaceutical supply house.
2 Distinguish between in-process inventory, safety stock inventory, and seasonal inventory.
3 Discuss the nature of the costs that affect inventory size.
4 Under which conditions would a plant manager elect to use a fixed–order quantity model as opposed to a fixed–time period model? What are the disadvantages of using a fixed–time period ordering system?
5 What two basic questions must be answered by an inventory-control decision rule?
6 Discuss the assumptions that are inherent in production setup cost, ordering cost, and carrying costs. How valid are they?
7 "The nice thing about inventory models is that you can pull one off the shelf and apply it so long as your cost estimates are accurate." Comment.
8 Which type of inventory system would you use in the following situations?
   a. Supplying your kitchen with fresh food.
   b. Obtaining a daily newspaper.
   c. Buying gas for your car.
   To which of these items do you impute the highest stockout cost?
9 Why is it desirable to classify items into groups, as the ABC classification does?

PROBLEMS

1   The local supermarket buys lettuce each day to ensure really fresh produce. Each morning any lettuce that is left from the previous day is sold to a dealer that resells it to farmers who use it to feed their animals. This week the supermarket can buy fresh lettuce for $4.00 a box. The lettuce is sold for $10.00 a box and the dealer that sells old lettuce is willing to pay $1.50 a box. Past history says that tomorrow's demand for lettuce averages 250 boxes with a standard deviation of 34 boxes. How many boxes of lettuce should the supermarket purchase tomorrow?

2   Next week, Super Discount Airlines has a flight from New York to Los Angeles that will be booked to capacity. The airline knows from past history that an average of 25 customers (with a standard deviation of 15) cancel their reservation or do not show for the flight. Revenue from a ticket on the flight is $125. If the flight is overbooked, the airline has a policy of getting the customer on the next available flight and giving the person a free round-trip ticket on a future flight. The cost of this free round-trip ticket averages $250. Super Discount considers the cost of flying the plane from New York to Los Angeles a sunk cost. By how many seats should Super Discount overbook the flight?

3   Ray's Satellite Emporium wishes to determine the best order size for its best-selling satellite dish (model TS111). Ray has estimated the annual demand for this model at 1,000 units. His cost to carry one unit is $100 per year per unit, and he has estimated that each order costs $25 to place. Using the EOQ model, how many should Ray order each time?

4   Dunstreet's Department Store would like to develop an inventory ordering policy of a 95 percent probability of not stocking out. To illustrate your recommended procedure, use as an example the ordering policy for white percale sheets.

Demand for white percale sheets is 5,000 per year. The store is open 365 days per year. Every two weeks (14 days) inventory is counted and a new order is placed. It takes 10 days for the sheets to be delivered. Standard deviation of demand for the sheets is five per day. There are currently 150 sheets on hand.

How many sheets should you order?

5   Charlie's Pizza orders all of its pepperoni, olives, anchovies, and mozzarella cheese to be shipped directly from Italy. An American distributor stops by every four weeks to take orders. Because the orders are shipped directly from Italy, they take three weeks to arrive.

Charlie's Pizza uses an average of 150 pounds of pepperoni each week, with a standard deviation of 30 pounds. Charlie's prides itself on offering only the best-quality ingredients and a high level of service, so it wants to ensure a 98 percent probability of not stocking out on pepperoni.

Assume that the sales representative just walked in the door and there are currently 500 pounds of pepperoni in the walk-in cooler. How many pounds of pepperoni would you order?

6   Given the following information, formulate an inventory management system. The item is demanded 50 weeks a year.

Item cost	$10.00	Standard deviation of weekly demand	25 per week
Order cost	$250.00	Lead time	1 week
Annual holding cost (%)	33% of item cost	Service probability	95%
Annual demand	25,750		
Average demand	515 per week		

a. State the order quantity and reorder point.

b. Determine the annual holding and order costs.

c. If a price break of $50 per order was offered for purchase quantities of over 2,000, would you take advantage of it? How much would you save annually?

7   Lieutenant Commander Data is planning to make his monthly (every 30 days) trek to Gamma Hydra City to pick up a supply of isolinear chips. The trip will take Data about two days. Before he leaves, he calls in the order to the GHC Supply Store. He uses chips at an average rate of five per day (seven days per week) with a standard deviation of demand of one per day. He needs a 98 percent service probability. If he currently has 35 chips in inventory, how many should he order? What is the most he will ever have to order?

8   Jill's Job Shop buys two parts (Tegdiws and Widgets) for use in its production system from two different suppliers. The parts are needed throughout the entire 52-week year. Tegdiws are used at a relatively constant rate and are ordered whenever the remaining quantity drops to the reorder level. Widgets are ordered from a supplier who stops by every three weeks. Data for both products are as follows:

ITEM	TEGDIW	WIDGET
Annual demand	10,000	5,000
Holding cost (% of item cost)	20%	20%
Setup or order cost	$150.00	$25.00
Lead time	4 weeks	1 week
Safety stock	55 units	5 units
Item cost	$10.00	$2.00

    a. What is the inventory control system for Tegdiws? That is, what is the reorder quantity and what is the reorder point?

    b. What is the inventory control system for Widgets?

9   Demand for an item is 1,000 units per year. Each order placed costs $10; the annual cost to carry items in inventory is $2 each. In what quantities should the item be ordered?

10 The annual demand for a product is 15,600 units. The weekly demand is 300 units with a standard deviation of 90 units. The cost to place an order is $31.20, and the time from ordering to receipt is four weeks. The annual inventory carrying cost is $0.10 per unit. Find the reorder point necessary to provide a 98 percent service probability.

    Suppose the production manager is asked to reduce the safety stock of this item by 50 percent. If she does so, what will the new service probability be?

11 Daily demand for a product is 100 units, with a standard deviation of 25 units. The review period is 10 days and the lead time is 6 days. At the time of review there are 50 units in stock. If 98 percent service probability is desired, how many units should be ordered?

12 Item X is a standard item stocked in a company's inventory of component parts. Each year the firm, on a random basis, uses about 2,000 of item X, which costs $25 each. Storage costs, which include insurance and cost of capital, amount to $5 per unit of average inventory. Every time an order is placed for more item X, it costs $10.

    a. Whenever item X is ordered, what should the order size be?

    b. What is the annual cost for ordering item X?

    c. What is the annual cost for storing item X?

13 Annual demand for a product is 13,000 units; weekly demand is 250 units with a standard deviation of 40 units. The cost of placing an order is $100, and the time from ordering to receipt is four weeks. The annual inventory carrying cost is $0.65 per unit. To provide a 98 percent service probability, what must the reorder point be?

    Suppose the production manager is told to reduce the safety stock of this item by 100 units. If this is done, what will the new service probability be?

14 In the past, Taylor Industries has used a fixed–time period inventory system that involved taking a complete inventory count of all items each month. However, increasing labor costs are forcing Taylor Industries to examine alternative ways to reduce the amount of labor involved in inventory stockrooms, yet without increasing other costs, such as shortage costs. Here is a random sample of 20 of Taylor's items.

ITEM NUMBER	ANNUAL USAGE	ITEM NUMBER	ANNUAL USAGE
1	$ 1,500	11	$13,000
2	12,000	12	600
3	2,200	13	42,000
4	50,000	14	9,900
5	9,600	15	1,200
6	750	16	10,200
7	2,000	17	4,000
8	11,000	18	61,000
9	800	19	3,500
10	15,000	20	2,900

    a. What would you recommend Taylor do to cut back its labor cost? (Illustrate using an ABC plan.)

    b. Item 15 is critical to continued operations. How would you recommend it be classified?

15   Gentle Ben's Bar and Restaurant uses 5,000 quart bottles of an imported wine each year. The effervescent wine costs $3 per bottle and is served only in whole bottles because it loses its bubbles quickly. Ben figures that it costs $10 each time an order is placed, and holding costs are 20 percent of the purchase price. It takes three weeks for an order to arrive. Weekly demand is 100 bottles (closed two weeks per year) with a standard deviation of 30 bottles.

    Ben would like to use an inventory system that minimizes inventory cost and will provide a 95 percent service probability.

    a. What is the economic quantity for Ben to order?

    b. At what inventory level should he place an order?

16   Retailers Warehouse (RW) is an independent supplier of household items to department stores. RW attempts to stock enough items for a 98 percent service probability.

    A stainless steel knife set is one item it stocks. Demand (2,400 sets per year) is relatively stable over the entire year. Whenever new stock is ordered, a buyer must assure that numbers are correct for stock on hand and then phone in a new order. The total cost involved to place an order is about $5. RW figures that holding inventory in stock and paying for interest on borrowed capital, insurance, and so on, adds up to about $4 holding cost per unit per year.

    Analysis of the past data shows that the standard deviation of demand from retailers is about four units per day for a 365-day year. Lead time to get the order is seven days.

    a. What is the economic order quantity?

    b. What is the reorder point?

17   Daily demand for a product is 60 units with a standard deviation of 10 units. The review period is 10 days, and lead time is 2 days. At the time of review there are 100 units in stock. If 98 percent service probability is desired, how many units should be ordered?

18   University Drug Pharmaceuticals orders its antibiotics every two weeks (14 days) when a salesperson visits from one of the pharmaceutical companies. Tetracycline is one of its most prescribed antibiotics, with average daily demand of 2,000 capsules. The standard deviation of daily demand was derived from examining prescriptions filled over the past three months and was found to be 800 capsules. It takes five days for the order to arrive. University Drug would like to satisfy 99 percent of the prescriptions. The salesperson just arrived, and there are currently 25,000 capsules in stock.

    How many capsules should be ordered?

19   Sally's Silk Screening produces specialty T-shirts that are primarily sold at special events. She is trying to decide how many to produce for an upcoming event. During the event itself, which lasts one day, Sally can sell T-shirts for $20 apiece. However, when the event ends, any unsold T-shirts are sold for $4 apiece. It costs Sally $8 to make a specialty T-shirt. Using Sally's estimate of demand that follows, how many T-shirts should she produce for the upcoming event?

DEMAND	PROBABILITY
300	0.05
400	0.10
500	0.40
600	0.30
700	0.10
800	0.05

20   Famous Albert prides himself on being the Cookie King of the West. Small, freshly baked cookies are the specialty of his shop. Famous Albert has asked for help to determine the number of cookies he should make each day. From an analysis of past demand he estimates demand for cookies as

DEMAND	PROBABILITY OF DEMAND
1,800 dozen	0.05
2,000	0.10
2,200	0.20
2,400	0.30
2,600	0.20
2,800	0.10
3,000	0.05

Each dozen sells for $0.69 and costs $0.49, which includes handling and transportation. Cookies that are not sold at the end of the day are reduced to $0.29 and sold the following day as day-old merchandise.

a. Construct a table showing the profits or losses for each possible quantity.

b. What is the optimal number of cookies to make?

c. Solve this problem by using marginal analysis.

21 Sarah's Muffler Shop has one standard muffler that fits a large variety of cars. Sarah wishes to establish a reorder point system to manage inventory of this standard muffler. Use the following information to determine the best order size and the reorder point:

Annual demand	3,500 mufflers	Ordering cost	$50 per order
Standard deviation of daily demand	6 mufflers per working day	Service probability	90%
Item cost	$30 per muffler	Lead time	2 working days
Annual holding cost	25% of item value	Working days	300 per year

22 Alpha Products, Inc., is having a problem trying to control inventory. There is insufficient time to devote to all its items equally. Here is a sample of some items stocked, along with the annual usage of each item expressed in dollar volume.

ITEM	ANNUAL DOLLAR USAGE	ITEM	ANNUAL DOLLAR USAGE
a	$ 7,000	k	$80,000
b	1,000	l	400
c	14,000	m	1,100
d	2,000	n	30,000
e	24,000	o	1,900
f	68,000	p	800
g	17,000	q	90,000
h	900	r	12,000
i	1,700	s	3,000
j	2,300	t	32,000

a. Can you suggest a system for allocating control time?

b. Specify where each item from the list would be placed.

23 After graduation, you decide to go into a partnership in an office supply store that has existed for a number of years. Walking through the store and stockrooms, you find a great discrepancy in service levels. Some spaces and bins for items are completely empty; others have supplies that are covered with dust and have obviously been there a long time. You decide to take on the project of establishing consistent levels of inventory to meet customer demands. Most of your supplies are purchased from just a few distributors that call on your store once every two weeks.

You choose, as your first item for study, computer printer paper. You examine the sales records and purchase orders and find that demand for the past 12 months was 5,000 boxes. Using your calculator you sample some days' demands and estimate that the standard deviation of daily demand is 10 boxes. You also search out these figures:

Cost per box of paper: $11.

Desired service probability: 98 percent.

Store is open every day.

Salesperson visits every two weeks.

Delivery time following visit is three days.

Using your procedure, how many boxes of paper would be ordered if, on the day the salesperson calls, 60 boxes are on hand?

24 A distributor of large appliances needs to determine the order quantities and reorder points for the various products it carries. The following data refer to a specific refrigerator in its product line:

Cost to place an order	$100
Holding cost	20 percent of product cost per year
Cost of refrigerator	$500 each
Annual demand	500 refrigerators
Standard deviation during lead time	10 refrigerators
Lead time	7 days

Consider an even daily demand and a 365-day year.
a. What is the economic order quantity?
b. If the distributor wants a 97 percent service probability, what reorder point, R, should be used?

25 It is your responsibility, as the new head of the automotive section of Nichols Department Store, to ensure that reorder quantities for the various items have been correctly established. You decide to test one item and choose Michelin tires, XW size 185 × 14 BSW. A perpetual inventory system has been used, so you examine this as well as other records and come up with the following data:

Cost per tire	$35 each
Holding cost	20 percent of tire cost per year
Demand	1,000 per year
Ordering cost	$20 per order
Standard deviation of daily demand	3 tires
Delivery lead time	4 days

Because customers generally do not wait for tires but go elsewhere, you decide on a service probability of 98 percent. Assume the demand occurs 365 days per year.
a. Determine the order quantity.
b. Determine the reorder point.

26 UA Hamburger Hamlet (UAHH) places a daily order for its high-volume items (hamburger patties, buns, milk, and so on). UAHH counts its current inventory on hand once per day and phones in its order for delivery 24 hours later. Determine the number of hamburgers UAHH should order for the following conditions:

Average daily demand	600
Standard deviation of demand	100
Desired service probability	99%
Hamburger inventory	800

27 DAT, Inc., produces digital audiotapes to be used in the consumer audio division. DAT lacks sufficient personnel in its inventory supply section to closely control each item stocked, so it has asked you to determine an ABC classification. Here is a sample from the inventory records:

ITEM	AVERAGE MONTHLY DEMAND	PRICE PER UNIT	ITEM	AVERAGE MONTHLY DEMAND	PRICE PER UNIT
1	700	$6.00	6	100	10.00
2	200	4.00	7	3,000	2.00
3	2,000	12.00	8	2,500	1.00
4	1,100	20.00	9	500	10.00
5	4,000	21.00	10	1,000	2.00

Develop an ABC classification for these 10 items.

28 A local service station is open 7 days per week, 365 days per year. Sales of 10W40 grade premium oil average 20 cans per day. Inventory holding costs are $0.50 per can per year. Ordering costs are $10 per order. Lead time is two weeks. Backorders are not practical—the motorist drives away.

   a. Based on these data, choose the appropriate inventory model and calculate the economic order quantity and reorder point. Describe in a sentence how the plan would work. Hint: Assume demand is deterministic.

   b. The boss is concerned about this model because demand really varies. The standard deviation of demand was determined from a data sample to be 6.15 cans per day. The manager wants a 99.5 percent service probability. Determine a new inventory plan based on this information and the data in *a*. Use Q_{opt} from *a*.

29 Dave's Auto Supply custom mixes paint for its customers. The shop performs a weekly inventory count of the main colors that are used for mixing paint. Determine the amount of white paint that should be ordered using the following information:

Average weekly demand	20 gallons
Standard deviation of demand	5 gallons/week
Desired service probability	98%
Current inventory	25 gallons
Lead time	1 week

30 A particular raw material is available to a company at three different prices, depending on the size of the order:

Less than 100 pounds	$20 per pound
100 pounds to 1,000 pounds	$19 per pound
More than 1,000 pounds	$10 per pound

   The cost to place an order is $40. Annual demand is 3,000 units. Holding (or carrying) cost is 25 percent of the material price.

   What is the economic order quantity to buy each time?

31 CU, Incorporated (CUI), produces copper contacts that it uses in switches and relays. CUI needs to determine the order quantity, Q, to meet the annual demand at the lowest cost. The price of copper depends on the quantity ordered. Here are price-break and other data for the problem:

Price of copper	$0.82 per pound up to 2,499 pounds
	$0.81 per pound for orders between 2,500 and 5,000 pounds
	$0.80 per pound for orders greater than 5,000 pounds
Annual demand	50,000 pounds per year
Holding cost	20 percent per unit per year of the price of the copper
Ordering cost	$30

Which quantity should be ordered?

CASE: HEWLETT-PACKARD—SUPPLYING THE DESKJET PRINTER IN EUROPE

The DeskJet printer was introduced in 1988 and has become one of Hewlett-Packard's (HP's) most successful products. Sales have grown steadily, now reaching a level of over 600,000. Unfortunately, inventory growth has tracked sales growth closely.

HP's distribution centers are filled with pallets of the DeskJet printer. Worse yet, the organization in Europe claims that inventory levels there need to be raised even further to maintain satisfactory product availability.

exhibit 17.12   HP DeskJet Supply Chain

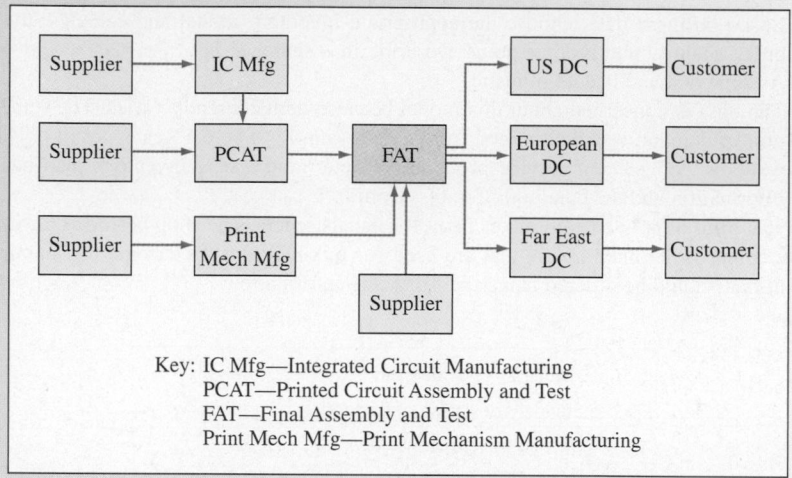

Key: IC Mfg—Integrated Circuit Manufacturing
PCAT—Printed Circuit Assembly and Test
FAT—Final Assembly and Test
Print Mech Mfg—Print Mechanism Manufacturing

THE DESKJET SUPPLY CHAIN

The network of suppliers, manufacturing sites, distribution centers (DCs), dealers, and customers for the DeskJet product make up the DeskJet supply chain (see Exhibit 17.12). HP in Vancouver does manufacturing. There are two key stages in the manufacturing process: (1) printed circuit assembly and test (PCAT) and (2) final assembly and test (FAT). PCAT involves the assembly and testing of electronic components (like integrated circuits, read-only memories, and raw printed circuit boards) to make logic boards used in the printer. FAT involves the assembly of other subassemblies (like motors, cables, keypads, plastic chassis, gears, and the printed circuit assemblies from PCAT) to produce a working printer, as well as the final testing of the printer. The components needed for PCAT and FAT are sourced from other HP divisions as well as from external suppliers worldwide.

Selling the DeskJet in Europe requires customizing the printer to meet the language and power supply requirements of the local countries, a process known as "localization." Specifically, the localization of the DeskJet of different countries involves assembling the appropriate power supply module, which reflects the correct voltage requirements (110 or 220) and power cord plug, and packaging it with the working printer and a manual written in the appropriate language. Currently, the final test is done with the actual power supply module included with the printer. Hence, the finished products of the factory are "localized" versions of the printer destined for all the different countries. For the European Union six different versions are currently produced. These are designated A, AA, AB, AQ, AU, and AY as indicated in the Bills of Materials shown in Exhibit 17.13.

The total factory throughput time through the PCAT and FAT stages is about one week. The transportation time from Vancouver to the European DC is five weeks. The long shipment time to Europe is due to ocean transit and the time to clear customs and duties at port of entry. The plant sends a weekly shipment of printers to the DC in Europe.

Globa

**Suppl
Chain**

exhibit 17.13   HP DeskJet Bill of Materials

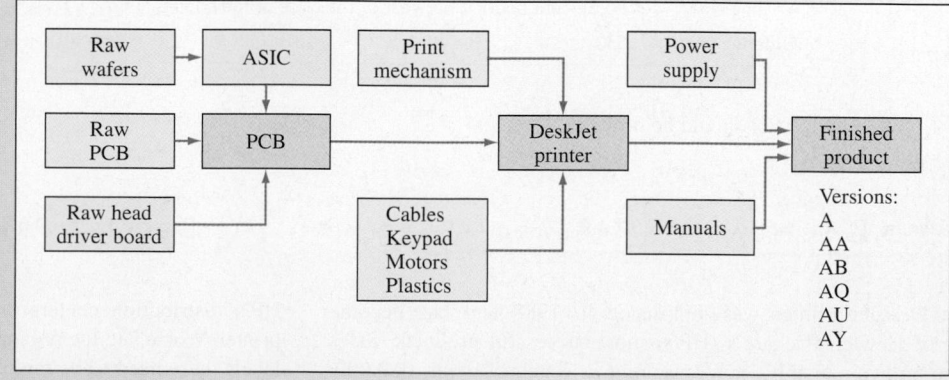

DeskJet Demand Data from Europe

exhibit 17.14

EUROPE OPTIONS	NOV.	DEC.	JAN.	FEB.	MAR.	APR.	MAY	JUN.	JUL.	AUG.	SEP.	OCT.
A	80	—	60	90	21	48	—	9	20	54	84	42
AB	20,572	20,895	19,252	11,052	19,864	20,316	13,336	10,578	6,095	14,496	23,712	9,792
AU	4,564	3,207	7,485	4,908	5,295	90	—	5,004	4,385	5,103	4,302	6,153
AA	400	255	408	645	210	87	432	816	430	630	456	273
AQ	4,008	2,196	4,761	1,953	1,008	2,358	1,676	540	2,310	2,046	1,797	2,961
AY	248	450	378	306	219	204	248	484	164	363	384	234
Total	29,872	27,003	32,344	18,954	26,617	23,103	15,692	17,431	13,405	22,692	30,735	19,455

**Excel:
HP Deskjet**

The printer industry is highly competitive. Resellers want to carry as little inventory as possible. Consequently there has been increasing pressure for HP as a manufacturer to provide high levels of availability at the DC. In response, management has decided to stock the DCs so that a high level of availability is maintained.

THE INVENTORY SERVICE CRISIS

To limit the amount of inventory throughout the DeskJet supply chain and at the same time provide the high level of service needed has been quite a challenge to Vancouver's management. The manufacturing group has been very successful in reducing the uncertainties caused by delivery to the European DC. Forecasting demand in Europe, though, is a significant problem. It has become common to have product shortages for model demands from some countries, while inventory of other models keeps piling up. In the past, the target inventory levels at the DCs were based on safety stocks that were a result of some judgmental rule of thumb. Specifically, target inventory levels, equal to one-month average sales, were set for each model carried in the DC. Now, however, it seems that the increasing difficulty of getting accurate forecasts means the safety stock rules should be revisited.

HP has put together a team of employees to help implement a scientifically based safety stock system that will be responsive to forecast errors and replenishment lead times. They are to recommend a method for calculating appropriate safety stock levels for the various DeskJet models carried in the European DC. The team has a good sample of demand data that can be used for developing the safety stock methodology (see Exhibit 17.14). HP hopes this new methodology will solve the inventory and service problem.

One issue that continually comes up is the choice of inventory carrying cost to be used in safety stock analyses. Estimates within the company range from 12 percent (HP's cost of debt plus some warehousing expenses) to 60 percent (based on the ROI expected of new product development projects). Management has decided to use 25 percent for this study. Assume that all printers cost an average of approximately $250 each to produce and ship to Europe. Another issue is the choice of safety stock probability for the model. The company has decided to use a probability of 98 percent, a number that marketing feels is appropriate.

THE DISTRIBUTION PROCESS

The DCs have traditionally envisioned their process as a simple, straight-line, standardized process. There are four process stops:

1 Receive (complete) products from various suppliers and stock them.
2 Pick the various products needed to fill a customer order.
3 Shrink-wrap the complete order and label it.
4 Ship the order via the appropriate carrier.

The DeskJet printer fits well into the standard process. In contrast, other products, such as personal computers and monitors, require special processing called "integration," which includes addition of an appropriate keyboard and manual for the destination country. Although this extra processing does not require much extra labor, it is difficult to accommodate in the standard process and disrupts the material flow. There is considerable frustration within DC management regarding the support of assembly processes. In general, DC management stresses the DCs' role as warehouses and the need to continue to do what they are best at—distribution.

Top management, though, feels that integration of the product at the warehouse is extremely valuable because it allows generic products to be sent to the DC with final configuration of the product done just prior to shipment to the customer. Rather than the factory making products specific to a country, generic products could be produced and shipped to Europe. Management is very interested in studying the value of this approach as it could be applied to the DeskJet printers.

QUESTIONS

1 Develop an inventory model for managing the DeskJet printers in Europe assuming that the Vancouver plant continues to produce the six models sold in Europe. Using the data in Exhibit 17.13, apply your model and calculate the expected yearly investment in DeskJet printer inventory in the Europe DC.
2 Compare your results from question 1 to the current policy of carrying one month's average inventory at the DC.

3   Evaluate the idea of supplying generic printers to the Europe DC and integrating the product by packaging the power supply and the instruction manual at the DC just prior to delivery to the European resellers. Focus on the impact on DC inventory investment in this analysis.

4   What is your recommendation to HP?

SUPER QUIZ

1   Model most appropriate for making a one-time purchase of an item.

2   Model most appropriate when inventory is replenished only in fixed intervals of time, for example, on the first Monday of each month.

3   Model most appropriate when a fixed amount must be purchased each time an order is placed.

4   Based on an EOQ-type ordering criterion, what cost must be taken to zero if the desire is to have an order quantity of a single unit?

5   Term used to describe demand that can be accurately calculated to meet the need of a production schedule, for example.

6   Term used to describe demand that is uncertain and needs to be forecast.

7   We are ordering T-shirts for the spring party and are selling them for twice what we paid for them. We expect to sell 100 shirts and the standard deviation associated with our forecast is 10 shirts. How many shirts should we order?

8   We have an item that we stock in our store that has fairly steady demand. Our supplier insists that we buy 1,200 units at a time. The lead time is very short on the item, since the supplier is only a few blocks away and we can pick up another 1,200 units when we run out. How many units do you expect to have in inventory on average?

9   For the item described in question 8, if we expect to sell approximately 15,600 units next year, how many trips will we need to make to the supplier over the year?

10 If we decide to carry 10 units of safety stock for the item described in questions 8 and 9, and we implemented this by going to our supplier when we had 10 units left, how much inventory would you expect to have on average now?

11 We are being evaluated based on the percentage of total demand met in a year (not the probability of stocking out as used in the chapter). Consider an item that we are managing using a fixed-order quantity model with safety stock. We decide to double the order quantity, but leave the reorder point the same. Would you expect the percent of total demand met next year to go up or down? Why?

12 Consider an item that we have 120 units currently in inventory. The average demand for the item is 60 units per week. The lead time for the item is exactly 2 weeks and we carry 16 units for safety stock. What is the probability of running out of the item if we order right now?

13 If we take advantage of a quantity discount, would you expect your average inventory to go up or down? Assume that the probability of stocking out criterion stays the same.

14 This is an inventory auditing technique where inventory levels are checked more frequently than one time a year.

1. Single-period model 2. Fixed–time period model 3. Fixed–order quantity model 4. Setup or ordering cost 5. Dependent demand 6. Independent demand 7. 100 shirts 8. 600 units 9. 13 trips 10. 610 units 11. Go up (we are taking fewer chances of running out) 12. 50 percent 13. Will probably go up if the probability of stocking out stays the same 14. Cycle counting

SELECTED BIBLIOGRAPHY

Brooks, R. B., and L. W. Wilson. *Inventory Record Accuracy: Unleashing the Power of Cycle Counting.* Essex Junction, VT: Oliver Wight, 1993.

Silver, E.; D. Pyke; and R. Peterson. *Decision Systems for Inventory Management and Production Planning and Control.* 3rd ed. New York: Wiley, 1998.

Sipper, D., and R. L. Bulfin Jr. *Production Planning, Control, and Integration.* New York: McGraw-Hill, 1997.

Tersine, R. J. *Principles of Inventory and Materials Management.* 4th ed. New York: North-Holland, 1994.

Vollmann, T. E.; W. L. Berry; D. C. Whybark; and F. R. Jacobs. *Manufacturing Planning and Control Systems for Supply Chain Management.* 5th ed. New York: McGraw-Hill, 2004.

Wild, T. *Best Practices in Inventory Management.* New York: Wiley, 1998.

Zipkin, P. H. *Foundations of Inventory Management.* New York: Irwin/McGraw-Hill, 2000.

FOOTNOTES

1 P is actually a cumulative probability because the sale of the nth unit depends not only on exactly n being demanded but also on the demand for any number greater than n.

2 As previously discussed, the standard deviation of a sum of independent variables equals the square root of the sum of the variances.

3 The Pareto principle is also widely applied in quality problems through the use of Pareto charts. (See Chapter 6.)

chapter 18

MATERIAL REQUIREMENTS PLANNING

FROM PUSH TO PULL

n the 1980s manufacturing led the national economy in the move from batch-oriented data processing systems to online transaction processing systems. The focus was MRP (initially material requirements planning, evolving to manufacturing resource planning), which later evolved into enterprise resource planning (ERP). It has been a long ride, and anyone who has been there for the duration deserves a rest.

However, the winds of change are blowing again as yet another new paradigm comes roaring through manufacturing. Specifically, we are speaking of the change in our economy from a build-to-stock to a build-to-order model of doing business.

After reading the chapter you will:

1. Describe what MRP is and where it is best applied.
2. Understand the source of the information used by the system.
3. Demonstrate how to do an MRP "explosion."
4. Explain how order quantities are calculated in MRP systems.

The weak link in the build-to-stock model is inventory management, and this can be traced to an even weaker link, reliance upon sales forecasts. A build-to-order model begins with the order, not the forecast. The old problem of coordinating the procurement of parts, production of the product, and shipping the product still exists.

Today the term *flow management* is used to describe new hybrid production planning systems that combine the information integration and planning capability of MRP with the response of a JIT kanban system. Major ERP software vendors such as Oracle, SAP, and i2 Technologies are selling these new systems.

Essentially, the idea behind flow management is to produce a constantly changing mix of products, a mix that is based on current orders, using a stream of parts that are supplied just-in-time. It's important not to be tricked into thinking that all these new words really represent something new. Actually, flow manufacturing just combines things that have been used for years. In this case the combination is JIT kanban logic, MRP logic for planning material requirements, and client–server ERP.

Material requirements planning (MRP)

Our emphasis here is on **material requirements planning (MRP)**, which is the key piece of logic that ties the production functions together from a material planning and control view. MRP has been installed almost universally in manufacturing firms, even those considered small. The reason is that MRP is a logical, easily understandable approach to the problem of determining the number of parts, components, and materials needed to produce each end item. MRP also provides the schedule specifying when each of these items should be ordered or produced.

MRP is based on dependent demand. Dependent demand is caused by the demand for a higher-level item. Tires, wheels, and engines are dependent demand items based on the demand for automobiles, for example.

Determining the number of dependent demand items needed is essentially a straightforward multiplication process. If one Part A takes five parts of B to make, then five parts of A require 25 parts of B. The basic difference in independent demand covered in the previous chapter and dependent demand covered in this chapter is as follows: If Part A is sold outside the firm, the amount of Part A that we sell is uncertain. We need to create a forecast using past data or do something like a market analysis. Part A is an independent item. However, Part B is a dependent part and its use depends on Part A. The number of B needed is simply the number of A times five. As a result of this type of multiplication, the requirements of other dependent demand items tend to become more and more lumpy as we go farther down into the product creation sequence. Lumpiness means that the requirements tend to bunch or lump rather than having an even dispersal. This is also caused by the way manufacturing is done. When manufacturing occurs in lots (or batches), items needed to produce the lot are withdrawn from inventory in quantities (perhaps all at once) rather than one at a time.

MASTER PRODUCTION SCHEDULING

Generally, the master schedule deals with end items and is a major input to the MRP process. If the end item is quite large or quite expensive, however, the master schedule may schedule major subassemblies or components instead.

All production systems have limited capacity and limited resources. This presents a challenging job for the master scheduler. Although the aggregate plan provides the general range of operation, the master scheduler must specify exactly what is to be produced. These decisions are made while responding to pressures from various functional areas such as the sales department (meet the customer's promised due date), finance (minimize inventory), management (maximize productivity and customer service, minimize resource needs), and manufacturing (have level schedules and minimize setup time).

To determine an acceptable feasible schedule to be released to the shop, trial master production schedules are run through the MRP program, which is described in the next section. The resulting planned order releases (the detailed production schedules) are checked to make sure that resources are available and that the completion times are reasonable. What appears to be a feasible master schedule may turn out to require excessive resources once the product explosion has taken place and materials, parts, and components from lower levels are determined. If this does happen (the usual case), the master production schedule is then modified with these limitations and the MRP program is run again. To ensure good master scheduling, the master scheduler (the human being) must

- Include all demands from product sales, warehouse replenishment, spares, and interplant requirements.
- Never lose sight of the aggregate plan.
- Be involved with customer order promising.
- Be visible to all levels of management.
- Objectively trade off manufacturing, marketing, and engineering conflicts.
- Identify and communicate all problems.

The upper portion of Exhibit 18.1 shows an aggregate plan for the total number of mattresses planned per month, without regard for mattress type. The lower portion shows a master production schedule specifying the exact type of mattress and the quantity planned for production by week. The next level down (not shown) would be the MRP program that develops detailed schedules showing when cotton batting, springs, and hardwood are needed to make the mattresses.

To again summarize the planning sequence, the aggregate operations plan, discussed in Chapter 16, specifies product groups. It does not specify exact items. The next level down in the planning process is the master production schedule. The **master production schedule (MPS)** is the time-phased plan specifying how many and when the firm plans to build each end item. For example, the aggregate plan for a furniture company may specify the total volume of mattresses it plans to produce over the next month or next quarter. The MPS goes

Master production schedule (MPS)

The Aggregate Plan and the Master Production Schedule for Mattresses

exhibit 18.1

Aggregate Production Plan for Mattresses

Month	1	2
Mattress production	900	950

Master Production Schedule for Mattress Models

	1	2	3	4	5	6	7	8
Model 327	200			400		200	100	
Model 538		100	100		150		100	
Model 749			100			200		200

exhibit 18.2   Master Production Schedule Time Fences

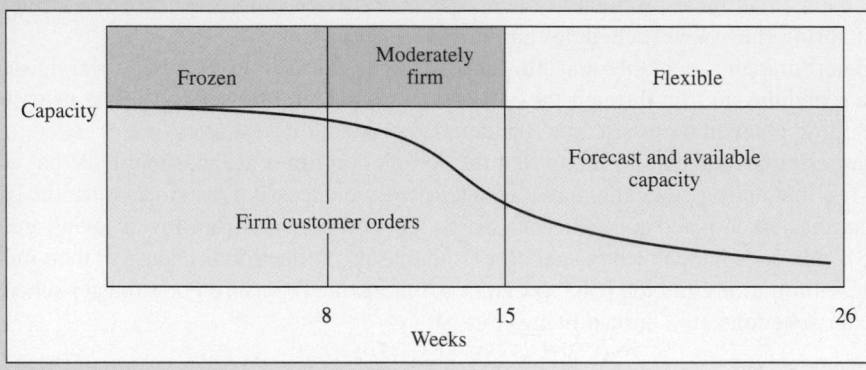

the next step down and identifies the exact size mattresses and their qualities and styles. All of the mattresses sold by the company would be specified by the MPS. The MPS also states period by period (usually weekly) how many and when each of these mattress types is needed.

Still further down the disaggregation process is the MRP program, which calculates and schedules all raw materials, parts, and supplies needed to make the mattress specified by the MPS.

TIME FENCES

The question of flexibility within a master production schedule depends on several factors: production lead time, commitment of parts and components to a specific end item, relationship between the customer and vendor, amount of excess capacity, and the reluctance or willingness of management to make changes.

The purpose of time fences is to maintain a reasonably controlled flow through the production system. Unless some operating rules are established and adhered to, the system could be chaotic and filled with overdue orders and constant expediting.

Exhibit 18.2 shows an example of a master production schedule time fence. Management defines *time fences* as periods of time having some specified level of opportunity for the customer to make changes. (The customer may be the firm's own marketing department, which may be considering product promotions, broadening variety, or the like.) Note in the exhibit that for the next eight weeks, this particular master schedule is frozen. Each firm has its own time fences and operating rules. Under these rules, *frozen* could be defined as anything from absolutely no changes in one company to only the most minor of changes in another. *Moderately firm* may allow changes in specific products within a product group so long as parts are available. *Flexible* may allow almost any variations in products, with the provisions that capacity remains about the same and that there are no long lead time items involved.

Available to promise   Some firms use a feature known as available to promise for items that are master scheduled. This feature identifies the difference between the number of units currently included in the master schedule and firm customer orders. For example, assume the master schedule indicates that 100 units of Model 538 mattress are going to be made during week seven. If firm customer orders now indicate that only 65 of those mattresses have actually been sold, the sales group has another 35 mattresses "available to promise" for delivery during that week. This can be a powerful tool for coordinating sales and production activities.

Industry Applications and Expected Benefits of MRP   **exhibit 18.3**

INDUSTRY TYPE	EXAMPLES	EXPECTED BENEFITS
Assemble-to-stock	Combines multiple component parts into a finished product, which is then stocked in inventory to satisfy customer demand. Examples: watches, tools, appliances.	High
Fabricate-to-stock	Items are manufactured by machine rather than assembled from parts. These are standard stock items carried in anticipation of customer demand. Examples: piston rings, electrical switches.	Low
Assemble-to-order	A final assembly is made from standard options that the customer chooses. Examples: trucks, generators, motors.	High
Fabricate-to-order	Items are manufactured by machine to customer order. These are generally industrial orders. Examples: bearings, gears, fasteners.	Low
Manufacture-to-order	Items are fabricated or assembled completely to customer specification. Examples: turbine generators, heavy machine tools.	High
Process	Includes industries such as foundries, rubber and plastics, specialty paper, chemicals, paint, drug, food processors.	Medium

WHERE MRP CAN BE USED

MRP is most valuable in industries where a number of products are made in batches using the same productive equipment. The list in Exhibit 18.3 includes examples of different industry types and the expected benefit from MRP. As you can see in the exhibit, MRP is most valuable to companies involved in assembly operations and least valuable to those in fabrication. One more point to note: MRP does not work well in companies that produce a low number of units annually. Especially for companies producing complex, expensive products requiring advanced research and design, experience has shown that lead times tend to be too long and too uncertain, and the product configuration too complex. Such companies need the control features that network scheduling techniques offer. These project management methods are covered in Chapter 10.

CATERPILLAR MANUFACTURES MORE THAN 300 PRODUCTS IN 23 COUNTRIES AND SERVES CUSTOMERS IN 200 COUNTRIES WORLDWIDE. "CAT" DEPENDS ON MRP FOR PLANNING ITS MANUFACTURING INVENTORY.

MATERIAL REQUIREMENTS PLANNING SYSTEM STRUCTURE

The material requirements planning portion of manufacturing activities most closely interacts with the master schedule, bill of materials file, inventory records file, and the output reports as shown in Exhibit 18.4.

Each facet of Exhibit 18.4 is detailed in the following sections, but essentially, the MRP system works as follows: the master production schedule states the number of items to be produced during specific time periods. A *bill of materials* file identifies the specific materials

exhibit 18.4   Overall View of the Inputs to a Standard Material Requirements Planning Program and the Reports Generated by the Program

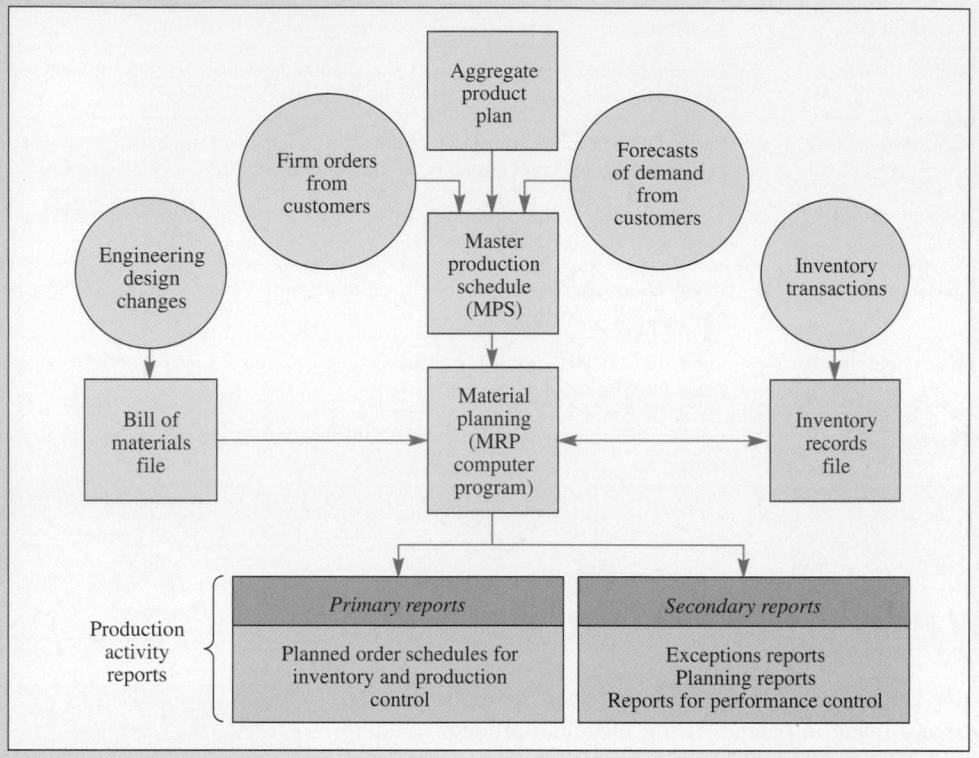

used to make each item and the correct quantities of each. The inventory records file contains data such as the number of units on hand and on order. These three sources—master production schedule, bill of materials file, and inventory records file—become the data sources for the material requirements program, which expands the production schedule into a detailed order scheduling plan for the entire production sequence.

DEMAND FOR PRODUCTS

Product demand for end items comes primarily from two main sources. The first is known customers who have placed specific orders, such as those generated by sales personnel, or from interdepartment transactions. These orders usually carry promised delivery dates. There is no forecasting involved in these orders—simply add them up. The second source is forecast demand. These are the normal independent-demand orders; the forecasting models presented in Chapter 15 can be used to predict the quantities. The demand from the known customers and the forecast demand are combined and become the input for the master production schedule, as described in the previous section.

In addition to the demand for end products, customers also order specific parts and components either as spares or for service and repair. These demands are not usually part of the master production schedule; instead, they are fed directly into the material requirements planning program at the appropriate levels. That is, they are added in as a gross requirement for that part or component.

BILL OF MATERIALS

Bill of materials (BOM)

The bill of materials (BOM) file contains the complete product description, listing not only the materials, parts, and components but also the sequence in which the product is created. This BOM file is one of the three main inputs to the MRP program. (The other two are the master schedule and the inventory records file.)

A. Bill of Materials (Product Structure Tree) for Product A

exhibit 18.5

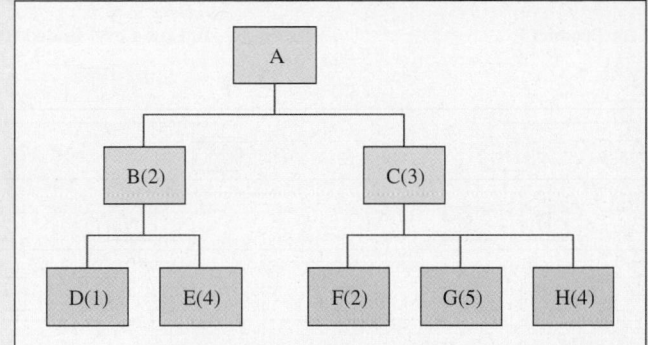

B. Parts List in an Indented Format and in a Single-Level List

INDENTED PARTS LIST			SINGLE-LEVEL PARTS LIST		
A			A		
					B(2)
	B(2)				C(3)
		D(1)	B		
		E(4)			D(1)
	C(3)				E(4)
		F(2)	C		
		G(5)			F(2)
					G(5)
		H(4)			H(4)

The BOM file is often called the *product structure file* or *product tree* because it shows how a product is put together. It contains the information to identify each item and the quantity used per unit of the item of which it is a part. To illustrate this, consider Product A shown in Exhibit 18.5A. Product A is made of two units of Part B and three units of Part C. Part B is made of one unit of Part D and four units of Part E. Part C is made of two units of Part F, five units of Part G, and four units of Part H.

Bills of materials often list parts using an indented structure. This clearly identifies each item and the manner in which it is assembled because each indentation signifies the components of the item. A comparison of the indented parts in Exhibit 18.5B with the item structure in Exhibit 18.5A shows the ease of relating the two displays. From a computer standpoint, however, storing items in indented parts lists is very inefficient. To compute the amount of each item needed at the lower levels, each item would need to be expanded ("exploded") and summed. A more efficient procedure is to store parts data in simple single-level lists. That is, each item and component is listed showing only its parent and the number of units needed per unit of its parent. This avoids duplication because it includes each assembly only once. Exhibit 18.5B shows both the indented parts list and the single-level parts list for Product A.

A *modular* bill of materials is the term for a buildable item that can be produced and stocked as a subassembly. It is also a standard item with no options within the module. Many end items that are large and expensive are better scheduled and controlled as modules (or subassemblies). It is particularly advantageous to schedule subassembly modules when the same subassemblies appear in different end items. For example, a manufacturer of cranes can combine booms, transmissions, and engines in a variety of ways to meet a customer's needs. Using a modular bill of materials simplifies the scheduling and control and also makes it

exhibit 18.6   Product L Hierarchy in (A) Expanded to the Lowest Level of Each Item in (B)

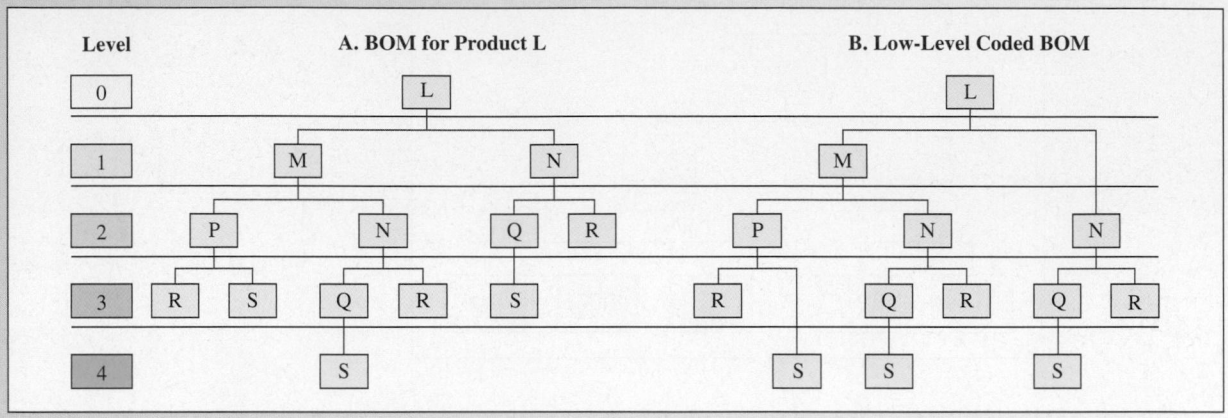

easier to forecast the use of different modules. Another benefit in using modular bills is that if the same item is used in a number of products, then the total inventory investment can be minimized.

A *super* bill of materials includes items with fractional options. (A super bill can specify, for example, 0.3 of a part. What that means is that 30 percent of the units produced contain that part and 70 percent do not.) Modular and super bills of materials are often referred to as planning bills of materials since they simplify the planning process.

Low-Level Coding   If all identical parts occur at the same level for each end product, the total number of parts and materials needed for a product can be computed easily. Consider Product L shown in Exhibit 18.6A. Notice that Item N, for example, occurs both as an input to L and as an input to M. Item N, therefore, needs to be lowered to level 2 (Exhibit 18.6B) to bring all Ns to the same level. If all identical items are placed at the same level, it becomes a simple matter for the computer to scan across each level and summarize the number of units of each item required.

INVENTORY RECORDS

The inventory records file can be quite lengthy. Exhibit 18.7 shows the variety of information contained in the inventory records. The MRP program accesses the *status* segment of the record according to specific time periods (called *time buckets* in MRP slang). These records are accessed as needed during the program run.

As we will see, the MRP program performs its analysis from the top of the product structure downward, calculating requirements level by level. There are times, however, when it is desirable to identify the parent item that caused the material requirement. The MRP program allows the creation of a *peg record* file either separately or as part of the inventory record file. Pegging requirements allows us to retrace a material requirement upward in the product structure through each level, identifying each parent item that created the demand.

Inventory Transactions File   The inventory status file is kept up to date by posting inventory transactions as they occur. These changes occur because of stock receipts and disbursements, scrap losses, wrong parts, canceled orders, and so forth.

MRP COMPUTER PROGRAM

The material requirements planning program operates using information from the inventory records, the master schedule, and the bill of materials. The process of calculating

The Inventory Status Record for an Item in Inventory

exhibit 18.7

Item master data segment	Part no.		Description		Lead time		Std. cost	Safety stock							
	Order quantity		Setup	Cycle		Last year's usage			Class						
	Scrap allowance		Cutting data		Pointers			Etc.							
Inventory status segment	Allocated		Control balance	Period								Totals			
				1	2	3	4	5	6	7	8				
	Gross requirements														
	Scheduled receipts														
	Projected available balance														
	Planned order releases														
Subsidiary data segment	Order details														
	Pending action														
	Counters														
	Keeping track														

the exact requirements for each item managed by the system is often referred to as the "explosion" process. Working from the top level downward in the bill of materials, requirements from parent items are used to calculate the requirements for component items. Consideration is taken of current on-hand balances and orders that are scheduled for receipt in the future.

The following is a general description of the MRP explosion process:

1. The requirements for level 0 items, typically referred to as "end items," are retrieved from the master schedule. These requirements are referred to as "gross requirements" by the MRP program. Typically, the gross requirements are scheduled in weekly time buckets.

2. Next, the program uses the current on-hand balance together with the schedule of orders that will be received in the future to calculate the "net requirements." Net requirements are the amounts that are needed week by week in the future over and above what is currently on hand or committed to through an order already released and scheduled.

3. Using net requirements, the program calculates when orders should be received to meet these requirements. This can be a simple process of just scheduling orders to arrive according to the exact net requirements or a more complicated process where requirements are combined for multiple periods. This schedule of when orders should arrive is referred to as "planned-order receipts."

4. Since there is typically a lead time associated with each order, the next step is to find a schedule for when orders are actually released. Offsetting the "planned-order receipts" by the required lead time does this. This schedule is referred to as the "planned-order release."

5. After these four steps have been completed for all the level zero items, the program moves to level 1 items.

6. The gross requirements for each level 1 item are calculated from the planned-order release schedule for the parents of each level 1 item. Any additional independent demand also needs to be included in the gross requirements.

7. After the gross requirements have been determined, net requirements, planned-order receipts, and planned-order releases are calculated as described in steps 2–4 above.

8. This process is then repeated for each level in the bill of materials.

The process of doing these calculations is much simpler than the description, as you will see in the example that follows. Typically, the explosion calculations are performed each week or whenever changes have been made to the master schedule. Some MRP programs have the option of generating immediate schedules, called *net change* schedules. **Net change systems** are "activity" driven and requirements and schedules are updated whenever a transaction is processed that has an impact on the item. Net change enables the system to reflect in "real time" the exact status of each item managed by the system.

Net change systems

AN EXAMPLE USING MRP

Ampere, Inc., produces a line of electric meters installed in residential buildings by electric utility companies to measure power consumption. Meters used on single-family homes are of two basic types for different voltage and amperage ranges. In addition to complete meters, some sub-assemblies are sold separately for repair or for changeovers to a different voltage or power load. The problem for the MRP system is to determine a production schedule to identify each item, the period it is needed, and the appropriate quantities. The schedule is then checked for feasibility, and the schedule is modified if necessary.

FORECASTING DEMAND

Demand for the meters and components originates from two sources: regular customers that place firm orders and unidentified customers that make the normal random demands for these items. The random requirements were forecast using one of the usual techniques described in Chapter 15 and past demand data. Exhibit 18.8 shows the requirements for meters A and B and Subassembly D for a three-month period (months three through five). There are some "other parts" used to make the meters. In order to keep our example manageable, we are not including them in this example.

DEVELOPING A MASTER PRODUCTION SCHEDULE

For the meter and component requirements specified in Exhibit 18.8, assume that the quantities to satisfy the known and random demands must be available during the first week of the month. This assumption is reasonable because management (in our example) prefers to produce meters in a single batch each month rather than a number of batches throughout the month.

| exhibit 18.8 | Future Requirements for Meters A and B and Subassembly D Stemming from Specific Customer Orders and from Random Sources |

	METER A		METER B		SUBASSEMBLY C	
MONTH	KNOWN	RANDOM	KNOWN	RANDOM	KNOWN	RANDOM
3	1,000	250	410	60	200	70
4	600	250	300	60	180	70
5	300	250	500	60	250	70

A Master Schedule to Satisfy Demand Requirements as Specified in Exhibit 18.8

exhibit 18.9

	Week								
	9	10	11	12	13	14	15	16	17
Meter A	1,250				850				550
Meter B	470				360				560
Subassembly D	270				250				320

Exhibit 18.9 shows the trial master schedule that we use under these conditions, with demand for months 3, 4, and 5 listed in the first week of each month, or as Weeks 9, 13, and 17. For brevity, we will work with demand through Week 9. The schedule we develop should be examined for resource availability, capacity availability, and so on, and then revised and run again. We will stop with our example at the end of this one schedule, however.

BILL OF MATERIALS (PRODUCT STRUCTURE)

The product structure for meters A and B is shown in Exhibit 18.10A in the typical way using low-level coding, in which each item is placed at the lowest level at which it appears in the

A. Product Structure for Meters A and B

exhibit 18.10

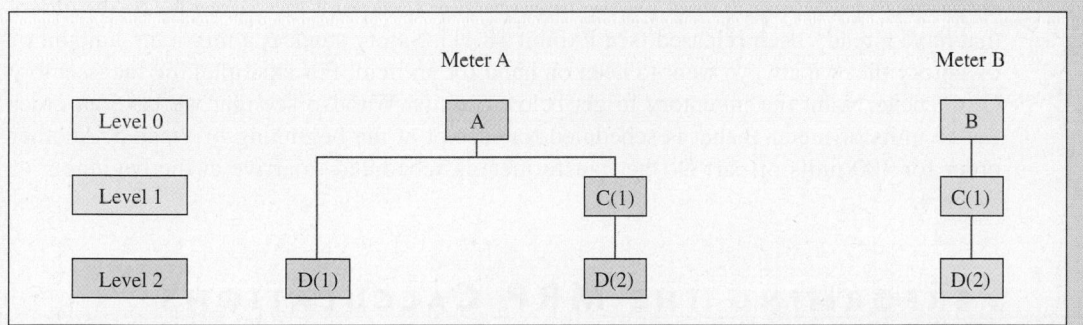

**Tutorial:
MRP**

B. Indented Parts List for Meter A and Meter B, with the Required Number of Items per Unit of Parent Listed in Parentheses

METER A				METER B		
A				B		
	D(1)					
	C(1)				C(1)	
			D(2)			D(2)

Exhibit shows the subassemblies and parts that make up the meters and shows the numbers of units required per unit of parent in parentheses.

Number of Units on Hand and Lead Time Data That Would Appear on the Inventory
Record File

ITEM	ON-HAND INVENTORY	LEAD TIME (WEEKS)	SAFETY STOCK	ON ORDER
A	50	2	0	
B	60	2	0	10 (week 5)
C	40	1	5	
D	200	1	20	100 (week 4)

structure hierarchy. Meters A and B consist of a common subassembly C and some parts that
include part D. To keep things simple, we will focus on only one of the parts, part D, which
is a transformer.

From the product structure, notice that part D (the transformer) is used in subassembly C (which is used in both meters A and B). In the case of meter A, an additional part D
(transformer) is needed. The "2" in parentheses next to D when used to make a C indicates
that two D's are required for every C that is made. The product structure, as well as the
indented parts list in Exhibit 18.10B, indicates how the meters are actually made. First,
subassembly C is made, and potentially these are carried in inventory. In a final assembly
process, meters A and B are put together, and in the case of meter A an additional part D
is used.

INVENTORY RECORDS

The inventory records data would be similar to that shown in Exhibit 18.7. As shown earlier in the chapter, additional data such as vendor identity, cost, and lead time also would be
included in these data. For this example, the pertinent data include the on-hand inventory
at the start of the program run, safety stock requirements, and the current status of orders
that have already been released (see Exhibit 18.11). Safety stock is a minimum amount of
inventory that we always want to keep on hand for an item. For example, for subassembly
C, we never want the inventory to get below 5 units. We also see that we have an order
for 10 units of meter B that is scheduled for receipt at the beginning of Week 5. Another
order for 100 units of part D (the transformer) is scheduled to arrive at the beginning of
Week 4.

PERFORMING THE MRP CALCULATIONS

Conditions are now set to perform the MRP calculations: End-item requirements have been
presented in the master production schedule, while the status of inventory and the order lead
times are available, and we also have the pertinent product structure data. The MRP calculations (often referred to as an explosion) are done level by level, in conjunction with the
inventory data and data from the master schedule.

Exhibit 18.12 shows the details of these calculations. The following analysis explains
the logic in detail. We will limit our analysis to the problem of meeting the gross requirements for 1,250 units of meter A, 470 units of meter B, and 270 units of transformer D, all
in Week 9.

An MRP record is kept for each item managed by the system. The record contains *gross
requirements, scheduled receipts, projected available balance, net requirements, planned
order receipts,* and *planned order releases* data. *Gross requirements* are the total amount
required for a particular item. These requirements can be from external customer demand
and also from demand calculated based on manufacturing requirements. *Scheduled receipts*

Material Requirements Planning Schedule for Meters A and B and Subassemblies C and D

exhibit 18.12

Tutorial: MRP

Item		Week 4	5	6	7	8	9
A LT = 2 weeks On hand = 50 Safety stock = 0 Order qty = lot-for-lot	Gross requirements						1250
	Scheduled receipts						
	Projected available balance	50	50	50	50	50	50
	Net requirements						1200
	Planned order receipts						1200
	Planned order releases				1200		
B LT = 2 weeks On hand = 60 Safety stock = 0 Order qty = lot-for-lot	Gross requirements						470
	Scheduled receipts		10				
	Projected available balance	60	60	70	70	70	70
	Net requirements						400
	Planned order receipts						400
	Planned order releases				400		
C LT = 1 week On hand = 40 Safety stock = 5 Order qty = 2000	Gross requirements				400+ 1200		
	Scheduled receipts						
	Projected available balance	35	35	35	35	435	435
	Net requirements				1565		
	Planned order receipts				2000		
	Planned order releases			2000			
D LT = 1 week On hand = 200 Safety stock = 20 Order qty = 5000	Gross requirements			4000	1200		270
	Scheduled receipts	100					
	Projected available balance	180	280	280	1280	80	80
	Net requirements			3720			190
	Planned order receipts			5000			5000
	Planned order releases		5000			5000	

represent orders that have already been released and that are scheduled to arrive as of the beginning of the period. Once the paperwork on an order has been released, what was prior to that event a "planned" order now becomes a *scheduled receipt. Projected available balance* is the amount of inventory that is expected as of the end of a period. This can be calculated as follows:

$$\text{Projected available balance}_t = \text{Projected available balance}_{t-1} - \text{Gross requirements}_t + \text{Scheduled receipts}_t + \text{Planned order receipts}_t - \text{Safety stock}$$

A *net requirement* is the amount needed when the *projected available* balance plus the *scheduled receipts* in a period are not sufficient to cover the *gross requirement*. The *planned order receipt* is the amount of an order that is required to meet a net requirement in the period. Finally, the *planned order release* is the planned order receipt offset by the lead time.

Beginning with meter A, the projected available balance is 50 units and there are no net requirements until Week 9. In Week 9, an additional 1,200 units are needed to cover the demand of 1,250 generated from the order scheduled through the master schedule. The order quantity is designated "lot-for-lot," which means that we can order the exact quantity needed to meet net requirements. An order, therefore, is planned for receipt of 1,200 units for the beginning of Week 9. Since the lead time is two weeks, this order must be released at the beginning of Week 7.

Meter B is similar to A, although an order for 10 units is scheduled for receipt in period 5. We project that 70 units will be available at the end of week 5. There is a net requirement for 400 additional units to meet the gross requirement of 470 units in Week 9. This requirement is met with an order for 400 units that must be released at the beginning of Week 7.

Item C is the subassembly used in both meters A and B. We need additional C's only when either A or B is being made. Our analysis of A indicates that an order for 1,200 will be released in Week 7. An order for 400 B's also will be released in Week 7, so total demand for C is 1,600 units in Week 7. The projected available balance is the 40 units on hand minus the safety stock of 5 units that we have specified, or 35 units. In Week 7, the net requirement is 1,565 units. The order policy for C indicates an order quantity of 2,000 units, so an order receipt for 2,000 is planned for Week 7. This order needs to be released in Week 6 due to the one-week lead time. Assuming this order is actually processed in the future, the projected available balance is 435 units in Weeks 7, 8, and 9.

Item D, the transformer, has demand from three different sources. The demand in Week 6 is due to the requirement to put D's into subassembly C. In this case two D's are needed for every C, or 4,000 units (the product structure indicates this two-to-one relationship). In the seventh week, 1,200 D's are needed for the order for 1,200 A's that are scheduled to be released in Week 7. Another 270 units are needed in Week 9 to meet the independent demand that is scheduled through the master schedule. Projected available balance at the end of Week 4 is 280 units (200 on hand plus the scheduled receipt of 100 units minus the safety stock of 20 units) and 280 units in Week 5. There is a net requirement for an additional 3,720 units in Week 6, so we plan to receive an order for 5,000 units (the order quantity). This results in a projected balance of 80 in Week 7 since 1,200 are used to meet demand. Eighty units are projected to be available in Week 8. Due to the demand for 270 in Week 9, a net requirement of 190 units in Week 9 results in planning the receipt of an additional 5,000-unit order in Week 9.

Step by Step

EXAMPLE 18.1: MRP Explosion Calculations

Juno Lighting makes special lights that are popular in new homes. Juno expects demand for two popular lights to be the following over the next eight weeks.

	Week							
	1	2	3	4	5	6	7	8
VH1-234	34	37	41	45	48	48	48	48
VH2-100	104	134	144	155	134	140	141	145

A key component in both lights is a socket that the bulb is screwed into in the base fixture. Each light has one of these sockets. Given the following information, plan the production of the lights and purchases of the socket.

	VH1-234	VH2-100	Light Socket
On hand	85	358	425
Q	200 (the production lot size)	400 (to production lot size)	500 (purchase quantity)
Lead time	1 week	1 week	3 weeks
Safety stock	0 units	0 units	20 units

SOLUTION

ITEM		WEEK							
		1	2	3	4	5	6	7	8
VH1-234	Gross requirement	34	37	41	45	48	48	48	48
Q = 200	Scheduled receipts								
LT = 1	Projected available balance	51	14	173	128	80	32	184	136
OH — 85	Net requirements			27				16	
SS = 0	Planned order receipts			200				200	
	Planned order releases		200				200		
VH2-100	Gross requirement	104	134	144	155	134	140	141	145
Q = 400	Scheduled receipts								
LT = 1	Projected available balance	254	120	376	221	87	347	206	61
OH = 358	Net requirements			24			53		
SS = 0	Planned order receipts			400			400		
	Planned order releases		400			400			
Socket	Gross requirement		600			400	200		
Q = 500	Scheduled receipts	500							
LT — 3	Projected available balance	905	305	305	305	405	205	205	205
OH = 425	Net requirements					95			
SS = 20	Planned order receipts					500			
	Planned order releases		500						

The best way to proceed is to work period by period by focusing on the projected available balance calculation. Whenever the available balance goes below zero, a net requirement is generated. When this happens, plan an order receipt to meet the requirement. For example, for VH1 we start with 85 units in inventory and need 34 to meet Week 1 production requirements. This brings our available balance at the end of Week 1 to 51 units. Another 37 units are used during Week 2, dropping inventory to 14. In Week 3, our project balance drops to 0 and we have a net requirement of 27 units that needs to be covered with an order scheduled to be received in Week 3. Since the lead time is one week, this order needs to be released in Week 2. Week 4 projected available balance is 128, calculated by taking the 200 units that are received in Week 3 and subtracting the Week 3 net requirement of 27 units and the 45 units needed for Week 4.

Since sockets are used in both VH1 and VH2, the gross requirements come from the planned order releases for these items: 600 are needed in Week 2 (200 for VH1s and 400 for VH2s), 400 in Week 5, and 200 in Week 6. Projected available balance is beginning inventory of 425 plus the scheduled receipts of 500 units minus the 20 units of safety stock. ●

LOT SIZING IN MRP SYSTEMS

The determination of lot sizes in an MRP system is a complicated and difficult problem. Lot sizes are the part quantities issued in the planned order receipt and planned order release sections of an MRP schedule. For parts produced in-house, lot sizes are the production quantities of batch sizes. For purchased parts, these are the quantities ordered from the supplier. Lot sizes generally meet part requirements for one or more periods.

Most lot-sizing techniques deal with how to balance the setup or order costs and holding costs associated with meeting the net requirements generated by the MRP planning process. Many MRP systems have options for computing lot sizes based on some of the more commonly used techniques. The use of lot-sizing techniques increases the complexity of running MRP schedules in a plant. In an attempt to save setup costs, the inventory generated with the larger lot sizes needs to be stored, making the logistics in the plant much more complicated.

Next we explain four lot-sizing techniques using a common example. The lot-sizing techniques presented are lot-for-lot (L4L), economic order quantity (EOQ), least total cost (LTC), and least unit cost (LUC).

Consider the following MRP lot-sizing problem; the net requirements are shown for eight scheduling weeks:

Cost per item	$10.00
Order or setup cost	$47.00
Inventory carrying cost/week	0.5%
Weekly net requirements:	

1	2	3	4	5	6	7	8
50	60	70	60	95	75	60	55

LOT-FOR-LOT

Lot-for-lot (L4L) is the most common technique. It

- Sets planned orders to exactly match the net requirements.
- Produces exactly what is needed each week with none carried over into future periods.
- Minimizes carrying cost.
- Does not take into account setup costs or capacity limitations.

Exhibit 18.13 shows the lot-for-lot calculations. The net requirements are given in column 2. Because the logic of lot-for-lot says the production quantity (column 3) will exactly match the required quantity (column 2), no inventory will be left at the end (column 4). Without any inventory to carry over into the next week, there is zero holding cost (column 5). However, lot-for-lot requires a setup cost each week (column 6). Incidentally, there is a setup cost each week because this is a work center where a variety of items are worked on each week. This is not a case where the work center is committed to one product and sits idle when it is not working on that product (in which case only one setup would result). Lot-for-lot causes high setup costs.

ECONOMIC ORDER QUANTITY

In Chapter 17 we already discussed the EOQ model that explicitly balances setup and holding costs. In an EOQ model, either fairly constant demand must exist or safety stock must be kept to provide for demand variability. The EOQ model uses an estimate of total annual demand, the setup or order cost, and the annual holding cost. EOQ was not designed for a system with discrete time periods such as MRP. The lot-sizing techniques used for MRP assume that part requirements are satisfied at the start of the period. Holding costs are then charged only to

exhibit 18.13   Lot-for-Lot Run Size for an MRP Schedule

(1) WEEK	(2) NET REQUIREMENTS	(3) PRODUCTION QUANTITY	(4) ENDING INVENTORY	(5) HOLDING COST	(6) SETUP COST	(7) TOTAL COST
1	50	50	0	$0.00	$47.00	$ 47.00
2	60	60	0	0.00	47.00	94.00
3	70	70	0	0.00	47.00	141.00
4	60	60	0	0.00	47.00	188.00
5	95	95	0	0.00	47.00	235.00
6	75	75	0	0.00	47.00	282.00
7	60	60	0	0.00	47.00	329.00
8	55	55	0	0.00	47.00	376.00

Economic Order Quantity Run Size for an MRP Schedule

exhibit 18.14

WEEK	NET REQUIREMENTS	PRODUCTION QUANTITY	ENDING INVENTORY	HOLDING COST	SETUP COST	TOTAL COST
1	50	351	301	$15.05	$47.00	$ 62.05
2	60	0	241	12.05	0.00	74.10
3	70	0	171	8.55	0.00	82.65
4	60	0	111	5.55	0.00	88.20
5	95	0	16	0.80	0.00	89.00
6	75	351	292	14.60	47.00	150.60
7	60	0	232	11.60	0.00	162.20
8	55	0	177	8.85	0.00	171.05

the ending inventory for the period, not to the average inventory as in the case of the EOQ model. EOQ assumes that parts are used continuously during the period. The lot sizes generated by EOQ do not always cover the entire number of periods. For example, the EOQ might provide the requirements for 4.6 periods. Using the same data as in the lot-for-lot example, the economic order quantity is calculated as follows:

$$\text{Annual demand based on the 8 weeks} = D = \frac{525}{8} \times 52 = 3,412.5 \text{ units}$$

$$\text{Annual holding cost} = H = 0.5\% \times \$10 \times 52 \text{ weeks} = \$2.60 \text{ per unit}$$

$$\text{Setup cost} = S = \$47 \text{ (given)}$$

$$\therefore \text{EOQ} = \sqrt{\frac{2DS}{H}} = \sqrt{\frac{2(3,412.5)(\$47)}{\$2.60}} = 351 \text{ units}$$

Exhibit 18.14 shows the MRP schedule using an EOQ of 351 units. The EOQ lot size in Week 1 is enough to meet requirements for Weeks 1 through 5 and a portion of Week 6. Then, in Week 6 another EOQ lot is planned to meet the requirements for Weeks 6 through 8. Notice that the EOQ plan leaves some inventory at the end of Week 8 to carry forward into Week 9.

LEAST TOTAL COST

The least total cost method (LTC) is a dynamic lot-sizing technique that calculates the order quantity by comparing the carrying cost and the setup (or ordering) costs for various lot sizes and then selects the lot in which these are most nearly equal.

The top half of Exhibit 18.15 shows the least cost lot size results. The procedure to compute least total cost lot sizes is to compare order costs and holding costs for various numbers of weeks. For example, costs are compared for producing in Week 1 to cover the requirements for Week 1; producing in Week 1 for Weeks 1 and 2; producing in Week 1 to cover Weeks 1, 2, and 3, and so on. The correct selection is the lot size where the ordering costs and holding costs are approximately equal. In Exhibit 18.15 the best lot size is 335 because a $38 carrying cost and a $47 ordering cost are closer than $56.75 and $47 ($9 versus $9.75). This lot size covers requirements for Weeks 1 through 5. Unlike EOQ, the lot size covers only whole numbers of periods.

On the basis of the Week 1 decision to place an order to cover five weeks, we are now located in Week 6, and our problem is to determine how many weeks into the future we can provide for from here. Exhibit 18.15 shows that holding and ordering costs are closest in the quantity that covers requirements for Weeks 6 through 8. Notice that the holding and ordering costs here are far apart. This is because our example extends only to Week 8. If the planning horizon were longer, the lot size planned for Week 6 would likely cover more weeks into the

exhibit 18.15   Least Total Cost Run Size for an MRP Schedule

WEEKS	QUANTITY ORDERED	CARRYING COST	ORDER COST	TOTAL COST	
1	50	$0.00	$47.00	$47.00	
1–2	110	3.00	47.00	50.00	
1–3	180	10.00	47.00	57.00	
1–4	240	19.00	47.00	66.00	1st order
1–5	335	38.00	47.00	85.00	← Least total cost
1–6	410	56.75	47.00	103.75	
1–7	470	74.75	47.00	121.75	
1–8	525	94.00	47.00	141.00	
6	75	0.00	47.00	47.00	
6–7	135	3.00	47.00	50.00	2nd order
6–8	190	8.50	47.00	55.50	← Least total cost

WEEK	NET REQUIREMENTS	PRODUCTION QUANTITY	ENDING INVENTORY	HOLDING COST	SETUP COST	TOTAL COST
1	50	335	285	$14.25	$47.00	$ 61.25
2	60	0	225	11.25	0.00	72.50
3	70	0	155	7.75	0.00	80.25
4	60	0	95	4.75	0.00	85.00
5	95	0	0	0.00	0.00	85.00
6	75	190	115	5.75	47.00	137.75
7	60	0	55	2.75	0.00	140.50
8	55	0	0	0.00	0.00	140.05

future beyond Week 8. This brings up one of the limitations of both LTC and LUC (discussed below). Both techniques are influenced by the length of the planning horizon. The bottom half of Exhibit 18.15 shows the final run size and total cost.

LEAST UNIT COST

The least unit cost method is a dynamic lot-sizing technique that adds ordering and inventory carrying cost for each trial lot size and divides by the number of units in each lot size, picking the lot size with the lowest unit cost. The top half of Exhibit 18.16 calculates the unit cost for ordering lots to meet the needs of Weeks 1 through 8. Note that the minimum occurred when the quantity 410, ordered in Week 1, was sufficient to cover Weeks 1 through 6. The lot size planned for Week 7 covers through the end of the planning horizon.

The least unit cost run size and total cost are shown in the bottom half of Exhibit 18.16.

CHOOSING THE BEST LOT SIZE

Using the lot-for-lot method, the total cost for the eight weeks is $376; the EOQ total cost is $171.05; the least total cost method is $140.50; and the least unit cost is $153.50. The lowest cost was obtained using the least total cost method of $140.50. If there were more than eight weeks, the lowest cost could differ.

The advantage of the least unit cost method is that it is a more complete analysis and would take into account ordering or setup costs that might change as the order size increases. If the ordering or setup costs remain constant, the lowest total cost method is more attractive because it is simpler and easier to compute; yet it would be just as accurate under that restriction.

Least Unit Cost Run Size for an MRP Schedule

exhibit 18.16

WEEKS	QUANTITY ORDERED	CARRYING COST	ORDER COST	TOTAL COST	UNIT COST	
1	50	$ 0.00	$ 47.00	$ 47.00	$0.9400	
1–2	110	3.00	47.00	50.00	0.4545	
1–3	180	10.00	47.00	57.00	0.3167	
1–4	240	19.00	47.00	66.00	0.2750	
1–5	335	38.00	47.00	85.00	0.2537	
1–6	410	56.75	47.00	103.75	0.2530	← 1st order
1–7	470	74.75	47.00	121.75	0.2590	Least unit cost
1–8	525	94.00	47.00	141.00	0.2686	
?	60	0.00	47.00	47.00	0.7833	2nd order
7–8	115	2.75	47.00	49.75	0.4326	← Least unit cost

WEEK	NET REQUIREMENTS	PRODUCTION QUANTITY	ENDING INVENTORY	HOLDING COST	SETUP COST	TOTAL COST
1	50	410	360	$18.00	$ 47.00	$ 65.00
2	60	0	300	15.00	0.00	80.00
3	70	0	230	11.50	0.00	91.50
4	60	0	170	8.50	0.00	100.00
5	95	0	75	3.75	0.00	103.75
6	75	0	0	0	0	103.75
7	60	115	55	2.75	47.00	153.50
8	55	0	0	0	0	$ 153.50

SUMMARY

Since the 1970s, MRP has grown from its original purpose of determining simple time schedules for production and material procurement to its present use as an integral part of enterprise resource planning that ties together all the major functions of a firm. MRP has proved to be a flexible platform that has been adapted to many different situations, including repetitive manufacturing using just-in-time systems.

In this chapter the basic concepts needed to understand MRP have been covered. The MRP engine takes information from a master schedule that is a detailed plan for future production. Depending on the needs of the firm, the master schedule can be stated in terms of individual products, generic products, or modules and subassemblies. Master scheduling is part of the sales and operations planning process that is critical to implementing the firm's operations strategy successfully.

The bill of materials depicts exactly how a firm makes the items in the master schedule. The "structure" of the bill of materials (sometimes referred to as the "product structure") captures how raw materials and purchased parts come together to form subassemblies and how those subassembles are brought together to make the items in the master schedule.

The MRP "explosion" process is the heart of the system. Using the master schedule and bill of materials, together with the current inventory status (amount on-hand and on-order) of each part in the bill of materials, detailed schedules are calculated that show the exact timing of needed parts in the future. In a typical company, this process can require a significant computation effort involving literally thousands of detailed schedules.

In this chapter, the important topic of how to consider inventory-related costs was addressed. A number of common MRP lot-sizing rules were described that consider the fixed cost and variable cost trade-off that can be significant in minimizing inventory costs.

KEY TERMS

Material requirements planning (MRP) The logic for determining the number of parts, components, and materials needed to produce a product. MRP also provides the schedule specifying when each of these materials, parts, and components should be ordered or produced.

Master production schedule (MPS) A time-phased plan specifying how many and when the firm plans to build each end item.

Available to promise A feature of MRP systems that identifies the difference between the number of units currently included in the master schedule and the actual (firm) customer orders.

Bill of materials (BOM) A computer file that contains the complete product description, listing the materials, parts, and components and the sequence in which the product is created.

Net change system An MRP system that calculates the impact of a change in the MRP data (the inventory status, BOM, or master schedule) immediately. This is a common feature in current systems.

SOLVED PROBLEMS

**Excel:
Solved
Problem**

SOLVED PROBLEM 1

Product X is made of two units of Y and three of Z. Y is made of one unit of A and two units of B. Z is made of two units of A and four units of C.

Lead time for X is one week; Y, two weeks; Z, three weeks; A, two weeks; B, one week; and C, three weeks.

a. Draw the bill of materials (product structure tree).

b. If 100 units of X are needed in week 10, develop a planning schedule showing when each item should be ordered and in what quantity.

Solution

a.

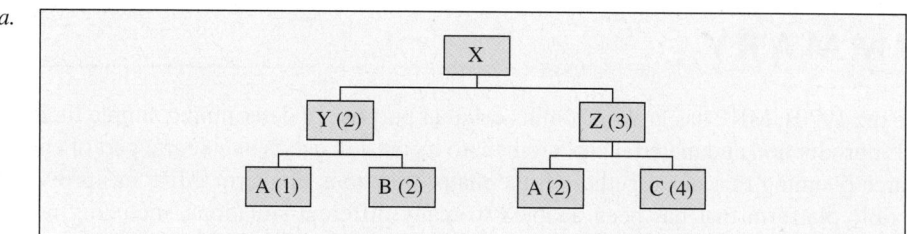

b.

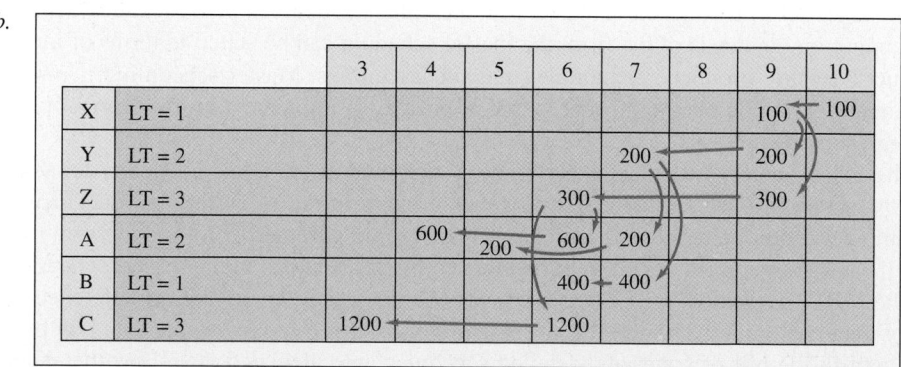

SOLVED PROBLEM 2

Product M is made of two units of N and three of P. N is made of two units of R and four units of S. R is made of one unit of S and three units of T. P is made of two units of T and four units of U.

a. Show the bill of materials (product structure tree).

b. If 100 M are required, how many units of each component are needed?

c. Show both a single-level parts list and an indented parts list.

Solution

a.

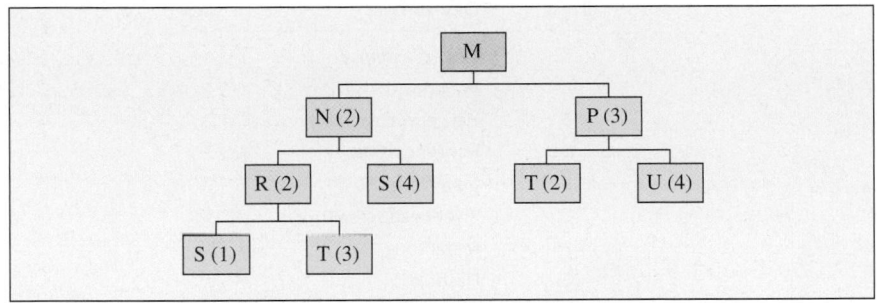

b.

M = 100	S = 800 + 400 = 1,200
N = 200	T = 600 + 1,200 = 1,800
P = 300	U = 1,200
R = 400	

c.

SINGLE-LEVEL PARTS LIST		INDENTED PARTS LIST		
M		M		
	N (2)	N(2)		
	P (3)		R(2)	
N				S (1)
	R (2)			T (3)
	S (4)		S (4)	
R		P (3)		
	S (1)		T (2)	
	T (3)		U (4)	
P				
	T (2)			
	U (4)			

REVIEW AND DISCUSSION QUESTIONS

1 Discuss the meaning of MRP terms such as *planned order release* and *scheduled order receipt*.

2 Many practitioners currently update MRP weekly or biweekly. Would it be more valuable if it were updated daily? Discuss.

3 What is the role of safety stock in an MRP system?

4 Contrast the significance of the term *lead time* in the traditional EOQ context and in an MRP system.

5 Discuss the importance of the master production schedule in an MRP system.

6 "MRP just prepares shopping lists. It does not do the shopping or cook the dinner." Comment.

7 What are the sources of demand in an MRP system? Are these dependent or independent, and how are they used as inputs to the system?

8 State the types of data that would be carried in the bill of materials file and the inventory record file.

PROBLEMS

1   Semans is a manufacturer that produces bracket assemblies. Demand for bracket assemblies (X) is 130 units. The following is the BOM in indented form:

ITEM	DESCRIPTION	USAGE
X	Bracket assembly	1
A	Wall board	4
B	Hanger subassembly	2
D	Hanger casting	3
E	Ceramic knob	1
C	Rivet head screw	3
F	Metal tong	4
G	Plastic cap	2

Below is a table indicating current inventory levels:

Item	X	A	B	C	D	E	F	G
Inventory	25	16	60	20	180	160	1000	100

    a. Using Excel, create the MRP using the product tree structure.

    b. What are the net requirements of each item in the MPS?

2   In the following MRP planning schedule for Item J, indicate the correct net requirements, planned order receipts, and planned order releases to meet the gross requirements. Lead time is one week.

ITEM J	0	1	2	3	4	5
			WEEK NUMBER			
Gross requirements			75		50	70
On-hand	40					
Net requirements						
Planned order receipt						
Planned order release						

3   Repeat Solved Problem 1 using current on-hand inventories of 20 X, 40 Y, 30 Z, 50 A, 100 B, and 900 C.

4   Assume that Product Z is made of two units of A and four units of B. A is made of three units of C and four D. D is made of two units of E.

    Lead times for purchase or fabrication of each unit to final assembly are: Z takes two weeks; A, B, C, and D take one week each; and E takes three weeks.

    Fifty units are required in Period 10. (Assume that there is currently no inventory on hand of any of these items.)

    a. Show the bill of materials (product structure tree).

    b. Develop an MRP planning schedule showing gross and net requirements and order release and order receipt dates.

5   *Note:* For Problems 5 through 10, to simplify data handling to include the receipt of orders that have actually been placed in previous periods, the following six-level scheme can be used. (A number of different techniques are used in practice, but the important issue is to keep track of what is on hand, what is expected to arrive, what is needed, and what size orders should be placed.) One way to calculate the numbers is as follows:

WEEK

Gross requirements
Scheduled receipts
Projected available balance
Net requirements
Planned order receipt
Planned order release

One unit of A is made of three units of B, one unit of C, and two units of D. B is composed of two units of E and one unit of D. C is made of one unit of B and two units of E. E is made of one unit of F.

Items B, C, E, and F have one-week lead times; A and D have lead times of two weeks.

Assume that lot-for-lot (L4L) lot sizing is used for Items A, B, and F; lots of size 50, 50, and 200 are used for Items C, D, and E, respectively. Items C, E, and F have on-hand (beginning) inventories of 10, 50, and 150, respectively; all other items have zero beginning inventory. We are scheduled to receive 10 units of A in Week 2, 50 units of E in Week 1, and also 50 units of F in Week 1. There are no other scheduled receipts. If 30 units of A are required in Week 8, use the low-level-coded bill of materials (product structure tree) to find the necessary planned order releases for all components.

6   One unit of A is made of two units of B, three units of C, and two units of D. B is composed of one unit of E and two units of F. C is made of two units of F and one unit of D. E is made of two units of D. Items A, C, D, and F have one-week lead times; B and E have lead times of two weeks. Lot-for-lot (L4L) lot sizing is used for Items A, B, C, and D; lots of size 50 and 180 are used for Items E and F, respectively. Item C has an on-hand (beginning) inventory of 15; D has an on-hand inventory of 50; all other items have zero beginning inventory. We are scheduled to receive 20 units of Item E in Week 2; there are no other scheduled receipts.

Construct simple and low-level-coded bills of materials (product structure tree) and indented and summarized parts lists.

If 20 units of A are required in Week 8, use the low-level-coded bill of materials to find the necessary planned order releases for all components. (See the note in Problem 5.)

7   One unit of A is made of one unit of B and one unit of C. B is made of four units of C and one unit each of E and F. C is made of two units of D and one unit of E. E is made of three units of F. Item C has a lead time of one week; Items A, B, E, and F have two-week lead times; and Item D has a lead time of three weeks. Lot-for-lot lot sizing is used for Items A, D, and E; lots of size 50, 100, and 50 are used for Items B, C, and F, respectively. Items A, C, D, and E have on-hand (beginning) inventories of 20, 50, 100, and 10, respectively; all other items have zero beginning inventory. We are scheduled to receive 10 units of A in Week 1, 100 units of C in Week 1, and 100 units of D in Week 3; there are no other scheduled receipts. If 50 units of A are required in Week 10, use the low-level-coded bill of materials (product structure tree) to find the necessary planned order releases for all components. (See the note in Problem 5.)

8   One unit of A is made of two units of B and one unit of C. B is made of three units of D and one unit of F. C is composed of three units of B, one unit of D, and four units of E. D is made of one unit of E. Item C has a lead time of one week; Items A, B, E, and F have two-week lead times; and Item D has a lead time of three weeks. Lot-for-lot lot sizing is used for Items C, E, and F; lots of size 20, 40, and 160 are used for Items A, B, and D, respectively. Items A, B, D, and E have on-hand (beginning) inventories of 5, 10, 100, and 100, respectively; all other items have zero beginning inventories. We are scheduled to receive 10 units of A in Week 3, 20 units of B in Week 7, 40 units of F in Week 5, and 60 units of E in Week 2; there are no other scheduled receipts. If 20 units of A are required in Week 10, use the low-level-coded bill of materials (product structure tree) to find the necessary planned order releases for all components. (See the note in Problem 5.)

9   One unit of A is composed of two units of B and three units of C. Each B is composed of one unit of F. C is made of one unit of D, one unit of E, and two units of F. Items A, B, C, and D have 20, 50, 60, and 25 units of on-hand inventory. Items A, B, and C use lot-for-lot (L4L) as their lot-sizing technique, while D, E, and F require multiples of 50, 100, and 100, respectively, to be purchased. B has scheduled receipts of 30 units in Period 1. No other scheduled receipts exist. Lead times are one period for Items A, B, and D, and two

periods for Items C, E, and F. Gross requirements for A are 20 units in Period 1, 20 units in Period 2, 60 units in Period 6, and 50 units in Period 8. Find the planned order releases for all items.

10   Each unit of A is composed of one unit of B, two units of C, and one unit of D. C is composed of two units of D and three units of E. Items A, C, D, and E have on-hand inventories of 20, 10, 20, and 10 units, respectively. Item B has a scheduled receipt of 10 units in Period 1, and C has a scheduled receipt of 50 units in Period 1. Lot-for-lot (L4L) is used for Items A and B. Item C requires a minimum lot size of 50 units. D and E are required to be purchased in multiples of 100 and 50, respectively. Lead times are one period for Items A, B, and C, and two periods for Items D and E. The gross requirements for A are 30 in Period 2, 30 in Period 5, and 40 in Period 8. Find the planned order releases for all items.

11   The MRP gross requirements for Item A are shown here for the next 10 weeks. Lead time for A is three weeks and setup cost is $10. There is a carrying cost of $0.01 per unit per week. Beginning inventory is 90 units.

	WEEK									
	1	2	3	4	5	6	7	8	9	10
Gross requirements	30	50	10	20	70	80	20	60	200	50

Use the least total cost and the least unit cost lot-sizing method to determine when and for what quantity the first order should be released.

12   Product A is an end item and is made from two units of B and four of C. B is made of three units of D and two of E. C is made of two units of F and two of E.

   A has a lead time of one week. B, C, and E have lead times of two weeks, and D and F have lead times of three weeks.

   a. Show the bill of materials (product structure tree).

   b. If 100 units of A are required in Week 10, develop the MRP planning schedule, specifying when items are to be ordered and received. There are currently no units of inventory on hand.

13   Product A consists of two units of Subassembly B, three units of C, and one unit of D. B is composed of four units of E and three units of F. C is made of two units of H and three units of D. H is made of five units of E and two units of G.

   a. Construct a simple bill of materials (product structure tree).

   b. Construct a product structure tree using low-level coding.

   c. Construct an indented parts list.

   d. To produce 100 units of A, determine the numbers of units of B, C, D, E, F, G, and H required.

14   The MRP gross requirements for Item X are shown here for the next 10 weeks. Lead time for A is two weeks, and setup cost is $9. There is a carrying cost of $0.02 per unit per week. Beginning inventory is 70 units.

	WEEK									
	1	2	3	4	5	6	7	8	9	10
Gross requirements	20	10	15	45	10	30	100	20	40	150

Use the least total cost and the least unit cost lot-sizing method to determine when and for what quantity the first order should be released.

15   Audio Products, Inc., produces two AM/FM/CD players for cars. The radio/CD units are identical, but the mounting hardware and finish trim differ. The standard model fits intermediate and full-size cars, and the sports model fits small sports cars.

   Audio Products handles the production in the following way. The chassis (radio/CD unit) is assembled in Mexico and has a manufacturing lead time of two weeks. The mounting hardware is purchased from a sheet steel company and has a three-week lead time. The finish trim is purchased from a Taiwan electronics company with offices in Los Angeles as prepackaged units consisting of knobs and various trim pieces. Trim packages have a two-week lead time. Final assembly time may be disregarded because adding the trim package and mounting are performed by the customer.

Audio Products supplies wholesalers and retailers, who place specific orders for both models up to eight weeks in advance. These orders, together with enough additional units to satisfy the small number of individual sales, are summarized in the following demand schedule:

| | WEEK | | | | | | | |
MODEL	1	2	3	4	5	6	7	8
Standard model				300				400
Sports model					200			100

There are currently 50 radio/CD units on hand but no trim packages or mounting hardware.

Prepare a material requirements plan to meet the demand schedule exactly. Specify the gross and net requirements, on-hand amounts, and the planned order release and receipt periods for the radio/CD chassis, the standard trim and sports car model trim, and the standard mounting hardware and the sports car mounting hardware.

CASE: BRUNSWICK MOTORS, INC.—AN INTRODUCTORY CASE FOR MRP

Recently, Phil Harris, the production control manager at Brunswick, read an article on time-phased requirements planning. He was curious about how this technique might work in scheduling Brunswick's engine assembly operations and decided to prepare an example to illustrate the use of time-phased requirements planning.

Phil's first step was to prepare a master schedule for one of the engine types produced by Brunswick: the Model 1000 engine. This schedule indicates the number of units of the Model 1000 engine to be assembled each week during the last 12 weeks and is shown below. Next, Phil decided to simplify his requirements planning example by considering only two of the many components that are needed to complete the assembly of the Model 1000 engine. These two components, the gear box and the input shaft, are shown in the product structure diagram shown on the next page. Phil noted that the gear box is assembled by the Subassembly Department and subsequently is sent to the main engine assembly line. The input shaft is one of several component parts manufactured by Brunswick that are needed to produce a gear box subassembly. Thus, levels 0, 1, and 2 are included in the product structure diagram to indicate the three manufacturing stages that are involved in producing an engine: the Engine Assembly Department, the Subassembly Department, and the Machine Shop.

The manufacturing lead times required to produce the gear box and input shaft components are also indicated in the product structure diagram. Note that two weeks are required to produce a batch of gear boxes and that all the gear boxes must be delivered to the assembly line parts stockroom before Monday morning of the week in which they are to be used. Likewise, it takes three weeks to produce a lot of input shafts, and all the shafts that are needed for the production of gear boxes in a given week must be delivered to the Subassembly Department stockroom before Monday morning of that week.

In preparing the MRP example Phil planned to use the worksheets shown on the next page and make the following assumptions:

1 Seventeen gear boxes are on hand at the beginning of week 1, and five gear boxes are currently on order to be delivered at the start of week 2.
2 Forty input shafts are on hand at the start of week 1, and 22 are scheduled for delivery at the beginning of week 2.

ASSIGNMENT

1 Initially, assume that Phil wants to minimize his inventory requirements. Assume that each order will be only for what is required for a single period. Using the following forms, calculate the net requirements and planned order releases for the gear boxes and input shafts. Assume that lot sizing is done using lot-for-lot.
2 Phil would like to consider the costs that his accountants are currently using for inventory carrying and setup for the gear boxes and input shafts. These costs are as follows:

PART	COST
Gear Box	Setup = $90/order
	Inventory carrying cost = $2/unit/week
Input Shaft	Setup = $45/order
	Inventory carrying cost = $1/unit/week

Given the cost structure, evaluate the cost of the schedule from (1). Assume inventory is valued at the end of each week.
3 Calculate a schedule using least-total-cost lot sizing. What are the savings with this new schedule?

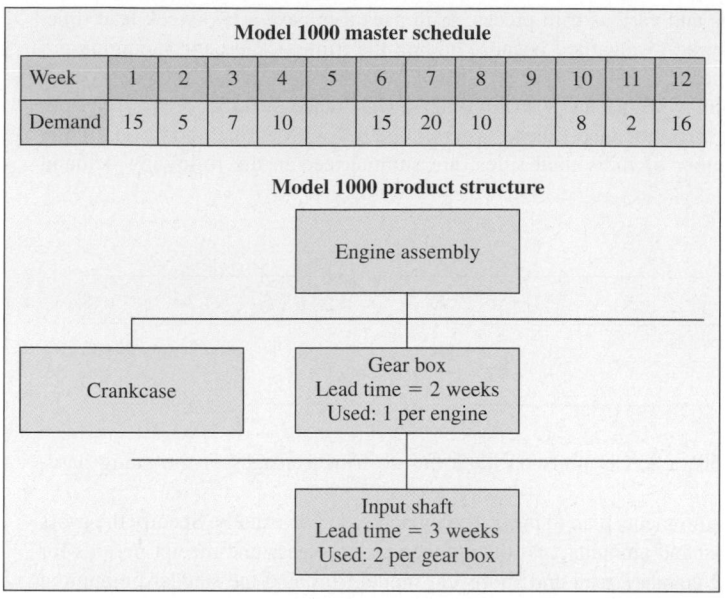

Model 1000 master schedule

Week	1	2	3	4	5	6	7	8	9	10	11	12
Demand	15	5	7	10		15	20	10		8	2	16

Model 1000 product structure

Engine assembly

Crankcase

Gear box
Lead time = 2 weeks
Used: 1 per engine

Input shaft
Lead time = 3 weeks
Used: 2 per gear box

Engine assembly master schedule

Week	1	2	3	4	5	6	7	8	9	10	11	12
Quantity												

Gear box requirements

Week	1	2	3	4	5	6	7	8	9	10	11	12
Gross requirements												
Scheduled receipts												
Projected available balance												
Net requirements												
Planned order release												

Input shaft requirements

Week	1	2	3	4	5	6	7	8	9	10	11	12
Gross requirements												
Scheduled receipts												
Projected available balance												
Net requirements												
Planned order release												

SUPER QUIZ

1   Logic used to calculate the needed parts, components, and other materials needed to produce an end item.

2   This drives the MRP calculations and is a detailed plan for how we expect to meet demand.

3   Period of time during which a customer has a specified level of opportunity to make changes.

4   This identifies the specific materials used to make each item and the correct quantities of each.

5   If an item is used in two places in a bill of material, say, level 3 and level 4, what low-level code would be assigned to the item?

6   One unit of Part C is used in item A and in item B. Currently, we have 10 A's, 20 B's, and 100 C's in inventory. We want to ship 60 A's and 70 B's. How many additional C's do we need to purchase?

7   These are orders that have already been released and are to arrive in the future.

8   This is the total amount required for a particular item.

9   This is the amount needed after considering what we currently have in inventory and what we expect to arrive in the future.

10 The planned order receipt and planned order release are offset by this amount of time.

11 These are the part quantities issued in the planned order release section of an MRP report.

12 Ordering exactly what is needed each period without regard to economic considerations.

13 None of the techniques for determining order quantity consider this important noneconomic factor that could make the order quantity infeasible.

1. Material requirements planning (MRP) 2. Master schedule 3. Time fence 4. Bill of materials 5. Level 4 6. Zero 7. Scheduled receipts 8. Gross requirements 9. Net requirements 10. Lead time 11. Lot sizes 12. Lot-for-lot ordering 13. Capacity

SELECTED BIBLIOGRAPHY

Orlicky, J. *Materials Requirements Planning.* 2nd ed. New York: McGraw-Hill, 1994. (This is the classic book on MRP)

Sheikh, K. *Manufacturing Resource Planning (MRP II) with Introduction to ERP, SCM, and CRM.* New York: McGraw-Hill, 2002.

Vollmann, T. E.; W. L. Berry; D. C. Whybark; and F. R. Jacobs. *Manufacturing Planning and Control Systems for Supply Chain Management.* 5th ed. New York: McGraw-Hill, 2004.

section 5

SCHEDULING

THE IMPORTANCE OF SCHEDULING

The argument has been made that the person in charge of scheduling is the person who is really managing the business. If you believe this, it stands to reason that if no one is in charge of scheduling, then no one is managing the business. Scheduling is the detailed plan for what is to be done in the short term. By short term, we mean two to three weeks into the future.

A schedule can be in the form of something as simple as your "to-do" list, or it can be much more complex and be a second-by-second chronicle of what is going to happen during the next two hours. As employees, we might look forward to the schedule to see when we are expected to work in the future. Airline pilots, for example, are scheduled for their flights each month based on a complex bidding procedure that considers their seniority with the airline. In some professions such as nursing work, schedules are developed that are equitable in terms of weekend and off-weekend days.

Another type of scheduling and what we consider to the greatest extent in this chapter is job scheduling. Here a firm has a number of work orders that need to be completed in the near term. Often the schedule is a prioritized list of the orders indicating what should be done first, second, and so on. The list should estimate when the order is expected to be completed. When many orders need to be completed using workers with different skill levels, different machines, and even possibly located in different places, scheduling can be amazingly complex.

chapter 19

SCHEDULING

HOSPITALS CUT ER WAITS—
NEW "FAST TRACK" UNITS,
HIGH-TECH IDs SPEED VISITS;
SEE A DOCTOR IN 17 MINUTES

A few years ago, Oakwood Hospital and Medical Center in Dearborn, Michigan, promised that anybody taken to the emergency department would be seen by a doctor within 30 minutes—or they would get a written apology and two free movie passes. It sounded like a cheap marketing ploy. Some employees cringed.

The 30-minute guarantee is a huge success. All four of Oakwood Healthcare System's hospitals rolled it out, and patient satisfaction levels soared. Less than 1 percent of the patients asked for free tickets.

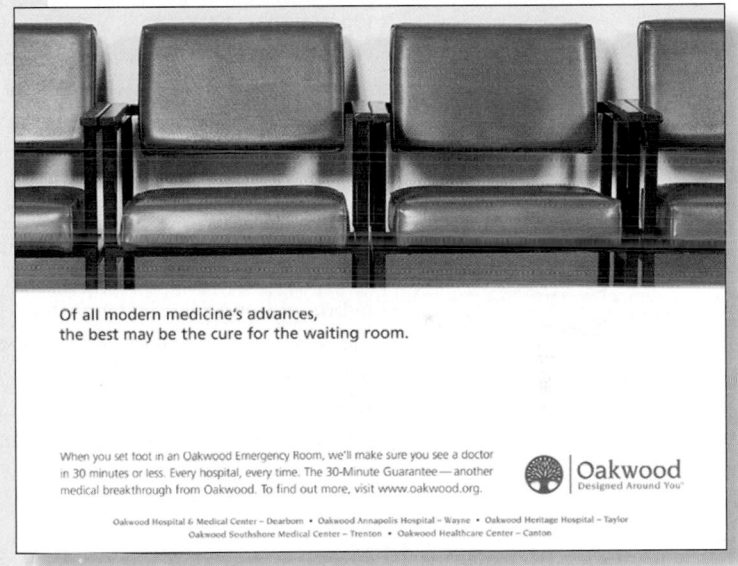
After reading this chapter you will:

1. Know what a Manufacturing Execution System production activity control is.

2. Understand typical priority scheduling rules and the impact they have on scheduling performance measures.

3. Recognize a simple job allocation procedure.

4. Explain the issues considered in employee scheduling.

Recently, the center announced a zero-wait program in the four hospital emergency departments and at Oakwood's health care center. Success with this precedent-setting service is not yet known, but processes were redesigned and some tricky scheduling of staff is being employed.

It's just one hospital system's response to the huge and prolonged problem of overcrowded emergency departments. One study showed it takes 47 minutes before a doctor sees a patient in a U.S. emergency room, but that's nothing compared with the hours upon hours that some patients end up waiting.

But the seemingly intractable problems of emergency room crowding are starting to spawn numerous attempts at solutions. A growing number of hospitals are putting patients with relatively minor ailments—those who previously would be left to languish in the waiting room—into "fast track" units to get them in and out of emergency beds quickly. Others are using sophisticated computer systems to give administrators a complete up-to-the-minute status report on every patient in every emergency bed. In some areas, medical identification cards are being used that can be swiped into a computer to speed up patient registrations and produce instant vital information to emergency doctors and nurses. Other changes needed to slash waiting times require reengineering billing, records, and laboratory operations; upgrading technical staff; and replacing the emergency physician group with a new crew willing to work longer hours.

Keep in mind that work flow equals cash flow, and scheduling lies at the heart of the process. A schedule is a timetable for performing activities, utilizing resources, or allocating facilities. In this chapter, we discuss short-run scheduling and control of orders with an emphasis on work centers. We also introduce some basic approaches to short-term scheduling of workers in services.

MANUFACTURING EXECUTION SYSTEMS

Service

Operations scheduling is at the heart of what is currently referred to as Manufacturing Execution Systems (MESs). An MES is an information system that schedules, dispatches, tracks, monitors, and controls production on the factory floor. Such systems also provide real-time linkages to MRP systems, product and process planning, and systems that extend beyond the factory, including supply chain management, ERP, sales, and service management. A number of software specialty houses develop and implement MESs as part of a suite of software tools.

Similar to an MES, a Service Execution System (SES) is an information system that links schedules, dispatches, tracks, monitors, and controls the customer's encounters with the service organization and its employees. Obviously, the extent to which each of these elements is brought into play is determined by the extent of the customer's physical involvement with the service organization, the number of stages in the service, and whether the service is standardized (e.g., a scheduled airline flight) or customized (e.g., a hospital visit). The common features of any large system are a central database that contains all the relevant information on resource availability and customers and a management control function that integrates and oversees the process.

THE NATURE AND IMPORTANCE OF WORK CENTERS

Work center

A **work center** is an area in a business in which productive resources are organized and work is completed. The work center may be a single machine, a group of machines, or an area where a particular type of work is done. These work centers can be organized according to function in a work-center configuration or by product in a flow, assembly line, or group technology cell (GT cell) configuration. Recall from the discussion in Chapter 6A that many firms have moved from the work-center configuration to GT cells.

In the case of the work center, jobs need to be routed between functionally organized work centers to complete the work. When a job arrives at a work center—for example, the drilling department in a factory that makes custom-printed circuit boards—it enters a queue to wait for a drilling machine that can drill the required holes. Scheduling, in this case, involves determining the order for running the jobs, and also assigning a machine that can be used to make the holes.

A characteristic that distinguishes one scheduling system from another is how capacity is considered in determining the schedule. Scheduling systems can use either infinite or finite

Infinite loading

loading. **Infinite loading** occurs when work is assigned to a work center simply based on what is needed over time. No consideration is given directly to whether there is sufficient capacity at the resources required to complete the work, nor is the actual sequence of the work as done by each resource in the work center considered. Often, a simple check is made of key resources to see if they are overloaded in an aggregate sense. This is done by calculating the amount of work required over a period (usually a week) using setup and run time standards for each order. When using an infinite loading system, lead time is estimated by taking a multiple of the expected operation time (setup and run time) plus an expected queuing delay caused by material movement and waiting for the order to be worked on.

A **finite loading** approach actually schedules in detail each resource using the setup and run time required for each order. In essence, the system determines exactly what will be done by each resource at every moment during the working day. If an operation is delayed due to a part(s) shortage, the order will sit in queue and wait until the part is available from a preceding operation. Theoretically, all schedules are feasible when finite loading is used.

Finite loading

Another characteristic that distinguishes scheduling systems is whether the schedule is generated forward or backward in time. For this forward–backward dimension, the most common is forward scheduling. **Forward scheduling** refers to the situation in which the system takes an order and then schedules each operation that must be completed forward in time. A system that forward schedules can tell the earliest date that an order can be completed. Conversely, **backward scheduling** starts from some date in the future (possibly a due date) and schedules the required operations in reverse sequence. The backward schedule tells when an order must be started in order to be done by a specific date.

Forward scheduling

Backward scheduling

A material requirements planning (MRP) system is an example of an infinite, backward scheduling system for materials. With simple MRP, each order has a due date sometime in the future. In this case, the system calculates parts needs by backward scheduling the time that the operations will be run to complete the orders. The time required to make each part (or batch of parts) is estimated based on historical data. The scheduling systems addressed in this chapter are intended for the processes required to actually make those parts and subassemblies.

Thus far, the term *resources* has been used in a generic sense. In practice, we need to decide what we are going to actually schedule. Commonly, processes are referred to as either machine limited or labor limited. In a **machine-limited process**, equipment is the critical resource that is scheduled. Similarly, in a **labor-limited process**, people are the key resource that is scheduled. Most actual processes are either labor limited or machine limited but, luckily, not both.

Machine-limited process
Labor-limited process
Dispatching

Exhibit 19.1 describes the scheduling approaches typically used for different manufacturing processes. Whether capacity is considered depends on the actual process. Available computer technology allows generation of very detailed schedules such as scheduling each job on each machine and assigning a specific worker to the machine at a specific point in time. Systems that capture the exact state of each job and each resource are also available. Using RFID or bar-coding technology, these systems can efficiently capture all of this detailed information.

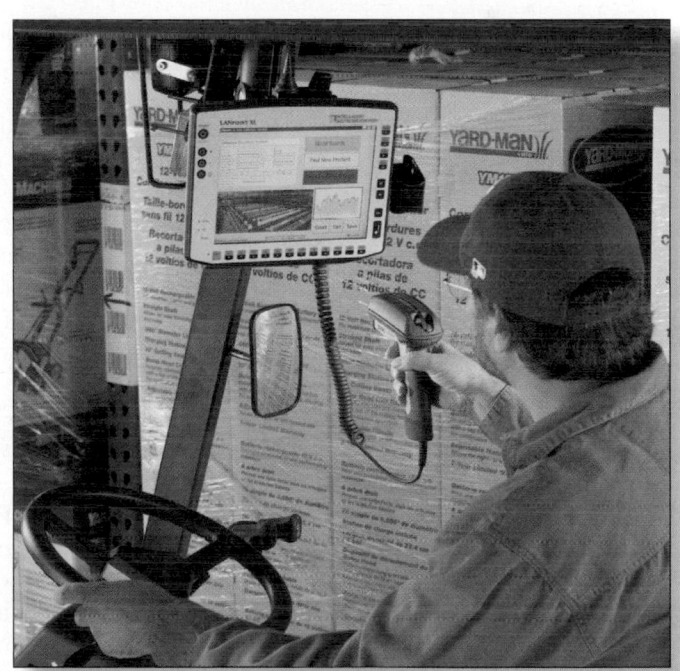

INTELLIGENT INSTRUMENTATION, A TEXAS INSTRUMENTS COMPANY, PRODUCES LAN POINT CE.NET VEHICLE MOUNT DATA COLLECTION TERMINALS. COMPANIES SUCH AS YARD-MAN USE THIS TOOL IN THEIR FULFILLMENT AND SHIPPING PROCESSES. THIS ENSURES FIFO INVENTORY MANAGEMENT CONTROL AND FASTER OPERATIONS.

TYPICAL SCHEDULING AND CONTROL FUNCTIONS

The following functions must be performed in scheduling and controlling an operation:

1. Allocating orders, equipment, and personnel to work centers or other specified locations. Essentially, this is short-run capacity planning.
2. Determining the sequence of order performance (that is, establishing job priorities).
3. Initiating performance of the scheduled work. This is commonly termed **dispatching** of orders.

exhibit 19.1   Types of Manufacturing Processes and Scheduling Approaches

TYPE	PRODUCT	CHARACTERISTICS	TYPICAL SCHEDULING APPROACH
Continuous process	Chemicals, steel, wire and cables, liquids (beer, soda), canned goods	Full automation, low labor content in product costs, facilities dedicated to one product	Finite forward scheduling of the process; machine limited
High-volume manufacturing	Automobiles, telephones, fasteners, textiles, motors, household fixtures	Automated equipment, partial automated handling, moving assembly lines, most equipment in line	Finite forward scheduling of the line (a production rate is typical); machine limited; parts are pulled to the line using just-in-time (kanban) system
Mid-volume manufacturing	Industrial parts, high-end consumer products	GT cells, focused minifactories	Infinite forward scheduling typical: priority control; typically labor limited, but often machine limited; often responding to just-in-time orders from customers or MRP due dates
Low-volume work centers	Custom or prototype equipment, specialized instruments, low-volume industrial products	Machining centers organized by manufacturing function (not in line), high labor content in product cost, general-purpose machinery with significant changeover time, little automation of material handling, large variety of product	Infinite, forward scheduling of jobs: usually labor limited, but certain functions may be machine limited (a heat-treating process or a precision machining center, for example); priorities determined by MRP due dates

4. Shop-floor control (or production activity control) involving
   a. Reviewing the status and controlling the progress of orders as they are being worked on.
   b. Expediting late and critical orders.[1]

A simple work-center scheduling process is shown in Exhibit 19.2. At the start of the day, the scheduler (in this case, a production control person assigned to this department) selects and sequences available jobs to be run at individual workstations. The scheduler's decisions would be based on the operations and routing requirements of each job, the status of existing jobs at each work center, the queue of work before each work center, job priorities, material availability, anticipated job orders to be released later in the day, and work-center resource capabilities (labor and/or machines).

To help organize the schedule, the scheduler would draw on job status information from the previous day, external information provided by central production control, process engineering, and so on. The scheduler also would confer with the supervisor of the department about the feasibility of the schedule, especially workforce considerations and potential bottlenecks. The details of the schedule are communicated to workers via dispatch lists shown on computer terminals, in hardcopy printouts, or by posting a list of what should be worked on in central areas. Visible schedule boards are highly effective ways to communicate the priority and current status of work.

OBJECTIVES OF WORK-CENTER SCHEDULING

The objectives of work-center scheduling are to (1) meet due dates, (2) minimize lead time, (3) minimize setup time or cost, (4) minimize work-in-process inventory, and (5) maximize machine or labor utilization. It is unlikely, and often undesirable, to simultaneously satisfy all of these objectives. For example, keeping all equipment and/or employees busy may result in having to keep too much inventory. Or, as another example, it is possible to meet 99 out of 100 of your due dates but still have a major schedule failure if the one due date that was missed was for a critical job or key customer. The important point, as is the case with other production activities, is to maintain a systems perspective to assure that work-center objectives are in sync with the operations strategy of the organization.

Typical Scheduling Process

exhibit 19.2

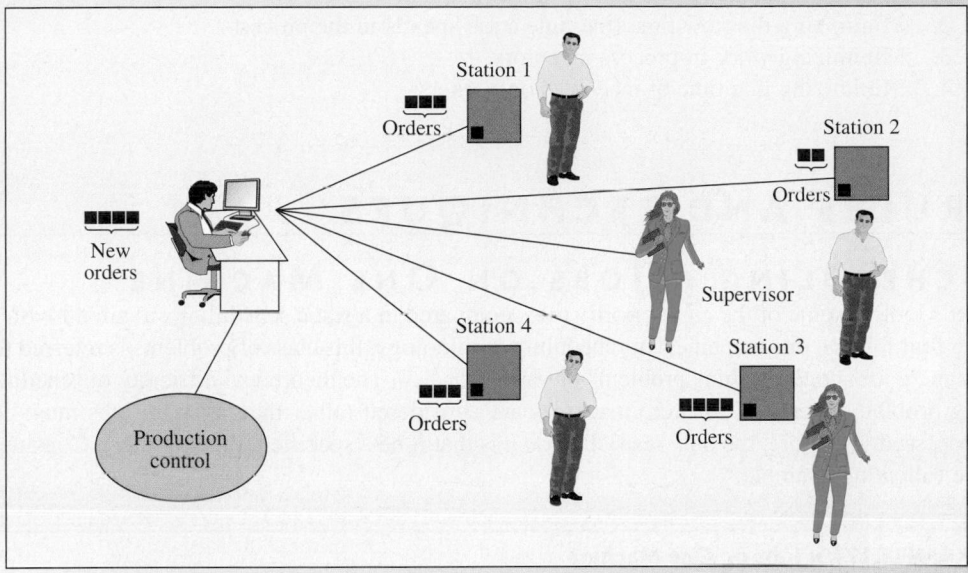

Priority Rules for Job Sequencing

exhibit 19.3

1 **FCFS** (first-come, first-served). Orders are run in the order they arrive in the department.

2 **SOT** (shortest operating time). Run the job with the shortest completion time first, next-shortest second, and so on. This is sometimes also referred to as SPT (shortest processing time). Often this rule is combined with a lateness rule to prevent jobs with longer times being delayed too long.

3 **EDD** (earliest due date first). Run the job with the earliest due date first.

4 **STR** (slack time remaining). This is calculated as the time remaining before the due date minus the processing time remaining. Orders with the shortest slack time remaining (STR) are run first.

> STR = Time remaining before due date − Remaining processing time

5 **STR/OP** (slack time remaining per operation). Orders with the shortest slack time per number of operations are run first.

> STR/OP = STR/Number of remaining operations

6 **CR** (critical ratio). This is calculated as the difference between the due date and the current date divided by the number of work days remaining. Orders with the smallest CR are run first.

7 **LCFS** (last-come, first-served). This rule occurs frequently by default. As orders arrive, they are placed on the top of the stack; the operator usually picks up the order on top to run first.

8 **Random** order or whim. The supervisors or the operators usually select whichever job they feel like running.

JOB SEQUENCING

The process of determining the job order on some machine or in some work center is known as **sequencing** or priority sequencing. **Priority rules** are the rules used in obtaining a job sequence. These can be very simple, requiring only that jobs be sequenced according to one piece of data such as processing time, due date, or order of arrival. Other rules, though equally simple, may require several pieces of information, typically to derive an index number such as the least-slack rule and the critical-ratio rule (both defined later). Still others, such as Johnson's rule (also discussed later), apply to job scheduling on a sequence of machines and require a computational procedure to specify the order of performance. Eight of the more common priority rules are shown in Exhibit 19.3.

Sequencing
Priority rules

The following standard measures of schedule performance are used to evaluate priority rules:

1. Meeting due dates of customers or downstream operations.
2. Minimizing the flow time (the time a job spends in the process).
3. Minimizing work-in-process inventory.
4. Minimizing idle time of machines or workers.

PRIORITY RULES AND TECHNIQUES

SCHEDULING *n* JOBS ON ONE MACHINE

Let's look at some of the eight priority rules compared in a static scheduling situation involving four jobs on one machine. (In scheduling terminology, this class of problems is referred to as an "*n* job—one-machine problem" or simply "*n*/1.") The theoretical difficulty of scheduling problems increases as more machines are considered rather than as more jobs must be processed; therefore, the only restriction on *n* is that it be a specified, finite number. Consider the following example.

Step by Step

EXAMPLE 19.1: *n* Jobs on One Machine

Mike Morales is the supervisor of Legal Copy-Express, which provides copy services for downtown Los Angeles law firms. Five customers submitted their orders at the beginning of the week. Specific scheduling data are as follows:

JOB (IN ORDER OF ARRIVAL)	PROCESSING TIME (DAYS)	DUE DATE (DAYS HENCE)
A	3	5
B	4	6
C	2	7
D	6	9
E	1	2

All orders require the use of the only color copy machine available; Morales must decide on the processing sequence for the five orders. The evaluation criterion is minimum flow time. Suppose that Morales decides to use the FCFS rule in an attempt to make Legal Copy-Express appear fair to its customers.

SOLUTION

FCFS RULE: The FCFS rule results in the following flow times:

	FCFS SCHEDULE		
JOB SEQUENCE	PROCESSING TIME (DAYS)	DUE DATE (DAYS HENCE)	FLOW TIME (DAYS)
A	3	5	$0 + 3 = 3$
B	4	6	$3 + 4 = 7$
C	2	7	$7 + 2 = 9$
D	6	9	$9 + 6 = 15$
E	1	2	$15 + 1 = 16$

Total flow time $= 3 + 7 + 9 + 15 + 16 = 50$ days

Mean flow time $= \dfrac{50}{5} = 10$ days

Comparing the due date of each job with its flow time, we observe that only Job A will be on time. Jobs B, C, D, and E will be late by 1, 2, 6, and 14 days, respectively. On average, a job will be late by $(0 + 1 + 2 + 6 + 14)/5 = 4.6$ days. ●

SOLUTION

SOT RULE: Let's now consider the SOT rule. Here, Morales gives the highest priority to the order that has the shortest processing time. The resulting flow times are

SOT SCHEDULE

JOB SEQUENCE	PROCESSING TIME (DAYS)	DUE DATE (DAYS HENCE)	FLOW TIME (DAYS)
E	1	2	$0 + 1 = 1$
C	2	7	$1 + 2 = 3$
A	3	5	$3 + 3 = 6$
B	4	6	$6 + 4 = 10$
D	6	9	$10 + 6 = 16$

Total flow time $= 1 + 3 + 6 + 10 + 16 = 36$ days

Mean flow time $= \dfrac{36}{5} = 7.2$ days

SOT results in a lower average flow time than the FCFS rule. In addition, Jobs E and C will be ready before the due date, and Job A is late by only one day. On average, a job will be late by $(0 + 0 + 1 + 4 + 7)/5 = 2.4$ days. ●

SOLUTION

EDD RULE. If Morales decides to use the EDD rule, the resulting schedule is

EDD SCHEDULE

JOB SEQUENCE	PROCESSING TIME (DAYS)	DUE DATE (DAYS HENCE)	FLOW TIME (DAYS)
E	1	2	$0 + 1 = 1$
A	3	5	$1 + 3 = 4$
B	4	6	$4 + 4 = 8$
C	2	7	$8 + 2 = 10$
D	6	9	$10 + 6 = 16$

Total flow time $= 1 + 4 + 8 + 10 + 16 = 39$ days
Mean flow time $= 7.8$ days

In this case, Jobs B, C, and D will be late. On average, a job will be late by $(0 + 0 + 2 + 3 + 7)/5 = 2.4$ days. ●

SOLUTION

LCFS, RANDOM, and STR RULES: Here are the resulting flow times of the LCFS, random, and STR rules:

JOB SEQUENCE	PROCESSING TIME (DAYS)	DUE DATE (DAYS HENCE)	FLOW TIME (DAYS)	
LCFS Schedule				
E	1	2	0 + 1 = 1	
D	6	9	1 + 6 = 7	
C	2	7	7 + 2 = 9	
B	4	6	9 + 4 = 13	
A	3	5	13 + 3 = 16	
Total flow time = 46 days				
Mean flow time = 9.2 days				
Average lateness = 4.0 days				
Random Schedule				
D	6	9	0 + 6 = 6	
C	2	7	6 + 2 = 8	
A	3	5	8 + 3 = 11	
E	1	2	11 + 1 = 12	
B	4	6	12 + 4 = 16	
Total flow time = 53 days				
Mean flow time = 10.6 days				
Average lateness = 5.4 days				
STR Schedule				*Slack*
E	1	2	0 + 1 = 1	2 − 1 = 1
A	3	5	1 + 3 = 4	5 − 3 = 2
B	4	6	4 + 4 = 8	6 − 4 = 2
D	6	9	8 + 6 = 14	9 − 6 = 3
C	2	7	14 + 2 = 16	7 − 2 = 5
Total flow time = 43 days				
Mean flow time = 8.6 days				
Average lateness = 3.2 days				●

Comparison of Priority Rules   Here are some of the results summarized for the rules that Morales examined:

RULE	TOTAL FLOW TIME (DAYS)	MEAN FLOW TIME (DAYS)	AVERAGE LATENESS (DAYS)
FCFS	50	10	4.6
SOT	36	7.2	2.4
EDD	39	7.8	2.4
LCFS	46	9.2	4.0
Random	53	10.6	5.4
STR	43	8.6	3.2

Here, SOT is better than the other rules in terms of mean flow time. Moreover, it can be shown mathematically that the SOT rule yields an optimal solution in the $n/1$ case for mean waiting time and average tardiness as well. In fact, so powerful is this simple rule that it has been termed "the most important concept in the entire aspect of sequencing."[2] It does have its shortcomings, however. The main one is that longer jobs may never be started if short jobs keep arriving at the scheduler's desk. To avoid this, companies may invoke what is termed a *truncated* SOT rule whereby jobs waiting for a specified time period are automatically moved to the front of the line.

SCHEDULING *n* JOBS ON TWO MACHINES

The next step up in complexity is the $n/2$ flow-shop case, where two or more jobs must be processed on two machines in a common sequence. As in the $n/1$ case, there is an approach that leads to an optimal solution according to certain criteria. The objective of this approach,

termed **Johnson's rule** or *Johnson's method* (after its developer), is to minimize the flow
time from the beginning of the first job until the finish of the last. Johnson's rule consists of
the following steps:

1. List the operation time for each job on both machines.
2. Select the shortest operation time.
3. If the shortest time is for the first machine, do the job first; if it is for the second machine, do the job last. In the case of a tie, do the job on the first machine.
4. Repeat Steps 2 and 3 for each remaining job until the schedule is complete.

EXAMPLE 19.2: *n* Jobs on Two Machines

We can illustrate this procedure by scheduling four jobs through two machines.

Step by Step

SOLUTION

Step 1: List operation times.

JOB	OPERATION TIME ON MACHINE 1	OPERATION TIME ON MACHINE 2
A	3	2
B	6	8
C	5	6
D	7	4

Steps 2 and 3: Select the shortest operation time and assign. Job A is shortest on Machine 2 and is assigned first and performed last. (Once assigned, Job A is no longer available to be scheduled.)

Step 4: Repeat Steps 2 and 3 until completion of the schedule. Select the shortest operation time among the remaining jobs. Job D is second shortest on Machine 2, so it is performed second to last. (Remember, Job A is last.) Now Jobs A and D are not available for scheduling. Job C is the shortest on Machine 1 among the remaining jobs. Job C is performed first. Now only Job B is left with the shortest operation time on Machine 1. Thus, according to Step 3, it is performed first among the remaining, or second overall. (Job C was already scheduled first.)

In summary, the solution sequence is C → B → D → A and the flow time is 25 days, which is a minimum. Also minimized are total idle time and mean idle time. The final schedule appears in Exhibit 19.4.

These steps result in scheduling the jobs having the shortest time in the beginning and end of the schedule. As a result, the concurrent operating time for the two machines is maximized, thus minimizing the total operating time required to complete the jobs. ●

Optimal Schedule of Jobs Using Johnson's Rule   **exhibit 19.4**

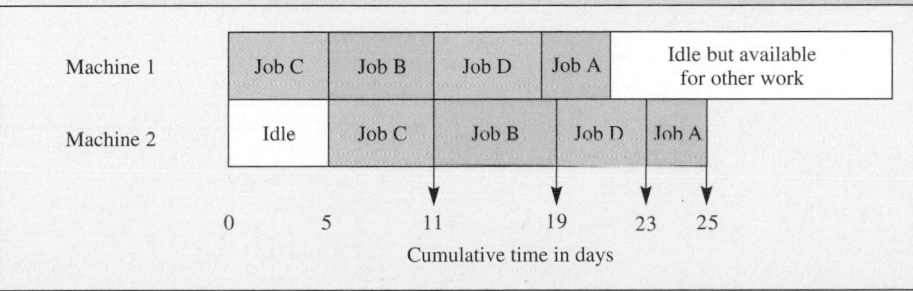

Johnson's method has been extended to yield an optimal solution for the $n/3$ case. When flow-shop scheduling problems larger than $n/3$ arise (and they generally do), analytical solution procedures leading to optimality are not available. The reason for this is that even though the jobs may arrive in static fashion at the first machine, the scheduling problem becomes dynamic, and waiting lines start to form in front of machines downstream. At this point, it becomes a multistage queuing problem, which is generally solved using simulation techniques such as those discussed in Chapter 19A.

SCHEDULING A SET NUMBER OF JOBS ON THE SAME NUMBER OF MACHINES

Some work centers have enough of the right kinds of machines to start all jobs at the same time. Here the problem is not which job to do first, but rather which particular assignment of individual jobs to individual machines will result in the best overall schedule. In such cases, we can use the assignment method.

Assignment method

The **assignment method** is a special case of the transportation method of linear programming. It can be applied to situations where there are n supply sources and n demand uses (such as five jobs on five machines) and the objective is to minimize or maximize some measure of effectiveness. This technique is convenient in applications involving allocation of jobs to work centers, people to jobs, and so on. The assignment method is appropriate in solving problems that have the following characteristics:

1. There are n "things" to be distributed to n "destinations."
2. Each thing must be assigned to one and only one destination.
3. Only one criterion can be used (minimum cost, maximum profit, or minimum completion time, for example).

Step by Step

EXAMPLE 19.3: Assignment Method

Suppose that a scheduler has five jobs that can be performed on any of five machines ($n = 5$). The cost of completing each job–machine combination is shown in Exhibit 19.5. The scheduler would like to devise a minimum-cost assignment. (There are 5!, or 120, possible assignments.)

SOLUTION

This problem may be solved by the assignment method, which consists of four steps (note that this also can be solved using the Excel Solver):

1. Subtract the smallest number in each *row* from itself and all other numbers in that row. (There will then be at least one zero in each row.)
2. Subtract the smallest number in each *column* from all other numbers in that column. (There will then be at least one zero in each column.)

exhibit 19.5

Assignment Matrix Showing Machine Processing Costs for Each Job

JOB	A	B	C	D	E
			MACHINE		
I	$5	$6	$4	$8	$3
II	6	4	9	8	5
III	4	3	2	5	4
IV	7	2	4	5	3
V	3	6	4	5	5

Procedure to Solve an Assignment Matrix

exhibit 19.6

Step 1: Row reduction—the smallest number is subtracted from each row.

JOB	A	B	C	D	E
I	2	3	1	5	0
II	2	0	5	4	1
III	2	1	0	3	2
IV	5	0	2	3	1
V	0	3	1	2	2

(MACHINE)

Step 2: Column reduction—the smallest number is subtracted from each column.

JOB	A	B	C	D	E
I	2	3	1	3	0
II	2	0	5	2	1
III	2	1	0	1	2
IV	5	0	2	1	1
V	0	3	1	0	2

(MACHINE)

Step 3: Apply line test—the number of lines to cover all zeros is 4; because 5 are required, go to step 4.

JOB	A	B	C	D	E
I	2	3	1	3	0
II	2	0	5	2	1
III	2	1	0	1	2
IV	5	0	2	1	1
V	0	3	1	0	2

(MACHINE)

Step 4: Subtract smallest uncovered number and add to intersection of lines. Using lines drawn in Step 3, smallest uncovered number is 1.

JOB	A	B	C	D	E
I	1	3	0	2	0
II	1	0	4	1	1
III	2	2	0	1	3
IV	4	0	1	0	1
V	0	4	1	0	3

(MACHINE)

Optimal solution—by "line test."

JOB	A	B	C	D	E
I	1	3	0	2	0
II	1	0	4	1	1
III	2	2	0	1	3
IV	4	0	1	0	1
V	0	4	1	0	3

(MACHINE)

Optimal assignments and their costs.

Job I to Machine E	$3
Job II to Machine B	4
Job III to Machine C	2
Job IV to Machine D	5
Job V to Machine A	3
Total cost	$17

3. Determine if the *minimum* number of lines required to cover each zero is equal to *n*. If so, an optimal solution has been found, because job machine assignments must be made at the zero entries, and this test proves that this is possible. If the minimum number of lines required is less than *n*, go to Step 4.
4. Draw the least possible number of lines through all the zeros. (These may be the same lines used in Step 3.) Subtract the smallest number not covered by lines from itself and all other uncovered numbers, and add it to the number at each intersection of lines. Repeat Step 3.

For the example problem, the steps listed in Exhibit 19.6 would be followed.

Note that even though there are two zeros in three rows and three columns, the solution shown in Exhibit 19.6 is the only one possible for this problem because Job III must be assigned to Machine C to meet the "assign to zero" requirement. Other problems may have more than one optimal solution, depending, of course, on the costs involved. ●

The nonmathematical rationale of the assignment method is one of minimizing opportunity costs.[3] For example, if we decided to assign Job I to Machine A instead of to Machine E, we would be sacrificing the opportunity to save $2 ($5 − $3). The assignment algorithm in effect performs such comparisons for the entire set of alternative assignments by means of row and column reduction, as described in Steps 1 and 2. It makes similar comparisons in Step 4. Obviously, if assignments are made to zero cells, no opportunity cost, with respect to the entire matrix, occurs.

SCHEDULING *n* JOBS ON *m* MACHINES

Complex work centers are characterized by multiple machine centers processing a variety of different jobs arriving at the machine centers intermittently throughout the day. If there are *n* jobs to be processed on *m* machines and all jobs are processed on all machines, then there are $(n!)^m$ alternative schedules for this job set. Because of the large number of schedules that exist for even small work centers, computer simulation (see Chapter 19A) is the only practical way to determine the relative merits of different priority rules in such situations.

Which Priority Rule Should Be Used?   We believe that the needs of most manufacturers are reasonably satisfied by a relatively simple priority scheme that embodies the following principles:

1. It should be dynamic, that is, computed frequently during a job to reflect changing conditions.
2. It should be based in one way or another on slack (the difference between the work remaining to be done on a job and the time remaining to do it).

Newer approaches combine simulation with human schedulers to create schedules.

SHOP-FLOOR CONTROL

Shop-floor (production activity) control

Scheduling job priorities is just one aspect of shop-floor control (now often called production activity control). The *APICS Dictionary* defines a *shop-floor control system* as

> A system for utilizing data from the shop floor as well as data processing files to maintain and communicate status information on shop orders and work centers.

The major functions of shop-floor control are

1. Assigning priority of each shop order.
2. Maintaining work-in-process quantity information.
3. Conveying shop-order status information to the office.
4. Providing actual output data for capacity control purposes.
5. Providing quantity by location by shop order for WIP inventory and accounting purposes.
6. Measuring efficiency, utilization, and productivity of manpower and machines.

GANTT CHARTS

Smaller job shops and individual departments of large ones employ the venerable Gantt chart to help plan and track jobs. As described in Chapter 10, the Gantt chart is a type of bar chart that plots tasks against time. Gantt charts are used for project planning as well as to coordinate a number of scheduled activities. The example in Exhibit 19.7 indicates that Job A is behind schedule by about four hours, Job B is ahead of schedule, and Job C has been completed, after a delayed start for equipment maintenance. Note that whether the job is ahead of schedule or behind schedule is based on where it stands compared to where we are now. In Exhibit 19.7, we are at the end of Wednesday, and Job A should have been completed. Job B has already had some of Thursday's work completed.

Gantt Chart

exhibit 19.7

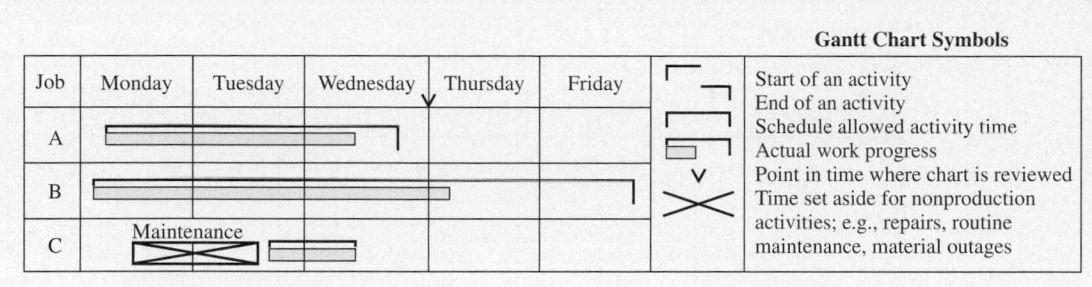

Job	Monday	Tuesday	Wednesday	Thursday	Friday
A					
B					
C	Maintenance				

Start of an activity
End of an activity
Schedule allowed activity time
Actual work progress
Point in time where chart is reviewed
Time set aside for nonproduction
activities; e.g., repairs, routine
maintenance, material outages

TOOLS OF SHOP-FLOOR CONTROL

The basic tools of shop-floor control are

1. The *daily dispatch list,* which tells the supervisor which jobs are to be run, their priority, and how long each will take. (See Exhibit 19.8A.)
2. Various *status and exception reports,* including
   a. The anticipated delay report, made out by the shop planner once or twice a week and reviewed by the chief shop planner to see if there are any serious delays that could affect the master schedule. (See Exhibit 19.8B.)
   b. Scrap reports.
   c. Rework reports.
   d. Performance summary reports giving the number and percentage of orders completed on schedule, lateness of unfilled orders, volume of output, and so on
   e. Shortage list.
3. An *input/output control report,* which is used by the supervisor to monitor the workload–capacity relationship for each workstation. (See Exhibit 19.8C.)

INPUT/OUTPUT CONTROL

Input/output (I/O) control is a major feature of a manufacturing planning and control system. Its major precept is that the planned work input to a work center should never exceed the planned work output. When the input exceeds the output, backlogs build up at the work center, which in turn increases the lead time estimates for jobs upstream. Moreover, when jobs pile up at the work center, congestion occurs, processing becomes inefficient, and the flow of work to downstream work centers becomes sporadic. (The water flow analogy to shop capacity control in Exhibit 19.9 illustrates the general phenomenon.) Exhibit 19.8C shows an I/O report for a downstream work center. Looking first at the lower or output half of the report, we see that output is far below plan. It would seem that a serious capacity problem exists for this work center. However, a look at the input part of the plan makes it apparent that the serious capacity problem exists at an upstream work center feeding this work center. The control process would entail finding the cause of upstream problems and adjusting capacity and inputs accordingly. The basic solution is simple: Either increase capacity at the bottleneck station or reduce the input to it. (Input reduction at bottleneck work centers, incidentally, is usually the first step recommended by production control consultants when job shops get into trouble.)

Input/output (I/O) control

DATA INTEGRITY

Shop-floor control systems in most modern plants are now computerized, with job status information entered directly into a computer as the job enters and leaves a work center.

exhibit 19.8   Some Basic Tools of Shop-Floor Control

A. Dispatch List

Work center 1501—Day 205

Start date	Job #	Description	Run time
201	15131	Shaft	11.4
203	15143	Stud	20.6
205	15145	Spindle	4.3
205	15712	Spindle	8.6
207	15340	Metering rod	6.5
208	15312	Shaft	4.6

B. Anticipated Delay Report

Dept. 24 April 8

Part #	Sched. date	New date	Cause of delay	Action
17125	4/10	4/15	Fixture broke	Toolroom will return on 4/15
13044	4/11	5/1	Out for plating—plater on strike	New lot started
17653	4/11	4/14	New part holes don't align	Engineering laying out new jig

C. Input/Output Control Report

Work center 0162

Week ending	505	512	519	526
Planned input	210	210	210	210
Actual input	110	150	140	130
Cumulative deviation	−100	−160	−230	−310
Planned output	210	210	210	210
Actual output	140	120	160	120
Cumulative deviation	−70	−160	−210	−300

Many plants have gone heavily into bar coding and optical scanners to speed up the reporting process and to cut down on data entry errors. As you might guess, the key problems in shop-floor control are data inaccuracy and lack of timeliness. When these occur, data fed back to the overall planning system are wrong, and incorrect production decisions are made. Typical results are excess inventory, stockout problems, or both; missed due dates; and inaccuracies in job costing.

Of course, maintaining data integrity requires that a sound data-gathering system be in place; but more important, it requires adherence to the system by everybody interacting with it. Most firms recognize this, but maintaining what is variously referred to as *shop discipline, data integrity,* or *data responsibility* is not always easy. And despite periodic drives to publicize the importance of careful shop-floor reporting by creating data integrity task forces, inaccuracies can still creep into the system in many ways: A line worker drops a part under the workbench and pulls a replacement from stock without recording either transaction. An

Shop Capacity Control Load Flow

exhibit 19.9

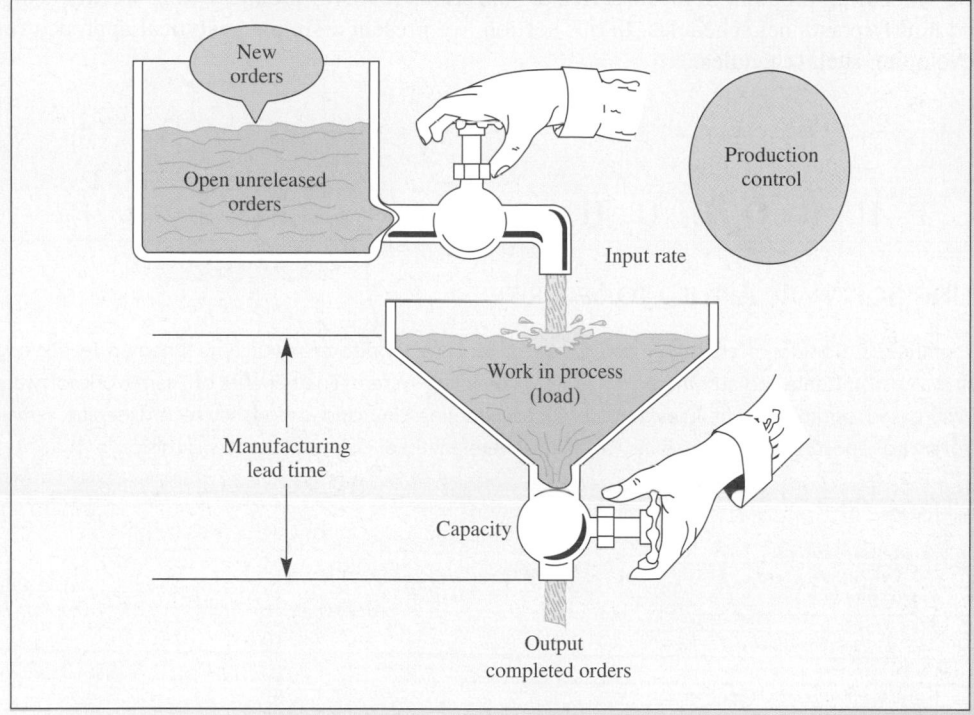

SOURCE: "TRAINING AID—SHOP FLOOR CONTROL," UNDATED. REPRINTED WITH PERMISSION OF APICS—THE EDUCATIONAL SOCIETY FOR RESOURCE MANAGEMENT. FALLS CHURCH, VA.

inventory clerk makes an error in a cycle count. A manufacturing engineer fails to note a change in the routing of a part. A department supervisor decides to work jobs in a different order than specified in the dispatch list.

PRINCIPLES OF WORK-CENTER SCHEDULING

Much of our discussion of work-center scheduling systems can be summarized in the following principles:

1. There is a direct equivalence between work flow and cash flow.
2. The effectiveness of any shop should be measured by speed of flow through the shop.
3. Schedule jobs as a string, with process steps back to back.
4. Once started, a job should not be interrupted.
5. Speed of flow is most efficiently achieved by focusing on bottleneck work centers and jobs.
6. Reschedule every day.
7. Obtain feedback each day on jobs that are not completed at each work center.
8. Match work-center input information to what the worker can actually do.
9. When seeking improvement in output, look for incompatibility between engineering design and process execution.
10. Certainty of standards, routings, and so forth, is not possible in a shop, but always work toward achieving it.

PERSONNEL SCHEDULING IN SERVICES

Service

The scheduling problem in most service organizations revolves around setting weekly, daily, and hourly personnel schedules. In this section, we present a simple analytical approach for developing such schedules.

BREAKTHROUGH

EMPLOYEE SCHEDULING SOFTWARE APPLIED TO SECURITY

ScheduleSource Inc. of Broomfield, Colorado, offers an integrated suite of tools for workforce management named TeamWork. At the heart of TeamWork is a customizable and automated employee scheduling system. The benefits of TeamWork software include features such as Web-based, optimized schedules; zero conflict scheduling; time and attendance recordkeeping; e-mail notifications; audit trail; advanced reporting; and accessibility from anywhere anytime. The way it works is this:

Step 1: Define labor requirements.

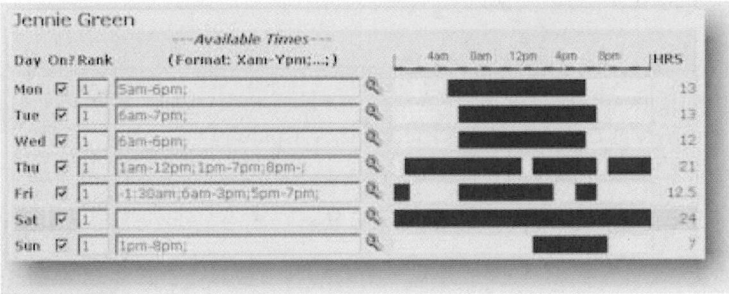

Step 2: Establish employee availability.

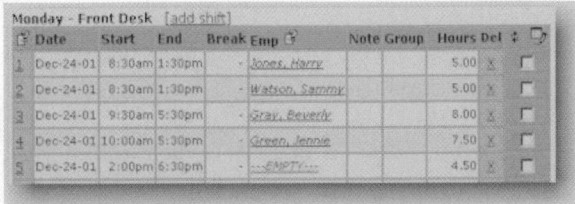

Step 3: Assign employees to particular skill sets and rank an employee's skill set level from 1 to 10 (1 being novice, 5 being average, and 10 being superlative).

Step 4: The TeamWork software automatically builds a schedule.

ScheduleSource customers include the Transportation Security Administration (TSA). ScheduleSource was successfully implemented to generate schedules for more than 44,000 federal airport security personnel at 429 airports. Over 30,000,000 individual shifts were scheduled in the airport security deployment.

SCHEDULING DAILY WORK TIMES

Service

We now show how bank clearinghouses and back-office operations of large bank branches establish daily work times. Basically, management wants to derive a staffing plan that (1) requires the fewest workers to accomplish the daily workload and (2) minimizes the variance between actual and planned output.

In structuring the problem, bank management defines inputs (checks, statements, investment documents, and so forth) as *products*, which are routed through different processes or *functions* (receiving, sorting, encoding, and so forth).

To solve the problem, a daily demand forecast is made by product for each function. This is converted to labor hours required per function, which in turn is converted to workers required per function. These figures are then tabled, summed, and adjusted by an absence and vacation factor to give planned hours. Then they are divided by the number of hours in the workday to yield the number of workers required. This yields the daily staff hours required. (See Exhibit 19.10.) This becomes the basis for a departmental staffing plan that lists the workers required, workers available, variance, and managerial action to deal with the variance. (See Exhibit 19.11.)

SCHEDULING HOURLY WORK TIMES

Services such as restaurants face changing requirements from hour to hour. More workers are needed for peak hours, and fewer are needed in between. Management must continuously adjust to this changing requirement. This kind of personnel scheduling situation can be approached by applying a simple rule, the *"first-hour"* principle. This procedure can be

---

Daily Staff Hours Required to Schedule Daily Work Times

exhibit 19.10

| | | FUNCTION | | | | | | | | |
| | | RECEIVE | | PREPROCESS | | MICROFILM | | VERIFY | | TOTALS |
PRODUCT	DAILY VOLUME	P/H	H_{std}	P/H	H_{std}	P/H	H_{std}	P/H	H_{std}	H_{std}
Checks	2,000	1,000	2.0	600	3.3	240	8.3	640	3.1	16.7
Statements	1,000	—	—	600	1.7	250	4.0	150	6.7	12.4
Notes	200	30	6.7	15	13.3		—			20.0
Investments	400	100	4.0	50	8.0	200	2.0	150	2.7	16.7
Collections	500	300	1.7			300	1.7	60	8.4	11.8
Total hours required			14.4		26.3		16.0		20.9	77.6
Times 1.25 (absences and vacations)			18.0		32.9		20.0		26.1	
Divided by 8 hours equals staff required			2.3		4.1		2.5		3.3	12.2

Note: *P/H* indicates production rate per hour; H_{std} indicates required hours.

Staffing Plan

exhibit 19.11

FUNCTION	STAFF REQUIRED	STAFF AVAILABLE	VARIANCE (±)	MANAGEMENT ACTIONS
Receive	2.3	2.0	−0.3	Use overtime.
Preprocess	4.1	4.0	−0.1	Use overtime.
Microfilm	2.5	3.0	+0.5	Use excess to verify.
Verify	3.3	3.0	−0.3	Get 0.3 from microfilm.

best explained using the following example. Assume that each worker works continuously for an eight-hour shift. The first-hour rule says that for the first hour, we assign a number of workers equal to the requirement in that period. For each subsequent period, assign the exact number of additional workers to meet the requirements. When in a period one or more workers come to the end of their shifts, add more workers only if they are needed to meet the requirement. The following table shows the worker requirements for the first 12 hours in a 24-hour restaurant:

	PERIOD											
	10 A.M.	11 A.M.	NOON	1 P.M.	2 P.M.	3 P.M.	4 P.M.	5 P.M.	6 P.M.	7 P.M.	8 P.M.	9 P.M.
Requirement	4	6	8	8	6	4	4	6	8	10	10	6

The schedule shows that four workers are assigned at 10 A.M., two are added at 11 A.M., and another two are added at noon to meet the requirement. From noon to 5 P.M. we have eight workers on duty. Note the overstaffing between 2 P.M. and 6 P.M. The four workers assigned at 10 A.M. finish their eight-hour shifts by 6 P.M., and four more workers are added to start their shifts. The two workers starting at 11 A.M. leave by 7 P.M., and the number of workers available drops to six. Therefore, four new workers are assigned at 7 P.M. At 9 P.M., there are 10 workers on duty, which is more than the requirement, so no worker is added. This procedure continues as new requirements are given.

	PERIOD											
	10 A.M.	11 A.M.	NOON	1 P.M.	2 P.M.	3 P.M.	4 P.M.	5 P.M.	6 P.M.	7 P.M.	8 P.M.	9 P.M.
Requirement	4	6	8	8	6	4	4	6	8	10	10	6
Assigned	4	2	2	0	0	0	0	0	4	4	2	0
On duty	4	6	8	8	8	8	8	8	8	10	10	10

Another option is splitting shifts. For example, the worker can come in, work for four hours, then come back two hours later for another four hours. The impact of this option in scheduling is essentially similar to that of changing lot size in production. When workers start working, they have to log in, change uniforms, and probably get necessary information from workers in the previous shift. This preparation can be considered as the "setup cost" in a production scenario. Splitting shifts is like having smaller production lot sizes and thus more preparation (more setups). This problem can be solved by linear programming methods described in the Nanda and Browne bibliographic reference.

SUMMARY

In manufacturing work centers, scheduling now relies heavily on simulation to estimate the flow of work through the system to determine bottlenecks and adjust job priorities. Various software packages are available to do this. In services, the focus is typically on employee scheduling using mathematical tools that can establish work schedules in light of expected customer demand. No matter what the scheduling situation is, it is important to avoid suboptimization—a schedule that works well for one part of the organization but creates problems for other parts or, most important, for the customer.

KEY TERMS

Work center An area in a business in which productive resources are organized and work is completed.

Infinite loading Work is assigned to a work center based on what is needed over time. Capacity is not considered.

Finite loading Each resource is scheduled in detail using the setup and run time required for each order. The system determines exactly what will be done by each resource at every moment during the working day.

Forward scheduling Schedules from now into the future to tell the earliest that an order can be completed.

Backward scheduling Starts from some date in the future (typically the due date) and schedules the required operations in reverse sequence. Tells the latest time when an order can be started so that it is completed by a specific date.

Machine-limited process Equipment is the critical resource that is scheduled.

Labor-limited process People are the key resource that is scheduled.

Dispatching The activity of initiating scheduled work.

Sequencing The process of determining which job to start first on a machine or work center.

Priority rules The logic used to determine the sequence of jobs in a queue.

Johnson's rule A sequencing rule used for scheduling any number of jobs on two machines. The rule is designed to minimize the time required to complete all the jobs.

Assignment method A special case of the transportation method of linear programming that is used to allocate a specific number of jobs to the same number of machines.

Shop-floor (production activity) control A system for utilizing data from the shop floor to maintain and communicate status information on shop orders and work centers.

Input/output (I/O) control Work being released into a work center should never exceed the planned work output. When the input exceeds the output, backlogs build up at the work center that increase the lead time.

SOLVED PROBLEMS

Joe's Auto Seat Cover and Paint Shop is bidding on a contract to do all the custom work for Smiling Ed's used car dealership. One of the main requirements in obtaining this contract is rapid delivery time, because Ed—for reasons we shall not go into here—wants the cars face-lifted and back on his lot in a hurry. Ed has said that if Joe can refit and repaint five cars that Ed has just received in 24 hours or less, the contract will be his. Following is the time (in hours) required in the refitting shop and the paint shop for each of the five cars. Assuming that cars go through the refitting operations before they are repainted, can Joe meet the time requirements and get the contract?

CAR	REFITTING TIME (HOURS)	REPAINTING TIME (HOURS)
A	6	3
B	0	4
C	5	2
D	8	6
E	2	1

Solution

This problem can be viewed as a two-machine flow shop and can be easily solved using Johnson's rule. The final schedule is B–D–A–C–E.

Manually, the problem is solved as follows:

	ORIGINAL DATA		JOHNSON'S RULE	
CAR	REFITTING TIME (HOURS)	REPAINTING TIME (HOURS)	ORDER OF SELECTION	POSITION IN SEQUENCE
A	6	3	4	3
B	0	4	1	1
C	5	2	3	4
D	8	6	5	2
E	2	1	2	5

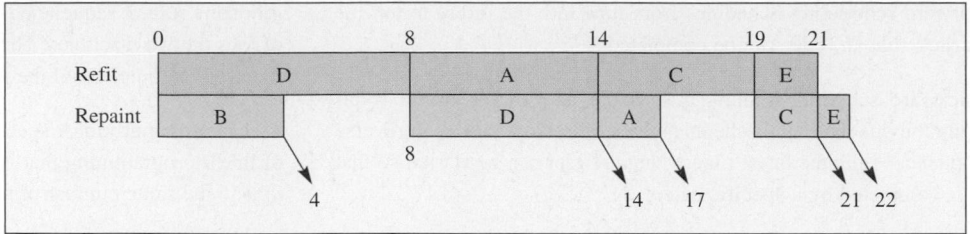

REVIEW AND DISCUSSION QUESTIONS

1   What are the objectives of work-center scheduling?
2   Distinguish between a work center, a GT cell, and a flow shop.
3   What practical considerations are deterrents to using the SOT rule?
4   What priority rule do you use in scheduling your study time for midterm examinations?
    If you have five exams to study for, how many alternative schedules exist?
5   The SOT rule provides an optimal solution in a number of evaluation criteria. Should the manager of a bank use the SOT rule as a priority rule? Why?
6   Data integrity is a big deal in industry. Why?
7   Why does batching cause so much trouble in work centers?
8   What job characteristics would lead you to schedule jobs according to "longest processing time first"?
9   Why is managing bottlenecks so important in work-center scheduling?
10 Under what conditions is the assignment method appropriate?
11 How might planning for a special customer affect the personnel schedule in a service?

PROBLEMS

1   The following table gives the operation times and due dates for five jobs which are to be processed on a machine. Assign the jobs according to the shortest operation time and calculate the mean flow time.

Job	Processing Time	Due Date (Days Hence)
101	6 days	5
102	7 days	3
103	4 days	4
104	9 days	7
105	5 days	2

2   The MediQuick lab has three lab technicians available to process blood samples and three jobs that need to be assigned. Each technician can do only one job. The table below represents the lab's estimate (in dollars) of what it will cost for each job to be completed. Assign the technicians to the jobs to minimize costs.

Job	Tech A	Tech B	Tech C
J-432	11	14	6
J-487	8	10	11
J-492	9	12	7

3   Christine has three cars that must be overhauled by her ace mechanic, Megan. Given the following data about the cars, use least slack per remaining operation to determine Megan's scheduling priority for each:

Car	Customer Pick-Up Time (Hours Hence)	Remaining Overhaul Time (Hours)	Remaining Operation
A	10	4	Painting
B	17	5	Wheel alignment, painting
C	15	1	Chrome plating, painting, seat repair

4   A hotel has to schedule its receptionists according to hourly loads. Management has identified the number of receptionists needed to meet the hourly requirement, which changes from day to day. Assume each receptionist works a four-hour shift. Given the following staffing requirement in a certain day, use the first-hour principle to find the personnel schedule:

	PERIOD											
	8 A.M.	9 A.M.	10 A.M.	11 A.M.	NOON	1 P.M.	2 P.M.	3 P.M.	4 P.M.	5 P.M.	6 P.M.	7 P.M.
Requirement	2	3	5	8	8	6	5	8	8	6	4	3
Assigned	2	1	2	3	2			6	2			1
On duty	2	3	5	8	8	7	5	8	8	8	8	3

5   Seven jobs must be processed in two operations: A and B. All seven jobs must go through A and B in that sequence—A first, then B. Determine the optimal order in which the jobs should be sequenced through the process using these times:

JOB	PROCESS A TIME	PROCESS B TIME
1	9	6
2	8	5
3	7	7
4	6	3
5	1	2
6	2	6
7	4	7

6   The following list of jobs in a critical department includes estimates of their required times:

JOB	REQUIRED TIME (DAYS)	DAYS TO DELIVERY PROMISE	SLACK
A	8	12	4
B	3	9	6
C	7	8	1
D	1	11	10
E	10	−10 (late)	−20
F	6	10	4
G	5	−8 (late)	−13
H	4	6	2

a. Use the shortest operation time rule to schedule these jobs.

   What is the schedule?

   What is the mean flow time?

b. The boss does not like the schedule in *a*. Jobs E and G must be done first, for obvious reasons. (They are already late.) Reschedule and do the best you can while scheduling Jobs E and G first and second, respectively.

   What is the new schedule?

   What is the new mean flow time?

7   The following matrix shows the costs in thousands of dollars for assigning Individuals A, B, C, and D to Jobs 1, 2, 3, and 4. Solve the problem showing your final assignments in order to minimize cost.

	JOBS			
INDIVIDUALS	1	2	3	4
A	7	9	3	5
B	3	11	7	6
C	4	5	6	2
D	5	9	10	12

8   A manufacturing facility has five jobs to be scheduled into production. The following table gives the processing times plus the necessary wait times and other necessary delays for each of the jobs. Assume that today is April 3 and the jobs are due on the dates shown:

JOB	DAYS OF ACTUAL PROCESSING TIME REQUIRED	DAYS OF NECESSARY DELAY TIME	TOTAL TIME REQUIRED	DATE JOB DUE
1	2	12	14	April 30
2	5	8	13	April 21
3	9	15	24	April 28
4	7	9	16	April 29
5	4	22	26	April 27

Determine *two* schedules, stating the order in which the jobs are to be done. Use the critical ratio priority rule for one. You may use any other rule for the second schedule as long as you state what it is.

9   Jobs A, B, C, D, and E must go through Processes I and II in that sequence (Process I first, then Process II). Use Johnson's rule to determine the optimal sequence in which to schedule the jobs to minimize the total required time.

JOB	REQUIRED PROCESSING TIME ON I	REQUIRED PROCESSING TIME ON II
A	4	5
B	16	14
C	8	7
D	12	11
E	3	9

10   In a work center, six machinists were uniquely qualified to operate any one of the five machines in the shop. The work center had considerable backlog, and all five machines were kept busy at all times. The one machinist not operating a machine was usually occupied doing clerical or routine maintenance work. Given the value schedule below for each machinist on each of the five machines, develop an optimal assignment. (Hint: Add a dummy column with zero cost values, and solve using the assignment method.)

			MACHINE		
MACHINIST	1	2	3	4	5
A	65	50	60	55	80
B	30	75	125	50	40
C	75	35	85	95	45
D	60	40	115	130	110
E	90	85	40	80	95
F	145	60	55	45	85

11   Joe has achieved a position of some power in the institution in which he currently resides and works. In fact, things have gone so well that he has decided to divide the day-to-day operations of his business activities among four trusted subordinates: Big Bob, Dirty Dave, Baby Face Nick, and Tricky Dick. The question is how he should do this in order to take advantage of his associates' unique skills and to minimize the costs from running all areas for the next year. The

following matrix summarizes the costs that arise under each possible combination of men and areas:

ASSOCIATE	AREA 1	2	3	4
Big Bob	$1,400	$1,800	$ 700	$1,000
Dirty Dave	600	2,200	1,500	1,300
Baby Face Nick	800	1,100	1,200	500
Tricky Dick	1,000	1,800	2,100	1,500

12 Joe has now been released from his government job. Based on his excellent performance, he was able to land a job as production scheduler in a brand-new custom refinishing auto service shop located near the border. Techniques have improved in the several years he was out of circulation, so processing times are considerably faster. This system is capable of handling 10 cars per day. The sequence now is customizing first, followed by repainting.

CAR	CUSTOMIZING TIME (HOURS)	PAINTING (HOURS)	CAR	CUSTOMIZING TIME (HOURS)	PAINTING (HOURS)
1	3.0	1.2	6	2.1	0.8
2	2.0	0.9	7	3.2	1.4
3	2.5	1.3	8	0.6	1.8
4	0.7	0.5	9	1.1	1.5
5	1.6	1.7	10	1.8	0.7

In what sequence should Joe schedule the cars?

13 The following table contains information regarding jobs that are to be scheduled through one machine:

JOB	PROCESSING TIME (DAYS)	DUE DATE
A	4	20
B	12	30
C	2	15
D	11	16
E	10	18
F	3	5
G	6	9

a. What is the first-come, first-served (FCFS) schedule?
b. What is the shortest operating time (SOT) schedule?
c. What is the slack time remaining (STR) schedule?
d. What is the earliest due date (EDD) schedule?
e. What are the mean flow times for each of the schedules above?

14 Schedule the following six jobs through two machines in sequence to minimize the flow time using Johnson's rule:

JOB	OPERATIONS TIME MACHINE 1	MACHINE 2
A	5	2
B	16	15
C	1	9
D	13	11
E	17	3
F	18	7

15   The following wait staff are needed at a restaurant. Use the first-hour principle to generate a personnel schedule. Assume a four-hour shift.

	PERIOD										
	11 A.M.	NOON	1 P.M.	2 P.M.	3 P.M.	4 P.M.	5 P.M.	6 P.M.	7 P.M.	8 P.M.	9 P.M.
Requirements	4	8	5	3	2	3	5	7	5	4	2
Assigned	4	4				3	2	2			
On duty	4	8	8	8	4	3	5	7	7	4	2

16   The following matrix contains the costs (in dollars) associated with assigning Jobs A, B, C, D, and E to Machines 1, 2, 3, 4, and 5. Assign jobs to machines to minimize costs.

	MACHINES				
JOBS	1	2	3	4	5
A	6	11	12	3	10
B	5	12	10	7	9
C	7	14	13	8	12
D	4	15	16	7	9
E	5	13	17	11	12

17   Bill Edstrom, managing partner at a biomedical consulting firm, has requested your expert advice in devising the best schedule for him for the following consulting projects, starting on February 2nd.

	DESCRIPTION OF CONSULTATION		CALL RECEIVED		DUE DATE (CLOSE
TASK	LENGTH	COMPANY	DATE	TIME	OF BUSINESS)
I	3 days	Novartis Corp.	February 1	9 a.m.	February 5
II	1 day	Reardon Biotech Corp.	February 1	10 a.m.	February 7
III	2 days	Vertex Pharmaceuticals	February 1	11 a.m.	February 7
IV	2 days	OSI Pharmaceuticals	February 1	1 p.m.	February 7

The consulting firm charges a flat rate of $4,000 per day. All four firms impose fines for lateness. Reardon Biotech charges a $500-per-day fine for each day that the completion of the consulting work is past the due date; Vertex Pharmaceuticals, Novartis, and OSI Pharmaceuticals all charge a fine of $1,500 per day for each day late.

Prepare alternative schedules based on the following priority rules: SOT, FCFS, EDD, STR, and another rule—longest processing time (LPT), which orders jobs according to longest assigned first, second longest assigned second, and so on. For the sake of simplicity, assume that consulting work is performed seven days a week. Which rule provides Bill with the best schedule? Why?

CASE: KEEP PATIENTS WAITING? NOT IN MY OFFICE

Good doctor–patient relations begin with both parties being punctual for appointments. This is particularly important in my specialty—pediatrics. Mothers whose children have only minor problems don't like them to sit in the waiting room with really sick ones, and the sick kids become fussy if they have to wait long.

But lateness—no matter who's responsible for it—can cause problems in any practice. Once you've fallen more than slightly behind, it may be impossible to catch up that day. And although it's unfair to keep someone waiting who may have other appointments, the average office patient cools his heels for almost 20 minutes, according to one recent survey. Patients may tolerate this, but they don't like it.

I don't tolerate that in my office, and I don't believe you have to in yours. I see patients *exactly* at the appointed hour more than

99 times out of 100. So there are many GPs (grateful patients) in my busy solo practice. Parents often remark to me, "We really appreciate your being on time. Why can't other doctors do that too?" My answer is "I don't know, but I'm willing to tell them how I do it."

BOOKING APPOINTMENTS REALISTICALLY

The key to successful scheduling is to allot the proper amount of time for each visit, depending on the services required, and then stick to it. This means that the physician must pace himself carefully, receptionists must be corrected if they stray from the plan, and patients must be taught to respect their appointment times.

By actually timing a number of patient visits, I found that they break down into several categories. We allow half an hour for any new patient, 15 minutes for a well-baby checkup or an important illness, and either 5 or 10 minutes for a recheck on an illness or injury, an immunization, or a minor problem like warts. You can, of course, work out your own time allocations, geared to the way you practice.

When appointments are made, every patient is given a specific time, such as 10:30 or 2:40. It's an absolute no-no for anyone in my office to say to a patient, "Come in 10 minutes" or "Come in a half-hour." People often interpret such instructions differently, and nobody knows just when they'll arrive.

There are three examining rooms that I use routinely, a fourth that I reserve for teenagers, and a fifth for emergencies. With that many rooms, I don't waste time waiting for patients, and they rarely have to sit in the reception area. In fact, some of the younger children complain that they don't get time to play with the toys and puzzles in the waiting room before being examined, and their mothers have to let them play awhile on the way out.

On a light day I see 20 to 30 patients between 9 A.M. and 5 P.M. But our appointment system is flexible enough to let me see 40 to 50 patients in the same number of hours if I have to. Here's how we tighten the schedule:

My two assistants (three on the busiest days) have standing orders to keep a number of slots open throughout each day for patients with acute illnesses. We try to reserve more such openings in the winter months and on the days following weekends and holidays, when we're busier than usual.

Initial visits, for which we allow 30 minutes, are always scheduled on the hour or the half-hour. If I finish such a visit sooner than planned, we may be able to squeeze in a patient who needs to be seen immediately. And, if necessary, we can book two or three visits in 15 minutes between well checks. With these cushions to fall back on, I'm free to spend an extra 10 minutes or so on a serious case, knowing that the lost time can be made up quickly.

Parents of new patients are asked to arrive in the office a few minutes before they're scheduled in order to get the preliminary paperwork done. At that time the receptionist informs them, "The doctor always keeps an accurate appointment schedule." Some already know this and have chosen me for that very reason. Others, however, don't even know that there *are* doctors who honor appointment times, so we feel that it's best to warn them on the first visit.

FITTING IN EMERGENCIES

Emergencies are the excuse doctors most often give for failing to stick to their appointment schedules. Well, when a child comes in with a broken arm or the hospital calls with an emergency Caesarean section, naturally I drop everything else. If the interruption is brief, I may just scramble to catch up. If it's likely to be longer, the next few patients are given the choice of waiting or making new appointments. Occasionally my assistants have to reschedule all appointments for the next hour or two. Most such interruptions, though, take no more than 10 to 20 minutes, and the patients usually choose to wait. I then try to fit them into the spaces we've reserved for acute cases that require last-minute appointments.

The important thing is that emergencies are never allowed to spoil my schedule for the whole day. Once a delay has been adjusted for, I'm on time for all later appointments. The only situation I can imagine that would really wreck my schedule is simultaneous emergencies in the office and at the hospital—but that has never occurred.

When I return to the patient I've left, I say, "Sorry to have kept you waiting, I had an emergency—a bad cut" (or whatever). A typical reply from the parent: "No problem, Doctor. In all the years I've been coming here, you've never made me wait before. And I'd surely want you to leave the room if *my* kid were hurt."

Emergencies aside, I get few walk-ins, because it's generally known in the community that I see patients only by appointment except in urgent circumstances. A nonemergency walk-in is handled as a phone call would be. The receptionist asks whether the visitor wants advice or an appointment. If the latter, he or she is offered the earliest time available for nonacute cases.

TAMING THE TELEPHONE

Phone calls from patients can sabotage an appointment schedule if you let them. I don't. Unlike some pediatricians, I don't have a regular telephone hour, but my assistants will handle calls from parents at any time during office hours. If the question is a simple one, such as "How much aspirin do you give a one-year-old?" the assistant will answer it. If the question requires an answer from me, the assistant writes it in the patient's chart and brings it to me while I'm seeing another child. I write the answer in—or she enters it in the chart. Then she relays it to the caller.

What if the caller insists on talking with me directly? The standard reply is "The doctor will talk with you personally if it won't take more than one minute. Otherwise you'll have to make an appointment and come in." I'm rarely called to the phone in such cases, but if the mother is very upset, I prefer to talk with her. I don't always limit her to one minute; I may let the conversation run two or three. But the caller knows I've left a patient to talk with her, so she tends to keep it brief.

DEALING WITH LATECOMERS

Some people are habitually late; others have legitimate reasons for occasional tardiness, such as a flat tire or "He threw up on me." Either way, I'm hard-nosed enough not to see them immediately if they arrive at my office more than 10 minutes behind schedule, because to do so would delay patients who arrived on time. Anyone who is less than 10 minutes late is seen right away, but is reminded of what the appointment time was.

When it's exactly 10 minutes past the time reserved for a patient and he hasn't appeared at the office, a receptionist phones his home to arrange a later appointment. If there's no answer and the patient arrives at the office a few minutes later, the receptionist says pleasantly, "Hey, we were looking for you. The doctor's had to go ahead with his other appointments, but we'll squeeze you in as soon as we can." A note is then made in the patient's chart showing the date, how late he was, and whether he was seen that day or given another appointment. This helps us identify the rare chronic offender and take stronger measures if necessary.

Most people appear not to mind waiting if they know they themselves have caused the delay. And I'd rather incur the anger of the rare person who *does* mind than risk the ill will of the many patients who would otherwise have to wait after coming in on schedule. Although I'm prepared to be firm with parents, this is rarely necessary. My office in no way resembles an army camp. On the contrary, most people are happy with the way we run it, and tell us so frequently.

COPING WITH NO-SHOWS

What about the patient who has an appointment, doesn't turn up at all, and can't be reached by telephone? Those facts, too, are noted in the chart. Usually there's a simple explanation, such as being out of town and forgetting about the appointment. If it happens a second time, we follow the same procedure. A third-time offender, though, receives a letter reminding him that time was set aside for him and he failed to keep three appointments. In the future, he's told, he'll be billed for such wasted time.

That's about as tough as we ever get with the few people who foul up our scheduling. I've never dropped a patient for doing so. In fact, I can't recall actually billing a no-show; the letter threatening to do so seems to cure them. And when they come back—as nearly all of them do—they enjoy the same respect and convenience as my other patients.

QUESTIONS

1 What features of the appointment scheduling system were crucial in capturing "many grateful patients"?

2 What procedures were followed to keep the appointment system flexible enough to accommodate the emergency cases, and yet be able to keep up with the other patients' appointments?

3 How were the special cases such as latecomers and no-shows handled?

4 Prepare a schedule starting at 9 A.M. for the following patients of Dr. Schafer:

Johnny Appleseed, a splinter on his left thumb.
Mark Borino, a new patient.
Joyce Chang, a new patient.
Amar Gavhane, 102.5 degree (Fahrenheit) fever.
Sarah Goodsmith, an immunization.
Tonya Johnston, well-baby checkup.
JJ Lopez, a new patient.
Angel Ramirez, well-baby checkup.
Bobby Toolright, recheck on a sprained ankle.
Rebecca White, a new patient.
Doctor Schafer starts work promptly at 9 A.M. and enjoys taking a 15-minute coffee break around 10:15 or 10:30 A.M.

Apply the priority rule that maximizes scheduling efficiency. Indicate whether or not you see an exception to this priority rule that might arise. Round up any times listed in the case study (e.g., if the case study stipulates 5 or 10 minutes, then assume 10 minutes for the sake of this problem).

SUPER QUIZ

1 This is the currently used term for a system that schedules, dispatches, tracks, monitors, and controls production.

2 This is when work is assigned to work centers based simply on when it is needed. Resources required to complete the work are not considered.

3 This is when detailed schedules are constructed that consider setup and run times required for each order.

4 This is when work is scheduled from a point in time and out into the future, in essence telling the earliest when the work can be completed.

5 This is when work is scheduled to tell the time work must be started so that it is completed by a specific date.

6 If we were to coin the phrase "dual constrained" relative to the resources being scheduled, we would probably be referring to what two resources?

7 For a single machine scheduling problem, what priority rule guarantees that the average (mean) flow time is minimized?

8 Consider the following three jobs that need to be run on two machines in sequence: A(3 1), B(2 2), and C(1 3), where the run time on the first and second machine are given in parenthesis. In what order should the jobs be run to minimize the total time to complete all three jobs?

9 According to APICS this is a system for utilizing data from the shop floor as well as data processing files to maintain and communicate status information on shop orders and work centers.

10 A resource that limits the output of a process by limiting capacity is called this.

1. Manufacturing Execution System 2. Infinite scheduling 3. Finite scheduling 4. Forward scheduling 5. Backward scheduling 6. Labor and equipment (machines) 7 Shortest operating time 8. C B A 9 Shop-floor (or production activity) control 10. Bottleneck

Selected Bibliography

Baker, K. R. *Introduction to Sequencing and Scheduling*. 2004. (Current edition is available from author.)

Blochlige, I. "Modeling Staff Scheduling Problems: A Tutorial." *European Journal of Operational Research* 158, no. 3 (November 1, 2004), p. 533.

Brucker, P. *Scheduling Algorithms*. 5th ed. Berlin: Springer Verlag, 2007.

Conway, R. W.; W. L. Maxwell; and L. W. Miller. *Theory of Scheduling*. Mineola, NY: Dover Publications, 2003.

Ernst, A. T.; H. Jiang; M. Krishnamoorthy; B. Owens; and D. Sier. "An Annotated Bibliography of Personal Scheduling and Rostering." *Annals of Operations Research* 127, nos. 1–4 (March 2004), pp. 21–25.

Gang, Y.; J. Pachon; B. Thengvall; D. Chandler; and A. Wilson. "Optimizing Pilot Planning and Training for Continental Airlines." *Interfaces* 34, no. 4 (July/August 2004), pp. 253–65.

Hollman, L. *Call Center Magazine* 16, no. 4 (April 2003), pp. 28–38.

Kirchmier, B., and G. I. Plenert. *Finite Capacity Scheduling*. New York: Wiley, 2002.

Nanda, R., and J. Browne. *Introduction to Employee Scheduling*. New York: Van Nostrand Reinhold, 1992.

Pinedo, M. *Scheduling: Theory, Algorithms, and Systems*. 2nd ed. Upper Saddle River, NJ: Prentice Hall, 2002.

Footnotes

1 Despite the fact that expediting is frowned on by production control specialists, it is nevertheless a reality of life. In fact, a typical entry-level job in production control is that of expeditor or "stock chaser." In some companies, a good expeditor—one who can negotiate a critical job through the system or can scrounge up materials that nobody thought were available—is a prized possession.

2 R. W. Conway, W. L. Maxwell, and L. W. Miller, *Theory of Scheduling* (Reading, MA: Addison-Wesley, 1967), p. 26. This is a classic book on the subject.

3 The underlying rationale of the procedure of adding and subtracting the smallest cell values is as follows: Additional zeros are entered into the matrix by subtracting an amount equal to one of the cells from all cells. Negative numbers, which are not permissible, occur in the matrix. To get rid of the negative numbers, an amount equal to the maximum negative number must be added to each element of the row or column in which it occurs. This results in adding this amount twice to any cell that lies at the intersection of a row and a column that were both changed. The net result is that the lined rows and columns revert to their original amounts, and the intersections increase by the amount subtracted from the uncovered cells. (The reader may wish to prove this by solving the example without using lines.)

SIMULATION

After reading this chapter you will:

1. Recognize key concepts related to discrete event simulation.
2. Understand how simulation models are constructed.
3. See examples of simulations developed using spreadsheets.
4. Compare the advantages and disadvantages of simulation.

Simulation has become a standard tool in business. In manufacturing, simulation is used to determine production schedules, inventory levels, and maintenance procedures; to plan capacity, resource requirements, and processes; and more. In services, simulation is widely used to analyze waiting lines and schedule operations. Often, when a mathematical technique fails, we turn to simulation.

Service

DEFINITION OF SIMULATION

Although the term *simulation* can have various meanings depending on its application, in business, it generally refers to using a computer to perform experiments on a model of a real system. Examples of other types of simulation are airplane flight simulators, video games, and virtual reality animation. Simulation experiments may be undertaken before a real system is operational, to aid in its design, to see how the system might react to changes in its operating rules, or to evaluate the system's response to changes in its structure. Simulation is particularly appropriate to situations in which the size or complexity of the problem makes the use of optimizing techniques difficult or impossible. Thus, job shops, which are characterized by complex queuing problems, have been studied extensively via simulation, as have certain types of inventory, layout, and maintenance problems (to name but a few). Simulation also can be used in conjunction with traditional statistical and management science techniques.

In addition, simulation is useful in training managers and workers in how the real system operates, in demonstrating the effects of changes in system variables, in real-time control, and in developing new ideas about how to run the business.

SIMULATION METHODOLOGY

Exhibit 19A.1 is a flowchart of the major phases in a simulation study. In this section, we develop each phase with particular reference to the key factors noted at the right of the chart.

PROBLEM DEFINITION

Problem definition for purposes of simulation differs little from problem definition for any other tool of analysis. Essentially, it entails specifying the objectives and identifying the relevant controllable and uncontrollable variables of the system to be studied. Consider the example of a fish market. The objective of the market's owner is maximizing the profit on sales of fish. The relevant controllable variable (that is, under the control of the decision maker) is the ordering rule; the relevant uncontrollable variables are the daily demand levels for fish and the amount of fish sold. Other possible objectives also could be specified, such as to maximize profit from the sale of lobsters or to maximize sales revenue.

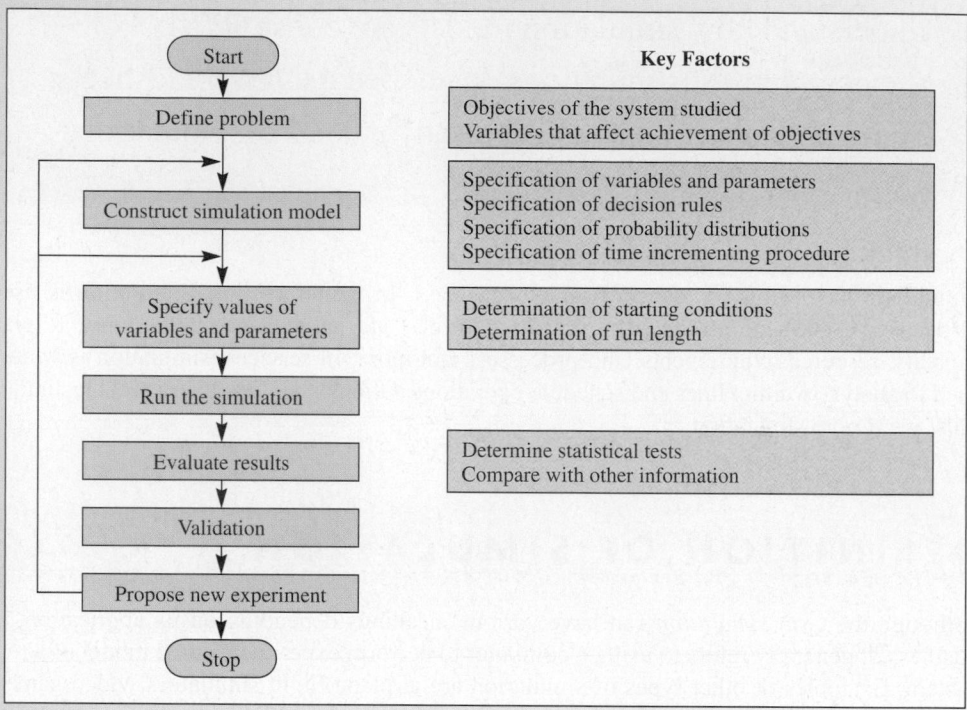

CONSTRUCTING A SIMULATION MODEL

A feature that distinguishes simulation from techniques such as linear programming or queuing theory is the fact that a simulation model must be custom built for each problem situation. (A linear programming model, in contrast, can be used in a variety of situations with only a restatement of the values for the objective function and constraint equations.) There are simulation languages that make the model building easier, however. We discuss this subject later in this chapter. The unique nature of each simulation model means that the procedures discussed later for building and executing a model represent a synthesis of various approaches to simulation and are guidelines rather than rigid rules.

Specification of Variables and Parameters   The first step in constructing a simulation model is determining which properties of the real system should be fixed (called **parameters**) and which should be allowed to vary throughout the simulation run (called **variables**). In a fish market, the variables are the amount of fish ordered, the amount demanded, and the amount sold; the parameters are the cost of the fish and the selling price of the fish. In most simulations, the focus is on the status of the variables at different points in time, such as the number of pounds of fish demanded and sold each day.

Parameters
Variables

Specification of Decision Rules   Decision rules (or operating rules) are sets of conditions under which the behavior of the simulation model is observed. These rules are either directly or indirectly the focus of most simulation studies. In many simulations, decision rules are priority rules (for example, which customer to serve first, which job to process first). In certain situations, these can be quite involved, taking into account a large number of variables in the system. For example, an inventory ordering rule could be stated in such a way that the amount to order would depend on the amount in inventory, the amount previously ordered but not received, the amount backordered, and the desired safety stock.

Decision rules

Actual Distribution of Demand and Normal Distribution with the Same Mean

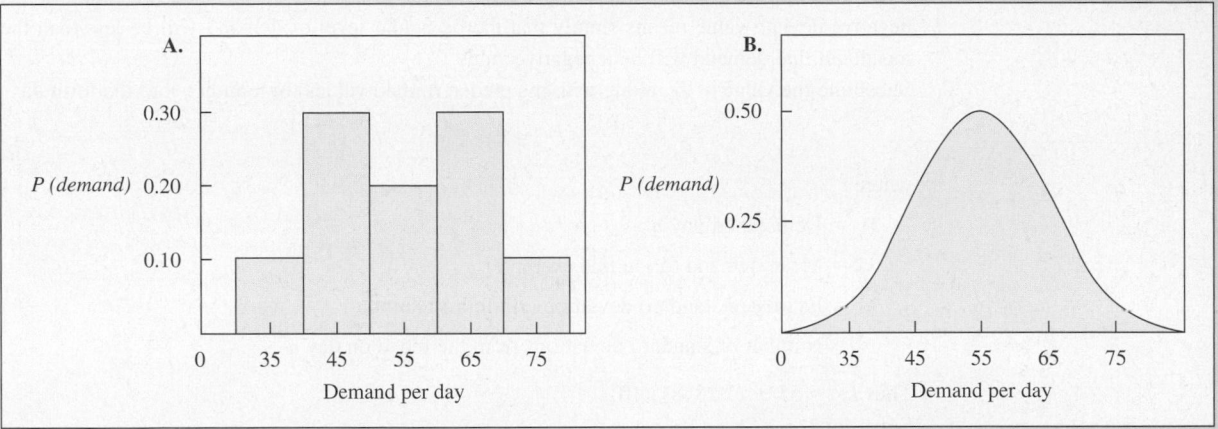

Specification of Probability Distributions   Two categories of distributions can be used for simulation: empirical frequency distributions and standard mathematical distributions. An empirical distribution is derived from observing the relative frequencies of some event, such as arrivals in a line or demand for a product. In other words, it is a custom-built demand distribution that is relevant only to a particular situation. It might appear like the one shown on the left side of Exhibit 19A.2. Such distributions have to be determined by direct observation or detailed analysis of records. (We show how to use these later in the waiting line simulation example.) But often demand, for example, can reasonably be assumed to closely approximate a standard mathematical distribution such as the normal or Poisson. This greatly simplifies data collection and computerization.

Distributions

EXAMPLE 19A.1: Relating Random Numbers to a Standard Distribution

To illustrate how to relate random numbers to a standard distribution, suppose that daily demand for newspapers from a vending machine is normally distributed with a mean of 55 and standard deviation of 10. (This distribution is shown on the right side of Exhibit 19A.2.) Under this assumption, the generation of daily demand would employ a table of randomly distributed normal numbers (or deviates) in conjunction with the statistical formula $D_n = \bar{x} + Z_n \sigma$ (terms defined later).[1]

Step by Step

SOLUTION

1.   Draw a five- or six-digit number from Exhibit 19A.3. The entries in this table are randomly developed deviate values that pertain to a normal distribution having a mean of 0 and a standard

Randomly Distributed Normal Numbers

1.23481	−1.66161	1.49673	−.26990	−.23812	.34506
1.54221	.02629	1.22318	.52304	.18124	.20790
.19126	1.18250	1.00826	.24826	−1.35882	.70691
−.54929	−.87214	−2.75470	−1.19941	−1.45402	.16760
1.14463	−.23153	1.11241	1.08497	−.28185	−.17022
−.63248	−.04776	.55006	.01196	1.16515	2.24938
.29988	.31052	−.49094	−.00926	−.28278	−.95339
−.32855	−.93166	−.04187	−.94171	1.64410	−.96893
.35331	.56176	−.98726	.82752	.32468	.36915
.72576					
.04406					

deviation of 1. The term *deviate* refers to the number of standard deviations some value is from the mean and, in this case, represents the number of standard deviations that any day's demand is from the mean demand. In the preceding formula for D_n, it would be the value for Z on day n. If we are simulating Day 1 and using the first entry in Exhibit 19A.3, then $Z_1 = 1.23481$. A negative deviate value means simply that the particular level of demand will be less than the mean, not that demand will be a negative value.

2. Substitute the value of Z_1, along with the predetermined values for x and σ, into the formula

$$D_n = \bar{x} + Z_n \sigma$$

where

D_n = Demand on day n

$\bar{x}$ = Mean demand (55 in this example)

σ = Estimated standard deviation (10 in this example)

z_n = Number of standard deviations from the mean on day n

Thus $D_n = 55 + (1.23481)(10)$.

3. Solve for D_n:

$$D_n = 55 + 12.3481$$
$$D_n = 67.3481$$

4. Repeat Steps 1 to 3, using different normal deviates from the table until the desired number of days have been simulated. ●

Time incrementing

Specification of Time-Incrementing Procedure   In a simulation model, time can be advanced by one of two methods: (1) fixed-time increments or (2) variable-time increments. Under both methods of **time incrementing**, the concept of a simulated clock is important. In the fixed-time increment method, uniform clock-time increments (such as minutes, hours, or days) are specified and the simulation proceeds by fixed intervals from one time period to the next. At each point in clock time, the system is scanned to determine if any events are to occur. If they are, the events are simulated and time is advanced; if they are not, time is still advanced by one unit.

In the variable-time increment method, clock time is advanced by the amount required to initiate the next event.

Which method is most appropriate? Experience suggests that the fixed-time increment is desirable when events of interest occur with regularity or when the number of events is large, with several commonly occurring in the same time period. The variable-time increment method is generally desirable, taking less computer run time, when there are relatively few events occurring within a considerable amount of time. It ignores time intervals where nothing happens and immediately advances to the next point when some event does take place.

SPECIFYING VALUES OF VARIABLES AND PARAMETERS

A variable, by definition, changes in value as the simulation progresses, but it must be given an initial starting value. The value of a parameter, remember, stays constant; however, it may be changed as different alternatives are studied in other simulations.

Determining Starting Conditions   Determining starting conditions for variables is a major tactical decision in simulation. This is because the model is biased by the set of initial starting values until the model has settled down to a steady state. To cope with this problem, analysts have followed various approaches such as (1) discarding data generated during the early parts of the run, (2) selecting starting conditions that reduce the duration of the warm-up period, or (3) selecting starting conditions that eliminate bias. To employ any of these alternatives, however, the analyst must have some idea of the range of output data expected. Therefore, in one sense, the analyst biases results. On the other hand, one of the unique features of simulation is that it allows judgment to enter into the design and analysis of the simulation; so if the analyst has some information that bears on the problem, it should be included.

Determining Run Length   The length of the simulation run (**run length** or **run time**) depends on the purpose of the simulation. Perhaps the most common approach is to continue the simulation until it has achieved equilibrium. In the fish market example, this would mean that simulated fish sales correspond to their historical relative frequencies. Another approach is to run the simulation for a set period such as a month, a year, or a decade and see if the conditions at the end of the period appear reasonable. A third approach is to set run length so that a sufficiently large sample is gathered for purposes of statistical hypothesis testing. This alternative is considered further in the next section.

Run length (run time)

EVALUATING RESULTS

The types of conclusions that can be drawn from a simulation depend, of course, on the degree to which the model reflects the real system, but they also depend on the design of the simulation in a statistical sense. Indeed, many analysts view simulation as a form of hypothesis testing, with each simulation run providing one or more pieces of sample data that are amenable to formal analysis through inferential statistical methods. Statistical procedures commonly used in evaluating simulation results include analysis of variance, regression analysis, and *t* tests.

In most situations, the analyst has other information available with which to compare the simulation results: past operating data from the real system, operating data from the performance of similar systems, and the analyst's own intuitive understanding of the real system's operation. However, information obtained from these sources is probably not sufficient to validate the conclusions derived from the simulation. Thus, the only true test of a simulation is how well the real system performs after the results of the study have been implemented.

VALIDATION

In this context, *validation* refers to testing the computer program to ensure that the simulation is correct. Specifically, it is a check to see whether the computer code is a valid translation of the flowchart model and whether the simulation adequately represents the real system. Errors may arise in the program from mistakes in the coding or from mistakes in logic. Mistakes in coding are usually easily found because the program is most likely not executed by the computer. Mistakes in logic, however, present more of a challenge. In these cases, the program runs but fails to yield correct results.

To deal with this problem, the analyst has three alternatives: (1) have the program print out all calculations and verify these calculations by separate computation, (2) simulate present conditions and compare the results with the existing system, or (3) pick some point in the simulation run and compare its output to the answer obtained from solving a relevant mathematical model of the situation at that point. Even though the first two approaches have obvious drawbacks, they are more likely to be employed than the third, because if we had a relevant mathematical model in mind, we would probably be able to solve the problem without the aid of simulation.

PROPOSING A NEW EXPERIMENT

Based on the simulation results, a new simulation experiment may be in order. We might like to change many of the factors: parameters, variables, decision rules, starting conditions, and run length. As for parameters, we might be interested in replicating the simulation with several different costs or prices of a product to see what changes would occur. Trying different decision rules would obviously be in order if the initial rules led to poor results or if these runs yielded new insights into the problem. (The procedure of using the same stream of random numbers is a good general approach in that it sharpens the differences among alternatives and permits shorter runs.) Also, the values from the previous experiment may be useful starting conditions for subsequent simulations.

Finally, whether trying different run lengths constitutes a new experiment rather than a replication of a previous experiment depends on the types of events that occur in the system operation over time. It might happen, for example, that the system has more than one stable level of operation and that reaching the second level is time dependent. Thus, while the first series of runs of, say, 100 periods shows stable conditions, doubling the length of the series may provide new and distinctly different but equally stable conditions. In this case, running the simulation over 200 time periods could be thought of as a new experiment.

COMPUTERIZATION

When using a computer model, we reduce the system to be studied to a symbolic representation to be run on a computer. Although it is beyond this book's scope to detail the technical aspects of computer modeling, some that bear directly on simulation are

1. Computer language selection.
2. Flowcharting.
3. Coding.
4. Data generation.
5. Output reports.
6. Validation.

We say more about simulation programs and languages at the end of this chapter.

Output Reports   General-purpose languages permit the analyst to specify any type of output report (or data) desired, providing one is willing to pay the price in programming effort. Special-purpose languages have standard routines that can be activated by one or two program statements to print out such data as means, variances, and standard deviations. Regardless of language, however, our experience has been that too much data from a simulation can be as dysfunctional to problem solving as too little data; both situations tend to obscure important, truly meaningful information about the system under study.

SIMULATING WAITING LINES

Waiting lines that occur in series and parallel (such as in assembly lines and work centers) usually cannot be solved mathematically. However, because waiting lines are often easily simulated on a computer, we have chosen a two-stage assembly line as our second simulation example.

EXAMPLE: A TWO-STAGE ASSEMBLY LINE

Consider an assembly line that makes a product of significant physical size such as a refrigerator, stove, car, boat, TV, or furniture. Exhibit 19A.4 shows two workstations on such a line.

The size of the product is an important consideration in assembly-line analysis and design because the number of products that can exist at each workstation affects worker performance. If the product is large, then the workstations are dependent on each other. Exhibit 19A.4, for example, shows Bob and Ray working on a two-stage line where Bob's output in Station 1 is fed to Ray in Station 2. If the workstations are adjacent, leaving no room for items between them, then Bob, by working slowly, would cause Ray to wait. Conversely, if Bob completes a product quickly (or if Ray takes longer to finish the task), then Bob must wait for Ray.

In this simulation, assume that Bob, the first worker on the line, can pull over a new item to work on whenever needed. We concentrate our analysis on the interaction between Bob and Ray.

Two Workstations on an Assembly Line

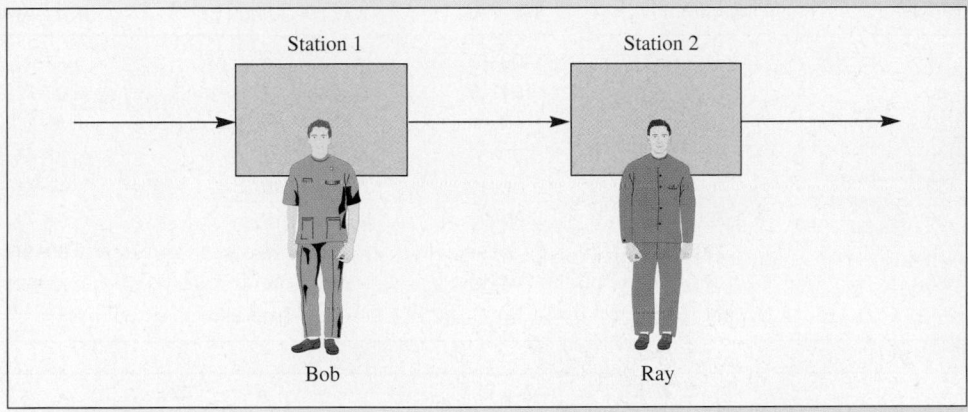

Objective of the Study   We would like to answer a number of questions about the assembly line from this study. A partial list would be

- What is the average performance time of each worker?
- What is the output rate of product through this line?
- How much time does Bob wait for Ray?
- How much time does Ray wait for Bob?
- If the space between the two stations were increased so that items could be stored there and give workers some independence, how would this affect output rates, wait times, and so on?

Data Collection   To simulate this system, we need the performance times of Bob and Ray. One way to collect these data is to divide the range of performance times into segments and then observe each worker. A simple check or tally mark in each of these segments results in a useful histogram of data.

Exhibit 19A.5 shows the data collection form used to observe the performances of Bob and Ray. To simplify the procedure, performance time was divided into 10-second intervals. Bob was observed for 100 repetitions of the work task and Ray was observed just 50 times. The number of observations does not have to be the same, but the more there are and the smaller the size of the time segments, the more accurate the study will be. The trade-off is that more observations and smaller segments take more time and more people (as well as more time to program and run a simulation).

Data Collection Form for Worker Observation

SECONDS TO COMPLETE TASK	BOB	TOTALS	RAY	TOTALS
5–14.99	IIII	4	IIII	4
15–24.99	ЖI	6	Ж	5
25–34.99	Ж Ж	10	ЖI	6
35–44.99	ЖЖЖЖ	20	Ж II	7
45–54.99	ЖЖЖЖЖЖЖЖ	40	ЖЖ	10
55–64.99	Ж ЖI	11	ЖIII	8
65–74.99	Ж	5	ЖI	6
75–84.99	IIII	4	IIII	4
		100		50

exhibit 19A.6   Random Number Intervals for Bob and Ray

SECONDS	TIME FREQUENCIES FOR BOB (OPERATION 1)	RN INTERVALS	TIME FREQUENCIES FOR RAY (OPERATION 2)	RN INTERVALS
10	4	00–03	4	00–07
20	6	04–09	5	08–17
30	10	10–19	6	18–29
40	20	20–39	7	30–43
50	40	40–79	10	44–63
60	11	80–90	8	64–79
70	5	91–95	6	80–91
80	4	96–99	4	92–99
	100		50	

exhibit 19A.7   Simulation of Bob and Ray—Two-Stage Assembly Line

| | BOB | | | | | | RAY | | | |
ITEM NUMBER	RANDOM NUMBER	START TIME	PERFORMANCE TIME	FINISH TIME	WAIT TIME	STORAGE SPACE	RANDOM NUMBER	START TIME	PERFORMANCE TIME	FINISH TIME	WAIT TIME
1	56	00	50	50		0	83	50	70	120	50
2	55	50	50	100	20	0	47	120	50	170	
3	84	120	60	180		0	08	180	20	200	10
4	36	180	40	220		0	05	220	10	230	20
5	26	220	40	260		0	42	260	40	300	30
6	95	260	70	330		0	95	330	80	410	30
7	66	330	50	380	30	0	17	410	20	430	
8	03	410	10	420	10	0	21	430	30	460	
9	57	430	50	480		0	31	480	40	520	20
10	69	480	50	530		0	90	530	70	600	10
			470		60				430		170

Exhibit 19A.6 contains the random number intervals assigned that correspond to the same ratio as the actual observed data. For example, Bob had 4 out of 100 times at 10 seconds. Therefore, if we used 100 numbers, we would assign 4 of those numbers as corresponding to 10 seconds. We could have assigned any four numbers, for example, 42, 18, 12, and 93. However, these would be a nuisance to search for, so we assign consecutive numbers, such as 00, 01, 02, and 03.

There were 50 observations of Ray. There are two ways we could assign random numbers. First, we could use just 50 numbers (say, 00–49) and ignore any numbers over that. However, this is wasteful because we would discard 50 percent of all the numbers from the list. Another choice would be to double the frequency number. For example, rather than assign, say, numbers 0–03 to account for the 4 observations out of 50 that took 10 seconds, we could assign numbers 00–07 to represent 8 observations out of 100, which is double the observed number but the same frequency. Actually, for this example and the speed of computers, the savings of time by doubling is insignificant.

Exhibit 19A.7 shows a hand simulation of 10 items processed by Bob and Ray. The random numbers used were from Appendix H, starting at the first column of two numbers and working downward.

Assume that we start out at time 00 and run it in continuous seconds (not bothering to convert this to hours and minutes). The first random number is 56 and corresponds to Bob's performance at 50 seconds on the first item. The item is passed to Ray, who starts at 50 seconds. Relating the next random number, 83, to Exhibit 19A.6, we find that Ray takes 70 seconds to complete the item. In the meantime, Bob starts on the next item at time 50 and takes 50 seconds (random number 55), finishing at time 100. However, Bob cannot start on the third item until Ray gets through with the first item at time 120. Bob, therefore, has a wait time of 20 seconds. (If there was storage space between Bob and Ray, this item could have been moved out of Bob's workstation, and Bob could have started the next item at time 100.) The remainder of the exhibit was calculated following the same pattern: obtaining a random number, finding the corresponding processing time, noting the wait time (if any), and computing the finish time. Note that with no storage space between Bob and Ray, there was considerable waiting time for both workers.

We can now answer some questions and make some statements about the system. For example,

The output time averages 60 seconds per unit (the complete time 600 for Ray divided by 10 units).

Utilization of Bob is $\frac{470}{530} = 88.7$ percent.

Utilization of Ray is $\frac{430}{550} = 78.2$ percent (disregarding the initial startup wait for the first item of 50 seconds).

The average performance time for Bob is $\frac{470}{10} = 47$ seconds.

The average performance time for Ray is $\frac{430}{10} = 43$ seconds.

We have demonstrated how this problem would be solved in a simple manual simulation. A sample of 10 is really too small to place much confidence in, so this problem should be run on a computer for several thousand iterations. (We extend this same problem further in the next section of this chapter.)

It is also vital to study the effect of item storage space between workers. The problem would be run to see what the throughput time and worker utilization times are with no storage space between workers. A second run should increase this storage space to one unit, with the corresponding changes noted. Repeating the runs for two, three, four, and so on, offers management a chance to compute the additional cost of space compared with the increased use. Such increased space between workers may require a larger building, more materials and parts in the system, material handling equipment, and a transfer machine, plus added heat, light, building maintenance, and so on.

These also would be useful data for management to see what changes in the system would occur if one worker position was automated. The assembly line could be simulated using data from the automated process to see if such a change would be cost justified.

SPREADSHEET SIMULATION

As we have stated throughout this book, spreadsheets such as Microsoft® Excel are very useful for a variety of problems. Exhibit 19A.8 shows Bob and Ray's two-stage assembly line on an Excel® spreadsheet. The procedure follows the same pattern as our manual display in Exhibit 19A.7.

The total simulation on Excel® passed through 1,200 iterations (shown in Exhibit 19A.9); that is, 1,200 parts were finished by Ray. Simulation, as an analytic tool, has an advantage over quantitative methods in that it is dynamic, whereas analytic methods show long-run average performance. As you can see in Exhibit 19A.9A, there is an unmistakable startup (or transient) phase. We could even raise some questions about the long-term operation of the line because it does not seem to have settled to a constant (steady state) value,

exhibit 19A.8   Bob and Ray Two-Stage Assembly Line on Microsoft Excel®

Excel: Two-Stage Assembly

		BOB					RAY						AVERAGE
ITEM	RN	START TIME	PERF. TIME	FINISH TIME	WAIT TIME	RN	START TIME	PERF. TIME	FINISH TIME	WAIT TIME	AVERAGE TIME/UNIT	TOTAL TIME	TIME IN SYSTEM
1	93	0	70	70	0	0	70	10	80	70	80.0	80	80.0
2	52	70	50	120	0	44	120	50	170	40	85.0	100	90.0
3	15	120	30	150	20	72	170	60	230	0	76.7	110	96.7
4	64	170	50	220	10	35	230	40	270	0	67.5	100	97.5
5	86	230	60	290	0	2	290	10	300	20	60.0	70	92.0
6	20	290	40	330	0	82	330	70	400	30	66.7	110	95.0
7	83	330	60	390	10	31	400	40	440	0	62.9	110	97.1
8	89	400	60	460	0	13	460	20	480	20	60.0	80	95.0
9	69	460	50	510	0	53	510	50	560	30	62.2	100	95.6
10	41	510	50	560	0	48	560	50	610	0	61.0	100	96.0
11	32	560	40	600	10	13	610	20	630	0	57.3	70	93.6
12	1	610	10	620	10	67	630	60	690	0	57.5	80	92.5
13	11	630	30	660	30	91	690	70	760	0	58.5	130	95.4
14	2	690	10	700	60	76	760	60	820	0	58.6	130	97.9
15	11	760	30	790	30	41	820	40	860	0	57.3	100	98.0
16	55	820	50	870	0	34	870	40	910	10	56.9	90	97.5
17	18	870	30	900	10	28	910	30	940	0	55.3	70	95.9
18	39	910	40	950	0	53	950	50	1000	10	55.6	90	95.6
19	13	950	30	980	20	41	1000	40	1040	0	54.7	90	95.3
20	7	1000	20	1020	20	21	1040	30	1070	0	53.5	70	94.0
21	29	1040	40	1080	0	54	1080	50	1130	10	53.8	90	93.8
22	58	1080	50	1130	0	39	1130	40	1170	0	53.2	90	93.6
23	95	1130	70	1200	0	70	1200	60	1260	30	54.8	130	95.2
24	27	1200	40	1240	20	60	1260	50	1310	0	54.6	110	95.8
25	59	1260	50	1310	0	93	1310	80	1390	0	55.6	130	97.2
26	85	1310	60	1370	20	51	1390	50	1440	0	55.4	130	98.5
27	12	1390	30	1420	20	35	1440	40	1480	0	54.8	90	98.1
28	34	1440	40	1480	0	51	1480	50	1530	0	54.6	90	97.9
29	60	1480	50	1530	0	87	1530	70	1600	0	55.2	120	98.6
30	97	1530	80	1610	0	29	1610	30	1640	10	54.7	110	99.0

even after the 1,200 items. Exhibit 19A.9A shows 100 items that pass through the Bob and Ray two-stage system. Notice the wide variation in time for the first units completed. These figures are the average time that units take. It is a cumulative number; that is, the first unit takes the time generated by the random numbers. The average time for two units is the average time of the sum of the first and second units. The average time for three units is the average time for the sum of the first three units, and so on. This display could have almost any starting shape, not necessarily what we have shown. It all depends on the stream of random numbers. What we can be sure of is that the times do oscillate for a while until they settle down as units are finished and smooth the average.

A. Average Time per Unit of Output
(Finish Time/Number of Units)

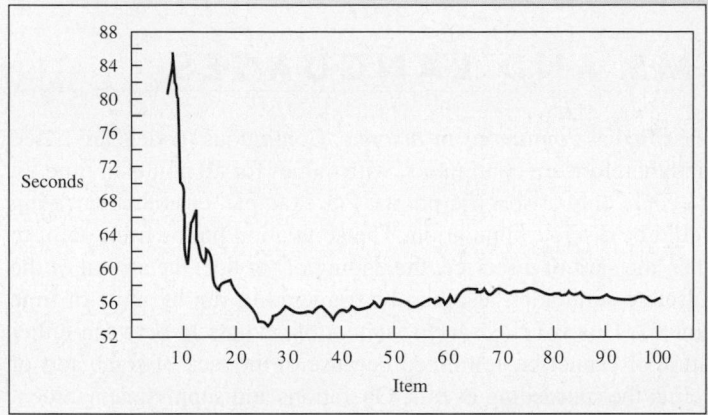

B. Average Time the Product Spends
in the System

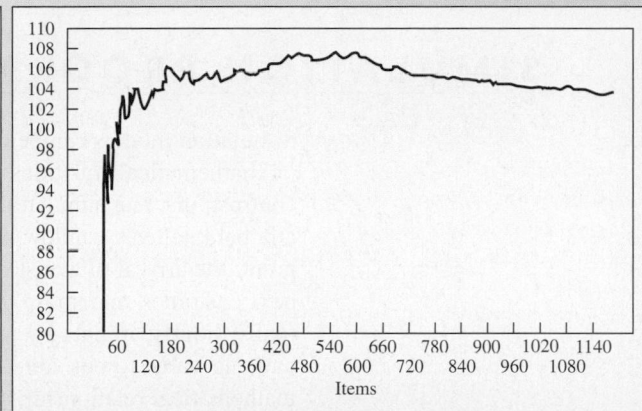

C. Results of Simulating 1,200 Units Processed by Bob and Ray

	BOB	RAY	UNIT
Utilization	0.81	0.85	
Average wait time	10.02	9.63	
Average performance time	46.48	46.88	
Average time per unit			57.65
Average time in system			103.38

Exhibit 19A.9B shows the average time that parts spend in the system. At the start, the display shows an increasing amount of time in the system. This can be expected because the system started empty and there are no interruptions for parts passing from Bob to Ray. Often parts enter the system and may have to wait between stages as work-in-process; this causes delays for subsequent parts and adds to the waiting time. As time goes on, however, stability should occur unless the capacity of the second stage is less than the first stage's. In our present case, we did not allow space between them. Therefore, if Bob finished first, he had to wait for Ray. If Ray finished first, he had to wait for Bob.

Exhibit 19A.9C shows the results of simulating Bob and Ray completing 1,200 units of product. Compare these figures to those that we obtained simulating 10 items by hand. Not too bad, is it? The average performance time for Bob is shown as 46.48 seconds. This is close to the weighted average of what you would expect in the long run. For Bob it is (10 × 4 + 20 × 6 + 30 × 10 etc.) 100 = 45.9 seconds. Ray's expected time is (10 × 4 + 20 × 5 + 30 × 6 etc.) 50 = 46.4 seconds.

The two-stage assembly line simulation is a good example of a specially designed spreadsheet for analyzing this problem. More general simulation programs built within Excel® are available. John McClain, professor of operations management at Cornell University, has developed two simulation spreadsheets that can be used to demonstrate a variety of common systems. These spreadsheets have been included on this book's Web site.

The first spreadsheet, titled "LineSim," is designed to analyze a simple serial production line. This is a system with a series of machines; the output of one machine goes to a storage area, which is the input to the next machine. The spreadsheet can be easily configured for

Excel: LineSim

Excel: CellSim

different numbers of machines, different buffer sizes, and numerous processing time distributions. In addition, machine breakdowns and repairs can be modeled. The second spreadsheet, "CellSim," is similar but allows machines to be arranged more generally. We thank Professor McClain for making these spreadsheets available.

SIMULATION PROGRAMS AND LANGUAGES

Simulation models can be classified as *continuous* or *discrete*. Continuous models are based on mathematical equations and therefore are continuous, with values for all points in time. In contrast, discrete simulation occurs only at specific points. For example, customers arriving at a bank teller's window would be discrete simulation. The simulation jumps from point to point: the arrival of a customer, the start of a service, the ending of service, the arrival of the next customer, and so on. Discrete simulation also can be triggered to run by units of time (daily, hourly, minute by minute). This is called *event simulation;* points in between either have no value to our simulation or cannot be computed because of the lack of some sort of mathematical relationship to link the succeeding events. Operations and supply management applications almost exclusively use discrete (event) simulation.

Simulation programs also can be categorized as general-purpose and special-purpose. General-purpose softwares allow programmers to build their own models. Examples are SLAM II, SIMSCRIPT II.5, SIMAN, GPSS/H, GPSS/PC, PC-MODEL, and RESQ. Special-purpose software simulation programs are specially built to simulate specific applications, for example, Extend and SIMFACTORY. In a specialized simulation for manufacturing, for example, provisions in the model allow for specifying the number of work centers, their description, arrival rates, processing time, batch sizes, quantities of work in process, available resources including labor, sequences, and so on. Additionally, the program may allow the observer to watch the animated operation and see the quantities and flows throughout the system as the simulation is running. Data are collected, analyzed, and presented in a form most suitable for that type of application. The software package called Extend is featured in the Breakthrough box titled "Animation and Simulation Software."

BREAKTHROUGH

ANIMATION AND SIMULATION SOFTWARE

Call centers are a good application for simulation. They are easy to model, and information is available about the service time, arrival rates, renege times, and the paths that the calls take through the center. In this call center, there are four types of calls arriving at random intervals and four types of agents who are able to answer the calls. Each agent type is specialized in a particular call type. However, some agents are able to answer calls of different types.

This was quickly modeled using Extend, a product of Imagine That! company. The product makes extensive use of animation so that the user can actually watch the call center operate. You can learn more about this product at http://www.imaginethatinc.com.

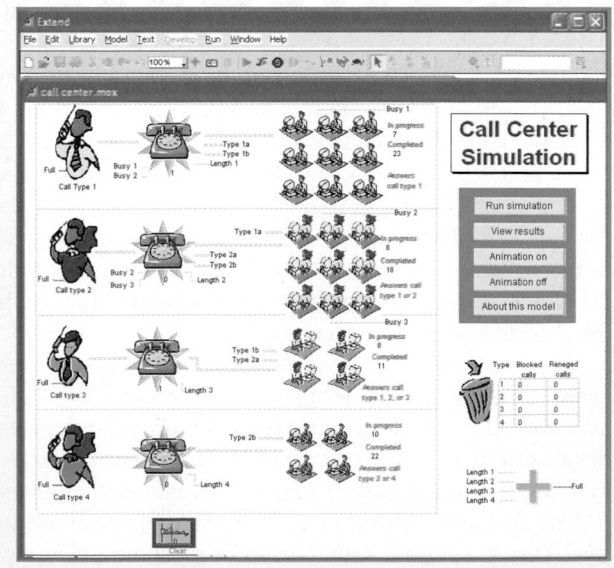

BREAKTHROUGH

HOSPITAL OVERCROWDING SOLUTIONS ARE FOUND WITH SIMULATION

Thanks to increased life expectancy through improved health care coupled with shifting population demographics, hospitals everywhere are becoming increasingly overcrowded. Limited health care budgets are forcing hospitals to explore creative solutions. But creative solutions can be risky, so they need to be carefully evaluated. From the standpoint of cost, the earlier a solution can be evaluated and either accepted or rejected, the better.

Along these lines, the outpatient laboratory at Bay Medical Center was experiencing serious capacity constraints. Adding to its difficulties, a renovation designed to improve efficiency actually added to the overcrowding problem. Dave Nall, a management engineer for Bay Medical Center, ran a study to evaluate several alternatives and make recommendations designed to reduce bottlenecks and improve patient flow through the outpatient laboratory. The objective of this study was to develop and evaluate alternative ways of reducing overcrowding at the outpatient laboratory.

SOLUTION

The key technology employed by Dave in conducting this analysis was computer simulation. Dave had used computer simulation numerous times in the past and had found that it was an efficient way to both gain insight into the problem and evaluate the solutions.

Through discussions with managers responsible for the outpatient laboratory, Dave built a network describing the patient's flow through the laboratory as it was currently configured. Then data were collected on the times required for patients to receive the various services they might need as well as the travel time between rooms where the services were provided. From this information, Dave constructed a computer simulation of the baseline laboratory configuration.

Dave then modified the computer simulation and used it to study issues relating to three categories of solutions to outpatient laboratory overcrowding: (1) changing staff, including both medical and administrative staff; (2) utilizing another clinic as an overflow laboratory; and (3) possibly redesigning the laboratory facility itself.

Service

With respect to staffing, the computer simulation verified that the medical staff currently employed was indeed the optimal number. However, Dave found that the administrative functions, if anything, were overstaffed and that a staff reduction could take place with no appreciable reduction in patient service. Staffing was not the key problem.

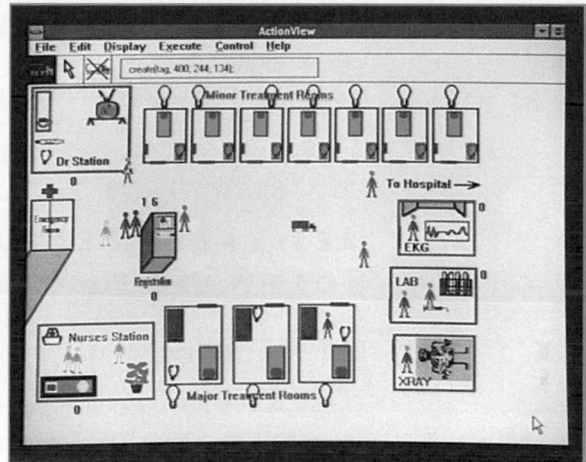

With respect to the option of utilizing another laboratory for overflow, there were significant opportunities for improving throughput if other patients could be enticed to use another laboratory. Although the simulation did not tell him how to get the patients to use an alternative laboratory, it did allow Dave to quantify the benefits of implementing policies that would increase alternative laboratory usage by 5 percent, 10 percent, and so on. With respect to redesign of the existing outpatient laboratory, Dave determined that, with a relatively minor redesign of the facility and a procedural change, the laboratory would become significantly more productive. Increased productivity would, of course, lead to better patient service.

BENEFITS

Individually, no one could have accurately guessed the impact of the different ways of addressing overcrowding at the outpatient laboratory at Bay Medical Center. Through the results of the simulation analysis and the insights gained, Dave was able to assess the relative merits of each alternative as well as predict their impact. With a small investment in Dave's time, Bay Medical Center was able to make informed decisions with an understanding of both costs and benefits. As a result, the right decisions were made, money was saved, and patients were better served.

SOURCE: MICRO ANALYSIS AND DESIGN MICRO SAINT SIMULATION SOFTWARE. © 2004 MICRO ANALYSES & DESIGN. USED WITH PERMISSION.

Service

Many software simulation programs are available. How, then, do you choose a program from a long list? The first step is to understand the different types of simulation. Then it becomes a matter of reviewing programs on the market to find one that fits your specific needs. (See the Breakthrough box titled "Hospital Overcrowding Solutions Are Found with Simulation" for a successful application of a commercial program.)

As a last comment on simulation programs, do not rule out spreadsheets for simulation. As you noticed, we simulated Bob and Ray on a spreadsheet in the preceding section. Spreadsheets are becoming quite user-friendly and are adding many features such as allowing random number generation and asking what-if questions. The simplicity in using a spreadsheet for simulation may well compensate for any needed reduction in the complexity of the problem in order to use the spreadsheet.

@RISK is an add-in program that works with Microsoft Excel®. The program adds many useful simulation-related functions to the spreadsheet. Using @RISK automates the process of taking random values from a specified distribution function, automates the recalculation of the spreadsheet with the new random values, and captures output values and statistics. @RISK simplifies the process of building and running spreadsheet simulations.[2]

DESIRABLE FEATURES OF SIMULATION SOFTWARE

Simulation software takes a while to learn to use. Once specific software is learned, the tendency is to stay with it for a long time, so the choice must be made carefully. Simulation software should

1. Be capable of being used interactively as well as allowing complete runs.
2. Be user-friendly and easy to understand.
3. Allow modules to be built and then connected. In this way, models can be worked on separately without affecting the rest of the system.
4. Allow users to write and incorporate their own routines; no simulation program can provide for all needs.
5. Have building blocks that contain built-in commands (such as statistical analysis or decision rules for where to go next).
6. Have macro capability, such as the ability to develop machining cells.
7. Have material flow capability. Operations involve the movement of material and people; the program should be able to model trucks, cranes, conveyers, and so on.
8. Output standard statistics such as cycle times, utilizations, and wait times.
9. Allow a variety of data analysis alternatives for both input and output data.
10. Have animation capabilities to display graphically the product flow through the system.
11. Permit interactive debugging of the model so the user can trace flows through the model and more easily find errors.[3]

ADVANTAGES AND DISADVANTAGES OF SIMULATION

The following is not intended as a comprehensive list of reasons why one should elect to use or not use simulation as a technique. Rather, we state some of the generally accepted advantages and disadvantages.

ADVANTAGES

1. Developing the model of a system often leads to a better understanding of the real system.
2. Time can be compressed in simulation; years of experience in the real system can be compressed into seconds or minutes.

3. Simulation does not disrupt ongoing activities of the real system.
4. Simulation is far more general than mathematical models and can be used where conditions are not suitable for standard mathematical analysis.
5. Simulation can be used as a game for training experience.
6. Simulation provides a more realistic replication of a system than mathematical analysis.
7. Simulation can be used to analyze transient conditions, whereas mathematical techniques usually cannot.
8. Many standard packaged models, covering a wide range of topics, are available commercially.
9. Simulation answers what-if questions.

DISADVANTAGES

1. Although a great deal of time and effort may be spent to develop a model for simulation, there is no guarantee that the model will, in fact, provide good answers.
2. There is no way to prove that a simulation model's performance is completely reliable. Simulation involves numerous repetitions of sequences that are based on randomly generated occurrences. An apparently stable system can, with the right combination of events—however unlikely—explode.
3. Depending on the system to be simulated, building a simulation model can take anywhere from an hour to 100 worker years. Complicated systems can be very costly and take a long time.
4. Simulation may be less accurate than mathematical analysis because it is randomly based. If a given system can be represented by a mathematical model, it may be better to use than simulation.
5. A significant amount of computer time may be needed to run complex models.
6. The technique of simulation, while making progress, still lacks a standardized approach. Therefore, models of the same system built by different individuals may differ widely.

SUMMARY

We could make the statement that anything that can be done mathematically can be done with simulation. However, simulation is not always the best choice. Mathematical analysis, when appropriate to a specific problem, is usually faster and less expensive. Also, it is usually provable as far as the technique is concerned, and the only real question is whether the system is adequately represented by the mathematical model.

Simulation, however, has nothing fixed; there are no boundaries to building a model or making assumptions about the system. Expanding computer power and memory have pushed out the limits of what can be simulated. Further, the continued development of simulation languages and programs—both general-purpose programs (SIMAN, SLAM) and special-purpose programs (Extend, Process Model, SIMFACTORY, Optima!)—have made the entire process of creating simulation models much easier.

KEY TERMS

Parameters Properties of a simulation model that are fixed.

Variables Properties of a simulation model that are allowed to vary throughout the simulation run. The results of the simulation are analyzed through these variables.

Decision rules Logic that controls the behavior of a simulation.

Distributions The probability distributions that are used to model the random events in a simulation.

Time incrementing The process of moving through time in a simulation.

Run length (or run time) The duration of a simulation in simulated time or number of events.

SOLVED PROBLEMS

SOLVED PROBLEM 1

To use an old statistical example for simulation, if an urn contains 100 balls, of which 10 percent are green, 40 percent are red, and 50 percent are spotted, develop a simulation model of the process of drawing balls at random from the urn. Each time a ball is drawn and its color noted, it is replaced. Use the following random numbers as you desire.

Simulate drawing 10 balls from the urn. Show which numbers you have used.

26768	66954	83125	08021
42613	17457	55503	36458
95457	03704	47019	05752
95276	56970	84828	05752

Solution

Assign random numbers to the balls to correspond to the percentage present in the urn.

	RANDOM NUMBER
10 green balls	00–09
40 red balls	10–49
50 spotted balls	50–99

Many possible answers exist, depending on how the random numbers were assigned and which numbers were used from the list provided in the problem.

For the random number sequence above and using the first two numbers of those given, we obtain

RN	COLOR	RN	COLOR
26	Red	17	Red
42	Red	3	Green
95	Spotted	56	Spotted
95	Spotted	83	Spotted
66	Spotted	55	Spotted

For the 10 there were 1 green, 3 red, and 6 spotted balls—a good estimate based on a sample of only 10!

SOLVED PROBLEM 2

A rural clinic receives a delivery of fresh plasma once each week from a central blood bank. The supply varies according to demand from other clinics and hospitals in the region but ranges between four and nine pints of the most widely used blood type, type O. The number of patients per week requiring this blood varies from zero to four, and each patient may need from one to four pints. Given the following delivery quantities, patient distribution, and demand per patient, what would be the number of pints in excess or short for a six-week period? Use simulation to derive your answer. Consider that plasma is storable and there is currently none on hand.

DELIVERY QUANTITIES		PATIENT DISTRIBUTION		DEMAND PER PATIENT	
PINTS PER WEEK	PROBABILITY	PATIENTS PER WEEK REQUIRING BLOOD	PROBABILITY	PINTS	PROBABILITY
4	0.15	0	0.25	1	0.40
5	0.20	1	0.25	2	0.30
6	0.25	2	0.30	3	0.20
7	0.15	3	0.15	4	0.10
8	0.15	4	0.05		
9	0.10				

Solution

First, develop a random number sequence; then simulate.

DELIVERY			NUMBER OF PATIENTS			PATIENT DEMAND		
PINTS	PROBABILITY	RANDOM NUMBER	BLOOD	PROBABILITY	RANDOM NUMBER	PINTS	RANDOM PROBABILITY	NUMBER
4	.15	00–14	0	.25	00–24	1	.40	00–39
5	.20	15–34	1	.25	25–49	2	.30	40–69
6	.25	35–59	2	.30	50–79	3	.20	70–89
7	.15	60–74	3	.15	80–94	4	.10	90–99
8	.15	75–89	4	.05	95–99			
9	.10	90–99						

WEEK No.	BEGINNING INVENTORY	QUANTITY DELIVERED		TOTAL BLOOD ON HAND	PATIENTS NEEDING BLOOD		PATIENT	QUANTITY NEEDED		NUMBER OF PINTS REMAINING
		RN	PINTS		RN	PATIENTS		RN	PINTS	
1	0	74	7	7	85	3	First	21	1	6
							Second	06	1	5
							Third	71	3	2
2	2	31	5	7	28	1		96	4	3
3	3	02	4	7	72	2	First	12	1	6
							Second	67	2	4
4	4	53	6	10	44	1		23	1	9
5	9	16	5	14	16	0				14
6	14	40	6	20	83	3	First	65	2	18
							Second	34	1	17
							Third	82	3	14
7	14									

At the end of six weeks, there were 14 pints on hand.

REVIEW AND DISCUSSION QUESTIONS

1 Why is simulation often called a technique of last resort?
2 What roles does statistical hypothesis testing play in simulation?
3 What determines whether a simulation model is valid?
4 Must you use a computer to get good information from a simulation? Explain.
5 What methods are used to increment time in a simulation model? How do they work?
6 What are the pros and cons of starting a simulation with the system empty? With the system in equilibrium?
7 Distinguish between known mathematical distributions and empirical distributions. What information is needed to simulate using a known mathematical distribution?
8 What is the importance of run length in simulation? Is a run of 100 observations twice as valid as a run of 50? Explain.

PROBLEMS

1 CLASSROOM SIMULATION: FISH FORWARDERS
This is a competitive exercise designed to test players' skills at setting inventory ordering rules over a 10-week planning horizon. Maximum profit at the end determines the winner.

Fish Forwarders supplies fresh shrimp to a variety of customers in the New Orleans area. It orders cases of shrimp from fleet representatives at the beginning of each week to meet a demand from its customers at the middle of the week. Shrimp are subsequently delivered to Fish Forwarders and then, at the end of the week, to its customers.

Both the supply of shrimp and the demand for shrimp are uncertain. The supply may vary as much as ±10 percent from the amount ordered, and, by contract, Fish Forwarders must purchase this supply. The probability associated with this variation is −10 percent, 30 percent of the time; 0 percent, 50 percent of the time; and +10 percent, 20 percent of the time. Weekly demand for shrimp is normally distributed with a mean of 800 cases and standard deviation of 100 cases.

Simulation Worksheet

(1)	(2)	(3)		(4)		(5)	(6)	(7)	(8)		(9)
		Orders placed		Orders received					Excess		
Week	Flash-frozen inventory	Regular	Flash-frozen	Regular	Flash-frozen	Available (regular and flash-frozen)	Demand (800 + 100Z)	Sales (minimum of demand or available)	Regular	Flash	Shortages
1											
2											
3											
4											
5											
6											
7		MARDI GRAS					*				
8											
9											
10											
Total											

*Flash-frozen only.

A case of shrimp costs Fish Forwarders $30 and sells for $50. Any shrimp not sold at the end of the week are sold to a cat-food company at $4 per case. Fish Forwarders may, if it chooses, order the shrimp flash-frozen by the supplier at dockside, but this raises the cost of a case by $4 and, hence, costs Fish Forwarders $34 per case.

Procedure for play. The game requires that each week a decision be made as to how many cases to order of regular shrimp and of flash-frozen shrimp. The number ordered may be any amount. The instructor plays the role of referee and supplies the random numbers. The steps in playing the game are as follows:

a. Decide on the order amount of regular shrimp or flash-frozen shrimp and enter the figures in column 3 of the worksheet. (See Exhibit 19A.10.) Assume that there is no opening inventory of flash-frozen shrimp.

b. Determine the amount that arrives and enter it under "Orders received." To accomplish this, the referee draws a random number from a uniform random number table (such as that in Appendix H) and finds its associated level of variation from the following random number intervals: 00 to 29 = −10 percent, 30 to 79 = 0 percent, and 80 to 99 = +10 percent. If the random number is, say, 13, the amount of variation will be −10 percent. Thus, if you decide to order 1,000 regular cases of shrimp and 100 flash-frozen cases, the amount you would actually receive would be 1,000 − 0.10(1,000), or 900 regular cases, and 100 − 0.10(100), or 90 flash-frozen cases. (Note that the variation is the same for both regular and flash-frozen shrimp.) These amounts are then entered in column 4.

c. Add the amount of flash-frozen shrimp in inventory (if any) to the quantity of regular and flash-frozen shrimp just received and enter this amount in column 5. This would be 990, using the figures provided earlier.

d. Determine the demand for shrimp. To accomplish this, the referee draws a random normal deviate value from Exhibit 19A.3 or Appendix H and enters it into the equation at the top of column 6. Thus, if the deviate value is −1.76, demand for the week is 800 + 100(−1.76), or 624.

e. Determine the amount sold. This will be the lesser of the amount demanded (column 6) and the amount available (column 5). Thus, if a player has received 990 and demand is 624, the quantity entered will be 624 (with 990 − 624, or 366, left over).

Profit from Fish Forwarders' Operations

Revenue from sales ($50 × Col. 7)	$_____
Revenue from salvage ($4 × Col. 8 reg.)	$_____
Total revenue	$_____
Cost of regular purchases ($30 × Col. 4 reg.)	$_____
Cost of flash-frozen purchases ($34 × Col. 4 flash)	$_____
Cost of holding flash-frozen shrimp ($2 × Col. 8 flash)	$_____
Cost of shortages ($20 × Col. 9)	$_____
Total cost	$_____
Profit	$_____

    f. Determine the excess. The amount of excess is simply that quantity remaining after demand for a given week is filled. Always assume that regular shrimp are sold before the flash-frozen. Thus, if we use the 366 figure obtained in *e*, the excess would include all the original 90 cases of flash-frozen shrimp.

    g. Determine shortages. This is simply the amount of unsatisfied demand each period, and it occurs only when demand is greater than sales. (Because all customers use the shrimp within the week in which they are delivered, backorders are not relevant.) The amount of shortage (in cases of shrimp) is entered in column 9.

Profit determination. Exhibit 19A.11 is provided for determining the profit achieved at the end of play. The values to be entered in the table are obtained by summing the relevant columns of Exhibit 19A.10 and making the calculations.

Assignment. Simulate operations for a total of 10 weeks. It is suggested that a 10-minute break be taken at the end of Week 5, allowing the players to evaluate how they may improve their performance. They might also wish to plan an ordering strategy for the week of Mardi Gras, when no shrimp will be supplied.

2   The manager of a small post office is concerned that the growing township is overloading the one-window service being offered. Sample data are collected on 100 individuals who arrive for service:

TIME BETWEEN ARRIVALS (MINUTES)	FREQUENCY		SERVICE TIME (MINUTES)	FREQUENCY
1	8		1.0	12
2	35		1.5	21
3	34		2.0	36
4	17		2.5	19
5	6		3.0	7
	100		3.5	5
				100

    Using the following random number sequence, simulate six arrivals; estimate the average customer waiting time and the average idle time for clerks.

       RN: 08, 74, 24, 34, 45, 86, 31, 32, 45, 21, 10, 67, 60, 17, 60, 87, 74, 96

3   Thomas Magnus, a private investigator, has been contacted by a potential client in Kamalo, Molokai. The call came just in time because Magnus is down to his last $10. Employment, however, is conditional on Magnus's meeting the client at Kamalo within eight hours. Magnus, presently at the Masters' residence in Kipahulu, Maui, has three alternative ways to get to Kamalo. Magnus may

    a. Drive to the native village of Honokahua and take an outrigger to Kamalo.

    b. Drive to Honokahua and swim the 10 miles across Pailolo Channel to Kamalo.

c. Drive to Hana and ask his friend T. C. to fly him by helicopter to Kamalo.

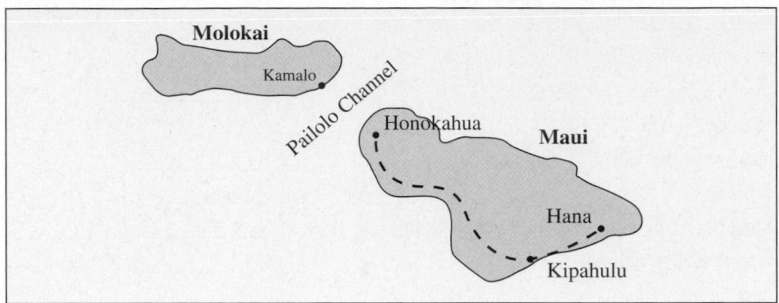

If option *a* is chosen, driving times to Honokahua are given in Distribution 1. Once at Honokahua, Magnus must negotiate with the friendly Tai natives. Negotiations always include a few Mai Tais, so if Magnus begins to negotiate, swimming becomes impossible. Negotiations center on how much each of the three outrigger crew members will be paid. Negotiation time, crew pay, and outrigger travel time are in Distributions 3, 4, and 5, respectively. You may assume each crew member is paid the same amount. If crew pay totals more than $10, Magnus is out of luck—trip time may then be taken to be infinity.

If option *b* is chosen, driving times to Honokahua and swimming times are given in Distributions 1 and 6.

If option *c* is chosen, driving times to Hana are given in Distribution 2. T. C., however, is at the airport only 10 percent of the time. If T. C. is not at the airport, Magnus will wait for him to arrive. Magnus's waiting time is given by Distribution 8. T. C. may refuse to fly for the $10 Magnus has available; Magnus puts the probability of T. C. refusing to fly for $10 at 30 percent. You may assume negotiation time is zero. If T. C. refuses, Magnus will drive to Honokahua via Kipahulu and swim to Kamalo. Helicopter flying times are given in Distribution 7.

Simulate each of the three alternative transportation plans *twice* and, based on your simulation results, calculate the average trip time for each plan. Use the following random numbers in the order they appear; do not skip any random numbers.

RN: 7, 3, 0, 4, 0, 5, 3, 5, 6, 1, 6, 6, 4, 8, 4, 9, 0, 7, 7, 1, 7, 0, 6, 8, 8, 7, 9, 0, 1, 2, 9, 7, 3, 2, 3, 8, 6, 0, 6, 0, 5, 9, 7, 9, 6, 4, 7, 2, 8, 7, 8, 1, 7, 0, 5

Distribution 1: Time to Drive from Kipahulu to Honokahua (Hours)

TIME	PROBABILITY	RN
1	.2	0–1
1.5	.6	2–7
2	.2	8–9

Distribution 2: Time to Drive from Kipahulu to Hana and Vice Versa (Hours)

TIME	PROBABILITY	RN
.5	.2	0–1
1	.7	2–8
1.5	.1	9

Distribution 3: Negotiation Time (Hours)

TIME	PROBABILITY	RN
1	.2	0–1
1.5	.3	2–4
2	.3	5–7
2.5	.2	8–9

Distribution 4: Outrigger Pay per Crew Member

PAY	PROBABILITY	RN
$2	.3	0–2
3	.3	3–5
4	.4	6–9

Distribution 5: Outrigger Travel Time from Honokahua to Kamalo (Hours)

TIME	PROBABILITY	RN
3	.1	0
4	.5	1–5
5	.4	6–9

Distribution 6: Time to Swim from Honokahua to Kamalo (Hours)

TIME	PROBABILITY	RN
5	.2	0–1
6	.6	2–7
7	.2	8–9

Distribution 7: Time to Fly from Hana to Kamalo (Hours)		
TIME	PROBABILITY	RN
1	.1	0
1.5	.7	1–7
2	.2	8–9

Distribution 8: Magnus's Waiting Time at Airport (Hours)		
TIME	PROBABILITY	RN
1	.1	0
2	.2	1–2
3	.4	3–6
4	.3	7–9

4   A bank of machines in a manufacturing shop breaks down according to the following interarrival time distribution. The time it takes one repairperson to complete the repair of a machine is given in the service time distribution:

INTERARRIVAL TIME (HOURS)	$P(X)$	RN	SERVICE TIME (HOURS)	$P(X)$	RN
.5	.30	0–29	.5	.25	0–24
1.0	.22	30–51	1.0	.20	25–44
1.5	.16	52–67	2.0	.25	45–69
2.0	.10	68–77	3.0	.15	70–84
3.0	.14	78–91	4.0	.10	85–94
4.0	.08	92–99	5.0	.05	95–99
	1.00			1.00	

Simulate the breakdown of five machines. Calculate the average machine downtime using two repairpersons and the following random number sequence. (Both repairpersons cannot work on the same machine.)

RN: 30, 81, 02, 91, 51, 08, 28, 44, 86, 84, 29, 08, 37, 34, 99

5   Jennifer Jones owns a small candy store she operates herself. A study was made observing the time between customers coming into the store and the time that Jones took to serve them. The following data were collected from 100 customers observed:

INTERARRIVAL TIME (MINUTES)	NUMBER OF OBSERVATIONS	SERVICE TIME (MINUTES)	NUMBER OF OBSERVATIONS
1	5	1	10
2	10	2	15
3	10	3	15
4	15	4	20
5	15	5	15
6	20	6	10
7	10	7	8
8	8	8	4
9	5	9	2
10	2	10	1

Simulate the system (all of the arrivals and services) until 10 customers pass through the system and are serviced.

How long does the average customer spend in the system? Use Appendix H to obtain random numbers.

6   A professional football coach has six running backs on his squad. He wants to evaluate how injuries might affect his stock of running backs. A minor injury causes a player to be removed from the game and miss only the next game. A major injury puts the player out of action for

the rest of the season. The probability of a major injury in a game is 0.05. There is at most one major injury per game. The probability distribution of minor injuries per game is

NUMBER OF INJURIES	PROBABILITY
0	.2
1	.5
2	.22
3	.05
4	.025
5	.005
	1.000

Injuries seem to happen in a completely random manner, with no discernible pattern over the season. A season is 10 games.

Using the following random numbers, simulate the fluctuations in the coach's stock of running backs over the season. Assume that he hires no additional running backs during the season.

RN: 044, 392, 898, 615, 986, 959, 558, 353, 577, 866, 305, 813, 024, 189, 878, 023, 285, 442, 862, 848, 060, 131, 963, 874, 805, 105, 452

7   At Tucson Mills, minor breakdowns of machines occur frequently. The occurrence of break-downs and the service time to fix the machines are randomly distributed. Management is concerned with minimizing the cost of breakdowns. The cost per hour for the machines to be down is $40. The cost of service repairpersons is $12 per hour. A preliminary study has produced the following data on times between successive breakdowns and their service times:

RELATIVE FREQUENCY OF BREAKDOWNS

Time between breakdowns (in minutes)	4	5	6	7	8	9
Relative frequency	.10	.30	.25	.20	.10	.05

RELATIVE FREQUENCY OF SERVICE TIMES

Service time (in minutes)	4	5	6	7	8	9
Relative frequency	.10	.40	.20	.15	.10	.05

Simulate 30 breakdowns under two conditions: with one service repairperson and with two service repairpersons.

Use the following random number sequence to determine time between breakdowns:

RN: 85, 16, 65, 76, 93, 99, 65, 70, 58, 44, 02, 85, 01, 97, 63, 52, 53, 11, 62, 28, 84, 82, 27, 20, 39, 70, 26, 21, 41, 81

Use the following random number sequence to determine service times:

RN: 68, 26, 85, 11, 16, 26, 95, 67, 97, 73, 75, 64, 26, 45, 01, 87, 20, 01, 19, 36, 69, 89, 81, 81, 02, 05, 10, 51, 24, 36

a. Using the results of the simulations, calculate
   (1) The total idle time for the service repairpersons under each condition.
   (2) The total delay caused by waiting for a service repairperson to begin working on a breakdown.
b. Determine the lowest-cost approach.

8   Jethro's service station has one gasoline pump. Because everyone in Kornfield County drives big cars, there is room at the station for only three cars, including the car at the pump. Cars arriving when three cars are already at the station drive on to another station. Use the following probability distributions to simulate the arrival of four cars to Jethro's station:

INTERARRIVAL TIME (MINUTES)	$P(X)$	RN	SERVICE TIME (MINUTES)	$P(X)$	RN
10	.40	0–39	5	.45	0–44
20	.35	40–74	10	.30	45–74
30	.20	75–94	15	.20	75–94
40	.05	95–99	20	.05	95–99

Use the following random number sequence:

RN: 99, 00, 73, 09, 38, 53, 72, 91

How many cars go to another station? What is the average time a car spends at the station?

9   You have been hired as a consultant by a supermarket chain to answer a basic question: How many items per customer should be permitted in the fast checkout line? This is no trivial question for the chain's management; your findings will be the basis for corporate policy for all 2,000 stores. The vice president of operations has given you one month to do the study and two assistants to help you gather the data.

In starting this study, you decide to avoid queuing theory as the tool for analysis (because of your concern about the reliability of its assumptions) and instead opt for simulation. Given the following data, explain in detail how you would go about your analysis, stating (1) the criteria you would use in making your recommendation, (2) what additional data you would need to set up your simulation, (3) how you would gather the preliminary data, (4) how you would set up the problem for simulation, and (5) which factors would affect the applicability of your findings to all of the stores.

Store locations	The United States and Canada
Hours of operation	16 per day
Average store size	9 checkout stands including fast checkout
Available checkers	7 to 10 (some engage in stocking activities when not at a checkout stand)

10 The saga of Joe from Chapter 19 (Problem 12, page 649) continues. Joe has the opportunity to do a big repair job for a local motorcycle club. (Their cycles were accidentally run over by a garbage truck.) The compensation for the job is good, but it is vital that the total repair time for the five cycles be less than 40 hours. (The leader of the club has stated that he would be very distressed if the cycles were not available for a planned rally.) Joe knows from experience that repairs of this type often entail several trips between processes for a given cycle, so estimates of time are difficult to provide. Still, Joe has the following historical data about the probability that a job will start in each process, processing time in each process, and transitional probabilities between each pair of processes:

PROCESS	PROBABILITY OF JOB STARTING IN PROCESS	PROCESSING TIME PROBABILITY (HOURS)			PROBABILITY OF GOING FROM PROCESS TO OTHER PROCESSES OR COMPLETION (OUT)			
		1	2	3	FRAME	ENGINE WORK	PAINTING	OUT
Frame repair	0.5	0.2	0.4	0.4	—	0.4	0.4	0.2
Engine work	0.3	0.6	0.1	0.3	0.3	—	0.4	0.3
Painting	0.2	0.3	0.3	0.4	0.1	0.1	—	0.8

Given this information, use simulation to determine the repair times for each cycle. Display your results on a Gantt chart showing an FCFS schedule. (Assume that only one cycle can be worked on at a time in each process.) Based on your simulation, what do you recommend Joe do next?

11 "Eat at Helen's" has decided to add a drive-up window to the restaurant. Due to limited capital, there is enough space for only two cars in the drive-up window lane (one being served and one waiting). Helen would like to know how many customers are bypassing her restaurant due to the limited space in the drive-up window lane. Simulate 10 cars as they attempt to use the drive-up window using the following distributions and random numbers:

TIME BETWEEN ARRIVALS (MINUTES)	PROBABILITY	SERVICE TIME (MINUTES)	PROBABILITY
1	0.40	1	0.20
2	0.30	2	0.40
3	0.15	3	0.40
4	0.15		

Use the following two-digit random numbers for this problem:

Arrivals: 37, 60, 79, 21, 85, 71, 48, 39, 31, 35
Service: 66, 74, 90, 95, 29, 72, 17, 55, 15, 36

12 Jane's Auto World has a policy of placing an order for 27 of the most popular model whenever inventory reaches 20. Lead time on delivery is two weeks, and 25 automobiles are currently on hand. Simulate 15 weeks' worth of sales using the following probabilities that were derived from historical information:

SALES PER WEEK	PROBABILITY	SALES PER WEEK	PROBABILITY
5	.05	10	.20
6	.05	11	.20
7	.10	12	.10
8	.10	13	.05
9	.10	14	.05

Use the following random numbers for sales: 23, 59, 82, 83, 61, 00, 48, 33, 06, 32, 82, 51, 54, 66, 55.

Does this policy appear to be appropriate? Explain.

13 A local newspaper vendor sells papers for $.50. The papers cost her $.40, giving her a $.10 profit on each one she sells. From past experience, she knows that

20% of the time she sells 100 papers
20% of the time she sells 150 papers
30% of the time she sells 200 papers
30% of the time she sells 250 papers

Assuming that she believes that the cost of a lost sale is $.05 and any unsold papers cost her $.25, simulate her profit outlook over 5 days if she orders 200 papers for each of the 5 days. Use the following random numbers: 51, 07, 55, 87, 53.

14 The daily demand for a high-energy drink from a given vending machine is 20, 21, 22, or 23 with probabilities 0.4, 0.3, 0.2, or 0.1, respectively. Assume the following random numbers have been generated: 08, 54, 74, 66, 52, 58, 03, 22, 89, and 85. Using these numbers, generate the daily drink sales for 10 days.

ADVANCED CASE: UNDERSTANDING THE IMPACT OF VARIABILITY ON THE CAPACITY OF A PRODUCTION SYSTEM

Excel: LineSim

This exercise, which uses LineSim, is an opportunity to study the impact that variability in processing time has on the capacity of a simple serial production system. Much more complex systems could be studied, but our hope is that by studying this simple system, you will gain insight that can be applied to more complex systems.

The system we are studying is similar to the two-stage assembly line discussed in this chapter; here we look at a three-stage assembly line. In practice, assembly lines have many more workstations, but completing an exercise with more workstations would take considerably longer. If you do not believe that your results can be generalized to a larger system, feel free to expand your study.

For this study, we use the Serial Line Simulator (LineSim) that is included on this book's Web site. This Microsoft Excel® spreadsheet simulates a simple serial production line. We are indebted to John McClain at the Johnson Graduate School of Management, Cornell University, for allowing us to use his innovative spreadsheet.

GOAL OF THIS EXERCISE

Our goal in this exercise is that you learn firsthand how variability can impact the performance of multistage production systems. A common approach used to reduce the impact of variability is through some type of buffering mechanism. To be more specific, in our system, variability exists in the amount of time that it takes to perform work at a workstation. In analyzing the system, we use the average time to complete each unit, so sometimes it takes longer and sometimes less time. It probably seldom takes exactly the average time.

When there is variability, production engineers put buffer stations between each workstation. These buffers allow the variability to be smoothed so that the variability in one workstation has less impact on the other workstations. An interesting question to study with simulation is if these buffers are eliminated, or if there are 100 units between each workstation, how would this change the performance of the system?

DETAILS OF THE EXERCISE

Start with the spreadsheet as Professor McClain configures it initially. Click the "Design" tab, and note that we have a three-station assembly line. The stations are named "Joe," "Next's," and "M2." There is a buffer area downstream from "Joe" with a capacity of one unit and another downstream from "Next's" with a capacity of one unit. The way this simulation is designed, "Joe" will always have something to work on and "M2" can always deposit finished work in a storage area.

Notice that the processing time distribution is Shifted Exponential with a mean of 5 and a standard deviation of 5. The shape of this distribution, described in the "Instructions" tab, shows that there is much process time variation. Answer the following question before going on to the next part of the exercise:

Question 1: How many units would you expect to be able to produce over 100 time periods?

Click the "Run" tab and, using the default values for "Run-In Time," "Run Length," and "Repetitions," run the simulation. Tabulate the average utilization at each machine based on the five repetitions, and tabulate the mean and standard deviation of the output of the system (these data are in the "Machine" worksheet).

Question 2: How many units did you actually produce per 100 time periods? Explain any difference between your simulation result and your estimate made in Question 1.

Next map the impact that increased buffer inventory has on the output of the system. You can change the buffer behind "Joe" and "Next's" by changing the inventory cell designated "Joe's Inventory" (this is on the "Design" worksheet) and then clicking "Make Storage Areas Like #1."

Question 3: Create a graph that shows the impact of changing the buffer stock on the output of the system. Consider buffer levels that vary from 0 to a maximum of 20 units. What can you conclude from your experiment?

Finally, experiment with the impact of a bottleneck in the system.

Question 4: What would be the impact on system performance if "M2" had a processing time that averaged 6 time units? (Assume that "Joe" and "Next's" still run at an average of 5.) What happens to the inventory after "Joe" and "Next's"? Does varying the size of these inventories have any impact?

Question 5: What happens if instead of "M2" being the bottleneck, "Joe" is the bottleneck? Do the buffers at "Joe" and "Next's" have any impact?

Keep your answers brief; your entire report, including graphs, should be no longer than two double-spaced pages.

SUPER QUIZ

1 This is a powerful tool that allows one to perform experiments using a computer model of a real system.
2 To allow the computer model to consider variability in such items as demand and processing times, these are used.
3 This is the logic that controls the behavior of the simulation.
4 This is the duration of simulation in simulation time or events.

5 This is the term used to check to see whether the computer code adequately represents the real system.
6 True/False: Simulation is most useful when a problem can be solved mathematically.
7 A simulation that jumps from one point in time directly to a second, and then to a third, and so on, is classified as this.

1. Simulation 2. Random numbers 3. Decision rules 4. Run length (or run time) 5. Validation 6. False 7. Discrete

SELECTED BIBLIOGRAPHY

Kelton, W. D. *Simulation with Arena.* 4th ed. New York: McGraw-Hill, 2006.

Ross, S. M. *Simulation.* 4th ed. Burlington, MA: Academic Press, Elsevier, 2006.

Winston, W. L. *Simulation Modeling Using @RISK.* Belmont, CA: Wadsworth, 2000.

FOOTNOTES

1 The basic formula is $Z = \frac{x - \mu}{\sigma}$, which when restated in terms of x appears as $x = \mu + Z\sigma$. We then substituted D_n for x and $\bar{x}$ for μ to relate the method more directly to the sample problem.

2 See W. L. Winston, *Simulation Modeling Using @RISK* (Belmont, CA: Wadsworth, 2000). @RISK is a product of Palisade Corporation (http://www.palisade.com).

3 S. W. Haider and J. Banks, "Simulation Software Products for Analyzing Manufacturing Systems," *Industrial Engineering* 18, no. 7 (July 1986), pp. 98−103.

chapter 20

CONSTRAINT MANAGEMENT

Scene: Alex Rogo is the plant manager at the Barrington Plant of UniWare, a Division of UniCo. He has had a lot of trouble with his plant in keeping schedules, reducing inventory, improving quality, and cutting costs, among other problems. Bill Peach, division vice president, just visited him and gave him three months to improve, or else the plant will be closed.

Alex's son Dave and his Boy Scout troop are taking a 20-mile overnight hike (10 miles to Devil's Gulch where they will camp for the night, returning the following morning). Alex had been coaxed by his wife and son to accompany the troop. They are now on the hike and way behind schedule. The line of scouts is spread way out with the fastest kids in front; Herbie, the slowest, lags way behind in the rear. Alex is trying to figure out how he can make the Boy Scouts stay together and move faster.

After reading this chapter you will:

1. Understand basic concepts of the Theory of Constraints (TOC) including the "Goal of the Firm" and "TOC—Performance Measures."

2. See how bottlenecks are controlled using TOC concepts.

3. Model processes using TOC concepts.

4. Compare MRP, JIT, and TOC concepts and see how they can complement one another.

5. Describe how TOC can be applied to areas other than production processes.

Up front, you've got Andy, who wants to set a speed record. And here you are stuck behind Fat Herbie, the slowest kid in the woods. After an hour, the kid in front—if he's really moving at three miles per hour—is going to be two miles ahead, which means you're going to have to run two miles to catch up with him.

Alex is thinking, "If this were my plant, Peach wouldn't even give me three months. I'd already be on the street by now. The demand was for us to cover 10 miles in five hours, and we've only done half of that. Inventory is racing out of sight. The carrying costs on that inventory would be rising. We'd be ruining the company."

"Okay," I say. "Everybody join hands."

They all look at each other.

"Come on! Just do it!" I tell them. "And don't let go."

SOURCE: E. M. GOLDRATT AND J. COX, *THE GOAL: A PROCESS OF ONGOING IMPROVEMENT*, 2ND REV. ED. (GREAT BARRINGTON, MA: NORTH RIVER PRESS, 1992), PP. 114–18.

Then I take Herbie by the hand and, as if I'm dragging a chain, I go up the trail, snaking past the entire line. Hand in hand, the rest of the troop follows. I pass Andy and keep walking. When I'm twice the distance of the lineup, I stop. What I've done is turn the entire troop around so that the boys have exactly the opposite order they had before.

"Now listen up!" I say. "This is the order you're going to stay in until we reach where we're going. Understood? Nobody passes anybody.

"The idea of this hike is not to see who can get there the fastest. The idea is to get there together. We're not a bunch of individuals out here. We're a team."

So we start off again. And it works. No kidding. Everybody stays together behind Herbie. I've gone to the back of the line so I can keep tabs, and I keep waiting for the gaps to appear, but they don't.

"Mr. Rogo, can't we put somebody faster up front?" asks a kid ahead of me.

"Listen, if you guys want to go faster, then you have to figure out a way to let Herbie go faster," I tell them.

One of the kids in the rear says, "Hey, Herbie, what have you got in your pack?"

Herbie stops and turns around. I tell him to come to the back of the line and take off his pack. As he does, I take the pack from him—and nearly drop it.

"Herbie, this thing weighs a ton," I say. "What have you got in here?"

"Nothing much," says Herbie.

I open it up and reach in. Out comes a six-pack of soda. Next are some cans of spaghetti. Then come a box of candy bars, a jar of pickles, and two cans of tuna fish. Beneath a raincoat and rubber boots and a bag of tent stakes, I pull out a large iron skillet.

"Herbie, look, you've done a great job of lugging this stuff so far. But we have to make you able to move faster," I say. "If we take some of the load off you, you'll be able to do a better job at the front of the line."

Herbie finally seems to understand.

Again we start walking. But this time, Herbie can really move. Relieved of most of the weight in his pack, it's as if he's walking on air. We're flying now, doing twice the speed as a troop that we did before. And we still stay together. Inventory is down. Throughput is up.

Dave and I share the same tent that night. We're lying inside it, both of us tired. Dave is quiet for a while. Then he speaks up.

He says, "You know, Dad, I was really proud of you today."

"You were? How come?"

"The way you figured out what was going on and kept everyone together, and put Herbie in front."

"Thanks," I tell him. "Actually, I learned a lot of things today."

"You did?"

"Yeah, stuff that I think is going to help me straighten out the plant," I say.

"Really? Like what?"

"Are you sure you want to hear about it?"

"Sure I am," he claims.

This is the beginning of Alex's successful turnaround of his plant—applying simple principles to the plant's operation.

Goldratt's Rules of Production Scheduling

exhibit 20.1

1   Do not balance capacity—balance the flow.

2   The level of utilization of a nonbottleneck resource is determined not by its own potential but by some other constraint in the system.

3   Utilization and activation of a resource are not the same.

4   An hour lost at a bottleneck is an hour lost for the entire system.

5   An hour saved at a nonbottleneck is a mirage.

6   Bottlenecks govern both throughput and inventory in the system.

7   The transfer batch may not and many times should not be equal to the process batch.

8   A process batch should be variable both along its route and in time.

9   Priorities can be set only by examining the system's constraints. Lead time is a derivative of the schedule.

Goldratt's Theory of Constraints (TOC)

exhibit 20.2

1   Identify the system constraints. (No improvement is possible unless the constraint or weakest link is found.)

2   Decide how to exploit the system constraints. (Make the constraints as effective as possible.)

3   Subordinate everything else to that decision. (Align every other part of the system to support the constraints even if this reduces the efficiency of nonconstraint resources.)

4   Elevate the system constraints. (If output is still inadequate, acquire more of this resource so it no longer is a constraint.)

5   If, in the previous steps, the constraints have been broken, go back to Step 1, but do not let inertia become the system constraint. (After this constraint problem is solved, go back to the beginning and start over. This is a continuous process of improvement: identifying constraints, breaking them, and then identifying the new ones that result.)

The story of Herbie is an analogy to the problems facing plant manager Alex Rogo and comes from a best-selling novel, *The Goal,* by Dr. Eli Goldratt.[1] Around 1980, Goldratt contended that manufacturers were not doing a good job in scheduling and in controlling their resources and inventories. To solve this problem, Goldratt and his associates at a company named Creative Output developed software that scheduled jobs through manufacturing processes, taking into account limited facilities, machines, personnel, tools, materials, and any other constraints that would affect a firm's ability to adhere to a schedule.

This was called *optimized production technology (OPT).* The schedules were feasible and accurate and could be run on a computer in a fraction of the time needed by an MRP system. This was because the scheduling logic was based on the separation of bottleneck and nonbottleneck operations. To explain the principles behind the OPT scheduling logic, Goldratt described nine production scheduling rules (see Exhibit 20.1). After approximately 100 large firms had installed this software, Goldratt went on to promote the logic of the approach rather than the software.

In broadening his scope, Goldratt developed his "Theory of Constraints" (TOC), which has become popular as a problem-solving approach that can be applied to many business areas. Exhibit 20.2 lists the "Five Focusing Steps of TOC." His Goldratt Institute (http://www.goldratt.com) teaches courses in improving production, distribution, and project management. The common thread through all of these courses is Goldratt's TOC concepts.

Before we go into detail on the theory of constraints, it is useful to compare it with two other popular approaches to continuous improvement: Six Sigma and lean manufacturing. Both Six Sigma and lean approaches focus on cost reduction through the elimination of waste and reduction of variability at every step in a process or component of a system. In contrast, the TOC five-step approach is more focused in its application. It concentrates its improvement efforts only on the operation that is constraining a critical process or on the weakest component that is limiting the performance of the system as a whole. If these elements are effectively managed, then it follows that better overall performance of the system relative to its goal is more likely to be achieved.

In this chapter, we focus on Goldratt's approach to manufacturing. To correctly treat the topic, we decided to approach it in the same way that Goldratt did: that is, first defining some basic issues about firms—purposes, goals, and performance measures—and then dealing with scheduling, providing buffer inventories, the influences of quality, and the interactions with marketing and accounting.

Synchronous manufacturing

Underlying Goldratt's work is the notion of synchronous manufacturing, which refers to the entire production process working in harmony to achieve the profit goal of the firm. When manufacturing is truly synchronized, its emphasis is on total system performance, not on localized measures such as labor or machine utilization.

GOAL OF THE FIRM

Goldratt has a very straightforward idea of the goal of a firm:

THE GOAL OF A FIRM IS TO MAKE MONEY.

Goldratt argues that although an organization may have many purposes—providing jobs, consuming raw materials, increasing sales, increasing share of the market, developing technology, or producing high-quality products—these do not guarantee long-term survival of the firm. They are means to achieve the goal, not the goal itself. If the firm makes money—and only then—it will prosper. When a firm has money, it can place more emphasis on other objectives.

PERFORMANCE MEASUREMENTS

To adequately measure a firm's performance, two sets of measurements must be used: one from the financial point of view and the other from the operations point of view.

FINANCIAL MEASUREMENTS
We have three measures of the firm's ability to make money:

1. *Net profit*—an absolute measurement in dollars.
2. *Return on investment*—a relative measure based on investment.
3. *Cash flow*—a survival measurement.

All three measurements must be used together. For example, a *net profit* of $10 million is important as one measurement, but it has no real meaning until we know how much investment was needed to generate that $10 million. If the investment was $100 million, this is a 10 percent *return on investment*. *Cash flow* is important because cash is necessary to pay bills for day-to-day operations; without cash, a firm can go bankrupt even though it is very sound in normal accounting terms. A firm can have a high profit and a high return on investment but still be short on cash if, for example, profit is invested in new equipment or tied up in inventory.

OPERATIONAL MEASUREMENTS
Financial measurements work well at the higher level, but they cannot be used at the operational level. We need another set of measurements that will give us guidance:

Throughput
Inventory

1. Throughput—the rate at which money is generated by the system through sales.
2. Inventory—all the money that the system has invested in purchasing things it intends to sell.

Operational Goal

exhibit 20.3

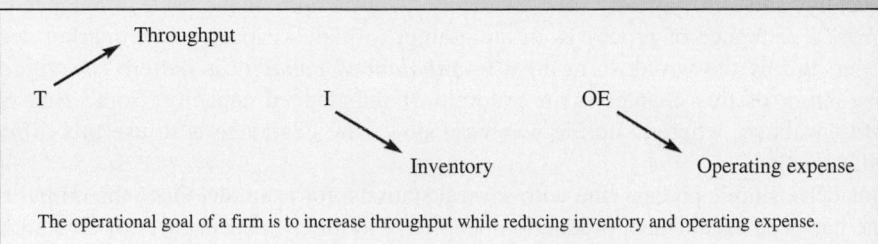

The operational goal of a firm is to increase throughput while reducing inventory and operating expense.

3. **Operating expenses**—all the money that the system spends to turn inventory into throughput.

Operating expenses

Throughput is specifically defined as goods *sold*. An inventory of finished goods is not throughput, but inventory. Actual sales must occur. It is specifically defined this way to prevent the system from continuing to produce under the illusion that the goods *might* be sold. Such action simply increases costs, builds inventory, and consumes cash. Inventory that is carried (whether work-in-process or finished goods) is valued only at the cost of the materials it contains. Labor cost and machine hours are ignored. (In traditional accounting terms, money spent is called *value added*.)

Although this is often an arguable point, using only the raw material cost is a conservative view. When the value-added method (which includes all costs of production) is used, inventory is inflated and presents some serious income and balance sheet problems. Consider, for example, work-in-process or finished goods inventory that has become obsolete, or for which a contract was canceled. A management decision to declare large amounts of inventory as scrap is difficult because it is often carried on the books as an asset even though it may really have no value. Using just raw materials cost also avoids the problem of determining which costs are direct and which are indirect.

Operating expenses include production costs (such as direct labor, indirect labor, inventory carrying costs, equipment depreciation, and materials and supplies used in production) and administrative costs. The key difference here is that there is no need to separate direct and indirect labor.

As shown in Exhibit 20.3, the objective of a firm is to treat all three measurements simultaneously and continually; this achieves the goal of making money.

From an operations standpoint, the goal of the firm is to

INCREASE THROUGHPUT WHILE SIMULTANEOUSLY REDUCING
INVENTORY AND REDUCING OPERATING EXPENSE.

PRODUCTIVITY

Typically, **productivity** is measured in terms of output per labor hour. However, this measurement does not ensure that the firm will make money (for example, when extra output is not sold but accumulates as inventory). To test whether productivity has increased, we should ask these questions: Has the action taken increased throughput? Has it decreased inventory? Has it decreased operational expense? This leads us to a new definition:

Productivity

PRODUCTIVITY IS ALL THE ACTIONS THAT BRING A COMPANY
CLOSER TO ITS GOALS.

UNBALANCED CAPACITY

Historically (and still typically in most firms) manufacturers have tried to balance capacity across a sequence of processes in an attempt to match capacity with market demand. However, this is the wrong thing to do—*unbalanced capacity* is better. The vignette at the beginning of this chapter is an example of unbalanced capacity. Some Boy Scouts were fast walkers, whereas Herbie was very slow. The challenge is to use this difference advantageously.

Consider a simple process line with several stations, for example. Once the output rate of the line has been established, production people try to make the capacities of all stations the same. This is done by adjusting machines or equipment used, workloads, skill and type of labor assigned, tools used, overtime budgeted, and so on.

In synchronous manufacturing thinking, however, making all capacities the same is viewed as a bad decision. Such a balance would be possible only if the output times of all stations were constant or had a very narrow distribution. A normal variation in output times causes downstream stations to have idle time when upstream stations take longer to process. Conversely, when upstream stations process in a shorter time, inventory builds up between the stations. The effect of the statistical variation is cumulative. The only way that this variation can be smoothed is by increasing work-in-process to absorb the variation (a bad choice because we should be trying to reduce work-in-process) or increasing capacities downstream to be able to make up for the longer upstream times. The rule here is that capacities within the process sequence should not be balanced to the same levels. Rather, attempts should be made to balance the flow of product through the system. When flow is balanced, capacities are unbalanced. This idea is further explained in the next section.

DEPENDENT EVENTS AND STATISTICAL FLUCTUATIONS

The term *dependent events* refers to a process sequence. If a process flows from A to B to C to D, and each process must be completed before passing on to the next step, then B, C, and D are dependent events. The ability to do the next process is dependent on the preceding one.

Statistical fluctuation refers to the normal variation about a mean or average. When statistical fluctuations occur in a dependent sequence without any inventory between workstations, there is no opportunity to achieve the average output. When one process takes longer than the average, the next process cannot make up the time. We follow through an example of this to show what could happen.

Suppose that we wanted to process five items that could come from the two distributions in Exhibit 20.4. The processing sequence is from A to B with no space for inventory in between. Process A has a mean of 10 hours and a standard deviation of 2 hours. This means that we would expect 95.5 percent of the processing time to be between 6 hours and 14 hours (plus or minus 2 sigma). Process B has a constant processing time of 10 hours.

We see that the last item was completed in 66 hours, for an average of 13.2 hours per item, although the expected time of completion was 60, for an average of 12 hours per item (taking into account the waiting time for the first unit by Process B).

Suppose we reverse the processes—B feeds A. To illustrate the possible delays, we also reverse A's performance times. (See Exhibit 20.5.) Again, the completion time of the last item is greater than the average (13.2 hours rather than 12 hours). Process A and Process B have the same average performance time of 10 hours, and yet performance is late. In neither case could we achieve the expected average output rate. Why? Because the time lost when the second process is idle cannot be made up.

This example is intended to challenge the theory that capacities should be balanced to an average time. *Rather than capacities being balanced, the flow of product through the system should be balanced.*

Processing and Completion Times, Process A to Process B

exhibit 20.4

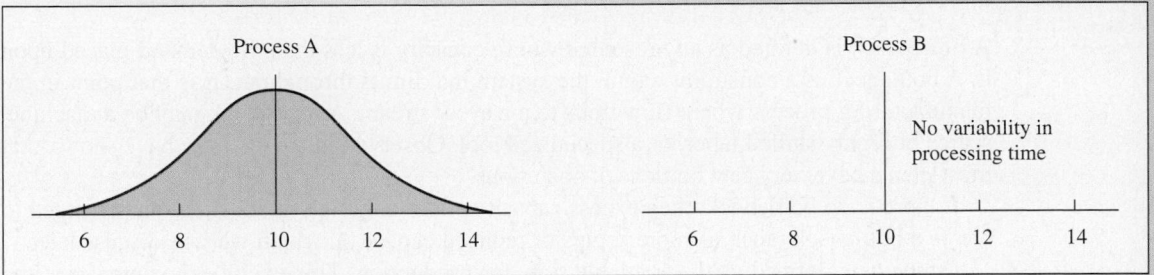

ITEM NUMBER	START TIME	PROCESSING TIME	FINISH TIME
1	0 hrs	14 hrs	14 hrs
2	14	12	26
3	26	10	36
4	36	8	44
5	44	6	50
	Average = 10 hours		

ITEM NUMBER	START TIME	PROCESSING TIME	FINISH TIME
1	14 hrs	10 hrs	24 hrs
2	26	10	36
3	36	10	46
4	46	10	56
5	56	10	66
	Average = 10 hours		

Here the flow is from Process A to Process B. Process A has a mean of 10 hours and a standard deviation of 2 hours; Process B has a constant 10-hour processing time.

Processing and Completion Times, Process B to Process A

exhibit 20.5

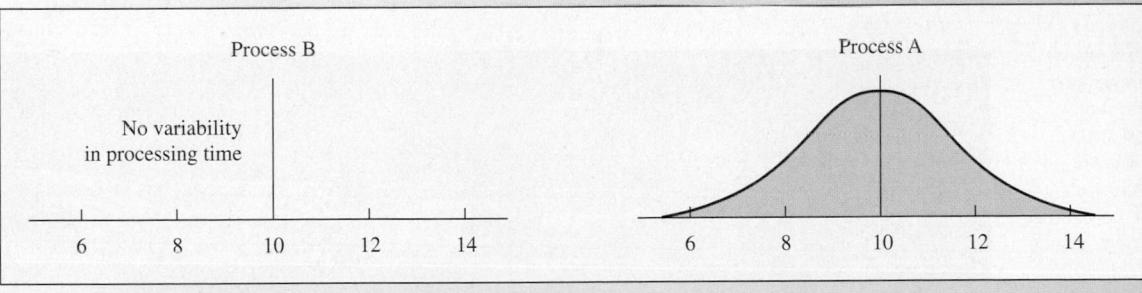

ITEM NUMBER	START TIME	PROCESSING TIME	FINISH TIME
1	0 hrs	10 hrs	10 hrs
2	10	10	20
3	20	10	30
4	30	10	40
5	40	10	50
	Average = 10 hours		

ITEM NUMBER	START TIME	PROCESSING TIME	FINISH TIME
1	10 hrs	6 hrs	16 hrs
2	20	8	28
3	30	10	40
4	40	12	52
5	52	14	66
	Average = 10 hours		

This is similar to Exhibit 20.4. However, the processing sequence has been reversed as well as the order of Process A's times.

BOTTLENECKS AND CAPACITY-CONSTRAINED RESOURCES

Bottleneck

A **bottleneck** is defined as any resource whose capacity is less than the demand placed upon it. A bottleneck is a constraint within the system that limits throughput. It is that point in the manufacturing process where flow thins to a narrow stream. A bottleneck may be a machine, scarce or highly skilled labor, or a specialized tool. Observations in industry have shown that most plants have very few bottleneck operations.

If there is no bottleneck, then excess capacity exists and the system should be changed to create a bottleneck (such as more setups or reduced capacity), which we will discuss later.

Nonbottleneck

Capacity is defined as the available time for production. This excludes maintenance and other downtime. A **nonbottleneck** is any resource whose capacity is greater than the demand placed on it. A nonbottleneck, therefore, should not be working constantly because it can produce more than is needed. A nonbottleneck contains idle time.

Capacity-constrained resource (CCR)

A **capacity-constrained resource (CCR)** is one whose utilization is close to capacity and could be a bottleneck if it is not scheduled carefully. For example, a CCR may be receiving work in a job-shop environment from several sources. If these sources schedule their flow in a way that causes occasional idle time for the CCR in excess of its unused capacity time, the CCR becomes a bottleneck when the surge of work arrives at a later time. This can happen if batch sizes are changed or if one of the upstream operations is not working for some reason and does not feed enough work to the CCR.

BASIC MANUFACTURING BUILDING BLOCKS

All manufacturing processes and flows can be simplified to four basic configurations, as shown in Exhibit 20.6. In Exhibit 20.6A, product that flows through Process X feeds into Process Y. In B, Y is feeding X. In C, Process X and Process Y are creating subassemblies, which are then combined, say, to feed the market demand. In D, Process X and Process Y are independent of each other and are supplying their own markets. The last column in the exhibit shows possible sequences of nonbottleneck resources, which can be grouped and displayed as Y to simplify the representation.

IN HIGHLY AUTOMATED PROCESS INDUSTRIES, INVENTORY AND THROUGHPUT ARE ALSO MONITORED WITH AUTOMATED SYSTEMS SUCH AS THIS CONTROL ROOM AT U.S. STEEL'S COLD REDUCTION MILL. ALL OPERATIONS FROM THE BLAST FURNACE THROUGH FINISHED ITEMS ARE CONTROLLED HERE, INCLUDING THE SPEED OF PROCESSING AT EACH STAGE.

The Basic Building Blocks of Manufacturing Derived by Grouping Process Flows

exhibit 20.6

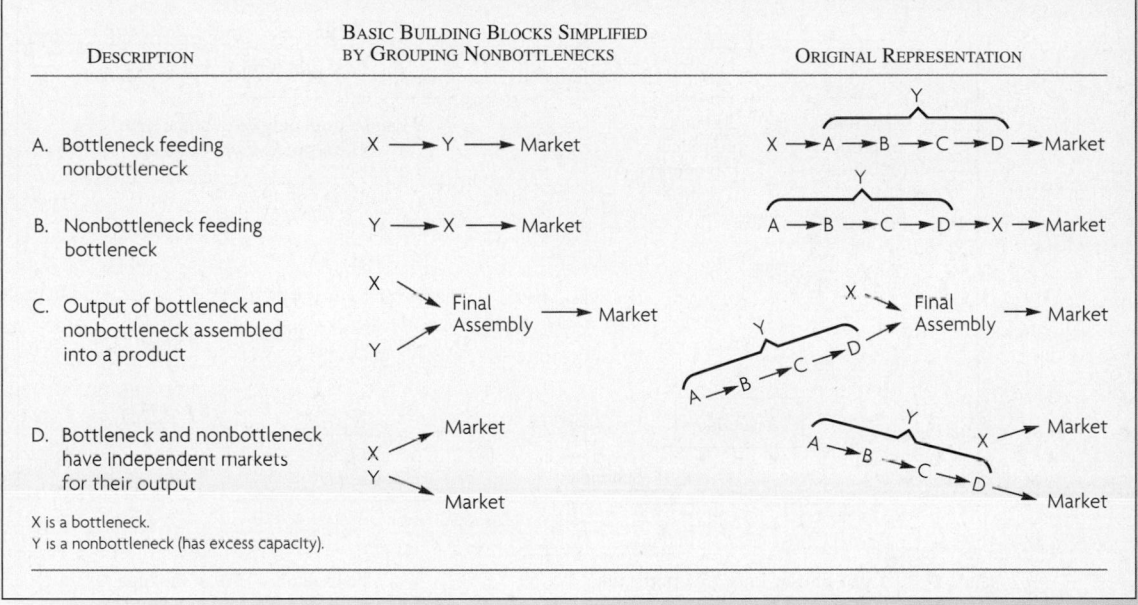

The value in using these basic building blocks is that a production process can be greatly simplified for analysis and control. Rather than track and schedule all of the steps in a production sequence through nonbottleneck operations, for example, attention can be placed at the beginning and end points of the building block groupings.

METHODS FOR CONTROL

Exhibit 20.7 shows how bottleneck and nonbottleneck resources should be managed.

Resource X and Resource Y are work centers that can produce a variety of products. Each of these work centers has 200 hours available per month. For simplicity, assume that we are dealing with only one product and we will alter the conditions and makeup for four different situations. Each unit of X takes one hour of production time, and the market demand is 200 units per month. Each unit of Y takes 45 minutes of production time, and the market demand is also 200 units per month.

Exhibit 20.7A shows a bottleneck feeding a nonbottleneck. Product flows from Work Center X to Work Center Y. X is the bottleneck because it has a capacity of 200 units (200 hours/1 hour per unit) and Y has a capacity of 267 units (200 hours/45 minutes per unit). Because Y has to wait for X and Y has a higher capacity than X, no extra product accumulates in the system. It all flows through to the market.

Exhibit 20.7B is the reverse of A, with Y feeding X. This is a nonbottleneck feeding a bottleneck. Because Y has a capacity of 267 units and X has a capacity of only 200 units, we should produce only 200 units of Y (75 percent of capacity) or else work-in-process will accumulate in front of X.

Exhibit 20.7C shows that the products produced by X and Y are assembled and then sold to the market. Because one unit from X and one unit from Y form an assembly, X is the bottleneck with 200 units of capacity and, therefore, Y should not work more than 75 percent or else extra parts will accumulate.

In Exhibit 20.7D, equal quantities of product from X and Y are demanded by the market. In this case we can call these products "finished goods" because they face independent

exhibit 20.7   Product Flow through Bottlenecks and Nonbottlenecks

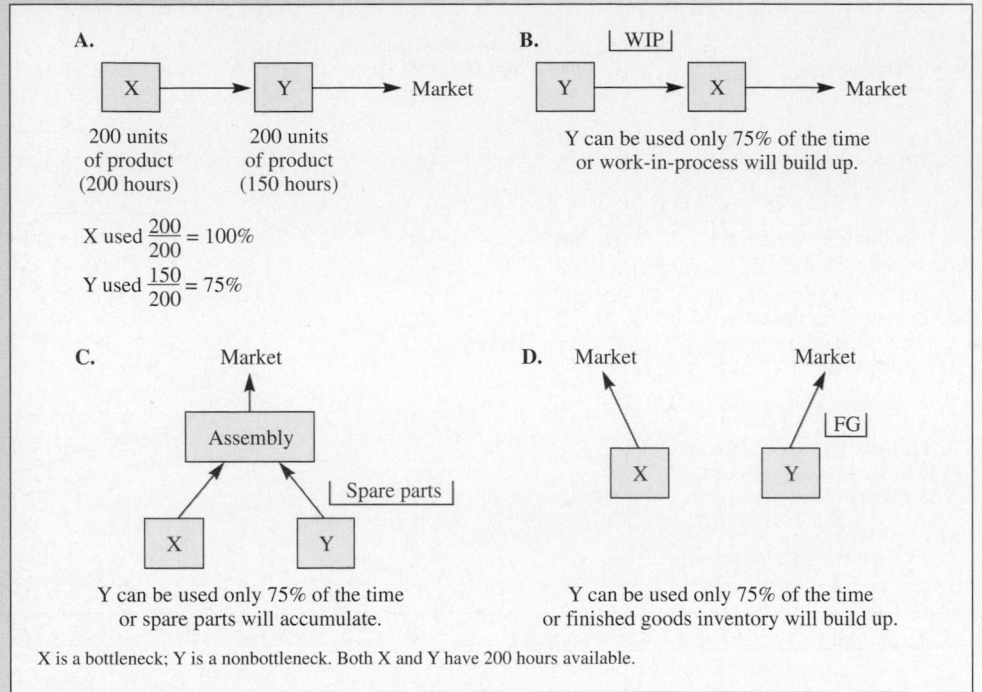

A.

X → Y → Market

200 units
of product
(200 hours)

200 units
of product
(150 hours)

X used $\frac{200}{200} = 100\%$

Y used $\frac{150}{200} = 75\%$

B. |WIP|

Y → X → Market

Y can be used only 75% of the time
or work-in-process will build up.

C. Market

Assembly

|Spare parts|

X   Y

Y can be used only 75% of the time
or spare parts will accumulate.

D. Market   Market

|FG|

X   Y

Y can be used only 75% of the time
or finished goods inventory will build up.

X is a bottleneck; Y is a nonbottleneck. Both X and Y have 200 hours available.

demands. Here Y has access to material independent of X and, with a higher capacity than needed to satisfy the market, it can produce more product than the market will take. However, this would create an inventory of unneeded finished goods.

The four situations just discussed demonstrate bottleneck and nonbottleneck resources and their relationships to production and market demand. They show that the industry practice of using resource utilization as a measure of performance can encourage the overuse of non-bottlenecks and result in excess inventories.

TIME COMPONENTS
The following kinds of time make up production cycle time:

1. *Setup time*—the time that a part spends waiting for a resource to be set up to work on this same part.
2. *Processing time*—the time that the part is being processed.
3. *Queue time*—the time that a part waits for a resource while the resource is busy with something else.
4. *Wait time*—the time that a part waits not for a resource but for another part so that they can be assembled together.
5. *Idle time*—the unused time, that is, the cycle time less the sum of the setup time, processing time, queue time, and wait time.

For a part waiting to go through a bottleneck, queue time is the greatest. As we discuss later in this chapter, this is because the bottleneck has a fairly large amount of work to do in front of it (to make sure that it is always working). For a nonbottleneck, wait time is the greatest. The part is just sitting there waiting for the arrival of other parts so that an assembly can take place.

Schedulers are tempted to save setup times. Suppose that the batch sizes are doubled to save half the setup times. Then, with a double batch size, all of the other times (processing time, queue time, and wait time) increase twofold. Because these times are doubled while saving only half of the setup time, the net result is that the work-in-process is approximately doubled, as is the investment in inventory.

FINDING THE BOTTLENECK

There are two ways to find the bottleneck (or bottlenecks) in a system. One is to run a capacity resource profile; the other is to use our knowledge of the particular plant, look at the system in operation, and talk with supervisors and workers.

A capacity resource profile is obtained by looking at the loads placed on each resource by the products that are scheduled through them. In running a capacity profile, we assume that the data are reasonably accurate, although not necessarily perfect. As an example, consider that products have been routed through Resources M1 through M5. Suppose that our first computation of the resource loads on each resource caused by these products shows the following:

M1	130 percent of capacity
M2	120 percent of capacity
M3	105 percent of capacity
M4	95 percent of capacity
M5	85 percent of capacity

For this first analysis, we can disregard any resources at lower percentages because they are nonbottlenecks and should not be a problem. With this list in hand, we should physically go to the facility and check all five operations. Note that M1, M2, and M3 are overloaded; that is, they are scheduled above their capacities. We would expect to see large quantities of inventory in front of M1. If this is not the case, errors must exist somewhere—perhaps in the bill of materials or in the routing sheets. Let's say that our observations and discussions with shop personnel showed that there were errors in M1, M2, M3, and M4. We tracked them down, made the appropriate corrections, and ran the capacity profile again:

M2	115 percent of capacity
M1	110 percent of capacity
M3	105 percent of capacity
M4	90 percent of capacity
M5	85 percent of capacity

M1, M2, and M3 are still showing a lack of sufficient capacity, but M2 is the most serious. If we now have confidence in our numbers, we use M2 as our bottleneck. If the data contain too many errors for a reliable data analysis, it may not be worth spending time (it could take months) making all the corrections.

SAVING TIME

Recall that a bottleneck is a resource whose capacity is less than the demand placed on it. Because we focus on bottlenecks as restricting *throughput* (defined as *sales*), a bottleneck's capacity is less than the market demand. There are a number of ways we can save time on a bottleneck (better tooling, higher-quality labor, larger batch sizes, reduction in setup times, and so forth), but how valuable is the extra time? Very, very valuable!

> AN HOUR SAVED AT THE BOTTLENECK ADDS AN EXTRA HOUR TO THE ENTIRE PRODUCTION SYSTEM.

How about time saved on a nonbottleneck resource?

> AN HOUR SAVED AT A NONBOTTLENECK IS A MIRAGE AND ONLY ADDS AN HOUR TO ITS IDLE TIME.

exhibit 20.8   Nonbottleneck Resources

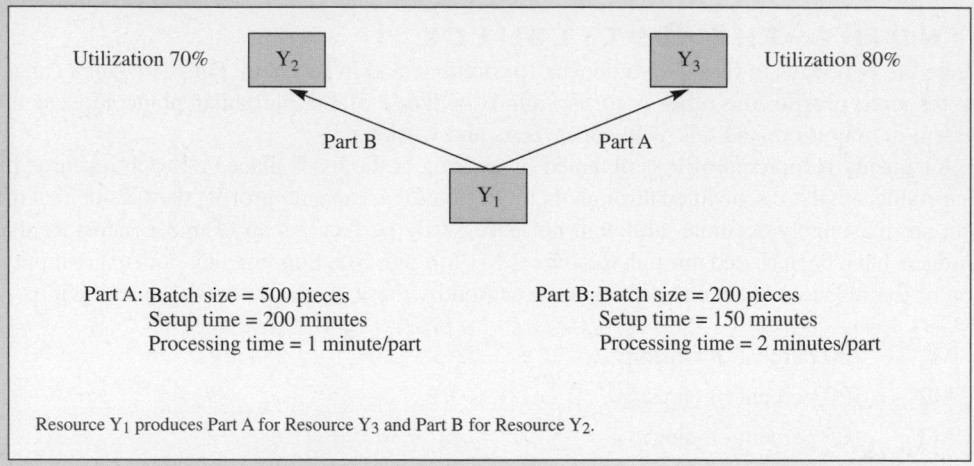

Part A: Batch size = 500 pieces
Setup time = 200 minutes
Processing time = 1 minute/part

Part B: Batch size = 200 pieces
Setup time = 150 minutes
Processing time = 2 minutes/part

Resource Y_1 produces Part A for Resource Y_3 and Part B for Resource Y_2.

Because a nonbottleneck has more capacity than the system needs for its current through-put, it already contains idle time. Implementing any measures to save more time does not increase throughput but only serves to increase its idle time.

AVOID CHANGING A NONBOTTLENECK INTO A BOTTLENECK

When nonbottleneck resources are scheduled with larger batch sizes, this action could create a bottleneck that we certainly would want to avoid. Consider the case in Exhibit 20.8, where Y_1, Y_2, and Y_3 are nonbottleneck resources. Y_1 currently produces Part A, which is routed to Y_3, and Part B, which is routed to Y_2. To produce Part A, Y_1 has a 200-minute setup time and a processing time of 1 minute per part. Part A is currently produced in batches of 500 units. To produce Part B, Y_1 has a setup time of 150 minutes and 2 minutes' processing time per part. Part B is currently produced in batches of 200 units. With this sequence, Y_2 is utilized 70 percent of the time and Y_3 is utilized 80 percent of the time.

Because setup time is 200 minutes for Y_1 on Part A, both worker and supervisor mistak-enly believe that more production can be gained if fewer setups are made. Let's assume that the batch size is increased to 1,500 units and see what happens. The illusion is that we have saved 400 minutes of setup. (Instead of three setups taking 600 minutes to produce three batches of 500 units each, there is just one setup with a 1,500-unit batch.)

The problem is that the 400 minutes saved served no purpose, but this delay did interfere with the production of Part B because Y_1 produces Part B for Y_2. The sequence before any changes were made was Part A (700 minutes), Part B (550 minutes), Part A (700 minutes), Part B (550 minutes), and so on. Now, however, when the Part A batch is increased to 1,500 units (1,700 minutes), Y_2 and Y_3 could well be starved for work and have to wait more time than they have available (30 percent idle time for Y_2 and 20 percent for Y_3). The new sequence would be Part A (1,700 minutes), Part B (1,350 minutes), and so on. Such an extended wait for Y_2 and Y_3 could be disruptive. Y_2 and Y_3 could become temporary bottlenecks and lose throughput for the system.

DRUM, BUFFER, ROPE

Every production system needs some control point or points to control the flow of product through the system. If the system contains a bottleneck, the bottleneck is the best place for control. This control point is called the *drum* because it strikes the beat that the rest of the system (or those parts that it influences) uses to function. Recall that a *bottleneck* is defined

Linear Flow of Product with a Bottleneck

exhibit 20.9

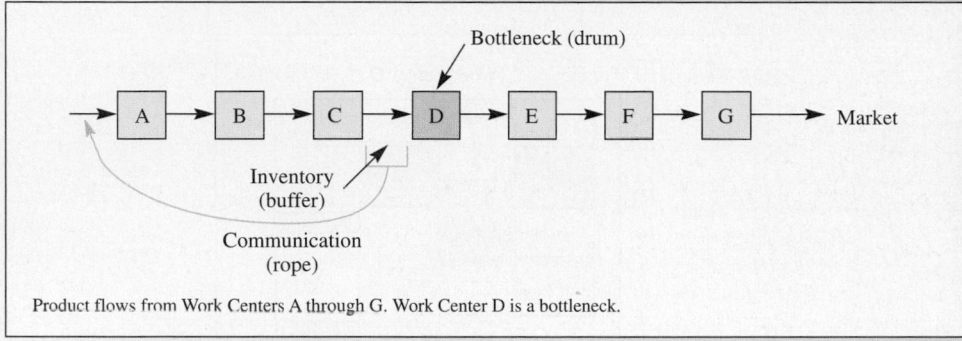

Product flows from Work Centers A through G. Work Center D is a bottleneck.

as a resource that does not have the capacity to meet demand. Therefore, a bottleneck is working all the time, and one reason for using it as a control point is to make sure that the operations upstream do not overproduce and build up excess work-in-process inventory that the bottleneck cannot handle.

If there is no bottleneck, the next-best place to set the drum would be a capacity-constrained resource (CCR). A capacity-constrained resource, remember, is one that is operating near capacity but, on the average, has adequate capability as long as it is not incorrectly scheduled (for example, with too many setups, causing it to run short of capacity, or producing too large a lot size, thereby starving downstream operations).

If neither a bottleneck nor a CCR is present, the control point can be designated anywhere. The best position would generally be at some divergent point where the output of the resource is used in several downstream operations.

Dealing with the bottleneck is most critical, and our discussion focuses on ensuring that the bottleneck always has work to do. Exhibit 20.9 shows a simple linear flow A through G. Suppose that Resource D, which is a machine center, is a bottleneck. This means that the capacities are greater both upstream and downstream from it. If this sequence is not controlled, we would expect to see a large amount of inventory in front of Work Center D and very little anywhere else. There would be little finished goods inventory because (by the definition of the term *bottleneck*) all the product produced would be taken by the market.

There are two things that we must do with this bottleneck:

1. Keep a *buffer* inventory in front of it to make sure that it always has something to work on. Because it is a bottleneck, its output determines the throughput of the system.
2. Communicate back upstream to A what D has produced so that A provides only that amount. This keeps inventory from building up. This communication is called the *rope*. It can be formal (such as a schedule) or informal (such as daily discussion).

The buffer inventory in front of a bottleneck operation is a *time buffer*. We want to make sure that Work Center D always has work to do, and it does not matter which of the scheduled products are worked on. We might, for example, provide 96 hours of inventory in the buffer as shown in the sequence A through P in Exhibit 20.10. Jobs A through about half of E are scheduled during the 24 hours of Day 1; Jobs E through a portion of Job I are scheduled during the second 24-hour day; Jobs I through part of L are scheduled during the third 24-hour day; and Jobs L through P are scheduled during the fourth 24-hour day, for a total of 96 hours. This means that through normal variation, or if something happens upstream and the output has been temporarily stalled, D can work for another 96 hours, protecting the throughput. (The 96 hours of work, incidentally, include setups and processing times contained in the job sheets, which usually are based on engineering standard times.)

exhibit 20.10   Capacity Profile of Work Center D (Showing Assigned Jobs A through P over a Period of Four 24-Hour Days)

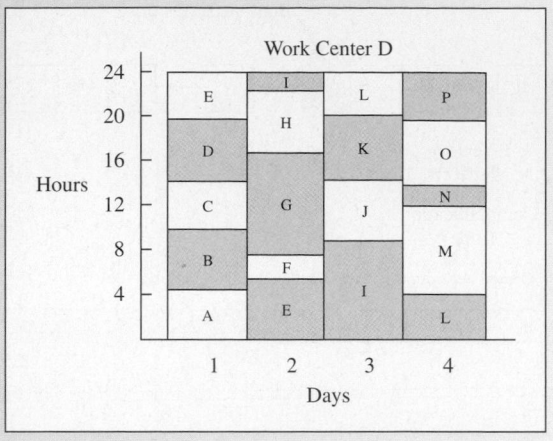

exhibit 20.11   Linear Flow of Product with a Capacity-Constrained Resource

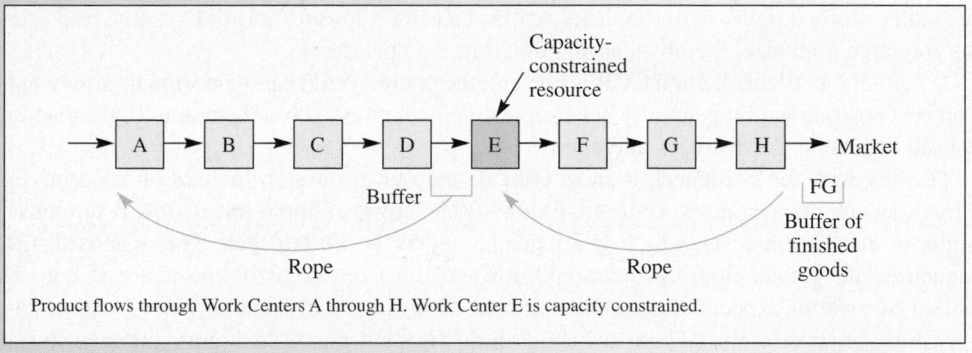

Product flows through Work Centers A through H. Work Center E is capacity constrained.

We might ask, How large should the time buffer be? The answer: As large as it needs to be to ensure that the bottleneck continues to work. By examining the variation of each operation, we can make a guess. Theoretically, the size of the buffer can be computed statistically by examining past performance data, or the sequence can be simulated. In any event, precision is not critical. We could start with an estimate of the time buffer as one-fourth of the total lead time of the system. Say, the sequence A to G in our example (Exhibit 20.9) took a total of 16 days. We could start with a buffer of four days in front of D. If, during the next few days or weeks, the buffer runs out, we need to increase the buffer size. We do this by releasing extra material to the first operation, A. On the other hand, if we find that our buffer never drops below three days, we might want to hold back releases to A and reduce the time buffer to three days. Experience is the best determination of the final buffer size.

If the drum is not a bottleneck but a CCR (and thus it can have a small amount of idle time), we might want to create two buffer inventories: one in front of the CCR and the second at the end as finished goods. (See Exhibit 20.11.) The finished-goods inventory protects the market, and the time buffer in front of the CCR protects throughput. For this CCR case, the market cannot take all that we can produce, so we want to ensure that finished goods are available when the market does decide to purchase.

Network Flow with One Bottleneck

exhibit 20.12

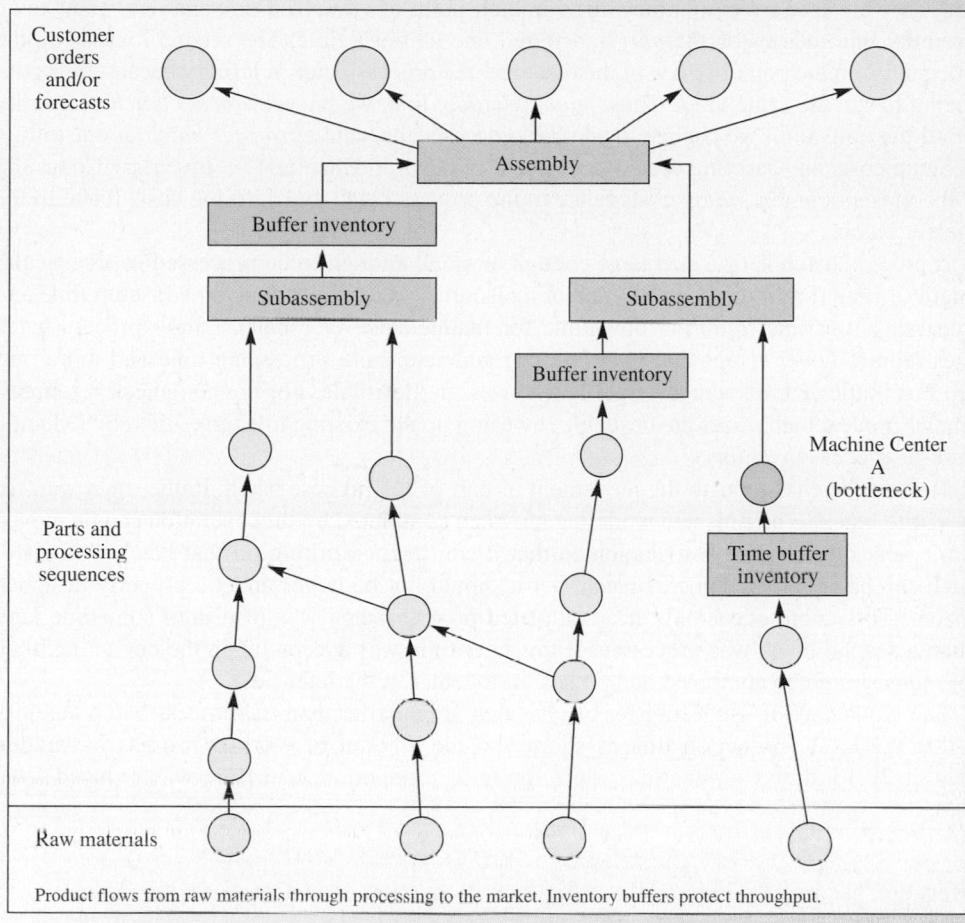

Product flows from raw materials through processing to the market. Inventory buffers protect throughput.

We need two ropes in this case: (1) a rope communicating from finished-goods inventory back to the drum to increase or decrease output and (2) a rope from the drum back to the material release point, specifying how much material is needed.

Exhibit 20.12 is a more detailed network flow showing one bottleneck. Inventory is provided not only in front of that bottleneck but also after the nonbottleneck sequence of processes that feed the subassembly. This ensures that the flow of product is not slowed down by having to wait after it leaves the bottleneck.

IMPORTANCE OF QUALITY

An MRP system allows for rejects by building a larger batch than actually needed. A JIT system cannot tolerate poor quality because JIT success is based on a balanced capacity. A defective part or component can cause a JIT system to shut down, thereby losing throughput of the total system. Synchronous manufacturing, however, has excess capacity throughout the system, except for the bottleneck. If a bad part is produced upstream of the bottleneck, the result is that there is a loss of material only. Because of the excess capacity, there is still time to do another operation to replace the one just scrapped. For the bottleneck, however, extra time does not exist, so there should be a quality control inspection just prior to the bottleneck to ensure that the bottleneck works only on good product. Also, there needs to be assurance downstream from the bottleneck that the passing product is not scrapped—that would mean lost throughput.

BATCH SIZES

In an assembly line, what is the batch size? Some would say "one" because one unit is moved at a time; others would say "infinity" because the line continues to produce the same item. Both answers are correct, but they differ in their point of view. The first answer, "one," in an assembly line focuses on the *part* transferred one unit at a time. The second focuses on the *process*. From the point of view of the resource, the process batch is infinity because it is continuing to run the same units. Thus, in an assembly line, we have a *process batch* of infinity (or all the units until we change to another process setup) and a *transfer batch* of one unit.

Setup costs and carrying costs were treated in depth in Chapter 17 ("Inventory Control"). In the present context, setup costs relate to the process batch and carrying costs relate to the transfer batch.

A process batch is of a size large enough or small enough to be processed in a particular length of time. From the point of view of a resource, two times are involved: setup time and processing run time (ignoring downtime for maintenance or repair). Larger process batch sizes require fewer setups and therefore can generate more processing time and more output. For bottleneck resources, larger batch sizes are desirable. For nonbottleneck resources, smaller process batch sizes are desirable (by using up the existing idle time), thereby reducing work-in-process inventory.

Transfer batches refer to the movement of part of the process batch. Rather than wait for the entire batch to be finished, work that has been completed by that operation can be moved to the next downstream workstation so that it can begin working on that batch. A transfer batch can be equal to a process batch, but it should not be larger under a properly designed system. This could occur only if a completed process batch was held until sometime later when a second batch was processed. If this later time was acceptable in the beginning, then both jobs should be combined and processed together at the later time.

The advantage of using transfer batches that are smaller than the process batch quantity is that the total production time is shorter so the amount of work-in-process is smaller. Exhibit 20.13 shows a situation where the total production lead time was reduced from

exhibit 20.13   Effect of Changing the Process Batch Sizes on Production Lead Time for a Job Order of 1,000 Units

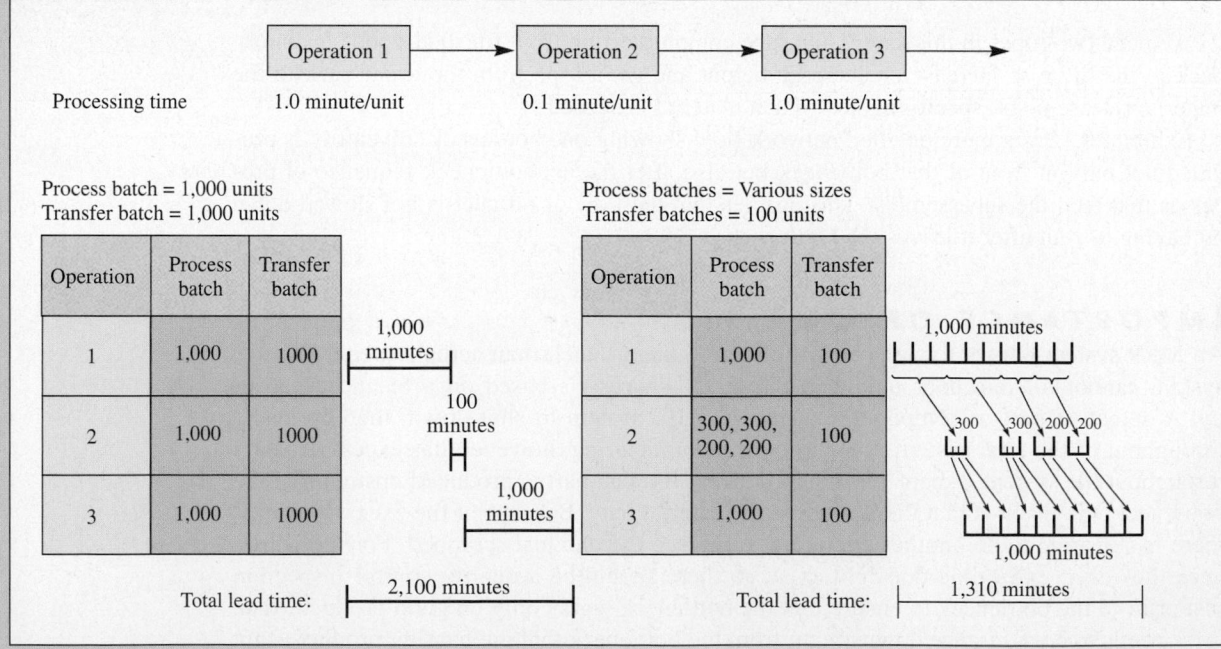

2,100 to 1,310 minutes by (1) using a transfer batch size of 100 rather than 1,000 and (2) reducing the process batch sizes of Operation 2.

How to Determine Process Batch and Transfer Batch Sizes   Logic would suggest that the master production schedule (however it was developed) be analyzed as to its effect on various work centers. In an MRP system, this means that the master production schedule should be run through the MRP and the CRP (capacity requirements planning program) to generate a detailed load on each work center. Srikanth states that from his experience, there are too many errors in the manufacturing database to do this.[2] He suggests using the alternative procedure of first identifying the probable CCRs and bottlenecks. There should be only one (or a few), and they should be reviewed by managers so that they understand which resources are actually controlling their plant. These resources set the drumbeat.

Rather than try to adjust the master production schedule to change resource loads, it is more practical to control the flow at each bottleneck or CCR to bring the capacities in line. The process batch sizes and transfer batch sizes are changed after comparing past performances in meeting due dates.

Smaller transfer batches give lower work-in-process inventory but faster product flow (and consequently shorter lead time). More material handling is required, however. Larger transfer batches give longer lead times and higher inventories, but there is less material handling. Therefore, the transfer batch size is determined by a trade-off of production lead times, inventory reduction benefits, and costs of material movement.

When trying to control the flow at CCRs and bottlenecks, there are four possible situations:

1. A bottleneck (no idle time) with no setup time required when changing from one product to another.
2. A bottleneck with setup time required to change from one product to another.
3. A capacity-constrained resource with a small amount of idle time, with no setup time required to change from one product to another.
4. A CCR with setup time required when changing from one product to another.

In the first case (a bottleneck with no setup time to change products), jobs should be processed in the order of the schedule so that delivery is on time. Without setups, only the sequence is important. In the second case, when setups are required, larger batch sizes combine separate similar jobs in the sequence. This means reaching ahead into future time periods. Some jobs will therefore be done early. Because this is a bottleneck resource, larger batches save setups and thereby increase throughput. (The setup time saved is used for processing.) The larger process batches may cause the early-scheduled jobs to be late. Therefore, frequent small transfer batches are necessary to try to shorten the lead time.

Situations 3 and 4 include a CCR without a setup and a CCR with setup time requirements. Handling the CCR would be similar to handling a nonbottleneck, though more carefully. That is, a CCR has some idle time. It would be appropriate here to cut the size of some of the process batches so that there can be more frequent changes of product. This would decrease lead time, and jobs would be more likely to be done on time. In a make-to-stock situation, cutting process batch sizes has a much more profound effect than increasing the number of transfer batches. This is because the resulting product mix is much greater, leading to reduced WIP and production lead time.

HOW TO TREAT INVENTORY

The traditional view of inventory is that its only negative impact on a firm's performance is its carrying cost. We now realize inventory's negative impact also comes from lengthening lead times and creating problems with engineering changes. (When an engineering change on a product comes through, which commonly occurs, product still within the production system often must be modified to include the changes. Therefore, less work-in-process reduces the number of engineering changes to be made.)

From a constraint management perspective, inventory is a loan given to the manufacturing unit. The value of the loan is based only on the purchased items that are part of the inventory. As we stated earlier, inventory is treated in this chapter as material cost only, without any accounting-type value added from production. If inventory is carried as a loan to manufacturing, we need a way to measure how long the loan is carried. One measurement is dollar days.

Dollar Days   A useful performance measurement is the concept of *dollar days,* a measurement of the value of inventory and the time it stays within an area. To use this measure, we could simply multiply the total value of inventory by the number of days inventory spends within a department.

Suppose Department X carries an average inventory of $40,000, and, on the average, the inventory stays within the department five days. In dollar days, Department X is charged with $40,000 times five days, or $200,000 dollar days of inventory. At this point, we cannot say the $200,000 is high or low, but it does show where the inventory is located. Management can then see where it should focus attention and determine acceptable levels. Techniques can be instituted to try to reduce the number of dollar days while being careful that such a measure does not become a local objective (that is, minimizing dollar days) and hurt the global objectives (such as increasing ROI, cash flow, and net profit).

Dollar days could be beneficial in a variety of ways. Consider the current practice of using efficiencies or equipment utilization as a performance measurement. To get high utilization, large amounts of inventory are held to keep everything working. However, high inventories would result in a high number of dollar days, which would discourage high levels of work-in-process. Dollar day measurements also could be used in other areas:

- Marketing—to discourage holding large amounts of finished-goods inventory. The net result would be to encourage sale of finished products.
- Purchasing—to discourage placing large purchase orders that on the surface appear to take advantage of quantity discounts. This would encourage just-in-time purchasing.
- Manufacturing—to discourage large work-in-process and producing earlier than needed. This would promote rapid flow of material within the plant.
- Project management—to quantify a project's limited resource investments as a function of time. This promotes the proper allocation of resources to competing projects. See the Breakthrough box on "Critical Chain Project Management" for Goldratt ideas for scheduling projects.

BREAKTHROUGH

CRITICAL CHAIN PROJECT MANAGEMENT

Critical Chain Project Management is the name of the approach that Eli Goldratt developed for scheduling and managing projects. The approach borrows many ideas from those used for manufacturing processes. The conventional critical path method was covered in Chapter 10, and Goldratt goes beyond those ideas by considering resource constraints and special time buffers in the project. The following are specific ideas included in his Critical Chain Project Management approach:

1 Schedules are level-loaded based on the limitations of available resources (constraints). This produces the "critical chain"—the longest set of sequential tasks (due to both task dependency and resource contention)—which dictates the shortest overall project duration.

2 Time buffers are inserted at strategic locations in the plan—at the end of the critical chain and at every point where a task interests the critical chain—to absorb the adverse effects of uncertainty without damaging performance. To create the buffers, some of the slack time built into tasks in planning is repositioned to these strategic locations.

3 Projects are "pipelined" or staged based on resource availability to combat the cascade effect of shared resources across projects and create viable multiproject plans.

4 Buffer management is used to dynamically set task priorities in execution. As uncertainty changes the original plan, tasks are prioritized based on the buffer burn rate (the amount of buffer consumed versus the percentage of the work complete). Tasks with critical buffer penetration take precedence over those with lower burn rates.

Learn more about Critical Chain Project Management at http://www.tocc.com.

COMPARING SYNCHRONOUS MANUFACTURING TO MRP AND JIT

MRP uses *backward scheduling* after having been fed a master production schedule. MRP schedules production through a bill of materials explosion in a backward manner—working backward in time from the desired completion date. As a secondary procedure, MRP, through its capacity resource planning module, develops capacity utilization profiles of work centers. When work centers are overloaded, either the master production schedule must be adjusted or enough slack capacity must be left unscheduled in the system so that work can be smoothed at the local level (by work center supervisors or the workers themselves). Trying to smooth capacity using MRP is so difficult and would require so many computer runs that capacity overloads and underloads are best left to local decisions, such as at the machine centers. An MRP schedule becomes invalid just days after it was created.

The synchronous manufacturing approach uses *forward scheduling* because it focuses on the critical resources. These are scheduled forward in time, ensuring that loads placed on them are within capacity. The noncritical (or nonbottleneck) resources are then scheduled to support the critical resources. (This can be done backward to minimize the length of time that inventories are held.) This procedure ensures a feasible schedule. To help reduce lead time and work-in-process, in synchronous manufacturing the process batch size and transfer batch size are varied—a procedure that MRP is not able to do.

Comparing JIT to synchronous manufacturing, JIT does an excellent job in reducing lead times and work-in-process, but it has several drawbacks:

1. JIT is limited to repetitive manufacturing.
2. JIT requires a stable production level (usually about a month long).
3. JIT does not allow very much flexibility in the products produced. (Products must be similar with a limited number of options.)
4. JIT still requires work-in-process when used with kanban so that there is "something to pull." This means that completed work must be stored on the downstream side of each workstation to be pulled by the next workstation.
5. Vendors need to be located nearby because the system depends on smaller, more frequent deliveries.

Because synchronous manufacturing uses a schedule to assign work to each workstation, there is no need for more work-in-process other than that being worked on. The exception is for inventory specifically placed in front of a bottleneck to ensure continual work, or at specific points downstream from a bottleneck to ensure flow of product.

Concerning continual improvements to the system, JIT is a trial-and-error procedure applied to a real system. In synchronous manufacturing, the system can be programmed and simulated on a computer because the schedules are realistic (can be accomplished) and computer run time is short.

RELATIONSHIP WITH OTHER FUNCTIONAL AREAS

The production system must work closely with other functional areas to achieve the best operating system. This section briefly discusses accounting and marketing—areas where conflicts can occur and where cooperation and joint planning should occur.

ACCOUNTING'S INFLUENCE

Sometimes we are led into making decisions to suit the measurement system rather than to follow the firm's goals. Consider the following example: Suppose that two old machines are currently being used to produce a product. The processing time for each is 20 minutes per part and, because each has the capacity of three parts per hour, they have the combined capacity of six per hour, which exactly meets the market demand of six parts per hour. Suppose that engineering finds a new machine that produces parts in 12 minutes rather than 20. However, the capacity of this one machine is only five per hour, which does not meet the market demand. Logic would seem to dictate that the supervisor should use an old machine to make up the lacking one unit per hour. However, the system does not allow this. The standard has been changed from the 20 minutes each to 12 minutes each and performance would look very bad on paper because the variance would be 67 percent $[(20 - 12)/12]$ for units made on the old machines. The supervisor, therefore, would work the new machine on overtime.

Problems in Cost Accounting Measurements   Cost accounting is used for performance measurement, cost determinations, investment justification, and inventory valuation. Two sets of accounting performance measurements are used for evaluation: (1) global measurements, which are financial statements showing net profit, return on investment, and cash flow (with which we agree); and (2) local cost accounting measurements showing efficiencies (as variances from standard) or utilization rate (hours worked/hours present).

From the cost accounting (local measurement) viewpoint, then, performance has traditionally been based on cost and full utilization. This logic forces supervisors to activate their workers all the time, which leads to excessive inventory. The cost accounting measurement system also can instigate other problems. For example, attempting to use the idle time to increase utilization can create a bottleneck, as we discussed earlier in this chapter. Any measurement system should support the objectives of the firm and not stand in the way. Fortunately, the cost accounting measurement philosophy is changing.

MARKETING AND PRODUCTION

Marketing and production should communicate and conduct their activities in close harmony. In practice, however, they act very independently. There are many reasons for this. The difficulties range from differences in personalities and cultures to unlike systems of merits and rewards in the two functions. Marketing people are judged on the growth of the company in terms of sales, market share, and new products introduced. Marketing is sales oriented. Manufacturing people are evaluated on cost and utilization. Therefore, marketing wants a variety of products to increase the company's position, whereas manufacturing is trying to reduce cost.

Data used for evaluating marketing and manufacturing are also quite different. Marketing data are "soft" (qualitative); manufacturing data are "hard" (quantitative). The orientation and experiences of marketing and production people also differ. Those in marketing management have likely come up through sales and a close association with customers. Top manufacturing managers have likely progressed through production operations and therefore have plant performance as a top objective.

Cultural differences also can be important in contrasting marketing and manufacturing personnel. Marketing people tend to have a greater ego drive and are more outgoing. Manufacturing personnel tend to be more meticulous and perhaps more introverted (at least less extroverted than their marketing counterparts).

The solution to coping with these differences is to develop an equitable set of measurements to evaluate performance in each area and to promote strong lines of communication so that they both contribute to reaching the firm's goals.

We now present two examples to show that different objectives and measurement criteria can lead to the wrong decisions. These examples also show that, even though you may have all the data required, you still may not be able to solve the problem—unless you know how!

Step by Step

EXAMPLE 20.1: What to Produce?

In this first example, three products (A, B, and C) are sold in the market at $50, $75, and $60 per unit, respectively. The market will take all that can be supplied.

Three work centers (X, Y, and Z) process the three products as shown in Exhibit 20.14. Processing times for each work center also are shown. Note that each work center works on all three products. Raw

Prices and Production Requirements for Three Products and Three Work Centers

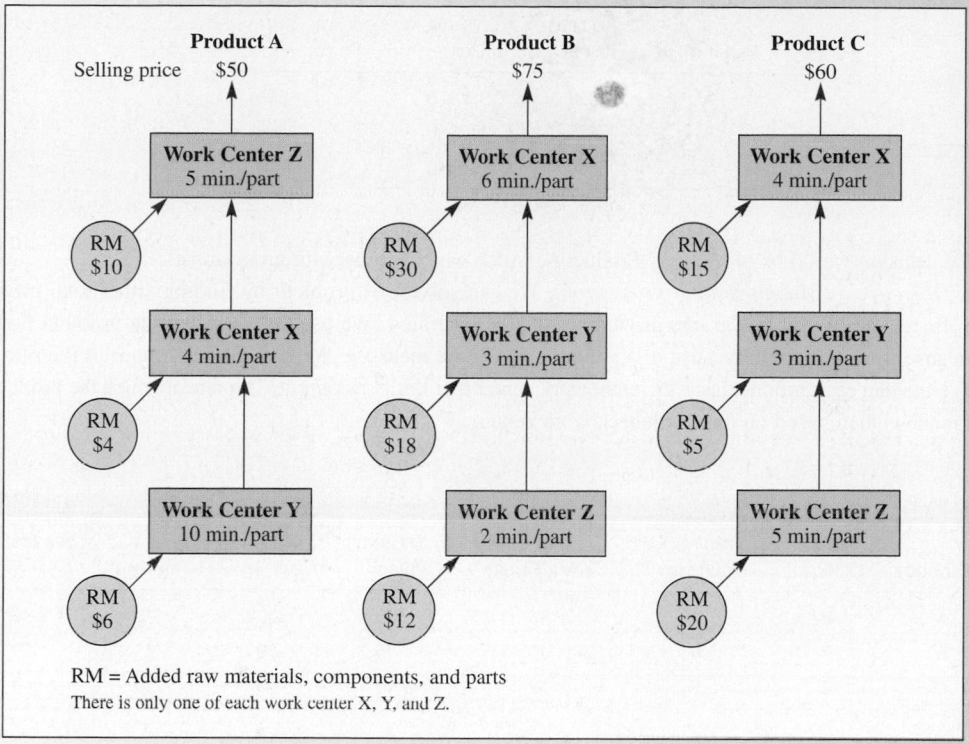

RM = Added raw materials, components, and parts
There is only one of each work center X, Y, and Z.

materials, parts, and components are added at each work center to produce each product. The per unit cost of these materials is shown as RM.

Which product or products should be produced?

SOLUTION

Three different objectives could exist that lead to different conclusions:

1. Maximize sales revenue because marketing personnel are paid commissions based on total revenue.
2. Maximize per unit gross profit.
3. Maximize total gross profit.

In this example, we use gross profit as selling price less materials. We also could include other expenses such as operating expenses, but we left them out for simplicity. (We include operating expenses in our next example.)

Objective 1: Maximize sales commission. Sales personnel in this case are unaware of the processing time required so, therefore, they will try to sell only B at $75 per unit and none of A or C. Maximum revenue is determined by the limiting resource as follows:

PRODUCT	LIMITING RESOURCE	TIME REQUIRED	NUMBER PRODUCED PER HOUR	SELLING PRICE	SALES REVENUE PER HOUR
A	Y	10 min	6	$50	$300
B	X	6 min	10	75	750
C	Z	5 min	12	60	720

Objective 2: Maximize per unit gross profit.

(1)	(2)	(3)	(4)
PRODUCT	SELLING PRICE	RAW MATERIAL COST	GROSS PROFIT PER UNIT (2) − (3)
A	$50	$20	$30
B	$75	$60	$15
C	$60	$40	$20

The decision would be to sell only Product A, which has a $30 per unit gross profit.

Objective 3: Maximize total gross profit. We can solve this problem by finding either total gross profit for the period or the rate at which profit is generated. We use rate to solve the problem both because it is easier and because it is a more appropriate measure. We use profit per hour as the rate.

Note that each product has a different work center that limits its output. The rate at which the product is made is then based on this bottleneck work center.

(1)	(2)	(3)	(4)	(5)	(6)	(7)	(8)
PRODUCT	LIMITING WORK CENTER	PROCESSING TIME PER UNIT (MINUTES)	PRODUCT OUTPUT RATE (PER HOUR)	SELLING PRICE	RAW MATERIAL COST	PROFIT PER UNIT	PROFIT PER HOUR (4) × (7)
A	Y	10	6	$50	$20	$30	$180
B	X	6	10	75	60	15	150
C	Z	5	12	60	40	20	240

From our calculations, and if we only consider a single product, Product C provides the highest profit of $240 per hour. Note that we get three different answers:

1. We choose B to maximize sales revenue.
2. We choose A to maximize profit per unit.
3. We choose C to maximize total profit.

Choosing Product C is obviously the correct answer for the firm if we restrict ourselves to making a single product. Profit can be improved to $280/hour by producing a mix of A-3, B-2 and C-8 units each hour. This solution can be obtained by solving the "product mix" problem described in Appendix A (see example A.1).

In this example, all work centers were required for each product and each product had a different work center as a constraint. We did this to simplify the problem and to ensure that only one product would surface as the answer. If there were more work centers or the same work center constraint in different products, the problem could still easily be solved using linear programming (as in Appendix A). ●

Step by Step

EXAMPLE 20.2: How Much to Produce?

In this example, shown in Exhibit 20.15, two workers are producing four products. The plant works three shifts. The market demand is unlimited and takes all the products that the workers can produce. The only stipulation is that the ratio of products sold cannot exceed 10 to 1 between the maximum sold of any one product and the minimum of another. For example, if the maximum number sold of any one of the products is 100 units, the minimum of any other cannot be fewer than 10 units. Workers 1 and 2, on each shift, are not cross-trained and can work only on their own operations. The time and raw material (RM) costs are shown in the exhibit, and a summary of the costs and times involved is on the lower portion of the exhibit. Weekly operating expenses are $3,000.

What quantities of A, B, C, and D should be produced?

Production Requirements and Selling Price of Four Products

exhibit 20.15

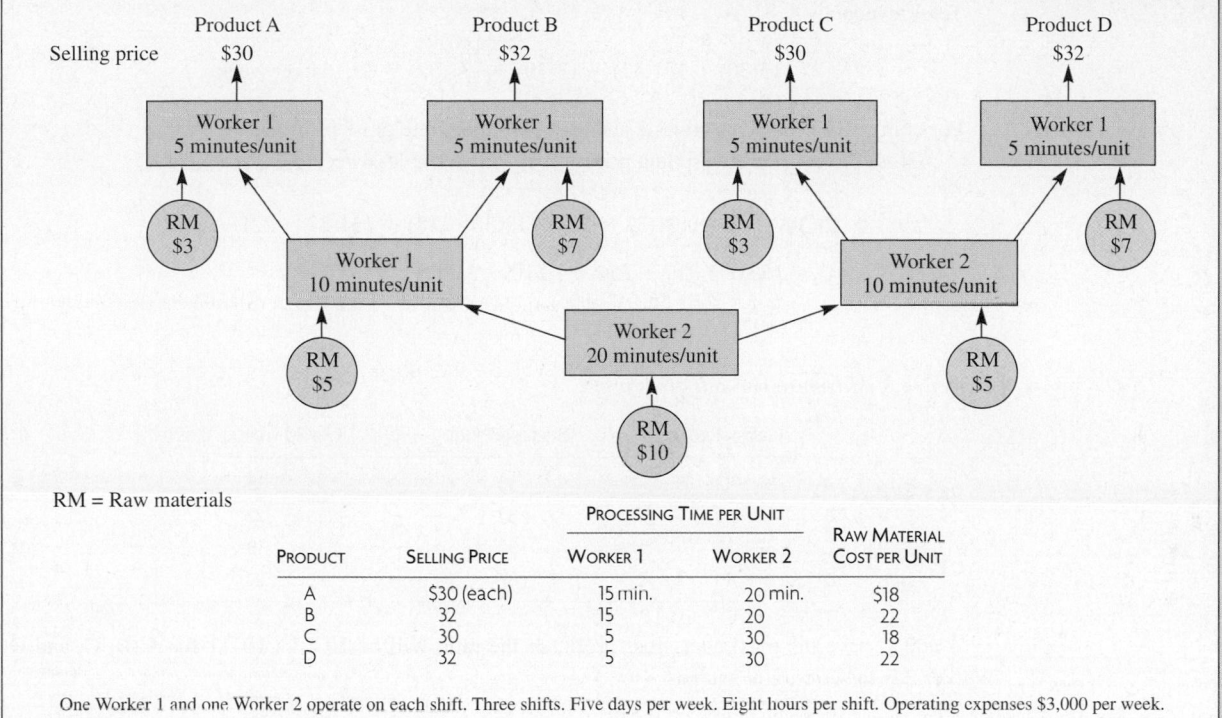

RM = Raw materials

		PROCESSING TIME PER UNIT		RAW MATERIAL
PRODUCT	SELLING PRICE	WORKER 1	WORKER 2	COST PER UNIT
A	$30 (each)	15 min.	20 min.	$18
B	32	15	20	22
C	30	5	30	18
D	32	5	30	22

One Worker 1 and one Worker 2 operate on each shift. Three shifts. Five days per week. Eight hours per shift. Operating expenses $3,000 per week.

SOLUTION

As in the previous example, there are three answers to this question, depending on each of the following objectives:

1. Maximize revenue for sales personnel, who are paid on commission.
2. Maximize per unit gross profit.
3. Maximize the utilization of the bottleneck resource (leading to maximum gross profit).

Objective 1: Maximize sales commission on sales revenue. Sales personnel prefer to sell B and D (selling price $32) rather than A and C (selling price $30). Weekly operating expenses are $3,000.

The ratio of units sold will be: 1A : 10B : 1C : 10D.

Worker 2 on each shift is the bottleneck and therefore determines the output. Note that if this truly is a bottleneck with an unlimited market demand, this should be a seven-day-per-week operation, not just a five-day workweek.

5 days per week × 3 shifts × 8 hours × 60 minutes = 7,200 minutes per week available

Worker 2 spends these times on each unit:

A   20 minutes   B   20 minutes   C   30 minutes   D   30 minutes

The ratio of output units is 1 : 10 : 1 : 10. Therefore,

$$1x(20) + 10x(20) + 1x(30) + 10x(30) = 7,200$$
$$550x = 7,200$$
$$x = 13.09$$

Therefore, the numbers of units produced are

$$A = 13 \qquad B = 131 \qquad C = 13 \qquad D = 131$$

Total revenue is

$$13(30) + 131(32) + 13(30) + 131(32) = \$9,164 \text{ per week}$$

For comparison with Objectives 2 and 3, we will compute gross profit per week.
Gross profit per week (selling price less raw material less weekly expenses) is

$$13(30 - 18) + 131(32 - 22) + 13(30 - 18) + 131(32 - 22) - 3,000$$

$$= 156 + 1,310 + 156 + 1,310 - 3,000$$

$$= (\$68) \text{ loss}$$

Objective 2: Maximize per unit gross profit.

	GROSS PROFIT	=	SELLING PRICE	−	RAW MATERIAL COST
A	12	=	30	−	18
B	10	=	32	−	22
C	12	=	30	−	18
D	10	=	32	−	22

A and C have the maximum gross profit, so the ratio will be 10 : 1 : 10 : 1 for A, B, C, and D. Worker 2 is the constraint and has

$$5 \text{ days} \times 3 \text{ shifts} \times 8 \text{ hours} \times 60 \text{ minutes} = 7,200 \text{ minutes available per week}$$

As before, A and B take 20 minutes, while C and D take 30 minutes. Thus

$$10x(20) + 1x(20) + 10x(30) + 1x(30) = 7,200$$

$$550x = 7,200$$

$$x = 13$$

Therefore, the number of units produced is

$$A = 131 \qquad B = 13 \qquad C = 131 \qquad D = 13$$

Gross profit (selling price less raw materials less \$3,000 weekly expense) is

$$131(30 - 18) + 13(32 - 22) + 131(30 - 18) + 13(32 - 22) - 3,000$$

$$= 1,572 + 130 + 1,572 + 130 - 3,000$$

$$= \$404 \text{ profit}$$

Objective 3: Maximize the use of the bottleneck resource, Worker 2. For every hour Worker 2 works, the following numbers of products and gross profits result:

(1) PRODUCT	(2) PRODUCTION TIME	(3) UNITS PRODUCED PER HOUR	(4) SELLING PRICE EACH	(5) RAW MATERIAL COST PER UNIT	(6) GROSS PROFIT PER HOUR (3) × [(4) − (5)]
A	20 minutes	3	\$30	\$18	\$36
B	20	3	32	22	30
C	30	2	30	18	24
D	30	2	32	22	20

Product A generates the greatest gross profit per hour of Worker 2 time, so the ratio is 10 : 1 : 1 : 1 for A, B, C, and D.

Available time for Worker 2 is the same as before:

$$3 \text{ shifts} \times 5 \text{ days} \times 8 \text{ hours} \times 60 \text{ minutes} = 7,200 \text{ minutes}$$

Worker 2 should produce 10 As for every 1 B, 1 C, and 1 D. Worker 2's average production rate is

$$10x(20) + 1x(20) + 1x(30) + 1x(30) = 7,200$$

$$280x = 7,200$$

$$x = 25.7$$

Therefore, the number of units that should be produced is

$$A = 257 \qquad B = 25.7 \qquad C = 25.7 \qquad D = 25.7$$

Gross profit (price less raw materials less $3,000 weekly expenses) is

$$257(30 - 18) + 25.7(32 - 22) + 25.7(30 - 18) + 25.7(32 - 22) - 3,000$$

$$= 3,084 + 257 + 308.4 + 257 - 3,000$$

$$= \$906.40$$

In summary, using three different objectives to decide how many of each product to make gave us three different results:

1. Maximizing sales commission resulted in a $68 loss in gross profit.
2. Maximizing gross profit gave us a profit of $404.
3. Maximizing the use of the capacity-constrained worker gave us the best gross profit, $906.40. ●

Both examples demonstrate that production and marketing need to interact. Marketing should sell the most profitable use of available capacity. However, to plan capacity, production needs to know from marketing what products could be sold.

EXAMPLE 20.3: TOC Applied to Bank Loan Application Processing[3]

In this example, Goldratt's theory of constraints five-step approach (see Exhibit 20.2) to removing bottlenecks is applied to a bank loan application process. As can be seen through the example, the ideas can be applied to all types of applications, including service processes.

Step by Step

Step 1: Identify the system's constraint. Assume that the bank is a private-sector institution and that its goal is to make more money now and in the future. Furthermore, suppose that the initial constraint is internal, namely, the loan officers are unable to carry out all of their responsibilities in a timely manner. That is, given the current demand for bank loan application processing, the loan officers are unable to perform all of the steps in the loan approval process in a responsive manner that is viewed as satisfactory by its customers.

Step 2: Decide how to exploit the system's constraint. Once a constraint is identified, management must effectively maximize the usage of the constraint's capacity and capability to fulfill the system's goal. By calculating the throughput yield per unit of time at the constraining resource, management has the information necessary to prioritize the work performed at the constraint. For example, the loan department manager could measure the throughput yield associated with each hour spent working on each type of loan request, such as home mortgage, automobile, and small business. The sequence of loans processed at the constraint would then be established by the "profitability" of the different types of loans so that the bank's goal can be expeditiously met. An optional approach to exploitation that complements prioritization is assuring that the constraint is always being effectively utilized. Thus, it may be possible to redesign the loan approval process so that some of the loan officers' current workload is offloaded to available personnel who are currently only being partially utilized.

Step 3: Subordinate everything else to the preceding decisions. Subordination involves aligning all of the nonconstraint resources in support of maximizing the performance of the constraint resource. In this case, the bank management would want to schedule appointments for potential customers seeking to complete their loan applications with bank agents so that there was always an abundant supply of completed loan requests waiting for the loan officers to process. Also, the manager of the bank's loan approval process would control the release of loan applications into the approval process so that the loan officers were not overwhelmed. Finally, the bank would have a non–fully occupied clerk assure that each application was complete and met process quality standards prior to being given to the loan officers. (Note that having a supply of finished applications available assured a highly productive usage of loan officer time; this approach to subordination would produce only a small increase in throughput. It would move the bank toward its goal; the constraint would remain with the loan officers.)

Step 4: Elevate the constraint. Elevating the constraining resource means adding enough new capacity so that the current constraint no longer limits system throughput. In contrast to the previous two steps, elevation often requires a monetary outlay or investment for new resources or capabilities. In the bank's loan subsystem illustration, despite increases in loan officer productivity that were presumed to result from steps 2 and 3, the system constraint has remained with the bank's loan officers. Thus, because these improvements were insufficient to break the constraint, it is necessary to address the constraining factor directly. The obvious step is to hire an additional loan officer. This action elevates the existing constraint by providing more than sufficient capacity to meet existing demand for processing loan applications. While this decision would produce a sizable increase in operating expenses, it could be justified by management as the best approach to meeting their process goal as well as the bank's overall goal.

Step 5: Return to step 1, but do not allow inertia to cause a system constraint. After the original constraint has been overcome in step 4, it is necessary to revisit all of the changes made in steps 2 and 3 to determine if they are still appropriate to effective process and system performance. In the loan example one more time, a review of the implemented changes in step 2 might show that offloading the responsibilities for assembling the loan package and some of the credit checking activities to bank clerical personnel was working well and that there is no need to go back to the original procedure. With regard to step 3, although the bank might still seek to aggressively schedule bank agents to meet with customers to help them complete their loan applications, it might not be possible to have a large inventory of loan requests in progress because the constraint in the loan application and approval process had shifted to the marketplace. Thus, it is appropriate to return to step 1 of the five-step focusing process.

Extending the process. Exhibit 20.16 shows how the application of the five-step focusing process might realistically unfold in managing the bank's loan application process over the next couple of years. Elevating the capacity of the original approval process constraint by hiring a new loan officer leads to a new constraint. This time it resides in the marketplace. Suppose this new constraint turns out to be a policy constraint, namely, bank management does not extend consumer loans to clients who do not use the bank's credit card services. Reconsideration of this policy leads to an exemption for a bank customer who has had any type of an account at the bank for at least the past year. Next, because there are insufficient monetary reserves to fund all of the approved loads, the new system constraint resides in the supply of capital. To address this new constraint, assume that the bank negotiates for additional funds from a wholesale lender and is now able to provide more loans than customers are currently demanding. Now, a new market constraint develops because the monetary supply of funds is greater than the demand in the marketplace. With some effort, the bank marketing team is able to break this constraint by creating a special loan product-service bundle to serve the needs of local university students. Finally in this example, the constraint shifts back inside the bank's loan approval process, where the loan officers and bank clerks are unable to process applications fast enough to keep up with demand. Bank management purchases a new software package that has been designed to augment loan application processing and fully trains the loan officer staff and clerical assistants on its use.

Sequential Application of the Five-Step Focusing Process in Managing the Bank's Loan Subsystem

exhibit 20.16

CONSTRAINT LOCATION	CONSTRAINT TYPE	CONSTRAINT IDENTIFICATION	APPROACH TO CONSTRAINT ALLEVIATION
Bank loan application process	Physical	Loan officers and bank clerks are unable to process all customer loan applications in a timely manner	Some loan officer tasks offloaded to clerks and additional loan officers hired. Now sufficient capacity exists in the loan application process.
Marketplace	Policy	Current bank policy: if a loan applicant does not have a credit card account with the bank, then he or she is not eligible to apply for consumer loan	New bank policy: every loan applicant must have some type of active account with the bank. Now demand for loans increases because more potential applicants qualify.
Supply	Physical	The availability of funds is insufficient to meet all approved customer loan requests	Bank negotiates for additional funds from wholesale lenders. Now capital reserves are greater than customers are demanding.
Marketplace	Policy	Loan markets are saturated relative to current loan products and excess funds are available to loan to qualified customers	Bank develops new loan product designed for local college students. Now total demand for loans in the marketplace increases.
Bank loan application process	Physical	Loan officers and bank clerks are unable to process all customer loan applications in a timely manner	Bank invests in the acquisition of a new software package to facilitate loan application processing. Now process capacity exceeds demand.

SOURCE: RICHARD A. REID, "APPLYING THE TOC FIVE-STEP FOCUSING PROCESS IN THE SERVICE SECTOR: A BANKING SUBSYSTEM," *MANAGING SERVICE QUALITY* 17, NO. 2 (2007), P. 223.

SUMMARY

The measurement system within a firm should encourage the increase of net profits, return on investment, and cash flow. The firm can accomplish this if, at the operations level, it rewards performance based on the amount of throughput, inventory, and operating expense created. This is essential for a firm's success.

To control throughput, inventory, and operating expense, the system must be analyzed to find bottlenecks and capacity-constrained resources. Only then can the company define a drum for control, buffers to ensure throughput, and ropes for communicating the correct information to the correct locations, while minimizing work-in-process everywhere else. Without this focus, problems are not correctly diagnosed and solution procedures are impossible.

Goldratt defined nine rules (Exhibit 20.1) to help guide the logic of an operating system and to identify the important points. These are basic to any operating system.

The underlying philosophy presented in this chapter—the vital importance of concentrating on system limitations imposed by capacity-constrained resources—has led Goldratt to broaden his view of the importance of system limitations and to develop his five-step "general theory of constraints."[4] (See Exhibit 20.2.)

Although the terms *bottleneck* and *constraint* can mean essentially the same thing, Goldratt uses *constraint* in the broadest sense to mean anything that limits the performance of a system and slows or prevents it from continuing to move toward its goal.

This general theory of constraints directs companies to find what is stopping them from moving toward their goals and find ways to get around this limitation. If, in a manufacturing environment, the limitation is insufficient capacity, then ways to break the constraint might be overtime, specialized tools, supporting equipment, exceptionally skilled workers, subcontracting, redesigning product or process, alternative routings, and so on. Point 5 (Exhibit 20.2) warns against letting biases in thinking prevent the search for further exploitation of constraints. For example, if a search and exploitation of a constraint has been conducted under the limitation of cost, make sure that this cost measure is not carried into the next search. Start clean each time.

One last summary comment on this chapter also serves well as a summary comment for this book: The key to competitive advantage through operations is for the firm to operate as a synchronized system, with all parts working in concert. Companies that do this effectively are well on their way to achieving the fundamental goal of the firm—profitability.

KEY TERMS

Synchronous manufacturing A production process coordinated to work in harmony to achieve the goals of the firm.

Throughput The rate at which money is generated by the system through sales (Goldratt's definition).

Inventory All the money that the system has invested in purchasing things it intends to sell (Goldratt's definition).

Operating expenses All the money that the system spends to turn inventory into throughput (Goldratt's definition).

Productivity All the actions that bring a company closer to its goals (Goldratt's definition).

Bottleneck Any resource whose capacity is less than the demand placed upon it (Goldratt's definition).

Nonbottleneck Any resource whose capacity is greater than the demand placed on it (Goldratt's definition).

Capacity-constrained resource (CCR) A resource whose utilization is close to capacity and could be a bottleneck if not scheduled carefully (Goldratt's definition).

SOLVED PROBLEM

Here is the process flow for Products A, B, and C. Products A, B, and C sell for $20, $25, and $30, respectively. There are only one Resource X and one Resource Y, which are used to produce A, B, and C for the numbers of minutes stated on the diagram. Raw materials are needed at the process steps as shown, with the costs in dollars per unit of raw material. (One unit is used for each product.)

The market will take all that you can produce.

a. Which product would you produce to maximize gross margin per unit?
b. If sales personnel are paid on commission, which product or products would they sell and how many could they sell?
c. Which and how many product or products should you produce to maximize gross profit for one week?
d. From c, how much gross profit would there be for the week?

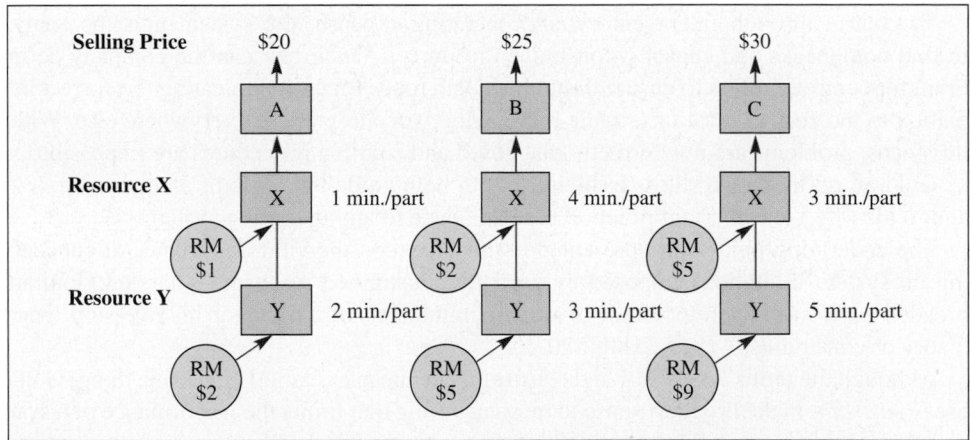

Solution

a. Maximizing gross margin per unit:

	GROSS MARGIN	=	SELLING PRICE	−	RAW MATERIAL COST
A	17	=	20	−	3
B	18	=	25	−	7
C	16	=	30	−	14

Product B will be produced.

b. Maximizing sales commission: Sales personnel would sell the highest-priced product, C (unless they knew the market and capacity limitations). If we assume the market will take all that we can make, then we would work 7 days/week, 8 hours/day. Y is the constraint in producing C. The number of C we can make in a week is

$$C = \frac{8 \text{ hours/day} \times 7 \text{ days/week} \times 60 \text{ minutes/hour}}{5 \text{ minutes/part}}$$

$$= 672 \text{ units}$$

c. To maximize profit, we need to compare profits per hour for each product:

(1) PRODUCT	(2) CONSTRAINT RESOURCE	(3) PRODUCTION TIME ON RESOURCE	(4) NUMBER OF UNITS OUTPUT PER HOUR	(5) SELLING PRICE ($)	(6) RM COST ($)	(7) GROSS PROFIT PER HOUR (4) × (5 − 6)
A	Y	2	30	20	3	$510
B	X	4	15	25	7	270
C	Y	5	12	30	14	192

If the constraining resource were the same for all three products, our problem would be solved and the answer would be to produce just A, and as many as possible. However, X is the constraint for B, so the answer could be a combination of A and B. To test this, we can see that the value of each hour of Y while producing B is

$$\frac{60 \text{ minutes/hour}}{3 \text{ minutes/unit}} \times (\$25 - 7) = \$360/\text{hour}$$

This is less than the $510 per hour producing A, so we would produce only A. The number of units of A produced during the week is

$$\frac{60 \text{ minutes/hour} \times 24 \text{ hours/day} \times 7 \text{ days/week}}{2 \text{ minutes/unit}} = 5,040$$

d. Gross profit for the week is 5,040 × $17 = $85,680.
Solved using profit per hour: $510 × 24 × 7 = $85,680.

REVIEW AND DISCUSSION QUESTIONS

1   State the global performance measurements and operational performance measurements and briefly define each of them. How do these differ from traditional accounting measurements?
2   Discuss process batches and transfer batches. How might you determine what the sizes should be?
3   Compare and contrast JIT, MRP, and synchronized manufacturing, stating their main features, such as where each is or might be used, amounts of raw materials and work-in-process inventories, production lead times and cycle times, and methods for control.
4   Compare the importance and relevance of quality control in JIT, MRP, and synchronous manufacturing.
5   Discuss what is meant by forward loading and backward loading.
6   Define and explain the cause or causes of a moving bottleneck.
7   Explain how a nonbottleneck can become a bottleneck.
8   What are the functions of inventory in MRP, JIT, and synchronous manufacturing scheduling?
9   Define *process batch* and *transfer batch* and their meaning in each of these applications: MRP, JIT, and bottleneck or constrained resource logic.
10   Discuss how a production system is scheduled using MRP logic, JIT logic, and synchronous manufacturing logic.
11   Discuss the concept of "drum–buffer–rope."
12   From the standpoint of the scheduling process, how are resource limitations treated in an MRP application? How are they treated in a synchronous manufacturing application?

13   What are operations people's primary complaints against the accounting procedures used in most firms? Explain how such procedures can cause poor decisions for the total company.

14   Most manufacturing firms try to balance capacity for their production sequences. Some believe that this is an invalid strategy. Explain why balancing capacity does not work.

15   Discuss why transfer batches and process batches many times may not and should not be equal.

PROBLEMS

1   For the four basic configurations that follow, assume that the market is demanding product that must be processed by both Resource X and Resource Y for Cases I, II, and III. For Case IV, both resources supply separate but dependent markets; that is, the number of units of output from both X and Y must be equal.

   Plans are being made to produce a product that requires 40 minutes on Resource X and 30 minutes on Resource Y. Assume that there is only one of each of these resources and that market demand is 1,400 units per month.

   How many hours of production time would you schedule for X and Y? What would happen if both were scheduled for the same number of hours?

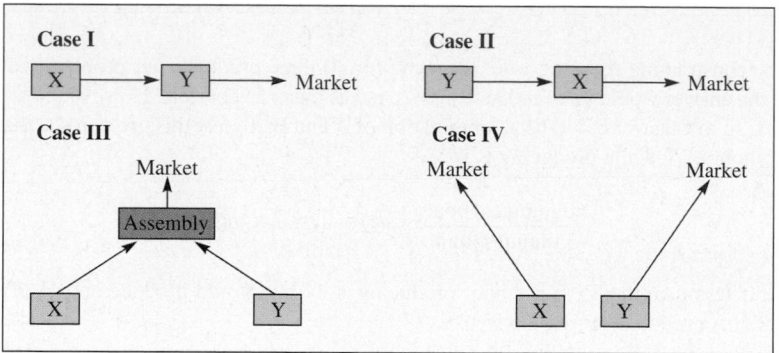

2   Following are the process flow sequences for three products: A, B, and C. There are two bottleneck operations—on the first leg and fourth leg—marked with an X. Boxes represent processes, which may be either machine or manual. Suggest the location of the drum, buffer, and ropes.

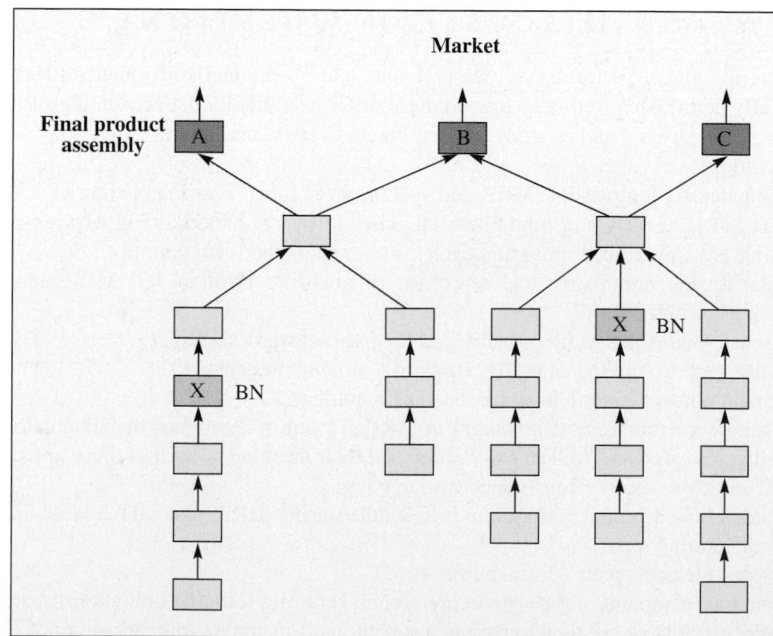

3 The accompanying figure shows a production network model with the parts and processing sequences. State clearly on the figure (1) where you would place inventory; (2) where you would perform inspection; and (3) where you would emphasize high-quality output. (Note: Operations may be shown either as rectangles as in Problem 2 or as circles as in Problem 3.)

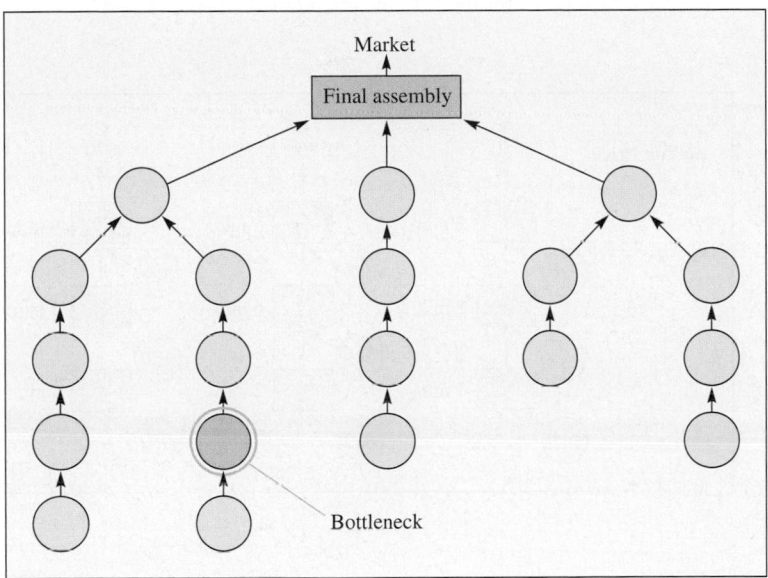

4 The following production flow shows Parts E, I, and N; Subassembly O; and final assembly for Product P:

A to B to C to D to E

F to G to H to I

J to K to L to M to N

E and I to O

N and O to P

B involves a bottleneck operation, and M involves a CCR.
   a. Draw the process flow.
   b. Where would you locate buffer inventories?
   c. Where would you place inspection points?
   d. Where would you stress the importance of quality production?

5 Here are average process cycle times for several work centers. State which are bottlenecks, nonbottlenecks, and capacity-constrained resources.

Processing time		Setup time

Processing time	Setup	Idle

Processing time	Setup	Idle

Processing time	Setup	Idle

Processing time	Setup	Idle

6 The following diagram shows the flow process, raw material costs, and machine processing time for three products: A, B, and C. There are three machines (W, X, and Y) used in the

production of these products; the times shown are in required minutes of production per unit. Raw material costs are shown in cost per unit of product. The market will take all that can be produced.

a. Assuming that sales personnel are paid on a commission basis, which product should they sell?

b. On the basis of maximizing gross profit per unit, which product should be sold?

c. To maximize total profit for the firm, which product should be sold?

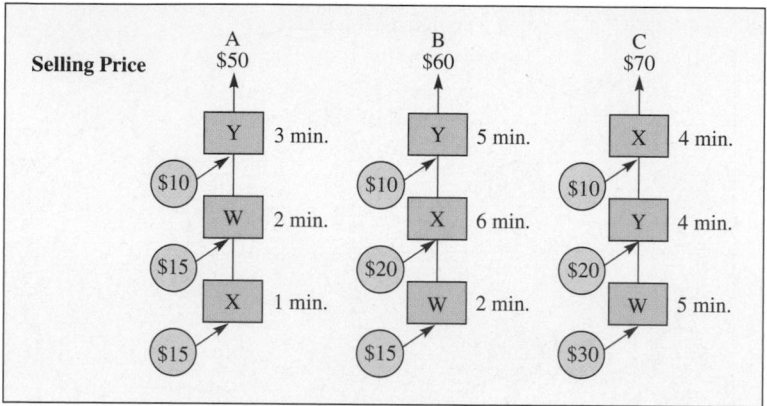

7   Willard Lock Company is losing market share because of horrendous due-date performance and long delivery lead times. The company's inventory level is high and includes many finished goods that do not match the short-term orders. Material control analysis shows that purchasing has ordered on time, the vendors have delivered on time, and the scrap/rework rates have been as expected. However, the buildable mix of components and subassemblies does not generally match the short-term and past-due requirements at final assembly. End-of-month expediting and overtime are the rule, even though there is idle time early in the month. Overall efficiency figures are around 70 percent for the month. These figures are regarded as too low.

   You have just been hired as a consultant and must come up with recommendations. Help the firm understand its problems. Specifically state some actions that it should take. The product flow is shown in the diagram below.

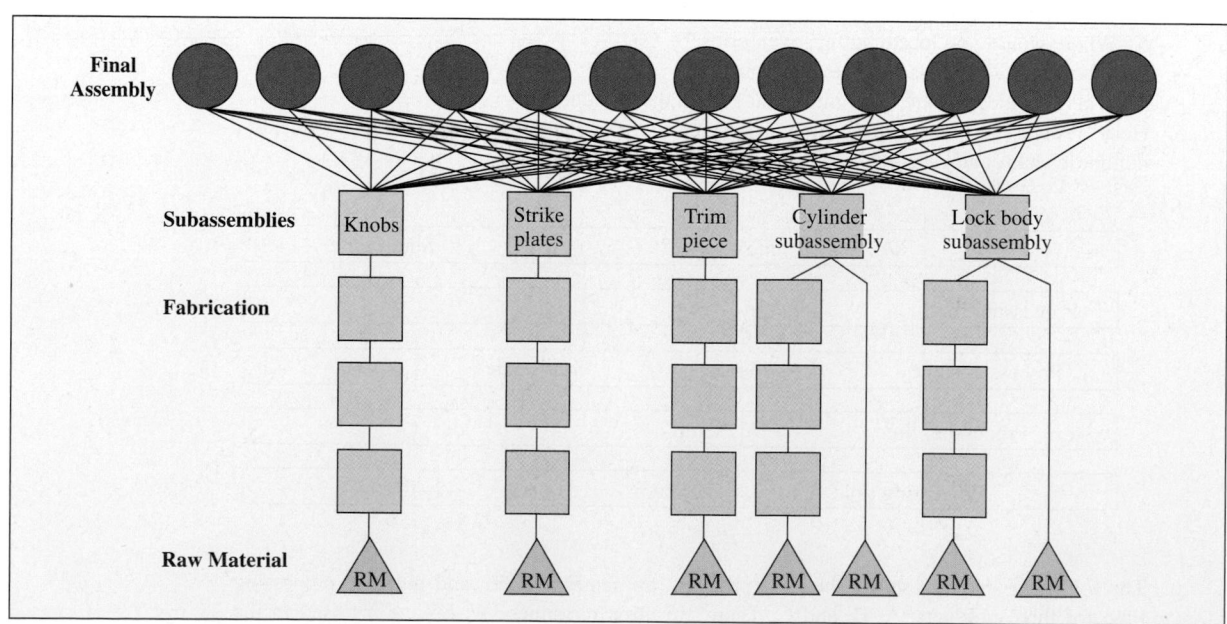

8   The M–N plant manufactures two different products: M and N. Selling prices and weekly market demands are shown in the following diagram. Each product uses raw materials with costs as shown. The plant has three different machines: A, B, and C. Each performs different tasks and can work on only one unit of material at a time.

Process times for each task are shown in the diagram. Each machine is available 2,400 minutes per week. There are no "Murphys" (major opportunities for the system to foul up). Setup and transfer times are zero. Demand is constant.

Operating expenses (including labor) total a constant $12,000 per week. Raw materials are not included in weekly operating expenses.

a. Where is the constraint in this plant?

b. What product mix provides the highest profit?

c. What is the maximum weekly profit this plant can earn?

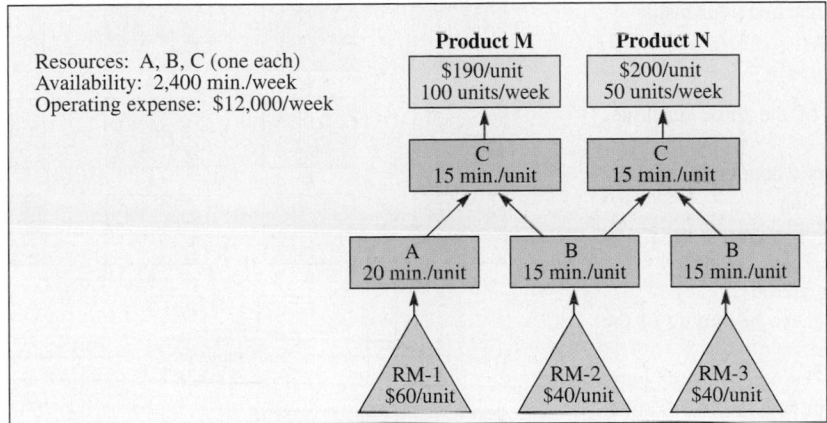

9   A steel product is manufactured by starting with raw material (carbon steel wire) and then processing it sequentially through five operations using machines A to E, respectively (see table below). This is the only use that the five machines are put to. The hourly rates for each machine are given in the table.

Operation:	1	2	3	4	5
Machine:	A	B	C	D	E
Hourly unit output rate:	100	80	40	60	90

Consider the following questions.

a. What is the maximum output per hour of the steel product?

b. By how much would the output be improved if B was increased to 90?

c. By how much would the output be improved if C was increased to 50?

d. By how much would the output be improved if C was increased to 70?

e. What is the effect on the system if machine A can only manage an output of 90 in one hour?

f. What is the effect on the system if machine C can only manage an output of 30 in one hour?

g. What is the effect on the system if machine B is allowed to drop to an output of 30 in one hour?

10 The following production flow shows parts O, Q, and T; Subassembly U; and final assembly for Product V.

M to N to O

P to Q

R to S to T

O and Q to U

U and T to V

N involves a bottleneck operation, and S involves a capacity-constrained resource. Draw the process flow.

CASE: SOLVE THE OPT QUIZ—A CHALLENGE IN SCHEDULING

Are you looking for a real scheduling challenge? This is a problem that was proposed by Dr. Eli Goldratt in a promotion for a factory-scheduling package called OPT (Optimized Production Technology). At the time Dr. Goldratt offered a $5,000 prize for the best schedule! See how good a schedule you can develop by applying the concepts described in this chapter to this problem.

THE TASK

The goal is to ship the most units, given the conditions listed below. Provide schedules on a Gantt chart for each of the three machines for the eight-week period to show how you reached your result.

CONDITIONS

1   There is one and only one of each of the three machines (A, B, and C).
2   A machine setup of 60 minutes occurs whenever a machine is switched from one operation to another.
3   The eight-week period consists of five-day weeks and 24-hour days with no breaks.
4   There is an unlimited supply of raw materials.
5   There is no inventory in the system at the beginning of the eight-week period.
6   To calculate the value of work-in-process and finished-parts inventory, assume each part has a value of $100 the moment it starts at the first operation. Once a set of four parts reaches assembly, the parts are assembled and shipped immediately. Raw material and completed units should not be included in the inventory calculation.

MINIMUM REQUIRED FOR A SOLUTION

1   The raw material value of work-in-process and finished-parts inventory may not exceed $50,000 at any given time.

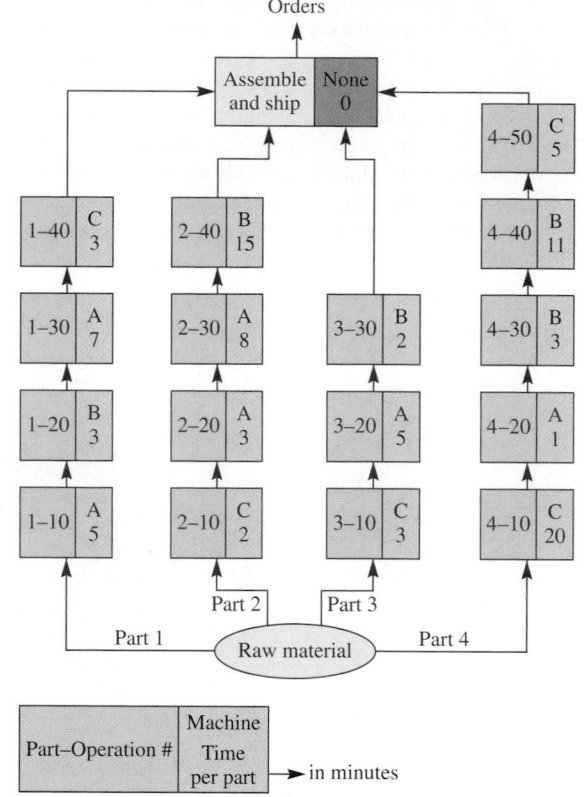

2   The minimum shipments of end items must be at least 140 units each week and at least 680 units by the end of the first four-week period.

Good luck!

SUPER QUIZ

1   According to Goldratt the goal of the firm is to do what?
2   At the operational level Goldratt suggests these three measures that should guide decisions.
3   The goal related to these three measures is this.
4   Goldratt argues that rather than capacity, this should be balanced.
5   This is any resource whose capacity is less than the demand placed on it.
6   Goldratt suggest that a production system should be controlled using these three mechanisms.
7   A bottleneck should have this placed in front of it to ensure that it never runs out of work.
8   A rope is used for this purpose in controlling a production system.
9   To pace the production system, this is used.
10   This is a measure of the value of inventory and the time it stays within an area.

1. Make money 2. Throughput, inventory, operating expenses 3. Increase throughput while simultaneously reducing inventory and reducing operating expense 4. Flow 5. Bottleneck 6. Drum, buffer, and rope 7. Buffer 8. Communication 9. Drum 10. Dollar days

SELECTED BIBLIOGRAPHY

Goldratt, E. *Critical Chain.* Croton-on-Hudson, NY: North River Press, 1997.

———. *The Haystack Syndrome: Sifting Information Out of the Data Ocean.* Croton-on-Hudson, NY: North River Press, 1990.

———. *Necessary but Not Sufficient.* Croton-on-Hudson, NY: North River Press, 2000.

———. *Theory of Constraints.* Croton-on-Hudson, NY: North River Press, 2000.

Goldratt, E. M., and J. Cox. *The Goal: Process of Ongoing Improvement.* 3rd rev. ed. Croton-on-Hudson, NY: North River Press, 2004.

Ricketts, J. *Reaching the Goal: How Managers Improve a Services Business Using Goldratt's Theory of Constraints.* New York: IBM Press, 2007.

Srikanth, M., and M. Umble. *Synchronous Management: Profit Based Manufacturing for the 21st Century.* Guilford, CT: Spectrum Publishing, 1997.

Goldratt, E. M., and R. E. Fox. *The Race for a Competitive Edge.* Milford, CT: Creative Output, 1986.

FOOTNOTES

1 Most of this chapter is based on the writings and teaching of Dr. Eliyahu M. Goldratt. Dr. Goldratt founded the Avraham Y. Goldratt Institute. The Institute's Web site is at http://www.rogo.com. We thank Dr. Goldratt for his permission to freely use his concepts, definitions, and other material.

2 M. L. Srikanth, *The Drum–Buffer–Rope System of Material Control* (New Haven, CT: Spectrum Publishing, 1987), pp. 25–37.

3 Adapted from Richard A. Reid, "Applying the TOC Five-Step Focusing Process in the Service Sector: A Banking Subsystem," *Managing Service Quality* 17, no. 2 (2007), pp. 209–34.

4 E. M. Goldratt, *The General Theory of Constraints* (New Haven, CT: Avraham Y. Goldratt Institute, 1989).

LINEAR PROGRAMMING USING THE EXCEL SOLVER

The key to profitable operations is making the best use of available resources of people, material, plant and equipment, and money. Today's manager has a powerful mathematical modeling tool available for this purpose with linear programming. In this appendix, we will show how the use of the Microsoft Excel Solver to solve LP problems opens a whole new world to the innovative manager and provides an invaluable addition to the technical skill set for those who seek careers in consulting. In this appendix, we use a product-planning problem to introduce this tool. Here we find the optimal mix of products that have different costs and resource requirements. This problem is certainly relevant to today's competitive market. Extremely successful companies provide a mix of products, from standard to high-end luxury models. All these products compete for the use of limited production and other capacity. Maintaining the proper mix of these products over time can significantly bolster earnings and the return on a firm's assets.

We begin with a quick introduction to linear programming and conditions under which the technique is applicable. Then we solve a simple product-mix problem. Other linear programming applications appear throughout the rest of the book.

INTRODUCTION

Linear programming (LP)

Linear programming (or simply **LP**) refers to several related mathematical techniques used to allocate limited resources among competing demands in an optimal way. LP is the most widely used of the approaches falling under the general heading of mathematical optimization techniques and has been applied to many operations management problems. The following are typical applications:

Aggregate sales and operations planning: Finding the minimum-cost production schedule. The problem is to develop a three- to six-month plan for meeting expected demand given constraints on expected production capacity and workforce size. Relevant costs considered in the problem include regular and overtime labor rates, hiring and firing, subcontracting, and inventory carrying cost.

Service/manufacturing productivity analysis: Comparing how efficiently different service and manufacturing outlets are using their resources compared to the best-performing unit. This is done using an approach called data envelopment analysis.

Product planning: Finding the optimal product mix where several products have different costs and resource requirements. Examples include finding the optimal blend of chemicals for gasoline, paints, human diets, and animal feeds. Examples of this problem are covered in this chapter.

Product routing: Finding the optimal way to produce a product that must be processed sequentially through several machine centers, with each machine in the center having its own cost and output characteristics.

Vehicle/crew scheduling: Finding the optimal way to use resources such as aircraft, buses, or trucks and their operating crews to provide transportation services to customers and materials to be moved between different locations.

Process control: Minimizing the amount of scrap material generated by cutting steel, leather, or fabric from a roll or sheet of stock material.

Inventory control: Finding the optimal combination of products to stock in a network of warehouses or storage locations.

Distribution scheduling: Finding the optimal shipping schedule for distributing products between factories and warehouses or between warehouses and retailers.

Plant location studies: Finding the optimal location of a new plant by evaluating shipping costs between alternative locations and supply and demand sources.

Material handling: Finding the minimum-cost routings of material-handling devices (such as forklift trucks) between departments in a plant, or hauling materials from a supply yard to work sites by trucks, for example. Each truck might have different capacity and performance capabilities.

Linear programming is gaining wide acceptance in many industries due to the availability of detailed operating information and the interest in optimizing processes to reduce cost. Many software vendors offer optimization options to be used with enterprise resource planning systems. Some firms refer to these as *advanced planning option, synchronized planning,* and *process optimization.*

For linear programming to pertain in a problem situation, five essential conditions must be met. First, there must be *limited resources* (such as a limited number of workers, equipment, finances, and material); otherwise there would be no problem. Second, there must be an *explicit objective* (such as maximize profit or minimize cost). Third, there must be *linearity* (two is twice as much as one; if three hours are needed to make a part, then two parts would take six hours and three parts would take nine hours). Fourth, there must be *homogeneity* (the products produced on a machine are identical, or all the hours available from a worker are equally productive). Fifth, there must be *divisibility:* Normal linear programming assumes products and resources can be subdivided into fractions. If this subdivision is not possible (such as flying half an airplane or hiring one-fourth of a person), a modification of linear programming, called *integer programming,* can be used.

When a single objective is to be maximized (like profit) or minimized (like costs), we can use linear programming. When multiple objectives exist, *goal programming* is used. If a problem is best solved in stages or time frames, *dynamic programming* is employed. Other restrictions on the nature of the problem may require that it be solved by other variations of the technique, such as *nonlinear programming* or *quadratic programming.*

THE LINEAR PROGRAMMING MODEL

Stated formally, the linear programming problem entails an optimizing process in which nonnegative values for a set of decision variables $X_1, X_2, \ldots, X_n$ are selected so as to maximize (or minimize) an objective function in the form

$$\text{Maximize (minimize) } Z = C_1X_1 + C_2X_2 + \cdots + C_nX_n$$

subject to resource constraints in the form

$$A_{11}X_1 + A_{12}X_2 + \cdots + A_{1n}X_n \leq B_1$$
$$A_{21}X_1 + A_{22}X_2 + \cdots + A_{2n}X_n \leq B_2$$
$$\vdots$$
$$A_{m1}X_1 + A_{m2}X_2 + \cdots + A_{mn}X_n \leq B_m$$

where C_n, A_{mn}, and B_m are given constants.

**Tutorial:
Intro to Solver**

Step by Step

Depending on the problem, the constraints also may be stated with equal signs (=) or greater-than-or-equal-to signs (≥).

EXAMPLE A.1: Puck and Pawn Company

We describe the steps involved in solving a simple linear programming model in the context of a sample problem, that of Puck and Pawn Company, which manufactures hockey sticks and chess sets. Each hockey stick yields an incremental profit of $2, and each chess set, $4. A hockey stick requires 4 hours of processing at machine center A and 2 hours at machine center B. A chess set requires 6 hours at machine center A, 6 hours at machine center B, and 1 hour at machine center C. Machine center A has a maximum of 120 hours of available capacity per day, machine center B has 72 hours, and machine center C has 10 hours.

If the company wishes to maximize profit, how many hockey sticks and chess sets should be produced per day?

SOLUTION

Formulate the problem in mathematical terms. If H is the number of hockey sticks and C is the number of chess sets, to maximize profit the objective function may be stated as

$$\text{Maximize } Z = \$2H + \$4C$$

The maximization will be subject to the following constraints:

$$4H + 6C \le 120 \quad \text{(machine center A constraint)}$$
$$2H + 6C \le 72 \quad \text{(machine center B constraint)}$$
$$1C \le 10 \quad \text{(machine center C constraint)}$$
$$H, C \ge 0 \; \bullet$$

This formulation satisfies the five requirements for standard LP stated in the first section of this appendix:

1. There are limited resources (a finite number of hours available at each machine center).
2. There is an explicit objective function (we know what each variable is worth and what the goal is in solving the problem).
3. The equations are linear (no exponents or cross-products).
4. The resources are homogeneous (everything is in one unit of measure, machine hours).
5. The decision variables are divisible and nonnegative (we can make a fractional part of a hockey stick or chess set; however, if this were deemed undesirable, we would have to use integer programming).

GRAPHICAL LINEAR PROGRAMMING

Graphical linear programming

Though limited in application to problems involving two decision variables (or three variables for three-dimensional graphing), graphical linear programming provides a quick insight into the nature of linear programming. We describe the steps involved in the graphical method in the context of Puck and Pawn Company. The following steps illustrate the graphical approach:

1. **Formulate the problem in mathematical terms.**   The equations for the problem are given above.
2. **Plot constraint equations.**   The constraint equations are easily plotted by letting one variable equal zero and solving for the axis intercept of the other. (The inequality portions of the restrictions are disregarded for this step.) For the machine center A constraint equation, when $H = 0$, $C = 20$, and when $C = 0$, $H = 30$. For the machine center B constraint equation, when $H = 0$, $C = 12$, and when $C = 0$, $H = 36$. For the machine center C constraint equation, $C = 10$ for all values of H. These lines are graphed in Exhibit A.1.
3. **Determine the area of feasibility.**   The direction of inequality signs in each constraint determines the area where a feasible solution is found. In this case, all inequalities

Graph of Hockey Stick and Chess Set Problem

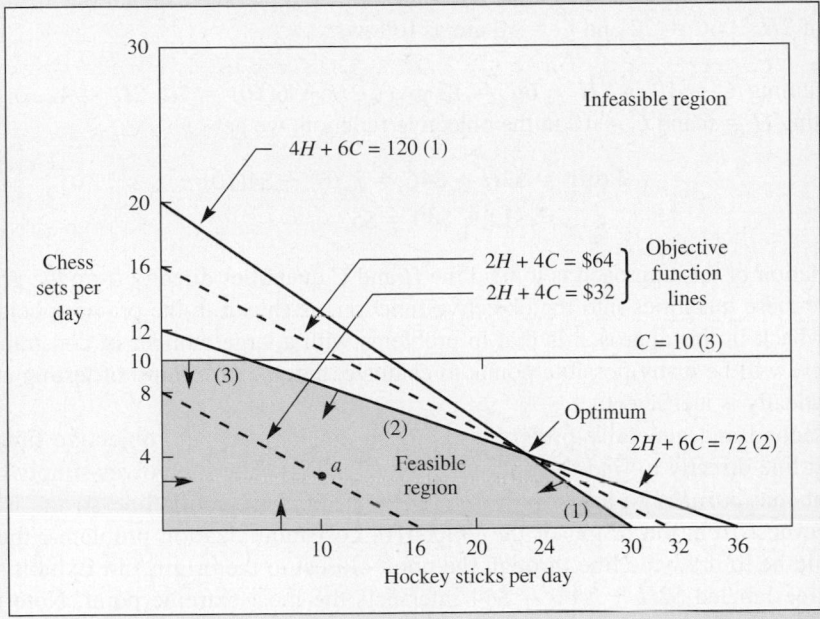

are of the less-than-or-equal-to variety, which means it would be impossible to produce any combination of products that would lie to the right of any constraint line on the graph. The region of feasible solutions is unshaded on the graph and forms a convex polygon. A convex polygon exists when a line drawn between any two points in the polygon stays within the boundaries of that polygon. If this condition of convexity does not exist, the problem is either incorrectly set up or is not amenable to linear programming.

4. **Plot the objective function.** The objective function may be plotted by assuming some arbitrary total profit figure and then solving for the axis coordinates, as was done for the constraint equations. Other terms for the objective function when used in this context are the *iso-profit* or *equal contribution line,* because it shows all possible production combinations for any given profit figure. For example, from the dotted line closest to the origin on the graph, we can determine all possible combinations of hockey sticks and chess sets that yield $32 by picking a point on the line and reading the number of each product that can be made at that point. The combination yielding $32 at point *a* would be 10 hockey sticks and three chess sets. This can be verified by substituting $H = 10$ and $C = 3$ in the objective function:

$$\$2(10) + \$4(3) = \$20 + \$12 = \$32$$

H	C	EXPLANATION
0	120/6 = 20	Intersection of Constraint (1) and C axis
120/4 = 30	0	Intersection of Constraint (1) and H axis
0	72/6 = 12	Intersection of Constraint (2) and C axis
72/2 = 36	0	Intersection of Constraint (2) and H axis
0	10	Intersection of Constraint (3) and C axis
0	32/4 = 8	Intersection of $32 iso-profit line (objective function) and C axis
32/2 = 16	0	Intersection of $32 iso-profit line and H axis
0	64/4 = 16	Intersection of $64 iso-profit line and C axis
64/2 = 32	0	Intersection of $64 iso-profit line and H axis

5. **Find the optimum point.** It can be shown mathematically that the optimal combination of decision variables is always found at an extreme point (corner point) of the convex polygon. In Exhibit A.1, there are four corner points (excluding the origin), and we

can determine which one is the optimum by either of two approaches. The first approach is to find the values of the various corner solutions algebraically. This entails simultaneously solving the equations of various pairs of intersecting lines and substituting the quantities of the resultant variables in the objective function. For example, the calculations for the intersection of $2H + 6C = 72$ and $C = 10$ are as follows:

Substituting $C = 10$ in $2H + 6C = 72$ gives $2H + 6(10) = 72$, $2H = 12$, or $H = 6$. Substituting $H = 6$ and $C = 10$ in the objective function, we get

$$\text{Profit} = \$2H + \$4C = \$2(6) + \$4(10)$$
$$= \$12 + \$40 = \$52$$

A variation of this approach is to read the H and C quantities directly from the graph and substitute these quantities into the objective function, as shown in the previous calculation. The drawback in this approach is that in problems with a large number of constraint equations, there will be many possible points to evaluate, and the procedure of testing each one mathematically is inefficient.

The second and generally preferred approach entails using the objective function or iso-profit line directly to find the optimum point. The procedure involves simply drawing a straight line *parallel* to any arbitrarily selected initial iso-profit line so the iso-profit line is farthest from the origin of the graph. (In cost minimization problems, the objective would be to draw the line through the point closest to the origin.) In Exhibit A.1, the dashed line labeled $\$2H + \$4C = \$64$ intersects the most extreme point. Note that the initial arbitrarily selected iso-profit line is necessary to display the slope of the objective function for the particular problem.[1] This is important since a different objective function (try Profit $= 3H + 3C$) might indicate that some other point is farthest from the origin. Given that $\$2H + \$4C = \$64$ is optimal, the amount of each variable to produce can be read from the graph: 24 hockey sticks and four chess sets. No other combination of the products yields a greater profit.

LINEAR PROGRAMMING USING MICROSOFT EXCEL

Spreadsheets can be used to solve linear programming problems. Microsoft Excel has an optimization tool called *Solver* that we will demonstrate by solving the hockey stick and chess problem. We invoke the Solver from the Data tab. A dialogue box requests information required by the program. The following example describes how our sample problem can be solved using Excel.

If the Solver option does not appear in your Data tab, click on Excel Options → Add-Ins, select the Solver Add-In, and then click OK. Solver should then be available directly from the Data tab for future use.

In the following example, we work in a step-by-step manner, setting up a spreadsheet and then solving our Puck and Pawn Company problem. Our basic strategy is to first define the problem within the spreadsheet. Following this, we invoke the Solver and feed it required information. Finally, we execute the Solver and interpret results from the reports provided by the program.

Step 1: Define Changing Cells   A convenient starting point is to identify cells to be used for the decision variables in the problem. These are H and C, the number of hockey sticks and the number of chess sets to produce. Excel refers to these cells as changing cells in Solver. Referring to our Excel screen (Exhibit A.2), we have designated B4 as the location for the number of hockey sticks to produce and C4 for the number of chess sets. Note that we have set these cells equal to 2 initially. We could set these cells to anything, but a value other than zero will help verify that our calculations are correct.

Step 2: Calculate Total Profit (or Cost)   This is our objective function and is calculated by multiplying profit associated with each product by the number of units produced. We have placed the profits in cells B5 and C5 ($2 and $4), so the profit is calculated by the following equation: B4*B5 + C4*C5, which is calculated in cell D5. Solver refers to this as the Target Cell, and it corresponds to the objective function for a problem.

Microsoft Excel Screen for Puck and Pawn Company

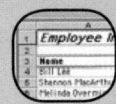

**Excel:
Solver LP**

Step 3: Set Up Resource Usage   Our resources are machine centers A, B, and C as defined in the original problem. We have set up three rows (9, 10, and 11) in our spreadsheet, one for each resource constraint. For machine center A, 4 hours of processing time are used for each hockey stick produced (cell B9) and 6 hours for each chess set (cell C9). For a particular solution, the total amount of the machine center A resource used is calculated in D9 (B9*B4 + C9*C4). We have indicated in cell E9 that we want this value to be less than the 120-hour capacity of machine center A, which is entered in F9. Resource usage for machine centers B and C is set up in the exact same manner in rows 10 and 11.

Step 4: Set Up Solver   Go to the Data tab and select the Solver option.

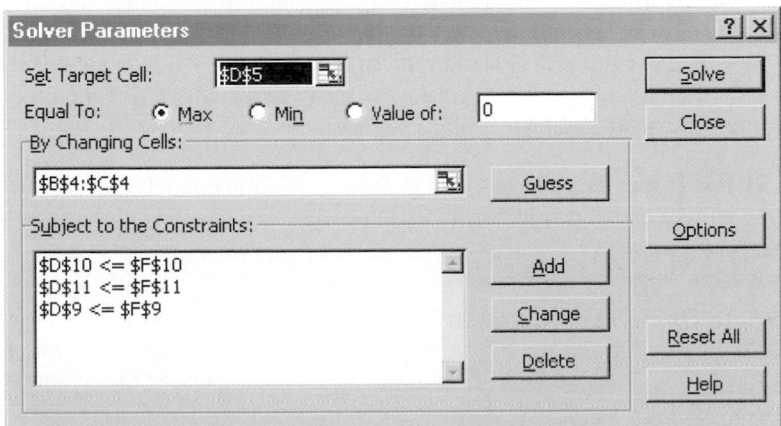

1.   Set Target Cell: is set to the location where the value that we want to optimize is calculated. This is the profit calculated in D5 in our spreadsheet.
2.   Equal To: is set to Max since the goal is to maximize profit.
3.   By Changing Cells: are the cells that Solver can change to maximize profit. Cells B4 through C4 are the changing cells in our problem.

4. Subject to the Constraints: corresponds to our machine center capacity. Here we click on Add and indicate that the total used for a resource is less than or equal to the capacity available. A sample for machine center A follows. Click OK after each constraint is specified.

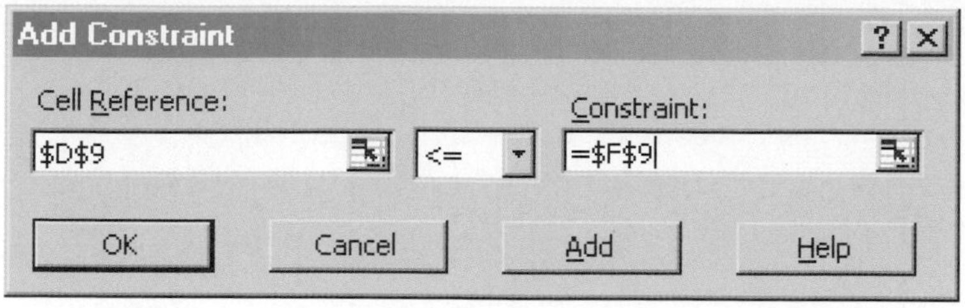

5. Clicking on Options allows us to tell Solver what type of problem we want it to solve and how we want it solved. Solver has numerous options, but we will need to use only a few. The screen is shown below.

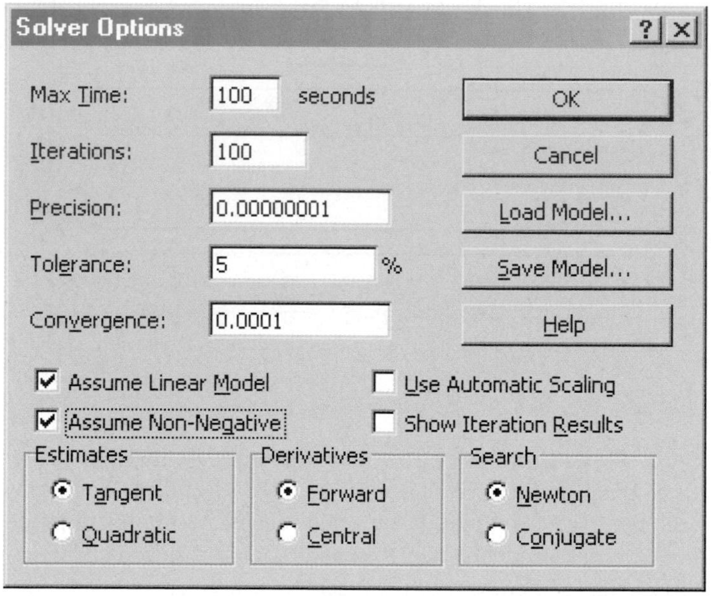

Most of the options relate to how Solver attempts to solve nonlinear problems. These can be very difficult to solve, and optimal solutions difficult to find. Luckily our problem is a linear problem. We know this since our constraints and our objective function are all calculated using linear equations. Click on Assume Linear Model to tell Solver that we want to use the linear programming option for solving the problem. In addition, we know our changing cells (decision variables) must be numbers that are greater than or equal to zero since it makes no sense to make a negative number of hockey sticks or chess sets. We indicate this by selecting Assume Non-Negative as an option. We are now ready to actually solve the problem. Click OK to return to the Solver Parameters box.

Step 5: Solve the Problem   Click Solve. We immediately get a Solver Results acknowledgment like that shown below.

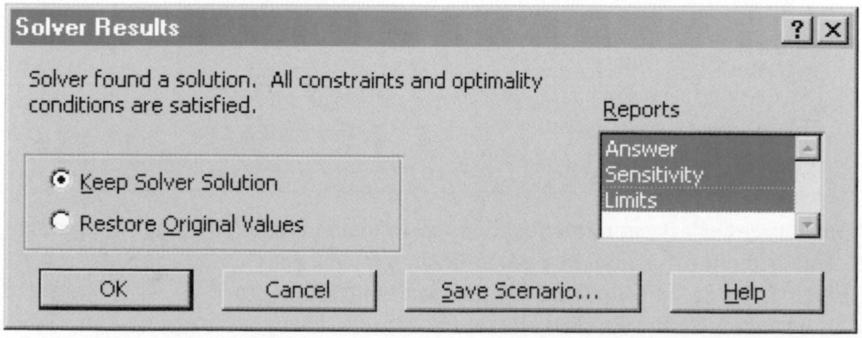

Excel Solver Answer and Sensitivity Reports

Answer Report

TARGET CELL (MAX)

CELL	NAME	ORIGINAL VALUE	FINAL VALUE
$D$5	Profit Total	$12	$64

ADJUSTABLE CELLS

CELL	NAME	ORIGINAL VALUE	FINAL VALUE
$B$4	Changing Cells Hockey Sticks	2	24
$C$4	Changing Cells Chess Sets	2	4

CONSTRAINTS

CELL	NAME	CELL VALUE	FORMULA	STATUS	SLACK
$D$11	Machine C Used	4	$D$11<=$F$11	Not Binding	6
$D$10	Machine B Used	72	$D$10<=$F$10	Binding	0
$D$9	Machine A Used	120	$D$9<=$F$9	Binding	0

Sensitivity Report

ADJUSTABLE CELLS

CELL	NAME	FINAL VALUE	REDUCED COST	OBJECTIVE COEFFICIENT	ALLOWABLE INCREASE	ALLOWABLE DECREASE
$B$4	Changing Cells Hockey Sticks	24	0	2	0.666666667	0.666666667
$C$4	Changing Cells Chess Sets	4	0	4	2	1

CONSTRAINTS

CELL	NAME	FINAL VALUE	SHADOW PRICE	CONSTRAINT R.H. SIDE	ALLOWABLE INCREASE	ALLOWABLE DECREASE
$D$11	Machine C Used	4	0	10	1E+30	6
$D$10	Machine B Used	72	0.333333333	72	18	12
$D$9	Machine A Used	120	0.333333333	120	24	36

Solver acknowledges that a solution was found that appears to be optimal. On the right side of this box are options for three reports: an Answer Report, a Sensitivity Report, and a Limits Report. Click on each report to have Solver provide these. After highlighting the reports, click OK to exit back to the spreadsheet. Three new tabs have been created that correspond to these reports.

The most interesting reports for our problem are the Answer Report and the Sensitivity Report, both of which are shown in Exhibit A.3. The Answer Report shows the final answers for the total profit ($64) and the amounts produced (24 hockey sticks and 4 chess sets). In the constraints section of the Answer Report, the status of each resource is given. All of machine A and machine B are used, and there are six units of slack for machine C.

The Sensitivity Report is divided into two parts. The first part, titled "Adjustable Cells," corresponds to objective function coefficients. The profit per unit for the hockey sticks can be either up or down $0.67 (between $2.67 and $1.33) without having an impact on the solution. Similarly, the profit of the chess sets could be between $6 and $3 without changing the solution. In the case of machine A, the right-hand side could increase to 144 (120 + 24) or decrease to 84 with a resulting $0.33 increase or decrease per unit in the objective function. The right-hand side of machine B can increase to 90 units or decrease to 60 units with the same $0.33 change for each unit in the objective function. For machine C, the right-hand side could increase to infinity (1E+30 is scientific notation for a very large number) or decrease to 4 units with no change in the objective function.

KEY TERMS

Linear programming (LP) Refers to several related mathematical techniques used to allocate limited resources among competing demands in an optimal way.

Graphical linear programming Provides a quick insight into the nature of linear programming.

SOLVED PROBLEMS

SOLVED PROBLEM 1

A furniture company produces three products: end tables, sofas, and chairs. These products are processed in five departments: the saw lumber, fabric cutting, sanding, staining, and assembly departments. End tables and chairs are produced from raw lumber only, and the sofas require lumber and fabric. Glue and thread are plentiful and represent a relatively insignificant cost that is included in operating expense. The specific requirements for each product are as follows:

RESOURCE OR ACTIVITY (QUANTITY AVAILABLE PER MONTH)	REQUIRED PER END TABLE	REQUIRED PER SOFA	REQUIRED PER CHAIR
Lumber (4,350 board feet)	10 board feet @ $10/foot = $100/table	7.5 board feet @ $10/foot = $75	4 board feet @ $10/foot = $40
Fabric (2,500 yards)	None	10 yards @ $17.50/yard = $175	None
Saw lumber (280 hours)	30 minutes	24 minutes	30 minutes
Cut fabric (140 hours)	None	24 minutes	None
Sand (280 hours)	30 minutes	6 minutes	30 minutes
Stain (140 hours)	24 minutes	12 minutes	24 minutes
Assemble (700 hours)	60 minutes	90 minutes	30 minutes

The company's direct labor expenses are $75,000 per month for the 1,540 hours of labor, at $48.70 per hour. Based on current demand, the firm can sell 300 end tables, 180 sofas, and 400 chairs per month. Sales prices are $400 for end tables, $750 for sofas, and $240 for chairs. Assume that labor cost is fixed and the firm does not plan to hire or fire any employees over the next month.

Required:

1 What is the most limiting resource to the furniture company?
2 Determine the product mix needed to maximize profit at the furniture company. What is the optimal number of end tables, sofas, and chairs to produce each month?

Solution

Define X_1 as the number of end tables, X_2 as the number of sofas, and X_3 as the number of chairs to produce each month. Profit is calculated as the revenue for each item minus the cost of materials (lumber and fabric), minus the cost of labor. Since labor is fixed, we subtract this out as a total sum. Mathematically we have $(400 - 100)X_1 + (750 - 75 - 175)X_2 + (240 - 40)X_3 - 75,000$. Profit is calculated as follows:

$$\text{Profit} = 300X_1 + 500X_2 + 200X_3 - 75,000$$

Constraints are the following:

Lumber: $10X_1 + 7.5X_2 + 4X_3 \leq 4,350$
Fabric: $10X_2 \leq 2,500$
Saw: $.5X_1 + .4X_2 + .5X_3 \leq 280$

Cut:	$.4X_2 \leq 140$
Sand:	$.5X_1 + .1X_2 + .5X_3 \leq 280$
Stain:	$.4X_1 + .2X_2 + .4X_3 \leq 140$
Assemble:	$1X_1 + 1.5X_2 + .5X_3 \leq 700$

Demand:

Table:	$X_1 \leq 300$
Sofa:	$X_2 \leq 180$
Chair:	$X_3 \leq 400$

Step 1: Define Changing Cells   These are B3, C3, and D3. Note that these cells have been set equal to zero.

E4		f_x =B4*$B$3+C4*$C$3+D4*$D$3-75000				
	A	B	C	D	E	F
1	Furniture Company					
2		End Tables	Sofas	Chairs	Total	Limit
3	Changing cells	0	0	0		
4	Profit	$300	$500	$200	-$75,000	
5						
6	Lumber	10	7.5	4	0	4350
7	Fabric	0	10	0	0	2500
8	Saw	0.5	0.4	0.5	0	280
9	Cut fabric	0	0.4	0	0	140
10	Sand	0.5	0.1	0.5	0	280
11	Stain	0.4	0.2	0.4	0	140
12	Assemble	1	1.5	0.5	0	700
13	Table Demand	1			0	300
14	Sofa Demand		1		0	180
15	Chair Demand			1	0	400
16						

Solved Problem

Ready   NUM

Step 2: Calculate Total Profit   This is E4 (this is equal to B3 times the $300 revenue associated with each end table, plus C3 times the $500 revenue for each sofa, plus D3 times the $200 revenue associated with each chair). Note the $75,000 fixed expense that has been subtracted from revenue to calculate profit.

Step 3: Set Up Resource Usage   In cells E6 through E15, the usage of each resource is calculated by multiplying B3, C3, and D3 by the amount needed for each item and summing the product (for example, E6 = B3*B6 + C3*C6 + D3*D6). The limits on these constraints are entered in cells F6 to F15.

Step 4: Set Up Solver   Go to Tools and select the Solver option.

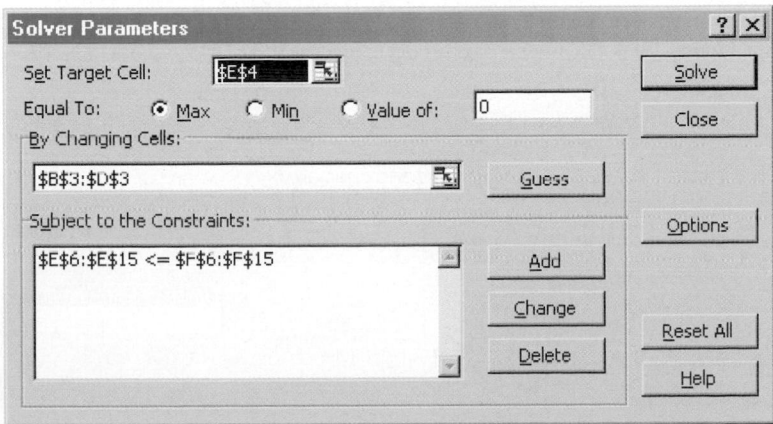

a.   Set Target Cell: is set to the location where the value that we want to optimize is calculated. This is the profit calculated in E4 in this spreadsheet.
b.   Equal To: is set to Max since the goal is to maximize profit.
c.   By Changing Cells: are the cells that Solver can change to maximize profit (cells B3 through D3 in this problem).
d.   Subject to the Constraints: is where a constraint set is added; we indicate that the range E6 to E15 must be less than or equal to F6 to F15.

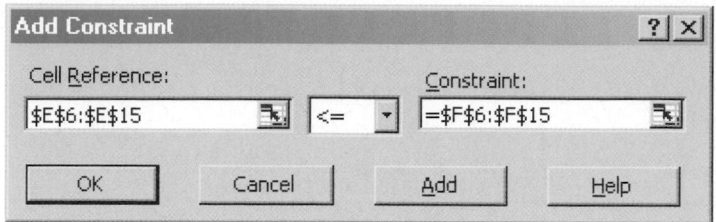

Step 5: Set Options   There are many options here, but for our purposes we just need to indicate Assume Linear Model and Assume Non-Negative. Assume Linear Model means all of our formulas are simple linear equations. Assume Non-Negative indicates that changing cells must be greater than or equal to zero. Click OK and we are ready to solve our problem.

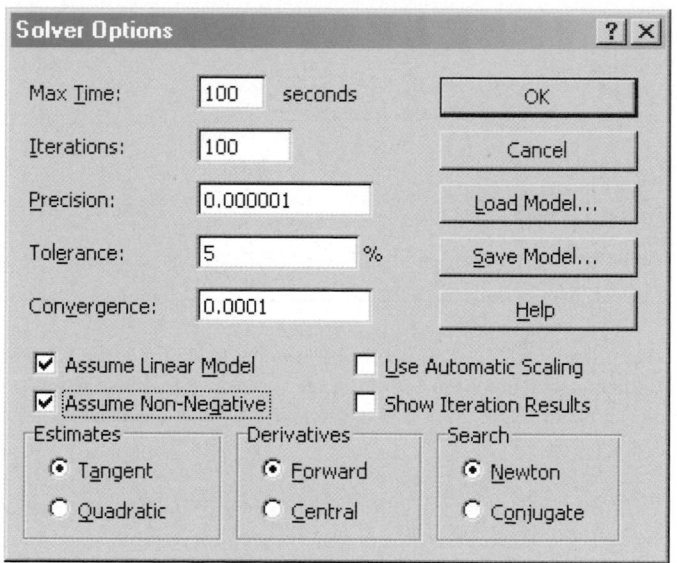

Step 6: Solve the Problem   Click Solve. We can see the solution and two special reports by highlighting items on the Solver Results acknowledgment that is displayed after a solution is found. Note that in the following report, Solver indicates that it has found a solution and all constraints and optimality conditions are satisfied. In the Reports box on the right, the Answer, Sensitivity, and Limits options have been highlighted, indicating that we would like to see these items. After highlighting the reports, click OK to exit back to the spreadsheet.

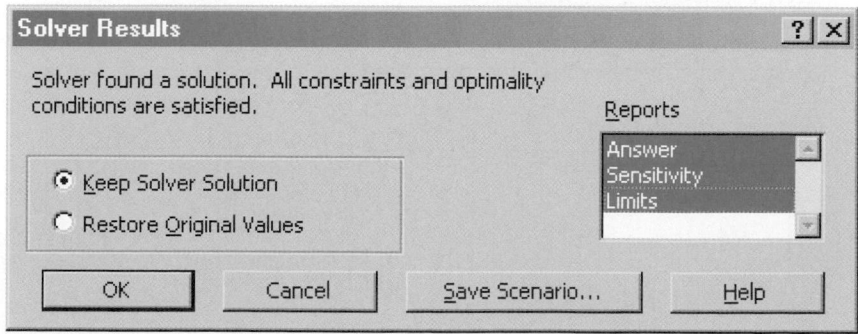

Note that three new tabs have been created: an Answer Report, a Sensitivity Report, and a Limits Report. The Answer Report indicates in the Target Cell section that the profit associated with this solution is $93,000 (we started at −$75,000). From the Target Cell section, we should make 260 end tables, 180 sofas, and no chairs. From the Constraints section, notice that the only constraints limiting profit are the staining capacity and the demand for sofas. We can see this from the column indicating whether a constraint is binding or nonbinding. Nonbinding constraints have slack, as indicated in the last column.

Target Cell (Max)

CELL	NAME	ORIGINAL VALUE	FINAL VALUE
$E$4	Profit Total	−$75,000	$93,000

Adjustable Cells

CELL	NAME	ORIGINAL VALUE	FINAL VALUE
$B$3	Changing cells End Tables	0	260
$C$3	Changing cells Sofas	0	180
$D$3	Changing cells Chairs	0	0

Constraints

CELL	NAME	CELL VALUE	FORMULA	STATUS	SLACK
$E$6	Lumber Total	3950	$E$6<=$F$6	Not Binding	400
$E$7	Fabric Total	1800	$E$7<=$F$7	Not Binding	700
$E$8	Saw Total	202	$E$8<=$F$8	Not Binding	78
$E$9	Cut fabric Total	72	$E$9<=$F$9	Not Binding	68
$E$10	Sand Total	148	$E$10<=$F$10	Not Binding	132
$E$11	Stain Total	140	$E$11<=$F$11	Binding	0
$E$12	Assemble Total	530	$E$12<=$F$12	Not Binding	170
$E$13	Table Demand Total	260	$E$13<=$F$13	Not Binding	40
$E$14	Sofa Demand Total	180	$E$14<=$F$14	Binding	0
$E$15	Chair Demand Total	0	$E$15<=$F$15	Not Binding	400

Of course, we may not be too happy with this solution since we are not meeting all the demand for tables, and it may not be wise to totally discontinue the manufacturing of chairs.

The Sensitivity Report (shown below) gives additional insight into the solution. The Adjustable Cells section of this report shows the final value for each cell and the reduced cost. The reduced cost indicates how much the target cell value would change if a cell that was currently set to zero were brought into the solution. Since the end tables (B3) and sofas (C3) are in the current solution, their reduced cost is zero. For each chair (D3) that we make, our target cell would be reduced $100 (just round these numbers for interpretation purposes). The final three columns in the adjustable cells section of the report are the Objective Coefficient from the original spreadsheet and columns titled Allowable Increase and Allowable Decrease. Allowable Increase and Decrease show by how much the value of the corresponding coefficient could change so there would not be a change in the changing cell values (of course, the target cell value would change). For example, revenue for each end table could be as high as $1,000 ($300 + $700) or as low as $200 ($300 − $100), and we would still want to produce 260 end tables. Keep in mind that these values assume nothing else is changing in the problem. For the allowable increase value for sofas, note the value 1E+30. This is a very large number, essentially infinity, represented in scientific notation.

Adjustable Cells

CELL	NAME	FINAL VALUE	REDUCED COST	OBJECTIVE COEFFICIENT	ALLOWABLE INCREASE	ALLOWABLE DECREASE
$B$3	Changing cells End Tables	260	0	299.9999997	700.0000012	100.0000004
$C$3	Changing cells Sofas	180	0	500.0000005	1E+30	350.0000006
$D$3	Changing cells Chairs	0	−100.0000004	199.9999993	100.0000004	1E+30

Constraints

CELL	NAME	FINAL VALUE	SHADOW PRICE	CONSTRAINT R.H. SIDE	ALLOWABLE INCREASE	ALLOWABLE DECREASE
$E$6	Lumber Total	3950	0	4350	1E+30	400
$E$7	Fabric Total	1800	0	2500	1E+30	700
$E$8	Saw Total	202	0	280	1E+30	78
$E$9	Cut fabric Total	72	0	140	1E+30	68
$E$10	Sand Total	148	0	280	1E+30	132
$E$11	Stain Total	140	749.9999992	140	16	104
$E$12	Assemble Total	530	0	700	1E+30	170
$E$13	Table Demand Total	260	0	300	1E+30	40
$E$14	Sofa Demand Total	180	350.0000006	180	70	80
$E$15	Chair Demand Total	0	0	400	1E+30	400

For the Constraints section of the report, the actual final usage of each resource is given in Final Value. The Shadow Price is the value to our target cell for each unit increase in the resource. If we could increase staining capacity, it would be worth $750 per hour. The Constraint Right-Hand Side is the current limit on the resource. Allowable Increase is the amount the resource could be increased while the shadow price is still valid. Another 16 hours' work of staining capacity could be added with a value of $750 per hour. Similarly, the Allowable Decrease column shows the amount the resource could be reduced without changing the shadow price. There is some valuable information available in this report.

The Limits Report provides additional information about our solution.

CELL	TARGET NAME	VALUE
$E$4	Profit Total	$93,000

CELL	ADJUSTABLE NAME	VALUE	LOWER LIMIT	TARGET RESULT	UPPER LIMIT	TARGET RESULT
$B$3	Changing cells End Tables	260	0	15000	260.0000002	93000
$C$3	Changing cells Sofas	180	0	3000	180	93000
$D$3	Changing cells Chairs	0	0	93000	0	93000

Total profit for the current solution is $93,000. Current value for B3 (end tables) is 260 units. If this were reduced to 0 units, profit would be reduced to $15,000. At an upper limit of 260, profit is $93,000 (the current solution). Similarly, for C3 (sofas), if this were reduced to 0, profit would be reduced to $3,000. At an upper limit of 180, profit is $93,000. For D3 (chairs), if this were reduced to 0, profit is $93,000 (current solution), and in this case the upper limit on chairs is also 0 units.

Acceptable answers to the questions are as follows:

1   *What is the most limiting resource to the furniture company?*
In terms of our production resources, staining capacity is really hurting profit at this time. We could use another 16 hours of capacity.

2   *Determine the product mix needed to maximize profit at the furniture company.*
The product mix would be to make 260 end tables, 180 sofas, and no chairs.

Of course, we have only scratched the surface with this solution. We could actually experiment with increasing staining capacity. This would give insight into the next most limiting resource. We also could run scenarios where we are required to produce a minimum number of each product, which is probably a more realistic scenario. This could help us determine how we could possibly reallocate the use of labor in our shop.

SOLVED PROBLEM 2

It is 2:00 on Friday afternoon and Joe Bob, the head chef (grill cook) at Bruce's Diner, is trying to decide the best way to allocate the available raw material to the four Friday night specials. The decision has to be made in the early afternoon because three of the items must be started now (Sloppy Joes, Tacos, and Chili). The table below contains the information on the food in inventory and the amounts required for each item.

FOOD	CHEESE BURGER	SLOPPY JOES	TACO	CHILI	AVAILABLE
Ground Beef (lbs.)	0.3	0.25	0.25	0.4	100 lbs.
Cheese (lbs.)	0.1	0	0.3	0.2	50 lbs.
Beans (lbs.)	0	0	0.2	0.3	50 lbs.
Lettuce (lbs.)	0.1	0	0.2	0	15 lbs.
Tomato (lbs.)	0.1	0.3	0.2	0.2	50 lbs.
Buns	1	1	0	0	80 buns
Taco Shells	0	0	1	0	80 shells

One other fact relevant to Joe Bob's decision is the estimated market demand and selling price.

	CHEESE BURGER	SLOPPY JOES	TACO	CHILI
Demand	75	60	100	55
Selling Price	$2.25	$2.00	$1.75	$2.50

Joe Bob wants to maximize revenue since he has already purchased all the materials that are sitting in the cooler.

Required:

1. What is the best mix of the Friday night specials to maximize Joe Bob's revenue?
2. If a supplier offered to provide a rush order of buns at $1.00 a bun, is it worth the money?

Solution

Define X_1 as the number of Cheese Burgers, X_2 as the number of Sloppy Joes, X_3 as the number of Tacos, and X_4 as the number of bowls of chili made for the Friday night specials.

$$\text{Revenue} = \$2.25\,X_1 + \$2.00\,X_2 + \$1.75\,X_3 + \$2.50\,X_4$$

Constraints are the following:

Ground Beef: $0.30 X_1 + 0.25 X_2 + 0.25 X_3 + 0.40 X_4 \leq 100$
Cheese: $0.10 X_1 + 0.30 X_3 + 0.20 X_4 \leq 50$
Beans: $0.20 X_3 + 0.30 X_4 \leq 50$
Lettuce: $0.10 X_1 + 0.20 X_3 \leq 15$
Tomato: $0.10 X_1 + 0.30 X_2 + 0.20 X_3 + 0.20 X_4 \leq 50$
Buns: $X_1 + X_2 \leq 80$
Taco Shells: $X_3 \leq 80$

Demand

Cheese Burger $X_1 \leq 75$
Sloppy Joes $X_2 \leq 60$
Taco $X_3 \leq 100$
Chili $X_4 \leq 55$

Step 1: Define the Changing Cells   These are B3, C3, D3, and E3. Note the values in the changing cell are set to 10 each so the formulas can be checked.

F7		ƒₓ =SUMPRODUCT($B$3:$E$3,B7:E7)						
	A	B	C	D	E	F	G	H
1								
2		Cheese Burger	Sloppy Joes	Taco	Chili			
3	Changing Cells	10	10	10	10			
4		>=	>=	>=	>=			
5	Demand	75	60	100	55			
6						Total		
7	Revenue	$ 2.25	$ 2.00	$ 1.75	$ 2.50	$ 85.00		
8								
9								
10	Food	Cheese Burger	Sloppy Joes	Taco	Chili	Total		Available
11	Ground Beef (lbs.)	0.3	0.25	0.25	0.4	12.00	<=	100
12	Cheese (lbs.)	0.1	0	0.3	0.2	6.00	<=	50
13	Beans (lbs.)	0	0	0.2	0.3	5.00	<=	50
14	Lettuce (lbs.)	0.1	0	0.2	0	3.00	<=	15
15	Tomato (lbs.)	0.1	0.3	0.2	0.2	8.00	<=	50
16	Buns	1	1	0	0	20.00	<=	80
17	Taco Shells	0	0	1	0	10.00	<=	80
18								

Step 2: Calculate Total Revenue   This is in cell F7 (this is equal to B3 times the $2.25 for each cheese burger, plus C3 times the $2.00 for a Sloppy Joe, plus D3 times the $1.75 for each taco, plus E3 times the $2.50 for each bowl of chili; the SUMPRODUCT function in Excel was used to make this calculation faster). Note that the current value is $85, which is a result of selling 10 of each item.

Step 3: Set Up the Usage of the Food   In cells F11 to F17, the usage of each food is calculated by multiplying the changing cells row times the per item use in the table and then summing the result. The limits on each of these food types are given in H11 through H17.

Step 4: Set Up Solver and Select the Solver Option

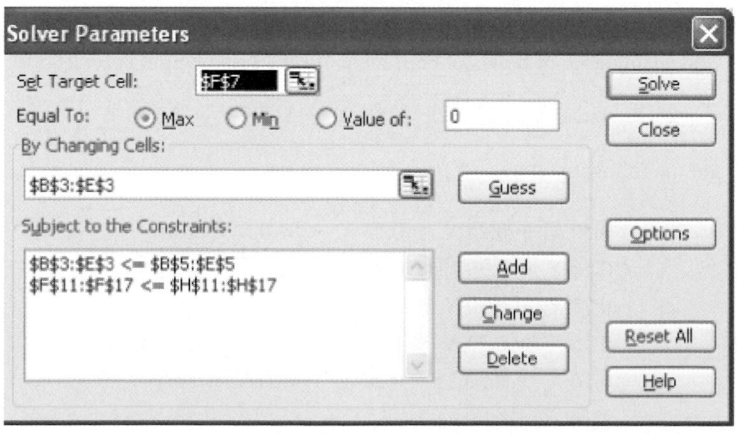

a. Set Target Cell: is set to the location where the value that we want to optimize is calculated. The revenue is calculated in F7 in this spreadsheet.

b. Equal to: is set to Max since the goal is to maximize revenue.

c. By Changing Cells: are the cells that tell how many of each special to produce.

d. Subject to the Constraints: is where we add two separate constraints, one for demand and one for the usage of food.

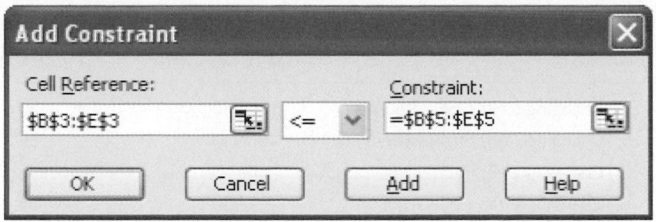

Step 5: Set Options   Click on Options. We will leave all the settings as the default values and only need to make sure of two changes: (1) check the Assume Linear Model option and (2) check the Assume Non-Negative option. These two options make sure that Solver knows that this is a linear programming problem and that all changing cells should be nonnegative. Click OK to return to the Solver Parameters screen.

Step 6: Solve the Problem   Click Solve. We will get a Solver Results box. Make sure it says that it has the following statement: "Solver found a solution. All constraints and optimality conditions are satisfied."

On the right-hand side of the box, there is an option for three reports: Answer, Sensitivity, and Limit. Click on all three reports and then click OK; this will exit you back to the spreadsheet, but you will have three new worksheets in your workbook.

The answer report indicates that the target cell has a final solution of $416.25 and started at $85. From the adjustable cells area we can see that we should make 20 cheese burgers, 60 Sloppy Joes, 65 tacos, and 55 bowls of chili. This answers the first requirement from the problem of what the mix of Friday night specials should be.

Target Cell (Max)

CELL	NAME	ORIGINAL VALUE	FINAL VALUE
$F$7	Revenue Total	$85.00	$416.25

Adjustable Cells

CELL	NAME	ORIGINAL VALUE	FINAL VALUE
$B$3	Changing Cells Cheese Burger	10	20
$C$3	Changing Cells Sloppy Joes	10	60
$D$3	Changing Cells Taco	10	65
$E$3	Changing Cells Chili	10	55

Constraints

CELL	NAME	CELL VALUE	FORMULA	STATUS	SLACK
$F$11	Ground Beef (lbs.) Total	59.25	$F$11<=$H$11	Not Binding	40.75
$F$12	Cheese (lbs.) Total	32.50	$F$12<=$H$12	Not Binding	17.5
$F$13	Beans (lbs.) Total	29.50	$F$13<=$H$13	Not Binding	20.5
$F$14	Lettuce (lbs.) Total	15.00	$F$14<=$H$14	Binding	0
$F$15	Tomato (lbs.) Total	44.00	$F$15<=$H$15	Not Binding	6
$F$16	Buns Total	80.00	$F$16<=$H$16	Binding	0
$F$17	Taco Shells Total	65.00	$F$17<=$H$17	Not Binding	15
$B$3	Changing Cells Cheese Burger	20	$B$3<=$B$5	Not Binding	55
$C$3	Changing Cells Sloppy Joes	60	$C$3<=$C$5	Binding	0
$D$3	Changing Cells Taco	65	$D$3<=$D$5	Not Binding	35
$E$3	Changing Cells Chili	55	$E$3<=$E$5	Binding	0

The second required answer was whether it is worth it to pay a rush supplier $1 a bun for additional buns. The answer report shows us that the buns constraint was binding. This means that if we had more buns, we could make more money. However, the answer report does not tell us whether a rush order of buns at $1 a bun is worthwhile. In order to answer that question, we have to look at the sensitivity report.

Adjustable Cells

CELL	NAME	FINAL VALUE	REDUCED COST	OBJECTIVE COEFFICIENT	ALLOWABLE INCREASE	ALLOWABLE DECREASE
$B$3	Changing Cells Cheese Burger	20	0	2.25	0.625	1.375
$C$3	Changing Cells Sloppy Joes	60	0.625	2	1E+30	0.625
$D$3	Changing Cells Taco	65	0	1.75	2.75	1.25
$E$3	Changing Cells Chili	55	2.5	2.5	1E+30	2.5

Constraints

CELL	NAME	FINAL VALUE	SHADOW PRICE	CONSTRAINT R.H. SIDE	ALLOWABLE INCREASE	ALLOWABLE DECREASE
$F$11	Ground Beef (lbs.) Total	59.25	0.00	100	1E+30	40.75
$F$12	Cheese (lbs.) Total	32.50	0.00	50	1E+30	17.5
$F$13	Beans (lbs.) Total	29.50	0.00	50	1E+30	20.5
$F$14	Lettuce (lbs.) Total	15.00	8.75	15	3	13
$F$15	Tomato (lbs.) Total	44.00	0.00	50	1E+30	6
$F$16	Buns Total	80.00	1.38	80	55	20
$F$17	Taco Shells Total	65.00	0.00	80	1E+30	15

We have highlighted the buns row to answer the question. We can see that buns have a shadow price of $1.38. This shadow price means that each additional bun will generate $1.38 of profit. We also can see that other foods such as ground beef have a shadow price of $0. The items with a shadow price of $0 add nothing to profit since we are currently not using all that we have now. The other important piece of information that we have on the buns is that they are only worth $1.38 up until the next 55 buns and that is why the allowable increase is 55. We also can see that a pound of lettuce is worth $8.75. It might be wise to also look for a rush supplier of lettuce so we can increase our profit on Friday nights.

Acceptable answers to the questions are as follows:

1 *What is the best mix of the Friday night specials to maximize Joe Bob's revenue?*
   20 cheese burgers, 60 Sloppy Joes, 65 tacos, and 55 bowls of chili.

2 *If a supplier offered to provide a rush order of buns at $1.00 a bun, is it worth the money?*
   Yes, each additional bun brings in $1.38, so if they cost us $1, then we will net $0.38 per bun. However, this is true only up to 55 additional buns.

PROBLEMS

1 Solve the following problem with Excel Solver:

$$\text{Maximize } Z = 3X + Y.$$
$$12X + 14Y \le 85$$
$$3X + 2Y \le 18$$
$$Y \le 4$$

2 Solve the following problem with Excel Solver:

$$\text{Minimize } Z = 2A + 4B.$$
$$4A + 6B \ge 120$$
$$2A + 6B \ge 72$$
$$B \ge 10$$

3 A manufacturing firm has discontinued production of a certain unprofitable product line. Considerable excess production capacity was created as a result. Management is considering devoting this excess capacity to one or more of three products: X_1, X_2, and X_3.
   Machine hours required per unit are

	PRODUCT		
MACHINE TYPE	X_1	X_2	X_3
Milling machine	8	2	3
Lathe	4	3	0
Grinder	2	0	1

The available time in machine hours per week is

	MACHINE HOURS PER WEEK
Milling machines	800
Lathes	480
Grinders	320

The salespeople estimate they can sell all the units of X_1 and X_2 that can be made. But the sales potential of X_3 is 80 units per week maximum.
   Unit profits for the three products are

	UNIT PROFITS
X_1	$20
X_2	6
X_3	8

a. Set up the equations that can be solved to maximize the profit per week.
b. Solve these equations using the Excel Solver.
c. What is the optimal solution? How many of each product should be made, and what should the resultant profit be?

    d. What is this situation with respect to the machine groups? Would they work at capacity, or would there be unused available time? Will X_3 be at maximum sales capacity?

    e. Suppose that an additional 200 hours per week can be obtained from the milling machines by working overtime. The incremental cost would be $1.50 per hour. Would you recommend doing this? Explain how you arrived at your answer.

4   A diet is being prepared for the University of Arizona dorms. The objective is to feed the students at the least cost, but the diet must have between 1,800 and 3,600 calories. No more than 1,400 calories can be starch, and no fewer than 400 can be protein. The varied diet is to be made of two foods: *A* and *B*. Food *A* costs $0.75 per pound and contains 600 calories, 400 of which are protein and 200 starch. No more than two pounds of food *A* can be used per resident. Food *B* costs $0.15 per pound and contains 900 calories, of which 700 are starch, 100 are protein, and 100 are fat.

    a. Write the equations representing this information.

    b. Solve the problem graphically for the amounts of each food that should be used.

5   Repeat Problem 4 with the added constraint that not more than 150 calories shall be fat and that the price of food has escalated to $1.75 per pound for food *A* and $2.50 per pound for food *B*.

6   Logan Manufacturing wants to mix two fuels, *A* and *B*, for its trucks to minimize cost. It needs no fewer than 3,000 gallons to run its trucks during the next month. It has a maximum fuel storage capacity of 4,000 gallons. There are 2,000 gallons of fuel *A* and 4,000 gallons of fuel *B* available. The mixed fuel must have an octane rating of no less than 80.

    When fuels are mixed, the amount of fuel obtained is just equal to the sum of the amounts put in. The octane rating is the weighted average of the individual octanes, weighted in proportion to the respective volumes.

    The following is known: Fuel *A* has an octane of 90 and costs $1.20 per gallon. Fuel *B* has an octane of 75 and costs $0.90 per gallon.

    a. Write the equations expressing this information.

    b. Solve the problem using the Excel Solver, giving the amount of each fuel to be used. State any assumptions necessary to solve the problem.

7   You are trying to create a budget to optimize the use of a portion of your disposable income. You have a maximum of $1,500 per month to be allocated to food, shelter, and entertainment. The amount spent on food and shelter combined must not exceed $1,000. The amount spent on shelter alone must not exceed $700. Entertainment cannot exceed $300 per month. Each dollar spent on food has a satisfaction value of 2, each dollar spent on shelter has a satisfaction value of 3, and each dollar spent on entertainment has a satisfaction value of 5.

    Assuming a linear relationship, use the Excel Solver to determine the optimal allocation of your funds.

8   C-town brewery brews two beers: Expansion Draft and Burning River. Expansion Draft sells for $20 per barrel, while Burning River sells for $8 per barrel. Producing a barrel of Expansion Draft takes 8 pounds of corn and 4 pounds of hops. Producing a barrel of Burning River requires 2 pounds of corn, 6 pounds of rice, and 3 pounds of hops. The brewery has 500 pounds of corn, 300 pounds of rice, and 400 pounds of hops. Assuming a linear relationship, use Excel Solver to determine the optimal mix of Expansion Draft and Burning River that maximizes C-town's revenue.

9   BC Petrol manufactures three chemicals at their chemical plant in Kentucky: BCP1, BCP2, and BCP3. These chemicals are produced in two production processes known as zone and man. Running the zone process for an hour costs $48 and yields three units of BCP1, one unit of BCP2, and one unit of BCP3. Running the man process for one hour costs $24 and yields one unit of BCP1 and one unit of BCP2. To meet customer demands, at least 20 units of BCP1, 10 units of BCP2, and 6 units of BCP3 must be produced daily. Assuming a linear relationship, use Excel Solver to determine the optimal mix of processes zone and man to minimize costs and meet BC Petrol daily demands.

10   A farmer in Wood County has 900 acres of land. She is going to plant each acre with corn, soybeans, or wheat. Each acre planted with corn yields a $2,000 profit; each with soybeans yields $2,500 profit; and each with wheat yields $3,000 profit. She has 100 workers and 150 tons of fertilizer. The table below shows the requirement per acre of each of the crops. Assuming a linear relationship, use Excel Solver to determine the optimal planting mix of corn, soybeans, and wheat to maximize her profits.

	CORN	SOYBEANS	WHEAT
Labor (workers)	0.1	0.3	0.2
Fertilizer (tons)	0.2	0.1	0.4

SELECTED BIBLIOGRAPHY

Anderson, D. R.; D. J. Sweeney; and T. A. Williams. *An Introduction to Management Science.* 11th ed. Mason, OH. South-Western, 2005.

Kelly, Julia, and Curt Simmons. *The Unofficial Guide to Microsoft Excel 2007.* New York: John Wiley & Sons, 2007.

Winston, W. L., and S. C. Albright. *Practical Management Science.* 3rd ed. Mason, OH: South-Western, 2006.

FOOTNOTE

1 The slope of the objective function is -2. If P = profit, $P = \$2H + \$4C$; $\$2H = P + \$4C$; $H = P/2 - 2C$. Thus, the slope is -2.

OPERATIONS TECHNOLOGY

Much of the recent growth in productivity has come from the application of operations technology. In services this comes primarily from soft technology—information processing. In manufacturing it comes from a combination of soft and hard (machine) technologies. Given that most readers of this book have covered information technologies in services in MIS courses, our focus in this supplement is on manufacturing.

TECHNOLOGIES IN MANUFACTURING

Some technological advances in recent decades have had a significant, widespread impact on manufacturing firms in many industries. These advances, which are the topic of this section, can be categorized in two ways: hardware systems and software systems.

Hardware technologies have generally resulted in greater automation of processes; they perform labor-intensive tasks originally performed by humans. Examples of these major types of hardware technologies are numerically controlled machine tools, machining centers, industrial robots, automated materials handling systems, and flexible manufacturing systems. These are all computer-controlled devices that can be used in the manufacturing of products. Software-based technologies aid in the design of manufactured products and in the analysis and planning of manufacturing activities. These technologies include computer-aided design and automated manufacturing planning and control systems. Each of these technologies will be described in greater detail in the following sections.

Hardware Systems *Numerically controlled (NC) machines* are comprised of (1) a typical machine tool used to turn, drill, or grind different types of parts and (2) a computer that controls the sequence of processes performed by the machine. NC machines were first adopted by U.S. aerospace firms in the 1960s, and they have since proliferated to many other industries. In more recent models, feedback control loops determine the position of the machine tooling during the work, constantly compare the actual location with the programmed location, and correct as needed. This is often called *adaptive control*.

Machining centers represent an increased level of automation and complexity relative to NC machines. Machining centers not only provide automatic control of a machine, they also may carry many tools that can be automatically changed depending on the tool required for each operation. In addition, a single machine may be equipped with a shuttle system so that a finished part can be unloaded and an unfinished part loaded while the machine is working on a part. To help you visualize a machining center, we have included a diagram in Exhibit B.1A.

Industrial robots are used as substitutes for workers for many repetitive manual activities and tasks that are dangerous, dirty, or dull. A robot is a programmable, multifunctional machine that may be equipped with an end effector. Examples of end effectors include a gripper to pick things up or a tool such as a wrench, a welder, or a paint sprayer. Exhibit B.1B examines the human motions a robot can reproduce. Advanced capabilities have been designed into robots to allow vision, tactile sensing, and hand-to-hand coordination. In addition, some models can be "taught" a sequence of motions in a three-dimensional pattern. As a worker moves the end of the robot arm through the required motions, the robot records this pattern in its memory and repeats it on command. Newer robotic systems can conduct

A. The CNC Machining Center

B. Typical Robot Axes
of Motion

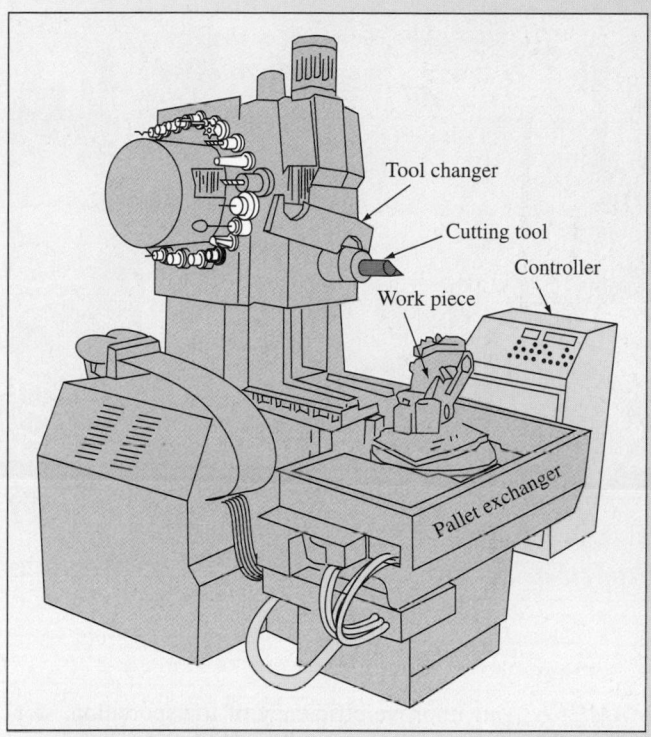

SOURCE: J. T. BLACK, *THE DESIGN OF THE FACTORY WITH A FUTURE* (NEW YORK: MCGRAW-HILL 1991), P. 39, WITH PERMISSION OF THE MCGRAW-HILL COMPANIES.

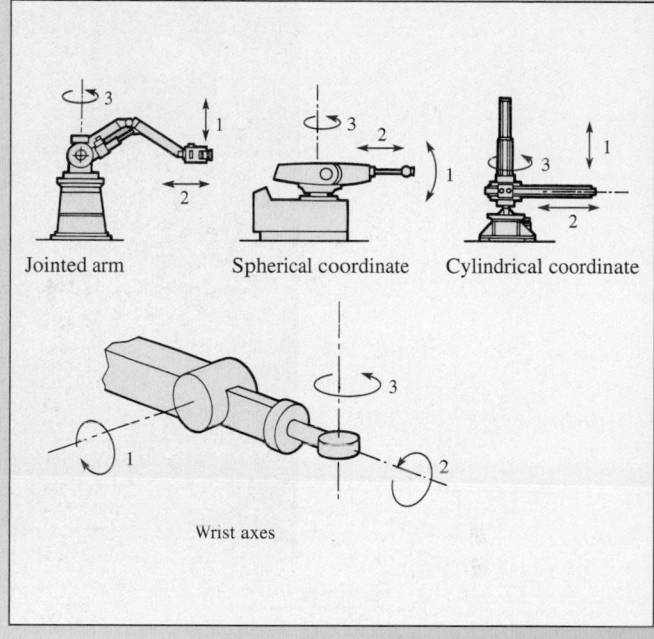

Jointed arm   Spherical coordinate   Cylindrical coordinate

Wrist axes

SOURCE: L. V. OTTINGER, "ROBOTICS FOR THE IE: TERMINOLOGY, TYPES OF ROBOTS," *INDUSTRIAL ENGINEERING*, NOVEMBER 1981, P. 30.

quality control inspections and then transfer, via mobile robots, those parts to other robots downstream. As shown in the box "Formula for Evaluating a Robot Investment," robots are often justified based on labor savings.

FORMULA FOR EVALUATING A ROBOT INVESTMENT

Many companies use the following modification of the basic payback formula in deciding if a robot should be purchased:

$$P = \frac{I}{L - E + q(L + Z)}$$

where

P = Payback period in years
I = Total capital investment required in robot and accessories
L = Annual labor costs replaced by the robot (wage and benefit costs per worker times the number of shifts per day)
E = Annual maintenance cost for the robot
q = Fractional speedup (or slowdown) factor
Z = Annual depreciation

Example:

I = \$50,000
L = \$60,000 (two workers $\times$ \$20,000 each working one of two shifts; overhead is \$10,000 each)
E = \$9,600 (\$2/hour $\times$ 4,800 hours/year)
q = 1.5 (robot works 150 percent as fast as a worker)
Z = \$10,000

then

$$P = \frac{\$50,000}{\$60,000 - \$9,600 + 1.5(\$60,000 + \$10,000)}$$

$$= 1/3 \text{ year}$$

ONE OF THE FOUR LARGE MACHINING CENTERS (SEE EXHIBIT B.2) THAT ARE PART OF THE FLEXIBLE MANUFACTURING SYSTEMS AT CINCINNATI MILACRON'S MT. ORAB, OHIO, PLANT.

Automated materials handing (AMH) systems improve efficiency of transportation, storage, and retrieval of materials. Examples are computerized conveyors and automated storage and retrieval systems (AS/RS) in which computers direct automatic loaders to pick and place items. Automated guided vehicle (AGV) systems use embedded floor wires to direct driverless vehicles to various locations in the plant. Benefits of AMH systems include quicker material movement, lower inventories and storage space, reduced product damage, and higher labor productivity.

These individual pieces of automation can be combined to form *manufacturing cells* or even complete *flexible manufacturing systems (FMS)*. A manufacturing cell might consist of a robot and a machining center. The robot could be programmed to automatically insert and remove parts from the machining center, thus allowing unattended operation. An FMS is a totally automated manufacturing system that consists of machining centers with automated loading and unloading of parts, an automated guided vehicle system for moving parts between machines, and other automated elements to allow unattended production of parts. In an FMS, a comprehensive computer control system is used to run the entire system.

A good example of an FMS is the Cincinnati Milacron facility in Mt. Orab, Ohio, which has been in operation for over 25 years. Exhibit B.2 is a layout of this FMS. In this system, parts are loaded onto standardized fixtures (these are called "risers"), which are mounted on pallets that can be moved by the AGVs. Workers load and unload tools and parts onto the standardized fixtures at the workstations shown on the right side of the diagram. Most of this loading and unloading is done during a single shift. The system can operate virtually unattended for the other two shifts each day.

Within the system there are areas for the storage of tools (Area 7) and for parts (Area 5). This system is designed to machine large castings used in the production of the machine tools made by Cincinnati Milacron. The machining is done by the four CNC machining centers (Area 1). When the machining has been completed on a part, it is sent to the parts washing station (Area 4), where it is cleaned. The part is then sent to the automated inspection station (Area 6) for a quality check. The system is capable of producing hundreds of different parts.

The Cincinnati Milacron Flexible Manufacturing System

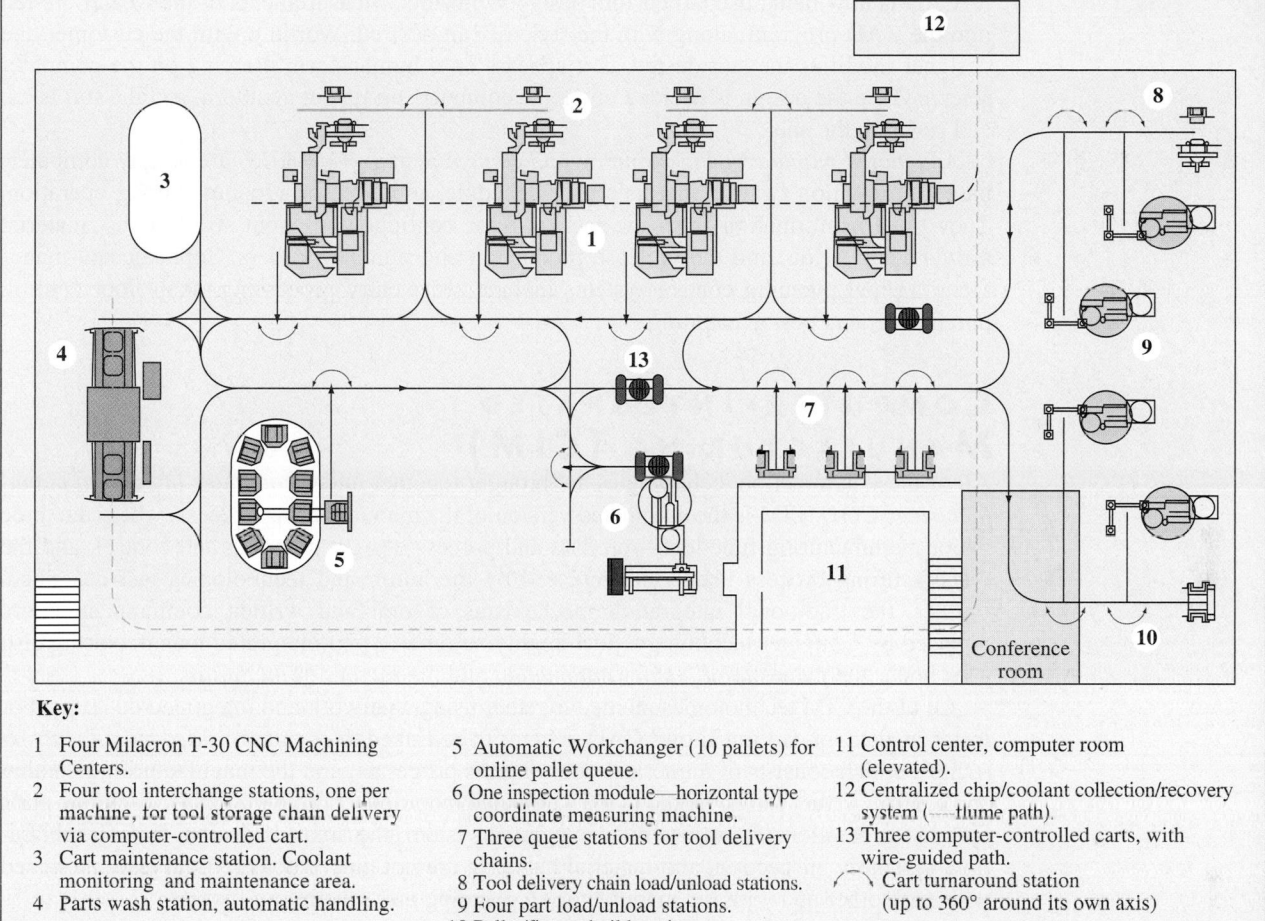

Key:

1 Four Milacron T-30 CNC Machining Centers.
2 Four tool interchange stations, one per machine, for tool storage chain delivery via computer-controlled cart.
3 Cart maintenance station. Coolant monitoring and maintenance area.
4 Parts wash station, automatic handling.

5 Automatic Workchanger (10 pallets) for online pallet queue.
6 One inspection module—horizontal type coordinate measuring machine.
7 Three queue stations for tool delivery chains.
8 Tool delivery chain load/unload stations.
9 Four part load/unload stations.
10 Pallet/fixture build station.

11 Control center, computer room (elevated).
12 Centralized chip/coolant collection/recovery system (——flume path).
13 Three computer-controlled carts, with wire-guided path.
⌒ Cart turnaround station (up to 360° around its own axis)

SOURCE: TOUR BROCHURE FROM THE PLANT.

Software Systems   *Computer-aided design (CAD)* is an approach to product and process design that utilizes the power of the computer. CAD covers several automated technologies, such as *computer graphics* to examine the visual characteristics of a product and *computer-aided engineering (CAE)* to evaluate its engineering characteristics. Rubbermaid used CAD to refine dimensions of its ToteWheels to meet airline requirements for checked baggage. CAD also includes technologies associated with the manufacturing process design, referred to as *computer-aided process planning (CAPP)*. CAPP is used to design the computer part programs that serve as instructions to computer-controlled machine tools and to design the programs used to sequence parts through the machine centers and other processes (such as the washing and inspection) needed to complete the part. These programs are referred to as *process plans*. Sophisticated CAD systems also are able to do on-screen tests, replacing the early phases of prototype testing and modification.

CAD has been used to design everything from computer chips to potato chips. Frito-Lay, for example, used CAD to design its O'Grady's double-density, ruffled potato chip. The problem in designing such a chip is that if it is cut improperly, it may be burned on the outside and soggy on the inside, be too brittle (and shatter when placed in the bag), or display other characteristics that make it unworthy for, say, a guacamole dip. However, through the use of CAD, the proper angle and number of ruffles were determined mathematically; the O'Grady's model passed its stress test in the infamous Frito-Lay "crusher" and made it to your grocer's shelf. But despite some very loyal fans, O'Grady's has been discontinued, presumably due to lack of sales.

CAD is now being used to custom design swimsuits. Measurements of the wearer are fed into the CAD program, along with the style of suit desired. Working with the customer, the designer modifies the suit design as it appears on a human-form drawing on the computer screen. Once the design is decided upon, the computer prints out a pattern, and the suit is cut and sewn on the spot.

Automated manufacturing planning and control systems (MP&CS) are simply computer-based information systems that help plan, schedule, and monitor a manufacturing operation. They obtain information from the factory floor continuously about work status, material arrivals, and so on, and they release production and purchase orders. Sophisticated manufacturing and planning control systems include order-entry processing, shop-floor control, purchasing, and cost accounting.

COMPUTER-INTEGRATED MANUFACTURING (CIM)

All of these automation technologies are brought together under *computer-integrated manufacturing (CIM)*. CIM is the automated version of the manufacturing process, where the three major manufacturing functions—product and process design, planning and control, and the manufacturing process itself—are replaced by the automated technologies just described. Further, the traditional integration mechanisms of oral and written communication are replaced by computer technology. Such highly automated and integrated manufacturing also goes under the names *total factory automation* and the *factory of the future*.

All of the CIM technologies are tied together using a network and integrated database. For instance, data integration allows CAD systems to be linked to *computer-aided manufacturing (CAM),* which consists of numerical-control parts programs; and the manufacturing planning and control system can be linked to the automated material handling systems to facilitate parts pick list generation. Thus, in a fully integrated system, the areas of design, testing, fabrication, assembly, inspection, and material handling are not only automated but also integrated with each other and with the manufacturing planning and scheduling function.

Evaluation of Technology Investments   Modern technologies such as flexible manufacturing systems or computerized order processing systems represent large capital investments. Hence, a firm has to carefully assess its financial and strategic benefits from a technology before acquiring it. Evaluating such investments is especially hard because the purpose of acquiring new technologies is not just to reduce labor costs but also to increase product quality and variety, to shorten production lead times, and to increase the flexibility of an operation. Some of these benefits are intangible relative to labor cost reduction, so justification becomes difficult. Further, rapid technological change renders new equipment obsolete in just a few years, making the cost–benefit evaluation more complex.

But never assume that new automation technologies are always cost-effective. Even when there is no uncertainty about the benefits of automation, it may not be worthwhile to adopt it. For instance, many analysts predicted that integrated CAD/CAM systems would be the answer to all manufacturing problems. But a number of companies investing in such systems lost money in the process. The idea was to take a lot of skilled labor out of the process of tooling up for new or redesigned products and to speed up the process. However, it can take less time to mill complex, low-volume parts than to program the milling machine, and programmer time is more expensive than the milling operator time. Also, it may not always be easy to transfer all the expert knowledge and experience that a milling operator has gained over the years into a computer program. CAD/CAM integration software has attained sufficient levels of quality and cost effectiveness that it is now routinely utilized even in high-variety low-volume manufacturing environments.

Benefits of Technology Investments   The typical benefits from adopting new manufacturing technologies are both tangible and intangible. The tangible benefits can be used in traditional modes of financial analysis such as discounted cash flow to make sound investment decisions. Specific benefits can be summarized as follows:

COST REDUCTION

Labor costs.   Replacing people with robots, or enabling fewer workers to run semiautomatic equipment.

Material costs.   Using existing materials more efficiently, or enabling the use of high-tolerance materials.

Inventory costs.   Fast changeover equipment allowing for JIT inventory management.

Quality costs.   Automated inspection and reduced variation in product output.

Maintenance costs.   Self-adjusting equipment.

OTHER BENEFITS

Increased product variety.   Scope economies due to flexible manufacturing systems.

Improved product features.   Ability to make things that could not be made by hand (e.g., microprocessors).

Shorter cycle times.   Faster setups and changeovers.

Greater product output.

Risks in Adopting New Technologies   Although there may be many benefits in acquiring new technologies, several types of risk accompany the acquisition of new technologies. These risks have to be evaluated and traded off against the benefits before the technologies are adopted. Some of these risks are described next.

TECHNOLOGICAL RISKS

An early adopter of a new technology has the benefit of being ahead of the competition, but he or she also runs the risk of acquiring an untested technology whose problems could disrupt the firm's operations. There is also the risk of obsolescence, especially with electronics-based technologies where change is rapid and when the fixed cost of acquiring new technologies or the cost of upgrades is high. Also, alternative technologies may become more cost-effective in the future, negating the benefits of a technology today.

OPERATIONAL RISKS

There also could be risks in applying a new technology to a firm's operations. Installation of a new technology generally results in significant disruptions, at least in the short run, in the form of plantwide reorganization, retraining, and so on. Further risks are due to the delays and errors introduced in the production process and the uncertain and sudden demands on various resources.

ORGANIZATIONAL RISKS

Firms may lack the organizational culture and top management commitment required to absorb the short-term disruptions and uncertainties associated with adopting a new technology. In such organizations, there is a risk that the firm's employees or managers may quickly abandon the technology when there are short-term failures or will avoid major changes by simply automating the firm's old, inefficient process and therefore not obtain the benefits of the new technology.

ENVIRONMENTAL OR MARKET RISKS

In many cases, a firm may invest in a particular technology only to discover a few years later that changes in some environmental or market factors make the investment worthless. For instance, in environmental issues, auto firms have been reluctant to invest in technology for making electric cars because they are uncertain about future emission standards of state and federal governments, the potential for decreasing emissions from gasoline-based cars, and the potential for significant improvements in battery technology. Typical examples of market risks are fluctuations in currency exchange rates and interest rates.

SUMMARY

Technology has played the dominant role in the productivity growth of most nations and has provided the competitive edge to firms that have adopted it early and implemented it successfully. Although each of the manufacturing and information technologies described here is a powerful tool by itself and can be adopted separately, their benefits grow exponentially when they are integrated with each other. This is particularly the case with CIM technologies.

With more modern technologies, the benefits are not entirely tangible and many benefits may be realized only on a long-term basis. Thus, typical cost accounting methods and standard financial analysis may not adequately capture all the potential benefits of technologies such as CIM. Hence, we must take into account the strategic benefits in evaluating such investments. Further, because capital costs for many modern technologies are substantial, the various risks associated with such investments have to be carefully assessed.

Implementing flexible manufacturing systems or complex decision support systems requires a significant commitment for most firms. Such investments may even be beyond the reach of small to medium-size firms. However, as technologies continue to improve and are adopted more widely, their costs may decline and place them within the reach of smaller firms. Given the complex, integrative nature of these technologies, the total commitment of top management and all employees is critical for the successful implementation of these technologies.

REVIEW AND DISCUSSION QUESTIONS

1 Do robots have to be trained? Explain.
2 How does the axiom used in industrial selling "You don't sell the product; you sell the company" pertain to manufacturing technology?
3 List three analytical tools (other than financial analysis) covered elsewhere in the book that can be used to evaluate technological alternatives.
4 The Belleville, Ontario, Canada, subsidiary of Atlanta-based Interface Inc., one of the world's largest makers of commercial flooring, credits much of its profitability to "green manufacturing" or "eco-efficiency." What do you believe these terms mean, eh? And how could such practices lead to cost reduction?
5 Give two examples each of recent process and product technology innovations.
6 What is the difference between an NC machine and a machining center?
7 The major auto companies are planning to invest millions of dollars in developing new product and process technologies required to make electric cars. Describe briefly why they are investing in these technologies. Discuss the potential benefits and risks involved in these investments.

SELECTED BIBLIOGRAPHY

Black, J. T. *The Design of the Factory with a Future.* New York: McGraw-Hill, 1991.

Groover, M. P. *Fundamentals of Modern Manufacturing.* 3rd ed. New York: Wiley, 2006.

Groover, M. P. *Automation, Production Systems, and Computer-Integrated Manufacturing.* 3rd ed. Upper Saddle River, NJ: Prentice Hall, 2007.

Hyer, N., and U. Wemmerlöv. *Reorganizing the Factory: Competing through Cellular Manufacturing.* Portland: OR; Productivity Press, 2002.

Kalpakjian, S., and S. Schmid. *Manufacturing, Engineering & Technology.* 5th ed. Upper Saddle River, NJ: Prentice Hall, 2005.

Melnyk, S. A., and R. Narasimhan. *Computer Integrated Manufacturing.* Homewood, IL: Irwin Professional Publishing, 1992.

FINANCIAL ANALYSIS

In this appendix we review basic concepts and tools of financial analysis for OSCM. These include the types of cost (fixed, variable, sunk, opportunity, avoidable), risk and expected value, and depreciation (straight line, sum-of-the-years'-digits, declining balance, double-declining balance, and depreciation-by-use). We also discuss activity-based costing and cost-of-capital calculations. Our focus is on capital investment decisions.

CONCEPTS AND DEFINITIONS

We begin with some basic definitions.

Fixed Costs A *fixed cost* is any expense that remains constant regardless of the level of output. Although no cost is truly fixed, many types of expense are virtually fixed over a wide range of output. Examples are rent, property taxes, most types of depreciation, insurance payments, and salaries of top management.

Variable Costs *Variable costs* are expenses that fluctuate directly with changes in the level of output. For example, each additional unit of sheet steel produced by USx requires a specific amount of material and labor. The incremental cost of this additional material and labor can be isolated and assigned to each unit of sheet steel produced. Many overhead expenses are also variable because utility bills, maintenance expense, and so forth, vary with the production level.

Exhibit C.1 illustrates the fixed and variable cost components of total cost. Note that total cost increases at the same rate as variable costs because fixed costs are constant.

Sunk Costs *Sunk costs* are past expenses or investments that have no salvage value and therefore should not be taken into account in considering investment alternatives. Sunk costs also could be current costs that are essentially fixed such as rent on a building. For example, suppose an ice cream manufacturing firm occupies a rented building and is considering making sherbet in

Fixed and Variable Cost Components of Total Cost

exhibit C.1

the same building. If the company enters sherbet production, its cost accountant will assign some of the rental expense to the sherbet operation. However, the building rent remains unchanged and therefore is not a relevant expense to be considered in making the decision. The rent is *sunk*; that is, it continues to exist and does not change in amount regardless of the decision.

Opportunity Costs   *Opportunity cost* is the benefit *forgone*, or advantage *lost*, that results from choosing one action over the *best-known alternative* course of action.

Suppose a firm has $100,000 to invest and two alternatives of comparable risk present themselves, each requiring a $100,000 investment. Investment A will net $25,000; Investment B will net $23,000. Investment A is clearly the better choice, with a $25,000 net return. If the decision is made to invest in B instead of A, the opportunity cost of B is $2,000, which is the benefit forgone.

Avoidable Costs   *Avoidable costs* include any expense that is *not* incurred if an investment is made but that *must* be incurred if the investment is *not* made. Suppose a company owns a metal lathe that is not in working condition but is needed for the firm's operations. Because the lathe must be repaired or replaced, the repair costs are avoidable if a new lathe is purchased. Avoidable costs reduce the cost of a new investment because they are not incurred if the investment is made. Avoidable costs are an example of how it is possible to "save" money by spending money.

Expected Value   Risk is inherent in any investment because the future can never be predicted with absolute certainty. To deal with this uncertainty, mathematical techniques such as expected value can help. Expected value is the expected outcome multiplied by the probability of its occurrence. Recall that in the preceding example the expected outcome of Alternative A was $25,000 and B, $23,000. Suppose the probability of A's actual outcome is 80 percent while B's probability is 90 percent. The expected values of the alternatives are determined as follows:

$$\text{Expected outcome} \times \genfrac{}{}{0pt}{}{\text{Probability that actual}}{\genfrac{}{}{0pt}{}{\text{outcome will be the}}{\text{expected outcome}}} = \text{Expected value}$$

Investment A: $25,000 \times 0.80 = $20,000
Investment B: $23,000 \times 0.90 = $20,700

Investment B is now seen to be the better choice, with a net advantage over A of $700.

Economic Life and Obsolescence   When a firm invests in an income-producing asset, the productive life of the asset is estimated. For accounting purposes, the asset is depreciated over this period. It is assumed that the asset will perform its function during this time and then be considered obsolete or worn out, and replacement will be required. This view of asset life rarely coincides with reality.

Assume that a machine expected to have a productive life of 10 years is purchased. If at any time during the ensuing 10 years a new machine is developed that can perform the same task more efficiently or economically, the old machine has become obsolete. Whether or not it is "worn out" is irrelevant.

The *economic life* of a machine is the period over which it provides the best method for performing its task. When a superior method is developed, the machine has become obsolete. Thus, the stated *book value* of a machine can be a meaningless figure.

Depreciation   Depreciation is a method for allocating costs of capital equipment. The value of any capital asset—buildings, machinery, and so forth—decreases as its useful life is expended. *Amortization* and *depreciation* are often used interchangeably. Through convention, however, *depreciation* refers to the allocation of cost due to the physical or functional deterioration of *tangible* (physical) assets such as buildings or equipment, whereas *amortization* refers to the allocation of cost over the useful life of *intangible* assets such as patents, leases, franchises, and goodwill.

Depreciation procedures may not reflect an asset's true value at any point in its life because obsolescence may at any time cause a large difference between true value and book value. Also, because depreciation rates significantly affect taxes, a firm may choose a particular method from the several alternatives with more consideration for its effect on taxes than its ability to make the book value of an asset reflect the true resale value.

Next we describe five commonly used methods of depreciation.

STRAIGHT-LINE METHOD

Under this method, an asset's value is reduced in uniform annual amounts over its estimated useful life. The general formula is

$$\text{Annual amount to be depreciated} = \frac{\text{Cost} - \text{Salvage value}}{\text{Estimated useful life}}$$

A machine costing $10,000 with an estimated salvage value of $0 and an estimated life of 10 years would be depreciated at the rate of $1,000 per year for each of the 10 years. If its estimated salvage value at the end of the 10 years is $1,000, the annual depreciation charge is

$$\frac{\$10,000 - \$1,000}{10} = \$900$$

SUM-OF-THE-YEARS'-DIGITS (SYD) METHOD

The purpose of the SYD method is to reduce the book value of an asset rapidly in early years and at a lower rate in the later years of its life.

Suppose that the estimated useful life is five years. The numbers add up to 15: $1 + 2 + 3 + 4 + 5 = 15$. Therefore, we depreciate the asset by $5 \div 15$ after the first year, $4 \div 15$ after the second year, and so on, down to $1 \div 15$ in the last year.

DECLINING-BALANCE METHOD

This method also achieves an accelerated depreciation. The asset's value is decreased by reducing its book value by a constant percentage each year. The percentage rate selected is often the one that just reduces book value to salvage value at the end of the asset's estimated life. In any case, the asset should never be reduced below estimated salvage value. Use of the declining-balance method and allowable rates are controlled by Internal Revenue Service regulations. As a simplified illustration, the preceding example is used in the next table with an arbitrarily selected rate of 40 percent. Note that depreciation is based on full cost, *not* cost minus salvage value.

YEAR	DEPRECIATION RATE	BEGINNING BOOK VALUE	DEPRECIATION CHARGE	ACCUMULATED DEPRECIATION	ENDING BOOK VALUE
1	0.40	$17,000	$6,800	$ 6,800	$10,200
2	0.40	10,200	4,080	10,880	6,120
3	0.40	6,120	2,448	13,328	3,672
4	0.40	3,672	1,469	14,797	2,203
5		2,203	203	15,000	2,000

In the fifth year, reducing book value by 40 percent would have caused it to drop below salvage value. Consequently, the asset was depreciated by only $203, which decreased book value to salvage value.

DOUBLE-DECLINING-BALANCE METHOD

Again, for tax advantages, the double-declining-balance method offers higher depreciation early in the life span. This method uses a percentage twice the straight line for the life span of the item but applies this rate to the undepreciated original cost. The method is the same as the declining-balance method, but the term *double-declining balance* means double the straight-line rate. Thus, equipment with a 10-year life span would have a straight-line depreciation rate of 10 percent per year and a double-declining-balance rate (applied to the undepreciated amount) of 20 percent per year.

DEPRECIATION-BY-USE METHOD

The purpose of this method is to depreciate a capital investment in proportion to its use. It is applicable, for example, to a machine that performs the same operation many times. The life of the machine is estimated not in years but rather in the total number of operations it may reasonably be expected to perform before wearing out. Suppose that a metal-stamping press has an estimated life of one million stamps and costs $100,000. The charge for depreciation per stamp is then $100,000 ÷ 1,000,000, or $0.10. Assuming a $0 salvage value, the depreciation charges are as shown in the following table:

YEAR	TOTAL YEARLY STAMPS	COST PER STAMP	YEARLY DEPRECIATION CHARGE	ACCUMULATED DEPRECIATION	ENDING BOOK VALUE
1	150,000	0.10	$15,000	$15,000	$85,000
2	300,000	0.10	30,000	45,000	55,000
3	200,000	0.10	20,000	65,000	35,000
4	200,000	0.10	20,000	85,000	15,000
5	100,000	0.10	10,000	95,000	5,000
6	50,000	0.10	5,000	100,000	0

The depreciation-by-use method is an attempt to gear depreciation charges to actual use and thereby coordinate expense charges with productive output more accurately. Also, because a machine's resale value is related to its remaining productive life, it is hoped that book value will approximate resale value. The danger, of course, is that technological improvements will render the machine obsolete, in which case book value will not reflect true value.

ACTIVITY-BASED COSTING

To know the costs incurred to make a certain product or deliver a service, some method of allocating overhead costs to production activities must be applied. The traditional approach is to allocate overhead costs to products on the basis of direct labor dollars or hours. By dividing the total estimated overhead costs by total budgeted direct labor hours, an overhead rate can be established. The problem with this approach is that direct labor as a percentage of total costs has fallen dramatically over the past decade. For example, introduction of advanced manufacturing technology and other productivity improvements has driven direct labor to as low as 7 to 10 percent of total manufacturing costs in many industries. As a result, overhead rates of 600 percent or even 1,000 percent are found in some highly automated plants.

This traditional accounting practice of allocating overhead to direct labor can lead to questionable investment decisions; for example, automated processes may be chosen over labor-intensive processes based on a comparison of projected costs. Unfortunately, overhead does not disappear when the equipment is installed and overall costs may actually be lower with the labor-intensive process. It also can lead to wasted effort because an inordinate amount of time is spent tracking direct labor hours. For example, one plant spent 65 percent of computer costs tracking information about direct labor transactions even though direct labor accounted for only 4 percent of total production costs.[1]

Activity-based costing techniques have been developed to alleviate these problems by refining the overhead allocation process to more directly reflect actual proportions of overhead consumed by the production activity. Causal factors, known as *cost drivers,* are identified and used as the means for allocating overhead. These factors might include machine hours, beds occupied, computer time, flight hours, or miles driven. The accuracy of overhead allocation, of course, depends on the selection of appropriate cost drivers.

Activity-based costing involves a two-stage allocation process, with the first stage assigning overhead costs to *cost activity pools.* These pools represent activities such as performing machine setups, issuing purchase orders, and inspecting parts. In the second stage, costs are assigned from these pools to activities based on the number or amount of pool-related activity required in their completion. Exhibit C.2 compares traditional cost accounting and activity-based costing.

Consider the example of activity-based costing in Exhibit C.3. Two products, A and B, are produced using the same number of direct labor hours. The same number of direct labor

Traditional and Activity-Based Costing

exhibit C.2

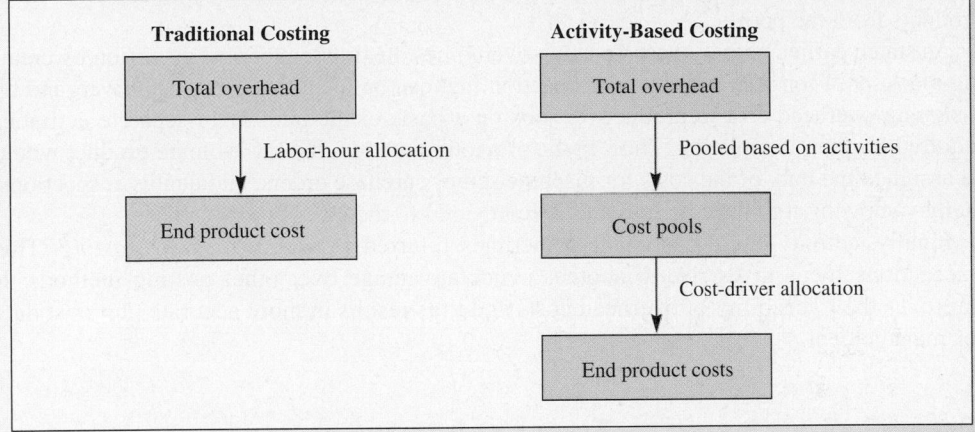

Overhead Allocations by an Activity Approach

exhibit C.3

BASIC DATA

ACTIVITY	TRACEABLE COSTS	EVENTS OF TRANSACTIONS		
		TOTAL	PRODUCT A	PRODUCT B
Machine setups	$230,000	5,000	3,000	2,000
Quality inspections	160,000	8,000	5,000	3,000
Production orders	81,000	600	200	400
Machine-hours worked	314,000	40,000	12,000	28,000
Material receipts	90,000	750	150	600
Number of units produced		25,000	5,000	20,000
	$875,000			

OVERHEAD RATES BY ACTIVITY

ACTIVITY	(a) TRACEABLE COSTS	(b) TOTAL EVENTS OR TRANSACTIONS	(a) ÷ (b) RATE PER EVENT OR TRANSACTION
Machine setups	$230,000	5,000	$46/setups
Quality inspections	160,000	8,000	$20/inspection
Production orders	81,000	600	$135/order
Machine-hours worked	314,000	40,000	$7.85/hour
Material receipts	90,000	750	$120/receipt

OVERHEAD COST PER UNIT OF PRODUCT

	PRODUCT A		PRODUCT B	
	EVENTS OR TRANSACTIONS	AMOUNT	EVENTS OR TRANSACTIONS	AMOUNT
Machine setups, at $46/setup	3,000	$138,000	2,000	$92,000
Quality inspections, at $20/inspection	5,000	100,000	3,000	60,000
Product orders, at $135/order	200	27,000	400	54,000
Machine-hours worked, at $7.85/hour	12,000	94,200	28,000	219,800
Material receipts, at $120/receipt	150	18,000	600	72,000
Total overhead cost assigned		$377,200		$497,800
Number of units produced		5,000		20,000
Overhead cost per unit, $\frac{\text{Total overhead}}{\text{No. of units}}$		$75.44		$24.89

SEE R. GARRISON, *MANAGERIAL ACCOUNTING*, 12TH ED. (NEW YORK: MCGRAW-HILL, 2007).

hours produces 5,000 units of Product A and 20,000 units of Product B. Applying traditional costing, identical overhead costs would be charged to each product. By applying activity-based costing, traceable costs are assigned to specific activities. Because each product required a different amount of transactions, different overhead amounts are allocated to these products from the pools.

As stated earlier, activity-based costing overcomes the problem of cost distortion by creating a cost pool for each activity or transaction that can be identified as a cost driver, and by assigning overhead cost to products or jobs on a basis of the number of separate activities required for their completion. Thus, in the previous situation, the low-volume product would be assigned the bulk of the costs for machine setup, purchase orders, and quality inspections, thereby showing it to have high unit costs compared to the other product.

Finally, activity-based costing is sometimes referred to as *transactions costing*. This transactions focus gives rise to another major advantage over other costing methods: It improves the traceability of overhead costs and thus results in more accurate unit cost data for management.

THE EFFECTS OF TAXES

Tax rates and the methods of applying them occasionally change. When analysts evaluate investment proposals, tax considerations often prove to be the deciding factor because depreciation expenses directly affect taxable income and therefore profit. The ability to write off depreciation in early years provides an added source of funds for investment. Before 1986, firms could employ an investment tax credit, which allowed a direct reduction in tax liability. But tax laws change, so it is crucial to stay on top of current tax laws and try to predict future changes that may affect current investments and accounting procedures.

CHOOSING AMONG INVESTMENT PROPOSALS

The capital investment decision has become highly rationalized, as evidenced by the variety of techniques available for its solution. In contrast to pricing or marketing decisions, the capital investment decision can usually be made with a higher degree of confidence because the variables affecting the decision are relatively well known and can be quantified with fair accuracy.

Investment decisions may be grouped into six general categories:

1. Purchase of new equipment or facilities.
2. Replacement of existing equipment or facilities.
3. Make-or-buy decisions.
4. Lease-or-buy decisions.
5. Temporary shutdowns or plant abandonment decisions.
6. Addition or elimination of a product or product line.

Investment decisions are made with regard to the lowest acceptable rate of return on investment. As a starting point, the lowest acceptable rate of return may be considered to be the cost of investment capital needed to underwrite the expenditure. Certainly an investment will not be made if it does not return at least the cost of capital.

Investments are generally ranked according to the return they yield in excess of their cost of capital. In this way, a business with only limited investment funds can select investment alternatives that yield the highest net returns. (*Net return* is the earnings an investment yields after gross earnings have been reduced by the cost of the funds used to finance the investment.) In general, investments should not be made unless the return in funds exceeds the marginal cost of investment capital. (*Marginal cost* is the incremental cost of each new acquisition of funds from outside sources.)

Determining the Cost of Capital   The cost of capital is calculated from a weighted average of debt and equity security costs. This average will vary depending on the financing strategy employed by the company. The most common sources of financing are short-term debt, long-term debt, and equity securities. A bank loan is an example of short-term debt. Bonds normally provide long-term debt. Finally, stock is a common form of equity financing. In the following, we give a short example of each form of financing, and then show how they are combined to find the weighted average cost of capital.

The cost of short-term debt depends on the interest rate on the loan and whether the loan is discounted. Remember that interest is a tax-deductible expense for a company.

$$\text{Cost of short-term debt} = \frac{\text{Interest paid}}{\text{Proceeds received}}$$

If a bank discounts a loan, interest is deducted from the face of the loan to get the proceeds. When a compensating balance is required (that is, a percentage of the face value of the loan is held by the bank as collateral), proceeds are also reduced. In either case, the effective or real interest rate on the loan is higher than the face interest rate owing to the proceeds received from the loan being less than the amount (face value) of the loan.

EXAMPLE OF SHORT-TERM DEBT

A company takes a $150,000, one-year, 13 percent loan. The loan is discounted, and a 10 percent compensating balance is required. The effective interest rate is computed as follows:

$$\frac{13\% \times \$150,000}{\$115,500} = \frac{\$19,500}{\$115,500} = 16.89\%$$

Proceeds received equal

Face of loan	$150,000
Less interest	(19,500)
Compensating balance (10% × $150,000)	(15,000)
Proceeds	$115,500

Notice how the effective cost of the loan is significantly greater than the stated interest rate.

Long term debt is normally provided through the sale of corporate bonds. The real cost of bonds is obtained by computing two types of yield: simple (face) yield and yield to maturity (effective interest rate). The first involves an easy approximation, but the second is more accurate. The nominal interest rate equals the interest paid on the face (maturity value) of the bond and is always stated on a per-annum basis. Bonds are generally issued in $1,000 denominations and may be sold above face value (at a premium) or below (at a discount, termed original issue discount, or OID). A bond is sold at a discount when the interest rate is below the going market rate. In this case, the yield will be higher than the nominal interest rate. The opposite holds for bonds issued at a premium.

The issue price of a bond is the par (or face value) times the premium (or discount).

$$\text{Simple yield} = \frac{\text{Nominal interest}}{\text{Issue price of bond}}$$

$$\text{Yield to maturity} = \frac{\text{Nominal interest} + \dfrac{\text{Discount (or premium)}}{\text{Years}}}{\dfrac{\text{Issue price} + \text{Maturity value}}{2}}$$

EXAMPLE OF LONG-TERM DEBT

A company issues a $400,000, 12 percent, 10-year bond for 97 percent of face value. Yield computations are as follows:

$$\text{Nominal annual payment} = 12\% \times \$400,000$$
$$= \$48,000$$
$$\text{Bond proceeds} = 97\% \times \$400,000$$
$$= \$388,000$$

$$\text{Bond discount} = 3\% \times \$400,000$$

$$= \$12,000$$

$$\text{Simple yield} = \frac{12\% \times \$400,000}{97\% \times \$400,000} = \frac{\$48,000}{\$388,000} = 12.4\%$$

$$\text{Yield to maturity} = \frac{\$48,000 + \dfrac{\$12,000}{10}}{\dfrac{\$388,000 + \$400,000}{2}} = \frac{\$48,000 + \$1,200}{\$394,000} = 12.5\%$$

Note that because the bonds were sold at a discount, the yield exceeds the nominal interest rate (12 percent). Bond interest is tax deductible to the corporation.

The actual cost of equity securities (stocks) comes in the form of dividends, which are not tax deductible to the corporation.

$$\text{Cost of common stock} = \frac{\text{Dividends per share}}{\text{Value per share}} + \text{Growth rate of dividends}$$

Here the value per share equals the market price per share minus flotation costs (that is, the cost of issuing securities such as brokerage fees and printing costs). It should be noted that this valuation does not consider what the investor expects in market price appreciation. This expectation is based on the expected growth in earnings per share and the relative risk taken by purchasing the stock. The capital asset pricing model (CAPM) can be used to capture this impact.[2]

EXAMPLE OF THE COST OF COMMON STOCK
A company's dividend per share is $10, net value is $70 per share, and the dividend growth rate is 5 percent.

$$\text{Cost of the stock} = \frac{\$10}{\$70} + 0.05 = 19.3\%$$

To compute the weighted average cost of capital, we consider the percentage of the total capital that is being provided by each financing alternative. We then calculate the after-tax cost of each financing alternative. Finally, we weight these costs in proportion to their use.

EXAMPLE OF CALCULATING THE WEIGHTED AVERAGE COST OF CAPITAL
Consider a company that shows the following figures in its financial statements:

Short-term bank loan (13%)	$1 million
Bonds payable (16%)	$4 million
Common stock (10%)	$5 million

For our example, assume that each of the percentages given above represents the cost of the source of capital. In addition to the above, we need to consider the tax rate of the firm because the interest paid on the bonds and on the short-term loan is tax deductible. Assume a corporate tax rate of 40 percent.

	PERCENT	AFTER-TAX COST	WEIGHTED AVERAGE COST
Short-term bank loan	10%	13% × 60% = 7.8%	.78%
Bonds payable	40%	16% × 60% = 9.6%	3.84%
Common stock	50%	10%	5%
Total	100%		9.62%

Keep in mind that in developing this section we have made many assumptions in these calculations. When these ideas are applied to a specific company, many of these assumptions may change. The basic concepts, though, are the same; keep in mind that the goal is to simply calculate the after-tax cost of the capital used by the company. We have shown the cost of capital for the entire company, though often only the capital employed for a specific project is used in the calculation.

Interest Rate Effects   There are two basic ways to account for the effects of interest accumulation. One is to compute the total amount created over the time period into the future as the *compound value*. The other is to remove the interest rate effect over time by reducing all future sums to present-day dollars, or the *present value*.

Compound Value of a Single Amount   Albert Einstein was quoted as saying that compound interest is the eighth wonder of the world. After reviewing this section showing compound interest's dramatic growth effects over a long time, you might wish to propose a new government regulation: On the birth of a child, the parents must put, say, $1,000 into a retirement fund for that child, available at age 65. This might reduce the pressure on Social Security and other state and federal pension plans. Although inflation would decrease the value significantly, there would still be a lot left over. At a 14 percent return on investment, our $1,000 would increase to $500,000 after subtracting the $4.5 million for inflation. That is still a 500-fold increase. (Many mutual funds today have long-term performances in excess of 14 percent per year.)

Spreadsheets and calculators make such computation easy. The box titled "Using a Spreadsheet" shows the most useful financial functions. However, many people still refer to tables for compound values. Using Appendix I, Table I.1 (compound sum of $1), for example, we see that the value of $1 at 10 percent interest after three years is $1.331. Multiplying this figure by $10 gives $13.31.

Compound Value of an Annuity   An *annuity* is the receipt of a constant sum each year for a specified number of years. Usually an annuity is received at the end of a period and does not earn interest during that period. Therefore, an annuity of $10 for three years would bring in $10 at the end of the first year (allowing the $10 to earn interest if invested for the remaining two years), $10 at the end of the second year (allowing the $10 to earn interest for the remaining one year), and $10 at the end of the third year (with no time to earn interest). If the annuity receipts were placed in a bank savings account at 5 percent interest, the total or compound value of the $10 at 5 percent for the three years would be

YEAR	RECEIPT AT END OF YEAR		COMPOUND INTEREST FACTOR $(1 + i)^n$		VALUE AT END OF THIRD YEAR
1	$10.00	×	$(1 + 0.05)^2$	=	$11.02
2	10.00	×	$(1 + 0.05)^1$	=	10.50
3	10.00	×	$(1 + 0.05)^0$	=	10.00
					$31.52

The general formula for finding the compound value of an annuity is

$$S_n = R[(1 + i)^{n-1} + (1 + i)^{n-2} + \cdots + (1 + i)^1 + 1]$$

where

S_n = Compound value of an annuity

R = Periodic receipts in dollars

n = Length of the annuity in years

USING A SPREADSHEET

We hope that you are all doing these calculations using a spreadsheet program. Even though the computer makes these calculations simple, it is important that you understand what the computer is actually doing. Further, you should check your calculations manually to make sure that you have the formulas set up correctly in your spreadsheet. There are many stories of the terrible consequences of making a wrong decision based on a spreadsheet with errors!

For your quick reference, the following are the financial functions you will find most useful. These are from the Microsoft Excel help screens.

PV (rate, nper, pmt)—Returns the present value of an investment. The present value is the total amount that a series of future payments is worth now. For example, when you borrow money, the loan amount is the present value to the lender. Rate is the interest rate per period. For example, if you obtain an automobile loan at a 10 percent annual interest rate and make monthly payments, your interest rate per month is 10%/12, or .83%. You would enter 10%/12, or .83%, or .0083, in the formula as the rate. Nper is the total number of payment periods in an annuity. For example, if you get a four-year car loan and make monthly payments, your loan has 4*12 (or 48) periods. You would enter 48 into the formula for nper. Pmt is the payment made each period and cannot change over the life of the annuity. Typically, this includes principal and interest but no other fees or taxes. For example, the monthly payment on a $10,000, four-year car loan at 12 percent is $263.33. You would enter 263.33 into the formula as pmt.

FV (rate, nper, pmt)—Returns the future value of an investment based on periodic, constant payments and a constant interest rate. Rate is the interest rate per period. Nper is the total number of payment periods in an annuity. Pmt is the payment made each period; it cannot change over the life of the annuity. Typically, pmt contains principal and interest but no other fees or taxes.

NPV (rate, value1, value2, . . .)—Returns the net present value of an investment based on a series of periodic cash flows and a discount rate. The net present value of an investment is today's value of a series of future payments (negative values) and income (positive values). Rate is the rate of discount over the length of one period. Value1, value2. . ., must be equally spaced in time and occur at the end of each period.

IRR(values)—Returns the internal rate of return for a series of cash flows represented by the numbers in *values*. (*Values* is defined below.) These cash flows do not have to be even, as they would be for an annuity. The internal rate of return is the interest rate received for an investment consisting of payments (negative values) and income (positive values) that occur at regular periods. *Values* is an array or a reference to cells that contain numbers for which you want to calculate the internal rate of return. Values must contain at least one positive value and one negative value to calculate the internal rate of return. IRR uses the order of values to interpret the order of cash flows. Be sure to enter your payment and income values in the sequence you want.

FROM MICROSOFT® EXCEL. COPYRIGHT © 2001 MICROSOFT CORPORATION.

Applying this formula to the preceding example, we get

$$S_n = R[(1 + i)^2 + (1 + i) + 1]$$
$$= \$10[(1 + 0.05)^2 + (1 + 0.05) + 1] = \$31.52$$

In Appendix I, Table I.2 lists the compound value factor of $1 for 5 percent after three years as 3.152. Multiplying this factor by $10 yields $31.52.

In a fashion similar to our previous retirement investment example, consider the beneficial effects of investing $2,000 each year, just starting at the age of 21. Assume investments in AAA-rated bonds are available today yielding 9 percent. From Table I.2 in Appendix I, after 30 years (at age 51) the investment is worth 136.3 times $2,000, or $272,600. Fourteen years later (at age 65) this would be worth $963,044 (using a hand calculator, because the table goes only to 30 years, and assuming the $2,000 is deposited at the end of each year)! But what 21-year-old thinks about retirement?

Present Value of a Future Single Payment   Compound values are used to determine future value after a specific period has elapsed; present value (PV) procedures accomplish just the reverse. They are used to determine the current value of a sum or stream of receipts expected to be received in the future. Most investment decision techniques use present value concepts rather than compound values. Because decisions affecting the future are made in the present, it is better to convert future returns into their present value at the time the decision is being made. In this way, investment alternatives are placed in better perspective in terms of current dollars.

An example makes this more apparent. If a rich uncle offers to make you a gift of $100 today or $250 after 10 years, which should you choose? You must determine whether the $250 in 10 years will be worth more than the $100 now. Suppose that you base your decision on the rate of inflation in the economy and believe that inflation averages 10 percent per year. By deflating the $250, you can compare its relative purchasing power with $100 received today. Procedurally, this is accomplished by solving the compound formula for the present sum, P, where V is the future amount of $250 in 10 years at 10 percent. The compound value formula is

$$V = P(1 + i)^n$$

Dividing both sides by $(1 + i)^n$ gives

$$P = \frac{V}{(1 + i)^n}$$

$$= \frac{250}{(1 + 0.10)^{10}} = \$96.39$$

This shows that, at a 10 percent inflation rate, $250 in 10 years will be worth $96.39 today. The rational choice, then, is to take the $100 now.

The use of tables is also standard practice in solving present value problems. With reference to Appendix I, Table I.3, the present value factor for $1 received 10 years hence is 0.386. Multiplying this factor by $250 yields $96.50.

Present Value of an Annuity   The present value of an annuity is the value of an annual amount to be received over a future period expressed in terms of the present. To find the value of an annuity of $100 for three years at 10 percent, find the factor in the present value table that applies to 10 percent in *each* of the three years in which the amount is received and multiply each receipt by this factor. Then sum the resulting figures. Remember that annuities are usually received at the end of each period.

YEAR	AMOUNT RECEIVED AT END OF YEAR		PRESENT VALUE FACTOR AT 10%		PRESENT VALUE
1	$100	×	0.909	=	$ 90.90
2	100	×	0.826	=	82.60
3	100	×	0.751	=	75.10
Total receipts	$300		Total present value	=	$248.60

The general formula used to derive the present value of an annuity is

$$A_n = R\left[\frac{1}{(1 + i)} + \frac{1}{(1 + i)^2} + \cdots + \frac{1}{(1 + i)^n}\right]$$

where

A_n = Present value of an annuity of n years

R = Periodic receipts

n = Length of the annuity in years

Applying the formula to the preceding example gives

$$A_n = \$100\left[\frac{1}{(1+0.10)} + \frac{1}{(1+0.10)^2} + \frac{1}{(1+0.10)^3}\right]$$

$$= \$100(2.487) = \$248.70$$

In Appendix I, Table I.4 contains present values of an annuity for varying maturities. The present value factor for an annuity of $1 for three years at 10 percent (from Table I.4) is 2.487. Given that our sum is $100 rather than $1, we multiply this factor by $100 to arrive at $248.70.

When the stream of future receipts is uneven, the present value of each annual receipt must be calculated. The present values of the receipts for all years are then summed to arrive at total present value. This process can sometimes be tedious, but it is unavoidable.

Discounted Cash Flow   The term *discounted cash flow* refers to the total stream of payments that an asset will generate in the future discounted to the present time. This is simply present value analysis that includes all flows: single payments, annuities, and all others.

Methods of Ranking Investments

Net Present Value   The net present value method is commonly used in business. With this method, decisions are based on the amount by which the present value of a projected income stream exceeds the cost of an investment.

A firm is considering two alternative investments. The first costs $30,000 and the second, $50,000. The expected yearly cash income streams are shown in this table:

	CASH INFLOW	
YEAR	ALTERNATIVE A	ALTERNATIVE B
1	$10,000	$15,000
2	10,000	15,000
3	10,000	15,000
4	10,000	15,000
5	10,000	15,000

To choose between Alternatives A and B, find which has the higher net present value. Assume an 8 percent cost of capital.

ALTERNATIVE A

3.993 (PV factor)
× $10,000   = $39,930
Less cost of investment = 30,000
Net present value   = $ 9,930

ALTERNATIVE B

3.993 (PV factor)
× $15,000   = $59,895
Less cost of investment = 50,000
Net present value   = $ 9,895

Investment A is the better alternative. Its net present value exceeds that of Investment B by $35 ($9,930 − $9,895 = $35).

Payback Period   The payback method ranks investments according to the time required for each investment to return earnings equal to the cost of the investment. The rationale is that the sooner the investment capital can be recovered, the sooner it can be reinvested in new revenue-producing projects. Thus, supposedly, a firm will be able to get the most benefit from its available investment funds.

Consider two alternatives requiring a $1,000 investment each. The first will earn $200 per year for six years; the second will earn $300 per year for the first three years and $100 per year for the next three years.

If the first alternative is selected, the initial investment of $1,000 will be recovered at the end of the fifth year. The income produced by the second alternative will total $1,000 after only four years. The second alternative will permit reinvestment of the full $1,000 in new revenue-producing projects one year sooner than the first.

Though the payback method is declining in popularity as the sole measure in investment decisions, it is still frequently used in conjunction with other methods to indicate the time commitment of funds. The major problems with payback are that it does not consider income beyond the payback period and it ignores the time value of money. A method that ignores the time value of money must be considered questionable.

Internal Rate of Return   The internal rate of return may be defined as the interest rate that equates the present value of an income stream with the cost of an investment. There is no procedure or formula that may be used directly to compute the internal rate of return—it must be found by interpolation or iterative calculation.

Suppose we wish to find the internal rate of return for an investment costing $12,000 that will yield a cash inflow of $4,000 per year for four years. We see that the present value factor sought is

$$\frac{\$12,000}{\$4,000} = 3.000$$

and we seek the interest rate that will provide this factor over a four-year period. The interest rate must lie between 12 and 14 percent because 3.000 lies between 3.037 and 2.914 (in the fourth row of Appendix I, Table I.4). Linear interpolation between these values, according to the equation

$$I = 12 + (14 - 12)\frac{(3.037 - 3.000)}{(3.037 - 2.914)}$$

$$= 12 + 0.602 = 12.602\%$$

gives a good approximation to the actual internal rate of return.

When the income stream is discounted at 12.6 percent, the resulting present value closely approximates the cost of investment. Thus, the internal rate of return for this investment is 12.6 percent. The cost of capital can be compared with the internal rate of return to determine the net rate of return on the investment. If, in this example, the cost of capital were 8 percent, the net rate of return on the investment would be 4.6 percent.

The net present value and internal rate of return methods involve procedures that are essentially the same. They differ in that the net present value method enables investment alternatives to be compared in terms of the dollar value in excess of cost, whereas the internal rate of return method permits comparison of rates of return on alternative investments. Moreover, the internal rate of return method occasionally encounters problems in calculation, as multiple rates frequently appear in the computation.

Ranking Investments with Uneven Lives   When proposed investments have the same life expectancy, comparison among them, using the preceding methods, will give a reasonable picture of their relative value. When lives are unequal, however, there is the question of how to relate the two different time periods. Should replacements be considered the same as the original? Should productivity for the shorter-term unit that will be replaced earlier be considered higher? How should the cost of future units be estimated?

No estimate dealing with investments unforeseen at the time of decision can be expected to reflect a high degree of accuracy. Still, the problem must be dealt with, and some assumptions must be made in order to determine a ranking.

SAMPLE PROBLEMS: INVESTMENT DECISIONS

Step by Step

EXAMPLE C.1: An Expansion Decision

William J. Wilson Ceramic Products, Inc., leases plant facilities in which firebrick is manufactured. Because of rising demand, Wilson could increase sales by investing in new equipment to expand output. The selling price of $10 per brick will remain unchanged if output and sales increase. Based on engineering and cost estimates, the accounting department provides management with the following cost estimates based on an annual increased output of 100,000 bricks:

Cost of new equipment having an expected life of five years	$500,000
Equipment installation cost	20,000
Expected salvage value	0
New operation's share of annual lease expense	40,000
Annual increase in utility expenses	40,000
Annual increase in labor costs	160,000
Annual additional cost for raw materials	400,000

The sum-of-the-years'-digits method of depreciation will be used, and taxes are paid at a rate of 40 percent. Wilson's policy is not to invest capital in projects earning less than a 20 percent rate of return. Should the proposed expansion be undertaken?

SOLUTION

Compute the cost of investment:

Acquisition cost of equipment	$500,000
Equipment installation costs	20,000
Total cost of investment	$520,000

Determine yearly cash flows throughout the life of the investment.

The lease expense is a sunk cost. It will be incurred whether or not the investment is made and is therefore irrelevant to the decision and should be disregarded. Annual production expenses to be considered are utility, labor, and raw materials. These total $600,000 per year.

Annual sales revenue is $10 \times 100,000$ units of output, which totals $1,000,000. Yearly income before depreciation and taxes is thus $1,000,000 gross revenue, less $600,000 expenses, or $400,000.

Next, determine the depreciation charges to be deducted from the $500,000 income each year using the SYD method (sum-of-years'-digits $= 1 + 2 + 3 + 4 + 5 = 15$):

YEAR	PROPORTION OF $500,000 TO BE DEPRECIATED		DEPRECIATION CHARGE
1	5/15 × $500,000	=	$166,667
2	4/15 × 500,000	=	133,333
3	3/15 × 500,000	=	100,000
4	2/15 × 500,000	=	66,667
5	1/15 × 500,000	=	33,333
Accumulated depreciation			$500,000

Find each year's cash flow when taxes are 40 percent. Cash flow for only the first year is illustrated:

Earnings before depreciation and taxes		$400,000
Deduct: Taxes at 40% (40% × 400,000)	$160,000	
Tax benefit of depreciation expense (0.4 × 166,667)	66,667	93,333
Cash flow (first year)		$306,667

Determine the present value of the cash flow. Because Wilson demands at least a 20 percent rate of return on investments, multiply the cash flows by the 20 percent present value factor for each year. The factor for each respective year must be used because the cash flows are not an annuity.

YEAR	PRESENT VALUE FACTOR		CASH FLOW		PRESENT VALUE
1	0.833	×	$306,667	=	$255,454
2	0.694	×	293,333	=	203,573
3	0.579	×	280,000	=	162,120
4	0.482	×	266,667	=	128,533
5	0.402	×	253,334	=	101,840
Total present value of cash flows (discounted at 20%) =					$851,520

Now find whether net present value is positive or negative:

Total present value of cash flows	$851,520
Total cost of investment	520,000
Net present value	$331,520

Net present value is positive when returns are discounted at 20 percent. Wilson will earn an amount in excess of 20 percent on the investment. The proposed expansion should be undertaken. ●

EXAMPLE C.2: A Replacement Decision

For five years Bennie's Brewery has been using a machine that attaches labels to bottles. The machine was purchased for $4,000 and is being depreciated over 10 years to a $0 salvage value using straight-line depreciation. The machine can be sold now for $2,000. Bennie can buy a new labeling machine for $6,000 that will have a useful life of five years and cut labor costs by $1,200 annually. The old machine will require a major overhaul in the next few months at an estimated cost of $300. If purchased, the new machine will be depreciated over five years to a $500 salvage value using the straight-line method. The company will invest in any project earning more than the 12 percent cost of capital. The tax rate is 40 percent. Should Bennie's Brewery invest in the new machine?

Step by Step

SOLUTION

Determine the cost of investment:

Price of the new machine		$6,000
Less: Sale of old machine	$2,000	
Avoidable overhaul costs	300	2,300
Effective cost of investment		$3,700

Determine the increase in cash flow resulting from investment in the new machine:

Yearly cost savings = $1,200

Differential depreciation

Annual depreciation on old machine:

$$\frac{\text{Cost} - \text{Salvage}}{\text{Expected life}} = \frac{\$4,000 - \$0}{10} = \$400$$

Annual depreciation on new machine:

$$\frac{\text{Cost} - \text{Salvage}}{\text{Expected life}} = \frac{\$6,000 - \$500}{5} = \$1,100$$

Differential depreciation = $1,100 − $400 = $700

Yearly net increase in cash flow into the firm:

Cost savings		$1,200
Deduct: Taxes at 40%	$480	
Add: Advantage of increase in depreciation (0.4 × $700)	280	200
Yearly increase in cash flow		$1,000

Determine total present value of the investment:

The five-year cash flow of $1,000 per year is an annuity.

Discounted at 12 percent, the cost of capital, the present value is

3.605 × $1,000 = $3,605

The present value of the new machine, if sold at its salvage value of $500 at the end of the fifth year, is

0.567 × $500 = $284

Total present value of the expected cash flows is

$3,605 + $284 = $3,889

Determine whether net present value is positive:

Total present value	$3,889
Cost of investment	3,700
Net present value	$189

Bennie's Brewery should make the purchase because the investment will return slightly more than the cost of capital.

Note: The importance of depreciation has been shown in this example. The present value of the yearly cash flow resulting from operations is

$$(\text{Cost savings} - \text{Taxes}) \times (\text{Present value factor})$$

$$(\$1,200 - \$480) \quad \times \quad (3.605) \quad = \$2,596$$

This figure is $1,104 less than the $3,700 cost of the investment. Only a very large depreciation advantage makes this investment worthwhile. The total present value of the advantage is $1,009:

$$(\text{Tax rate} \times \text{Differential depreciation}) \times (\text{PV factor})$$

$$(0.4 \times \$700) \quad \times \quad (3.605) \quad = \$1,009 \ \bullet$$

Step by Step

EXAMPLE C.3: A Make-or-Buy Decision

The Triple X Company manufactures and sells refrigerators. It makes some of the parts for the refrigerators and purchases others. The engineering department believes it might be possible to cut costs by manufacturing one of the parts currently being purchased for $8.25 each. The firm uses 100,000 of these parts each year. The accounting department compiles the following list of costs based on engineering estimates:

Fixed costs will increase by $50,000.
Labor costs will increase by $125,000.
Factory overhead, currently running $500,000 per year, may be expected to increase 12 percent.
Raw materials used to make the part will cost $600,000.

Given the preceding estimates, should Triple X make the part or continue to buy it?

SOLUTION

Find the total cost incurred if the part were manufactured:

Additional fixed costs	$ 50,000
Additional labor costs	125,000
Raw materials cost	600,000
Additional overhead costs = 0.12 × $500,000	60,000
Total cost to manufacture	$835,000

Find the cost per unit to manufacture:

$$\frac{\$835,000}{100,000} = \$8.35 \text{ per unit}$$

Triple X should continue to buy the part. Manufacturing costs exceed the present cost to purchase by $0.10 per unit. ●

SELECTED BIBLIOGRAPHY

Bodie, Z.; A. Kane; and A. Marcus. *Investments*. 6th ed. New York: McGraw-Hill/Irwin, 2004.

Helfert, E. *Techniques of Financial Analysis: A Modern Approach.* 11th ed. New York: Irwin/McGraw-Hill, 2002.

Poterba, J. M., and L. H. Summers. "A CEO Survey of U.S. Companies' Time Horizons and Hurdle Rates." *Sloan Management Review,* Fall 1995, pp. 43–53.

FOOTNOTES

1 T. Johnson and R. Kaplan, *Relevance Lost: The Rise and Fall of Management Accounting* (Boston: Harvard Business School Press, 1987), p. 188.

2 A description of capital asset pricing is included in many finance textbooks; see, for example, Z. Bodie, A. Kane, and A. Marcus, *Investments*, 6th ed. (New York: McGraw-Hill/Irwin, 2004).

ANSWERS TO SELECTED PROBLEMS

CHAPTER 2

4. Productivity (hours)
   Deluxe   0.20
   Limited   0.20
   Productivity (dollars)
   Deluxe   133.33
   Limited   135.71

CHAPTER 3

No solved problems.

CHAPTER 4

3. No. Must consider demand in fourth year.
5. Expected NPV—Small
   $4.8 million
   Expected NPV—Large
   $2.6 million

CHAPTER 4A

3. *LR* labor, 80%
   LR parts, 90%
   Labor = 11,556 hours
   Parts = $330,876
7. 4,710 hours
11. *a.* 3rd = 35.1 hours
    b. Average = 7.9 hours each; well worth it

CHAPTER 5

3. Traditional method 20 min. setup + 10 × 2 = 40 min. total scan/retrieve system. 1 min. setup + 10 × 5 = 51 min. total. Traditional method is best.
5. *a.* The market can be served only at 3 gals/hr. In 50 hours bathtub will overflow.
   b. The average amount being served is only 2.5 gal/hr, so that is the output rate.

CHAPTER 5A

2. *a.* 1.35 minutes
   b. 1.51 minutes
   c. $48. The worker would not make the bonus.
6. *a.* NT = 0.9286 minute/part
   b. ST = 1.0679 minutes/part
   c. Daily output = 449.50
      Day's wages = $44.49

CHAPTER 6

6. *a.* 20,000 books
   b. higher
   c. lower
12. 80 units/hour

CHAPTER 6A

3. *b.* 120 seconds
   d. 87.5%
9. *a.* 33.6 seconds
   b. 3.51, therefore 4 workstations
   d. AB, DF, C, EG, H
   e. Efficiency = 70.2%
   f. Reduce cycle time to 32 seconds and work $6\frac{2}{3}$ minutes overtime
   g. 1.89 hours overtime; may be better to rebalance

CHAPTER 7

No solved problems.

CHAPTER 7A

5. W_s = 4.125 minutes
   L_q = 4.05 cars
   L_s = 4.95 car
9. *a.* L = 0.22 waiting
   b. W = 0.466 hour
   c. D = 0.362
10. *a.* 2 people
    b. 6 minutes
    c. 0.2964
    d. 67%
    e. 0.03375 hour
18. *a.* 0.833
    b. 5 documents
    c. 0.2 hour
    d. 0.4822
    e. L_1 = tends to infinity

CHAPTER 8

No solved problems.

CHAPTER 9

No solved problems.

CHAPTER 9A

1. *a.* Not inspecting cost = $20/hr. Cost to inspect = $9/hr. Therefore, inspect.
   b. $0.18 each
   c. $0.22 per unit
6. $\bar{\bar{X}}$ = 999.1
   UCL = 1014.965
   LCL = 983.235
   $\bar{R}$ = 21.733
   UCL = 49.551
   LCL = 0
   Process is in control
9. *a.* n = 31.3 (round sample size to 32)
   b. Random sample 32; reject if more than 8 are defective.
12. $\bar{X}$ = 0.499
   UCL = 0.520
   LCL = 0.478
   R = 0.037
   UCL = 0.078
   LCL = 0.000
   Process is in control

CHAPTER 10

5. *b.* A-C-F-G-I and A-D-F-G-I
   c. C: one week
       D: one week
       G: one week
   d. Two paths: A-C-F-G-I; and A-D-F-G-I; 16 weeks
10. *a.* Critical path is A-E-G-C-D
    b. 26 weeks
    c. No difference in completion date
11. *a.* Critical path is A-C-D-F-G

   b.

Day	Cost	Activity
First	$1,000	A
Second	1,200	C
Third	1,500	D (or F)
Fourth	1,500	F (or D)
	$5,200	

CHAPTER 11

1. Taiwan $84,442.11
   In-house $149,427.14
   Purchase from Taiwanese supplier
3. Average inventory turn = 148.6
   Days of supply = 2.46 days

CHAPTER 12

1. C_X = 176.7
   C_Y = 241.5
2. C_X = 374
   C_Y = 357

CHAPTER 13

1. 5 kanban card sets
5. 5 kanban card sets

CHAPTER 13A

No solved problems.

CHAPTER 14

No solved problems.

CHAPTER 15

3. *a.* February 84
       March 86
       April 90
       May 88
       June 84
   b. MAD = 15

7.

Quarter	Forecast
9	232
10	281
11	239
12	231

11. *a.* April to September = 130, 150, 160, 170, 160, 150
    b. April to September = 136, 146, 150, 159, 153, 146
    c. Exponential smoothing performed better.
15. MAD = 104
    TS = 3.1
    The high TS value indicates the model is unacceptable.
19. *a.* MAD = 90
        TS = −1.67
    b. Model okay since tracking is −1.67.

CHAPTER 16

2. Total cost = $413,600
5. Total cost = $413,750

CHAPTER 17

5. q = 713
8. *a.* Q = 1,225
       R = 824
   b. q = 390 − Inventory on hand
12. *a.* Q = 89
    b. $224.72
    c. $222.50
14. *a.* A(4, 13, 18);
        B (2, 5, 8, 10, 11, 14, 16);
        C (remainder)
    b. Classify as A.
17. q = 691
26. 729 hamburgers
31. 5,000 pounds

CHAPTER 18

4.

11. Least total cost method: Order 250 units in Period 1 for Periods 1–8;
    Least unit cost method: Order 450 units in Period 1 for Periods 1–9.

13. *c.* .A
         .B(2)
              .E(4)
              .F(3)
         .C(3)
              .D(3)
              .H(2)
                      .E(5)
                      .G(2)
         .D(1)

    d. Level 0   100 units of A
        Level 1   200 units of B
                       300 units of C
        Level 2   600 units of F
                       600 units of H
                     1000 units of D
        Level 3   3800 units of E
                     1200 units of G

CHAPTER 19

5. Job order: 5, 6, 7, 3, 1, 2, 4
7. A to 3, B to 1, C to 4, D to 2; cost = $17,000
8. Critical ratio schedule: 5, 3, 2, 4, 1
   Earliest due date, job priority: 2, 5, 3, 4, 1
   Shortest processing time (including delay time): 2, 1, 4, 3, 5
9. E, A, B, D, C
14. C, B, D, F, E, A

CHAPTER 19A

2. Average customer waiting time = $\frac{1}{6}$ minute
   Average teller idle time = $\frac{4}{6}$ minute

7. *a.*

	Condition 1	Condition 2
(1)	Idle 18 min.	76 + 134 = 210 min.
(2)	Delay 87 min.	0 min.

b.

	Condition 1	Condition 2
Cost of repairperson	$ 38.80	$ 77.20
Cost of machine down	175.33	117.33
	$214.13	$194.53 (Total Cost)

    Lowest cost is Condition 2.
11. One car bypasses.

CHAPTER 20

1. Case I: X used = 933.3 hours
                      Y used = 700 hours
       Case II: Y = 700 hours
                      X = 933.3 hours
       Case III: X = 933.3 hours
                      Y = 700 hours
       Case IV: X = 933.3 hours
                      Y = 700 hours
       Otherwise:
       Case I: No problem
       Case II: Excess WIP
       Case III: Excess spare parts
       Case IV: Excess finished goods
8. *a.* Machine B is the constraint.
   b. All of M; as many N as possible
   c. $600 (100 M and 30 N)

APPENDIX A

2. Optimal combination is $B = 10$, $A = 15$, and $Z = 70$.
4. *a.* $600A + 900B \leq 3,600$
        $600A + 900B \geq 1,800$
        $200A + 700B \leq 1,400$
        $400A + 100B \geq 400$
        $A \leq 2$
        Minimize $.75A + .15B$
   b. $A = 0.54$
        $B = 1.85$
        Obj = 0.68

PRESENT VALUE TABLE

Present Value of $1

YEAR	1%	2%	3%	4%	5%	6%	7%	8%	9%	10%	12%	14%	15%
1	.990	.980	.971	.962	.952	.943	.935	.926	.917	.909	.893	.877	.870
2	.980	.961	.943	.925	.907	.890	.873	.857	.842	.826	.797	.769	.756
3	.971	.942	.915	.889	.864	.840	.816	.794	.772	.751	.712	.675	.658
4	.961	.924	.889	.855	.823	.792	.763	.735	.708	.683	.636	.592	.572
5	.951	.906	.863	.822	.784	.747	.713	.681	.650	.621	.567	.519	.497
6	.942	.888	.838	.790	.746	.705	.666	.630	.596	.564	.507	.456	.432
7	.933	.871	.813	.760	.711	.665	.623	.583	.547	.513	.452	.400	.376
8	.923	.853	.789	.731	.677	.627	.582	.540	.502	.467	.404	.351	.327
9	.914	.837	.766	.703	.645	.592	.544	.500	.460	.424	.361	.308	.284
10	.905	.820	.744	.676	.614	.558	.508	.463	.422	.386	.322	.270	.247
11	.896	.804	.722	.650	.585	.527	.475	.429	.388	.350	.287	.237	.215
12	.887	.788	.701	.625	.557	.497	.444	.397	.356	.319	.257	.208	.187
13	.879	.773	.681	.601	.530	.469	.415	.368	.326	.290	.229	.182	.163
14	.870	.758	.661	.577	.505	.442	.388	.340	.299	.263	.205	.160	.141
15	.861	.743	.642	.555	.481	.417	.362	.315	.275	.239	.183	.140	.123
16	.853	.728	.623	.534	.458	.394	.339	.292	.252	.218	.163	.123	.107
17	.844	.714	.605	.513	.436	.371	.317	.270	.231	.198	.146	.108	.093
18	.836	.700	.587	.494	.416	.350	.296	.250	.212	.180	.130	.095	.081
19	.828	.686	.570	.475	.396	.331	.276	.232	.194	.164	.116	.083	.070
20	.820	.673	.554	.456	.377	.312	.258	.215	.178	.149	.104	.073	.061
25	.780	.610	.478	.375	.295	.233	.184	.146	.116	.092	.059	.038	.030
30	.742	.552	.412	.308	.231	.174	.131	.099	.075	.057	.033	.020	.015

YEAR	16%	18%	20%	24%	28%	32%	36%	40%	50%	60%	70%	80%	90%
1	.862	.847	.833	.806	.781	.758	.735	.714	.667	.625	.588	.556	.526
2	.743	.718	.694	.650	.610	.574	.541	.510	.444	.391	.346	.309	.277
3	.641	.609	.579	.524	.477	.435	.398	.364	.296	.244	.204	.171	.146
4	.552	.516	.482	.423	.373	.329	.292	.260	.198	.153	.120	.095	.077
5	.476	.437	.402	.341	.291	.250	.215	.186	.132	.095	.070	.053	.040
6	.410	.370	.335	.275	.227	.189	.158	.133	.088	.060	.041	.029	.021
7	.354	.314	.279	.222	.178	.143	.116	.095	.059	.037	.024	.016	.011
8	.305	.266	.233	.179	.139	.108	.085	.068	.039	.023	.014	.009	.006
9	.263	.226	.194	.144	.108	.082	.063	.048	.026	.015	.008	.005	.003
10	.227	.191	.162	.116	.085	.062	.046	.035	.017	.009	.005	.003	.002
11	.195	.162	.135	.094	.066	.047	.034	.025	.012	.006	.003	.002	.001
12	.168	.137	.112	.076	.052	.036	.025	.018	.008	.004	.002	.001	.001
13	.145	.116	.093	.061	.040	.027	.018	.013	.005	.002	.001	.001	.000
14	.125	.099	.078	.049	.032	.021	.014	.009	.003	.001	.001	.000	.000
15	.108	.084	.065	.040	.025	.016	.010	.006	.002	.001	.000	.000	.000
16	.093	.071	.054	.032	.019	.012	.007	.005	.002	.001	.000	.000	
17	.080	.060	.045	.026	.015	.009	.005	.003	.001	.000	.000		
18	.069	.051	.038	.021	.012	.007	.004	.002	.001	.000	.000		
19	.060	.043	.031	.017	.009	.005	.003	.002	.000	.000			
20	.051	.037	.026	.014	.007	.004	.002	.001	.000	.000			
25	.024	.016	.010	.005	.002	.001	.000	.000					
30	.012	.007	.004	.002	.001	.000	.000						

Using Microsoft Excel®, these are calculated with the equation: $(1 + interest)^{-years}$.

APPENDIX F

NEGATIVE EXPONENTIAL DISTRIBUTION: VALUES OF e^{-x}

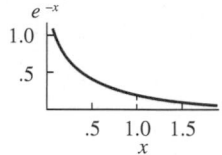

X	e^{-x} (VALUE)	X	e^{-x} (VALUE)	X	e^{-x} (VALUE)	X	e^{-x} (VALUE)
0.00	1.00000	0.50	0.60653	1.00	0.36788	1.50	0.22313
0.01	0.99005	0.51	.60050	1.01	.36422	1.51	.22091
0.02	.98020	0.52	.59452	1.02	.36060	1.52	.21871
0.03	.97045	0.53	.58860	1.03	.35701	1.53	.21654
0.04	.96079	0.54	.58275	1.04	.35345	1.54	.21438
0.05	.95123	0.55	.57695	1.05	.34994	1.55	.21225
0.06	.94176	0.56	.57121	1.06	.34646	1.56	.21014
0.07	.93239	0.57	.56553	1.07	.34301	1.57	.20805
0.08	.92312	0.58	.55990	1.08	.33960	1.58	.20598
0.09	.91393	0.59	.55433	1.09	.33622	1.59	.20393
0.10	.90484	0.60	.54881	1.10	.33287	1.60	.20190
0.11	.89583	0.61	.54335	1.11	.32956	1.61	.19989
0.12	.88692	0.62	.53794	1.12	.32628	1.62	.19790
0.13	.87809	0.63	.53259	1.13	.32303	1.63	.19593
0.14	.86936	0.64	.52729	1.14	.31982	1.64	.19398
0.15	.86071	0.65	.52205	1.15	.31664	1.65	.19205
0.16	.87514	0.66	.51685	1.16	.31349	1.66	.19014
0.17	.84366	0.67	.51171	1.17	.31037	1.67	.18825
0.18	.83527	0.68	.50662	1.18	.30728	1.68	.18637
0.19	.82696	0.69	.50158	1.19	.30422	1.69	.18452
0.20	.81873	0.70	.49659	1.20	.30119	1.70	.18268
0.21	.81058	0.71	.49164	1.21	.29820	1.71	.18087
0.22	.80252	0.72	.48675	1.22	.29523	1.72	.17907
0.23	.79453	0.73	.48191	1.23	.29229	1.73	.17728
0.24	.78663	0.74	.47711	1.24	.28938	1.74	.17552
0.25	.77880	0.75	.47237	1.25	.28650	1.75	.17377
0.26	.77105	0.76	.46767	1.26	.28365	1.76	.17204
0.27	.76338	0.77	.46301	1.27	.28083	1.77	.17033
0.28	.75578	0.78	.45841	1.28	.27804	1.78	.16864
0.29	.74826	0.79	.45384	1.29	.27527	1.79	.16696
0.30	.74082	0.80	.44933	1.30	.27253	1.80	.16530
0.31	.73345	0.81	.44486	1.31	.26982	1.81	.16365
0.32	.72615	0.82	.44043	1.32	.26714	1.82	.16203
0.33	.71892	0.83	.43605	1.33	.26448	1.83	.16041
0.34	.71177	0.84	.43171	1.34	.26185	1.84	.15882
0.35	.70469	0.85	.42741	1.35	.25924	1.85	.15724
0.36	.69768	0.86	.42316	1.36	.25666	1.86	.15567
0.37	.69073	0.87	.41895	1.37	.25411	1.87	.15412
0.38	.68386	0.88	.41478	1.38	.25158	1.88	.15259
0.39	.67706	0.89	.41066	1.39	.24908	1.89	.15107
0.40	.67032	0.90	.40657	1.40	.24660	1.90	.14957
0.41	.66365	0.91	.40252	1.41	.24414	1.91	.14808
0.42	.65705	0.92	.39852	1.42	.24171	1.92	.14661
0.43	.65051	0.93	.39455	1.43	.23931	1.93	.14515
0.44	.64404	0.94	.39063	1.44	.23693	1.94	.14370
0.45	.63763	0.95	.38674	1.45	.23457	1.95	.14227
0.46	.63128	0.96	.38289	1.46	.23224	1.96	.14086
0.47	.62500	0.97	.37908	1.47	.22993	1.97	.13946
0.48	.61878	0.98	.37531	1.48	.22764	1.98	.13807
0.49	.61263	0.99	.37158	1.49	.22537	1.99	.13670
0.50	.60653	1.00	.36788	1.50	.22313	2.00	.13534

Using Microsoft Excel®, these values are calculated with the equation: 1 — EXPONDIST(x, 1, TRUE).

AREAS OF THE CUMULATIVE STANDARD NORMAL DISTRIBUTION

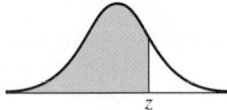

An entry in the table is the proportion under the curve cumulated from the negative tail.

z	G(z)	z	G(z)	z	G(z)
−4.00	0.00003	−1.30	0.09680	1.40	0.91924
−3.95	0.00004	−1.25	0.10565	1.45	0.92647
−3.90	0.00005	−1.20	0.11507	1.50	0.93319
−3.85	0.00006	−1.15	0.12507	1.55	0.93943
−3.80	0.00007	−1.10	0.13567	1.60	0.94520
−3.75	0.00009	−1.05	0.14686	1.65	0.95053
−3.70	0.00011	−1.00	0.15866	1.70	0.95543
−3.65	0.00013	−0.95	0.17106	1.75	0.95994
−3.60	0.00016	−0.90	0.18406	1.80	0.96407
−3.55	0.00019	−0.85	0.19766	1.85	0.96784
−3.50	0.00023	−0.80	0.21186	1.90	0.97128
−3.45	0.00028	−0.75	0.22663	1.95	0.97441
−3.40	0.00034	−0.70	0.24196	2.00	0.97725
−3.35	0.00040	−0.65	0.25785	2.05	0.97982
−3.30	0.00048	−0.60	0.27425	2.10	0.98214
−3.25	0.00058	−0.55	0.29116	2.15	0.98422
−3.20	0.00069	−0.50	0.30854	2.20	0.98610
−3.15	0.00082	−0.45	0.32636	2.25	0.98778
−3.10	0.00097	−0.40	0.34458	2.30	0.98928
−3.05	0.00114	−0.35	0.36317	2.35	0.99061
−3.00	0.00135	−0.30	0.38209	2.40	0.99180
−2.95	0.00159	−0.25	0.40129	2.45	0.99286
−2.90	0.00187	−0.20	0.42074	2.50	0.99379
−2.85	0.00219	−0.15	0.44038	2.55	0.99461
−2.80	0.00256	−0.10	0.46017	2.60	0.99534
−2.75	0.00298	−0.05	0.48006	2.65	0.99598
−2.70	0.00347	0.00	0.50000	2.70	0.99653
−2.65	0.00402	0.05	0.51994	2.75	0.99702
−2.60	0.00466	0.10	0.53983	2.80	0.99744
−2.55	0.00539	0.15	0.55962	2.85	0.99781
−2.50	0.00621	0.20	0.57926	2.90	0.99813
−2.45	0.00714	0.25	0.59871	2.95	0.99841
−2.40	0.00820	0.30	0.61791	3.00	0.99865
−2.35	0.00939	0.35	0.63683	3.05	0.99886
−2.30	0.01072	0.40	0.65542	3.10	0.99903
−2.25	0.01222	0.45	0.67364	3.15	0.99918
−2.20	0.01390	0.50	0.69146	3.20	0.99931
−2.15	0.01578	0.55	0.70884	3.25	0.99942
−2.10	0.01786	0.60	0.72575	3.30	0.99952
−2.05	0.02018	0.65	0.74215	3.35	0.99960
−2.00	0.02275	0.70	0.75804	3.40	0.99966
−1.95	0.02559	0.75	0.77337	3.45	0.99972
−1.90	0.02872	0.80	0.78814	3.50	0.99977
−1.85	0.03216	0.85	0.80234	3.55	0.99981
−1.80	0.03593	0.90	0.81594	3.60	0.99984
−1.75	0.04006	0.95	0.82894	3.65	0.99987
−1.70	0.04457	1.00	0.84134	3.70	0.99989
−1.65	0.04947	1.05	0.85314	3.75	0.99991
−1.60	0.05480	1.10	0.86433	3.80	0.99993
−1.55	0.06057	1.15	0.87493	3.85	0.99994
−1.50	0.06681	1.20	0.88493	3.90	0.99995
−1.45	0.07353	1.25	0.89435	3.95	0.99996
−1.40	0.08076	1.30	0.90320	4.00	0.99997
−1.35	0.08851	1.35	0.91149		

Using Microsoft Excel®, these probabilities are generated with the NORMSDIST(z) function.

UNIFORMLY DISTRIBUTED RANDOM DIGITS

56970	10799	52098	04184	54967	72938	50834	23777	08392
83125	85077	60490	44369	66130	72936	69848	59973	08144
55503	21383	02464	26141	68779	66388	75242	82690	74099
47019	06683	33203	29603	54553	25971	69573	83854	24715
84828	61152	79526	29554	84580	37859	28504	61980	34997
08021	31331	79227	05748	51276	57143	31926	00915	45821
36458	28285	30424	98420	72925	40729	22337	48293	86847
05752	96045	36847	87729	81679	59126	59437	33225	31280
26768	02513	58454	56958	20575	76746	40878	06846	32828
42613	72456	43030	58085	06766	60227	96414	32671	45587
95457	12176	65482	25596	02678	54592	63607	82096	21913
95276	67524	63564	95958	39750	64379	46059	51666	10433
66954	53574	64776	92345	95110	59448	77249	54044	67942
17457	44151	14113	02462	02798	54977	48340	66738	60184
03704	23322	83214	59337	01695	60666	97410	55064	17427
21538	16997	33210	60337	27976	70661	08250	69509	60264
57178	16730	08310	70348	11317	71623	55510	64750	87759
31048	40058	94953	55866	96283	40620	52087	80817	74533
69799	83300	16498	80733	96422	58078	99643	39847	96884
90595	65017	59231	17772	67831	33317	00520	90401	41700
33570	34761	08039	78784	09977	29398	93896	78227	90110
15340	82760	57477	13898	48431	72936	78160	87240	52710
64079	07733	36512	56186	99098	48850	72527	08486	10951
63491	84886	67118	62063	74958	20946	28147	39338	32109
92003	76568	41034	28260	79708	00770	88643	21188	01850
52360	46658	66511	04172	73085	11795	52594	13287	82531
74622	12142	68355	65635	21828	39539	18988	53609	04001
04157	50070	61343	64315	70836	82857	35335	87900	36194
86003	60070	66241	32836	27573	11479	94114	81641	00496
41208	80187	20351	09630	84668	42486	71303	19512	50277
06433	80674	24520	18222	10610	05794	37515	48619	62866
39298	47829	72648	37414	75755	04717	29899	78817	03509
89884	59651	67533	68123	17730	95862	08034	19473	63971
61512	32155	51906	61662	64430	16688	37275	51262	11569
99653	47635	12506	88535	36553	23757	34209	55803	96275
95913	11085	13772	76638	48423	25018	99041	77529	81360
55804	44004	13122	44115	01601	50541	00147	77685	58788
35334	82410	91601	40617	72876	33967	73830	15405	96554
57729	88646	76487	11622	96297	24160	09903	14047	22917
86648	89317	63677	70119	94739	25875	38829	68377	43918
30574	06039	07967	32422	76791	30725	53711	93385	13421
81307	13114	83580	79974	45929	85113	72268	09858	52104
02410	96385	79067	54939	21410	86980	91772	93307	34116
18969	87444	52233	62319	08598	09066	95288	04794	01534
87863	80514	66860	62297	80198	19347	73234	86265	49096
08397	10538	15438	62311	72844	60203	46412	65943	79232
28520	45247	58729	10854	99058	18260	38765	90038	94209
44285	09452	15867	70418	57012	72122	36634	97283	95943
86299	22510	33571	23309	57040	29285	67870	21913	72958
84842	05748	90894	61658	15001	94005	36308	41161	37341

INTEREST TABLES

Compound Sum of $1

table I.1

YEAR	1%	2%	3%	4%	5%	6%	7%	8%	9%
1	1.010	1.020	1.030	1.040	1.050	1.060	1.070	1.080	1.090
2	1.020	1.040	1.061	1.082	1.102	1.124	1.145	1.166	1.188
3	1.030	1.061	1.093	1.125	1.158	1.191	1.225	1.260	1.295
4	1.041	1.082	1.126	1.170	1.216	1.262	1.311	1.360	1.412
5	1.051	1.104	1.159	1.217	1.276	1.338	1.403	1.469	1.539
6	1.062	1.126	1.194	1.265	1.340	1.419	1.501	1.587	1.677
7	1.072	1.149	1.230	1.316	1.407	1.504	1.606	1.714	1.828
8	1.083	1.172	1.267	1.369	1.477	1.594	1.718	1.851	1.993
9	1.094	1.195	1.305	1.423	1.551	1.689	1.838	1.999	2.172
10	1.105	1.219	1.344	1.480	1.629	1.791	1.967	2.159	2.367
11	1.116	1.243	1.384	1.539	1.710	1.898	2.105	2.332	2.580
12	1.127	1.268	1.426	1.601	1.796	2.012	2.252	2.518	2.813
13	1.138	1.294	1.469	1.665	1.886	2.133	2.410	2.720	3.066
14	1.149	1.319	1.513	1.732	1.980	2.261	2.579	2.937	3.342
15	1.161	1.346	1.558	1.801	2.079	2.397	2.759	3.172	3.642
16	1.173	1.373	1.605	1.873	2.183	2.540	2.952	3.426	3.970
17	1.184	1.400	1.653	1.948	2.292	2.693	3.159	3.700	4.328
18	1.196	1.428	1.702	2.026	2.407	2.854	3.380	3.996	4.717
19	1.208	1.457	1.754	2.107	2.527	3.026	3.617	4.316	5.142
20	1.220	1.486	1.806	2.191	2.653	3.207	3.870	4.661	5.604
25	1.282	1.641	2.094	2.666	3.386	4.292	5.427	6.848	8.623
30	1.348	1.811	2.427	3.243	4.322	5.743	7.612	10.063	13.268

YEAR	10%	12%	14%	15%	16%	18%	20%	24%	28%
1	1.100	1.120	1.140	1.150	1.160	1.180	1.200	1.240	1.280
2	1.210	1.254	1.300	1.322	1.346	1.392	1.440	1.538	1.638
3	1.331	1.405	1.482	1.521	1.561	1.643	1.728	1.907	2.067
4	1.464	1.574	1.689	1.749	1.811	1.939	2.074	2.364	2.684
5	1.611	1.762	1.925	2.011	2.100	2.288	2.488	2.932	3.436
6	1.772	1.974	2.195	2.313	2.436	2.700	2.986	3.635	4.398
7	1.949	2.211	2.502	2.660	2.826	3.185	3.583	4.508	5.629
8	2.144	2.476	2.853	3.059	3.278	3.759	4.300	5.590	7.206
9	2.358	2.773	3.252	3.518	3.803	4.435	5.160	6.931	9.223
10	2.594	3.106	3.707	4.046	4.411	5.234	6.192	8.594	11.806
11	2.853	3.479	4.226	4.652	5.117	6.176	7.430	10.657	15.112
12	3.138	3.896	4.818	5.350	5.936	7.288	8.916	13.216	19.343
13	3.452	4.363	5.492	6.153	6.886	8.599	10.699	16.386	24.759
14	3.797	4.887	6.261	7.076	7.988	10.147	12.839	20.319	31.691
15	4.177	5.474	7.138	8.137	9.266	11.974	15.407	25.196	40.565
16	4.595	6.130	8.137	9.358	10.748	14.129	18.488	31.243	51.923
17	5.054	6.866	9.276	10.761	12.468	16.672	22.186	38.741	66.461
18	5.560	7.690	10.575	12.375	14.463	19.673	26.623	48.039	85.071
19	6.116	8.613	12.056	14.232	16.777	23.214	31.948	59.568	108.89
20	6.728	9.646	13.743	16.367	19.461	27.393	38.338	73.864	139.38
25	10.835	17.000	26.462	32.919	40.874	62.669	95.396	216.542	478.90
30	17.449	29.960	50.950	66.212	85.850	143.371	237.376	634.820	1645.5

Using Microsoft Excel®, these are calculated with the equation: $(1 + interest)^{years}$.

table I.2

Sum of an Annuity of $1 for *N* Years

YEAR	1%	2%	3%	4%	5%	6%	7%	8%
1	1.000	1.000	1.000	1.000	1.000	1.000	1.000	1.000
2	2.010	2.020	2.030	2.040	2.050	2.060	2.070	2.080
3	2.030	3.060	3.019	3.122	3.152	3.184	3.215	3.246
4	4.060	4.122	4.184	4.246	4.310	4.375	4.440	4.506
5	5.101	5.204	5.309	5.416	5.526	5.637	5.751	5.867
6	6.152	6.308	6.468	6.633	6.802	6.975	7.153	7.336
7	7.214	7.434	7.662	7.898	8.142	8.394	8.654	8.923
8	8.286	8.583	8.892	9.214	9.549	9.897	10.260	10.637
9	9.369	9.755	10.159	10.583	11.027	11.491	11.978	12.488
10	10.462	10.950	11.464	12.006	12.578	13.181	13.816	14.487
11	11.567	12.169	12.808	13.486	14.207	14.972	15.784	16.645
12	12.683	13.412	14.192	15.026	15.917	16.870	17.888	18.977
13	13.809	14.680	15.618	16.627	17.713	18.882	20.141	21.495
14	14.947	15.974	17.086	18.292	19.599	21.051	22.550	24.215
15	16.097	17.293	18.599	20.024	21.579	23.276	25.129	27.152
16	17.258	18.639	20.157	21.825	23.657	25.673	27.888	30.324
17	18.430	20.012	21.762	23.698	25.840	28.213	30.840	33.750
18	19.615	21.412	23.414	25.645	28.132	30.906	33.999	37.450
19	20.811	22.841	25.117	27.671	30.539	33.760	37.379	41.446
20	22.019	24.297	26.870	29.778	33.066	36.786	40.995	45.762
25	28.243	32.030	36.459	41.646	47.727	54.865	63.249	73.106
30	34.785	40.568	47.575	56.085	66.439	79.058	94.461	113.283

YEAR	9%	10%	12%	14%	16%	18%	20%	24%
1	1.000	1.000	1.000	1.000	1.000	1.000	1.000	1.000
2	2.090	2.100	2.120	2.140	2.160	2.180	2.200	2.240
3	3.278	3.310	3.374	3.440	3.506	3.572	3.640	3.778
4	4.573	4.641	4.770	4.921	5.066	5.215	5.368	5.684
5	5.985	6.105	6.353	6.610	6.877	7.154	7.442	8.048
6	7.523	7.716	8.115	8.536	8.977	9.442	9.930	10.980
7	9.200	9.487	10.089	10.730	11.414	12.142	12.916	14.615
8	11.028	11.436	12.300	13.233	14.240	15.327	16.499	19.123
9	13.021	13.579	14.776	16.085	17.518	19.086	20.799	24.712
10	15.193	15.937	17.549	19.337	21.321	23.521	25.959	31.643
11	17.560	18.531	20.655	23.044	25.733	28.755	32.150	40.238
12	20.141	21.384	24.133	27.271	30.850	34.931	39.580	50.985
13	22.953	24.523	28.029	32.089	36.786	42.219	48.497	64.110
14	26.019	27.975	32.393	37.581	43.672	50.818	59.196	80.496
15	29.361	31.772	37.280	43.842	51.660	60.965	72.035	100.815
16	33.003	35.950	42.753	50.980	60.925	72.939	87.442	126.011
17	36.974	40.545	48.884	59.118	71.673	87.068	105.931	157.253
18	41.301	45.599	55.750	68.394	84.141	103.740	128.117	195.994
19	46.018	51.159	63.440	78.969	98.603	123.414	154.740	244.033
20	51.160	57.275	72.052	91.025	115.380	146.628	186.688	303.601
25	84.701	93.347	133.334	181.871	249.214	342.603	471.981	898.092
30	136.308	164.494	241.333	356.787	530.312	790.948	1181.882	2640.916

Using Microsoft Excel®, these are calculated with the function: FV(interest, years, −1).

Present Value of $1

table I.3

YEAR	1%	2%	3%	4%	5%	6%	7%	8%	9%	10%	12%	14%	15%
1	.990	.980	.971	.962	.952	.943	.935	.926	.917	.909	.893	.877	.870
2	.980	.961	.943	.925	.907	.890	.873	.857	.842	.826	.797	.769	.756
3	.971	.942	.915	.889	.864	.840	.816	.794	.772	.751	.712	.675	.658
4	.961	.924	.889	.855	.823	.792	.763	.735	.708	.683	.636	.592	.572
5	.951	.906	.863	.822	.784	.747	.713	.681	.650	.621	.567	.519	.497
6	.942	.888	.838	.790	.746	.705	.666	.630	.596	.564	.507	.456	.432
7	.933	.871	.813	.760	.711	.665	.623	.583	.547	.513	.452	.400	.376
8	.923	.853	.789	.731	.677	.627	.582	.540	.502	.467	.404	.351	.327
9	.914	.837	.766	.703	.645	.592	.544	.500	.460	.424	.361	.308	.284
10	.905	.820	.744	.676	.614	.558	.508	.463	.422	.386	.322	.270	.247
11	.896	.804	.722	.650	.585	.527	.475	.429	.388	.350	.287	.237	.215
12	.887	.788	.701	.625	.557	.497	.444	.397	.356	.319	.257	.208	.187
13	.879	.773	.681	.601	.530	.469	.415	.368	.326	.290	.229	.182	.163
14	.870	.758	.661	.577	.505	.442	.388	.340	.299	.263	.205	.160	.141
15	.861	.743	.642	.555	.481	.417	.362	.315	.275	.239	.183	.140	.123
16	.853	.728	.623	.534	.458	.394	.339	.292	.252	.218	.163	.123	.107
17	.844	.714	.605	.513	.436	.371	.317	.270	.231	.198	.146	.108	.093
18	.836	.700	.587	.494	.416	.350	.296	.250	.212	.180	.130	.095	.081
19	.828	.686	.570	.475	.396	.331	.276	.232	.194	.164	.116	.083	.070
20	.820	.673	.554	.456	.377	.312	.258	.215	.178	.149	.104	.073	.061
25	.780	.610	.478	.375	.295	.233	.184	.146	.116	.092	.059	.038	.030
30	.742	.552	.412	.308	.231	.174	.131	.099	.075	.057	.033	.020	.015

YEAR	16%	18%	20%	24%	28%	32%	36%	40%	50%	60%	70%	80%	90%
1	.862	.847	.833	.806	.781	.758	.735	.714	.667	.625	.588	.556	.526
2	.743	.718	.694	.650	.610	.574	.541	.510	.444	.391	.346	.309	.277
3	.641	.609	.579	.524	.477	.435	.398	.364	.296	.244	.204	.171	.146
4	.552	.516	.482	.423	.373	.329	.292	.260	.198	.153	.120	.095	.077
5	.476	.437	.402	.341	.291	.250	.215	.186	.132	.095	.070	.053	.040
6	.410	.370	.335	.275	.227	.189	.158	.133	.088	.060	.041	.029	.021
7	.354	.314	.279	.222	.178	.143	.116	.095	.059	.037	.024	.016	.011
8	.305	.266	.233	.179	.139	.108	.085	.068	.039	.023	.014	.009	.006
9	.263	.226	.194	.144	.108	.082	.063	.048	.026	.015	.008	.005	.003
10	.227	.191	.162	.116	.085	.062	.046	.035	.017	.009	.005	.003	.002
11	.195	.162	.135	.094	.066	.047	.034	.025	.012	.006	.003	.002	.001
12	.168	.137	.112	.076	.052	.036	.025	.018	.008	.004	.002	.001	.001
13	.145	.116	.093	.061	.040	.027	.018	.013	.005	.002	.001	.001	.000
14	.125	.099	.078	.049	.032	.021	.014	.009	.003	.001	.001	.000	.000
15	.108	.084	.065	.040	.025	.016	.010	.006	.002	.001	.000	.000	.000
16	.093	.071	.054	.032	.019	.012	.007	.005	.002	.001	.000	.000	
17	.080	.060	.045	.026	.015	.009	.005	.003	.001	.000	.000		
18	.069	.051	.038	.021	.012	.007	.004	.002	.001	.000	.000		
19	.060	.043	.031	.017	.009	.005	.003	.002	.000	.000			
20	.051	.037	.026	.014	.007	.004	.002	.001	.000	.000			
25	.024	.016	.010	.005	.002	.001	.000	.000					
30	.012	.007	.004	.002	.001	.000	.000						

Using Microsoft Excel®, these are calculated with the equation: $(1 + interest)^{-years}$.

table I.4

Present Value of an Annuity of $1

YEAR	1%	2%	3%	4%	5%	6%	7%	8%	9%	10%
1	0.990	0.980	0.971	0.962	0.952	0.943	0.935	0.926	0.917	0.909
2	1.970	1.942	1.913	1.886	1.859	1.833	1.808	1.783	1.759	1.736
3	2.941	2.884	2.829	2.775	2.723	2.673	2.624	2.577	2.531	2.487
4	3.902	3.808	3.717	3.630	3.546	3.465	3.387	3.312	3.240	3.170
5	4.853	4.713	4.580	4.452	4.329	4.212	4.100	3.993	3.890	3.791
6	5.795	5.601	5.417	5.242	5.076	4.917	4.766	4.623	4.486	4.355
7	6.728	6.472	6.230	6.002	5.786	5.582	5.389	5.206	5.033	4.868
8	7.652	7.325	7.020	6.733	6.463	6.210	6.971	5.747	5.535	5.335
9	8.566	8.162	7.786	7.435	7.108	6.802	6.515	6.247	5.985	5.759
10	9.471	8.983	8.530	8.111	7.722	7.360	7.024	6.710	6.418	6.145
11	10.368	9.787	9.253	8.760	8.306	7.887	7.449	7.139	6.805	6.495
12	11.255	10.575	9.954	9.385	8.863	8.384	7.943	7.536	7.161	6.814
13	12.134	11.348	10.635	9.986	9.394	8.853	8.358	7.904	7.487	7.103
14	13.004	12.106	11.296	10.563	9.899	9.295	8.745	8.244	7.786	7.367
15	13.865	12.849	11.938	11.118	10.380	9.712	9.108	8.559	8.060	7.606
16	14.718	13.578	12.561	11.652	10.838	10.106	9.447	8.851	8.312	7.824
17	15.562	14.292	13.166	12.166	11.274	10.477	9.763	9.122	8.544	8.022
18	16.398	14.992	13.754	12.659	11.690	10.828	10.059	9.372	8.756	8.201
19	17.226	15.678	14.324	13.134	12.085	11.158	10.336	9.604	8.950	8.365
20	18.046	16.351	14.877	13.590	12.462	11.470	10.594	9.818	9.128	8.514
25	22.023	19.523	17.413	15.622	14.094	12.783	11.654	10.675	9.823	9.077
30	25.808	22.397	19.600	17.292	15.373	13.765	12.409	11.258	10.274	9.427

YEAR	12%	14%	16%	18%	20%	24%	28%	32%	36%
1	0.893	0.877	0.862	0.847	0.833	0.806	0.781	0.758	0.735
2	1.690	1.647	1.605	1.566	1.528	1.457	1.392	1.332	1.276
3	2.402	2.322	2.246	2.174	2.106	1.981	1.868	1.766	1.674
4	3.037	2.914	2.798	2.690	2.589	2.404	2.241	2.096	1.966
5	3.605	3.433	3.274	3.127	2.991	2.745	2.532	2.345	2.181
6	4.111	3.889	3.685	3.498	3.326	3.020	2.759	2.534	2.339
7	4.564	4.288	4.039	3.812	3.605	3.242	2.937	2.678	2.455
8	4.968	4.639	4.344	4.078	3.837	3.421	3.076	2.786	2.540
9	5.328	4.946	4.607	4.303	4.031	3.566	3.184	2.868	2.603
10	5.650	5.216	4.833	4.494	4.193	3.682	3.269	2.930	2.650
11	5.988	5.453	5.029	4.656	4.327	3.776	3.335	2.978	2.683
12	6.194	5.660	5.197	4.793	4.439	3.851	3.387	3.013	2.708
13	6.424	5.842	5.342	4.910	4.533	3.912	3.427	3.040	2.727
14	6.628	6.002	5.468	5.008	4.611	3.962	3.459	3.061	2.740
15	6.811	6.142	5.575	5.092	4.675	4.001	3.483	3.076	2.750
16	6.974	6.265	5.669	5.162	4.730	4.033	3.503	3.088	2.758
17	7.120	6.373	5.749	5.222	4.775	4.059	3.518	3.097	2.763
18	7.250	6.467	5.818	5.273	4.812	4.080	3.529	3.104	2.767
19	7.366	6.550	5.877	5.316	4.844	4.097	3.539	3.109	2.770
20	7.469	6.623	5.929	5.353	4.870	4.110	3.546	3.113	2.772
25	7.843	6.873	6.097	5.467	4.948	4.147	3.564	3.122	2.776
30	8.055	7.003	6.177	5.517	4.979	4.160	3.569	3.124	2.778

Using Microsoft Excel®, these are calculated with the function: PV(interest, years, −1).

PHOTO CREDITS

Note: Page numbers followed by *n* refer to footnotes.

Student Operations Management Video DVD

Fifteen Full Length Video Segments

- Project Management at Six Flags, New Jersey

- Service Processing at BuyCostumes.com

- Six Sigma at Caterpillar

- Green Manufacturing at Xerox

- Burton Snowboards – Manufacturing Design

- Honda – Green Product Design and PHILL

- FedEx – Logistics and Customer Service

- DHL – Global Delivery Service

- Ford – Total Supply Chain Management

- Ford – Supplier Relationships – Fords CAP Supplier Campus featuring SY

- Flexible Manufacturing: Featuring Ford – Chicago Assembly Plant

- The Product Process Matrix

- Queuing – Featuring Disney World

- Louisville Slugger Aluminum Bats – Plant Tour

- Noodles & Company – Service Process Design